PERGAMON GENERAL PSYCHOLOGY SERIES
EDITORS
Arnold P. Goldstein, Syracuse University
Leonard Krasner, Stanford University & SUNY at Stony Brook

THE CLINICAL PSYCHOLOGY
HANDBOOK
(PGPS-120)

Titles of Related Interest

THE CLINICAL PSYCHOLOGY HANDBOOK

Second Edition

Edited by

MICHEL HERSEN
University of Pittsburgh School of Medicine

ALAN E. KAZDIN
Yale University

ALAN S. BELLACK
Medical College of Pennsylvania at Eastern
Pennsylvania Psychiatric Institute

PERGAMON PRESS
Member of Maxwell Macmillan Pergamon Publishing Corporation
New York • Oxford • Beijing • Frankfurt
São Paulo • Sydney • Tokyo • Toronto

Pergamon Press Offices:

U.S.A.	Pergamon Press, Inc., Maxwell House, Fairview Park, Elmsford, New York 10523, U.S.A.
U.K.	Pergamon Press plc, Headington Hill Hall, Oxford OX3 0BW, England
PEOPLE'S REPUBLIC OF CHINA	Pergamon Press, Xizhimenwai Dajie, Beijing Exhibition Centre, Beijing, 100044, People's Republic of China
GERMANY	Pergamon Press GmbH, Hammerweg 6, D-6242 Kronberg, Germany
BRAZIL	Pergamon Editora Ltda, Rua Eça de Queiros, 346, CEP 04011, Paraiso, São Paulo, Brazil
AUSTRALIA	Pergamon Press Australia Pty Ltd., P.O. Box 544, Potts Point, NSW 2011, Australia
JAPAN	Pergamon Press, 8th Floor, Matsuoka Central Building, 1-7-1 Nishishinjuku, Shinjuku-ku, Tokyo 160, Japan
CANADA	Pergamon Press Canada Ltd., Suite 271, 253 College Street, Toronto, Ontario M5T 1R5, Canada

---

Copyright © 1991 Pergamon Press, Inc.

All rights reserved. No part of this publication may be reproduced, stored in a retrieval system or transmitted in any form or by any means: electronic, electrostatic, magnetic tape, mechanical, photocopying, recording or otherwise, without permission in writing from the publishers.

Library of Congress Cataloging in Publication Data

The Clinical psychology handbook / edited by Michel Hersen, Alan
E. Kazdin, and Alan S. Bellack. -- 2nd ed.
     p.   cm. -- (Pergamon general psychology series 120)
     Includes bibliographical references.
     Includes indexes.
     ISBN 0-08-036441-1 (alk. paper) :
     1. Clinical psychology--Handbooks, manuals, etc. I. Hersen,
Michel. II. Kazdin, Alan E. III. Bellack, Alan S. IV. Series.
     [DNLM: 1. Psychology, Clinical.   WM 105 C6417]
RC467.2.C55 1991
616.89--dc20
DLC
for Library of Congress   90-7981
                                                  CIP
Printing: 1 2 3 4 5 6 7 8 9   Year: 1 2 3 4 5 6 7 8 9 0

Printed in the United States of America

∞™ The paper used in this publication meets the minimum
requirements of American National Standard for Information
Sciences—Permanence of Paper for Printed Library Materials,
ANSI Z39.48-1984

Dedication

To the memory of our friend and editor, Jerry Frank.

CONTENTS

EVALUATION AND TREATMENT

Part IV. ASSESSMENT AND DIAGNOSIS

Part V. TREATMENT

PREFACE

In 1981, when we first undertook the task of outlining the contents for the first edition of *The Clinical Psychology Handbook,* we were struck most by how the number of activities clinical psychologists pursued had increased dramatically since the 1960s. This, of course, was something that we endeavored to underscore in that original volume. It should not be surprising, then, that the field has burgeoned again. Who could have predicted in 1965, when Benjamin B. Wolman published a handbook on clinical psychology, the spectacular advances in the field—structured psychotherapies, diagnosis, structured interviewing, behavioral assessment, biological and genetic influences of behavior, psychopharmacology, prevention, ethical and legal issues, multivariate statistics, single-case research, psychopathology in the minorities, and the political and legislative impact of clinical psychology? In 1965 Wolman's book represented the state of the art. Today only a computer search can keep us abreast of the exciting developments in all facets of clinical psychology.

In considering the marked changes since 1965 and since publication of the first edition of our handbook in 1983, we present the reader with a review of contemporary theory, research, and practice. But we also have done our best to preserve the important and classic contributions of the past. Each of our authors is fully aware of the rich legacy of our eminent predecessors in clinical psychology. The historic basis for present-day thinking has been fully acknowledged throughout this edition.

Our handbook is divided into six major sections. The first, "General Issues," deals with history, theoretical foundations, clinical training, roles, and mental health policy. The second is concerned with the spectrum of personality theories and models. The third involves an examination of research issues and problems facing the field. The fourth covers diagnosis, interviewing, personality assessment, intellectual evaluation, neuropsychological evaluation, behavioral assessment, psychophysiological assessment, and medical assessment. The fifth encompasses the major treatment approaches that are carried out today. The sixth addresses issues including primary prevention, community consultation, and the brief psychotherapies. Finally, the editors present an afterword that underscores progress in the field.

The second edition of *The Clinical Psychology Handbook* is expanded from 38 to 41 chapters. Five chapters are totally new, and two that appeared in the first edition have been omitted. The remainder are either totally revised or have been written by authors whose expertise reflects the developments that have occurred.

We each carried out our fair share of the editorial burden. But we must acknowledge the contributions of numerous individuals who eagerly participated in the development and completion of this project—first and foremost our eminent contributors who cheerfully agreed to carry out their tasks. We are grateful to them for sharing their thinking about their respective areas of expertise. Next, we sincerely thank our secretaries (Mary H. Newell, Mary Anne Frederick, and Joan Gill) who typed and retyped many parts of the manuscript. We thank the people at Pergamon Press for their herculean effort to put this large manuscript into readable form. Finally, we acknowledge the support of our late editor at Pergamon Press, Jerome B. Frank, who was not only a good friend, but a tireless and infinitely patient taskmaster. Without Jerry none of this could have happened.

Michel Hersen, Pittsburgh
Alan E. Kazdin, New Haven
Alan S. Bellack, Philadelphia

PART I

GENERAL ISSUES

EDITOR'S COMMENTS

When compared with the other major helping professions, the history of clinical psychology appears to be brief. Most of the important findings in the field appeared after World War I, and the bulk after World War II. Despite the brevity of its existence, clinical psychology has a rich heritage, with various roots in philosophy, psychophysics, the early testing movement, early behaviorism, and psychoanalysis. Although clinical psychology has had multifaceted influences, as a unique discipline it has developed its own character. The area is consistently increasing in scope, with its practitioners carrying out numerous tasks and functions on a daily basis. Its popularity within the general field of psychology is still extending, as evidenced by the large enrollments in all programs focusing on this specialty. Thus, there is no doubt that the field is alive and healthy. But as a result of its exponential growth, it has also become more complex. Such complexity is amply documented in this handbook.

In this part of the handbook we provide the reader with an overview of clinical psychology in addition to outlining important issues that affect the discipline at this time. In chapter 1, Brendan A. Maher presents an incisive review of the history of clinical psychology that, as the title indicates, is highly personalized. His views on the scientific and political developments within clinical psychology are clearly articulated. Notwithstanding these views Maher ends the chapter with a call for increased knowledge for the purpose of more effectively dealing with the psychological problems presented to clinical psychologists. In chapter 2, Irving B. Weiner considers the theoretical foundations of clinical psychology with emphasis on psychoanalytic, learning, and humanistic theory. He evaluates the trend toward eclecticism, documenting its popularity on the basis of recent surveys. He also notes that despite the self-avowed label of being "eclectic," many therapists do operate from "a preferred theoretical" framework. Barry A. Edelstein and William S. Brasted, in chapter 3, examine in detail the clinical training of psychologists from the historical perspective and in terms of current issues. Future perspectives are considered as well, with attention to funding, computerization, and the role in prevention. Also underscored are the future needs for training in psychoneuroimmunology, neurophysiology, psychopharmacology, and the biological sciences in general. Steven T. Fishman and Barry S. Lubetkin, in chapter 4, share their expertise in

1

developing a successful group practice of clinical psychology that has survived the vicissitudes of changes in third party payments, the emergence of health maintenance organizations (HMOs), and challenges from other professional groups offering comparable client services. The complete spectrum of issues involving private practice are delineated in the form of guidelines for the new practitioner. Charles A. Kiesler, Celeste G. Simpkins, and Teru L. Morton, in chapter 5, consider the various research issues in mental health policy. Trends at the state and federal level are considered with considerable emphasis on the underlying economic factors. Jerry J. Sweet and Ronald H. Rozensky, in chapter 6, examine the issue of professional relationships in clinical psychology. Much emphasis is given to the need to maintain strong ties within the field of clinical psychology, in addition to fostering relationships with the other subdivisions of psychology, the consumers of psychological services who are in the community, and, of course, with the parallel helping disciplines. In chapter 7, Kenneth S. Pope carefully examines how ethical and legal factors affect the activities of clinical psychologists. These ethical and legal factors are discussed with respect to administrative, legislative, and judicial considerations. Finally, in chapter 8, Patrick H. DeLeon, Gary R. VandenBos, Michael R. Pollard, Andrea L. Solarz, and Richard B. Weinberg bring us up to date on clinical psychology and the political scene. The vast federal legislative accomplishments of clinical pychology over the last two decades are documented, especially with respect to its practitioners being recognized as viable health care providers who can function independently.

CHAPTER 1

A PERSONAL HISTORY OF CLINICAL PSYCHOLOGY

Brendan A. Maher

This chapter is intended to be a personal history of clinical psychology.[1] With this comes a dangerous temptation to write as though the personal experience of the author has been systematically representative of the main themes that would be discerned in a comprehensive nonpersonal history of the field. At its worst this approach can mislead the reader into thinking that an anecdotal memoir is an adequate history; at best, it can employ personal experience to illuminate some of the main themes of the history. It can serve to describe not only what happened, but to give the flavor of what it was like to be involved in these happenings.

Clinical psychology is a creature that lives uneasily in the twin domains of academic science and the social world of the professions (especially psychiatry) in which political and economic factors play a significant role. Science does not develop free from the influence of nonintellectual factors; the professions, being conducted in the larger society, are even more subject to social movements and pressures. No history of clini-

cal psychology, not even a personal one such as this, can be coherent without frequent reference to events lying outside the narrow boundaries of psychology itself. It has fallen to the lot of clinical psychologists of my own generation to witness far-reaching changes in the conception of clinical psychology. These changes have elicited different reactions. For some they have represented progress on the professional front; for others they represent an abandonment of valued goals. Few who have taken part in the field during these changes remain indifferent to them. The kind of history that is written inevitably reflects the reaction of the writer of the history. This is true of this chapter. Hence, in what follows, I have tried to weave together personal experience, aspects of the formal history of clinical psychology, and descriptions of the social milieu in which they occurred; I have also tried to make my own judgments clear where they exceed a simple description of events.

A personal beginning: My first opportunity to study

---

[1]The reader interested in more systematic histories of clinical psychology and of psychopathology may wish to turn to other sources such as Hilgard (1987), Kendall & Norton-Ford (1982), Kirsch & Winter (1983), Maher & Maher (1979), Maher W. B. & Maher B. A. (1985), Maher B. A. & Maher W. B. (1985), Maher (1988), and Matarazzo (1985).

psychology came and went when an occupational therapist suggested that I might while away my time as a plastic surgery patient in a Royal Naval Hospital by studying something. The year was 1945, World War II was over in Europe, and wounds received while minesweeping had removed me from the scene long enough to give time for reflection. Correspondence courses were offered to military patients by a government and college consortium; each of us could choose two. I chose psychology first, with meteorology as the alternate. Psychology proved to be oversubscribed, so I was assigned the meteorology course instead. By the time the first lesson was due to arrive, the authorities had moved me to another hospital, thereby terminating my prospects of becoming acquainted with either psychological systems or storm systems for the time being. It was not until I entered the University of Manchester two years later, in 1947, that I began to find out what psychology was all about.

MANCHESTER, 1947 TO 1950

Here psychology was one of the options from the list of subjects that could be studied in the freshman year. With English, history, and logic, it constituted my schedule for the first term. By the end of that term I had refined my interests down to English and psychology. Deciding to apply to take the honors curriculum in one or the other, I went to the English department, only to find that it was closed for lunch. As the passage of the war years had given me a sense of urgency about the future, I went directly to the psychology department. It was not closed for lunch, and so in this seemingly accidental fashion I entered the field that was to be the basis of my professional life. It was not an accident that I ever had real reason to regret.

The department of psychology at Manchester was dominated in its curriculum by its head, Professor Thomas H. Pear. Pear had studied at Wurzburg and was much influenced by the conceptions of that school of thought. Although he had written a small monograph on shell shock many years before, he was chiefly a social psychologist. His social psychology, and therefore ours, was informed by the writings of Gordon Allport, Margaret Mead, Ruth Benedict, and the social anthropologists generally. Pear's most visible interest was in the relationship between voice and personality—the most concrete interpretation of this being the link between accent and social class. He had conducted a large-scale survey with the aid of the BBC, in which radio listeners were asked to estimate the social background of speakers, each of whom read an identical passage from a scientific text. Impressive percentages of the British listening public correctly identified a Church of England vicar, a police officer, and so forth. An attempt by Pear to replicate this in the United States in collaboration with Gordon Allport had failed; it appeared that the boundaries of social class there were less indelibly marked than in the United Kingdom.[2]

No one in the department taught psychopathology or courses with a serious clinical content. A short series of visiting lectures on abnormal psychology was given by a faculty member from the Medical School. We were introduced briefly to the Rorschach cards in a session of a course defined as experimental laboratory psychology (the rest of that course was devoted to finding the "hot" and "cold" spots on the back of each other's hands) and to introspecting aloud to see if we could trap an imageless thought from time to time. Pear, we were told, had an antipathy to animal psychology of any kind and would not permit laboratory animals in the department. Hence—except for Thorndike—the works of Hull, Tolman, and the American behaviorists were largely unknown to us, although an intrepid junior lecturer once showed a short American-made film of rats running a maze, the accompanying commentary being delivered by him *sotto voce,* as if apprehensive that even the photographic image of the prohibited rodent would provoke professorial wrath. Nonetheless, even the most cursory examination of the shelves of the university libraries, or of the readings lists distributed in lectures, indicated that the most significant work in psychology was occurring in the United States.

We were, however, thoroughly exposed to the British school of intelligence testing and to the psychometric tradition generally. We read Spearman, became familiar with the concept of "g," and gave each other the Raven's Matrices test. Continuing study in philosophy and physiology forming part of the honors requirement in psychology, we spent time making nerve-muscle preparations under the benevolent eye of Professor Walter Schlapp and watching the wonders of a primitive syllogism computer developed by Wolfe Mayes of the philosophy department.[3] Whatever the strengths and weaknesses of that kind of

---

[2]This theme, of course, had inspired Shaw's *Pygmalion* and its later musical version, *My Fair Lady.*
[3]Turing was at Manchester at that time, and a colleague of Mayes, but the significance of all of this was, I regret to say, lost on this naive undergraduate.

instruction, it left an indelible impression that psychology was a science with bonds to both biology and philosophy and that this was to be welcomed rather than seen as a source of intellectual conflict.

Any understanding of the experience of those times is incomplete without reference to the world outside the university. A Labour government had come to power in Britain with a large majority of seats in the House of Commons and with an agenda intended to put right many of the grosser social and economic injustices of the prewar years. A keystone of the new social edifice was the National Health plan, and close to that was the intention to reform those aspects of the educational system that prevented all but a few children from entering the college preparatory high school system. Times were hard in Britain. Although the war had been over for two years, rationing of many commodities was still in force, especially of heating fuel, clothing, and some foods. Rental housing was almost nonexistent, more than half a million homes having been destroyed by air raids and by other consequences of war. Manchester had been heavily bombed in the Christmas air raids of 1940, and new building was slow to take place.

The social purpose of the times was in keeping with the historical ambience of the university and of the city of Manchester itself. Engels's "classic slum," Salford, lay just across the city boundary. The black grime that coated every building in the city, including those of the university, was a silent reminder that this was one of the first centers of the Industrial Revolution in the Western world, and a reminder of the human horrors that had been created in the name of commercial success. Peterloo, the murder of protesting citizens by militia cavalry in St. Peter's Square in the city center in 1819, was permanently lodged in the communal memory of the city.

For many ordinary Britons, especially in the industrial North of England, there had been two war aims. The first was to defeat Hitler and the apparatus of fascism; the second was to bring into being a society in Britain that would distribute opportunity and power more evenly. The postwar electoral defeat of Winston Churchill, such a stunning surprise to the rest of the world, was less a surprise in a Britain in which this charismatic war leader had failed to understand that success in achieving the first war aim would not compensate for refusal to undertake the second.

The combination of the prospect of a brave new future of social justice, and the sharing of current hardships, combined to prolong the spirit of camaraderie of the war years. Psychology in this context offered a chance to contribute to the improvement of human life. As students of psychology, it seemed to most of us that we were engaged in a worthwhile human enterprise that would enable us to follow an interesting vocation with social meaning. One of the most applicable parts of psychology seemed to be clinical psychology—a helping profession.

Manchester University was also the first British university to establish a chair in American studies, the initial incumbent being a former Manchester graduate returning from Columbia University, Professor Kandel. Assisted by one junior lecturer, he gave courses ranging from the Federalist papers to the Federal Reserve Bank, from the geography of the Great Divide to the economics of the Great Depression, and from the politics of the Gilded Age to the music of the Jazz Age. Curiosity about America and the Americans had been stimulated in me by experience in joint operations with the U.S. Navy during the war, so I took the courses that were offered. Kandel was a wonderful teacher, sharpening one's interest in the culture of the United States although, as I discovered later, never fully managing to convey the effects of large distances and enormous variety that so influence American life.

During the final year of undergraduate study, it was necessary for us to face the issue of a postbaccalaureate career. Serious but brief further training in clinical psychology in Britain was available at the Institute of Psychiatry at the Maudsley Hospital in London and, to some extent, with J. C. Raven in Scotland. In both cases the training lasted little more than a year, emphasized personality assessment, and did not include the award of a higher degree. A more commonly available alternative was direct entry into the hospital system of the newly established National Health Service, where on-the-job training was provided on the apprenticeship model. Promotion through the higher grades would follow from length of service and demonstrated competence. The duties of clinical psychologists, however trained, were predominantly in the field of assessment and research. Psychotherapy by psychologists was essentially unknown, although this fact should be considered in the light of the parallel paucity of psychotherapeutic activities by psychiatrists in Britain.

Due to distinctions made between the practice of psychotherapy and the activity of child guidance, British psychologists employed within the educational system did practice techniques designed to change the behavior of children of school age, but this was not officially regarded as child psychotherapy—although it rather obviously met all of the definitional criteria for that activity.

All of this made it clear that if thorough graduate education in clinical psychology was to be found, it would be necessary to go to the United States to find it. A fellowship from the Fulbright Commission and the English-Speaking Union combined to make it possible to do this. The letter bearing the news told me that I was bound for Ohio State University in Columbus; it is now a matter of retrospective embarrassment to me that I had to go to the atlas to find not only Columbus, but to find Ohio. Professor Kandel was not helpful in the matter, remarking only that the university there had a great football team. He was right about the football team. What he could not know was that circumstances were sending me to a center of intellectual ferment and debate in psychology that would have a critical influence on my own thinking for the rest of my professional career. I debarked from the Cunard liner *Mauretania* in August 1950, one of a group of such students on board, each of us struck by the incredible Manhattan skyline and many of us, unwittingly, a tiny part of the stream that was accompanying the shift of the intellectual center of influence of the Western world from Europe to the United States.

OHIO STATE UNIVERSITY, 1950 TO 1954

The department of psychology at Ohio State was large. Clinical psychology in 1950 consisted of a group of faculty including Julian Rotter, George Kelly, and Boyd McCandless. Paul Mussen and Alvin Scodel were to join the clinical faculty shortly thereafter. The rest of the department included, among others, Harold Burtt, the chairman, Paul Fitts, Donald Meyer, Harold Pepinsky, Herbert Toops, Robert Wherry, and Delos Wickens. Shortly before, Donald Campbell had departed for Northwestern University and Carl Rogers for Chicago. These were losses, but it was a department in its prime; I was lucky to be there.

The doctoral program in clinical psychology was designed explicitly to fit what was already being called the "Boulder model." In 1949, the year before my own arrival in Columbus, a major conference on the problems of doctoral training in clinical psychology had been held by the American Psychological Association (APA) at Boulder, Colorado. It recommended a model of doctoral training in which competence in the subject matter of general psychology and particularly in research design and statistics was an essential component of the training of clinical psychologists at the doctoral level, as well as training in clinical skills. Acceptance of this scientist-practitioner model was widespread in the leading universities in the country.

The Boulder conference itself was the outcome of earlier reports of APA committees in 1945 and 1947. These had proposed a four-year doctoral program to include one year of clinical internship to be taken either before or after the dissertation had been completed but before the degree could be awarded. A major impetus for these reports had been requests to the APA by the Veterans Administration (VA) and the National Institute of Mental Health (NIMH) for help in setting standards to be applied in their award of funds to doctoral programs designed to train clinical psychologists. By the early 1920s the shell shock of World War I had been recognized as a psychological response to stress. This had led to a greater emphasis on the provision of psychological services for veterans than had been the case in previous wars. World War II produced many more American casualties of all kinds than had World War I. This naturally created heavy demands on the services of the VA. Many new hospitals and clinics were being built in addition to the older structures established after World War I. Mental health professionals of all kinds were scarce, and it was necessary to train them if the needs of the patients were to be met.

In practice the application of the Boulder model at Ohio State meant that the first two years of doctoral training were spent in a mixture of courses and seminars in learning theory, physiological psychology, statistics, and so forth on the one hand, and courses in personality theory and clinical psychology plus practica in intelligence and personality testing on the other. The third year was generally spent as a clinical intern, and the fourth year was spent on the dissertation. Students being trained and supported by the VA generally alternated academic work and clinical assignments at a VA clinic or hospital in a sequence that provided the required total internship experience in a cumulative manner over the four-year span of graduate study. But much more important than the mechanics of scientist-practitioner training was the intellectual atmosphere in which it was conducted.

The fabric of clinical psychology graduate training presented a texture woven from several distinct strands. First and most important of these was a faith in the potential of behavioral science to put clinical practice on a firm base. The commitment to becoming a scientist-practitioner was not merely acquiescence in the long-standing academic requirement that the Doctor of Philosophy degree be a testimony to scientific and scholarly competence. It was due to a firm belief that then-current clinical techniques did not, in fact, possess adequate justification in scientific terms. This, it was felt, could be rectified by the systematic application of the scientific method and sophisticated measurement procedures to the development of better techniques. Along with this went the observation that the training of psychiatrists in normal psychological science and in research methods was negligible.

If there were to be real improvements in clinical practice, they would have to come from a group of scientifically trained persons with firsthand experience of the clinical problems that were to be solved. These were to be the scientist-practitioner clinical psychologists. As the patients could not be expected to wait until the scientists had come up with effective procedures, the duty of the clinical psychologist was to apply what was available as skillfully as possible, but to do so with a conscious recognition that this was a temporary expedient, to be replaced with something much better as soon as possible. Creating the "something better" was a higher duty than mastering the techniques at hand.

One inevitable consequence of this was that entry into private practice was regarded as an undesirable career choice. Private practice appeared to border on the mildly unethical as it involved selling services of dubious adequacy and diverted the clinical psychologist from the main task of developing better methods. Indeed, too big a career investment in private practice might dispose the practitioner to reduce dissonance by defending the use of inadequate techniques rather than improving them.

A second thread on the loom of our experience was a sense of camaraderie. We were all engaged, we thought, in a great social enterprise. Scientific psychology would contribute to the postwar world; those of us involved in developing this psychology were joint contributors. By present-day standards, academic competition between us was minimal. Graduate students studied together, helped each other with shared notes, abstracts of required readings, and a host of other things designed to overcome the hurdles set by the curriculum; with a few exceptions we did not try to trip others so as to ensure that we got over the hurdles sooner or higher than our fellow students. Much of this was due, no doubt, to the fact that many of us were veterans and used to this way of life. But it was equally true of those who had not served in the military; the common theme was scientific optimism and the expectation of a useful collaborative future career in research, teaching, and clinical work. The emphasis was usefulness, not affluence. Recognition, if it came, was to be the result of genuine contributions, not of skilled public relations.

Third, there came an acquired indifference to the problem of diagnosis in psychopathology. Although we were exposed to the classic psychiatric diagnostic categories, it was implied that they were not really relevant to the understanding of abnormal behavior. From Julian Rotter we learned that maladaptive behavior could be understood in terms of social learning processes and that behavior change could be achieved by changing the client's expectancies. George Kelly was at work developing his theory of personal constructs and impressed on us the need to gain insight into the way in which clients perceived themselves and their social worlds. From both we learned that the task at hand was to develop a comprehensive theory of human personality and that the clinical implications would necessarily follow. Although our testing practica took us into the closed wards of the local state psychiatric hospital and the state school for the mentally handicapped, our experiences there were rarely linked systematically to the theoretical programs of the psychology department. Nor did the work of our mentors ever turn to consider the scientific problems of schizophrenia, the psychoses in general, or the classic neurotic syndromes.

Experimental studies of major psychopathology played little part in our graduate training at Ohio State, but there was opportunity and encouragement to undertake experimental work in the spectrum of psychology generally. It was because of this spirit that I was fortunate to obtain supervision and instruction from Donald Meyer as an assistant in experimental studies of the functions of the visual areas of the rat brain. Under the primitive conditions then prevailing, I was taught the techniques of cortical ablation and the conduct of experimental procedures for the investigation of discrimination learning in laboratory animals. Stereotaxic localization of the lesions was not then available. Errors in placement were determined by postmortem microscopic examination of the relevant brain sections. None of this had direct relevance to the clinical psychology or personality psychology that was then being provided in the doctoral program but was very much in keeping with my undergraduate education, in which physiology, psychology, and philosophy were assumed naturally to go hand in hand. Technical skills came first, and their theoretical integration would come later.

Psychoanalysis was dealt with critically at Ohio State. Its fatal shortcomings as a science were discussed, and we were in this way armed for the follies that we understood would await us when the clinical internship would bring us into daily contact with psychiatry—which in its academic medical settings was then effectively dominated by Freudian thinking and its variants. The arrival of Alvin Scodel did bring a more positive exposition of psychodynamic concepts, but they remained generally on the edge of the main intellectual core of the clinical program.

In 1950 I met a fellow graduate student, Winifred Barbara Brown, then pursuing a demanding doctoral program in both clinical psychology and experimental psychology. From the outset she was, and has remained, my true companion and best friend. She provided for me an example of genuine and wide-ranging intellectual curiosity and personal and intellectual integrity. From Barbara I first learned the intricacies of Hullian learning theory as well as instruction in the habits and customs of American life, academic and otherwise. Our initial meeting at a department barn dance was followed by interactions in a testing course, in which the writer was required to simulate some syndrome of psychological handicap. From these and from evenings spent together studying and writing reports, our affections developed to the point at which we decided to marry in August 1952, at the beginning of the third year of graduate study, the time at which we were to enter internship. George Kelly, whose understanding of the constructs of others was not confined to theory, supported our applications for internship appointment at the Illinois Neuropsychiatric Institute in Chicago, where the department of psychology was directed by David Shakow. His support led to our acceptance together, and saw us, three days after the wedding, arriving in Chicago in a 1937 Chevrolet, hauling a rental trailer loaded with used furniture and books, accompanied by a Siamese cat and a mixture of enthusiasm and apprehension about the real world of clinical experience that lay just ahead.

David Shakow is undoubtedly one of the major figures in the history of clinical psychology in the United States. Born in 1901, Shakow had studied psychology at Harvard as an undergraduate. On graduation, financial need led him to obtain a position as a research assistant at the Worcester State Hospital in Massachusetts. Returning to Harvard as a graduate student in experimental psychology, he commenced work on a dissertation on subliminal perception under the supervision of E. G. Boring. The dissertation was unsuccessful, and Shakow returned to Worcester State

Hospital in 1928. Here he began a major series of experimental investigations in the psychopathology of schizophrenia, many of them centering on the role of reaction time as an index of attentional deficit in schizophrenic patients. He did receive his doctoral degree from Harvard after the war, this time submitting a dissertation on schizophrenia.

Shakow's presence at Worcester State created a setting in which young psychologists could obtain internship experience during the prewar years.[4] His own professional mixture of quantitative experimentation and his personal psychoanalysis provided an early example of the values expected of the scientist-practitioner. In 1946, Shakow moved from Worcester State to Chicago, taking up a professorial appointment at the College of Medicine of the University of Illinois, of which the Illinois Neuropsychiatric Institute formed a component unit.

When we arrived in 1952, Shakow had assembled a talented group of colleagues in his department. Ann Magaret, Alan Rosenwald, and Charles Wenar provided training and supervision for five interns. Shakow's own work included the analysis of a large quantity of reaction time data from his earlier investigations at Worcester State Hospital.[5] However, he had also begun preparations for an ambitious project—the study of psychoanalytic therapy via film recording of actual therapeutic sessions.[6] This project required that a room be set aside for therapeutic sessions, equipped with lighting adequate to movie making. Although the recording of sessions was to be done with the knowledge and consent of both therapist and client, Shakow judged it advisable to render the camera unobtrusive. Hence, the room had been decorated with wallpaper, the design of which contained many whorls somewhat reminiscent of camera lenses, and one of which was. Nothing definitive appears to have come out of this study or subsequent studies at NIMH. The massive quantity of data was recalcitrant to analysis, and no conclusions were reached.

Ironically, in 1952, portents of future difficulties for the psychoanalytic hegemony of psychiatry were already present in several guises. One took the form of the traveling representatives of pharmaceutical com-

---

[4]One of these was Julian Rotter, who warned us that Shakow would expect not only dedication to the work of the internship but a willingness to take part in occasional performances of the operettas of Gilbert and Sullivan in his home. The warning proved correct on both counts.

[5]Shakow depended heavily in this work on the statistical skills of his research assistant, Jean Paulsen. We were delighted to be able to attend her wedding to Loren Chapman during that year.

[6]Hilgard (1987) described Shakow's studies as involving the videotaping of therapy sessions. This may have been the case at the NIMH, but his Chicago study employed a movie camera, video cameras and recorders being entirely absent from the department of psychology at that time.

panies. They were to be found in the lobbies and corridors of the hospital, distributing samples of the new drugs reserpine and chlorpromazine. Psychology interns wore long white coats while on duty, and being thus indistinguishable from residents in psychiatry received unsolicited samples of various drugs from detail men who did not feel obliged to ask us to show medical credentials. The psychopharmacological revolution had begun, and these were its first heralds.

Even as David Shakow was preparing his room for the study of psychoanalytic therapy, the *Journal of Consulting Psychology* published the now famous article by Eysenck (1952) reporting that patients treated psychoanalytically fared worse than those treated supportively by general practitioners, who in turn fared less well than those not treated at all. Eysenck's article was flawed by many problems related to the noncomparability of the groups treated and other such matters. Nonetheless, one conclusion was indubitable: namely that psychotherapy, especially psychoanalytic psychotherapy, had been applied for many years with neither any real evidence that it was effective nor any recognition that such evidence was essential to justify it. The paper provoked vigorous controversy within the ranks of psychotherapists generally, although the self-assurance of the psychoanalysts at the Neuropsychiatric Institute was such that its implications were largely ignored when it first appeared.

If developments in pharmacology and in the analysis of the outcome of psychotherapy stirred few ripples in the Neuropsychiatric Institute, the third portent of the early 1950s attracted even less attention. This was the rapid growth of knowledge of the neurobiology of consciousness, knowledge that would effectively demolish the belief that the study of conscious and unconscious mental life required an exclusive reliance on verbal behavior and other introspective techniques of the kind that formed the stock-in-trade of psychotherapy.

Each of these three beginnings has had lasting effects on the scientific study of psychopathology and hence on contemporary clinical work. In 1952, they appeared as clouds no bigger than a person's hand. Instead, we had the task of mastering the art of psychological assessment of both inpatients and outpatients. Projective testing, the Rorschach, and Thematic Apperception Test (TAT) being the primary instruments used, and intelligence testing with emphasis on the clinical interpretation of signs of pathology in responses to the Wechsler-Bellevue Scale, together with writing reports on the basis of these tests, formed the main part of our days. Regular

seminars and journal meetings were interspersed with attendance at weekly staff meetings, these being conducted in the grand style.

Psychiatry at the Neuropsychiatric Institute was dominated by psychoanalysts, members for the most part of the Chicago Psychoanalytic Institute. The senior psychiatrists were all distinguished analysts; young psychiatrists in residency training were obliged de facto, if not de jure, to undergo a training analysis if they had hopes of a career in academic psychiatry later on. Franz Alexander, already famous for his psychoanalytic studies of psychosomatic disorders, was perhaps the leading light in this group of analysts, which included Roy Grinker, Beulah Bosselman, and Harold Solomon among others.

Wednesday staff meetings were attended by everyone. Residents, psychology interns, social work students, medical students, psychiatric nurses, and others filled an amphitheater looking down toward a central stage. Here sat the resident in charge of the case to be staffed, the psychology intern, and the social work student—in short the team responsible for assessing and treating the patient. In the front row sat the analytic professorate, the ultimate oracles in all professional and scientific matters. When the team members had finished their individual presentations, the audience listened to the opinions of the occupants of the front row. The consensus of opinion from that source determined the proper understanding of the case.

Experience of these meetings confirmed suspicions about the worth of the psychoanalytic enterprise conducted in this way. One staff meeting was spent discussing why a young female patient would be unlikely to leave the hospital in the near future due to some complicated intrapsychic factors. At the close of the meeting the resident remarked diffidently that the patient had already left the hospital to join her husband who had now found a job in another city; the meeting had been an exercise in futility, and the diagnosis was irrelevant to the factors that determined the patient's behavior. None of this disturbed the senior staff, who remained equally serene when asserting that sibling rivalry was the cause of disturbance in a patient who was an only child, and when providing a plausible psychodynamic account of a patient whose laboratory tests proved him to have brucellosis.

Here too, formal diagnosis was ignored except for statistical reporting purposes. It was necessary to assign some diagnostic label to each patient, and so the categories of the *Diagnostic and Statistical Manual of Mental Disorders* (DSM) were employed but had little role in the actual conceptualization of cases by the clinicians who applied them. Perhaps the most consistent diagnostic decision related to a dichotomy of organic versus nonorganic. Tests for organicity were crude. Electroencephalography was available but was prone to many false negatives and false positives; X-ray methods were even less informative; and clinical neurological examinations were of limited validity. Under these conditions, support for the diagnosis of organicity was sought from psychological tests such as the Goldstein-Scheerer series and the subscale analysis of the Wechsler-Bellevue Scale. These formed prominent parts of the neuropsychological battery, and we spent much time in mastering the principles of their interpretation.

Rotation through the pediatric clinic gave experience in rapid clinical assessment of intelligence in children, three or four such assessments per day being a normal load. A month's assignment to the Cook County Psychopathic Hospital across the street gave first-hand experience of the overcrowding, understaffing, and generally inadequate services that were the lot of so many psychiatric patients—a stark contrast with the comfortable conditions prevailing in the Neuropsychiatric Institute.

There was also some time for research. Ralph Gerard was then director of the research laboratories at the Institute, symbolically placed in the basement that lay beneath the separate towers that housed psychiatry and neurology. With his encouragement and material support, it was possible to conduct a study of frontal lobe function in rats—a study stimulated in part by the then-current unfortunate wave of interest in psychosurgical intervention in the frontal lobes of psychiatric patients. A study of the Lowenfeld's Mosaic productions of arteriosclerotic patients in another institution, conducted collaboratively with a fellow intern, Anthony Martin, was also completed during the year.

Psychosurgery was not practiced at the Institute during our time there, although much interest in it had been engendered by the Columbia Greystones (Mettler, 1949, 1952) study of the outcome of psychosurgery. Electroconvulsive therapy (ECT) was in use and was applied to a wider range of patients than the depressive patients to whom it is now administered. Other than being assigned to observe the application of ECT, we had no direct involvement in the assessment decisions that led to its use in individual cases.

All in all, the internship year left lasting impressions. One was the reinforcement of the belief that technical advances were necessary and would not come without new knowledge. Psychopathology was the obvious discipline within which new knowledge would be organized, and hence the clinical psychologist must become a psychopathologist. A second impression was that as a contributing discipline to psychopathology, psychoanalysis was scientifically bankrupt, and that its clinical rituals had little relevance to the woes of the kind of patients who found their way into the wards of the Institute.

The question of psychotherapy provoked a kind of ambivalence that took some time to resolve. Psychotherapy at the Institute meant psychoanalytically based forms of treatment. Behavior therapy and nondirective forms of therapy were not employed. It was clear that the status differential between psychiatrists and psychologists in the Institute centered on who was judged competent to perform psychotherapy. Superior status was not based on a greater knowledge of scientific psychology, for the psychologists were well ahead of the psychiatrists on that score. The scientific contributions of David Shakow are with us still, but he was of lower status in the Institute hierarchy than were any of the psychoanalysts, whose contributions have long since been forgotten.

Nor was it due to the presumed ability of medically trained psychiatrists to provide medical services to psychiatric patients, for the medical problems of patients at the Institute were always handled by consultant physicians from the appropriate branch of medicine, not by psychiatrists. Some of the most embarrassing failures to realize that an apparently psychological problem had a major neuropathological basis were attributable to the hubris of psychiatrists; the clinical psychologists were much too aware of their own ignorance to take any risks. Medical training as such clearly had little relevance to the daily activities of psychiatrists.[7]

All of this being the case, why was psychotherapy forbidden territory to the psychologist? Much of the reason had to do with the policies of the psychoanalytic institutes in the United States, and much had to do with the fear that nonmedical psychotherapy would be the beginning of a movement that, by demedicalizing treatment, would lead to the ultimate exclusion of

---

[7]Given the psychoanalytic emphasis of the Institute, it was ironic to discover that Freud had suggested that medical training was unnecessary to the practice of psychoanalysis. What the psychiatric residents did have, which many psychologists did not, was extensive clinical experience of the mentally ill, but this was something that could be easily equalized without any concessions to the relevance of medical training.

psychiatry from the ancillary benefits of membership in the medical profession. Ambivalence about all this arose from a paradox. The paradox was that while admission to the practice of psychotherapy promised to diminish status differentials that had no justifiable basis in differential competence, this fact itself was a reflection of a more disturbing fact: namely, that there was no reason in evidence to support the notion that anyone should be doing psychotherapy. It was not at all clear how one person could be a more competent therapist than another unless there were skills to be learned that had a demonstrable relationship to successful outcome. No evidence of this existed. Someone had once defined psychotherapy as an indescribable technique applied to indefinable problems followed by unknown outcomes, adding the ironic comment, "For this rigorous training is required!" Thus, to lobby for the reduction of status differentials by demanding the right to do something irrelevant seemed silly and intellectually demeaning.

There were, of course, other solutions to the problem. Problem-specific treatments based on the systematic application of empirically validated psychological principles were being developed by the behaviorists, but these were still known more by rumor than by published report. Mention of them around the Institute elicited dismissive assurances that the only possible result of such approaches would be symptom substitution and that for that reason they were probably rather unethical.

However, there were already developments in the search for independent status as mental health professionals. In 1946, psychologists had become eligible for state certification in Virginia, and in 1951 a state licensing law had been enacted by the state of Georgia. None of this affected Illinois or Ohio at this time. For most clinical psychologists the most available and significant postdoctoral certification was voluntary and was provided by the diploma of the American Board of Examiners in Professional Psychology. Large-scale licensing was yet to come. Our own first identification with organized scientific-professional psychology came with our student affiliate membership of the APA in 1952. It gave us great pride and a consequent depth of disappointment in later years as the scientific purposes of the Association were so overwhelmed by the guild functions that it would gradually assume.

1953 saw Barbara and me homeward bound for Columbus and the final year of graduate study, confirmed in our beliefs about the irrelevance of psychoanalysis and in the attractions and challenge of the scientific mission of psychology. Our dissertations were directed at problems of the disruptive effects of anxiety on cognitive functioning, mine on the interaction of induced anxiety and personality factors on flexibility in problem solving and hers on the effects of trait anxiety on interference in verbal learning and recall. Graduation in June 1954 and the coincident expiration of my student visa sent me back to Britain immediately, where I was scheduled to be interviewed for a position as psychologist in an unspecified government department. Barbara, now expecting our first child, remained in Columbus to finish data collection, joining me in England in the fall of the year. Having reversed the traditional epic of the emigrant who leaves his home country penniless and returns to buy a Rolls Royce, I had returned to England with even less money in hand than the few pounds with which I had embarked on the *Mauretania* four years before. There was a pressing need for a job. I was able to satisfy the Civil Service interviewers that I was eligible for appointment to a psychologist position, but as days turned into weeks nothing was forthcoming about where the job would be and when it would begin.

BRITAIN, 1954 TO 1955

In the meantime I was offered a post as clinical psychologist at the Graylingwell Hospital in Chichester at a salary of £450 per annum, this being a 1-year increment over the starting salary for newly appointed BA apprentices, the increment being granted in recognition of the year's internship. It was accompanied by the gloomy prophecy of a local real estate agent that we might find housing in the area if someone should happen to emigrate, as there was nothing otherwise available. Martin Roth was the senior psychiatrist at Graylingwell at that time, and the post might have been attractive were it not for the fact that living would be difficult and that the kind of independent research activity that the doctoral program had prepared me for would not be available in the British hospital system. Hurried inquiry of the Civil Service brought the message that I had been appointed psychologist to Her Majesty's Prison in Birmingham, with an immediate assignment to the prison in Wakefield, Yorkshire, for a period of orientation to the work. A night train from Chichester to Manchester, and then on to Wakefield, and I was at last on the job and no longer a student. Due to the complexities of government regulations, I was regarded as officially working away from my home post of Birmingham, and hence received a significant additional salary allowance for the purely hypothetical disruption of residence. It came at the right time.

Wakefield Prison was a dark, castellated fortress, blackened by the same industrial grime that disfigured Manchester and most cities of the industrial North of England. Its visual grimness was somewhat alleviated by the daily sight of groups of prisoners, unescorted by guards, knocking at the main gate to be let inside after a day's work off the premises. The prison was atypical in that its inmate population included prisoners who had unsuccessfully pled the McNaghten defense to murder, but whose nonetheless evident psychiatric disability had led the Home Secretary to recommend to the Queen that their death sentences be commuted to life imprisonment. Not being legally insane, they could not be sent to any of the Broadmoor institutions designed for that purpose, but were imprisoned in a "normal" prison as the law required. Other prisoners at Wakefield had committed crimes that had some diagnostic implications, such as incest, child sexual abuse, and the "crime" of homosexual behavior—the law on that matter not yet having been repealed. Yet others seemed to have been sent to Wakefield as what the chief medical officer called the "Black sheep syndrome"—namely, that they came from the kind of upper socioeconomic background whose members rarely serve prison time for breaches of the law. One of these was the atom spy Klaus Fuchs, then nearing the end of his sentence. A silent man, he mixed little with other prisoners, was taciturn in our interview, and departed promptly for East Germany when released.

Little in my clinical training had prepared me for this work. An initial expectation that most of my clients would prove to be actually innocent, to have entered a criminal life as the victims of social injustice, or to have committed their crimes for reasons that lay deep in their psychopathology was quickly disappointed. True, some warranted the diagnosis of psychopathy, but of the others some were weak men driven to a single crime by unbearable frustration, and others were callously evil in the banal way described by Hannah Arendt.[8] Yet others were professional burglars and car thieves for whom occasional imprisonment was an occupational hazard, much as limb fracture is to a movie stunt person. All this was new to me. It was necessary to improvise on my clinical training if I were to develop any framework for understanding what was before my eyes. This, however, never came to pass. In March 1955, a few months after arriving in Wakefield, a cable from

George Kelly inquired whether we could return to Ohio State immediately to replace a new young faculty member who had just been drafted.[9] And so, with our new baby daughter and our suitcases, we embarked on the aging Cunard liner *Samaria* at Southampton, rolled through a full gale off the coast of Nova Scotia, and arrived in New York just in time to begin the spring quarter at the university.

OHIO STATE, 1955 TO 1956

By 1955, the theoretical activities of both Julian Rotter and George Kelly had borne fruit in the form of major books. Rotter's *Social Learning and Clinical Psychology* was published in 1954 by Prentice-Hall. Kelly's two volumes, *The Psychology of Personal Constructs,* appeared in the following year, published by Norton. These works served as texts for the groups of students who worked with Rotter and Kelly respectively. Both books achieved for their authors greater visibility in clinical psychology as both, in different ways, offered systematic alternatives to the theoretical formulations then prevailing in clinical psychology. With the end of the academic year 1955 to 1956 my temporary appointment at Ohio State came to an end, and we left Columbus for the last time. I had received an appointment as Assistant Professor of Psychology at Northwestern University in Evanston, Illinois.

The years at Columbus had brought me into contact with a group of fellow students who were destined for later prominence: Rue Cromwell, Walter Mischel, and Lee Sechrest stand out, but there were many others both then and in the years that followed our departure.

NORTHWESTERN, 1956 TO 1958

Northwestern University in 1956 had a small but impressive department of psychology. Clinical psychology was staffed by Janet Taylor (later Janet Spence), Robert I. Watson, and myself, together with William Hunt, who was also department chairman. Other colleagues included Donald Campbell, Lester Clark, Carl Duncan, Donald Lewis, Benton Underwood, Leonard Diamond, and John Cotton. This was a collegial group, small enough to get together at coffee time each morning to discuss matters to do with psychology and science generally. Two topics came

---

[8]Hannah Arendt's well-known term for the psychological state of many of the people who operated the Nazi death camps.
[9]Jerome Kagan.

up repeatedly. One was the question of the epistemology of psychology and the related question of measurement. Campbell was the spark plug of these discussions, and our general interest in the matter led to lively colloquium presentations by visitors such Herman Feigl and Michael Scriven. MacCorquodale and Meehl (1948) had published their paper on the distinction between hypothetical constructs and intervening variables, and this distinction had provided an impetus for extensive examination of the philosophical bases of psychological science.

Our other discussions often centered on the importance of experimental psychopathology as the base of clinical psychology. Janet Taylor, then an assistant professor, was already a leading figure in that field, a visibility that had been initiated by her experimental work on anxiety and the development of the Taylor Manifest Anxiety Scale. Hull-Spence theory provided a framework for the study of psychopathological phenomena conceptualized as the product of drive (usually anxiety), the effects of reinforcement, generalization and extinction, and especially the interaction of the various kinds of inhibition (proactive, retroactive, and reactive). With this model in hand, the verbal behavior of schizophrenic patients was understandable as due to the interfering or facilitating effects of associations, the paired-associate learning task being the ideal vehicle for the investigation of this. Other schizophrenic anomalies lent themselves to interpretation as instances of an excessive range of stimulus generalization. Sarnoff Mednick had completed his doctoral dissertation at Northwestern on this topic.

Hullian influence was not confined to our studies of human behavior. Under the influence of the work of Neal Miller and his associates at Yale (e.g., Miller, 1948; Murray & Berkun, 1955), the employment of animal analogs to investigate the sequelae of conflict had become a significant element in our work. Beginning from the paradigmatic approach-avoidance conflict in rats, we looked at escape, displacement, the generalization of extinction (as therapy), and the like, together with the influence of early exposure to trauma (loud noise) on the adaptive capacity of the adult animal to produce these behaviors. The behaviors for which we sought animal analogues were drawn mainly from the catalog of psychoanalytic defense mechanisms and had evolved as a product of the famous seminar at Yale at which a synthesis of psychoanalysis and conditioning theory had been unsuccessfully attempted by Hull, Dollard, and others of their group. Although the immediate stimulus for the adoption of this strategy was the work at Yale, it is clear that the early work of Pavlov, and especially the

production of experimental neurosis by Shenger-Krestovnikovna, were the real historical antecedents.

Implicit in the ready transition from human to animal and back again was the assumption that similar mechanisms were involved in all vertebrate species. This, in turn, meant that we had accepted, tacitly or overtly, the centrality of psychobiological processes in psychopathology. With this came additional questions, such as the effectiveness of psychosurgery and of the new tranquilizers in modifying conflict-induced behavior in animals. Looking back at that period with the benefit of hindsight, I am struck by the readiness with which we accepted a view of the unity of science. We did not worry much about the problems of biological reductionism, nor about any assumed conflict between social ("psychological") explanations and biological explanations of abnormal behavior. The task was to solve some definable human problems with whatever concepts and techniques proved to be relevant.

Perhaps the most important advantage of the intellectual community in the department at Northwestern was an atmosphere in which it was taken for granted that we were all psychologists first, and clinicians, social psychologists, or experimental psychologists second. Furthermore, as psychologists we were assumed to have not only a commitment to scientific psychology, but to have an interest in the other sciences generally.

LOUISIANA STATE, 1958 TO 1960

In 1958 we moved to Louisiana State University where, now an associate professor, I was to be responsible for the direction of the psychological clinic and the doctoral program in clinical psychology. The university was engaged in a major effort to recruit new faculty and to expand its programs, and this was particularly evident in psychology. Louisiana provided our first exposure to real segregation, to the many bizarre policies that had arisen to prolong it and the equally strange subterfuges that had to be developed to circumvent it. New Orleans was the main island of an archipelago placed in the surrounding sea of Southern conservatism; Louisiana State University was another, although there was a long road to be traveled before it could reach the present state of affairs. Consulting and supervisory duties required that I travel throughout the region, from Shreveport in the north to Gulfport, Mississippi, in the south, and reminded me again, as at Wakefield, how little I knew about the life circumstances of most people, and how confined our psychology was to understanding the psychological workings of the minds of urban, middle-class, white adults.

In 1958, psychologists in Louisiana could be certified by a nonstatutory body. However, the state had recognized a need for trained psychologists when it inaugurated a program of fellowships for graduate students from anywhere in the country to study clinical psychology in any approved program in the country, provided that the fellow agreed to work in a mental health facility in Louisiana for a number of years after graduation. This program, together with the expansion of the faculty, brought a number of good students to the university. Several were to become leading figures in the direction of clinical psychology programs in the South, notably Henry Adams, Charles Noblin, and Roger McIntyre.

During this period several new developments were occurring at the national level. Behavior therapy was beginning to emerge as a force within clinical psychology. Wolpe's book, *Psychotherapy by Reciprocal Inhibition,* appeared in 1958, and Skinner had already described the possible uses of operant conditioning methods in the treatment of behavior deviations. My own research continued to explore the use of animal analogs. I saw nothing anomalous about my daily schedule, which typically included some hours in the animal laboratory followed by appointments with clients in the university clinic, together with teaching experimental psychopathology and psychological test interpretation. The hyphen in scientist-practitioner was a firm bond, and there was no good reason to try to pry it loose.

HARVARD, 1960 TO 1964

In the fall of 1960 we moved to Cambridge, Massachusetts where I had been appointed to a position as lecturer in the department of social relations. Robert White was the chairman, David McClelland directed the doctoral program in clinical psychology, and my immediate colleagues included Walter Mischel, Herbert Kelman, Irving Gottesman, Timothy Leary, and Richard Alpert. Our offices were located in a Victorian frame house at 5 Divinity Avenue, known as the Center for Research in Personality. It had once been the home of Walter Cannon, I was told. My own appointment was intended to provide a teaching replacement for Richard Solomon, who had recently moved to the University of Pennsylvania, leaving a gap in the provision of instruction in experimental and physiological psychology within the department. There were, of course, experimental and physiological psychologists in the department of psychology, but

at that time the separation between the departments of social relations and of psychology was sharp, and hence Solomon had acted as resident experimental psychologist for the former. Thus, my teaching assignments included Theories of Learning, Proseminar in General Psychology (cotaught with Irving Gottesman), as well as a course that I had developed entitled Somatic Bases of Behavior and Its Pathology. Personality assessment was taught by Walter Mischel, and clinical practica were mainly in the hands of Justin Weiss at the Massachusetts Mental Health Center, or at the Veterans Hospital on Longwood Avenue, under the direction of Donald Ramsdell. Gottesman provided expertise in the Minnesota specialties of genetics studied via the twin method and the use of the Minnesota Multiphasic Personality Inventory (MMPI) and actuarial assessment procedures generally.

Clinical psychology at Harvard had been shaped by the influence of Henry Murray. Murray defined himself as a personologist. He was interested in the study of personality in normal individuals, his approach being informed by the concepts of psychoanalytic psychology much modified by his own theoretical framework of needs and presses. The approach to understanding an individual was essentially hermeneutic, having in it the portents of contemporary psychobiography and owing as much to the influence of the humanities as it did to behavioral science.

Social relations had been created for several reasons. Some of these had to do with the abrasive nature of relations between certain senior faculty members in the original departments from which it drew its founding members, but much of it grew from intellectual aspirations for a kind of unified study of human beings at all levels from the anthropological on down to the individual personality. In this respect, the work of Murray and his colleagues formed an important level in the edifice.

Unfortunately, there were serious problems inherent in the entire plan. One major problem lay in the fact that were no analogous departments of social relations at other universities. Students graduating with the doctorate from socal relations went on to develop academic careers in traditional departments of psychology, sociology, or anthropology elsewhere. In turn, there were no major journals of social relations, no grants for research given under a social relations heading, and no learned society devoted to it. Publication, grant applications, and society memberships were all firmly anchored under the traditional departmental rubrics. Hence, the realities of the academic and scientific worlds encouraged both student and faculty member to retain a disciplinary identity.

This meant that, by 1960, the department of social relations had developed into a de facto federation of Balkan states, held together rather loosely by certain department-wide requirements, but with no strongly held commitment to a central theoretical framework. For those of us in it, the arrangement had certain advantages. Interaction with anthropologists and sociologists on various committees, including thesis committees, created an opportunity for joint collaboration in research to an extent not often found within single departments. In my case it led to joint research into aspects of juvenile delinquency with a group of investigators coordinated by Stanton Wheeler, including James Q. Wilson, then at MIT, Walter Miller, Irving Zola of Brandeis University, and many others (Wheeler, 1968). Another collaboration involved work with the newly developed General Inquirer computer program. With this program, Philip Stone and others provided the means to categorize and analyze large quantities of verbal material; this meant that the detailed study of language utterances by psychotic patients was now possible and marked for me the beginning of a research enterprise that has continued ever since.

Others who were in the department in the period beginning in 1947, its early years (e.g., Korchin, 1983), describe it as more interdisciplinary than it appeared 13 years later. Gordon Allport, one of the founders of the department, continued to express throughout his career both the hope and the expectation that the social relations idea would be taken up elsewhere. By 1960 it was clear that this was not going to happen. In 1972, the department dissolved into its constituent parts and the experiment was over.

For clinical psychology, the organization of the department presented special problems, most of which arose from the fact that the personological approach with its emphasis on normal individuals had diminished the attention given to real-world clinical problems. No senior faculty member in the program had had significant clinical experience in a psychiatric setting. The clinical training of graduate students was left to adjunct faculty members in the associated hospitals and clinics of Harvard Medical School. There were clinically experienced senior faculty members such as the psychiatrist John Spiegel in the department, but they played no part in clinical training.

In 1962, Robert White concluded his term of office as chairman of the department, being replaced by David McClelland. Since McClelland was no longer available to direct the clinical psychology training program, I was asked to undertake the responsibility and was appointed chairman of the Center for Research in Personality. When I came into that office, the field of clinical psychology was on the verge of major changes.

THE 1960s, ANTIPSYCHIATRY, AND PROFESSIONALISM IN CLINICAL PSYCHOLOGY

This period was one in which the rise of what came to be called the antipsychiatry movement began. Erving Goffman published *Asylums* in 1961. Thomas Szasz published *The Myth of Mental Illness* in the same year, and other works were to follow in short order. Contained in this movement was a central message: Mental illness does not exist, in the sense that those who receive psychiatric diagnoses are not biologically ill in the way that people who receive a diagnosis of cancer or tuberculosis are ill. Terms such as *illness, hospital,* and *therapy* arise from the medicalization of what are essentially deviations from social, ethical, or legal norms of behavior. These problems would, and should, be treated differently were they not defined medically. However, the initial deviations are exacerbated by hospitalization in large total institutions which produce behavior that is a reaction to the hospital milieu. Reactions thus produced seem bizarre when viewed against the norm of the behavior of nonhospitalized persons, and so the initial diagnosis is confirmed, although it is the treatment that has led to the new "symptoms" that now appear.

From these basic propositions, several conclusions followed. One was that the use of coercive or biological therapies for mental illness (restraints, ECT, psychosurgery) were fundamentally misconceived. They might even be thought of as constituting punishment for deviant behavior, albeit disguised as treatment. Psychotherapy and psychopharmacology were seen as merely another form of restraint, subtler by virtue of the fact that they place the restraints inside the patient rather than outside. Another conclusion was that psychiatric patients, particularly involuntary inpatients, were victims of deprivation of civil rights, whose plight was in need of a political solution on a par with those then being sought for ethnic minorities. Ethical more than scientific matters lay at the root of these criticisms.

Yet a further implication of all this was that psychiatry itself, no matter how well intentioned its practitioners, functioned as a repressive force. To the obvious question "What is being repressed, and why is it being repressed?" an answer was offered in its most explicit form by Ronald Laing (e.g., Laing, 1960). His answer was that psychosis, and especially schizophrenia, could best be understood as an inevitable consequence of the hypocrisies of family life in a capitalist society. Schizophrenic patients, he asserted, perceive the fundamental dishonesty of the social situation and are unable to enter into the self-deceptions that are necessary to adapt to it. Schizophrenics are therefore best understood as imprisoned dissenters from the prevailing dishonest ethos of their society. Just as the Soviet Union was using psychiatry to stifle dissent, so, according to the antipsychiatrists, did the Western world. Patients should be discharged from hospitals and readmitted, if at all, only voluntarily and briefly. Abuses abounded and were well documented by the antipsychiatrists. Reform was needed, but its nature was unclear, for the critics were at their best in pointing to problems, but less forthcoming about the solutions.

There were, of course, some answers to these complaints. Szasz's assertion that the major mental illnesses had no biological basis was premature and tantamount to the confirmation of the null hypothesis. None of the critics had spent much time looking into the history of the fate of the mentally ill before the establishment of the contemporary mental hospital to discover what their civil rights had been then. One little-noted response to the antipsychiatry movement was that it provided a convenient pretext for spending less money on the care of the mentally ill. From this perspective it could be seen as a refusal of the more affluent to contribute to the welfare of the poor.

At first, none of this had any discernible impact on the practical conduct of clinical psychology in the 1960s. However, it did reflect and contribute to a climate of opinion that was growing with the deepening involvement of the country in the undeclared Vietnam war. Established authority, many people now believed, was willing to override individual rights and to subvert democratic processes in the pursuit of its own goals. Appeals to patriotism, to communal duties, to obedience to the law, indeed to any conventional standard were seen as devices intended to keep people in order while those in power pursued their own immoral aims. Indeed, some concluded that if moral purposes were to be achieved by the individual, it would be by illegal actions such as the burning of draft records, the obstruction of research that had possible military applications, and the disruption of speeches by those who supported the establishment.

Some clinical psychologists concluded that the proper approach to mental health lay in preventive work in the social settings in which maladjustment developed. This view gave rise to the concept of community psychology. In 1963 Congress had enacted a bill (the Community Mental Health Centers Act) to establish a national network of community mental health centers. Two thousand of them were planned to be in place by 1975. This was in part an attempt to move the locus of treatment out of the hospitals and into neighborhood centers, but the implication was that the rationale for and types of treatment would remain unchanged. While this promised large-scale opportunities for the employment of psychologists, the continuance of traditional psychiatric approaches to mental health was a source of concern—hence, the movement for involvement in the community directly, via community psychology (e.g., Bennett et al., 1967).

For the most part, clinical psychologists in the 1960s were preoccupied with the need to secure professional independence from psychiatry. The act that had established the mental health centers had arisen from Congressional reports that also foresaw the introduction of a national health insurance system. This, in turn, meant that a crucial question would arise—namely, who would be entitled to direct reimbursement for the delivery of psychological services, psychologists in independent practice or psychologists working under medical supervision? Autonomous practice would require a legal definition of who was to be qualified to practice, and this meant that the motive to establish state licensing laws had become urgent.

As the opportunities for employment in clinical settings increased, there was an accompanying debate about the proper training for the clinical psychologist of the future. The debate turned on the necessity of the continuance of the scientist component of the scientist-practitioner model. Proponents of the abandonment of the model argued that research played little or no part in the responsibilities of psychologists in clinical settings and that the time spent in studying it could be better spent in getting more clinical experience. Those who recognized the necessity of research training in the curriculum for a Doctor of Philosophy degree proposed that a new degree be created, the Doctor of Psychology. Implicit in this latter suggestion was that there now existed a body of clinical techniques that were of proven effectiveness and that the mastery of them warranted the granting of a doctoral degree of some kind. In the discussions on the need for a separate degree, no significant data were presented relevant to this matter.

THE NEW THERAPIES: BEHAVIOR THERAPY AND HUMANISTIC THERAPY

The complex of influences that converged during the 1960s included not only antipsychiatry, antiestablishment attitudes, and pressures for professional autonomy. Equally prominent were the rise of the behavior therapies and the rise of the so-called humanistic therapies. Behavior modification had been applied to the training of the mentally retarded in the 1950s and was already in active use under the direction of Norman Ellis at the State Colony in Alexandria, Louisiana, during my own time at the University in Baton Rouge. However, the first event of note was the appearance of Wolpe's (1958) account of systematic desensitization, *Psychotherapy by Reciprocal Inhibition*. Although Dollard and Miller (1950) had attempted to formulate a learning theory translation of psychoanalytic concepts, it was no more than a translation and provided no significant new technique for the therapist. By the early 1960s, the operant conditioning approach had been applied to the modification of symptomatic behavior in chronic schizophrenic patients, with notable success.

At Harvard at that time there were no behavior therapists, and I was not to meet any until I moved to Wisconsin in 1964. However, James Holland of the department of psychology and I did give a joint graduate seminar in learning theory to students in that Department[10] and in this seminar Holland introduced us to the work of Allyon and his colleagues (Allyon & Houghton, 1962; Allyon & Michael, 1959).

Nor was there any specific exposure to the emerging range of new therapies, often referred to as humanistic. Serious discussion of the philosophical and methodological underpinnings of psychotherapy had been preempted by the unusual activities of my colleagues Timothy Leary and Richard Alpert. Space does not permit the full description of this period that it deserves; suffice it to say here that the notion of instant chemical access to insight and to ecstasy as opposed to the harder, longer grind required to master the profession and science of clinical psychology appealed to some students and repelled others. Leary and Alpert left the department of social relations at the end of the spring term 1963, Leary of his own accord[11] and Alpert by dismissal.

In my own case, the growing divide between the science and profession prompted me to start work on a textbook on psychopathology (Maher, 1966). From the beginning of my graduate studies I had been puzzled by the fact that textbooks on abnormal psychology, written by psychologists for psychology students, made no significant reference to psychological science. They were, by and large, watered-down expositions of Freudian psychoanalysis with a few case histories thrown in and a mandatory chapter on organic psychoses. On the other hand, the scientific journals devoted to abnormal psychology were amply supplied with articles describing experimental psychological and other quantitative investigations of patient samples. The Boulder model of training had not yet penetrated into the books that were to present the scientific material most central to our work.

WISCONSIN AND BRANDEIS, 1964 TO 1972

In August 1964 we moved to Madison, Wisconsin, where I had been appointed a professor of psychology. The department of psychology was strong in experimental and biological psychology; the roster of my colleagues included Wulf Brogden, David Grant, Harry Harlow, Fred Mote, and Michael Posner in experimental psychology, Leonard Berkowitz and Vernon Allen in social psychology, and Mavis Hetherington, Peter Lang, Barclay Martin, Albert Marston, and myself in clinical psychology. Carl Rogers had left Wisconsisn for the West Coast shortly before our arrival. It appeared that he had been unhappy with his move from Chicago to Wisconsin, feeling strongly that his students interested in clinical psychology, by

---

[10]Sometime after my arrival in Cambridge, Harvard had decided that the separation of psychology into two departments had adverse consequences for the curriculum, so I was one of four members of social relations then additionally appointed to the department of psychology as part of a plan to rectify this. Ironically my contribution to the department of psychology was to teach learning theories—a subject neglected in a department in which the operant paradigm dominated all alternative conceptions of the relationship of stimuli to responses. Thus in the process of teaching neo-Hullian ideas to the psychologists in Memorial Hall, I was first exposed to the literature of behavior modification, by an experimental psychologist. No such exposure occurred in the department of social relations.

[11]Most accounts of this episode state that Leary was fired by Harvard for his activities. In fact he simply left the campus, and his obligations, before the end of the spring term, 1963. He was granted leave without pay for the rest of the term, at which point his 5-year appointment as lecturer expired as scheduled.

which he meant the humanistic psychology of his own kind, were being faced with difficult and irrelevant requirements created by the experimental psychological culture of the Wisconsin department. Before departing he had communicated these concerns in a memorandum addressed to his colleagues, including myself still at Harvard.

There were concrete requirements in statistics and experimental design for all students, including clinical students. There was also a functioning psychological clinic in the department in which each clinical faculty member took responsibililty for the supervision of students. It was, in my judgment, a good example of the continuance of the Boulder model and intellectually congenial. However, Rogers's memorandum was another straw blowing in the wind, portending changes in clinical training at the national level. One year after our arrival in Madison, a conference was held in Chicago, the Conference on the Professional Preparation of Clinical Psychologists. I was invited to submit a position paper for the conferences and did so. It read, in part, as follows:

1. The most important functions of the clinical psychologist are in the areas known as behavior pathology, behavior deviation, etc. Derivative areas such as management counseling and motivational training are important in their own right; they are not central to the role of the clinical psychologist.
2. The basic purposes of the clinical psychologist are the prevention and cure of mental illness in both serious and minor forms.
3. Current psychological techniques of diagnosis and therapy are inadequate on two counts. First, the wealth of research evidence now available has cast grave doubts on their efficacy and validity; second, their application is too costly in manpower to support the belief that they may provide satisfactory solutions to the social evils of behavior pathology.
4. This technical inadequacy has generated two serious problems. One of these is the current state of low morale and doubt among clinical psychologists themselves. The other is the mounting pressure on the part of nonclinical psychologists to place clinical training in some other department or school, and to award some degree other than the Doctor of Philosophy on graduation.
5. Parallel problems exist in psychiatry where too early acceptance of psychoanalytic theory and therapy has produced a serious impasse . . . we must (therefore) attempt to expose the student to certain kinds of intellectual attitude. He should see his role as a potential innovator—not as a practitioner of existing techniques. He should be encouraged to develop an interest in problems, not methods . . . we should not be producing

experts in the Rorschach or any other single technique. We need Jonas Salks, not Dr. Kildares. (Maher, 1965, p. 53)

The outcome of the conference was an endorsement in principle of the Boulder model, but with an important modification. While the clinical psychology student should be exposed to a series of topics, including research, it was necessary only that the student master a subset of them. In effect, the research requirement was now reduced to simple exposure, not mastery.

At Wisconsin the clinical faculty were attracted to the possibilities of the behavior therapies. They were deduced from a clear theoretical base, were consistent with what we knew of general psychological principles, and seemed to have a much better cure rate than the competing psychotherapies. Peter Lang was a central figure in this work. Our joint interest led us to take part in forming Section III of Division 12, the clinical division of the APA, the purposes of the section being to support presentations in the areas of behavior therapy and experimental psychopathology at the annual meetings of the Association. At this point we remained convinced that the steady drift of clinical psychology from its base in behavioral science need not continue and that a return to first principles could be achieved within the framework of the Association.

Others, more prescient, were less sanguine. The foundation of Psychonomic Society had already taken place a few years earlier, a response by an increasing group of research psychologists to what was seen as the gradual erosion of scientific values from the APA and an accompanying shift toward the protection of the guild interests of the clinical psychologist.

Several of us also took part in a 2-day workshop on behavior therapy given for the Wisconsin Psychological Association. By coincidence, the hotel at which the workshop was given was also the site of the annual meeting of the Wisconsin Psychiatric Association. It was immediately agreed that members of either society could attend either set of meetings. Consequently, our workshop audience now included a substantial number of psychiatrists, mostly in private practice. As a presenting speaker at the workshop, I was struck by the visible enthusiasm of the psychiatrists for the possibilities inherent in behavior therapy, in contrast to the defensive hostility shown by some of the psychologist-psychotherapists in private practice. It was a reminder that individuals whose daily living comes from the application of a specific technique are unlikely to examine it critically and equally unlikely to be hospitable to competing alternatives.

Discussions within the department of psychology frequently turned to the question of the possible appointment of a new faculty member in clinical psychology with full-time responsibility for clinical supervision and clinical teaching, but whose salary increments and promotions would not require evidence of a solid research contribution. The idea was that such an individual would replace the expected investment of time in research with an additional investment of time in clinical supervision. A broad spectrum of the department members was supportive of this idea; the allegedly anticlinical experimental psychologists were sympathetic to the need to be flexible in managing a clinical facility within an academic department. I gather that such an appointment was tried out, but this was after I had left Wisconsin for Brandeis, and I was not on hand to observe the success of the plan. To me, however, it was plain that Rogers had underestimated the support that the Wisconsin department would give to a scientific clinical psychology and perhaps overestimated the support that his own brand of humanistic psychology could command.

In the fall of 1966, with the textbook now in print, we traveled to Copenhagen where I was to be a Special Fellow of the National Institutes of Health (NIH) appointed to the Institute of Clinical Psychology at the university there. Professor Lise Østergård was the senior faculty member in clinical psychology and had a long-standing interest in language and thought disorder in schizophrenia. Several American psychologists were active in Copenhagen at that time. Sarnoff Mednick and Fini Schulsinger were deeply involved in the early stages of their longitudinal study of children at high risk for schizophrenia. Melvin Zax was in Copenhagen on sabbatical leave from Rochester, as was Oscar Parsons from Oklahoma, my office mate at the Institute. It was a congenial and productive year; it established a lasting affection for Danes and things Danish and a basis for two subsequent visits in later years.

In addition to collecting language samples from Danish subjects, I completed a short book on research methods in psychopathology (Maher, 1970) and an article to an early issue of *Psychology Today,* then newly published. During my time in the department of psychology in Memorial Hall at Harvard, I had made the acquaintance of George Reynolds, then a junior faculty member. George, Nicholas Charney, and another colleague were at that point formulating the concept that led to the founding of *Psychology Today;* it was to be for the educated layperson interested in

psychology what the *American Scientist* is to the same kind of audience interested in the sciences generally. In its early years it managed to live up to that standard, although a major investment in elegant and creative color illustrations hinted at the possibility that concessions to popularity might someday outweigh faithfulness to science. Nonetheless, I was pleased with the article when it appeared until the discovery that the final rather flamboyant paragraphs had been added by a house editor.

While in Copenhagen I received an invitation to return to Massachusetts to take up a professorship at Brandeis. George Kelly had moved to Brandeis and was eager to establish a clinical program there in which the scientist-practitioner model would be maintained. Not long after accepting a formal offer from the university, I received from the department chairman Ricardo Morant a letter with the melancholy news that George had died. And so in the fall of 1967 we returned to New England to settle down in our present home after many years of academic and geographic moves, but without the much admired colleague whose presence in Brandeis had made the move attractive.

Brandeis was and is a small university. The department of psychology was therefore small in size and, of necessity, spread its faculty appointments across the range of specialties necessary to offer a satisfactory curriculum. At this time the dominant figure in the department was Abraham Maslow, then at the height of his career. His emphasis on the values of personal growth, and especially his concept of self-actualization, had wide appeal. By 1967 his reputation had placed him in the position of de facto leader of the humanistic psychology in the United States. Although the department did not have an APA approved program in clinical psychology, many of our graduate students had clinical interests. Courses and seminars, together with placements in clinical field settings, produced a small but steady stream of graduate students who went on to later positions of significance in clinical psychology and psychopathology. Douglas Whitman of Wayne State and Cathy Widom of Indiana provide obvious examples; the list could be expanded considerably with the names of Brandeis undergraduates who entered graduate clinical training programs elsewhere.

Other graduate students and some faculty were committed to the humanistic approach to psychology. The emphasis on the expression of personal feelings unconstrained by notions of tact, the rejection of personal privacy as a value in social life, and (as it has appeared to me) the essential narcissism of the personal growth movement made an uneasy fit with the requirements of scholarship and research in a PhD program. Something of the spirit of the time has remained encapsulated for me in an incident in which a graduate student came to object vehemently to the grade of D that I had given to his exceptionally shoddy and ill-written term paper. "I deserve an A," he said angrily, "I had an A quality experience writing that paper." "No doubt," I responded, "but I had a D experience reading it, and that is what counts." But my satisfaction at the reply was irrelevant in an atmosphere where standards of competence or mastery were seen as oppressive and where the primacy of personal experience was taken for granted.

In some areas of clinical psychology the spirit was evident in the tacit decision that the demand for objective evidence of the efficacy of psychotherapy could safely be ignored. The experiences in therapy sessions were what therapy was all about—not some later outcome that was supposed to arise as a result of the therapy. The challenges of the statisticians and the behavior therapists could be safely ignored so long as the clients kept coming. Clients, in turn, could move from therapy to therapy until they found one that was congenial. The number of therapies now on the national scene increased steadily, and new labels proliferated. Thus, the primal scream, rolfing, and Gestalt therapy took their places in a kind of psychological supermarket, with issues of efficacy simply ignored.

The antipsychiatry movement continued to develop through the end of the decade. One controversial contribution to it was a paper by Rosenhan (1973) reporting a study in which it was said that a number of normal volunteer subjects managed to get themselves admitted to psychiatric hospitals by presenting minimal symptoms of auditory hallucinations, followed by perfectly normal behavior on the ward. The report stated that only the other patients recognized the normal subjects as normal, the staff failing to do so. After this report was published a flurry of debate in the professional journals followed quickly. Unfortunately, most of the questions raised could only be answered by inspection of the actual data of the study, and these have not been made available by the author in the subsequent 20 years. That the paper was so often cited in later years is perhaps a tribute to the strength of feeling about psychiatric diagnosis rather than the impact of convincing data.

However, events on the academic scene nationally were beginning to preempt concern. The second half of the decade was marked by student protests, mostly about the worsening Vietnam war, but also about the

policies and practices of universities. So it was at Brandeis, and in the turmoil following the occupation of a building by minority students, that I was asked in 1969 to become dean of the graduate school. This was followed by appointment as dean of the faculty from 1971 to 1972. My personal involvement in clinical psychology diminished as a result of this, although I was able to maintain a continuing research effort in psychopathology. In 1972 I was invited to return to Harvard as professor, and thus entered my present position.

HARVARD, 1972 TO 1989

In 1972 the department of social relations had dissolved, and the department of psychology and social relations formed from the psychologists from the two separate departments. Sociologists had reestablished the department of sociology, and the social anthropologists had returned to join other anthropologists in their own department. The first chairman of the unified department of psychology was Gardner Lindzey, who had moved from the University of Texas at Austin to take over. Circumstances led him to leave Harvard as the first academic year was coming to a close, before the administrative task of making the paper unification of the department into an actual unity could properly be begun. Acting on the assumption that anyone who has been a dean should be able to administer a department, the president called on me to replace Lindzey as chairman, which I did in the spring of 1973.

By 1972, the formal doctoral program in clinical psychology was in the final stages of a phaseout. Not being present as a witness to the scene, my account of this is based on the reports of others. During the period from 1964 onward, the program had been permitted to run down in terms of faculty strength. In light of this, the university had agreed to appoint two new senior faculty members in clinical psychology, one to have a main emphasis on research and the other (to be appointed when the first was in place) to have a more clinical practical emphasis. Norman Garmezy was offered the first position and accepted it with the proviso that the program would be strengthened by one or more junior appointments. The department of social relations agreed to this condition—a necessary one if the program was to be restored to even minimal levels of strength. Apparently the first of the intended junior appointments was filled by a nonclinician at the instigation of the then chairman of the department, Garmezy not being consulted in the matter. Garmezy then resigned, naturally, and elected to stay at Minnesota. At this point the senior members of the department decided that the whole area of clinical psychology had become too problematic to be continued and began to dismantle it.

My own responsibilities as chairman were to create a unified department. They occupied much of my time. Coincident with my return to Harvard, I had accepted the editorship of the *Journal of Consulting and Clinical Psychology (JCCP)* for a 5-year period beginning in 1973.[12] This task, together with the chairmanship, meant that any serious effort at reestablishing clinical psychology in the new department would have to wait. There were enough potentially divisive matters within the department faculty without introducing an additional one.

In 1975 there began a steady decline in federal support for graduate training in psychology. As most doctoral programs were heavily dependent on this kind of support, the loss of stipends and associated expenses meant an inevitable reduction in the number of students. Coupled with this decline was a gradual tightening in the academic job market. In part a consequence of the completion of the expansion of universities that had taken place during the postwar period, it was exacerbated by an age distribution in the faculty skewed toward youth—with a consequent diminution of the percentage of retirements in the 1960s and onward. This has been the state of affairs up to the present time, although there are clear signs that matters will shortly improve.

While the number of entering graduate students in nonclinical psychology declined steadily, the total number of doctorates granted did not—the difference made up by the continuing rapid increase in production of PhD clinical psychologists. This increase antedated the 1970s, but the sharp increase in the ratio of clinical to nonclinical degrees did not begin until the mid-1970s. At Harvard, these events were reflected in a reduction of the entering class from 30 or more in 1972, to 12 to 14 at the present time. An inevitable consequence of the shortage of academic positions was that more and more doctoral graduates sought employment outside the academic and research fields, and that those already in nontenure academic positions were under greater pressure to obtain tenure.

This latter factor led to a steady increase in the submission of manuscripts to the *JCCP*. Between the years 1969 and 1972, submissions had declined slightly, from 708 to 624, a reduction of 11%. By 1977, total submissions had increased to 938, an increase of fractionally over 50%. Rejection rates stayed essentially steady at 80%, the overwhelmingly common reason for rejection being major methodological errors in the research reported. From the Editor's Annual Report for 1976, I quote the following paragraph:

> A reading of many manuscripts and all of the reviews strongly suggests that recent entrants into the field of clinical psychology are poorly educated in research design and statistics. Gaffes of a kind that were relatively rare in submitted articles in the late 1960s are now common and, more disturbing, correspondence with aggrieved authors suggests that many contributors are unaware of many of the most common criteria for validity, reliability, sampling, controls, etc. (p. 4)

In response to this problem we published a special methodological edition of the journal in 1978, which appears to have been widely used as a text. However, the proliferation of PsyD programs in free-standing professional schools and the reduced requirements for research training in many PhD programs constitute a tide against which no adequate dam could be erected, and there are no current signs of improvement in the general level of scientific sophistication in newly trained clinical psychologists in all but a few graduate programs.

By 1977, the department began serious consideration of the reestablishment of clinical psychology. What we had in mind was the scientist-practitioner model. As we looked into the requirements for APA accreditation, it became clear to us that the kinds of accommodation in our curriculum that would have to be made to meet these requirements could seriously compromise the intellectual adequacy of our doctoral standards. Matters had changed in the field of clinical psychology. Already more than half of the newly graduated clinical psychologists in the country were entering private practice as a main career activity. The APA itself no longer appeared to serve our scientific interests, and many of us were discussing the need for reorganization of the Association if we were to remain in it.

For me the decision to withdraw from the Association was finally determined by its purchase of *Psy-*

---

[12]Due to the untimely death of my editorial predecessor, Jules Holzberg, before the end of his term, I had accepted responsibility for the remainder of that period, beginning the editorial office in 1972.

chology Today.[13] Catering to a perceived public need for sensationalized psychology, its ownership by the APA demeaned the image of a learned and professional society. At the time of purchase, the Association expressed the intention of improving the scientific quality and integrity of the articles. Unfortunately, this intention was futile when pitted against the hard fact that the necessity to publish between 80 and 100 such articles a year inevitably means that quality cannot be maintained. Psychology does not produce annually a sufficient number of new findings of general public interest to support this requirement. Instead, there was a continuing financial need to publish whatever was available—a concession to commercial aspects of psychology that was also evident in other areas of clinical psychology.[14] I withdrew sadly. My membership in 1952 had been a matter of some pride, and my disappointment correspondingly deep.

MARKET ASPECTS OF CLINICAL PSYCHOLOGY

With the increased emphasis on private practice, clinical psychology in the late 1970s moved toward a conscious attempt to market mental health. Some of this took the form of a growing literature in the psychological journals on the ways in which psychological services might be promoted. By the 1980s new journals had been formed devoted exclusively to the market interests of private practitioners. As a holder of a Massachusetts license, I found myself on the mailing lists of various derivative commercial enterprises devoted to the marketing of psychological services, or of services to psychologists designed to improve their marketing. Into my mail came letters such as the following: "Dear fellow professional: If your practice isn't where you would like it to be, now you can learn of a unique and exciting opportunity. My very first effort grossed $4800 working 1½ hours weekly for 16 weeks. That's $200 per hour." Yet another brochure offered me the opportunity to buy a franchise to provide an unspecified treatment for cocaine abusers, the cost of the franchise being based on the known

average income level of the territory to be assigned. In case I did not understand the commercial advantages of franchising, the brochure included a simple account of the operation of McDonald's fast food service.

While the marketing of psychological services provided one way in which the practitioner could hope to increase income, the main source of payment for therapeutic services has been the payments provided by health insurance carriers.

Health Insurance

Most histories of clinical psychology attach importance to the resolution of the issue of the entitlement of psychologists to receive independent reimbursement for the provision of psychological services covered by health insurance systems. The major event in this history was the success of the Virginia Psychological Association in its court action to require the Blue Cross–Blue Shield organization to include clinical psychologists in its reimbursement policies when they are acting as independent health providers. The public argument of clinical psychologists was not that it opened the door to a significant source of income, but that it gave the client freedom to choose the mental health professional he or she preferred, and that the existence of licensing laws for psychologists meant that quality was assured.

Politically, this suit arrayed clinical psychologists against psychiatrists, who had been the only mental health professionals to receive insurance reimbursement as independent practitioners. However, the argument that by excluding psychologists from independent practice psychiatrists were acting in ways that limited competition was a double-edged sword. For example, in 1982, a new Florida licensing law was about to be enacted to replace a previous law that had expired in 1979. The APA, the Florida Psychological Association, and others lobbied extensively for passage of the new law. They were then sued by other mental health professionals (including social workers and other counselors) for having lobbied for a law that would reduce competition. The suit failed, but the implications were clear enough—namely, that the

---

[13]I was particularly disaffected by this action. Some years earlier, during my editorship of *JCCP*, the Association had distributed to a large sample of the membership a first issue of a proposed competing magazine to be produced by the APA. I received a copy. With the copy came a request for a vote on whether or not the Association should go ahead with the proposed magazine. The membership did not support the idea, and so it was dropped. Hence the decision to purchase *Psychology Today* seems to me to have been a clear rejection of what was known of membership sentiment on such matters.

[14]Public taste must have been underestimated, as the enterprise appears to have lost significant sums of money for the Association.

argument that competition must be opened up may be extended indefinitely to cover many other professional groups. Exclusion of these groups can only be justified if it can be shown empirically that their services are less effective, or their professional behavior less ethical than is the case with psychologists and psychiatrists. This has yet to be shown reliably.

At the time of writing, the policy of reimbursement of psychologists in independent practice has been extended widely. A more controversial issue, and one in which I was to become involved directly in a minor way, is the issue of mandatory coverage of outpatient psychotherapy in health insurance coverage. While the details vary somewhat from place to place, the mandatory provision in Massachusetts law then required all health insurance carriers to include at least $500 of coverage annually for outpatient psychotherapy. This provision, of course, does not specify who shall provide the psychotherapy, and hence psychiatrists and psychologists alike stand to benefit from the increased pool of dollars now set aside for their services. Before passage of the relevant act, coverage of outpatient psychotherapy was an option, chosen by the policyholder and, like all insurance options, subject to an increased annual premium.

In response to an article by McGuire (1981) I wrote a critical analysis of the whole concept of mandatory insurance coverage of psychotherapy (Maher, 1982). The core of the criticism is that unlike medical illnesses, the need for psychotherapy is determined mainly by the client; there is no independent laboratory test to determine the reality of the client's need (as there is in the case of tuberculosis, for example) and no assessor to decide that an insurable loss has actually occurred, as there is in the case of fire insurance. In brief, the fundamental requirement of insurance that the determination of need not be left in the hands of the policyholder is absent in the case of psychotherapy. While strongly in favor of the existence of voluntary optional add-ons of coverage for psychotherapy, I was, and am, opposed to mandatory coverage; it has seemed ironic that as clinical psychologists our insistence that insured persons should be free to choose between psychiatrists and psychologists has not been extended as logic requires to include the choice not to have coverage for psychotherapy at all.

There is no need to go into the details of the argument here; clinical psychologists of good will may have genuinely differing opinions on the merits of the matter. What was of more interest was the response that the article provoked. One letter writer (Reed, 1982) voiced his objections to the article. His letter ended as follows: "Such counterproductive, ruminative and misleading material is not appropriate for a journal representing an organization of professional and politically active clinical psychologists. Another such article and my council votes and those of a number of my associates will be applied to another division" (p. 17). Apart from the unusual notion that dissenting voices should not be heard in a professional journal, the writer had expressed his own right to discontinue his support for something that he did not wish to support—but that this right was to be denied to those consumers who did not wish to support the costs of psychotherapy.

It was clear that clinical psychology had evolved in a direction of which Albee (1970) had warned:

> The truly crippling sources of cognitive dissonance in the professional psychologist . . . are the fundamental differences between the scientist and the professional. . . . Science is open, and its knowledge is public. . . . Incisive mutual and self-criticism, replication, debate and argument over procedures . . . is ever present. In sharp contrast a profession must jealously guard its secrets. . . . Secrecy and mystery are essential. (pp. 1074–1075)

That the professional interests had now come to outweigh the scientific aspects of clinical psychology is evidenced by certain simple statistics, some of which are as follows:

1. In 1968 there was one professional PsyD program (at the University of Illinois); in 1982 there were 24 (McNett, 1982).
2. In 1968, 41.8% of all new PhDs awarded in psychology were in clinical psychology; in 1982 the percentage had risen to 52.6%.
3. In 1972 the percentage of all doctorate holders in the clinical behavioral sciences[15] who described themselves as self-employed was 11.9; in 1981 the comparable percentage had more than doubled to 26, while the absolute numbers had risen from 1,251 to 6,196 (Institute of Medicine, 1983).

---

[15]These figures are taken from the 1983 *Report of the Institute of Medicine, Personnel Needs and Training for Biomedical and Behavioral Research*. Clinical behavioral science in this report includes school psychology, counseling, and guidance as well as clinical psychology. Clinical psychologists form the large bulk of these numbers; the numbers do not include PsyD graduates, and hence the true numbers of private practitioners in 1981 are likely to have been much higher.

4. The research activities of clinical psychologists were surveyed in 1974 by Garfield and Kurtz (1974) and in 1981 by Norcross and Prochaska (1982). During the 8-year period between these surveys, certain trends were evident. The increasing opportunities for women in clinical psychology are indicated by an increase in the percentage from 16 to 21. The percentage of time reportedly spent in doing psychotherapy rose from 31 to 35, while the percentage of time reportedly spent in research remained low at a little over 7. Of this time, only 38% was spent on actually conducting research—the rest being described as "supervising research" or "scholarly writing." Thus, the percentage of working time actually spent in the conduct of research by clinical psychologists was 3, or roughly an hour and a half per the 48 hours that most reported as their normal working week. Clinical psychology as a field has continued to attract increasing proportions of women graduate students. In 1988 the number of doctorates awarded in all fields of psychology showed a ratio of 1,675/1,383 for women to men. The percentage increase has been greatest in clinical (46.4), counseling (183.7), and business (253.3).[16]

CLINICAL PSYCHOLOGY IN THE NEAR FUTURE

Because professional interests have come to predominate in the activities and policies of the APA, many of those members dedicated to the values of science and teaching reluctantly concluded that reform within the Association was impossible and that the time had come to form a new organization which would take up the functions that had been so eroded within the APA. Thus, the American Psychological Society (APS) came into being, with a first annual conference in 1988 and an initial membership of several thousand. Some clinical and other psychologists with serious research interests in behavior pathology formed the society for Research in Psychopathology as a forum for the presentation and discussion of scientific contributions to psychopathology. The first annual conference of this organization was held at Harvard in 1986, the fourth (1989) meeting being held at the University of Miami. At the time of this writing a new organization, the American Association of Applied and Preventive Psychology, is in the process

of formation intended to support and preserve the original purposes of the field of clinical psychology.

For the time being at least, it seems clear that the scientific interests of the clinical psychologist are likely to be focused in the main in organizations outside the APA. Indeed, the proliferation of specialized societies for various subdisciplines of psychology in general has increased steadily in recent decades and appears to reflect the perception of scientific psychologists that their interests will best be served outside the APA. The interests of the practitioner seem to be solidly established within the APA.

With regard to the practice of psychotherapy, it is possible that economic forces will reduce the number of psychiatrists involved in this, leaving it largely to clinical psychologists and an array of other mental health professionals. Economic forces include the increased competition for what is not a bottomless fund of potential client payments, but more to the point, the fact that psychotherapy is hourly paid. As medical financial policies are such that payment for a procedure is the norm (a simple appendectomy generally costing a certain amount regardless of the time taken to do it), the economics of psychiatric practice provide a disincentive toward hourly payment and a positive incentive to the use of procedures such as the prescription of medication. As psychiatry moves increasingly toward a biological approach to psychopathology, this trend is supported by its effect in bringing psychiatry closer to its medical heritage and further from the psychosocial influences that were predominant in the 1930s to 1960s. Recent advances in biobehavioral measurement, exemplified by the development of brain scan methods, and the rapid expansion of neuropsychology testify to the emphases that we may expect to see in the immediate future.

The events covered in this personal history of clinical psychology have not altered the fact that there are many human beings with serious psychological problems and that their effective treatment still awaits the accumulation of greater knowledge. To gain that knowledge requires a continued and arduous effort, and the task remains as one of the most important to face the clinical psychologist.

REFERENCES

Albee, G. W. (1970). The uncertain future of clinical psychology. *The American Psychologist, 25,* 1071–1080.

---

[16]Figures from the National Science Foundation, as reported in the *APS Observer,* 1989, 2, p. 7.

Allyon, T., & Houghton, E. (1962). Control of the behavior of schizophrenic patients by food. *Journal of the Experimental Analysis of Behavior, 5*, 343–352.

Allyon, T., & Michael, J. (1959). The psychiatric nurse as a behavioral engineer. *Journal of the Experimental Analysis of Behavior, 2*, 323–336.

Bennett, C. C., Anderson, L. S., Cooper, S., Hassol, L., Klein, D. L., & Rosenblum, G. (Eds.). (1967). *Community psychology*. Boston: Boston University Press.

Dollard, J., & Miller, N. E. (1950). *Personality and psychotherapy*. New York: McGraw-Hill.

Eysenck, H. J. (1952). The effects of psychotherapy: An evaluation. *Journal of Consulting Psychology, 16*, 319–324.

Garfield, S. L., & Kurtz, R. M. (1974). A survey of clinical psychologists: Characteristics, activities and orientations. *The Clinical Psychologist, 28* (1), 7–10.

Goffman, E. (1961). *Asylums*. New York: Anchor-Doubleday.

Hilgard, E. R. (1987). *Psychology in America: A historical survey*. San Diego, CA: Harcourt Brace Jovanovich.

Institute of Medicine. (1983). *Personnel needs and training for biomedical and behavioral research*. Washington, DC: National Academy Press.

Kendall, P. C., & Norton-Ford, J. D. (1982). *Clinical psychology: Scientific and professional dimensions*. New York: John Wiley & Sons.

Kirsch, I., & Winter, C. (1983). A history of clinical psychology. In C. E. Walker (Ed.), *The handbook of clinical psychology: Theory, research and practice* (Vol. 1, pp. 3–30). Homewood, IL: Dow-Jones Irwin.

Korchin, S. J. (1983). The history of clinical psychology: A personal view. In M. Hersen, A. E. Kazdin, & A. S. Bellack (Eds.), *The clinical psychology handbook* (pp. 5–19). Elmsford, NY: Pergamon Press.

Laing, R. D. (1960). *The divided self*. London: Tavistock.

MacCorquodale, K., & Meehl, P. E. (1948). On the distinction between hypothetical constructs and intervening variables. *Psychological Review, 85*, 99–107.

Maher, B. A. (1965). The clinician as a research-psychopathologist. *Preconference materials: Conference on professional preparaton of clinical psychologists*. Washington, DC: American Psychological Association.

Maher, B. A. (1966). *Principles of psychopathology: An experimental approach*. New York: McGraw-Hill.

Maher, B. A. (1970). *Introduction to research in psychopathology*. New York: McGraw-Hill.

Maher, B. A. (1976). *Journal of Clinical and Consulting Psychology*, Editor's Annual Report to the American Psychological Association. Unpublished document.

Maher, B. A. (1982). Mandatory insurance coverage for psychotherapy: A tax on the subscriber and a subsidy to the practitioner. *The Clinical Psychologist, 35* (2), 9–12.

Maher, B. A. (1988). Abnormal and clinical psychology. In E. R. Hilgard (Ed.), *Fifty years of psychology: Essays in honor of Floyd Ruch* (pp. 153–168). Glenview, IL: Scott Foresman.

Maher, B. A., & Maher, W. B. (1979). Psychopathology. In E. Hearst (Ed.), *The first century of experimental psychology* (pp. 561–621). Hillsdale, NJ: Lawrence Erlbaum Associates.

Maher, B. A., & Maher, W. B. (1985). Psychopathology: II. From the eighteenth century to modern times. In G. A. Kimble & K. Schlesinger (Eds.), *Topics in the history of psychology* (pp. 295–329). Hillsdale, NJ: Lawrence Erlbaum Associates.

Maher, W. B., & Maher, B. A. (1985). Psychopathology: I. From ancient times to the eighteenth century. In G. A. Kimble & K. Schlesinger (Eds.), *Topics in the history of psychology* (pp. 251–294). Hillsdale, NJ: Lawrence Erlbaum Associates.

Matarazzo, J. D. (1985). Psychotherapy. In G. A. Kimble & K. Schlesinger (Eds.), *Topics in the history of psychology* (pp. 219–250). Hillsdale, NJ: Lawrence Erlbaum Associates.

McGuire, T. C. (1981). Compulsory insurance for psychotherapy. *The Clinical Psychologist, 34*, 13–14.

McNett, I. (1982). Psy.D. fills the demand for practitioners. *APA Monitor, 13*, 10–11.

Mettler, F. A. (Ed.). (1949). *Selective partial ablation of the frontal cortex*. New York: Hoeber-Harper.

Mettler, F. A. (Ed.). (1952). *Psychosurgical problems*. New York: Blakiston.

Miller, N. E. (1948). Theory and experiment relating psychoanalytic displacement to stimulus response generalization. *Journal of Abnormal and Social Psychology, 43*, 155–178.

Murray, E. J., & Berkun, M. M. (1955). Displacement as a function of conflict. *Journal of Abnormal and Social Psychology, 51*, 47–56.

Norcross, J. C., & Prochaska, J. O. (1982). A national survey of clinical psychologists: Characteristics and activities. *The Clinical Psychologist, 35* (2), 1–8.

Reed, M. R. (1982). Letter to the editor. *The Clinical Psychologist, 36*, 16–17.

Rosenhan, D. L. (1973). On being sane in insane places. *Science, 179*, 250–258.

Szasz, T. (1961). *The myth of mental illness*. New York: Hoeber-Harper.

Wheeler, S. (1968). *Controlling delinquents*. New York: John Wiley & Sons.

Wolpe, J. (1958). *Psychotherapy by reciprocal inhibition*. Palo Alto: Stanford University Press.

CHAPTER 2

THEORETICAL FOUNDATIONS OF CLINICAL PSYCHOLOGY

Irving B. Weiner

Contemporary thinking and practice in clinical psychology have mainly been shaped by three lines of theory: psychoanalytic theory, learning theory, and humanistic theory. As elaborated in Part II of this handbook, each of these frames of reference includes diverse schools of thought and shades of emphasis; in fact, groups of psychoanalytic, learning, and humanistic theorists sometimes differ as much among themselves as from each other (Ewen, 1988; Eysenck & Martin, 1987; Hall & Lindzey, 1978; Munroe, 1955; Shaffer, 1978; Wilson & Franks, 1982; Wyss, 1973). These broad lines of theory have nevertheless fostered three distinctive approaches to the conceptualization, assessment, and amelioration of abnormal behavior. Psychoanalytic theories have generated various *dynamic* approaches in clinical practice and research; learning theories have provided the basis for numerous *behavioral* approaches; and humanistic theories have given rise to several *experiential* approaches.

This chapter summarizes the basic postulates of these three approaches, identifies their distinctive emphases, and comments on their abiding influences on clinical psychology. The discussion then turns to some lines of convergence among these approaches, especially in relation to threads of cognitive emphasis, and describes alternative ways in which clinicians have attempted to accommodate such communalities. Ecumenical revisions in the major theories that undergird clinical psychology have increased lines of convergence among approaches since the first edition of this handbook, and the chapter concludes by addressing the implications of these developments for the emergence of eclectic clinical perspectives and a growing literature written from an integrationist point of view.

DYNAMIC APPROACHES

Dynamic approaches in clinical psychology derive from the belief that human behavior is determined by the interplay of psychological forces. As formulated by Freud (1923/1961, 1926/1959, 1933/1964b) in his structural model of personality functioning, these forces include (a) basic needs, wishes, and impulses, many of which lie outside of conscious awareness (*id*); (b) capacities for thinking, feeling, and acting in ways that express or gratify needs, wishes, and impulses (*ego*); (c) a sense of propriety or conscience concerning whether particular needs, wishes, and impulses should be expressed or gratified (*superego*);

and (d) the opportunities for self-expression or gratification that exist in the external environment (*reality*).

From the dynamic perspective, the balance that is struck among the frequently contradictory demands and constraints of id, ego, superego, and reality shapes an individual's personality style and preferred action patterns. Failure or inability to resolve conflicts among these four agencies generates anxiety, which is a painful affect that people seek to reduce or eliminate. Maladaptive efforts to minimize anxiety produce various forms of psychopathology, which are regarded as inadequate or immature defensive reactions to distress stemming from unresolved psychological conflicts (Cameron, 1963; Fenichel, 1945; Holzman, 1970).

Dynamic formulations of psychopathology lead to an emphasis in personality assessment on two questions. First, with respect to personality dynamics, what are the conflicting thoughts and feelings that are causing an individual to experience anxiety? Second, with respect to personality structure, what are the preferred coping styles that account for why the individual is dealing with his or her anxiety in certain adaptive or maladaptive ways (Allison, Blatt, & Zimet, 1988; Pope, 1979; Rapaport, Gill, & Schafer, 1968; Spitzer & Endicott, 1973; Weiner, 1966; Wiens, 1983)?

In treatment, dynamic approaches seek to help people gain increased understanding of why they are anxious and how they are coping ineffectively with their anxiety. Interpretations are used to expand patient awareness of underlying concerns and maladaptive response styles. This expanded awareness allows troubled people to reflect more rationally than before on their unresolved conflicts and to opt for more effective coping behaviors (Chessick, 1974; Dewald, 1971; Greenson, 1967; Langs, 1973; Menninger & Holzman, 1973; Weiner, 1975).

Distinctive Emphases

Dynamic approaches to assessment and treatment involve three distinctive emphases. First, dynamic approaches are based on *inferred processes*. Behavior is explained in terms of underlying aspects of personality structure and dynamics that are considered to account for it. The answer to why a disturbed person displays a particular symptom, gives a particular test response, or shows a particular reaction in psychotherapy is to be found in personality characteristics that exist independently of whatever behavior is being manifest.

Second, dynamic approaches stress *intellectual processes* as the highest order of human functioning. Psychoanalytic formulations address the part that inappropriate, excessive, or ambivalent affects play in psychological maladjustment. In the end, however, progress in traditional dynamic psychotherapy depends on the patient's being able to gain understanding and impose reason on emotion. Only when reason prevails can people manage stress effectively and find satisfaction in their work and interpersonal relationships. Freud (1933/1964b) expressed the importance of mastering the irrational by saying, "Where id was, there shall ego be" (p. 80).

Third, dynamic approaches emphasize *historical processes*. Psychological difficulties are believed to originate in stressful developmental experiences that leave a residue of unresolved conflicts and maladaptive coping styles. Assessment and therapy in this framework are exploratory efforts to unearth the nature of such past experiences, to allow them to be reexperienced or reevaluated in the critical light of current perspectives. The following illustrative interpretation captures these emphases in the dynamic approach on inferred, intellectual, and historical approaches in the dynamic approach: "From what we have learned about you, we can see that now, as an adult with children of your own, you still tend to respond to women as you did to your mother when you were a child."

Abiding Influences

The abiding influences of dynamic approaches in clinical psychology are closely entwined with the historical influence of the psychoanalytic movement. As elaborated by Shakow and Rapaport (1964), Freud's formulations have left their stamp on virtually all of psychology, and especially on the areas of abnormal, developmental, personality, and social psychology. Probably most significant in each of these areas is the lasting impact of Freud's insistence that all behavior—no matter how strange, irrational, self-defeating, or seemingly incomprehensible—can be understood in psychological terms.

Some of Freud's proposals have stood the test of time and validation better than others (Fisher & Greenberg, 1977; Masling, 1983, 1986). Substantial revisions of his notions have been promulgated even by theorists committed to a traditional psychoanalytic point of view, especially ego-analytic clinicians who have placed less emphasis than Freud on instinctual determinants of the human condition and more emphasis on coping capacities and styles of adapting to environmental influence (Erikson, 1950; A. Freud,

1936/1946; Hartmann, 1939/1958; Rapaport, 1967). Nevertheless, any of Freud's early works—including a chapter on psychotherapy he wrote for *Studies on Hysteria* (Breuer & Freud, 1893–1895/1955), his *Psychopathology of Everyday Life,* (1901/1960), and *The Interpretation of Dreams* (1900/1953a)—remain as influential today as they were originally in establishing the following: (a) that potentially understandable psychological factors determine human behavior, and (b) that this psychological determination provides avenues for alleviating emotional disorder through psychological interventions.

BEHAVIORAL APPROACHES

Behavioral approaches in clinical psychology are based on the conviction that all behavior, normal and abnormal, is learned. Various patterns of psychopathology result when people learn maladaptive ways of coping with their experience, and poor psychological adjustment accordingly consists of bad habits (Eysenck, 1959; Kanfer & Phillips, 1970; Wolpe, 1958; Yates, 1970). In this frame of reference the manifest symptoms of psychological disorder constitute the disorder and their removal constitutes its cure: "There is no neurosis underlying the symptom, but merely the symptom itself. Get rid of the symptom . . . and you have eliminated the neurosis" (Eysenck & Rachman, 1965, p. 10).

Whereas dynamic approaches to assessment seek to account for why people behave as they do, assessment from the behavioral perspective focuses on how people actually behave in particular situations or in response to various reinforcement contingencies. Assessment data are derived as much as possible from observations of behavior in natural settings, with special attention to antecedent and consequent events that elicit and sustain overt response patterns. When naturalistic observations cannot be made and assessment situations must be contrived, every effort is made to use methods that will yield a representative sample of what the actual behavior would be (Barlow, 1981; Bellack & Hersen, 1988; Ciminero, Calhoun, & Adams, 1986; Goldfried, 1983; Mash & Terdal, 1988; Nelson & Hayes, 1986).

The central treatment strategy in behavioral approaches consists of exposing people to new learning situations that will modify their maladaptive response patterns. The therapist's task is to implement reinforcement contingencies that will inhibit pathological habits and expand a person's repertoire of adaptive coping patterns—sometimes through pairing pleasant experience with previously painful situations (systematic desensitization), sometimes through pairing painful experience with undesirable behavior (aversion therapy), sometimes through fostering and rewarding specific types of constructive action patterns (operant conditioning), and sometimes through education in more effective ways of dealing with experience (modeling). If the therapist can provide a corrective set of reinforcements, the client's abnormal behavior can be expected to change for the better (Bandura, 1969; Goldstein & Foa, 1980; Lichstein, 1988; Nathan, Witte, & Langenbucher, 1983; Rimm & Masters, 1979; Rosenthal & Bandura, 1978).

Distinctive Emphases

In contrast to the emphasis in dynamic approaches on inferred, intellectual, and historical processes, behavioral approaches are first of all concerned with *observable processes.* The appropriate subject of the clinician's attention is what people can actually be observed to do, not possible explanations of their actions in terms of underlying personality characteristics.

Second, the central focus in this approach is on *behavioral processes,* not thoughts or feelings. What is real about people is how they act. The behavioral tradition recognizes that disturbed people may experience troubling thoughts and painful affects. If, however, they can be helped to act differently, their progress toward more effective behavior patterns will ameliorate their distressing thoughts and feelings.

Third, behaviorally oriented clinicians concentrate on *ahistorical processes.* Learning theorists believe that a person's preferred behavior patterns are shaped by prior experiences that have produced a hierarchy of habits of various strengths. However, clinical work from the behavioral perspective consists not of uncovering such prior experiences, but instead of establishing a present set of reinforcement contingencies that will alter the existing habit-strength hierarchy. This traditional emphasis on observable, behavioral, and ahistorical processes in the behavioral approach is summarized as follows by Eysenck and Rachman (1965):

> All treatment of neurotic disorders is concerned with habits existing at present; the historical development is largely irrelevant. Cures are achieved by treating the symptom itself. . . . Interpretation, even if not completely subjective and erroneous, is irrelevant. Symptomatic treatment leads to permanent recovery (p. 12).

Abiding Influences

Whereas psychoanalytic theorists have had their major impact on clinical psychology by establishing that psychopathology can be understood, learning theorists have had their most abiding influence by insisting that psychopathology must be objectified. The inferred processes inherent in dynamic approaches are difficult to translate into reliably measurable variables for research purposes. Although increasingly sophisticated methodology has begun to surmount this difficulty, definitive empirical confirmation of psychoanalytic postulates remains in its infancy (Blatt & Lerner, 1983; Luborsky & Spence, 1978; Silverman, 1983; Silverman & Weinberger, 1985). Too often, moreover, dynamically oriented clinicians have written and taught as if their convictions were sufficient to document their conclusions, no matter what research workers report.

Historically, the impressionistic and self-validating stance taken by most psychoanalytic theorists alienated psychologists, who regard their discipline as a behavioral science. The impact of learning theory on clinical psychology served to reduce this alienation. By objectifying the content of clinical psychology for research purposes, behavioral approaches fostered the accumulation of verifiable knowledge. By increasing the interest of experimentally oriented psychologists in clinical problems and also by encouraging dynamically oriented clinicians to think in more objective terms, behaviorally oriented clinicians brought clinical pursuits into the mainstream of psychology and enriched the field with new ideas, new methods, and a new generation of teachers, scholars, and practitioners.

As a second abiding influence, behavioral approaches have expanded the range of problems that clinical psychologists believe they can and should address. Dynamic psychotherapy calls for active participation in an intellectual process of gaining insight into one's problems. Depending on how well they can participate in such a process, some people will profit more from the treatment than others, and people with some kinds of disorders have traditionally been considered unlikely to derive any benefit at all.

By contrast, the behavioral focus on manifest symptoms rather than underlying disorder creates the potential for any problem to be ameliorated through psychological intervention. If the clinician can present reinforcement contingencies that will shape more desirable behavior, the client's adjustment will be improved—even if he or she happens to be autistic, retarded, neurologically impaired, psychopathic, addicted, elderly, physically ill, or nonverbal, to choose some characteristics often regarded as contraindicating psychotherapy or any major treatment role for clinical psychologists. The work of behaviorally oriented therapists with people who have such characteristics has substantially broadened the scope of substantive concerns, professional activities, and work settings that define contemporary clinical psychology (Kazdin, 1978, 1979a; Leitenberg, 1976; Turner, Calhoun, & Adams, 1981).

Like psychoanalytic formulations, learning theories of behavior have prompted numerous proposals for revision since they were first articulated. Analogous to ego-analytic extensions of orthodox psychoanalysis, traditional behaviorism has been embellished by the emergence of a mediational perspective. Mediational theorists advance two basic postulates: first, that reinforcement contingencies exert their maximum influence on learning and behavior only when people recognize and understand the events by which they are being influenced; second, that emotional and behavioral disturbances are shaped not only by learned bad habits, but also by maladaptive beliefs, expectations, and ways of processing information (Bandura, 1977; Hollon & Beck, 1986; Meichenbaum, 1977). From this perspective, traditional behavioral formulations placed too much emphasis on observable events and too little emphasis on how people perceive and evaluate these events: "Environmental events *per se*, although important, are not of *primary* importance; rather what the client says to himself about those events influences his behavior" (Meichenbaum, 1977, p. 108).

This mediational perspective has provided the basis for cognitive and social learning formulations that, although not well received by traditional behaviorists (Skinner, 1977; Wolpe, 1978), may have become more widely endorsed and employed than traditional behavioral approaches. In similar fashion, despite reservations in orthodox quarters, ego-analytic clinicians may have become more numerous than classical psychoanalytic theorists and practitioners. Should these conjectures be correct, it is the revisions brought forward by ego-analytic and mediational theorists, rather than the basic postulates of psychoanalytic and learning theories of normal and abnormal behavior, that currently constitute the theoretical foundations of mainstream dynamic and behavioral approaches in clinical psychology. Because ego-analytic dynamicism and mediational behaviorism have more in common than orthodox psychoanalytic and traditional learning theory, their ascendance compels further consideration of how contemporary theoretical developments have increased lines of convergence among originally disparate points of view. Before such consideration is given, however, the influence of humanistic theories must be brought into this discussion.

EXPERIENTIAL APPROACHES

Experiential approaches in clinical psychology depart from dynamic and behavioral frameworks in two significant respects. First, people are not regarded as passive products of a balance that is struck between conflicting forces or of reinforcements that shape habit hierarchies. Instead, people are seen as inherently active, self-affirming organisms who forge their own destiny and have enormous capacity for positive personal growth. Progress toward improved adjustment is conceived not as an effort to throw off the shackles of previously determined psychological handicaps, but as a future-oriented pursuit of self-fulfillment (Allport, 1937, 1961; Kelly, 1955, 1980; Maslow, 1962; May, Angel, & Ellenberger, 1958).

Second, the humanistic tradition from which experiential approaches emerged is an *idiographic* psychology. There is no place in this orientation for principles of behavior that address prevalent or recurrent patterns among groups of people. Rather, humanism is concerned with the uniqueness of each individual person, with how people differ from each other instead of with how they are alike (Mahrer, 1978; Pervin, 1984). Maslow (1966) expresses this attention to human individuality by saying, "I must approach a person as an individual unique and peculiar, the sole member of his class" (p. 10).

From this perspective, people are by nature inclined to develop into kind, friendly, self-accepting, socially engaged human beings. Maladjustment encroaches on their existence only when they must live in an atmosphere that interferes with their personal growth. Psychopathology consists neither of maladaptive efforts to manage anxiety stemming from intrapsychic conflicts nor of learned maladaptive habits, but rather of the reduced expression of human potential and a loss of congruence with one's internal self-experience. To be precise, however, it is not psychopathology of which experientially oriented clinicians prefer to speak, but rather problems in living—difficulties in experiencing oneself, inability to find pleasure and fulfillment in one's activities, and failure to make meaningful contact with others (Jourard, 1964; Rogers, 1961).

Consistent with an idiographic emphasis, experiential assessment seeks to identify the unique and individual meanings that people attach to their experience. Experientially oriented clinicians are not concerned with assessing personality structures or habit systems, nor have they traditionally endorsed attempts to classify people in terms of diagnostic labels, shared personality traits, or quantitative positions along various dimensions of behavior. Such classification is rejected as a dehumanizing procedure that strips people of their dignity and self-respect. The proper focus in assessment is a *qualitative* study of the individual case, with special attention to the ways in which a person is interacting with and feeling about his or her environment. Foremost in these assessments is concern with each individual's consciousness and inner experience, rather than with the influence on behavior of guiding dispositions or external events (Brown, 1972; Dana & Leech, 1974; Jourard, 1968, 1971; Kelly, 1955, chaps. 5 & 6; Landfield & Epting, 1987).

The treatment aim in experiential approaches is to promote positive personal growth, maximal self-awareness, and a clear understanding of how one is relating to one's world. Heightened consciousness in these respects is expected to expand a person's possibilities for richer and more meaningful living and greater realization of his or her human potential. By being helped to come into closer contact with what they are experiencing, clients gain greater freedom to choose rewarding commitments to other people and to creative endeavors.

The specific techniques employed by experientially oriented therapists vary across four major types of experiential therapy: client-centered therapy, existential therapy, gestalt therapy, and personal construct therapy. These varieties of experiential therapy share two themes in common. First, the essence of the therapists' role is not what they should do, as in providing interpretations or reinforcements, but how they should be, in order to provide an atmosphere in which clients can grow and seek their own solutions to their problems in living. Second, psychotherapy is regarded less as a treatment conducted by the therapist than as a personal encounter used by clients to increase their capacity to relate to themselves, to others, and to their own needs, talents, and future prospects (Bannister, 1975; Bugental, 1978; Landfield & Leitner, 1980; Mahrer, 1983; Neimeyer & Neimeyer, 1987; Perls, Hefferline, & Goodman, 1951; Polster & Polster, 1973; Rogers, 1951, 1961; Wright, Everett, & Roisman, 1986).

Distinctive Emphases

In experiential approaches to working with troubled people, neither the inferred processes formulated by dynamically oriented clinicians nor the observable processes stressed by behaviorally oriented clinicians are particularly relevant, primarily because both reflect the clinician's perspective on the client. In the humanistic tradition behavior can be understood only from the client's perspective. Accordingly, *subjective processes,* as experienced and reported by the client, identify what a person is like and whether he or she can be helped to change.

For similar reasons, experiential approaches stress *emotional processes* instead of intellectual or behavioral processes. It is not what people think or do that is important, but how they feel. The way in which individuals experience their life is a function of how they feel about it, and the personal growth by which people overcome problems in living while in psychotherapy requires an interaction in which meanings are intensely felt.

Finally, experiential approaches emphasize *ahistorical processes* in both the origin and the treatment of problems in living. Psychological maladjustment consists of current difficulties in finding self-fulfillment and a comfortable way of being in the world, and therapy succeeds to the extent that present encounters with a clinician can help people construct for themselves new and more rewarding ways of being.

Abiding Influences

Humanistic theorists have influenced clinical psychology most by insisting that difficulties in living should be personalized. Instead of asking what causes certain kinds of psychopathology, experientially oriented clinicians ask how individual people are failing to come to terms with themselves or their environment. This frame of reference has heightened psychologists' sensitivity to unique feelings and attitudes of clients that differ from or even run counter to how most people usually think and feel.

Instead of asking how psychopathy, schizophrenia, motivation, intelligence, social class, and other client characteristics might affect the outcome of psychotherapy, experiential clinicians ask how the therapy environment can liberate each client's inherent potential for personal growth. This humanistic perspective has encouraged researchers and practitioners to look closely at therapist as well as client variables in psychotherapy. Of special importance in this regard is the attention that experiential clinicians have called to the help therapists give their clients, not by their skills as interpreters or reinforcers of behavior, but by their qualities as human beings, their sharing of their own experience, and their skill in sustaining a personal encounter.

Historically, in addition, the optimistic and person-centered tone of experiential approaches attracted to clinical work psychologists for whom dynamic and behavioral approaches held little appeal. Dynamic psychology, its diversity notwithstanding, has a legacy of pessimism in which neurotic conflicts are believed to persist or recur despite extensive increments in self-understanding. In one of his last major works, Freud (1937/1964a) concluded that "A normal ego . . . is, like normality in general, an ideal fiction" (p. 235). Analysis, he continued, may thus be "the third of those 'impossible' professions in which one can be sure beforehand of achieving unsatisfying results. The other two, which have been known much longer, are education and government" (p. 248).

Behavioral approaches, their evolution over the years also notwithstanding, share a legacy in which techniques are administered by therapists to clients independently of any relevant personal relationship between them. The therapist operates mechanically, as a "reinforcement machine," and "personal relations are not essential for cures of neurotic disorders, although they may be useful in certain circumstances" (Eysenck & Rachman, 1965, p. 12). Many psychologists who found the dynamic tradition too pessimistic and the behavioral tradition too impersonal were drawn by the experiential perspective into making valuable contributions to theory and practice in clinical psychology.

THEORETICAL DEVELOPMENTS AND LINES OF CONVERGENCE AMONG APPROACHES

Table 2.1 summarizes the central differences among dynamic, behavioral, and experiential approaches in clinical psychology. Although these differences reflect contrasting theoretical positions, they are less discrete than they may appear or are sometimes believed to be. Diversity of opinion within each approach blurs the boundaries among them, as was noted earlier, and common threads run through the assessment and intervention practices espoused by each. For example, despite differences in whether they are concerned mainly with intellectual, behavioral, or emotional processes, clinicians of all persua-

Table 2.1. Central Differences among Approaches in Clinical Psychology

	DYNAMIC APPROACHES	BEHAVIORAL APPROACHES	EXPERIENTIAL APPROACHES
Nature of psychopathology	Maladaptive efforts to minimize anxiety stemming from unresolved psychological conflicts	Learned maladaptive habits	Difficulties in finding pleasure and fulfillment in relating to oneself and one's environment
Assessment question	Why do people behave as they do?	How do people behave in particular situations?	What unique and individual meanings do people attach to their experience?
Treatment aim	Promote increased self-understanding through interpretation	Modify maladaptive response patterns through corrective reinforcement contingencies	Facilitate positive personal growth through providing an atmosphere that expands self-awareness
Distinctive emphases	Inferred processes Intellectual processes Historical processes	Observable processes Behavioral processes Ahistorical processes	Subjective processes Emotional processes Ahistorical processes
Focal influence	Psychopathology can be understood	Psychopathology must be objectified	Psychopathology should be personalized

sions address the totality of how people think, feel, and act. Together with many such long-standing but frequently overlooked similarities among different approaches, ongoing evolution in the theories from which they derive has narrowed the gaps among them. Numerous aspects of each approach can consequently be identified in the other two.

Behavioral and Experiential Aspects of the Dynamic Approach

Personality assessment as currently practiced within the dynamic tradition attends to many of the concerns of behaviorally and experientially oriented clinicians. Contemporary applications of the Rorschach test, for example, conceptualize the inkblots as a perceptual-cognitive task and stress the sampling of representative behavior in order to minimize levels of inference. In this way of looking at the Rorschach, subjects are given a problem to solve ("What might this be?"), and the manner in which they respond indicates how they are likely to respond in other situations that call for perceptual-cognitive structuring and problem-solving behavior (Exner, 1983; Exner & Weiner, 1982, chap. 1; Goldfried, Stricker, & Weiner, 1971, chap. 13; Weiner, 1983).

Turning to experiential concerns, adequate assessment within a dynamic frame of reference attends just as much to how people differ from each other as to how they are alike. Traditional psychodiagnosticians

regard idiographic and nomothetic evaluations as complementary, not mutually exclusive, and they consistently emphasize humanistic considerations in applying their findings (Appelbaum, 1976; Shevrin & Shectman, 1973; Sugarman, 1978).

In addition, contemporary developments in psychoanalytic theory have directed many dynamically oriented clinicians toward a fuller assessment of how people view themselves and their relations with others. In particular, emerging concepts of developmental ego psychology, object relations theory, and self-psychology have placed greater emphasis than either traditional or ego-oriented psychoanalytic theory on early life events, especially parent-child interactions, and the manner in which people subsequently structure their interpersonal world and their sense of themselves. Dynamically oriented clinicians who are pursuing these new theoretical directions report being drawn to an increasingly experiential focus in their utilization of psychological test data (Lerner, 1984).

Although current trends toward idiography in dynamic approaches must be given their just due, concern with the unique meanings that people attach to their experience has characterized psychoanalytic theory since Freud (1900/1953a) wrote in *The Interpretation of Dreams,* "I . . . am prepared to find that the same piece of content may conceal a different meaning when it occurs in various people or in various contexts" (p. 105). Because dream analysis is so often identified with psychoanalytic therapy (correctly), and because universal meanings of symbols are so often attributed to Freudian psychology (erroneously), it is noteworthy that Freud's idiographic stance has continued to the present day to mark the literature on dream interpretation. Bonime (1962) wrote, "Dream symbols arise out of the specific life history of each individual, and it is only from the individual's life history that we can derive the meanings of his dream symbols" (p. 32). Weiss (1986) confirms, "A dream consists of symbols that are unique to the individual" (p. 92).

In treatment, the efforts of dynamically oriented clinicians to promote self-understanding do not preclude attention to behavior change. To the contrary, dynamic psychotherapy has always shared with behavioral approaches the goal of behavior change, including relief from emotional distress and modification of maladaptive ways of acting. While self-understanding is considered to be the most effective means of achieving such goals, it does not constitute an end in itself (Marmor & Woods, 1980; Weiner, 1975, chap. 1).

Along with traditionally being concerned with behavior change, dynamic approaches in psychotherapy have had a behaviorally pragmatic cast at least since the advent of interest in short-term analytic therapy. Building on the then radical suggestion by Alexander and French (1946) that "corrective emotional experience" can considerably shorten the time necessary for psychoanalytic therapy to achieve a satisfactory outcome, numerous authors have described techniques for implementing brief, problem-focused dynamic psychotherapy (Bauer & Kobos, 1987; Malan, 1976; Sifneos, 1979; Small, 1979). Luborsky (1984) and Strupp and Binder (1984) have provided manuals for conducting even time-limited treatment within a psychoanalytic frame of reference.

Most recently, psychoanalytic theory and dynamic psychotherapy have been moved in behavioral directions by increased attention to cognitive determinants of normal and abnormal behavior. Strupp and Binder (1984), for example, assert in the context of a dynamic formulation of psychotherapy that maladaptive behaviors stem from dysfunctional beliefs people form about themselves and others. Other currently influential psychoanalytic texts have similarly embraced such cognitive perspectives as the notion that psychopathology derives from pathogenic beliefs and can be alleviated by helping people modify or give up these beliefs (Horowitz, 1988; Weiss & Sampson, 1986). These present-day elaborations of ego-analytic theory seem clearly to be treading the same path as the previously noted mediational formulations that are shaping contemporary behavioral approaches.

In common with experiential approaches, dynamic psychotherapy has traditionally addressed how people can realize a greater sense of personal freedom, human relatedness, and self-fulfillment (Strupp, 1980; Sugarman, 1976). Strupp (1975) commented specifically that "analytic therapy is an education for optimal personal freedom in the context of social living" (p. 135). The emergence of object relations and self-theory from the contributions of Fairbairn, Klein, Mahler, Winnicott, Kernberg, and Kohut has further graced psychoanalytic theory with a more positive view of human nature than was held by Freud. Explicit as well in these theoretical developments are increased attention to subjective experience and a greater inclination to believe that people can control their own destiny (Blanck & Blanck, 1974; Cashdan, 1988; Eagle, 1984a, 1984b; Kahn, 1985).

The experiential clinician's concern with the client-therapist relationship has long had a prominent place in dynamic formulations of the treatment process. Freud (1917/1963) himself anticipated the interpersonal thrust of most contemporary psychoanalytic thinking about psychotherapy by arguing that "what turns the scale" in a patient's struggle to resolve neurotic conflicts "is not his intellectual insight . . . but simply and solely his relation to the doctor" (p. 445). Many dynamically oriented clinicians have similarly endorsed the power of here-and-now analysis of the treatment relationship as a tool for identifying and correcting maladaptive ways of thinking and feeling (Bordin, 1979; Greenson, 1967, chap. 3; Sullivan, 1954; Weiner, 1975, chap. 10).

Finally, some new psychoanalytic postulates concerning the nature of truth and meaning would point dynamic approaches in an experiential direction. Psychoanalysis has traditionally sought to uncover past experiences that have led to present dysfunction. Reviewing and reevaluating the nature of events that have had untoward psychological consequences is expected to provide an opportunity for patients to undo these consequences. In contrast to this "archeological" focus on unearthing historical truth (i.e., an accurate reconstruction of past events), Spence (1982) and Strupp and Binder (1984) proposed that only a "narrative" truth (i.e., an adaptive construction of reality with which the person feels comfortable, whether historically accurate or not) is necessary for working successfully to resolve adjustment difficulties. Such attention to how people construct events in their lives, rather than to what actually has transpired, embodies the characteristic emphasis of humanistic theorists on the meanings people attach to their experience.

Dynamic and Experiential Aspects of the Behavioral Approach

In behavioral as in traditional assessment, good clinical practice attends to distinctive as well as shared features of how people respond to their experience. Along with this humanistic component, behavioral assessment has in common with dynamic approaches an inescapable need to make inferential interpretations. Only rare circumstances make it possible to answer an assessment question by samplng behavior in a perfectly representative situation. Instead, behavioral and traditional assessors alike regularly find it necessary to consider how representative their data are, how great an inferential leap they must make to derive conclusions from these data, and how reliable their conclusions are consequently likely to be. Since its principles were first formulated, behavioral assessment has come increasingly to involve clinical interviews, personality inventories, self-report measures, and role-playing exercises—all of which require inferential processes to yield conclusions about real-life behavior outside of the assessment situation (Kanfer, 1985; Nelson & Hayes, 1986; Strosahl & Linehan, 1986).

The advent of mediational perspectives within behavioral approaches and the resulting emergence of cognitive and social learning formulations have further narrowed the gap between traditional and behavioral assessors in the issues they face and the practices they employ. Cognitive behaviorists assess not only what people can be observed to do, but also what kinds of feelings, fantasies, expectations, and beliefs they seem to harbor. They focus less on the match between the content of an assessment procedure and a response tendency to be measured (which involves the traditional concern of behavioral assessors with face validity) than on how well a test can measure a particular cognitive process (which involves the kind of construct validity traditionally of concern to dynamic assessors). As a further deviation from the behavioral tradition, cognitive assessors report that simple procedures closely tied to observable events do not necessarily guarantee conclusions; for example, observations of behavior in contrived situations appear to be less predictive of behavior than subjects' self-reports of how they have behaved in the past (Ciminero, Calhoun, & Adams, 1986; Kendall & Hollon, 1981; Segal & Shaw, 1988; Strosahl & Linehan, 1986).

In therapy many behaviorally oriented therapists have come over the years to endorse the role of client attitudes and the treatment relationship in fostering and sustaining behavior change. In the view of these clinicians, maximally effective treatment occurs only when clients understand the manner in which reinforcement contingencies have determined and can modify their behavior; when they develop improved internal capacities for self-control and self-determination; and when they hold a positive view of the helping potential of the treatment relationship (Goldfried & Merbaum, 1973; Goldfried & Robins, 1982; Lazarus, 1971; Mahoney & Arnkoff, 1978; Sweet, 1984; Wilson & Evans, 1977).

Contemporary developments in cognitive behavior therapy are also infusing learning-based approaches with dynamic and experiential perspectives. Most dramatic in this regard as a departure from traditional behaviorism has been the position taken by Meichenbaum and Gilmore (1984) that the introduction of cognition into behavioral formulations necessitates attention to unconscious events. Like psychoanalytic theorists, these authors argue that behavior cannot be adequately explained without recourse to concepts extending beyond conscious mental experience. Borrowing further from nonbehavioral approaches, cognitive-behavioral theorists place considerable emphasis on the needs for clients to become emotionally aroused and gain insight and for therapists to provide a warm and understanding environment (Dobson & Block, 1988; D'Zurilla, 1986; Thompson & Spana, 1986). Mahoney (1988, p. 376) described this view of cognitive-behavior therapy as follows: "The therapeutic relationship entails a safe, caring, and intense contact in and from which the client can explore and develop relationships with self and world."

Dynamic and Behavioral Aspects of the Experiential Approach

Over the years experiential approaches in clinical psychology have more often influenced than been influenced by dynamic and behavioral approaches. Nevertheless, two developments within this frame of reference have served to increase its communality with other approaches.

First, despite their humanistic orientation, experiential clinicians have begun to encourage scientific validation of their procedures and some degree of objectivity in applied work. Dana (1982) endorsed the use of such traditional assessment instruments as the Rorschach and Thematic Apperception Test (TAT) in the context of an interactive consideration by client and examiner of what the results mean, and he adduced a large body of experimental work to provide empirical justification for relying on these instruments. Bugental (1987) similarly argued that experiential psychotherapy, however idiographic, can be enhanced by drawing on shared clinical experience and the implications of empirical findings: "The artistry of master therapists shows in their ability selectively to blend the subjective with the objective, their art with their science" (p. ix). Speaking more generally, Rychlak (1988) argued compellingly in *The Psychology of Rigorous Humanism* that psychological theory can at the same time be humanistic and scientifically rigorous.

Second, like their dynamic and behavioral colleagues, experientially oriented clinicians have come to attach importance to the role of cognitive processes in promoting personal growth. Some client-centered theorists, for example, supplement their traditional stress on personal growth through openness to experience with the conviction that clients must understand as well as experience life situations. From this perspective the ability to achieve and sustain a richer existence is measured by how adequately people can acquire and organize information about themselves and their world (Anderson, 1974; Bohart, 1982; Wexler, 1974; Zimring, 1974).

This cognitive-experiential trend is particularly evident in the rational-emotive therapy developed by Ellis (Ellis, 1962; Ellis & Dryden, 1987). The basic assumption in rational-emotive therapy is that emotional distress and self-defeating behavior result from misperceptions and mistaken beliefs, and the treatment consists of directives and exercises intended to modify what people think and say to themselves. Although Ellis's formulations played a part in the emergence of contemporary cognitive-behavior therapy, Ellis himself regards specialized rational-emotive therapy as a humanistic psychotherapy that aims at helping clients become maximally self-accepting (Ellis, 1980). His work can thus be seen as having added a cognitive component to experiential approaches.

The cognitive emphasis that has characterized developments in dynamic, behavioral, and experiential approaches has been suggested by some theorists to constitute a distinct approach to clinical psychology in its own right. From this perspective psychological adjustment can be fully understood and described in terms of cognitive-representational processes: Maladjustment or problems in living derive from irrational fears, beliefs, or expectations, and clinical work consists of a cognitive process of identifying thoughts, wishes, and feelings and making psychological connections among them (Beck, 1976; Bieber, 1980; Emery, Hollon, & Bedrosian, 1981; Mahoney, 1977; Raimy, 1975). At the same time, Hollon and Beck

(1986) pointed out that legitimate questions remain whether cognitive approaches add anything to purely behavioral approaches, whether they work differently from other modes of intervention, and even whether they are instrumental in producing cognitive change. Hence, it must be left to future work to determine whether cognitive formulations will continue to be refined as a bridge among dynamic, behavioral, and experiential approaches or whether instead, supported by theoretical and research developments in cognitive psychology, they will become established as a fourth major approach in clinical psychology.

ACCOMMODATING LINES OF CONVERGENCE

Clinicians have responded in several different ways to the lines of convergence among dynamic, behavioral, and experiential approaches. Some have chosen simply to ignore or deny their existence. Clinicians who adopt this stance adhere strictly to a single point of view, as if it were the revealed truth, and seldom consider the possibility that other frames of reference might contribute to the understanding and treatment of psychological disorder. Such stonewallers typically reinforce their convictions by listening only to colleagues who share their narrow outlook. In accounting for this reluctance to recognize lines of convergence, Frank (1976) observed that "little glory derives from showing that the particular method one has mastered with so much effort may be indistinguishable from other methods in its effects" (p. 74).

To their credit, most clinicians combine some theoretical preference with a supportive or at least tolerant attitude toward other approaches. Setting a good example in this regard, Freud (1904/1953b), while unequivocal in his view that "the analytic method of psychotherapy is the one that penetrates most deeply and carries furthest" (p. 260), also observed that "there are many ways and means of practicing psychotherapy. All that lead to recovery are good" (p. 259).

Although Freud's followers and disciples of other theorists have not always been so open-minded, parochial dogmatism seems presently on the wane. Experienced clinicians have come increasingly to respect each other's views and to endorse treatment strategies of demonstrated effectiveness, whatever their theoretical origin (Garfield, 1982; Goldfried & Newman, 1986; Norcross, 1987; Parloff, London, & Wolfe, 1986). Despite some persistent stonewalling, clinical psychology appears to be reaching a point of agreement with the present author that "effective psychotherapy is defined not by its brand name, but by how well it meets the needs of the patient" (Weiner, 1975, p. 44).

A second response to lines of convergence has been an effort to accommodate them through *reformulation,* which consists of translating the concepts of other theoretical formulations into the language of some preferred frame of reference. As cases in point, both psychoanalytic and client-centered methods have been presented in the conceptual language of social learning theory (Dollard & Miller, 1950; Martin, 1972). Such efforts at reformulation, although intellectually challenging and sometimes comforting to theorists into whose language the work of others is being translated, often prove to be sterile exercises. The robustness of one approach may be demonstrated by its capacity to absorb the concepts of other approaches, but the ensuing result does little to enrich theoretical perspectives on human behavior or expand the scope of clinical methods.

Another accommodation of the lines of convergence among approaches in clinical psychology has consisted of efforts at *amalgamation.* From an amalgamation perspective the distinctive theoretical formulations associated with different schools of thought are merely window dressing. Although they may provide a professionally supportive sense of identity with some theoretical tradition, they have less bearing on how clinical psychology is actually practiced than do lessons learned from experience. In this frame of reference, all roads lead to Rome. Talented and experienced clinicians will end up working with their clients in the same ways, regardless of the theories they espouse. Advances in knowledge in clinical psychology will accordingly come not from comparative theoretical analyses, but instead from identifying common principles of behavior change that transcend all variations in theoretical language.

In discussing the possible amalgamation of theories that have influenced clinical practice, numerous writers have called attention to general factors that promote positive behavior change in any psychotherapy relationship. These general factors include the opportunity for catharsis that all forms of psychotherapy provide the client; the expectations of change that clients bring into psychotherapy or develop from their therapist's willingness to work with them; regular occasions for clients to talk with another person who respects their dignity and is trying to understand and be helpful; and reinforcing effects of how and when therapists respond to positive aspects of what their clients say and do. These general factors foster increments in well-being independently of specific treatment techniques prescribed by one or another theoret-

ical stance, such as interpretation, modeling, and self-disclosure (Frank, 1971; Kazdin, 1979c; Lambert, 1986; Lazarus, 1980; Strupp, 1970, 1973; Strupp & Hadley, 1979; Weiner & Bordin, 1983).

Support for the argument that different approaches in clinical psychology should be amalgamated requires evidence that general factors account fully for behavior change in psychotherapy, while specific theory-driven procedures produce neither enhanced nor distinctive results. In addition, it should be demonstrable that experienced therapists of all persuasions do in fact conduct therapy in essentially the same way.

With respect to the first kind of evidence, Lambert (1986) drew the following conclusions from available outcome research: Approximately 40% of the improvement in psychotherapy patients is attributable to spontaneous remission, which occurs when environmental events and client characteristics independent of participation in therapy foster recovery; 45% of improvement is attributable to common factors in all psychological therapies, such as expectancy effects and the impact of the treatment relationship; and the remaining 15% is attributable to technical procedures specific to particular therapies. While thus documenting the substantial contribution of general factors to psychotherapy outcome, these data also establish the place of specific therapist interventions in promoting positive behavior change.

Moreover, in all therapies certain technical procedures must be employed to breathe life into the general factors that produce improvement. For example, experienced therapists recognize that a salutary therapeutic environment, including reciprocal and empathic bonding between patient and therapist, cannot be created unless the therapist has acquired considerable skill in conducting treatment sessions: that is, knowing what kinds of things to say and do, when, and how. Not surprisingly, then, evidence continues to emerge that specific techniques predict treatment outcome in certain circumstances, and many researchers who stress the importance of general factors in promoting change also urge adequate attention to technical operations in the conduct of psychotherapy (Jones, Cumming, & Horowitz, 1988; Lambert, Shapiro, & Bergin, 1986; Orlinsky & Howard, 1986; Strupp, 1979). Regardless of how important general factors are in predicting psychotherapy outcome, then, psychologists must be adequately trained to make these factors operable, and they should continue to seek, learn, and teach specific treatment techniques that can enhance and accelerate the therapy process beyond what general factors alone can achieve.

Turning to distinctive results, available evidence

indicates that various approaches in therapy are about equally effective when a broad spectrum of clients is considered in general. When specific kinds of disorders are examined, however, some differences appear in how likely they are to respond favorably to particular treatment methods. Although much definitive research remains to be done concerning distinctive outcomes, there is growing empirical support for applying certain specific therapies to specific problems (Frank, Hoehn-Saric, Imber, Liberman, & Stone, 1978; Lambert, Shapiro, & Bergin, 1986; Luborsky, Singer, & Luborsky, 1975; Luborsky & Spence, 1978; Smith, Glass, & Miller, 1980; Stiles, Shapiro, & Elliott, 1986).

Clinically, in addition, there is almost universal endorsement for preceding psychological intervention with an evaluation designed to identify the form of therapy best suited to meet a particular patient's needs. Implicit in such differential treatment planning is the conviction born of experience that different kinds of patients, like different kinds of problems, call for different types of treatment. The previously mentioned superiority of behavioral over dynamic approaches in working with some seriously disturbed and organically impaired patients illustrates this point. Some authors have concluded from the generally similar effectiveness of different treatment approaches that "psychoanalytic, behavioristic, and humanistic forms of psychotherapy are, in the final analysis, interchangeable" (Strong & Claiborn, 1982, p. 211). With respect to specific case circumstances, this is definitely not the case.

As for the conduct of therapy in actual practice, some early research reports suggested that therapists of all persuasions endorse many of the same basic treatment strategies, such as providing a warm and accepting atmosphere and engaging their clients in corrective experiences, and display more similarities than differences in the tactics of what they actually say to their clients (Fiedler, 1950; Marmor, 1976; Wrenn, 1960). Subsequently, however, accumulating evidence has indicated otherwise: Therapists with different orientations view their clients' needs differently, provide distinctive kinds of treatment, and differ in many technical aspects of how they conduct psychotherapy sessions (Bruinink & Schroeder, 1979; Cohen & Oyster-Nelson, 1981; Staples, Sloane, Whipple, Cristol, & Yorkton, 1975).

To elaborate this important finding, therapists espousing different theoretical orientations have been observed to vary systematically in how active they are during treatment sessions, how much direct guidance they provide, how close or distant a personal relationship they maintain with their clients, and how they deal with issues involving the treatment relationship (Altshuler & Rush, 1984). They differ in the number of statements they make during a session, the length of their statements, and the complexity of the language they use (Meara, Shannon, & Pepinsky, 1979). These variations among therapists are found to be consistent with the theories to which they adhere, and different forms of therapy can be distinguished from each other by observers listening to brief taped segments (Luborsky, Woody, McLellan, O'Brien, & Rosenzweig, 1982). Hence, the once postulated tactical equivalence of therapies has not stood the test of empirical verification; experienced therapists do not all do the same thing, and their orientation is at least as influential as their level of experience in determining their clinical behavior (Norcross, 1985; Stiles et al., 1986).

On balance, then, efforts to amalgamate approaches in clinical psychology cannot be supported by empirical data. Numerous communalities among approaches can be identified at the level of clinical strategies, such as providing a warm relationship and corrective experiences in psychotherapy. At the level of clinical tactics, however, differences in theory are much more than window dressing. The evidence indicates that the theoretical orientations to which psychologists subscribe influence them to employ many clearly distinctive methods and techniques in their clinical work.

In recognition of these facts, a fourth approach to dealing with lines of convergence among approaches stresses *complementarity*. From this point of view, dynamic, behavioral, and experiential perspectives on assessment and intervention complement each other and enrich the ability of clinicians to understand and work effectively with their clients. The complete clinician is one who appreciates the lessons taught by various theories and can draw on the concepts and methods of many different approaches in delivering psychological services. Pursuit of such complementarity has given rise to numerous eclectic perspectives in clinical psychology, a brief summary of which will provide the conclusion to this discussion of theoretical foundations.

EMERGING ECLECTIC PERSPECTIVES

Pointing as they do toward complementarity, the lessons learned from comparative study of diverse approaches in clinical psychology have prompted the emergence of eclectic perspectives. Like its theoretical forebears, eclecticism has not come forth all of one piece. Instead, groups of clinicians have opted for varieties of eclecticism that share the spirit of complementarity but lead in some substantially different directions.

One major variety of eclecticism extends in an ecumenical vein the earlier efforts to accommodate convergence through reformulation. Rather than merely seeking to sanctify one theory or another by translating other theories into its language, eclectic reformulators advocate a common language that will embrace the postulates of diverse theories without imposing any one on the others. Opinions differ, however, concerning what language this should be. Responding to the cognitive directions of recent dynamic, behavioral, and experiential theorizing, some eclecticists propose rewriting the distinctive formulations of these three approaches in the language of cognitive psychology; others propose using the language of interpersonal theory or social psychology for this purpose (Goldfried & Padawer, 1982; Norcross, 1987; Strong & Claiborn, 1982).

Still other eclectic theorists question the desirability of using any extant technical language to encompass diverse approaches and favor instead formulations couched in general, nontechnical language that describe in neutral terms the communalities among them. In the area of psychotherapy, such intent to describe in nontechnical, pantheoretical terms the basic processes common to all forms of psychological therapy is exemplified by Beitman's (1987) *The Structure of Individual Psychotherapy,* Beutler's (1983) *Eclectic Psychotherapy,* and Prochaska and DiClemente's (1984) *The Transtheoretical Approach.*

This contemporary type of reformulation is generally referred to as *synthetic eclecticism* or *integrationism.* Despite being on the cutting edge of today's theorizing about clinical psychology, integrationism is not without its critics. Some opposition to efforts at integration comes from clinicians who take issue with the notion of convergence in the first place, at least at the basic conceptual level. These critics argue from a variety of theoretical vantage points that differences between dynamic, behavioral, and experiential approaches in how people and their problems are viewed are so great as to preclude any integration of them into a single frame of reference (Dreikurs, 1987; Messer, 1983, 1986; Yates, 1986). This conclusion is in turn refuted by integrationists, who consider it empirically unwarranted and conceptually linked to traditional rather than contemporary psychoanalytic, learning, and humanistic theory (Murray, 1983, 1986; Wachtel, 1977, 1983). Nevertheless, the fact remains that integrationism is currently a controversial approach and not a universally endorsed distillate of clinical psychological theories.

Other objections to integrationism have been raised from within the eclectic camp by theorists who are concerned lest the whole ends up being less than the sum of its parts. As pointed out by Norcross (1986), all integrationists are eclectic in their orientation, but not all eclecticists favor integrationism. This latter group fears that turning to any one common language will sacrifice needlessly the richness of the terminology with which distinctive notions have been expressed in traditional approaches and the sophistication these terms have brought to understanding and communicating about human behavior. Instead of total divorce from previously familiar concepts, which may leave us with a host of new competing theoretical systems, and retard rather than accelerate development of knowledge, these authors urge professionals to be multilingual in their approach to clinical work (Goldfried, 1987; Goldfried & Safran, 1986).

Being multilingual involves building on the early efforts to accommodate convergence not by reformulation but through amalgamation. Without suggesting that all approaches are basically the same, multilingualism consists of drawing on their communalities and distinctiveness alike to establish an approach to practice that combines the advantages of each.

Among psychologists who speak many languages and choose procedures to meet circumstances, regardless of the theoretical origins of these procedures, some do so without holding any theoretical preference or feeling any need for an overarching theory. This type of amalgamation is usually referred to as *atheoretical eclecticism.* Although clinically serviceable when the procedures chosen have been proved effective in the kinds of circumstances to which they will be applied, atheoretical eclecticism is a risky business. It brings with it a persistent danger that being eclectic will justify a superficial, chaotic approach to assessment and intervention in which practitioners improvise, their open-mindedness and lack of commitment to any single point of view concealing ignorance of any of the theoretical formulations that provide a necessary guide to clinical work.

When eclecticism masks the absence of a cohesive frame of reference, clients rarely reap the benefits of cumulative clinical wisdom, and knowledge seldom advances through definitive research designs. Without a coherent point of view, clinical skills can be exceedingly difficult to teach and learn, and interventions consisting of a mélange of techniques unconnected to any uniform conceptualization of how and why these techniques work limit the capacities of therapists to meet their patients' needs. For these reasons many eclectic clinicians prefer to work from a

Table 2.2. Theoretical Orientations of Clinical Psychologists

THEORETICAL ORIENTATION	PERCENTAGE	
	DIVISION 12[a]	DIVISION 29[b]
Eclectic	29	30.2
Dynamic (psychoanalytic, psychodynamic)	23	29.2
Behavioral	16	5.6
Experiential (existential, gestalt, humanistic, client-centered)	12	16.1
Cognitive	13	8.3
Other	7	10.6

a. Based on survey of 579 members of APA Division of Clinical Psychology (Norcross, Prochaska, & Gallagher, in press).
b. Based on survey of 410 members of APA Division of Psychotherapy (Prochaska & Norcross, 1983).

preferred theoretical frame of reference within which they utilize procedures drawn from diverse approaches. Lazarus's (1976) multimodal behavior therapy has been a leading example of this type of eclecticism, usually referred to as *systematic* or *technical eclecticism*. Systematic eclecticism is far removed from an intuitive, nonconceptual approach to clinical work. It represents instead the willingness and capacity of clinicians with some preferred conceptual frame of reference to acknowledge, understand, and utilize in their work the postulates of theorists with other preferences and the empirical data generated by theorists of all preferences.

Surveys of psychologists in the American Psychological Association (APA) Division of Clinical Psychology and Division of Psychotherapy who regard themselves as eclectic indicate that 62% to 65% favor synthetic eclecticism, 4% to 11% atheoretical eclectics, and 27% to 31% technical eclecticism (Norcross & Prochaska, 1988; Prochaska & Norcross, 1983). As shown in Table 2.2, these eclectic perspectives taken together constitute the most frequent theoretical orientation among these survey respondents, followed closely by adherence to dynamic frames of reference. A behavioral orientation is next most frequent among clinical division members, whereas an experiential perspective is the third most frequent preference of psychotherapy division members.

How adequately these two division samples represent clinical psychologists in general is uncertain. The diverse views held by contemporary clinicians are reflected in the presence of other APA divisions such as Humanistic Psychology and Psychoanalysis, and many clinicians identify with other groups such as the Association for Advancement of Behavior Therapy and the Society for the Exploration of Psychotherapy Integration. Still others may study, practice, and teach clinical psychology without belonging to any formal association. Despite all of the communalities among different theories and the pronounced convergence among approaches, diversity remains the most prominent characteristic of theoretical foundations of clinical psychology.

REFERENCES

Alexander, F., & French, T. M. (1946). *Psychoanalytic therapy*. New York: Ronald Press.

Allison, J., Blatt, S. J., & Zimet, C. N. (1988). *The interpretation of psychological tests* (2nd ed.). New York: Hemisphere.

Allport, G. W. (1937). *Personality: A psychological interpretation*. New York: Holt, Rinehart & Winston.

Allport, G. W. (1961). *Pattern and growth in personality*. New York: Holt, Rinehart & Winston.

Altshuler, K. Z., & Rush, A. J. (1984). Psychoanalytic and cognitive therapies: A comparison of theory and tactics. *American Journal of Psychotherapy, 38,* 4–16.

Anderson, W. (1974). Personal growth and client-centered therapy: An information processing view. In D. A. Wexler & L. N. Rice (Eds.), *Innovations in client-centered therapy* (pp. 121–148). New York: John Wiley & Sons.

Appelbaum, S. A. (1976). Objections to diagnosis and diagnostic psychological testing diagnosed. *Bulletin of the Menninger Clinic, 40,* 559–564.

Bandura, A. (1969). *Principles of behavior modification*. New York: Holt, Rinehart & Winston.

Bandura, A. (1977). *Social learning theory*. Englewood Cliffs, NJ: Prentice-Hall.

Bannister, D. (1975). Personal construct theory psychotherapy. In D. Bannister (Ed.), *Issues and approaches in the psychological therapies* (pp. 121–146). New York: John Wiley & Sons.

Barlow, D. H. (Ed.). (1981). *Behavioral assessment of adult disorders*. New York: Guilford Press.

Bauer, G. P., & Kobos, J. C. (1987). *Brief therapy: Short-term psychodynamic intervention*. New York: Aronson.

Beck, A. T. (1976). *Cognitive therapy and the emotional disorders*. New York: International Universities Press.

Beitman, B. D. (1987). *The structure of individual psychotherapy*. New York: Guilford Press.

Bellack, A. S., & Hersen, M. (1988). *Behavioral assessment: A practical handbook* (3rd ed). Elmsford, NY: Pergamon Press.

Beutler, L. E. (1983). *Eclectic psychotherapy*. Elmsford, NY: Pergamon Press.

Bieber, I. (1980). *Cognitive psychoanalysis*. New York: Aronson.

Blanck, G., & Blanck, R. (1974). *Ego psychology: Theory and practice*. New York: Basic Books.

Blatt, S. J., & Lerner, H. (1983). Investigations in the psychoanalytic theory of object relations and object representations. In J. Masling (Ed.), *Empirical studies of psychoanalytical theories* (Vol. 1, pp. 189–250). Hillsdale, NJ: Lawrence Erlbaum Associates.

Bohart, A. C. (1982). Similarities between cognitive and humanistic approaches in psychotherapy. *Cognitive Therapy and Research, 6*, 245–250.

Bonime, W. (1962). *The clinical use of dreams*. New York: Basic Books.

Bordin, E. S. (1979). The generalizability of the psychoanalytic concept of the working alliance. *Psychotherapy: Theory, Research and Practice, 16*, 252–259.

Breuer J., & Freud, S. (1955). Studies on hysteria. *Standard Edition* (Vol. II, pp. 1–306). London: Hogarth (Original work published 1883–1895).

Brown, E. C. (1972). Assessment from a humanistic perspective. *Psychotherapy: Theory, Research and Practice, 9*, 103–106.

Bruinink, S. A., & Schroeder, H. E. (1979). Verbal therapeutic behavior of expert psychoanalytically oriented, Gestalt, and behavior therapists. *Journal of Consulting and Clinical Psychology, 47*, 567–574.

Bugental, J. T. F. (1978). *Psychotherapy and process: The fundamentals of an existential humanistic approach*. Reading, MA: Addison-Wesley.

Bugental, J. T. F. (1987). *The art of the psychotherapist*. New York: W W Norton.

Cameron, N. (1963). *Personality development and psychopathology: A dynamic approach*. Boston: Houghton Mifflin.

Cashdan, S. (1988). *Object relations therapy*. New York: W W Norton.

Chessick, R. D. (1974). *Technique and practice of intensive psychotherapy*. New York: Aronson.

Ciminero, A. R., Calhoun, K. S., & Adams, H. E. (Eds.). (1986). *Handbook of behavioral assessment* (2nd ed.). New York: John Wiley & Sons.

Cohen, L. H., & Oyster-Nelson, C. K. (1981). Clinician's evaluations of psychodynamic psychotherapy: Experimental data on psychological peer review. *Journal of Consulting and Clinical Psychology, 49*, 583–589.

Dana, R. H. (1982). *A human science model for personality assessment with projective techniques*. Springfield, IL: Charles C Thomas.

Dana, R. H., & Leech, S. (1974). Existential assessment. *Journal of Personality Assessment, 38*, 428–435.

Dewald, P. (1971). *Psychotherapy: A dynamic approach* (2nd ed.). New York: Basic Books.

Dobson, K. S., & Block, L. (1988). Historical and philosophical bases of the cognitive-behavioral therapies. In K. S. Dobson (Ed.), *Handbook of cognitive-behavioral therapies* (pp. 3–38). New York: Guilford Press.

Dollard, J., & Miller, N. E. (1950). *Personality and psychotherapy*. New York: McGraw-Hill.

Dreikurs, R. (1987). Are psychological schools of thought outdated? *Individual Psychology: Journal of Adlerian Theory, Research & Practice, 43*, 265–272.

D'Zurilla, T. D. (1986). *Problem-solving therapy*. New York: Springer.

Eagle, M. N. (1984a). *Recent developments in psychoanalysis*. New York: McGraw-Hill.

Eagle, M. N. (1984b). Psychoanalysis and modern psychodynamic theories. In N. S. Endler & J. McV. Hunt (Eds.), *Personality and the behavior disorders* (2nd ed., pp. 73–112). New York: John Wiley & Sons.

Ellis, A. (1962). *Reason and emotion in psychotherapy*. New York: Lyle Stuart.

Ellis, A. (1980). Rational-emotive therapy and cognitive behavior therapy: Similarities and differences. *Cognitive Therapy & Research, 4*, 325–340.

Ellis, A., & Dryden, W. (1987). *The practice of rational emotive therapy*. New York: Springer.

Emery, G., Hollon, S. D., & Bedrosian, R. C. (1981). *New directions in cognitive therapy*. New York: Guilford Press.

Erikson, E. H. (1950). *Childhood and society*. New York: W W Norton.

Ewen, R. B. (1988). *An introduction to theories of personality*. Hillsdale, NJ: Lawrence Erlbaum Associates.

Exner, J. E. (1983). Rorschach assessment. In I. B. Weiner (Ed.), *Clinical methods in psychology* (2nd ed., pp. 58–99). New York: John Wiley & Sons.

Exner, J. E., & Weiner, I. B. (1982). *The Rorschach: A Comprehensive system, Vol. 3. Assessment of children and adolescents*. New York: John Wiley & Sons.

Eysenck, H. J. (1959). Learning theory and behavior therapy. *Journal of Mental Science, 105*, 61–75.

Eysenck, H. J., & Martin, I. (1987). *Theoretical foundations of behavior therapy*. New York: Plenum Publishing.

Eysenck, H. J., & Rachman, S. (1965). *The causes and cures of neurosis*. San Diego: Knapp.

Fenichel, O. (1945). *The psychoanalytic theory of neurosis*. New York: W W Norton.

Fiedler, F. E. (1950). A comparison of therapeutic relationship in psychoanalytic, nondirective, and Adlerian therapy. *Journal of Consulting Psychology, 14,* 436–445.

Fisher, S., & Greenberg, R. P. (1977). *The scientific credibility of Freud's theories and therapy.* New York: Basic Books.

Frank, J. D. (1971). Therapeutic factors in psychotherapy. *American Journal of Psychotherapy, 25,* 351–361.

Frank, J. D. (1976). Restoration of morale and behavior change. In A. Burton (Ed.), *What makes behavior change possible?* (pp. 73–95). New York: Brunner/Mazel.

Frank, J. D., Hoehn-Saric, R., Imber, S. D., Liberman, B. L., & Stone, A. R. (1978). *Effective ingredients of successful psychotherapy.* New York: Brunner/Mazel.

Freud, A. (1946). *The ego and the mechanisms of defence.* New York: International Universities Press (Original work published 1936).

Freud, S. (1953a). *The interpretation of dreams. Standard edition* (Vols. IV and V). London: Hogarth (Original work published 1900).

Freud, S. (1953b). *On psychotherapy. Standard edition* (Vol. VII, pp. 252–270). London: Hogarth (Original work published 1904).

Freud, S. (1959). *Inhibitions, symptoms, and anxiety. Standard edition* (Vol. XX, pp. 87–172). London: Hogarth (Original work published 1926).

Freud, S. (1960). *The psychopathology of everyday life. Standard edition* (Vol. VI). London: Hogarth (Original work published 1901).

Freud, S. (1961). *The ego and the id. Standard edition* (Vol. XIX, pp. 13–59). London: Hogarth (Original work published 1923).

Freud, S. (1963). *Introductory lectures on psycho-analysis. Standard edition* (Vols. XV and XVI). London: Hogarth (Original work published 1917).

Freud, S. (1964a). *Analysis terminable and interminable. Standard edition* (Vol. XXIII, pp. 216–254). London: Hogarth (Original work published 1937).

Freud, S. (1964b). *New introductory lectures on psycho-analysis. Standard edition* (Vol. XXII, pp. 7–184). London: Hogarth (Original work published 1933).

Garfield, S. L. (1982). Eclecticism and integration in psychotherapy. *Behavior Therapy, 13,* 610–623.

Goldfried, M. R. (1983). Behavioral assessment. In I. B. Weiner (Ed.), *Clinical methods in psychology* (2nd ed., pp. 233–281). New York: John Wiley & Sons.

Goldfried, M. R. (1987). A common language for the psychotherapies: Commentary. *International Journal of Eclectic Psychotherapy, 6,* 200–204.

Goldfried, M. R., & Merbaum, M. (Eds.). (1973). *Behavior change through self-control.* New York: Holt, Rinehart & Winston.

Goldfried, M. R., & Newman, C. (1986). Psychotherapy integration: An historical perspective. In J. C. Norcross (Ed.), *Handbook of eclectic psychotherapy* (pp. 25–61). New York: Brunner/Mazel.

Goldfried, M. R., & Padawer, W. (1982). Current status and future directions in psychotherapy. In M. R. Goldfried (Ed.), *Converging themes in psychotherapy* (pp. 3–50). New York: Springer.

Goldfried, M. R., & Robins, C. (1982). On the facilitation of self-efficacy. *Cognitive Therapy and Research, 6,* 361–379.

Goldfried, M. R., & Safran, J. D. (1986). Future directions in psychotherapy integration. In J. C. Norcross (Ed.), *Handbook of eclectic psychotherapy* (pp. 463–483). New York: Brunner/Mazel.

Goldfried, M. R., Stricker, G., & Weiner, I. B. (1971). *Rorschach handbook of clinical and research applications.* Englewood Cliffs, NJ: Prentice-Hall.

Goldstein, A., & Foa, E. B. (Eds.). (1980). *Handbook of behavioral interventions.* New York: John Wiley & Sons.

Greenson, R. R. (1967). *The technique and practice of psychoanalysis.* New York: International Universities Press.

Hall, C. S., & Lindzey, G. (1978). *Theories of personality* (3rd ed.). New York: John Wiley & Sons.

Hartmann, H. (1958). *Ego psychology and the problem of adaptation.* New York: International Universities Press. (Original work published 1939).

Hollon, S. D., & Beck, A. T. (1986). Cognitive and cognitive-behavioral therapies. In S. L. Garfield & E. A. Bergin (Eds.), *Handbook of psychotherapy and behavior change* (3rd ed., pp. 443–482). New York: John Wiley & Sons.

Holzman, P. S. (1970). *Psychoanalysis and psychopathology.* New York: McGraw-Hill.

Horowitz, M. J. (1988). *Introduction to psychodynamics: A new synthesis.* New York: Basic Books.

Jones, E. E., Cumming, J. D., & Horowitz, M. J. (1988). Another look at the nonspecific hypothesis of therapeutic effectiveness. *Journal of Consulting and Clinical Psychology, 56,* 48–55.

Jourard, S. M. (1964). *The transparent self: Self-disclosure and well-being.* New York: Van Nostrand Reinhold.

Jourard, S. M. (1968). *Disclosing man to himself.* New York: Van Nostrand Reinhold.

Jourard, S. M. (1971). *Self-disclosure: An experimental analysis of the transparent self.* New York: John Wiley & Sons.

Kahn, E. (1985). Heinz Kohut and Carl Rogers: A timely comparison. *American Psychologist, 40,* 893–904.

Kanfer, F. H. (1985). Target selection for clinical change programs. *Behavioral Assessment, 7,* 7–20.

Kanfer, F. H., & Phillips, J. (1970). *Learning foundations of behavior therapy.* New York: John Wiley & Sons.

Kazdin, A. E. (1978). The application of operant techniques in treatment, rehabitation, and education. In S. L. Garfield & A. E. Bergin (Eds.), *Handbook of psychotherapy and behavioral change* (2nd ed., pp. 549–590). New York: John Wiley & Sons.

Kazdin, A. E. (1979a). Fictions, factions, and functions of behavior therapy. *Behavior Therapy, 10,* 629–654.

Kazdin, A. E. (1979b). Situational specificity: The two-edged sword of behavioral assessment. *Behavioral Assessment, 1,* 57–76,

Kazdin, A. E. (1979c). Nonspecific treatment factors in psychotherapy outcome research. *Journal of Consulting and Clinical Psychology, 47,* 846–851,

Kelly, G. A. (1955). *The psychology of personal constructs.* New York: W W Norton.

Kelly, G. A. (1980). A psychology of the optimal man. In A. W. Landfield & L. M. Leitner (Eds.), *Personal construct psychology.* New York: John Wiley & Sons.

Kendall, P. C., & Hollon, S. D. (Eds.). (1981). *Assessment strategies for cognitive-behavioral interventions.* New York: Academic Press.

Lambert, M. J. (1986). Implications of psychotherapy outcome research for eclectic psychotherapy. In J. C. Norcross (Ed.), *Handbook of eclectic psychotherapy* (pp. 436–462). New York: Brunner/Mazel.

Lambert, M. J., Shapiro, D. A., & Bergin, A. E. (1986). The effectiveness of psychotherapy. In S. L. Garfield & A. E. Bergin (Eds.), *Handbook of psychotherapy and behavior change* (3rd ed., pp. 157–211). New York: John Wiley & Sons.

Landfield, A. W., & Epting, F. R. (1987). *Personal construct psychology: Clinical and personality assessment.* New York: Human Sciences Press.

Landfield, A. W., & Leitner, L. M. (Eds.). (1980). *Personal construct psychology.* New York: John Wiley & Sons.

Langs, R. (1973). *The technique of psychoanalytic psychotherapy.* New York: Aronson.

Lazarus, A. A. (1971). *Behavior therapy and beyond.* New York: McGraw-Hill.

Lazarus, A. A. (1976). *Multi-modal behavior therapy.* New York: Springer.

Lazarus, A. A. (1980). Toward delineating some causes of change in psychotherapy. *Professional Psychology, 11,* 863–870.

Leitenberg, H. (Ed.). (1976). *Handbook of behavior modification and behavior therapy.* Englewood Cliffs, NJ: Prentice-Hall.

Lerner, P. M. (1984). Projective techniques and personality assessment: The current perspective. In N. S. Endler & J. McV. Hunt (Eds.), *Personality and the behavior disorders* (2nd ed., pp. 283–312). New York: John Wiley & Sons.

Lichstein, K. L. (1988). *Clinical relaxation strategies.* New York: John Wiley & Sons.

Luborsky, L. (1984). *Principles of psychoanalytic psychotherapy.* New York: Basic Books.

Luborsky, L., Singer, B., & Luborsky, L. (1975). Comparative studies of psychotherapies. *Archives of General Psychiatry, 32,* 995–1008.

Luborsky, L., & Spence, D. P. (1978). Quantitative research on psychoanalytic therapy. In S. L. Garfield & A. E. Bergin (Eds.), *Handbook of psychotherapy and behavior change* (2nd ed., pp. 331–368). New York: John Wiley & Sons.

Luborsky, L., Woody, G. E., McLellan, A. T., O'Brien, C. P., & Rosenzweig, J. (1982). Can independent judges recognize different psychotherapies? *Journal of Consulting and Clinical Psychology, 50,* 49–62.

Mahoney, M. J. (1977). Reflections on the cognitive learning trend in psychotherapy. *American Psychologist, 32,* 5–13.

Mahoney, M. J. (1988). The cognitive sciences and psychotherapy: Patterns in a developing relationship. In K. S. Dobson (Ed.), *Handbook of cognitive-behavioral therapies* (pp. 357–386). New York: Guilford Press.

Mahoney, M. J., & Arnkoff, D. (1978). Cognitive and self-control therapies. In S. L. Garfield & A. E. Bergin (Eds.), *Handbook of psychotherapy and behavior change* (2nd ed., pp. 689–722). New York: John Wiley & Sons.

Mahrer, A. R. (1978). *Experiencing: A humanistic theory of psychology and psychiatry.* New York: Brunner/Mazel.

Mahrer, A. R. (1983). *Experiential psychotherapy.* New York: Brunner/Mazel.

Malan, D. (1976). *The frontier of brief psychotherapy.* New York: Plenum Publishing.

Marmor, J. (1976). Common operational factors in diverse approaches to behavior change. In A. Burton (Ed.), *What makes behavior change possible?* (pp. 3–12). New York: Brunner/Mazel.

Marmor, J., & Woods, S. (1980). *The interface between the psychodynamic and behavioral therapies.* New York: Plenum Publishing.

Martin, D. G. (1972). *Learning-based client-centered therapy.* Monterey, CA: Brooks/Cole.

Mash, E. J., & Terdal, L. G. (Eds.). (1988). *Behavioral assessment of childhood disorders* (2nd ed.). New York: Guilford Press.

Masling, J. (Ed.). (1983). *Empirical studies of psychoanalytical theories* (Vol. 1). Hillsdale, NJ: Analytic Press.

Masling, J. (Ed.). (1986). *Empirical studies of psychoanalytical theories* (Vol. 2). Hillsdale, NJ: Analytic Press.

Maslow, A. H. (1962). *Toward a theory of being.* Princeton, NJ: Van Nostrand Reinhold.

Maslow, A. H. (1966). *The psychology of science: A reconnaissance.* New York: Harper & Row.

May, R., Angel, E., & Ellenberger, H. F. (Eds.). (1958). *Existence: A new dimension in psychiatry and psychology.* New York: Basic Books.

Meara, N. M., Shannon, J. W., & Pepinsky, H. B. (1979). Comparison of the stylistic complexity of the language of counsel and client across three theoretical orientations. *Journal of Counseling Psychology, 26,* 181–189.

Meichenbaum, D. (1977). *Cognitive-behavior modification.* New York: Plenum Publishing.

Meichenbaum, D., & Gilmore, J. B. (1984). The nature of unconscious processes: A cognitive-developmental perspective. In K. S. Bowers & D. Meichenbaum (Eds.), *The unconscious reconsidered* (pp. 273–298). New York: John Wiley & Sons.

Menninger, K. A., & Holzman, P. S. (1973). *Theory of psychoanalytic technique* (2nd ed.). New York: Basic Books.

Messer, S. B. (1983). Integrating psychoanalytic and behaviour therapy: Limitations, possibilities and trade-offs. *British Journal of Clinical Psychology, 22*, 131–132.

Messer, S. B. (1986). Eclecticism in psychotherapy: Underlying assumptions, problems, and trade-offs. In J. Norcross (Ed.), *Handbook of eclectic psychotherapy* (pp. 379–397). New York: Brunner/Mazel.

Munroe, R. L. (1955). *Schools of psychoanalytic thought*. New York: Dryden Press.

Murray, E. J. (1983). Beyond behavioural and dynamic therapy. *British Journal of Clinical Psychology, 22*, 127–128.

Murray, E. J. (1986). Therapeutic integration and visions of reality. *International Journal of Eclectic Psychotherapy, 5*, 127–133.

Nathan, P. E., Witte, G., & Langenbucher, J. W. (1983). Behavior therapy and behavior modification. In I. B. Weiner (Ed.), *Clinical methods in psychology* (2nd ed., pp. 509–571). New York: John Wiley & Sons.

Neimeyer, R. A., & Neimeyer, G. J. (Eds.). (1987). *Personal construct therapy casebook*. New York: Springer.

Nelson, R. O., & Hayes, S. C. (Eds.). (1986). *Conceptual foundations of behavioral assessment*. New York: Guilford Press.

Norcross, J. C. (1985). In defense of theoretical orientations for clinicians. *Clinical Psychologist, 38*, 13–17.

Norcross, J. C. (1986). Eclectic psychotherapy: An introduction and overview. In J. C. Norcross (Ed.), *Handbook of eclectic psychotherapy* (pp. 3–24). New York: Brunner/Mazel.

Norcross, J. C. (1987). Toward a common language for psychotherapy: Introduction. *International Journal of Eclectic Psychotherapy, 6*, 165–167.

Norcross, J. C., & Prochaska, J. O. (1988). A study of eclectic (and integrative) views revisited. *Professional Psychology, 19*, 170–174.

Norcross, J. C., Prochaska, J. O., & Gallagher, K. M. (in press). Clinical psychologists in the 1980s: II. Theory, research, and practice. *Clinical Psychologist*.

Orlinsky, D. E., & Howard, K. I. (1986). Process and outcome in psychotherapy. In S. L. Garfield & A. E. Bergin (Eds.), *Handbook of psychotherapy and behavior change* (pp. 311–384). New York: John Wiley & Sons.

Parloff, M. B., London, P., & Wolfe, B. (1986). Individual psychotherapy and behavior change. *Annual Review of Psychology, 37*, 321–349.

Perls, F., Hefferline, R., & Goodman, P. (1951). *Gestalt therapy*. New York: Julian Press.

Pervin, L. A. (1984). Idiographic approaches to personality. In N. S. Endler & J. McV. Hunt (Eds.), *Personality and the behavior disorders* (2nd ed., pp. 261–282). New York: John Wiley & Sons.

Polster, E., & Polster, M. (1973). *Gestalt therapy integrated*. New York: Brunner/Mazel.

Pope, B. (1979). *The mental health interview*. Elmsford, NY: Pergamon Press.

Prochaska, J. O., & DiClemente, C. C. (1984). *The transtheoretical approach: Crossing traditional boundaries of therapy*. Homewood, IL: Dow Jones-Irwin.

Prochaska, J. O., & Norcross, J. C. (1983). Contemporary psychotherapists: A national survey of characteristics, practices, orientations, and attitudes. *Psychotherapy: Theory, Research and Practice, 20*, 161–173.

Raimy, V. (1975). *Misunderstandings of the self: Cognitive psychotherapy and the misconception hypothesis*. San Francisco: Jossey-Bass.

Rapaport, D. (1967). *The collected papers of David Rapaport*. New York: Basic Books.

Rapaport, D., Gill, M. M., & Schafer, R. (1968). *Diagnostic psychological testing* (rev. ed.). New York: International Universities Press.

Rimm, D. C., & Masters, J. C. (1979). *Behavior therapy* (2nd ed.). New York: Academic Press.

Rogers, C. R. (1951). *Client-centered therapy*. Boston: Houghton Mifflin.

Rogers, C. R. (1961). *On becoming a person: a therapist's view of psychotherapy*. Boston: Houghton Mifflin.

Rosenthal, T., & Bandura, A. (1978). Psychological modeling: Theory and practice. In S. L. Garfield & A. E. Bergin (Eds.), *Handbook of psychotherapy and behavior change* (2nd ed., pp. 621–658). New York: John Wiley & Sons.

Rychlak, J. F. (1988). *The psychology of rigorous humanism* (2nd ed.). New York: New York University Press.

Segal, Z. V., & Shaw, B. F. (1988). Cognitive assessment: Issues and methods. In K. S. Dobson (Ed.), *Handbook of cognitive-behavioral therapies* (pp. 39–81). New York: Guilford Press.

Shaffer, J. B. P. (1978). *Humanistic psychology*. Englewood Cliffs, NJ: Prentice-Hall.

Shakow, D., & Rapaport, D. (1964). *The influence of Freud on American psychology*. New York: World Publishing Co.

Shevrin, H., & Shectman, F. (1973). The diagnostic process in psychiatric evaluations. *Bulletin of the Menninger Clinic, 37*, 451–494.

Sifneos, P. (1979). *Short-term dynamic psychotherapy*. New York: Plenum Publishing.

Silverman, L. H. (1983). The subliminal psychodynamic activation method: Overview and comprehensive listing of studies. In J. Masling (Ed.), *Empirical studies of psychoanalytical theories* (pp. 69–100). Hillsdale, NJ: Analytic Press.

Silverman, L. H., & Weinberger, J. (1985). Mommy and I are one: Implications for psychotherapy. *American Psychologist, 40*, 1296–1308.

Skinner, B. F. (1977). Why I am not a cognitive psychologist. *Behaviorism, 5*, 1–10.

Small, L. (Ed.). (1979). *The briefer psychotherapies* (rev. ed.). New York: Brunner/Mazel.

Smith, M. L., Glass, G. V., & Miller, T. I. (1980). *The benefits of psychotherapy*. Baltimore, MD: Johns Hopkins University Press.

Spence, D. P. (1982). *Narrative truth and historical truth: Meaning and interpretation in psychoanalysis*. New York: W W Norton.

Spitzer, R. L., & Endicott, J. (1973). The value of the

interview for the evaluation of psychopathology. In M. Hammer, K. Salzinger, & S. Sutton (Eds.), *Psychopathology: Contributions from social, behavioral, and biological sciences* (pp. 397–408). New York: John Wiley & Sons.

Staples, F. R., Sloane, R. B., Whipple, K., Cristol, A. H., & Yorkton, N. J. (1975). Differences between behavior therapists and psychotherapists. *Archives of General Psychiatry, 32*, 1517–1522.

Stiles, W. B., Shapiro, D. A., & Elliott, R. (1986). Are all psychotherapies equivalent? *American Psychologist, 41*, 165–180.

Strong, S. R., & Claiborn, C. D. (1982). *Change through interaction: Social psychological processes of counseling and psychotherapy*. New York: John Wiley & Sons.

Strosahl, K. D., & Linehan, M. M. (1986). Basic issues in behavioral assessment. In A. R. Ciminero, K. S. Calhoun, & H. E. Adams (Eds.), *Handbook of behavioral assessment* (2nd ed., pp. 12–46). New York: John Wiley & Sons.

Strupp, H. H. (1970). Specific vs. nonspecific factors in psychotherapy and the problem of control. *Archives of General Psychiatry, 23*, 393–401.

Strupp, H. H. (1973). On the basic ingredients of psychotherapy. *Journal of Consulting and Clinical Psychology, 1*, 1–8.

Strupp, H. H. (1975). Psychoanalysis, "focal psychotherapy," and the nature of the therapeutic influence. *Archives of General Psychiatry, 32*, 127–135.

Strupp, H. H. (1979). A psychodynamicist looks at modern behavior therapy. *Psychotherapy: Theory, Research and Practice, 16*, 124–131.

Strupp, H. H. (1980). Humanism and psychotherapy: A personal statement of the therapist's essential values. *Psychotherapy: Theory, Research and Practice, 17*, 396–400.

Strupp, H. H., & Binder, J. L. (1984). *Psychotherapy in a new key: A guide to time-limited dynamic psychotherapy*. New York: Basic Books.

Strupp, H. H., & Hadley, S. W. (1979). Specific vs nonspecific factors in psychotherapy: A controlled study of outcome. *Archives of General Psychiatry, 36*, 1125–1136.

Sugarman, A. (1976). Psychoanalysis as a humanistic psychology. *Psychotherapy: Theory, Research and Practice, 14*, 204–211.

Sugarman, A. (1978). Is psychodiagnostic assessment humanistic? *Journal of Personality Assessment, 42*, 11–21.

Sullivan, H. S. (1954). *The psychiatric interview*. New York: W W Norton.

Sweet, A. A. (1984). The therapeutic relationship in behavior therapy. *Clinical Psychology Review, 4*, 253–272.

Thompson, J. K., & Spana, R. E. (1986). An interpersonally based cognitive-behavioral psychotherapy. *International Journal of Eclectic Psychotherapy, 5*, 179–191.

Turner, S. M. Calhoun, K. S., & Adams, H. E. (Eds.). (1981). *Handbook of clinical behavior therapy*. New York: John Wiley & Sons.

Wachtel, P. L. (1977). *Psychoanalysis and behavior therapy: Toward an integration*. New York: Basic Books.

Wachtel, P. L. (1983). Integration misunderstood. *British Journal of Clinical Psychology, 22*, 129–130.

Weiner, I. B. (1966). *Psychodiagnosis in schizophrenia*. New York: John Wiley & Sons.

Weiner, I. B. (1975). *Principles of psychotherapy*. New York: John Wiley & Sons.

Weiner, I. B. (1983). The future of psychodiagnosis revisited. *Journal of Personality Assessment, 47*, 451–461.

Weiner, I. B., & Bordin, E. S. (1983). Individual psychotherapy. In I. B. Weiner (Ed.), *Clinical methods in psychology* (2nd ed., pp. 333–388). New York: John Wiley & Sons.

Weiss, J., & Sampson, H. (1986). *The psychoanalytic process*. New York: Guilford Press.

Weiss, L. (1986). *Dream analysis in psychotherapy*. Elmsford, NY: Pergamon Press.

Wexler, D. A. (1974). A cognitive theory of experiencing, self-actualization, and therapeutic process. In D. A. Wexler & L. N. Rice (Eds.), *Innovations in client-centered therapy* (pp. 49–116). New York: John Wiley & Sons.

Wiens, A. N. (1983). The assessment interview. In I. B. Weiner (Ed.), *Clinical methods in psychology* (pp. 3–57). New York: John Wiley & Sons.

Wilson, G. T., & Evans, I. M. (1977). The therapist-client relationship in behavior therapy. In A. S. Gurman & A. M. Razin (Eds.), *Effective psychotherapy: A handbook of research*. Elmsford, NY: Pergamon Press.

Wilson, G. T., & Franks, C. M. (Eds.). (1982). *Contemporary behavior therapy: Conceptual and empirical foundations*. New York: Guilford Press.

Wolpe, J. (1958). *Psychotherapy by reciprocal inhibition*. Stanford, CA: Stanford University Press.

Wolpe, J. (1978). Cognition and causation in human behavior and its therapy. *American Psychologist, 33*, 437–446.

Wrenn, R. L. (1960). Counselor orientation: Theoretical or situational. *Journal of Counseling Psychology, 7*, 40–45.

Wright, L., Everett, F., & Roisman, L. (1986). *Experiential psychotherapy with children.* Baltimore, MD: Johns Hopkins University Press.

Wyss, D. (1973). *Psychoanalytic schools from the beginning to the present*. New York: Aronson.

Yates, A. J. (1970). *Behavior therapy*. New York: John Wiley & Sons.

Yates, A. J. (1986). Behaviour therapy and psychodynamic psychotherapy: Basic conflict or reconciliation and integration? *British Journal of Clinical Psychology, 212*, 107–125.

Zimring, F. (1974). Theory and practice of client-centered therapy: A cognitive view. In D. A. Wexler & L. N. Rice (Eds.), *Innovations in client-centered therapy* (pp. 117–138). New York: John Wiley & Sons.

CHAPTER 3

CLINICAL TRAINING

Barry A. Edelstein
William S. Brasted

In 1896, Lightner Witmer established the first psycho logical clinic to offer professional services (Korchin, 1976) and coined the term *clinical psychologist* (Strickland, 1988). Within 15 years, five additional clinics were established, four of which were associated with psychology departments. During the early 1900s, clinical practicum and internship training occurred in clinics and such clinical settings as the Vineland New Jersey Training School, Boston Psychopathic Hospital, and the Worcester State Hospital (Pottharst, 1976). The nature of clinical training varied across psychology programs, and many individuals who were to become identified as clinical psychologists received general psychology training followed by an internship. As the need for psychologists expanded, so did the number of psychologists who identified themselves as clinical psychologists.

In 1919, clinical psychologists persuaded the American Psychological Association (APA) to form a clinical section. In 1924, the clinical section of the APA recommended that clinical psychologists have a PhD in psychology and 4 years of experience, one of which was to be under supervision (Kendall & Norton-Ford, 1982; Reisman, 1981). This recommendation also supported a scientist-practitioner model of training, in which a balance of research and clinical

training was recommended. Later, in 1931, the APA committee on standards of training for clinical psychologists was formed, and their report was published in 1935. Though recommendations were beginning to come forth, there seemed to be little or no attempt to insure adherence to any of the recommendations. In 1938, the first volume of the *Journal of Consulting Psychology* carried articles discussing the training of clinical psychologists and the recommended 1-year internship (Derner, 1965). In the same year, Shakow (1938) presented his now archetypal recommendations for an internship year in a psychiatric hospital.

Poffenberger (1938) recommended that the doctoral degree be a prerequisite for membership in the newly formed American Association of Applied Psychology (Derner, 1965). The doctorate described by Poffenberger was the Doctor of Psychology (PsyD) degree, which emphasized preparation for clinic service and, to a lesser extent, academic research. The awarding of this degree continues to spark controversy as a function of the imbalance of emphasis between research and practice. In the third volume of the *Journal of Consulting Psychology,* Rogers (1939) also described an approach for clinical training and supported Shakow's appeal for a required internship.

Though the foregoing events helped to shape early

notions of clinical training, or what it should be, it was World War II that yielded the first apparent attempts to arrive at some consensus regarding the nature of acceptable clinical psychology training. Assessment and testing were the principal activities of clinical psychologists prior to World War II, with the greatest emphasis being on children and their mothers. Following the war, psychologists were called on to deliver a full range of psychological services to all age groups. The United States was filled with returning veterans whose needs for psychological services far exceeded the mental health manpower of the time. It was estimated that 4,700 new clinical psychologists were needed to provide psychological assessment and therapy in Veterans Administration (VA) facilities (Kendall & Norton-Ford, 1982). The VA and the United States Public Health Service approached the APA with the task of specifying the nature of adequate clinical psychology training and eventually identifying programs that met these criteria. Carl Rogers, then president of the APA, asked David Shakow to chair a committee on training in clinical psychology. The committee report, presented in September of 1947, was entitled "Recommended Graduate Training Program in Clinical Psychology," and became known as the Shakow report. The report stated 14 general principles in three major areas: diagnostics, research, and therapy. Most important, the report emphasized both the scientific and the professional aspects of clinical psychology. Programs were encouraged to graduate well-balanced clinical psychologists who could provide clinical services and continue to contribute to the field of psychology in their research efforts. By 1947, 22 universities had training programs in clinical psychology (Reisman, 1981).

Two years after publication of the Shakow report, 71 representatives of the profession met in Boulder, Colorado, to discuss training (Raimy, 1950). The scientist-professional model was again endorsed, and approximately 70 propositions were considered. It is important to note that the Boulder conference was supported financially by the VA and the U.S. Public Health Service, a fact that could have substantially affected the general outcome of the meeting (Sarason, 1981). The importance of funding for clinical training and its influence on the directions of the field began here and has continued to the present. Based on the recommendations of the Boulder conference and the stated needs of the VA and U.S. Public Health Service, the APA formed an education and training board to monitor the training of clinical psychologists and accredit graduate and internship training through its committee on accreditation.

The next major clinical training conference to follow the Boulder conference was entitled the Institute on Education and Training for Psychological Contributions to Mental Health. The conference was held over a 4-day period at Stanford University and is sometimes referred to as the Stanford conference (Strother, 1956). According to Lloyd and Newbrough,

> Three factors which led to this conference were: (a) the trend toward specialization manifested in the Boulder, Northwestern, and Thayer Conferences and its implications for graduate training, (b) the recommendation of the Boulder Conference to review the policies and procedures that it developed, and (c) the rapid growth of the mental hygiene movement. (1966, p. 127)

The major contribution of this conference was attention to the training needs of psychologists in community mental health programs, who would adopt broader roles than those addressed at the Boulder conference.

In December 1958, a training conference on graduate education was held in Miami Beach (Roe, Gustad, Moore, Ross, & Skodak, 1959). The conference addressed five major issues that pertained to graduate education in psychology in general. Among many issues, the conference addressed fieldwork experiences, alternative degree in place of the PhD, standards for internship and postdoctoral programs, subdoctoral training programs, and accreditation (Lloyd & Newbrough, 1966). Lloyd and Newbrough noted that there was a strong consensus that doctoral education in psychology "should continue to educate doctoral psychologists as broadly as possible, limited only by the major aspects of the type of position to which the student is initially oriented" (Roe et al., 1959). There was also considerable agreement that the PhD should remain a research degree and that a nonresearch degree did not demand attention at that time (Lloyd & Newbrough, 1966).

In August 1965, the Chicago Conference on the Professional Preparation of Clinical Psychologists was held (Hoch, Ross, & Winder, 1966). Bernstein and Nietzel (1980) noted that this conference broke two traditions: "It was held in a city with a less than thrilling climate, and it was the first conference to seriously consider some alternative models of clinical training" (p. 474). In their summary of the conference, the conferees agreed that:

> Clinical psychology includes the following broad functions: Psychological analysis and assessment for

decision-making purposes; psychotherapy and other forms of behavior modification; psychological investigation (research and evaluation); training and education; consultation; administration. It was understood that any individual clinical psychologist need not be equally competent in all these functions, but that a comprehensive training program should introduce him to each of them and prepare him well for several of them. (Hoch et al., 1966, p. 92)

The conferees also strongly recommended diversification of training opportunities, with the objective of providing opportunity for different students to stress different knowledge and methods in their professional preparation (Roe et al., 1959). Therefore, programs could experiment with different models as long as their primary emphasis was on the training of scientist-professionals. They were free to explore the potential value of greater emphasis on the professional model of training.

The Miami conference was followed by the Vail conference, held in Vail, Colorado, in the summer of 1973. The plans for this conference originated in 1969 with the joint appointment by the APA Board of Professional Affairs and the Education and Training Board of an ad hoc committee on professional training (Darley, 1973). The Vail conference was entitled the National Conference on Levels and Patterns of Professional Training in Psychology. After 5 days the conferees passed approximately 150 resolutions. The resolutions could be summarized in the context of the following major themes (Korman, 1974): professional training models, multilevel training, desirable characteristics of professional training, doctoral training, Master's level training, training at Bachelor's level and below, continuing professional training, minority groups, professional training and women, service delivery systems, and the social context.

According to Korman (1974), "The conference explicitly endorsed professional training programs as one type of heuristic model to guide those programs defining themselves by a basic service orientation" (p. 19). At the same time, the conferees reaffirmed the need to emphasize basic psychological content and methodology as the root of training and education. They continued to reaffirm empiricism and scientific endeavors. The conferees noted that some programs might decide to adopt primarily professional training programs and that they would support such enterprises as long as the roots in basic psychological content and methodology were retained. The conferees also recognized the acceptability of the PsyD degree when the primary emphasis of training was on the direct delivery of professional services and the evaluation and improvement of those services (Korman, 1974).

An important result of the Vail conference was attention to the professional trained at the Master's level. The conferees stated that "many of the psychological services currently performed by Ph.D., and Ed.D., or Psy.D. degree holders could be performed equally well by personnel trained at the Master's or lower levels. The real cost of such services to the public could be appreciably lowered by training such personnel to provide them directly" (Korman, 1974, p. 25). It was also suggested that a psychologist trained at the Master's level be given full APA membership and be called a psychologist, a position that the APA currently does not support.

Another major theme of the conference, continuing professional development, was an important feature of this conference in contrast to previous conferences. It is clear that as the emphasis on professional training increased, the apparent need for continuing professional development and education was becoming a greater issue. The strong emphasis on professional training at the Vail conference yielded a concomitant emphasis on continuing education.

The most recent major training conference was held in Salt Lake City, Utah, in 1987 and entitled the National Conference on Graduate Education in Psychology (see Bickman, 1987). The 10 issues discussed at the conference were based on the products of the Planning Conference on University-based Graduate Education and Training in Psychology held in Morgantown, West Virginia, in 1985 and cosponsored by West Virginia University and APA. While the Utah conference dealt with graduate education in psychology in general, several issues were discussed and resolutions passed that addressed clinical psychology training. These included three hotly debated recommendations: (a) All psychologists should be trained in a core of psychology (unspecified by the conferees); (b) training should occur in university or university-affiliated settings (to the chagrin of freestanding clinical training programs); and (c) the distinction between and legitimacy of the PsyD and PhD degrees should be maintained. In the case of the latter resolution, debates were concerned primarily with whether the PsyD degree should be supported. A compromise evolved in which conferees supported the need for the integration of science and practice regardless of the degree granted. The issue of what constitutes the most appropriate training model was not resolved at this conference. In January of 1990, a National Conference on Scientist-Practitioner Education and Training for the Professional Practice of Psychology was held at the University of Florida under the sponsorship of the Association of Scientist-

Practitioner Psychologists and the Department of Clinical and Health Psychology of the University of Florida. The Conference was also cosponsored by twenty formal organizations representing the major educating, training, and credentialing groups in psychology. The 62 delegates reaffirmed the scientist-practitioner model of training and clarified its essential characteristics. The Conference recommendations included descriptions of basic principles, components for the preparation of the scientist-practitioner, a didactic practice core, a scientific experiential component, a professional practice experiential core, the integration of all education and training, and system characteristics. One of the many important points agreed upon was the need to emphasize domains of knowledge and skills rather than a listing of required courses.

ACCREDITATION

"Accreditation implies quality in education, training, and professional service. It is both a process and a status by which institutions or programs are publicly recognized as having met certain criteria or standards of performance" (Nelson & Aletky, 1987, p. 231). All of the conferences discussed in the foregoing section have influenced the nature of clinical training since the 1940s, when criteria for acceptable programs were sought by the APA following prompts and financial support from the VA and the U.S. Public Health Service. The accreditation of doctoral programs has occurred since the education and training board of the APA adopted the report of the Boulder conference as a basis for their initial accreditation criteria. Both predoctoral clinical psychology graduate programs and predoctoral clinical psychology internships are accredited by the APA. In early 1989 there were 158 accredited predoctoral training programs and 354 accredited internships.

The APA committee on accreditation operates under the auspices of the education and training board. The committee

> exercises professional judgment in making decisions on programs being considered for accreditation by APA under the current *Accreditation Criteria and Procedures*. It also develops guidance documents and data gathering instruments necessary to carry out this function, institutes programs for the training of site visitors and provides a consultation to programs. (APA, 1981, p. 8)

In 1973, the committee on accreditation published the *Accreditation Procedures and Criteria*. These were revised between 1978 and 1980, resulting in publication of the *Accreditation Handbook* in 1980. Publication of the handbook was a monumental step. It contains detailed descriptions of the accreditation process for graduate programs and internships, current accreditation criteria, instructions for site visitors who evaluate training programs, and various suggestions for guiding the accreditation process from perspectives of both the training program and site visitors. It was a much needed document for training programs that previously had no explicit criteria with which to guide their development and prepare for evaluations by accreditation site visitors.

The second accreditation criterion, addressing training models and curricula, includes statements of principles that are considered basic to sound training in professional psychology. A portion of that section reads as follows:

A. It is the responsibility of the faculty to integrate practice with theory and research early in the program.
B. Students should form an early identification with their profession. Faculty should be available to demonstrate and model the behaviors that students are expected to learn. A close working relationship between faculty and students is essential.
C. The foundation of professional practice in psychology is the evolving body of knowledge in the discipline of psychology. While programs will vary in emphasis and in available resources, sound graduate educaton in general psychology is therefore essential in any program. The curriculum shall encompass the equivalent of a minimum of three academic years of full-time resident graduate study. Instruction in scientific and professional ethics and standards, research design and methodology, statistics, psychological measurement, and history, and systems of psychology must be included in every doctoral program in professional psychology. The program shall further require each student to demonstrate competence in each of the following substantive content areas:
(1) biological bases of behavior (e.g., physiological psychology, comparative psychology, neuropsychology, sensation, psychopharmacology),
(2) cognitive-affective bases of behavior (e.g., learning, memory, perception, cognition, thinking, motivaton, emotion),
(3) social bases of behavior (e.g., social psychology, cultural, ethnic, and group processes; sex roles, organizational and systems theory), and
(4) individual behavior (e.g., personality theory, human development, individual differences, abnormal psychology).
Competence may be demonstrated in a number of ways: by passing suitable comprehensive exami-

nations in each of the four areas, succesful completion of at least three or more graduate semester hours (or equivalent quarter hours) in each of the four areas, or by other suitable means. These curriculum requirements represent the necessary core but not a sufficient number of graduate hours for a degree in professional psychology. All professional training programs in psychology will, in addition, include course requirements in specialty areas. (APA, 1980, p. 5)

The section goes on to elaborate training in specific skills, APA policies, ethical standards, APA standards for providers of psychological services, and APA standards for educational and psychological tests, among others. Access to training in related fields is emphasized, as are research training, the canons of science, and scholarship. Further, programs are required to develop comprehensive evaluation systems.

These accreditation criteria provide standards for training while permitting considerable flexibility for program innovation and specialization. Thus, training programs offer a variety of didactic courses and seminars on approaches to intervention, assessment, and program evaluation. Other courses frequently deal wth various psychological disorders and current research relating to their etiology and treatment. Clinical practica also vary considerably across training programs. Students may see clients in a psychology department or university-based clinic and/or in community agencies. Clinical practica with a greater emphasis on the community and social systems are also offered in some programs. These afford the student opportunities to evaluate and influence large systems.

Since its inception, the APA education and training board has continued to revise its policies and procedures for accreditation as the field of clinical psychology has evolved. In 1984 the APA board of directors authorized the education and training board to appoint a task force to conduct a major review of the APA accreditation practices, with attention to the scope of future criteria for accreditation and other procedural issues which might be implicated. The task force on reviewing the scope and criteria for accreditation began meeting in 1986 and has continued to meet, discuss, and make recommendations regarding several issues, particularly with regard to the following: (a) access to the accreditation process for doctoral education and training programs in specialty areas of professional psychology in addition to those currently recognized (clinical, counseling, and school psychology): for example, clinical neuropsychology, applied developmental psychology, mental retardation, health

psychology, pediatric psychology; and (b) access to the accreditation process for certain types of postdoctoral training programs in professional psychology. A major issue facing the task force is how to differentiate emerging specialties seeking accreditation from those currently being accredited. Virtually all of the activities proposed for these emerging specialties are being performed by practitioners within the current three specialties.

In summary, accreditation is a highly desirable process sought by clinical training programs. The accreditation process insures that clinical training programs undergo annual self-evaluations and also external evaluations at least every 5 years. This results in accredited programs graduating individuals who have met acceptable standards of the field.

INTERNSHIP TRAINING

The vast majority of doctoral programs require students to be enrolled for 4 years of full-time education. Most programs require the PhD candidate to fulfill either 1 year full time or 2 years of half-time internship. Curiously, the history of the internship is longer than that of the other predoctoral curricula, because prior to the Boulder conference all clinical training occurred in internship-like settings (Korchin, 1976, p. 72). Perhaps for this reason, Shakow (1938) placed significant emphasis on the internship as an integral part of clinical training. Therefore, among Shakow's recommendations was the suggested requirement of a full-year internship experience as part of overall training. The internship was to provide four basic functions: (a) to develop further "facility with already acquired techniques," (b) to "saturate the student with experience in the practical aspects of psychopathology," (c) to "further develop the students' experimental-objective attitude," and (d) to "get the student acquainted with the types of thinking and attitudes of his colleagues in other disciplines" (Shakow, 1938, pp. 74–76).

To satisfy these functions, the APA developed accreditation standards for internships that have remained virtually unchanged for the subsequent 30 years. The current standards still mirror Shakow's recommendations and involve such criteria as a 1-year full-time or 2-year half-time requirement, access to numerous role models, and the development of several abilities such as research, therapeutic, and interpersonal skills.

Although the establishment of accreditation guidelines was somewhat effective in standardizing internship training experiences, there remained concern for several years that this was an insufficient solution to the problem of internship regulation. Subsequently, because of the increasing numbers of internship settings and the somewhat vague guidelines determining their functions and structure, the APA established a committee that evolved in 1968 into the Association of Psychology Internship Centers (APIC). The purpose of APIC was to provide a clearinghouse for internship information and centralization for issues related to APA. Among the various functions that APIC has fulfilled are the establishment of uniform procedures for tendering internship offers, the annual publication of a directory of internship centers, and the provision of a formal liaison between internship centers and the education and training board of the APA (A. G. Burstein, personal communication, February, 1981).

Since its inception, APIC also has moved gradually toward greater control of the structure and evaluation of internship training. For example, in 1977 a committee was appointed to determine standards for internship matriculation such that a minimum competency level could be required prior to both entrance and completion of the internship experience. Unfortunately, the committee has been unable to resolve this issue completely because of the high degree of variation in evaluation methodology evidenced across internship. APIC has, however, succeeded in providing suggestions for both entrance and exit requirements for internships, as well as methods for evaluating intern performance in relation to these criteria.

The diversity and the occasional complete lack of specific evaluative criteria for intern performance found by the APIC committee is suggestive of the current scarcity of data on internship training. In general, the available research has taken the form of surveys targeted either at internship directors' attitudes toward preinternship preparation of students (e.g., Petzel & Berndt, 1980; Shemberg & Keeley, 1970; Shemberg & Leventhal, 1981), or at interns' satisfaction with their internship experience (e.g., Khol, Matefy, & Turner, 1972; Rosenkrantz & Holmes, 1974). Surprisingly, there is a dearth of research directed toward the systematic evaluation of either the specific learning experiences occurring at internship relative to APA recommendation (e.g., Kirk, 1970; Tucker, 1970), or intern performance relative to minimum competency standards.

The internship evaluation literature, while lacking, has pointed out some important issues that are likely to affect future trends in training. For example, several studies have indicated that although interns view their experiences as beneficial in areas such as assessment, research, and therapy, there is less satisfaction with training in administrative and consultative skills (e.g., Miller, 1977; Stout, Holmes, & Rothstein, 1977).

In response to the need for greater attention to internship training, a National Conference on Internship Training in Psychology was held in Gainesville, Florida, in 1987. This was a particularly exciting and notable event, since no other conference had been singularly devoted to internship training. The conference was sponsored by the APIC and the University of Florida, which fortunately removed it from the influence of any accrediting, governing, or granting agency and left it free to address current issues without many of the attending political pressures one might expect with such an event. While many issues were considered by the conferees, the principal recommendations were that (a) the internship be a 2-year process (1 year predoctoral and 1 year postdoctoral); (b) all training occur within APA-accredited internship programs; (c) all interns be funded at a level commensurate with experience; and (d) internship training occur only after a student has an accepted dissertation proposal and has completed all coursework and supervised practice. Though most of the Gainesville conference recommendations have been met with general acceptance, the Council of University Directors of Clinical Psychology voted unanimously to oppose a 2-year internship. Such a requirement was considered to be an unnecessary and financially burdensome addition for students based on opinion rather than empirical evaluative data. While the Gainesville conference took a significant step forward in recommending the raising of training standards for internship training, it remains to be seen how such standards can be implemented. The Gainesville conference raised the perennial question of when graduate programs and internships will establish specific training and education criteria for purposes of graduate and internship program evaluation, as well as student evaluation for admission to internships. Many of the issues raised in the various training conferences discussed in this chapter could be addressed effectively if educational and training criteria and evaluative data were available (Edelstein & Berler, 1987).

RECENT TRENDS

In the preceding sections the historical development of graduate training and internships and issues relevant to the APA's impact on such training has been discussed. Some of the more recent trends in clinical training are discussed in the following sections.

Specialization

Perhaps the most notable change in the field of clinical psychology in the past 2 decades has been the shift toward increased specialization. Numerous areas now boast their own distinctive sets of problems and problem-solving techniques in terms of both research and clinical practice. This has resulted in the fractionalization of both academic and internship training programs such that increasing numbers of graduates are being trained in one specific area of clinical psychology rather than in general clinical practice. The following section briefly reviews some of the major new areas and the issues related to graduate training in these areas.

Health Psychology

The most dramatic transition toward a distinctive specialty area has occurred in a field that has been called health psychology, medical psychology, and behavioral medicine. The continually expanding job market for health psychologists (Gentry & Matarazzo, 1981; Lubin, Nathan, & Matarazzo, 1978) has ultimately triggered formal recognition of the area, as evidenced by the establishment of the behavioral medicine special-interest group within the Association for Advancement of Behavior Therapy in 1977, APA Division 38 (Health Psychology) in 1978 (and its journal, *Health Psychology,* in 1982), the Council of Directors of Health Psychology Training Programs in 1984, the birth of both the Society of Behavioral Medicine and *The Journal of Behavioral Medicine* in 1978, and a recent move toward the establishment of a professional board of health psychology.

The rather rapid establishment of this area has raised several issues pertaining to graduate education, particularly since health psychology was the label used by both basic researchers and health service providers. Virtually all of the graduate education issues identified in 1983 were thoroughly discussed at the National Working Conference on Education and Training in Health Psychology held at Arden House in Harriman, New York (see Stone, 1983). Issues addressed included, but were not limited to, the definition of health psychology, the graduate training model to be followed, core training in psychology, interdisciplinary breadth of training, ethical and legal problems unique to health settings, relationship to clinical psychology, and credentialing and accreditation. The conferees agreed unanimously on the value of the scientist-practitioner model for training health psy-

chologists. Scientific training was deemed essential for health psychology practitioners so that they could critically evaluate research and develop and evaluate new applications. Contact with practical problems was also deemed desirable for basic scientists to enable them to discover vitally significant new areas of application (Miller, 1983). Core training in psychology was also considered desirable so that health psychologists may have a solid and broad foundation in all aspects of psychology, ranging from social psychology to physiological psychology.

The relationship between health psychology and clinical psychology was difficult to resolve. The conferees concluded that "considerable knowledge of clinical psychology is essential for those who provide care as health psychologists, and at least some knowledge is highly desirable for those whose emphasis is research. Nevertheless, the special requirements for training in health psychology are such that this field should become an independent specialty" (Miller, 1983, p. 13). Consequently, individuals pursuing training in health psychology may do so within the context of many clinical programs offering health psychology specializations, or within the context of an independent health psychology program.

The Arden House conference was a monumental event, the resolutions of which set the course for pre- and postdoctoral training in health psychology and continue to influence significantly the development of training programs and the refinement of existing ones.

Child Clinical and Pediatric Psychology

A second area that has experienced a period of rapid expansion is clinical child psychology. In spite of the growth, too few psychologists have been trained adequately to deal with child and adolescent mental health needs (Ollendick, 1985). The number of doctoral level programs offering specialties in clinical child psychology rose steadily from fewer than 10 in 1968 (Ross, 1972) to 34 formal programs in 1978. In addition, 52 others offered informal child training experiences (Fischer, 1978) at that time. No more recent data are available. However, Mannarino and Fischer (1982) found that 88 individuals trained formally and 93 trained informally in child clinical psychology receive doctorates each year. Although the increase has been dramatic, VandenBos (1979) estimated that the number of trained psychologists would still be 80% less than the projected demand for child specialists over the next decade.

Using the Mannarino and Fischer data, we should

have only two thirds of the number needed in 1989 (Tuma, 1985).

Until recently, many issues have been raised, ranging from training criteria and models (Erickson, 1978) to definitions of emerging subareas. These issues and many more were discussed in depth at the Conference on the Training of Clinical Child Psychologists that met at Hilton Head Island in 1985 (Tuma, 1985). Among the goals of the conference was to strengthen the professional preparation of clinical child psychologists. Issues addressed included whether and how specialty training should occur, roles and responsibilities of clinical child psychologists, boundaries between other child professionals (e.g., school psychologists, pediatric psychologists, applied developmental psychologists), the appropriate curriculum, training models, credentialing and licensing, and implementation of the conference recommendations.

Twenty-five recommendations resulted from the conference. Among the recommendations were endorsement of the scientist-practitioner model of training; required courses in lifespan developmental psychology; student acquisition of minimal competencies in assessment, psychopathology, and intervention with children, youth, and families; and continuing education for all clinical child psychologists. While the recommendations of the conference might not appear startling, they represented a milestone for clinical psychology and the many psychologists who have fought hard to establish criteria for training competent clinical child psychologists.

Community Psychology

Community psychology is yet another area that is frequently considered within the field of clinical psychology and that has developed into a distinct specialty area. Although numerous definitions have been proposed for the area (e.g., Bennett, Anderson, Hassol, Klein, & Rosenblum, 1966; Bloom, 1973; Rappaport, 1977; Zax & Specter, 1974), the consensus is that community psychology is an approach emphasizing social-systems–level analyses and interventions designed to alleviate societal problems as opposed to emphasizing individual solutions for "individual troubles" (Bloom, 1973, p. 8).

The specific structure of this area and the training for practice began to be delineated in 1965 at the Boston conference (Bennett et al., 1966) and continued to be further distinguished and organized at subsequent conferences, such as the Austin conference in 1967 (Iscoe & Spielberger, 1970), the Vail conference in 1973 (Korman, 1974), and the National

Training Conference on Community Psychology in 1975 (Bloom, 1977; Iscoe, Bloom, & Spielberger, 1977). Throughout this period, community psychology has moved continually closer to becoming a distinctive entity, in addition to moving further away from the more traditional emphasis on the individual. For example, at the Boston conference, areas such as (a) the individual's interaction with the physical and social environment, (b) the individual's reaction to community change, and (c) the relationship between social and cultural conditions and individual personality functioning were among those discussed as essential research concerns for community psychology (Bennett et al., 1966). Yet, 10 years later at the National Training Conference in 1975, the emphasis had clearly moved toward the understanding of social issues, theory, and research methodology devoted to intervention at the community level (Reiff, 1977) and a general social-system orientation for the field (Kelly, 1977). Further, Sarason (1977) called for the establishment of community psychology as a distinct and separate field from clinical psychology, with its own training opportunities and curricula.

Although these conferences have failed to provide a final definitive statement concerning the identity of the field (Barton, Andrulis, Grove, & Sponte, 1976), they have engendered a significant increase in the training opportunities available in community psychology. For example, Meyer and Gerrard (1977) noted that in 1962, Golann, Wurm, and Magoon (1964) found only one program reporting a distinguishable community psychology curriculum; by 1977 the number had increased to 62.

Clinical psychology programs have been loath to incorporate community psychology into their curricula. Zolik (1983) attributed this to "the ideological conflict posed for many between a preventive orientation and the palliative-salvage approach underlying the deficit reparative orientation of traditional training programs" (p. 276).

Prevention has become an important area of training. It has traditionally been tucked away in community psychology programs and received less acknowledgement than has been deserved. This is no longer the case (see Buckner, Trickett, & Corse, 1985; Edelstein & Michelson, 1986; Felner, Jason, Moritsugu, & Farber, 1983). Prevention efforts have spread from systems to individuals, including such foci as schizophrenia (e.g., Watt, 1986), developmental disorders (e.g., Ornitz, 1986), achievement deficits (e.g., Lloyd & De Bettencourt, 1986), marital problems (e.g., L'Abate, 1986), crime and delinquency (e.g., Nietzel & Himelein, 1986), substance abuse (e.g., Milgram & Nathan, 1986), and various health disorders (e.g., cancer and cardiovascular disease). The research literature has burgeoned to the point that a relatively recent annotated bibliography of prevention in mental health listed 1,008 publications since 1960.

The Task Force on Prevention of the President's Commission on Mental Health saw the move toward preventive mental health as "the fourth revolutionary change in society's approach for the mentally ill" (Murphy & Frank, 1979, p. 182). However, although prevention has been identified as a desirable approach to health and mental health problems, there is much more discussion of the topic than there is substantive research work (Cowen, 1977). The paucity of research literature on prevention yields concomitant problems in determining what should be taught to students who wish to embrace this orientation. New journals, such as the *Journal of Primary Prevention,* collate the available work, but functional curricula are sparse. Only Albee and his colleagues at the University of Vermont seem to be attempting to disseminate a prevention educational curriculum.

The future of training in prevention is unclear, muddled primarily by the political realities of this orientation and the lack of research. The need for training in this area is clear, but the opportunities are severely limited.

Clinical Gerontology

A fourth area of specialization that has been receiving increasing attention is clinical gerontology (Carstensen & Edelstein, 1987). While the demand for clinical gerontologists is growing with the increasingly large geriatric population, the training of clinical gerontologists is unfortunately not progressing at a rate that will enable us to meet the mental health needs of the elderly. In spite of the great need for specialists in clinical gerontology, "training is woefully lacking" (Reveron, 1982, p. 82). In 1979, only two doctoral programs offered formal programs or subspecialties in this area (Reveron, 1982, p. 82). Only 22 of 97 clinical internship programs surveyed offered formal training with elderly clients. A point of even greater concern is that "nearly 70% of psychologists serve no older adults and over half of doctoral programs offer no training in gerontology and geriatrics" (Gatz & Pearson, 1986, p. 5). This is a shocking figure in light of the number of elderly to be served.

Two relatively recent events have brought more visibility to the plight of the elderly and their mental health needs, as well as recommendations for the training of gerontologists. The White House Conference on Aging, held in 1981, raised many issues and heightened the awareness of professionals and the general public regarding the needs and problems of the elderly. Second, the APA sponsored a conference on training psychologists for work in aging (Santos & VandenBos, 1981) in Boulder, Colorado. This conference, sometimes referred to as the "Older Boulder Conference," formulated recommendations regarding the training of psychologists for work with the elderly. The conferees' recommendations were detailed and specific, covering the topics of training, curriculum, continuing education, retraining, in-service education, recruitment and retention of faculty, service and settings, sociopsychological knowledge base, biopsychological knowledge base, and professional, educational, and public information on geropsychology. It seems that recruitment of faculty and exposure of students to problems of the elderly are the principal training concerns for the area of clinical gerontology. Until more faculty appreciate the unique needs and challenges of working with the elderly, we will continue to train clinical psychologists who are ill equipped to deal with the problems of an ever-growing and vastly underserved population.

Clinical Neuropsychology

Clinical neuropsychology has rapidly gained popularity, as evidenced by the increasingly large number of positions available for clinical neuropsychologists, formation of the clinical neuropsychology division of APA (Division 40), designation as a specialty area by the American Board of Professional Psychology, and the large number of journals dedicated to this specialty (e.g., *International Journal of Clinical Neuropsychology, Clinical Neuropsychology, Archives of Clinical Neuropsychology,* and *The Clinical Neuropsychologist*). Although neuropsychological screening has been performed by clinical psychologists for many years, development of and dissemination of more sophisticated neuropsychological batteries (e.g., Halstead-Reitan, Luria-Nebraska) has expanded the role of the clinical neuropsychologist, which now includes such activities as diagnosing neurological disorders, diagnosing psychiatric disorders, localizing brain lesions, evaluating the effects of physical disease on neuropsychological functioning (e.g., Golden, Strider, Ariel, & Golden, 1986), and rehabilitating traumatically brain injured individuals (e.g., Grimm & Bleiberg, 1986). The increased interest in this area can in part be attributed to the increased publication of books addressing screening for brain impairment (e.g., Berg, Franzen, & Wedding, 1987; Franzen & Berg, 1989), the demand for neuropsychological assessment in a variety of settings, and the increased accuracy and reliability (see Franzen, 1989) with which one can assess neuropsychological functioning.

Training in clinical neuropsychology is quite varied. Sheer and Lubin (1980) conducted a survey of 627 members of the International Neuropsychological Society and received 178 responses. The survey was conducted to obtain information about the training activities, areas of concentration, course work, research training, clinical training, faculty, students, and so on. The respondents expressed a need for more organized and extensive training in the area. According to the survey, students receive training in neuropsychology through one of four general avenues: (a) minimal training associated with primary service functions on practica or internships; (b) internship programs specifically designed for training in clinical neuropsychology; (c) standard PhD programs, usually in clinical psychology (some programs are also offering specializations in clinical neuropsychology for students entering predoctoral programs other than clinical); and (4) separate formal training in clinical neuropsychology.

A survey by Golden and Kuperman (1980) of 65 APA-approved clinical programs indicated that 32 offered neuropsychology courses and encouraged students interested in neuropsychology to apply to their program. Twenty-eight of the programs offered neuropsychology but did not systematically encourage students to apply if they were specifically interested in that area. Eighteen of the 32 programs that encouraged applications from students offered specializations in clinical neuropsychology. These data clearly indicate a strong trend toward increased training in neuropsychology.

In response to the growing demand for guidance in the training of clinical neuropsychologists, the International Neuropsychological Society and Division 40 (Neuropsychology) of the APA established a task force on education, accreditation, and credentialing of clinical neuropsychologists, resulting in a set of guidelines for doctoral training programs in clinical neuropsychology (INS/APA, 1987). The guidelines suggest that doctoral training in clinical neuropsychology could be accomplished "through a Ph.D. programme in Clinical Neuropsychology offered by a Psychology Department or Medical Faculty or through the completion of a Ph.D. programme in a related specialty area (e.g., Clinical Psychology) which offers sufficient specialization in clinical neu-

ropsychology" (INS/APA, 1987, p. 29). Thus, clinical neuropsychology was identified as an independent specialty, like health psychology, which could be approached as such or as a specialty within clinical psychology. While this approach is, in principle, reasonable, difficulties are encountered when one begins to draw the line between the practices of consultants and licensed human service providers.

The INS/APA task force report specified five elements of an adequate training program, including (a) a generic psychology core, (b) a generic clinical core, (c) specialized training in the neurosciences and basic human and animal neuropsychology, (d) specific training in clinical neuropsychology, and (e) an 1,800-hour internship preceded by appropriate practicum experience.

Guidelines for postdoctoral training in clinical neuropsychology were also issued, which contained training criteria that should prepare the student for eligibility for certification in clinical neuropsychology by the American Board of Professional Psychology.

The opportunities for neuropsychologists appear almost unlimited at this point. Moreover, the merging of neuropsychological evaluation and behavioral approaches to rehabilitation of brain-injured individuals offers an exciting future (Goldstein, 1979) and a burgeoning area of training for the clinical psychologist.

Legal and Forensic Psychology

Psychologists have been working with or studying the judicial system for at least 90 years. Stern (1939) reported work he performed on the memory of experts offering testimony as far back as 1901. Over the past several years, the legal system has evidenced a growing recognition of the potential roles for psychologists, although the debate about the proper role of social scientists in adjudication continues to rage (Nietzel & Dillehay, 1986). Psychologists have found applications for their knowledge and skills within the correctional system (e.g., Nietzel & Moss, 1972; Twain, McGree, & Bennett, 1973), the criminal justice system (e.g., Brodsky, 1973; Fowler & Brodsky, 1978; Twain et al., 1973), and the field of civil law (e.g., Levine, Wilson, & Sales, 1980). Subsequently, there has been a dramatic increase in service-oriented and research activities involving the roles for psychology in law (Tapp, 1977). Although interest is rapidly increasing, training programs have been somewhat slow to integrate forensic issues into program curricula (Poythress, 1979):

Since the Jenkins case in 1962 the movement has been snowballing, but 17 years later few graduate programs offer extensive (if any) coursework in forensic psychology, and as yet there is no division of the APA that recognizes this specialty coursework in forensic psychology, and as yet there is no division of the APA that recognizes this specialty area. (Poythress, 1979, p. 613)

This situation has changed somewhat with the introduction of the American Board of Forensic Psychology, which holds a contractual relationship with the American Board of Professional Psychology. While such boards do not specify the nature of training required or recommended at the doctoral level, they do afford a check on the competence of individuals seeking board certification.

In response to the aforementioned training issues, several training models have been elucidated by professionals interested in legal and forensic psychology. For example, a few universities (e.g., the Universities of Nebraska and Maryland) offer joint JD-PhD programs that enable graduates to practice in either field. However, as Poythress (1979) noted, such programs may discourage students who would have to meet admission and completion requirements for two fields rather than one, or who may find much of the material irrelevant for their needs.

Another approach has been to design specific legal and forensic course sequences to be provided within psychology programs. Examples of such courses have been presented by Poythress (1979) and Fernster, Litwach, and Seymonds (1975). Taking this concept several steps further, some programs offer training specifically within the legal and forensic field. For example, Fowler and Brodsky (1978) described a new program at the University of Alabama that prepares psychology students to work within any area of the legal system, although in this particular program the most intensive training takes place in the correctional system.

One factor that has enhanced the development of such programs has been the rapid expansion of literature in the area. For example, journals such as *Law and Psychology Review, Criminal Justice and Behavior, Law and Human Behavior,* and *Criminal Justice and Behavior* have become sources for relevant information, along with several books on legal and forensic psychology (e.g., Brodsky, 1973; Nietzel & Dillehay, 1986; Sales, 1981; Ziskin, 1981). In light of the rapid growth in both interest and literature, forensic psychology has clearly become a distinct area of specialization both within and outside clinical psychology.

CURRENT ISSUES

Training Models

No issue has sparked more controversy with respect to clinical training than that of the relative weight given to research and professional practice. Ever since the Boulder conference (Raimy, 1950), this controversy has grown in intensity. Critics have argued that current programs that attempt to implement the Boulder model of training ignore the mental health manpower needs of the nation (Adler, 1972), are disparaging of clinical psychology as a profession, are using relatively inexperienced and untrained individuals to provide clinical training, are not providing an adequate theoretical background for integrating theory, research, and practice, are not providing many of the vital courses for clinical practice (Matulef & Rothenberg, 1968), and are not training students to "realize their research potential within a practice-oriented work setting" (Goldfried, 1984, p. 477). Goldfried suggested that faculty members make attempts to integrate clinical and research work and serve as role models for their students. This can be accomplished by teaching both single-subject methodologies for evaluating interventions and a cybernetic model for reflecting on one's own assessment and intervention practices (Alberts & Edelstein, 1990a). An act that has further fired the controversy over professional training was the endorsement by the Vail conferees (Korman, 1974) of professional programs that would train students primarily as service deliverers. The conferees distinguished between the PsyD degree for service training and the PhD degree for training in the development of new knowledge. No reason was presented in the report why the PsyD degree was needed (Stricker, 1975). The PsyD degree and professional training was again recognized at the Salt Lake City Conference on Graduate Education and Training (Bickman, 1987), where "the distinction and legitimacy of both the Psy.D. and Ph.D. degrees" was affirmed (p. 10).

Peterson (1968, 1976), who began the first PsyD program while at the University of Illinois, has been an eloquent advocate of professional training. Peterson argued that the current need for professional psychologists is not being met by the PhD programs, that "there is no way to train professional psychologists thoroughly except through explicitly professional programs" (1976, p. 795), that current PhD programs do not support the value of professional work, that there is no way to restructure the current

PhD programs so that a student could receive adequate professional training in the 4 or 5 years we have allotted for training, and that there is an issue of professional identity raised for practitioners receiving the PhD degree, which he viewed as a research degree.

The degree requirements of the various professional psychology programs differ considerably. Some PsyD degree programs require a dissertation while others require a "doctoral paper," which is usually something less than a traditional dissertation document. Other programs have no dissertation requirement and may instead require comprehensive examinations and defense of one's clinical competence and scientific proficiency (McNett, 1982, p. 11). One might argue that there is as much variety in curriculum and doctoral requirements between programs offering the PsyD degree as there is between many of the PsyD and PhD programs. In fact, several of the earliest concerns regarding the relatively poor professional preparation of clinical PhD students have been addressed by the new APA accreditation criteria. For example, a minimum number of hours of practicum experience and direct supervision are specified. Whether these criteria elevate the professional training in the PhD programs to a level that is adequate for the demands of the profession is perhaps largely dependent on the quality of the supervision, instruction, and breadth of experiences provided on each practicum and in the classroom. At the present time there are, unfortunately, no formal criteria for quality assurance for students practicing their skills as clinical psychologists (Bent, 1982). A movement in this direction, however, is evidenced by the Professional Psychology Quality Control Conference (La Jolla Conference) held in 1981 and the published results of a national self-study survey of professional schools (Callan, Peterson, & Stricker, 1986), which have advanced our efforts in the quality assurance domain. In spite of these advances, it continues to be difficult to determine the nature and amount of training necessary to produce a competent professional clinical psychologist. In the absence of suitable criteria and evaluation methods, we are merely guessing about what and how much is needed (Edelstein & Berler, 1987).

Master's Degree Level Training

The role of Master's level training in clinical psychology has been an issue for more than 30 years, in spite of the fact that the proportion of educational institutions offering Master's degrees is increasing. In the 1986 *Graduate Study in Psychology*, 196 institu-

tions offered a Master's-only degree program. This constitutes an 82% increase from the number of such programs listed in the 1972–1973 *Graduate Study in Psychology* (Quereshi & Kuchan, 1988). These figures are probably conservative, since not all programs are necessarily listed in this volume and some doctoral-granting psychology departments also offer terminal Master's degrees. Several general issues continue to fuel the debate of whether to offer terminal Master's level clinical training. The first involves the question of whether Master's level training is sufficient to ensure competent provision of psychological services by graduates. Though the APA has set fairly rigorous criteria for evaluation of doctoral level training, it has as yet failed to determine or adopt such criteria for Master's degree programs (Havens, 1979; Perlman & Lane, 1981). This possibility is again under consideration by the APA committee on graduate education. Therefore, terminal Master's programs have been forced to determine their own standards for training, with one consequence being a rather large degree of variation across programs (Jones, 1979). Adding to this problem is the fact that Master's degrees are frequently awarded as "consolation prizes" to students who fail to complete their doctorates (Havens, 1979). This has resulted in a bimodal population, including those who are specifically and intensively trained as Master's level practitioners, and those who receive only the initial training. In response to this issue, several authors have proposed specific models for the training of Master's level psychologists (e.g., Havens & Dimond, 1978; Kelly, 1957) that would ensure a minimum standard of competence. The first guidelines were prepared by Kelly (1957) and included suggestions for a minimum of 2 years for training and the combination of core course work, including psychopathology, research design, diagnostics, and supervised practicum experiences. Although these guidelines have failed to be formally recognized (Woods, 1971), other authors have continued to propose criteria that might be acceptable to the APA (e.g., Havens, 1979; Jones, 1979). For example, one model recommends a curriculum sequence of core courses providing a background in psychopathology and treatment, a practicum sequence, and an internship (Jones, 1979). Upon completion of such training, the trainee would be designated as a "psychological specialist" and would be considered to be at a level somewhat analogous to a physician's assistant or nurse practitioner in the medical field.

Integration of such guidelines would appear to resolve two basic issues in Master' level training: competency and labeling. The labeling issue stems from the question of who can call themselves psychologists. As Periman and Lane (1981) indicated, it is somewhat confusing from the consumer's standpoint that individuals holding PhD and Master's degrees are entitled to the same professional title. Currently, Master's level psychologists have been entitled with different professional labels across the country ranging from psychological examiner to psychologist, depending on the state in which one practices (Dale, 1988; Periman & Lane, 1981). Such a variety of labels can only increase consumer confusion.

In spite of these issues, the future of Master's level training appears bright. More than 24,000 Master's level psychologists are currently delivering services around the United States, and the market does not appear to be showing signs of saturation.

The principal issue that continues to demand attention is a set of standardized criteria for evaluating and accrediting these programs. While the public is protected to some extent through the accreditation of doctoral programs, no such safeguards exist for Master's level programs. The accreditation process could enhance current training practices and provide some standard against which the public and licensing boards could measure the adequacy of training provided in Master's degree programs.

A second issue is the granting of Master's degrees for individuals who fail to complete doctoral level training programs. One solution, suggested by Havens (1979) and Jones (1979), would involve eliminating the Master's degree as a step toward the PhD. Consideration of such a practice would undoubtedly lead to extensive debate. Nevertheless, the competence to practice as a psychologist, psychological examiner, psychological assistant, and so forth should be determined before Master's level graduates of doctoral programs are unleashed on a credulous public that has difficulty discriminating psychiatrists from clinical psychologists, much less a variety of Master's level training programs.

Training in Assessment Techniques

For the past 3 decades, psychologists have debated the importance of training clinicians in the use of traditional psychodiagnostic techniques. The ongoing dialogue has involved numerous issues ranging from the scientific credibility of both objective and projective techniques, to legal and institutional demands for the continued use of these devices, to the determination of which particular tests should be taught in the PhD programs. In this section, we briefly review some of the relevant issues that have affected and will

continue to influence the structure of training in clinical psychology. This section focuses on issues involving training in personality and psychopathology assessment, as it appears to be the most hotly contested assessment issue. For a thorough review and discussion of issues concerning the latter forms of assessment, refer to *American Psychologist*, 1981, 36(10), whole issue.

Perhaps the most important issue involving traditional assessment is the utility of objective and projective tests. Numerous evaluations of these tests have continued to demonstrate their inadequacy in terms of reliability and validity (e.g., Meehl, 1956; Mischel, 1968), and yet advocates of traditional assessment continue to suggest that such studies fail to evaluate the intricacies in personality structure that are illuminated by testing (e.g., McCully, 1965; Sarason, 1966). Although strong arguments have been presented for both sides of this issue, in general it appears that psychologists' attitudes toward the utility of traditional tests are becoming more negative (e.g., Thelan, Varble, & Johnson, 1968).

Contributing to the negative trend in attitudes toward traditional forms of assessment is the increasing dissatisfaction with the medical model role for psychologists as diagnosticians (Mischel, 1968). As psychological therapeutic techniques have gained a continually sounder empirical base, psychologists have vied for increasing independence from traditional roles. The original function of testing was to assist in the diagnosis of psychological disorders. Since publication of the *Diagnostic & Statistical Manual of Mental Disorders, Third Edition* (DSM-III) and its revision, the utility of testing for diagnosis has diminished because of the greater specificity of behavioral criteria available in the DSM-III. Thus, the recent and greater emphasis on behavioral components of disorders appears to have affected practitioners' attitudes toward the utility of personality tests.

This shift in attitudes and behaviors is also becoming evident in university settings. For example, surveys by Shemberg and Keeley (1970), Thelan and Ewing (1973), and Jackson and Wohl (1966) have found a decreasing trend in the emphasis placed on testing by training programs, especially with projective tests. More specifically, the surveys have indicated that in established university programs, emphasis on projective testing has declined significantly while emphasis on objective assessment techniques has increased. Further, in newer, less established programs, there is a marked decrease in emphasis on both forms of testing as compared to older programs (Shemberg & Keeley, 1970). Yet the authors state that in general there remains a significant emphasis on testing.

The obvious question raised by these issues is, To what degree can testing be deemphasized? A partial answer stems from the psychology marketplace. Wade and Baker (1977) found that clinical psychologists reported that approximately 35% of their professional time was spent administering and evaluating tests. Further, among the most common reasons provided for engaging in these activities were satisfaction of institutional demands and legal requirements, provision of psychologists with a specialty, and the enhancement of employability. Thus, it may be undesirable not to provide sufficient training in testing skills if it is likely to reduce a student's subsequent survival in the marketplace.

Since institutional and economic pressures currently (and presumably will continue to) demand testing skills from psychologists, it is apparent that training in testing will retain its significance in the curricula of graduate programs, at least in the foreseeable future. But this, too, raises several questions. If the psychometric properties of most traditional assessment devices are questionable at best (e.g., Goldfried & Kent, 1972; Kanfer & Saslow, 1965), then what specific tests are to be taught? Surveys have indicated that practicing clinicians report that students should learn at least one test (Wade & Baker, 1977). Further, the four most commonly suggested tests recommended in this survey were, respectively: the Rorschach Inkblot Test, Thematic Apperception Test (TAT), the Wechsler Adult Intelligence Scale (WAIS), and the Minnesota Multiphasic Personality Inventory (MMPI). It is interesting that the two frequently suggested tests are among the least psychometrically sound (Anastasi, 1982; Mischel, 1968). Moreover, only 18.5% of the professionals who recommended training in these devices stated that they used standardized procedures for administering and scoring the tests. The remaining 81.5% stated that they used personalized procedures developed through personal clinical experience. This latter group intimated that use of such individualized procedures alleviated the problems associated with the poor psychometric properties of the testing devices. Unfortunately, research has suggested that such clinically determined criteria are even less predictive than the mechanical standardized procedures provided for testing (Sawyer, 1966).

Training institutions are therefore faced with a dilemma. The economic marketplace currently requires that graduates in psychology be skilled in testing, and yet the tests that are available and frequently recommended are replete with inadequacies. In light of this problem, Wade and Baker (1977) suggested that graduate training be directed toward assessment theory and evaluation of psychometric properties, in lieu of specific testing skills. It is unlikely, however, that programs will cease training in specific test devices. It is more probable that there will be a continuation of the current trend in the direction of objective diagnostic procedures and away from projective devices (Shemberg & Keeley, 1970).

Continuing Education

It was previously noted that continuing professional development and education have become more significant issues as clinical psychology as a profession has developed. Various reasons for the need for continuing education have been advanced. These include the increasing knowledge base of clinical psychology, maintenance of high standards of practice, maintenance of public confidence in the profession (Vitulano & Copeland, 1980; Welch, 1976), obsolescence of skills (Jensen, 1979), and the emergence of service needs for which psychologists were not trained (Jensen, 1979; Webster, 1971). It has been estimated that 50% of a psychologist's knowledge is outmoded within 10 to 12 years (Dubin, 1972). That is a startling notion, even if one allows for some inaccuracy in the estimate.

In recent years, the APA has become involved in continuing education. The APA Council of Representatives endorsed the current continuing education sponsor approval system in January 1979. National standards for continuing education in psychology have been articulated, and sponsors have been identified who meet the APA standards for continuing education. The APA maintains a continuing education registry of credits obtained by individuals under the sponsorship of the APA continuing education approval system. In addition, the APA provides a calendar and clearinghouse for continuing education information and events. As the sponsor approval system has developed, so have private enterprises that provide continuing education approved by the APA. Moreover, at least one excellent demonstration project has emerged at Pennsylvania State University (Lindsay, Crowe, & Jacobs, 1987) in which a practice-oriented model for continuing professional education for clinical psychology was developed and evaluated. Several states require continuing education for relicensure or recertification. The first state to require continuing education for relicensure was Maryland in July 1957; however, 18 years elapsed before the next state, New

Mexico, required continuing education. The amount of continuing education required varies from state to state. Credit-hour requirements range from five credit-hours per 2 years to 50 credit-hours per year.

The current issues in continuing education center on the amount of credit-hours that should be required, the nature of the training and credit determination, training methods, evaluation methods, who should be permitted to offer training, and criteria for satisfactory performance. Training opportunities range from convention institutes and workshops to home education programs developed by private enterprises and sponsored by educational institutions. There appears to be no consensus regarding what kinds of educational experiences are most desirable or acceptable, the method of determining credits, how one should be evaluated (if at all), or whether anyone should be permitted to offer continuing education credits. At present, each state that requires continuing education determines the guidelines that pertain to the foregoing issues. It would seem, however, that the ultimate criterion of professional development and continuing education should at least be a positive change in professional behavior and in the care of mental health clients (Brown & Uhl, 1970). It is unclear how long it will take the field to get its educational house in order.

Evaluation of Clinical Training

Perhaps the most important and overlooked issue in clinical training is evaluation. It is ironic that psychologists whose job is primarily that of training have paid so little attention to the valid evaluation of clinical training. In a review of research on the training of counselors and clinicians, Ford (1979) concluded that "research investigating the effects of different training curricula, curriculum content sequences, and curricular materials, is, unfortunately, non-existent in the counselor/clinician training literature" (p. 87). There is ample evidence that one can train specific clinical skills (see Alberts & Edelstein, 1990a, 1990b; Ford, 1979; Matarazzo, 1978, for reviews); however, few researchers and educators have bothered to evaluate or gather empirical support for their training practices.

Although few would dispute the need for adequate evaluation of training, little is being done (Stevenson & Norcross, 1987). A handful of articles have appeared that suggest a slight trend toward the empirical evaluation of clinical training. Hill, Charles, and Reed (1981), for example, conducted a longitudinal study of changes in counseling skills among graduate students being trained in counseling psychology. The authors analyzed brief counseling sessions of students

for each of the 3 years of training. The results revealed that "students increased their use of minimal encouragers and decreased use of questions and maintained acceptable levels of activity, anxiety, and quality" (p. 428). From a consumer perspective, Walfish, Kaufman, and Kinder (1980) conducted a program evaluation in which they surveyed 316 graduates from APA-approved doctoral programs in clinical psychology and asked them to rate the adequacy of their training in a variety of skill areas. The authors concluded that "for the most part, respondents were relatively satisfied with their training and were most satisfied with traditional skills in therapy and assessment" (p. 1040). These data were consistent with the results of a survey by Garfield and Kurtz (1976), who found that 77% of those surveyed indicated "some degree of satisfaction" with their graduate training.

Two relatively recent articles (Stevenson, Norcross, King, & Tobin, 1984; Walsh et al., 1985) have described psychology clinic evaluation programs which provide fine models for other programs pursuing evaluative information.

Other recent demonstrations include reports of student clinical competence evaluation (Dienst & Armstrong, 1988), a survey of the utility of various components of graduate training by past graduates (Tyler & Clark, 1987), and the use of goal-attainment models to evaluate program goal-related objectives and hypotheses (Guydish & Markley, 1986). In spite of recent attempts to evaluate programs in general and training in particular, little research exists that points the way to effective clinical skills.

There are several possible reasons for the paucity of research on the evaluation of clinical training. There is little agreement about what skills a clinical graduate student should be taught, what should form the knowledge base for learning these skills, the level of skills that should be expected, and the criteria that should be used for judging skills. The problem is similar to that of establishing outcome criteria for psychotherapy research (see Kazdin, 1981; Strupp, 1981). The sheer diversity of training approaches and orientations makes the development of commonly acceptable outcome measures a formidable task at best. The fact that we are moderately ignorant of the most effective ingredients of our many approaches to intervention further complicates the issue of what is to be taught and evaluated.

Regardless of the impediments to evaluation, it must be done. As research points the way toward effective skills and relevant information, clinical training programs may incorporate the newly acquired information into their training. It is clear that our data base for building effective training programs and evaluating them is sadly limited at this time. In many cases, clinical training programs can graduate very skilled clinical psychologists; one can, however, rarely articulate how it was accomplished. Although the field is safe because of the former, its future is still in question because of the latter.

FUTURE DIRECTIONS

Formal training in clinical psychology has been with us but a few decades, and yet we have witnessed tremendous changes in the role of clinical psychologists and concomitant changes in the nature of their training. One might even argue that the training has not kept pace with the changing roles of clinical psychologists. Indeed, this is part of the argument made by advocates of increased professional training for clinical psychologists in lieu of the extensive research training required. The gap between training and practice extends well beyond this more general criticism. Clinical psychologists are becoming involved in anything and everything that involves human behavior in its normal and abnormal forms. It is this fact that makes it particularly difficult to predict the future directions of clinical training. The field has no bounds.

Although the distant future of clinical training is difficult to predict, the more immediate future is amenable to intelligent guesses. First, further specialization is inevitable with the growth of our knowledge and its applications. Clinical psychology appears to be following in the footsteps of allied health fields by becoming more specialized as the knowledge base and sheer number of skills required increase. Some specializations have already demonstrated exceptional growth in just a matter of years. Health psychology, for example, is growing quickly and will probably continue to do so as more and more of our health and illness is shown to be related to our behavior. Moreover, training specializations within health psychology (e.g., psychoneuroimmunology) have even developed, and postdoctoral training programs exist in these areas. The manner in which clinical training programs obtain funds for training will certainly contribute to the shape of training. As clinical training grants continue to diminish in number and funding level, more students will be faced with the prospect of poverty. They will acquire loans when possible and part-time jobs when classes and practica permit. In addition, the rapid specialization within clinical psychology is driving students to seek postdoctoral training, particularly in clinical neuropsychology and

health psychology. It is our fear that, over time, training programs will be shaped away from the provision of sound scientific and clinical training as they chase financial support that is tied to services that are only tangentially related to acceptable clinical practice. The clinical researcher and scientist-practitioner will probably suffer the most, since the repayment of loans will be much more difficult for those who will hold poorer-paying public service and academic research positions. Those who will seek clinical practice, particularly in the private sector, will be most able to weather the hardships of 5 to 7 years of full-time clinical training with limited financial support. The possible effects this could have on the future contributions to the field of clinical psychology should be of considerable concern to directors of clinical training as well as others who are in a position to influence its directions.

The future of clinical training will undoubtedly include training in the use of computers, which are currently used not only as a tool for controlling elaborate experiments and analyzing data but also as a means for providing analog training experiences that test and teach. Competency-based criterion-referenced training will become commonplace as we identify effective clinical behaviors or practices. Computers are already used to simulate client problems for evaluating professional competence of counseling psychology students (e.g., Berven, 1987; Berven & Scofield, 1980). The computer will be used for self-assessment, both by students and by professionals who are engaged in graduate or continuing education. This has already been done on a limited basis at meetings of the Association for Advancement of Behavior Therapy.

The clinical psychologist of the future will undoubtedly require a broader knowledge base in the biological sciences. As evidence of biological contributions to psychological disorders mounts and the emphasis on health psychology grows, the need to take such factors into consideration in training and practice will surely increase. Future clinical psychologists will also require more training in the use of information derived from sophisticated electronic diagnostic instruments. As our technology for measuring nervous system functions continues to develop, it will become necessary for graduate students to understand and utilize information obtained from measures of cerebral blood flow, CAT scans, magnetic resonance devices, and tests of event-related cortical potentials.

The clinical psychologists of the future may require additional training in neurophysiology and psychopharmacology. The U.S. Army, for example, is currently pursuing the possibility of prescribing privileges for clinical psychologists.

Increasingly, training to perform psychosocial interventions may be guided by treatment manuals as more therapists develop standard manuals that permit reliable implementation of effective interventions. As a consequence, clinical training may place a greater emphasis on matching the clinician, treatment, and intervention techniques.

Increased postdoctoral training for clinical psychologists appears inevitable as more specialties develop within clinical psychology, with concomitant increases in the breadth and depth of knowledge needed to function at the cutting edge of a specialty area. Both neuropsychologists and health psychologists have advocated postdoctoral training in their respective training recommendations.

Finally, we hope that the future holds more promise for training in primary prevention. The potential impact on mental and physical health through prevention is, in our estimation, almost unlimited. Although our current knowledge base is limited, the existing evidence for the efficacy of the approach is compelling. Training in primary prevention could begin now as an approach that is unencumbered by the disease model; our professional behavior could be controlled by health rather than by disease.

REFERENCES

Adler, P. T. (1972). Will the Ph.D. be the death of professional psychology? *Professional Psychology, 3,* 69–72.

Alberts, G., & Edelstein, B. (1990a). Therapist training: A critical review of skill training studies. *Clinical Psychology Review, 10*(5), 497–512.

Alberts, G., & Edelstein, B. (1990b). Training in behavior therapy. In A. Bellack, M. Hersen, & A. Kazdin (Eds.), *International handbook of behavior modification and therapy* (2nd ed., pp. 213–226). New York: Plenum Publishing.

American Psychological Association. (1980). *Accreditation handbook.* Washington, DC: APA.

American Psychological Association. (1981). *APA Monitor, 2,* 11.

Anastasi, A. (1982). *Psychological testing.* New York: Macmillan.

Barton, A. K., Andrulis, D. P., Grove, W. P., & Sponte, J. G. (1976). A look at community psychology in the seventies. *American Journal of Community Psychology, 4,* 1–11.

Bennett, C. C., Anderson, L. S., Hassol, L., Klein, D., & Rosenblum, B. (Eds.). (1966). *Community psychology: A report of the Boston conference on the education of psychologists for community mental health.* Boston:

Boston University and South Shore Mental Health Center.

Bent, R. J. (1982). The quality assurance process as a management method for psychology training programs. *Professional Psychology, 13,* 98–104.

Berg, R., Franzen, M., & Wedding, D. (1987). *Screening for brain impairment: A manual for mental health practice.* New York: Springer.

Bernstein, D. A., & Nietzel, M. T. (1980). *Introduction to clinical psychology.* New York: McGraw-Hill.

Berven, N. L. (1987). Improving evaluation in counselor training and credentialing through standardized simulations. In B. Edelstein & E. Berler (Eds.), *Evaluation and accountability in clinical training* (pp. 203–230). New York: Plenum Publishing.

Berven, N. L., & Scofield, M. E. (1980). Evaluation of professional competence through standardized simulations: A review. *Rehabilitation Counseling Bulletin, 23,* 178–202.

Bickman, L. (Ed.). (1987). Proceedings of the National Conference on Graduate Education in Psychology, University of Utah, Salt Lake City, June 13–19 [Special issue]. *American Psychologist, 42* (12).

Bloom, B. L. (1973). The domain of community psychology. *American Journal of Community Psychology, 1,* 8–11.

Bloom, B. L. (1977). The rhetoric and some views of reality. In I. Isco, B. L. Bloom, & C. D. Spielberger (Eds.), *Community psychology in transition: Proceedings of the national conference on training in community psychology.* Washington, DC: Hemisphere.

Brodsky, S. L. (Ed.). (1973). *Psychologists in the criminal justice system.* Chicago: University of Illinois Press.

Brown, C. R., & Uhl, H. S. (1970). Mandatory continuing education: Sense or nonsense? *Journal of the American Medical Association, 213,* 1660–1668.

Buckner, J. C., Trickett, E. J., & Corse, S. J. (1985). *Primary prevention in mental health: An annotated bibliography.* Rockville, MD: NIMH.

Burstein, A. G. (1981). Standards for evaluation and training. *APIC Newsletter, 7,* 20–24.

Callan, J. E., Peterson, D. R., & Stricker, G. (1986). *Quality in professional psychology training: A national conference and self-study.* National Council of Schools of Professional Psychology.

Carstensen, L. L., & Edelstein, B. A. (1987). *Handbook of clinical gerontology.* Elmsford, NY: Pergamon Press.

Cowen, E. L. (1977). Baby steps primary prevention. *American Journal of Community Psychology, 5,* 1–22.

Dale, R. H. I. (1988). State psychological associations, licensing criteria, and the master's issue. *Professional Psychology: Research and Practice, 19,* 589–593.

Darley, J. G. (1973). Opening address: Psychology: Science? Profession? In M. Korman (Ed.), *Levels and patterns of professional training in psychology.* Washington, DC: APA.

Derner, G. F. (1965). *Graduate education in clinical psy-*

chology. In B. B. Wolman (Ed.), *Handbook of clinical psychology.* New York: McGraw-Hill.

Dienst, E. R., & Armstrong, P. M. (1988). Evaluation of students' clinical competence. *Professional Psychology: Research and Practice, 19,* 339–341.

Dubin, S. S. (1972). Obsolescence of lifelong education: A choice for the professional. *American Psychologist, 27,* 486–498.

Edelstein, B. A., & Berler, E. (1987). *Evaluation and accountability in clinical training.* New York: Plenum Publishing.

Edelstein, B. A., & Michelson, L. (1986). *Handbook of prevention.* New York: Plenum Publishing.

Erickson, M. D. (1978). Letter to the office of APA Educational Affairs on training. *Journal of Clinical Child Psychology, 9,* 91.

Felner, R. D., Jason, L. A., Moritsugu, J. N., & Farber, S. S. (1983). *Preventive psychology: Theory, research, and practice.* Elmsford, NY: Pergamon Press.

Fernster, A. C., Litwach, T. R., & Seymonds, M. (1975). The making of a forensic psychologist: Needs and goals for doctoral training. *Professional Psychology, 6,* 457–467.

Fischer, C. T. (1978). Graduate programs in clinical child psychology and related fields. *Journal of Clinical Child Psychology, 9,* 91.

Ford, J. D. (1979). Research on training counselors and clinicians. *Review of Educational Research, 49,* 87–130.

Fowler, R. D., & Brodsky, S. L. (1978). Development of a correctional-clinical psychology program. *Professional Psychology, 9,* 440–447.

Franzen, M. D. (1989). *Reliability and validity in neuropsychological assessment.* New York: Plenum Publishing.

Franzen, M. D., & Berg, R. (1989). *Screening children for brain impairment.* New York: Springer.

Garfield, S. L., & Kurtz, R. (1976). Clinical psychologists in the 1970s. *American Psychologist, 31,* 1–9.

Gatz, M., & Pearson, C. G. (1986). Training clinical psychology students in aging. *Gerontology and Geriatrics Education, 6,* 15–25.

Gentry, W. D., & Matarazzo, J. D. (1981). Medical psychology: Three decades of growth and development. In C. K. Prokop & L. A. Bradley (Eds.), *Medical psychology: Contributions of behavioral medicine.* New York: Academic Press.

Golann, S. E., Wurm, L. A., & Magoon, T. M. (1964). Community mental health content of graduate programs in departments of psychology. *Journal of Clinical Psychology, 20,* 518–522.

Golden, C. J., & Kuperman, S. K. (1980). Graduate training in clinical neuropsychology. *Professional Psychology, 11,* 55–63.

Golden, C. J., Strider, M. A., Ariel, R., & Golden, E. E. (1986). Neuropsychology and medical disorders. In S. B. Filskov & T. J. Boll (Eds.), *Handbook of clinical neuropsychology: Vol. 2* (pp. 257–279). New York: John Wiley & Sons.

Goldfried, M. R. (1984). Training the clinician as scientist-

professional. *Professional Psychology: Research and Practice, 15,* 477–481.

Goldfried, M. R., & Kent, R. N. (1972). Traditional versus behavioral personality assessment: A comparison of methodological and theoretical assumptions. *Psychological Bulletin, 77,* 409–420.

Goldstein, G. (1979). Methodological and theoretical issues in neuropsychological assessment. *Journal of Behavioral Assessment, 1,* 23–41.

Grimm, B. H., & Bleiberg, J. (1986). Psychological rehabilitation in tramautic brain injury. In S. B. Filskov & T. J. Boll (Eds.), *Handbook of clinical neuropsychology* (Vol. 2, pp. 495–560). New York: John Wiley & Sons.

Guydish, J., & Markley, R. P. (1986). Evaluation of psychology training: A goal oriented approach. *Evaluation and Program Planning, 9,* 153–159.

Havens, R. A. (1979). A brief review of the current M.A. controversy. *Professional Psychology, 10,* 185–188.

Havens, R. A., & Dimond, R. E. (1978). A proposed education and training model for clinical psychologists. *Teaching of Psychology, 5,* 3–6.

Hill, C. E., Charles, D., & Reed, K. G. (1981). A longitudinal analysis of changes in counseling skills during doctoral training in counseling psychology. *Journal of Counseling Psychology, 28,* 428–436.

Hoch, E. L., Ross, A. O., & Winder, C. L. (Eds.). (1966). *Professional preparation of clinical psychologists.* Washington, DC: APA.

INS/APA. (1987). Reports of the INS-Division 40 Task Force on Education, Accreditation, and Credentialing. *The Clinical Neuropsychologist, 1,* 29–34.

Iscoe, I., Bloom, B. L., & Spielberger, C. D. (Eds.). (1977). *Community psychology in transition: Proceedings of the national conference on training in community psychology.* Washington, DC: Hemisphere.

Iscoe, I., & Spielberger, D. C. (Eds.). (1970). *Community psychology: Perspectives in training and research.* New York: Appleton-Century-Crofts.

Jackson, C. W., Jr., & Wohl, J. (1966). A survey of Rorschach teaching in the university. *Journal of Projective Techniques and Personality Assessment, 30,* 115–134.

Jensen, R. E. (1979). Competent professional service in psychology: The real issue behind continuing education. *Professional Psychology, 10,* 381–389.

Jones, A. C. (1979). Model for psychological practice for Ph.D. and M.A. professionals. *Professional Psychology, 10,* 189–194.

Kanfer, F. H., & Saslow, G. (1965). Behavioral analysis: An alternative to diagnostic classification. *Archives of General Psychiatry, 12,* 529–538.

Kazdin, A. E. (1981). Methodology of psychotherapy outcome research: Recent developments and remaining limitations. In J. H. Harvey & M. M. Parks (Eds.), *Psychotherapy research and behavior change. The master lecture series* Vol. 1. Washington, DC: APA.

Kelly, J. (1977). Varied educational settings for community psychology. In I. Iscoe, B. L. Bloom, & C. D. Spielberger (Eds.), *Community psychology in transition: Proceedings of the national conference on training in community psychology*. Washington, DC: Hemisphere.

Kelly, N. (1957). A current look at issues in subdoctoral education in psychology. Task Committee on Subdoctoral Education, American Psychological Association.

Kendall, P. C., & Norton-Ford, J. D. (1982). *Clinical psychology: Scientific and professional dimensions*. New York: John Wiley & Sons.

Khol, T., Matefy, R., & Turner, J. (1972). Evaluation of APA internship programs: A survey of clinical psychology interns. *Journal of Clinical Psychology, 28*, 562–569.

Kirk, B. A. (1970). Internship in counseling psychology: Goals and issues. *Journal of Counseling Psychology, 17*, 88–90.

Korchin, S. J. (1976). *Modern clinical psychology: Principles of intervention in the clinic and community*. New York: Basic Books.

Korman, M. (1974). National conference on levels and patterns of professional training in psychology: The major themes. *American Psychologist, 29*, 441–449.

L'Abate, L. (1986). Prevention of marital and family problems. In B. Edelstein & L. Michelson (Eds.), *Handbook of prevention* (pp. 177–194). New York: Plenum Publishing.

Levine, D., Wilson, K., & Sales, B. A. (1980). An exploratory assessment of APA internship with legal/forensic experiences. *Professional Psychology, 11*, 64–71.

Lindsay, C. A., Crowe, M. B., & Jacobs, D. F. (1987). Continuing professional education for clinical psychology: A practice-oriented model. In B. Edelstein and E. Berler (Eds.), *Evaluation and accountability in clinical training* (pp. 331–363). New York: Plenum Publishing.

Lloyd, D. N., & Newbrough, J. R. (1966). Previous conferences on graduate education in psychology: A summary and review. In E. L. Hoch, A. O. Ross, & C. L. Winder (Eds.), *Professional preparation of clinical psychologists*. Washington, DC: APA.

Lloyd, J. W., & De Bettencourt, L. U. (1986). Prevention of achievement deficits. In B. Edelstein & L. Michelson (Eds.), *Handbook of prevention* (pp. 117–132). New York: Plenum Publishing.

Lubin, B., Nathan, R. G., & Matarazzo, J. D. (1978). Psychologists in medical education. *American Psychologist, 33*, 339–343.

Mannarino, A. P., & Fischer, C. (1982). Survey of graduate training in clinical child psychology. *Journal of Clinical Child Psychology, 11*, 22–26.

Matarazzo, R. G. (1978). Research on the teaching and learning of psychotherapeutic skills. In S. L. Garfield & A. E. Bergin (Eds.), *Handbook of Psychotherapy and Behavior Change: An empirical analysis* (pp. 941–966). New York: John Wiley & Sons.

Matulef, N. J., & Rothenberg, P. J. (1968). The crisis in clinical training: Apathy and action. *Special Bulletin, National Council on Graduate Education in Psychology, 2*(1).

McCully, R. S. (1965). Current attitudes about projective techniques in APA-approved internship training centers. *Journal of Projective Techniques and Personality Assessment, 27*, 271–280.

McNett, I. (1982). Psy. D. fills demand for practitioners. *APA Monitor, 13*, 10–11.

Meehl, P. E. (1956). Wanted—A good cookbook. *American Psychologist, 11*, 263–272.

Meyer, M. L., & Gerrard, M. (1977). Graduate training in community psychology. *American Journal of Community Psychology, 5*, 155–162.

Milgram, G. G., & Nathan. P. E. (1986). Efforts to prevent alcohol abuse. In B. Edelstein & L. Michelson (Eds.), *Handbook of prevention* (pp. 243–262). New York: Plenum Publishing.

Miller, N. E. (1983). Some main themes and highlights of the conference. In G. Stone (Ed.), National working conference on education and training in health psychology. *Health Psychology, 2*(5), supplement.

Mischel, W. (1968). *Personality and assessment*. New York: John Wiley & Sons.

Murphy, L. B., & Frank, C. (1979). Prevention: The clinical psychologist. In M. R. Rosenweign & L. W. Porter (Eds.), *Annual Review of Psychology* (Vol. 30). Palo Alto, CA: Annual Reviews.

Nelson, P. D., & Aletky, P. J. (1987). Accreditation: A link between training and practice. In B. Edelstein & E. Berler (Eds.), *Evaluation and accountability in clinical training* (pp. 231–251). New York: Plenum Publishing.

Nietzel, M. T., & Dillehay, R. C. (1986). *Psychological consultation in the courtroom*. Elmsford, NY: Pergamon Press.

Nietzel, M. T., & Himelein, M. J. (1986). Prevention of crime and delinquency. In B. Edelstein & L. Michelson (Eds.), *Handbook of prevention* (pp. 195–222). New York: Plenum Publishing.

Nietzel, M. T., & Moss, C. S. (1972). The psychologist in the criminal justice system. *Professional Psychology, 3*, 259–270.

Ollendick, T. H. (1985). Summary report on the national conference on the training of clinical child psychologists. *Journal of Child and Adolescent Psychotherapy, 2*, 311–312.

Ornitz, E. M. (1986). Prevention of developmental disorders. In B. Edelstein & L. Michelson (Eds.), *Handbook of prevention* (pp. 75–116). New York: Plenum Publishing.

Periman, B., & Lane, R. (1981). The clinical master's degree. *Teaching of psychology, 8*, 72–77.

Peterson, D. R. (1968). The doctor of psychology program at the University of Illinois. *American Psychologist, 23*, 511–516.

Peterson, D. R. (1976). Need for the doctor of psychology degree in professional psychology. *American Psychologist, 31*, 792–798.

Petzel, T. P., & Berndt, D. J. (1980). APA internship selection criteria: Relative importance of academic and clinical preparation. *Professional Psychology, 11,* 792–796.

Poffenberger, A. T. (1938). The training of a clinical psychologist. *Journal of Consulting Psychology, 1,* 1–6.

Pottharst, K. E. (1976). A brief history of the professional model of training. In M. Korman (Ed.), *Levels and patterns of professional training in psychology.* Washington, DC: APA.

Poythress, N. G., Jr. (1979). A proposal for training in forensic psychology. *American Psychology, 34,* 612–621.

Quereshi, M. Y., & Kuchan, A. M. (1988). The master's degree in clinical psychology: Longitudinal program evaluation. *Professional Psychology: Research and Practice, 19*(6), 594–599.

Raimy, V. C. (Ed.). (1950). *Training in clinical psychology.* Englewood Cliffs, NJ: Prentice-Hall.

Rappaport, J. (1977). *Community psychology: Values, research, and action.* New York: Holt, Rinehart & Winston.

Reiff, R. (1977). Ya gotta believe. In I. Iscoe, B. L. Bloom, & C. D. Spielberger (Eds.), *Community psychology in transition: Proceedings of the national conference on training in community psychology.* Washington, DC: Hemisphere.

Reisman, J. (1981). History and current trends in clinical psychology. In C. E. Walker (Ed.), *Clinical practice of psychology.* Elmsford, NY: Pergamon Press.

Reveron, D. (1982). Aged are a mystery to most psychologists. *APA Monitor, 13,* 9.

Roe, A., Gustad, J. W., Moore, B. V., Ross, S., & Skodak, M. (Eds.). (1959). *Graduate education in psychology.* Washington, DC: APA.

Rogers, C. R. (1939). Needed emphasis in the training of clinical psychologists. *Journal of Consulting Psychology, 3,* 141–143.

Rosenkrantz, A. L., & Holmes, G. R. (1974). A pilot study of clinical internship at the William S. Hall Psychiatric Institute. *Journal of Clinical Psychology, 25,* 417–419.

Ross, A. O. (1972). The clinical child psychologist. In B. B. Wolman (Ed.), *Manual of child psychopathology.* New York: McGraw-Hill.

Sales, B. D. (Ed.). (1981). *Perspectives in law and psychology: Vol. 2. The trial process.* New York: Plenum Publishing.

Santos, J. F., & VandenBos, G. R. (1981). *Psychology and the older adult: Challenges for training in the 1980s.* Washington, DC: APA.

Sarason, I. G. (1966). *Personality: An objective approach.* New York: John Wiley & Sons.

Sarason, S. B. (1977). Community psychology, network, and Mr. Everyman. In I. Iscoe, B. L. Bloom, & C. D. Spielberger (Eds.), *Community psychology in transition: Proceedings of the national conference on training in community psychology.* Washington, DC: Hemisphere.

Sarason, S. B. (1981). An asocial psychology and misdirected clinical psychology. *American Psychologist, 36,* 827–836.

Sawyer, J. (1966). Measurement and prediction, clinical and statistical. *Psychological Bulletin, 66,* 178–200.

Shakow, D. (1938). An internship year for psychologists (with special reference to psychiatric hospitals). *Journal of Consulting Psychology, 2,* 73–76.

Sheer, D. E., & Lubin, B. (1980). Survey of training programs in clinical neuropsychology. *Journal of Clinical Psychology, 36,* 1035–1039.

Shemberg, K., & Keeley, S. (1970). Psychodiagnostic training in the academic setting: Past and present. *Journal of Consulting and Clinical Psychology, 34,* 205–211.

Shemberg, K. M., & Leventhal, D. B. (1981). Attitudes of internship directors toward preinternship training and clinical training models. *Professional Psychology, 12,* 639–646.

Stern, W. (1939). The psychology of testimony. *Journal of Abnormal and Social Psychology, 34,* 3–20.

Stevenson, J. F., & Norcross, J. C. (1987). Current status of training evaluation in clinical psychology. In B. Edelstein & E. Berler (Eds.), *Evaluation and accountability in clinical training* (pp. 77–111). New York: Plenum Publishing.

Stevenson, J. F., Norcross, J. C., King, J. T., & Tobin, K. G. (1984). Evaluating clinical training programs: A formative effort. *Professional Psychology: Research and Practice, 15,* 218–239.

Stone, G. (Ed.). (1983). National working conference on education and training in health psychology. *Health Psychology, 2*(5), supplement.

Stout, A. L., Holmes, G. R., & Rothstein, W. (1977). Responses by graduates to memory of their internship in clinical psychology. *Perceptual and Motor Skills, 45,* 863–870.

Stricker, G. (1975). On professional schools and professional degrees. *American Psychologist, 30,* 1062–1066.

Strickland, B. R. (1988). Clinical psychology comes of age. *American Psychologist, 43,* 104–107.

Strother, C. R. (Ed.). (1956). *Psychology and mental health.* Washington, DC: APA.

Strupp, H. H. (1981). The outcome problem in psychotherapy: Contemporary perspectives. In J. H. Harvey & M. M. Parks (Eds.), *Psychotherapy research and behavior change. The master lecture series,* Vol. 1. Washington, DC: APA.

Tapp, J. L. (1977). Psychology and law: Look at interface. In B. D. Sales (Ed.), *Psychology and the legal process.* New York: Spectrum.

Thelan, M. H., & Ewing, D. R. (1973). Attitudes of applied clinicians toward roles, functions, and training in clinical psychology: A comparative survey. *Professional Psychology, 4,* 28–34.

Thelan, M. H., Varble, D. L., & Johnson, J. (1968). Attitudes of academic clinical psychologists toward projective techniques. *American Psychologist, 23,* 517–521.

Tucker, R. L. (1970). Strangers in paradise. *Journal of Clinical Psychology, 34,* 140–143.

Tuma, J. M. (1985). *Proceedings of the Conference on*

Training Clinical Child Psychologists. Washington, DC: APA.

Twain, D., McGree, R., & Bennett, L. A. (1973). Functional areas of psychological activity. In S. L. Brodsky (Ed.), *Psychologists in the criminal justice system.* Chicago: University of Illinois Press.

Tyler, J. D., & Clark, J. A. (1987). Clinical psychologists reflect on the usefulness of various components of graduate training. *Professional Psychology: Research and Practice, 18,* 381–384.

VandenBos, G. R. (1979). *APA input to NIMH regarding planning for mental health personnel development.* Washington, DC: APA.

Vitulano, L., & Copeland, B. (1980). Trends in continuing education and competency demonstration. *Professional Psychology, 11,* 891–897.

Wade, T. C., & Baker, T. B. (1977). Opinions and use of psychological tests: A survey of clinical psychologists. *American Psychologist, 32,* 874–882.

Walfish, S., Kaufman, K., & Kinder, B. N. (1980). Graduate training in clinical psychology: A view from the consumer. *Journal of Clinical Psychology, 36,* 1040–1045.

Walsh, J. A., Wollersheim, J. P., Bach, P. J., Bridgwater, C. A., Klentz, B. A., & Steblay, N. M. (1985). Program evaluation as applied to the goals of a psychology department clinic. *Professional Psychology: Research and Practice, 16,* 661–670.

Watt, N. F. (1986). Prevention of schizophrenic disorders. In B. Edelstein & L. Michelson (Eds.), *Handbook of prevention* (pp. 223–242). New York: Plenum Publishing.

Webster, T. F. (1971). National priorities for the continuing education of psychologists. *American Psychologist, 26,* 1016–1019.

Welch, C. E. (1976). Professional licensure and hospital delineation of clinical privileges: Relationship to quality assurance. In R. H. Egdahl & P. M. Gertman (Eds.), *Quality assurance in health care.* Germantown, MD: Aspen Systems.

Woods, P. J. (1971). A history of APA's concern with the master's degree: Or "discharged with thanks." *American Psychologist, 26,* 696–707.

Zax, M., & Specter, G. (1974). *An introduction to community psychology.* New York: John Wiley & Sons.

Ziskin, J. (1981). *Coping with psychiatric and psychological testimony* (3rd ed). Venice, CA: Law and Psychology Press.

Zolik, E. S. (1983). Training for preventive psychology. In R. D. Felner, L. A. Jason, J. N. Moritsugu, & S. S. Farber (Eds.), *Preventive psychology: Theory, research and practice.* Elmsford, NY: Pergamon Press.

CHAPTER 4

PROFESSIONAL PRACTICE

Steven T. Fishman
Barry S. Lubetkin

When clinical psychologists contemplate establishing a professional practice, they assume that their graduate didactic and practicum training has prepared them for service delivery, but very few, if any, psychology graduate programs incorporate the requisite skills for practice development and management. Countless decisions must be made and numerous problems must be resolved before one pencils in his or her first appointment.

In this chapter we draw on our 20 years of experience in professional practice and review some of the fine resources that have been published of late to aid the neophyte practitioner, and we address the issues necessary to establish and maintain a viable professional practice.

FULL-TIME VERSUS PART-TIME PRACTICE

One of the first questions facing new practitioners is how much of their professional time they would like to devote to their professional practice. An ancillary but more relevant question concerns how much time is actually practical and functional and what percentage of allocated time is "dead time." Even though an

individual may be eager to launch a career as a practitioner, it is certainly more practical to commence one's practice in a modest way: that is, on a part-time basis. The reasoning for this recommendation is as follows:

1. The overhead and operational costs in an established office can be prohibitively high for a practitioner just beginning.
2. Building a practice is not an easy matter; there are many mental health workers in various disciplines with various orientations competing for the same psychotherapy dollar.
3. Functioning in another professional setting, whether it be an academic setting, a community health center, or a hospital, affords the neophyte clinician both the experience of working with a clinical population, but, even more so, the exposure to potential referral sources.
4. Income is not immediately forthcoming, and the pressure of having to generate income for office maintenance or support of one's family can impose undue stress on new clinicians, such that every phone call (i.e., cancellations or new referrals) can take on catastrophic proportions. In other words, it

can have an emotional toll on new clinicians if they must rely solely on their evolving practice for financial support.

GENERALIST VERSUS SPECIALIST

Another question that must be addressed but is usually influenced by one's graduate and practicum training concerns how one presents oneself professionally—as a practitioner with a particular orientation functioning as a generalist, thereby promoting the orientation; as a specialist with a particular treatment approach (e.g., hypnosis, cognitive therapy, etc.); or as specialist with expertise with a particular problem area or population (e.g., obsessive-compulsive disorders, anorexia, adolescents).

The opinions on the generalist versus specialist question are mixed at best. In our opinion, when one is trying to develop a practice, one should take on all patients in order to build a following and a referral network. In the nascent stages of practice development, one cannot afford to limit one's practice in any way, but can develop an expertise that can be marketed at a later point. Specialization is an excellent way of distinguishing oneself from the masses of mental health workers, but it is a luxury until one has an established practice.

The other viewpoint is that developing an area of expertise enables one to command referrals because of having more knowledge in a certain area or with a certain population.

SOLE PRACTITIONER VERSUS GROUP PRACTICE

Another question concerns whether a clinician starting out should do so alone or join with a group of practitioners to (a) share the expense of operating the office, (b) have monies available for a more aggressive promotional effort in developing the practice, and (c) share in the emotional burden of the vicissitudes of everyday practice (a point that we elaborate on later in this chapter).

There are several models in which one can structure a practice. Specifically, one can function as a sole practitioner either in an independent office or in an agency. (For example, one can practice in a university or hospital setting that allows for such independent practices, or practice from one's home or apartment.) One can operate within a group format with other practitioners or as an independent that hires other practitioner assistants or employees.

Practice formats can be as varied as working out of one's home with no support staff and relying on a telephone answering machine for contacts, to a large group practice with many practitioner associates with diverse specialties in a multioffice suite sharing operating expenses for the facility and the support staff.

As Chapman (1990) pointed out, there are a number of advantages and disadvantages to solo practice:

1. One can make one's own hours depending on one's preference, as well as take time off when one feels it is necessary.
2. There is a greater potential for income, but there is much greater risk for a declining income due to referral sources "drying up," a depressed economic climate, delays in third party payments, and so on.
3. One is personally responsible for one's own decisions, professional ethics, and actions. One has to be comfortable with that degree of independent responsibility.
4. One is responsible for any and all business aspects of the practice, such as collection, submission of insurance forms, as well as attending to aspects of the development and marketing of the practice.
5. Sole practitioners have to procure their own benefits.
6. Most important is the emotional toll and liabilities of practicing alone. One is much more susceptible to personal and professional isolationism.

In a group practice, even though most hours are spent in direct patient contact, merely knowing that peers are in the same office helps. Professional or social conversations with one's peers helps to counteract the feeling of isolation.

Group practice counters many of the disadvantages of solo practice. Specifically, overhead is shared so there is less exposure to the individual; it provides a more collegial environment where professional issues and problems can be shared; and an aggregate of practitioners can provide a wider range of evaluation and treatment services. The principal problem, however, is having to work closely with other professionals, which can lead to competitiveness and personality clashes. Individuals must weigh their own temperament and need for support from others in order to determine whether a solo or group practice is more suitable.

A word about in-home practices warrants our consideration. The principal advantage of operating one's practice out of one's home is holding down operating expenses as well as functioning in a more comfortable climate. But, in our opinion, the disadvantages of home practice far outweigh the advantages, in that patients are more exposed to one's personal life and family. In some known cases, this can lead to danger, harassment, or even impact on the psychotherapeutic process because of greater familiarity.

SETTING FEES

Setting and receiving fees for services rendered establishes one as a professional with all of the implied ramifications of professional functioning.

The charging of fees for service delivery engenders a conflict for many psychologists who embarked on their graduate careers with the humanitarian ideal of wanting to help people. Charging fees for their service contradicts this ideal, but as Canter and Freudenberger (1990) aptly stated, "it becomes a matter of balancing idealism with realism" (p. 217). One has operating expenses, one must support a family, one must repay loans for graduate education, and one spent 8 to 9 years of a college education and training to prepare for mental health delivery services.

Another issue closely allied to the previous one is that charging fees for service is imbued with excess meaning for some novice clinicians. It is more acceptable for them not to charge for their services; they feel less accountable for the quality of treatment that they are delivering. Charging considerably less than the patient can afford can also have a telling impact on the treatment itself. In all likelihood, patients will value their treatment less and will not be as motivated to carry out prescriptions of the therapist.

Because the charging of fees in the service of helping others evokes numerous emotional problems for some psychologists, it is an issue that requires considerable self-exploration. This process should involve consideration of such issues as one's attitude toward money in general. For instance, some professionals view money as an indicator of self-worth, and particularly self-worth as a professional with respect to the quality of care that one is extending to patients. As Canter and Freudenberger (1990) pointed out, "Often one finds that psychotherapists disavow the importance of money, claiming that they are really functioning as professionals, and that the professionals are not 'in business'" (p. 218). These authors continue to say that "it is important to point out that the independent practitioner is in business—in the business of being a professional—and that therapists who are uncomfortable with money issues really need some self-exploration" (p. 218).

Besides a therapist's own feelings about charging

fees for helping "suffering" people, as well as the meaning that money has for them personally, the whole issue of how fee setting and collection impacts upon the course of therapy itself requires examination. The degree of respect patients have for therapists is often measured by what therapists charge for their services. If therapists undercharge (undervalue) their psychotherapy, then patients may do so as well. If therapists charge too little or are too liberal about collection of fees, they are acting as a "superior being" (Freudenberger, 1987) and fostering dependency in their patients, which runs contrary to the expressed purpose of psychotherapy—personal growth and autonomous functioning.

Assuming one can work one's way through the emotional subtleties and attitudes of charging for professional services, one must consider a number of variables in setting fees for the spectrum of services offered. One must charge fees that are in line with other practitioners in the same discipline and that reflect one's breadth of training and education, years of experience in service delivery, credentials (i.e., degree, certificates of specialized training, National Health Register, diplomas from the American Board of Professional Psychology [ABPP], and the market or geographic area in which the practice is operating.

COLLECTING FEES

Fee collecting is the mainstay of a professional practice. Prompt payment and a good collection procedure are central for the maintenance of a viable practice.

A schedule of fees must be established for each therapy segment, whether it be a 30-, 45-, or 50-minute session, and for each type of service offered: individual, group, couples, family, testing, consultation, court appearances, and so on. It has been our experience that patients appreciate therapists being direct and matter-of-fact in their discussion pertaining to fees. It is inappropriate for a therapist to surprise a patient with the cost of any service rendered.

Costs for each service should be discussed in the initial sessions and should be printed in some format that the patient can read and then sign. Charges for additional services, such as calling other professionals on the patient's behalf, telephone sessions or contacts, report writing, and consulting with the patient's work or school, must be discussed and agreed on by each patient.

Some therapists establish a policy to charge for extra services, as attorneys do. Others feel that such services are part of their professional responsibility to the patient. Our position is that time is a therapist's most precious commodity and must be protected and used judiciously. For many of the services provided for the patient (e.g., report writing, phoning other professionals that are involved with the same patient, and limited between-session contacts), there are no extra charges. But when any one of these involvements becomes too time consuming or when a patient is taking advantage of or abusing these privileges, then the patient should be forewarned and subsequently charged for the therapist's time, prorated on the basis of the hourly rate.

There are a number of other ancillary issues about fees for which practitioners must set specific policies. When are fees to be paid? A poll conducted by *Psychotherapy Finances Newsletter* indicated that approximately 26% of therapists collect fees immediately after each treatment session. We have established this policy and have found that it minimizes losses and curtails the expense of billing, postage, and so on. Moreover, it minimizes cash flow problems, particularly when one has a high operating expense. If for some unforeseen reason patients cannot pay or forget their check or payment, they are asked to drop it in the mail to be received before their subsequent session. No patient is seen if he or she is more than two session payments in arrears, unless there are extenuating circumstances that are discussed in advance with the therapist. If some other family member or agency other than the insurance company is responsible for payment, then that person or agency is contacted and asked to submit payment in advance for scheduled sessions.

Does one offer a range of fees or a sliding scale depending on the patient's ability to pay for service? Some therapists do offer a sliding scale depending on the patient's income, while others charge their standard fee but maintain lists of resources where patients can receive treatment at affordable fee levels. We do the latter, because we have a number of associates and fellows in training, which allows us to offer a range of fees contingent on the experience level of each therapist.

Is there a time when fees are reduced after the initial determination? On some occasions, particularly when a patient's financial situation changes because of a loss of job, change in marital status, or insurance coverage, the fee is reduced to some negotiated manageable level, with the stipulation that once the economic level is restored the fee will revert back to its original level.

CANCELLATION POLICY

The loss of a session through cancellation or a missed appointment is costly. A clear policy must be established and communicated to all new patients to minimize such loss of income. There are many ways of addressing this situation. Some clinicians charge a patient either half or the whole fee, regardless of the reason for the cancellation. Indeed, when patients contract with therapists for treatment, they purchase the therapists' time and are responsible for payment irrespective of whether they use it each week. Other therapists charge a percentage of the fee (either 50% or 100%) for missed sessions, depending on how much advance notice is given for the cancelled appointment. Our own policy has been to charge a half fee for missed appointments unless informed 48 hours in advance of the appointed time. No-shows without explanation are charged the full fee.

Harari (1990) considered fee collection from three standpoints: practical issues; therapeutic issues; and ethical, moral, and legal issues. Regarding practical issues, a clear policy statement must be established and agreed on in the opening sessions on such matters as missed appointments, lateness, vacations, and legal holidays. As long as policy is clearly communicated and proceeds accordingly, collection of fees has little impact on the course of therapy.

Fees become a therapeutic issue when a patient becomes delinquent in payment and begins to accumulate a large balance. Build-up of arrears seems to occur most often when significant others are paying for treatment or when an assignment is accepted from a third party payer. Such delinquencies must be raised with the patient to discern whether the delinquency is an oversight, a function of some change in the patient's financial circumstance, or some form of resistance where the nature of the relationship has changed between patient and therapist. It also may be a direct reflection of the patient's motivation for treatment and particularly for change.

One of the greatest problems in collecting delinquent accounts occurs once the patient has terminated. Standard routine would be to send a bill or monthly statement followed up with a phone call. The former patient is more likely to respond to a phone call from the therapist than from an administrative assistant regarding periodic payments to clear up outstanding balances.

Therapists' feelings about the use of a collection agency are mixed at best. Some feel that turning over a patient for collection to an agency is tantamount to violation of confidentiality. The collection agency typically pursues an individual until some movement toward payment is made. The agency is representing the therapist, but the therapist has little control over how it functions. If the therapist elects to hire a collection agency for truant accounts, this must be specified in the policy statement that the patient agrees to and signs prior to beginning treatment.

THIRD PARTY PAYMENT: INSURANCE

Since insurance reimbursement is filtered through a bureaucratic network, a number of simple steps suggested by Jones (1982) should be followed in order to insure payment:

There is a wide variability in the rules and procedures from state to state, from one insurance company to another, and even variability in plans within the same company. So, it is imperative that you get clarification from a company's representative:

1. Make sure that you are eligible for reimbursement, that you have the necessary credentials, and that you have filed the necessary forms to be eligible for various insurance plans.
2. Clarify with your patient about his [or her] expectations regarding fees and insurance coverage, in particular.
3. Be very clear as to what your policy states regarding insurance reimbursement: that is, whether you will accept assignment or whether you or your administrative staff will fill out and file forms for their reimbursement, or whether the patient will be expected to pay their fees each session or whether you will accept partial payment (i.e., co-payment) plus assignment.
4. Make sure that all information required on forms submitted on behalf of the patient is completed. Otherwise, considerable turn around time can be lost, which of course will have an effect upon the cash flow situation or will be looked upon with disdain by the patient. It is best, however, to supply information only that is required. Providing excessive documentation is unnecessary and can delay reimbursement. When you are not the primary therapist, or the patient has been referred to you by another therapist, it is best to carry over the same diagnosis from the previous therapist. (pp. 184–193)

CoPayment

In some instances insurance plans require the patient to pay a portion of the therapist's fee, referred to as a copayment. This charge is in addition to the deductible charged at the beginning of the calendar year or the anniversary date of the policy. There are many plans that allow the provider to accept a copayment. But there are others that insist that the patient be reimbursed through some insurance plan and that the provider accept as full payment a customary and reasonable charge for services. This stipulation is particularly true of state or federal government plans, such as CHAMPUS or Medicare, but some private plans like Blue Cross & Blue Shield do the same.

A practitioner must keep abreast of the constantly changing picture on reimbursement of mental health services, concerning both eligibility status and actual percentages reimbursed.

Frequently, insurance plans present an ethical dilemma for practitioners in that the company requires information which, under ordinary circumstances, would be considered a violation of confidentiality. But the patient signs a release, which acts as a blanket statement of permission to the insurance carrier to inquire about the legitimacy of the claim, the treatment, and the provider. Conversely, the provider is ethically bound to comply with any request by their patient to release information or records about them to their insurance carrier.

Howard Cohen (1990) offered a word of advice about billing third party payers: Under all circumstances be forthright in billing, and if you have a question about the decision, contact the company. Cohen referred to a number of circumstances whereby patients would like to take advantage of the fact that mental health services are covered partially or totally. Some patients ask therapists either to inflate fees or to indicate more sessions than they received on their insurance forms in order to compensate for any copayment that they are required to pay. This, of course, is never recommended.

On the other hand, clinicians feel that they should be compensated for lost income due to missed sessions, which in most cases are not covered by private insurance carriers. Or they would like to charge either for telephone sessions or prolonged telephone calls due to a crisis. Carriers may or may not reimburse for such exceptions to the conventional treatment hour. We recommend that a procedural code be used to cover the rendered service, with hopes of being reimbursed. Falsifying insurance forms is considered fraud and is punishable by both prosecution and loss of license.

Another important issue that often arises, particularly in group practices when the group supervises junior staff or training fellows, is that supervising licensed practitioners are reqested to sign insurance forms of patients seen by their supervisees. Such an enterprise is referred to as lending one's license. Indeed, this practice is not allowable both on legal and ethical grounds and can lead to denial of benefits to the patient, as well as possible loss of license and the criminal prosecution of the practitioner. Only those clinicians that personally rendered professional services are eligible to sign insurance forms.

Peer review for continuity of benefits payment has become a commonplace practice. Currently over 98% of the population of the United States has some form of health coverage. Increased recognition of the financial loss from emotional or substance abuse problems means that a greater portion of the health dollar will be assigned to mental health benefits. Those delivering professional services will be scrutinized closely. Such accountability, as burdensome as it may be for the independent practitioner, assures greater quality control in service delivery.

The future will probably bring greater prospective review of intended treatment for a predetermined period of time. A review of proposed treatment must be approved by an independent agency hired by insurance carriers for increments of 10 sessions.

MARKETING AND DEVELOPING A PRACTICE

Marketing one's therapy practice requires a time-consuming effort which should last throughout the life of the clinical practice. Over the past 20 years we have experimented with a host of marketing strategies at our facility in New York City. Our needs have been somewhat different than those of the typical solo practice because in our group practice we employ approximately 25 part-time and full-time staff psychologists. Naturally, we must ensure a continuing flow of referrals.

In the following sections, we have included five of the most effective marketing and promotional strategies that we have employed. Some were more effective during the nascent phase of our practice; others have been useful during our slower periods when we needed to revitalize our practice.

Trade Names

Early on in our practice we made a fundamental decision that affected the direction of our efforts. By taking on a trade name, we were able to recruit more colleagues and establish a professional center in which we could function in more ways than just individual practice. We have found that potential patients are often more attracted to group practices than to individual practitioners for a number of reasons. They often believe that in a group practice clinicians are more competent because of collegial interaction and that they are on the cutting edge of developments within their specialty. Referring professionals, as well, hold similar views, believing that patients will receive more comprehensive care in a group practice.

Advertisements under an assumed name for a group practice can usually be more flexible (promoting the particular expertise of each member) and promoting more specific programs (e.g., aerophobia clinic, stress management training, adult children of alcoholics) than is possible for an individual practitioner. This comprehensive image is appealing to the average consumer of psychological services.

Creative Networking with Colleagues

As we have indicated in countless workshops that we have offered in private practice development, a solid, trusting relationship with one referring professional is worth far more than a year's worth of advertising. Yet it continually amazes us how little extra time and effort are actually expended by psychotherapists nurturing these relationships.

In the early stages of the development of our group practice, we established a board of advisors. Our board was composed of family physicians, neurologists, attorneys, dentists, psychiatrists, and other professionals to whom we were going to refer. We met with each board member briefly, explained the goals of our practice, and described the kinds of individuals we might need to refer to them. By establishing these ties without engaging in a hard sell, we had made ourselves known to important referral sources within the community. To this day, we regularly contact other professionals in the community and apprise them of our work.

It is important not to neglect any opportunity to promote one's practice with other professionals. For example, telephone consultations with a patient's attorney about a legal matter provide an opportunity to mention what you have done on behalf of other patients as well.

Make it a habit to acknowledge every referral from colleagues with a thank-you note and a brief report of the consultation, including a description of future interventions. The form of the report is outlined in Table 4.1. Such reports must protect the confidential relationship with the client, and the client should sign an informed consent form.

For many years, we have regularly mailed out to referring colleagues or potential referral sources copies of research or clinical reports that we believed would be of interest to them. They have come to rely on our Center as an ongoing source of relevant information in the mental health field, which also keeps our name before them several times each year. Thereby, we ensure continued support of our practice. We have also regularly disseminated newsletters with articles written by our staff members to potential referral sources—a subtle but effective strategy for promoting our practice to other professionals.

Affiliation with Self-Help Groups

As a consequence of soaring medical and therapy costs, large numbers of potential therapy consumers are turning to self-help programs in order to receive the support and guidance they require. Since the vast majority of such groups provide rather pat formulas for emotional growth and could not possibly respond to individual needs, many of their members eventually seek professional help. It is important, then, for clini-cians to work with self-help groups in order to increase their exposure to this potential pool of patients.

The two most productive ways to become a re-source clinician for self-help groups are through (a) individual contacts with members and by joining their professional advisory boards, and (b) making presen-tations at their regional meetings or by submitting relevant articles for their newsletters.

Use of the Media

It has been our experience that appearances on radio and television (either local or national presentations) have proved to be ineffectual in furthering our prac-tice. We have found the same to hold true for national magazine coverage. For example, after we had been interviewed numerous times by national magazines, aside from a few letters from readers, these articles did little more than fill a scrapbook.

There is, however, one form of media coverage that has proved to be consistently effective in generating interest in our practice: local newspaper coverage. Such coverage can be in the form of interviews with interesting professional personalities in the commu-nity, quotations about important psychological issues, or articles about particular areas of clinical interest (e.g., contemporary sex therapy, biofeedback for headache management, therapy for shyness). Because opinion polls generally conclude that the public views reports in newspapers as a credible source of news, it is not surprising that articles will generate many inquiries from the public. Science and feature editors of local newspapers are usually interested in covering new developments in the field of psychology. For any practitioner that is providing an innovative commu-nity service, it is likely that science editors will request an interview. To be more action oriented, practitio-ners can expedite the process by writing a brief synopsis of their work in the form of a press release and mail it to editors of the newspapers in the geo-graphic areas in which they are practicing. Appropri-ate disclaimers and qualifiers should be included.

Advertising

Since the late 1970s, we have seen a tremendous change in the policy and attitudes toward advertising from both the professional and private sectors. This movement began with a series of antitrust rulings from the Federal Trade Commission that permitted lawyers to advertise their services in a variety of ways. We have since witnessed many professionals breaking

---

Table 4.1. Consultation and Future Goals Report

1. Findings from your consultation
2. Overt behavioral problems (e.g., specific assertion deficits)
3. Covert (thought and image) problems (e.g., dichotomous thinking)
4. Other problems (e.g., depressed affect)
5. Patient's stated goals and expectations of therapy
6. Therapist's decision concerning goal priorities
7. Recommended interventions with approximate time periods for completion
8. Special instructions to referring colleagues if they are also maintaining professional relationships with their patients (e.g., encourage patients to attempt relaxation exercises despite the fact that they will continue to be responsible for chemotherapy)
9. Dates of future follow-up notes to be expected by referring colleagues

from the traditional conservative posture of little or no use of the media for advertising their professional services to actively advertising their practices. Radio and television commercials, newspaper advertisements, and the like are now commonplace for attorneys, medical specialists, and other professionals. In our experience, it appears that the most successful professional advertising is both repetitive and tasteful. Once practitioners have segmented the market to which they wish to direct their advertising, they should repeat this announcement in the same medium rather than switching to another medium.

The various mental health professions have issued clear guidelines concerning advertising that should be adhered to as closely as possible. This not only protects the clinical psychologist from unprofessional conduct charges, but it also ensures that the profession is portrayed in the best possible light.

Some portion of the public sector finds disfavor with professionals who advertise, but they particularly dislike professionals who advertise in a nonprofessional manner. It has been our experience that the most effective advertising medium for our services consistently has been the Yellow Pages of the telephone directory.

More self-referred patients come from the Yellow Pages than any other source. This population possesses some distinctive characteristics when compared to individuals referred by professionals or other patients. Yellow Page referrals tend to stay in therapy for a significantly shorter period of time, tend to be no-shows for first appointments, and generally can afford only lower- to medium-priced consultations. They also generally tend to be less sophisticated about the therapy endeavor.

Notwithstanding these characteristics, for a high-volume practice such as ours, Yellow Page advertising has proved to be invaluable over the life of our practice. Group practices may want larger ads with boldface type, red borders, and even photographs or powerful graphics. It is recommended that the advertisement be interactive: that is, you may offer a free brochure describing your practice or offer a recorded announcement providing useful information. Of course, information providing hours, location, insurance acceptability, problems treated, and years of experience should appear as well.

Finally, we have found that advertising in newspapers, on the radio, or on television bears little fruit in recruiting new patients, unless such advertising is done on an ongoing basis. However, the expense of continual advertising is enormous.

ALTERNATIVES TO CONVENTIONAL MENTAL HEALTH DELIVERY SYSTEMS

The changing economic climate in this country that was evinced in the mid- to late 1970s (which led to the mushrooming costs for health delivery) came at a time when employers were searching for ways of reducing their general operating costs. Alternatives to conventional health insurance plans were sought that would ensure greater cost containment and cost-effectiveness. More emphasis was also placed on preventive programs, such as wellness and fitness programs. From this climate were born three new alternative mental health delivery systems which address the aforementioned needs of both large and small businesses: Health Maintenance Organizations (HMOs), Preferred Provider Organizations (PPOs), and Employee Assistance Programs (EAPs).

According to Borowy, Buffone, and Kaplan (1985), clinicians must begin to develop and devote at least a portion of practice and promotional time to becoming involved as a service provider in these new systems. In our opinion, their position is an overstatement at the present time, but it does warrant attention. If new practitioners would like to have alternatives with which to build their practice, then they should get involved in such programs, for adaptability must be a key ingredient in the growth and maintenance of an independent practice.

Health Maintenance Organizations (HMOs)

Of the three alternatives, the HMOs, particularly those administered by large insurance complexes, seem to be prospering. As of a few years ago there were approximately 300 HMOs serving 13.6 million people; at present HMOs serve people in at least 42 states.

An HMO is a health care plan that delivers comprehensive and coordinated medical services to voluntarily enrolled members on a prepaid basis. Premiums are paid monthly by either the subscriber or more typically by employers. There are no deductibles that must be met by the subscriber, but subscribers may be responsible for a minimal copayment.

Employers usually pay a predetermined amount (capitation basis) for their employees whether they utilize the plan or not. An HMO is serviced by a group staff of practitioners from a hospital or clinic or by a group of practitioners that are recruited by the HMO to service their subscribers.

Kaplan (1986) pointed out the advantages and disadvantages of the HMO system to both the practitioners and providers as well as to the subscribers of such plans. Providers can expect to deliver their services at a rate less than their normal rate, but since the provider is paid on a capitation basis the income will be consistent whether or not patients are seen. Patients and subscribers receive treatment without filing claim forms, as would be the practice with a major medical insurance plan. They receive a comprehensive medical package which covers nearly all health and mental health care services with no deductibles to be satisfied. The major disadvantage is that subscribers are limited in their choice of professional providers and can select only from the panel of providers included in their particular HMO plan. More precisely, the specialty areas that include all mental health service providers must be chosen by the gatekeeper or the primary care physician (i.e., usually the family physician). If, however, subscribers are dissatisfied with the quality of care, then they can seek out a professional of their own choice. Subscribers assume the cost for same, unless they are covered by a traditional insurance plan as well.

The main advantage to the psychologist who is a member of the HMO provider panel is that it will increase the flow of patients into the practice if the HMO flow is viable. But there is no way of predetermining the flow of patients at any particular time. Because providers are remunerated in a steady and regular manner, they must provide service to all patients regardless of numbers or types of problems.

Preferred Provider Organizations (PPOs)

A PPO is a group or panel of independent health care providers contractually offering their services to third party payers (insurance companies, employers, and unions) at a rate that is less than their usual and customary fees. One of the important characteristics (and of distinct advantage to the payers) is that the PPO has some form of utilization review or claims review, so that employers are kept abreast of the cost-effectiveness of each provider. The principal advantage to consumers is that they have the privilege of selecting their own providers either within the provider panel or outside of the provider group.

Unlike an HMO, a PPO has no set model or prototype and is formatted in various ways among professionals, hospitals, clinics, and insurance carriers from state to state.

The advantages are clear to the consumer and patient in terms of cost containment, but the question remains as to whether the quality of health care is compromised. Since PPOs are a business, they engender a certain amount of suspicion among consumers.

The benefit to psychologists is that despite somewhat reduced rates for their services, there is little or no delay in payment. This allays cash flow and accounts receivable problems. In many plans, particularly the larger commercial plans administered by insurance firms, there is a medical gatekeeper who is responsible for referring subscribers to other professionals. Frequently, this practice will limit referrals to psychologists in favor of psychiatrists. If indeed a psychologist's practice is increased, then with the need for greater accountability, one of the hallmarks of PPOs is that practitioners work harder for less money to see more patients.

Employee Assistance Programs (EAPs)

An EAP is a legal entity that contracts with various businesses and organizations to provide cost-free assistance to troubled employees and their families. The services provided by EAPs vary but typically involve the evaluation and subsequent referral to a treatment facility for brief individual therapy (usually 10 sessions or less). Most identified patients are self-selected or referred by supervisory personnel for emotional or behavioral problems that are interfering with the employee's job performance. The majority of presenting problems tend to be for alcohol or substance abuse.

According to Kaplan (1986), presently more than 55% of companies with 5,000 employees or more offer EAP services, whereas 70% of *Fortune* 500 companies maintain EAP services. Such programs are looked on with considerable favor by large businesses that are concerned about maintaining their manpower worker efficiency. Reported success rates with EAPs range anywhere from 50% to 80% in both identifying, treating, and returning employees to the work force.

Psychologists can become involved in EAP programs in several ways: (a) developing and administering on-site programs; (b) serving as a resource for psychometrics or therapy either in-house or in one's office; or (c) doing post-EAP therapy for employees requiring more extensive treatment.

Summarizing these alternative mental health plans, Ramsey (1990) pointed out in a recent edition of the *National Health Register* newsletter,

> The geography of the mental health map is rapidly changing as insurers, hospitals, provider groups,

unions, and others are carving up, re-shaping the topography of the mental health map. In the 70's it was the individual health care subscriber that "hired" or "fired" health care professionals and facilities. Income for psychologists was relatively predictable and stable, even though many in the field were restrained in other ways (i.e., freedom of choice). (p. 6)

Unquestionably, HMOs and PPOs have changed and continue to change the mental health care landscape in significant ways. Managed care has penetrated the marketplace significantly. Despite the problems of many managed care HMOs and PPOs, the overall growth in numbers of subscribers and the volume of dollars spent for such programs continues to grow and stabilize. Fortunately or unfortunately, depending on one's particular perspective or position, managed care is here to stay.

According to Ramsey (1990), there now seems to be a separation or a "carving out" of the mental health service delivery portion from the general health care portion, with the former being managed by mental health care specialists in mental health and substance abuse.

BURNOUT AND OTHER LIABILITIES OF PROFESSIONAL PRACTICE

As we have indicated earlier, independent professional practice has many rewards, financially, intellectually, and creatively. It offers a variety of experiences, such as practice, supervision, writing, and teaching, and additionally some degree of prestige. However, a word of caution is necessary. Clinical practice, particularly with a difficult population of patients over many years, can have a devastating toll on therapists, especially when such factors as personal, health, and financial problems begin to encroach. Such occurrences, unless checked, can lead to depression, isolationism, boredom, and general feelings of disenchantment with life. Freudenberger (1980, 1983) has attached the singular label of *burnout* to this insidious condition. Freudenberger views this phenomenon as an exhaustion of an individual's mental and physical resources attributed to his or her prolonged, yet unsuccessful, striving toward unrealistic expectations (internally or externally derived).

Burnout occurs as, over years of practice, one's fulfillment of success, as determined by the amount of intellectual stimulation, financial reward, prestige, and relationships with patients and colleagues, is no longer meaningful. Some practitioners fail to maintain their earlier level of commitment and enthusiasm for their clinical practice and for the field of psychology in general.

Clinicians often become trapped in their own feelings of loneliness and isolation, which are known to be components of practice. They are invested in evincing only the most competent behavior and must maintain the facade of being in charge (Freudenberger, 1983; Smith, 1990).

Some of the stresses inherent in professional practice that may have a toll on the practicing psychologist are as follows:

1. The population of patients that therapists may see in their practice. Infantile, depressed, hostile, suicidal, and borderline and dependent patients require considerable attention, nurturance, support, compassion, and understanding, to the point where the therapist is emotionally spent. These patients require incredible amounts of intellectual and emotional resources.
2. The natural roller coaster effect of clinical practice.
3. The development of alternative systems of mental health delivery, like HMOs or PPOs.
4. The increased reliance of patients on third party payment and their demand for assignment or reduced fees.
5. Increased overhead or other operating expenses, both personally and in the professional setting.
6. Threats of malpractice suits.

Besides diminished interest in one's practice, the burned out clinician may turn to some form of substance abuse as a means of relief from the everyday pressures of practice, or may be more inclined to stretch the ethical boundaries of a sound practice.

Freudenberger (1984) recommended that clinicians recognize burnout as a real phenomenon and that they take precautions in preventing its occurrence. He suggested that the following prophylactic measures be taken:

1. Vary one's clinical commitment by involving oneself in other professional areas, like teaching, supervising, research, attachment to an agency, hospital, or hotline.
2. Organize and develop peer supervision and support groups to share experiences and sharpen skills. These also afford the clinician the opportunity to discuss problematic cases, to air frustrations, and to discuss ethical dilemmas.
3. Determine what activities, involvements, or types of patients are personally draining and invoke

some limitations on this type of activity or taking on a particular type of patient.

4. Take short vacations, limit the number of hours of work, engage in various desirable recreational diversions, and say no to some professional commitments (i.e., be more discriminating).
5. Pay particular attention to one's health, nutrition, and exercise. Exercise is an excellent way to alleviate mental stress.
6. Be honest with yourself about your emotional state. If you are emotionally spent, then seek out professional help.

Freudenberger (1984) pointed out that not only are the more senior therapists vulnerable to burnout, but novice therapists can also develop symptomatology, albeit for different reasons. In young professionals, symptoms of stress and burnout may occur if they are not constitutionally or emotionally suited for psychotherapy. They may find themselves overidentifying with their clients and virtually adopting their patients' suffering and feelings of helplessness. Another difficulty occurs, particularly in the early stages of therapists' careers, when they feel ill prepared, lacking in sufficient knowledge to help patients, or that interventions used are ineffective. The feeling of impotency in administering psychotherapy can be emotionally devastating for a new clinician.

THE FUTURE OF PROFESSIONAL PRACTICE

Some practitioners and authors (Borowy, Buffone, & Kaplan, 1985; Kaplan, 1986) have sounded the death knell for clinical practice as we know it, but it is our feeling that any rumors of its demise may be premature. In all likelihood, however, with the proliferation of more organized alternative mental health service delivery plans, the 1990s will yield greater modifications of the landscape of clinical practice.

The key words of the 1990s will be cost containment, cost-efficiency, and accountability in all treatment. As we have pointed out, industry will rely more heavily on mental health plans that are an alternative to the traditional insurance plans—HMOs, PPOs, and EAPs.

In our opinion, independent or group practitioners in the 1990s will not only have to compete with mental health workers from other disciplines and orientations, but will also have to compete with these organized plans that can offer treatment for less and will have more monies for the promotion of their programs. The independent practitioner will have to work harder to get a slice of the mental health market and will have to be more innovative in diversifying services offered, but private practice will endure. It will endure because there are substantial portions of the patient pool that will continue to select their own psychotherapists.

Because of the ever-changing rules for reimbursement from third party payers, it appears that there will be a greater need to justify treatment plans retrospectively through peer review. The field seems to be moving in the direction of the prospective evaluation of treatment plans for the individual patient. It would appear that insurers or other such contractors will favor the more time-limited, problem-centered approaches (e.g., cognitive therapy and/or behavior therapy) for reimbursement.

REFERENCES

Borowy, T., Buffone, G., & Kaplan, S. J. (1985). *EAP's PPO's, HMO's: A growing opportunity for private practice*. Workshop presented at the Southeastern Psychological Association, Atlanta, GA.

Canter, M. B., & Freudenberger, H. (1990). Fee scheduling and monitoring. In E. Margenau (Ed.), *The encyclopedic handbook of private practice* (pp. 217–232). New York: Gardner Press.

Chapman, R. (1990). Sole proprietorship. In E. Margenau (Ed.), *The encyclopedic handbook of private practice* (pp. 5–17). New York: Gardner Press.

Cohen, H. (1990). Third party payments. In E. Margenau (Ed.), *The encyclopedic handbook of private practice* (pp. 233–242). New York: Gardner Press.

Freudenberger, H. (1980). *Burnout: The high cost of high achievement*. New York: Doubleday.

Freudenberger, H. (1983). Hazards of psychotherapeutic practice. *Psychotherapy in Private Practice I, 1,* 83–89.

Freudenberger, H. (1984). Impaired clinicians: Coping with "burnout." In P. A. Keller & L. L. Ritt (Eds.), *Innovations in clinical practice: A source book.* (Vol. 3, pp. 221–228). Sarasota, FL: Professional Resource Exchange.

Freudenberger, H. (1987). Chemical abuse among psychologists: Symptoms, dynamics, and treatment issues. In R. R. Kilburg, P. E. Nathan, & R. W. Thoresun (Eds.), *Professionals in distress* (pp. 135–152). Washington, DC: APA.

Harari, C. (1990). Collections. In E. Margenau (Ed.), *The encyclopedic handbook of private practice* (pp. 243–249). New York: Gardner Press.

Jones, S. E. (1982). How to collect insurance reimbursement. In P. A. Keller & L. L. Ritt (Eds.), *Innovations in clinical practice: A sourcebook*. (Vol. 1, pp. 184–193). Sarasota, FL: Professional Resource Exchange.

Kaplan, S. J. (1986). *The private practice of behavior therapy*. New York: Plenum Publishing.

Ramsey, C. (1990). "Carve-out" of the mental health market. *National Health Register Newsletter, 16*(1), 6.

Smith, L. B. (1990). Boredom and burnout: How to avoid them. In E. Margenau (Ed.), *The encyclopedic handbook of private practice* (pp. 799–806). NY: Gardner Press.

CHAPTER 5

RESEARCH ISSUES IN MENTAL HEALTH POLICY

Charles A. Kiesler
Celeste G. Simpkins
Teru L. Morton

Most psychological research and practice is relevant to national mental health policy. However, psychologists have not been very involved in either the development of national mental health policy or its evaluation. The task panel on Planning and Review of the Presidents' Commission on Mental Health (PCMH) says more generally "that mental health professionals, except for public employees in delivery management systems, play almost no role in developing the policy other than the protection of their turf" (Allerton, 1978, p. 270). The task panel spoke prophetically, since the legislation implementing the recommendations of the PCMH—the Mental Health Systems Act—produced a similar competition among professions for resources (Rochefort, 1987).

Mental health policy not only determines both the context and limits of professional practice, but also has serious implications for research funding. For example, the decision in 1981 to decrease sharply National Institute of Mental Health (NIMH) funding for basic behavioral research was a policy decision based on perceived national needs in mental health.

We describe later how health policy strongly and often unwittingly influences mental health policy. We anticipate that the current health care revolution will

have a powerful effect on mental health issues. Further, the private sector is becoming an increasingly dominant force in health care delivery, and this corporate influence will have effects throughout the mental health system (see Kiesler & Morton, 1988b).

All of this argues that psychologists should be interested in mental health policy and, because of their scientific background, particularly in research in mental health policy. Let us first define what we mean by mental health policy, set the stage for a discussion of current issues with some historical perspective, and then move to a review of the research literature.

We define mental health policy as

> the de facto or de jure aggregate of laws, practices, social structures, or actions occurring within our society, the intent of which is improved mental health of individuals or groups. A study of such policy includes the descriptive parameters of the aggregate, the comparative assessment of particular techniques, the evaluation of a system and its subparts, human resources available and needed, cost-benefit analyses of practices or actions, and the cause and effect relationship of one set of policies, such as mental health, to others, such as welfare and health, as well as the study of institutions or groups seeking to affect such policy. (Kiesler, 1980, p. 1066)

The literature review for this chapter was completed in February, 1989.

This definition has both de facto and de jure components. In essence, we advocate a top-down approach to policy analysis. We inquire first what is done in the name of mental health in the United States, at what cost, and with what effects or outcomes.

Mental health policy research, like all public policy research, is inherently interdisciplinary (Task Force on Psychological and Public Policy, 1986). Important research that is directly relevant to the study of mental health policy exists not only in the fields of psychiatry and clinical psychology, but also epidemiology, psychiatric statistics, biostatistics, mental health and health economics, medical sociology, demography, political science, and law. The field of mental health policy should be important for psychologists, and they should play a central role in its development and study.

One might chauvinistically argue that psychologists should dominate research in mental health policy because of the centrality of psychology's concerns with human behavior, both abnormal and normal. However, psychology does not dominate this field and never has. It will become obvious in this chapter that only a small minority of the important research studies reported here have been carried out by psychologists and/or published in psychological journals (with the possible exception of the *American Psychologist*). By an informal count of our citations in this chapter (and excluding citations of our own work), less than 20% of the work cited had a psychologist involved, and less than 10% was published in psychology journals.

HISTORICAL ISSUES

Concern with madness has been with us throughout recorded history. For example, Eaton (1980) reported that depression was systematically studied in Greece in the fifth century B.C. The first mental health policy was articulated in fifth century B.C. Rome, where one of 12 tables of Roman law dealt with how one's goods were disposed of if one were "raving mad." Although insane asylums date from Bagdad in the 8th century, the treatment of the insane was generally one of benign neglect until the 16th century (Eaton, 1980). In the Age of Reason, incarceration became the treatment of choice, and in the Great Confinement of 1656, 1% of the population of Paris was locked up at one time (Foucault, 1973).

In Colonial America, punishment was the treatment of choice.

While the violently insane went to the whipping post and into prison dungeons or, as sometimes happened,

burned at the stake or hanged, the pauper insane often roamed the country side as wild men and from time to time were pilloried, whipped, and jailed . . . or . . . auctioned off as free labor . . . a form of slavery. (*Action for Mental Health,* 1961, p. 26)

The Pennsylvania Hospital was the first in the U.S. to admit patients (18th century), and punishment was an integral part of treatment (Deutsch, 1949).

The history of mental health policy for the last 150 years has centered around "mental hospitalization: yea or nay?" Parry (1989) identified three distinct cycles in the literature: (a) the moral treatment period of the 19th century; (b) the mental hygiene movement of the early 20th century; and (c) the community mental health movement of the 1950s and 1960s (Goldman & Morrissey, 1985; Rochefort, 1988; Sharfstein, 1987). For much of the 19th century, patient populations were largely acute cases institutionalized for less than a year. The elderly were seldom sent to mental institutions.

In the latter part of the 19th century, Dr. John Gray, as editor of the *American Journal for Insanity,* became spokesman for the point of view that rejected the concept of moral treatment and held that insanity involved an incurable brain disease. Custodial care became the treatment of choice (Kiesler & Sibulkin, 1987). By 1923, more than half of all patients had been institutionalized for over 5 years, and more than 80% of the beds were occupied by chronic patients (Grob, 1987a).

The National Mental Health Act in 1946 established NIMH. Not only did this legislation provide financial and institutional support for research, but it also promoted a social model of mental disease and emphasized community rather than institutional treatment of the mentally ill (Grob, 1987b). A Joint Commission on Mental Illness and Health (JCMIH) in the late 1950s recommended the establishment of community mental health clinics to augment services offered by mental hospitals and to provide services to those who otherwise had their needs unmet. The Kennedy Administration translated the requested clinics to community mental health centers (CMHCs) and intended them ultimately to replace mental institutions (Grob, 1987b). The late 1950s saw the beginnings of the deinstitutionalization movement from state mental hospitals, although no programs existed then, and few today, to pay for and/or treat such deinstitutionalized patients (Bachrach, 1976; Kiesler & Sibulkin, 1987).

The establishment of Medicare and Medicaid was a significant factor in reducing hospital populations (Grob, 1987b). This legislation stimulated the growth of nursing homes, thus affecting hospitalization but not necessarily institutionalization. State officials were enthusiastic about the legislation since it transferred fiscal responsibility for many elderly individuals to the federal government (cost shifting). Third party reimbursement plans also stimulated the development of both inpatient and outpatient psychiatric services in general.

Many of these historical concerns continue as contemporaneous issues in mental health policy research, and will be discussed here. For example, health policy (particularly as represented in federal legislation) has always dominated mental health policy. The so-called health care revolution, having as antecedent a concern with cost containment, will have as consequence a potentially powerful effect on mental health policy (Kiesler & Morton, 1988b). Changes in Medicare legislation, particularly those creating the prospective payment system (PPS) for medical and psychiatric services, are reverberating through the mental health system (Kiesler & Morton, 1988a).

At the same time there is no clear federal policy for coordinating treatment of mentally disturbed persons, but rather 50 separate state policies (Bachrach, Talbott, & Meyerson, 1987; Parry, 1989). President Carter's Presidential Commission on Mental Health (PCMH) was an attempt to develop a coherent federal policy, but the primary legislation coming out of the commission, the Mental Health Systems Act, was vetoed by then incoming President Reagan. The failure of this Act can be traced partly to its process of development, which Rochefort (1987) characterized as involving a splintering of interest, competition for resources, and disagreements over recommendations and the scope of the legislation.

The Reagan Administration further undercut the development of federal policy for mental health with the Omnibus Budget Reconciliation Act of 1981 (Public Law [PL] 93-35), which eliminated the services component of NIMH and created block grants to states along with the authority to specify program priorities for them.

In spite of these federal shifts (and ironically to some extent because of them), research in mental health policy and mental health services has begun to flourish. This chapter can, of course, only scratch the surface of mental health policy research. We will sketch the current state of research on some issues that seem to be of more central concern to psychologists as well as other issues which, independent of the concern of psychologists, represent in our opinion the most important ones of empirical and conceptual debate. The latter issues, less traditional in nature but central to the future development of mental health policy, warrant psychology's close attention.

De Facto and De Jure Mental Health Policy

As with most national policies, mental health policy is not a carefully planned and coordinated set of laws resting on the best of scientific knowledge (Mechanic, 1987b). Mental health policy is strongly influenced by financing streams, reimbursement rules, and organizational alignments (Mechanic, 1987b). Kiesler (1980) used the terms *de facto* and *de jure policy* to distinguish between unintended and intended national public policy. De jure public policy is what we intend to accomplish as a nation through appropriate legislation and agency practices. Our de facto policy is the whole system of what is done in the name of mental health whether it is intended or not. Indeed, in mental health, there are unintended consequences of our de facto policy that undercut our de jure policy.

For the last 25 years, the two major threads of our national de jure policy have been deinstitutionalization of patients from mental hospitals and the development of outpatient care, particularly through the CMHC system. Our de facto policy is dominated to a considerable extent by insurance mechanisms that undercut the de jure policy of nonhospitalization and outpatient care. About 70% of the national mental health dollar is spent on hospitalization. The largest such program is Medicaid, although Medicare and private insurance programs are important ingredients of the de facto policy as well (Kiesler & Sibulkin, 1987). The general issues of incentives, alternative insurance plans, and their costs on patient utilization are important policy research questions. We will bring them up as appropriate during this chapter.

RESEARCH ISSUES

Scope of the Problem

The field of psychiatric epidemiology focuses on both the incidence and prevalence of mental disorders (Dohrenwend et al., 1980). *Prevalence* refers to the number of cases existing in the population at a given time. *Incidence* refers to the number of new cases during a specified period of time. Some early attempts at psychiatric epidemiology included professional interviews by psychiatrists of entire communities (e.g., Hagnell, 1966). More recent research has centered around the use of various psychiatric screening devices (see Mechanic, 1980).

Older studies led professionals to agree that about 15% of the population is in need of mental health services at any one time. Both the task panel on the scope of the problem for the PCMH and a related paper by senior staff at NIMH independently reported this percentage (Mechanic, 1978; Regier, Goldberg, & Taube, 1978). Dohrenwend et al. (1980) found a substantial proportion of the population not fitting established clinical categories but nonetheless showing severe psychological and somatic distress. They found that an additional 13% of the population was in this category, with severe distress but without a diagnosable psychiatric disorder.

Dohrenwend et al. (1980) thoroughly reviewed the evidence related to the then current state of psychiatric epidemiology. They concluded that the true prevalence of psychiatric disorders varied sharply as a function of age, sex, community, and region of the country, socioeconomic class, and race. They also found a substantially larger fraction of the population with serious psychiatric disorders than have others. Further, they highlighted the phenomenon of people who do not fit into psychiatric categories but nonetheless have severe psychological distress.

Myers et al. (1984) reported 6-month prevalence rates for selected *Diagnostic and Statistical Manual of Mental Disorders, Third Edition* (DSM-III) psychiatric disorders based on community surveys in New Haven, Baltimore, and St. Louis. As part of the Epidemiologic Catchment Area program (ECA), data were gathered on more than 9,000 adults, using the Diagnostic Interview Schedule to generate a diagnosis. The most common disorders found were phobias, alcohol abuse and/or dependence, dysthymia, and major depression. Excluding phobias, 6-month prevalence roles in the three cities varied between 11.6% and 13.2%, with at least one of the DSM-III disorders, and from 14.8% to 22.5% when phobias were included. Lifetime prevalence rates were 23% to 25.2%. Rates were compared for two time periods (1975 to 1976 and 1980 to 1981) for the New Haven site and were found to be reasonably stable for the two periods. Data from this project found that 16% of the ECA population met the criteria for a DSM-III disorder, and an additional 12% met the criteria at some prior time.

Although overall rates in lifetime prevalence were similar in the cities (if phobias are excluded), there were significant differences in specific disorders by site. One must be cautious about extrapolating from a survey of several cities to a national prevalence rate, but one can conclude at minimum from this study and others that the prevalence rate for mental disorders in the United States is substantial and deserves serious national attention. Indeed, Kiesler and Sibulkin (1983b) found that about a quarter of all hospital days for all disorders in the United States are for mental disorders.

The clear interrelationship between physical and mental disorders further complicates epidemiological estimates of mental disorders. Goplerud (1981) provided a comprehensive discussion of these issues. For example, in one stratified sample of a Florida community, Schwab, Bell, Warheit, and Schwab (1979) found that 28% of the population had emotional problems, 39% had one or more physical illnesses, and 26% reported psychosomatic disorders, such as nervous stomach, hypertension, and colitis. Ten percent of the sample reported all three categories of disorder, and another 11% reported two of the three.

The bilateral linkages between physical and emotional disorders are increasingly recognized by researchers (Eastwood, 1975; Goplerud, 1981), but apparently not by physician practitioners. Hoeper (1980) found that general practitioners were able to detect only 3% of psychiatric cases, when the diagnoses were independently assessed.

Much remains to be done in the field of psychiatric epidemiology. There is not a good national data base, and differences between cities and regions of the country are not well explained. Part of the problem is that the psychiatric diagnoses are less reliable than the typical medical (epidemiologic) ones, particularly when performed by a nonpsychiatric physician. Pressures for reliability make the cost of a plausible data base prohibitive. The data base is sufficient to conclude that the problem of mental disorders is a substantial one for the nation, but insufficient for building treatment strategies, training mechanisms, and outcome assessments.

Services Needed and Number of Providers Available

Whichever estimate of prevalence and incidence one accepts for mental disorders, all agree that few people needing specialty services actually receive them. Regier, Goldberg, and Taube (1978) estimated that only about 15% of people needing services actually receive them from the mental health specialty sector. Since 15% to 25% of the population are in need of mental health services at any one time and only 15% of those contact the specialty sector, we can conclude that only about 2% to 3% of the overall population are receiving services at any time from the specialty mental health sector. Other estimates concur with this from an entirely different perspective. Cummings (1986) concluded that when mental health services are added to insurance programs, only about 2% to 4% of the insured population use them.

Kiesler (1980) made the point that the number of providers available is sufficiently small so that they can only provide a fraction of the services needed by the country as a whole. He estimated that there is only one doctoral-level service provider (psychiatrist or clinical psychologist) available for every 660 people in need, and that each person needing service could conceivably obtain at maximum 2 hours of service for his or her problems during a year.

Policy research questions become clearer in this view. Traditional psychotherapy, for example, could only be expected to provide a minor part of the solution to national needs. Therefore, research is needed to inform policies concerning alternative modes of treatment, the development of other potential providers and paraprofessionals, the relative efficacy of various treatment modalities, and the enhancement of the potential of voluntary organizations and alternative helping groups, such as social networks and families.

This is a good example of the difference between top-down and bottom-up policy approaches. From the bottom up, it appears that we would need to continue to refine therapeutic techniques, increase the number of service providers, develop the capacity for outpatient services, and the like. From that view it looks like we are continuing to improve our efforts over time to address national needs. That is a reasonable and accurate view. On the other hand, the view from the top down can appear quite different. The top-down view says that despite a steady track record of continued improvement in the delivery of services, the current approach to the overall national policy problem cannot succeed. We could never hope (nor probably aspire) to have a sufficient number of M.D. or Ph.D.-level mental health service providers to provide traditional mental health services to the number of people who actually need them. The top-down view leads us to put greater attention on alternative service providers, preventive techniques, and community support networks.

Mental Hospitalization

Kiesler and Sibulkin (1987) reviewed the existing literature on mental hospitalization. They argued that the national data on mental hospitalization lead to conclusions different than what most professionals believe.

Inpatient Episodes

The total number of inpatient episodes in the United States is almost 3 million, about 60% more than is typically reported in the literature. The difference is due to how inpatient episodes get counted in general (nonfederal short-stay) hospitals. Previously, in deriving the national totals, only episodes occurring in mental hospitals or within psychiatric units were counted. In total, 60% of the hospital episodes for mental disorders in this country occurred in general hospitals, but less than half (40%) of those were seen in specialized psychiatric units. Kiesler and Sibulkin concluded that the remaining 60% of inpatient episodes in general hospitals were being treated in "scatter beds" in hospitals without psychiatric units. A more detailed analysis of the Hospital Discharge Survey (HDS) by Kiesler, Simpkins, and Morton (1989), however, leads to different conclusions. Previous analyses had been unable to ascertain in a national sample how many people were treated in a specialty chemical dependency unit and how many were treated in specialized but short-term general hospitals. In a substantial refinement of the HDS, Kiesler et al. (1989) concluded that the majority of patients treated in general hospitals (62%) are in fact treated in specialized units. Further, the decision to place patients with mental disorders in general hospitals without units and even outside the specialized unit in those hospitals that do have them appears to be based on rational considerations. For example, secondary diagnoses of physical disorders and less serious psychiatric disorders lead to inpatient treatment outside a specialized unit.

Episodic Rate of Mental Hospitalization

Until recently, it was believed that the rate of mental hospitalization per 100,000 population in the United States was stable. Kiesler and Sibulkin (1984, 1987) used previously unpublished data from the HDS for general hospitals to calculate that, in fact, the episodic rate of mental hospitalization had increased rather rapidly over a 15-year period—a total rate increase of 60% over that time period. Previous estimates had included only inpatient treatment within the specialized psychiatric units of general hospitals. Kiesler and Sibulkin used the totals for the general hospitals whether treatment occurred in the psychiatric unit or not. They concluded that the increase in the national episodic rate of mental hospitalization was due to treatment in general hospitals without psychiatric units.

The more recent work of Kiesler, Simpkins, and Morton (1989) shows that the picture is much more complicated than that. First, their independent estimates agreed with those from NIMH about the number of people treated in psychiatric units of general hospitals—approximately 660,000, or 39% of the total treated in short-term hospitals. However, they also found what had been previously unascertainable from the HDS data: namely, that an additional 23% of the total patients were being treated in a short-term specialty hospital or a chemical dependency unit. Thus, as mentioned, 62% of the total patients treated in short-term hospitals were actually treated in specialized units. However, the remainder were not necessarily treated in general hospitals without any specialized unit—approximately 10% of the total were treated in hospitals with specialized units, but outside of the unit. Goldman, Taube, and Jencks (1987) found that 80% of the mental disorder episodes for which Medicare paid in 1984 occurred in general hospitals, and almost half of these occurred in hospitals without psychiatric units or outside the units. Kiesler and Sibulkin (1987) found that the number of people treated outside the psychiatric unit in general hospitals had grown enormously. How the specific treatment sites other than the psychiatric unit relate to that growth pattern is unknown at the present time. Certainly, severe mental disorders have become an increasing proportion of general hospital psychiatric episodes, and general hospital care seems to be replacing care previously provided by state mental hospitals (Thompson, Burns, & Taube, 1988).

Length of Stay for Inpatient Treatment

Kiesler and Sibulkin (1983a) reviewed the national evidence on length of stay for inpatient care in the U.S. from 1969 to 1984. They found that for most treatment sites the length of stay was stable. However, length of stay had substantially decreased in that time period in the state mental hospital and the Veterans Administration (VA), while still remaining long in both places. Thus, when investigators previously concluded that length of stay for mental hospitalization had decreased, they were technically accurate in the overall sense. However, they were unaware that it had decreased only in the two treatment sites that have traditionally been the most custodially oriented in treatment philosophy. In the remaining treatment sites (which currently treat 75% to 80% of the patients), the length of stay was stable from 1969 to 1984.

More recently, the PPS in Medicare for both general medical treatment and psychiatric inpatient care has had a clear effect on the length of stay. We will discuss this more recent effect in our subsequent discussion of PPS.

Impact of Treatment for Mental Disorders on Total Hospital Care

Cost containment in general inpatient care has been subject to much public discussion for well over a decade. It is not unusual to read in newspapers and magazines that the total number of inpatient days in general hospitals has decreased over a 15-year period. Kiesler and Sibulkin (1983b) were able to ascertain that this decrease was almost totally due to the decrease in hospital days spent for mental disorders. Further, within the treatment of mental disorders, the decrease in total days was due specifically to the decrease in the VA hospitals and state mental hospitals. If one removes the effect of the treatment for mental disorders from the total national statistics, total inpatient treatment for physical disorders has remained stable. Even with the decrease in days of treatment for mental disorders, such treatment still accounted for almost a quarter of total hospital days spent in the United States. Kiesler and Sibulkin (1987) estimated that in the early 1950s, approximately one half of the total hospital days in the United States were accounted for by a primary diagnosis of mental disorder.

There is an interesting inconsistency here between data bases. Kiesler and Sibulkin (1983b) found that approximately one quarter of all hospital days in the U.S. are for mental disorders. Yet investigators such as Cummings (1986) found that when mental health services are added to an existing insurance program, only 2% to 4% of the insured population use them. Part of the discrepancy can be attributed to the demographic characteristics of an insured population. A newly insured population would not include those on Medicaid, Medicare, or the 30 to 40 million people without any insurance. If, for example, one excludes from national data those from VA hospitals, state mental hospitals, CMHCs, and residential treatment centers, then the proportion of residual inpatient days due to mental disorders falls to 7.9% in 1978 (instead of 25%). If one emphasizes the insured in the residual, the percentage falls dramatically. For example, we have the 1980 data from general hospitals (Kiesler, Sibulkin, Morton, & Simpkins, in press). In 1980, by our calculations derived especially for this paper, only about one third of the days for mental disorder (Major Diagnostic Category [MDC] 19) in general hospitals were covered by Blue Cross and Blue Shield (BC/BS) or other private insurance. If one takes this into account, the percentage of total days falls to 4.1%. If we limited days considered in private mental hospitals to those covered by commercial insurance, the percentage would fall even more. Thus, the two conclusions are not inconsistent. It is clear that the vast majority of hospital days for mental disorders are not covered by private insurance. Obviously, private insurance covers a subset of the total population apparently less in need of inpatient mental health services.

Mental Hospitalization versus Alternative Care

Where mental patients are most efficaciously and cost-effectively treated continues to be an issue of considerable discussion. The number of studies reported in the literature in which patients with serious mental disorders are randomly assigned to traditional inpatient care versus care outside the hospital continues to increase. Kiesler (1982) reported details of 10 such studies, and Kiesler and Sibulkin (1987) added four other studies to this total. In general, these studies consistently find that an organized system of care outside a mental hospital is, on average, more effective and typically less expensive than is traditional care inside a hospital (even when the latter is well organized and funded).

The work of Stein and Test (1985), with their model of Training in Community Living (TCL), continues to have a growing impact on public policy. The model became the basis of the community support program for the state of Wisconsin. One principal element in the Wisconsin experience is incentives to reduce inpatient care. The state of Wisconsin funnels all of its money through counties, and thus it is in the interest of the principal mental health center in each county to handle its funds efficiently. As Stein and Diamond (1985) stated:

> Dane county has a philosophy and commitment to work with all the chronically mentally ill (CMI) persons in the community who require services . . . the goal is to insure that patients have as few relapses as possible, that they live as stable a life as possible, that they live as independently as they can, and that they enjoy a decent quality of life. . . . if goals are not kept in mind, and the resources are not husbanded carefully, just one part of the CMI population could use all the resources, and other patients would be left with no treatment at all. (p. 30)

In the Mendota Mental Health Center, with effective care outside of the hospital and careful husbanding of resources, hospitalization can be "virtually eliminated for all but 15–25% of these individuals" (Test, 1981, p. 82).

The array of services they offer continues to expand. Stein and Diamond (1985) described the Mobile Community Treatment (MCT) program, which is an outreach program to work with the most difficult and treatment resistant schizophrenic patients within the CMI program in Dane County. The MCT program, treating only the most difficult chronic patients, has a readmission rate of approximately 25%, which is less than half of the national average. That figure is more striking considering that only the most severely mentally ill are hospitalized in the first place in Dane County. Further, although nationally over 70% of the mental health dollar goes for inpatient care, in Dane County only 17% of the mental health dollar goes for inpatient care while 83% supports community-based services. "From our experience, one could argue that there is already enough money in the national system to provide good care if only that money were distributed more rationally" (Stein & Diamond, 1985, p. 38).

Witheridge and Dincin (1985) described their implementation of a version of the TCL program in urban Chicago for CMI patients. Their approach is to prevent readmission of severely disturbed patients, using TCL techniques. Employing a team of home visiting resource coordinators, they found that the average number of admissions per client per year dropped from 3.3 in the year before to 1.9 in the year after. The corresponding reduction in the average number of days hospitalized within the year was even more dramatic, dropping from 87.1 to 36.6, leading to an average savings of $5,742 per year per patient.

A somewhat different incentive system for outpatient care was instituted by the state of Texas, in response to two federal class action lawsuits (Miller & Rago, 1988). For the mentally ill, local areas are paid $35.50 per day for each patient they maintain in the community, rather than referring to the state hospital. Profits are retained by, and losses absorbed by, the local areas.

The debate over inpatient care versus alternative services continues but is typically ideological in nature and often acrimonious (Gudeman & Shore, 1984). It seems clear that the principal element in an effective alternative care program is the provision of incentives to prevent hospitalization (Kiesler & Sibulkin, 1987; Mechanic, 1987b). The number of geographical areas that provide such incentives by funneling funds through a central resource is growing (Wisconsin, Chicago, Texas, Australia) but at a rate which seriously lags behind the knowledge base. Medicare reforms that would reallocate hospital savings to community programs offering managed care could provide the type of incentive necessary (Aiken, Sommers, & Shore, 1986).

Some of the debate centers on whether the appropriate treatment model should be rehabilitation or treatment of disease (Mechanic, 1987b). The practice of medicine is oriented more toward the diagnosis and treatment of disease rather than toward its prevention, however, and the organization of its incentive system (fee for service) reflects that orientation (Katz & Hermalin, 1987). Outside the potential for Medicare and Medicaid reform, there is little federal direction or organized policy in this area (Bachrach, Talbott, & Meyerson, 1987). Patients at risk for psychiatric hospitalization make only limited use of outpatient service, partly because insurers have restricted outpatient mental health benefits to control utilization (Goldstein & Horgan, 1988).

Community support programs continue to show potential for cost-effectiveness, with one report claiming a savings of about $3,000 per client (Dickstein, Hanig, & Grosskopf, 1988). Although not all alternative care programs are less expensive (Glick et al., 1986), patients and families do regard alternative care more favorably (e.g., Lehman, Possidente, & Hawker, 1986).

Insuring Mental Health Care

PPS

PPS was introduced to Medicare in 1983 under PL 98-21. Under the regulations of this law, medical diagnoses are grouped first into MDCs, of which two are applicable to mental disorders (MDC 19, for mental disorders; and MDC 20 for alcohol and drug abuse). Within an MDC, diagnoses are further grouped into diagnostically related groups (DRGs). With certain reasonably well-specified exceptions, prospective payment under Medicare is fixed for a given DRG. This program is also having a dramatic effect on general medical care outside Medicare, since other insurance programs often look to Medicare as an exemplar (DeLeon & VandenBos, 1980). Some states now require all health insurance programs to pay for hospital care using DRGs (Ellis & McGuire, 1986), and even Blue Cross plans in at least nine states now use DRGs (Short & Goldfarb, 1987).

PPS has stirred much controversy in psychiatry and psychology (see Kiesler & Morton, 1988b for a discussion of both sides of this debate). Specialized hospitals and psychiatric units may petition for exemption from PPS. All specialty psychiatric hospitals have successfully done so (Uyeda & Moldawsky, 1986), and by the end of 1985 two thirds of the psychiatric units in general hospitals had also been declared exempt (Taube, Lave, Rupp, Goldman, & Frank, 1988). More recently (October, 1987), the potential of exemption from PPS for facilities specializing in alcohol and drug abuse was removed. Further, children's hospitals, originally exempt from PPS, requested to be removed from exemption through the National Association of Children's Hospitals and Related Institutes (NACHRI), which had developed a sufficiently improved patient classification system to predict reliably the length of stay for children's hospitalization.

There is no question that PPS decreases length of stay for general medical patients (Jencks, Horgan, & Taube, 1987) and for psychiatric patients when the hospital is not exempt (Frank, Lave, Taube, Rupp, & Goldman, 1986). Further, hospitals' profit margin for Medicare business is still twice as high as that for overall hospital operations (Jencks, Horgan, Goldman, & Taube, 1987).

Research issues regarding the use of PPS for psychiatric care abound, including the predictability and meaning of length of stay (Kiesler, Simpkins, & Morton, 1990), whether readmissions increase (Jencks, Horgan, & Taube, 1987), whether a fixed payment threatens the quality of care (Fuchs, 1986), whether hospital systems will attempt to develop alternative delivery products that do not come under PPS (Johnson, 1987), and how the homeless and indigent others can be treated under a PPS system (Mechanic, 1985). The reader is referred to Kiesler and Morton (1988b) for a more extensive discussion of the research issues involved in the pros and cons of PPS.

The Rand Experiment

In the Rand Health Insurance experiment (HIE), families were randomly assigned to different levels of insurance coverage for ambulatory mental health services (Keeler, Wells, Manning, Rumpel, & Hanley, 1986). The HIE enrolled a large representative sample of the nonelderly in six cities and collected data regarding service utilization over a 3-to-5-year period. Experimental insurance variations included co-insurance rates varying from 0% (free care) to 95%. To focus the experiment on the effect of incentives on demand for care, each experimental variation had a cap on annual family expense beyond which care was free.

There are a number of important findings of this comprehensive study. Keeler et al. (1986) found that outpatient mental health use is more responsive to price than is medical use. Those with no insurance coverage spent about one quarter as much on mental health care as did those with free care. Those with 50% co-insurance spent about 40% as much as those with free care. When users exceeded the cap (and therefore subsequent care was free), use increased. When a new accounting year started (and co-insurance began again), use dropped sharply.

Co-insurance had little effect on the duration and intensity of use within a mental health episode but sharply reduced the number of episodes within a year. However, the cap itself had a significant effect, and Keeler et al. estimated that spending in the HIE would have been 45% less for mental health if there had been no cap beyond which care were free. A $150 annual individual outpatient deductible did not affect the use of mental health providers, since almost all mental health users exceeded the deductible. However, the deductible did substantially reduce other outpatient medical care. Interestingly, users with free care were more likely to choose a psychiatrist as provider and more likely to use psychotropic drugs. Few users had more than one episode of treatment in a year, but those with multiple episodes spent no more on average than those with only one.

The use of mental health services was strongly related to symptoms of psychological distress (especially depression), but not to the level of positive psychological affect. An interesting policy question is the degree to which attempts to raise the degree of positive affect in the population as a method of prevention would have any effect on the use of mental health services. These data suggest not. Factors other than documented need also had a strong effect on the use of services, including gender, age, site, and education.

In this experiment, the utilization of outpatient mental health services was responsive to cost sharing and price. Moving from no insurance to full insurance (free care) quadrupled the expenses for mental health care. Over the range of 50% to 95% co-insurance, sheer price response for mental health care was twice as large as that for medical care. With lower co-insurance, the two services had about the same response to price.

Similar to other studies, Keeler et al. found that mental health care within a total system was not very expensive, about $32 per enrollee—about 4% of the cost of all health care. Further, relatively few people used the outpatient services; only 4.5% used any mental health care within a year, and only 14% over a 5-year period. Based on their data, Keeler et al. concluded that a typical insurance policy of 25% co-insurance for outpatient medical care and 50%

co-insurance for mental health care is reasonable. For each, such insurance produces about a 50% increase in demand over that of the uninsured. On the other hand, they pointed out that mental health care is a small part of the overall health care financial burden, and efforts to contain the cost of general medical care will not find much savings in the mental health arena. Further, cost containment in mental health care may, they noted, have the unintended consequences of disguised mental health care (possibly by unqualified providers) and the long-term implications of unmet needs.

Patterns of Insurance

Beginning with the Reagan Administration, the federal government has attempted to contain health care costs by adopting a so-called "marketing strategy," which involves promoting competition in the marketplace and capping reimbursement, particularly within the Medicare system. It has also encouraged Health Maintenance Organizations (HMOs) through new limits in tax laws and favorable tax treatment. Health care providers within HMO systems are required to provide comprehensive health care on a prospective per capita basis and are assumed to be more economical and efficient than traditional costing schemes. In 1983, the Civilian Health and Medical Program of the Uniformed Services (CHAMPUS) imposed a 60-day cap on inpatient psychiatric services and, more recently, proposed reimbursement limits on residential treatment facilities (Dougherty, 1988). Federal efforts to reduce the number of recipients of mental health services under Medicaid have been very controversial (Bazzoli, 1986; Mechanic, 1986).

Growth patterns of insurance coverage for mental health services have largely been limited to inpatient psychiatric care (Rubin, 1987). By 1984 almost all firms, except the smallest, provided some type of employee inpatient coverage for mental disorders. The coverage was offered on the same basis as for any other illness in about half of these patient plans. Most of the firms also provided some form of psychiatric outpatient coverage, but for over 90% the coverage was more restricted and/or with higher copayments than for other illnesses. Patient benefits are even more restricted in Medicare and other public programs. Clearly, current insurance patterns provide incentives to inpatient care and little or no opportunity for exchanging inpatient expenditures with outpatient treatment costs (Rubin, 1987). Research issues for the future of care for the severely mentally ill will depend on how the nation attacks the problem of the 37 million people uninsured in the United States, how it modifies Medicaid, and how it handles Social Security Disability Insurance (SSDI), Social Security Supplemental Income (SSI), and housing issues (Bazzoli, 1986; Mechanic, 1986; Rubin, 1987).

Perhaps the biggest change in insurance patterns is occurring in America's corporations (Kiesler & Morton, 1988a). The self-insured corporations are a relatively new phenomenon. Under the Employee Retirement Income Security Act (ERISA), large companies may insure themselves for health and mental health while being legally relieved of some of the reserve and other requirements of insurance companies. By 1983, 17.5% of the private health insurance market was accounted for by self-insured corporations (Higgins & Meyers, 1986). There is also a modified form of self-insurance for smaller corporations that do not satisfy all the requirements under ERISA. These companies can contract with outside insurance companies to provide billing and other administrative services and to insure the corporation against large claims. By 1983, this method of insurance accounted for another 14.3% of the health care market. Higgins and Meyers estimated that it may currently be as much as 50% of the health care market.

These corporate changes are an integral part of the so-called health care revolution, and their full effects have yet to be felt in mental health. As Kiesler and Morton (1988a) stated:

> Overall, immense changes are taking place. We predict that public and private cost-containment efforts, in tandem with rapid restructuring of the industry and growing consensus about the limits of free marketplace competition, should lead to declining provider autonomy, increasing integration of services, increasing emphasis on treatment outcomes, increasing management purview and control, changing power bases and (eventually) more consumer control via government and administrative decree. (p. 997)

These corporate changes may well have more effect on mental health care in the coming decades than will the federal government, treatment providers, or third party payers. In other words, the health care system will be dominated by those who pay for health care rather than those who provide it (Sharfstein, Krizay, & Muszynski, 1988).

The roots for this corporate concern are very clear. Medicare and Medicaid were established in 1965, and national health care costs were $38 billion then, or 6% of the gross national product (GNP). By 1982, costs had risen to $355 billion (almost 11% of the GNP), and Flinn, McMahon, and Collins (1987) projected them to rise to $750 billion (or 12% of the GNP) by 1990. From 1979 to 1982, hospital costs increased 19.2% per year (Uyeda & Moldawsky, 1986). By 1984, when Medicare introduced PPS, American corporations were paying more for health insurance premiums than they were to shareholders in dividends (Califano, 1986). Recently, 20% of the growth in the federal budget has been in Medicare and Medicaid (Short & Goldfarb, 1987).

This has led corporations, such as the Chrysler group chaired by Califano (1986), to look closely at health care costs in other countries. America spends almost 11% of the GNP on health care, compared to 8% to 9% of Canadian and West German GNP that went to providers and 6% of GNP for providers in the United Kingdom and Japan.

The effects of the health care revolution on mental health care and policy seem inevitable, and Kiesler and Morton (1988a) pointed to needed research regarding outcome studies, service systems research, resource allocations, and needs assessment.

Medicare and Medicaid

Medicare continues to have a number of important changes, with considerable potential impact on mental health treatment. Of course, the change most discussed is that of prospective payment, in which a hospital receives reimbursement for a specific DRG (Kiesler & Morton, 1988a). There are certain exceptions, such as extra payment for long-term stays that can be justified, and modifications of payment such as an indirect medical education adjustment for teaching hospitals. Reimbursement limits for psychiatric inpatient care under Medicare had already been in the process of change through PL 97-248, the Tax Equity and Fiscal Responsibility Act of 1982 (TEFRA), which offered incentives to reduce costs and length of stay by offering hospitals a share of the savings. The TEFRA provision made it more difficult to test the immediate effects of PPS.

Children's hospitals were also originally exempt from PPS. However, as mentioned, an improved patient classification system based on research and combining the variables of birth weight and time on a respirator led to a restructured and more precise DRG system. At the request of NACHRI, the Health Care Finance Administration (HCFA) removed their exemption (Jencks & Goldman, 1987).

The possibility of PPS for psychiatric care has sparked a lively controversy, with the professional organizations largely opposed to the system (Kiesler & Morton 1988b; Jencks, Horgan, Goldman, & Taube, 1987; Jencks, Horgan, & Taube, 1987).

Kiesler and Morton (1988b) described some of the research issues salient as a function of which side of the debate one assumes.

Medicaid is also an important aspect of our system of public mental health care. In fiscal 1985, Medicaid spent $710 million through state agencies. Half of the beneficiaries of Medicaid (11 million) are dependent children, and these benefits to children represent 55% of all the public health funds spent on children (Dougherty, 1988). Most of the Medicaid funds spent through state mental health agencies went for state mental hospital care ($558 million), leaving only about 20% for community-based services (Dougherty, 1988).

A growing problem are the 30 to 40 million Americans who have no health insurance (13% to 15% of the population: Goldsmith, 1986). These are people who are not eligible for either Medicare or Medicaid and have no access to private insurance. Many are employed full time but have an income near the poverty line. In Medicare, demonstrations are currently planned that will pool funds for inpatient and outpatient care for a defined population. A single public entity will establish systems of managed care for that population and develop waivers for care (Mechanic, 1987a).

Sites of Mental Health Service Delivery

Over the past 40 years or so, the emphasis in psychology in terms of mental health care delivery has been on a one-to-one patient relationship with a service provider (Kiesler, 1980). However, discussions of changes for new public policy in mental health are removed from psychotherapy. The emphasis in health and mental health policy is on systems of care (Kiesler & Morton, 1988b).

One important aspect of systems of care is the physical locale for the delivery of services. Discussions of mental health service delivery, even by sophisticated professionals, often unwittingly concentrate on only three: the private psychiatric hospital, the state mental hospital, and the office of the psychotherapist.

Approximately 70% of the cost of mental health services in the United States is due to inpatient care (Kiesler & Sibulkin, 1987). However, the site of inpatient care has changed dramatically in the last 2 decades. Now, the majority of inpatient episodes occur in general hospitals (Kiesler & Sibulkin, 1984), and the fastest moving site for care is treatment in a general hospital but outside of a psychiatric unit.

The CMHC has been a centerpiece of federal policy making for a long time. However, the Omnibus Budget Reconciliation Act of 1981 cut off direct federal support for CMHCs and forced states through the block grant program to establish internal priorities. The block grant program did not have an immediate negative effect on CMHCs (Kiesler et al., 1983). However, lack of federal data gathering makes it difficult to assess the current national impact of CMHCs and the degree to which they are integrated into an overall system. One original intent of the CMHC program was deinstitutionalization, but Gronfein (1985) suggested that Medicaid had a much stronger effect on deinstitutionalization than the CMHC program and that the structure of reimbursement schedules rather than the philosophy of community care was more decisive in promoting deinstitutionalization. The CMHC program was set up by the federal government independent of influence by, or consultation with, states (Mechanic, 1980). Because of that, there has always been friction between the state authorities and the community mental health centers, and CMHCs have never played the role in deinstitutionalization that the federal government originally envisioned (Mechanic, 1980).

CMHCs were a site for delivery of care, but they also were associated with a movement and a philosophy (Bachrach, 1976, 1985). The disagreements between proponents of hospital-based and community-based care have often been more philosophically than empirically based. According to Stein (1988),

> both are absolutely essential elements in a comprehensive and integrated system of care for persons with long-term mental illness. We should be searching for what each can do best for the benefit of the patient, and that question should be answered by data not by hocus pocus. (p. 1029)

Gudeman and Shore (1984) used the Massachusetts Mental Health Center as a basis for proposing a new class of facilities for the care of the mentally ill. Their services include a day hospital, an intensive care unit to stabilize acute episodes, and a inn-type of temporary residence for transition to community living. There is, as well, a continuing care program of graduated levels of community living, a day treatment program, a psychiatric and geriatric nursing home program, and an outreach program for those receiving care in nursing homes.

Gudeman and Shore found that some patients do not benefit from any of these services even after 5 years of the full range of service and, according to them, would be better placed in a more restrictive and specialized environment. These five types of patients (about 6% of the patient population) were (a) elderly patients suffering from a combination of dementia, psychosis, and medical illness which make them dangerous to themselves or others; (b) mentally retarded individuals with concomitant psychiatric illness and assaultive and aggressive behavior; (c) patients with serious loss of impulse control due to brain damage from head injuries or degenerative diseases; (d) schizophrenics who are unremittingly assaultive, suicidal, relentlessly obstreperous, and oppositional; and (e) chronic schizophrenic patients who are not acutely dangerous to themselves or others but exhibit behavior that makes them vulnerable to exploitation.

It is interesting to note that in this proposal for a new class of facilities there is no long-term treatment facility (all state hospital patients were transferred to the center). In short, Gudeman and Shore (1984) found that only about 6% of the patients had difficulty responding to an array of treatment that did not include a long-term facility. In designing a national mental health policy, an important and integral aspect of future policy would rest on the need for long-term inpatient care and the resources necessary to fund such care. If only 6% of the patients require such care, the savings could go a long way toward funding the remaining array of services that Gudeman and Shore described as necessary.

There has also been an upsurge of interest in recent years in general hospital psychiatry (e.g., Bachrach, 1985; Detre & Kupfer, 1975; Flamm, 1979; Keill, 1986; Schulberg & Burns, 1985; Summergrad & Hackett, 1987). In this view, the general hospital is seen as the core of the mental health services system (Keill, 1981) for short-term acute care. Diagnosis and treatment are hindered by the high rates of comorbidity—psychiatric and substance abuse problems in medical and surgical cases, and medical illness in psychiatric cases (Barlow, DiNardo, Vermilyea, Vermilyea, & Blanchard, 1986; Bunce, Jones, Badger, & Jones, 1982; Cavanaugh, 1986; Dulit, Strain, & Strain, 1986; Dvoredsky & Cooley, 1986; Fulop, Strain, Vita, Lyons, & Hammer, 1987). Attention has been focused on the general hospital emergency room and the diagnostic and case management problems of its psychiatrically complex and comorbid cases (Baker, 1985; Fulop & Strain, 1986; Hillard, Slomowitz, & Levi, 1987; Schwartz, Braverman, & Roth, 1987). There has been continuing concern over the inability of primary care physicians to detect and treat psychiatric problems, and the need for psychiatrists to play a role in educating primary care physicians (Strain, Pincus, Gise, & Houpt, 1986; Thomp-

son & Thomas, 1985; Wise, 1985). Models for the interface of psychiatry and primary care in the general hospital, such as triage or team approaches, or consultation-liaison psychiatry, have been proposed (Fink, 1985; Pincus, 1987; Wallen, Pincus, Goldman, & Marcus, 1987). The advantages and disadvantages of segregating psychiatrically comorbid patients in psychiatric wards, psychiatric medical units, and medical psychiatric units have been discussed (Breen, 1979; Fogel, 1985; Fogel, Stroudemire, & Houpt, 1985), as have the pros and cons of nonsegregation of psychiatric patients in a general hospital (Reding & McGuire, 1973; Smith, 1979).

There has been a recent increase in beds in nongovernment general hospitals and a decrease in beds in state hospitals. Thompson et al. (1988) found that referrals to state hospitals were rare in 1980 while they were predominant in 1970. Indeed, referrals to other hospitals from psychiatric units in general hospitals, although unusual, are more frequent than such referrals from treatment outside the psychiatric unit (Friedman, 1985; Kiesler et al., in press).

Richman and Harris (1985) found considerable differences in general hospital psychiatry between the U.S. and Canada on the one hand and England, Trieste, Italy, and Australia on the other. They described most hospital services in North America as being dependent on a mental hospital as a backup, with few psychiatric divisions being able to provide a broad range of treatment and care through linkages to other community services. In Trieste and Britain, the clearly stated policy was to phase out mental hospitals, and the general hospital became the central focal point in the care system. Even though this plan has not been fully realized in Britain, Richman and Harris found the intended role and function to be clear for a general hospital there.

Meanwhile, the investor-owned hospital corporations have had a powerful impact on the U.S. marketplace. In 1983, hospital chains owned nearly 15% of all the general care facilities in the United States and managed 5% of the rest. Eisenberg (1986) projected this to rise to 60% by 1995. In the late 1960s, the first investor-owned psychiatric multihospital systems were established. By 1980 such systems owned 41 of the 130 proprietary psychiatric hospitals, and by 1986 they owned 86 (Eisenberg, 1986).

Eisenberg (1986) described how the unique financing of this marketplace can have an indirect impact on the cost of the delivery of mental health services. According to Eisenberg, when Hospital Corporation of America (HCA) purchased Hospital Affiliates International (HAI) for $885 million (in stock, borrowed funds, and assumption of debt), costs increased by $55 million during the first year due to increased interest and increased depreciation from necessary declaration of capital appreciation. Allowable costs that could be charged to Medicare increased by $272 million following the purchase. Thus, any leveraged buyout, in which the new corporation incurs the debt borrowed in order to purchase it, would have a substantial and legal impact on the use of public funds.

HMOs continue to be an important aspect of mental health policy, although good data are hard to come by. Psychologists worry about mental health benefits decreasing in HMOs, particularly in HMOs of marginal financial stability. The earlier studies of medical offsets as a result of mental health intervention were disproportionately HMO efforts (Jones & Vischi, 1980). More recently, Seltzer (1988) described a study based on ChoiceCare of Cincinnati. The study involved a variation of the limits on inpatient care and the number of outpatient visits. Under a pilot program, patients were allowed a greater number of outpatient visits, but with the copayments increased after the limit was reached. Inpatient care could also be extended beyond the limit, as long as a written request was made before the limit expired. Both potential extensions were reviewed by treatment review committees. Seltzer found that these extensions of prior service limits did not increase overall medical costs. The reason is that for the individual patients who were granted extensions, there was a significant decrease in medical costs to the plan following the extended treatments.

Children's Mental Health Policy

Problems related to children's mental health policy continue to plague planners, and the overall effort is not well coordinated. Dougherty (1988) described the current situation very well:

> At least 12%, or 7.5 million of the nation's children suffer from emotional or other problems that warrant mental health treatment. Untold others—the 14 million children living in poverty, (U.S. Congress, Congressional Research Service [CRS], 1985); the 7 million children of alcoholic parents (Russell, Hendersen, & Blume, 1984) and the 1 million who are neglected or abused (U.S. Department of Health and Human Services, 1981)—are at serious risk of developing mental health problems. Only 20% to 30% of these children may be getting appropriate mental health services (U.S. Congress, Office of Technology Assessment, 1986). (p. 811)

Saxe, Cross, and Silverman (1988) described a recent report on the state of children's mental health policy for the Office of Technology Assessment. They found that less than half of the children needing services receive any form of treatment, and for those who do receive it, it often is inappropriate treatment.

Less attention has been focused on discovering the needs of children, and research on children's mental health issues is more poorly funded than that on adults (National Academy of Sciences, 1982). There is encouraging recent evidence on the effectiveness of certain kinds of therapies for certain problems of children (Saxe et al., 1988). However, Saxe et al., in their original Office of Technology Assessment report (1986), described the most important trend—the care taking place in the private sector and a general increase in use of psychiatric hospitalization. They pointed to substantial increases in the use of private hospitals and specialized hospital facilities for children. One primary site of treatment is the residential treatment center (RTC). While the evidence for the effectiveness of the RTC is sparse, the average length of stay in a residential treatment center exceeds 1 year, and the average costs may be in excess of $50,000 (Kiesler & Sibulkin, 1987).

The Child and Adolescent Service System Program was initiated by NIMH to coordinate mental health care and encourage interagency efforts in states to serve severely disturbed children. However, although it is enthusiastically endorsed by all, this program represents only seed money.

One of the principal problems in children's mental health policy is the tendency to see children's problems as merely duplicative of adults. As Senator Inouye (1988) stated:

> We must stop treating our children like miniature adults; instead we must recognize their special needs. Children's mental health treatment is often more complex, and therefore more costly than treatment for adults. . . . our policies and funding practices need to focus on the special and complex requirements of children. (p. 816)

We have made decent progress in research on mental health policy and services in the few years since the publication of the first edition of this handbook (1983). Arguably, children's mental health policy is more important to the nation than adult mental health policy. Yet legislation, theory, research, and thoughtful consideration of the alternatives have lagged behind in children's issues.

Mental Health Policy Issues for the Elderly

Research regarding the mental problems and policies for the elderly continues to expand. The current and expected continuing increase in the number of the elderly is well known. That the problems of the elderly seem to receive greater legislative and public attention than those of children is partly a function of the increasing sophistication of political action groups reprsenting the elderly, such as the American Association for Retired People (AARP). Catastrophic health insurance bills are disproportionately oriented toward the problems of the elderly (Goldsmith, 1986) but are at the same time perhaps the most expensive form of health insurance (Zook, Moore, & Zeckhauser, 1981).

Liptzin (1987) described some of the ways by which assessment or treatment of the elderly is complicated. They tend to have hearing impairments, visual impairments, cognitive impairments, ambulatory difficulties, physical illnesses, altered physical states that make psychotropic drugs stay in the body longer (with concomitant potentially powerful clinical and toxic effects), less willingness to discuss personal problems, and clinical presentations that may be different than those of younger patients. In addition, many of the serious mental disorders (such as schizophrenia and organic brain syndrome) are age linked, and consequently the number of people who are at risk for such disorders is both increasing and predictable (Kramer, 1983).

The previous discussion of issues regarding Medicaid and Medicare applies to the elderly specifically as a special population. In terms of overall medical care in the U.S., those over age 65 now account for more than 40% of all hospital days, and the federal government currently finances about two thirds of all health care expenditures of older people (DeSario, 1987). One can expect nursing facilities, home health care services, and hospice programs to continue expanding. One of the driving forces behind the shifting of patients from state mental hospitals to nursing homes is the economic advantages for the state in transferring costs from their own mental health budgets to federal programs.

Controversies over the quality of care and the access to care within nursing homes continue to abound. Lack of access to specialty mental health providers in nursing homes is well documented, as well as the relative inability of general practitioners to recognize mental disorders. In one study, diagnoses made by a group of family physicians were compared with those generated by the Diagnostic Interview Schedule (DIS). Even though all physicians had satisfactorily completed a psychiatry curriculum designed for family physicians, 79% of the DIS diagnoses went undetected (Jones, Badger, Ficken, Leeper, & Anderson, 1987). Indeed, even among psychiatrists, Loring and Powell (1988) found considerable unreliability in psychiatric diagnoses as a function of the match between the gender and race of the psychiatrist and those of the patient.

Kiesler and Sibulkin (1987) reviewed the evidence concerning the effects of deinstitutionalization on the rapidly increasing population of mentally disabled in nursing homes. First, they concluded that the number of people in nursing homes with mental disorders has increased dramatically in recent years, far in excess of the increase in the number of the elderly. They found the increase to be true of each age group beyond age 65. They closely inspected admissions and discharge rates of state mental hospitals over a 20-year period, as well as admissions rates and discharge rates for nursing homes (including deaths in both cases).

They concluded that the increase in the mentally disabled in nursing homes cannot be accounted for either by discharges from state mental hospitals or by a change in institutionalization practices in state mental hospitals. For example, over 90% of the net releases from state mental hospitals have consistently been under age 65 (since 1964). On the other hand, only 5% or less of total nursing home residents have been under 65. Thus, the discharges from state mental hospitals can account for little of the increase in the mentally disabled in nursing homes. Further, of the increase in the mentally disabled in nursing homes, only about 16% can be accounted for by the increase in sheer numbers of people over 65 in the country at large. Kiesler and Sibulkin (1987) concluded that the increase of the mentally disabled in nursing homes is a new national phenomenon that needs direct research attention.

It is clear that nursing home residents in need of mental health services rarely receive it (Shadish, Silber, & Bootzin, 1984). Further, what treatment is received is typically drug treatment with little active involvement by the attending physician, and patients are subject to widely varying normative practices by physicians. In one study, 14% of the physicians in a sample of nursing homes accounted for 81% of the antipsychotic drugs prescribed (Ray, Federspiel, & Schaffner, 1980).

The Homeless

National attention continues to focus on the homeless. The best general review of these issues is the report *Homelessness, Health and Human Needs* by the National Academy of Sciences (1988). Estimates of the number of the homeless vary widely, from 250,000 to 2,200,000, and estimates of the percentage of the homeless with mental disorders vary widely as well.

There has also been a spate of important federal legislation to aid the homeless that should interest mental health policy researchers. The Food Security Act of 1985 (PL 99-198) requires state welfare offices to provide food stamps to people without a permanent address. The Homeless Eligibility Clarification Act (PL 99-570) allowed food stamp eligibility for shelter residents and allowed their use within the shelter. It also allowed Aid to Families with Dependent Children (AFDC), SSI, Medicaid, and veterans' benefits for the homeless (they were previously required to have a permanent address). The Homeless Assistance Act of 1987 (PL 100-77) was an omnibus bill providing funds for a homeless interagency council, emergency food and shelter programs, literacy programs, housing, and mental health services. Research is badly needed, and research opportunities have increased with this legislation.

State Mental Health Systems

State mental health systems continue to evolve and change, but disproportionately due to changes in federal policy (such as the Omnibus Budget Reconciliation Act of 1981). Mechanic (1987b) described recent changes in state mental health systems. In general, state mental hospitals have been transformed from custodial care institutions to acute care institutions, although there is extraordinary variation among states in the extent in which their systems of care are institutionally based. By 1982, the average state hospital had 529 inpatients, 807 employees, and an average expense per patient of $31,000. Currently, approximately two thirds of state expenditures for mental health are used to support state hospitals.

The Wisconsin system is perhaps the best known for funneling state funds through the counties, forcing the counties to assess trade-offs between community care and inpatient care and to seek alternatives to hospitalization (Stein & Ganser, 1983; Stein & Test, 1985). But even in Wisconsin the results have been uneven throughout the state (Mechanic, 1987b). The resistance to change of state mental hospital systems depends on how well established the hospital system is, how dependent communities are on the hospitals for economic benefits, and how well organized and unionized the employees of the hospitals are.

The state of Arizona has recently moved to a system similar to that of Wisconsin, but as the outcome of a lawsuit brought in 1981 by the Arizona Center for Law in the Public Interest (Santiago, 1987; Santiago, Gittler, Beigel, Stein, & Brown, 1986). This led to revised standards that require the provision of unified mental health programs that include the functions of both the state mental hospital and community mental health services. Arizona statutes give the county the sole authority and responsibility for providing medical care for its indigent residents. It is interesting that the suit was based on Bachrach's (1978, 1981, 1982, 1986) model of continuity of care for chronic mental patients.

Prevention

We recommend to the reader the report of the task panel on prevention of the PCMH. Both the quantity and quality of research and prevention have probably been undervalued. The support among professionals and the funding from federal agencies for research and prevention have never been strong—a topic worthy of investigation itself. There is a developing body of literature regarding prevention of mental disorders in populations at risk (see Albee, 1980).

In some ways the notion of prevention in mental health does not match up well with the history of prevention in general medicine. Prevention in public health is almost a century old and originated with special concerns about the control of infectious diseases (Katz & Hermalin, 1987). The public health concept distinguishes three levels of prevention: primary, secondary, and tertiary. Primary prevention means preventing disease before it occurs. Secondary prevention refers to detecting disease and treating it early before it worsens. Tertiary prevention refers to the treatment of apparent disease to prevent serious later complications (Katz & Hermalin, 1987).

Katz and Hermalin (1987) applied the three levels of prevention to schizophrenia as an example. Since it is not known how to prevent many varieties of schizophrenia, there is no primary prevention. However, at the secondary level one can detect the beginning stages of schizophrenia and bring people to earlier remedial and supportive treatment. At the tertiary level, the individual disability in functions could be ameliorated and thus prevent further physical and psychosocial deterioration.

Morell (1987) described the special difficulties specific to prevention in mental health: (a) In mental health, prevention is not as generally accepted as with other types of health programs; (b) There is less faith that prevention efforts could have any worthwhile consequence; (c) The data on the efficacy of prevention rely on the social and behavioral sciences which (according to Morell) lack credibility in many people's eyes; (d) Except for dramatic situations such as suicide, heavy substance abuse, or homelessness, it is difficult to make a convincing case that mental health issues present serious public health or social welfare problems. Swift and Weirich (1987) argued that an applied research process has to be an integral part of the prevention planning implementation, and that research must be a meaningful and useful component of each stage of prevention development.

Methodological Issues in Mental Health Policy Research

Mental health policy is relatively unique among national policies. The national data base that is policy relevant is small compared to other national policy areas, in spite of substantial recent activity. The interaction of public programs and their effect on service delivery, such as Medicare, Medicaid, SSI, nursing home legislation, and the like, have been insufficiently investigated. In addition, mental health policy can be seen as dominated both by health policy and the perspectives that underlie health policy. That domination includes professional, financial, and metaphorical aspects of policy. There is great resistance to a detached view that considers the potential independence of mental health policy and the ways in which mental health policy might affect health policy to its benefit. There are considerable barriers to effective knowledge use in mental health policy, and often considerable dispute about what we know that is relevant to policy (Kiesler, 1981).

To be applauded is the recent application of regression techniques typically used in economic research to mental health services research (Ellis & McGuire, 1986; Frank et al., 1986; McGuire, Dickey, Shively, & Strumwasser, 1987; Short & Goldfarb, 1987). There is also some use of computer simulation techniques (Short & Goldfarb, 1987). Some alternative methods of handling messy data sets have been accomplished (Kiesler et al., 1990 & 1989; McGuire, 1981). McGuire's (1981) elegant cleaning up in the Marmor, Scheidermandel, and Kanns (1975) survey of psychiatric private practice provides an excellent example of this potential. Frank's (1981) application of the same method to the effect of state freedom-of-choice laws on psychiatric fees provides another good example. Broskowski, Marks, and Budman (1981) reviewed several approaches to the study of the linkages between health and mental health issues.

Computer simulation holds considerable promise to enhance the study of mental health policy. Ultimately, if we understand our policy and the interworkings of its various components, we should be able to demonstrate our understanding by simulating a national

policy in a computer model. Simulation of such a policy would force us first to consider the total policy at a given time, which is now only rarely accomplished. It would allow us, further, to consider the implementation or change of various policy alternatives. If we could successfully simulate the policy, then we could look at the potential direct and indirect implications of various policy alternatives. For example, we could inspect the impact on the system as a whole resulting from increased insurance incentives for services delivered in HMOs. One positive side effect of computer simulation is that it clearly demonstrates that we do indeed understand our national policy as a whole.

The computer simulation of judgmental and decision processes could also be helpful. A good deal of the practice of delivering mental health services is analogous to judgments and decisions under uncertainty and risk, an area in which computer simulation has been utilized effectively. These studies demonstrate that human beings often inadequately conceptualize their own decision-making and judgmental processes (Tversky & Kahneman, 1974). The various weights given to variables entering into a decision are frequently misconstrued by the individual making the decision. Thus, decisions relating to diagnosis, treatment regimens, and the choice between inpatient and outpatient care could all be simulated to considerable benefit.

Both of these uses of computer simulation relate to the fact that there has been little direct study of overall mental health policy. There are considerable methodological, statistical, and empirical problems in attempting to deal with the system as a whole, partly because of the informal nature of a good deal of the implicit system (such as volunteer groups). Research in mental health policy should be more oriented toward the evaluation of the outcomes of specific aspects of policy. Meta-analysis in particular, and secondary analyses and evaluation research in general, are useful in attempting to ascertain what we already know about specific aspects of the treatment of mental disorders. Increased methodological sophistication and further refinement of these techniques for use in mental health issues are desirable. Closely related are the techniques of cost-benefit and cost-effectiveness analysis, more typically used in economics. These techniques are more difficult to apply to such processes as psychotherapy than would seem apparent at first blush, with questionable assumptions often being made on both the cost and the benefit side of the formula (cf. Saxe, 1980).

Research regarding the effects of psychotherapy on

medical utilization and absenteeism, for example, suggests the importance of careful consideration in casting a broad enough net in order to capture benefits of mental health services, including some that are far removed from the immediate service setting. The marginal utility of psychological services is closely related to cost-benefit analysis. Typically, we should not consider the effects of psychological services in isolation, but rather their marginal utility when added to an existing system. We do have well-developed and well-organized systems of welfare and health, and psychological services must be considered as additions to those systems. Whether the services reduce the costs of the total given system is a reasonable policy question. The marginal utility of such services is often the principal public policy question, even though it might be a secondary or tertiary scientific question.

The meaning of epidemiological instruments used with large populations is still open to question (Mechanic, 1980). The ECA program conducted by NIMH produced useful data, but it is difficult to extrapolate from the design of that program to national epidemiological estimates. There has always been a disturbingly large range in the outcomes of epidemiological studies in mental health that is not due simply to sampling problems.

These differences in epidemiological projections become astonishingly important when considering national policy alternatives. For example, we typically see a range between 15% and 25% of the population being seen as in need of mental health services. That range is still 10%, and it can be startling to realize that we are speaking of 10% of the U.S. population or about 25 million people, about whom we are apparently uncertain whether they need mental health services.

On the other hand, there is often an implicit assumption that service need is functional: that the services, if used, would be effective. One could as well look at this question from the opposite point of view: carefully inspect which services are effective for which populations, and then calculate the ranges of people in those categories who could be effectively helped. Mental health services need more analogies such as the common cold. One can present epidemiological data on the common cold, but there is no known cure for it (although there are some easily applicable techniques of ameliorating the symptoms). Some prevention techniques can be discussed, but without an adequate cure, no national policy regarding treatment is necessary.

Many mental health problems apparently go away by themselves as well. We do need better analogies to the common cold, forcing us to describe which mental health problems are more likely to be cured with time alone, and which need professional care for effective treatment. There is often an assumption in mental health that a self-perceived problem by a potential patient is sufficient grounds for using public funds to pay a professional caregiver. We need to distinguish better and more precisely those problems that (a) appear to the public and to legislators as important public problems, and (b) have well-documented, clearly effective treatment(s). Some problems can be effectively treated, but no one would want to spend public money on them. Other problems, such as alcoholism, have clear public policy ramifications in terms of traffic fatalities, child and spouse abuse, absenteeism from the workplace, and the like. Statements of need should carefully consider questions of outcome and effectiveness of mental health services.

In the last 5 years there has been more research specifically related to national public policy in mental health than in the previous decade. However, the research effort is not well balanced across policy needs or issues. A good deal of the research has been driven by particular questions raised by legislation, such as prospective payment and other aspects of Medicare legislation (e.g., TEFRA). This is neither unexpected nor to be deplored and is not dissimilar to what takes place in other public policy areas with abrupt shifts in federal policy. Further, the research produced by these efforts is good and has produced cumulative knowledge directly applicable to public policy issues. Given the large and pressing research needs of related mental health policy, this recent body of research has addressed only a narrow slice of the array of important policy questions. Still, the interest in these issues has certainly fueled an increase in federal funding for research on mental health services—most of which is directly related to important mental health policy questions.

OTHER ISSUES

Space requirements led us to review only a selected subset of the potential issues worthy of study in mental health policy. Issues that we have not discussed here but that are certainly worthy of consideration and research include the clash of (a) public policy needs (regarding services and their organization), and (b) citizen needs (regarding privacy, confidentiality, and rights to commitment proceedings). Outcome data continue to be needed for mental health services. In addition, the mental health benefits and liabilities, intended or not, of various facets of other coexisting systems (e.g., employment, health, education, and welfare) are research areas rich in promise. There is a great need for such data, but at the same time available methods of obtaining them raise serious problems with issues of privacy and confidentiality.

We have not discussed the optimal use of volunteers, paraprofessionals, self-help groups, and community networks. Such research topics would include comparisons of paraprofessional and professional services aimed at a mental disorder as a matter of course. However, the potential mental health benefits of activities not usually associated with mental health, such as neighborhood improvement programs, child care services, participation in team sports, and hobby groups, should also be considered. We have also omitted discussing the potential cost-effectiveness of strengthening the family and other naturally existing support groups, and the changes that would take place if family-centered policies were substituted for policy currently oriented toward the individual. These issues and many others often found in the community psychology or the prevention literature could enrich our understanding of alternatives to traditional mental health service.

We have focused this chapter on the formal, organized service delivery system, at the same time noting that the size of the nation's mental health problem vastly overpowers the capacity of the organized service sector as we know it.

We have not described research regarding the public's attitude toward mental illness. The public continues to accept mental hospitalization and supports it in various ways, suggesting perhaps that the perceived dangerousness and unpredictability of the mentally disabled continue to play a prominent role in the public's attitude toward public policy alternatives.

We also have not discussed the critical issue of knowledge use and knowledge utilization (Kiesler, 1981). Mental health policy continues to be an area in which fairly traditional policies have existed for decades, without due regard for the rapid increase in knowledge about human behavior and the treatment of mental disorders (Kiesler, 1982).

We have not discussed how research issues in mental health policy can or should affect how psychologists are trained (see Kiesler & Morton, 1988b). Clearly, little traditional training in psychology, clinical or otherwise, is related either to the analysis of existing policy or to techniques of research in public policy. Further, although there has been a flurry of recent research related to mental health policy, psy-

chologists have not played much of a role in spite of their heavy research backgrounds.

SUMMARY AND CONCLUSIONS

We have reviewed the primary areas of mental health policy, attempting to characterize research findings in each area, as they relate to policy alternatives. Innumerable issues for policy-relevant research remain. To refresh the reader, we summarize as follows:

- Available evidence suggests a high incidence and prevalence of mental disorder in this country, complicated by physical comorbidity, variation by geographic region, and unreliability of diagnoses. Mental disorder is clearly a substantial national problem, but additional epidemiological research is necessary for the design of optimal training, treatment, and evaluation strategies.
- It is unrealistic to expect the supply of doctoral mental health professionals to meet more than a fraction of the mental health needs in this country. A top-down analysis shifts attention to making the best possible use of specialists, utilizing alternative providers and systems (e.g., families, social networks, volunteers, and self-help groups), maximizing the mental health benefits of coexisting systems (e.g., health, education, and welfare), and evaluating the relationship between mental health and such factors as work conditions, lifestyle, and family functioning.
- Contrary to popular thought, the rate of mental hospitalization is high—entailing mostly specialized psychiatric treatment—and length of stay has not decreased (except in those public facilities traditionally devoted to long-term custodial care). Given the high cost and questionable value of hospitalization, more attention to alternative care systems is needed.

  Several important demonstration projects have shown that correctly employing economic disincentives for unnecessary hospitalization, and incentives for outpatient care and community support programs, is successful across a wide range of outcomes. The potential for innovative, policy-shaping research in the alternative care arena is vast, albeit hindered by reluctance to replace the medical model with a rehabilitative one.
- The greatest changes in mental health care delivery in this decade are the result of policy developments in the insurance arena. Utilization of outpatient mental health care has proven responsive to cost

sharing and price through various alternative insurance schemes. Federal policy in mental health remains inconsistent and weak. Issues needing policy-relevant research include conflicting incentive structures for both cost containment and use of hospitalization, coordination of Medicare and Medicaid policies with those of Social Security, housing and welfare, and the growing uninsured population.

The most significant influence in future mental health funding will be, we predict, the rapid emergence of the self-insured corporations. Private sector cost-containment efforts may have more impact than de jure public policy on the overall quality and quantity of mental health care. This sector will probably investigate closely which funding bases determine the quality of services provided.

- The bulk of mental health dollars continues to be spent on hospitalization, although the dominant site has shifted from long-term hospitals to general hospitals. CMHCs, established with the original intent to foster more community-based care, have more recently been ignored by the federal government. Research continues to demonstrate the utility of community-based care for the vast majority of mental patients. There has been a notable increase in investor-owned psychiatric hospitals and in HMOs. The ways in which economic incentives shape the character and quality of care in different sites are rich research topics.
- The mental health needs of children are not being met, and policy here remains inadequate in conceptualization and coordination.
- The number of elderly mentally disabled continues to grow, particularly in nursing homes. Existing findings indicate poor quality of nursing homes and overreliance on drug treatment. The number of elderly with mental disorders in nursing homes far exceeds that projected from their recent growth in the population. Research concerns for both children and the elderly revolve around appropriate treatment strategies and sites.
- State mental health systems have changed, largely as a function of federal policy. State mental hospitals remain the costly kingpins of these systems, by and large, although their functions have typically shifted from custodial to acute care. Several states have successfully reduced reliance on hospitalization by providing financial incentives to the local community to treat patients there. There is great variation between states, and policy research issues include common elements in resistance to change and alternative methods of successful organizational change.
- Prevention is given lip service, but there has been little recent research activity. Greater public recognition of the value of prevention in mental health is needed, which in turn depends on more convincing outcome research.
- Given the broad scope and interdisciplinary nature of mental health policy research, it is not unexpected that a wide range of methodologies, particularly drawn from economics and epidemiology, are useful. Regression analyses, decision and judgment models, and cost-benefit and cost-effectiveness approaches appear especially useful in evaluating policy questions in mental health. It is increasingly recognized that a wide range of independent and dependent variables must be considered if therapeutic need and benefit are to be assessed meaningfully. Accurate epidemiological projections are still needed and will be meaningful to the degree that they target treatable and treatment-worthy problems. Computer simulation research holds immense promise for evaluating the impact of a given policy and its alternatives. It is also an excellent means of evaluating our understanding of national policy as a whole. Research activity and research funding in mental health policy have accelerated in recent years, and we can expect the application of these and other methods to a rapidly expanding array of research issues.

Mental health policy has existed implicitly for at least 150 years; indeed, in Eaton's (1980) view, 2,500 years. Research related to mental health policy is as least as old as the history of scientific psychology and psychiatry. However, research that is openly directed toward the assessment of policy and the consideration of public policy alternatives is a relatively recent phenomenon. It involves looking at the overall policy, both explicit and implicit, a perspective to which we still seem unaccustomed. It involves research techniques and the accumulation of data that are not traditional. The time is right for rapid growth in the study of mental health policy, but it is unclear how involved psychologists will be in that effort. We hope that this chapter has captured for readers some of the flavor of how such policy study can be conducted, as well as some of the intellectual excitement that is inherent in mental health policy research.

REFERENCES

Aiken, L. H., Sommers, S. A., & Shore, M. F. (1986). Private foundations in health affairs: A case study of the development of a national initiative for the chronically mentally ill. *American Psychologist, 41,* 1290–1295.

Albee, G. W. (1980). A competency model to replace the defect model. In L. A. Bond & J. C. Rosen (Eds.), *Competence and coping during adulthood* (pp. 75–104). Hanover, NH: University Press of New England.

Allerton, W. (Coordinator). (1978). *Report of the Task Panel on Planning and Review*. (President's Commission on Mental Health, Vol. 2). Washington, DC: U.S. Government Printing Office.

Bachrach, L. (1976). *Deinstitutionalization: An analytical review and sociological perspective*. Washington, DC: U.S. Government Printing Office. Mental Health Statistics Series D, No. 4. DHEW No. (ADM) 79-351.

Bachrach, L. L. (1978). A conceptual approach to deinstitutionalization. *Hospital and Community Psychiatry, 29,* 573–578.

Bachrach, L. L. (1981). Continuity of care for chronic mental patients: A conceptual analysis. *American Journal of Psychiatry, 138,* 1449–1456.

Bachrach, L. L. (1982). Assessment of outcomes in community support systems: Results, problems, and limitations. *Schizophrenia Bulletin, 8,* 39–61.

Bachrach, L. L. (1985). General hospital psychiatry and deinstitutionalization: A systems view. *General Hospital Psychiatry, 7,* 239–248.

Bachrach, L. L. (1986). The challenge of service planning for chronic mental patients. *Community Mental Health Journal, 22,* 189–197.

Bachrach, L. L., Talbott, J. A., & Meyerson, A. T. (1987). The chronic psychiatric patient as a "difficult" patient: A conceptual analysis. In A. T. Meyerson (Ed.), *Barriers to treating the chronic mentally ill* (pp. 35–50). New Directions for Mental Health Services, No. 33. San Francisco: Jossey-Bass.

Baker, F. M. (1985). ER "capture" of the skid-row alcoholic. *General Hospital Psychiatry, 7,* 138–143.

Barlow, D. H., DiNardo, P. A., Vermilyea, B. B., Vermilyea, J., & Blanchard, E. B. (1986). Comorbidity and depression among the anxiety disorders: Issues in diagnosis and classification. *Journal of Nervous and Mental Disease, 174,* 63–72.

Bazzoli, G. W. (1986). Health care for the indigent: Overview of critical issues. *Health Services Research, 21,* 353–393.

Breen, H. (1979). The benefits of placing medical surgical patients on a psychiatric ward. *Hospital and Community Psychiatry, 30,* 634–635.

Broskowski, A., Marks, E., & Budman, S. H. (1981). *Linking health and mental health*. Beverly Hills, CA: Sage Publications.

Bunce, D. F. M., Jones, L. R., Badger, L. W., & Jones, S. E. (1982). Medical illness in psychiatric patients: Barriers to diagnosis and treatment. *Southern Medical Journal, 75,* 941–944.

Califano, J. A. (1986). A corporate Rx for America: Managing runaway health costs. *Issues in Science and Technology, 2*(3), 81–90.

Cavanaugh, S. V. A. (1986). Depression in the hospitalized inpatient with various medical illnesses. *Psychotherapy and Psychosomatics, 45,* 97–104.

Cummings, N. A. (1986). The dismantling of our health system: Strategies for the survival of psychological practice. *American Psychologist, 41,* 426–431.

DeLeon, P. H., & VandenBos, G. R. (1980). Psychotherapy reimbursement in federal programs: Political sector. In G. R. VandenBos (Ed.), *Psychotherapy: Practice, research, policy* (pp. 247–285). Beverly Hills, CA: Sage Publications.

DeSario, J. (1987). Health issues and policy options. *PS, 20,* 226–231.

Detre, T. P., & Kupfer, D. J. (1975). General hospital psychiatric services. In D. X. Freedman & J. E. Dryud (Eds.), *American Handbook of Psychiatry* (pp. 607–617). New York: Basic Books.

Deutsch, A. (1949). *The mentally ill in America: A history of their care and treatment from Colonial times*. New York: Columbia University Press.

Dickstein, D., Hanig, D., & Grosskopf, B. (1988). Reducing treatment costs in a community support program. *Hospital and Community Psychiatry, 39,* 1033–1035.

Dohrenwend, B. P., Dohrenwend, B. S., Gould, M. S., Link, B., Neugebaur, R., & Wunsch-Hitzig, R. (1980). *Mental illness United States: Epidemiological estimates*. New York: Praeger.

Dougherty, D. (1988). Children's mental health problems and services: Current federal efforts and policy implications. *American Psychologist, 43,* 808–812.

Dulit, R. A., Strain, J. J., & Strain, J. J. (1986). The problem of alcohol in the medical/surgical patient. *General Hospital Psychiatry, 8,* 81–85.

Dvoredsky, A. E., & Cooley, H. W. (1986). Comparative severity of illness in patients with combined medical and psychiatric diagnoses. *Psychosomatics, 27,* 625–630.

Eastwood, M. R. (1975). *The relation between physical and mental illness*. Toronto: University of Toronto Press.

Eaton, W. W. (1980). *The sociology of mental disorders*. New York: Praeger.

Eisenberg, L. (1986). Health care: For patients or for profits? *American Psychiatric Association, 143,* 1015–1019.

Ellis, R. P., & McGuire, T. G. (1986). Cost sharing and patterns of mental health care utilization. *The Journal of Human Resources, 21,* 359–379.

Fink, P. J. (1985). Psychiatry and primary care: Can a working relationship develop? *General Hospital Psychiatry, 7,* 205–209.

Flamm, G. H. (1979). The expanding roles of general hospital psychiatry. *Hospital and Community Psychiatry, 30,* 190–192.

Flinn, D. E., McMahon, T. C., & Collins, M. F. (1987). Health maintenance organizations and their implications for psychiatry. *Hospital and Community Psychiatry, 38,* 255–262.

Fogel, B. S. (1985). A psychiatric unit becomes a psychiatric-medical unit. Administrative and clinical implications. *General Hospital Psychiatry, 7,* 26–35.

Fogel, B. S., Stroudemire, A., & Houpt, J. L. (1985).

Contrasting models for combined medical and psychiatric inpatient treatment. *American Journal of Psychiatry, 142*, 1085–1089.

Foucault, M. (1973). *Madness and civilization: A history of insanity in the age of reason*. New York: Random House.

Frank, R. G. (1981). *Pricing and location of physician services in mental health*. Unpublished doctoral dissertation, Boston University.

Frank, R. G., Lave, J. R., Taube, C. A., Rupp, A., & Goldman, H. H. (1986). *The impact of Medicare's prospective payment system on psychiatric patients treated in scatter beds* (Working Paper No. 2030). Cambridge, MA: National Bureau of Economic Research.

Friedman, L. (1985). *Caring for the mental patient in the general hospital: A comparison of hospitals with and without psychiatric units*. Unpublished doctoral dissertation, University of Pittsburgh.

Fuchs, V. R. (1986). Has cost containment gone too far? *The Milbank Quarterly, 64*, 479–488.

Fulop, G., & Strain, J. J. (1986). Psychiatric emergencies in the general hospital. *General Hospital Psychiatry, 8*, 425–431.

Fulop, G., Strain, J. J., Vita, J., Lyons, J. S., & Hammer, J. S. (1987). Impact of psychiatric comorbidity on length of hospital stay for medical surgical patients: A preliminary report. *American Journal of Psychiatry, 144*, 878–882.

Glick, I. D., Fleming, L., DeChillo, N., Meyerkopt, N., Muscara, D., & Good-Ellis, M. (1986). A controlled study of transitional day care for non-chronically-ill patients. *American Journal of Psychiatry, 143*, 1551–1556.

Goldman, H. H., & Morrissey, J. P. (1985). The alchemy of mental health policy: Homelessness and the fourth cycle of reform. *American Journal of Public Health, 75*, 727–731.

Goldman, H. H., Taube, C. A., & Jencks, S. F. (1987). The organization of the psychiatric inpatient services system. *Medical Care, 25*(Suppl. 9), S6–S21.

Goldsmith, J. C. (1986). The U.S. health care system in the year 2000. *Journal of the American Medical Association, 256*, 3371–3375.

Goldstein, J. M., & Horgan, C. M. (1988). Inpatient and outpatient psychiatric services: Substitutes or complements? *Hospital and Community Psychiatry, 39*, 632–636.

Goplerud, E. N. (1981). The tangled web of clinical and epidemiological evidence. In A. Broskowski, E. Marks, & S. H. Budman (Eds.), *Linking health and mental health* (pp. 59–76). Beverly Hills, CA: Sage Publications.

Grob, G. N. (1987a). The forging of mental health policy in America: World War II to New Frontier. *Journal of the History of Medicine, 42*(4), 410–446.

Grob, G. N. (1987b). Mental health policy in post-world war II America. In D. Mechanic (Ed.), *Improving mental health services: What the social sciences can tell us* (pp. 15–32). New Directions for Mental Health Services, No. 36. San Francisco: Jossey-Bass.

Gronfein, W. (1985). Incentives and intentions in mental health policy: A comparison of the medicaid and community mental health programs. *Journal of Health and Social Behavior, 26*, 192–206.

Gudeman, J. E., & Shore, M. F. (1984). Beyond deinstitutionalization: A new class of facilities for the mentally ill. *New England Journal of Medicine, 311*, 832–836.

Hagnell, O. (1966). *A prospective study of the incidence of mental disorder*. Stockholm: Svenska Bokforlaget Norstedts-Bonniers.

Higgins, C. W., & Meyers, E. D. (1986). The economic transformation of American health insurance: Implications for the hospital industry. *Health Care Management Review, 11*(4), 21–27.

Hillard, J. R., Slomowitz, M., & Levi, L. S. (1987). A retrospective study of adolescents' visits to a general hospital psychiatric emergency service. *American Journal of Psychiatry, 144*, 432–436.

Hoeper, E. W. (1980). Observations on the impact of psychiatric disorders upon primary medical care. In D. L. Parron & F. Solomon (Eds.), *Mental health services in primary care settings* (pp. 88–96). Washington, DC: U.S. Government Printing Office. DHHS Publication No. (ADM) 80-995.

Inouye, D. K. (1988). Children's mental health issues. *American Psychologist, 43*, 813–816.

Jencks, S. F., & Goldman, H. H. (1987). Implications of research for psychiatric prospective payment. *Medical Care, 25*(Suppl. 9), S42–S51.

Jencks, S. F., Horgan, C., Goldman, H. H., & Taube, C. A. (1987). The problem. *Medical Care, 25*(Suppl. 9), S1–S5.

Jencks, S. F., Horgan, C., & Taube, C. A. (1987). Evidence on provider response to prospective payment. *Medical Care, 25*(Suppl. 9), S37–S41.

Johnson, S. C. (1987). Commentary. *Inquiry, 24*, 181–182.

Joint Commission on Mental Illness and Health (1961). *Action for Mental Health*. New York: Basic Books.

Jones, L. R., Badger, L. W., Ficken, R. P., Leeper, J. D., & Anderson, R. L. (1987). Inside the hidden mental health network: Examining mental health care delivery of primary care physicians. *General Hospital Psychiatry, 9*, 287–293.

Jones, K., & Vischi, T. (1980). Impact of alcohol, drug abuse, and mental health treatment of medical care utilization: Review of the research literature. *Medical Care, 12*(Suppl. 17), 1–82.

Katz, A. H., & Hermalin, J. (1987). Self-help and prevention. In J. Hermalin & J. A. Morell (Eds.), *Prevention planning in mental health* (pp. 151–190). Sage Studies in Community Mental Health, Vol. 9. Newbury Park, CA: Sage Publications.

Keeler, E. B., Wells, K. B., Manning, W. G., Rumpel, J. D., & Hanley, J. M. (1986). *The demand for episodes of mental health services*. Santa Monica, CA: Rand Corporation.

Keill, S. L. (1981). The general hospital as the core of the mental health services system. *Hospital and Community Psychiatry, 32*, 776–778.

Keill, S. L. (1986). The changing patient population in

general hospital psychiatric services. *General Hospital Psychiatry, 8,* 350–358.

Kiesler, C. A. (1980). Mental health policy as a field of inquiry for psychology. *American Psychologist, 35,* 1066–1080.

Kiesler, C. A. (1981). Barriers to effective knowledge use in mental health policy. *Health Policy Quarterly, 1,* 201–215.

Kiesler, C. A. (1982). Mental hospitals and alternative care: Noninstitutionalization as potential public policy for mental patients. *American Psychologist, 37,* 349–360.

Kiesler, C. A., McGuire, T., Mechanic, D., Mosher, L., Nelson, S. S., Newman, F., Rich, R., & Schulberg, H. C. (1983). Federal mental health policy making: An assessment of deinstitutionalization. *American Psychologist, 38,* 1292–1297.

Kiesler, C. A., & Morton, T. L. (1988a). Prospective payment system for inpatient psychiatry: The advantages of controversy. *American Psychologist, 43,* 141–150.

Kiesler, C. A., & Morton, T. L. (1988b). Psychology and public policy in the "health care revolution." *American Psychologist, 43,* 993–1003.

Kiesler, C. A., & Sibulkin, A. E. (1983a). Episodic length of hospital stay for mental disorders. In G. M. Stephenson & J. H. Davis (Eds.), *Progress in Applied Social Psychology* (Vol. 2, pp. 31–61). New York: John Wiley & Sons.

Kiesler, C. A., & Sibulkin, A. E. (1983b). Proportion of inpatient days for mental disorders: 1969–1978. *Hospital and Community Psychiatry, 34,* 606–611.

Kiesler, C. A., & Sibulkin, A. E. (1984). Episodic rate of mental hospitalization: Stable or increasing? *American Journal of Psychiatry, 141,* 44–48.

Kiesler, C. A., & Sibulkin, A. E. (1987). *Mental Hospitalization: Myths and Facts About a National Crisis.* Beverly Hills, CA: Sage Publications.

Kiesler, C. A., Sibulkin, A. S., Morton, T. L., & Simpkins, C. G., (In Press). Characteristics of psychiatric discharges from nonfederal, short-term specialty hospitals and general hospitals with and without psychiatric and chemical dependency units: The HDS data. *HSR: Health Services Research.*

Kiesler, C. A., Simpkins, C. G., & Morton, T. L. (1990). Predicting hospital length of stay for psychiatric inpatients: The HDS data. *Hospital and Community Psychiatry, 41*(2), 149–154.

Kiesler, C. A., Simpkins, C. G., & Morton, T. L. (1989). Who is treated in psychiatric scatter beds in general hospitals? An imputational algorithm. *Professional Psychology: Research and Practice, 20,* 236–243.

Kramer, M. (1983). The continuing challenge: The rising prevalence of mental disorders, associated chronic diseases and disabling conditions. *American Journal of Social Psychiatry, 3*(4), 13–24.

Lehman, A., Possidente, S., & Hawker, F. (1986). The quality of life of chronic patients in a state hospital and in community residences. *Hospital and Community Psychiatry, 37,* 901–907.

Liptzin, B. (1987). The geriatric patient and general hospital psychiatry. *General Hospital Psychiatry, 9,* 198–202.

Loring, M., & Powell, B. (1988). Gender, race and DSM-III: A study of the objectivity of psychiatric diagnostic behavior. *Journal of Health and Social Behavior, 29,* 1–22.

Marmor, J., Scheidermandel, P. L., & Kanns, C. K. (1975). *Psychiatrists and their patients.* Washington, DC: American Psychiatric Association.

McGuire, T. G. (1981). *Financing psychotherapy: Costs, effects, and public policy.* Cambridge, MA: Ballinger.

McGuire, T. G., Dickey, B., Shively, E., & Strumwasser, I. (1987). Differences in resource use and cost among facilities treating alcohol, drug abuse, and mental disorders: Implications for design of a prospective payment system. *American Journal of Psychiatry, 144,* 616–620.

Mechanic, D. (Coordinator). (1978). *Report of the task panel on the nature and scope of the problem.* (President's Commission on Mental Health, Vol. 2). Washington, DC: U.S. Government Printing Office.

Mechanic, D. (1980). *Mental health and social policy* (rev. ed). Englewood Cliffs, NJ: Prentice-Hall.

Mechanic, D. (1985). Mental health and social policy: Initiatives for the 1980s. *Health Affairs, 4,* 75–88.

Mechanic, D. (1986). Health care for the poor: Some policy alternatives. *Journal of Family Practice, 22,* 283–289.

Mechanic, D. (1987a). Correcting misconceptions in mental health policy: Strategies for improved care of the seriously mentally ill. *Milbank Memorial Fund Quarterly, 65*(2), 203–289.

Mechanic, D. (1987b). Evolution of mental health services and areas for change. In D. Mechanic (Ed.), *Improving mental health services: What the social sciences can tell us* (pp. 3–13). New Directions in Mental Health Services, No. 36. San Francisco: Jossey-Bass.

Miller, G. E., & Rago, W. V. (1988). Fiscal incentives to development of services in the community. *Hospital and Community Psychiatry, 39,* 595–597.

Morell, J. A. (1987). Planning in prevention: Implications from a general model. In J. Hermalin & J. A. Morell (Eds.), *Prevention planning in mental health* (pp. 9–20). Sage Studies in Community Mental Health, Vol. 9. Newbury Park, CA: Sage Publications.

Myers, J. K., Weissman, M. M., Tischler, G. L., Holzer, C. E., Leaf, P. J., Orvaschel, H., Anthony, J. C., Boyd, J. H., Burke, J. D., Kramer, M., & Stoltzman, R. (1984). Six-month prevalence of psychiatric disorders in three communities. *Archives of General Psychiatry, 41,* 959–967.

National Academy of Sciences. (1982). *Making policies for children.* Washington, DC: National Academy Press.

National Academy of Sciences. (1988). *Homelessness, health and human needs.* Washington, DC: National Academy Press.

Parry, C. D. H. (1989). *The chronic mentally ill: Public policy considerations for the 90s.* Unpublished manuscript, University of Virginia, Department of Psychology, Charlottesville, VA.

Pincus, H. A. (1987). Patient oriented models for linking

primary care and mental health care. *General Hospital Psychiatry, 9,* 95–101.

Ray, W. A., Federspiel, C. F., & Schaffner, W. (1980). A study of antipsychotic drug use in nursing homes: Epidemiologic evidence suggesting misuse. *American Journal of Public Health, 70,* 485–491.

Reding, G. R., & McGuire, B. (1973). Nonsegregated acute psychiatric admissions to general hospitals—continuity of care within the community hospital. *New England Journal of Medicine, 289,* 185–189,

Regier, D. A., Goldberg, I. D., & Taube, C. A. (1978). The de facto U.S. mental health services system: a public health perspective. *Archives of General Psychiatry, 35,* 685–693.

Richman, A., & Harris, P. (1985). General hospital psychiatry: Are its roles and functions adjunctive or pivotal? *General Hospital Psychiatry, 7,* 258–266.

Rochefort, D. A. (1987). The political context of mental health care. In D. Mechanic (Ed.), *Improving mental health services: What the social sciences can tell us* (pp. 93–105). New Directions for Mental Health Services, No. 36. San Francisco: Jossey-Bass.

Rochefort, D. A. (1988). Policymaking cycles in mental health: Critical examination of the conceptual model. *Journal of Health Politics, Policy & Law, 13,* 129–153.

Rubin, J. (1987). Financing care for the seriously mentally ill. In D. Mechanic (Ed.), *Improving mental health services: What the social sciences can tell us* (pp. 107–116). New Directions for Mental Health Services, No. 36. San Francisco: Jossey-Bass.

Russell, M., Henderson, D., & Blume, S. B. (1984). *Children of alcoholics: A review of the literature.* New York: Children of Alcoholics Foundation.

Santiago, J. M. (1987). Reforming a system of care: The Arizona experiment. *Hospital and Community Psychiatry, 38*(3), 270–273.

Santiago, J. M., Gittler, A., Beigel, A., Stein, L., & Brown, P. J. (1986). Changing a state mental health system through litigation: The Arizona experiment. *American Journal of Psychiatry, 143,* 1575–1579.

Saxe, L. (1980). *The efficacy and cost-effectiveness of psychotherapy.* Office of Technology Assessment, Congress of the U.S. Washington, DC: U.S. Government Printing Office.

Saxe, L., Cross, T., & Silverman, N. (1988). Children's mental health: The gap between what we know and what we do. *American Psychologist, 43,* 800–807.

Schulberg, H. C., & Burns, B. J. (1985). The nature and effectiveness of general hospital psychiatric services. *General Hospital Psychiatry, 7,* 249–257.

Schwab, J. J., Bell, R. A., Warheit, G., & Schwab, R. B. (1979). *Social order and mental health.* New York: Brunner/Mazel.

Schwartz, G. M., Braverman, B. G., & Roth, B. (1987). Anxiety disorders and psychiatric referral in the general medical emergency room. *General Hospital Psychiatry, 9,* 87–93.

Seltzer, D. A. (1988). Limitations on HMO services and the emerging redefinition of chronic mental illness. *Hospital and Community Psychiatry, 39,* 137–139.

Shadish, W. R., Silber, B. G., & Bootzin, R. R. (1984). Mental patients in nursing homes: Their characteristics and treatment. *International Journal of Partial Hospitalization, 2,* 153–163.

Sharfstein, S. S. (1987). Reimbursement resistance to treatment and support for the long-term mental patient. In A. T. Meyerson (Ed.), *Barriers to treating the chronic mentally ill* (pp. 75–85). New Directions for Mental Health Services, No. 33. San Francisco: Jossey-Bass.

Sharfstein, S. S., Krizay, J., & Muszynski, I. L. (1988). Defining and pricing psychiatric care "products." *Hospital and Community Psychiatry, 39,* 372–375.

Short, T., & Goldfarb, M. G. (1987). Redistribution of revenues under a prototypical prospective payment system: Characteristics of winners and losers. *Journal of Policy Analysis and Management, 6,* 385–401.

Smith, P. R. (1979). Nonsegregation of psychiatric patients in a general hospital. *Journal of Psychiatric Nursing and Mental Health Services, 17,* 20–24.

Stein, L. I. (1988). Taking Issue: "It's the focus, not the locus." Hocus-pocus! *Hospital and Community Psychiatry, 39,* 1029.

Stein, L. I., & Diamond, R. J. (1985). A program for difficult-to-treat patients. In L. I. Stein & M. A. Test (Eds.), *The training in community living model: A decade of experience* (pp. 29–39). New Directions in Mental Health Services, No. 26. San Francisco: Jossey-Bass.

Stein, L. I., & Ganser, L. J. (1983). Wisconsin's system for funding mental health services. In J. A. Talbott (Ed.), *Unified mental health systems: Utopia unrealized* (pp. 25–32). New Directions in Mental Health Services, No. 18. San Francisco: Jossey-Bass.

Stein, L. I., & Test, M. A. (1985). *The training in community living model: A decade of experience.* New Directions in Mental Health Services, No. 26. San Francisco: Jossey-Bass.

Strain, J. J., Pincus, H. A., Gise, L. H., & Houpt, J. L. (1986). The role of psychiatry in the teaching of primary care physicians. *General Hospital Psychiatry, 8,* 372–385.

Summergrad, P., & Hackett, T. P. (1987). Alan Gregg and the rise of general hospital psychiatry. *General Hospital Psychiatry, 9,* 439–445.

Swift, M., & Weirich, T. W. (1987). Prevention planning as social and organizational change. In J. Hermalin & J. A. Morell (Eds.), *Prevention planning in mental health* (pp. 21–50). Sage Studies in Community Mental Health, Vol. 9. Newbury Park, CA: Sage Publications.

Task Force on Psychological and Public Policy (1986). Psychology and public policy. *American Psychologist, 41,* 914–921.

Taube, C. A., Lave, J. R., Rupp, A., Goldman, H. H., & Frank, R. G. (1988). Psychiatry under prospective payment: Experience in the first year. *American Journal of Psychiatry, 145,* 210–213.

Test, M. A. (1981). Effective treatment of the chronically mentally ill: What is necessary? *Journal of Social Issues, 37,* 71–86.

Thompson, J. W., Burns, B. J., & Taube, C. A. (1988). The severely mentally ill in general hospital psychiatric units. *General Hospital Psychiatry, 10,* 1–9.

Thompson, T. L., & Thomas, M. R. (1985). Teaching psychiatry to primary care internists. *General Hospital Psychiatry, 7,* 210–213.

Tversky, A., & Kahneman, D. (1974). Judgment under uncertainty: Heuristics and biases. *Science, 185*(1), 121–124.

U. S. Congress, Congressional Research Service. (1985). *Summary of poor children: A study of trends and policy, 1968–1984.* Washington, DC: Author.

U. S. Congress, Office of Technology Assessment. (1986). *Children's mental health: Problems and services.* Washington, DC: U.S. Government Printing Office.

U. S. Department of Health and Human Services, Office of Human Development Services, Administration for Children, Youth and Families, Children's Bureau, National Center on Child Abuse and Neglect. (1981). *Study findings: National study of incidence and severity of child abuse and neglect.* Washington, DC: Author.

Uyeda, M. K., & Moldawsky, S. (1986). Prospective payment and psychological services. *American Psychologist, 41,* 60–63.

Wallen, J., Pincus, H. A., Goldman, H. H., & Marcus, S. E. (1987). Psychiatric consultations in short-term general hospitals. *Archives of General Psychiatry, 44,* 163–168.

Wise, T. N. (1985). Commentary: Psychiatry and primary care. *General Hospital Psychiatry, 7,* 202–204.

Witheridge, T. F., & Dincin, J. (1985). The Bridge: An assertive outreach program in an urban setting. In L. I. Stein & M. A. Test (Eds.), *The training in community living model: A decade of experience* (pp. 65–76). New Directions in Mental Health Services, No. 26. San Francisco: Jossey-Bass.

Zook, C. J., Moore, F. D., & Zeckhauser, R. J. (1981). "Catastrophic" health insurance—a misguided prescription? *The Public Interest, 62,* 66–81.

CHAPTER 6

PROFESSIONAL RELATIONS

Jerry J. Sweet
Ronald H. Rozensky

While demanding for themselves freedom of inquiry and communication, psychologists accept the responsibility this freedom requires: competence, objectivity in the application of skills, and *concern for the best interests of clients, colleagues, students, research participants, and society.* [italics added] (Excerpt from preamble to *Ethical Principles of Psychologists,* American Psychological Association, 1981a)

As the number of practicing clinical psychologists grows, there is an increasing need to consider the implications and importance of professional relations. Whereas the emphasis to date in the clinical psychology literature has been on the application of skills and development of competence (as mentioned in the first portion of the foregoing preamble), the evolution of the profession of psychology in the direction of clinical practice, as well as the ever-changing practice environment, has resulted in growing concern regarding professional relations. This concern affects both the individual psychologist and the profession as a whole.

The current health care marketplace seems destined to (a) increase competitiveness both within and between disciplines, (b) increase monitoring of both practice and economics by colleagues and third party payers, and (c) provide incentives for group practice in agencies and institutions, rather than isolated office practices. Among the effects of such changes is the need for psychologists to interact on a regular basis with a greater number of psychology and nonpsychology colleagues, consumers, and individuals involved with the delivery of health care.

In this chapter the many varied aspects of professional relations that are an increasingly important part of a clinical psychologist's daily life will be discussed. For the purposes of discussion within this chapter, professional relations will be considered to include any relationships of a professional nature between a clinical psychologist and his or her consumers (i.e., referral sources, patients, media, general public), clinical and research colleagues, employers, employees, third party payers, students, and professional organizations (e.g., state psychological associations, American Psychological Association [APA]).

FOUNDATIONS OF PROFESSIONAL RELATIONS

A Data-Based Orientation: Accountability as Both a Professional Zeitgeist and a Personal Philosophy

Our identity as clinical psychologists and the relations and communications that we have with others must be founded on some basic definitions of knowledge and practice. The historical, political, economic, and emotional arguments regarding the scientist-practitioner (Boulder) or professional (Vail) models of training and practice have been addressed elsewhere (Frank, 1984; Stern, 1984; Tyler & Spiesman, 1967; Strickland, 1985). The discussion at hand concerns the basis, quality, and presentation of professional communications and the structure of knowledge on which that communication is based.

Psychology is a science that presupposes the rules of the other natural sciences and like them continues to look for explanations (Piaget & Kamii, 1978). The clinical psychologist, through training and experience, combines the nomothetic and idiographic approaches within the questioning attitude of the scientist tempered by the sensitivity of the humanist (Shakow, 1976). The science of psychology, in its clinical application, should be based on explanations and formulations that are "clear, coherent, and parsimonious" (Feigl, 1959, p. 122). Additionally, it is the clinical psychologist's comfort with the scientific model and hypothesis testing in general that allows the accurate presentation of research data and clinical hypotheses (either diagnoses or treatment plans). Comfort with the probabilistic nature of the relationship between the true state and judged states of nature is most likely maximized by those with the "mathematical wherewithal to reason quantitatively" (Kleinmuntz, 1984, p. 122).

It is the discipline of the scientific method, the "better monitoring by a system that mobilizes criticism" (Weed, 1970, p. 4) and the preparation of the research-based thesis that prepares the scientist in developing a respect for order, logic, and consistency (Weed, 1970). In the clinical environment (of the psychologist, in this case) there is in effect not a single thesis, according to Weed, but thousands of them with "variables that are exceptionally difficult to enumerate and control" (p. 5). Disciplined thinking, trained by the scientific method, and the inherent comfort with being hypothesis testers prepare clinicians to organize and challenge their own clinical thinking.

It is one's training as an empiricist, with an orientation toward accountability, comfort with and training in measuring effectiveness of interventions, and an objectivity in presenting data that defines the field of clinical psychology. The clear presentation of organized clinical data, diagnostic impressions, treatment plans, and/or treatment outcomes is the product of the clinical psychologist. The sharing of this product with our professional colleagues, clients, and students forms the basis of our professional relations (Rozensky, Sweet, & Tovian, 1991).

Ethical Principles and Professional Relations

The Ethical Principles of Psychologists (APA, 1981a) provides an excellent source of information regarding establishment and maintenance of relationships with other psychologists, as well as with other professionals outside psychology. These principles are available in pamphlet form from the central APA office (1200 Seventeenth St., N.W., Washington, DC 20036). In addition, each year in the archival issue (typically the June issue) of the *American Psychologist,* the journal provided to all APA members, there is a discussion of cases pertaining to ethical principles. This discussion is presented in an article entitled, "Casebook for Providers of Psychological Services" (cf. Board of Professional Affairs, 1987). One of the stated goals of that article is to provide clarification of the "specialty guidelines for the delivery of services by clinical psychologists" (APA, 1981b). A casebook of illustrative ethical cases is also available from the central APA office (*Casebook on Ethical Principles of Psychologists,* APA, 1987).

Of particular relevance to this chapter is Principle 7—Professional Relationships:

> Psychologists act with due regard for the needs, special competencies, and obligations of their colleagues in psychology and other professions. They respect the prerogatives and obligations of the institutions or organizations with which these other colleagues are associated. (APA, 1981a, p. 636)

The foregoing principle is further elaborated to include the following specific aspects of relationships.

Competence of Other Professionals

Psychologists are supposed to understand and respect the areas of competence of other professionals with whom they may have contact. While this can represent a formidable challenge, it is important that psychologists understand the competencies of medical, legal, and other professionals. It is only with this knowledge that psychologists can truly provide the most thoughtful and effective services to those who, in turn, trust in their competence. Knowledge of specific competencies and specific practices of fellow mental health practitioners is crucial. For example, if a patient explains during a psychological evaluation that he or she is currently in therapy with a psychotherapist who is not a psychologist, it is incumbent on the psychologist to avoid presentation of conflictive information or recommendations in a manner that would be at odds with, or interfere with, the treatment already in progress. Since full cooperation with other professionals is expected, psychologists must be familiar with the practices of other professionals. This knowledge of professional practices can typically be obtained through active pursuit of professional literature written by, and personal communications with, members of other disciplines.

Beyond avoiding negative interactions with other professionals, the psychologist also must be aware of potential opportunities for positive interactions with members of other disciplines. In the case of an evaluation of a patient already in treatment, which can often take place at the request of a third party (e.g., the patient's family physician, who may not know of the ongoing therapy with another practitioner), the psychologist can offer to provide a copy of the evaluation report to the patient's psychotherapist, especially if it becomes apparent that it would be relevant or helpful to the psychotherapist. Further, if the patient is already receiving psychological services, the psychologist does not offer services directly to that individual, and proceeds cautiously and with sensitivity in balancing the client's welfare with the need to avoid interfering with the client's relationships with other professionals.

Employment, Supervision, and Training of Other Professionals

Psychologists who employ or train other professionals have responsibilities regarding the professional development of these individuals. These responsibilities include the provision of explicit agreements with the individuals regarding the nature of their working relationship (e.g., hours, pay, duties, number of hours of supervision provided, manner in which supervision is to be given). Whether written or verbal in nature, the responsibility for following through on these agreements is clear. Feedback, given by the psychologist, on the performance of duties should be timely and constructive. When negative feedback is necessary, care should be taken not to be unduly harsh or critical. Since the intent of such feedback is typically to improve future performance, sensitivity and tact are often needed to ensure that a working relationship will still be possible. Along these lines, objective feedback, rather than personal attack, is indicated.

Exploitation of Relationships

Regardless of the specific relationship, psychologists do not exploit or take advantage, by the nature of whatever authority they possess in a professional relationship, of other individuals. This includes relationships with patients, supervisees, students, employees, and research participants. Sexual exploitation of these individuals is expressly forbidden. In addition, sexual harassment (e.g., of female students by male psychologists in the role of supervisors) is considered unethical. For the purposes of ethical considerations, sexual harassment is defined as "deliberate or repeated comments, gestures, or physical contacts of a sexual nature that are unwanted by the recipient" (APA, 1981a).

Relationship Aspects of Research

Given the nature of psychological research, psychologists often conduct their research in institutions, agencies, or organizational settings. These settings typically require formal submission and review of research proposals by research and human subject review committees. Psychologists carrying out research must be aware of the potential impact of their investigations on future researchers. The psychologist must obtain proper authorization to carry out research from the designated authorities within the institution, and carry out the research in a manner that safeguards the privacy and the well-being of the participants using full voluntary informed consent. Host institutions are to be given proper acknowledgment for their role in supporting the research. Publication credit is to be assigned in proportion to the degree of professional contribution to the research. Major contributions result in joint authorship, while minor contributions are noted in footnotes. The majority of disputes regarding assignment of authorship can be avoided by explicit negotiation of research responsibilities and duties, as well as commensurate explicit agreement of authorship rank, at the outset of the research study.

It is particularly important that psychologists do not assume that professionals from other disciplines understand the training, areas of competence, and nature of psychological practice and psychological research. When working in institutions within which organized research activities take place and that are not the exclusive domain of psychology (i.e., hospitals), psychologists must actively seek out opportunities to be part of research and human subject committees. Membership on such committees can lead to increased awareness of, and acceptance of, psychologists as credible and capable researchers.

Response to Ethical Violations by Other Psychologists

All psychologists have a professional responsibility to respond to ethical violations by other psychologists, even though this type of professional relationship might potentially be fraught with emotional distress and hardship for both parties. When a psychologist discovers that another psychologist has engaged in unethical behavior, a typical initial response would be to attempt to resolve the issue informally by direct communication with the psychologist. Especially in cases of a minor nature, or cases that might represent inadvertent misconduct (e.g., due to lack of knowledge), such informal resolutions are often appropriate. However, in cases of a serious nature or cases in which an informal response seems unlikely to bring about the desired result, psychologists are also obliged to bring the matter to the attention of the appropriate state and/or national committees on professional ethics and conduct. In cases of serious misconduct, applicable state and federal laws might take priority in determining the psychologist's response (e.g., sexual mistreatment of children), such that the unethical behavior is expediently reported to appropriate legal authorities, both criminal and regulatory (e.g., statutory licensure boards; see the annual archival *American Psychologist* issue for listing of state boards).

In addition to Principle 7, several other ethical principles are relevant to the establishment and maintenance of professional relationships. For example, Principle 1, Responsibility, section (b), discusses the need for psychologists to avoid establishing research relationships within institutions that would create conflict of interest. Similarly, Principle 6, Welfare of the Consumer, section (a), describes the need to avoid dual relationships with clients, students, and subordinates that could impair professional judgment or increase the possibility of exploitation. Principle 8, Assessment Techniques, section (f), discourages using teaching and supervisory relationships to allow or encourage use of psychological assessment techniques by unqualified individuals. The remaining principles abound with references to aspects of professional relationships that are too numerous to discuss here. Clearly, in a person-oriented profession such as psychology, professional relationships are the most important commodity.

Common Sense

In addition to the guidelines available from a well-conceived personal theoretical perspective, as well as on the basis of ethical principles, many of the guidelines for establishing and maintaining good professional relations are based on common sense. For example, it is difficult to imagine a professional in any discipline being well received if his or her professional behavior is insensitive, discourteous, or disrespectful of others. This includes behavior that has the effect of acting to eschew, distance, or deny meaningful interaction with peers, clients, students, or subordinates. Similarly, a demeanor which conveys elitism or exclusive access to knowledge is destructive. Unfortunately, professional behavior between psychologists who have specialized in different areas (e.g., academic psychologists versus clinical practitioners, clinical versus educational and counseling psychologists) has provided some notorious examples of inappropriate professional behavior. Ironically, it is likely that most readers have either experienced or observed numerous examples of these types of intradisciplinary relationship problems.

Especially when interacting with professionals outside psychology, there is a need to be aware of the inappropriate knowledge or lack of knowledge other professionals may have about psychologists. One cannot assume that other professionals are familiar with either the training or typical modes of practice of psychologists. In particular, it is probably best to assume that most professionals in other disciplines, unless they have had extensive contact with practicing clinical psychologists, do not know of the practice limitations of psychologists. For example, physicians who are not psychiatric specialists may ask a psychologist to recommend a specific brand name and dosage of medication for a patient who has been evaluated, simply because the psychologist, in evaluating the patient, has recommended consideration of referral for medication evaluation. As another example, one of the authors (J. J. S.) was once asked by a medical colleague to perform a biofeedback procedure that would have required application of electrodes near the genital area while the female patient was disrobed. Even after an extensive working relationship with the psychologist, or perhaps because of the comfortable long-term professional relationship, the physician had overlooked the distinction in professional boundaries between the two disciplines.

There is virtually no limit to the net positive effects that can stem from the application of common sense in the conduct of professional relationships. Conversely, there is no limit to the sometimes irrevocable harmful effects that can emanate from a lack of thoughtfulness and common sense in relationships with other professionals. These issues will be discussed further in the following section.

RELEVANCE TO SPECIFIC CLINICAL ENDEAVORS

Patients and Families

The present chapter focuses on the individual clinical psychologist's relations with other professionals. While the sine qua non of professional relations is with patients and their families (see the preamble at the beginning of this chapter), space does not allow an adequate discussion of the intricacies of these important ethical and clinical issues. Instead, the reader is referred to relevant chapters in this volume.

Other Health Care Providers

Psychologists

Korchin (1976) described a number of differences between various specialties of psychologists. With regard to differences between clinicians and nonclinicians, he noted that a basic manner of thinking—the clinical attitude—is the key difference, rather than particular techniques or subject matter. He stated:

> It is in the import of psychological knowledge to the lives of *persons in particular* that the clinical attitude is revealed. Clinicians are concerned with understanding and *helping* individuals in psychological distress. In this pursuit, they engage directly with particular persons in their actual functioning, in their natural life situations, or more usually in the miniaturized life situations of the clinic. They intervene in individual human lives, respecting their complexity and uniqueness. (p. 23)

As alluded to earlier in this chapter, relationships of psychologists with one another have often been among the most difficult. Brought about largely by rivalries between academicians and practitioners, different specialty areas (clinical vs. counseling), different affiliations within universities (psychology vs. education departments), and different models of clinical training (Boulder vs. Vail, and affiliated degrees; PhD vs. PsyD), these intradisciplinary relationship difficulties continue to exist. In fact, the current increasingly competitive health care climate may serve to increase these intradisciplinary difficulties. However, on the brighter side, the APA is currently involved in attempting a restructuring, which is intended to result in a more cohesive and better integrated professional organization for the many diverse elements now represented within APA (cf. *Monitor,* March, 1988). Perhaps the eventual reorganization of APA will bring about a new era for psychologists in which they seek a stronger and more unified definition, rather than simply the coexistence of disagreeable factions. Whether or not this occurs, psychologists will need to improve their intradisciplinary relationships, especially as they affect their public image, if clinical psychologists are to remain viable in the marketplace as health care providers.

Until further developments within organized psychology clarify the solutions to practice (i.e., turf), training, and assorted identity problems within the profession, common sense and guidelines based on ethical standards appear to provide the best source of appropriate and professional behavior when interacting with other psychologists. These ideas can be summarized as behaviors to avoid and behaviors to promote, as follows.

When interacting with other psychologists, do not:
1. assume your training background is superior to that of your colleagues, regardless of the type of specialty training completed or the type of degree granted;
2. be narrow-minded with regard to the type of theoretical orientation, clinical techniques, or modes of practice that you publicly state are acceptable;
3. be unduly or overly critical with regard to peer review of research or clinical activities of your colleagues;
4. procrastinate or otherwise passively obstruct the work of colleagues when asked to perform some type of peer review function;
5. resist or obstruct the attempts of patients or representatives of the patient as they seek second opinions in either clinical or forensic situations.

Conversely, when interacting with other psychologists, do seek to:
1. establish comfortable and truly collegial working relationships through objective and respectful interactions;
2. provide reasoned and thoughtful public statements regarding alternative theoretical orientations, competence, clinical techniques, and modes of practice;
3. apply appropriate and generally accepted standards in evaluating the scientific and clinical endeavors of colleagues;
4. provide timely and constructive feedback to colleagues when evaluating their research and clinical activities;
5. cooperate fully, by providing appropriate information or records when consent is given, with patients or legal representatives of the patient as they seek second opinions in either clinical or forensic situations.

Among clinical psychologists who do research, the frequent requests for reprints of research studies presented at conventions provide a good example of an opportunity for promotion of good professional relations. As Knight (1987) noted of his experience in requesting reprints, a frustrating experience that many of us have shared, as few as 1 in 10 individuals at an APA convention may actually respond to reprint requests from colleagues.

Other Mental Health Professionals

Colleagues in mental health include psychiatrists, social workers, psychiatric nurses, and pastoral counselors. With various training backgrounds outside of psychology, these professionals nevertheless typically have a high degree of familiarity with the training and traditional practice areas of psychologists. Therefore, compared to nonpsychiatric physicians, for instance, these professionals generally do not need much, if any, educative information about psychologists. However, even among colleagues in related mental health disciplines, one should not assume a prior understanding of, or exposure to, recently developed specialty practice areas, such as health psychology or neuropsychology.

The majority of relationship conflicts that arise between psychologists and other mental health professionals are likely to involve turf issues. As might be surmissed from the guidelines for positive interactions with fellow psychologists listed earlier, there are no exact formulas that allow one to avoid or resolve these types of issues. Another way to think about this is that with the exception of state licensing acts, which delimit the exclusive practice areas of psychologists, practice areas can overlap to a large extent with that of other health professionals, particularly mental health professionals. Most of the guidelines mentioned earlier with regard to interacting with other psychologists also apply to relationships with other mental health professionals. Of these, it is particularly important not to act in a manner that conveys a sense of superiority. For example, it is best to ask whether a colleague is familiar with a specific psychological test or biofeedback procedure, rather than simply assuming a lack of knowledge and launching into a lecture on the subject.

Medical and Allied Health Care Providers

Practitioners outside of mental health with whom psychologists have contact include physicians in various medical practice areas (e.g., internal medicine, neurology, neurosurgery, obstetrics-gynecology, physiatry, orthopedic surgery, pediatrics), speech therapists, occupational therapists, physical therapists, nurses, dentists, and others. Schenkenberg, Peterson, Wood, and DaBell (1981) surveyed 112 physicians who used psychologists for consultation and liaison services to determine the positive characteristics sought by physicians. Among the personal characteristics that physicians reported as important when using psychologists were pleasant demeanor, compassion, interest, availability, effective communication, cooperation, intelligence, openness, and common sense. Among the professional qualifications of a psychologist rated highly by the physicians were knowledge, background in medical illness, verbal and written communication skills, testing skills, knowledge of local psychological resources, and diagnostic acumen. While it is not possible to know whether these appraisals of psychologists apply to all practice in medical settings or whether they remain stable across time in the ever-changing health care environment, such personal and professional characteristics seem to have a great deal of face validity for clinical psychologists practicing in medical settings.

When interacting with non-mental-health professionals, one should keep in mind that unless there has been extensive previous contact with psychologists, there may be a significant need for educative information pertaining to training and practice areas. For example, in our experience a fair number of physicians do not know that psychologists have not received 4 years of medical school training (or for that matter even the first 2 years of basic sciences shared by physicians and dentists).

Much less difficulty can be expected related to turf issues, although occasionally psychologists practicing in specialty areas may experience this problem with other allied health professionals. For example, neuropsychologists, speech therapists, and occupational therapists sometimes find that their practices overlap with respect to evaluation and remediation of brain-injured individuals. In such situations, it is typically possible to have all parties agree that no practitioner should be excluded, and that to avoid redundancy and to highlight the strengths of each professional, services to the patient are apportioned by content area (e.g., language and academic skills by the speech therapist, visual and motor skills by the occupational therapist, and memory and other higher cognitive skills by the neuropsychologist) or by some other logical means. Along these lines, William Lynch, a neuropsychologist active in the field of cognitive retraining, has suggested that the field is not developed well enough to mandate or legislate who will provide cognitive retraining services. Thus, until controls arise from within the field, no discipline should be excluded (personal communication, April 20,

1988). Dr. Lynch's position is a constructive one that will no doubt build and facilitate interdisciplinary relationships.

Belar, Deardorff, and Kelly (1987, chap. 3) presented an excellent discussion of some of the salient points for psychologists working in medical settings. Among these points are: (a) Do not overidentify with the traditional medical model; (b) place concrete patient care goals as the priority when faced with the occasional aversive interaction with a physician; (c) provide prompt follow-through with both service to the patient and communication back to the physician after accepting a referral; and (d) understand local referral customs (e.g., who is allowed to refer, when patients are to be given feedback by the consultant).

The Insurance Industry

A relatively new area of professional relations for psychologists is with health insurance representatives, often claims representatives or nurses. These individuals are employed by insurance carriers to monitor and manage cases that may involve protracted and potentially costly claims to the carrier. As clinical psychology has expanded into broader practice areas, such as rehabilitation, and as the insurance industry increasingly has sought to decrease expenses, the likelihood of direct contacts between insurance representatives and psychologists has increased. These contacts may range from requests for specific information regarding assessment procedures billed, to summaries of treatment plans, progress and goals in treatment, and prognosis. In some states, such as Illinois, Worker's Compensation law may require that all treatment records and reports be made available to the insurance carrier on request. Even the choice of selecting which psychologist is to perform evaluation or treatment for such cases may be within the legal powers of the insurance carrier. Thus, from the outset, in these types of cases the psychologist must conduct clinical activities, maintain clinical records, and inform the patient accordingly.

The relatively recent growth of the insurance plan known as a health maintenance organization (HMO) has also increased monitoring and management of mental health benefits relevant to psychologists. In those plans that allow psychologists to provide assessment or treatment to HMO patients, often by requiring the psychologist to join a preferred provider organization (PPO), monitoring and repeated written justification to the primary physician or HMO utilization of care coordinator are routine. Much education of the HMO personnel may be needed to correct gross misconceptions in expectations for treatment (e.g., biofeedback for headaches is not expected to be of any benefit if only one or two sessions are allowed).

The Legal System

Attorneys

As the professional activities of psychologists become more visible in communities and in medical settings, greater interaction with the legal system is a natural consequence. Thus, contact with attorneys in the form of providing expert consultation or expert witness testimony is to be expected for many psychologists. In fact, enough clinical psychologists perform such duties regularly to have prompted the American Board of Professional Psychology to begin granting a Diplomate in Forensic Psychology in 1986. At this point, numerous authors have provided basic information pertaining to the unique world of involvement in legal cases (Boyer, 1983; Schwitzgebel & Schwitzgebel, 1980). In this section we will consider the general nature of relationships with attorneys.

While attorneys know about the basic qualifications of psychologists (e.g., that psychologists are not physicians), one would be prudent to assume that a particular attorney who requests a psychologist's expert opinion does not know the finer points of expertise or limitations of training and practice of a clinical psychologist, particularly one who specializes. When first contacted by an attorney, a number of points should be clarified, including (a) fees and arrangements for payment (e.g., monthly or at the conclusion of the legal proceeding), (b) who is responsible for payment (e.g., patient, insurance carrier, defendant's attorney, plaintiff's attorney, the state); and (c) whether the psychologist is to provide consultation only or is actually expected to appear in court. As Boyer (1983) noted, it is best to inform attorneys at the time psychological services are enlisted of the need to present an unbiased, independent opinion, rather than simply endorsing the position most favorable to the attorney's side of the case. Since all written materials of the expert witness will be scrutinized, as will all formal verbal statements made on the record by all interested parties, it is the psychologist's responsibility to make statements that are professionally responsible and can be defended in court. Even though many cases never make it to court, it is not possible to determine which cases will.

Logistical arrangements for giving expert testimony, via deposition or in court, are often difficult.

Psychologists should expect that many of the scheduled events may be postponed or cancelled, even at the last moment. Most attorneys will be willing to hold depositions in the psychologist's office at his or her convenience, whereas timing of court appearances is beyond anyone's ability to predict or control. Typically, schedule problems can be minimized by informing the attorney in advance of schedule limitations, asking for confirmations of events as the expected dates approach, and keeping in contact with the attorney's office as the schedule develops. Despite all efforts, agreeing to be an expert witness will at times prove exasperating, stressful, inconvenient, and intrusive.

Elected Officials (Public Policy)

Bismarck said that one should avoid watching the making of both "policy and sausage." That view, if carried out by professional psychology during the last few decades, would have greatly limited research funding, clinical training grants, professional practice, and ultimately the public good. Kelly, Garrison, and DeLeon (1987) noted that a large number of psychologists have become involved in legislative and public policy issues. Both the APA's Office of Legislative Affairs and Office of Professional Practice reflect organized psychology's professional relationship with public policy and the legislative system. Activities carried out by individual psychologists reflect the impact psychologists can have on these issues (Kelly et al., 1987).

Ebert-Flattau (1980) prepared a legislative guide that can help psychologists understand the legislative policy process. The *Monitor, The American Psychologist,* and *The Clinical Psychologist* can keep the reader abreast of changes on the national level. Membership in state psychological associations and subscription to relevant newsletters can keep psychologists current on local policy and legislative issues.

Reppucci and Aber (1987) suggested that interest in public policy bridges the scientist, scientist-practitioner, and practitioner differences often discussed in clinical psychology today. While individual foci may differ given one's place of employment or interests, involvement has affected various areas. Clinical training (Strickland & Calkins, 1987), national health policy (DeLeon, 1977), women's issues (Russo, 1987), and research (Kelly et al., 1987) are among those topics influenced by psychologists' involvement in public policy. Kiesler and Morton (1987) suggested that "psychologists be trained in policy analysis and health/mental health economics" (p. 31). Zuckerman

(1987) urged psychologists to share their expertise "clearly, persuasively, and succinctly to a nonpsychologist" (p. 40) as a meaningful part of a professional relationship with the legislative system and the community at large.

The School System

When working with the school system, the clinical psychologist should be viewed as a consultant. The consultative role can be aimed directly to the school as an agent for the school, or for a child and his or her parents if requested by them in consultation to the school. This distinction should be made clear at the outset to avoid any ethical dilemmas that could compromise the psychologist's clinical role and input.

In Alpert's (1985) vision of school psychology, that specialty of psychology is seen as serving a central role within the educational and community system. Using skills in systems analysis, knowledge of learning and educational theory, and training in mental health, the school psychologist should serve as a natural point of contact for the clinical psychologist who has been asked to consult either with individual children and families or on broader school and community issues. The clinical psychologist who is consulting within a school district should respect the knowledge and boundaries of school psychologist colleagues with an appropriate understanding of their professional qualifications, skills, and responsibilities (cf. APA, 1981b).

In preparing evaluations for school personnel, teachers, administrators, school social workers, or school psychologists, the language of reports should avoid jargon and provide a practical understanding of a child's intellectual and/or emotional status. Recommendations should be clear and attainable within the school milieu. In this respect, psychological evaluations in a school setting must meet the same requirements of evaluations provided in any clinical context (Sweet, 1991). A series of articles reflecting trends in school consultation issues (Gallessich, 1976) present many practical ideas for the clinician who works with school personnel. In one of those articles, Alpert (1976) related the story of a school principal who felt that her school was her house and as "master" she was entitled to "information and respect and a sense of responsibility" (p. 623) about and for the work of the consultant. When preparing data about children that are to be used by teachers, one must remember that while the psychologist may have spent several hours testing and analyzing data or hours in therapy sessions with a child and family, the teacher has spent days and weeks living in that "house" of education with the child. The teacher should be accorded respect for that time and the professional viewpoint developed therefrom.

Professional Training Programs

One of the first professional relationships in which the student clinician becomes involved is that of supervisor-supervisee. The purposes of that relationship include modeling of appropriate professional and therapeutic behavior, providing a practical translation of theoretical models of diagnosis and treatment, teaching actual diagnostic and therapeutic skills, assisting the supervisee with their reactions (countertransference) to patients, and assuring quality of care to the patient being treated.

Despite the importance of this relationship, little is known about the supervisory process (Matarazzo, 1978). Few clinicians actually receive direct training in supervisory skills (Styczynski, 1980). It has been suggested that clinical psychology may even take the supervisory relationship for granted (Hess, 1987). Following their review of the available literature, Lambert and Arnold (1987) concluded that the gains resulting from training and supervision in specific psychotherapy skills are maintained over time and generalize to the practical setting. Given the role, goal, and impact of this professional relationship, certain issues deserve discussion here.

In reviewing the literature on the ideal supervisory relationship, Carifio and Hess (1987) concluded that supervisors should exhibit those characteristics inherent in the good psychotherapeutic relationship: respect, empathy, concreteness, and appropriate self-disclosure. Although not shown empirically, Carifio and Hess suggested that flexibility, concern, attention, investment, curiosity, and openness describe desired traits of the good supervisor.

Operationalization of the successful supervisory relationship includes a supervisor with therapy experience (Carifio & Hess, 1987), the setting of explicit and meaningful goals (Archer & Peake, 1984; Fox, 1983), and a clear discussion of criteria of evaluation (Freeman, 1985). While therapist-like in style, Carifio and Hess (1987) concluded that the ideal supervisor avoids conducting psychotherapy during the supervisory sessions. Supervisory style is maximized where the feedback is given objectively, timely, clearly, and in a manner offering useful alternatives to a given problem (Freeman, 1985).

To be truly effective in this important professional relationship, the supervising clinician must take seriously the clinical and ethical import and implications of supervision. All psychologists experience supervision in their graduate training and during their working years. Similarly, a large portion of professional time may be spent in doing direct supervision and training (Hess, 1987). Therefore, the profession in general must see to it that clinicians, while still trainees, receive training in the theoretical and practical issues that surround this most basic of professional relationships (Dodds, 1986).

PSYCHOLOGISTS AND THE MASS MEDIA

Psychologists are called on in increasing numbers and frequency to relate to the popular media. This is true in their role as both clinicians (Bouhoutsos, Goodchilds, & Huddy, 1986; Klonoff, 1983) and as scientists (McCall, 1988). As the field matures, the media looks to psychologists for information that, if presented in a professional manner, will enhance psychologists' image with the public (Pryzwansky & Wendt, 1987), while at the same time contributing to the best interests of society.

Whatever the motivation to become involved with the media, be it seeking referrals or status, answering the needs of consumers (Klonoff, 1983), or imparting relevant and meaningful information (Freudenberger, 1983), the psychologist's professional relationship with the media is guided by a specific ethical principle.

Prior to the 1981 revision, the APA *Ethical Principles* specifically forbade a professional relationship with the media, the use of psychological techniques for entertainment (APA, 1953, p. 84), or the provision of psychological services or advice by means of public lectures or demonstration, newspaper or magazine articles, radio or television programs, mail, or similar media (APA, 1977, Principle 4-i). Presently, however, the psychologist's professional relationship with the media has been more broadly defined.

> Individual psychological services are provided in the context of a *professional psychological relationship* [italics added]. When professional advice is given by means of public lectures or demonstrations, newspaper or magazine articles, radio or television programs, mail, or similar media, the psychologist utilizes the most current relevant data and exercises the highest level of professional judgment. (APA, 1981a, p. 635)

Klonoff (1983) cautioned the psychologist that the term *advice* involves some level of diagnostic thinking in order to generate recommendations. She further cautioned the field of its need to better define the vague and ambiguous nature of this principle such that the psychologist is not free to use "current relevant data" (p. 852) that is elsewhere contradicted.

Caveat emptor clearly does not apply here in light of ethical standards. The following guidelines offered by Freudenberger (1983) provide a set of rules that help to assure that the consumer is best served by the psychologist's professional relationship with the media.

1. When speaking to the media consumer-public do so more in terms of giving information, rather than advice.
2. Seek to stimulate interest in your area of expertise through thought provoking questions.
3. Do not seek to comment on an area wherein you have limited knowledge. Referring to sources is an excellent way of transmitting information.
4. Understand and come to grips with a possible conflict that may arise between your own personal and professional ethics, as opposed to the demands of a studio or radio station. They may become more interested in the sensational, than you are willing, or ought to provide.
5. Be aware of the seduction that may occur once you are on camera and before a live audience. Self monitoring is always appropriate as a guide to appropriate demeanor.
6. Seek to walk the narrow line between the desire to be a commercial success and your ethics and values.
7. Seek to present your material in a clear and concise manner. The public is not interested in a psychologist who is subtly talking down to them in language not understood.
8. While presenting and identifying yourself as a psychologist, re-identify for the public all the contributions that we as psychologists have made. (p. 5)

For those psychologists involved in research as well as direct service activities, it would appear that the foregoing rules should also be noted. Dunwoody and Scott (1982) reported that social and behavioral scientists are 39% more likely than scientists from other disciplines to be contacted by the media.

In general, the media reporting of scientific results is considered as accurate (McCall, 1988). Thus, researchers should not be dissuaded from presenting their findings in the popular press. Most scientists are not trained in handling the journalistic interview and should be aware of the pitfalls of the unprepared statement as well as the advantages of properly educating the general public. Avoiding "disastrous phraseologies" and saying their piece correctly to the jouranlist ensures proper reporting in the press (McCall, 1988, p. 89). Benjamin (1987) pointed out that Hall, Watson, and James, among others, wrote articles for the popular press to educate the public about their new science. Benjamin, in requesting cooperation in disseminating material to the media via the APA convention, pointed out that federal budgetary cuts to psychological research programs were a function of the field's unwillingness to share its findings with the general public.

In studying the effects of radio call-in psychology programming, Bouhoutsos et al. (1986) found that 49% of a sample of shopping mall patrons reported, on inquiry, that they listen to or watch these types of programs. Among those, 78% said they tune in more often during times when their lives are "worse." Forty one percent of listeners found the programming helpful, and 31% considered it educational. In a sample of actual program callers, these same authors reported that callers were most distressed by problems of an interpersonal nature and had sought psychological or psychiatric assistance at least once.

Media psychology has the chance to reach a large segment of the population who may rely on the efficacy of the media presented advice. Psychologists should take their relationship with media seriously, realizing that they are ultimately responsible for the advice given or statements made (Pryzwansky & Wendt, 1987). Similarly, those who speak to the public should be reminded that they are representatives of the entire field (Klonoff, 1983). As Shakespeare wrote, "Good name in man and woman, is the immediate jewel of their souls. Who steals my purse steals trash; but he that filches from me my good name, robs me of that which not enriches him, and makes me poor indeed."

PSYCHOLOGISTS' RELATIONSHIP WITH THE PROFESSION

In the extended family of professional psychology, psychologists can choose to relate to their peers on a local, state, national, and international level. Many of the forces in the broader aspects of professional development, practice, research, education, and politics seen in the world at large may well be reflected in the microcosm of the psychologist's university, hospital, consulting firm, community, or private office setting. Awareness of and involvement in professional relationships in general helps to prepare the psychologist for day-to-day events as well as offering a chance to make an impact on one's students, colleagues, or the field.

There are over 45 national professional organizations that represent various factions of the field of psychology. Many of those organizations are described and discussed by Pryzwansky and Wendt (1987). Membership in these organizations and local professional organizations can provide journals and/or newsletters, as well as a variety of personal contacts, that offer a medium for exchange of professional information.

Membership in the APA brings with it on a monthly basis the journal *American Psychologist* and the newspaper *The APA Monitor*. This range of readings helps one relate to the field's organizational issues and current events, as well as popular, scientific, and professional issues. Membership in one of the APA's 45 divisions or subscription to one or more of the 20 plus APA or division sponsored journals can provide psychologists with a network of written materials enhancing their relationship with the field. Attendance at the national APA convention or divisional meetings can bring about the reestablishment of old friendships or the building of new professional relationships through the formality of the lecture room or the casualness of the hotel coffee shop. Very few notables in the field will turn down students for a discussion of their work, if approached in a professional manner.

The changing face of the APA reflects changes in the field. A smaller proportion of psychologists is being trained in the research subfields, as organized psychology focuses increasingly on its health service provider role (Howard et al., 1986). Reorganization of the APA is being discussed in order to balance the relationship of the applied and scientific schools of activities (Fisher, 1987). The history of the organization shows a split in 1937 with the clinicians leaving APA to join the American Association of Applied Psychology, followed by a 1944 APA reorganization designed to include both the scientific and applied or professional concerns. The recently organized Assembly for Scientist-Practitioner Psychologists is an attempt by some clinical psychologists to bridge the schism in the field.

Knowledge of local political information is an important component of one's relationship with the profession. Certification or licensure and the clinical privileges inherent therein are determined by statute, and maintaining those privileges helps the profession continue its recognition and autonomy (Phillips,

1982). Sunset legislation designed to trim governmental bureaucracy caused organized psychology to step forward to defend the gains it had made legislatively in previous years (Kilburg & Ginsberg, 1983), as states focused their sunset rulings on professional and occupational regulatory activities. A flurry of information ensured that psychologists could relate to each other, to the field in general, and to the government in an organized manner in order to meet the challenge. Dorken (1981) and Ebert-Flattau (1980) offered steps in relating to government in a professional manner. In the areas of hospital privileges (Tanney, 1983) and insurance reimbursement (Buie, 1988b), for example, this type of professional organization has begun to show results.

In our global village, psychologists' relationship with the profession now can be only a few computer key strokes and a modem away. The APA offers a computerized data bank of information on subjects that range from professional competency to legislative information (Buie, 1988). The relative ease of attaining this type of information points to a future in which knowledge of current events and maintenance of collegial contacts will help psychologists relate to the profession in an effective manner.

SUMMARY

In recent years clinical psychology has grown significantly. As would be expected, one net effect of growth in a person-oriented, service delivery field is a need to develop and maintain strong professional relations within clinical psychology, with other areas of psychology, with consumers and the community at large, and with other disciplines. While difficult, the establishment of viable professional relations is a basic ingredient to continued professional growth, both on an individual level as well as for the profession itself. Ethical guidelines have been, and will no doubt continue to be, useful in providing basic foundations in professional relations, but need to be augmented by sound judgment and common sense.

REFERENCES

Alpert, J. L. (1976). Conceptual bases of mental health consultation in the schools. *Professional Psychology, 7,* 619–626.

Alpert, J. L. (1985). Change within a profession: Change, future, prevention, and school psychology. *American Psychologist, 40,* 1112–1121.

American Psychological Association. (1953). *Ethical standards of psychologists.* Washington, DC: Author.

American Psychological Association. (1977). *Ethical standards of psychologists*. Washington, DC: Author.

American Psychological Association. (1981a). *Ethical principles of psychologists*. Washington, DC: Author.

American Psychological Association. (1981b). Specialty guidelines for delivery of services by clinical psychologists. *American Psychologists, 36,* 640–651.

American Psychological Association. (1987). *Casebook on ethical principles of psychologists*. Washington, DC: Author.

Archer, R., & Peake, T. (1984). Learning and teaching psychotherapy: Signposts and growth stages. *The Clinical Supervisor, 2,* 61–74.

Belar, C. D., Deardorff, W. D., & Kelly, K. E. (1987). *The practice of clinical health psychology*. Elmsford, NY: Pergamon Press.

Benjamin, L. T. (1987). We need the press; they need us. *The APA Monitor, 18,* 3.

Board of Professional Affairs, Committee on Professional Standards. (1987). Casebook for providers of psychological services. *American Psychologist, 42,* 704–711.

Bouhoutsos, J. C., Goodchilds, J. D., & Huddy, L. (1986). Media psychology: An empirical study of radio call-in psychology programs. *Professional Psychology: Research and Practice, 17,* 408–414.

Boyer, J. (1983). Law and the practice of clinical psychology. In C. E. Walker (Ed.), *The handbook of clinical psychology: Theory, research, and practice*. Vol. II (pp. 1389–1419). Homewood, IL: Dorsey.

Buie, J. (1988a). Data you can bank on. *The APA Monitor, 19,* 13–14.

Buie, J. (1988b). Psychology wins place in health insurance bill. *The APA Monitor, 19,* 12.

Carifio, M. S., & Hess, A. K. (1987). Who is the ideal supervisor? *Professional Psychology: Research and Practice, 18,* 244–250.

DeLeon, P. H. (1977). Implications of national health policies for professional psychology. *Professional Psychology, 8,* 263–268.

Dodds, J. B. (1986). Supervision of psychology trainees in field placements. *Professional Psychology: Research and Practice, 17,* 296–300.

Dorken, H. (1981). Coming of age legislatively: In 21 steps. *American Psychologist, 36,* 165–173.

Dunwoody, S., & Scott, B. T. (1982). Scientists as mass media sources. *Journalism Quarterly, 59,* 52–59.

Ebert-Flattau, P. (1980). *A legislative guide*. Washington, DC: APA.

Feigl, H. (1959). Philosophical embarrassment of psychology. *The American Psychologist, 14,* 115–128.

Fisher, K. (1987). Group on restructuring asked to fine-tune plan. *The APA Monitor, 18,* 1, 5.

Fox, R. (1983). Contracting in supervision: A goal oriented process. *The Clinical Supervisor, 1,* 37–49.

Frank, G. (1984). The Boulder Model: History, rationale, and critique. *Professional Psychology: Research and Practice, 15,* 417–435.

Freeman, E. (1985). The importance of feedback in clinical supervision: Implications for direct practice. *The Clinical Supervisor, 1,* 5–26.

Freudenberger, H. J. (1983). Making mental health public— How you as a psychologist, can function more effectively in the media. *The Independent Practitioner, 3,* 5.

Gallessich, J. (1976). Conceptual bases of school consultation models: Introduction. *Professional Psychology, 7,* 618.

Hess, A. K. (1987). Advances in psychotherapy supervision: Introduction. *Professional Psychology: Research and Practice, 18,* 187–188.

Howard, A., Pion, G. M., Gottfredson, G. D., Flattau, P. E., Oskamp, S., Pfafflin, S. M., Bray, D. W., & Burstein, A. G. (1986). The changing face of American psychology: A report from the committee on employment and human resources. *American Psychologist, 41,* 1311–1327.

Kelly, D. M., Garrison, E. G., and DeLeon, P. (1987). Psychology and public policy: Why get involved? *The Clinical Psychologist, 40,* 28.

Kennard, B. D., Stewart, S. M., and Gluck, M. R. (1987). The supervision relationship: Variables contributing to positive versus negative experiences. *Professional Psychology: Research and Practice, 18,* 172–175.

Kiesler, C. A., and Morton, T. (1987). Responsible public policy in a rapidly changing world. *The Clinical Psychologist, 40,* 28–31.

Kilburg, R. R., and Ginsberg, M. R. (1983). Sunset and psychology or how we learned to love a crisis. *American Psychologist, 38,* 1227–1231.

Kleinmuntz, B. (1984). The scientific study of clinical judgment in psychology and medicine. *Clinical Psychology Review, 4,* 111–126.

Klonoff, E. A. (1983). A star is born: Psychologists and the media. *Professional Psychology: Research and Practice, 14,* 847–854.

Korchin, S. J. (1976). *Modern clinical psychology: Principles of intervention in the clinic and community*. New York: Basic Books.

Knight, J. A. (1987). Reprints: Are they an all-too-rare professional courtesy? *The APA Monitor, 18,* 3.

Lambert, M. J., and Arnold, R. C. (1987). Research and the supervisory process. *Professional Psychology: Research and Practice, 18,* 217–224.

Matarazzo, R. C. (1978). Research on the teaching and learning of psychotherapeutic skills. In S. Garfield & A. Bergin (Eds.), *Handbook of psychotherapy and behavior change* (2nd ed., pp. 941–966). New York: John Wiley & Sons.

McCall, R. B. (1988). Science and the press: Like oil and water? *American Psychologist, 43,* 87–94.

Phillips, B. M. (1982). Regulation and control in psychology: Implications for certification and licensure. *American Psychologist, 37,* 919–926.

Piaget, J., & Kamii, C. (1978). What is psychology? *The American Psychologist, 7,* 648–652.

Pryzwansky, W. B., & Wendt, R. N. (1987). *Psychology as*

a profession: Foundations of practice. Elmsford, NY: Pergamon Press.

Reppucci, N. D., & Aber, M. (1987). Views of public policy psychologists. *The Clinical Psychologist, 40,* 36–38.

Rozensky, R. H., Sweet, J. J., & Tovian, S. M. (1991). Toward program development: An integration of science and service in medical settings. In J. J. Sweet, R. H. Rozensky, & S. M. Tovian (Eds.), *Handbook of clinical psychology in medical settings.* (pp. 285–289). New York: Plenum Publishing.

Russo, N. (1987). Women and mental health policy: Opportunities and strategies. *The Clinical Psychologist, 40,* 34–36.

Schenkenberg, T., Peterson, D., Wood, D., & DaBell R. (1981). Psychological consultation/liaison in a medical and neurological setting: Physician's appraisal. *Professional Psychology, 12,* 309–317.

Schwitzgebel, R. L., & Schwitzgebel, R. K. (1980). *Law and psychological practice.* New York: John Wiley & Sons.

Shakow, D. (1976). What is clinical psychology? *American Psychologist, 30,* 553–560.

Staff. (1988). Reorganization plan to be sent to members. *The APA Monitor, 19,* 1.

Stern, S. (1984). Professional training and professional competence: A critique of current thinking. *Professional Psychology: Research and Practice, 2,* 230–243.

Strickland, B. R. (1985). Over the Boulder(s) and through the Vail. *The Clinical Psychologist, 38,* 52–56.

Strickland, B. R., and Calkins, B. J. (1987). Public policy and clinical training. *The Clinical Psychologist, 40,* 31–34.

Styczynski, L. E. (1980). The transition from supervisee to supervisor. In A. K. Hess (Ed.), *Psychotherapy supervision* (pp. 29–40). New York: John Wiley & Sons.

Sweet, J. J. (1991). Psychological evaluation and testing services in a medical setting. In J. J. Sweet, R. H. Rozensky, & S. M. Tovian (Eds.), *Handbook of clinical psychology in medical settings.* New York: Plenum Publishing.

Tanney, F. (1983). Hospital privileges for psychologists: A legislative model. *American Psychologist, 38,* 1232–1237.

Tyler, F. B., and Spiesman, J. C. (1967). An emerging scientist-professional role in psychology. *American Psychologist, 22,* 839–847.

Weed, L. L. (1970). *Medical records, medical education, and patient care.* Cleveland: Case Western Reserve.

Zuckerman, D. (1987). Uncle Sam wants you: How psychologists can get involved in public policy. *The Clinical Psychologist, 40,* 38–40.

CHAPTER 7

ETHICAL AND LEGAL ISSUES IN CLINICAL PRACTICE

Kenneth S. Pope

We practice in an era of increasing accountability. Complaints to the American Psychological Association (APA) Ethics Committee are increasing, malpractice premiums are rising to cover proliferating jury awards and settlements, and licensing boards are becoming increasingly active. So diverse and complex are the interrelated ethical, legal, and clinical issues that even a brief discussion of each is beyond the scope of any chapter. The more modest aim of this chapter is to review some of the major causes of malpractice suits, licensing disciplinary actions, and ethics complaints against psychologists and to suggest some principles by which psychologists can avoid placing their clients at risk for harm and themselves at risk for formal complaint.

CURRENT LAWS, STANDARDS, AND GUIDELINES

An initial step toward practicing in accordance with the highest ethical, legal, and clinical standards is to understand the concepts on which those standards are based and to become familiar with the most widely accepted standards.

Ethical standards have been conceptualized in a variety of frameworks. The APA (1990), for example, sets forth 10 diverse topic areas: (a) responsibility, (b) competence, (c) moral and legal standards, (d) public statements, (e) confidentiality, (f) welfare of the consumer, (g) professional relationships, (h) assessment techniques, (i) research with human participants, and (j) care and use of animals. As another example, which serves as an alternative to topic areas, Redlich and Pope (1980; see also Pope, Tabachnick, & Keith-Spiegel, 1987, 1988) suggested seven basic principles governing professional practice, the first five of which are from the ancient Hippocratic Oath: (a) avoiding harm, (b) competence, (c) avoiding exploitation, (d) respect, (e) confidentiality, (f) informed consent, and (g) social equity justice. APA (1990, 1981, 1986, 1987; see also *Standards for educational and psychological tests,* 1985) publishes several documents setting forth ethical and related professional standards. The reader is particularly referred to "Trends in Ethics Cases, Common Pitfalls, and Published Resources" (APA Ethics Committee, 1988), a review article that discusses patterns of complaints, the actions (or failures to act) by psychologists that tend to elicit formal complaints, and useful readings.

Legal standards come from sources as diverse as criminal and civil legislation, malpractice case law, and administrative law. Perhaps of most concern to psychology practitioners are the malpractice standards. The basic concept of malpractice is often explained in terms of the "four D's." First, there must exist a duty. Any time a psychologist maintains a professional relationship with a patient or client, there exists a variety of such duties. Second, there is a dereliction of duty. The psychologist either does something he or she is not supposed to do, or fails to perform a mandated duty. Third, there must be damage. The individual (generally a client or patient, but in some cases third parties) to whom the duty is owed is somehow harmed. Fourth, the damage is a direct result of the psychologist's dereliction of duty. Psychologists need to devise ways of staying abreast of the constantly evolving state and federal legal standards applicable to clinical practice.

Clinical standards seem to evolve at a more rapid pace than either ethical or legal standards. For example, both Fowler (1988), then president of the APA, and Weiner (1988), editor of the *Journal of Personality Assessment,* have stressed that our understanding of, procedures for, and empirical norms for psychological testing change so constantly that to practice according to the norms and procedures of even 5 years ago would be considered malpractice in light of the current state of the field. Many of the other chapters in this volume will help readers to ensure that they are familiar with current clinical knowledge, approaches, and standards. In addition, subscribing to and reading academic and professional journals, attending inservice training and continuing education courses, participating in scientific meetings and professional conventions, obtaining individual or group supervision, making use of such programs as the American Board of Professional Psychology's Post-Graduate Institute courses, and forming a small peer-education group with respected colleagues are other examples of ways in which psychologists can help ensure that their training and expertise is based on current clinical knowledge, procedures, and approaches.

AN OVERVIEW OF MALPRACTICE, LICENSING, AND ETHICS BOARD ACTIONS

A second step toward practicing in accordance with the highest ethical, legal, and clinical standards is to become familiar with the most common formal complaints filed against psychologists. The actual proportion of such complaints in various arenas (e.g., licensing boards, ethics committees, the civil courts) provides an empirical basis for identifying high-risk areas of practice. The diversity of issues leading to formal complaints becomes apparent in the following arrays of data compared and contrasted by Pope (1989). Table 7.1 presents the causes of licensing disciplinary actions recorded by the American Association of State Psychology Boards for the period January 16, 1986, through July 1, 1988. Table 7.2 presents the major bases for complaints filed with the APA Ethics Committee over the past 5 years. Table 7.3 presents the 27 major sources of costs for malpractice suits against psychologists handled by APA's carrier from February, 1976, through May, 1988.

CONFLICTING STANDARDS

A third important step is for psychologists to reflect on the various sets of standards and other factors governing the practice of psychology, to identify areas of possible conflict, and to develop for themselves a way to resolve those conflicts. In some instances, state or federal legislation may be in conflict with APA's ethical standards. In other instances, governmental directives or the demands of one's employing organization may be perceived by a psychologist to endanger client safety or welfare. Interested readers are referred to Simon's (1978) case study and analysis of the firing of a Veterans Administration (VA) psychologist who

Table 7.1. Causes of Licensing Disciplinary Actions Recorded by the American Association of State Psychology Boards for the Period January 16, 1986, through July 1, 1988

36%	Dual relationships (both sexual and nonsexual)	2%	Disciplinary action in another jurisdiction
11%	Unprofessional conduct		
10%	Conviction of a felony	2%	Ethical violations
8%	Failure to comply with a board order	2%	Unreported
8%	Improper billing practices	1%	Confidentiality
6%	Incompetent manner of practice	1%	Misrepresentation of competence
3%	Mental incompetence	1%	Child abuse
3%	Fraud in application for license	1%	Failure to report child abuse

Table 7.2. Percentages of Major Complaints Filed with APA Ethics Committee over a 5-Year Period (1983 to 1987)

23%	Principle 6a (sexual and nonsexual dual relationships)
16%	Principle 3d (violating various APA standards and guidelines related to practice and research or governmental laws and institutional regulations)
8%	Principle 3c (acting in a way that violates or diminishes the legal or civil rights of others)
4%	Principle 5a (failing to preserve appropriate confidentiality of information concerning clients, students, etc.)

objected, first internally and later publicly, to VA policies that he believed jeopardized the health and well-being of his patients, and of the responses of the VA, the Civil Service Commission, professional associations, and various individuals to this incident. In still other instances, the formal ethical and legal standards themselves may be in conflict with the psychologist's own deeply held values. A national study found that a majority of psychologists had intentionally broken the law or formal ethical principle in light of the psychologist's own values (Pope & Bajt, 1988). Almost half (48%) of these instances involved keeping or breaking confidentiality: Twenty-one percent involved refusing to make a legally mandated report of child abuse, 21% involved illegally divulging confidential information, and 6% involved refusing to make legally mandated warnings regarding dangerous clients.

COMPETENCE

A fourth step toward practicing in accordance with the highest ethical, legal, and clinical standards is to remain within one's areas of expertise. The *Ethical Principles* (APA, 1990) state this standard clearly: This responsibility is to provide of their services only within the bounds of competence.

Whether from pride (failure to realize that we are less than omniscient and omni talented), from financial considerations (an acute reluctance to refer a potential client—one who can pay a full fee—to someone else), from lack of appreciation or concern for the immense damage that can be done by a blundering clinician, or from other causes, many psychologists find it difficult to restrict their practice to areas in which they have adequate training and experience, and hence expertise. The figures cited previously indicate that incompetent manner of practice is the sixth most frequent cause of licensing disciplinary actions and that incorrect treatment (a cause of action directly related to competence) is the third most frequent cause of successful malpractice suits against psychologists. As prominent as these figures are, they appear to understate the problem. About one fourth of psychologists on a national basis

Table 7.3. The 27 Major Sources of Costs for Malpractice Suits Against Psychologists Handled by APA's Carrier from February, 1976, through May, 1988

53.2%	Sexual impropriety	0.7%	Defamation: Libel/slander
11.2%	Suicide of patient	0.6%	Failure to warn
8.4%	Incorrect treatment	0.5%	Violation of legal regulations
7.9%	Undetermined	0.4%	Undue influence
3.7%	Diagnosis: Failure to diagnose or incorrect diagnosis	0.3%	Failure to supervise properly
		0.2%	Loss of child custody or visitation
2.6%	Loss from evaluation	0.2%	Licensing or peer review
2.0%	Improper death of patient or others	0.1%	Abandonment
1.6%	Bodily injury	0.1%	Breach of contract
1.5%	Assault and battery	0.1%	Poor results
1.3%	Countersuit for fee collection	0.1%	Premise liability
1.3%	Breach of confidentiality or privacy	0.1%	False imprisonment or arrest
1.1%	Violation of civil rights	0.1%	Failure to refer
0.8%	Miscellaneous	0.1%	Failure to treat

indicate that they have provided services outside areas of competence (Pope, Tabachnick, & Keith-Spiegel, 1987, 1988).

Psychologists who move from one area of specialization to another need to ensure that their education, training, and supervised work experience in the new area adequately establish their competence. At its 1976 meeting (January 23 to 25), the APA Council of Representatives formally adopted a "Policy on Training for Psychologists Wishing to Change Their Specialty." The policy, which should be carefully reviewed by anyone moving to a new area of specialization, includes the following two sections:

4. With respect to subject matter and professional skills, psychologists taking such training must meet all requirements of doctoral training in the new specialty, being given due credit for relevant course work or requirements they have previously satisfied.
5. It must be stressed, however, that merely taking an internship or acquiring experience in a practicum setting is not, for example, considered adequate preparation for becoming a clinical, counseling, or school psychologist when prior training has not been in the relevant area.

In reaffirming and extending the 1976 policy, the APA Council, at its 1982 meeting (January 22 to 24), adopted the following policy:

The American Psychological Association holds that respecialization education and training for psychologists possessing the doctoral degree should be conducted by those academic units in regionally accredited universities and professional schools currently offering doctoral training in the relevant specialty, and in conjunction with regularly organized internship agencies where appropriate. Respecialization for purposes of offering services in clinical, counseling, or school psychology should be linked to relevant APA approved programs.

DUAL RELATIONSHIPS

The Nature and Scope of the Problem

Dual relationships occur whenever a psychologist engages in a professional and at least one other formal or substantial relationship with an individual. Thus, when one serves as a therapist as well as employer, or engages in a sexual relationship as well as a professional relationship (such as teacher, supervisor, or therapist), one is engaging in a dual relationship. Borys and Pope (1989) review the prohibitions against

dual relationships and the finding of a national survey of clinicians' attitudes and behaviors in regard to dual relationships.

As Tables 7.1, 7.2, and 7.3 make clear, dual relationships are by far the major cause of formal complaints against psychologists. There are over three times as many licensing disciplinary actions due to dual relationships (36%) as there are for the second most frequent basis (unprofessional conduct—11%) of action. Nearly one fourth of all ethics complaints involve charges of dual relationships. But it is in the realm of malpractice suits that dual relationships are most prominent. Over half (53%) of all monies paid out to plaintiffs by APA's professional liability carrier are due to sexual dual relationships alone. This major cause is almost five times as prevalent as the second most costly basis of suits.

The formal complaints, however, appear to underestimate the prevalence of dual relationships. Table 7.4 (adapted from Pope & Bouhoutsos, 1986, p. 34) presents the prevalence studies conducted during the past 2 decades. The varying methods of sample selection, survey instrument construction, and so forth make comparison of the data difficult and uncertain. However, it is clear that male therapists report engaging in sexual intimacies with their clients at rates about four or five times higher than female therapists. Unadjusted for sample size, the aggregate averages from these studies are an 8.3% rate for male therapists and a 1.7% rate for female therapists.

As with other forms of sexual abuse and exploitation, such as rape, incest, and child sex abuse, the perpetrators tend to engage in this form of sexual activity with more than one individual. Holroyd and Brodsky (1977) found that 80% of those who reported sexual activity with a patient indicated that the activity was with more than one patient.

Sexual involvement with patients is not limited to adult patients. Bajt and Pope (1989) found that a significant number of instances of therapist-patient sexual intimacies involved child and adolescent patients. Slightly less than half (44%) of the patients in this study were boys of average age 12, ranging from 7 to 16. The girls had a mean age of 13, ranging from 3 to 17.

Avoiding Dual Relationships

Because a psychologist is more likely to be the object of a licensing disciplinary action, ethics complaint, or malpractice suit alleging a dual relationship than any other cause, the issue warrants great care. The following principles may be of use to psycholo-

Table 7.4. Frequency Studies of Therapist-Client Sexual Intimacy

REF. NO.	PUB. DATE	PROFESSION	LOCATION	RETURN RATE	M	F
1	1973	Psychiatrists	L.A. Cty.	46%	10.0%	n/a
2	1976	Psychiatrists	CA & NY	33%	n/a	0.0
3	1977	Psychologists	National	70%	12.1	2.6
4	1979	Psychologists	National	48%	12.0	3.0
5	1985	Social workers	National	54%	3.8	0.0
6	1986	Psychologists	National	59%	9.4	2.5
7	1986	Psychiatrists	National	26%	7.1	3.1
8	1987	Psychologists	National	46%	3.6	0.5

Reference key: 1. Kardener, Fuller, and Mensch; 2. Perry; 3. Holroyd and Brodsky; 4. Pope, Levenson, and Schover; 5. Gechtman and Bouhoutsos; 6. Pope, Keith-Spiegel, and Tabachnick; 7. Gartrell, Herman, Olarte, Feldstein, and Localio; 8. Pope, Tabachnick, and Keith-Spiegel
Note. Adapted from Pope and Bouhoutsos, 1986, p. 34.

gists in ensuring that all aspects of their work have been carefully thought through to avoid difficulties with both sexual and nonsexual dual relationships.

1. *It is always and without exception the psychologist's responsibility to avoid engaging in a dual relationship with a patient, a student, or a supervisee.* Too often, psychologists futilely try to avoid licensing, ethics, or civil sanctions by claiming, for example, that the patient initiated or at least did not object to a sexualized dual relationship (see Pope, 1990b). Such demonstrable lack of understanding does not tend to help the psychologist's case.
2. *Dual relationships can result in harm that is deep, lasting, and pervasive.* An understanding of the damage that can occur as a consequence of dual relationships may serve to make clinicians especially careful to avoid endangering those with whom they work in this way.

Perhaps the most extensive study of nonsexual dual relationships was conducted by Borys (1988), who investigated the practices of 4,800 clinicians. Her study confirmed the frequently made comparison of dual relationships to incest in terms of dynamics and consequences. The "role boundaries and norms in the therapeutic relationship, just as those in the family, serve a protective function" (Borys, 1988, p. 182).

The sequelae of sexual dual relationships in therapy tend to form a distinct syndrome, with similarities to rape response syndrome, battered spouse syndrome, reaction to incest, response to child abuse, and post-Traumatic stress disorder (PTSD). Aspects of therapist-patient sex syndrome (Pope, 1985, 1986b, 1988b) include (a)

ambivalence, (b) a sense of guilt, (c) feelings of emptiness and isolation, (d) sexual confusion, (e) impaired ability to trust, (f) identity, boundary, and role confusion, (g) emotional lability (frequently involving severe depression and acute anxiety), (h) suppressed rage, (i) substantially increased suicidal risk, and (j) cognitive dysfunction (especially in the areas of attention and concentration, frequently involving flashbacks, nightmares, intrusive thoughts, and unbidden images). Among the most frequently cited research studies of harm are those by Feldman-Summers and Jones (1984), Durre (1980), and Bouhoutsos, Holroyd, Lerman, Forer, and Greenberg (1983).

One reflection of the seriousness of the consequences is the fact that a number of states (e.g., Colorado, Minnesota, Wisconsin) have passed criminal statutes raising therapist-patient sexual relationships to the status of a felony (see Pope 1990b & 1990c).

3. *Engaging in sexual relations with a client after termination does not legitimize or make safe the exploitation of a client.* Civil courts, ethics committees, and licensing boards have all imposed sanctions on therapists who attempted to use termination as a defense to charges of improper sexual activities. The APA Ethics Committee (1988, p. 568) summarized some of the many factors that support the prohibition against sexual activity with clients after termination: (a) critical reviews and analyses of the research and theory concerning sexual intimacies after termination (Brodsky, 1988; Gabbard & Pope, 1988; Gilbert & Scher, in press); (b) professional liability suits (e.g., *Whitesell v. Green*, 1973) finding malpractice when the sexual contact was initiated only after passage of

time after termination; (c) the analysis of disciplinary actions by state psychology licensing boards and state ethics committees that found "that psychologists asserting *that* sexual relationship had occurred only after termination of the therapeutic relationship were more likely to be found in violation than those not making that claim" (Sell, Gottlieb, & Schoenfeld, 1986, p. 504); (d) the current APA malpractice coverage, which applies the cap on coverage with regard to sex with both former and current clients; (e) studies demonstrating not only that patients develop an internalized "image of their therapist but also that the vividness and use of this image after termination is correlated with measures of improvement (Geller, Cooley, & Hartley, 1981–1982); (f) studies demonstrating that even in successfully terminated therapies there tends to be "a gradual working through of unresolved transference issues with passage of time following treatment" and that the "5-10-year period following therapy" would "seem to be a critical time in the post-therapeutic development" (Buckley, Karasu, & Charles, 1981, p. 304); (g) the national studies that conclude by affirming a prohibition against any sexual activity with clients after termination (Herman, Gartrell, Olarte, Feldstein, & Localio, 1987; Sell et al., 1986); and (h) ethics texts containing clear prohibitions against sexual involvement with patients prior to or after termination, such as Dyer's (1988) summary of "the most *un*ambiguous point" that "the prohibition about sex with patients (and of course former patients since transferences endure in time) is of crucial importance" (pp. 33–34).

State legislatures appear to be providing leadership in protecting clients after termination just as they have for clients prior to termination. For example, Florida Chapter 21U-12.004 states, "For purposes of determining the existence of sexual misconduct as defined herein, the psychologist-client relationship is deemed to continue in perpetuity."

4. *Certain factors may increase or decrease the risk of a therapist becoming sexually involved with a client.* Perhaps the clearest trend emerging from the research is that engaging in a dual relationship greatly increases the probability of engaging in subsequent dual relationships. It has already been noted that about 80% of psychologists who engage in sexual dual relationships with clients do so with more than one client (see California Department of Consumer Affairs, 1990; Pope, 1990a). However, there is also research evidence that individuals who, as students, become sexually involved with faculty or staff in their graduate training programs or internships are more likely to engage, once they become therapists, in sexual intimacy with their clients (Pope, Levenson, & Schover, 1979; see also Glaser & Thorpe, 1986; Robinson & Reid, 1985). Furthermore, Borys's (1988) research has revealed that engaging in a nonsexual dual relationship is predictive, in 78% of the cases, of also engaging in sexual dual relationships with clients. Borys found "an increased risk of a therapy relationship becoming sexualized when there are nonsexual boundary violations during therapy." Thus, "[a]s with familial incest, sexual involvement between therapist and client" appears to be "the culmination of a more general breakdown in roles and relationship boundaries which begin on a non-sexual level. This link was predicted by the systems perspective, which views disparate roles and behaviors within a relationship system as interrelated. Changes in one arena are expected to affect those in other realms of behavior" (p. 182).

A lack of adequate training in the issue of sexual attraction to clients may leave therapists ill equipped to recognize, accept, and handle professionally their own erotic feelings about those whom they serve. A national study found that while most (87%) psychologists experience attraction to some of their clients, most (63%) felt "guilty, anxious, or confused" about the attraction (Pope, Keith-Spiegel, & Tabachnick, 1986). Less than 10% had had adequate training regarding this issue, and, for one out of five, the subject was so taboo that they did not ever mention their attraction to anyone else but kept it a complete secret. So inadequate is the training regarding sexual feelings about clients—whether or not acted on—that a number of apparently senior psychologists in a national study used "client welfare" as the rationale for engaging in sex with their clients (Pope & Bajt, 1988).

General administrative and supervisory responsibilities will be discussed in a later section; however, it is important to note here that anyone with administrative responsibilities who becomes aware that an employee, supervisee, or other therapist within the sphere of the administrative responsibility has attempted or engaged in sexual intimacies with a client has the following responsibilities: (a) to ensure that the client is adequately informed about the nature of therapist-client sexual intimacies and has available adequate resources for assessment, treatment, and support (see, e.g., California Department of Consumer Affairs, 1990); (b) that a careful determination be made, in the least intrusive and disruptive manner possible consistent with the clients' right to privacy, concerning whether other clients seen by the therapist have been sexually exploited; (c) that other clients not be placed at risk for abuse by the therapist; and (d) that any reporting requirements be observed. The APA Insurance Trust (1990) has noted that "the recidivism rate for sexual misconduct is substantial" (p. 3). Moreover, the executive directors for the California licensing boards for psychologists, social workers, and marriage and family counselors reviewed extensive efforts to rehabilitate perpetrators and concluded that for therapists who become sexually intimate with a patient, "prospects for rehabilitation are minimal and it is doubtful that they should be given the opportunity to ever practice psychotherapy again" (Callanan & O'Connor, 1988, p. 11).

In light of the varied issues and responsibilities in this area, clinical psychologists need to maintain awareness of the evolving research, theory, and legal standards. General reviews are provided by Gabbard (1989) and Pope (1990b & 1990c). More specific topics are addressed by Bates and Brodsky (1989), Bouhoutsos and Brodsky (1985), Chesler

(1972), Dahlberg (1971), Davidson (1977), Freeman and Roy (1976), Freud (1915/1963), Holroyd and Bouhoutsos (1985), Plaisil (1985), Sonne (1987, 1989), and Sonne, Meyer, Borys, and Marshall (1985).

5. *Dual relationships occur in a variety of forms.* Psychologists may be unaware of the great variety of dual relationships; Borys (1988), for example, provided examples of over 15 types of nonsexual dual relationships. An awareness of the diverse ways in which such relationships come about can help enable psychologists to be alert to the subtle beginnings of unethical and harmful practices. Table 7.5 provides a list of the 10 most frequent types of sexual relationships between therapists and patients.

FEES

An Explicit Fee Policy

Clients have a right to fee arrangements that are clearly set forth by the psychologist in advance of the service (APA, 1990). Practices that are routine in clinical work may surprise many patients. For example, 72% of psychologists indicate that they raise the fee during the course of therapy, and 88% charge for

Table 7.5. Ten Common Scenarios

SCENARIO	CRITERION
1. Role trading	Therapist becomes the "patient," and the wants and needs of the therapist become the focus of the treatment.
2. Sex therapy	Therapist fraudulently presents therapist-client sexual intimacy as a valid treatment for sexual or other kinds of difficulties.
3. As if . . .	Therapist treats positive transference as if it were not the result of the therapeutic situation.
4. Svengali	Therapist creates and exploits an exaggerated dependence on the part of the client.
5. Drugs	Therapist uses cocaine, alcohol, or other drugs as part of the seduction.
6. Rape	Therapist uses physical force, threats, and/or intimidation.
7. "True love"	Therapist uses rationalizations that attempt to discount the professional nature of the relationship with its attendant responsibilities and dynamics.
8. It just got out of hand	Therapist fails to treat the emotional closeness that develops in therapy with sufficient attention, care, and respect.
9. Time out	Therapist fails to acknowledge and take account of the fact that the therapeutic relationship does not cease to exist between scheduled sessions or outside the therapist's office.
10. Hold me	Therapist exploits client's desire for nonerotic physical contact and client's possible difficulties distinguishing erotic and nonerotic contact.

Note. Adapted from Pope and Bouhoutsos, 1986, p. 4.

missed appointments (Pope et al., 1987, 1988); such practices need to be spelled out to prospective patients. Pope (1988a) recommended that therapists ensure that each of the following six points are clearly understood by all patients: (a) the amount of the fee; (b) the duration of the therapy sessions; (c) when the fee is due (e.g., at each session, within 10 days of receiving a monthly bill); (d) charges for other services (e.g., phone contacts, consultation, preparing reports or other documents); (e) policies for missed or canceled sessions; and (f) what happens if the client does not or cannot pay the bill.

Billing and Collecting from Insurance Companies

The APA Ethics Committee (1988) has identified seven prohibited practices that may lead to loss of license and criminal penalties as well as ethical sanctions:

The following practices must be avoided:
(a) Billing for services that have not been rendered by the psychologist signing the form. This included signing forms for supervisees without the supervisee's cosignature. Kovacs (1987) noted that "such behavior constitutes insurance fraud, requires perjury to commit (there is a sworn statement at the bottom of the claim form), and, if done as part of a plan concocted with the knowledge and consent of the client may constitute conspiracy as well."
(b) Billing insurance carriers for missed or uncanceled sessions.
(c) Changing the date of the onset of the client's episode or of the beginning of therapy to fit third-party reimbursement criteria.
(d) Changing diagnoses to fit reimbursement criteria.
(e) Billing couple, family, or group services as individual sessions with each client.
(f) Failing to clarify provider status. If a psychological assistant, intern, or other unlicensed person is providing the service, claims submitted to third parties must clearly indicate who provided the service (rather than just listing the supervisor, which implies that the supervisor actually provided the service) *and* a title indicating the licensing status.
(g) Waiving the client's co-payments without informing a third-party source one is doing so. Kovacs (1987) noted that "recent court cases in New York and California have made it eminently clear that the insurance companies will not tolerate such practices and will bring suit—successfully." In guidelines formulated in 1983, the Ethics Committee noted that this billing practice can constitute "a violation of the Preamble to Principle 3 and Principle 3c when it causes the Insurance Carrier to pay more than the Insurance Carrier would have paid had it known the actual payment schedule or procedures." (p. 569)

Unpaid Bills

Psychologists should be aware that in some instances allowing a patient to run up a large unpaid bill has been viewed as financially exploitive and an abuse of the dependence of the patient (*Geis v. Landau*, 1983). Any lateness in paying fees should be promptly attended to by the therapist as a possible clinical issue. In some cases, of course, the financial status of the patient changes and the patient is no longer able to pay. If it is important that such a patient, although temporarily or permanently unable to pay, continue receiving services from the therapist, psychologists may wish to observe ethical principle 6d (APA, 1990), which states that psychologists perform a portion of their work pro bono.

Bartering Services for Therapy

Bartering services creates a nonsexual dual relationship, a topic discussed previously in this chapter. However, the topic is of such importance that it is worth stressing that such dual relationships are a violation of ethical, malpractice, and licensing standards. At its 1982 meeting (February 18 to 20), the APA Ethics Committee formally approved a policy statement that "bartering of personal services is a violation of Principle 6a." Their interpretation is that bartering is per se an ethical violation. Rick Imbert (personal communication, August 1988), president of the American Professional Agency (which provides professional liability coverage to APA members), notes not only that bartering is a great risk for malpractice suits but also that it is excluded from APA coverage due to both exclusion e ("disputes concerning fees") and exclusion n ("any claim arising out of a business relationship or venture with any prior or current client"). Crawford (1987) highlighted a landmark California licensing case, as a matter of public record, in which the psychologist "was suspended from practice" and otherwise sanctioned "because of a relationship in which he provided therapy in return for construction work around his home to be done by the patient" (pp. 3–4).

Contingency Fees

In certain instances, contingency fees may create an actual or apparent conflict of interest for psychologists and thus violate ethical, malpractice, or licensing standards. The standard textbooks in forensic psychology, for example, prohibit conducting forensic work for contingency fees. Shapiro (1984) wrote:

"The expert witness should never, under any circumstances, accept a referral on a contingent fee basis" (p. 95). Similarly, Blau (1984) wrote: "The psychologist should never accept a fee contingent upon the outcome of a case" (p. 336).

DOCUMENTATION

The documentation—forms for informed consent, assessments of the client's status, a written treatment plan, chart notes regarding each treatment session, and so on—are a primary and often pivotal basis on which formal complaints against psychologists are judged. Generally, juries and other deliberative bodies infer that if a procedure or intervention is not recorded, it was not performed (or, in forensic slang, "if it's not down, it's not done").

Inadequate notes showing careful attention to a client's treatment and welfare may lead to inferences of inadequate treatment. As one court stated,

> We find that said record did not conform to the standards . . . and that the inadequacies in this record militated against proper and competent psychiatric and ordinary medical care. . . . Therefore, to the extent that . . . [the chart] develops information for subsequent treatment, it contributed to the inadequate treatment this claimant received . . . in our opinion, it was so inadequate that even a layman could determine that fact. (*Whitree v. State*, 1968, p. 49)

Psychologists bear two major responsibilities in regard to their written records of clinical work. First, procedures must ensure that such records remain confidential (see principle 5c, APA, 1990). Second, psychologists must maintain records for at least 15 years unless statutes or regulations specify a longer period (see APA, 1981).

DUTIES RELATED TO SUICIDAL AND HOMICIDAL PATIENTS

Attempts to Define the Duties

Ever since 1974, when the California Supreme Court held that therapists had a duty to warn intended victims of possible violence by a patient, the nebulous and quickly evolving responsibilities concerning patients potentially violent toward self or others have been a prominent concern for many psychotherapists. Subsequent rulings in California alone have been inconsistent and frequently confusing. Two years after the original Tarasoff ruling, the Supreme Court abolished its 1974 ruling and replaced it with a duty to

protect third parties (*Tarasoff v. Regents*, 1976). A year later, an appellate court held that the Tarasoff duty did not apply to suicidal patients: "Tarasoff requires only that a therapist disclose the contents of a confidential communication where the risk to be prevented thereby is the danger of violent assault, and not where the risk of harm is self-inflicted harm or mere property damage" (*Bellah v. Greenson*, 1977, p. 95).

In 1980, the Supreme Court returned from the duty to protect back to the duty to warn and held that the duty did not exist unless the therapist could readily identify the potential victim: "Within this context and for policy reasons the duty to warn depends upon and arises from the existence of a prior threat to a specific identifiable victim" (*Thompson v. County of Alameda*, 1980, p. 739).

In 1983, the Supreme Court held that the therapist had a duty not only to an identifiable third party, but also to anyone who is likely to be near to the intended victim at the time of the attack.

> It is equally foreseeable when a therapist negligently fails to warn a mother of a patient's threat of injury to her, and she is injured as a proximate result, that her young child will not be far distant and may be injured or, upon witnessing the incident, suffer emotional trauma. Nor is it unreasonable to recognize the existence of a duty to persons in close relationship to the object of a patient's threat, for the therapist must consider the existence of such persons both in evaluating the seriousness of the danger posed by the patient and in determining the appropriate steps to be taken to protect the named victim. (*Hedlund v. Superior Court of Orange County*, 1983, p. 46)

In the same year, the U.S. Court of Appeals upheld "findings of [a California VA hospital's] malpractice [that] concerned a failure to record and communicate [a] warning by the police, the failure to secure [the patient's] prior records, and the failure to warn [the intended victim]" (*Jablonski v. U.S.*, 1983, p. 397).

The confusion, anxiety, and unpredictability generated by such decisions led, in California, to the adoption of APA's model legislation defining therapists' duties vis-à-vis potentially violent patients. In 1986, Civil Code 43.92, consisting of only two sentences, became law. The first sentence clearly limited the circumstances under which a therapist had a duty to warn or protect:

> There shall be no monetary liability on the part of, and no cause of action shall arise against, any person who is a psychotherapist . . . in failing to warn of and protect from a patient's threatened violent behavior except where the patient has communicated to the psychotherapist a serious threat of physical violence against a reasonably identifiable victim or victims.

The second sentence specified exactly how such a duty could be discharged:

> If there is a duty to warn and protect under the limited circumstances specified above, the duty shall be discharged by the psychotherapist making reasonable efforts to communicate the threat to the victim or victims and to a law enforcement agency.

It must be stressed that the legislation and case law governing duties in regard to suicidal and homicidal patients differ from state to state, and that psychologists must remain knowledgeable about the current and evolving status of these requirements within their state. Psychologists practicing in states in which fundamental issues have not been decided by the courts, or in which the case law seems in need of improvement, may wish to consider the possibility of supporting either APA's model legislation or an alternate legislative remedy.

Assessing Dangerousness toward Self or Others

Regardless of the legally imposed duties, psychologists must attempt an adequate assessment of the likelihood that their patients are at risk for suicide or homicide. Consequently, they must be aware of the factors that research has found to be associated with suicide and homicide. The following factors, for example, appear to be systematically associated with increased or decreased suicidal risk (Pope, 1986a):

- direct verbal warning
- a plan
- history of suicidal attempts
- indirect statements of intent and behavioral signs
- clinical depression
- other specific clinical syndromes
- hopelessness
- intoxication
- sex
- age
- race
- religion
- living alone
- bereavement
- unemployment
- health status
- impulsivity
- rigid thinking
- stressful life events
- release from hospitalization.

Discussions of such risk factors are also available for homicide (e.g., Beck, 1985; Monahan, 1981). However, because homicide is significantly more rare than suicide, the low base rate phenomenon becomes a major obstacle to useful or effective prediction.

> Assume that one person out of a thousand will kill. Assume also that an exceptionally accurate test is created which differentiates with 95% effectiveness those who will kill from those who will not. If 100,000 people were tested, out of the 100 who would kill, 95 would be isolated. Unfortunately, out of the 99,900 who would not kill, 4,995 people would also be isolated as potential killers. (Livermore, Malmquist, & Meehl, 1968, p. 81).

Thus, in any circumstance in which the base rate of a predicted behavior is low, assessments designed to identify those who will engage in the behavior must be undertaken with the greatest of caution and with awareness of limitations.

ADMINISTRATIVE AND SUPERVISORY DUTIES

Even psychologists who are scrupulously careful regarding their ethical, legal, and clinical responsibilities to patients may sometimes be less attentive to administrative and supervisory duties. Psychologists are often surprised to learn, on reading their policy, that the current APA professional liability coverage explicitly states that it does not apply "to wrongful acts of a managerial or administrative nature, except wrongful acts of the Insured as a member of a formal accreditation or professional review board of a hospital or professional society, or professional licensing board" (American Professional Association, 1990, p. 3).

Among the most important responsibilities of psychologists whose work has administrative or supervisory aspects are the following:

1. *Developing precise, useful, and written job descriptions that fit into an explicit description of what the unit is attempting to accomplish* (APA, 1987).
2. *Carefully screening all applicants.* Virtually any aspect of one's education, training, work experience, publication record, honors, positions held, and so forth can be favorably distorted, elliptically presented (leaving out, for instance, a training program one was forced to leave due to cheating, a job from which one was let go due to sexual exploitation of patients, a year during which one served time in jail due to possession and use of

cocaine), or completely made up. Psychologists bear a serious responsibility to avoid negligence in screening applicants. An adequate screening includes (but may not be limited to): (a) verifying an applicant's degrees, internships, employment positions, and so on; (b) obtaining at least three letters of recommendation overall and at least one letter regarding each major time period and/or educational or employment setting; (c) speaking by phone with either the authors of the recommendation letters or with others in a position to know the applicant's talents and character well; (d) obtaining adequate information about any apparent gaps in the applicant's curriculum vitae; (e) arranging interviews with the applicant; and (f) following up on any areas in which there are—or should be—doubts, questions, or concerns.

3. *Ensuring that clear procedures guide the activities on the unit and that all individuals clearly understand the procedures* (APA, 1987).

4. *Ensuring that there is adequate supervision or peer review for all individuals.* In many cases, it has become obvious in hindsight that a particular clinician in a hospital, clinic, or group practice was insufficiently supervised and that even minimal program evaluation or case monitoring could have prevented harm to clients (see Pope, 1990a).

CONCLUSION

Seen in the worst possible light, the administratively (i.e., licensing board), legislatively, and judicially imposed standards and sanctions are the frequently clumsy and sometimes misplaced attempts of external social institutions to regulate a psychology profession that frequently declines to regulate itself effectively. Yet the attempts of both psychology and external institutions to set standards are a crucial aspect of ensuring effective accountability and of minimizing the harm that clients suffer from incompetent, negligent, exploitive, or otherwise hazardous clinicians.

The myriad standards represent a consensus or at least an authoritative statement about what constitutes minimally acceptable behavior and about what abuses must be avoided no matter what the rationale. For most clinicians, the standards provide no easy answers and address only certain aspects of clinical and ethical behavior. For conscientious clinicians, they provide the context for creative thought rather than a replacement for it. They steer clinicians toward better questions and preclude certain thoughtless, careless, or exploitive approaches toward their work and toward those whom they serve.

REFERENCES

American Professional Agency. (1990). Professional Liability Policy. Amityville, NY: author.

American Psychological Association. (1981). *Specialty guidelines for the delivery of services: Clinical psychologists, counseling psychologists, industrial/organizational psychologists, school psychologists.* Washington, DC: Author.

American Psychological Association. (1986). *Guidelines for computer-based tests and interpretations.* Washington, DC: Author.

American Psychological Association. (1987). *General guidelines for providers of psychological services.* Washington, DC: Author.

American Psychological Association. (1990). Ethical principles of psychologists. *American Psychologist, 45,* 390–395.

American Psychological Association Insurance Trust. (1990). *Bulletin: Sexual misconduct and professional liability claims.* Washington, DC: author.

Bajt, T. R., & Pope, K. S. (1989). Therapist-patient sexual intimacy involving children and adolescents. *American Psychologist, 44,* 455.

Bates, C.M., & Brodsky, A.M. (1989). *Sex in the therapy hour: A case of professional incest.* New York: Guilford.

Beck, J. C. (1985). *The potentially violent patient and the Tarasoff decision in psychiatric practice.* Washington, DC: American Psychiatric Press.

Bellah v. Greenson, 73 Cal. App. 3d 892, 1977.

Blau, T. H. (1984). *The psychologist as expert witness.* New York: John Wiley & Sons.

Borys, D. S. (1988). *Dual relationships between therapist and client: A national survey of clinicians' attitudes and practices.* Unpublished doctoral dissertation, University of California, Los Angeles.

Borys, D.S., & Pope, K.S. (1989). Dual relationships between therapist and client: A national study of psychologists, psychiatrists, and social workers. *Professional Psychology: Research and Practice, 20,* 283–293.

Bouhoutsos, J., & Brodsky, A. M. (1985). Mediation in therapist-client sex: A model. *Psychotherapy, 22,* 189–193.

Bouhoutsos, J., Holroyd, J., Lerman, H., Forer, B., & Greenberg, M. (1983). Sexual intimacy between psychologists and patients. *Professional Psychology, 14,* 185–196.

Brodsky, A. M. (1988, January). *Is it ever o.k. for a therapist to have a sexual relationship with a former patient?* Paper presented at the mid-winter meeting of Division 12, San Diego, California.

Buckley, P., Karasu, T. B., & Charles, E. (1981). Psychotherapists view their personal therapy. *Psychotherapy: Theory, Research and Practice, 18,* 299–305.

California Department of Consumer Affairs. (1990). *Professional therapy never includes sex*. (Available from Board of Psychology, 1430 Howe Avenue, Sacramento, CA 95825).

Callanan, K., & O'Connor, T. (1988). *Staff comments and recommendations regarding the report of the Senate Task Force on Psychotherapist and Patients Sexual Relations*. Sacramento, CA: Board of Behavioral Science Examiners and Psychology Examining Committee.

Chesler, P. (1972). *Women and madness*. New York: Avon Books.

Crawford, W. C. (1987, August). State licensing laws and accountability. Paper presented at the annual meeting of the American Psychological Association, New York City.

Dahlberg, C. C. (1971). Sexual contact between client and therapist. *Medical Aspects of Human Sexuality, 5*, 34–56.

Davidson, V. (1977). Psychiatry's problem with no name. *American Journal of Psychoanalysis, 37*, 43–50.

Durre, L. (1980). Comparing romantic and therapeutic relationships. In K. S. Pope (Ed.), *On love and loving: Psychological perspectives on the nature and experience of romatic love* (pp. 228–243). San Francisco: Jossey-Bass.

Dyer, A. R. (1988). *Ethics and psychiatry*. Washington, DC: American Psychiatric Press.

Ethics Committee of the American Psychological Association. (1988). Trends in ethics cases, common pitfalls, and published resources. *American Psychologist, 43*, 564–572.

Feldman-Summers, S., & Jones, G. (1984). Psychological impacts of sexual contact between therapists or other health care practitioners and their clients. *Journal of Consulting and Clinical Psychology, 52*, 1054–1061.

Fowler, R. (1988, August). Discussion of symposium on *Doing valid and useful clinical assessments* presented at the annual meeting of the American Psychological Association, Atlanta.

Freeman, L., & Roy, J. (1976). *Betrayal*. New York: Stein and Day.

Freud, S. (1963). Further recommendations in the technique of psychoanalysis: Observations on transference-love. In P. Rieff (Ed.), *Freud: Therapy and technique* (pp. 167–180). New York: Collier Books (Original work published 1915).

Gabbard, G. O. (Ed.) (1989). *Sexual exploitation in professional relationships*. Washington, DC: American Psychiatric Press.

Gabbard, G. O., & Pope, K. S. (1988). Sexual intimacies after termination: Clinical, ethical and legal aspects. *Independent Practitioner, 8*, 21–26.

Gartrell, N., Herman, J., Olarte, S., Feldstein, M., & Localio, R. (1986). Psychiatrist-patient sexual contact: Results of a national survey, I: Prevalence. *American Journal of Psychiatry, 143*, 1126–1131.

Gechtman, L., & Bouhoutsos, J. (1985, October). *Sexual intimacy between social workers and clients*. Paper presented at the annual meeting of the Society for Clinical Social Workers, Universal City, California.

Geis v. Landau, N.Y. City Civil Court, N.Y.S. 2d 1000, 1983.

Geller, J. D., Cooley, R. S., & Hartley, D. (1981–1982). Images of the psychotherapist: A theoretical and methodological perspective. *Imagination, Cognition, and Personality, 1*, 123–146.

Gilbert, L. A., & Scher, M. (in press). The power of an unconscious belief. *Professional Practice of Psychology*.

Glaser, R. D., & Thorpe, J. S. (1986). Unethical intimacy: A survey of sexual contact and advances between psychology educators and female graduate students. *American Psychologist, 41*, 43–51.

Hedlund v. Superior Court of Orange County, 669 P. 2d 41 (Cal. 1983).

Herman, J. L., Gartrell, N., Olarte, S., Feldstein, M., & Localio, R. (1987). Psychiatrist-patient sexual contact: Results of a national survey, II. Psychiatrists' attitudes. *American Journal of Psychiatry, 144*, 164–169.

Holroyd, J. C., & Bouhoutsos, J. (1985). Sources of bias in reporting effects of sexual contact with patients. *Psychotherapy: Research and Practice, 16*, 701–709.

Holroyd, J. C., & Brodsky, A. M. (1977). Psychologists' attitudes and practices regarding erotic and nonerotic physical contact with patients. *American Psychologist, 32*, 843–849.

Jablonski v. United States, 712 F. 2d 391 (1983).

Kardener, S. H., Fuller, M., & Mensch, I. N. (1973). A survey of physicians' attitudes and practices regarding erotic and nonerotic contact with patients. *American Journal of Psychiatry, 130*, 1077–1081.

Kovacs, A. L. (1987). Insurance billing: The growing risks of lawsuits against psychologists. *Independent Practitioner, 7*, 21–24.

Livermore, J., Malmquist, C., & Meehl, P. (1968). On the justifications for civil commitment. *University of Pennsylvania Law Review, 117*, 75–96.

Monahan, J. (1981). *Predicting violent behavior: An assessment of clinical techniques*. Beverly Hills: Sage Library of Social Research.

Perry, J. A. (1976). Physicians' erotic and nonerotic involvement with patients. *American Journal of Psychiatry, 133*, 838–840.

Plaisil, E. (1985). *Therapist*. New York: St. Martin's.

Pope, K. S. (1985, August). *Diagnosis and treatment of therapist-patient sex syndrome*. Paper presented at the annual meeting of the American Psychological Association, Los Angeles.

Pope, K. S. (1986a) Assessment and management of suicidal risk. *Independent Practitioner, 6*, 17–23.

Pope, K. S. (1986b, May). *Therapist-patient sex syndrome: Research findings*. Paper presented at the annual meeting of the American Psychiatric Association, Washington, DC.

Pope, K. S. (1987). Preventing therapist-patient sexual

intimacy: Therapy for a therapist at risk. *Professional Psychology: Research and Practice, 18,* 624–628.

Pope, K. S. (1988a). Fee policies and procedures: Causes of malpractice suits and ethics complaints. *Independent Practitioner, 8,* 24–29.

Pope, K. S. (1988b). How clients are harmed by sexual contact with mental health professionals: The syndrome and its prevalence. *Journal of Counseling and Development, 67,* 222–226.

Pope, K. S. (1989). Malpractice suits, licensing actions, and ethics cases: Frequencies, causes, and costs. *Independent Practitioner, 9,* 22–26.

Pope, K. S. (1990a). Ethical and malpractice issues in hospital practice. *American Psychologist, 45,* 1066–1070.

Pope, K. S. (1990b). Therapist-patient sex as sex abuse: Six scientific, professional, and practical dilemmas in addressing victimization and rehabilitation. *Professional Psychology: Research and Practice, 21,* 227–239.

Pope, K. S. (1990c). Therapist-patient sexual involvement: A review of the research. *Clinical Psychology Review, 10,* 477–490.

Pope, K. S., & Bajt, T. R. (1988). When laws and values conflict: A dilemma for psychologists. *American Psychologist, 43,* 828–829.

Pope, K. S., & Bouhoutsos, J. C. (1986). *Sexual intimacy between therapists and patients.* New York: Praeger.

Pope, K. S., Keith-Spiegel, P., & Tabachnick, B. G. (1986). Sexual attraction to clients: The human therapist and the (sometimes) inhuman training system. *American Psychologist, 41,* 147–158.

Pope, K. S., Levenson, H., & Schover, L. S. (1979). Sexual intimacy in psychology training: Results and implications of a national survey. *American Psychologist, 34,* 682–689.

Pope, K. S., Tabachnick, B. G., & Keith-Spiegel, P. (1987). Ethics of practice: The beliefs and behaviors of psychologists as therapists. *American Psychologist, 42,* 993–1006.

Pope, K. S., Tabachnick, B. G., & Keith-Spiegel, P. (1988). Good and poor practices in psychotherapy: A national survey of the beliefs of psychologists. *Professional Psychology: Research and Practice, 19,* 547–552.

Redlich, F. C., & Pope, K. S. (1980). Ethics of mental health training. *Journal of Nervous and Mental Disease, 168,* 709–714.

Robinson, W. L., & Reid, P. T. (1985). Sexual intimacies in psychology revisited. *Professional Psychology, 16,* 512–520.

Sell, J. M., Gottlieb, M. C., & Schoenfeld, L. (1986). Ethical considerations of social/romantic relationships with present and former clients. *Professional Psychology: Research and Practice, 17,* 504–508.

Shapiro, D. L. (1984). *Psychological evaluation and expert testimony: A practical guide to forensic work.* New York: Van Nostrand Reinhold.

Simon, G. C. (1978). The psychologist as whistle-blower: A case study. *Professional Psychology, 9,* 322–340.

Sonne, J. L. (1987). Therapist/patient sexual intimacy: Understanding and counseling the patient. *Medical Aspects of Human Sexuality, 11,* 18–23.

Sonne, J. L. (1989). An example of group therapy for victims of therapist-client sexual intimacy. In G.O. Gabbard (Ed.), *Sexual exploitation in professional relationships* (pp. 101–127). Washington, DC: American Psychiatric Press.

Sonne, J., Meyer, C. B., Borys, D., & Marshall, V. (1985). Clients' reactions to sexual intimacy in therapy. *American Journal of Orthopsychiatry, 55,* 183–189.

Standards for educational and psychological testing. (1985). Washington, DC: APA.

Tarasoff v. Regents for the University of California, 551 P. 2d 334 at 347 (Sup. Ct. Cal. 1976).

Thompson v. County of Alameda, 614 Pacific Reporter, 2d Series, 728 (1980).

Walker, E., & Young, T. D. (1986). *A killing cure.* New York: Holt, Rinehart & Winston.

Weiner, I. (1988, August). *Can psychology do what we think it can?* Paper presented at the annual meeting of the American Psychological Association, Atlanta.

Whitesell v. Green, Hawaii District Court, Honolulu Docket No. 38745, November 19, 1973.

Whitree v. State, 290 N.Y.S. 2nd 486 (Ct. Cal. 1968).

CHAPTER 8

CLINICAL PSYCHOLOGY AND THE POLITICAL SCENE

Patrick H. DeLeon
Gary R. VandenBos
Michael R. Pollard
Andrea L. Solarz
Richard B. Weinberg

Applied clinical psychology has evolved from a relatively small psychological testing specialty to one of the major health care professions during the last 45 years. This evolution has been accelerating in recent years. Recognition of the profession of psychology has been achieved through an unprecedented growth of qualified scientists and practitioners; through an increasing orientation to policy by the national organization, the American Psychological Association (APA); and through educational efforts of universities to develop interest in the political process.

During the 1970s and 1980s, psychologists increasingly have been recognized as fully legitimate scientists and bona fide health care practitioners by the public, by the country's policy makers, and under federal regulations written by the Executive Branch. A review of the recent federal legislative accomplishments demonstrates continued expansion into a wide range of areas (DeLeon, Forsythe, & VandenBos, 1986; DeLeon, VandenBos, & Kraut, 1984; DeLeon, VandenBos, & Kraut, 1986).

As the field of psychology has matured and as significant numbers of graduates are trained, psychology is faced with new societal responsibilities and

clinical opportunities (DeLeon, 1986a, 1988). The policy initiatives taken by organized psychology to advance science and the profession must be done in a manner that addresses and solves pressing national problems.

In this chapter, we briefly trace the increasing public recognition of modern clinical psychology over the last 45 years and the beginnings of public policy involvement by psychologists. We then discuss the current status of clinical psychology and its federal legislative accomplishments in professional practice, recognition of the profession by the judicial system and the courts, and inclusion of psychology in federal health training initiatives. Because the public policy process is never ending and ever changing, psychologists must be continually aware of developments in the political arena—in the structure, concerns, and interests of the nation's legislature. Thus, we examine the structure and composition of Congress and its staff, what roles psychologists can play in the public policy process, and how best psychologists can train for such roles. We conclude with a case study of the Federal Trade Commission (FTC), as a regulatory agency whose efforts have opened some markets for clinical psychology and other health care services.

Historical Beginnings of Public Policy Involvement by Psychologists

Development of modern clinical psychology over the last 45 years—including establishment of a training model and a system for accrediting standardized training, achieving recognition of professional practice through licensure or certification, and working toward economic recognition by third party insurance carriers and government agencies—is essentially a case study of one profession's struggle for professional autonomy and recognition (Cummings, 1979; Cummings & VandenBos, 1983).

Psychology was primarily an academically based discipline before World War II, engaged in university teaching and research to understand basic human behavior, function, and experience. In the 1940s, the military played a significant role in stimulating the growth of clinical psychology. In the 1950s, the beginning of much legal recognition of professional psychologists was undertaken.

In the late 1950s, the National Clinical Liaison Committee, a group of psychologists primarily from New York, circulated material warning clinical psychologists that psychotherapy in the United States soon would be financed by third party payment, and that if psychology were not recognized as a primary mental health provider by the government and by insurance carriers, the profession would suffer economic extinction.

By the 1960s, professional psychologists worked forcefully on a range of health insurance reimbursement issues, particularly on freedom-of-choice legislation. However, much of this involvement in public policy included random opportunities, piecemeal efforts, or local initiatives of a few concerned practitioners rather than a nationally organized endeavor.

Efforts to move the APA into an active policy role were largely unsuccessful from the late 1950s through the early 1970s. Because of APA's unresponsiveness, a small group of psychologists created the Council for the Advancement of the Psychological Professions and Sciences (CAPPS) in 1970. This organization became a self-sustained organization, but it soon became embroiled in APA internal politics. It was CAPPS's successor, the Association for the Advancement of Psychology (AAP), formed in 1974, that finally realized CAPPS's goal to move organized psychology more clearly into the arena of public policy.

During the 1970s, professional psychologists consolidated many of their early legislative initiatives: universal state-level licensure and certification, large-scale adoption of freedom-of-choice legislation, and extensive federal recognition (Cummings & VandenBos, 1983). By the late 1970s, increasing numbers of psychologists were becoming aware of the important role that state legislation played in the recognition and practice of health professions. It also became clear that it would become increasingly important for significant interaction to occur between the various state psychological associations and the APA. In 1977, the APA State Associations Program was founded within the APA Office of Professional Affairs as a means to provide a focal point for state associations to use the resources and expertise of the APA Central Office (Ginsberg, Kilburg, & Buklad, 1983). In 1979, a staff member was added who could travel to the states to aid in the development of the organization and operation of state associations.

In 1985, professional psychologists realized that they needed a more sophisticated network for exchanging information on policy efforts. A resolution was introduced before APA's Council of Representatives expressing the need for APA to give proactive leadership to state advocacy organizations, and a special assessment for all licensed psychologists to receive income from practice was authorized. This special assessment gave professional psychologists the economic resources to build a professional staff and a nationwide technological network. In 1987, the APA Practice Directorate was established, and shortly thereafter the state association office was expanded to better assist in the organization of state programs and policy agendas (Welch, 1989).

In the last 2 decades, clinical psychology accomplished a number of legislative objectives that put the profession in a good position to significantly influence our nation's health care and social policies.

STATUS AND RECOGNITION OF CLINICAL PSYCHOLOGY

Practice Accomplishments in the Legislature

The sine qua non of an autonomous profession is its scope of practice act. To those who establish our nation's health policies and priorities (that is, to our elected and appointed public officials), licensure is one of the critical aspects for the recognition of a profession. It is our nation's legislatures (both state and federal) that ultimately determine the appropriate scope of practice for any profession. In 1945, Connecticut became the first state in the nation to recognize psychology formally (DeLeon, Donahue, & VandenBos, 1984). Some 3 decades later, in 1977, when the state of Missouri enacted its practice act, psychologists finally became statutorily recognized as independent providers in every state in the nation (Cummings & VandenBos, 1983).

Psychology's federal legislative accomplishments over the past 2 decades illustrate the evolving nature of the field. Without question, psychology has made major advances at the federal level.

The Internal Revenue Service (IRS) clarified the personal federal income tax instructions, in 1973, to indicate expressly that the services of psychologists may qualify under the medical expenses deduction provision of the Internal Revenue Code (26 U.S.C. Sections 162 and 213).

A federal freedom-of-choice provision was enacted—Public Law (PL) 93-363—in 1974, which legislatively ensured that when mental health services were made available to the approximately 9 million federal employees, annuitants, and their dependents who participate in the Federal Employee Health Benefit Program (FEHBP), they would have a statutory right to select a psychologist, rather than a psychiatrist, if they so desired. This freedom-of-choice success at the federal level has now been emulated at the state level in 42 states, which represent approximately 94.7% of the U.S. population.

CHAMPUS

During the mid-1970s, psychology made significant progress in obtaining administrative and legislative inclusion as autonomous providers under the Department of Defense's Civilian Health and Medical Program of the Uniformed Services (CHAMPUS) initiative. The history of this success had at least two parallel, but essentially independent, components. Several leaders within professional psychology (in particular, Charles A. Thomas, Gene Shapiro, John McMillan, and Jack Wiggins) began negotiations with the Pentagon about the possibility of having psychology administratively recognized as independent providers under CHAMPUS. About the same time, the Senate Appropriations Committee began including similar directives in its annual report to the Department, including adoption of formal legislative language during its deliberations on the Fiscal Year 1976 Appropriations bill (PL 94-212). During the latter years of the 1970s, it was necessary for the Senate Appropriations Committee to reiterate its strong support for psychology's autonomous recognition. However, over time, psychology has come to be routinely included in all CHAMPUS initiatives, including inpatient, outpatient, residential treatment, and partial hospitalization care.

Medicare and Medicaid

Medicare and Medicaid were enacted into public law in 1965. Medicare is a nationwide health insurance entitlement program that covers health care for the nation's elderly and disabled. It offers uniform benefits nationwide and is composed of two separate programs. Part A consists of a program of mandatory hospitalization and extended care insurance and is 100% federally financed. Part B, Supplemental Medical Insurance, covers physician's services and other related services independent of hospital care, and while Part B is voluntary, nearly 96% of the eligible population participates. It is financed by a combination of federal payments and participant premiums.

Medicaid is a medical assistance program that is targeted to needy and low-income persons. It is state operated and state administered, with each individual state having broad discretion to develop its own programmatic priorities. The federal government pays approximately 56% of the costs of the Medicaid program. Historically, it has been Medicaid (and not Medicare) that has been the major source of financial support for our nation's nursing homes.

Medicare and Medicaid combined account for nearly 90% of the federal government's health care expenditures, and the implementing regulations promulgated by the Health Care Financing Administration (HCFA) have a major impact on the standards adopted by all segments of our nation's health delivery system, both public and private, including staffing and administrative requirements (Uyeda, DeLeon, Perloff, & Kraut, 1986).

From its inception, Congress and the Administration have made clear their intention that Medicare and Medicaid were to be health—not social—welfare programs. Accordingly, there has traditionally been a deliberate medical orientation, as demonstrated by the statutory requirement that only medically necessary services were to be provided. Further, the Senate report accompanying the original Social Security Amendments of 1965 (PL 89-97) expressly stated that "the committee's bill provides that the physician is to be the key figure in determining utilization of health services" (Sen. Rpt. 89-404). When the Department of Health, Education, and Welfare (DHEW, now the Department of Health and Human Services) issued its congressionally mandated recommendations on the proposed status of psychology and other types of nonphysician health care providers (PL 90-248), it made clear that, in its judgment, psychological services were to be reimbursed only when provided in an organized setting and when there had been physician referral and physician establishment of a plan for the patient's total care, including overall medical responsibility for patient management (Cohen, 1968).

Psychology achieved its initial statutory recognition under Medicare in 1972, when the Secretary of DHEW authorized to determine "whether the services of clinical psychologists may be made more generally available to persons eligible . . . in a manner consistent with quality of care and equitable and efficient administration" (PL 92-603). This legislation eventually led to the formal hearings before the Senate Finance Committee in August, 1978 (Government Printing Office [GPO], 1978) and to the Colorado Medicare Study (Bent, Willens, & Lassen, 1983; Inouye, 1983).

The first significant Medicare success directly benefitting psychology was inclusion of language in the Deficit Reduction Act of 1984 (PL 98-369) that authorized coverage for psychologists as autonomous providers under the risk-sharing health maintenance organization (HMO) provisions of the Act. By definition, this proposal could not result in increased costs to the government, and it was viewed as merely providing greater administrative flexibility to HMOs, similar to that provided for their utilizing nurse practitioners in 1982. Soon thereafter, the Social Security Disability Benefits Reform Act of 1984 (PL 98-460) contained similar statutory language, this time authorizing "qualified psychologists" to evaluate mental impairments for purposes of determining whether a beneficiary should be eligible for disability benefits and also including "psychological abnormalities" as a bona fide case of pain.

During the congressional deliberations on the Omnibus Budget Reconciliation Act of 1987 (PL 100-203), psychology also obtained recognition under both the Rural Health Clinic provisions of Medicare and Medicaid, as well as under an APA Practice Directorate proposed initiative that established a new Part B Community Mental Health Center provision of the law. After the Health Care Financing Administration (HCFA) and the American Psychiatric Association objected to psychology being reimbursed at off-site community mental health center locations, a subsequent technical amendment package specifically authorized such payment (PL 100-647).

Psychologists became recognized under Part A of the Act as a provision of the Omnibus Budget Reconciliation Act of 1987 (PL 100-203). Part A pays for inpatient hospital costs—but inpatient professional services (such as those a physician or psychologist might provide) are to be reimbursed under Part B. However, the key to ultimate independent recognition under Medicare has always been to be included under Part B (physician's services) of the Act, which provides for the reimbursement of the type of professional services that psychologists provide. During the closing hours of the first session of the 101st Congress, psychology was finally successful in obtaining direct reimbursement under Part B of Medicare (Welch, 1990), as a provision of the Omnibus Budget Reconciliation Act of 1989 (PL 101-239).

Even with the major success in the 101st Congress, it is still necessary for psychology to continue working closely with members of the congressional committees having jurisdiction over the Social Security Act to ensure that the profession becomes statutorily recognized under the other relevant programs of Medicare and Medicaid. Organized medicine's attempts to have the federal government mandate direct physician involvement (i.e., supervision or referral) in services being rendered by nonphysician health care providers has received little support during the 1980s. For the past several legislative sessions, the medical community had been steadily moving toward requesting the more generic and diffuse phrase "in collaboration with a physician" to continue legislative support of their proffered unique medical expertise. This requirement did not previously exist for any of the other nonphysician providers (other than clinical nursing). It may be deleted over the next several years, based on the policy argument that this is an area historically deemed as a state scope of practice responsibility, but not one appropriately determined by the federal government.

There is further legislative work to do with Medicare and Medicaid to assure full access to psychological services. Psychology will probably not be deemed currently eligible for reimbursement under the Hospice program, Rehabilitation program, Medical Educational initiative, or the newly authorized Rural Health Medication Education demonstration projects. Similarly, it will also be necessary to address the various administrative restrictions still contained within Medicare (e.g., the present prohibition on psychologists being appointed medical directors of state mental institutions, requirements of the Hospital Conditions of Participation that mandate physician involvement in the care of Medicare and Medicaid inpatients, and the effective prohibition on use of the diagnostic skills of psychologists by skilled nursing homes).

Judicial Accomplishments in the Legislature and Courts

Psychology succeeded in the 1980s to modify through legislation every relevant federal criminal justice statute. Those sections of the federal criminal codes that address the issue of mental competence were specifically amended in order to ensure that psychology's diagnostic and treatment expertise was appropriately recognized. Prior to 1982, only physicians were recognized under federal law (and the implementing court rules) as possessing diagnostic, evaluative, and treatment competence. With enactment of President Reagan's Comprehensive Crime Control Acts of 1982 and 1984 (PL 98-473), psychologists were recognized as fully qualified to provide diagnostic and treatment functions for federal courts. Although the federal judicial rules are not binding on the various state courts, there can be little question that they have major precedent value—judicially, legislatively, and in the education of the next generation of lawyers.

The legal procedures within the military have been modified recently to recognize psychology more fully. In March 1987, President Reagan issued Executive Order 12586, which modified the Department of Defense (DOD) Manual for Court-Martial to ensure that psychological expertise would be appropriately utilized. Following up on this directive, psychology was also successful in having all other relevant military regulations appropriately modified, such as ensuring that psychologists can serve on boards that determine whether an individual is considered mentally incapable of managing his or her own affairs.

Other enacted legislation provided psychology with appropriate stature under the Federal Rules of Civil Procedure (PL 100-690), notwithstanding organized psychiatry's vocal objection. Psychology was able to elicit positive policy positions regarding its expertise from the American Bar Association, the National Conference of Commissioners on Uniform State Laws, and the Committee on Rules of Practice and Procedure of the Judical Conference of the United States (DeLeon & Donahue, 1983; DeLeon, Donahue, & VandenBos, 1984).

The policy concepts inherent in freedom-of-choice statutes were the basis of the landmark *Virginia Blues* case (Dorken & DeLeon, 1986; Enright, Resnick, DeLeon, Sciara, & Tanney, in press; Overcast, Sales, & Pollard, 1982). This litigation, which began in the late 1970s, went directly to the underlying policy issue of whether the courts, for public health reasons, should find a "quality of care" basis for requiring psychology's practitioners to be supervised or overseen by members of the medical profession. The eventual favorable holding for psychology by the federal court of appeals also expressly noted that "psychologists and psychiatrists do compete" (Bersoff, 1983, p. 1239). This particular judicial finding was a significant factor in the Joint Commission on Accreditation of Hospitals' (now the Joint Commission on Accreditation of Healthcare Organizations) subsequent decision to modify its standards in order to provide individual hospitals with the flexibility to permit nonphysician staff membership, when expressly authorized by relevant state statutes (Zaro, Batchelor, Ginsberg, & Pallak, 1982).

Educational Accomplishments in the Legislature

Psychology has historically relied almost exclusively on the National Institute of Mental Health (NIMH) and the Veterans Administration (VA) for its clinical training support. However, the U.S. Public Health Service Act's Title VII (health professions) legislation has been the primary forum since the early 1960s for the federal government's health training initiatives for the professions of medicine, osteopathy, dentistry, veterinary medicine, optometry, podiatry, pharmacy, and public health (MODVOPPP).

The clinical training resources available within Medicare and Medicaid far surpass that available to psychology under the auspices of NIMH. For example, in Fiscal Year 1989 psychology obtained approximately $2 million of the NIMH's clinical training account. Yet, at the same time (in January, 1989), the General Accounting Office (GAO) released a report entitled *Medicare: Indirect Medical Education Payments Are Too High,* which reported that, in 1986, the additional payments to teaching hospitals for compensation for higher patient care costs associated with providing graduate medical education were approximately $2.1 billion—of which $1 billion was for direct medical education costs. The report further described "direct medical education costs" as consisting of "salaries and fringe benefits for residents and teaching physicians, the cost of conference and classroom space, the cost of additional equipment and supplies, and allocated overhead costs" (GAO, 1989,

p. 11). If psychology is going to function as a bona fide health care profession, psychology training programs must seek eligibility for their fair share of this $2.1 billion in training resources.

In the late 1970s psychology was included under the MODVOPPP project grant authority, and the 1979 Departmental Allied Health Personnel Report to Congress contained a specific section on clinical psychology. During the 1980s, psychology steadily obtained recognition under an ever-widening range of the Title VII programs—including the health professions data collection section, eligibility for the Individual Federal Insured Loan Program (or the Health Assistance Loan [HEAL] Program), and the National Health Service Corps Scholarship program. Psychologists are now authorized to serve in the U.S. Public Health Service Regular Corps, which is the sole statutory requirement for being appointed by the President to the position of Surgeon General of the United States. Psychology is recognized under the Indian Education Act Fellowship provisions and the Health Careers Opportunity Program (Educational Assistance to Individuals from Disadvantaged Backgrounds).

During the 100th Congress, the Health Omnibus Programs Extension Act of 1988 (PL 100-607) provided a major opportunity for psychology's educational establishment to appreciate the importance of Title VII by expanding the composition of the National Advisory Council on Health Professions Education to mandate that a psychologist be appointed (Buie, 1989). The same statute also completed the process of legislatively removing psychology from the statutory designation of allied health, and enumerated psychology as one of the MODVOPPP professions. In fact, with the sole exception of the Health Professions Student Loan (HPSL) Program—and legislation did pass the U.S. Senate during a previous Congress to provide psychology with this eligibility—psychology is now eligible for every major Title VII initiative.

Public Law 100-607 also included a provision that represents an entirely new frontier for psychology—one that emphasizes the importance of interdisciplinary cooperation and the active policy involvement of psychology's training institutions (DeLeon, Wakefield, Schultz, Williams, & VandenBos, 1989). This legislation provides authority for an annual appropriation of $5 million for innovative health professions and service delivery projects for rural America. This interdisciplinary rural health initiative provides significant economic incentives and administrative flexibility to address creatively the health care needs of rural America. It is intended to be interdisciplinary and nonphysician oriented; a major priority is behavioral science expertise and prevention. International health offers another arena in which psychology could play a major role in conceptualizing and implementing interdisciplinary behavioral health programming (Raymond, DeLeon, VandenBos, & Michael, in press).

Few psychology departments have sought jointly funded positions or actual clinical control over treatment facilities. This should receive greater legislative attention from organized psychology soon, if for no other reason than these administrative positions do, in fact, set day-to-day health policies within the various state and federal agencies. A provision contained within the Omnibus Budget Reconciliation Act of 1989 (PL 101-239) modified the Social Security Act to allow dentists to serve as medical directors of hospitals, if permitted under state law. It is not a major policy leap to expect that psychologists should similarly be authorized to serve as medical directors of state institutions.

Psychology has been somewhat slow to work for special recognition of the educational status of its members working in the public sector. Most psychologists are not aware of the extent to which the medical profession has been successful in legislatively recognizing the educational credentials of its public sector members. For example, with enactment of the 1990 Department of Defense Reauthorization Act (PL 101-189), individual military physicians will be eligible for annual incentive pay bonuses up to $59,000, in addition to their basic salary. During the late 1980s, federal legislation was enacted providing authority for special pay bonuses for psychologists who have obtained their board certification (diplomates) from the American Board of Professional Psychology (ABPP). The first provision enacted was for VA psychologists in 1984 (PL 98-528), but this has not yet been implemented. Later provisions for providing bonuses for psychologists within the U.S. Public Health Service (PL 100-140) and the Department of Defense (PL 101-189) have met with less administrative resistance. The actual psychology bonus ranges from $2,000 to $5,000 annually, based on years of federal experience.

Developments such as the aforementioned related to the educational arena can be viewed, from a public policy frame of reference, as reflecting a developing view among our nation's health policy experts that professional psychology represents something qualitatively more than merely a mental health specialty (and in particular, more than junior psychiatrists). However, how much more has yet to be determined

(Fox, Kovacs, & Graham, 1985; Rodgers, 1980). But there are growing signs that this evolution is occurring. For example, in late 1989, after more than a decade of urging by the Senate Appropriations Committee, the Health Resources and Services Administration (HRSA) announced that it would no longer collect information solely on "psychiatric shortage areas." It would instead begin to seek information on more generic "mental health manpower shortage areas." In announcing this policy modification in the *Federal Register* (August 8, 1989), HRSA stated:

> The research reviewed . . . indicates that, despite their significant differences, the four core mental health service provider types often perform similar roles, especially in the provision of verbal psychotherapy and the treatment of less severe conditions. The research . . . also suggests that the different disciplines make similar diagnoses and have similar therapeutic results. (p. 32,461)

As clinical psychology has matured, and as its knowledge base and clinical expertise have expanded, psychology must become more intimately involved in the public policy and political process.

THE POLITICAL PROCESS

Structure and Composition of Federal Legislature and Staff

Much of the actual federal decision making that affects psychology nationwide occurs in the U.S. Congress, and it occurs in committees and subcommittees so numerous that almost all members of Congress are in a position to influence laws related to psychology.

Our nation's legislatures are organized on a committee basis, with individual members actively seeking appointment to those committees that have jurisdiction over subject matters that either hold considerable personal interest to them, or significant interest to perceived critical constituents (DeLeon, 1983). Under the committee system, it is difficult for an elected official to modify significantly the course of legislation if he or she does not serve on the committee with relevant jurisdiction. But for an area as diverse and complex as health care, which represents the third largest industry in our nation, one soon finds that there are many legislative targets of opportunity (DeLeon, 1983; Dorken, 1981).

For example, if one considers the Senate committees that have jurisdiction over our nation's health delivery system, the committees on appropriations,

budget, finance, and labor and human resources readily come to mind. The Committee on Governmental Affairs has jurisdiction over the Federal Employees Health Benefit Program (FEHBP), as well as the conditions of employment for many federal psychologists. The Committee on Armed Services has jurisdiction over the Department of Defense health care initiatives (including CHAMPUS); the Committee on Commerce, Science, and Transportation has jurisdiction over the FTC, not to mention elements of the insurance industry. The Committee on Foreign Relations has jurisdiction over our international health activities, such as those of the Agency for International Development (AID); the Committee on Small Business has potential jurisdiction over almost every aspect of the health delivery system; and the Committee on Veterans Affairs, the Select Committee on Indian Affairs, and the Special Committee on Aging have major legislative and public policy responsibilities for their unique beneficiary populations. Further, the Committee on Agriculture, Nutrition, and Forestry continues to present a formidable claim over all programs (including health care) affecting the 56 million Americans residing in rural America. Each of the 13 subcommittees of the Senate Appropriations Committee have traditionally acted independently of the parent full Committee, not to mention the aforementioned various authorization committees.

It is unreasonable, however, for psychologists to assume that their elected officials possess an in-depth knowledge of, or appreciation for, the intricacies of health and mental health care delivery. If one looks at the composition of the Congress of the United States, it is evident that those policy makers with personal health care backgrounds are in the minority. For example, during the 101st Congress (1989 to 1990), only one member of the U.S. Senate could be considered a health care professional, and she was a clinical social worker. By contrast, 67 of her colleagues in the Senate possessed law degrees. Similar statistics exist for the composition of the House of Representatives—where there were one dentist, one optometrist, one pharmacist, and two physicians.

Capitol Hill staff are also not generally health professionals. Less than 1% of congressional staff are scientists (Scribner, 1978). Of the staff assigned to health care issues, Grupenhoff (1983) reported that most were relatively young (60% were under the age of 29; 96% were under the age of 40) and had nonspecialized college training. A review of the Senate telephone directory for the 101st Congress revealed that, out of a total of approximately 5,650 staff named, only six were physicians—two of whom were clearly engaged exclusively in the delivery of clinical services. Only 2% of congressional staff are generally found to have formal training in any of the health professions, with only 11 individuals possessing doctorate degrees. Further, the turnover rate of these professional staff was high—40% had worked less than 2 years in Congress, and 79% had worked 5 years or less.

As we have emphasized in this chapter, enhanced autonomy, recognition, and respect for the profession are accompanied by increasing obligations and responsibilities. A broader perspective on social issues, coupled with more organized efforts in influencing public policy, are essential for clinical psychology to affect our increasingly specialized and politicized society. Psychologists must be adequately trained to develop better awareness, understanding, and appreciation of the political process.

Becoming a Profession Capable of Influencing Policy

Psychologists, by virtue of their interests and education, possess a unique expertise in understanding human behavior that is combined with an emphasis on scientific rigor, verifiable knowledge, and an awareness of social and cultural relativism. Psychologists can therefore synthesize information about human behavior to provide a complete consideration of alternative policies. Unfortunately, due to their unfamiliarity with the policy process, the technical skills and perspectives of psychologists have not been effectively utilized in developing solutions to our social problems.

A profession must possess a critical mass of members before it can fully participate in the political process and influence public policy. There were, in 1976, approximately 25,000 doctoral-level health care psychologists and 26,000 psychiatrists (Dorken & Whiting, 1976). By mid-1985, there were 45,536 licensed psychologists (Dorken, Stapp, & Vanden-Bos, 1986). It is estimated that, in 1990, there are approximately 56,000 licensed psychologists in the United States. Thus, there are more psychological practitioners than those in optometry, podiatry, clinical nursing (i.e., pediatric nurse practitioners and certified nurse midwives), or psychiatry.

Psychologists are also more effectively organized to influence public policy than ever before. The APA, the largest scientific and professional organization representing psychology in the United States, provides outstanding educational information and policy analyses to Congress. Psychology departments and professional schools have begun to offer specialized training programs to encourage public policy involvement. Several graduate training programs in community psychology and applied social psychology also actively encourage research and action directly related to public policy matters (Serrano-Garcia, 1983). Participation of the APA in the American Association for the Advancement of Science (AAAS) Congressional Science Fellow Program provides excellent training for psychologists to be directly involved in legislative policy making.

However, psychology is a relative newcomer to the ranks of professions involved systematically in policy issues. The potential for psychology's contribution to a broad range of national issues is great. Psychologists must work vigilantly to ensure that the potential contribution is better understood and recognized by federal policy makers. Psychologists must become acquainted with our nation's policy leadership and must become more active in the political process at all levels (DeLeon, O'Keefe, VandenBos, & Kraut, 1982).

Roles Psychologists Can Play in the Public Policy Process

The APA's Task Force on Psychology and Public Policy (1986), for purposes of sensitizing the profession, has outlined the stages of the public policy process and has identified ways by which psychologists can exert their influence at each stage. There are five stages that remain similar, whether the process is conceptualized from a top-down or a bottom-up perspective. In practice, these stages do not always occur in an orderly sequence; they tend to be complex and are characterized by numerous feedback loops. If psychologists are to have more impact on public policy, they must bring their skills to bear at each stage of the process.

The first stage is problem identification and definition (i.e., social problems worthy of recognition and action must be identified and defined). Psychologists can help policy makers (top-down) and program recipients (bottom-up) to select and define issues. They can do this by questioning assumptions about human behavior and presenting alternative definitions and approaches, by data collection through scientific surveys that will expand and validate current thinking, and by obtaining information from involved constituencies or representative groups.

The second stage is policy formation, which involves developing a plan, method, or prescription for acting on a problem. Psychologists can assist by critically reviewing and analyzing relevant social science literature, by surveying or interviewing knowledgeable parties, by bringing parties with divergent perspectives together to decide on an optimal plan of action, or by designing programs to implement, evaluate, and compare, on a pilot basis, what appear to be the best possible policies.

In the third stage, policy adoption, the goal is to gain sanction from relevant officials for a plan of action. Psychologists can contribute their skills in organization, networking, group dynamics, and other types of communication and interpersonal influence to gain adoption of the measure. Additionally, data collection on optimal strategies and expert testimony by psychologists (or through their assistance) are also critical ways of securing policy adoption.

The fourth stage, policy implementation, involves ensuring that the designated plan of action is delivered as intended to the targeted constituents. Psychologists are of course directly affected when they are part of the programs to be implemented. Here, interpersonal influence and communication skills and a thorough understanding of the issues relating to the new programs are crucial for psychologists. Clinical supervision and organizational consultation are examples of direct involvement.

Finally, the fifth stage, policy impact, involves determining the effectiveness of the program in meeting its goals and whether unintended consequences of the policy developed in the course of implementation. Psychologists' evaluation skills are particularly relevant in assessing efficacy of program procedures and outcomes, and their translation skills are useful in transmitting findings and suggested modifications to program managers (Task Force on Psychology and Public Policy, 1986).

Training Psychologists for Public Policy Participation

Psychology as an organized body, and in collaboration with its training institutions, must work collectively in furthering national legislative and administrative goals it has set for itself as a means of contributing to the solution of national problems. Because most policy makers have limited understanding of psychology and the behavioral sciences, educational institutions must train leaders to develop a public policy orientation (i.e., psychologists who will want to work with policy makers and take on public policy careers). As noted earlier, there is still much to do in further educating policy makers on what impor-

tant contributions psychologists and behavioral experts can make to specific problem areas.

Understanding the political process must become an integral element of graduate education (DeLeon & VandenBos, 1987). Unfortunately, formal training for students interested in public policy is not generally offered in psychology departments, and there are few faculty members who actively engage in public policy activities to serve as role models. Most of the formal training programs in public policy outside psychology are offered at the master's level with public affairs, public administration, political science, and public policy programs. A few specialized training programs in psychology that encourage public policy have recently emerged (Serrano-Garcia, 1983). But these programs are relatively recent and have produced only a few graduates. What needs to be identified and built into psychology training programs is a core of public policy skills and knowledge involving an interdisciplinary perspective that can provide guidelines for future development of professionals and training programs, as well as systematic ways to acquire these skills (Task Force on Psychology and Public Policy, 1986).

One example of a university-based program to train psychologists to contribute to the policy process is the predoctoral psychology internship within the Florida Mental Health Institute (FMHI) at the University of South Florida (Florida Mental Health Institute, 1989; Solomon, 1989). The APA-accredited internship provides training in public sector psychology. Interns are exposed to a variety of community intervention programs, trained in agency consultation, and can participate in a 4-month rotation (in the FMHI department of epidemiology and policy analysis) where they learn how public mental health services evolve through various phases of policy development, planning, funding, and implementation.

Interns are offered a variety of training opportunities in the policy analysis unit. For example, interns gain familiarity with the mental health epidemiology literature, learn how to conduct epidemiological research, and see how these data are used by mental health administrators and legislators in planning for the future. They can participate in APA's consultation activities through involvement in community-based mental health advocacy groups. Interns can observe how important decisions are made in appropriating funds to various constituencies and learn how to influence this process by serving on citizen committees. Finally, interns can see how these decisions are implemented (for example, by attending meetings where determinations are made regarding children's institutional placements, and what data are used in deciding how individual children will be served by the state). Thus, interns learn about public mental health policy development in a variety of ways under the guidance and supervision of experienced psychologists. Organized psychology needs more such predoctoral policy-relevant training experiences.

Postdoctoral policy training opportunities are also needed. Real-world, hands-on political experience is critical. Psychologists can become directly involved in the federal legislative process through participation in the APA Congressional Science Fellowship Program (American Association for the Advancement of Science, 1987). The majority of psychologists now working on Capitol Hill first came to Congress as Fellows.

The APA has participated in the Congressional Science Fellowship Program since 1974. Each year two Fellows are selected through a national competition for 1-year assignments to staff positions on Capitol Hill. A 1-year stipend and a travel allowance are provided. The Fellowship year begins with an intensive 2-week orientation that exposes Fellows to various aspects of the legislative process, current issues before Congress, and introduces them to agencies and organizations interacting with Congress. Fellows eventually secure a position in a congressional office for their fellowship year. APA does not place the Fellows in certain offices; Fellows interview with offices just as they would for any job. Each of these positions provides different experiences.

Fellows serving on personal staffs are responsible for monitoring many different pieces of legislation and are closely involved in the often hectic day-to-day process of law making. Tasks include preparing briefing memos, face-to-face briefings with the Member, assisting in legislative debates on the floor of the House or Senate, and representing the Member at meetings with lobbyists and constituents.

Positions as committee staff are more likely to capitalize on a Fellow's substantive knowledge and expertise. Legislation is generally developed within congressional committees, and a Fellow on a committee staff will be responsible for developing a particular piece of legislation. Tasks include developing background information for the legislation, communicating with experts in the field of concern, planning and conducting hearings on the legislation, briefing the Committee Chair on the issues, and authoring portions of the final legislative report.

Working on Capitol Hill can be challenging and exciting (DeLeon, 1986b; Vincent, 1990). Whether APA Fellows stay on Capitol Hill, return to their former jobs, or enter new policy positions, they have gained invaluable experience (DeLeon, Frohboese, & Meyers, 1984). Fellows who remain on the Hill will help increase the psychological expertise available in the legislative structure. Fellows returning to academic settings will have critical insights into developing policy-relevant research and in making research results useful and accessible to legislators.

Without question, there has been increasing institutional involvement by psychology in the public policy and political process (Albee, 1982; Bevan, 1980, 1982; Hosticka, Hibbard, & Sundberg, 1983; Miller, 1969)—both as evidenced by APA programs and initiatives and by the development of innovative training modules within academic settings (Forman & O'Malley, 1984). Nevertheless, there still remains considerably more that can be accomplished, especially by the profession's training institutions (DeLeon, 1989; Payton, 1984).

Conceptualizing Future Policy Initiatives

Psychology has much that it can offer society, but to do so it must become more intimately involved in public policy. Because the political process is ongoing and ever changing, psychology must continually be part of this process to ensure that its views and expertise are consistently considered. As psychology becomes more intimately involved in the process, it will learn that each accomplishment opens the door for future opportunities (Weick, 1984). The profession will never complete its legislative agenda, for it is impossible to predict accurately what opportunities lie ahead. To achieve such overall goals, psychology will need to pursue legislative agendas on two levels (DeLeon, VandenBos, & Kraut, 1986). Its first agenda must stress immediate, short-term agendas (i.e., psychology must systematically strive to ensure that its practitioners and scientists are included in every appropriate phase of every legislative development). The second approach is for psychology to generate its own legislative agenda. As successes are demonstrated at the local level, they must be parlayed at the national level, and vice versa. For example, now that psychology has obtained complete parity with medicine throughout the federal judicial system, similar progress (using the federal code as a model) must be accomplished at the local level.

There are numerous areas in which psychology can play a major role. For example, the U.S. population is rapidly aging, and the elderly possess many unique health and mental health needs around which psychology could take the lead—such as in developing quality nursing home care and its alternatives (U.S. Senate, 1988), as well as developing other effective programs targeted toward this segment of society. Similarly, the teenage pregnancy rate in the U.S. far exceeds that of any other industrialized nation (Carnegie Council, 1989); again, psychology must develop appropriate clinical responses. As evidence continues to demonstrate the critical importance of the psychosocial aspects of physical health care (DeLeon & Vanden-Bos, 1983; Hamburg, Elliott, & Parron, 1982; Lalonde, 1974; Matarazzo, 1982, 1984; U.S. DHEW, 1979; Yates, 1984), psychology must be in the forefront of developing effective interdisciplinary clinical and research protocols. Training institutions must be willing to accept clinical responsibility for establishing model treatment programs for the elderly, the disabled, or those who are chronically or terminally ill. Psychology must decide about the role of psychotropic medication in the practice of psychology (Burns, DeLeon, Chemtob, Welch, & Samuels, 1988). Several other issues, such as developing programs for the homeless and improving employee productivity, should be important concerns for psychology. The ultimate goal is to make behavioral health an integral component in the health care agenda of Congress and to integrate clinical psychology's agenda with the national agenda in order to serve mutual concerns and interests (DeLeon & Vanden-Bos, 1984).

To collaborate successfully with federal officials on public policy issues, psychology must systematically expand its participation within those entities that provide policy guidance to Congress and to various state legislatures (DeLeon & VandenBos, 1984, 1987). It is psychology's responsibility to make the legislative bodies and the Administration aware of what the profession can offer. For example, psychology must play a more active role in ensuring that its collective voice is heard during the deliberations of such agencies as the Office of Technology Assessment (OTA), the GAO, the Institute of Medicine (IOM), and especially congressionally mandated advisory committees. For psychology's voice to be heard, the profession must understand current problems facing our nation, as well as be familiar with prior policy responses. It is also critical that the leadership of psychology learn and appreciate, on a first-hand basis, how national and local policies are established (DeLeon et al., 1982). Above all, we

psychologists must remember that the public policy and political process is a never-ending one.

A special aspect of government regulation of the professions involves promoting competition in the public interest. This is the responsibility of the FTC and of the various state regulatory bodies. Following is a brief review of the enforcement activities of the FTC and their implications for clinical psychology.

CASE STUDY: REGULATION IN THE PUBLIC INTEREST

Under our chosen form of constitutional government, it has long been established that one of government's primary responsibilities is to protect the public from a variety of potential harms. In the health arena, this means unqualified practitioners. At the state level, this responsibility is embodied in each profession's state practice act, which includes the establishment of a governmental body (typically a state psychology board) charged with the administrative responsibility, through promulgated rules and regulations, of protecting the public. Such state regulatory bodies are not an arm of psychology—or of the state psychological association. The sole purpose and mission of a state licensing body is to protect the public and enhance the public good.

Admittedly, state psychology boards are typically composed of those who possess psychological expertise and are local professionals. However, each board's authority comes from the specific wording of its underlying psychology practice act. Thus, all promulgated rules and regulations must be demonstrably consistent with this legislative charge. In a similar manner, the code of ethics of any profession should first and foremost serve and protect the public.

Over the years, the U.S. has evolved an intricate balance of state and federal responsibilities (or powers). Issues surrounding a profession's appropriate scope of practice traditionally have been left to the state authorities, with the federal government establishing national standards only in areas in which the states have been grievously deficient. However, the ethical codes of professions are national in scope, and they are generally concerned at the federal level.

The FTC

The FTC is an independent regulatory agency, established by Congress in 1914, to enforce various antitrust and consumer protection statutes. During the 1970s, at a time when there was growing interest in fostering competition in the health care sector as a means of increasing consumer options and controlling prices charged by providers through the operation of market forces, the FTC (1979) became involved in a series of cases and rule makings that challenged restrictions imposed by organized medicine and dentistry on the business practices of health professionals. FTC cases against the American Medical Association (AMA), the American Dental Association, the California Medical Association, and several national medical societies rocked the medical establishment and forced major changes in how these professional groups regulated not only their own members but also members of other professional groups with whom they compete, including clinical psychologists.

Antitrust Enforcement and Professional Services

In 1975, the Supreme Court struck down a mandatory minimum fee schedule imposed by a local bar association in the landmark case of *Goldfarb v. Virginia State Bar* (1975). The Court rejected the argument that the professions are exempt from the antitrust laws because they are not trade or commerce—both of which are critical elements in the competitive analysis that underlies antitrust enforcement. Instead, the Court made it clear, for the first time, that Congress had not intended to exempt the professions when it enacted the antitrust laws.

The *Goldfarb* case and others that followed laid the foundation for a series of investigations by the FTC, the Department of Justice, and several state attorneys general. At one time, these three antitrust enforcement arms of government had investigations of architects, civil engineers, accountants, lawyers, real estate brokers, physicians, dentists, and veterinarians.

As early as 1975, the FTC staff began investigating the role of the medical profession in accrediting and structuring physician education. The theory behind these inquiries was that organized medicine was using accreditation as a means for limiting the number of new physicians who could enter the market for health care services and thereby limit their competition for patients.

One of the most controversial cases brought by the FTC was a complaint against the AMA and two state medical societies charging them with unfairly restricting competition among physicians by banning advertising (*American Medical Association*, 1979). Activities designed to refer patients to a particular

practitioner or group of physicians were forbidden by AMA. The FTC's decision in the AMA case reviewed these and other restrictions on the ability of physicians to engage in truthful advertising and held that these restrictions were not only unreasonable but also had significant anticompetitive effects.

In light of the price-fixing focus on the *Goldfarb* case, the FTC also investigated two widespread medical fee-setting practices—the development and use of relative value scales and control of Blue Shield insurance plans by state and local medical societies. Relative value scales in and of themselves are not illegal, but when groups of competing physicians agree on what these relative values for their services should be and then seek to enforce them when it comes to obtaining payment from insurers, questions can be raised about the competitive effects of such practices. Medical control of third party payers, like Blue Shield, raises another set of antitrust concerns, particularly when that control affects the level of payments other health professionals may receive or the methods through which those payments are made (*Virginia Academy of Clinical Psychologists v. Blue Shield of Virginia*, 1980).

Challenges to Professional Licensure

At the time that the FTC was bringing antitrust cases against professionals for enforcing ethical codes or professional standards with anticompetitive effects, the Commission was also conducting a series of rule makings that challenged similar restrictions imposed by state licensing boards, comprised overwhelmingly of members of the regulated professions. These rule makings sought to invalidate restrictions on a wide array of business practices such as advertising, location in a commercial area (such as a shopping center), use of technicians or paraprofessionals for routine tasks, or requiring one professional group to be supervised by another profession. The FTC's rule-making investigations centered on optometrists, ophthalmologists, opticians, dental hygientists, and nurse midwives.

In 1978, the FTC adopted a trade regulation rule allowing truthful advertising for eyeglasses and vision care services. This action opened up the market and greatly lowered the prices for eye examinations and eyeglasses. The rule was in effect for 18 months but was subsequently overturned by the District of Columbia Court of Appeals and remanded to the FTC (*American Optometric Association v. FTC*, 1980).

Efforts to Curtail the FTC's Enforcement Activities

The fact that the Commission was beginning to make inroads against professional restraints on competition did not go unnoticed by the affected professional associations. In 1979, Senators James McClure (R-Idaho) and John Melcher (D-Montana) introduced an amendment to the FTC's authorization legislation that stated: "The Federal Trade Commission shall not have any authority to use any funds . . . for the purpose of investigating, or taking any action against, or promulgating any rule or regulation . . . with respect to any legal, dental, medical, or other state regulated profession, or with respect to its state or national professional associations." The American Dental Association provided the impetus for the introduction of this amendment, which was the beginning of a 4-year struggle by the Commission. A coalition of numerous professional and consumer groups (including psychology) worked to convince Congress to maintain the Commission's authority over the professions. The fight spanned the tenures of three FTC chairmen and garnered the unanimous support of all sitting commissioners, Democratic and Republican alike.

In 1980, the McClure and Melcher Amendment gained support from the AMA, the American Optometric Association, the American Veterinary Medical Association, the American Bar Association, and several state bar associations. A similar amendment was introduced in the House of Representatives by Congressmen Thomas Luken (D-Ohio) and Gary Lee (R-New York) (Pollard & Schultheiss, 1983). While the FTC ultimately prevailed in retaining its jurisdiction over the professions, it emerged a weakened agency—lacking support from its traditional backers on Capitol Hill and viewed as a political liability by the Reagan White House.

Just at the point where the natural progression of the FTC's enforcement activities involving the professions would have pointed to psychology, the agency was beleaguered by a massive lobbying campaign to strip it of all its authority over the professions. The goal of senior staff and the Commission itself became preservation of the agency's jurisdictional authority and not to take on new, controversial cases or rule makings. The psychology profession was one of the prime movers in the coalition to save the FTC's authority over the professions. Ultimately, the FTC prevailed in the battle over its authority, but it was a hollow victory because the authority was preserved only for it to be used at a later time, when the political climate might be more favorable to the kinds of reforms that the FTC had unleashed in the 1970s (FTC, 1979; Overcast et al., 1982; Pollard & Leibenluft, 1981).

In 1985, psychology's ethical principles began to be examined by the FTC. Ultimately, the APA approved an FTC agreement to settle allegations that some of APA's ethical principles constituted unreasonable restraint of trade (APA, 1990). Under the agreement, the APA elimitated seven ethical provisions that were viewed as unduly general and broad and as possibly restricting appropriate professional competition. The APA developed more narrow and appropriate ethical provisions to protect vulnerable populations and restrict deceptive practices.

SUMMARY

In this chapter we have provided a fairly detailed description of clinical psychology's federal legislative accomplishments, particularly over the past 2 decades. With enactment during the 101st Congress of legislation that provided for the field's independent recognition under Part B (physician's services) of Medicare, nearly every federal health care initiative currently provides for appropriate recognition of psychology's clinical expertise.

However, as the field of clinical psychology has matured and obtained professional recognition and status, it has taken on significant societal responsibilities and clinical opportunities. No longer can its training institutions afford to operate in a societal vacuum. No longer can the field rely on ad hoc training for administrative skills and public policy and political expertise.

Clinical psychology must institutionally accept its responsibility for developing effective clinical and research responses to evolving national needs. To accomplish this end, its scientists and practitioners must become personally involved in developing relevant health policy recommendations for our nation's elected and appointed public officials and then in implementing them. Psychology must develop the public policy knowledge base required—for example, through the expansion of the APA Congressional Science Fellowship program and innovative graduate school training initiatives, such as that at the University of Florida.

Above all, psychology must understand that the public policy and political process is an ongoing one. The profession must continue to be intimately involved in order to take advantage of evolving opportunities and, most importantly, to serve the nation.

REFERENCES

Albee, G. W. (1982). Preventing psychopathology and promoting human potential. *American Psychologist, 37*, 1043–1050.

American Association for the Advancement of Science. (1987). *Program description: Congressional science and engineering fellow program.* Washington, DC: American Association for the Advancement of Science.

American Medical Association, 94 FTC 701 (1979), aff'd. 638 F.2d 443 (2d Cir. 1980), aff'd. by an equally divided Court, 455 U.S. 676 (1982).

American Optometric Association v. FTC, 626 F.2d 896 (D.C. Cir. 1980).

American Psychological Association. (1990). APA OKs agreement on ethics with the FTC. *APA Monitor, 21*, 4.

American Psychological Association Task Force on Psychology and Public Policy, Board of School and Ethical Responsibility for Psychology. (1986). Psychology and public policy. *American Psychologist, 41*, 914–921.

Bent, R. J., Willens, J. G., & Lassen, C. L. (1983). The Colorado clinical psychology/expanded mental health benefits experiment: An introductory commentary. *American Psychologist, 38*, 1274–1278.

Bersoff, D. N. (1983). Hospital privileges and the antitrust laws. *American Psychologist, 38*, 1238–1242.

Bevan, W. (1980). On getting in bed with a lion. *American Psychologist, 35*, 779–789.

Bevan, W. (1982). A sermon of sorts in three parts. *American Psychologist, 37*, 1303–1322.

Burns, S. M., DeLeon, P. H., Chemtob, C. M., Welch, B. L., & Samuels, R. M. (1988). Psychotropic medication: A new technique for psychology? *Psychotherapy: Theory, Research, Practice and Training, 25*, 508–515.

Buie, J. (1989). Fox appointed to HHS training advisory panel. *APA Monitor, 20*, 26.

Carnegie Council on Adolescent Development. (1989). *Turning points: Preparing American youth for the 21st century.* New York: Carnegie Corp.

Cohen, W. J. (1968). *Independent practitioners under Medicare: A report to the Congress.* Washington, DC: Department of Health, Education, and Welfare.

Cummings, N. A. (1979). Mental health and national health insurance: A case history of the struggle for professional autonomy. In C. A. Kiesler, N. A. Cummings, & G. R. VandenBos (Eds.), *Psychology and national health insurance. A sourcebook* (pp. 5–16). Washington, DC: APA.

Cummings, N. A., & VandenBos, G. R. (1983). Relations with other professions. In C. Eugene Walker (Ed.), *The handbook of clinical psychology: Theory, research, and practice* (Vol. 2, pp. 1301–1327). Homewood, IL: Dow Jones-Irwin.

DeLeon, P. H. (1983). The changing and creating of legislation: The political process. In B. Sales (Ed.), *The professional psychologist's handbook* (pp. 601–620). New York: Plenum Publishing.

DeLeon, P. H. (1986a). Increasing the societal contribution of organized psychology. *American Psychologist, 41*, 466–474.

DeLeon, P. H. (1986b). A psychologist on Capitol Hill: Evolving changes in our profession. *Psychotherapy in Private Practice, 4*(3), 1–10.

DeLeon, P. H. (1988). Public policy and public service: Our professional duty. *American Psychologist, 43*, 309–315.

DeLeon, P. H. (1989). New roles for "old" psychologists. *The Clinical Psychologist, 42*(1), 8–11.

DeLeon, P. H., & Donahue, J. (1983). Overview: The growing impact of organized psychology in the judicial area. *Psychotherapy in Private Practice, 1*(1), 109–121.

DeLeon, P. H., Donahue, J., & VandenBos, G. R. (1984). The interface of psychology and the law. In J. R. McNamara (Ed.), *Critical issues, developments, and trends in professional psychology* (Vol. 2, pp. 235–256). New York: Praeger

DeLeon, P. H., Forsythe, P., & VandenBos, G. R. (1986). Federal recognition of psychology in rehabilitation programs. *Rehabilitation Psychology, 31*, 47–56.

DeLeon, P. H., Frohboese, R., & Meyers, J. C. (1984). Psychologist on capitol hill: A unique use of the skills of the scientist/practitioner. *Professional Psychology: Research and Practice, 15*, 697–705.

DeLeon, P. H., O'Keefe, A. M., VandenBos, G. R., & Kraut, A. G. (1982). How to influence public policy: A blueprint for political activism. *American Psychologist, 37*, 476–485.

DeLeon, P. H., & VandenBos, G. R. (1983). The new federal health care frontiers—Cost containment and "wellness." *Psychotherapy in Private Practice 1*(2), 17–32.

DeLeon, P. H., & VandenBos, G. R. (1984). Public health policy and behavioral health. In J. D. Matarazzo, S. M., Weiss, J. A. Herd, N. E. Miller, & S. M. Weiss (Eds.), *Behavioral health: A handbook of health enhancement and disease prevention* (pp. 150–163). New York: John Wiley & Sons.

DeLeon, P. H., & VandenBos, G. R. (1987). Health psychology and health policy. In G. C. Stone, S. M. Weiss, J. D. Matarazzo, N. E. Miller, J. Rodin, C. D. Belar, M. J. Follick, & J. E. Singer (Eds.), *Health psychology: A discipline and a profession* (pp. 175–187). Chicago: University of Chicago Press.

DeLeon, P. H., VandenBos, G. R., & Kraut, A. G. (1984). Federal legislation recognizing psychology. *American Psychologist, 39*, 933–946.

DeLeon, P. H., VandenBos, G. R., & Kraut, A. G. (1986). Federal recognition of psychology as a profession. In H. Dorken and Associates (Eds.), *Professional psychology in transition: Meeting today's challenges* (pp. 99–117). San Francisco: Jossey-Bass.

DeLeon, P. H., Wakefield, M., Schultz, A. J., Williams, J., & VandenBos, G. R. (1989). Rural America: Unique opportunities for health-care delivery and health-services research. *American Psychologist, 44*, 1298–1306.

Dorken, H. (1981). Coming of age legislatively: In 21 steps. *American Psychologist, 36*, 165–173.

Dorken, H., & DeLeon, P. H. (1986). Cost as the driving force in health care reform. In H. Dorken et al. (Eds.), *Professional psychology in transition: Meeting today's challenges* (pp. 313–349). San Francisco: Jossey-Bass.

Dorken, H., Stapp, J., & VandenBos, G. R. (1986). Licensed psychologists: A decade of major growth. In H. Dorken & Associates (Eds.), *Professional psychology in transition: Meeting today's challenges* (pp. 3–19). San Francisco: Jossey-Bass.

Dorken, H., & Whiting, F. (1976). Psychologists as health service providers. In H. Dorken & Associates (Eds.), *The professional psychologist today: New developments in law, health insurance, & health practice* (pp. 1–18). San Francisco: Jossey-Bass.

Enright, M. F., Resnick, R., DeLeon, P. H., Sciara, A. D., & Tanney, M. F. (in press). The practice of psychology in hospital settings. *American Psychologist*.

Federal Trade Commission. (1979, June). *Health services policy review session*. Washington, DC: Federal Trade Commission.

Florida Mental Health Institute. (1989). *Conference proceedings: Children's mental health services and policy: Building a research base*. Tampa: Florida Mental Health Institute.

Forman, S. G., & O'Malley, P. O. (1984). A legislative field experience for psychology graduate students. *Professional Psychology: Research and Practice, 15*, 324–332.

Fox, R. E., Kovacs, A. L., & Graham, S. R. (1985). Proposals for a revolution in the preparation and regulation of professional psychologists. *American Psychologist, 40*, 1042–1050.

Ginsberg, M. R., Kilburg, R. R., & Buklad, W. (1983). State-level legislative and policy advocacy: An introduction and systemic review. *American Psychologist, 38*, 1206–1209.

Goldfarb v. Virginia State Bar, 421 U.S. 773 (1975).

Government Printing Office (GPO). (1978). *Proposals to expand coverage of mental health under Medicare-Medicaid* (Hearing before Subcommittee on Health, Committee on Finance, U.S. Senate). Washington, DC: U.S. Government Printing Office.

Grupenhoff, J. T. (1983). Profile of congressional health legislative aides. *Mount Sinai Journal of Medicine, 50*, 1–7.

Hamburg, D. A., Elliott, G. R., & Parron, D. L. (Eds.). (1982). *Health and behavior: Frontiers of research in the biobehavioral sciences*. Washington, DC: National Academy Press.

Hosticka, C. J., Hibbard, M., & Sundberg, N. D. (1983). Improving psychologists' contributions to the policy-making process. *Professional Psychology: Research and Practice, 14*, 374–385.

Inouye, D. K. (1983). Mental health care: Access, stigma, and effectiveness. *American Psychologist, 38*, 912–917.

Lalonde, M. (1974). *A new perspective on the health of Canadians: A working document*. Ottawa: Government of Canada.

Matarazzo, J. D. (1982). Behavioral health's challenge to academic, scientific and professional psychology. *American Psychologist, 37*, 1–14.

Matarazzo, J. D. (1984). Behavioral health: A 1990 challenge for the health sciences professions. In J. D. Matarazzo, S. M. Weiss, J. A. Herd, N. E. Miller, & S. M. Weiss (Eds.), *Behavioral health: A handbook of health enhancement and disease prevention* (pp. 1–40). New York: John Wiley & Sons.

Miller, G. A. (1969). Psychology as a means of promoting human welfare. *American Psychologist, 24*, 1063–1075.

Overcast, T. D., Sales, B. D., & Pollard, M. R. (1982). Applying antitrust laws to the professions. *American Psychologist, 37*, 517–525.

Payton, C. R. (1984). Who must do the hard things? *American Psychologist, 39*, 391–397.

Pollard, M. R., & Leibenluft, R. (1981, July). *Antitrust and the health professions: Policy planning issues paper*. Washington, DC: Federal Trade Commission.

Pollard, M. R., & Schultheiss, P. (1983). FTC and the professions: Continuing controversy. *Nursing Economics, 1*(3), 158–163.

Raymond, J. S., DeLeon, P. H., VandenBos, G. R., & Michael, J. M. (in press). Policy issues influencing behavioral medicine: An international analysis. In G. R. Caddy & D. G. Byrne (Eds.), *International Perspectives in Behavioral Medicine* (Vol II). Norwood, NJ: Albex.

Rodgers, D. A. (1980). The status of psychologists in hospitals: Technicians or professionals. *The Clinical Psychologist, 33*(4), 5–7.

Scribner, R. A. (1978). Congressional science fellows: A bridge to better understanding and public policy. *Grants Magazine, 3*, 206–217.

Serrano-Garcia, I. (1983). Education and training for psychologists in public policy. Unpublished manuscript. (Available from the American Psychological Association, Office of Social and Ethical Responsibility, 1200 Seventeenth St., N. W., Washington, DC.)

Solomon, E. (1989). *Training mental health professionals to meet the needs of the Florida public mental health system*. Unpublished manuscript, Florida Mental Health Institute, University of South Florida, Tampa.

U.S. Department of Health, Education, and Welfare (DHEW). (1979). *Healthy people: The surgeon general's report on health promotion and disease prevention*. DHEW Pub. No. (PHS) 79-55071. Washington, DC: U.S. Government Printing Office.

U.S. General Accounting Office. (1989). *Medicare: Indirect medical education payments are too high*. (GAO/HRD-89-33). Washington, DC: U.S. Government Printing Office, p. 16.

U.S. Senate Special Committee on Aging. (1988). *The rural health care challenge* (Serial No. 100-N; Sen. Rpt. 100-145). Washington, DC: U.S. Government Printing Office.

Uyeda, M. K., DeLeon, P. H., Perloff, R., & Kraut, A. G. (1986). Financing mental health services: A comparison of two federal programs. *American Behavioral Scientist, 30,* 90–110.

Vincent, T. A. (1990). A view from the Hill: The human element in policy making on Capitol Hill. *American Psychologist, 45,* 61–64.

Virginia Academy of Clinical Psychologists v. Blue Shield of Virginia, 624 F.2d 476 (4th Cir. 1980), cert. denied, 450 U.S. 916 (1981).

Weick, K. E. (1984). Small wins: Redefining the scale of social problems. *American Psychologist, 39,* 40–49.

Welch, B. (1989). Practice Directorate dons advocacy role. *APA Monitor, 20,* 14–15.

Welch, B. (1990). Medicare win demonstrates bill's strength in Congress. *APA Monitor, 21,* 18.

Yates, B. T. (1984). How psychology can improve effectiveness and reduce costs of health services. *Psychotherapy, 21,* 439–451.

Zaro, J. S., Batchelor, W. F., Ginsberg, M. R., & Pallak, M. S. (1982). Psychology and the JCAH: Reflections on a decade of struggle. *American Psychologist, 37,* 1342–1349.

PART II

PERSONALITY THEORIES AND MODELS

EDITOR'S COMMENTS

Personality lies at the core of clinical psychology. In many respects, it is the focus of almost all research and clinical activity. It should not be surprising, therefore, that it is one of the most controversial issues as well. There is substantial disagreement over the utility of the entire concept, how it should be defined and assessed, and how the laws governing it function. Early efforts at understanding and explaining personality often involved macro theories, such as psychoanalytic theory, which attempted to cover all aspects of behavior. More recently, emphasis has been on micro theories, which deal with only one or a few particular issues. However, while the global theories have not and cannot be validated in toto, several remain powerful influences on the field. They serve as guiding perspectives, shaping peoples' values and approaches to clinical or research activity. The chapters in this part provide an overview of current thinking in the most influential perspectives.

Sidney J. Blatt and Howard Lerner (chapter 9) discuss the psychodynamic perspective. They examine the evolution of psychoanalytic theory and describe the most significant current issues, including the concept of self, which is a central concern in contemporary psychoanalysis. In chapter 10, Howard Rachlin and A. W. Logue present an overview of issues in learning, emphasizing how they apply to human psychological problems. The critical need for cross-fertilization between learning theorists and applied behavioral researchers is underscored. In chapter 11, Robert C. Carson delineates the social-interactional viewpoint, documenting how recently this approach to personality has had a pervasive influence on the field. In chapter 12, Hugh B. Urban writes on the phenomenological and humanistic approaches, considering some of the newer developments, including D. Ford's Living Systems Framework. In addition to describing these perspectives, he contrasts the phenomenological way of thinking about the subject matter with the traditional scientific approach.

CHAPTER 9

PSYCHODYNAMIC PERSPECTIVES ON PERSONALITY THEORY

Sidney J. Blatt
Howard Lerner

It is important to consider the development of psychoanalytic theory and dynamic psychology over the past century in a broad theoretical context. In 1978 Blatt discussed psychoanalysis as part of a major scientific revolution that began around the middle of the 19th century. He pointed out that around 1850, mathematicians (Gauss, Riemann, Lobachevski, & Bolyai) realized that the conception of the universe based on Euclidean geometry and rectilinear Cartesian coordinates was only one particular way among a number of alternatives to conceptualize the universe. With development of non-Euclidean geometries and concepts of curvilinearity of space, it became possible to conceptualize the universe in a number of equally valid ways. These discoveries led, in part, to the realization that all experience and any conception of reality are influenced by the relative position and assumptions of the observer. As reflected in the formulations of Kant and Cassirer, there was increasing awareness that nature was not simply observed but rather was a construction based on a particular vantage point. Thus, it was no longer possible to simply accept the manifest, surface appearance of phenomena as valid, since there were multiple ways of describing manifest characteristics. It was recognized that in order to understand phenom-

ena, one had to identify the structure and the organization principles that underlie surface appearances. Such emphasis on internal structure became, in Foucault's term, a major "cultural episteme" of our time. This emphasis on structuralism has been a central focus in multiple fields of endeavor. There has been a search in numerous fields for identification of the inherent principles of organization that define relationships among elements and their potential transformations in hierarchically organized systems. Interest in underlying structural principles of organization has been a major emphasis in the physical and biological sciences, as well as in the humanities (e.g., literature, linguistics, anthropology, and the history of art) (Blatt & Blatt, 1984). In all these disciplines there has been increasing emphasis on the need to identify and understand principles of structural organization that define interrelationships and potential transformations of elements that determine variations of surface phenomena. Despite this emphasis on internal structure in many fields throughout the 20th century, a large segment of psychology and psychiatry still maintains an exclusive interest in manifest behavior and overt symptomatology: for example, the *Diagnostic and Statistical Manual of Mental Disorders,* Third

Edition and (DSM III), and the *Diagnostic and Statistical Manual of Mental Disorders,* Third Edition, Revised (DSM III-R). There have been notable exceptions, of course, and these exceptions have made major contributions to the understanding of some of the structural principles inherent in human behavior. These include Gestalt analyses of perception, contemporary approaches to cognitive processes (including the work of Piaget, Werner, Bartlett, and others), and psychoanalytic theory (Blatt, 1978).

Attempts in the human sciences to identify principles of structural organization that underlie manifest behavior have emphasized two dimensions fundamental to the human condition: (a) humans' capacity for complex symbolic activity, and (b) recognition of the importance of the complex interpersonal matrix within which we evolve and exist. These two factors are unique to the human condition and must be accounted for in any understanding of the structural principles that underlie manifest behavior (Blatt, 1978).

Emphasis on complex symbolic activity and the interpersonal matrix in human functioning is consistent with the cognitive revolution in psychology (Gardner, 1984) and the increasing interest of psychologists in cognitive processes and issues of mental representation (Blatt, 1990). Contemporary psychology and many of its subareas (e.g., clinical, cognitive developmental, personality, and social) have begun to investigate systematically how individuals establish cognitive structures—schema, plans, scripts, and templates—and how these cognitive structures guide and influence behavior. Psychology has also moved beyond a primarily hedonic theory of motivation to an appreciation of the powerful motivational forces of

> bonding, attachment, exploration, play and curiosity that develop relatively independently of basic biological needs and drives. And increasing attention . . . [is] given to the role of caring interpersonal relationships in psychological development and . . . the building of cognitive structures that determine much of human behavior. . . . We now recognize that an essential part of human functioning involves the establishment and construction of meaning. . . . This emphasis on cognitive structures and meaning systems in psychology is consistent with the contemporary emphasis in a number of other disciplines on structuralism and semiotics as basic philosophic and conceptual models. . . . This new emphasis in psychology is also highly congruent with aspects of psychoanalytic theory which, since its inception, has sought to identify cognitive structures and how complex systems of meaning are established and result in adaptive and maladaptive functioning. Psychoanalysis from the very beginning has been a structuralist theory interested in semiotics and the functioning of the mind. (Blatt, 1991, in press).

THEORETICAL REVIEW

Since its inception as a field of scientific inquiry at the threshold of the 20th century, psychoanalytic theory has gone through a number of important revisions, elaborations, and extensions. Freud's monumental discoveries in *The Interpretation of Dreams* (1899 to 1900) established the importance of the unconscious as a system of the mind and stressed illogical, drive-laden, primary process thinking as an important form of mentation. In this work, Freud laid the basis for his metapsychology and his clinical theory, which he was to revise and elaborate through the next 40 years. Initially, he was interested in understanding the impact of the drives, especially infantile sexuality, on the development of the psychic apparatus, and their role in the onset of psychopathology. Freud (1905/1957d) explicated his concepts of infantile sexuality in his *Three Essays on the Theory of Sexuality* as he discovered the importance of the oedipal complex in normal development and its role in the onset of neurosis. Subsequent focus in psychoanalysis was on the modulating or control functions of the ego—the defenses—and their interaction with drives. Interest in the defensive functions of the ego was later broadened to include the ego's external, reality-oriented adaptive functions. Freud established a basis for an ego psychology, a psychology concerned with the defensive and adaptive functions, and one's adaptation in reality. These formulations of a structural theory were articulated in *The Ego and the Id* (Freud, 1923/1961b) and in the reformulation of the theory of anxiety in *Inhibitions, Symptoms and Anxiety* (Freud, 1926/1961c).

Up to this point, psychoanalysis had focused primarily on innate biological forces, how these predispositions toward discharge and control unfolded in normal personality development, and how disruptions of their interactions could result in personality disturbances. The concepts of ego psychology were consolidated and expanded by Anna Freud (1936) in *Ego and the Mechanisms of Defense*, by Heinz Hartmann (1958) in *Ego Psychology and the Problem of Adaptation*, and by David Rapaport (1940) in *Organization and Pathology of Thought*. The psychoanalytic ego psychologists, from 1940 to 1960, were interested in the metatheory of psychoanalysis—its economic, topographic, and structural models of the mind—and in the study of ego functions such as impulse-defense configurations, affect modulation and regulation, and the organization of thought processes and other adaptive ego functions.

In the past 30 years, there have been further significant revisions and extensions of psychoanalytic theory, which have taken place primarily through integrating the traditional concepts of psychoanalysis with concepts of object relations theory (Blatt, 1974; Blatt, Wild, & Ritzler, 1975; Fairbairn, 1954; Guntrip, 1969; Winnicott, 1965c), with a broadened, psychodynamically based, developmental theory (Blatt & Wild, 1976; Fraiberg, 1969; A. Freud, 1965; Jacobson, 1964; Mahler, 1968, Mahler, Pine, & Bergman, 1975), and a systemic psychology of the self (Balint, 1952; Kohut, 1971, 1977; Winnicott, 1971). These recent developments within psychoanalytic theory are an integral part of an attempt to extend the experience-distant metapsychology, which uses concepts of structures, forces, and energies to describe the functioning of the mind—concepts based primarily on a model related to the natural sciences, to a more experience-near clinical theory (Klein, 1976). This clinical theory is primarily concerned with concepts of the self and others in a representational world (Jacobson, 1964; Sandler & Rosenblatt, 1962) seen as a central psychological process within a model based primarily on hermeneutics (Home, 1966; Klein, 1976; Steele, 1979), which emphasizes meaning and interpretation rather than forces and counterforces. In psychoanalytic theory there have been attempts to extend beyond an exclusive focus on ego structures, such as impulse-defense configurations and cognitive styles, to include a fuller consideration of the experiences of an individual in an interpersonal matrix as expressed in representations of the self and the object world (Blatt & Lerner, 1983a).

Interest in the study of object relations and in self and object representations evolved as Freud's interest extended beyond basic biological predispositions to include factors of the cultural context and their influence on psychological development. Freud (1914/1961d, 1917/1957c) began to discuss issues of object relations and the superego in his papers *On Narcissism* and *Mourning and Melancholia*, and he later extended these concepts in *The Ego and the Id* (Freud, 1923/1961b) and *Civilization and Its Discontents* (Freud, 1938/1961c). His interest in the superego as the internalization of cultural prohibitions and values led to a fuller appreciation of the family as a major mediating force in the transmission of cultural values. There was increasing interest in the role of parents in shaping psychological development. Psychological growth and development were viewed as a consequence of the care-giving patterns of significant people in the child's early environment. These patterns interact with the child's evolving libidinal and aggressive drives and the modulating and adaptive functions of the ego. Interpersonal interactions with significant, consistent, care-giving figures were now seen as major factors in the formation of cognitive-affective

structures, defined primarily in terms of evolving concepts of the self and of others in the object world (Jacobson, 1964). Such structures were seen as the result of the complex interaction between the child's biological endowment and predispositions and the interpersonal matrix of the family and culture. Knowledge gained from psychoanalytic work with children and the observation of the normal and disrupted development of infants and children contributed to the further appreciation and understanding of early development sequences, their role in normal personality development, and the occurrence of psychopathology throughout the life cycle.

Freud (1923/1961b, 1938/1961c), in his formulations about the development of the superego, discussed the process of internalization and how

> a portion of the external world, has, at least partially, been abandoned as an object and has instead, by identification, been taken into the ego and thus become an integral part of the internal world. This new psychical agency continues to carry on the functions which have hitherto been performed by the people (the abandoned objects) in the external world. (Freud, 1938/1961e, p. 205)

The conceptualization of internalization was subsequently extended beyond superego formation to include all processes in which interactions with the environment are transformed into inner regulators and are assimilated as characteristics of the self (Behrends & Blatt, 1985; Blatt and Behrends, 1987; Hartmann, 1958; Hartmann & Lowenstein, 1962; Schafer, 1968). Internalization of object relations provides one of the primary bases for the development of intrapsychic structures (Blatt, 1974; Blatt, Wild, & Ritzler, 1975; Fenichel, 1945; A. Freud, 1952; Glover, 1950; Gouin-Decarie, 1965; Hartmann, 1958; Hartmann, Kris, & Lowenstein, 1949; Hoffer, 1952; Jacobson, 1964; Kernberg, 1966, 1972; Loewald, 1951, 1960, 1973; Mahler, 1968; Parens, 1971; Schafer, 1968; Stierlin, 1970). Object relations, through the processes of internalization, result in the formation of intrapsychic structures (ego functions and cognitive structures such as object and self-representations) that regulate and direct behavior. Psychoanalytic theory and research have progressively focused on the complex interactions among early formative interpersonal relationships and how these transactions result in the formation of intrapsychic structures that are best understood in terms of the quality of the representational world. These concepts or representations of self and others in turn shape and direct subsequent interpersonal relationships.

An understanding of the development of the concept of the object (of the self and others) can be greatly facilitated by an integration of psychoanalytic theory with the contribution of cognitive developmental psychology, particularly the formulations of Jean Piaget and Heiz Werner. Piaget and Werner traced the development of cognitive schemata (sensorimotor, preoperational, and concrete and formal operations) through which children come to know and think about their world in increasingly sophisticated and symbolic form. Development for Piaget (1954) and Werner (1948) consists of a progressive unfolding of cognitive structures according to innate principles of functioning in which the construction of new cognitive schemata evolve out of earlier cognitive structures. The child's relationship to his or her reality becomes increasingly integrated. The child comes to know the world as a product of his or her actions on objects, and through the relationship of these actions to his or her symbolic representation of actual and potential actions and interactions.

Formulations of cognitive developmental psychologists about children's development of cognitive schemata have been based primarily on the study of children in states of relative quiescence and as they respond primarily to inanimate objects. In contrast, psychoanalytic theorists offer formulations of children's development of cognitive structures based on the study of children in states of relative comfort and discomfort within an interpersonal relationship (Wolff, 1967). According to Jacobson (1964), Mahler et al. (1975), A. Freud (1965), Fraiberg (1969), and others, representations of self and of others are initially vague and variable and only develop gradually to become consistent, relatively realistic representations. Based initially on pleasurable and unpleasurable experiences of frustration and gratification, the child begins to build stable representations of the self and of others and to establish enduring investments and affective commitments. At the earliest stage, the self, the object, and interpersonal experiences are all one undifferentiated, affective, sensorimotor experience of pleasure or displeasure. As discussed by Mahler, in early autistic and symbiotic stages the infant is in a state of undifferentiated fusion and attachment to the mother. The infant slowly begins to perceive need satisfaction as coming from the mother, and there is a corresponding shift from the internal experience of pleasure to an awareness of a need-satisfying object. The object is recognized at first primarily in terms of its need-gratifying functions and actions. Slowly, the child becomes able to differentiate representations of self and of others. With development, these representations become more stable and constant and begin to coalesce into an increasing sense of identity.

Mental schemata or structures are transmitted to the child in an interpersonal matrix—in the relationship between the child and its caring aspects and in the child's relationship to the culture at large (see also Parsons & Bales, 1955; Vygotsky, 1962). The child initially internalized the orderly, predictable regularity of the mother-child, care-taking relationship. Basic differentiations of reality are subsequently extended and elaborated in further interpersonal relationships and experiences within the culture. But it is the basic caring relationship that provides the primary differentiations in reality that are internalized as the earliest and most fundamental principles of cognitive organization. The relatively predictable sequences of frustration and gratification in the caring relationship provide the child with the foundations for a sense of order and coherence. The infant's experiences of the mother's love and care are essential for the development of a capacity for reality adaptation (Winnicott, 1945). The mother's consistent and reliable care provides the infant with a sense of reality that is predictable and structured. Internalization of the mother's predictability and organization enables the child to tolerate delay that is externally imposed. This eventually develops into the capacity for internal delay, the establishment of psychological structures that permit the postponement of discharge, and the development of the capacity for anticipation, planning, and transformation. It must be stressed, however, that the amount of structure and organization that the environment must provide for these processes to develop will vary from child to child, depending on the child's biological constitution and temperament (Thomas, Chess, & Birch, 1968). What may be an appropriate degree and form of organization for one child may be insufficient or excessive for another. Further, the degree and nature of the organization and structure provided by the environment must change in response to the child's development. But it is the internalization of the caring agents' organized and structured responses that provide the basis for the establishment of the cognitive-affective structures of the representational world (Blatt, 1978).

Broadly defined, object representation refers to the conscious and unconscious mental schemata—including cognitive, affective, and experiential components—of significant interpersonal encounters. Beginning as vague, diffuse, variable, sensorimotor experiences of pleasure and unpleasure, schemata gradually develop into differentiated, consistent, relatively realistic representations of the self and the object world. Earlier forms of representations are based on action sequences associated with need gratification; intermediate forms are based on specific perceptual and functional features; and the higher forms are more symbolic and conceptual (Blatt, 1974). There is a constant and reciprocal interaction between past and present interpersonal relations and the development of representations. Schemata evolve from the internalization of object relations, and new levels of object and self representations provide a revised organization for subsequent interpersonal relationships (Blatt, 1974).

This conceptualization of the development of object representation is based on a broadened definition of psychoanalytic theory that integrates the concepts of drive, defense, and adaptation in a developmental model that focuses primarily on the child's evolving interactions with care-giving agents. In particular, this expanded theory had implications for clinical practice and research and has facilitated the study of psychotic, borderline, and narcissistic disorders. It has also resulted in formulations about the mutative forces in psychoanalysis. There is increased emphasis on directly relevant experiential dimensions in both theory and practice (Mayman, 1976; Schafer, 1968) and a renewed interest in the psychoanalytic context, the role of interpretation, and analytic relationship as important factors in the therapeutic action of psychoanalysis (Loewald, 1960). The expanded conceptualization of psychoanalytic theory has also led to new approaches to research, such as the microanalysis of infant-parent interaction, the study of the development of language and concepts of the self and objects, and the differential impairment of these processes in various forms of psychopathology. Research has also begun to focus on the processes within the psychoanalytic context that facilitate development of concepts of the self and the capacity to establish meaningful, effective, personally satisfying interpersonal relationships (Blatt & Shichman, 1983). Thus, one of the primary currents in contemporary psychoanalytic thought is the emphasis on the quality of interpersonal interactions (object relationships) throughout the life cycle, their role in normal development, and their impairments in psychopathology. The ground work for this approach was established by the ego psychologists, such as Hartmann and Rapaport, and developmental psychoanalysts, such as Anna Freud, Edith Jacobson, and Margaret Mahler. Important statements in object relations theory include the work of Klein, Winnicott, Fairbairn, Balint, and Guntrip, who provided understanding of the processes of internalization and the establishment of the representational structures—the concepts of the self and the object world. These contributions have led to the work of Kohut and Kernberg and to current interest in very early childhood experiences and severe forms of psychopathology—the psychosis, borderline conditions, and narcissistic disorders. In this chapter, we will review the development of object-relations theory evolving from the early work of Freud, Ferenczi, and Abraham, articulated more fully by Melanie Klein, given further shape and definition by the British Object Relations Theorists, and culminating in the contemporary theoretical and clinical efforts of Kohut and Kernberg.

CURRENT ISSUES

The pioneering work of Freud, Ferenczi, and Abraham led to the development of an object-relations theory in psychoanalysis, as seen primarily in the work of Klein, Fairbairn, Balint, Winnicott, and Guntrip. In this approach, the focus is on the quality of interpersonal relationships and the internalization of these experiences resulting in the construction of an internal world. Central are the care-taking experiences of the early mother-child relationship and the quality of the interaction with other significant caring figures. These care-taking interactions result in the construction of cognitive and affective structures, which in turn shape and direct the nature of subsequent interpersonal experiences. Thus, interpersonal relations and the establishment of cognitive and affective structures proceed in complex interaction.

The historical antecedents of the British Object Relations Theorists (Sutherland, 1980) can be seen in Karl Abraham's (1924, 1927) discussion of the differences in object relations in melancholia and obsessional neuroses. Abraham (1924) described the different qualities of interpersonal relatedness in the oral, anal, and phallic stages of psychosexual development and their implications for the nature of psychopathology.

One of the central figures in the development of object-relations theory was Melanie Klein, who was particularly attentive to the influence of drives, especially aggression and anxiety in children. Klein discussed the differences between "paranoid persecutory anxieties" and the "depressive anxieties" and guilt that result from the child's fantasized destruction of significant care-giving objects. Inborn aggression in the "paranoid-schizoid" and "depressive" positions lead to the development of fragmented internal objects. But this internal world also provides the basis for the child's subsequent perceptions and interpersonal relations.

Internal objects develop, according to Klein, from extreme experiences of good and bad that are attributed to fragmented part properties of the maternal object, such as the mother's breast. These representations become increasingly differentiated, integrated, and realistic. Internal objects are not exact replicas of external objects and experiences but are always embellished by the infant's drives and fantasies, which are externalized (projected) and reinternalized (introjected). This process of successive projections and introjections enables internal objects to become increasingly integrated and realistic. Good and bad fragmented part properties eventually become integrated into realistic representation, as drive-dominated part objects gradually become more accurate images of realistic, integrated figures.

Klein's formulations of the paranoid-schizoid and depressive positions extended and enriched Freud's structural theory of the mind (id, ego, and superego). In the developmentally earlier paranoid-schizoid position, anxiety is primarily experienced around preserving a sense of intactness in a hostile, persecutory world, while anxiety in the latter depressive position is aimed at the preservation of a sense of an integrated good object with which the individual is identified. In the paranoid-schizoid position, the child's inner world is filled with split-off, overstated, fragmented part objects. Anxiety and fear are focused on extremely menacing, persecutory external part objects that can invade and destroy the individual. There is an attempt to preserve and protect the overstated, fragmented, all-good part objects that have been tentatively internalized. The aim of the paranoid phase is ruthlessly to possess an ideal object and to project and ward off bad persecutory objects and destructive impulses.

The depressive position begins when objects are no longer experienced as exaggerated, split-off, and fragmented, but rather part properties of the object are integrated into a conception of a whole person with both good and bad properties. The persecutory anxiety of the paranoid position is replaced by feelings of guilt, remorse, and more modulated feelings of sadness about object loss. Resolution of the depressive position is a developmental achievement that ushers in a number of other developmental advances, including the capacity to experience and tolerate ambivalent feelings, the development of symbol formation, the capacity to identify with an integrated, realistic object, and a shift in anxiety from concerns about primitive aggression and destruction to concerns about fears of losing the love and respect of a good object.

Klein's interest in the child's building of internal objects stresses the symbolizing activity of the child. There is an inextricable link between the experiences of love and hate in object relations and the development of cognitive process. According to Melanie Klein (1975),

> The analysis of very young children has taught me that there is no individual urge, no anxiety situation, no mental process which does not include object, external or internal, in other words, object relations are at the center of emotional life. Furthermore, love and hatred, fantasies, anxieties, and defenses are also operative from the beginning and are ad initio indivisibly linked with object relations. This insight showed the many phenomena in a new light. (pp. 52–53)

Klein's distinctions between the paranoid-schizoid and the depressive position provide another basis for differentiating between psychotic and neurotic processes. The transition between these two positions also describes aspects of borderline phemonena. Klein's formulations have contributed to the widening scope of psychoanalysis by extending the range of understanding to patients often considered unsuitable for psychoanalysis—psychotic, borderline, and narcissistic individuals. Understanding of paranoid-schizoid mechanisms—the primitive defenses, unconscious fantasies, and the quality of internal objects—has provided the basis for a psychoanalytic approach to these more disturbed patients. Klein's articulation of the resolution of the depressive position has also provided a conceptual model for assessing progress toward achieving an integrated sense of one's self and of others.

Klein reminds us that we live in two worlds, including an internal world that is as real and as central as the external world (Meltzer, 1981). This internal world is a *place*, a life space, in which meaning is generated. The reality of this internal world is the origin of personal meaning, which is then expressed in the quality of interpersonal relationships established in the external world.

Michael Balint (1952) stressed that psychological growth and development do not proceed from an initial, objectless, primary narcissism and autoeroticism; rather, at birth the infant has an intense, dependent relatedness to its environment. Balint (1968) discussed severe psychopathology as related to a "basic fault," to "something missing" inside that is universal and that affects the entire functioning of an individual. This sense of fault or of something missing originates from a fundamental "failure of fit" (Sutherland, 1980, p. 832) between the infant's needs and the mother's responses.

Balint considers all psychological processes as originating in a basic two-person structure of the individual (subject) and the primary care-giving person (object). The individual struggles to cling to the object for security while at the same time seeking autonomy from such vulnerability. These two tendencies define two types of object relations that can serve as a defense against the effects of environmental failures. Balint's formulations of these two tendencies are similar to Mahler's emphasis on separation-individuation (Mahler, Pine, & Bergman, 1975) and the importance of the "need-fear dilemma" (Burnham, Gladstone, & Gibson, 1969) in severe psychopathology.

Balint's observations of a "basic fault" describes a developmental arrest that is fundamental to severe psychopathology. Verbal interpretations fail to alter this fundamental fault; what is needed in the treatment of regressed states is "the opportunity to make good a deficiency" (Sutherland, 1980, p. 833) or to establish a "new beginning" (Balint, 1952, 1968). The analyst, in his neutrality, becomes an object in a new environment around which the patient can discover his or her way in the object world. The quality of the therapeutic relationship and the analyst's understanding of the patient's inner world provide the basis for mending a primary developmental deficiency so that the individual can begin to relate to others in more effective and satisfying ways.

Balint contrasts a "benign regression," which has the potential for a "new beginning," with a "malignant regression," in which failures of empathy re-create in the treatment the lack of fit between infant and mother and lead to expressions of insatiable demands for instinctual gratification. Balint's emphasis on the primacy of object relatedness in psychological development and his articulation of the importance of a failure of fit in the maternal experience has had an important influence in the development of an object-relations theory. Balint's formulations are consistent with Winnicott's conceptions of the "true" and "false" self and the importance of a "holding environment," as well as Kohut's emphasis on the importance of empathy in the therapeutic process.

Donald Winnicott, because of his dual interests in pediatrics and psychoanalysis, made a distinctive contribution to object-relations theory based on this appreciation of both child development and the experiences of the mother. His interests in the earliest stages of development enabled him to explore, in a poetic and evocative way, preverbal experiences (Dare, 1976). His theoretical formulations remained close to the phenomenological and the experiential, and he eschewed jargon and technical language. Terms such as "ordinary devoted mother" or "good-enough mother," "holding environment," "true and false self," and "transitional object" and "transitional space" capture important personal experiences. Winnicott was especially interested in the momentum toward growth, maturity, and creativity. Instincts and impulses are seen as not just destructive and dangerous, but also as the source of spontaneity, creativity,

and productivity. Winnicott maintained a positive view of the person and was interested in the "facilitating environment" that encouraged emotional growth. He was interested in the individual as well as the environment, and especially the interaction between child and mother in facilitating growth and development. "One half of the theory of the parent-infant relationship," according to Winnicott (1960), concerns the infant and the infant's journey from absolute dependence, through relative dependence, to independence. The other half of the parent-infant relationship concerns the qualities and changes in the mother that are responsive to specific developing needs of her infant. For Winnicott (1965b), there was no such thing as the baby alone; the infant always existed as an essential part of a relationship. Winnicott focused on the experiencing individual within an interpersonal matrix. But eventually, "the experience of being alone while someone else is present" leads to the capacity to be alone (Winnicott, 1965a). Because Winnicott's concepts remain close to phenomenological experiences, his contributions appear somewhat unsystematic, but they are not without an underlying structure. His formulations are equally applicable to child development, to an understanding of adult psychopathology, and of the psychotherapeutic process.

Winnicott (1960) noted that the complete physical helplessness of the infant indicates the importance of attending to the "facilitating environment" and "the maternal care which together with the infant forms a unit." The infant's innate potential for growth is manifested in numerous spontaneous gestures. "If the inherited potential is to have a choice to become actual in the sense of manifesting itself in the individual person, then the environmental provision must be adequate. It is convenient to use a phrase like 'good-enough mothering' to convey an unidealized view of the maternal function" (Winnicott, 1965a, p. 44). The mother responds to the infant's spontaneous gestures through the development of a "primary maternal preoccupation"—a special psychological condition of the mother in the weeks before and after birth, a particular kind of identification or empathy that "gives the mother her special ability to do the right thing" (Winnicott, 1960, p. 585).

The "fit" between the infant's gesture and the mother's "good-enough" response to the infant's spontaneous gestures facilitates the development of an infantile omnipotence. Empathy, responsiveness, and "holding" provide a predictable "continuity of being" (Winnicott, 1960); excessive frustration stunts development and impedes the inherent capacity of the true self for relatedness. Excessive and repeated frustration at the hands of a not-good-enough mother impinges upon the infant's omnipotence, creating a negative experience of compliance that subsequently becomes organized to form a false self. In its extreme and malignant form, severe failures in mothering give rise to what Winnicott (1960) terms the "unthinkable anxieties" of going to pieces and losing orientation to oneself and others. Consistent with Balint's (1968) "basic fault," Winnicott considers that experiences assimilated into the true and false self are not based on instinctual gratification but rather on the quality of the relationship between infant and mother. For Winnicott, the study of psychological development of the infant is inextricably related to the study of maternal relationships.

With experiences of "ordinary good-enough mothering," the infant establishes a sense of wholeness, a conviction about the goodness of reality, and a fundamental "belief in" the world as a secure place. This sensorimotor integration provides the foundation for the emergence of the "true self," initially in the form of an increased repertoire of activity and subsequently in the actualization of "joyful" relations with others. Confidence in the mother allows the infant to relinquish the infantile omnipotence. This process of "disillusionment" is accompanied by intense affects of love and hate. But the "me" of the infant becomes separate from the "not-me" of the mother, and the infant begins a lifelong journey from absolute dependence, to relative dependence, to what Winnicott (1960) referred to as "interdependence" or "mature dependence."

Winnicott (1960) described psychological growth as a series of overlapping maturational achievements of integration, personalization, and object relations proceeding from absolute to relative dependence. Early experiences of adequate "holding" facilitate the infant's development of an integrated sense of "I am"—a sense of subjective continuity that persists despite temporary experiences of disintegration. This sense of "I am" eventually develops into the "capacity to be alone," "one of the most important signs of maturity in emotional development" (Winnicott, 1965a, p. 29).

Winnicott (1960) also discussed the process of "personalization" through which the infant develops a sense of "me" and "not me" based on sensorimotor experiences of an inner-outer body boundary between oneself and others. Personalization creates the sense of a whole body and of an inner world as a psychic reality. As discussed by Winnicott (1960) and others (e.g., Blatt & Wild, 1976; Federn, 1952; Freud, 1930/1961a; Lidz & Lidz, 1952; Tausk, 1950), disruption of boundaries is most apparent in the impaired

reality testing and distorted object relations of psychosis. The establishment of the first sense of the other ("object presenting") emerges out of the symbiotic fusion of "subject-object" (Winnicott, 1965b). It is important to note that Winnicott stressed that the infant's initiation of action is crucial to psychological development. "Too much" or "not enough" maternal response can interfere with the emergence of the self and the object out of the fusion of the symbiotic "subject-object."

Winnicott has an essentially positive view of human nature. He discussed the natural unfolding of the infant's potential for growth and how maternal care within a facilitating environment leads to the development of cognitive and affective structures. There is a gradual awareness of a "me" and a "not me" and the development of the capacity for objectivity and for active participation in a world experienced as relatively stable and permanent in time and space. Winnicott (1958) is particularly attentive to the transitional phases in this developmental process, as the child attempts to bridge the gap between fantasy and reality:

> part of the life of the human being . . . is an intermediate area of experiencing, to which inner reality and external life both contribute. . . . I am here staking a claim for an intermediate state between a baby's inability and his growing ability to recognize and accept reality. I am therefore studying the substance of illusion, that which is allowed to the infant, and which in adult life is inherent in art and religion, and yet becomes the hallmark of madness when an adult puts too powerful a claim on the credulity of others (pp. 230–231).

The illusion to which Winnicott referred is the illusion of omnipotence. Without it, "it is not possible for the infant to begin to develop a capacity to experience a relationship to external reality or even form a conception of external reality" (Winnicott, 1958, p. 239). From earliest infancy and within the confines of a "subject object" relationship, there is "something, some activity or sensation in between the infant and the mother." It is in this in-between area or "space" that fantasy and reality join and omnipotence is experienced. In this space the inner and outer worlds overlap in such a way that the infant discovers his or her creation of an outer, "not-me" world. The retaining of an illusion of omnipotence to some degree allows reality to be experienced with a potential sense of joy. This sense of illusion or "potential space" (Winnicott, 1958) occurs through the child's "first 'not-me' possession"—a "transitional object" such as a toy or blanket or a piece of wool (Winnicott, 1958). The child's relationship to the transitional object is marked by a decrease in omnipotence. The relationship established with the transitional object takes on a reality of its own, combining the qualities of being paradoxically created and discovered (Winnicott, 1971, p. 233):

> Its fate is to be gradually allowed to be decathected, so that in the course of years it becomes not so much forgotten as relegated to limbo. . . . It is forgotten and it is not mourned. It loses meaning, and this is because the transitional phenomena have become diffused, have become spread out over the whole intermediate territory between "inner psychic reality" and "the external world as perceived by two persons in common," that is to say, over the whole cultural field.

Winnicott (1971) stressed the importance of play in establishing the illusion and the creation of the transitional object in the "potential space" between infant and mother. Play is a facilitator of growth, separation-individuation, symbol formation, and communication. For Winnicott (1971), playing is a creative activity in normal development and even in psychotherapy—it is only through play that one can creatively discover the self (Sutherland, 1980).

W. R. D. Fairbairn developed a consistent and systematic object-relations theory of personality based on a developmental model of internalization. Fairbairn, like Klein, was especially influenced by experiences with seriously disturbed, schizoid patients. He stressed the primacy of the paranoid-schizoid position and how a profound detachment and withdrawal evolves from the failure of the infant to experience a sense of "being loved for himself." For Fairbairn (1954), personality development evolves not from instinctual gratification, but from experiences of being a person, valued and enjoyed "for his own sake, as a person in his own right." "Libido is not primarily pleasure-seeking, but object seeking" (Fairbairn, 1954, p. 137). Fairbairn was interested in the "personal" rather than the biological dimensions of Freud's formulations. As Jones (1954) noted in his forward to Fairbairn's (1954) book, *Object Relations Theory of Personality:*

> Instead of starting as Freud did, from stimulation of the nervous system proceeding from excitation of various erotogenic zones and internal tension arising from gonadic activity, Dr. Fairbairn starts at the centre of the personality, the ego, and depicts its strivings and difficulties in its endeavour to reach an object where it may find support. . . . This constitutes a fresh approach in psychoanalysis. (p. v)

At birth, the infant begins a libidinal search to establish an infantile dependence with a need-gratifying object. The erogenous zones are the channels through which objects are sought. Libido, in contrast to Freud's concepts of discharge and pleasure seeking through the erogenous zones, is reality oriented and directed toward establishing an attachment to the maternal object. Freud's concepts of psychosexual development are supplemented by concepts of the quality of dependence in object relations. The earliest stage of infantile dependence is characterized by primary identification (fusion) and an incorporative attitude. The gradual separation from the primary object constitutes a transitional stage from which the individual emerges with a capacity for mature dependence; the object and self are fully differentiated as separate individuals with independent identities. In his search for security, the individual must deal with frustrating experiences and malevolent interactions, and try to maintain relations with benevolent figures. Without a secure sense of self, the innate longings for object relations are blunted. It is too frightening to approach others because of fears of rejection. Instead, the individual develops a compensatory inner world of fantasized relationships.

The representations of figures in the environment provide the intrapsychic structures that are expressed in relatively stable and enduring patterns of experiencing and behaving. The representation of objects becomes the enduring features and patterns of personality organization. The quality of these object representations are expressed in dreams, symptoms, and interpersonal relationships. Personality development is a function of the quality of the caring environment. Loving and supportive interactions with a maternal figure facilitate growth, as the individual evolves in a process of differentiation. For Fairbairn, good object relations promote good development (Guntrip, 1974, p. 837). The infant attempts to cope with an unpredictable reality by internalizing external experiences and objects. Frustrating experiences and objects are internalized as an attempt to master and contain those negative experiences that cannot be tolerated in reality.

The earliest internalization of frustrating experiences develop around separation anxiety. According to Fairbairn, the nucleus of psychopathology rests on the extent to which there is a split in the ego. "Two aspects of the internalized object, viz. its exciting and its frustrating aspects, are split off from the main core of the object and repressed by the ego" (Fairbairn, 1963, p. 224). The exciting, gratifying aspects are termed the "libidinal object" and the frustrating, rejecting, prohibiting aspects are called the "antilibidinal object." Fairbairn (1963) continued: "there comes to be constituted two repressed internal objects, viz. the exciting (libidinal) and the rejecting (antilibidinal) object." This fundamental internal situation represents the schizoid position. Fairbairn noted that "the original ego is split into three egos—a central (conscious) ego attached to the ideal object (ego-ideal), a repressed libidinal ego attached to the exciting (or libidinal) object, and a repressed antilibidinal ego attached to the rejecting (or antilibidinal) object" (1963, p. 224).

The vicissitudes of object relations account for normal development, and deviations from the normal internalization of object relations account for the development of psychopathology. Fairbairn discussed four neurotic conditions: hysteric, phobic, obsessive, and nonpsychotic paranoid states. These four neurotic conditions correspond to four groups of good and bad, external and internal objects. Hysteria is the prototype of all neurotic psychopathology. In hysteria, good objects are projected into the outer world where the libidinal ego appears to them for help against its bad objects, which are experienced as internal persecutors. Obsessional states represent an attempt to maintain internal control over all good and all bad internalized objects. In phobic states the libidinal ego takes flight from bad objects to safe good ones, all of which are projected and seen as part of outer reality. In nonpsychotic paranoid states, the good object is internal while bad objects are projected into the outer world and hated. These four psychoneurotic conditions are regarded by Fairbairn as psychological modes of relating and particular patterns of internalized object relations.

Harry Guntrip was influenced by Fairbairn and Winnicott. Guntrip's contributions to object-relations theory stem directly from Fairbairn's formulations and from Guntrip's clinical experience with schizoid patients (Guntrip, 1961, 1969). Guntrip has contributed to object-relations theory by emphasizing the epistemological significance of subjective phenomena and the necessity of conceptualizing clinical phenomena as psychological, dynamic, and personal, rather than as biological, neurological, or sociological. For Guntrip, clinical experience must provide the data for theoretical formulations.

Guntrip's (1961, 1969) emphasis is on the quality of personal life. He discussed the schizoid patient's need to regress, not in search of satisfactions, but rather in search of "recognition as a person." The experience of being accepted and understood enables the patient to feel hopeful and to be "born again" (Guntrip, 1969). The regressed states of schizoid patients feature a massive withdrawal from relation-

ships and a morbid sense of inner deadness. Guntrip discussed how the patient takes flight from all object relations in an attempt to recapture the safety of the intrauterine milieu. The regressive flight toward ultimate security is juxtaposed by the experience of terrifying anxiety involving a loss of self, total isolation, and an apathetic abyss that is equated with death. Guntrip viewed most forms of psychopathology as defensive attempts to hold the self together against this terror of annihilation. The ultimate therapeutic problem is aiding the patient to cope with these primal anxieties. Rather than emphasizing the vicissitudes of libidinal instincts and primitive aggression, Guntrip focused on the profound fears of intolerable helplessness and weakness that characterize the infant, especially in an experience of deprivation.

Guntrip (1969) discussed how the schizoid individual "hovers between two opposite fears, the fear of isolation in independence with loss of his ego in a vacuum of experience, and the fear of bondage to, of imprisonment or absorption in the personality of whomsoever he rushes to for protection" (1969, p. 274). The schizoid patient perpetually oscillates between nearness and distance, dependence and independence, trust and mistrust, and the maintenance and fear of the therapeutic relationship. A permanent compromise midway between the extremes of absorption and isolation constitutes the nature of treatment stalemates with disturbed patients. Guntrip noted that this schizoid compromise is an essential intermediate phase through which the regressed patient must progress. The pathway to effective treatment involves establishing a terrifying passive dependence. Successful treatment involves the resolution of the struggle against this passive dependence.

Contributions of Kernberg and Kohut

The contributions of the object-relations theorists have led to an extension of psychoanalytic concepts and practice, including a shift from an emphasis on mental functioning to an interest in experiencing (Lichtenberg, 1979). Basic psychoanalytic concepts of drive and defense have been supplemented by an interest in subjective experiences and concepts of the representational world. A key question facing contemporary psychoanalysis is "can psychoanalytic theory conceptualize the individual's total experience, his ever shifting yet generally stable sense of self, and his sense of the world of people and things, actual and illusory?" (Lichtenberg, 1979, p. 376). Psychoanalytic concepts now include an interest in the vicissitudes of the instincts, defensive and adaptive functions of the ego, and a concern with the early mother-child interaction and its impact upon the development of object relations and concepts of the self and the object world.

From a historical perspective, Freud (1914/1961d), in his pivotal paper *On Narcissism*, raised many questions about the development of narcissistic and object libido, about the development of feelings and concepts about the self and of significant others. Freud's early formulations have been refined and extended to include a consideration of the self as the conscious, preconscious, and unconscious representation of the total person, the processes through which self and object representations are internalized as enduring structures, the consideration of self as structure and as experience, the importance of the internal world in psychological functioning, and the importance of a narcissistic object choice as an attempt to correct a deficit in psychological structure (Teicholz, 1978). These elaborations of psychoanalytic theory have contributed to the attempts to broaden the scope of psychoanalytic practice beyond the treatment of the neuroses, in which there are conflicts over sexual and aggressive impulses, to an interest in the treatment of disorders in which the personality is seriously malformed or arrested—the narcissistic borderline and psychotic conditions.

The emphasis on object-relations theory in the past decade has led to a marked increase in interest in borderline and narcissistic disorders. Some investigators consider borderline and narcissistic disorders as a unique diagnostic category, while others regard them as part of a continuum of psychopathology (e.g., Horner, 1980; Kernberg, 1975; Settlage, 1977). The term *borderline* is often used to designate an intermediate area of psychopathology—a diagnosis applied to patients who could be classified as neither neurotic nor psychotic, but who exhibit some features of both. Some (e.g., Green, 1977) argued that, like the hysteric of Freud's time, the borderline patient is the problem of our time. Pruyser (1975) asserted that the concept has become a "star word."

Two primary figures in this expanding scope of psychoanalytic theory and practice are Heinz Kohut (1971, 1977) and Otto Kernberg (1975, 1976). Kernberg's work derives from psychoanalytic ego psychology and object-relations theory, especially Melanie Klein and the developmental psychology of Jacobson and Mahler. Kernberg examined the role of aggression and primitive defenses in borderline and narcissistic psychopathology. Kohut, on the other hand, focused on a psychology of the self and the developmental transformation that takes place as the concepts of the self move from archaic psychological states to more mature levels.

Kohut is particularly interested in the narcissistic patient and found that the classical theory of drives and defenses, which is useful in understanding neuroses, has relatively little to contribute to the understanding of narcissistic disorders. Neurosis has its origins later in childhood, when self-object differentiations and the structures of the mind (id, ego, and superego) are well established. Libidinal and aggressive drives are experienced as dangerous, anxiety is mobilized, defenses are only partially successful, and neurotic symptoms are a compromise for the tensions between impulse and defense. In psychoanalytic treatment, neurotic patients develop a transference neurosis in which the analyst is experienced as a version of the parents, to whom libidinal and aggressive urges are directed. By contrast, self-pathology begins much earlier in development, at a time when psychological structures are still in the process of formation. Symptoms occur when an insecurely established self is threatened by dangers of psychological disintegration, fragmentation, and devitalization. Because of the absence of a firm cohesive sense of self, the treatment relationship initially is a holding environment that serves as a protective container; it permits consolidation of the self so that eventually a therapeutic alliance can be established and a more classical analysis of conflicts, defenses, and transference can take place (Topin & Kohut, 1980).

A weakened or defective self, the core of psychopathology in narcissistic patients, is created by an empathic failure in early parent-child relationships. According to Kohut (1971, 1977), an authentic, capable, and vital self can be erected only when the "mirroring" and "idealizing" needs of the child are responded to by parents. Without an adequate sense of self, the child is unable to separate from primitive experiences of the parents as self-objects. The child retains an archaic grandiosity and the wish to continue the fusion with an omnipotent self-object in order to maintain an archaic sense of self as a defense against painful states of anxiety (fragmentation) and depression (devitalization, depletion). Narcissistic disturbances are viewed as primarily structural rather than dynamic disturbances; that is, the patients suffer from a developmental arrest rather than a conflict between drive and defense. Kohut articulated the need of narcissistic patients to reexperience a "self-object transference" ("mirror" or "idealizing") in order to correct their developmental arrest. The primary factor in therapy is the therapist's empathy rather than the interpretation of drives. According to Kohut and

Wolff (1978), the patient needs to become aware of, express, and experience the unfulfilled narcissistic needs of childhood in order to develop the basis of an adequate sense of self.

Kohut posited a separate developmental line for narcissism, and traced transformations of narcissism from primitive to mature forms. In normal development, the equilibrium of primary narcissism is disturbed by failures of maternal care, and the child attempts to maintain the narcissistic perfection by establishing grandiose and exhibitionistic images of the self or by attributing the narcissistic perfection onto an omnipotent self-object—the idealized parent image. In normal development, the "grandiose self" and "idealized parent image" are the precursors of mature ambitions, enjoyment, and self-esteem. With inevitable, natural, phase-appropriate failures, misunderstandings, and delays on the part of the mothering agent, the infant gradually withdraws libido from the archaic images of narcissistic perfection and slowly acquires increments of inner psychological structure that gradually take over the mother's function of maintaining narcissistic equilibrium. Gradual and tolerable disappointments in narcissistic equilibrium lead to the development of internal structure and the capacity for self-soothing and tension tolerance.

Serious failures in empathy on the part of the mother, however, may result in narcissistic trauma and a disillusionment with the idealized object. This may lead to a quest for a perfect, idealized external object (and a consequent failure in superego development), or the development of a hypercathected "grandiose self." The "grandiose self" represents "another approach to attempt to recapture the original all embracing narcissism by concentrating perfection and power on the (grandiose) self, and by turning away disdainfully from an outside to which all imperfections have been assigned (Kohut, 1971, p. 106). The grandiose self and idealized parent image remain unintegrated in the developing personality.

A chronic frustration of legitimate childhood needs interferes with the development of psychological structure, and the self perceptions of these patients are fragmented, discontinuous, and unreal. External objects are used as a replacement for psychological structures (Teicholz, 1978). Depending on the quality of interaction with the self-object during development, the adult self may emerge "in states of varying degrees of coherence, from cohesion to fragmentation; in states of varying degrees of vitality, from vigor to enfeeblement; and in states of varying degrees of functional harmony, from order to chaos. Significant failure to achieve cohesion, vigor or harmony, or a

significant loss of these qualities after they have been tentatively established, may be said to constitute a stage of 'self-disorders' " (Kohut and Wolff, 1978, p. 414).

Kohut and Wolff (1978) described specific syndromes of "self pathology" as a consequence of developmental failures. An "understimulated self" develops from a lack of stimulation in childhood. As children, these patients may have exhibited head banging; later, compulsive masturbation and in adolescence, daredevil activities. A "fragmented self" develops as a consequence of an absence of integrating responses from a caring agent. States of fragmentation vary in degree, and more malignant manifestations include profound anxiety and hypochondriacal worry, which can be quasi-delusional. States of fragmentation are frequently induced in empathic failure or rebuff, and often disappear when an empathic response is reestablished. An "overstimulated self" stems from nonempathic, excessive, and phase-inappropriate parental responses to the child's grandiose-exhibitionistic strivings. Unrealistic fantasies of greatness lead to tension, anxiety, and painful inhibitions. Such individuals tend not to perform up to their potential because they are frightened of their intense ambition, perfectionistic tendencies, and archaic grandiose fantasies. An "overburdened self" has been deprived of the opportunity to merge with self-objects representing soothing and calmness. These individuals have failed to internalize a self-soothing modality and insistently dread the trauma of unbridled emotionality, especially anxiety. In order to avoid the dangers of noxious stimuli, these individuals develop chronic attitudes of irritability, suspiciousness, and paranoia.

Kohut and Wolff (1978) also delineated specific self disorders or personality types associated with the narcissistic character or psychopathology within the "narcissistic realm." "Mirror-hungry personalities" seek attention exhibitionistically in order to counterbalance intense feelings of worthlessness and lack of self-esteem. "Ideal-hungry personalities" want others to admire their prestige, power, beauty, and intelligence. They can only experience a sense of positive self-esteem while relating to idealized self-objects; but, because of their structural defect, they continually find defects in the idealized other and are inevitably disappointed. "Alter-ego-hungry personalities" experience a profound inner void that can only be filled by a twinship hollowed by conformity to the self's appearance, values, and ideas, with an awareness that the other is separate and distinct. The alter-ego-hungry personality is prone to feel alienated and estranged. The three narcissistic character types—mirror-hungry, ideal-hungry, and alter-ego-hungry—tend to look relentlessly for self-objects. The mirror-hungry personality manifests a compelling need to control the self-object in an effort to obtain self-structure. The need to merge dominates the clinical picture, the particular type of merger (mirroring, idealizing, or alter-ego) is secondary to structural defects in the self and the need for a self-object in lieu of self-structure. Because of fluidity in the self-other boundary, the merger-hungry personality is intolerant of the self-object's independence, they are acutely sensitive to separations, and they demand the immediate and continuous presence of self-objects. As a reciprocal to the merger-hungry type, "contact-shunting personalities" avoid social contact and isolate themselves as a defense against deep-seated apprehensions that they will be swallowed up and devoured by the symbiotic yearnings for an all-encompassing union.

The work of Otto Kernberg, beginning in 1966, has had a primary influence on psychoanalytic thinking about borderline phenomena. Kernberg's contributions are based on an integration of basic psychoanalytic concepts, psychoanalytic ego psychology, and the object-relations theories of Klein, Fairbairn, and Winnicott. Kernberg discusses specific and nonspecific ego defects and failures of integration that result from disruptions of the internalization of object relations (Kernberg, 1976). Kernberg placed his concepts of the borderline personality development within a conceptual model of normal development, and he was specifically concerned about the relation of borderline pathology to issues of pathological narcissism.

Psychological structure is determined by the vicissitudes of internalized object relations, which constitute a crucial determinant of ego integration. Abnormalities in internalization of object relations, regardless of etiology (constitutional or environmental), determine various types of psychopathology (Kernberg, 1975, 1976, 1978). Kernberg (1975) discussed four stages in the internalization of object relations, which range from primary narcissism at the beginning of the developmental continuum to object constancy at the highest level.

In the first 3 months of infancy there is a primary, undifferentiated self-object matrix based on the pleasurable, gratifying experiences of the infant in interaction with the mother. This undifferentiated self-object representation of gratifying experiences within the infant-mother matrix is juxtaposed with a representation of an undifferentiated, "all-bad" self-object representation based on painful and frustrating experiences. Good and bad or pleasure and pain are the primary differentiations at this stage, and there is no differentiation between self and nonself. Self and object representations become differentiated only with perceptual and cognitive development. Ego boundaries are stabilized, and self representation gradually becomes separate from object representation. Around 1 to 2 years of age, good and bad self-images coalesce into an integrated self-concept. Good and bad object images are also integrated in more realistic representation of others. Affects become more differentiated, integrated, and modulated.

In borderline psychopathology, there is a basic and rudimentary differentiation between self and other, but it is based on an extreme juxtaposition and primitive aggression that facilitates the differentiation of "me" and "not me." The active struggle to maintain a differentiation based on contradictory images results in massive anxiety and the ego's use of "splitting" as a major defensive operation. The pathological use of splitting becomes the primary characteristic of the borderline personality.

Borderline pathology is characterized by powerful, untamed affects: a reliance on a constellation of primitive defenses centered in splitting; a lack of impulse control and anxiety tolerance; and premature sexualization of relationships. There is little evidence of internal control and there is an overreliance on external sources for reassurance, praise, and punishment. These characteristics of borderline psychopathology define, according to Kernberg (1975), "a specific, stable, pathological personality organization," well demarcated from both neurosis and psychosis on the one hand, and with a typical constellation of symptoms, defense operations, instinctual vicissitudes, and quality of self and object representation on the other hand.

The treatment goal with borderline patients includes overcoming developmental arrests, the integraton of part-object representations into total-object representations, the development of object constancy, and the achievement of an integrated self-object. The therapist's maintenance of technical neutrality and the interpretation of splitting and other primitive defenses assists the patient to relinquish a contradictory representation of both an overtly idealized and a ruthlessly depreciated therapist. Idealization and depreciation are both attempts to defend against the dread of emptiness and aloneness (Kernberg, 1975, 1976, 1982). Improvement in therapy is a function of the ego strength of the patient and the therapist's skill and empathy in establishing a therapeutic alliance and modulating the patient's primitive aggression. According to Kernberg (1982, p. 26):

In the severe psychopathologies (including border-line personalities), early, primitive units of internalized object relations are directly manifest in the transference as conflicting drive derivatives reflected in contradictory ego states. In these cases, the predominance of a constellation of early defense mechanisms centering on primitive dissociation or splitting, immediately activates contradictory, primitive but conscious intrapsychic conflicts in the transference. What appear to be inappropriate, chaotic character traits and interpersonal interactions, impulsive behavior, and affect storms are actually reflections of the fantastic early object-relations-derived structures. . . . These highly fantastic, unrealistic precipitates of early object relations, which do not directly reflect the real object relations of infancy and childhood and must be interpreted until the more realistic aspects of the developmental history emerge, determine the characteristics of primitive transference.

While symptoms and pathological character traits reflect intrapsychic conflict, these conflicts are dynamically structured into relatively stable patterns of organization based on the quality of internalized object relations. At severe levels of psychopathology, such as the borderline personality organization, the interpretation of primitive defenses and transference manifestations fosters integration and the transformation of primitive transference into more advanced, neurotic transferences. Relationships based on distorted representations of part properties are replaced by relationships based on more realistic and comprehensive representations of self and others (Kernberg, 1975, 1976, 1982).

This approach to the treatment of borderline patients is part of the widening scope of psychoanalysis in that it extends psychoanalytic concepts and methods to the treatment of more severely disturbed patients. It introduces modifications of basic psychoanalytic methods that focus on the primitive transference as the major locus of therapeutic action. The focus of treatment shifts from a traditional emphasis on the content of free associations to a fuller appreciation of the patient-therapist interaction as expressed in the dynamics of the transference. Interpretations of the therapeutic relationship, as expressed through the transference, are made in terms of the patient's predominant level of self and object representations. With seriously disturbed patients, the therapeutic relationship can become a "holding environment" (Winnicott) and the therapist a "container" (Bion, 1959) for the early forms of object relations established by the patient. The therapist's cognitive and affective tolerance provides an integrative function for the patient's chaotic experiences. The interpretation of the primitive borderline defenses of splitting, pro-

jective identification, denial, idealization, and devaluation contributes to the gradual development of a capacity to be more observant and reflective. The interpretation of defensive resistance and transference is a major aspect of the treatment process with borderline patients. Kernberg also noted the important role of powerful countertransference reactions in the treatment of borderline patients and the need to use these emotional reactions in the therapeutic process.

The extensive recent developments in psychoanalytic thought embodied in object relations theory, self-psychology, and developmental psychoanalysis have been countered by rebuttal from what might be termed modern structural theory or what many critics regard as classical psychoanalytic theory. Taking as its starting point Freud's (1923/1961b) tripartite model of id, ego, and superego (independent of earlier concepts of psychic energy from libido theory of Freud's earlier topographical model), modern structural theory tried to reestablish itself as the "mainstream hypothesis of modern psychoanalysis" (Boesky, 1988, p. 172) by reasserting the ubiquitous nature of internal, intrapsychic conflict and the view that this conflict can best be conceptualized in the terms of the interaction of the id, ego, and superego. Charles Brenner (1983) has been one of the more articulate spokesmen for this point of view. According to Brenner, psychic conflict is at the heart of psychoanalytic theory and treatment—the components and interaction of this conflict result in "compromise formations." All thoughts, actions, plans, fantasies, and symptoms are compromise formations that are multidetermined by the components of conflict. Specifically, all compromise formations represent a combination of a drive derivative (a specific personal and unique wish of the individual, originating in childhood, for gratification); of an unpleasure in the form of anxiety or depressive affect and their ideational contents of object loss, loss of love, or castration associated with the drive; of defense that functions to minimize unpleasure; and various manifestations of superego functioning such as guilt, self-punishment, remorse, and atonement. According to Brenner, compromise formations are the observational base for the study of all psychic functioning; that is, they are the data of observation when one applies the psychoanalytic method to observing all psychological phenomena. Brenner (1986) notes that

To say everything is a compromise formation, means everything. Not just symptoms, not just neurotic character traits, not just the slips and errors of daily living, but everything. The normal as well as the pathological. Just as nothing is ever just defense or only wish-fulfillment, so nothing is ever only "realistic" as opposed to "neurotic." One of the principal contributions of psychoanalysis to human psychology is precisely this. The various components of conflict over wishes of childhood play as important a part in normal psychic functioning as they do in pathological psychic functioning. (p. 41)

From this perspective, important questions to be asked in understanding all psychological phenomena are as follows: (a) What wishes of childhood are being gratified? (b) What unpleasure (anxiety and depressive affect) is being aroused? (c) What are the defenses utilized? (d) What are the superego expressions? The answers to these questions, according to Brenner, provide a distinctive psychoanalytical understanding of all mental phenomena in the treatment situation and guide the timing and nature of therapeutic interventions. From a developmental perspective, conflict and compromise formation are a significant part of normal as well as pathological functioning and development. Knowledge of the components of conflict and of the consequent compromise formations is as essential to an understanding of normal functioning as it is to an understanding of psychopathology.

Although contemporary structural theorists in psychoanalytic thought acknowledge the importance of preoedipal conflicts, they stress the importance of oedipal-phase experiences and superego conflicts even in determining severe psychological disorders such as borderline and narcissistic psychopathology. With specific reference to borderline psychopathology, modern structural theory takes issue with formulations based on Mahler's concepts of separation-individuation as well as Kernberg's theory of primitive defenses. Adherents to modern structural theory take issue with formulations about the specificity of very early developmental stages in the evolution of psychopathology, specifically borderline phenomena and narcissism. They believe it premature, in view of current knowledge, to attribute etiological significance to failures in very early development during specific phases in the life cycle. According to Abend, Parder, and Willick (1983),

On the whole, we have been led to adopt a far more skeptical attitude toward the validity of constructs based largely upon theories of early psychic development than have many other analysts. We believe that much of what they propose is based on speculative interpretation of necessarily sketchy data. However plausible such constructions may be, they are difficult if not impossible to substantiate with analytic data gathered from clinical work with adults. (p. 222)

The aforementioned authors are critical of formulations involving the study of mental activities in adult patients as if they represent direct and modified continuations of early, preverbal phases of development; specifically as these conceptualizations are applied to understanding ego functions, object relations, and defenses. The view of Abend, Parder, and Willick (1983) is that the disturbances or impediments in borderline patients vary along a quantitative continuum of different degrees of severity, and in turn they favor a formulation and treatment of these patients as related to that of the neuroses. In essence, these authors conceptualized borderline patients utilizing classical psychoanalytic theory, with an emphasis on libidinal and aggressive drives, conflict, and structural theory, postulating that the diverse clinical phenomena and transferences in these more disturbed patients are not qualitatively different from that of neurotic patients. They disagreed with the view that the borderline diagnosis indicates a common, pathognomonic set of underlying structures, such as the formulations of Kernberg, who discussed the borderline personality organization in terms of a constellation of primitive defenses and pathological internalized object relations derived from the fundamental utilization of the specific defense mechanism of splitting. It is within the context of these divergent perspectives (that is, the classical rebuttal to object-relations theory and self-psychology) that some of the more lively debates within psychoanalysis are currently taking place.

FUTURE DIRECTIONS

The concept of self in psychoanalysis, according to Grossman (1982) stands at the crosscurrents of several traditional philosophical and psychoanalytic issues, which can be formulated along two axes. The first axis encompasses the everyday, personal experience of self; that is, self-awareness, self-consciousness, self-esteem, and will—and the philosophical issues of mind and body, free will, and the relations between the self and world of things. The other axis, according to Grossman (1982), is the psychoanalytic dimension based on events of the clinical situation and the subjective experience of the patient at one end and systematic, theoretical concepts at the other end of the continuum. A concept of self requires a coordination of these different perspectives. The essential tension in any theory of the self is between the subjective and objective perspectives.

The concept of the self has, in recent years, emerged as a central concern in psychoanalysis. The origins of the concept in psychoanalysis can be traced to Freud's ambiguous use of the word *ich*. He used *ich* to refer to both a particular psychic agency of the mind (the ego) and to a personal, subjectively experienced sense of self. With Strachey's imprecise translation of *ich* as ego, usage focused more on the impersonal, intrapsychic, systemic meaning of the term. Hartmann (1950/1964) was the first psychoanalyst to distinguish clearly the concept of ego from self. By redefining narcissism as the libidinal investment not of the ego but of the self, Hartmann separated the subjective and personal from the objective and impersonal. Hartmann's formulations, however, were somewhat ambiguous in that he used the term *self* to refer to the whole person, including both bodily and psychological components, as well as to the aggregation of self-representations, implying that such an aggregate was a subcategory of the ego's representational function.

Subsequent contributions to a psychoanalytic theory of self include Spiegel (1959) on the concept of identity and George Klein (1976) on the self-schema. Currently there are three lines of psychoanalytic theorizing about the self. One line, represented by Grossman (1982), regards the self as a fantasy formation. From this vantage point, the self is seen as a compromise of drive and defense forces and is regarded as a fantasy, but with mythic elements. Whereas the ego is a structural term for classifying behavior, fantasies, defenses, and so on, the self, by contrast, is a phenomenological term of significance for the individual in that it provides an organization or frame of reference for inner experience. A second line regards the self as an integrated structure of self-representations with particular reference to introjection. Following Hartmann (1950/1964), Kernberg (1975) described the self as "an intrapsychic structure consisting of multiple self-representations and related affect dispositions. Self-representations are affective-cognitive structures reflecting the person's perception of himself in real and fantasized interactions with others" (pp. 315–316). In this frame of reference, the self is regarded as part of the ego.

The third line of theorizing about the self is that of Kohut, who conceived of the self as a superordinate, unified, coherent constellation with drives and defenses that evolve out of an independently defined developmental line of narcissism. The self essentially emerges from the emphatic mirroring and idealizing activities of parental figures. Initially Kohut (1971) limited his view of the self to a developmental outcome of narcissism, and as such, his view was consistent with what Freud more traditionally described as the transformation of infantile narcissism into the ego ideal. Kohut accepted Freud's narrow concept of the self as the content of the agencies of the mental apparatus, that is, as mental representations of the id, ego, and superego. Kohut (1977) subsequently took a broader perspective in which the self was conceptualized as a superordinate structure subsuming within it the id, ego, and superego. Kohut's dissatisfaction with the earlier, narrower concept of the self was based on clinical rather than theoretical grounds. He suggested that an understanding of narcissism required a concept of the self. The mental content of narcissism is the self and the content of disordered narcissism is a disordered concept of self. Therefore, according to Kohut, when narcissistic disorders are closely examined, conflicts and fixations that are traditionally understood in structural terms of the agencies of the mind (id, ego, superego) are more readily understood as secondary to disorders of the self. Kohut repeatedly distinguished between the self as experience-near and the structural entities of the mind as experience-distant, implying that the self occupies a different level of conceptual and experiential organization. Beyond clinical-empirical reasons, both Meissner (1986) and Blatt (1974; Blatt & Behrends, 1987) pointed out that an experience-near concept of the self provides a place in psychoanalytic theory for considering a personal self as the active, originating source for the construction of personal meaning. Identification of the processes involved in this capacity for the construction of meaning allows for a more complete account of complex experiential states as well as offering a conceptual point of reference for formulating a theory of object relations as well as a way of conceptualizing various personal qualities and capacities that are superordinate to and yet based on various substructures of the personality.

One of the important current debates in contemporary psychoanalysis and dynamic psychology concerns the concept and very nature of narcissism and its role in normal development, in psychopathology, and in the therapeutic process. Kohut (1971) discussed narcissism as an independent developmental line (A. Freud, 1965); impairments in this developmental process create unique forms of pathology. "Narcissism has a development of its own, a pathology of its own, and requires a treatment of its own. . . . Narcissism and object love have side-by-side existences and development that are mutually exclusive" (Goldberg, 1974, p. 245). Kernberg, in contrast, viewed narcissistic disturbances as part of borderline personality organization. Narcissistic disturbances involve the primitive defenses of splitting and dissociation—the defenses of borderline patients. But, in addition, as "compensation" for the lack of a normal, integrated self-concept, narcissistic patients become grandiose, extremely self-centered, and lack an interest in and an empathy for others, even though they are eager to have the admiration and approval of others (Kernberg, 1975, p. 228). Narcissistic patients have better impulse control and social functioning, including a capacity for work and achievement, than borderline patients because of this compensatory, but pathologically integrated, grandiose self-concept.

There are important theoretical and clinical implications for considering narcissistic disturbances either as specific forms of psychopathology that evolve from a separate developmental line (Kohut, 1971, 1977) or as a subtype of borderline phenomena that evolves out of disruptions in the development of object relations (Kernberg, 1975). The differences in theoretical orientation have significant clinical implications for how one views the role of interpretation, the importance of transference, and the therapeutic alliance in the treatment process. For Kohut, treatment of narcissistic patients involves recognition of the patient's inability to perceive and experience the analyst as a separate person. Therapy involves accepting, for long periods of time, the idealization of the patient as externalizations and projections of the patient's grandiose self. Gradually in treatment, through a series of transmuting internalizations, the narcissistic grandiose self is modified and concepts of the self begin to develop normally and become integrated into the total personality organization. Kernberg, in contrast, views narcissistic structures (grandiose self and idealization) as defenses against primitive oral rage, envy, paranoid fears, and loneliness. Expression of this repressed primitive rage in treatment is a prerequisite for structural change, and this can occur only through the active interpretation of the grandiose and idealizing transferences that are seen as defenses against the underlying rage and negative transference. Kernberg maintains continuity with traditional psychoanalysis in his primary emphasis on the mutative power of interpreting conflicts and defenses (resistances) as experienced in the transference.

Kohut, in contrast, emphasized the special quality of the interpersonal relationship that the patient seeks to establish with the therapist and how important it is to be very attentive to the experiential dimensions of the patient-analyst relationships. Kohut is particularly interested in how the patient constructs concepts of self and others out of the neutrality and implicit support of the therapeutic relationship. The narcissistic patient has difficulties perceiving the analyst as a separate person, and only gradually, through a process of transmuting internalizations, can this type of patient relinquish primitive forms of narcissism and allow the self-concept to develop in a more realistic form and be coordinated with a developing capacity for object love. Kohut stressed the experiential dimensions of the therapeutic alliance and the mutative role of the unique interpersonal relationship established. He also stressed the manner in which the alliance provides the basis for a sense of transmuting internalizations that result in the establishment of more realistic and appropriate concepts of the self and of others.

Blatt and Behrends (1987), in a discussion of therapeutic action from the perspective of processes of separation and individuation, provided a theoretical model of therapeutic action based on integration of the interpretation of conflict and defense as well as transmuting internalizations. They pointed out that transmuting internalizations can occur only after there has been significant resolution of prior, pathological internalizations (Blatt & Erlich, 1982). Recognition and relinquishing of pathological introjects that seriously distorted concepts of self and others can come about only through the interpretation of conflict and defense. While this process is essential for therapeutic change, it is not sufficient. Interpretations enable the patient to recognize the power of pathological internalizations and eventually resolve them. The relinquishing of these well-established but distorted introjects provides the patient with the opportunity to establish new and hopefully more constructive internalizations. These new internalizations occur, initially at least, in the context of the therapeutic alliance. The benign support implicit in the analyst's neutrality enables the patient to explore new concepts of self and of others and new conceptions of actual and potential interpersonal interactions. Establishment of these new, transmuting internalizations consolidates the patient's relinquishing prior, pathological introjects. The therapeutic process of interpretation and internalization is the mutative force not only in the treatment of narcissistic and borderline pathology but is an essential dimension in all dynamically oriented psychotherapy and psychoanalysis (Blatt & Behrends, 1987; Blatt & Erlich, 1982).

These contemporary considerations about the etiology and treatment of severe psychopathology—the debate between Kernberg and Kohut—indicate an emerging emphasis in psychoanalytic thought on experiential dimensions and the inclusion of a phenomenological point of view. Phenomenological considerations supplement Freud's biological, drive-discharge theory—the economic point of view. There has been substantial criticism of the economic theory of psychoanalysis (Apfelbaum, 1965; Arlow, 1975; Blatt, Wild, & Ritzler, 1975; Dahl, 1968; Holt, 1965, 1967, 1976; Klein, 1976; Peterfreund, 1971; Rubinstein, 1967; Stolorow & Atwood, 1979) as based on outmoded concepts of physiology and physics that are inconsistent with current neurophysiological knowledge. Also, the drive theory postulates impersonal, quasi-physiological forces that ignore personal meaning and motivational dynamics. Likewise, there has been considerable controversy about Freud's "structural theory"—the concepts of id, ego, and superego and how they are often used as reifications and personifications rather than considerations of the individual as an integrated organism with a synthesized orchestration of multiple levels of meanings and motivations. Numerous alternatives have been suggested as replacements for the metapsychological superstructure of psychoanalysis (the economic and structural points of view), including a "protoneurophysiological" theory (Rubinstein, 1967, 1976), a model of information processing and systems theory (Kubie, 1975, Peterfreund, 1971, 1975), and a phenomenological approach that considers issues of intention, meanings, reasons, and subjective experiences (Gill, 1976; Home, 1966; Klein, 1976; Schafer, 1976).

It is our belief that the most important of these alternatives is the development of a phenomenological point of view. In the phenomenological approach, concepts of cause, effect, impulse, energy, and drive are supplemented by aspects of subjective experiences such as intentions, decisions, and actions for avowed and disavowed reasons (Anscombe, 1981; Schafer, 1976). Personal meanings and subjective experiences can form the basis of a clinical theory that examines the whys of human experiences rather than the hows (Sandler & Joffe, 1969). This clinical theory uses what Mayman (1976) called a "middle-level language" that focuses on subjective meaning, intentions, aims, and motives emerging from "cognitive-emotional schemata" (Klein, 1976) of the representational world (Sandler & Rosenblatt, 1962). These representational configurations have cognitive and affective components and evolve with development and assume "functional significance" (Klein, 1976) in guiding and directing behavior (Blatt, 1974; Blatt et al., 1975). These cognitive affective representational structures of the self and the object world can be considered not only from a psychoanalytic perspective but also as they intersect with developmental, cognitive, and social-psychological theory.

This new orientation in psychoanalysis—this addition of a phenomenological point of view—need not replace, but rather it can serve to supplement prior psychoanalytic points of view. The emerging emphasis on a phenomenological point of view in psychoanalysis can be seen in many aspects of contemporary psychoanalytic research. Greater attention is being given to the study of infant-mother transaction, such as research on the early, preverbal development of the infant that emerges in significant care taking (e.g., Beebe, 1982). The emphasis on interpersonal interactions in development can also be seen in investigations of the psychoanalytic situation (e.g., Gill & Hoffman, 1981; Hartley & Strupp, 1982; Sampson & Weiss, 1982), on the quality of object and self-representations (e.g., Blatt, Brenneis, Schimek, & Glick, 1976; Blatt & Lerner, 1983a; Blatt, Wein, Chevron, & Quinlan, 1979; Mayman, 1967; Unst, 1977), and on the subliminal stimulation of fundamental interpersonal experiences (Weinberger & Silverman, 1990). In fact, a large proportion of articles in a newly developed annual on empirical investigations of psychoanalytic concepts (Masling, 1982a, 1982b) deal with phenomenological issues such as self-deception, self-esteem, and depression (Sackeim, 1982), the definition and assessment of meaning (Dahl, 1982), interests as objects relations (Eagle, 1982), orality and interpersonal behavior (Masling, 1982b), needs for fusion and differentiation (Greene, 1982), and on hopelessness and hope (Freedman, 1982).

CONCLUSION

In this review we have sought to describe recent developments in dynamic theories of personality and especially the increased emphasis on interpersonal relationships and phenomenological experiences as a fundamental data base for the development of a clinical theory of psychoanalysis. The development of a phenomenological point of view in psychoanalytic theory has resulted in a broadening of the scope of psychoanalysis to include interest in more severe forms of psychopathology, including narcissistic disturbances and the borderline and psychotic conditions, an interest in specifying the mutative forces of therapeutic action—the forces that create change in psychoanalysis and psychotherapy—an interest in very early, preverbal development, the normal development of concepts of self and other (the representational world) and their impairment in psychopathology, and the study of a wide range of phenomenological experiences such as hope and hopelessness, wishes, interests, intentions, interpersonal relationships, and the early experiences of dependency, orality, and fusion. This phenomenological orientation has had a profound impact on clinical practice, theory, and research. It has provided a closer link between the basic data base of psychoanalysis—observations made in the clinical context of the psychoanalytic process—and theoretical formulations. This closer tie between psychoanalytic data and theory will continue to have a significant impact on the nature of clinical practice, and it will facilitate empirical investigation of important dimensions of human experience.

REFERENCES

Abend, S. M., Parder, M. J., & Willick, M. D. (1983). *Borderline patients: Psychoanalytic perspectives.* New York: International Universities Press.

Abraham, K. (1924). A short study of the development of the libido. In *Selected papers on psychoanalyses.* London: Hogarth Press.

Abraham, K. (1927). Notes on the psychoanalytical investigation and treatment of manic-depressive insanity and allied conditions. In *Selected papers on psychoanalysis.* London: Hogarth Press.

Anscombe, R. (1981). Referring to the unconscious. A philosophical critique of Schafer's action language. *International Journal of Psychoanalysis.* 62, 225–241.

Apfelbaum, B. (1965). Ego psychology, psychic energy, and the hazards of quantitative exploration in psychoanalytic theory. *International Journal of Psychoanalysis.* 46, 168–182.

Arlow, J. (1975). The structural hypothesis—Theoretical considerations. *Psychoanalytic Quarterly,* 44, 509–525.

Balint, M. (1952). *Primary love and psychoanalytic technique.* London: Hogarth Press.

Balint, M. (1968). *The basic fault.* London: Tavistock Press.

Beebe, B. (1982). Mother-infant mutual influence and precursors of self and object representation. In J. Masling (Ed.), *Empirical studies of psychoanalytic theories* (Vol. II, pp. 27–48). Hillsdale, NJ: Lawrence Erlbaum Associates.

Behrends, R. S., & Blatt, S. J. (1985). Internalization and psychological development throughout the life cycle. *Psychoanalytic Study of the Child, 40,* 11–39.

Bion, W. (1959). Attack on linking. *International Journal of Psychoanalysis, 40,* 308–315.

Blatt, S. J. (1974). Levels of object representation in anaclitic and introjective depression. *Psychoanalytic Study of the Child, 29,* 107–157.

Blatt, S. J. (1978, May). *Paradoxical representations and their implications for the treatment of psychosis and borderline states.* Paper presented at a meeting of the Institute for Psychoanalytic Research and Training, New York City.

Blatt, S. J. (1990). The Rorschach: A test of perception or an evaluation of representation. *Journal of Personality Assessment, 55,* 394–416.

Blatt, S. J., & Behrends, R. (1987). Internalization, separation-individuation, and the nature of therapeutic action. *International Journal of Psychoanalysis, 68,* 279–297.

Blatt, S. J., & Blatt, E. S. (1984). *Cultural continuity and change in art: The development of modes of representation.* Hillsdale, NJ: Lawrence Erlbaum Associates.

Blatt, S. J., Brenneis B., Schimek, J. G., & Glick, M. (1976). Normal development and psychopathological impairment of the concept of the object on the Rorschach. *Journal of Abnormal Psychology, 85,* 364–373.

Blatt, S. J., & Erlich, H. S. (1982). Levels of resistance in the psychotherapeutic process. In P. L. Wachtel (Ed.), *Resistance: Psychodynamic and behavioral approaches* (pp. 69–91). New York: Plenum Publishing.

Blatt, S. J., & Lerner, H. (1983a). Investigations in the psychoanalytic theory of object relations and object representations. In J Masling (Ed.), *Empirical studies of psychoanalytic theories* (pp. 189–249). Hillsdale, NJ: Analytic Press.

Blatt, S. J., & Lerner, H. (1983b). The psychological assessment of object representations. *Journal of Personality Assessment, 47,* 7–28.

Blatt, S. J., & Schichman, S. (1983). Two primary configurations of psychotherapy. *Psychoanalysis and Contemporary Thought, 6,* 187–254.

Blatt, S. J., Wein, S. J., Chevron, E., & Quinlan, D. (1979). Parental representations and depression in normal young adults. *Journal of Abnormal Psychology, 78,* 388–397.

Blatt, S. J., & Wild, C. M. (1976). *Schizophrenia: A developmental analysis.* New York: Academic Press.

Blatt, S. J., Wild, C. M., & Ritzler, B. A. (1975). Disturbances of object representations in schizophrenia. *Psychoanalysis and Contemporary Science, 4,* 235–288.

Boesky, D. (1988). A discussion of evidential criteria for therapeutic change. In A. Rothstein (Ed), *How does treatment help: Models of therapeutic action of psychoanalytic therapy.* Madison, CT: International Universities Press.

Brenner, C. (1983). *The mind in conflict.* New York: International Universities Press.

Brenner, C. (1986). Reflections. In A. Richards & M. S. Willich (Eds.). *Psychoanalysis: The science of mental conflict. Essays in honor of Charles Brenner.* Hillsdale, NJ: Analytic Press.

Burnham, D., Gladstone, A., & Gibson, R. (1969). *Schizophrenia and the need fear dilemma.* New York: International Universities Press.

Dahl, H. (1968). Panel on "Psychoanalytic theory of the instinctual drives in relation to recent developments." *Journal of the American Psychoanalytic Association, 16,* 629–632.

Dahl, H. (1982). On the definition and measurement of wishes. In J. Masling (Ed.). *Empirical studies of psychoanalytical theories,* (Vol. I). Hillsdale, NJ: Lawrence Erlbaum Associates.

Dare, C. (1976). Psychoanalytic theories. In M. Rutter & L. Hersou (Eds.). *Child psychiatry: Modern approaches.* Oxford, England: Blackwell.

Eagle, M. (1982). Interest as object relations. In J. Masling (Ed.). *Empirical studies of psychoanalytical theories* (Vol I, pp. 159–187). Hillsdale, NJ: Lawrence Erlbaum Associates.

Fairbairn, W. R. (1963). Synopsis of an object-relations theory of the personality. *International Journal of Psychoanalysis, 44*, 224–226.

Fairbairn, W. R. D. (1954). *An object relations theory of the personality.* New York: Basic Books.

Federn, P. (1952). *Ego psychology and the psychoses.* New York: Basic Books.

Fenichel, O. (1945). *The psychoanalytic theory of neurosis.* New York: W W Norton.

Fraiberg, S. (1969). Libidinal object constancy and mental representation. *Psychoanalytic Study of the Child, 24,* 9–47.

Freedman, N. (1982). On depression: From hopelessness to hope. In J. Masling (Ed.). *Empirical studies of psychoanalytical theories* (Vol. II). Hillsdale, NJ: Lawrence Erlbaum Associates.

Freud, A. (1936). *Ego and the mechanisms of defense.* New York: International Universities Press.

Freud, A. (1952). The mutual influences in the development of ego and id. *Psychoanalytic Study of the Child, 7,* 42–50.

Freud, A. (1965). *Normality and pathology in childhood. Assessments of developments* (Vol. VI). New York: International Universities Press.

Freud, A. (1969a). The assessment of borderline cases. Research at the Hampstead Child Therapy Clinic and other papers. *The writings of Anna Freud, 1956, 5,* 301–314. New York: International Universities Press.

Freud, A. (1969b). Assessment of pathology in childhood. In A. Freud (Ed.). Research at the Hampstead Child Therapy Clinic and Other Papers. *The writings of Anna Freud, 1956, 5.* New York: International Universities Press.

Freud, A. (1981). Psychopathology seen against the background of normal development. In *Psychoanalytic psychology of normal development.* (Vol. VIII). New York: International Universities Press.

Freud, S. (1957a). Instincts and their vicissitudes. *Standard edition* (Vol. 14). London: Hogarth Press. (Original work published 1915)

Freud, S. (1957b). The interpretation of dreams. *Standard Edition.* (Vol. 5). London: Hogarth Press. (Original work published 1900)

Freud, S. (1957c) Mourning and melancholia. *Standard edition* (Vol. 14). London: Hogarth Press. (Original work published 1917)

Freud, S. (1957d). Three essays on the theory of sexuality. *Standard Edition.* London: Hogarth Press. (Original work published 1905)

Freud, S. (1961a). Civilization and its discontents. *Standard edition.* (Vol. 21). London: Hogarth Press. (Original work published 1930)

Freud, S. (1961b). The ego and the id. *Standard edition* (Vol. 19). London: Hogarth Press. (Original work published 1923)

Freud, S. (1961c). Inhibitions, symptoms and anxiety. *Standard edition* (Vol. 20). London: Hogarth Press. (Original work published 1926)

Freud, S. (1961d). On narcissism. *Standard edition* (Vol. 14). London: Hogarth Press. (Original work published 1914)

Freud, S. (1961e). An outline of psychoanalysis. *Standard edition* (Vol. 23). London: Hogarth Press. (Original work published 1938)

Gardner, H. (1984). *The mind's new science: A history of the cognitive revolution.* New York: Basic Books.

Gill, M. M. (1976). Metapsychology is not psychology. In M. Gill & P. Holzman (Eds.), *Psychology versus metapsychology. Psychological issues,* Monograph, 36. New York: International Universities Press.

Gill, M. M., & Hoffman, I. (1981). *Analysis of transference* (Vol. I & II). New York: International Universities Press.

Glover, E. (1950). Functional aspects of the mental apparatus. *International Journal of Psychoanalysis, 31,* 125–131.

Goldberg, A. (1974). On the prognosis and treatment of narcissism. *Journal of the American Psychoanalytic Association, 22,* 243–254.

Gouin-Decarie, T. G. (1965). *Intelligence and affectivity in early childhood.* New York: International Universities Press.

Green, A. (1977). The borderline concept. In P. Hartocollis (Ed.), *Borderline personality disorders.* New York: International Universities Press.

Greene, L. (1982). Idiosyncratic needs for fusion and differentiation in groups. In J. Masling (Ed.), *Empirical studies of psychoanalytic theories* (Vol. II). Hillsdale, NJ: Lawrence Erlbaum Associates.

Grossman, W. I. (1982). The self as fantasy: Fantasy as theory. *Journal of the American Psychoanalytic Association, 30,* 919–938.

Guntrip, H. (1961). *Personality structure and human interaction.* New York: International Universities Press.

Guntrip, H. (1969). *Schizoid phenomena object relations and the self.* New York: International Universities Press.

Guntrip, H. (1974). Psychoanalytic object relations theory: The Fairbairn-Guntrip approach. In S. Aneti (Ed.), *American handbook of psychiatry* (Vol. I). New York: Basic Books.

Hartley, D., & Strupp, H. (1982). The therapeutic alliance: Its relationship to outcome in brief psychotherapy. In J. Masling (Ed.), *Empirical studies of psychoanalytical theories:* (Vol. 1, pp. 1–37). Hillsdale, NJ, Lawrence Erlbaum Associates.

Hartmann, H. (1958). *Ego psychology and the problem of adaptation.* New York: International Universities Press.

Hartmann, H. (1964). Comments on the psychoanalytic theory of the ego. In H. Hartman (Ed.), *Essays on ego psychology, selected problems in psychoanalytic theory* (pp. 113–141). New York: International Universities Press. (Original work published 1950)

Hartmann, H., Kris, E., & Lowenstein, R. M. (1949). Notes on the theory of aggression. *The Psychoanalytic Study of the Child, 4*, 9–36. New York: International Universities Press.

Hartmann, H., & Loewenstein, R. M. (1962). Notes on the superego. *The Psychoanalytic Study of the Child, 17*, 42–81. New York: International Universities Press.

Hoffer, W. (1952). The mutual influences in the development of ego and id. Earliest stages. *The Psychoanalytic Study of the Child, 7*, 31–41. New York: International Universities Press.

Holt, R. (1965). A review of some of Freud's biological assumptions and their influence on his theories. In N. Greenfield & W. Lewis (Eds.), *Psychoanalysis and current biological thought* (pp. 93–124). Madison: University of Wisconsin Press.

Holt, R. (1967). On freedom, autonomy, and the redirection of psychoanalytic theory: A rejoinder. *International Journal of Psychiatry, 6*, 524–536.

Holt, R. (1976). Drive or wish? A reconsideration of the psychoanalytic theory of motivation. In M. Gill & P. Holzman (Eds.), *Psychology versus metapsychology: Psychological Issues*, Monograph 36 (pp. 158–197). New York: International Universities Press.

Home, H. (1966). The concept of mind. *International Journal of Psychoanalysis, 47*, 43–49.

Horner, A. (1980). *Object relations and the developing ego in therapy*. New York: Jason Aronson.

Jacobson, E. (1964). *The self and the object world*. New York: International Universities Press.

Jones, E. (1954). Preface In W. R. D. Fairbairn (Ed.). *An object relations theory of the personality*. New York: Basic Books.

Kernberg, O. (1966). Structural derivatives of object relationships. *International Journal of Psychoanalysis, 47*, 236–253.

Kernberg, O. (1972). Early ego integration and object relations. *Annual of the New York Academy of Science, 193*, 233–247.

Kernberg, O. (1975). *Borderline conditions and pathological narcissism*. New York: Jason Aronson.

Kernberg, O. (1976). *Object relations theory and clinical psychoanalysis*. New York: Jason Aronson.

Kernberg, O. (1978). Contrasting approaches to the treatment of borderline conditions. In J. Masterson (Ed.). *New perspectives in psychotherapy of the borderline adult*. New York: Brunner/Mazel.

Kernberg, O. (1982). The theory of psychoanalytic psychotherapy. In S. Slipp (Ed.). *Curative factors in dynamic psychotherapy* (pp. 1–21). New York: McGraw-Hill.

Klein, G. S. (1976). *Psychoanalytic theory*. New York: International Universities Press.

Klein, M. (1975). *The writings of Melanie Klein* (Vol III). London: Hogarth Press.

Kohut, H. (1971). *The analysis of the self*. New York: International Universities Press.

Kohut, H. (1977). *The restoration of the self*. New York: International Universities Press.

Kohut, H., & Wolff, E. (1978). The disorders of the self and their treatment. An outline. *International Journal of Psychoanalysis, 59*, 413–425.

Kubie, L. (1947). The fallacious use of quantitative concepts in dynamic psychology. *Psychoanalytic Quarterly, 16*, 507–518.

Kubie, L. (1975). The language tools of psychoanalysis: A search for better tools drawn from better models. *International Review of Psychoanalysis, 2*, 11–24.

Lichtenberg, H. (1979). Factors in the development of the sense of the object. *Journal of the American Psychoanalytic Association, 27*, 375–386.

Lidz, T., and Lidz, R. (1952). Therapeutic considerations arising from the intensive symbiotic needs of schizophrenic patients. In E. Brody & F. C. Redlich (Eds.), *Psychotherapy with schizophrenics*. New York: International Universities Press.

Loch, W. (1977). Some comments on the subect of psychoanalysis and trust. In J. Smith (Ed.), *Psychiatry and the humanities* (Vol. 2). New Haven: Yale University Press.

Loewald, H. (1951). Ego and reality. *International Journal of Psychoanalysis, 32*, 10–18.

Loewald, H. (1960). On the therapeutic action of psychoanalysis. *International Journal of Psychoanalysis, 41*, 16–33.

Loewald, H. (1970). Psychoanalytic theory and the psychoanalytic process. In *The psychoanalytic study of the child* (pp. 45–68). New York: International Universities Press.

Loewald, H. (1973). On internalization. *International Journal of Psychoanalysis, 54*, 9–17.

Loewald, H. (1979). Reflections on the psychoanalytic process and its therapeutic potential. In *The psychoanalytic study of the child*. New Haven: Yale University Press.

Luborsky, L. (1962). Clinician's judgments of mental health: A proposed scale. *Archives of General Psychiatry, 7*, 407–417.

Mahler, M. (1968). *On human symbiosis and the vicissitudes of individuation*. New York: International Universities Press.

Mahler, M., Pine, F., & Bergman, A. (1975). *The psychological birth of the human infant*. New York: Basic Books.

Masling, J. (Ed.). (1982a). *Empirical studies of psychoanalytical theories* (Vol. I). Hillsdale, NJ: Lawrence Erlbaum Associates.

Masling, J. (1982b). Orality, psychopathology, and interpersonal relations. In J. Masling (Ed.), *Empirical studies on psychoanalytical theories* (Vol. II, pp. 73–106). Hillsdale, NJ: Lawrence Erlbaum Associates.

Mayman, M. (1967). Object representations and object relationships in Rorschach responses. *Journal of Projective Techniques and Personality Assessment, 31*, 17–24.

Mayman, M. (1976). Psychoanalytic theory in retrospect and prospect. *Bulletin of the Menninger Clinic, 40*, 199–210.

Meissner, W. (1986). Can psychoanalysis find itself? *Journal of the American Psychoanalytic Association, 34*, 379–400.

Meltzer, D. (1981). The Kleinian expansion of Freud's metapsychology. *International Journal of Psychoanalysis, 62*, 177–185.

Modell, A. (1981). Does metapsychology still exist? *International Journal of Psychoanalysis, 62*, 391–402.

Parens, H. (1971). A contribution of separation-individuation to the development of psychic structures. In J. B. McDevitt & C. F. Settlage (Eds.), *Separation-individuation: Essays in honor of Margaret S. Mahler* (pp. 100–112). New York: International Universities Press.

Parsons, T., & Bales, R. (1955). *Family socialization and interaction process.* Glencoe, IL: Free Press.

Peterfreund, E. (1971). *Information, symptoms, and psychoanalysis: An evolutionary biological approach to psychoanalytic theory. Psychological Issues.* Monograph 25/26. New York: International Universities Press.

Peterfreund, E. (1975). The need for a new general theoretical frame of reference for psychoanalysis. *Psychoanalytic Quarterly, 44*, 534–549.

Piaget, J. (1954). *The construction of reality.* New York: Basic Books.

Pruyser, P. (1975). What splits in splitting? *Bulletin of the Menninger Clinic, 39*, 1–46.

Rapaport, D. (1940). *Organization and pathology of thought.* New York: Columbia University Press.

Rubinstein, B. (1967). Exploration and more description: A metascientific examination of certain aspects of the psychoanalytic theory of motivation. In R. Holt (Ed.), *Motives and thought: Psychoanalytic essays in honor of David Rapaport. Psychological issues*, Monograph 18/19. New York: International Universities Press.

Rubinstein, B. (1976). On the possibility of a strictly clinical psychoanalytic theory: An essay on the philosophy of psychoanalysis. In M. Gill & P. Holzman (Eds.), *Psychology versus metapsychology. Psychological issues.* Monograph 36 (pp. 229–264). New York: International Universities Press.

Sackeim, H. (1982). Self deception, self esteem, and depression: The adaptive value of lying to oneself. In J. Masling (Ed.), *Empirical studies of psychoanalytic theories* (Vol. I). Hillsdale, NJ: Lawrence Erlbaum Associates.

Sampson, H., & Weiss, J. (1982). Testing alternative psychoanalytic explanations of the therapeutic process. In J. Masling (Ed.), *Empirical studies of psychoanalytic theories* (Vol. II). Hillsdale, NJ: Lawrence Erlbaum Associates.

Sandler, J., & Joffe, W. (1969). Toward a basic psychoanalytic model. *International Journal of Psychoanalysis, 50*, 74–90.

Sandler, J., & Rosenblatt, B. (1962). The concept of the representational world. *Psychoanalytic study of the child* (pp. 128–145). New York: International Universities Press.

Schafer, R. (1968). *Aspects of internalization.* New York: International Universities Press.

Schafer, R. (1976). *A new language for psychoanalysis.* New Haven: Yale University Press.

Spiegel, L. (1959). The self, the sense of self and perception. *Psychoanalytic Study of the Child, 14*, 81–109.

Settlage, C. (1977). The psychoanalytic understanding of narcissistic and borderline disorders: Advances in developmental theory. *J. Amer. Psychoanalytic Assn., 25*, 805–833.

Steele, R. (1979). Psychoanalysis and hermeneutics. *International Review of Psycho-analysis, 6*, 389–412.

Stierlin, H. (1970). The function of inner objects. *International Journal of Psycho-analysis, 51*, 321–329.

Stolorow, R., & Atwood, G. (1979). *Faces in a cloud: Subjectivity in personality theory.* New York: Jason Aronson.

Sutherland, J. (1980). The British object relation theorists: Balint, Winnicott, Fairbairn, Guntrip. *Journal of the American Psychoanalytic Association, 28*, 829–60.

Tausk, V. (1950). On the origin of the "influencing machine" in Schizophrenia. In R. Fliess (Ed.), *The Psycho-Analytic Reader* (pp. 31–64). London: Hogarth Press. (Original work published 1919)

Teicholz, J. G. (1978). A selective review of the psychoanalytic literature on theoretical conceptualization of narcissism. *Journal of the American Psychoanalytic Association, 26*, 831–862.

Thomas, R., Chess, S., & Birch, H. (1968). *Temperament and behavior disorders in children.* New York: New York University Press.

Topin, M., & Kohut, H. (1980). The disorders of the self: The psychopathology of the first years of life. In S. I. Greenspan & G. H. Pollock (Eds.), *The course of life: Psychoanalytic contributions toward understanding personality development.* (Vol. 1). *Infancy and early childhood.* Washington, DC: NIMH.

Unst, J. (1977). The Rorschach test and the assessment of object relations. *Journal of Personality Assessment, 41*, 3–9.

Vygotsky, L. (1962). *Thought and language.* E. Hanfmann & G. Vakar (Trans.). Cambridge, MA: MIT Press.

Weinberger, J., & Silverman, L. (1990). Testability and empirical verification of psychoanalytic dynamic propositions through subliminal psychodynamic activation. *Psychoanalytic Psychology, 7*, 299–339.

Werner, H. (1948). *Comparative psychology of mental development.* New York: International Universities Press.

Winnicott, D. W. (1945). Primitive emotional development. *International Journal of Psychoanalysis, 26*, 137–143.

Winnicott, D. W. (1958). Transitional objects and transitional phenomena. *Collected papers: Through pediatrics to psychoanalysis.* New York: Basic Books.

Winnicott, D. W. (1960). The theory of the parent-infant relationship. *International Journal of Psychoanalysis, 41*, 585–595.

Winnicott, D. W. (1964). What do we mean by a normal child? In D. W. Winnicott (Ed.), *The child, the family, and the outside world.* London: Penguin Books.

Winnicott, D. W. (1965a). The capacity to be alone. In D. W. Winnicott (Ed.), *The maturational processes and the facilitating environment.* New York: International Universities Press.

Winnicott, D. W. (1965b) Ego integration in child development. *The maturational processes and the facilitating environment*. London: Hogarth Press.

Winnicott, D. W. (1965c). Growth and development in immaturity. In D. W. Winnicott (Ed.), *The maturational processes and the facilitating environment*. London: Hogarth Press.

Winnicott, D. W. (1971). *Playing and reality*. New York: Basic Books.

Winnicott, D. W. (1980). The use of an object and relating through identifications. In D. W. Winnicott (Ed.), *Playing and reality* (pp. 85–94). London: Penguin Books.

Wolff, P. H. (1967). Cognitive reconsiderations for a psychoanalytic acquisition. In R. Holt (Ed.), *Motives and thought* (pp. 300–343). New York: International Universities Press.

CHAPTER 10

LEARNING

Howard Rachlin
A. W. Logue

The study of learning has frequently played a role in clinical psychology and in understanding personality. As long ago as the 1920s, Pavlov reported that he could mimic human neuroses in his animal learning laboratory by exposing his subjects, dogs, to increasingly difficult discriminations (Pavlov, 1927). The dogs became irritable and then began to show many symptoms characteristic of human neurotics. They barked, squealed, whined, and trembled, bit and tore at the apparatus, and lost the ability to make even the easier, previously mastered, discriminations. This was one of the first attempts to model clinical phenomena in the learning laboratory. Another early example is Watson's (Watson & Rayner, 1920) experiments on learned fears in infants.

The relevance of laboratory learning theory to clinical psychology has rested on three assumptions. The first is that human behavior is at least to some extent learned. There have been no serious quarrels with this assumption. The second assumption is that experiments performed in laboratory settings can have relevance for real life. This assumption has been subject to much criticism, particularly by ethologists, who frequently claim that organisms' natural behavior can be studied only in "natural" surroundings (see,

e.g., Houston & McNamara, 1988; Johnston, 1981; Johnston & Pietrewicz, 1985). The argument about this issue continues to rage with much bitter commentary on both sides. It is our belief (King & Logue, 1988; Logue, 1981a; Rachlin, 1981, 1988) that while an animal's normal activities can be discovered only in a particular ecological niche, the limits of these activities can be tested only in the laboratory. Laboratory experiments, unlike observations of learning in the field, allow the experimenter to control critical variables. For example, in the laboratory, it is possible to deprive subjects of food or water to a predetermined level, to isolate them from extraneous noises or lights, and to have a full record of their previous environmental histories. Furthermore, in the laboratory, the experimenter is much less likely to succumb to the illusion that he or she intuitively understands the subject (animal or person) and is much more likely to rely on the data.

The third assumption is similar to the second in that it also concerns the generality of laboratory experiments. Just as the applicability of the experimental study of learning necessitates the assumption that results obtained from laboratory experiments are relevant for the real world, so it also often necessitates the assumption that results obtained from nonhuman subjects are relevant for humans. Again, there has been much criticism of this assumption (e.g., Lowe & Horne, 1988; Seligman, 1970; Shimoff & Catania, 1988). Clearly, rats are very different from humans, and so it has been difficult for some psychologists to see any relevance of animal-learning experiments for human behavior. This issue will be discussed in the section of this chapter entitled, "General Laws of Learning and Their Biological Limits," but for now it suffices to say that the comparative study of learning has revealed many similarities between species (see, e.g., Gustavson, 1977; Logue, 1988).

Keeping these three assumptions in mind, much of what occurs in learning laboratories is of potential relevance for clinical psychology. The bulk of this chapter presents some of the general issues and specific topics of current interest in the field of learning. The general issues are presented without regard for clinical application. In discussing some specific topics, however, we briefly indicate how they may be applied. Finally, some brief observations on the successes, failures, and prospects for clinical application of laboratory work are presented.

RECENT ISSUES WITHIN LEARNING THEORY

Molecular and Molar

A problem for any science concerns the level at which information should be examined and principles constructed. In learning theory a molecular approach usually involves analyzing data and constructing principles at the level of individual responses, such as lever presses or key pecks, often determining the effects of reinforcement on the actual sequence of responses (see, e.g., Watson, 1924/1970). A molar approach usually involves analyzing data and constructing principles using units of data that are composed of many individual responses, such as the number of responses in an experimental session, or the number of times that an animal correctly negotiates a maze, or the proportion of an animal's responses on each of two response alternatives during a session (e.g., Herrnstein, 1970; Tolman, 1948).

The reason for concern with the molecular versus molar issue is that anyone who claims that organisms learn something at a molar level is promptly faced with a counterargument that some regularity, the real cause of the regular behavior seen at the molar level, must exist at a more molecular level. But molar level

learning may occur where there is no apparent regularity at a more molecular level (Baum, 1981).

Recent models at all points of the molecular-molar spectrum have contributed much to our understanding of learning. The issue is not which approach, molecular or molar, is the best one, but which is best to answer a particular question. It will always be possible to describe an organism's behavior in terms of smaller units up to the limits of our physical knowledge. The most truthful level of analysis is, by pragmatic definition, the most useful.

Classical and Instrumental

One of the oldest issues in learning theory is whether there are two kinds of learning or just one. Most of the prominent learning theorists of the 1940s, including Skinner (1938), believed that there are two kinds of learning: classical and instrumental. The first consists of the association of a formerly neutral stimulus (a conditioned stimulus) with a reflex (an unconditioned stimulus and its resulting response); the second consists of the positive and negative laws of effect—the strengthening of a response (or operant) by its favorable consequences (positive reinforcement) and the weakening of a response by its unfavorable consequences (punishment).

While many theorists agree that both kinds of learning are possible, it has been argued that all classical conditioning is really instrumental conditioning (Zener, 1937), and that all instrumental conditioning is really classical conditioning (Moore, 1973). The groundwork of the former argument was actually laid by Pavlov (1927), who asserted that classical conditioning always worked so as to better suit the subject to its environment. Presumably when classical conditioning is maladaptive it is less stable.

The main thrust of the argument that classical conditioning is instrumental is anti-Pavlovian—it comes from the frequent finding of a difference between conditioned and unconditioned responses. For example, in heart rate conditioning, with electric shock as the unconditioned stimulus, the conditioned response, a decrease in heart rate, is actually the opposite of the unconditioned response—an increase (Black, 1971). It is frequently the case that where the conditioned response differs from the unconditioned response the former seems to be a form of preparation for the conditioned or the unconditioned stimulus. For instance, if a rat is shown another rat and then fed, the second rat comes to elicit a conditioned response in the first rat. But this conditioned response is social contact, not biting, which is the unconditioned response to the food (Timberlake & Grant, 1975).

The opposite argument holds that instrumental conditioning is a form of classical conditioning. This argument has gained strength with the finding of autoshaping—that pigeons readily learn keypecking as a conditioned response (Brown & Jenkins, 1968). Simple pairing of a lit key with food generates keypecking. Many other so-called instrumental responses are also susceptible to autoshaping (i.e., can be conditioned responses). Even the various forms of the supposedly arbitrary response of brushing against a pole learned by cats in the famous experiments of Guthrie and Horton (1946) may well be conditioned responses, the unconditioned response being nuzzling against the leg of the experimenter once out of the puzzle box (see Gardner & Gardner, 1988).

It is hoped that findings and arguments such as the aforementioned will lead, eventually, to a satisfactory unified theory of learning, particularly given the fact that most instances of learning involve both classical and operant conditioning (Domjan & Burkhard, 1986). Meanwhile, however, most researchers still distinguish between classical and instrumental procedures.

Reinforcement and Maximization

Within instrumental conditioning there is currently some controversy about the way that reinforcement acts. One group of theorists holds to the view of Thorndike (1911/1965), Hull (1943), and Skinner (1938) that positive reinforcement acts automatically to strengthen any response that happened to precede it. This automatic action is perhaps epitomized by Skinner's concept of superstition. According to this view, a given environment will frequently provide random reinforcers to a given organism. Such reinforcers may adventitiously strengthen whatever behavior happens to occur just before their delivery. Each subsequent reinforcer delivery strengthens the behavior more— thus generating idiosyncratic, superstitious responses. Whatever mechanism is responsible for strengthening the superstitious responses is also responsible for strengthening normal instrumentally conditioned responses, except in the latter case it is usually arranged in the environment (by the contingencies of reinforcement) that only a particular response may precede reinforcement.

Another approach to understanding the effects of instrumental conditioning (Rachlin & Burkhard, 1978) derives from the work of Premack (1965) on the relativity of reinforcers, the work of Herrnstein (1970)

on choice, and the work of Staddon (1979) on allocation of time. Instrumental conditioning is seen as an allocation of time to various activities (the instrumental response, consumption of the reinforcer, other behavior) so as to maximize the overall value of the group of behaviors together. The response is seen as no more important than its context (consisting of other responses occurring before and after the target response). Learning is a reallocation of behavior. A change of contingencies is a change of constraints on behavior. For instance, imagine a hungry rat put in a Skinner box for an hour with a dish of food freely available and a bar that can be pressed or not pressed at will. The rat might spend 10 minutes eating, half a minute pressing the bar, and the other 49.5 minutes in performing other activities (grooming, scratching, sleeping, etc.). Imagine that a ratio contingency is now imposed that demands 10 presses of the lever for each 5-second availability of the food dish (say it takes the rat 5 seconds to make the 10 presses) so that now the rat must spend as much time pressing the bar as it does eating. How will the rat reallocate its time? That, according to a form of maximization theory derived from economics (Rachlin, Kagel, & Battalio, 1980), depends on the degree to which the other activities (grooming, etc.) are substitutable for eating. To the extent that other available responses are substitutable for eating, eating will be reduced. To the extent that other responses are not substitutable for eating, eating will remain rigidly constant. Perhaps surprisingly, experiments with hungry rats show considerable substitutability of these "leisure" activities for food. Similar analyses have been made of the behavior of children playing with toys, adding or removing available toys, and making availability of one toy contingent on playing with another. Again, allocation depends on the degree of substitutability of one behavior for another (Rachlin & Burkhard, 1978).

Maximization theory is currently in its early stages of development. It remains to be seen whether it will prove as durable or as fruitful as reinforcement theory.

General Laws of Learning and Their Biological Limits

Pavlov thought of himself as a neurophysicist rather than as a psychologist, so, from the beginning, he saw learning in biological terms. It was not surprising to Pavlov that stomach secretions should follow food inserted in the mouth. The nervous system may well connect receptors in the mouth with glands that secrete digestive juices—what could be more natural? But when Pavlov discovered that what seemed to be completely arbitrary stimuli, such as bells and lights, would also generate secretions ("psychic" secretions), it was tempting to suppose (although Pavlov himself did not) that all stimuli could serve equally well as conditioned stimuli with a given unconditioned stimulus.

Skinner also began his career in a neurophysiology laboratory (with Crozier at Harvard) and used the Skinner box initially only as a way of indexing the eating behavior of rats. But when he discovered the powerful effects of schedules of reinforcement on behavior, it was natural to suppose (although Skinner himself did not) that all reinforcers could serve equally well to strengthen a given response.

Subsequent research has shown that these natural suppositions are only partly true. Certain kinds of conditioned stimuli will simply not work (will not result in conditioning) with certain kinds of reflexes. Certain reinforcers will not work with certain responses. Nowhere is this affinity more clear than with taste aversion learning, to be discussed later in detail. Briefly, when a visual or auditory stimulus is paired with sickness, animals easily learn to avoid the taste. Thus, there are boundaries, determined by the biological characteristics of the organism, to the degree of arbitrariness with which a given pair of conditioned or unconditioned stimuli may be selected. Nevertheless, within these boundaries, there is still a degree of arbitrariness regarding conditioned and unconditioned stimuli, responses, and reinforcers. It may be that tastes must be paired with illness for conditioning to occur easily, but there is a wide range of such tastes.

Given the biological limits on learning the question arises whether Pavlov, Skinner, and other learning theorists were correct in supposing that there exist general laws of learning that transcend biological limits. Are there any such general laws?

Data from several other areas of learning have bolstered the emphasis that taste aversion learning has placed on the biological origins of behavior. For example, Bolles (1970) noted the predisposition of animals to make certain responses, and not others, in response to aversive stimuli. He called these responses species-specific defense reactions. Another example of biological influence is autoshaping—the finding that pigeons' key pecks are not arbitrary responses that experimenters happened to have chosen to reinforce, but can be elicited by the presence of food (Gamzu & Schwartz, 1973). In fact, pigeons will even keep pecking when their pecking postpones food (Schwartz & Williams, 1972). Further, key pecks consistently followed by food are topographically different from key pecks consistently followed by

water, although such differences may never have been reinforced (Wolin, 1968). The key pecks followed by food look more like eating pecks, and the key pecks followed by water look more like drinking pecks.

Such results cast suspicion on generalizations from animal learning experiments. The stimuli and responses studied in these experiments were apparently not arbitrary, and the laws of learning appear to be different for at least some of these predisposed responses. Some authors have gone so far as to say that the learning of each type of task in each species might be described by different laws (Rozin & Kalat, 1971).

Of course, as indicated earlier, learning theorists have not been totally unaware of species and task differences in learning. The following quote from Skinner (1959) demonstrates this point:

> Pigeon, rat, monkey, which is which? It doesn't matter. Of course, these three species have behavioral repertoires which are as different as their anatomies. But once you have allowed for the ways in which they act upon the environment, what remains of their behavior shows astonishingly similar properties. (pp. 374–375)

Skinner, like many learning theorists (see, e.g., Thorndike, 1932), was well aware that the laws of learning are not exactly the same for every organism and every situation. But Skinner chose to investigate some of the myriad aspects of learning that do appear to be general across different species and tasks. Some examples of such general aspects of learning are (a) better learning the shorter the delay between the conditioned stimulus (CS, or the response) and the reinforcer, (b) stimulus generalization, (c) the eventual disappearance of learning following the removal of reinforcement (extinction), and (d) better learning with a more intense unconditioned stimulus, or US (Logue, 1979).

There are good evolutionary reasons for general aspects of learning. Since every species has been shaped by evolution and since certain selection pressures, such as the uniformity of rules of future prediction, are common to all organisms, species-general behaviors could and should result (Lockhard, 1971; Revusky, 1977; Rozin & Kalat, 1971); further, phyletic closeness (Lockhard, 1971) or economy of the neural wiring of the organism (Rozin & Kalat, 1971) could also result in general laws of learning (Logue, 1979). Species and task-specific aspects of learning do not have a corner on natural selection. Every law has its limits. But the other side of this coin is that every law has its sphere. So within biological limits, general laws of learning do exist and can be studied.

MAJOR TOPICS IN LEARNING

The Rescorla-Wagner Model of Classical Conditioning

There have been several noteworthy recent attempts to construct learning theories that are either distinctly molecular or distinctly molar. A molecular learning theory that has received much attention since its inception is the Rescorla-Wagner model of learning (Rescorla & Wagner, 1972).

The original object of this model was to account for Pavlovian conditioning with more than one conditioned stimulus. One reason for its success is that researchers have come to realize that it is impossible to present only one CS. For example, if a tone is presented as a CS, that tone must be heard by the subject against a background of ambient noise, ambient illumination, ambient smells, tastes, and so on. These stimuli constitute the backround (or context) against which the putative CS is presented. As long as the background remains constant between conditioning trials, it can be considered a single stimulus. Thus, the standard Pavlovian classical conditioning procedure can be viewed as an alternation between (a) the background alone during the intertrial intervals (without the US); and (b) the background plus the CS during the trials (with the US). Thus, the Rescorla-Wagner model is applicable to all classical conditioning procedures.

The theory itself (as originally formulated) contains two critical assumptions. First, the strength gained by the CS on a reinforced trial (a trial with the US) is proportional to the difference between the strength of conditioning prior to the trial and the asymptotic strength of conditioning. Unreinforced trials (extinction trials) are treated just like conditioning trials except that the asymptote is zero. This assumption implies the standard negatively accelerated learning and extinction curves. The second critical assumption of the theory is that the strength of conditioning of a compound stimulus (more than one CS) is the sum of the strengths of the individual components. Thus, on a reinforced trial with a compound stimulus, the two conditioned stimuli both contribute to the pretrial level of conditioning. This level determines the amount gained on a specific trial, given a particular US. Both conditioned stimuli also share (according to their relative salience) in the added conditioning from the trial itself.

An important consequence of the model is that if a component CS that has already obtained high conditioning strength (through previous reinforced trials with that stimulus alone) is paired with a new stimulus that has no conditioning strength and the compound is reinforced, the reinforcement (the US) will have little effect; the strength of the compound will be incremented slightly if at all. (This occurs because the strength of the compound must be at least as high as the strength of the first conditioned component.) In consequence, the new conditioned stimulus component, the one that had not previously been conditioned, can gain little or no conditioning strength. Thus, the Rescorla-Wagner model explains the phenomenon of blocking. Now suppose that the first CS is the background alone and the second CS is the background plus an explicit signal such as a sound or light: The model implies that if the US is first presented during the intertrial interval (paired with the background alone), the conditioning thus imparted to the background will block further conditioning to any signal (CS) superimposed on it. This is indeed the case.

The Rescorla-Wagner model has been challenged and modified considerably during the last 15 years, but today it is the reference point for almost all theory and practice in classical conditioning. It accounts for an otherwise vast and confusing mass of experimental findings with a pair of simple, plausible assumptions. It applies to disruption of rats' lever pressing by shock, rabbits blinking their nictitating membranes, and pigeons pecking keys, as well as to dogs salivating. In other words, it is a general law of learning.

A model as general as this is likely to have clinical implications. Let us briefly consider a fairly obvious one, in which classical conditioning is deliberately applied as therapy. Suppose a therapist is trying to condition relaxation during previously stressful situations. The conditioned stimuli used in relaxation therapy are often a series of graded verbal statements of increasing threat. The unconditioned and conditioned responses are both relaxation. Consideration of the Rescorla-Wagner model brings our attention immediately to the background of this conditioning situation. What occurs in the therapist's office before and between conditioning sessions? If, as is certainly possible, the therapist's office (the background) itself becomes a CS for deep relaxation, stimuli superimposed on this background (the graded series of statements) are unlikely to gain conditioning strength. The patient may well relax in the therapist's office during conditioning sessions but in everyday life, outside of the office, the conditioned stimuli will be presented away from the background, which has the greatest share of conditioning strength. It is then that the inherent weakness of these conditioned stimuli as elicitors of relaxation will be made evident. The therapist who wants to condition a given response in a therapeutic setting and intends that conditioning to carry over into everyday life must take care not to condition the response initially to the therapeutic setting itself. Care must be taken, in general, not to make the therapeutic setting the place where any kind of desirable behavior first appears. The very conditioning of such behavior would make transfer to everyday life more difficult; conditioning to the therapist's office as background would block conditioning to other stimuli superimposed on that background. In light of the Rescorla-Wagner model, the therapist may be better advised to try to transfer elements from those (perhaps few) everyday life situations where behavior is still normal into the therapeutic situation, and from there into those situations where behavior is most dysfunctional.

The Matching Law

The matching law (Herrnstein, 1961) states that animals distribute their responses in proportion to the distribution of reinforcers. For instance, if a pigeon receives twice as much food for pecking one key as another, it will peck that key twice as often. Thus,

$$\frac{B_1}{B_2} = \frac{R_1}{R_2} \qquad [1]$$

(Baum & Rachlin, 1969) where B_1 and B_2 correspond to the number of responses made on alternatives 1 and 2, and R_1 and R_2 correspond to the number of reinforcers obtained for responses on alternatives 1 and 2. Equation 1 has been confirmed many times with many species (de Villiers, 1977) including humans (see, e.g., Bradshaw, Ruddle, & Szabadi, 1981; McDowell, 1988).

The matching law is a rule of allocation. As such, it has been derived from maximization theory (Rachlin et al., 1980). There is some debate now whether the fundamental principle by which animals allocate time and effort to various activities is maximization of utility or whether the fundamental principle is matching. It may be that animals have inherited a tendency to match, because matching conforms so frequently to maximization, and that in those few instances where matching and maximizing behaviors diverge, animals match. Much research is now being directed toward this question (Commons, Herrnstein & Rachlin, 1982; Heyman & Herrnstein, 1986; Rachlin, Green, & Tormey, 1988). However the issue is decided, the important fact remains that matching is a widely pervasive empirical finding (Williams, 1988).

As with the Rescorla-Wagner model, the matching law derives its wide applicability from its consider-ation of background (or context) of reinforcement. The scope of the matching law was demonstrated by Herrnstein (1970), who extended what was previously a description of choice behavior to a general principle of all instrumental behaviors. If B_1 of equation 1 is any particular response, then B_2 may be considered the background of that response—all other reinforcement obtained in the experimental situation. That is, the strength of a response is directly proportional to reinforcement dependent on that response and inversely proportional to the overall level of reinforcement.

This principle implies that there are many ways to vary the frequency of (or the time spent at) any behavior. A response may be directly increased in frequency by increasing reinforcement of that response; this is well known. But a response may also be increased in frequency indirectly, by decreasing reinforcement for (or punishing) another response, or by decreasing the background reinforcement. Symmetrically, a response may be directly decreased in frequency by decreasing the reinforcement for (or punishing) that response. But a response may also be indirectly decreased in frequency by increasing the reinforcement for another response or increasing the background reinforcement.

An important caveat to the foregoing comes from maximization theory, which says that the indirect methods work only to the extent that the indirect reinforcer is substitutable for the direct reinforcer. If the indirect and direct reinforcers are not mutually substitutable (food and water, for example) the exact opposite results will occur. Increasing water reinforcement for a response on which water delivery depends will tend to increase the rate of any responses on which food delivery depends.

The importance of these indirect methods for clinical practice is obvious. Often direct methods of dealing with behavior are impossible either because the behavior is difficult to observe or infrequent or is deliberately hidden by the patient. The therapist, nevertheless, may alter the frequency of such behaviors by reinforcing or punishing other behaviors, or by working to increase or decrease the overall level of other reinforcers substitutable for the reinforcers of the response in question (see, e.g., McDowell, 1982, 1988).

SELF-CONTROL

The matching law, as previously stated, describes choice in a situation in which responses produce reinforcers at two separate rates. An expanded form of the matching law is as follows (Rachlin, 1974):

$$\frac{B_1}{B_2} = \frac{R_1\, A_1\, D_2}{R_2\, A_2\, D_1}\, . \qquad [2]$$

B_1, B_2, R_1, and R_2 are defined as they were in equation 1. A_1 and A_2 correspond to the size, or the amount, of reinforcers obtained for responses on alternatives 1 and 2 and D_1 and D_2 to the delay between a response and receipt of a reinforcer on alternatives 1 and 2. Equation 2 states that behavior is directly proportional to the frequency and amount of reinforcement and inversely proportional to its delay. In situations in which R_1 is equal to R_2, equation 2 reduces to

$$\frac{B_1}{B_2} = \frac{A_1\, D_2}{A_2\, D_1} \qquad [3]$$

Equation 3 can be used to model self-control. Self-control as defined here is really just one kind of choice, the choice of a larger, more delayed reinforcer over a smaller, less delayed reinforcer; the opposite of self-control, choosing the smaller, less delayed reinforcer, is impulsiveness (Logue, 1988; Rachlin, 1974).

Equation 3 has been quite successful at describing pigeons' choices in self-control experiments: that is, experiments in which a choice must be made between a smaller, less delayed reinforcer and a larger, more delayed reinforcer (e.g., Green, Fisher, Perlow, & Sherman, 1981). Suppose, in equation 3, that A_1 is larger than A_2 but also that D_1 is greater than D_2. Thus A_1 and D_1 constitute the larger, more delayed reinforcer. If B_1 is greater than B_2 the animal is defined as showing self-control. Otherwise, the animal is showing impulsiveness.

B_1 and B_2 are entirely determined by the physical values of A_1, A_2, D_1, and D_2. Therefore, according to equation 3, given two reinforcers of specific sizes and delays, all subjects should make the same choice between these two reinforcers. Nevertheless, we know that individuals within a species, and across different species, show varying amounts of self-control in similar situations. Equation 3 clearly needs modification in order to express degrees of difference in self-control.

As self-control develops within or across species or within or across individuals, animals come to choose more in accordance with amounts (A_1 and A_2) and less in accordance with delays (D_1 and D_2). Suggested modifications of equation 3 provide new parameters in the equation, the variation of which would cause delays to be more or less heavily weighted. One suggested modification of equation 3 (Logue, Rodriguez, Pena-Correal, & Mauro, 1984) is

$$\frac{B_1}{B_2} = \left[\frac{A_1}{A_2}\right]^{S_A} \cdot \left[\frac{D_2}{D_1}\right]^{S_D}. \qquad [4]$$

Individual differences in self-control may be expressed as individual differences in the exponent of equation 4. From equation 4 it can be seen that if the delay exponent, s_D, is very small (i.e., approaching zero), the ratio $(D_2/D_1)^{S_D}$ will approach 1.0 and behavior will mostly be a function of the amounts of the reinforcers. In such cases the subject would be more likely to choose the larger reinforcer irrespective of the reinforcer delays, thus showing more self-control. In the other direction, if s_D were very large, reinforcer delays would affect behavior more strongly than reinforcer amounts, thus reducing self-control. Animals' experiences, and perhaps their genes, could affect the size of s_D.

Examples of individual differences in self-control as a result of past conditioning history have been shown by Logue and her colleagues (Logue & Mazur, 1981; Logue & Pena-Correal, 1984; Mazur & Logue, 1978). These researchers trained some pigeons to show increased self-control by first giving them a choice between equally delayed large and small reinforcers, and then very slowly fading that choice to one between a delayed large reinforcer and an immediate small reinforcer. The experimental pigeons exposed to this procedure continued to choose the large, delayed reinforcer significantly more often than control subjects that had not been exposed to this fading procedure. Such learning does appear to generalize to other situations (Logue et al., 1984). Logue and Mazur (1981) showed further that colored lights used to illuminate the experimental chamber during reinforcer delays were crucial to the experimental subjects' maintenance of self-control, these lights possibly functioning as conditioned reinforcers. Finally, they showed that the effects of the fading procedure were stable over time.

The implication of this finding for clinical practice is its suggestion that within biological limits self-control may be learned in a specific setting. Mischel (1966) showed that self-control in children may differ considerably across age, sex, occupation, and wealth. For instance, children are generally impulsive in laboratory settings, whereas with laboratory studies of adult humans self-control is the predominant finding (King & Logue, 1987; Logue, Pena-Correal, Rodriguez, & Kabala, 1986; Rodriguez & Logue, 1988). Because adult humans often behave impulsively outside of the laboratory, it appears likely that self-control within the laboratory setting is due to some characteristic of the testing environment (such as lack of meaningful programmed reward, desire to appear mature in the eyes of the experimenter, tediousness of the experimental task, or lack of rewarding alternatives during waiting periods) rather than any unique characteristic of adult humans. It is hoped that further research will sort out these variables.

The model represented by equation 4 may thus be one way in which individual differences in self-control can be measured and described. At least at the qualitative level, this model does appear to be an improvement over equation 3, and it is consistent with other research on choice (see, e.g., Baum, 1974; Green & Snyderman, 1980; Wearden, 1980). Future research on self-control will be directed at testing the predictions and implications of this model while concurrently improving methods for teaching self-control. Mazur (1987) suggested that an alternative delay discount function, $B_i = A_i/(1 + kD_i)$, better accounts for choice between different amounts and delays of reward. Individual differences in self-control would here be expressed by differences in the constant, k. An advantage of Mazur's discount function is that at zero delays $B_i = A_i$ rather than approaching infinity as it does in equation 4.

Learned Helplessness

Some recent approaches to learning are based on the supposition that organisms can learn correlations between their responses and the occurrences, or nonoccurrences, of reinforcers; no close contiguity between the responses and reinforcers need occur. The implication is that if the data are reexamined at the level of individual responses and reinforcers, little regularity will be found; the only way that learning can be observed is by looking at large groups of responses at once, a molar approach.

One recent example of the theories falling within this group is Seligman's (1975) learned helplessness model. The data that initially led Seligman to this model consisted of observations of dogs' behavior following inescapable shock (Overmier & Seligman, 1967; Seligman & Maier, 1967). Dogs strapped in a hammock were given shock regardless of their behavior. Later, it proved extremely difficult to train the dogs to jump to the other side of a shuttle box in order to avoid shock. Seligman and his colleagues concluded that the dogs had learned that they could not avoid shock; they had learned helplessness. Subsequent experiments were designed (more or less successfully) to show that the results had not been caused by the dogs learning to tense in a certain way to ameliorate shock while in the hammock or other spurious factors (Seligman, 1975).

Besides describing in a general way how animals can learn that their behavior has no effect on aversive events in their environment, Seligman's learned helplessness theory has been specifically applied to cases of human reactive depression (see Seligman, 1975, for a general discussion on this subject). Seligman and his colleagues have postulated that people who cannot control the aversive events in their lives become depressed. In fact, Seligman believes that the symptoms of depression are themselves the symptoms of learned helplessness. He suggested a common biochemical basis for the two phenomena and attempted to distinguish between chronic and acute depressions (Abramson, Seligman, & Teasdale, 1978; Seligman, 1975).

Several similar approaches to learning, but concerning positive rather than aversive stimuli, have also recently been proposed. One has been termed "learned laziness" (Engberg, Hansen, Welker, & Thomas, 1973). Engberg et al. showed that pigeons periodically given food regardless of their behavior learned to be lazy; they learned that their behavior was not connected to food delivery. When pigeons are exposed to Engberg et al.'s procedure, it is subsequently more difficult to train them to peck for food.

Mackintosh (1973, 1974) proposed a general term that encompasses Seligman's and Engberg et al.'s findings: *learned irrelevance*. According to Mackintosh, organisms can learn that their responses are uncorrelated with environmental events in general. Mackintosh's primary purpose in identifying this type of learning was to challenge the Rescorla-Wagner model (Rescorla & Wagner, 1972), which, in its original form, could not account for learned irrelevance. However, Mackintosh's concept has proved to have much broader implications than that because it provides a formal description of a certain type of learning by organisms at the molar level.

Taste Aversion Learning

Taste aversion learning, also known as food aversion learning, occurs when an organism eats a food, becomes ill (usually with a gastrointestinal illness), and subsequently develops an aversion to the food. The terminology of classical conditioning is typically employed to describe taste aversion learning; whatever causes the illness being termed the US, and the particular aspect or aspects of the food that become aversive (e.g., the food's taste or smell) called the CS.

Several characteristics of taste aversion learning appear unusual. First, taste aversions can be learned with very long delays, up to 24 hours, between the CS and the US (Etscorn & Stephens, 1973). This seemed at odds with traditional studies of learning that claimed to obtain learning only with delays of up to a few seconds (Kimble, 1961). Attempts to explain taste aversion learning data by postulating food after-tastes or taste restimulation through vomiting have proved futile (Revusky & Garcia, 1970). It has been noted that long-delay aversion learning appears quite adaptive given that it may take some time before an ingested poison causes illness (see, e.g., Rozin & Kalat, 1971).

Second, rats, the most commonly used subjects in taste aversion experiments, appear to form aversions more easily to the taste of a food than its visual appearance: hence the name taste aversion learning (Garcia, McGowan, Ervin, & Koelling, 1968). As previously noted, this characteristic also seemed discordant with traditional views of learning that seemed to assume that any CS should be equally associable with any US (Thorndike, 1911/1965).

Third, there appear to be species differences in the predisposition of various types of stimuli to become associated with illness. For example, while rats tended to associate tastes with illness, quail appeared to more easily associate visual stimuli with illness (Wilcoxin, Dragoin, & Kral, 1971). One explanation of this difference between rats and quail might be that the quail's visual system is far superior to that of rats. But guinea pigs learn both taste and visual aversions well, although their visual system is no better developed than that of rats (Braveman, 1974, 1975). A more satisfactory explanation is that the manner in which the members of a species hunt for food predicts what stimuli will most easily be associated with illness for that species; both quail and guinea pigs search for their food in the daytime using their visual systems, while rats tend to search for food at night using gustation and olfaction (Braveman, 1974, 1975).

Thus, all of the peculiar characteristics of taste aversion learning seem well suited to help organisms deal with poisons, and particularly poisons in their own ecological niche. Clearly, if feeding were to be understood and properly investigated, each species' own evolutionary history would have to be taken into account (Rozin & Kalat, 1971).

As this issue was examined over a number of years, however, it seemed as if those who had advocated taste aversion learning as something truly unique were too hasty. While there are differences between taste aversion learning and more traditional laboratory learning tasks, these differences appear to be differences of degree, not of kind (Logue, 1979). For example, it is possible to observe learning with more

than a few seconds between the stimuli and responses in traditional learning procedures (Lett, 1977). However, no paradigm has equalled the 24-hour CS-US delays found with taste aversion learning. As additional examples, recent research has suggested that taste does play a role in the learning of food aversions for every species (Gustavson, 1977; Lett, 1980) and that humans learn taste aversions in much the same ways that other animals do (Logue, 1988; Logue, Ophir, & Strauss, 1981).

Cognition and Learning

Human and animal studies of cognition have been oriented around the notion of representation and representational systems. That is, some aspect of the environment is said to be represented in coded form in the mind (or, in less dualistic conceptions, the nervous system) of the organism. Subsequent behavior is then said to be a function, not of the environment directly, but of the encoded representation or system of representations.

Many of the early psychology experiments in the United States were attempts to investigate the "mental life" of animals so as to complement ongoing investigations of the mental life of humans. The first study of rats in mazes (Small, 1901) was such an attempt. Small made observations of the "cognitions" as well as the overt behavior of his subjects. The behaviorist movement (Watson, 1913) grew out of the fact that although overt behavior of rats in mazes was clearly observable and verifiable from one day, one experimenter, one laboratory to the next, the cognitions of the rats seemed not to be thus observable or verifiable. Behaviorists such as Watson (and later Hull, 1943) assumed that complex behavior of rats in mazes (and, by extension, behavior of humans in everyday life) could be reduced to a series of observable stimulus-response connections. However, Tolman (1948), with a series of ingenious studies of the behavior of rats in mazes, showed that a rat's behavior could be so complex (while, at the same time, systematic) that immediate observable stimulus-response connections could not reasonably account for that behavior. Tolman suggested that the rat learned a representation of the maze, which he called a mental map or "cognitive map," to which the rat referred while traversing the maze. Tolman felt that he could avoid the problems of nonobservability and nonverifiability by rigidly defining the concept "mental map" in behavioral terms—not as immediate behavior, but as long-term behavior that takes into account the spatial and temporal context of a given experimental trial. The focus on immediate behavior in its context is a molar approach. Tolman (1932) thus referred to himself as a molar behaviorist.

Hull and his followers reacted to Tolman's experiments and arguments by postulating another sort of representation: a representation of the stimulus-response connection itself in the nervous system of the animal (Hull, 1952). They called this representation a "fractional anticipatory goal response" $(r_g\text{-}s_g)$. The argument between Hullians and Tolmanians was thus not one of cognitive psychology versus behavioral psychology; both camps agreed on the necessity for discussing representation, and therefore, both were cognitive psychologists. The argument was whether those representations were to be more molecular $(r_g\text{-}s_g)$ or more molar (cognitive maps). It was Skinner ("Are Theories of Learning Necessary?" 1950) who rejected the notion of internal representations entirely on the grounds that representations not defined in behavioral terms suffered from nonobservability and nonverifiability. But once a representation was defined in behavioral terms, the behavior, not the representation, must be the proper object of study.

Recent theory and practice on the relation between cognition and learning has increased and has taken several intertwining paths, all relying on the notion of internal representations of aspects of the external environment. We are unable to explore any of these paths in detail here, or even to label them all. Instead, we will briefly describe some current work with nonhuman subjects.

Response Sequences

In a series of experiments by Olton and his colleagues (e.g., Olton & Samuelson, 1976), rats were placed in a maze containing a central chamber and a number of arms (usually eight) radiating outward from the central chamber. At the outer ends of the arms were goal boxes, some of which contained food. Rats were then trained to choose arms in a specific order, say arms 1, 3, and 7 in three successive trials. After learning had proceeded to criterion, a transfer test was performed (for example, by rotating the arms relative to the central area). Rats in this experiment, using cues external to the maze (visually open to the experimental room) entered the rotated arms so as to arrive at the same series of spatial locations as before. Further, they were able to keep track of which spatial locations they visited (and removed food from) because they tended not to return to a spatial location once it had been emptied of food even though their sequence of

responses (and, presumably, stimulus-response connections) had been interrupted. In these experiments the rats are said to form a cognitive map of the maze and to refer to this map when making choices among arms.

Another series of experiments with pigeons shows that they can learn to peck a series of differently colored keys (say, red-green-blue-yellow) in a specific order regardless of the spatial location of the keys. Pigeons continued to peck the keys in the specified order even when the sequence was interrupted by removing one of the intermediate colors (Straub, Seidenberg, Bever, & Terrace, 1979). Here the pigeon's representation cannot be spatial but is said to be more abstract.

The general nature of these experiments involves transfer tests of various kinds to determine what is learned and, usually, to show that what is learned cannot be mere stimulus-response connections. These experiments follow in the tradition of Tolman and his students. For instance, Macfarlane (1930) taught rats to run through a maze for food and then flooded the maze and found that the rats could now swim correctly through the maze, which shows that they must have learned something other than a series of chained movements; they learned something general about the maze.

Matching-to-sample

In a simple matching-to-sample experiment with pigeons, a "stimulus sample" is presented by lighting the response key with a particular color. When the pigeon pecks the key, the light is extinguished and two other keys are lit, one with the same color as the sample, the other with a different color. If the pigeon pecks the same colored key, it gets a brief food delivery. If the pigeon pecks a different colored key, no food is delivered. Variations on this procedure involve inserting a delay between the offset of the sample and the onset of the comparison stimuli or changing the relation of the correct comparison stimulus to the sample (by making the nonmatching color correct, by varying the number of comparison stimuli, or by specifying some specific relationship between the sample and the correct comparison such as, "If the sample is red, the correct comparison is blue; if the sample is blue, the correct comparison is yellow"). In a still more complex version of matching-to-sample (e.g., Maki & Hegvik, 1980) the presentation of the comparison stimuli is delayed from the offset of the sample but, immediately after the sample, a brief signal is given. If the signal has one value (a "re-member" signal), the comparison stimuli are pre-sented as scheduled. But if the signal has another value (a "forget" signal), the comparison stimuli are not presented. When, contrary to usual procedure, the forget signal is followed by the comparison stimuli, the pigeons seem to have forgotten the sample stimu-lus—their performance is poor.

Here the representation is said to be the rule that regulates reinforcement: "Peck blue if sample was red. Peck yellow if sample was blue. Forget sample if "forget" stimulus is presented," and so on.

Complex Discriminations

Recent experiments by Herrnstein and others (Bhatt, Wasserman, Reynolds, & Knauss, 1988; Herrn-stein & de Villiers, 1980; Herrnstein, Loveland, & Cable, 1976; Honig & Stewart, 1988; Vaughan & Herrnstein, 1987; Wasserman, Kiedinger, & Bhatt, 1988) take the following form: a library of slides is formed, half of which, positive slides, contain a picture of an object or a substance (say, a person or water) in many different actual forms; the second, half, called negative slides, do not contain a picture of the object or substance. The slides are projected in random order and the subject (a pigeon) is rewarded by a food delivery for pecking at the positive slides and is not rewarded for pecking at the negative slides. A given pigeon never sees the same slide twice. As far as has been determined, no discrimination can be formed on the basis of lightness, color, texture, or any feature of the slide other than the concept (for exam-ple, person or water) itself. Pigeons quickly learn to discriminate between positive and negative slides, pecking the positive slides rapidly and the negative slides slowly. In other words, the pigeons learn the concept. In this case, it is clear that although the concept can be represented by an internal rule such as "Peck slides containing water," the postulation of the rule is not useful in understanding what the pigeons are doing. The question that still remains to be an-swered is, How do the pigeons learn to discriminate between the two groups of slides?

Modification of Cognitions

These three areas of research, again, represent only a sample of the work currently being done in nonhu-man cognitive psychology, only a fraction of the work in cognitive psychology in general. The resemblance between this work and the clinical practice of cogni-tive behavior therapy, like the relation among the

various areas of cognitive psychology, rests on their common notions of representation and representa-tional systems. In the case of cognitive behavior therapy, the representations postulated are sometimes said to consist of rules for behavior such as, "Ev-eryone must like me for everything I do," and some-times to consist of sentences or phrases people actu-ally say to themselves. To the extent that these rules are not identifiable with sets of overt behaviors, the problems of observability and verifiability that origi-nally caused the behaviorist revolt still remain. In nonhuman and human experiments no adequate method has been found to change representations without changing the overt behavior that initially defines those representations. This is not to say that representations of external events do not exist in the nervous system (or the mind) or that people do not talk to themselves; such events may well play a central role in overt behavior. It nevertheless seems to us an illusion that identification and modification of repre-sentations will provide a short cut to identification and modification of reinforcers in the environment and modification of overt dysfunctional behavior.

Future Directions

There are several directions in which we believe learning theory will move in the near future. First, controversial issues that are of recent concern, such as the biological boundaries of learning and the cognitive versus behavioral approaches to learning, will proba-bly become less clear-cut. There will be fewer adher-ents of extreme positions on these issues. Historically, progress in science has been characterized by a group of scientists adopting an extreme position precipitat-ing a theoretical crisis. The crisis is eventually re-solved as most scientists adopt a more moderate position, one that is somewhat different from the original, precrisis position (Kuhn, 1962). Psycholo-gists who felt that individual laws of learning would be necessary for every species and every task, and those who felt that cognitive psychology would completely revolutionize the study of learning in nonhuman sub-jects, are examples of scientists whose extreme opin-ions precipitate theoretical crisis and change but who are probably not representative of future opinions.

A present trend in learning that will probably continue is the development of complex, mathemati-cal models. As experimental techniques become more precise, as psychologists become more sophisticated in mathematics and continue to model physics or other natural sciences, these models will proliferate. Whether they will ultimately prove a great use to learning theorists is not clear. Hull's (1943) famous elaborate mathematico-deductive learning theory grew so complex that it became unwieldy and untestable and ultimately died a quiet death. There is always a danger that this will happen to present and future mathematical models of learning in psychology. Nevertheless, the success of some of the present models bodes well for mathematical models in the future.

Until now learning theorists have not paid much attention to individual differences. An example of how individual differences could be dealt with was already given with respect to self-control. In the future there will probably be a greater number of similar attempts in other areas. Finally, the future will undoubtedly see increased application to humans of learning theory obtained from work with nonhumans. Most researchers are concerned about the applications of their work. As the study of learning gains depth, the number of clinical applications of learning studies should increase. For example, because the properties of taste aversion learning have been worked out in great detail in rats (see Logue, 1979, for a review) and because further studies have shown that humans learn taste aversions much as rats do (e.g., Bernstein, 1978; Garb & Stunkard, 1974; Logue, 1988; Logue et al., 1981), it is now possible to take advantage of that knowledge to improve experimental manipulations resulting in or removing taste aversions in humans. These developments may then be applied to treatments of alcoholism, cancer, anorexia, and other clinical conditions involving excessive cravings or avoidance of specific foods (Bernstein & Borson, 1986; Logue, Logue, & Strauss, 1983).

SUMMARY AND CONCLUSIONS

Studies performed by learning theorists as far back as 1920 (e.g., Watson & Rayner's [1920] work on conditioning fears in Little Albert) still have impact for present-day work on human psychological problems (see Harris, 1979). Such impact will undoubtedly continue, allowing clinical psychologists and personality theorists to gain a better understanding of their own areas. However, this will only happen if those researchers in the more applied areas understand the work being done by learning theorists. In the past there has been poor communication between the two groups. For example, some therapists (see Wiens, Montague, Manaugh, & English, 1976) have attempted to treat alcoholism using a taste aversion paradigm by first making the patients ill, waiting until the patients were actually vomiting, and then giving the patients an alcoholic beverage to drink. As anyone

familiar with research on learning could have predicted, this procedure was not very effective. Presenting the US prior to the CS, known as backward conditioning, is much less effective than forward conditioning, presenting the CS first (Mackintosh, 1974).

In other cases, perhaps too enthusiastic and too crude application of results obtained in the laboratory has made for poor clinical practice. The use of punishment without proper attention to its side effects is one example. The use of tokens without proper attention to their context is another (Levine & Fasnacht, 1974). Perhaps most surprising to the learning theorist is the expectation among some clinicians that reinforcement and punishment procedures, having only a temporary effect in the laboratory—a performance rather than a learning effect—will have a more permanent effect in therapy. Thus, patients are "cured" in the clinic and returned to the environments where the contingencies of reinforcement and punishment that originally generated dysfunctional behavior are reimposed. When, as laboratory results predict, the dysfunctional behavior returns, the therapeutic procedures are said to be faulty. But such procedures are demonstrably effective. They do not need to be replaced by "deeper" methods, cognitive or psychoanalytic. Rather, they need to be modified along lines suggested earlier so as to take context and background into account—to shift control from the clinic to the everyday environment.

What are such techniques? We have suggested a few possibilities here, but we do not believe that it is possible to take a laboratory procedure and apply it straightforwardly to the clinic. No applied science can take the developments of a laboratory science and simply use them. Physicists learned much more about physics from steam engines than engineers learned about steam engines from physics. Theory, in this respect, is limited. It can provide a common language and can relate one applied procedure to another, apparently dissimilar, one. But it cannot prescribe. The theorist has more to learn from the clinician than vice versa. For this reason we deplore the current tendency toward compartmentalization in psychology.

REFERENCES

Abramson, L. Y., Seligman, M. E. P., & Teasdale, J. D. (1978).Learned helplessness in humans: Critique and reformulation. *Journal of Abnormal Psychology, 87*, 49–74.
Baum, W. M. (1974). On two types of deviation from the

matching law: Bias and undermatching. *Journal of the Experimental Analysis of Behavior, 22*, 231–242.

Baum. W. M. (1981). Optimization and the matching law as accounts of instrumental behavior. *Journal of the Experimental Analysis of Behavior, 36*, 387–403.

Baum, W. M., & Rachlin, H. C. (1969). Choice as time allocation. *Journal of the Experimental Analysis of Behavior, 12*, 861–874.

Bernstein, I. L. (1978). Learned taste aversions in children receiving chemotherapy. *Science, 200*, 1302–1303.

Bernstein, I. L., & Borson, S. (1986). Learned food aversion: A component of anorexia syndromes. *Psychological Review, 93*, 462–472.

Bhatt, R. S., Wasserman, E. A., Reynolds, W. F., & Knauss, K. S. (1988). Conceptual behavior in pigeons: Categorization of both familiar and novel examples from four classes of natural and artificial stimuli. *Journal of Experimental Psychology: Animal Behavior Processes, 14*, 219–234.

Black, A. H. (1971). Autonomic aversive conditioning in infrahuman subjects. In F. R. Brush (Ed.), *Aversive conditioning and learning*. New York: Academic Press.

Bolles, R. C. (1970). Species-specific defense reactions and avoidance learning. *Psychological Review, 77*, 32–48.

Bradshaw, C. M., Ruddle, H. V., & Szabadi, E. (1981). Studies of concurrent performance in humans. In C. M. Bradshaw, E. Szabadi, & C. F. Lowe (Eds.), *Quantification of steady-state operant behaviour* (pp. 79–90). Amsterdam: Elsevier/North-Holland Biomedical Press.

Braveman, N. S. (1974). Poison-based avoidance learning with flavored or colored water in guinea pigs. *Learning and Motivation, 5*, 182–194.

Braveman, N. S. (1975). Relative salience of gustatory and visual cues in the formation of poison-based food aversions by guinea pigs (*Cavia porcellus*). *Behavioral Biology, 14*, 189–199.

Brown, P. L., & Jenkins, H. M. (1968). Auto-shaping of the pigeon's key-peck. *Journal of the Experimental Analysis of Behavior, 11*, 1–8.

Commons, M. L., Herrnstein, R. J., & Rachlin, H. (Eds.). (1982). *Quantitative analyses of behavior: Vol. 2. Matching and maximizing accounts*. Cambridge, MA: Ballinger.

de Villiers, P. (1977). Choice in concurrent schedules and a quantitative formulation of the law of effect. In W. K. Honig & J. E. R. Staddon (Eds.), *Handbook of operant behavior* (pp. 233–287). Englewood Cliffs, NJ: Prentice-Hall.

Domjan, M., & Burkhard, B. (1986). *The principles of learning and behavior* (2nd ed.). Monterey, CA: Brooks/Cole.

Engberg, L. A., Hansen, G., Welker, R. L., & Thomas, D. R. (1973). Acquisition of key-pecking via autoshaping as a function of prior experience: "Learned laziness"?, *Science, 178*, 1002–1004.

Etscorn, F., & Stephens, R. (1973). Establishment of conditioned taste aversions with 24-hour CS-US interval. *Physiological Psychology, 1*, 251–253.

Gamzu, E., & Schwartz, B. (1973). The maintenance of key pecking by stimulus-contingent and response-independent food presentation. *Journal of the Experimental Analysis of Behavior, 19*, 65–73.

Garb, J. L., & Stunkard, A. J. (1974). Taste aversions in man. *American Journal of Psychiatry, 131*, 1204–1207.

Garcia, J., McGowan, B. K., Ervin, F. R., & Koelling, R. A. (1968). Cues: Their relative effectiveness as a function of the reinforcer. *Science, 160*, 794–795.

Gardner, R. A., & Gardner, B. T. (1988). Truth or consequences. *Behavioral and Brain Sciences, 11*, 479–493.

Green, L., Fisher, E. B., Perlow, S., & Sherman, L. (1981). Preference reversal and self control: Choice as a function of reward amount and delay. *Behaviour Analysis Letters, 1*, 43–51.

Green, L., & Snyderman, M. (1980). Choice between rewards differing in amount and delay: Toward a choice model of self control. *Journal of the Experimental Analysis of Behavior, 34*, 135–147.

Gustavson, C. R. (1977). Comparative and field aspects of learned food aversions. In L. M. Barker, M. R. Best, & M. Domjan (Eds.), *Learning mechanisms in food selection* (pp. 23–43). Waco, TX: Baylor University Press.

Guthrie, E. R., & Horton, G. P. (1946). *Cats in a puzzle box*. New York: Holt, Rinehart & Winston.

Harris, B. (1979). Whatever happened to Little Albert? *American Psychologist, 34*, 151–160.

Herrnstein, R. J. (1961). Relative and absolute strength of response as a function of frequency of reinforcement. *Journal of the Experimental Analysis of Behavior, 4*, 267–272.

Herrnstein, R. J. (1970). On the law of effect. *Journal of the Experimental Analysis of Behavior, 13*, 243–266.

Herrnstein, R. J., & de Villiers, P. A. (1980). Fish as a natural category for people and pigeons. In G. H. Bower (Ed.), *The psychology of learning and motivation* (Vol. 14, pp. 59–95). New York: Academic Press.

Herrnstein, R. J., Loveland, D. H., & Cable, C. (1976). Natural concepts in pigeons. *Journal of Experimental Psychology: Animal Behavior Processes, 2*, 285–311.

Heyman, G. M., & Herrnstein, R. J. (1986). More on concurrent interval-ratio schedules: A replication and review. *Journal of the Experimental Analysis of Behavior, 46*, 331–351.

Honig, W. K., & Stewart, K. E. (1988). Pigeons can discriminate locations presented in pictures. *Journal of the Experimental Analysis of Behavior, 50*, 541–551.

Houston, A. I., & McNamara, J. M. (1988). A framework for the functional analysis of behavior. *Behavioral and Brain Sciences, 11*, 117–164.

Hull, C. L. (1943). *Principles of behavior*. New York: Appleton-Century-Crofts.

Hull, C. L. (1952). *A behavior system*. New Haven: Yale University Press.

Johnston, T. D. (1981). Contrasting approaches to a theory of learning. *The Behavioral and Brain Sciences, 4*, 125–173.

Johnston, T. D., & Pietrewicz, A. T. (Eds.). (1985). *Issues in the ecological study of learning.* Hillsdale, NJ: Lawrence Erlbaum Associates.

Kimble, G. A. (1961). *Hilgard and Marquis' conditioning and learning.* New York: Appleton-Century-Crofts.

King, G. R., & Logue, A. W. (1987). Choice in a self-control paradigm with human subjects: Effects of change-over delay duration. *Learning and Motivation, 18,* 421–438.

King, G. R., & Logue, A. W. (1988). Norms of behavior: Balancing generality with testability. *Behavioral and Brain Sciences, 11,* 138.

Kuhn, T. S. (1962). *The structure of scientific revolutions.* Chicago: University of Chicago Press.

Lett, B. T. (1977). Long delay learning in the T-maze: Effect of reward given in the home cage. *Bulletin of the Psychonomic Society, 10,* 211–214.

Lett, B. T. (1980). Taste potentiates color-sickness associations in pigeons and quail. *Animal Learning and Behavior, 8,* 193–198.

Levine, F. M., & Fasnacht, G. (1974). Token rewards may lead to token learning. *American Psychologist, 29,* 817–820.

Lockhard, R. B. (1971). Reflections on the fall of comparative psychology: Is there a message for us all? *American Psychologist, 26,* 168–179.

Logue, A. W. (1979). Taste aversion and the generality of the laws of learning. *Psychological Bulletin, 86,* 276–296.

Logue, A. W. (1981a, November). *Effects of experience on self-control.* Paper presented at the meeting of the Psychonomic Society, Philadelphia.

Logue, A. W. (1981). Species differences and principles of learning: Informed generality. *The Behavioral and Brain Sciences, 4,* 150–151.

Logue, A. W. (1988). A comparison of taste aversion learning in humans and other vertebrates: Evolutionary pressures in common. In R. C. Bolles & M. D. Beecher (Eds.), *Evolution and learning* (pp. 97–116). Hillsdale, NJ: Lawerence Erlbaum Associates.

Logue, A. W. (1988). Research on self-control: An integrating framework. *Behavioral and Brain Sciences, 11,* 665–679.

Logue, A. W., Logue, K. R., & Strauss, K. E. (1983). The acquisition of taste aversions in humans with eating and drinking disorders. *Behaviour Research & Therapy, 21,* 275–289.

Logue, A. W., & Mazur, J. E. (1981). Maintenance of self-control acquired through a fading procedure: Follow-up on Mazur and Logue (1978). *Behaviour Analysis Letters, 1,* 131–137.

Logue, A. W., Ophir, I., & Strauss, K. E. (1981). The acquisition of taste aversions in humans. *Behaviour Research and Therapy, 19,* 319–333.

Logue, A. W., & Pena-Correal, T. E. (1984). Responding during reinforcement delay in a self-control paradigm. *Journal of the Experimental Analysis of Behavior, 41,* 267–277.

Logue, A. W., Pena-Correal, T. E., Rodriguez, M. L., & Kabela, E. (1986). Self-control in humans: Variation in positive reinforcer amount and delay. *Journal of the Experimental Analysis of Behavior, 46,* 159–173.

Logue, A. W., Rodriguez, M. L., Pena-Correal, T. E., & Mauro, B. C. (1984). Choice in a self-control paradigm: Quantification of experience-based differences. *Journal of the Experimental Analysis of Behavior, 41,* 53–67.

Lowe, C. F., & Horne, P. J. (1988). On the origins of selves and self-control. *Behavioral and Brain Sciences, 11,* 689–690.

Macfarlane, D. A. (1930). The role of kinesthesis in maze learning. *University of California Publications in Psychology, 4,* 227–305.

Mackintosh, N. J. (1973). Stimulus selection: Learning to ignore stimuli that predict no change in reinforcement. In R. A. Hinde & J. Stevenson-Hinde (Eds.), *Constraints on learning* (pp. 75–100). New York: Academic Press.

Mackintosh, N. J. (1974). *The psychology of animal learning.* New York: Academic Press.

Maki, W. J., & Hegvik, D. (1980). Directed forgetting in pigeons. *Animal Learning and Behavior, 8,* 567–574.

Mazur, J. E. (1987). An adjusting procedure for studying delayed reinforcement. In M. L. Commons, J. E. Mazur, J. A. Nevin, & H. Rachlin (Eds.), *Quantitative analyses of behavior: Vol. 5. The effect of delay and of intervening events on reinforcement value* (pp. 55–73). Hillsdale, NJ: Lawrence Erlbaum Associates.

Mazur, J. E., & Logue, A. W. (1978). Choice in a "self-control" paradigm: Effects of a fading procedure. *Journal of the Experimental Analysis of Behavior, 30,* 11–17.

McDowell, J. J. (1982). The importance of Herrnstein's mathematical statement of the law of effect for behavior therapy. *American Psychologist, 37,* 771–779.

McDowell, J. J. (1988). Matching theory in natural environments. *The Behaviorist Analyst, 11,* 95–109.

Mischel, W. (1966). Theory and research on the antecedents of self-imposed delay of reward. In B. A. Maher (Ed.), *Progress in experimental research* (Vol. 3, pp. 85–132). New York: Academic Press.

Moore, B. R. (1973). The role of directed Pavlovian reactions in simple instrumental learning in the pigeon. In R. A. Hinde & J. Stevenson-Hinde (Eds.), *Constraints on learning* (pp. 159–188). London: Academic Press.

Olton, D. S., & Samuelson, R. J. (1976). Remembrance of places past: Spatial memory in rats. *Journal of Experimental Psychology: Animal Behavior Processes, 2,* 97–116.

Overmier, J. B., & Seligman, M. E. P. (1967). Effects of inescapable shock upon subsequent escape and avoidance learning. *Journal of Comparative and Physiological Psychology, 63,* 23–33.

Pavlov, I. P. (1927). *Conditioned reflexes* (G. P. Anrep, Trans.). London: Oxford University Press.

Premack, D. (1965). Reinforcement theory. In D. Levine (Ed.), *Nebraska symposium on motivation: 1965* (pp. 123–179). Lincoln: University of Nebraska Press.

Rachlin, H. (1974). Self-control. *Behaviorism, 2,* 94–107.

Rachlin, H. (1981). Learning theory in its niche. *Behavioral and Brain Sciences, 4*, 155–156.

Rachlin, H. (1988). Biological relevance. *Behavioral and Brain Sciences, 11*, 114.

Rachlin, H., & Burkhard, B. (1978). The temporal triangle: Response substitution in instrumental conditioning. *Psychological Review, 85*, 22–48.

Rachlin, H., Green, L., & Tormey, B. (1988). Is there a decisive test between matching and maximizing? *Journal of the Experimental Analysis of Behavior, 50*, 113–123.

Rachlin, H., Kagel, J. H., & Battalio, R. C. (1980). Substitutability in time allocation. *Psychological Review, 87*, 355–374.

Rescorla, R. A., & Wagner, A. R. (1972). A theory of Pavlovian conditioning: Variations in the effectiveness of reinforcement and nonreinforcement. In A. H. Black and W. F. Prokasy (Eds.), *Classical conditioning II* (pp. 64–99). New York: Appleton-Century-Crofts.

Revusky, S. H. (1977). Learning as a general process with an emphasis on data from feeding experiments. In N. W. Milignam, L. Krames, & T. M. Alloway (Eds.), *Food aversion learning* (pp. 1–51). New York: Plenum Publishing.

Revusky, S. H., & Garcia, J. (1970). Learned associations over long delays. In G. H. Bower & J. T. Spence (Eds.), *The psychology of learning and motivation: Advances in theory and research* (Vol. 4, pp. 1–84). New York: Academic Press.

Rodriguez, M. L., & Logue, A. W. (1988). Adjusting delay to reinforcement: Comparing choice in pigeons and humans. *Journal of Experimental Psychology: Animal Behavior Processes, 14*, 105–117.

Rozin, P., & Kalat, J. W. (1971). Specific hungers and poison avoidance as adaptive specializations of learning. *Psychological Review, 78*, 459–486.

Schwartz, B., & Williams, P. R. (1972). Two different kinds of key-peck in the pigeon: Some properties of response maintained by negative and positive response-reinforcer contingencies. *Journal of the Experimental Analysis of Behavior, 18*, 201–216.

Seligman, M. E. P. (1970). On the generality of the laws of learning. *Psychological Review, 77*, 406–418.

Seligman, M. E. P. (1975). *Helplessness*. San Francisco: W H Freeman.

Seligman, M. E. P., & Maier, S. F. (1967). Failure to escape traumatic shock. *Journal of Experimental Psychology, 74*, 1–9.

Shimoff, E., & Catania, A. C. (1988). Self-control and the panda's thumb. *Behavioral and Brain Sciences, 11*, 665–709.

Skinner, B. F. (1938). *The behavior of organisms*. New York: Appleton-Century-Crofts.

Skinner, B. F. (1950). Are theories of learning necessary? *Psychological Review, 57*, 193–216.

Skinner, B. F. (1959). A case history in scientific method. *American Psychologist, 11*, 359–379.

Small, W. S. (1901). Experimental study of the mental processes of the rat. *American Journal of Psychology, 12*, 218–220.

Staddon, J. E. R. (1979). Operant behavior as an adaption to constraint. *Journal of Experimental Psychology: General, 108*, 48–67.

Straub, R. O., Seidenburg, M. S., Bever, T. G., & Terrace, H. S. (1979). Serial learning in the pigeon. *Journal of the Experimental Analysis of Behavior, 32*, 137–148.

Thorndike, E. L. (1965). *Animal intelligence*. New York: Hafner. (Original work published 1911).

Thorndike, E. L. (1932). *The fundamentals of learning*. New York: Bureau of Publications, Teacher's College.

Timberlake, W., & Grant, D. L. (1975). Autoshaping in rats to the presentation of another rat predicting food. *Science, 190*, 690–692.

Tolman, E. C. (1932). *Purposive behavior in animals and men*. New York: Appleton-Century-Crofts.

Tolman, E. C. (1948). Cognitive maps in rats and men. *Psychological Review, 20*, 158–177.

Vaughan, W., & Herrnstein, R. J. (1987). Choosing among natural stimuli. *Journal of the Experimental Analysis of Behavior, 47*, 5–16.

Wasserman, E. A., Kiedinger, R. E., & Bhatt, R. S. (1988). Conceptual behavior in pigeons: Categories, subcategories, and pseudocategories. *Journal of Experimental Psychology: Animal Behavior Processes, 14*, 235–246.

Watson, J. B. (1913). Psychology as the behaviorist views it. *Psychological Review, 20*, 158–177.

Watson, J. B. (1970). *Behaviorism*. New York: W W Norton. (Original work published 1924)

Watson, J. B., & Rayner, R. (1920). Conditioned emotional reactions. *Journal of Experimental Psychology, 3*, 1–14.

Wearden, J. H. (1980). Undermatching on concurrent variable-interval schedules and the power law. *Journal of the Experimental Analysis of Behavior, 33*, 149–152.

Wiens, A. W., Montague, J. R., Manaugh, T. S., & English, C. J. (1976). Pharmacological aversive counter-conditioning to alcohol in a private hospital: One-year follow-up. *Journal of Studies on Alcohol, 37*, 1320–1324.

Wilcoxin, H. C., Dragoin, W. B., & Kral, P. A. (1971). Illness-induced aversions in rat and quail: Relative salience of visual and gustatory cues. *Science, 171*, 826–828.

Williams, B. A. (1988). Reinforcement, choice, and response strength. In R. C. Atkinson, R. J. Herrnstein, G. Lindzey, & R. D. Luce (Eds.), *Stevens' handbook of experimental psychology: Vol. 2. Learning and cognition* (pp. 167–244). New York: John Wiley & Sons.

Wolin, B. R. (1968). Difference in manner of pecking a key between pigeons reinforced with food and with water. In A. C. Catania (Ed.), *Contemporary research in operant behavior* (pp. 286–287). Glenview, IL: Scott Foresman and Company.

Zener, K. (1937). The significance of behavior accompanying conditioned salivary secretion for theories of the conditioned response. *American Journal of Psychology, 50*, 384–403.

CHAPTER 11

THE SOCIAL-INTERACTIONAL VIEWPOINT

Robert C. Carson

The ideas considered in this chapter constitute neither a theory nor a model of personality in any reasonable sense of those terms, which in proper use imply a degree of systematization or even elegance not in evidence in a survey of this particular domain. In the personality field, such terms are also frequently associated with identifiable and universal ideologic positions on the nature of humankind, ones that tend not to be amenable to empirical verification and even less to falsification. These more dubious qualities are also for the most part missing from social-interactional accounts of personhood and its aberrations, which lends them a relatively high degree of adaptability in the face of expanding knowledge. What follows, therefore, is relatively modest in scope—although continually developing—and is perhaps best considered a particular perspective or viewpoint. It is, however, one that clinicians increasingly find helpful in their work, regardless of their primary theoretical predilections (e.g., Strupp & Binder, 1984) or their familiarity with the finer details of the material to be discussed.

ORIGINS

The roots of this social-interactional perspective go back at least to Alfred Adler, one of the early defectors from Freud's inner circle. Horney, Fromm, and Erickson, also trained originally in the psychoanalytic camp, departed from that tradition in the direction of reduced emphasis on the vicissitudes of instinctual energies and the assigning of greater weight to social and interpersonal variables in personality development and functioning. Excellent summaries (e.g., Hall & Lindzey, 1978) of the thinking of these psychoanalytic expatriates are readily available, and no attempt will be made here to review these relatively well-known revisions of basic Freudian doctrine. Instead, we take as our point of departure the work of Harry Stack Sullivan (1892 to 1949).

Sullivan's (1953) original leanings were also strongly influenced by Freudian doctrine. Eventually, however, he too took an oppositional stance toward major elements of psychoanalytic theory, based largely on his considerable familiarity with the emerging American social science and psychology of his day. He was encouraged in this from within his own profession of psychiatry by mentors such as Adolf Meyer and William Alanson White, both of whom were practical men with an antipathy to doctrinaire approaches. While there are obvious similarities to both G. H. Mead and C. H. Cooley in much of Sullivan's thought, the major social science influence on him was doubtless the work of Edward Sapir (see, e.g., Sapir, 1949).

It was also clear that Sullivan was familiar with, and influenced by, the psychological writings of William James. Finally, it is certain that he was acquainted with the field-theoretical gestalt notions imported into American psychology from Germany, probably through the early work of Kurt Lewin, who would have found absurd the person versus situation controversy that so recently dominated much American personality and social psychology. It is thus fair to say that Sullivan's connection with the intellectual origins of contemporary clinical psychology is more direct than in the case of any of the other major personality theorists mentioned. This connectedness may account to some extent for the relative ease with which Sullivanian thinking has, almost unnoticed, become a pervasive presence in much personality research, as well as clinical psychological practice, in this country.

Despite a style of communicating that many have found turgid and impenetrable, Sullivan's basic ideas were relatively simple and straightforward. They may be summarized in contemporary language as follows:

1. The most important origins of personality and of psychopathology are to be found in the nature of the interactions with others that characterize the individual's social history.
2. These early interactions lay down memory traces (e.g., personifications), often affect-laden, imprecise, inarticulable, and schematic in quality, that are activated by current interpersonal situations and determine to a greater or lesser extent both experience and behavior in those situations. Therefore, a person's personality is essentially the record of important prior interactions as manifested in current ones, including current ones with purely fantasied others. Indeed, personality is manifested only in interpersonal relations.
3. Because of the inevitable imperfections of parents and other significant others, the meeting of one's fundamental needs (for tenderness, intimacy, sex, etc.) is likely to collide with requirements for security and self-esteem (which are the inverse of the experience of anxiety), leading to the deployment of security operations that complicate, distort, and render highly problematic the simple coming together of persons in pursuit of mutual satisfaction. The casualties seen in clinical practice are merely the victims of an especially malignant interpersonal history in these respects.

Except among a small group of devotees, Sullivanian ideas were largely ignored by the first large wave of clinical psychologists—mostly veterans of the military—emerging from our universities in the years immediately following World War II. Somewhat anomalous in retrospect, this was the heyday of Freudian psychoanalysis in clinical psychology, bolstered by the ready applicability of the psychoanalytic orientation to the extraordinarily popular projective techniques then in widespread use in personality assessment and diagnosis. The emerging views of Carl Rogers offered the only serious competition, and few in that era discerned the considerable affinity between Rogerian and Sullivanian views of personality and its development (cf. Rogers, 1959). Through the later 1950s, then, Sullivan's status in psychology was at best that of a minor personality theorist whose name might be encountered by students in an examination. His elevation to a position of far greater importance began in 1957 with the publication of Timothy Leary's *Interpersonal Diagnosis of Personality*.

In *Interpersonal Diagnosis* Leary summarized the work he and his colleagues at the Kaiser Foundation in California had been doing on a new system of personality assessment, one that was explicitly undergirded by Sullivan's ideas. The book described what was at once a radical departure from tradition and a highly developed, original, and sensitive operationalization of Sullivan's approach to the understanding of persons. Published more than 3 decades ago, it can be read with profit even now, and its perusal frequently produces an experience of enlightenment in young clinicians struggling to get a grasp on what is happening between themselves and their clients. The book was undoubtedly the single most important factor leading to Leary's appointment to the Harvard faculty. The remainder of that story is well known and is of little consequence here, except that subsequent developments in Leary's interests and career terminated any substantial personal involvement in extending the work begun so well in *Interpersonal Diagnosis*.

A central element in what is sometimes called the Leary system is the now familiar "interpersonal circle," a circular model of descriptors systematically arranged around the bipolar orthogonal axes of "hate–love" and "dominance–submission." The space thus defined is essentially Cartesian. The segments of the circle, which, depending on purpose, may be relatively fine grained or coarse in extent (i.e., in degrees of the circle subsumed), were conceived as defining in a relatively exhaustive manner the entire realm of behaviors one person might direct toward another.

While Leary and his colleagues appear to have arrived at this conception intuitively, it was and continues to be concordant with empirical evidence relating to the manner in which interpersonal behavior is in fact organized. This evidence also suggests compellingly that the circle has the technical psychometric properties of a true circumplex (Carson, 1969; Foa, 1961; Gifford & O'Connor, 1987; Wiggins, 1968; Wiggins, Phillips, & Trapnell, 1989).

The discovery of such formal regularity and order in a human behavioral domain is somewhat amazing and would in itself justify the high regard accorded Leary's major work. But a second major advance in interpersonal thinking can also be traced to the Kaiser Foundation group—namely, the notion that any interpersonal act constrains to some extent the range of reactions it is likely to elicit. That is, the act constitutes a provocation or pull for a certain type of response from the other, and moreover the response of the other can be predicted within limits from circle-relevant information contained within the original act. This idea—that there is an above-baseline probability that the target person's reaction will often be controlled in predictable fashion by the type of behavior the actor deploys—was not only a highly original extension of Sullivan's thought, but it also brilliantly clarified the security operation role of a person's characteristic repertoire of interpersonal behaviors.

In short, one maintains one's security (in the Sullivanian sense of the term) in large part by controlling—even if usually inadvertently—the feedback one receives from one's interaction partners. A distinguishing characteristic of the psychologically disturbed person is a more or less exclusive reliance on a narrow range of interpersonal behaviors, or interpersonal security operations. As Leary warned, however, this constricted repertoire is often deployed with "magnificent finesse" by disturbed persons, who as a group are both well practiced and intensely motivated in the management of their interpersonal environments.

Despite the intuitive appeal and potential power of these ideas, they languished in relative obscurity for a number of years following the publication of Leary's book. An exception to this general neglect was the ongoing work of Lorr and McNair (1963, 1965; Lorr, Bishop & McNair, 1965) on the development of an interpersonal circumplex-based assessment instrument. While this was an independent effort, it profited from and shared many features with the earlier Kaiser Foundation work. The most recent version of the assessment instrument, called the Interpersonal Style Inventory (ISI), is now commercially available (Lorr,

1986). It yields measurements on a profile of trait variables that are largely interpersonal in nature, many of them appearing to be of the same genre as those representing particular segments of the Leary circle and its closely related successors. However, the circular format has been abandoned in the current ISI, and there are substantial departures from the original concept in other ways as well. The present ISI may thus be considered an early offshoot of the developmental direction under discussion, one whose independence from the latter has actually increased over time.

The rediscovery of the Leary system in the 1970s probably had multiple causes, among them the fact that it provided a plausible alternative to those psychologists (and there were many) unwilling to decide for either person (i.e., dispositions) or situation in the silly exclusionary debate about what causes behavior, which extended through the whole of that decade and well into the next. A landmark appears to have been the publication in 1969 of Carson's *Interaction Concepts of Personality*. In this work the author attempted to update the Sullivanian perspective by integrating it with the advances made by the Kaiser Foundation group, with certain contemporary trends in social psychology—especially the social exchange notions of Thibaut and Kelley (1959)—and with varied concepts and findings derived from clinical research. The enthusiastic reception accorded the book was surprising, at least to its author, and in retrospect seems to have appeared at a particularly auspicious time—one characterized by the decline of psychoanalysis (except in some northeast metropolitan centers), the rise of behaviorism, and the not unrelated ferment generated by the aforementioned person-situation controversy.

Whatever the immediate precipitants, the 1970s and 1980s were witness to a widespread renaissance of the interpersonal perspective in clinical psychology. It is to these newer developments that we now turn.

RECENT THEORY AND RESEARCH

As with any viewpoint still in its nascent stage of development and struggling to define itself, the interpersonal perspective seems to be moving forward on several different fronts simultaneously in a somewhat disorganized and nonlinear fashion. The several areas of active development may be somewhat loosely categorized under the following rubics: (a) questions of measurement, taxonomy, and the related interface with psychiatric diagnosis; (b) the nature of interbehavioral influence or contingency; (c) impact of the cognitive revolution; and (d) developing rapprochements with other conceptual and theoretical traditions.

Psychometric Considerations

Precision and efficiency in communication are dependent on a shared framework for differentiating a realm of observation into conceptually valid constituents and shared criteria for the identification, description, and quantification of those constituents. As we have seen, the Leary circle pointed the way for a potentially powerful means of achieving this sort of consensus in the realm of interpersonal behavior. By today's standards, however, it was a relatively unvalidated classificatory system, particularly in its segmental details, and the assessment instruments developed to operationalize its principal constructs, such as the Interpersonal Check List (ICL), have proven to have decided psychometric deficiencies.

There is little doubt that one of the intents of Leary's group was to offer their system as an alternative to—possibly even a substitute for—standard psychiatric diagnosis. As was regretfully noted by Adams (1964) early on, however, this somewhat radical proposal did not initially fare well. A similar attempt to redirect attention to the proposal by McLemore and Benjamin (1979) 15 years later attracted more interest, in part because it contained a pointed critique of the fundamental assumptions of the *Diagnostic and Statistical Manual of Mental Disorders, Third Edition* (DSM-III), but it too failed to generate any widespread rejection of the DSM approach in favor of an interpersonally based one.

Revisions of the Circle

Suggested revisions of Leary's original circle, largely minor in character (e.g., modest changes in the trait adjectives or their particular placements around the circle's circumference) have been relatively common over the years. Three of these revisionary efforts deserve special attention because of the extent of the background investigation that preceded them and because their originators have continued to utilize them productively in sustained efforts to examine their properties and extend their applications. I refer here to the ongoing work of Jerry Wiggins (Wiggins et al., 1989), Donald Kiesler (1988), and Lorna Benjamin (1986a).

Wiggins's version of the circle derives from his original (1979) Interpersonal Adjective Scales (IAS), whose eight 16-item self-description scales had intercorrelations clearly reflecting the circumplex ordering of decreasing and then increasing correlations in departure from and return to any point on the hypothetical circumference. The latest revision of the instrument, the IAS-R (Wiggins et al., 1989) consists of 64 adjectives on which subjects rate self-descriptiveness using a Likert-type scale. The yield is a measure of trait strength or intensity on each of eight scales that array themselves in counterclockwise circular order (beginning at 3:00, with degree equivalents in parentheses) as follows: Warm-Agreeable (0), Gregarious-Extraverted (45), Assured-Dominant (90), Arrogant-Calculating (135), Cold-Hearted (180), Aloof-Introverted (225), Unassured-Submissive (270), and Unassuming-Ingenuous (315). An especially promising aspect of this particular approach is the opening it provides to formal geometric models in the processing of assessment data, as illustrated in Wiggins et al. (1989).

Kiesler (1983) presented his "1982 Interpersonal Circle" following successive, data-based revision of earlier approximations. In its self-report form it is based on frequency of endorsement of questionnaire items designed to tap each of 16 types of interpersonal behavior, which also array themselves in the familiar circular pattern. For ease of comparison with the aforementioned Wiggins model they are presented here in corresponding sequence with intermediate trait descriptors indicated by italics: Friendly, *Sociable*, Exhibitionistic, *Assured*, Dominant, *Competitive*, Mistrusting, *Cold*, Hostile, *Detached*, Inhibited, *Unassured*, Submissive, *Deferent*, Trusting, and *Warm*. Allowing for a certain amount of method variance and idiosyncrasy in choice of terms, the Wiggins and Kiesler circles appear to have substantial overlap, as they should if fundamental considerations of validity are to be met. In keeping with Leary's original version, Kiesler supplied comparable lists of descriptors to indicate the more extreme intensities of each of these qualitative distinctions, usually depicted as farther out (i.e., signifying a more extended vector) from the circle's center. Thus, Friendly at this outer range becomes Devoted-Indulgent. Kiesler (1988) went on to provide a systematic listing of behavioral acts (the "Acts Version") corresponding to his circle descriptors, enhancing its ease of use by observers.

With introduction of her Structural Analysis of Social Behavior (SASB) model in 1974, Lorna Benjamin embarked on a closely related but in many ways far more ambitious project, one that immediately expanded the concerns addressed to certain developmental issues and to the previously neglected dimension of autonomy versus interdependence in interpersonal relations. In doing so, she resurrected the affection, control, and inclusion triad that Schutz (1958) had earlier proposed in his concept of Fundamental Interpersonal Relations Orientation (FIRO).

In Benjamin's scheme the pictorial graphic form is retained, but the shape is no longer circular, nor can it be captured in a single space or surface. Instead, three interrelated diamond-shaped surfaces are proposed. The first two depict separately the behaviors of the subject-person (self) and those of the interaction partner (other). The third surface represents the hypothetical internal response, or introject, activated by the behavior of the interaction partner, who is assumed to be in a parent- or therapist-like role vis-à-vis the subject. Corresponding points on each of the three surfaces bear a complementary relation to each other. For example, behavior of the other characterized by the expression "Abandon, leave in lurch" is complementary to "Detach, weep alone" behavior on the part of the subject and is thought to evoke the intrapsychic response of "Reckless." All of these behaviors, incidentally, represent the intensity extremes of a common vector path originating at the diamond's center.

The SASB model retains through all three surfaces the same horizontal hate–love dimension as the Leary circle and its successors. The vertical dimension, however, is altered to accommodate the new complexity introduced when consideration is given to the degree of autonomy or separateness of two interaction partners and the differential statuses they are assumed to occupy. In effect, the old dominance–submission dimension of the circle is represented in the other (dominant) and self (submissive) surfaces. Thus, the other stance of "Abandon, leave in lurch," while both dominant and hostile, also invites (demands?) the self to assume a degree of autonomy, not submission. The opposite (both psychologically and graphically) stance of "Protect, back up," on the other hand, is not only more loving but also assumes a hierarchical mutuality. On the Self surface of the SASB, then, the polar opposite of "Yield, submit, give in" is not Dominate but rather "Freely come and go," the complement of the other's (also affectionally neutral) stance of "Endorse freedom." Benjamin (1986a) added tentative suggestions of characteristic affects and cognitions thought to be associated with the various surface positions.

As even this brief description demonstrates, Benjamin's (1974, 1982, 1986a) SASB is a decidedly more complicated interpersonal behavioral model than is envisaged by the circle, although it is not fundamentally incompatible with the latter. As might be expected, the assessment paraphernalia associated with the SASB, originating with data from multiple questionnaires or observer codings, is also far more daunting in time, effort, and level of sophistication required for maximally productive use. However, much of the burden has been eased through computerization—in the case of individual assessment under the trade name Intrex (Benjamin, 1980)—and in any event it is probably illusory to believe that clinical understanding will ever come cheaply. The system is also backed by a massive array of empirical data (e.g., Benjamin, 1986a) attesting to its reliability and validity and illustrating its often intriguing clinical applications. In this author's judgment, Benjamin's SASB is a major achievement, one that deserves far more attention among clinical psychologists than it has thus far garnered.

Applications to Formal Diagnosis

The basic idea that the most essential manifestations of psychopathology are to be found in the interpersonal realm goes back to Sullivan. However, his accounts of how one translates into interpersonal terms the disorders that were then recognized are sketchy and unsystematic at best: more illustrations than algorithms. Interpersonalists have since offered a more articulate set of proposals in this area, but the effort itself is seriously hampered by the persistent tendency of framers of diagnostic systems (e.g., DSM-III-R) to conceive of disorder as existing entirely within persons in the manner of medical diseases. There is, of course, a considerable politico-economic dimension to this practice, one not likely to yield readily to mere empirical reality or logic. In consequence, some, including this author, take the position that we must construct an interpersonal diagnostic taxonomy that is independent of the DSM-III-R (and any similarly based successors) and for the foreseeable future remain not unduly concerned with translation between it and the highly corruptible (Millon, 1986; Rothblum, Solomon, & Albee, 1986) DSMs. The recent work of Horowitz and colleagues (e.g., Horowitz & Vitkus, 1986) suggesting an integrative prototypal approach to interpersonal problems on the one hand and psychiatric symptoms on the other is, from this point of view, encouraging.

The modern interpersonal conception of psychopathology, as it has evolved from Leary (1957) through Carson (1969, 1982), Kiesler (1986a, 1986b), Wiggins (Wiggins et al., 1989), and others is rather straightforward. It may be summarized as follows. Psychopathology consists of a defect in the repertoire of an individual's interpersonal behavior, either qualitative or quantitative in nature, and frequently both.

Qualitatively, the defect is seen in a persistent absence, or inhibition, of a given type of interpersonal behavior (which may be defined in terms of a segment of the circle) in situations in which it would be appropriate and adaptive. This deficit in repertoire is in turn accompanied by a relatively inflexible, rigid display of interpersonal behavior that tends to be qualitatively opposite (again in terms of the circle) of the behavior that is missing. Quantitatively, the disordered person typically displays interpersonal behavior of exaggerated, inappropriate intensity within some segment of the circle, normally the same segment that is deployed with excessive frequency. Normality, then, is simply the flexible and adaptive deployment, within moderate ranges of intensity, of behaviors encompassing the entire circle, as varied interpersonal situations dictate. While these propositions seem reasonable on their face and consistent with much clinical lore and literature, they have also garnered impressive support in formal empirical analyses (e.g., Wiggins et al., 1989).

Despite the inevitable frustrations of attempting to deal with DSM-defined disorders as noted previously, some intrepid interpersonalists have made the effort, not without a measure of success. Major credit in this regard goes to Lorna Benjamin and to Donald Kiesler.

Kiesler (1986a, 1986b) noted correctly that, of the various Axes of DSM-III, Axis II, dealing (in adults) with so-called Personality Disorders, shows the greatest a priori promise of yielding to redefinition in interpersonal terms. Reviewing the available evidence, which (partly owing to the notorious unreliability of Axis II disorders) is to date not very impressive, Kiesler (1986a) offered a kind of translation table whereby the 11 Axis II diagnoses can be projected onto the interpersonal circle, focusing on his own 1982 version of the latter. The effort is variably successful depending chiefly on the internal coherence of the several diagnoses and the extent to which they specify overt rather than inferred criteria. To my mind, there is a danger in this practice (one Kiesler successfully avoided) of assuming that the Axis II diagnoses constitute a worthwhile criterion for evaluating the validity of interpersonal diagnosis, when in fact the basic validity of those diagnoses is far more suspect than the circle variables to which they are compared. It would be a tragic error, after all, to reify current Personality Disorder diagnoses and assume that they are substantive improvements over character descriptions that have been part of common human experience and language for centuries.

Benjamin (1986a) took on the decidedly more challenging task of relating interpersonal assessment to DSM-III Axis I disorders. In fact, the challenge was greater than had been anticipated because of serious difficulty in arriving at reliable, mutually exclusive Axis I diagnoses when rigorous patient selection criteria were employed. While only incomplete results of Benjamin's large-scale project in this area are as yet available, these results are quite startling in showing the extent to which specific profiles of aberrant interpersonal functioning are embedded within patient behaviors that result in particular Axis I diagnoses. In fact, systematic nurse observations using Benjamin's system resulted in only slightly less overall accuracy in DSM-III diagnosis allocations than their systematic reports of classical symptoms (classical symptoms are, of course, the stuff of which DSM-III diagnoses are made). As expected, diagnostic accuracy using SASB varied across the different diagnoses. Among the Axis I disorders studied, it was best for uncomplicated (i.e., without psychosis) major depression (86.7%) and worst for chronic undifferentiated schizophrenia (25.0%). Although such results must be considered tentative pending cross-validation, they appear promising.

The striking findings reported by Benjamin (1986a), of which the foregoing includes only a notably germane portion, are subject to the same caveat as was earlier suggested for Kiesler's work with Axis II disorders. That is, there is no good reason to assume that DSM-III (or its revision) is correct, although it appears that for the present we shall have to settle for this particular view of the mental disorder domain. Given its manifest deficiencies in arbitrary decision rules and the like, however, it cannot reasonably serve as a scientifically adequate validity criterion in respect to other approaches. In this author's view, Benjamin may be correct.

Behavioral Aspects of Sex and Gender

While somewhat peripheral to our main focus, there is some work on gender-related behavior and possible sex differences in personality organization that is sufficiently pertinent to the measurement of interpersonal behavior to warrant brief mention. Paulhus (1987), in a largely critical review of research purporting to measure behavioral variations associated with gender role, observed that certain standard scales employed in this undertaking could more appropriately be interpreted as assessing nodal variables on the interpersonal circle. Wiggins (1979, 1980; Wiggins & Holzmuller, 1978) made virtually the same suggestion nearly a decade earlier. Conceivably there is an important relationship here with gender differences in the incidence profiles for various disorders. While this would appear to be a promising approach to furthering our understanding of gender-related behavior, especially in light of the confused state of the pertinent literature (cf. Carson, 1989), the matter apparently has not been pursued in a serious way.

Interbehavioral Contingencies

Interbehavioral contingency means the tendency for a given individual's interpersonal behavior to be constrained or controlled in more or less predictable ways by the behavior received from an interaction partner. As we have seen, this idea was a key element in the conceptions developed by Leary (1957) and his group, and it is a prominent feature in the thinking of most contemporary interpersonalists. That such contingencies, sometimes considered as conditional or transitional probabilities, exist is hardly subject to question (Anchin, 1982). What we have lacked until recently is detailed knowledge about the nature of these regularities, and what we still lack to some extent is an understanding of the factors producing unpredictability or exceptions (e.g., Orford, 1986) to the transactional principles holding for at least most clinical situations.

The Concept of Complementarity

These transactional principles are usually subsumed under the concept of complementarity. In interpersonal circle terms complementarity exists essentially when the behavior of interaction partners occupies the same vertical bisection or semicircle and the opposite horizontal ones. That is, partners are in a complementary relation when both are emitting hostile or friendly behavior and when their behaviors are reciprocal with respect to dominance–submission. In Kiesler's (1986a, 1986b) version, complementarity is maximized when intensity levels on the hate–love dimension approach equality. It is hypothesized that relationships are least problematical when a condition of complementarity obtains, and therefore that, other things being equal, both partners of a dyad are motivated to achieve and maintain this state of affairs (Carson, 1969; Kiesler, 1986a, 1986b). The "other things being equal" qualification is of course an important one and may in reality be a rare happenstance. Hence, the partner whose agenda is more strongly motivated, or who is more powerful, more skillful, and so on may be in a position to recruit complementarity pressures to his or her own service,

inducing the other to occupy an originally nonpreferred position. To anticipate, much of interpersonally based therapy consists of the strategic management of these influences.

As we have also seen, the complementarity concept plays a central role in Benjamin's (1974) SASB model. Here, however, complementarity exists between corresponding points on the three SASB surfaces. Complementarity with respect to the power and love dimensions is, so to speak, built in, as it is also for the additional variable of autonomy–interdependence (which, like love, is a matter of correspondence in interactant positions on that axis). Translatability between the circle and the SASB diamond in regard to the principle of complementarity is widespread, as is most obviously seen in Benjamin's simplified quadrant versions of the surfaces. In the latter, the other surface, reading clockwise from the upper left, consists of "Invoke hostile autonomy," "Encourage friendly autonomy," "Friendly influence," and "Hostile power." The corresponding, and complementary, positions on the self surface are "Take hostile autonomy," "Enjoy friendly autonomy," "Friendly accept," and "Hostile comply." In the SASB system complementarity is also extended to the relationship between the other and introject surfaces, where as earlier noted the latter is conceived as the self's intrapsychic reaction to the initiatives of the other. These introjects, presented in the same order, are "Reject self," "Accept, enjoy self," "Manage, cultivate self," and "Oppress self."

In line with a suggestion originally advanced by Carson (1969), both the Kiesler (1983) and the Benjamin (1974) systems specify "anticomplementarities," or what Benjamin referred to as "antidotes" or "antitheses." These are behavioral positions vis-à-vis the actor that disrupt or block a proffered transaction. In the Carson and Kiesler version, anticomplementary reactions are those that disqualify both the control and love components of the initiator's behavior, as, for example, where a detached-aloof (hostile-submissive) overture is followed by warm-pardoning (loving-submissive) response. For Benjamin, an antithetical response is simply one that is the opposite of the complement (or alternatively the complement of the opposite) of the behavior proffered. Using the quadrant form of the SASB, for example, the antithesis to a "Hostile comply" action (one associated with an "Oppress self" introject) would be an "Encourage friendly autonomy" reaction. As the example implies, the antithetical response would tend to pull for a response opposite to the action originally deployed (i.e., "Enjoy friendly autonomy").

Therapeutic Considerations

The most important principles of psychotherapy as they have evolved within the interpersonal perspective involve issues of complementarity. Cashdan (1973) offered an early but relatively systematic account of how therapeutic change is accomplished within this framework. Provided it is not regarded as a single-route roadmap of how to get from here to there, which would be an absurd undertaking from any perspective, this work remains a valuable and insightful outline of the challenges (whether recognized or not) likely to be faced in any therapeutic relationship, and it suggests tactical therapeutic operations to overcome the common pitfalls and roadblocks to progress. It also describes the kind of vigorous and proactive therapeutic management that most interpersonalists recommend be instituted at critical points in order to induce change in problematic client behaviors. As we shall see, an updated version of it intersects directly with the dominant object-relations thrust in contemporary psychodynamic theory (Cashdan, 1988).

For most interpersonal therapists, the core of their work, the essential element in initiating therapeutic change, lies in the skillful and timely deployment of anticomplementary (or antithetical) responses. An exception appears to be the Harvard-Yale "Interpersonal Therapy of Depression" approach (Klerman, Weissman, Rounsaville, & Chevron, 1984), which focuses on client relationships outside of therapy. In any case, several studies have confirmed clinical observations in showing positive relationships between level of therapeutic outcome and optimal use by therapists of anticomplementary tactics (Andrews, 1973, 1983; Brokaw, 1983; Celani, 1974; Dietzel & Abeles, 1975). But, of course, disruptive operations of this sort are not to be undertaken lightly and are in most circumstances best preceded by complementary or acomplementary ("asocial," in the language of Beier, 1966) therapist behaviors until such time as a solid therapeutic relationship is established (Kiesler, 1988). Indeed, as Kiesler suggested, the therapist can hardly avoid a position complementary to that of the client at the relationship's outset.

As was suggested earlier, the question of whose preferred mode of transactional complementarity is to obtain in a given relationship is not unaffected by the motivations and skills the interactants bring to the relationship. Normally, the novice or inexperienced therapist is at a decided disadvantage here, inasmuch as the client is both more powerfully motivated to create certain effects and extremely well practiced in doing so (Carson, 1982). Hence, it is considered vital that the therapist be able to recognize the relationship ensnarements deployed by the client in order to be in a position to counter them. Failure to do so leads to a protracted recapitulation in therapy of the client's characteristic interpersonal problems, rather than the new experience (Young & Beier, 1982) therapy at its best is supposed to provide. Kiesler (1986a, 1986b, 1988), in particular, focused attention on the crucial importance of the therapist's discerning the often subtle impact the client's behavior generates, where this information can be used to guide therapeutic planning and, on suitable occasions, to provide constructive confrontative feedback.

The Cognitive Interface

What has been called the cognitive revolution through a vast region of psychology's domain has also produced appreciable reverberations in the interpersonal area. Before sampling some of this work, however, it seems appropriate to note how—once again—Sullivan was well ahead of his time.

A convincing argument can be made that the central conception of mind that Sullivan entertained was that of an information-processing system. His invention of the concepts of personification and parataxic distortion, as Carson (1982) pointed out, was undoubtedly inspired by his insight that person-information entering on the input side of a person's receptor apparatus seemed frequently to be transformed dramatically by the time its influence could be discerned at the manifest behavioral output side. Clearly, then, some important things were happening inside the black box, these things being in concept remarkably similar to the stuff of which contemporary cognitive psychology is largely made. Also to be noted here is the ease with which the important Sullivanian notion of selective inattention can be translated into the modern concepts of cue selection and encoding processes insofar as they pertain to person perception and the construal of interpersonal events (see, e.g., Golding, Valone, & Foster, 1980).

In the paper just noted, Carson (1982) attempted to employ a largely cognitive model to account for the commonly observed persistence of patently maladaptive interpersonal behavior. In brief, he postulated an unbroken causal loop among expectancies concerning others' behavior, enactment of behavior consistent with those expectancies, and expectancy-confirming reactions generated in the interpersonal environment. Recently, Andrews (1989) productively employed a similar but more detailed model in an important theoretical treatise expanding on the interpersonal dynamics of depression as originally proposed by Coyne (1976).

Related to this general theme is an earlier speculation by Carson (1979) that the rigid and unduly circumscribed interpersonal repertoires of disturbed persons, as discussed earlier, should result in sometimes severe constraints on the behavior they observe in others, thus affecting their generalized expectancies about the nature of the interpersonal world. Using circle quadrants for illustration, he suggested, for example, that the rigidly loving-submissive person experiences all others as more powerful, but in either a loving or a hostile way. It thus becomes a matter of some importance to the person to probe persistently for information that would clarify the latter issue, but of course these endless probes may often themselves determine the outcome and confirm the person's helplessness. As another example, the rigidly hostile-dominant person should experience the interpersonal world as (ultimately) uniformly hostile, but as consisting of winners and losers within that affective constraint. It is not difficult to imagine how such an experience-based view of the nature of things will operate as a self-fulfilling prophecy (Jones, 1986). Dodge and Coie (1987) showed a similar mechanism in operation among excessively aggressive boys.

The concept of person schematas or prototypes—imprecisely organized elements of memory relating to our social history—is central to such thinking and is in fact central to much research and theorizing in the person perception area (e.g., Hastie et al., 1980). We tend to think about others in prototypic terms (Cantor & Mischel, 1977, 1979a, 1979b). Relatedly, Wiggins (1979, 1980, 1982) pointed out that our cognitive organizations relating to persons seem—in common with other cognitive organizations—to be composed of categories that have indistinct cores and boundaries, what have been called "fuzzy sets." This observation is inconsistent with all manner of personality typologies, including those of DSM-III-R (Cantor, Smith, French, & Mezzich, 1980), that posit sharply demarcated classes of behavior. It is entirely in keeping, however, with a circumplexly ordered taxonomy of trait-descriptive terms that are not sharply separated at the edges, but rather blend into one another in continuous fashion in the manner suggested by the interpersonal circle. Probing this idea of prototypal or analogic (Watzlawick, Beavin, & Jackson, 1967) mentation from a Sullivanian perspective yields the interesting conclusion that our thinking about persons, including our own troubled selves (Horowitz, et al., 1982), may involve decidedly parataxic operations.

Rapprochement with Other Views

As was suggested earlier, evidence of Sullivan's influence on clinical practice and theory is pervasive but often remains curiously unacknowledged. His relative anonymity among the elite of psychiatric and psychoanalytic circles may be explained in part by the fact that during his professional lifetime he was something of an embarrassment to these establishments (Alexander, 1990), a condition that his notorious irascibility probably did little to dispell. In any event, it is clear that the current interest in object relations among American psychoanalysts owes something to ideas originally proposed by Sullivan, although historic credit is usually assigned to the British school of Melanie Klein, W. R. D. Fairbairn, D. W. Winnicott, and Harry Guntrip. Fine's (1979) A History of Psychoanalysis provides a more balanced picture of the development of the interpersonal viewpoint within American psychoanalysis and gives due credit to Sullivan's contribution. Cashdan (1973), who made an earlier noted contribution to psychotherapeutic theory within the interpersonal framework, recast that theory (1988) into an explicit object-relations formulation—demonstrating in the process the high level of translatability that has probably always existed between these two supposedly diverse approaches.

Pointing to another bridge, Wachtel's (1977) already classic work attempting to integrate psychoanalysis and behavior therapy presents a model of the former that is very active in its interpersonal aspect, reminiscent of the transference management type of psychoanalysis advocated by Alexander and French (1946) 3 decades earlier. In announcing the behaviorist manifesto that was shortly to become a dominant force in American clinical psychology, Krasner (1962) described the therapist as a "social reinforcement machine." That manifesto, however, contained in fact very little that could be described as social and essentially nothing of the more restrictive domain of interpersonal relations as understood within the present context and as is seemingly envisaged in Wachtel's (1977) integration. The early (circa 1960) behavior therapists apparently did indeed think of themselves for the most part as impersonal technicians who delivered objective treatment packages intended to alter the equally impersonal problematic behaviors of their clients. But they did not do so for long. In due course, they discovered such problems as client noncompliance and other irrational disruptions of their carefully programmed interventions, leading to a rash of publications dealing with problems of the relationship in behavior therapy. Such loss of innocence was appropriately accompanied by a developing interest in, and growing sophistication about, the use of the client-therapist relationship in maximizing the effectiveness of more technical therapeutic operations. Thus, by 1974 Rimm and Masters would write: "Any would-be practitioner who chooses to be a behavior therapist because he finds it difficult to put clients at ease . . . is advised to rethink his professional goals" (p. 35).

The implications of a thoroughgoing interpersonal analysis of behavior therapy go well beyond considerations of relationship building and other nonspecific therapeutic factors, however. For example, the original notion of social reinforcement, which seems to involve little more than direct praise or commendation, is from an interpersonal perspective naive at best, if only because such praise would be anathema, an aversive stimulus, to clients with certain types of aberrant interpersonal functioning. The other side of the coin is that some therapist behaviors not generally considered to have positive hedonic value would in fact function as positive reinforcers for certain clients and might therefore be employed in the shaping of new responses (Brokaw & McLemore, 1983; DeVoge & Beck, 1978). In an interesting twist, many contemporary behavior therapists concern themselves with attempts at direct revision of the interpersonal repertoires of their clients in what is called social skills training, although few if any such programs at present explicitly incorporate complementarity (or anticomplementarity) principles. The oversight seems unfortunate.

Examples of the interpenetration of the interpersonal and the newer cognitive-behavioral perspectives are abundant and widespread. Besides those already mentioned, the cognitive restructuring work that is advocated in such major systematic approaches to treatment as those of Beck (Beck, Emery, & Greenberg, 1985; Beck, Rush, Shaw, & Emery, 1979) and Ellis (1970) is involved primarily with the manner in which various interpersonal situations are construed. And even cursory examination of the clinical material used to illustrate these approaches reveals that most of it can rather readily be mapped onto the templates provided by the interpersonal circle or the SASB variation of it. This conclusion seems entirely consistent with the fact that client complaints, when decomposed according to the methods of Horowitz and his associates (Horowitz et al., 1982), usually turn out to have a strongly interpersonal focus—often of the form: "I can't [do something interpersonal]." In addition to these relatively general observations, Safran

(1984a, 1984b) made a convincing case that the interpersonal and the cognitive must be seen as inextricably interwoven in managing the cognitive therapy relationship and in the planning of appropriate cognitive interventions.

CURRENT STATE OF THE FIELD

As the foregoing demonstrates, the interpersonal perspective in clinical psychology is not only alive and well but growing and expanding at a rate exceeded by few if any other approaches to an understanding of persons as psychosocial (as opposed to biological) entities.

Accomplishments

Accomplishments to date include at least the following:

1. The approach to personality and psychopathology originally proposed by Sullivan has proven to be a seminal one. It is rich enough to be a continuing source of new hypotheses and flexible enough to accommodate to new findings that emerge from the testing of those hypotheses as well as from work in cognate areas.
2. We now have the beginnings of an understanding of the structure of interpersonal behavior. In turn, this understanding has shed new light on such venerable problems as the classification of psychopathological conditions and the nature of interpersonal influence.
3. The interpersonal approach has contributed importantly to a productive redefinition of psychotherapy and of therapist as participant-observer, thereby pointing the way for a planfully active form of managing client experience in a corrective direction.
4. Therapists have a growing sophistication concerning the relationship between the presenting complaints and symptoms of clients and the interpersonal meaning and function of those expressed disablements.
5. The concepts of Sullivan relating to the manner in which humans process information, particularly person information, have proven strikingly prophetic in the light of modern cognitive psychology. In fact, the work of investigators of interpersonal construal processes or person perception, where progress has been notably slow and uncertain, would probably benefit from a greater appreciation of what Sullivan called parataxis.

6. Interpersonalists have been in the forefront in urging the abandonment of the naive but widespread notion of unidirectional causality in attempts to understand the socially significant behavior of persons. In so doing they have pointed to a richer appreciation of how personality traits, adaptive and maladaptive, are maintained.

7. The interpersonal perspective has spawned a variety of new and imaginative psychotherapeutic techniques and strategies, for a sampling of which the reader is referred to the Anchin and Kiesler (1982) *Handbook*.

Considered in the context of Meehl's (1978) painfully accurate observation about the "slow progress of soft psychology" (p. 806), this summary of accomplishments is relatively impressive. But, of course, hardly anything in life or psychology is all sweetness and light.

Remaining Issues and Problems

In the version of this chapter prepared for the first edition of *The Clinical Psychology Handbook,* I pointed to three general problem areas: (a) limitations of available assessment instruments pertinent to the area; (b) our ignorance concerning temporal factors and change in the interpersonal realm, due in part to the unavailability of appropriate analytical techniques; and (c) the phenomenological impasse, which is by no means unique to this particular psychological domain. As will be seen, only the first of these roadblocks has diminished appreciably in the interim, and then with qualifications.

Problems of Assessment

Much has happened in the interpersonal assessment arena in recent years. Already mentioned in this regard is the commercial availability of Lorr's (1986) ISI, the development of which has involved lengthy and sophisticated empirical analyses through various of its stages. The ISI appears to be a solidly based individual assessment tool. Unfortunately, as previously noted, the organizing concepts of principal axes, circumplex ordering, and the like seem largely to have been abandoned at some stage in the development process. As a result, it is not immediately apparent how ISI data would map onto the spaces envisaged by the structural conceptions so central to much of the work described herein. The seriousness of this failing, if it is one, can be estimated only by data that are yet to be gathered.

Also appearing since the writing of the first edition of this chapter have been Kiesler's (1983) 1982 circle and variations (1988) and the revised version of Wiggins's (1989) Interpersonal Adjective scales. Both remain solidly within the conceptual tradition originating with Leary (1957) and his colleagues, and both are sophisticated instruments with a history of extensive background research. In neither case, however, has the questionnaire paraphernalia associated with these instruments been made available as yet for general use, and potential users may therefore experience some inconvenience in obtaining copies of them.

The same difficulty faces potential users of Benjamin's (1986a) increasingly elaborate SASB assessment system, with the added constraint that the more impressive types of yield from these instruments is dependent on specialized computer software created by the author. (Advice on obtaining access to the latter is contained in Benjamin, 1986a.) For some applications, in addition, specialized training may be mandatory. It is a sad commentary that, owing to funding shortages, progress on this important work has been seriously hampered.

Temporal Factors, Partner Variance, and Change

With the exception of Benjamin's SASB system, the formal assessment devices currently available refer only to the present point in time and are not readily adapted to description in terms of particular interaction partners. By and large, they focus on a generalized self in relation to a generalized other. The SASB system additionally involves description of self in relation to parents and significant others and includes attention to earlier time periods and to variation in mood (best and worst). It is therefore capable, in principle, of providing far more differentiated results and predictions of future behavior.

The latter qualities of the SASB more closely approximate the real world of interpersonal behavior. There is, after all, something of a paradox embedded in any attempt to measure interpersonal behavior where a trait-like approach undergirds the effort. One of the cardinal principles of the interpersonal perspective is that a person's behavior in an interpersonal situation is to a significant extent determined by the behavior of the interaction partner; indeed, where that is not the case it raises the question of mental disorder, as we have seen. The basic assessment issue, therefore, is that of determining what regularities exist between the individual's behavioral output on the one hand and the various challenges presented by his or her interpersonal environment on the other. Not even the mentally disordered respond in the same way to every such variation. If assessment is limited to the measurement of general propensities toward the display of certain kinds of interpersonal behavior, then it will be necessary to concede fairly large error terms for the predictions we make.

Much of what we have learned about interpersonal behavior is based on observation of relatively short-term relationships, and we commonly make the assumption that the behavior of the individuals in those relationships does not change appreciably by virtue of experience in those relationships. Such an assumption violates both common sense and the premises on which psychotherapy is based. Making the reasonable assumption that most people do change in consequence of at least their more important relationships with others, we are confronted with the unpleasant reality that we know little about the details involved in such change. Nor is it certain at present that we can fashion methods adequate to the task of overcoming this ignorance. Analysis of change at this level appears to fall within the domain of stochastic processes, one variety of which—Markov chains—has already seen limited use in the area (Benjamin, 1979; Rausch, 1972). The problem, however, remains a methodologically intimidating one for which a general solution continues to be elusive.

The Phenomenological Impasse

As recent work like that of Andrews (1989) on the self-perpetuating nature of depression shows, interpersonal theory is becoming increasingly cognitive in its focus—a development Sullivan would doubtless have approved. Further movement in this direction, however, will at some point confront us with what has always been psychology's most vexing problem: the problem of individual experience. It is evidently difficult to observe one's own cognitive processes (e.g., Nisbett & Wilson, 1977). The requirement that we observe and reliably measure the fundamentally private cognitions of others threatens to tax our ingenuity to its limits. When we ask a person to describe (typically in the English linguistic code) his or her experience of self or of another person, we do not obtain anything closely correspondent with primary impressions. Yet it is difficult to imagine making much progress in the cognitive direction without being able reliably to tap into exactly this sort of data. Sweeping the problem under the rug, a time-honored stratagem in psychology generally, will not produce a satisfactory solution in the domain of interpersonal relations, if indeed it has anywhere in psychology.

The foregoing observations do not necessarily justify an attitude of hopelessness and despair. It is the case, after all, that the broader field of cognitive psychology per se faces precisely the same challenges and has managed to fabricate some ingenious techniques and analytical methods for circumventing them, albeit with perhaps excessive dependence on computer modeling. With some exceptions, the same level of ingenuity is hardly to be found in the realm of interpersonal processes. That will change as more young investigators find excitement in the story as already unfolded.

CONCLUSION

During his professional lifetime the author has been privileged to observe the transformation of the interpersonal perspective from a minor entry in the competition among sweeping theories of personality to a central theme in clinical psychology, one whose influence pervades the entire field. That is gratifying for one steeped in the Sullivanian approach virtually from the outset. Yet there is a certain poignancy that comes with reflecting on this history—the realization that acceptance has come slowly, and that major movements in the field, such as DSM-III-R and the now rampant neo-Kraepelinianism of contemporary psychiatry, can still ignore the essential message that human beings are above all else social animals. Clearly, we still have a long way to go.

REFERENCES

Adams, H. B. (1964). "Mental illness" or interpersonal behavior? *American Psychologist, 19*, 191–197.

Alexander, F., & French, T. M. (1946). *Psychoanalytic therapy*. New York: Ronald.

Alexander, I. E. (1990). *Personology: Method and content in personality assessment and psychobiography* (chap. 6). Durham, NC: Duke University Press.

Anchin, J. C. (1982). Sequence, pattern, and style: Integration and treatment implications of some interpersonal concepts. In J. C. Anchin & D. J. Kiesler (Eds.), *Handbook of interpersonal psychotherapy* (pp. 95–131). Elmsford, NY: Pergamon Press.

Anchin, J. C., & Kiesler, D. J. (Eds.). (1982). *Handbook of interpersonal psychotherapy*. Elmsford, NY: Pergamon Press.

Andrews, J. (1973). Interpersonal challenge: A source of growth in laboratory training. *Journal of Applied Behavioral Science, 9*, 514–533.

Andrews, J. (1983). *Interpersonal challenge in psychotherapy.* San Diego: University of California, San Diego, Psychological and Counseling Services. Unpublished manuscript.

Andrews, J. D. W. (1989). Psychotherapy of depression: A self-confirmation model. *Psychological Review, 96,* 576–607.

Beck, A. T., Emery, G., & Greenberg, R. L. (1985). *Anxiety disorders and phobias: A cognitive perspective.* New York: Basic Books.

Beck, A. T., Rush, A. J., Shaw, B., & Emery, G. (1979). *Cognitive therapy of depression.* New York: Guilford Press.

Beier, E. G. (1966). *The silent language of psychotherapy.* Chicago: Aldine

Benjamin, L. S. (1974). Structural analysis of social behavior. *Psychological Review, 81,* 392–425.

Benjamin, L. S. (1979). Use of structural analysis of social behavior (SASB) and Markov chains to study dyadic interactions. *Journal of Abnormal Psychology, 88,* 303–313.

Benjamin, L. S. (1980). *INTREX users manual.* Madison, WI: INTREX Interpersonal Institute.

Benjamin, L. S. (1982). Use of structural analysis of social behavior (SASB) to guide intervention in psychotherapy. In J. C. Anchin & D. J. Kiesler (Eds.), *Handbook of interpersonal psychotherapy* (pp. 190–212). Elmsford, NY: Pergamon Press.

Benjamin, L. S. (1986a). Adding social and intrapsychic descriptors to Axis I of DSM-III. In T. Millon & G. L. Klerman (Eds.), *Contemporary directions in psychopathology: Toward the DSM-IV* (pp. 599–638). New York: Guilford Press.

Benjamin, L. S. (1986b). Use of structural analysis of social behavior (SASB) for operational definition and measurement of some dynamic concepts. *Psychiatry, 47,* 104–129.

Brokaw, D. (1983). *Markov chains and master therapists: An interpersonal analysis of psychotherapy process.* Unpublished doctoral dissertation, Fuller Theological Seminary.

Brokaw, D., & McLemore, C. W. (1983). Toward a more rigorous definition of social reinforcement: Some interpersonal clarifications. *Journal of Personality and Social Psychology, 44,* 1014–1020.

Cantor, N., & Mischel, W. (1977). Traits as prototypes: Effects on recognition memory. *Journal of Personality and Social Psychology, 35,* 38–48.

Cantor, N., & Mischel, W. (1979a). Categorization processes in the perception of people. In L. Berkowitz (Ed.), *Advances in experimental social psychology.* New York: Academic Press.

Cantor, N., & Mischel, W. (1979b). Prototypicality and personality: Effects on free recall and personality impressions. *Journal of Research in Personality, 13,* 187–205.

Cantor, N., Smith, E., French, R. de S., & Mezzich, J. (1980). Psychiatric diagnosis as prototype categorization. *Journal of Abnormal Psychology, 89,* 181–193.

Carson, R. C. (1969). *Interaction concepts of personality.* Chicago: Aldine.

Carson, R. C. (1979). Personality and exchange in developing relationships. In R. L. Burgess & T. L. Huston (Eds.), *Social exchange in developing relationships* (pp. 247–269). New York: Academic Press.

Carson, R. C. (1982). Self-fulfilling prophecy, maladaptive behavior, and psychotherapy. In J. C. Anchin & D. J. Kiesler (Eds.), *Handbook of interpersonal psychotherapy* (pp. 64–77). Elmsford, NY: Pergamon Press.

Carson, R. C. (1989). Personality. In M. R. Rosenzweig & L. W. Porter (Eds.), *Annual Review of Psychology, 40,* 227–248. Palo Alto, CA: Annual Reviews, Inc.

Cashdan, S. (1973). *Interactional psychotherapy.* New York: Grune & Stratton.

Cashdan, S. (1988). *Object relations therapy: Using the relationship.* New York: W W Norton.

Celani, D. P. (1974). *The complementarity hypothesis: An exploratory study.* Unpublished doctoral dissertation, University of Vermont.

Coyne, J. C. (1976). Depression and the response of others. *Journal of Abnormal Psychology, 55,* 186–193.

DeVoge, J. T, & Beck, S. (1978). The therapist-client relationship in behavior therapy. In M. Hersen, R. M. Eisler, & P. M. Miller (Eds.), *Progress in behavior modification* (Vol. 6). New York: Academic Press.

Dietzel, C., & Abeles, N. (1975). Client-therapist complementarity and therapeutic outcome. *Journal of Counseling Psychology, 22,* 264–272.

Dodge, K. A., & Coie, J. D. (1987). Social-information-processing factors in reactive and proactive aggression in children's peer groups. *Journal of Personality and Social Psychology, 53,* 1146–1158.

Ellis, A. (1970). *Reason and emotion in psychotherapy.* New York: Lyle Stuart.

Fine, R. (1979). *A history of psychoanalysis.* New York: Columbia University Press.

Foa, U. G. (1961). Convergences in the analysis of the structure of interpersonal behavior. *Psychological Review, 68,* 341–353.

Gifford, R., & O'Connor, B. (1987). The interpersonal circumplex as a behavioral map. *Journal of Personality and Social Psychology, 52,* 1019–1026.

Golding, S. L., Valone, K., & Foster, S. W. (1980). Interpersonal construal: An individual differences framework. In N. Hirschberg (Ed.), *Multivariate methods in the social sciences: Applications.* Hillsdale, NJ: Lawrence Erlbaum Associates.

Hall, C. S., & Lindzey, G. (1978). *Theories of personality* (3rd ed.). New York: John Wiley & Sons.

Hastie, R., Ostrom, T. M., Ebbeson, E. G., Wyer, R. S., Hamilton, D. L., & Carlston, D. E. (Eds.). (1980). *Person memory: The cognitive basis of social perception.* Hillsdale, NJ: Lawrence Erlbaum Associates.

Horowitz, L., & Vitkus, J. (1986). The interpersonal basis of psychiatric symptoms. *Clinical Psychology Review, 6,* 443–469.

Horowitz, L. M., Smith, R. de S. Lapid, J. S., & Weckler, D. A. (1982). Symptoms and interpersonal problems: The prototype as an integrating concept. In J. C. Anchin & D. J. Kiesler (Eds.), *Handbook of interpersonal psychotherapy* (pp. 168–189). Elmsford, NY: Pergamon Press.

Jones, E. E. (1986). Interpreting interpersonal behavior: The effects of expectancies. *Science, 234,* 41–46.

Kiesler, D. J. (1983). The 1982 interpersonal circle: A taxonomy for complementarity in human transactions. *Psychological Review, 90,* 185–214.

Kiesler, D. J. (1986a). The 1982 interpersonal circle: An analysis of DSM-III personality disorders. In T. Millon & G. L. Klerman (Eds.), *Contemporary perspectives in psychopathology: Toward the DSM-IV* (pp. 571–598). New York: Guilford Press.

Kiesler, D. J. (1986b). Interpersonal methods of diagnosis and treatment. In R. Michels & J. O. Cavenar (Eds.), *Psychiatry.* Philadelphia: J B Lippincott.

Kiesler, D. J. (1988). *Therapeutic communication: Therapist impact disclosure as feedback in psychotherapy.* Palo Alto, CA: Consulting Psychologists Press.

Klerman, G. L., Weissman, M. M., Rounsaville, B. J., & Chevron, E. S. (1984). *Interpersonal psychotherapy of depression.* New York: Basic Books.

Krasner, L. (1962). The therapist as a social reinforcement machine. In H. H. Strupp & L. Luborsky (Eds.), *Research in psychotherapy* (Vol. II, pp. 61–94). Washington, DC: APA.

Leary, T. (1957). *Interpersonal diagnosis of personality.* New York: Ronald.

Lorr, M. (1986). *Interpersonal style inventory (ISI) manual.* Los Angeles: Western Psychological Services.

Lorr, M., Bishop, P. F., & McNair, D. M. (1965). Interpersonal types among psychiatric patients. *Journal of Abnormal Psychology, 70,* 468–472.

Lorr, M., & McNair, D. M. (1963). An interpersonal behavior circle. *Journal of Abnormal and Social Psychology, 67,* 68–75.

Lorr, M., & McNair, D. M. (1965). Expansion of the interpersonal behavior circle. *Journal of Personality and Social Psychology, 2,* 823–830.

McLemore, C. W., & Benjamin, L. S. (1979). Whatever happened to interpersonal diagnosis: A psychosocial alternative to DSM-III. *American Psychologist, 34,* 17–34.

Meehl, P. E. (1978). Theoretical risks and tabular asterisks: Sir Karl, Sir Ronald, and the slow progress of soft psychology. *Journal of Consulting and Clinical Psychology, 46,* 806–834.

Millon, T. (1986). On the past and future of the DSM-III: Personal recollections and projections. In T. Millon & G. L. Klerman (Eds.), *Contemporary directions in psychopathology: Toward the DSM-IV* (pp. 29–70). New York: Guilford Press.

Nisbett, R. E., & Wilson, T. D. (1977). Telling more than we can know: Verbal reports on mental processes. *Psychological Review, 84,* 231–259.

Orford, J. (1986). The rules of interpersonal complementarity: Does hostility beget hostility and dominance, submission? *Psychological Review, 93,* 365–377.

Paulhus, D. L. (1987). Effects of group selection on correlations and factor patterns in sex role research. *Journal of Personality and Social Psychology, 53,* 314–317.

Rausch, H. L. (1972). Process and change: A Markov model of interaction. *Family Process, 11,* 275–298.

Rimm, D. C., & Masters, J. C. (1974). *Behavior therapy: Techniques and empirical findings.* New York: Academic Press.

Rogers, C. R. (1959). A theory of therapy, personality, and interpersonal relationships as developed in the client-centered framework. in S. Koch (Ed.), *Psychology: A study of a science* (Vol. 3, pp. 184–266). New York: McGraw-Hill.

Rothblum, E., Solomon, L. J., & Albee, G. W. (1986). A sociopolitical perspective of DSM-III. In T. Millon & G. L. Klerman (Eds.), *Contemporary directions in psychopathology: Toward the DSM-IV* (pp. 167–189). New York: Guilford Press.

Safran, J. D. (1984a). Assessing the cognitive-interpersonal cycle. *Cognitive Therapy and Research, 8,* 333–348.

Safran, J. D. (1984b). Some implications of Sullivan's interpersonal theory for cognitive therapy. In M. A. Reda & M. J. Mahoney (Eds.), *Cognitive psychotherapies: Recent developments in theory, research, and practice.* Cambridge, MA: Ballinger.

Sapir, E. (1949). *Selected writings of Edward Sapir in language, culture, and personality.* Berkeley: University of California Press.

Schutz, W. C. (1958). *FIRO: A three-dimensional theory of interpersonal behavior.* New York: Holt, Rinehart & Winston.

Strupp, H. H., & Binder, J. L. (1984). *Psychotherapy in a new key: A guide to time-limited dynamic psychotherapy.* New York: Basic Books.

Sullivan, H. S. (1953). *The interpersonal theory of psychiatry.* New York: W W Norton.

Thibaut, J. W., & Kelley, H. H. (1959). *The social psychology of groups.* New York: John Wiley & Sons.

Wachtel, P. L. (1977). *Psychoanalysis and behavior therapy: Toward an integration.* New York: Basic Books.

Watzlawick, P., Beavin, J. H., & Jackson, D. D. (1967). *Pragmatics of human communication.* New York: W W Norton.

Wiggins, J. S. (1968). Personality structure. In P. R. Farnsworth, M. R. Rozenzweig, & J. T. Polefka (Eds.), *Annual Review of Psychology, 19,* 293–350. Palo Alto, CA: Annual Reviews, Inc.

Wiggins, J. S. (1979). A psychological taxonomy of trait-descriptive terms: The interpersonal domain. *Journal of Personality and Social Psychology, 37,* 395–412.

Wiggins, J. S. (1980). Circumplex models of interpersonal behavior. In L. Wheeler (Ed.), *Review of personality and social psychology* (Vol. 1, pp. 265–294). Beverly Hills: Sage Publications.

Wiggins, J. S. (1982). Circumplex models of interpersonal behavior in clinical psychology. In P. C. Kendall & J. N. Butcher (Eds.), *Handbook of research methods in clinical psychology*. New York: Wiley Interscience.

Wiggins, J. S., & Holzmuller, A. (1978). Psychological androgyny and interpersonal behavior. *Journal of Consulting and Clinical Psychology, 46*, 40–52.

Wiggins, J. S., & Holzmuller, A. (1981). Further evidence on androgyny and interpersonal flexibility. *Journal of Research in Personality, 15*, 67–80.

Wiggins, J. S., Phillips, N., & Trapnell, P. (1989). Circular reasoning about interpersonal behavior: Evidence concerning some untested assumptions underlying diagnostic classification. *Journal of Personality and Social Psychology, 56*, 296–305.

Young, D. M., & Beier, E. G. (1982). Being asocial in social places: Giving the client a new experience. In J. C. Anchin & D. J. Kiesler (Eds.), *Handbook of interpersonal psychotherapy* (pp. 262–273). Elmsford, NY: Pergamon Press.

CHAPTER 12

HUMANIST, PHENOMENOLOGICAL, AND EXISTENTIAL APPROACHES

Hugh B. Urban

In the period following the end of World War II, many were captured by the observations of the eminent and influential scientist Sir Charles P. Snow (1959), who had observed that an ominous gap had developed between two strong investigative traditions within British and American universities—the arts and humanities on the one hand, and the sciences and engineering on the other. Both of these traditions had remained centered on a study of the human condition, and both had maintained their search for ways in which the circumstances of people might be enhanced and improved. But, in Snow's view, a separation had formed such that two cultures had developed, sufficiently different from one another that useful communication and exchange between them had virtually ceased to occur.

Drawing an analogy to the manner in which ethnic cultures can follow divergent paths of development when pursued in disparate portions of the world, Snow proposed that the traditions had evolved from different philosophical and ideological foundations, followed different paradigms and models, developed their own languages, fashioned their own tools, and adhered to their own conventions of communications and commerce within their own groups. He recognized that the divergencies had been both long-standing and progressive, but that by the time he chose to comment the cultural gaps had become very large. Sharp and sustained disagreements existed between the traditions as to the important things to be emphasized about the human condition, stemming from the philosophical differences on which they stood. Languages had become sufficiently different that attempts to communicate across cultural lines had become burdensome, frustrating, and typically abandoned. Investigators stayed increasingly within their own cultural boundaries, contenting themselves with their own literature with which they felt compatible, neglecting to stay abreast of inquiry in neighboring areas, and failing to relate their own discoveries to what might be unfolding elsewhere. Finally, barriers to exchange had become formed within the academic community, inhibiting the free movement of persons between the two traditions; sanctions were used to discourage those considered disloyal to their cultural traditions; varied hindrances were formed to render collaboration across boundaries more difficult; and the inevitable suspicions and animosities that can develop between segmented human groups had come into being and exerted a dissuasive effect.

Snow regarded the situation as unfortunate for a number of reasons. A major concern, of course, is the jeopardy in which the larger society is placed when deep divisions, increasingly difficult to reconcile, become formed within it. This is especially the case when those divisions form within the intellectual leadership on which the society has come to rely. Moreover, such divisions are unfortunate whenever valuable and/or significant ideas needed for the full development of both fail to be freely exchanged, or when solutions to human problems require cross cultural collaboration in order to be found. Each culture, as well as the larger society of which it is a part, becomes impoverished as a result.

Commentators were quick to point out that Snow's characterization of the two cultures within the intellective circles of our societies—like all broad analogies—was somewhat overdrawn. It was not difficult to find exceptions or to point to areas of rapprochement. Yet many came to agree that his observations held considerable merit, that his concerns were well founded, and that attempts to remedy the situation were indicated. Thus, one of the foremost historians of science (Sarton, 1962) agreed, observing that the humanities without scientific education are essentially incomplete, but that without history, philosophy, art, and letters, and without a living faith, human life on this planet ceases to be worthwhile.

There proved to be greater agreement regarding the diagnosis of the difficulty than in coming up with some form of corrective treatment. Many remedies were suggested and tried. Committees, workshops, and conferences were convened; modifications in undergraduate and graduate degree programs were considered; and two-culture dialogues became an institutional fixture on some campuses. Most such attempts, however, met with indifferent success, and the two cultures appear to be maintaining a relatively peaceful, if uneasy, coexistence.

It is tempting to suggest that something akin to all of this has taken place within the arena of psychology and psychiatry as well. We are referring in this instance to the apparently large discrepancies seen between the humanist-phenomenological-existential perspectives regarding the proper study of humans and their behavior, in contrast to the more prevalent posture, known as scientific psychology. The parallels with Snow's characterization of two cultures within the larger realm of academia appear on the surface to be close. Inspection reveals that the philosophical positions from which the two streams have developed are not only at great variance with one another, but also that the antinomies that exist between them have been with humankind since earliest times. With variant proposals about the nature of being in general (ontology), as well as divergent views concerning the nature of knowledge and how we come to know what we think we know (epistemology), the two streams of thought have emerged with sharply different models for characterizing the nature of the human person, as well as very different notions as to the methods and means required to understand humans and to render their behavior intelligible.

Separated domains of investigation do seem to have developed. Psychologists with an existential orientation, for example, naturally maintain contact with others of similar persuasion, tend to read the materials written by others working along comparable lines, and are constrained by the limitations of time and energy from remaining conversant with markedly different views and approaches. The same can be said of their more laboratory-based colleagues, for whom the business of staying abreast of developments in their own areas of emphasis is equally seductive and demanding. However, even if time and circumstance permitted a greater degree of interplay between persons operating within these different perspectives, productive exchanges would be bothersome. With their differences lying at the most basic paradigmatic levels, it is not surprising that productive communication across these lines has proven to be so difficult, that conceptual units and their definitional terminologies require such lengthy periods of time to share, or that generalizations and conclusions about events generated by one set of models and observational procedures can be viewed as nonpersuasive from an alternate perspective.

Separation exists in other respects as well. Persons working within one perspective tend to be concentrated in the world of practice, the other within the academic world. The writings of representatives of these two perspectives are found in different sources and in different professional journals. Professional conferences that attract the members of one perspective find few participants who reflect the other. Separate professional associations have become formed. Cross-fertilization of ideas between the two perspectives are difficult to discern; one can look in vain in the literature of one for references to the findings or discoveries of the other. Often, the two perspectives do not appear in juxtaposition to one another, except in comprehensive compendia such as the present volume. As a consequence, remaining bilingual has become difficult for contemporary psychologists and psychiatrists.

The suggestion that two cultures are operative

within the human sciences is made with considerable diffidence, for several reasons. Not only is it likely that the analogy, like that of C. P. Snow, is an overstated one, but there is also a question as to whether people and their points of view can be legitimately grouped in such a fashion. Writers within the humanistic, phenomenological, or existentialist traditions, for example, are numerous, and important differences are discernible between and among them. It is more proper to regard these as points of view rather than as systematic models around which consensus has developed. The citation of commonalities within each of these groupings, insofar as they are discernible, will invariably be found to have done an injustice to the writings of a particular theorist. Furthermore, the legitimacy of clustering the humanist, phenomenological, and existential perspectives within a common framework is open to challenge, since important differences exist between these perspectives as well.

At the same time, a number of commonalities can be identified. Writers within these theoretic streams have cited instances in which their position is comparable to that of others. Certain compatibilities have been noted as, for example, when Sartre (1947) argued forcefully that existentialism is a humanism, or when Perls (1973) asserted that the phenomenalism in his gestalt approach is existential in character. Finally, the view has become prevalent that a confluence among these approaches has taken place, and that with the passage of time they have become progressively more similar to one another in the manner in which they are represented (Pervin, 1960).

At the risk, therefore, of misrepresenting the points of view of individual theorists, and with the foreknowledge that the variability they collectively represent cannot be accommodated within a single overarching paradigmatic frame, an attempt will be made to fashion a broad outline of the characteristics of one of the cultures so as to explicate and expose the nature and extent to which it differs from the other. It is hoped that the deficiencies in the way each tends to characterize the other will become apparent, as will the recognition that critiques of one by the other can only occur from the vantage point of their own philosophical posture. In order to accomplish this task, it will be necessary first to treat the historical contexts from which the perspectives have emerged.

HISTORICAL ANTECEDENTS

The seminal origins of all three lines of thought with which we are concerned are older than the titles by which they have come to be known.

The Humanist Tradition

The ingredients that have come to form the humanist point of view can be traced as far back as the fifth century B.C. Protagoras is cited as having enunciated the fundamental principle underlying this perspective: "Man is the measure of all things; of those that are, that they are; of those that are not, that they are not." In classical literature, Socrates is also linked with this perspective, because he eschewed the study of physical nature as a means of dependable insight into the understanding of the human and the development of human knowledge, or of developing a satisfactory basis for intellectual and moral value. He looked instead to a study of people in search of a rational basis for human thought and action.

The preeminence of a theistic view tended to obscure this viewpoint throughout the Middle Ages. It underwent a revival, however, in Italy in the latter part of the 14th century, a revival that rapidly spread throughout the Western world, with Petrarch and Erasmus constituting the principal figures in this movement. It was at this time that the term *Humanism* was explicitly adopted as a way of asserting a clear break from the sterile, authoritarian intellectual traditions that had accumulated within scholastic philosophy and theology. It featured a return to, and renewed study of, the classical Greek and Roman writers as a source of inspiration and guidance. Classical Humanism is considered to have been the parent of all modern philosophical, scientific, or social developments.

The current view is that Humanism as a perspective contains three major divisions: (a) Classical Humanism, which is exemplified in some college and university circles that have retained a focus on the study of great literature; (b) Christian Humanism, which is a God-centered form of Humanism, of which the neo-Thomist Jacques Maritain is illustrative; and (c) Scientific Humanism, which seeks to wed the contributions of scientific inquiry to the protection and enrichment of humankind's circumstances on earth by liberating the latent potentialities within human nature. It has, in common with the other Humanist divisions, affirmed a positive attitude toward the development and preservation of human life, the dignity and value of each individual person, and the salience of humans' most distinctive characteristic— rationality. It also supports change and growth in order to enhance the quality of human living, asserts the priority of human needs and values over material things, espouses the necessity for freedom from want and constraint to enable people to maximize their personal aspirations and accomplishments within the course of their individual lives, and emphasizes the significance of each person's contribution to the lives and welfare of all those who follow (Frank, 1977).

The obvious counterpart to the Humanist position is Naturalism, which advocates the study of objects, people, and events through reliance on the combined use of empirical observation and rationality and which seeks to explain their origins and functions within the general context of the natural world. There are many varieties of the Naturalist position. Those who are persuaded that all energies, forces, and occurrences can be reduced to events comprising the subject matter of physics and chemistry hold a view referred to as Physicalism, or Materialism.

Humanists as a group take strong exception to most versions of the Naturalist position, which they regard as dehumanizing in both its manner of approach and its effects. They would emphasize instead the distinctiveness of humans from the remainder of the natural order. Although they acknowledge that there are continuities between humans and their capabilities and the biological and physical worlds, they also insist that there are large-scale differences, that these differences are the most significant aspects of humans on which attention needs to be focused, and that an explication of these characteristics and what they enable humans to do can only be discovered by a study of humans themselves. Explanatory extrapolations of human action derived from a study of other species would be regarded as biocentric and spuriously metaphorical in character.

Likewise associated with the Humanist position has been the assertion of the legitimacy of the concept of mind, a concept that is anathema to a thoroughgoing materialist. Attributes of mind judged particularly significant include the human capacity for conscious apprehension of the directly experienced world, for the imposition of order and coherence on the contents of experience, for transcending immediate experience, for intentionality and the pursuit of valued purposes and goals, and for exercising freedom and choice, leading to the necessity for democratic institutions for moral and social behavior.

In keeping with their long tradition, Humanists also maintain a broad-gauged appreciation of the multiplicity of actions in which humans are everywhere found to engage: art, music, poetry, dance, drama, history, philosophical thought, and religious practice. Significant insights and understandings are recognized to arise from the exercise of these pursuits, insights that augment and clarify the characteristics of human nature above and beyond what the more restricted scientific approach might be able to contribute. Reliance on scientific methods of inquiry alone is referred to as Scientism, which Humanists view as a narrow and potentially damaging approach to humans and their world. The discoveries achieved through the scientific method constitute only a small part of the overall knowledge base concerning humans and their capabilities. Appreciation of individuals as a whole must capitalize on knowledge and understandings drawn from the entire spectrum of human activity, not merely from the scientific investigations carried out by a small segment of humankind.

Finally, a hallmark of the Humanist tradition has been the consistent emphasis placed throughout the ages on the classic human virtues (attributes of excellence), the attainability of these attributes by each and every person, the importance of ensuring that the necessary conditions for their acquisition and development are available to all, and the benefits to humans—collectively as well as individually—that can thereby be expected to follow. This is the normative aspect of Humanism, where *norm* is used in the classical sense of constituting the idealized standard. In contrast to the cynic who supposes that most people are no more capable of grand passion than they are of grand opera, the Humanist remains optimistic, adhering to the notion of the perfectibility of humans through the collective exercise of their own resources. Illustrations of the form in which such normative statements tend to occur are found not only in the classical literature from earliest Greek and Roman times up to the present but also in contemporary humanist views, such as Maslow's (1950) characterization of self-actualizing people, Roger's definition of the fully functioning person (1961), and Jahoda's (1958) description of healthy functioning from a mental health point of view.

To attempt a listing of people who have made important contributions to American psychology within the Humanist tradition is a hazardous undertaking. There are the inherent risks in categorizing people and their ideas, the indistinct nature of the categorical boundaries, and the inevitable omissions that rankle and annoy. However, William James and John Dewey are typically cited as among the more important earlier theorists; Charlotte Buhler (1959, 1964; Buhler & Massarik, 1968) and Eric Erikson (1963, 1968, 1975) are ordinarily included as significant figures; Maddi (1963) has shown how both Gordon Allport and Henry Murray stand within this tradition; and of course Abraham Maslow (1954, 1968) has explicitly labeled his approach as Humanist in character. Many theorists who are typically grouped with the related traditions of phenomenology or existentialism, such as Adler (1924, 1927), Rogers (1951, 1961), Perls (1973), or Frankl (1962, 1967), can be identified with many of the elements of the Humanist view. It is to one of these related traditions that we turn next.

Phenomenological Tradition

The problem of the correspondence between objects and events in the world and our comprehension of them has been with philosophy and science since their beginnings. The ingredients of the phenomenological tradition are as old as that of the Humanist tradition.

In ordinary language, the term *phenomenon* refers to a thing, an event, or a process of occurrences that is noted and observed through the senses. From the outset of human thought it has been distinguished from the thing or the process itself.

A variety of postures have been adopted over the centuries in an effort to address the problem of the relationship between the phenomenal appearance of such objects and events and the objects and happenings themselves. One view has been characterized as the Realist position, sometimes referred to as Presentationism, which is exemplified in the writings of John Locke (Boring, 1929). In this view, objects are said to have the capabilities of directly affecting other objects (the senses), and hence the phenomenal experience of such objects serves as a faithful indication of the objects themselves. Realism asserts that the intellect conforms to and apprehends objects just as they exist. There is the attraction of simplicity to this theory of knowledge, and it is said that most people—lay and professional—behave in accordance with it on a day-to-day basis. Detractors call it Naive Realism.

An alternative view has followed the pattern established by Plato, who noted that if we simply accepted all that we see at face value, and if the comprehension we reached permitted all that we required, there would be no need to search for principles and understandings that lie behind or beyond the surface of things. But, from a phenomenal standpoint, what we encounter is a world of constant change; to rely on the changing objects of the senses is to notice the inevitable tendency of all things to come into being, to exist for a period of time, and subsequently to pass away. In addition, the senses often turn out to be "bad witnesses." With this second line of thought, it has been customary since Plato to conceive of at least two worlds—the world as we experience it, and the world and its objects as they exist independently of our mind's grasp and the structuring of them in our knowledge. From this perspective we are operating in relation to the objects and events in our world, but our intellect does not have direct and immediate contact with the events as they are, in and of themselves. We apprehend them as they are affected by our ways of perceiving and understanding them. We draw on our collective phenomenal experiences, and through the application of reason we proceed to develop increasingly closer approximations of things as we infer they must be. What we generate are representations, or constructions of our world, that have greater or lesser merit depending on what it is that they enable us to do. The position is sometimes called Representationism.

Still a third resolution of the problem has been to assert the reality and stability of the phenomena themselves; indeed, to assert that it is only such phenomena on which one can safely rely. An early spokesman of this point of view was Berkeley, an 18th-century English philosopher whose work was elaborated, developed, and refined by David Hume in the same period. The posture espoused by these writers is known as Phenomenalism, and asserts that what exists is only that which occurs when the senses experience it. Phenomenalists do not presume the existence of a reality independent of human observers to apprehend it. Rather, they affirm that what is known, perhaps directly, is sense experience itself. As a consequence, reality is whatever observers sense, or construe it to be. Reality, then, is constructed by persons out of the sense experiences of themselves and others. For Hume, objects external to the person viewing them have the appearance of substance, with qualities that appear to be inherent in them. However, these same appearances, which constitute the real world for the realist, and the real world to be approximated by the representationist, are fictions for Hume. What is real, or at least existent, are the sense impressions that occur, which in turn lead to the formation of ideas about them. Phenomenalists claim sensation, sense experience, or sense contents. They do not say what they are; they simply occur, and out of them one constructs one's view of physical reality (Eacker, 1972).

What came to be called phenomenology began as a philosophical movement devoted to the descriptive analysis and interpretation of existences as they show themselves in the pure form of conscious life. Edmund Husserl was the first to apply the label to an entire system of philosophy that was intended to develop into an exact, universal, and radical science, capable of serving as a matrix for all theoretical knowledge. The point of view became increasingly influential throughout Europe and the Latin American world, introduced for example to the Spanish-speaking countries by Ortega y Gasset. It sought to give all categories of experience independent and adequate description. Its rather obscure and esoteric method was one of intuitive abstraction, which sought to identify the essential elements of conscious experience so as to discover the manner in which relations, developed between external events, and subjective awareness became generative of meaning.

The translation of this point of view into a study of individual people occurred early in this century, taking place initially at the hands of figures such as Adler (1924) and Rank (1945), and later undergoing explicit development with the work of Snygg and Combs (1949) and Rogers (1951, 1961). The Ansbachers' (1956) representation of Adler's essentially phenomenological position, and the significance it played in his break from his mentor, Freud, is a penetrating and important analysis. Most of the emphases that have come to characterize the phenomenological posture in the study of personality (the state of quality of being a person) were reflected in Adler's approach and were subsequently echoed in the work of those who followed. Several of the more important emphases can be cited.

The search for explanations of human behavior must be centered on individual people rather than on collectivities of people grouped according to some arbitrary set of categorical arrangements. Information must be sought by means of a detailed analysis of the person's inner nature, since the principal determinants of what a person comes to do are events that take place within the mind rather than events that occur externally. The primary events of concern are those with which people perceive, interpret, and thereby construe their world and themselves; what people elect to do is guided by the particular constructions concerning themselves and their surroundings. Thus, the behavior of the person, and of people in general, is guided and directed by perceptions, images, and thoughts, which are interpretations of actual events but are not isomorphic with them. Consequently, they are fictional rather than real. Important among these fictions are the person's constructions about future events or consequences, which the person judges to be attainable. From among a wide variety of such futures deemed possible of occurrence, those the person chooses as desirable and worthy of pursuit take on the character of objectives or goals. It is an inherent characteristic of people to order their actions not only in terms of the way in which they construe the present, but also in terms of their current constructions as to the future conditions they seek to bring about. It is toward the latter that a large proportion of human energy becomes directed.

The person in whom these events occur has direct and immediate access to them. Access to these inner events by others external to the person can only be accomplished by indirection, primarily by means of the verbal report about them made by the person in whom they occur. Accordingly, the primary method for studying individual people (and thus, human behavior) is to view it from the vantage point of the behaving individual, the subject, in whom they occur. Reliance is necessarily placed on the observations of the subject by the subject and the sharing of these observations by means of verbal report. Attempts to formulate a framework of understanding from the vantage point of an outside observer (e.g., the behavior analyst) will generate spurious accounts. Through the use of a posture of empathic understanding, however, the analyst of behavior can approximate the position of the person to be understood, thereby coming to at least a partial comprehension of the bases for the person's behavior and some indication of what it is that the person may or may not be likely to do. Initial understandings of the operation of human thought and action must be built on such intensive studies of the individual case (idiographic analysis). Only after an acceptable number of such studies will it be possible to identify when commonalities appear, thereby permitting one to formulate a limited number of statements that are descriptive of people in general (nomothetic analysis). However, although such generalizations can be informative and useful, they remain limited since they cannot sufficiently account for the behavior of any individual person. Each person in the last analysis constitutes a unique constellation and organization (Ford & Urban, 1963).

It is the phenomenological concern with the analysis of consciousness and the role of conscious events in the regulation and control of human action that has become a hallmark of 20th-century existentialism. Indeed, to many observers, the phenomenological posture has been the intellectual forebear of this tradition.

The Existential Tradition

Despite its frequent depiction as a philosophy, a theory, or a system of thought, existentialism is more correctly seen to be an attitude or a way of construing human beings and their world. As such, it has existed since humans confronted their frailty and sought to formulate some meaning for their existence (Commerchero, 1970). Job, bemoaning his fate amidst the ashes but nonetheless asserting the reality of his existence to his rationalizing would-be comforters, was being existential. The writer of Ecclesiastes, sorrowing over the futilities of the everyday world, yet seeking meaning in life, was speaking from an existential view. Dostoyevsky has shown the confrontation between the existential Christ and the institutions of his day and all subsequent institutionalized forms of religion. Hamlet's soliloquies bespeak a tormented struggle to discover value and purpose for living. To be consciously aware of happenings, to be anguished by perplexities, to glory in possibilities, to savor sensations and prize experiences, is to operate within an existential mode. More importantly, however, to recognize that no one can borrow value, truth, or meaning from without but must create them from within, and that they must be a product of one's ongoing experiential existing and being, is to be truly existential. Naive, uncritical acceptance of the frameworks of others—no matter how elegantly or persuasively they may be presented—is to depart from the necessarily honest and authentic position in which all humans are inevitably placed. Life is an unclear gift; there are no useful truths that can serve as unerring guidelines for living; systems of thinking (Christian, Marxist, Psychoanalytic, or Behaviorist) advocated by others are from the standpoint of the individual person a fraud. Life is a burden pressed on each as a result of one's inevitable confrontation with the ultimate concerns of individual existence: isolation, meaninglessness, responsibility, death. Freedom to experience, freedom to choose, indeed, freedom to exist is the truth with which each person must come to terms, and along with it must come an acceptance of responsibility for the form that one's existence comes to assume. Not "The Truth shall set you free," but "You are free" is the truth. From an existentialist point of view, when one has said that humans exist, and that in their existence they are free—compelled to freedom, ceaselessly free—one has exhausted all useful generalizations about humans (Comerchero, 1970; Finkelstein, Wenegrat, & Yalom, 1982; Stevenson, 1974).

To say, therefore, that one is an existentialist can be seen to be a contradiction in terms. To do so is to order and abrogate, to fix experience into categories, whereas experience by its very nature is ongoing, fluid, not a thing but a process. A biography is not to be confused with the person it purports to represent; to formulate generalizations about people is to seek smothering simplicities, tidy proprieties, and packaged answers, which one can only formulate by pruning away all that is irregular and inconvenient to the illusion of regularity. Pressed to its limits, existentialism is thus a radical perspective—radical in the sense of getting to the root of something, or focusing

on something that is thought to be fundamental. The fundamental questions for each and every individual person are: Who am I? What can my existence represent? What should my existence represent? What shall I do with my freedom?

A large number of writers have come to be called, or call themselves, existentialists. Given the foregoing discussion, however, one would not expect them to constitute a coherent group, nor to evidence a great deal of commonality. The contemporaries, Nietzsche and Kierkegaard, were perhaps most influential in articulating the characteristics of this posture toward oneself, one's life, and one's world and prompted a wealth a subsequent writers to explore its multiple ramifications. But there were significant differences between them: Nietzsche's Zarathustra declared that "God is dead," thereby emphasizing that humans are ultimately alone; whereas Kierkegaard insisted that all sense and meaning must begin with an initial "leap of faith," emerging with an opposite conclusion. Likewise, one encounters the contrast between Jean-Paul Sartre, who sought to reconcile his existentialist views with Marxism, and Albert Camus, who scathingly denounced Marxist efforts to represent human behavior as determined in character.

It should be clear, however, that the existentialist perspective shares with humanist and phenomenological traditions an intense antipathy to an ontological naturalism or an epistemological realism. The naturalist view of humans, with its attempts to use the procedures of empirical science to analyze and explain human beings as natural objects like any other, eliminates from consideration the very characteristics that render humans distinctive—namely, their awareness of their own existence and their freedom to choose what they will become. Moreover, explanatory generalizations developed by science about human action are inappropriate; they are only possible for objects and events that are determined, not for those that are free. Attempts to use statistical analyses of human behavior cannot unravel causal effects; they can only make things appear to be determined, after the fact. To the thoroughgoing existentialist, such exercises are not scientific; they are merely scholastic. The radical existentialist can also be antiintellectual, since systems of thought developed by others victimize people with spurious truth, whenever they are imposed on, or adopted by, people who have abdicated their freedom and responsibility for architecting their own development. When this happens, the person is no longer the measure of all things, and meaning is no longer something with which they invest things and experience. People are thus emptied of their own experiential content and become a passive receptacle for the ideas of others, and both they and the world become something that is interpreted for them. Such a process, for the existentialist, destroys human responsibility, which in turn destroys human potentiality, and in so doing destroys humans themselves.

One would not have expected the existentialist viewpoint to enter into the realm of psychology in its most radical form. It appears to have become introduced through a development in European psychiatry, which sought to combine the assumptions of the existential view about the nature and circumstance of human beings with the phenomenological viewpoint and its associated methodology. The historical factors leading up to this development are briefly reviewed in Ford and Urban (1963). Its impetus was a desire to be of greater assistance to troubled people. It sought to develop a more satisfactory understanding of humans, particularly their problems and dilemmas, than was thought to be provided by the standard psychoanalytic, behaviorist, and scientific viewpoints available within Western thought. Influential in this movement have been writers such as Heidegger (1962), Binswanger (1956), and Boss (1958, 1963) writing from a continental vantage, with May (1961, 1969) representing the foremost American contributor. The movement came to be called Existential Analysis. Subsequent influential contributors to this general movement have been Berne (1972), Frankl (1962, 1967, 1969, 1975), Lowen (1970), and Perls (1973), and the more recent writings of Carl Rogers have become more explicitly influenced by the viewpoint as time has gone on.

Although remarkably different in many ways, these writers appear to share a set of principles concerning the nature of humans and the appropriate means for comprehending what they are like and what they can and will do. Humans are distinct from other entities within the natural world. One does not simply exist in some state of being; rather, one is in a constant state of becoming something other than what one presently is. The human is an instance of constant activity and change. Moreover, people have the capability for conscious awareness, comprised not only of direct, personal experiences that enable one to be aware of one's immediate surroundings, but also of oneself, and of what one is doing. Thus, people are capable of being self-conscious and of developing a sense of personal identity. The process is burdensome; it entails a constant struggle to come to terms with one's own experience and to render it intelligible. However, the awareness also enables one to be selective to what one elects to respond and how one chooses to act. As a consequence, one is able to make decisions about these things and to take responsibility for oneself. In doing so, one creates oneself with one's worlds. What one proceeds to become will be the result of one's inborn potentialities, the opportunities that present themselves, and the choices one makes in the succession of situations that are continuously presented. By the actions chosen, one continually expresses one's innate behavioral possibilities, molding one's environment to oneself and oneself to one's environment, thereby actualizing what had earlier been potential. Finally, humans have the capacity to transcend the immediacy of the present and to envision alternate future states and possibilities. This presents one with the opportunity to invest meaning into one's existence, and specifically to formulate intention, purpose, sense, and significance into the pursuit of one's life. To be authentically human is to become increasingly open to experience, to accept the inherent freedom associated with one's fate, to assume fully the responsibility for constantly developing and refashioning one's identity, one's personal commitments, and one's life. To attribute responsibility to factors outside oneself is to deny and distort the essential quality of human existence. Everything of significance with regard to this entire process occurs within the inner or subjective experience of the individual. Comprehension by others of what and where each individual may be operating with respect to the life task can only be approximate. The method by which it becomes approximated is necessarily phenomenological in character.

SOME COMMON FRAMEWORKS AND THEMES

If it is hazardous to try to identify commonalities among writers within these several long-standing traditions of thought; to attribute commonalities across those traditions is even more problematic. Affinities between them are noticeable; in particular instances, similarities are detectable. However, a combination of the multiplicity of viewpoints contributed by the many people working within these several traditions is something that can only be effected by eliding their numerous differences and choosing to emphasize the commonalities instead. To emphasize the similarities as opposed to the differences is akin to choosing to look through one end of a telescope as opposed to the other. The use of the metaphor of culture is thought to be helpful in this regard, since the concept of culture allows for widespread heterogeneity among the ideas and attitudes of its many members. Few cultures can boast of singular, mono-lithic systems of thought and action to which even a majority of its members subscribe. A pluralism of ideas is the norm. It has been in keeping with the concept of culture that terms such as system, theory, or model have been deliberately avoided in the depic-tion of these several traditions; it is preferable to speak of perspectives or points of view. Without intending, therefore, to suggest that there is anything like an ethnic character to a humanist-phenomenological-existential type of culture, pursuit of the metaphor of two cultures leads to the attempt to identify at least some of the common stock of ideas within the frame-work of which the study of human nature and behavior takes place. Accordingly, it is proposed that across these several traditions of thought a common set of emphases has tended to develop, some of which can be more readily discerned than others. It is understood that the complexities involved will not permit such a list to be exhaustive.

Distinctive Character of Humans and Their Behavior

One can discern, first of all, the prevailing assertion that the human person, human attributes, and human actions need to be viewed as distinct from all other entities in nature and all other forms of life. As Frankl (1962) expressed it, the human is not seen to be one thing among others, not merely a mechanism or a biological organism, nor a member of a herd; rather, the human retains properties and capabilities that are distinctive to the human and to no other creature. To Allport (1955), the human is so unique that attempts to understand human functioning by relying on informa-tion gained from a study of lower species of animals are virtually useless. Similarly, Murray (1954) chal-lenged the "audacious assumption of species equiva-lence" (p. 11). Ideas about humans drawn from a study of other objects and things are suggestive at best, misleading and damaging at their worst. It follows that any attempt to comprehend the nature of humans and their behavior must derive from an anal-ysis of humans themselves, with particular emphasis placed on those characteristics that render humans distinctive.

Significance of the Individual

A second major emphasis has been placed on the value and the significance of each and every individ-ual person. All are viewed as equally important, no one showing any inherent merit over any other, all with a legitimate posture and perspective with respect to themselves, their life, and the world of others. Each person is singular, unique, and therefore unrepeatable and irreplaceable. This has led to the methodological tendency to generate knowledge about humans and their behavior from a detailed analysis of individual people, taken singly and one at a time. Useful conclu-sions about people cannot be gained by looking at that person as a representative of a species, as a particular kind of machine, or as an element in a social or cultural organization. Rather, one must approach that person as an autonomous entity, operating in and through the particular arrangements afforded by that person's peculiar characteristics and environmental opportunities.

It has been the existentialists who have argued most forcefully for this view; it is conceived by Tillich (1952) to be the essence of the existentialist ap-proach—understanding the human situation from the standpoint of, and as experienced by, the individual. Existentialists are concerned with the person under scrutiny rather than with developing generalized the-ories about that person. Generalizations about humans are said to leave out what is the single most important feature of each—namely, one's uniqueness. Others, such as Allport (1955), have taken a similar position, to the effect that each person is an idiom. Allport argued for the development of idiographic methods capable of providing a personal representation of the individual so as to permit the understanding and development of predictions in regard to the individual case. He characterized general principles in regard to people at large to be merely convenient fictions of only occasional utility when they turn out to resemble the characteristics and attributes of some people. Still others, such as Murray (1954) or Maslow (1968), took a broader view, construing humans as comprised of characteristics, aspects of which are species-constant, but others of which are specific and unique to each individual.

Characterizations of persons can be effected in terms of both, as long as the uniqueness of the individual does not become lost in the process. The emphasis on the individuality and uniqueness of peo-ple is also reflected in the extent to which variability between and within individuals becomes stressed by this group of writers. To many, humans are so exceed-ingly variable in their modes of thought and action that most any sort of generalization one might seek to formulate concerning them will have the ring of plausibility, despite the dubious validity associated with them.

Organizational Complexity of the Individual

There would also appear to be a common disposition across these traditions to find ways to account for the enormous complexity that any given person seems to represent. The observation is repeatedly made that individuals retain a large number of different and changing intentions, values, patterns, and styles of behaving, and that these can be manifested in a great variety of ways, depending on the person's circumstance and the nature of the environmental context within which he or she is functioning. There is a recurrent inclination to be critical of efforts to minimize this complexity or to reduce matters to simpler structure. Such attempts are judged to follow from the fallacy of reductionism and result in spurious oversimplification.

However, despite this enormous complexity, each person is simultaneously judged to be functioning in a unified and organized fashion. To Allport (1961), the person's behavior routinely displays integration, complex and intricate though it may be. Allport suggested an inherent "pressing" for unification of one's self and one's life to be operative within each. The proposal echoes Rogers's notion of an organizing principle underlying human functioning, or Adler's notion of an innate movement toward self-consistency within each person, leading to the formation of the individual's unique lifestyle. Likewise, Murray (1959) chose to argue that each person operates as a temporal whole; one is capable of unified and concerted action at a given point in time but also capable of long-range enterprises that can take weeks, months, or even years of sustained effort to complete (Murray, 1951). Thus, despite the huge number of subsidiary elements that may comprise humans and their actions, it is necessary to recognize that the person always functions as a unit and operates as an integrated whole. Our knowledge concerning persons at any one time may be incomplete and fragmentary, but the person cannot be understood in terms of such fragments. Ways must be found to encompass the complex whole, even if conceptions of a high order of abstraction must be used.

Plasticity of the Individual Person

It has been remarked that two basic postures with respect to the notion of change have been operative throughout the history of Western thought. One of these sees stability as the norm, and change is seen as a perturbation of some kind that serves to deflect things away from a condition of stasis, requiring the exercise of corrective action in order to reinstate the norm. From this standpoint, the world (and people) is geared toward equilibrium and the maintenance of similar states (homeostasis). The alternative view regards activity and change as the norm (heterostasis); conditions of only relative stability are possible and occur only as a consequence of some artificial (and often undesirable) interference with an otherwise ongoing and active process.

If such is the case, the viewpoints we have been considering could be said to favor heterostasis. Once again, using the existentialists as the more convenient group with which to emphasize this point, the individual person and everything that he or she represents is an existence, and therefore a continuing process, rather than something fixed and static. This helps to account for the proclivity for using a particular set of terms. *Being* has traditionally been used to refer to what is actual, or already existent. However, since not existents are present and available at any one time, the concept is accompanied by a second, *becoming*, to reflect the process of things constantly coming into being that were not available earlier. Moreover, we have had to find a way to represent not only what does, but also what will or can exist. This has led traditionally to the concept of potential. Those entities or states that are not now actual, but will or might become so, are postulated to exist now, but only in a state of potentiality. The processes by which what exists as potential becomes existent (actual) is called actualization.

The Western world is indebted to Aristotle for this basic framework, one that has been an important ingredient in the thinking of the writers we are currently considering. Rogers (1959) followed the lead of a number of others in placing heavy reliance on the process of conversion of the potential into the actual. He postulated an actualizing tendency to be an inherent characteristic of the individual, constituting a kind of master motive around which all activity of the person becomes organized; this actualizing tendency is a particularized form of the more general processes whereby the potentialities of the person undergo progressive development and behavioral expression. Use of the concept of self-actualization has been equally important to others. Maslow (1954) proposed that each person proceeds in relation to an inner nature: intrinsic, given, to some extent unique, constituting an essential core of that person, susceptible to being overpowered or suppressed, but never disappearing entirely and persisting underground, forever pressing for actualization.

If one construes the person as standing in the midst of constant change, where one aspect becomes another, one state changes into another, and the form of the person's being (existence) is an unfolding succession of potentialities that become transformed into actualities, one construes the person as an instance of Becoming, as both Allport (1955) and Rogers (1959) did in the titles of their writings. Moreover, one stands in expectation of the essential unpredictability of the person over any extended period of time. Only proximal predictions could be expected, based on a thorough knowledge of where the person was at a given instant in anticipation of an immediate instant to follow, or where artificial constraints have been imposed on, or adopted by, the person as a way of forestalling the unfolding process. Cyclical regularities may describe the operation of the planets and the seasons; reversion to steady states may characterize the physical and biological worlds. Not so with the process of human living, it is said, unless that process becomes stifled by human action. Imposition of blind consistency and regulation on the process is seen to be the road to ill health.

If one adds to the foregoing the notion that the human is equipped with volition and choice as well, and that each has the freedom to change at any instant, then the states of the person will be seen to differ from one to another, from day to day, and from hour to hour, and the individual personality remains essentially unpredictable (Frankl, 1962).

Significance of Conscious Experience

In the opinions of this group of writers we have been considering, there are a variety of characteristics that are peculiar to the human person, whose operation and functioning must be recognized and understood if an intelligible view of people is to be formed. However, among the more important would appear to be the emphasis on conscious experience.

With this phrase, reference is ordinarily made to the capabilities of humans to be awake and aware for extended periods of time and inwardly sensible of things and happenings. The condition and capability for consciousness was introduced early in American psychology by William James but has undergone a period of benign neglect by academic and experimental psychology for much of the past century. To James, consciousness constituted an inherent capability with certain important characteristics. He considered it to be invariably personal (individual in character); forever changing such that no conscious state that had once occurred could ever recur as the exact same state; sensibly continuous and thereby producing the impression of continuity of experience despite time gaps as in sleep; and inherently selective in that it provided a vehicle for the exercise of choice—the contents of consciousness being governed by the judged relevance of incoming and potential experience to the accomplishment of personal ends (Boring, 1929).

The centrality of consciousness for understanding human behavior was echoed by the Functionalists, of whom John Dewey and J. R. Angell were the foremost spokesmen, and the theme was maintained by writers in the humanist tradition, such as Allport and Murray, who provided in their theories for an active and influential consciousness (Maddi, 1963).

The concept of experience has been one for which a variety of other writers have shown a preference. This has been particularly true for those writing within the phenomenological (e.g., Rogers, 1951; Sullivan, 1953) and also the existential traditions (e.g., Binswanger, 1956; May, 1961). The term *awareness* has been preferred by others (Perls, 1973). *Experience* as a term is ordinarily used to refer to the collectivity of the person's impressions or apprehensions (usually conscious) of the world of occurrences, whether these be of an external, bodily, or psychic sort. Experiences are said to accumulate with the passage of time, and an individual's experience at any given time is thought to be the product of happenings personally encountered, undergone, or lived through.

It is difficult to overemphasize the significance these writers have attached to the role of conscious experience for humans and their behavior. It has been customary to start with the observation that the contents of experience are multiple, varied, and rapidly changing. In particular, the infant is pictured as entering a world that has the phenomenal appearance of being one big booming confusion. The inherent instability and uncertainty that the phenomenal world represents is in principle intolerable, but it is confronted by the inherent hunger within each person for constancy and certitude, and the confluence of these two tendencies initiates a search within the person for some form of order and stability in the midst of change. A process directed toward the institution of order and organization within the person continues in association with the person's development and persists throughout the course of the person's life. In the process, however, each person operates in isolation. Each will form some manner of organization that will prove to be more or less serviceable. However, since no two people are precisely identical, since the extent of experiences undergone will vary from one person to the next, and since the manner in which the experiences are ordered in relationship to one another will necessarily be different, the experiential organization with which each person proceeds becomes personal and individual and in principle unique. It is this inner organization of subjective experiences that is said to constitute reality from the vantage point of the individual and is thought to exert the principal influence on the manner in which people construe themselves and their surroundings, and therefore what they subsequently come to be and to do.

Among several writers there has been considerable interest in trying to identify the elements of conscious experience—for example, the capabilities for attention and awareness (selective in their functioning), perception and the categorization of experience, imagery, affect (as distinct from emotion), conception and thought, recollection, anticipation and foresight, symbolization and language, and a set of capabilities thought to permit interpersonal cohesion, variously referred to as projection, empathy, altruism, or social interest (Adler, 1927; Rogers, 1959; Sullivan, 1953; and others). There has also been interest in characterizing what are referred to as modes of experience. This is an approach that seeks to define larger and more inclusive patterns of interaction developed by people to order the complexities of their experiences. Illustrations of such proposals would be the prototaxic, parataxic, and syntaxic modes of experiencing by Sullivan (1953), or the modes-of-being-in-the-world suggested by existential writers to constitute different patterns of organization evolved by different persons, including the singular, dual, or plural existential modes, or the modes of *umwelt*, *mitwelt*, and *eigenwelt* (May, Angel, & Ellenberger, 1958). Understanding people in terms of such larger experimental organizations has been thought to be particularly helpful.

The centrality of conscious experience is recognizable in several additional ways. The proposition is typically advanced that consciousness necessarily has an object; it is always consciousness of something other than itself. This gives rise to another peculiarly human capability: of being aware of the phenomenon of awareness within experience, and in a sense to "see" that one can see. The ability to sense oneself as a self is asserted to be a power and a possibility exclusive to humans (Pervin, 1960). It is this capability that permits people to behave as observers and, when appropriate, as reporters about themselves to others concerning the myriad thoughts, wishes, beliefs, attitudes, memories, sensations, and aspirations that apparently occur continuously during waking experience. It is also suggested that the capability for self-awareness is responsible for the distinctly human process that leads to the idea of a self. It led William James, for example, to propose the concept of self as a stream of thought derived from conscious experience, comprised of all those experiences related to oneself as perceptually differentiated from externals (the me versus the not-me), and out of this was fashioned one's personal identity. Rogers opted for the term *self-concept*, thought to be an organized configuration of perceptions (experiences) of one's being and functioning that are admissible to the person's awareness (1951, 1959). One's self-concept is who one construes oneself to be, and it constitutes the frame of reference from which all else is observed, interpreted, and comprehended by the person. The process leads to an awareness of oneself as a unique person of many qualities and values, with an associated feeling of personness. Existentialists have argued that as a consequence of the selectivity of experience, each person continually reformulates and thereby recreates what one is and what one comes to be. In this way, the self is not only a product but is also a producer of experience, serving as the framework within which opportunities are chosen and future experiences are selectively undergone (Combs, Avila, & Purkey, 1971). There has developed an immense literature on the notion of the self, as well as various subsidiary selves that observers have suggested are useful: the perceived as opposed to the idealized self (Rogers, 1951); the stable self (Snygg & Combs, 1949); the mutable self (Zurcher, 1972); the acceptable self (Berne, 1972); the subjective, objective, and social self (Arkoff, 1968). These do not exhaust the alternatives.

Finally, the centrality of experience is reflected in related proposals concerning health and wholeness. A common theme continually recurs. Problems in human behavior are said to arise when incongruities between self and experience are allowed to develop. Jung (1964) observed that modern humans' troubles stem from an excessive and debilitating overemphasis on rationality, with the simultaneous denial of the intuitive, expressive, and esthetic aspects of their nature. Fromm (1955, 1956) characterized modern humans as alienated from themselves, as well as from their fellow humans and from nature. To Maslow (1962), the denial or suppression of one's inner nature constitutes a crime against one's self—it makes people despise themselves, feel worthless and unlovable because they know that they are guilty of failing to do with their lives all that they know to be possible. *Authenticity* is an important term for existential writers, for to remain authentic is to function in accordance with the actuality of one's experience; to be nonauthentic is to practice self-deception. To attempt to escape anguish by pretending one is not free, by trying to convince oneself that one's attitudes and actions are determined by what has been done by others, by situations outside oneself, by the roles to which one has been consigned in life, or anything other than oneself and the choices and decisions one has made, is the epitome of self-deception (Sartre, 1947). Denial of experience to awareness, or distortion of the characteristics of experience by means of faulty symbolization, is the avenue to human misery (Rogers, 1951, 1959).

Correspondingly, by being aware of the myriad transactions between oneself and one's environment on a moment-to-moment basis, one can make the discovery that one is actually making multiple decisions that govern the course of one's life (Perls, 1973). The more people are conscious (aware) of what it is that they are (angry or proud), the more they are not just angry or proud but also more capable of becoming something else by effecting a change or transformation of themselves. Reclamation from misery can occur when people are led to widen and broaden their fields of awareness so that the entire spectrum of meaning and value becomes accessible to the person's conscious experience. People can be led to become aware of the multiplicity of forces acting on them, to realize their competencies and capabilities, to comprehend the range of available possibilities and opportunities, and to accept the responsibility associated with the process of living (Frankl, 1962, 1969).

Self-Regulatory Properties of Human Activity

The review of cross-cultural differences we have been pursuing could be continued at considerable length. We must content ourselves with a focus on a final characteristic that should not be overlooked because of the critical role it tends to play in the overall view of the culture we have been describing.

The importance of the several ingredients of conscious experience, or "internal proceedings" as Murray (1951) described them, has been emphasized in the foregoing section. It is these "inner characteristics" that are seen to be the most important aspects of the person and, in turn, lead to one's characteristic patterns of thought and action (Allport, 1961). Among these "internal proceedings" are the human capabilities for directing the course that action will follow, for maintaining direction and sustained activity in the face of barriers and obstacles that inevitably arise, and for

exercising overall supervisory control over the behavior in which the person elects to engage. Each person is construed to be an ongoing, self-regulatory entity.

This is an additional feature, therefore, seen to distinguish the human from all other objects or species in the natural world (i.e., the capability for instigating transactions with the environment in relation to one's thoughts, values, interests, wants, and anticipations of outcomes deemed to be desirable). The depiction of the person as proactive, rather than reactive, was made by Murray (1959) in an effort to designate the manner in which human activity is initiated spontaneously from within, rather than by a confronting external situation. It was Murray's (1959) view that people's activity cannot adequately be explained with reference to factors outside the person. He strongly objected to the Freudian view that tends to make the person almost wholly a reactive product of contending forces. His objection to a behaviorist view was equally strong. Murray was impressed with the manner in which humans can organize themselves so as to identify goals and objectives judged worthy of pursuit, to initiate and sustain action intended to lead to the attainment of those goals, and to pursue their interests and purposes so as to enhance themselves and their development in ways that they judge to be useful. To Allport (1961), the self-initiating characteristics of humans were equally impressive. He postulated the operation of inner dispositions that have the capability for initiating and guiding consistent forms of adaptive and stylistic behavior.

We have here an emphasis on the overwhelming importance of the human's orientation toward future states of being. The outlook of the person is seen to be essentially prospective in nature. Attempts to account for humans' efforts and actions by focusing on early fixations, habits, or instincts all seek to trace the behavior of the person in reference to the past; all are misdirected, because the person is continuously straining toward the future instead (Allport, 1955).

The directiveness associated with human behavior arises from the capability of humans not only to be future oriented, but also to be purposive and intentional in operation (Allport, 1961). Each person, it is said, initiates behavioral action for reasons other than simply to achieve and maintain a homeostatic balance, or simply to survive. Rather, people pursue dispositions to construct and create new and useful thoughts, objects, and procedures (Murray, 1959), to acquire greater competence and capability (White, 1952), or to implement a philosophy of living (Allport, 1961). These purposes and goals will vary greatly from one person to the next; they may be proximal or remote, they may be few or many, and they may be segmented or ordered into a sequence of subsidiary goals (Murray, 1959). For most the variety of goals becomes integrated into a coherent cluster of life goals, reflecting the inherent tendency within the person toward an organized integration of the various elements of which he or she is composed (Allport, 1955). This emphasis on the teleonomic or purposive nature of the human, and its importance in rendering human behavior intelligible, is echoed in Adler's depiction of the goal directedness of human action (1927) and Buhler's emphasis on the study of life goals (1964). The functioning of people is seen as governed by such conscious characteristics of personality as plans of action, long-range goals, and philosophies of life.

To the existentialist writers, the development of purpose that can provide value and significance to one's existence constitutes the critical task for each person to accomplish. To Sartre (1957), there is no ultimate meaning or purpose inherent in human life; in this sense, life is absurd; we are forlorn, abandoned in the world, and must look after ourselves completely. We have not come into being for any purpose, neither created by God, nor predisposed by our biological ancestry, nor by anything else. We simply find ourselves existing, and each must decide what to make of himself or herself. It is through the exercise of free choice that we decide what will be the purposes and conditions under which we shall live. Frankl (1969), on the other hand, perceived a purpose or meaning to be inherent in each person's life. Human life is basically purposive, but the meaning or purpose of each individual is unique and specific and can be discovered and fulfilled by that one person and by none other. Everyone has his or her specific vocation (calling) or mission in life; each must carry out a concrete assignment that demands fulfillment. In this respect, no person can be replaced; nor can another's life be repeated. Each individual's task is as unique as the specific opportunities one has to implement it. The specific purpose or meaning for a person's life cannot be invented or contrived; it can only be encountered and discovered through the process of living. Frankl's position shows a number of similarities with those of others, such as Maslow (1950, 1968) and Rogers (1951), who asserted that tendencies toward actualization of personal potentialities are inherent, basic, and primitive and impel the person forward in a search for accomplishment, growth, and human fulfillment (Butler & Rice, 1963).

Critical to the exercise of direction and control is the notion of volition and decisional choice. It is the existential writers who have emphasized the significance of choice to the greatest degree. The term *freedom* is one they have elected to use in dealing with the decisional capabilities they consider to be the premier human feature. Freedom has traditionally meant the absence of outside influence in the action of a thing, such that in the development of its capabilities no block, barrier, or impediment becomes imposed on the exercise of those capabilities. More specifically, freedom is the power to exercise regulatory control without outside interference, to be or act so that things may be other than they presently are. In this sense, only a god can be fully free. With humans it has been customary to speak in relative terms; one is more or less free in regard to one or more conditions, since one's knowledge and existence are finite, and one is always subject to, and to some extent governed by, forces, actions, and situations surrounding oneself. To the extentialist, the human is free; it is a freedom not in the sense of indeterminacy, but in the sense of being able to govern the course of one's development and destiny by means of the decisions (choices) made in the "center of one's Being" (Tillich, 1952). To the freedom to envision alternate future possibilities within the contents of consciousness is added the freedom to initiate action to try to actualize them. To be conscious is to be free, although one is not free to cease being free. Humans may not be able to free themselves from any or all conditions; by the same token, however, they are not unwitting victims of such conditions, since it is always possible to take a stand toward them and thereby choose what one's existence will be and what it will become in the next moment. Every moment requires new or renewed choice; no motive or past resolution entirely determines what one does in the now. There is the inevitable responsibility for one's fate and the inherent unpredictability of the consequences of one's choices that is the source of so much subjective anguish—the painful awareness of our freedom and the frequent wish to avoid it.

The setting of objectives and goals, selecting a pattern of effort to attain those objectives from among alternate courses of action, the initiation and maintenance of that activity until such time as the objectives have been achieved, the decision as to whether achievement is sufficient to warrant a shift in direction toward additional goals and objectives—all imply the operation of some kind of command post, or central executive unit within the person whereby such activities can be sensibly coordinated. For this purpose, a variety of suggestions have been made. Murray (1959) found the concept of ego useful, characterizing it as the rational, differentiated, and governing establishment of the person, with multiple capacities and functions, including the organization of perceptions into an apperceptive complex, the exercise of intellective operations, the development of serial programs and schedules, the coordination of action, and the exercise of decision. Allport (1955) suggested the concept of the proprium, a component thought to serve an organizing and integrating role and responsible for producing a sense of body, self-identity, self-image, self-esteem, self-extension, rational coping, and propriate striving. The concept of self has enjoyed a long history in this regard; William James used it to refer to an instrumental process of functional utility in regulating and governing the person's entire psychobiophysical functioning. The concept has been a popular vehicle for writers of both phenomenological and existential persuasions. Whether construed as ego, self, or as some other type of component, there would appear to be no alternative to some such conceptualization, if indeed the person is to be seen as the self-initiating, self-guiding, self-directing, self-maintaining, self-regulating, and self-organizing entity that our group of writers construe each individual to be.

TWO-CULTURES DIALOGUE

One of the defining characteristics of a culture is the existence and operation of a common ideology, or network of belief, around which its members tend to coalesce, the main outlines of which attract their allegiance. Ideologies serve as guidelines for thought and action, providing a common set of conceptions as to the preferred way to look at things and a set of customary practices that enable the participant members to function in collective fashion.

The foregoing materials suggest such a development, with the implication that it is around such an ideology that a large number of people dealing with humans and their behavior have tended to congregate. It must be left to the reader to decide whether a sufficient number of commonalities have been identified to warrant the attribution of an ideology common to the humanist, phenomenological, and existential writers, and whether at least these ingredients of a culture can be legitimately said to exist. A preoccupation with the task of describing the ideological elements of one culture precluded a comparable itemization of a suggested cultural counterpart (loosely referred to as scientific psychology), although some of the latter's characteristics are implied in the description of the views of the first.

Critical exchanges between representatives of these two cultures have, of course, been taking place since earliest times, and these have continued up to present. Since the philosophical positions from which they are derived are at such variance, each has found much to criticize in the other's position. The differences are basically philosophical in nature for essentially two reasons: (a) They stem from different answers to the most fundamental questions that can be asked, since they speak to one's conceptions of reality (metaphysics) and humans' capabilities for apprehending it (epistemology); and (b) the questions are unlikely to be resolved through the exercise of reason alone.

The number of derivatives that follow from the basic positions adopted on these issues are, as one might expect, large in number; consequently, their specific criticisms of one another are too numerous to catalog. The essential character of the criticisms has not changed over the decades. Moreover, the main outlines of the respective critiques have by now become well known. Thus, a point-by-point account of the critical exchange will not be attempted. However, since indications of the many critical views maintained by the humanist-phenomenological-existential group toward the other culture have been cited in earlier pages, some of the elements of the counter-critique deserve mention. A number of telling points are frequently made.

While the intent, and conceivably the effect of, the humanist-phenomenological-existential approach to the person may be positive and optimistic, its effect on scientific study is considered negative. What, for example, does one do with the processes of consciousness and its successive experiences if one wishes to understand them, other than to fix them photographically through their successive states? How productive can such qualitative, post hoc descriptions prove to be?

Even if one grants that the operations of both mental and bodily events are important, and that the mind controls much of what the body does and hence assumes preeminence, this should not lead to a neglect of the physical and physiological properties of the person nor to the blithe disregard of the difficulties occasioned by a dualistic position on the mind versus body problem.

By the same token, emphasis on the characteristics of the individual person should not lead to an accompanying neglect of environmental factors, both physical and social, nor to the evident effect of sociocultural factors on the behavior of both individuals and groups.

Adherence to the notion of discontinuity within human behavior and its development, both within each person from one occasion to the next and between each person from one situation to the next, condemns one to an inherently descriptive posture of analysis; it precludes the possibilities of explanation, prediction, and the prospects for management and control, all of which are made possible by alternate methods of analysis, for which empirical support has been accumulated.

If each event and each integrate of events (i.e., the person) is truly unique, then the prospect of developing general laws across an array of humans would appear to be impossible. Writers who advocate such a view and simultaneously generalize about human nature and behavior are contradicting themselves.

The formal properties of the several viewpoints (even those that have undergone more detailed development) are typically deficient, with conspicuous failure to distinguish between axiomatic presumptions and empirical propositions. As a result, they have not as a group proved to be generative of propositions that can be satisfactorily tested. From an empirical point of view, many are both speculative and sterile.

Reliance on subjective report as a means of access to the subjective experience said to be so critical precludes the satisfactory study of all people in whom the capabilities for such reports is limited (e.g., infants or the mentally retarded), impaired (e.g., senile conditions), or otherwise distorted (e.g., drug-induced psychoses).

The reader will recognize that most of the foregoing criticisms and others like them speak more to what the opposition fails to do rather than to what it attempts to do and manages to accomplish. The rejoinders and countercriticisms by their opposite numbers tend to be of the same order, as, for example, the criticisms of what a reductionist, determinist, materialist position leaves out of consideration in its attempts to render peoples's lives intelligible. Because of their fundamental underlying differences, the broad outlines of the dialogue tend to continue and show no signs of abating.

IN SEARCH OF A SYNTHESIS

An instructive series of articles appeared during the 1970s that addressed comparable difficulties in the literature of developmental psychology. These articles relied on the concept of models. Reese and Overton (1970) characterized models as man-made tools, originating in metaphor, that become constructed in a search for the most effective means for representing categories of events to permit the development of understanding, prediction, and control over events. Following the lead initiated by Kuhn (1962), they noted that models can be said to exist on levels, ranging from all-inclusive metaphysical models to narrowly circumscribed models of specific theories. First-order models that endeavor to map the world of concrete experience both imply and can be shown to derive from a more general second-order model, which in turn is related to a more encompassing model at a still higher level—up to the most general order of representation, termed "meta-models" by Reese and Overton, or "paradigms" or world views in the language of Kuhn.

Consensus had been developing that most approaches to the study of human development tended to fall into one of two dominant metamodel frames, one called an organismic model, whose origins lay within the European tradition, and the other called a mechanistic model, considered more distinctively American. Reese and Overton (1970) and Overton and Reese (1973) developed the view that these two paradigms served as the major bases for most representations of the developmental processes in humans. By a careful explication of the metaphysical and epistemological propositions of these paradigms, they succeeded in exposing the multiple ways in which the respective metamodels remained incompatible with one another. Moreover, since the differences related to such fundamental issues as the criteria for defining truth itself, it could be demonstrated that the paradigms and the subordinate models developed in relation to them remained in two entirely separate realms of discourse and were therefore essentially irreconcilable.

In subsequent writings, Looft (1973) and Lerner (1976) agreed. Although later both commentators emphasized that lower order models derived from these more general paradigms do not always dovetail with the metamodels implicit within them, they nonetheless succeeded in categorizing most developmental theories into one or the other and concluded that it was in the metamodel structures—organismic and mechanistic—where one could discern the principal elements of their respective representations of the nature of humans. They sought to enumerate these differences by listing issues considered fundamental to any paradigmatic model that might attempt to represent human development. They differed only in the number of issues they thought necessary to include. In Lerner's (1976) characterization of these differences, the mechanistic paradigm is described as a natural science position, emphasizing quantitative change, continuity, reductionism, a preference for physicochemical representations of events, and concerned with additive effects; whereas the organismic paradigm is described as an epigenetic position, emphasizing qualitative change, discontinuity, emergence, and concerned with multiplicative and interactive effects.

Such a listing reveals a striking parallel between what has been taking place in studies of human development on the one hand and the study of human personality on the other. Indeed, one of the ways in which the differences between the two groups under consideration could have been formulated would have been to characterize them as alternate and competing world views, or paradigms. There are several reasons for eschewing such an approach. There is first the need to establish that the phenomenological, humanist, and existential positions do indeed derive from a common paradigmatic frame. It has been suggested that in many respects they do; however, the analysis can hardly be said to have been adequately accomplished. A second and more compelling reason is that to inspect alternate views from the standpoint of models and metamodels is to adopt the representational epistemology from the outset, and this does immediate violence to one of the views (i.e., the one developed from the phenomenalist posture). Finally, use of the notion of paradigm does not adequately connote the extensive social and professional differences extant in the behavior of the adherents of these opposing views and the extraordinary difficulties attendant on their efforts to communicate usefully with one another. It is for reasons such as these that the metaphor of culture has been used instead.

After reviewing the situation in the domain of developmental psychology, Reese and Overton remained sanguine over the possibility of reconciling views that stood at such variance with one another. They concluded that there is no foreseeable way in which the differences could be bridged as long as the metamodels remain cast in their current terms. To attempt such a reconciliation, using the language in which they are currently presented would require the capitulation by one into the terms of the other. This, or course, has been frequently tried, with advocates of one model attempting to co-opt the viewpoint of the other by translating its representations and recasting them into its own terms. However, as Overton and Reese (1973) were able to demonstrate, this cannot be legitimately done without violating many of the paradigmatic assumptions on which the second is based.

An alternate route is to seek larger and more encompassing paradigms within which the two may be subsumed. The search for newer synthetic viewpoints to incorporate those that have gone before is, of course, motivated by profit. Syntheses are designed to capitalize on the capabilities of the respective elements on which they become constructed. They aspire to more adequate representations that promise to generate more adequate information than has been earlier possible. In developmental theory, Riegel (1975, 1976) pursued this course, proposing that the mechanist and organismic metamodels could in turn be conceptualized as thesis and antithesis, making it possible to architect a dialectic synthesis at more abstract levels of conceptualization. Looft (1973) likewise argued for the development of a new metamodel, reflecting a different set of developmental models, with more powerful concepts, propositions, methods of inquiry, and generative information.

Addressing a parallel problem in the domain of behavior theory, Hilgard (1980) applauded the revival of interest throughout the field of psychology in such areas as consciousness, attention, volition, and choice and expressed the view that a cognitive paradigm might prove to be sufficient, with its derivative theoretic formulations in information processing, decision theory, serial program analyses, and the like.

The search for useful synthetic viewpoints must continue. Were it not for the extraordinary strengths and accomplishments of these respective cultures, there would be a poor basis for such a synthesis; one would be discarded in preference for the other, or both would be discarded to be replaced by a third. However, the capabilities displayed by these respective cultures have earned them a strong measure of admiration and support. The humanist-phenomenological-existential viewpoint, for example, has proven extremely valuable in clinical and counseling practice and has been one on which many procedures for effectively helping troubled people has been based. Its emphasis on the worth of the individual, its positive attitude toward human potential, its promotion of freedom and expressiveness, rights and choices, and its advocacy of authentic personalities that reflect candor, honesty, altruism, caring, respect, and empathy toward others have been requisite elements in effective service. However, the generation of information concerning the physical and physiological aspects of people through the methodologies of experimental science has been equally valuable, as well as the insights provided by disciplines that have emphasized the sociocultural contexts within which people function and develop.

Formulating such syntheses is no small task. As indicated earlier, the problem is not simply one of reconciliation between antithetic viewpoints. Not only is each incomplete without ingredients drawn from the other, but it also remains unclear how either paradigm or culture, in combination with the other, can succeed in representing the complexities of human life, the intricacies of human organization and its continuous modification and change in relation to the multiplicity of influences that affect the person, the various ways in which the person in turn affects the environment, the person's goal-oriented and planful undertakings, or the person's complex and inevitable participations in social groups. A position of detachment from both paradigmatic frames discloses that each can provide only partial characterization of the complexities of human life; the criticisms they level at one another are telling.

It is likely that such syntheses will need to eschew the present frameworks, terminologies, and associated methods of inquiry in order to emerge with a framework of analysis of more adequate scope (White, 1952). In the writer's view, approaches that utilize a systems perspective show the greatest promise in this regard at the present time. The systems perspective is an integrate of many elements. As Grinker (1967) emphasized, and persons such as Laszlo (1972) and Sutherland (1973) developed, the systems perspective encompasses an alternative paradigm or world view (the systems view). At a more particularized level it constitutes a set of models by which the functioning and operation of organized occurrences can be conceptualized and descriptively represented so as to lead to orderly prediction and control (systems theory). It is finally a set of strategies whereby extant systems can undergo investigation and where novel systems can become designed (systems approach).

The systems perspective has been strongly endorsed as a replacement for established modes of thought. For some, like Bertalanffy (1968), its attraction lies in its potentiality for overcoming the inadequacies of mechanistic models as a framework for science; for Rapoport (1966), for counteracting the fragmentation of science into isolated specialties; for Ashby (1958), for addressing problems of complexity; for Boulding (1956), for the construction of new and more useful metatheoretic frameworks; and for Grinker (1967) and Urban (1978), for serving as a unifying framework for the study of human activity and human development.

The recent publication of D. Ford's (1987) Living Systems Framework (LSF) is an excellent illustration of the kind of synthesis that is possible. The LSF takes its place alongside earlier efforts to characterize humans in systems terms (e.g., Gray, Duhl, & Rizzo, 1969; Grinker, 1967, 1975; Menninger, Mayman, & Pruyser, 1963; Miller, 1978; Powers, 1973; Urban, 1978) and shares a number of their basic themes. It construes the person as a network (system) of interrelated and interacting subsidiary units (components) that are organized in a way that enables the person to operate in a unified and integrated fashion. It provides a way of taking into account all aspects of the person—physical, physiological, psychological, and social—and for representing the multiple ways in which these facets of human functioning are simultaneously operative in governing what a person is like, what a person proceeds to do, and what a person can and will become. It builds on the core elements of the control-system unit as a heuristic device for construing not only the operation of the many subsidiary units of which the person is composed but the operation of the person as a whole as well. There is a strong emphasis on the selective (purposive) aspects of human functioning at all levels of organization. This leads to a characterization of human action in terms of outcomes (effects) that become generated in the person as a consequence of the person's own activity, directed toward the attainment of certain effects. The person is understood to be organized in a way calculated to achieve and/or maintain as close a correspondence between effects sought and effects gained as possible. The necessity for including environmental conditions within any analysis of human functioning is similarly stressed because of the manner in which behavioral occurrences and environmental events are inherently intertwined. Finally, there is a significant emphasis placed on the self-constructing characteristics of living systems (autopoesis) that render people capable of building, elaborating, and modifying both their physical structures and their behavioral functions over the course of time. The publication of the LSF was accompanied by a companion volume (Ford & Ford, 1987), which undertook to demonstrate the applicability of the approach in research and practice and the significant changes in conventional modes of thinking (e.g., in the analysis of pathology [Urban, 1987] and in established methods of inquiry [e.g., Nesselroade & Ford, 1987]), which the perspective indicates to be needed.

The systems world view and its associated theories and methods appear to be sufficiently comprehensive to meet the integrative and synthetic requirements for bridging the cultural gap that we described earlier. It appears capable of providing for most of the ingredients that advocates of both cultures consider to be critical. A demonstration that it can succeed in doing so to everyone's satisfaction, however, is a task that remains to be done.

REFERENCES

Adler, A. (1924). *The practice and theory of individual psychology*. New York: Harcourt Brace Jovanovich.

Adler, A. (1927). *Understanding human nature*. New York: Greenberg Publishers.

Allport, G. W. (1955). *Becoming: Basic considerations for a psychology of personality*. New Haven: Yale University Press.

Allport, G. W. (1961). *Pattern and growth in personality*. New York: Holt, Rinehart & Winston.

Ansbacher, H., & Ansbacher, R. (1956). *The individual psychology of Alfred Adler*. New York: Basic Books.

Arkoff, A. (1968). *Adjustment and mental health*. New York: McGraw-Hill.

Ashby, W. R. (1958). General systems theory as a new discipline. *General Systems, 3*, 1–8.

Berne, E. (1972). *What do you say after you say hello?* New York: Grove Press.

Bertalanffy, L. V. (1968). *General system theory: Foundation, development, applications*. New York: Braziller.

Binswanger, L. (1956). Existential analysis and psychotherapy. In F. Fromm-Reichmann & J. L. Moreno (Eds.), *Progress in psychotherapy* (pp. 144–148). New York: Grune & Stratton.

Boring, E. G. (1929). *A history of experimental psychology*. New York: Appleton-Century-Crofts.

Boss, M. (1958). *The analysis of dreams*. New York: Philosophical Library.

Boss, M. (1963). *Daseinsanalyse and psychoanalysis*. New York: Basic Books.

Boulding, K. E. (1956). General system theory: The skeleton of science. *Management Science, 2*, 197–208.

Buhler, C. (1959). Theoretical observations about life's basic tendencies. *American Journal of Psychotherapy, 13*, 561–581.

Buhler, C. (1964). The human course of life and its goal aspects. *Journal of Humanistic Psychology, 4*, 1–18.

Buhler, C., & Massarik, F. (1968). *The course of human life*. New York: Springer.

Butler, J. M., & Rice, L. N. (1963). Adience, self-actualization and drive theory. In J. M. Wepman & R. W. Heine (Eds.), *Concepts of personality* (pp. 79–110). Chicago: Aldine de Gruyter.

Combs, A. W., Avila, D. L., & Purkey, W. W. (1971). *Helping relationships: Basic concepts for the helping professions*. Boston: Allyn & Bacon.

Commerchero, V. (Ed.). (1970). *Values in conflict*. New York: Appleton-Century-Crofts.

Eacker, J. N. (1972). On some elementary philosophical problems of psychology. *American Psychologist, 27*, 553–565.

Erikson, E. H. (1963). *Childhood and society* (2nd ed.). New York: W W Norton.

Erikson, E. H. (1968). *Identity, youth and crisis*. New York: W W Norton.

Erikson, E. H. (1975). *Life history and the historical moment*. New York: W W Norton.

Finkelstein, P., Wenegrat, B., & Yalom, I. (1982). Large group awareness training. In M. R. Rosenzweig & L. W. Porter (Eds.), *Annual review of psychology* (Vol. 33, pp. 515–540). Palo Alto, CA: Annual Reviews.

Ford, D. H. (1987). *Humans as self-constructing living systems: A developmental perspective on behavior and personality*. Hillsdale, NJ: Lawrence Erlbaum Associates.

Ford, D. H., & Ford, M. E. (1987). *Humans as self-constructing living systems: Putting the framework to work*. Hillsdale, NJ: Lawrence Erlbaum Associates.

Ford, D. H., & Urban, H. B. (1963). *Systems of psychotherapy: A comparative approach*. New York: John Wiley & Sons.

Frank, J. D. (1977). Nature and functions of belief systems: Humanism and transcendental religion. *American Psychologist, 32*, 555–559.

Frankl, V. E. (1962). *Man's search for meaning: An introduction to logotherapy*. Boston: Beacon Press.

Frankl, V. E. (1967). *Psychotherapy and existentialism*. New York: Washington Square Press.

Frankl, V. E. (1969). *The will to meaning*. New York: World Publishing Co.

Frankl, V. E. (1975). *The unconscious god*. New York: Simon & Schuster.

Fromm, E. (1955). *The sane society*. New York: Holt, Rinehart, & Winston.

Fromm, E. (1956). *The art of loving*. New York: Harper & Row.

Gray, W., Duhl, F. J., & Rizzo, N. D. (Eds.). (1969). *General systems theory and psychiatry*. Boston: Little Brown.

Grinker, R. R., Sr. (Ed.). (1967). *Toward a unified theory of human behavior* (2nd ed.). New York: Basic Books.

Grinker, R. R., Sr. (1975). *Psychiatry in broad perspective*. New York: Behavioral Publications.

Heidegger, M. (1962). *Being and time*. London: SCM Press.

Hilgard, E. R. (1980). Consciousness in contemporary psychology. *Annual Review of Psychology, 31*, 1–26.

Jahoda, M. (1958). *Common concepts of mental health*. New York: Basic Books.

Jung, C. G. (Ed.). (1964). *Man and his symbols*. London: Aldus.

Kuhn, T. S. (1962). *The structure of scientific revolutions*. Chicago: University of Chicago Press.

Laszlo, E. (1972). *Introduction to systems philosophy*. New York: Harper Torchbooks.

Lerner, R. (1976). *Theories and concepts of human development*. Reading, MA: Addison-Wesley.

Looft, W. R. (1973). Socialization and personality throughout the life-span: An examination of contemporary psychological approaches. In P. B. Baltes & K. W. Schaie

(Eds.), *Life-span developmental psychology: Personality and socialization* (pp. 26–52). New York: Academic Press.

Lowen, A. (1970). *Pleasure*. Baltimore: Penguin Books.

Maddi, S. R. (1963). Humanistic psychology: Allport and Murray. In J. M. Wepman & R. W. Heine (Eds.), *Concepts in personality* (pp. 162–205). Chicago: Aldine de Gruyter.

Maslow, A. H. (1950). Self actualizing people: A study of psychological health. In W. Wolff (Ed.), *Personality symposium*, No. 1 (pp. 207–216). New York: Grune & Stratton.

Maslow, A. H. (1954). *Motivation and personality*. New York: Harper & Row.

Maslow, A. H. (1962). *Toward a psychology of living*. Princeton, N.J.: Van Nostrand.

Maslow, A. H. (1968). *Toward a psychology of being*. (2nd ed.). New York: Van Nostrand Reinhold.

May, R. (Ed.) (1961). *Existential psychology*. New York: Random House.

May, R. (1969). *Love and will*. New York: W W Norton.

May, R., Angel, E., & Ellenberger, M. F. (Eds.). (1958). *Existence: A new dimension in psychiatry and psychology*. New York: Basic Books.

Menninger, K., Mayman, M., & Pruyser, P. (1963). *The vital balance: The life process in mental health and illness*. New York: Viking Press.

Miller, J. G. (1978). *Living systems*. New York: McGraw-Hill.

Murray, H. A. (1951). Some basic psychological assumptions and conceptions. *Dialectica*, *5*, 266–292.

Murray, H. A. (1954). Toward a classification of interaction. In T. Parsons & E. A. Shils (Eds.), *Toward a general theory of action* (pp. 3–29). Cambridge, MA: Harvard University Press.

Murray, H. A. (1959). Preparations for the scaffold of a comprehensive system. In S. Koch (Ed.), *Psychology: A study of science* (Vol. 3, pp. 7–54). New York: McGraw-Hill.

Murray, H. A., & Kluckhohn, C. (1956). Outline of a conception of personality. In C. Kluckhohn, H. A. Murray, & D. M. Schnieder (Eds.), *Personality in nature, society and culture* (2nd ed., pp. 3–32). New York: Alfred A. Knopf.

Nesselroade, J. R., & Ford, D. H. (1987). Methodological considerations in modeling living systems. In D. H. Ford & M. E. Ford (Eds.), *Humans as self-constructing living systems: Putting the framework to work* (pp. 47–79). Hillsdale, NJ: Lawrence Erlbaum Associates.

Overton, W. R., & Reese, H. W. (1973). Models of development: Methodological implications. In J. R. Nesselroade & H. W. Reese (Eds.), *Life-span developmental psychology: Methodological issues* (pp. 65–86). New York: Academic Press.

Perls, F. (1973). *The Gestalt approach and eyewitness to therapy*. Palo Alto, CA: Science and Behavior Books.

Pervin, L. A. (1960). Existentialism, psychology, and psychotherapy. *American Psychologist*, *15*, 305–309.

Powers, W. T. (1973). *Behavior: The control of perception*. Chicago: Aldine de Gruyter.

Rank, O. (1945). *Will therapy and truth and reality*. New York: Alfred A Knopf.

Rapoport, A. (1966). Mathematical aspects of general systems analysis. *General Systems*, *11*, 3–12.

Reese, H. W., & Overton, W. F. (1970). Models of development and theories of development. In L. R. Goulet & P. B. Baltes (Eds.), *Life-span developmental psychology: Research and theory* (pp. 116–145). New York: Academic Press.

Riegel, K. F. (1975). Toward a dialectical theory of development. *Human Development*, *18*, 50–64.

Riegel, K. F. (1976). The dialectics of human development. *American Psychologist*, *31*, 689–700.

Rogers, C. R. (1951). *Client-centered therapy*. Boston: Houghton Mifflin.

Rogers, C. R. (1959). A theory of therapy, personality and interpersonal relationships, as developed in the Client-Centered framework. In S. Koch (Ed.), *Psychology: A study of science*. Vol 11. *General systematic formulations, learning and special processes* (pp. 184–256). New York: McGraw-Hill.

Rogers, C. R. (1961). *On becoming a person*. Boston: Houghton Mifflin.

Sarton, G. (1962). *The history of science and the new humanism*. Cambridge, MA: Harvard University Press.

Sartre, J.-P. (1947). *Existentialism*. New York: Philosophical Library.

Sartre, J.-P. (1957). *Being and nothingness* (H. Barnes, Trans.). Secaucus, NJ: Citadel Press.

Snow, C. P. (1959). *The two cultures and the scientific revolution*. New York: Cambrige University Press.

Snygg, D., & Combs, A. W. (1949). *Individual behavior*. New York: Harper & Row.

Stevenson, L. (1974). *Seven theories of human nature*. New York: Oxford University Press.

Sullivan, H. S. (1953). *The interpersonal theory of psychiatry*. New York: W W Norton.

Sutherland, J. W. (1973). *A general systems philosophy for the social and behavioral sciences*. New York: Braziller.

Tillich, P. (1952). *The courage to be*. New Haven: Yale University Press.

Urban, H. B. (1978). The concept of development from a systems perspective. In P. B. Baltes (Ed.), *Life-span development and behavior*. (Vol 1, pp. 45–83). New York: Academic Press.

Urban, H. B. (1987). Dysfunctional systems: Understanding pathology. In D. H. Ford & M. E. Ford (Eds.), *Humans as self-constructing living systems: Putting the framework to work* (pp. 315–346). Hillsdale, NJ: Lawrence Erlbaum Associates.

White, R. W. (1952). *Lives in progress*. New York: Dryden Press.

White, R. W. (1959). Motivation reconsidered: The concept of competence. *Psychological Review*, *66*, 297–333.

Zurcher, L. A. (1972). The mutable self. *The Futurist*, *6*, 171–185.

PART III

RESEARCH ISSUES AND PROBLEMS

EDITOR'S COMMENTS

Advances in clinical psychology have been achieved in part because of developments in research methodology, assessment, and experimental design. Expansion of the range of design options, assessment strategies, and methods of data evaluation have affected the type of research that is completed and the substantive yield. With the progress in design has come a clearer focus on the problems and issues that need to be addressed and resolved in future research. The chapters in this section detail advances in clinical research methods and their impact on theory and clinical work and substantive areas of personality, psychopathology, and psychotherapy.

In chapter 13, Steven C. Hayes and Christoph Leonhard discuss single-case research design strategies and their contribution to knowledge in clinical work. Single-case designs and alternative assessment strategies can provide empirically based methods for evaluating interventions with individual clients. In this chapter, characteristics of alternative designs, the rationale for their use, and the role of the individual case in the utility and consumption of knowledge in clinical work are elaborated.

In chapter 14, John F. Kihlstrom and Susan M. McGlynn discuss experimental research in clinical psychology. They consider laboratory models of psychopathology as illustrated with specific disorders. Psychological deficits in psychopathology, the development of cognitive neuropsychology, and other experimental underpinnings of clinical research are elaborated.

In chapter 15, Norman S. Endler and James D. A. Parker consider advances in personality research. The impact of methodology on conceptual advances in personality research is evident in the discussion of alternative models of personality and research that integrates diverse positions. The chapter discusses key issues in personality including the consistencies and inconsistencies of behavior over time and the impact of trait and situational factors in explaining performance.

In chapter 16, Scott M. Monroe and John E. Roberts trace advances in psychopathology research. Genetic and biological research, brain imaging techniques, and developments in cognitive psychology are discussed. The evaluation of community and nonpatient samples, longitudinal studies, and research on comorbidity are used to illustrate recent substantive and methodological developments.

In chapter 17, Alan E. Kazdin examines research issues in relation to the investigation of psychotherapy. Alternative treatment evaluation strategies and methodological issues in relation to assessment and design in therapy outcome research are presented. Several methodological issues are addressed including treatment integrity, clinical significance, and statistical power of treatment outcome research.

In chapter 18, Bruce E. Wampold and Richard D. Freund discuss the integration of experimental design and statistical evaluation. The evaluation of alternative statistical tests, clinical and statistical significance, and statistical evaluation of single-case studies are key topics. Models of research other than traditional hypothesis testing are presented in relation to clinical research.

CHAPTER 13

THE ROLE OF THE INDIVIDUAL CASE IN CLINICAL SCIENCE AND PRACTICE

Steven C. Hayes
Christoph Leonhard

For clinicians, the individual is almost always the relevant level of analysis. Clients are individuals acting within a physical and social context. This orientation can be contrasted with sciences that hold the group as the relevant level of analysis. Sociologists, for example, are dealing with the group level of analysis when they study, say, Russian culture. When clinicians deal with groups, the group is typically considered either as a context for action or as a means for behavior change. The individual is ultimately the focus.

Given the centrality of the individual to clinical science and practice, it should not be surprising that some of the most influential clinical literature is based on analyses of individual cases. Classic case studies, such as Little Hans or Anna O., have provided a foundation for major clinical orientations. Multiple clinical replications (e.g., Masters & Johnson, 1970; Wolpe, 1958) have provided the empirical basis for highly influential clinical treatments. Collections of unsystematic case descriptions organized around a central theme (e.g., Haley, 1984) are still among the most widely read forms of clinical literature.

This central quality of clinical psychology has created a certain tension between clinical practice and

much of the scientific literature said to be relevant to clinical issues. Ever since statistical inferential tools moved from agriculture to the behavioral sciences and began to dictate design decisions, psychology has largely relied on group comparison designs. Although there are some exceptions, such as the experimental analysis of behavior (e.g., Johnston & Pennypacker, 1981; Sidman, 1960), the hegemony of group comparison designs in most areas of psychology is so great that the scientific method itself is often virtually identified with them.

Research is a process to be put to use, and in clinical psychology most applications of research are applications to individual people. It is not possible to translate the group level of analysis directly to the individual level of analysis. To know what Americans do is not to know what a particular American does. Thus, the outcome of much of the scientific literature in psychology cannot be translated directly into the level required for its use by clinicians. The cost of this poor fit between the practice of clinical psychology and the dominant methods in psychology has been very high. It has (a) helped drive a wedge between clinical practice and research; (b) cut off the practicing clinician from input into the legitimate knowledge base of the field; and (c) produced research that is not maximally applicable to the clinical situation.

DISTINGUISHING GROUP-LEVEL AND INDIVIDUAL-LEVEL RESEARCH

It seems worthwhile to defend the claim that the individual level of analysis cannot normally be abstracted from group comparison research. First, the difference between individual and group levels of analysis has almost nothing to do with the number of subjects examined. Failing to distinguish issues of numerosity from these of the most appropriate level of analysis has needlessly hindered the adoption of designs appropriate to the individual level of analysis. Researchers interested in the individual level of analysis have themselves failed to emphasize the distinction, for example, in their terminology. The phrase *single-subject design* is misleading (for that reason we will also occasionally use the more informative synonym *time-series design* to describe these approaches). No one claims that we can learn as much by studying a few as we do by studying many. Rather, the claim can be made that we will learn something different by studying many where the information applies only to the level of the many, versus studying many where the information applies to the level of the few.

To see what a group level of analysis means, we can consider the logic of the archetypal group study. A group of clients is randomly assigned to two groups. All clients receive a pretest. One of the group then receives treatment; the other does not. All clients receive a posttest. The differences between pre- and posttest scores are calculated for each subject. The distribution of these difference scores within each group is mathematically examined. The mean differences between the two groups are then assessed relative to certain mathematical aspects of their distributions.

Each of these steps is designed to deal with the most fundamental reason for all forms of experimental design. Experimentation exists to distinguish three sources of variation over scores: measurement error or inconsistency, extraneous factors, and treatment-related factors. Measurement error is false variation due to sloppy or inconsistent measurement. For example, an assessor might unknowingly measure the phenomenon of interest under different levels of social demand for improvement. Extraneous factors produce real change, but the presence of these factors is uncontrolled. For example, a depressed person's critical mother may take a trip, and the client's mood may improve. Treatment-related factors are the specific and nonspecific influences contained within the treatment itself. If we could easily distinguish these three sources of variability, there would be no reason for experimental design.

If distinguishing these three sources of variability is the raison d'être of design, how does the aforementioned archetypal group design deal with them? The ideas is as follows: We cannot say why a given individual improved from pre to post. It could be due to any of these three sources of variation, or all three in some unknown combination. However, if we randomly assigned subjects to groups, we can assume that measurement error and extraneous factors are equally likely in each group. Since within each group our treatment was the same for each individual, the variability within a group between individuals must be due to measurement error and extraneous factors. Thus, we can use the degree of within-group variability as a kind of rubber ruler against which to measure the meaningfulness of the mean differences between the groups. Statistical inferential tools have been developed to stretch the rubber ruler the proper amount in a given instance (more variability = more stretching).

This basic idea is understood by every psychology student. The reasoning is impeccably logical, though we will note later that its logical requirements are rarely met. What is often not appreciated, however, is that this logic applies only to the group level of analysis. It is only when considering the group as a whole that the three sources of variation can be distinguished. Thus, for example, it is illegitimate to say who improved due to treatment. Using such a design, we cannot know. Person X may have improved from pre to post because mother moved out. Person Y may have improved the same amount because of measurement error. Person Z may have improved an identical amount because of the treatment supplied. Which individuals improved due to treatment is a meaningful question only at the level of the individual. That is, it is meaningful only when the three sources of variation are distinguishable for persons X, Y, and Z. In the archetypal group study, all we can say is whether treatment worked, relative to the other factors assumed to be participating, considering the group as a whole.

The need for case analysis is usually argued on the basis of the possibility that it suggests hypotheses for examination in true experimental (i.e., group comparison) research. We will argue that because of the unique goals of clinical psychology, case analyses are not only useful but necessary. Far from being the weak sister in the clinical research enterprise, case analyses are (in practice if not in the models of methodologists) at its core. It is case analysis that embraces the correct level of analysis, given the purposes of the clinical sciences.

ROLE OF THE INDIVIDUAL CASE IN THE PRODUCTION OF CLINICAL KNOWLEDGE

It has long been recognized that practicing clinicians contribute relatively little to the research base of clinical psychology (Garfield & Kurtz, 1976; Kelly, Goldberg, Fiske, & Kilkowski, 1978; Levy, 1962). A number of arguments have been advanced about this, from defending it as necessary, to blaming clinicians for some inherent weakness, to chastising academics for their lack of interest in the clinical environment (e.g., see Leitenberg, 1974; Meehl, 1971; Peterson, 1976; Raush, 1969, 1974; Rogers, 1973; Shakow, 1976). The role and nature of research training is still a controversial issue in clinical areas (e.g., Frank, 1986; Howard, 1985, 1986; Ivanoff, Robinson, & Blythe, 1987; Peterson, 1985).

Consider, however, the methodological tools clinicians have been given. Not only are they unwieldy, but they also tend not to produce the kind of knowledge base that clinical psychology needs because the level of analysis is incorrect. Clinicians themselves say that inappropriate research methods are a major reason they fail to do research (Haynes, Lemsky, & Sexton-Radek, 1987).

An explosion of interest has occurred in methodological tools that are built on an analysis at the level of the individual. This interest has been especially prominent in the clinical disciplines, from clinical psychology to social work (e.g., Barlow, Hayes, & Nelson, 1984; Barlow & Hersen, 1984; Browning & Stover, 1971; Chassan, 1967, 1979; Hayes, 1981; Jayaratne & Levy, 1979; Kazdin, 1978, 1980, 1982; Kratochwill, 1978; Leitenberg, 1973; Miller, 1985; Svenson & Chassan, 1967). These tools are not only scientifically defensible, they are much more applicable to the clinical environment than are group comparison designs.

FUNDAMENTALS OF SINGLE-CASE ANALYSIS

In the next several sections we will examine the fundamentals of single-case analysis. The essentials of the treatment-related analysis of the individual case parallel the essentials of good clinical practice. They involve accurate and repeated assessment, careful analysis of trends in client progress, specification of the treatment plan and adherence to it, and a readiness to change directions when the client's program indicates that that is what is needed.

Accurate and Systematic Assessment

All valid clinical knowledge is based on systematic observation. For example, if what is observed is a function of the needs, biases, or wants of the clinician (i.e., because of countertransference) and not client behavior, the information gleaned from the case will necessarily be faulty. Anecdotal information has a place in single-case analysis, but the threats to accuracy are so large that little can be learned without going the extra step to assess the client in a systematic way (Kazdin, 1981a). This is good clinical practice. The nature of the observation may include systematic interviews, testing, self-monitoring, direct observation, or other procedures (see Nelson, 1981, or Barlow et al., 1984, for a short review of clinically practical measures). The measures should be practical and taken under consistent and specifiable conditions.

Repeated Measurement

Repeated measurement is essential to single-case analysis and also parallels rules of clinical practice. Practical clinical guides often exhort clinicians to "examine regularly and consistently whether therapy is being helpful" (Zaro, Barach, Nedelmann, & Dreiblatt, 1977, p. 157). In clinical practice, repeated measurements should start early, using several measures if possible. Often, when normal assessment ends, the clinician will have a systematically collected baseline. The use of repeated measurement, more than any other single factor, allows knowledge to be drawn from the individual case, because it eliminates or restricts the plausibility of measurement error or extraneous factors as a source for the effects seen at the level of the individual.

Specification of Conditions

The product of research is a verbal description of a relation among events. If the verbal description itself is vague, the clinical community cannot share in the knowledge gained. We must be able to replicate what the researcher actually did sufficiently well that the same results are likely. There is good evidence in the clinical literature that specification of conditions is a major problem (Peterson, Homer, & Wonderlich,

1982; Yeaton & Sechrest, 1981). Recently, attempts have been made to develop ways of assessing the adequacy of procedural descriptions (Thomas, Bastien, Stuebe, Bronson, & Yaffe, 1987). The need for procedural specification is familiar to practicing clinicians. Without a clear treatment plan—one that is documented and followed—it is impossible to know what has been tried. Clinical agencies spend a great deal of time on the development and documentation of treatment plans, in part for that reason.

Replication

All valid knowledge should be replicable. Replication is the mechanism used in clinical science to rule out the many threats to validity. All single-case designs make contact with the issue of replication.

Establishment of the Degree of Variability

We cannot know if treatment had an effect unless we have an accurate estimate of the pretreatment course of a problem. Measures should be taken long enough and be stable enough to allow us to know where the problem is going and to see treatment effects, should they occur. These are not absolute qualities—it depends on what we know about the problem and its treatment. If treatment effects are expected to be large, considerable variability can be tolerated. If the problem is so variable that no effects can be seen, why proceed? In some situations, we know enough about the problem to assume a fair amount of stability, and we may need only a few assessments. An extremely academically deficient child, for example, is unlikely to improve or deteriorate rapidly over short periods of time.

If the measures are too variable, three clinically defensible options are open. First, one could wait to see if a clearer picture emerges. Second, one can search for the events that are causing variability. It may be sloppy measurement, or it could be real and a clue to the actual events influencing the problem. Third, the temporal unit of analysis may be too small. Perhaps the overall pattern is unclear because the specific measures are being examined in terms of days, when weeks make more clinical sense; hours when days make more sense, and so on.

The need for clarity about the course of a problem is again not just a reflection of abstract research concerns. Clinicians, too, must attend carefully to the improvement or deterioration of the client's problem.

Investigative Play and Creative Use of Single-Case Logic

The investigation of the individual case should be a dynamic enterprise, produced by the interaction of continuously collected clinical information and ongoing therapeutic actions. When unanticipated effects are seen, the clinician must be ready to abandon previous decisions and to let the client's data be the guide. This is also good clinical practice. Clinicians are told to "be prepared to alter your style of dealing with a client in response to new information" and "be prepared to have many of your hypotheses disproved" (Zaro et al., 1977, p. 28). This is the single greatest difference between group comparison approaches and time-series analyses.

Unfortunately, even the users of time-series designs may have fallen into this trap, as might be indicated by the literature's emphasis on complete designs rather than on design elements. All single-case analyses are built on a few core elements. The specific arrangement of elements should be dictated by clinical needs, not by formal categorization of complete designs. One is trying to use these elements to determine if treatment is needed and useful. The present chapter is thus organized around elements, not completed designs.

In summary, a methodology for the production of clinical knowledge based on the individual case must accord itself with fundamental values of good clinical practice: accurate and repeated assessment; establishment of clinical need; specification of treatment; continuous sensitivity to the needs of clients; and establishment of the role of treatment in client improvement. Whether the knowledge developed will be valid and useful will depend on the degree to which these recommendations are followed. Only the last recommendation is somewhat foreign to trained clinicians, although it is implicit in clinical decision making.

DESIGN ELEMENTS IN SINGLE-SUBJECT ANALYSIS

Following the format described in Hayes (1981) and Barlow et al. (1984), the present chapter describes single-case experimental designs in terms of a few core units, organized by the nature of stability estimates and the logic of the data comparisons. These core elements are put together as the needs of the case analysis dictate. The elements can be organized into three types: between, within, and combined series. A more detailed treatment can be found in Barlow et al. (1984).

Within-Series Elements

The within-series elements draw their estimates of stability, level, and trend within a series of data points organized into a temporal sequence. Stability, level, and trend are estimated under a constant condition, termed a *phase*. Changes are then made in the conditions impinging on the client, and stability, level, or trend of the sequential data points in the new phase is estimated. It is the difference between the stability, level, or trend of the data in one phase versus another that is the source of information about client change. Because changes seen within a series of data points across time are the main source of clinical information, we term these design elements *within-series elements*.

There are two classes of within-series elements. In the simple phase change, the within-series comparison is made one or more times between two conditions (for example, baseline and treatment). In the complex phase change, there is an overall coordinating strategy that dictates a particular sequence of three or more conditions. In either case, there is always only one condition per phase.

Perhaps the most common example of a within-series element is the A-B design (by tradition, A always stand for baseline, B for the first treatment element, C for the second, and so on). The A-B represents a simple case study (but with repeated measurement and careful specification of treatment) in which a period of assessment is followed by a single treatment strategy. If the stability, level, or trend of the data taken in the assessment phase changes when treatment is implemented, our confidence increases that treatment is responsible, especially if the change is marked, sudden, and consistent.

Often, however, we can think of other reasons for the change, such as the effect of extraneous events or the effects of assessment itself (see Barlow & Hersen, 1984; Campbell & Stanley, 1963; Kazdin, 1982), so we need to replicate the effect. A simple way is to repeat the phase change in reverse order (an A-B-A) and then perhaps to repeat it again in the original order (an A-B-A-B). Each time changes in the data coincide with phase changes, our confidence in the effect increases. This type of design answers the question: Does treatment work for this client?

The alternation of phase changes can continue indefinitely, each sequence constituting a type of completed design. The two conditions could be two treatments (e.g., B-C-B-C), or elements of a treatment package (e.g., B-B + C-B). The logic of these spe-cific types is identical; only the questions being asked and the extent of comparisons differ owing to the specific content of the phases and the number of alternations. In a B-C-B-C design, for example, the question being asked is: Which treatment works best for this client?

When components of a treatment package are being compared, the sequence is called an interaction element. It answers the question: What are the combined effects of two treatment components compared to one alone? A number of specific sequences are possible (e.g., B-B + C-B-B + C or B + C-C-B + C).

Several types of complex phase change elements exist. An example is an A-B-A-C-A sequence. A simple phase change comparing two treatments (e.g., a B-C-B-C) does not show that either works relative to baseline. If this is not already known, and if the clinician still wants to compare the two treatments, it can be done by combining simple phase-change strategies for determining the effectiveness of each treatment. The sequence A-B-A-C-A combines an A-B-A with an A-C-A. This allows us to ask if treatments B and C are effective, and if they are differentially effective. Because order effects are possible and noncontiguous data are being compared (B and C), it is best for other subjects also to receive an A-C-A-B-A sequence. If the conclusions are the same, then the believability of the treatment comparison is strengthened. For a clinical example of this type of design, see Harmon, Nelson, and Hayes (1980).

Another complex phase-change element termed a *changing criterion* is available when a criterion can be set beforehand of the type of behavior that must be seen in the phase to achieve a given outcome (Hartmann & Hall, 1976). If the behavior repeated changes to match a sequence of criterion changes, the therapeutic conditions can be said to be responsible.

This element is often used when changes can only occur in one direction, either for ethical or for practical reasons. The logic of the maneuver, however, allows for criterion reversals when the behavior is reversible. The criteria usually relate to the level of the behavior seen, but the logic of a changing criterion also applies to criteria based on stability, trend, relationship to initiating conditions, and the like. The weakness of the element is that it is not always clear when observed behavior is tracking criterion shifts. This problem can be alleviated by altering the length, magnitude, or direction of criterion shifts.

Other complex strategies are possible but are seen infrequently in clinical research. For example, the intensity of treatment might be systematically increased and then decreased in a series of phases (see Sidman, 1960). This might be written A-B-B'-B''-B'''-B''-B'-A. The design is most frequently seen in research on dose-related drug responses.

A strategy that draws on similar logic is the periodic treatments element (Barlow et al., 1984; Hayes, 1981). If the frequency of measurement is high (much more often than treatment) and if actual treatment is confined to periodic sessions (e.g., 1-hour outpatient visits), then a consistent relationship between the periodicity of behavior change and that of treatment may indicate a treatment effect. This is particularly so if the sessions are irregularly spaced and if the behavior changes that follow are rapid and stable.

Between-Series Elements

In the between-series elements the estimates of stability level and trend of the data are made in a series of measures taken concurrently with other measurement series. Assessments are organized first by specific condition and then by time. This is different than the within-series design elements, in which phases are defined by the condition in place over a period of time. Because within-series designs are based on phases, data series can be organized in a simple temporal sequence. In the between-series elements, effects are assessed by looking for differences between two or more of these series.

There are two basic types. One type is an alternating treatment design element, or ATD (Barlow & Hayes, 1979; Barlow et al., 1984). The ATD is based on the rapid alternation of two or more conditions, in which there is one potential alternation of condition per measurement unit. Since a single data point associated with one condition may be preceded and followed by measurements associated with other conditions, there are no phases. Rather, measurements associated with each condition are put into separate series. If there is a clear separation between the series, differences among conditions are inferred.

Order effects are usually minimized by random or semirandom alternation of conditions. The conditions may or may not include baseline, depending on the question being asked. The strategy is especially useful for comparing two or three treatments or treatment elements. One could think of the ATD as a rapid simple phase change, but the estimates of variability and source of treatment comparisons are different, and it can easily incorporate three or even more conditions into a single comparison sequence (see Barlow & Hayes, 1979).

Discriminations between treatment conditions can be enhanced by supplying a specific stimulus associated with each condition (Barlow & Hayes, 1979), but no stimulus is logically required. For example, one could do an alternating treatments design comparing an effect medication with a placebo. A specific stimulus for each condition is usually unavoidable, however.

The ATD is particularly useful for comparing two or more treatments or when measurement is cumbersome or lengthy (e.g., an entire Minnesota Multiphasic Personality Inventory, or MMPI). Only four data points are absolutely needed (two in each condition), though more are desirable. Alternations may be made after weeks or months, so that a given data point may incorporate many treatment sessions; or on the other extreme, it might occur several times per session (e.g., Hayes, Hussian, Turner, Anderson, & Grubb, 1983). Rapid alternation refers only to the rate of treatment alternation relative to the rate of measurement.

The ATD is subject to multiple treatment interference. That is, the effect of a treatment may differ by virtue of its comparison with another. It is known, for example, that the frequency of alternation can itself alter the effects of treatment (McGonigle, Rojahn, Dixon, & Strain, 1987). So far, no one has found that the direction of the differences can be affected, so it is probably safe to assume that differences found in an ATD are real.

The only other true between-series element is the simultaneous treatment design (Browning, 1967). It requires the simultaneous availability of two or more treatments, while the client controls which treatment is actually applied. Thus, a true instance of this design can only measure treatment preference, and it is used little in the applied literature.

Combined-Series Elements

Several elements use comparisons both between and within data series to draw conclusions. One is built on several repetitions of a single simple phase change, each with a new data series, in which the length of the first phase and the timings of the phase change differ at each repetition. This strategy might best be termed a *multiple phase change*, but it is universally known as a *multiple baseline* (whether or not baseline is one of the conditions).

The different series might be based on different behaviors, different individuals, different situations, or combinations of these. By replication across different series, the multiple baseline corrects for major deficiencies of a simple phase change, that effects could be due to coincidental extraneous events, assessment, and so on. If the effects are replicated, but with different lengths of baseline for each replication (a strategy that controls for the amount of baseline assessment or mere maturation) and with the actual time of the phase change arbitrarily altered (to reduce the possibility of correlated extraneous events), the conclusions are correspondingly strengthened.

As with many of these design elements, the literature on the multiple baseline contains many rules that seem unnecessary. It was originally asserted that the additional series must be built on variation along a single dimension (person, place, or behavior; see Baer, Wolf, & Risley, 1968). The logic of the comparison does not require this, although the breadth of the question differs if it is violated. For example, if an effect shown in behavior A in person B and situation C is replicated across behavior A in person X and situation Z, it tests both the person and situation generality of the results.

In each sequential phase change in a multiple baseline, the same first condition must yield to the same second condition, since we are controlling for alternative explanations for a specific phase-change effect. The logic of the comparison does not require a baseline. A series of B-C phase changes could easily be arranged into a multiple baseline.

No set number of phase-shift replications is required in a multiple-baseline element, but each additional series strengthens our confidence that much more. The same is true of the differences in initial phase length. If one series has an initial phase that is only slightly longer or shorter than the other, it is less satisfactory than if there are large differences.

If a phase shift is accompanied by changes between as well as within series, either effect is due to extraneous variables (not treatment), or the effects of treatment are generalized across series. For this reason, the design element is most useful when the series are independent (Kazdin & Kopel, 1975). If several series are being compared, some interdependence can be tolerated (see Hayes & Barlow, 1977; Hersen & Bellack, 1976, for examples), without undoing the design (Barlow et al., 1984; Kazdin, 1980).

Another combined-series strategy, termed a *crossover*, is based on two concurrent phase changes on separate series, one the reverse of the other. A crossover has essentially the same logic as a true reversal design (Leitenberg, 1973). By changing phases at the same time, this strategy equalizes alternative sources

of control that might have produced an apparent phase-change effect (e.g., maturation, phase length). Consistent within-series effects in both series provided some evidence of the superiority of one condition over the other. The controls are fairly weak (e.g., for order effects), so additional replications are needed.

A final combined-series element is the baseline-only control. This is simply an uninterrupted series that can be compared to other manipulated series, allowing a between-series comparison in addition to whatever within-series comparisons are possible. Changes occurring elsewhere and not in the baseline-only control series are more likely to have been produced by treatment (see Campbell & Stanley's [1963] equivalent time samples design). The logic of this is identical to the between-series comparisons in a multiple baseline.

CONDUCTING A CASE ANALYSIS

The level of scientific product in a given single-case analysis depends on the degree to which reasonable alternative explanations can be ruled out. For some clinical issues, careful interviewing or formal assessment may be enough to arrive at valid conclusions. For example, a particular view of depression may claim that a special type of client history or attitude is necessary for depression to occur. Even a single credible instance where this is not true may in itself make a contribution.

In treatment research (as in clinical treatment itself), more is usually required. Accurate and systematic assessment will almost always be needed. Repeated measurement is needed when we do not have certain knowledge of the stability and trend of the behavior of interest. If we are certain that a given disorder is stable and accurately measured, then even a single measurement before treatment and after treatment may add to our knowledge base (Jayaratne & Levy, 1979), especially if it is repeated in several cases. For example, a person shown to have acquired immune deficiency syndrome (AIDS) may not need to be reassessed over and over in research on a new AIDS treatment. The course of AIDS is known, and long-term spontaneous remissions apparently do not happen. Few such situations exist in the clinical sciences. In order to project trends against which effects can be evaluated, we usually need to measure repeatedly. Another exception occurs when treatment is strong. If most individuals improve significantly, a simple pre and post measurement may be sufficient.

Once repeated and accurate measurement is occurring, case studies are single-case designs. There is no clear division between them. The level of scientific product will vary from one case study to another, but this is not just due to issues of design. It depends heavily on the context in which the information is viewed (what we know about the behavior, etc.).

The most influential case analyses in clinical psychology (e.g., Little Albert) amount to variations of single-case designs, as described earlier. They may at times seem relatively uncontrolled, but they rely on the same logical structure.

The fit between single-case methodology and clinical practice is assured because rules of good clinical practice are fundamentally based on the same logic (Hayes, 1981). Of course, the amount of knowledge gleaned from a case or series of cases depends on how precise the analysis can be. Rather than a dichotomy (e.g., research versus practice), the amount of knowledge gained from a case lies on a continuum.

In this section we will describe how single-case methodology fits clinical decision making. Further, we will attempt to show that treatment-related case analysis is actually a form of single-case experimental analysis. The use of within-series and combined strategies provides a good example of this. The following sections describe the sequence of events a clinician might follow in conducting such an analysis.

Within- and Combined-Series Elements in Actual Practice

The clinician typically begins a therapeutic relationship with a period of assessment. If repeated measures are taken, this period amounts to a baseline phase. In order to establish estimates of stability, level, and trend, at least three measurement points are needed, although more are desirable and may be needed in a given case to discern a trend. Shorter periods of assessment may be justified when there is other information available about the problem being measured. For example, the clinical disorder may have a known history and course (e.g., the social withdrawal of a chronic schizophrenic), or archival baselines may be available (e.g., family reports, records from school). Note that this issue is a clinical one ("Do I know the nature and course of the problem?"), not an arbitrary addition of single-case methodology.

Even though a baseline would be useful, sometimes treatment must be begun immediately. In this case, scientifically valid information may still be gained by design elements that do not require a baseline (e.g., an ATD), or by replication (e.g., in other cases or later in the same case).

When a baseline is taken, it may show the problem to be improving, deteriorating, or staying the same. In general, if substantial improvement is occurring it is not time to change course (i.e., to shift phases and to start treatment). This advice is the same on clinical grounds (Why interfere with a good thing?) as it is on methodological grounds (How can you see if you have had an effect?).

Suppose the problem is deteriorating or staying the same. At this point, the clinician may be ready to implement treatment. Before doing so, the clinician may want to see if there is a variable that needs to be controlled first. For example, if the client seems susceptible to mild interventions such as family support, positive therapeutic expectations, and social encouragement (especially if the treatment is dangerous, difficult, or costly), it might be worth trying the less difficult treatment first. If it is not effective, the meaningfulness of subsequent therapeutic effects may be enhanced.

When starting treatment, it should ideally be implemented in a powerful way. Excessively gradual implementation will make real effects more difficult to see (Thomas, 1978), although even this would not necessarily be lethal to the scientific value of the resulting analysis.

When the second phase is implemented, only three outcomes are possible: no change, deterioration, or improvement. If there is no change, the clinician can either wait and see if there is a delayed effect or try another strategy. It is typically assumed that a phase producing no change can be (with caution) considered part of the previous phase (e.g., $A = B\text{-}C$). There are limits to this, of course. An $A = B = C = C = E\text{-}F\text{-}E\text{-}F$ design would not be convincing and would need to be replicated, but this is true in normal clinical work. If we seem to find the key to a case after extensive floundering, we usually are not sure that we really have it until we try it out with others. Sometimes the new strategies we try are modifications or additions to previous ones (e.g., $A = B = B + C = B + C + D\text{-}B + C + D + E$). The methodological considerations here are the same. If treatment produces deterioration, the clinician should withdraw treatment (creating an $A\text{-}B\text{-}A$). If the behavior improves, an iatrogenic effect is shown, which itself may be a significant (if somewhat disturbing) contribution to the field.

The final possible effect is improvement. Several courses are then opened up: (a) to continue to completion and (perhaps) to try it with similar cases, (b) to try the intervention in other areas of the client's life, if appropriate; or (c) to withdraw treatment briefly, with an eye toward reimplementation. Since this (an *A-B*) is the cornerstone of clinical case evaluation, these alternatives will be discussed in some detail.

Continue to Completion

An *A-B* design by itself often produces useful clinical knowledge. This is particularly true if the effects are marked. It makes it unlikely that such things as assessment effects or regression to the mean are responsible (Kazdin, 1981a). It is, of course, always possible that the effects are due to maturation or some extraneous environmental event. This may be more or less likely depending on the nature of the problem, its chronicity, past history of treatment, the identification of sudden changes in the client's world, and rapidity and consistency of improvement in various areas of functioning. In favorable circumstances, a single *A-B* can produce fairly believable demonstrations of treatment impact because the overall pattern of results significantly undermines competing explanations.

The only way to know for sure is through replication, either within the same client or between different clients. If the *A-B* can be repeated in other clients, a natural multiple baseline will almost always be formed. This is probably one of the clearest examples of natural design elements that arise in clinical practice. Nothing could be more natural to clinical work than an *A-B*. Individual cases will naturally have different lengths of baseline (often widely so), and sequential cases usually lead to a multiple baseline across people.

Some of the earliest applied literature on the multiple baseline (e.g., Baer, Wolf, & Risley, 1968) stated that multiple baselines across persons should always be one at the same time in the same setting with the same behavior. Saving cases, with perhaps periods of months or even years separating each, violates this rule, but fortunately the logic of the strategy does not require it (see Harris & Jenson, 1985; Hayes, 1985, for argument and counterargument on this point). If the time of the phase shift differs in real time from client to client, it is unlikely that important external events could repeatedly coincide with the phase changes. It is true that the external events that were present with case *X* are not simultaneously present in case *Y*, but this additional control is unimportant if the effects are clear and replicable.

The multiple baseline controls for the effects of assessment, maturation, and similar effects by varying the lengths of baseline. Multiple *A-B*s retain much of this protection as long as the reasons for changing phases at the precise moment are described, vary from case to case, seem unlikely to be related to sudden improvement, and (ideally) are at times somewhat arbitrary. Thus, while multiple *A-B*s have been described as case studies (Kazdin, 1981a), they seem to be legitimate experimental designs.

The clinicians must report all cases attempted, not just those showing the desired effect. If the effect is not seen in some, the clinician should attempt to find out why (e.g., by adding phases to those clients showing an *A* = *B* effect). A careful examination of the variables accounting for differences between clients may lead to knowledge about mechanisms of change and boundary conditions.

The multiple baseline across cases also provides a home for those cases in which treatment only is given (*B* only), and in which treatment is never given (baseline-only control). As anchors in a series of cases, they can provide evidence of the effectiveness of treatment even when no baseline is taken (*B* only)—thus controlling for an unlikely order effect caused by baseline assessment—or of the likelihood of change when no treatment is given (baseline-only control).

A related use of these multiple *A-B*s is multiple clinical replications (Barlow, 1980). In this use, the focus is on the numbers of cases showing effects of particular types at the *A-B* shift. While the method of presentation differs, if the baseline lengths differ substantially, this amounts to a method of summarizing multiple-baseline data, more than a new design.

Conduct a Multiple Baseline within the Case

Multiple baselines often form naturally across behaviors because of the tendency for practicing clinicians to tackle subsets of problems sequentially rather than all at once (e.g., Brownell, Hayes, & Barlow, 1977). Multiple baselines across settings are less common but also naturally occur when clinicians treat problem behavior shown in one specific condition first (e.g., Hayes & Barlow, 1977). If the client has shown a good response to treatment with one problem or in one situation, the clinician should consider trying the same strategy with remaining difficulties. If so, a multiple baseline will be formed.

Withdrawal

Withdrawal of an apparently effective treatment raises ethical issues, client fees issues, potential client morale problems, and possible neutralization of subsequent treatment effects. However, it often seems justified and even clinically useful. It also frequently occurs naturally.

First, a withdrawal can avoid the unnecessary use of ineffective treatment. Physicians recognize this issue in the common practice of drug holidays (i.e., withdrawals) to assess the continued need for treatment. Second, withdrawals often present themselves naturally in treatment in the form of vacations, holidays, sickness, temporary treatment dropouts, or in terms of clinical reassessment, attention to unrelated clinical issues, and the like. When using these kinds of withdrawals, the reasons for the phase change should be described and some interpretive caution should be used, since changes seen could be due to the events causing the natural withdrawal, not to withdrawal per se.

Third, withdrawals can be short and given a good rationale. It this is well done, the client may be helped regardless of the outcome. If a short withdrawal is associated with deterioration, clients may become more convinced of the need for treatment. Greater patient involvement may result. Conversely, withdrawals associated with maintenance can lead to greater confidence on the client's part that the problem is now under better control.

If treatment is withdrawn, the behavior will show no change, deterioration, or continued improvement. If it deteriorates, treatment should be reimplemented (an *A-B-A-B*). If it shows no change (but there is room to improve), treatment could be started again to see if improvement will then occur. If the behavior continues to improve, the case can be saved and the same thing tried again later (forming a multiple baseline).

Between Series in Actual Practice

The possibilities for using ATD elements in clinical evaluation are great but usually require more planning. One of the advantages of an ATD is its ability to produce information rapidly. When the clinician wants to know if condition *B* works better than *C*, there are few finer ways to find out. A situation where this is common is when difficult treatment-related assessment decisions exist. Suppose, for example, that a client is presenting with depression. The clinician may have a difficult time determining if the client is more likely to respond to cognitive-therapy procedures or skills-training procedures. Rather than guess, the clinician might do both, in an alternating-treat-

ments fashion. The better treatment may quickly be revealed, and all treatment effort could then go in this direction. We have recently conducted such a clinical series (McKnight, Nelson, Hayes, & Jarrett, 1984) and were able to show that the ATD reliably categorized cognitive responders and skills responders in ways that corresponded with pretreatment assessment data.

Combining Elements

Case analysis is an exploration into the world of an individual. This kind of exploration calls for dynamic and creative uses of clinical tools: assessment, intervention, and evaluation. Designs should not be a framework into which clinical procedures are injected; rather, design elements should be used to support clinical decision making. In the ebb and flow of hypotheses that emerge in a clinical case, design tools should be used as needed and discarded as quickly when they are no longer useful. Table 13.1 presents examples of the use of various design elements to answer specific clinical questions. Which design tool is used in any row is determined by which is most feasible in terms of the kind of behavior being analyzed and the situation in treatment.

Group Comparisons and Time-Series Designs

The time-series design tradition is not incompatible with group comparison designs. As was emphasized earlier, the issue is not "few versus many," but the level of analysis. There may be times when the researcher is interested in both levels of analysis. If enough subjects are examined with intensive, single-subject designs, these can often be combined into groups and comparisons made at that level. For example, a series of *A-B-A-B* designs could be collapsed into a repeated measures group design (see Redd et al., 1987, for a recent example). Similarly, a series of *A-B* and *A-C* designs could also be examined as a two-group, pre–post design.

We have argued that time-series designs fit well with the clinical environment and can be the basis for the production of new knowledge from clinical settings. But that is not the primary reason to value clinical research at the level of the individual; it is because the proper consumption of clinical knowledge depends on knowledge that is applicable to the individual. We now turn to that topic.

Table 13.1. Examples of the Use of Design Elements to Answer Specific Types of Clinical Questions

CLINICAL QUESTION	DESIGN TYPE		
	WITHIN SERIES	BETWEEN SERIES	COMBINED SERIES
Does a treatment work?	A-B-A-B-.... B-A-B-A-.... A-B (see combined designs) Periodic treatments design Changing criterion design	Alternating treatments (comparing A and B)	Multiple baseline across settings, behaviors, or persons comparing A and B Replicated crossovers (comparing A and B)
Does one treatment work better than another, given that we already know they work?	B-C-B-C-.... C-B-C-B-....	Alternating treatments (comparing B and C)	Replicated crossovers (comparing B and C) Multiple baselines (comparing B and C and controlling for order)
Does one treatment work, does another work, and which works better?	A-B-A-C-A combined with A-C-A-B-A Or combine any element from row A with any element from row B	Alternating treatments (comparing A and B and C)	Multiple baseline (comparing A and B and C and controlling for order)
Are there elements within a successful treatment that make it work?	B-B + C-B B + C-B-B + C C-B + C-C B + C-C-B + C	Alternating treatments (comparing, for example, B and B + C)	Multiple baseline (comparing B and B + C, and C and B + C) Replicated crossovers (comparing B and B + C, and C and B + C)
Does the client prefer one treatment over another?		Simultaneous treatments (comparing B and C)	
Does a treatment work, and if it does, what part of it makes it work?	Combine any elements from rows A or C with any element from row D		
What level of treatment is optimal?	Ascending/descending design B-B'-B-B'	Alternating treatments (comparing B and B')	Multiple baseline (comparing B and B' and controlling for order) Replicated crossovers (comparing B and B')

ROLE OF THE INDIVIDUAL CASE IN THE CONSUMPTION OF CLINICAL KNOWLEDGE

The applicability of findings is a critical issue to the practicing clinician. For practitioners, the ultimate question is (Paul, 1969) which treatment delivered in what way is likely to be most effective for this client with this set of problems and characteristics. We will call this the *clinical question*. The clinical question is fundamentally a question of the external validity of our knowledge, whether that knowledge is based on formal research data, direct clinical experience, reports from the clinical experience of others, or even just common sense.

The consumption of research does not depend solely on the kinds of concerns that are critical to the proper design of an experiment. In the real world, no amount of care in experimental design will ensure that the findings will be relevant, because studies do not possess external validity as a matter of logical necessity (Birnbrauer, 1981).

Group comparison research does promise external validity as an outgrowth of internal validity. This promise, however, cannot be kept, and even if it could, the kind of resulting external validity would be irrelevant to the kind required by the clinical question.

The basis of the claim for external validity as a logical outgrowth of experimental design is random selection and assignment. Suppose we could randomly draw from the population called schizophrenics and then randomly assign these subjects to treatment x, treatment y, or no treatment. We might then be able to say that the particular treatments have particular effects on the population known as schizophrenics. If, furthermore, a new set of patients also constituted a random sample of the population, then one could know at some level of probability that the results would likely apply to those patients, considered as a group. Given all of these requirements, it would be possible to say that an experiment possessed external validity as a matter of logical necessity.

Unfortunately, there are three problems: (a) We are never, or perhaps almost never, able to select randomly from a known population: some clients do not come in for treatment, and we do not have access to all that do; (2) even if we solved the first problem, we cannot force all patients to participate in treatment, much less in research; and (3) even if we could resolve the second problem, the kind of resultant external validity logically applies only to additional random samples from the population, not to nonrandom samples (e.g., only rich clients, or only clients that like

therapist x). The kind of external validity demanded by the clinical question is not the validity of results as applied to other random samples of the population. Clinicians' client loads are not random samples. Clients go to particular clinicians for particular reasons. For these reasons, studies do not possess useful generality by virtue of statistical necessity.

The Intensive Correlational Strategy

If external validity is not a direct result of internal validity, how will answers be developed for the clinical question? One way might be to correlate client and therapist characteristics with improvement. In this way, the relation between characteristics of individual clients and therapists and particular therapeutic activities could be developed (Kazdin, 1981b).

This is a good strategy. It requires refinement, however. First, it can only be efficiently used if our knowledge is based on an intensive analysis of the individual, repeated many times. We will term this the *intensive correlational strategy*. In the typical group comparison study we cannot say which individuals improved because of treatment. Correlations between patient characteristics and treatment outcome will thus necessarily be reduced or distorted because we are relating client characteristics to a mixture of treatment effects and all other sources of variability.

The advantage of the intensive correlational strategy is that variability due to sources other than treatment can be identified at the level of the individual, and thus more reliable rules can be generated that relate particular therapist, patient, and setting characteristics to treatment outcomes. The total number of clients needed may be as large as in group comparison research, however, and because the analyses are more intensive, the total amount of work may be greater. This fact brings us to the second major point about the intensive correlational strategy: As a practical matter it cannot be mounted through the normal channels of funding and conducting research. Most clinical research is conducted by academic clinicians, or those based in research institutes. Much of this research is driven by grants, academic tenure and promotion, and other such considerations.

The intensive correlational strategy requires many intensive analyses. By definition, most of the work should replicate known treatment methods—not develop new ones—or its usefulness in answering the clinical question will be limited. Considered as a whole, an intensive correlational strategy, even in a limited clinical area, would be enormously expensive for a granting institution to undertake. Considered piecemeal, there are few incentives for academic clinicians to mount the program.

Only the practicing clinician has the needed access to clients. Only practicing clinicians can develop the needed numbers of analyses. A properly funded clearinghouse of such information tied to a broad clinical base could begin to develop the needed data base. Thus, while the intensive correlational strategy seems well positioned to help answer the clinical question, it probably is not feasible unless practitioners can be harnessed to it. It is the practical requirements for the consumption of clinical knowledge that provide the best argument for including practitioners in the efforts to produce such knowledge.

Factors to Examine in the Consumption of Clinical Research

In the meantime, how can clinicians consume psychological research? The clinician must attempt to assess the degree to which the functionally important characteristics in one's own situation are the same as those the research presented. Sources of potential functional importance are (a) setting, (b) patient, (c) treatment, (d) therapist, and (e) methodological issues.

Setting

If the piece of research experimentally tested situational differences that might be related to the impact of treatment, these differences can be examined for their similarity to the situation at hand. For example, if it has been shown that a given treatment works better in an inpatient than an outpatient setting, then the clinician should consider this dimension.

It is probably unwise simply to look for research done in the same setting as one's own. This is so for two reasons: First, it may greatly reduce the amount of research that can be examined for relevance to the current situation. Second, the issue is not structural similarity but functional similarity. In the absence of other information, however, findings within the same situation, structurally defined, should be given weight.

Patient Characteristics

If the patients are described in detail, a clinician can examine one's own patients and see if they seem similar in respects that are probably important (or that are known to be important) to treat outcome. It is even better if the study examined whether patient character-

istics were related to treatment outcome. The research is then more relevant if the patient currently under consideration shares the characteristics of those who were treated most successfully.

Unfortunately, most clinical research does not include intensive analyses of individuals, often relying only on group means for the description of results. This kind of research is difficult to consume, for reasons already described. If the results are reported in group form, are there at least percentages of individuals showing the effect reported? Are clinically significant data included? If so, these data can provide a more useful guide to research consumption.

Treatment

The procedures must be described in sufficient detail for clinicians to do what was done in all respects that seem important to treatment outcome. On this basis, much of the clinical literature must be questioned. It also shows most clearly the difference between internal and external validity. Without specification we may know for sure that an effect occurred, but we can only apply it if we know how it was produced (see Cook & Campbell's [1979] description of construct validity).

If the researchers checked on the integrity of their treatment (for example, by having others observe and code the application of the particular procedure or technique, particularly with complicated clinical techniques), its applicability is probably greater. Such specification includes the conditions (therapist, therapy environment) under which treatment was applied.

Therapist

If therapist characteristics are spelled out or are specifically related to clinical outcome, the research should be assumed to be more applicable to the degree that these characteristics are shared. If clinicians have tried out these procedures and achieved similar results, then external validity has already been shown, to a degree.

Methodological Issues

If measures are taken repeatedly across time so that an adequate individual sample is obtained, then the results will probably be more likely to apply to similar clients. If there is not one universally accepted measure, studies that show similar results with several different measures are probably more replicable.

If the results have been replicated, especially by others, external validity is more likely. If the replications are done by several different people in several different settings and if the findings are relatively consistent, then a certain degree of generality has already been shown.

Another important dimension is the strength of results. Researchers often examine the level of statistical significance and forget the magnitude of the effect shown. It seems likely, however, that strong effects will be more generalizable than weak ones.

Most importantly, is the study internally valid? Are competing explanations for the results unlikely? Are the results analyzed correctly? These questions underline the importance of other considerations that are often neglected in discussions of the consumption of research. Only when findings are internally valid will they have any hope of generalizing to other situations.

SUMMARY

In this chapter, we have argued that the nature of clinical psychology puts a fundamental emphasis on the individual for both the consumption and the production of clinical knowledge. Multiple analyses of the individual case should be a major source of clinical knowledge. The logic applied to this effort should be the logic inherent in rules of good clinical practice. By articulating that logic, the dichotomy between case studies and single-case experimental design is replaced by a gradual continuum of certainty of knowledge; the distinction between research and practice turns out to be essentially artificial, and practicing clinicians are legitimized in their role as producers as well as consumers of clinical knowledge.

REFERENCES

Baer, D. M., Wolf, M. M., & Risley, T. R. (1968). Some current dimensions of applied behavior analysis. *Journal of Applied Behavior Analysis, 1*, 91–97.

Barlow, D. H. (1980). Behavior therapy: The next decade. *Behavior Therapy, 11*, 315–328.

Barlow, D. H., & Hayes, S. C. (1979). Alternating treatments design: One strategy for comparing the effects of two treatments in a single subject. *Journal of Applied Behavior Analysis, 12*, 199–210.

Barlow, D. H., Hayes, S. C., & Nelson, R. O. (1984). *The scientist-practitioner: Research and evaluation in clinical and educational settings*. Elmsford, NY: Pergamon Press.

Barlow, D. H., & Hersen, M. (1984). *Single-case experi-* *mental designs: Strategies for studying behavior change* (2nd ed.). Elmsford, NY: Pergamon Press.

Birnbrauer, J. S. (1981) External validity and experimental investigation of individual behavior. *Analysis and Intervention in Developmental Disabilities, 1*, 117–132.

Brownell, K. D., Hayes, S. C., & Barlow, D. H. (1977). Patterns of appropriate and deviant arousal: The behavioral treatment of multiple sexual deviations. *Journal of Consulting and Clinical Psychology, 45*, 1144–1155.

Browning, R. M. (1967). A same-subject design for simultaneous comparison of three reinforcement contingencies. *Behavior Research and Therapy, 5*, 237–243.

Browning, R. M., & Stover, D. O. (1971). *Behavior modification in child treatment: An experimental and clinical approach*. Chicago: Aldine de Gruyter.

Campbell, D. T., & Stanley, J. C. (1963). *Experimental and quasi-experimental designs for research*. Chicago: Rand McNally.

Chassan, J. (1967). *Research design in clinical psychology and psychiatry*. New York: Appleton-Century-Crafts.

Chassan, J. B. (1979). *Research design in clinical psychology and psychiatry*. (2nd ed.). New York: Irvington.

Cook, T. D., & Campbell, D. T. (Eds.). (1979). *Quasi-experimental: Design and analysis issues for field settings*. Chicago: Rand McNally.

Frank, G. (1986). The Boulder model revisited: The training of the clinical psychologist for research. *Psychological Reports, 58*, 579–585.

Garfield, S. L., & Kurtz, R. (1976). Clinical psychologists in the 1970's. *American Psychologist, 31*, 1–9.

Haley, J. (1984). *Ordeal Therapy*. San Francisco: Jossey-Bass.

Harmon, T. M., Nelson, R. O., & Hayes, S. C. (1980). Self-monitoring of mood versus activity by depressed clients. *Journal of Consulting and Clinical Psychology, 48*, 30–38.

Harris, F. N., & Jenson, W. R. (1985). Comparisons of multiple-baseline across persons designs and AB designs with replication: Issues and confusion. *Behavioral Assessment, 7*, 121–129.

Hartmann, D. P., & Hall, R. V. (1976). The changing criterion design. *Journal of Applied Behavior Analysis, 9*, 527–532.

Hayes, S. C. (1981). Single-case experimental design and empirical clinical practice. *Journal of Consulting and Clinical Psychology, 49*, 193–211.

Hayes, S. C. (1985). Natural multiple baselines across persons: A reply to Harris and Jenson. *Behavioral Assessment, 7*, 129–132.

Hayes, S. C., & Barlow, D. H. (1977). Flooding relief in a case of public transportation phobia. *Behavior Therapy, 8*, 742–746.

Hayes, S. C., Hussian, R. A., Turner, A. E., Anderson, N. B., & Grubb, T. D. (1983). The effect of coping statements on progress through a desensitization hierarchy. *Journal of Behavior Therapy and Experimental Psychiatry, 14*, 117–129.

Haynes, S. N., Lemsky, C., & Sexton-Radek, K. (1987). Why clinicians infrequently do research. *Professional Psychology: Research and Practice, 18*, 515–519.

Hersen, M., & Bellack, A. S. (1976). A multiple baseline analysis of social skills training in chronic schizophrenics. *Journal of Applied Behavior Analysis, 9*, 527–532.

Howard, G. S. (1985). Can research in the human sciences become more relevant to practice? *Journal of Counseling and Development, 63*, 539–544.

Howard, G. S. (1986). The scientist-practitioner in counseling psychology: Toward a deeper integration of theory, research, and practice. *The Counseling Psychologist, 14*, 61–105.

Ivanoff, A., Robinson, E. A. R., & Blythe, B. J. (1987). Empirical clinical practice from a feminist perspective. *Social Work, 32*, 417–423.

Jayaratne, S., & Levy, R. L. (1979). *Empirical clinical practice*. New York: Columbia University Press.

Johnston, J. M., & Pennypacker, H. S. (1981). *Strategies and tactics of human behavioral research*. Hillsdale, NJ: Lawrence Erlbaum Associates.

Kazdin, A. E. (1978). Methodological and interpretive problems of single-case experimental designs. *Journal of Consulting and Clinical Psychology, 46*, 629–642.

Kazdin, A. E. (1980). *Research design in clinical psychology*. New York: Harper & Row.

Kazdin, A. E. (1981a). Drawing valid inferences from case studies. *Journal of Consulting and Clinical Psychology, 49*, 183–192.

Kazdin, A. E. (1981b). External validity and single-case experimentation: Issues and limitations (A response to J. S. Birnbrauer). *Analysis and Intervention in Developmental Disabilities, 1*, 133–143.

Kazdin, A. E. (1982). *Single-case research designs: Methods for clinical and applied settings*. New York: Oxford University Press.

Kazdin, A. E., & Hartmann, D. P. (1978). The simultaneous-treatment design. *Behavior Therapy, 9*, 912–922.

Kazdin, A. E., & Kopel, S. A. (1975). On resolving ambiguities of the multiple-baseline design: Problems and recommendations. *Behavior Therapy, 6*, 601–608.

Kelly, E. L., Goldberg, L. R., Fiske, D. W., & Kilkowski, J. M. (1978). Twenty-five years later. *American Psychologist, 33*, 746–755.

Kratochwill, T. F. (1978). *Single-subject research: Strategies for evaluating change*. New York: Academic Press.

Leitenberg, H. (1973). The use of single case methodology in psychotherapy research. *Journal of Abnormal Psychology, 82*, 87–101.

Leitenberg, H. (1974). Training clinical researchers in psychology. *Professional Psychology: Research and Practice, 5*, 59–69.

Levy, L. H. (1962). The skew in clinical psychology. *American Psychologist, 17*, 244–249.

Masters, W. H., & Johnson, V. E. (1970). *Human sexual inadequacy*. Boston: Little Brown.

McGonigle, J. J., Rojahn, J., Dixon, J., & Strain, P. S.

(1987). Multiple treatment interference in the alternating treatments design as a function of the intercomponent interval length. *Journal of Applied Behavior Analysis, 20*, 171–178.

McKnight, D. L., Nelson, R. O., Hayes, S. C., & Jarrett, R. B. (1984). Importance of treating individually-assessed response classes in the amelioration of depression. *Behavior Therapy, 15*, 315–335.

Meehl, P. E. (1971). A scientific, scholarly, non-research doctorate for clinical practitioners: Arguments pro and con. In R. R. Holt (Ed.), *New horizons for psychotherapy: Autonomy as a profession* (pp. 37–54). New York: International Universities Press.

Miller, M. J. (1985). Analyzing client change graphically. *Journal of Counseling and Development, 63*, 491–494.

Nelson, R. O. (1981). Realistic dependent measures for clinical use. *Journal of Consulting and Clinical Psychology, 49*, 168–182.

Paul, G. L. (1969). Behavior modification research: Design and tactics. In C. M. Franks (Ed.), *Behavior therapy: Appraisal and status* (pp. 29–62). New York: McGraw-Hill.

Peterson, D. R. (1976). Need for the doctor of psychology degree in professional psychology. *American Psychologist, 31*, 792–798.

Peterson, D. R. (1985). Twenty years of practitioner training in psychology. *American Psychologist, 40*, 441–451.

Peterson, L., Homer, A. L., & Wonderlich, S. A. (1982). The integrity of independent variables in behavior analysis. *Journal of Applied Behavior Analysis, 15*, 477–492.

Raush, H. L. (1969). Naturalistic method and the clinical approach. In E. P. Willems & H. L. Raush (Eds.), *Naturalistic viewpoints in psychological research* (pp. 122–146). New York: Holt, Rinehart & Winston.

Raush, H. L. (1974). Research, practice, and accountability. *American Psychologist, 29*, 678–681.

Redd, W. H., Jacobsen, P. B., Die-Trill, M., Dermatis, H., McEvoy, M., & Holland, J. C. (1987). Cognitive/attentional distraction in the control of conditioned nausea in pediatric cancer patients receiving chemotherapy. *Journal of Consulting and Clinical Psychology, 55*, 391–395.

Rogers, C. R. (1973). Some new challenges. *American Psychologist, 28*, 379–387.

Shakow, D. (1976). What is clinical psychology? *American Psychologist, 31*, 553–560.

Sidman, M. (1960). *Tactics of scientific research*. New York: Basic Books.

Svenson, S. E., & Chassan, J. B. (1967). A note on ethics and patient consent in single-case design. *Journal of Nervous and Mental Disease, 145*, 206–207.

Thomas, E. J. (1978). Research and service in single-case experimentation: Conflicts and choices. *Social Work Research and Abstracts, 14*, 20–31.

Thomas, E. J., Bastien, J., Stuebe, D. R., Bronson, D. E., & Yaffe, J. (1987). Assessing procedural descriptive-

ness: Rationale and illustrative study. *Behavioral Assess-
    ment, 9,* 43–56.
Wolpe, J. (1958). *Psychotherapy by reciprocal inhibition.*
    Stanford, CA: Stanford University Press.
Yeaton, W. H., & Sechrest, L. (1981). Critical dimensions
    in the choice and maintenance of successful treatments:
Strength, integrity, and effectiveness. *Journal of Con-
    sulting and Clinical Psychology, 49,* 156–167.
Zaro, J. S., Barach, R., Nedelmann, D. J., & Dreiblatt, I. S.
    (1977). *A guide for beginning psychotherapists.* Cam-
    bridge, MA: Cambridge University Press.

CHAPTER 14

EXPERIMENTAL RESEARCH IN CLINICAL PSYCHOLOGY

John F. Kihlstrom
Susan M. McGlynn

Psychopathology, as the branch of psychology concerned with abnormalities in mental functioning, consists of three main branches. Descriptive psychopathology seeks to characterize and organize the symptoms and syndromes of mental illness. Clinical psychopathology attempts to devise effective techniques for their diagnosis, treatment, and prevention. Experimental psychopathology applies the methods and principles of psychological science to understanding their nature and origins. Obviously, the three enterprises are closely related. Without good description, experimentalists do not know what to investigate; and systematic research is predicated on the existence of a reliable and valid diagnostic system, which in turn is based on systematic description. Basic research on the nature and origins of psychopathology will inevitably contribute to a refined diagnostic system, as it uncovers subtle differences among superficially similar syndromes and features that unite categories that seem different on the surface. It should also yield a new generation of assessment devices, more firmly grounded in the paradigms and procedures of modern experimental psychology (Kihlstrom & Nasby, 1981; Nasby & Kihlstrom, 1986). Ultimately, of course, an important aim of experimental psychopathology is to lead to advances in treatment and prevention analogous to those achieved elsewhere in scientific medicine.

Experimental psychopathology has two main components: Laboratory models of psychopathology develop simulations of the symptoms and syndromes of mental illness in subjects who are not otherwise at risk for mental illness, and in nonhuman animals; research on psychological deficits studies defects in the functioning of basic psychological processes that presumably account for abnormal and maladaptive patterns of experience, thought, and action. The purpose of the present chapter is to give a brief overview of both lines of experimental research on psychopathology and to suggest directions for future activity.

This chapter is based in part on a review commissioned by the Senior Consultants Panel, Behavioral Sciences and Mental Health Review, National Institute of Mental Health (Kihlstrom, 1983). Preparation of this paper was supported in part by Grants #MH-35856 and #MH-44739 from the National Institute of Mental Health.

LABORATORY MODELS OF PSYCHOPATHOLOGY

Laboratory models of psychopathology attempt to create, in otherwise normal individuals, conditions resembling various psychopathological states. These models are rarely exact replicas of naturally occurring mental illness, but rather represent a laboratory phenomenon, or cluster of phenomena, that mimics a particular syndrome or symptom. In a sense, a laboratory model is a formal theory of mental illness, in that it assumes that the causal agents manipulated in the laboratory somehow parallel those that operate in the real world; and that the laboratory phenomenon can be analyzed to suggest hypotheses about previously unobserved features of the clinical syndrome, and employed to test proposals for treatment and prevention.

In an important paper, Abramson and Seligman (1977) listed the standards against which any laboratory model of psychopathology should be evaluated. Such models should, first and foremost, preserve the essential features of the symptom or syndrome observed in the clinic. That is, a proper laboratory model of phobia, depression, or schizophrenia would produce symptoms in normal subjects that parallel those observed in diagnosed patients.

This requirement presents a serious problem for the erstwhile modeler, because it is not always clear what the essential symptoms are. Psychiatric diagnoses traditionally have been construed in terms of the classical view of categorization: that a diagnostic category may be defined by the singly necessary and jointly sufficient features that define a proper set (Cantor & Genero, 1986; Cantor, Smith, French, & Mezzich, 1980). Thus, a patient might have to present with each of Bleuler's (1911/1950) "four As" (associative disturbance, anhedonia, autism, and ambivalence) in order to be labeled schizophrenic; and any patient presenting these four symptoms would be labeled schizophrenic, regardless of any other presenting symptoms. In contrast, Cantor and her colleagues (1980) argued cogently that the diagnostic categories are fuzzy sets of features that are correlated with, but not singly necessary or jointly sufficient for, category membership. The principal result of this situation is considerable heterogeneity among category members, such that they are related by family resemblance more than any set of common defining features. That is, Schizophrenic A may have some symptoms in common with Schizophrenic B, and B may have some symptoms in common with Schizophrenic C, but A and C might have no features in common.

Heterogeneity within syndromes is a fact of diagnostic life, at least for the major psychoses such as schizophrenia and affective disorder, and it wreaks havoc with the laboratory modeling enterprise. Unless we know the essential features of a syndrome, we can hardly try to reproduce those features in the laboratory. One solution to this problem is to forswear any attempt to model syndromes of psychopathology, but to model specific symptoms such as thought disorder or hallucinations instead (Costello, 1970). This solves the problem of within-category heterogeneity of features but raises the question of the degree to which superficially similar symptoms are in fact identical across syndromes. For example, hallucinations are common features in schizophrenia, depression, and organic brain syndrome, but it is not at all clear that an adequate laboratory model of one would serve as a satisfactory explanation of the other.

Whether the investigator is modeling single symptoms or whole syndromes, Abramson and Seligman (1977) argued further that a proper laboratory model of psychopathology must also demonstrate commonalities with the clinical phenomenon in terms of causes, cures, and preventative strategies. For example, the experimental manipulations known to produce the laboratory model should have their counterparts in the life histories of clinical patients. If one is to adopt a classical conditioning model of phobia, one had better find evidence of aversive conditioning experiences in the lives of phobics. Similarly, effective treatment regimens ought to be predicted by experimental manipulations that successfully reverse the laboratory model. Finally, there should be similarities in terms of underlying biological structures and processes. If certain genetic or hormonal factors mediate the response of experimental subjects to the independent variables, the same factors should be involved in the vulnerability of patients at risk for true psychopathology.

Few laboratory models, if any, would meet all of these standards. In fact, Abramson and Seligman (1977) argued cogently that many of the classic laboratory models—such as Masserman's (1943) and Maier's (1949) studies of frustration and conflict, Watson and Rayner's (1920) case of Little Albert, Osmond and Smithies's (1952) proposed mescaline models of psychosis—are not at all compelling when subjected to close scrutiny. Aside from the limitations of any particular research program, Abramson and Seligman (1977) argued that the success of the laboratory modeling enterprise in general is constrained by three considerations: (a) Ethical considerations, especially (though not exclusively) as applied to models developed in human subjects, may prevent the production of full-blown symptoms and syndromes in otherwise undisturbed individuals; (b) even given an exhaustive description of some symptom or syndrome of psychopathology, the experimenter may not have any idea how to produce it in the laboratory; and (c) most laboratory models, as will be seen, are developed on nonhuman animal subjects—thus effectively precluding the expression through language of the cognitive and experiential symptoms that are some of the most central features of psychopathology.

Nevertheless, this state of affairs has not prevented a large number of investigators from pursuing the laboratory modeling approach in the study of a wide variety of conditions, ranging from phobia to schizophrenia (for authoritative reviews of many major lines of investigation, see Maser & Seligman, 1977). Laboratory models have the advantage over other experimental approaches to psychopathology because, at least in principle, they can go beyond the description of the psychological differences between patients and nonpatients and get at issues of cause. In this section, we provide brief sketches of some of the more salient of these attempts.

Experimental Neurosis

In a historical sense, perhaps the most prominent laboratory model of psychopathology is the work on experimental neurosis initiated in Pavlov's (1927) laboratory and continued by others (for overviews, see Mineka & Kihlstrom, 1978; Thomas & Dewald, 1977). Following Pavlov's (1927) classic report, other experimenters successfully induced neurotic behavioral disorders in a wide variety of animals (sheep, goats, pigs, and cats as well as dogs) by means of a wide variety of procedures: difficult discriminations, variable intervals, and punishment of appetitive responses. These and other procedures (see Mineka & Kihlstrom, 1978, for fuller descriptions) generally led to the replacement of some previously adaptive response, innate or acquired, by some uncharacteristic behavior (hypersensitivity, howling, rapid respiration, piloerection, muscular tension, mydriasis; or passivity, lethargy, and anorexia), often accompanied by signs of autonomic arousal. In other words, the behavioral consequences of experimental neurosis roughly paralleled the symptoms of anxiety and depression.

While the various procedures used to induce experimental neurosis have a number of consequences in common, it has proved difficult to find any common thread that runs through these demonstrations that could explain the effects. Mineka and Kihlstrom (1978) proposed that in each case, environmental

events of vital importance to the organism (e.g., obtaining food or escaping shock) become unpredictable, uncontrollable, or both. Their reanalysis of the classic demonstrations of experimental neurosis showed that many of the phenomena of experimental neurosis are mirrored in the behavioral effects of unpredictable and/or uncontrollable shock (see also Thomas & Dewald, 1977), and that important elements of unpredictability and/or uncontrollability could be found in the procedures employed in the classic investigations. Interestingly, anxiety has often been related to the occurrence of unpredictable events, while depression has been related to learned helplessness and the lack of control (Alloy, Kelly, Mineka & Clements, 1989; Mineka & Kelly, 1989). Thus, although the commonalities between experimental and human neurosis are far from perfect at the level of symptoms, there are salient parallels between the apparent sources of experimental neuroses and factors presumed to be of causative significance in the clinical syndromes.

Phobias, Obsessions, Compulsions, and Anxiety

Another historically prominent modeling enterprise has been concerned with fears, phobias, and other aspects of anxiety (Marks, 1969, 1987; Rachman, 1978; Rachman & Hodgson, 1980; Wolpe, 1958). This line of research has its origins in the work on experimental neurosis just described and also in the classic case of Little Albert described by Watson and Rayner (1920; for critiques of both the case and subsequent accounts of it, see Harris, 1979; Samelson, 1980). Conventional thought in this area equated phobias with classically conditioned fear responses and compulsions with avoidance responses, while anxiety states were attributed to generalization of fear conditioning. The model was extremely heuristic—it led directly to the development of systematic desensitization and flooding (implosion) therapies (for example, Yates, 1970), but recent work has added several layers of theoretical sophistication (Mineka, 1985a, 1985b, 1987).

Mineka (1985a, 1987) provided the most thorough statement and analysis of the animal models of phobias, obsessive-compulsive disorders, and generalized anxiety states; for reasons of space, we limit our discussion to phobias. Mineka (1985a) argued, at the outset, that any model of anxiety-based disorders must confront the apparent fact that fear, whether normal or pathological, has three aspects—cognitive, behavioral, and psychophysiological—that are at least partly dissociable (Lang, 1968; Rachman, 1978).

Nevertheless, she cogently argued that recent work on fear conditioning and avoidance in rats and monkeys forms the basis for an animal model of phobia that successfully encompasses symptomatology, etiology, maintenance, and therapy.

To begin with, Mineka (1985a) noted that simple classical conditioning models of phobia—in which a phobic object, such as an animal, serves as a conditioned stimulus (CS) for an aversive unconditioned stimulus (US), such as an animal bite—fail because of the simple fact that phobias are notoriously difficult to extinguish, whereas most classically conditioned fears extinguish over a moderate number of trials. On this ground alone, avoidance learning would seem to fare somewhat better. Unfortunately, as Seligman (1971) noted, phobics avoid the CS, while animals in avoidance situations avoid the US, and there have been few if any successful attempts to train them to avoid the CS. These and other considerations have prompted a return to a fear-conditioning model of phobia, but with two important revisions. First, the selectivity of phobias is accounted for by the concept of preparedness (Seligman, 1971), in which the most common phobic objects are seen as representing a class of stimuli that were dangerous to our evolutionary forebears. Finally, the fact that many phobics apparently lack a history of traumatic experience with their phobic objects—perhaps the most serious difficulty with conditioning models (Jacobs & Nadel, 1985)—is accounted for in terms of observational and vicarious conditioning.

Mineka's (1985a, 1985b, 1987) own work on fear conditioning provides the best example of the model in action. She begins with the fact that fear of snakes in wild-reared rhesus monkeys is intense, persistent, and difficult to modify. Although such a fear would seem to be natural and thus innate, rhesus monkeys reared under ordinary laboratory conditions show no significant fear of snakes: Thus, snake fear appears to be acquired through experience. Of course, it would not be too difficult to show that monkeys that are bitten by vipers or squeezed by pythons fear snakes subsequently. Much more interestingly, in an elegant series of studies, Mineka (1987) and her colleagues showed that fear of snakes can be acquired quickly by laboratory monkeys solely on the basis of observing a wild-reared counterpart react fearfully to an objectively harmless snake. Moreover, when the lab-reared animals were given 12 sessions of implosion therapy, they quickly became able to reach past the snake to grasp food. Despite this reduction in one component of fear, however, the animals continued to show other signs of gross behavioral disturbance.

Thus, animal models of phobic disorder seem to be a particularly promising experimental vehicle for asking questions about the origins, maintenance, and treatment of psychopathology. There are unresolved questions about social phobias and agoraphobia, but overall the line of research has proved productive. Unfortunately, as Mineka (1985a) noted, analogous models for the remaining anxiety-based disorders have not received much attention (Beck & Emery, 1985; Dollard & Miller, 1950; Eysenck, 1979; Eysenck & Rachman, 1965). Avoidance appears to provide a good start for obsessive-compulsive behavior (Carr, 1974; Teasdale, 1974; but for a more thoroughly cognitive approach see Reed, 1985), while the experimental neurosis literature lays the basis for an analysis of anxiety disorder (Mineka & Kelly, 1989), but work in both areas has only just begun.

Hysteria and Hypnosis

Laboratory models of psychopathology are not limited to experiments involving nonhuman animals. For example, another historically important laboratory model of psychopathology has been offered by hypnosis (Kihlstrom, 1979). Hypnosis is a social interaction in which one person (the subject) responds to suggestions offered by another person (the hypnotist) for various kinds of imaginative experiences. In the classical instance, as represented by the responses of highly hypnotizable individuals, these experiences are accompanied by a degree of subjective conviction bordering on delusion (Kihlstrom & Hoyt, 1988) and feelings of involuntariness bordering on compulsion. Thus, two of the cardinal phenomena of hypnosis are also important symptions of psychopathology—thus creating the rationale for hypnosis as a laboratory model of certain forms of mental illness.

In the late 19th and early 20th centuries, clinical and experimental interest in hypnosis was largely motivated by the apparent similarities between its phenomena and the symptoms of hysteria (for a detailed history, see Ellenberger, 1970; Perry & Laurence, 1984). Both states involve subjectively compelling disruptions and anomalies in conscious awareness and control—blindness, deafness, amnesia, paralysis, compulsive automatisms, and the like—in the absence of any evidence of brain insult, injury, or disease. The fact that phenomena closely resembling hysterical symptomatology could be induced in (selected) normal subjects, simply by means of the hypnotist's spoken word, led Janet, Freud, and others to propose psychogenic theories of hysteria as correctives to the somatogenic view that had prevailed up to the time of Charcot, and to develop a wide variety of "talking cures" for its treatment.

More recently, hypnosis has been employed as a vehicle for experimental research on divisions in consciousness and the relations between conscious and nonconscious mental processes that seem to be involved in hysteria (Hilgard, 1977; Kihlstrom, 1984, 1987, 1989, 1990a, 1990b). For example, hysterical patients frequently give evidence of intact perception and memory, in apparent contradiction to their presenting complaints. Thus, a patient might claim to be blind yet navigate successfully around an unfamiliar room (Sackeim, Nordlie, & Gur, 1979) or claim a loss of identity while simultaneously displaying personal knowledge. Similar contradictions occur in hypnosis. For example, subjects experiencing hypnotic analgesia nevertheless may show unaltered psychophysiological responses to painful stimuli, and amnesic subjects commonly show intact priming effects of their forgotten experiences. While such paradoxes have sometimes been taken as evidence that both hysterical and hypnotic subjects are engaged in role enactment (Sarbin & Coe, 1979), more recent experimental analyses have linked both states to a broad range of phenomena of implicit cognition, in which certain aspects of perception, memory, thought, learning, and action are dissociated from phenomenal awareness (Kihlstrom, 1987, 1989, 1990b). This experimental research, in turn, suggests a common mechanism underlying functional disorders of memory, sensory-perceptual, and motor function—a suggestion which, if proved correct, would indicate that the conversion disorders classified by *The Diagnostic and Statistical Manual of Mental Disorders, Third Edition, Revised* (DSM-III-R) as somatoform in nature are more properly regarded as a subcategory of dissociative disorder (Kihlstrom, 1990a).

PSYCHOLOGICAL DEFICIT IN PSYCHOPATHOLOGY

The study of psychological deficits has a long tradition, beginning with the studies by Jung on word associations, Kraepelin on continuous performance, Shakow on attention, and Goldstein on concept attainment. The classic review of studies of psychological deficit by Hunt and Cofer (1944) indicates that by midcentury a great variety of procedures familiar to academic experimental psychologists had been applied to clinical patients, covering such diverse topics as sensory thresholds, perceptual processes reaction time, reflex functions, eye movements, motor performance, word associations, startle response, conditioning, memory, language, and thought. This tradition continued after the war, and the vast amount of research in this area was authoritatively summarized by Buss (1966), Maher (1966), Costello (1970), and Yates (1966, 1970). With the exception of a few systematic programs of inquiry (e.g., Eysenck, 1955; Lindsley & Skinner, 1954; Wishner, 1955), however, it seems fair to say that experimental psychopathology in that era was guided more by phenomena than by theory. Investigators were concerned with differences between patients and nonpatients in performance on psychological tasks, but these tasks seem to have been selected almost arbitrarily, with little theoretical motivation and little effort expended in linking the positive findings in one domain with those in others.

What was needed was an overarching theoretical conception of psychological functions that would link a variety of findings and direct research toward fundamental rather than peripheral topics. This goal came into view with the formal emergence of cognitive psychology, which for the first time brought diverse studies of attention, perception, learning, memory, thought, and language under a single rubric—the information-processing approach (e.g., Atkinson & Shiffrin, 1968; Newell & Simon, 1972). Within a few years, from 1967 to 1973, this model became widely accepted within academic experimental psychology and began to filter down to clinical psychology to guide the work of experimental psychopathologists. Emblematic of this transition is the review of psychological deficits in schizophrenia by Chapman and Chapman (1973a), which devoted most of its pages to classical approaches but included a chapter on information processing. Only 6 years later, a whole book appeared on the latter topic, in which the earlier approaches received hardly a mention (Matthysse, Spring & Sugarman, 1979). A similar shift is apparent in research on depression. Before 1967, depression was generally considered to be a purely emotional disorder, involving as it does dysphoria as its primary symptom, and studies of cognitive deficits were largely nonexistent (Miller, 1975). However, the work of Beck (1967) and Seligman (1975) drew attention to the cognitive deficits characteristic of depressed patients, opening up a whole new line of inquiry on perception and cognition in the affective disorders (Ingram & Reed, 1986). For a further treatment of developments in information-processing theory and their implications for experimental psychopathology, see Kihlstrom (1983) and Ingram (1986).

Schizophrenia

As suggested earlier, the longest and most vigorously pursued line of research on psychological deficit has focused on schizophrenia (for reviews, see Chapman & Chapman, 1973a; Magaro, 1980; Matthysse et al., 1979; Neale & Oltmanns, 1980; Nuechterlein & Dawson, 1984; Oltmanns & Neale, 1982; Saccuzzo, 1986; Schwartz, 1978, 1982; Spaulding & Cole, 1984; Widlocher & Hardy-Doyle, 1989). Much of this research has focused on problems of language and communication, since that is how schizophrenic thought disorder typically manifests itself (Kasanin, 1944). Using tasks derived from experimental psycholinguistics, the nature of schizophrenic language might be analyzed for various hypothesized phonological, syntactic, and semantic deficits (for reviews, see Maher, 1972; Schwartz, 1978, 1982). Thus, for example, schizophrenics might experience difficulties in the organization and production of speech, in the application of grammatical rules, in the network of associations making up semantic memory, or in the use of context to comprehend ambiguous utterances. Although it is the universal experience of clinicians that it is difficult to communicate with schizophrenics—Kraepelin (1896) referred to their language problem as "schizophasia"—the results of formal studies have largely failed to reveal any uniform deficits in language processing (e.g., Schwartz, 1982).

This is not to suggest that everything is all right with schizophrenic cognition. However, Schwartz (1982) and many other investigators have proposed that the locus of psychological deficit in schizophrenia lies at some other aspect of the cognitive system. Such a deficit, it is argued, would in turn account for the manifest disorders in thinking and language observed in schizophrenia. Much of this research on schizophrenic information processing has been inspired by McGhie and Chapman's (1961) classic interview study, which underscored the problems experienced by schizophrenics in deploying and maintaining selective attention and has been more or less explicitly based on a generic multistore model of information processing. In this model, information flows between various storage structures (sensory registers, primary memory, secondary memory), in the process of which it is subject to various manipulations and transformations subjected by various control processes (e.g., pattern recognition, attention, rehearsal). Thus, appropriately designed experimental tasks could, in principle, detect selective deficits in the operation of one or more storage structures and control processes.

A good example of this sort of research is an experiment by Saccuzzo, Hirt, and Spencer (1974) employing a backward-masking paradigm to study information-processing speed (for a review, see Saccuzzo, 1986). In their experiment, subjects were presented with a visual array of 16 letters and then asked to report which of two targets had been presented in the matrix. Presentation of the array was followed by a meaningless masking stimulus, used to control the amount of time a representation of the array was held in iconic memory. By varying the interval between array and mask, Saccuzzo et al. (1974) were able to show that schizophrenics read information out of iconic memory and into primary memory more slowly than controls. Other results from their study indicated that schizophrenics' iconic memories may be degraded to begin with and persist longer than those of normals.

Subsequent research by Knight and his colleagues, using similar sorts of paradigms, clarified the role of schizophrenic subtype (e.g., good vs. poor premorbid adjustment) in the experiment of Saccuzzo et al. (1974) and identified a further problem at the stage of primary memory (Knight, Elliott, & Freedman, 1985; for a review, see Knight, 1984). They showed that poor premorbid schizophrenics gave similar responses to pattern and cognitive masks, while normals and good premorbid schizophrenics responded differently to them (depending on the interval between array and mask). The entire pattern of results indicates that the principal difficulty in schizophrenics' visual information processing is not at the level of the icon per se, or even in readout from the icon, but rather in certain automatic perceptual processes interposed between iconic and short-term visual memory. This deficit in perceptual organization may, in turn, be responsible for some of the problems apparent in schizophrenic speech and language (Knight & Sims-Knight, 1982); somewhat paradoxically, it also leads to superior performance by schizophrenics on tasks (e.g., judgments of numerosity) where the operation of these organizational processes (e.g., gestalt principles of similarity or proximity) cause poor performance in normals (Place & Gilmore, 1980).

Affective Disorder

In contrast to the long history of experimental studies of schizophrenia, the affective disorders have been much less frequently studied from the perspective of psychological deficit. In the earliest review of this literature, Miller (1975) attributed this state of affairs to a general tendency to construe depression as a disorder of emotion rather than cognition and a corresponding belief that depressives would show few performance deficits on the kinds of affectively neutral perceptual, cognitive, and motor tasks studied in schizophrenia. Nevertheless, Miller (1975) did find evidence of psychological deficit in severe, mild, and subclinical forms of affective disorder.

The wide acceptance of Schacter and Singer's (1962) cognitive-attributional theory of emotion, coupled with the publication of Beck's (1967) seminal monograph on depression, changed this situation considerably. Schachter and Singer argued that emotional states were cognitively constructed, while Beck argued that specific modes of thought predisposed individuals to depressive forms of mental illness. The next decade saw the progressive evolution of helplessness and hopelessness theories of depression in the hands of Seligman, Abramson, Alloy, and their associates (e.g., Abramson & Sackeim, 1977; Abramson, Seligman, & Teasdale, 1978; Abramson, Metalsky, & Alloy, 1988; Mineka, 1982; Seligman, 1975), plus a growing appreciation of the reciprocal effects of depression on cognitive processes in memory and thought (e.g., Bower, 1981; Ellis & Ashbrook, 1988; Isen, 1984; Kuiken, 1989; Mayer, 1986; Singer & Salovey, 1988; Tobias, Schacter, & Kihlstrom, 1990). Thus, either because cognitive processes influenced mood, or mood influenced cognitive processes, or both, it has made sense to search for psychological deficits among patients with affective disorder (Alloy, 1988; Blaney, 1977; Coyne & Gotlib, 1983; Ingram & Reed, 1986; Miller, 1975).

In contrast to most work in schizophrenia, much recent research has focused on identifying various cognitive styles, as opposed to deficits per se, that may be characteristic of depression. For example, Abramson, Alloy, Seligman, and their colleagues have identified a tendency for depressives, or normals at risk for depression, to make global, stable attributions concerning the causes of important negative life events, despite the actual pattern of consensus, consistency, and distinctiveness information available to them (e.g., Metalsky, Halberstadt, & Abramson, 1987; Peterson & Seligman, 1984). Such a pattern is depressogenic in that it predisposes the person to react in a depressive manner to the occurrence of negative life events or the absence of positive ones: It is the diathesis, which when combined with a negative event stressor leads to depression. When the person is also disposed to make internal causal attributions, the depression is accompanied by lowered self-esteem. Of course, nondepressives also show attributional biases, as evidenced by the fundamental attribution error (Nisbett & Ross, 1980; Ross, 1977), so it is not proper to consider depressives' errors as evidence of a psychological deficit.

Moreover, some research has identified aspects of performance in which depressives are, at least in some

sense, superior to normals. A good example is the assessment of covariation between events (Crocker, 1981). Alloy and Abramson (1979) compared depressed and nondepressive subjects on a task in which button-pressing behavior sometimes, but not always, led to the illumination of a light. Both Beck's (1967) cognitive theory and the original learned-helplessness theory of depression predict that depressives would underestimate the covariation between act and outcome. In fact, depressives proved to be more accurate than nondepressives. The finding has been replicated under a number of different conditions (Alloy & Tabachnik, 1984) and has given rise to the concept of depressive realism: While normal individuals may be subject to an illusion of predictability and control, depressives accurately perceive when events are random and uncontrollable—thus, in some sense depressives are sadder but wiser than their nondepressed counterparts.

No fully satisfactory theoretical account of depressive realism has yet been proposed (Alloy & Abramson, 1988; Kayne & Alloy, 1988). The phenomenon may reflect merely an inability of current laboratory paradigms to capture the cognitive distortions and errors suffered by depressives. Alternatively, depressives, far from possessing specific depressogenic schemata (Beck, 1967), may lack certain organized cognitive structures that promote the illusion of control and predictability in normals and that protect normals from depression. In any event, psychological deficit in depression appears to pose a paradox: Whereas schizophrenics appear to be more vulnerable than normals to certain distortions and errors, depressives are less prone to them. In other words, the psychological deficit in depressives may be that they lack precisely the biases and distortions that keep the rest of us sane.

The development of cognitive models of depression, and the corresponding revival of inquiry on psychological deficits in the affective disorders, has stimulated new developments in treatment (e.g., Beck, 1976; Mahoney, 1974; Meichenbaum, 1977). Moreover, as with laboratory models of hysteria, research on psychological deficits in depression has laid the foundation for revisions in diagnosis. Thus, Abramson et al. (1988) have postulated the existence of a "hopelessness subtype" (p. 43) of depression. Thus, feelings of hopelessness are held to be sufficient, but not necessary, to cause depression; but when such feelings occur, they will necessarily lead to a specific form of depression whose characteristic symptoms, prognosis, and preferred treatment may be quite different from other forms of depression that may have other proximal causes. The reasoning is not tautological, any more than it is to assert that hypothyroidism is a necessary but not sufficient cause of mental retardation and that when hypothyroidism occurs it will lead to the specific syndrome of cretinism.

Linking Laboratory Models with Psychological Deficits: The Case of Psychopathy

Research on psychopathy, or antisocial personality disorder, illustrates how the development of a convincing laboratory model of psychopathology can breathe new life into studies of psychological deficit and how studies of psychological deficit can influence both the classification of psychopathology and our understanding of normal mental processes. The enduring tendency of psychopaths to engage in antisocial behavior, and their persistent failure to respond to punishment, led to extensive research comparing psychopaths and controls on measures of response to aversive stimulation, avoidance learning and punishment, psychophysiological arousal, and the like (for reviews, see Hare, 1970; Hare & Schalling, 1978). All of this work was in the classic pattern of psychological deficit research and seemed to implicate some sort of deficit in the arousal system—either underarousal or an enhanced ability to modulate arousal.

Somewhat later, Gorenstein and Newman (1980) noted the strong similarities between the behavior of psychopaths and that of rats with lesions in the septal area. Thus, animals with septal lesions do not freeze when punished; although they do not show a generalized learning deficit, they are rather poor at passive avoidance and delay of gratification; they show a steep temporal gradient of fear arousal and have difficulty acquiring conditioned fear responses. In short, these animals show performance deficits where they are required to suppress or alter habitual responses in order to avoid aversive consequences: They are impulsive. Without specifically proposing that psychopaths suffer brain damage in the limbic system, these investigators used the septal animal model to generate both an alternative theoretical explanation of psychopathic personality and an innovative line of empirical research.

The parallels between psychopathic humans and septal animals offer two alternative possibilities for research: testing psychopaths for behavioral patterns characteristic of septal animals, and testing septal animals for patterns characteristic of psychopaths. Newman and his associates have pursued the former

line of inquiry in an extensive series of studies (for a review, see Patterson & Newman, 1987). This research shows that the characteristic behavior of psychopathic individuals results not from any lack of arousal, but rather from an emotional response to frustration, especially in mixed-motive situations. When the appetitive behavior of nonpsychopathic individuals is interrupted by an aversive event, their most likely response is to pause and collect information about the changed situation. By contrast, psychopathic individuals respond to the changed circumstances with increased effort, which effectively prohibits such reflectivity. One prediction is that psychopaths can learn to modulate their behavior if forced to pause and reflect on its consequences, and research by Newman's group indicates that this is so.

Based on this approach, Patterson and Newman (1987; see also Newman, 1987) proposed that the entries in DSM-III-R may hide a heretofore unrecognized group of syndromes of disinhibition, just as other clusters of syndromes are organized around themes of schizophrenia, depression, and anxiety. Such a category might include, in addition to psychopathy, borderline personality disorder, attention deficit disorder, histrionic personality disorder, somatization disorders, early onset alcoholism, and the current miscellaneous category of disorders of impulse control not otherwise classified (e.g., pathological gambling and kleptomania). These syndromes of psychopathology are linked to normal personality features such as Type A personality and extraversion by an underlying proneness to disinhibition. Evidence in support of this proposal comes from studies showing that normal extraverts and hyperactive children respond in a manner similar to psychopaths on a variety of experimental tasks—tasks derived, at the outset, from behavioral studies of rats with septal lesions. Thus, work in experimental psychopathology, drawing on studies of both laboratory models and psychological deficits, has had an impact on the organization of descriptive and clinical psychopathology.

Problem of Differential Deficit

One problem that stands in the way of progress in investigating psychological deficits in psychopathology is the diagnostic system itself. Despite advances in the rigor and reliability of the diagnostic process, the nosological categories remain heterogeneous. There is little at the level of the observable symptom that unites one schizophrenic or manic depressive with another (Cantor et al., 1980; Cantor & Genero, 1986).

Without a diagnostic system for reliably segregating cases of psychopathology into distinct, relatively homogeneous categories, there will be too much noise in the data to permit firm conclusions about the nature of the disorders in mental functioning implicated in clinical psychopathology.

Even with fairly homogeneous diagnostic categories, however, and reliable procedures for sorting patients into them, the study of psychological deficit is plagued by a subtle but thorny problem: the discriminating power of tests of psychological deficit (Chapman & Chapman, 1973b, 1978). As Chapman and Chapman (1973b) noted, the favored paradigm in studies of psychological deficit involves documenting differential deficits (this is sometimes called the logic of dissociation; see Schacter & Tulving, 1982). In the simplest exemplar of this logic, two groups—for example, schizophrenics and normals—are compared on two different tests of mental performance, such as digit span forward and backward. Assume that the two groups are found to differ on digits backward but not on digits forward—a standard two-way interaction. Under ordinary circumstances, the temptation would be to conclude that schizophrenics suffer a deficit in whatever underlying psychological process is known or presumed to differentiate between the two tasks. Thus, it might be concluded that schizophrenics have a deficit in attention but not in short-term memory capacity.

The problem with this logic is that differences in task performance depend not only on differences between groups in mental ability but also on differences between tests in discriminating power. The discriminating power of mental tests, in turn, is determined by such factors as their mean item difficulties, the dispersion of item difficulties around the mean, the number of items, and their average covariance. If the two tests in question are not matched on these psychometric properties, any group differences observed may well be artifactual. This is because patients with major psychopathology generally show generalized cognitive deficits—that is, they score lower than nonpatients on almost any cognitive test. Such subjects must show greater performance deficits on the more discriminating tests, regardless of the actual presence of differential psychological deficits, even if they are actually equivalent on the abilities measured by the tests in question. In principle, any finding of differential deficit (such as the foregoing comparison between digits forward and digits backward) could be reversed simply by altering the properties of the tests in question.

A similar problem arises in a variant on the differential deficit design, in which two groups are administered two tests, each under two conditions manipulated by the experimenter. Thus, to extend the preceding example, tests of digit span forward and backward might be administered under two levels of ambient noise level. If so, a triple interaction might be found such that schizophrenics and normals differ on digits forward under high- but not low-noise conditions, and that the group difference on digits backward is exacerbated by high noise levels. Unfortunately, the manipulation of any experimental variable that affects accuracy will yield a greater performance deficit on the more discriminating test, even though there is no effect on the specific mental ability presumably tapped by the test.

Chapman and Chapman (1973b) argued that these problems cannot be corrected by any obvious statistical means, such as analysis of covariance or the use of residualized error scores. Nor can the direction of the artifact be predicted in advance, such that conservative tests could be devised. The only guaranteed solution to the problem is extensive pretesting, using a standardization sample of normal subjects with widely varying abilities, to match the tests in question in terms of reliability, difficulty, and number of items. Given tests that are equivalent on these psychometric properties, the possibility of statistical artifact may be ruled out, and any group differences in test scores or effects of experimental manipulations can be safely attributed to differential psychological deficits.

The problem of discriminating power, and its solution, is nicely illustrated in a classic study by Oltmanns and Neale (1975) on digit span. It was already known that schizophrenics perform worse than normals on such short-term memory tasks, and the deficit is especially severe under distracting conditions. However, almost by definition, a task performed under conditions of distraction is more difficult than the same task performed alone—so the interaction is difficult to interpret in terms of schizophrenics' differential vulnerability to distraction rather than overall cognitive inefficiency. Oltmanns and Neale (1975) found through pretesting with normals that a five-digit distractor task and a six-digit control task were equally difficult, as were a six-digit distractor task and seven- or eight-digit control tasks (recall that the capacity of short-term memory is approximately seven items). Comparing schizophrenics and nonschizophrenics on the six-digit control and distractor tasks, they found the usual interaction. However, the interaction disappeared when the six-digit neutral task was compared to the difficulty-matched five-digit distractor task, raising the problem of differential difficulty. Evidence of differential deficit was obtained only when the six-digit distractor task was compared to the seven- and eight-digit neutral task. The overall pattern of results confirmed a differential vulnerability to distraction among schizophrenics, but the conditions under which the interaction was obtained indicated that the locus of the attentional difficulty was at the stage of memory encoding rather than sensory-perceptual processing. In the present context, the point is that neither of these conclusions would have been legitimate without careful matching of experimental and control tasks.

Unfortunately, more than a decade after Chapman and Chapman (1973b) drew attention to this problem, many investigators in the field of psychopathology, mental retardation, child development, aging, and neuropsychology continue to draw conclusions concerning differential deficits based on tests that have not been properly equated for discriminating power. The appropriate corrective measures are expensive and time consuming, but failure to employ them poses a serious threat to the validity of conclusions from experimental results.

COGNITIVE NEUROPSYCHOLOGY AND PSYCHOPATHOLOGY

Cognitive neuropsychology represents the merging of two previously distinct subdisciplines within psychology, cognitive psychology and neuropsychology, and has flourished as a scientific enterprise in its own right over the past 15 years. According to Ellis and Young (1988), the two main goals of cognitive neuropsychology are (a) to account for patterns of impaired and preserved cognitive performance in terms of disruption to particular components of an information processing theory or model; and (b) to increase our knowledge of normal cognitive processes based on the patterns of cognitive deficits and intact abilities observed in brain-damaged patients. We propose that the conceptual framework of cognitive neuropsychology may serve as a useful model for investigating and interpreting the psychological deficits observed in various psychopathological populations. In this section we will briefly review the basic concepts and assumptions of cognitive neuropsychology, describe examples from the cognitive neuropsychological literature, and discuss potential applications of this model to the study of psychological deficit in psychopathology.

An important concept in cognitive neuropsychology is the dissociation of a specific process or function from another. For example, if a brain-injured patient has severe difficulty reading words but exhibits intact writing abilities, we may conclude that there is a dissociation between reading and writing. In other words, there appear to be different cognitive processes involved in reading and writing words that permit differential disruption of the two functions. An even more convincing argument for this kind of conclusion is derived from a double dissociation. That is, if in addition to observing cases where reading is impaired but writing is intact, we find individuals who exhibit preserved reading ability in the presence of impaired writing, we would have a much stronger case for concluding that the two tasks involve different cognitive processes.

Dissociations are generally interpreted within a modular framework for the mind (see Fodor, 1983; Marr, 1982). This view of cognitive organization suggests that multiple cognitive processors or modules operate relatively independently; hence, any particular module can theoretically malfunction in isolation without affecting other modules in the total cognitive system. Furthermore, modules are considered to be impenetrable by higher order influences such as beliefs, motivations, and expectations. This property of modules has been referred to by Fodor (1983) as informational encapsulation. For example, there may be a group of modules responsible for different aspects of object recognition, another group involved in facial recognition, and so on. Disruption of particular perceptual modules involved in these functions may result in specific kinds of recognition impairments. Modules are also assumed to be domain specific (Fodor, 1983); that is, each module can only process one kind of input such as visual, auditory, or tactile information. In contrast to the modular structure of input processors, Fodor (1983) proposed that more complex mental operations involving higher order processing of output from individual modules are driven by central processes that do not follow the principles of modularity and are not amenable to investigation. The important difference between modules and central processes in Fodor's model is that modules are restricted to a particular type of information and are resistant to top-down cognitive influences, whereas central processes can receive and integrate information across many domains and from many different directions, which makes them difficult to study. However, Ellis and Young (1988) argued that by examining the kinds of errors made by patients with disorders of higher mental functions and the types of difficulties they experience on various tasks, we may be able to elucidate the ways in which these complex operations can go awry as well as learn something about how these higher mental processes normally operate.

Recently, Moscovitch and Umilta (in press) proposed that the study of higher order disturbances in cognition provides critical evidence for the issue of informational encapsulation. They argued that if a particular function remains intact despite generalized intellectual deterioration, one can assume that it is informationally encapsulated since the malfunctioning of a central cognitive system has no effect on that function. For example, patients with Alzheimer's disease exhibit widespread intellectual deficits, yet they retain the ability to read, to repeat, and correct grammatically incorrect sentences (Schwartz, Marin, & Saffran, 1979). Thus, specific domains of preserved function in the context of generalized intellectual deterioration provide support for the notion of informational encapsulation (i.e., modular organization of those spared functions).

Specific examples of how dissociations are interpreted within the modular framework of cognitive neuropsychology illustrate the value of this approach for understanding the nature of deficits in brain-damaged patients as well as for increasing our knowledge of normal cognitive functioning.

Recognition of Faces and Objects

Several striking dissociations have been reported in the literature concerned with prosopagnosia, referring to disorders of face recognition, and object agnosia or impaired object recognition. Prosopagnosic patients are unable to recognize any familiar faces including famous faces, friends, family, and their own faces when seen in a mirror (Hecaen & Angelergues, 1962). Interestingly, however, prosopagnosia may occur in the absence of any obvious difficulty with recognizing objects and, conversely, severe object agnosia has been observed in patients without prosopagnosia (Ellis & Young, 1988). This double dissociation between face recognition and object recognition suggests that the two tasks involve different cognitive and perceptual processes such that disruption of one function can occur in isolation from the other.

Dissociable impairments within each of these categories of recognition disorders have also been reported. For example, neuropsychological findings of face processing disorders suggest that impairments involving familiar face recognition can be doubly dissociated from impairments involving identification of facial expression or unfamiliar face matching (Bruce & Young, 1986). These kinds of dissociations imply that different functional components are in-

volved in various aspects of face processing and consequently can malfunction independently of one another. These findings, combined with results from studies of normal subjects, have played an integral role in the development of functional models of face processing (e.g., Bruce & Young, 1986).

Anosognosia and Unilateral Neglect

Damage to the posterior right cerebral hemisphere of the brain frequently produces a constellation of neuropsychological symptoms. Patients sustaining injury to this region may exhibit hemiplegia (paralysis of the left side of the body), unilateral neglect (inattention to the left side of space), hemianopia (visual field defect), and somatosensory impairment on the left side. In addition, these patients often appear entirely unaware of one or more of these deficits. Unawareness of a neuropsychological deficit is referred to as anosognosia and may occur in relation to any or all of the aforementioned defects. Some investigators have suggested that this group of behavioral changes reflects disruption of a common underlying mechanism, or at least disruption of closely related mechanisms (for review see McGlynn & Schacter, 1989); however, little systematic research has been devoted to this issue.

An important study by Bisiach and his colleagues (Bisiach, Vallar, Perani, Papagno, & Berti, 1986) investigated the relation between anosognosia for hemiplegia, anosognosia for hemianopia, unilateral neglect, and various other neurological disturbances in patients with damage to the right hemisphere. Results revealed a double dissociation between unawareness of motor impairment and unilateral neglect. Some patients who completely ignore the affected side of the body may be fully aware of their motor defect. Others who continue to deny their hemiplegia, even when confronted with evidence to the contrary, may attend normally to the left side. Another striking finding was a double dissociation between unawareness of hemiplegia and somatosensory impairment, suggesting that a somatosensory disturbance is not an essential condition for the development of unawareness of hemiplegia. Bisiach, Meregalli, and Berti (1985) developed a cognitive model of the awareness disorder, viewing unawareness phenomena as modality-specific disorders of thought resulting from disruption of specific mechanisms that normally monitor the output of individual perceptual and cognitive modules. Interpretation of the former dissociations within an information processing model has heuristic value, in that we are now in a position to investigate systematically, based on the model, specific hypotheses regarding organization of function.

Amnesic Syndromes

Amnesic syndromes occur as a consequence of various types of neurological impairment involving lesions to medial temporal or diencephalic brain regions (Schacter & Tulving, 1982; Squire, 1986). Amnesic patients typically have normal or near-normal intellectual, linguistic, and perceptual function but are unable to remember recent events and learn many types of new information. Graf and Schacter (1985, 1987; Schacter & Graf, 1986a, 1986b) distinguished between two kinds of memory, referred to as explicit and implicit memory. The former type is what we generally think of as remembering and involves conscious recollection of a recent event. However, memory can also be expressed implicitly, as a facilitation of task performance without conscious recollection. Although amnesic individuals fail to demonstrate explicit recall or recognition of recent episodes, their performance on tests of implicit memory indicates that some new information and skills can be acquired without conscious awareness of the prior learning episode(s) (e.g., Graf & Schacter, 1985; McAndrews, Glisky, & Schacter, 1987; Schacter, McAndrews, & Moscovitch, 1988). For example, the well-studied patient H. M. could acquire motor skills such as pursuit rotor and mirror tracing, even though he did not remember explicitly that he had previously performed the task (Milner, 1962; Milner, Corkin, & Teuber, 1968). Similarly, amnesic patients can learn and retain complex computer knowledge and a variety of computer operations without any recollection of encountering a computer previously (e.g., Glisky & Schacter, 1986). These kinds of findings with amnesic patients have had a significant impact on current theoretical accounts of memory organization and function (for review see Schacter, 1987) and stimulated a large body of cognitive research with normal subjects.

The striking dissociations between implicit and explicit memory in amnesic patients have been paralleled in cognitive research with normal subjects. For example, several studies have shown that variations in level or type of study processing have differential effects on implicit and explicit memory for familiar words or word pairs (e.g., Jacoby & Dallas, 1981; Schacter & McGlynn, 1989). Explicit memory is influenced by type of study processing, with better recall or recognition performance following elaborative study tasks than nonelaborative study tasks. In contrast, implicit memory is unaffected by the study task manipulation. A variety of paradigms, such as the levels of processing manipulation, used to study dissociations between implicit and explicit memory in normal subjects can easily be adopted for examining the nature of memory impairment in amnesic patients.

The cognitive and neuropsychological literature concerned with dissociations in memory provides an excellent illustration of how the study of neurological patients can facilitate our understanding of normal information processing and how the paradigms and theories of cognitive psychology can be applied to the study of neuropsychological impairments.

Cognitive Neuropsychology as a Model for Studying Psychological Deficit

Of central importance in the former demonstrations is the attempt to interpret the patterns of impaired and intact cognitive abilities in terms of disrupted components of an information-processing model and to infer from these disturbances how normal cognitive processes are organized. The general concepts and methodology of cognitive neuropsychology may be fruitfully applied to the study of psychological deficit in so-called functional disorders. Consider, for example, how the delusions of schizophrenia may be investigated based on the assumption of modular structure of cognitive functions. Several investigators (e.g., Kihlstrom & Hoyt, 1988; Maher & Ross, 1984) view delusions as the product of disordered perceptual and attentional processes. By this account, schizophrenic patients engage in relatively normal, intact information processing to explain their anomalous perceptual experiences, suggesting that the disruption occurs at the level of specific perceptual modules. If this is a viable account, it follows that schizophrenics should exhibit reasonably intact higher order mental functions or central processes involved in judgment, inference, and problem-solving abilities. In order to firmly establish that the particular processes disrupted in delusions are modular in nature, one would want to follow the principle discussed by Moscovitch and Umilta (in press) and obtain evidence that the converse case also exists; that is, patients with gross impairment of judgment, inference, and problem solving in conjunction with intact perceptual modules. Interestingly, two subtypes of schizophrenics have been identified that exhibit dramatically different patterns of psychological deficit (Andreasen & Olsen, 1982). One group exhibits primarily positive symptoms consisting of delusions, hallucinations, formal thought disorder, and bizarre behavior. The other group is characterized by negative symptoms such as affective flattening, alogia, avolition, anhedonia, and attentional impairment. These two groups may provide a useful context for investigating dissociations and drawing conclusions about where in the model of normal cognitive functioning specific breakdowns are occurring.

In addition to postulating dysfunction of particular perceptual modules in schizophrenia, there is evidence to suggest that certain higher order or central processes may be disturbed in this population. Several investigators have suggested that some aspects of the schizophrenic syndrome could be explained by a self-monitoring deficit, whereby patients fail to use feedback to alter their cognitive performance (Brown, 1980; Cohen, 1978; Feinberg, 1978; Goldberg, Weinberger, Berman, Pliskin, & Podd, 1987). In addition to being unable to monitor their own cognitive behavior, schizophrenics appear to be deficient in the ability to monitor and correct ongoing motor behavior on the basis of internal, self-generated cues (Malenka, Angel, Hampton, & Berger, 1982). Interestingly, Malenka et al. (1982) found that schizophrenics were no different than normal subjects and alcoholics in terms of their ability to initiate correct responses on a complex tracing task that prevented the use of the exteroceptive cues. However, the schizophrenic patients differed from the other two groups in an important respect: They were significantly less likely to recognize and reverse false responses. The authors ruled out the possible contribution of nonspecific factors to the performance of schizophrenics and concluded that schizophrenic subjects exhibit an impaired ability to monitor ongoing motor behavior on the basis of internal cues.

From a cognitive neuropsychological perspective, one might hypothesize that a central process, in this case some kind of executive function, may be disrupted in schizophrenia such that a wide variety of behaviors (e.g., motor, cognitive, social) are performed without an adequate error-detecting and error-correcting mechanism in operation. The important dissociation to be examined in this context would be between the specific modules involved in the motor or cognitive functions of interest and the central process responsible for monitoring the output of these modules. For example, Malenka et al. (1982) indicated that schizophrenics initiated correct motor responses equally often as normal subjects, suggesting that the relevant modules involved in producing the correct response were intact, whereas patients were impaired in their ability to correct inaccurate responses which

may rely on a higher order process. The application of a cognitive neuropsychological framework to this kind of problem stimulates a number of interesting questions that could be pursued and offers a variety of methodological techniques for investigating the relevant dissociations.

From a practical perspective, increased understanding of how the cognitive system of schizophrenics is receiving and processing information will prove crucial for developing effective rehabilitation programs. Recent approaches to rehabilitation have focused on alleviating social skill and community support deficits among the chronically mentally ill. However, Erickson and Binder (1986) argued that many of these patients suffer from subtle cognitive deficits that prevent them from learning and generalizing social and vocational skills to the real world. The cognitive limitations of these patients need to be taken into account when developing intervention programs, and the goal of treatment should be to maximize the preserved abilities and minimize the impact of disrupted functions.

Although we have focused on the psychological deficits of schizophrenia in this section, the principles of cognitive neuropsychology as a model for studying psychological deficit could just as easily be imposed on other types of psychopathology be it affective disorders, eating disorders, or anxiety disorders. In all of these categories, there exists some degree of disturbed information processing along with many intact cognitive components. By viewing the pattern of psychological deficits and preserved functions within a modular framework, research may progress in a more organized and theoretically important direction. The practical implications in terms of developing more effective treatment and rehabilitation programs for patients with various kinds of disturbances may be far-reaching.

PROSPECTS FOR EXPERIMENTAL PSYCHOPATHOLOGY

The present review of the literature on experimental psychopathology has been highly selective. Due to necessary constraints on space, we have attempted to give the reader only the flavor of recent trends in the area. Many syndromes and paradigms have been omitted—substance abuse and infantile autism, for example, and computer simulation and psychophysiology. Nevertheless, it seems clear that after more than a half century of sustained activity, the experimental study of psychopathology appears to be alive and well. New generations of laboratory models, involving both nonhuman and human subjects, have offered new perspectives on the origins, maintenance, and treatment of phobia, anxiety, depression, psychopathy, and the dissociative disorders. The adoption of contemporary information-processing paradigms has shed new light on the cognitive, emotional, and motivational deficits that underlie the syndromes of psychopathy, depression, and schizophrenia.

One salutary aspect of the field today is the apparent convergence of its two main constituents, laboratory models and psychological deficit. Early signs of this are to be found in the literature on depression, where the learned helplessness model, derived directly from animal research (Maier, Seligman, & Solomon, 1969), led to the concept of hopelessness and empirical work on depressogenic attributional style and depressive realism. The links are even more tightly developed in the area of psychopathy, where a virtual renaissance in psychological deficit research has been instigated by the septal rat model. A further convergence is between psychological deficit in psychopathology and the neuropsychological study of brain-damaged patients. Similarly, we detect the beginnings of an injection of neuropsychological methods into the study of a wide variety of symptoms in schizophrenia and the potential of the neuropsychological model for the study of language disorders in that syndrome. The septal model suggests that the neuropsychological study of psychopathy and other syndromes of disinhibition might well be productive.

Another positive development is the rapid adoption by experimental psychopathologists of new concepts and paradigms, as they have been developed in research on normal mental life (Kihlstrom, 1983). For example, laboratory models of phobias and other anxiety-based disorders have kept abreast of trends within conditioning theory, as evidenced both by their emphasis on cognitive concepts of predictability and controllability and their use of evolutionary and psychobiological concepts related to preparedness and other biological boundaries on learning. While the information-processing view began to be widely adopted within cognitive psychology about the time of Neisser's (1967) seminal monograph and was well consolidated 5 years later (Newell & Simon, 1972), it made its entrance into the study of psychological deficit between 1973 and 1979.

However, other developments have been slow to catch on. Research on language in schizophrenia, for example, has yet to take full advantage of the vast panoply of concepts and methods offered by experimental psycholinguistics. We wonder what would be produced, for example, if experimental psychopathologists would take seriously the implications of Kraepelin's (1896) notion of schizophasia and approach schizophrenic speech and language in the manner that cognitive neuropsychologists have studied the communication disorders in brain-damaged patients. Similarly, we note that classical models of judgment and decision making based on formal, logical reasoning are threatened by the judgment heuristics approach (for reviews, see Hastie, 1983; Kahneman, Slovic, & Tversky, 1982; Kahneman & Tversky, 1984) that emphasizes the limitations of the human information-processing system and people's reliance on a set of cognitive shortcuts that permit judgment under uncertainty but also increase the probability of judgmental error. Our impression is that these theoretical developments have not been systematically incorporated into studies of thought disorder in schizophrenia, although this situation may be beginning to change (e.g., Chapman & Chapman, 1988; Kihlstrom & Hoyt, 1988; Maher, 1988).

In this regard, investigators of psychological deficit should be aware of recent trends within cognitive psychology that mark the progressive abandonment of the traditional multistore models of human information processing and their possible replacement by variants known collectively as connectionism or parallel distributed processing (PDP; McClelland & Rummelhart, 1986; Rummelhart & McClelland, 1986). By postulating the existence of a large number of domain-specific processing units, or modules, working in parallel to perform various cognitive operations and passing information back and forth between them, PDP models undercut the discrete-stage, serial-processing models that have traditionally offered the best hope of determining the locus of psychological deficit in syndromes such as schizophrenia (Kihlstrom, 1983). Although connectionist models of human information processing remain controversial (Pinker & Mehler, 1988; Smolensky, 1988), issues of connectionism and modularity have already made their way into cognitive neuropsychology, and experimental psychopathologists would do well to consider their implications sooner rather than later.

Despite the difficulties posed by actual and potential paradigm shifts, experimental psychopathology continues to offer a unique and valuable perspective on the nature of mental illness. Historically, human science has progressed along two parallel tracks, constituting two different levels of explanation. At the cultural level, events are explained in terms of social, historical, and economic forces. Thus, the incidence of mental illness may be related to socioeconomic status, or the content of delusions to the culture in which the patient lives. At the physical level, the same events are explained in terms of biological and chemical processes. Thus, individuals may be at risk for depression by virtue of the genetic endowment, and imbalances among neurotransmitters may be linked to schizophrenia.

Psychology in general, and experimental psychopathology in particular, attempts to explain these same events at a third, intermediate level of individual mental processes—of the person's percepts, memories, beliefs, thoughts, emotions, and motives. Each level of explanation is perfectly appropriate—sociologists are not obligated to explain thoughts and action in biological terms, and psychology is not something to do until the neurochemist comes—and each, when applied properly, relies on and informs the others. Experimental psychopathology at its best, combining the three approaches of laboratory modeling, psychological deficit, and cognitive neuropsychology, provides a way of linking the symptoms of individual mental patients, or classes of patients, with both their biological endowment and the sociocultural context in which they live.

REFERENCES

Abramson, L.Y., Metalsky, G. I., & Alloy, L. B. (1988). The hopelessness theory of depression: Does the research test the theory? In L. Y. Abramson (Ed.), *Social cognition and clinical psychology: A synthesis* (pp. 33–65). New York: Guilford Press.

Abramson, L. Y., & Sackeim, H. A. (1977) A paradox in depression: Uncontrollability and self-blame. *Psychological Bulletin, 84,* 838–851.

Abramson, L. Y., & Seligman, M. E. P. (1977). Modeling psychopathology in the laboratory: History and rationale. In J. P. Maser & M. E. P. Seligman (Eds.), *Psychopathology: Experimental models* (pp. 1–26). San Francisco: W H Freeman.

Abramson, L. Y., Seligman, M. E. P., & Teasdale, J. D. (1978). Learned helplessness in humans: Critique and reformulation. *Journal of Abnormal Psychology, 87,* 49–74.

Alloy, L. B. (1988). *Cognitive processes in depression.* New York: Guilford Press.

Alloy, L. B., & Abramson, L. Y. (1979). Judgment of contingency in depressed and nondepressed students: Sadder but wiser? *Journal of Experimental Psychology: General, 108,* 441–485.

Alloy, L. B., & Abramson, L. Y. (1988). Depressive realism: Four theoretical perspectives. In L. B. Alloy (Ed.), *Cognitive processes in depression* (pp. 223–265). New York: Guilford Press.

Alloy, L. B., Kelly, K. A., Mineka, S., & Clements, C. M. (1989). Comorbidity in anxiety and depressive disorders:

A helplessness/hopelessness perspective. In J. D. Maser & C. R. Cloninger (Eds.), *Comorbidity in anxiety and mood disorders* (pp. 499–543). Washington, DC: American Psychiatric Press.

Alloy, L. B., & Tabachnik, N. (1984). Assessment of covariation by humans and animals: The joint influence of prior expectations and current situational information. *Psychological Review, 91,* 112–149.

Andreasen, N. C., & Olsen, S. (1982). Negative vs. positive schizophrenia. *Archives of General Psychiatry, 39,* 789–794.

Atkinson, R. C., & Shiffrin, R. M. (1968). Human memory: A proposed system and its control processes. In K. W. Spence and J. T. Spence (Eds.), *The psychology of learning and motivation* (Vol. 2, pp. 89–125). New York: Academic Press.

Beck, A. T. (1967). *Depression: Clinical, experimental, and theoretical aspects.* New York: Harper & Row.

Beck, A. T. (1976). *Cognitive therapy and the emotional disorders.* New York: International Universities Press.

Beck, A. T., & Emery, G. (1985). *Anxiety disorder and phobias: A cognitive perspective.* New York: Basic Books.

Bisiach, E., Meregalli, S., & Berti, A. (1985, June). *Mechanisms of production-control and belief-fixation in human visuospatial processing. Clinical evidence from hemispatial neglect.* Paper presented to the Eighth Symposium on Quantitative Analyses of Behavior, Harvard University.

Bisiach, E., Vallar, G., Perani, D., Papagno, C., & Berti, A. (1986). Unawareness of disease following lesions of the right hemisphere: Anosognosia for hemiplegia and anosognosia for hemianopia. *Neuropsychologia, 24,* 471–482.

Blaney, P. H. (1977). Contemporary theories of depression: Critique and comparison. *Journal of Abnormal Psychology, 86,* 203–233.

Bleuler, E. (1950). *Dementia praecox, or the group of schizophrenias.* New York: International Universities Press. (Original work published 1911)

Bower, G. H. (1981). Mood and memory. *American Psychologist, 36,* 129–148.

Brown, T. A. (1980). The microgenesis of schizophrenic thought. *Archive Für Psychologie, 48,* 215–237.

Bruce, V., & Young, A. W. (1986). Understanding face recognition. *British Journal of Psychology, 77,* 305–327.

Buss, A. M. (1966). *Psychopathology.* New York: John Wiley & Sons.

Cantor, N., & Genero, N. (1986). Psychiatric diagnosis and natural categorization: A close analogy. In T. Millon & G. Klerman (Eds.), *Contemporary issues in psychopathology* (pp. 223–256). New York: Guilford Press.

Cantor, N., Smith, E. E., French, R. D., & Mezzich, J. (1980). Psychiatric diagnosis as prototype categorization. *Journal of Abnormal Psychology, 89,* 181–193.

Carr, A. (1974). Compulsive neurosis: A review of the literature. *Psychological Bulletin, 81,* 311–318.

Chapman, L. J., & Chapman, J. P. (1973a). *Disordered thought in schizophrenia*. Englewood Cliffs, NJ: Prentice-Hall.

Chapman, L. J., & Chapman, J. P. (1973b). Problems in the measurement of cognitive deficit. *Psychological Bulletin, 79,* 380–385.

Chapman, L. J., & Chapman, J. P. (1978). The measurement of differential deficit. *Journal of Psychiatric Research, 14,* 303–311.

Chapman, L. J., & Chapman, J. P. (1988). The genesis of delusions. In T. F. Oltmanns & B. A. Maher (Eds.), *Delusional beliefs* (pp. 167–183). New York: Wiley-Interscience.

Cohen, B. D. (1978). Self-editing deficits in schizophrenia. *Journal of Psychiatric Research, 14,* 267–273.

Costello, C. G. (1970). *Symptoms of psychopathology: A handbook*. New York: John Wiley & Sons.

Coyne, J. C., & Gotlib, I. H. (1983). The role of cognition in depression: A critical appraisal. *Psychological Bulletin, 94,* 472–505.

Crocker, J. (1981). Judgments of covariation by social perceivers. *Psychological Bulletin, 90,* 272–292.

Dollard, J., & Miller, N. E. (1950). *Personality and psychotherapy*. New York: McGraw-Hill.

Ellenberger, H. F. (1970). *The discovery of the unconscious: The history and evolution of dynamic psychiatry*. New York: Basic Books.

Ellis, H. A., & Ashbrook, P. J. (1988). Resource allocation model of the effects of depressed mood states on memory. In K. Fiedler & J. Forgas (Eds.), *Affect, cognition, and social behavior* (pp. 25–43). Toronto: Hogrefe.

Ellis, A. W., & Young, A. W. (1988). *Human cognitive neuropsychology*. Hillsdale, NJ: Lawrence Erlbaum Associates.

Erickson, R. C., & Binder, L. M. (1986). Cognitive deficits among functionally psychotic patients: A rehabilitative perspective. *Journal of Clinical and Experimental Neuropsychology, 8,* 257–274.

Eysenck, H. J. (1955). *Psychology and the foundations of psychiatry*. London: Lewis.

Eysenck, H. J. (1979). The conditioning model of neurosis. *Behavioral and Brain Sciences, 2,* 155–199.

Eysenck, H. J., & Rachman, S. (1965). *Causes and cures of neurosis*. London: Routledge & Kegan Paul.

Feinberg, I. (1978). Efference copy and corollary discharge: Implications for thinking and its disorders. *Schizophrenia Bulletin, 4,* 636–640.

Fodor, J. (1983). *The modularity of the mind*. Cambridge, MA: MIT Press.

Glisky, E. L., & Schacter, D. L. (1986). Remediation of organic memory disorders: Current status and future prospects. *The Journal of Head Trauma Rehabilitation, 1,* 54–63.

Goldberg, T. E., Weinberger, D. R., Berman, K. F., Pliskin, N. H., & Podd, M. H. (1987). Further evidence for dementia of the prefrontal type in schizophrenia? *Archives of General Psychiatry, 44,* 1008–1114.

Gorenstein, E. E., & Newman, J. P. (1980). Disinhibitory psychopathology: A new perspective and a model for research. *Psychological Review, 87,* 301–315.

Graf, P., & Schacter, D. L. (1985). Implicit and explicit memory for new associations in normal and amnesic subjects. *Journal of Experimental Psychology: Learning, Memory, and Cognition, 11,* 501–518.

Graf, P., & Schacter, D. L. (1987). Selective effects of interference on implicit and explicit memory for new associations. *Journal of Experimental Psychology: Learning, Memory, and Cognition, 13,* 45–53.

Hare, R. D. (1970). *Psychopathy: Theory and research*. New York: John Wiley & Sons.

Hare, R. D., & Schalling, D. (Eds.). (1978). *Psychopathic behavior: Approaches to research*. New York: John Wiley & Sons.

Harris, B. (1979). Whatever happened to Little Albert? *American Psychologist, 34,* 151–160.

Hastie, R. (1983). Social inference. *Annual Review of Psychology, 34,* 511–542.

Hecaen, H., & Angelergues, R. (1962). Agnosia for faces (prosopagnosia). *Archives of Neurology, 7,* 92–100.

Hilgard, E. R. (1977). *Divided consciousness: Multiple controls in human thought and action*. New York: Wiley-Interscience.

Hunt, J. M., and Cofer, C. N. (1944). Psychological deficit. In J. M. Hunt (Ed.), *Personality and the behavior disorders* (Vol. 2, pp. 971–1032). New York: Ronald.

Ingram, R. E. (1986). *Information processing approaches to clinical psychology*. Orlando, FL: Academic Press.

Ingram, R. E., & Reed, M. R. (1986). Information encoding and retrieval processes in depression: Findings, issues, and future directions. In R. E. Ingram (Ed.), *Information processing approaches to clinical psychology* (pp. 131–150). Orlando, FL: Academic Press.

Isen, A. M. (1984). Toward understanding the role of affect in cognition. In R. S. Wyer & T. K. Srull (Eds.), *Handbook of social cognition* (Vol. 3, pp. 179–236). Hillsdale, NJ: Lawrence Erlbaum Associates.

Jacobs, W. J., & Nadel, L. (1985). Stress-induced recovery of fears and phobias. *Psychological Review, 92,* 512–531.

Jacoby, L. L., & Dallas, M. (1981). On the relationship between autobiographical memory and perceptual learning. *Journal of Experimental Psychology: General, 110,* 306–340.

Kahneman, D., Slovic, P., & Tversky, A. (1982). *Judgment under uncertainty: Heuristics and biases*. Cambridge, England: Cambridge University Press.

Kahneman, D., & Tversky, A. (1984). Choices, values, and frames. *American Psychologist, 39,* 341–350.

Kasanin, J. S. (1944). *Language and thought in schizophrenia*. Berkeley: University of California Press.

Kayne, N. T., & Alloy, L. B. (1988). Clinician and patient as aberrant actuaries: Expectation-based distortions in assessment of covariation. In L. Y. Abramson (Ed.), *Social cognition and clinical psychology: A synthesis* (pp. 295–365). New York: Guilford Press.

Kihlstrom, J. F. (1979). Hypnosis and psychopathology:

Retrospect and prospect. *Journal of Abnormal Psychology*, *88*, 459–473.

Kihlstrom, J. F. (1983). Mental health implications of information processing: Studies of perception and attention. In *Behavioral sciences research in mental health: An assessment of the state of the science and recommendations for research directions* (pp. I1–I65). Rockville, MD: National Institute of Mental Health.

Kihlstrom, J. F. (1984). Conscious, subconscious, unconscious: A cognitive perspective. In K. S. Bowers & D. Meichenbaum (Eds.), *The unconscious reconsidered* (pp. 149–211). New York: Wiley-Interscience.

Kihlstrom, J. F. (1987). The cognitive unconscious. *Science*, *237*, 1445–1452.

Kihlstrom, J. F. (1989). Cognition, unconscious processes. In G. Adelman (Ed.), *Neuroscience year: Supplement 1 to the Encyclopedia of neuroscience* (pp. 34–36). Boston: Birkhauser.

Kihlstrom, J. F. (1990a). Dissociative disorders. In P. B. Sutker & H. E. Adams (Eds.), *Comprehensive handbook of psychopathology* (2nd ed.). New York: Plenum Publishing.

Kihlstrom, J. F. (1990b). The psychological unconscious. In L. Pervin (Ed.), *Handbook of personality theory and research* (pp. 445–464). New York: Guilford Press.

Kihlstrom, J. F., & Hoyt, I. P. (1988). Hypnosis and the psychology of delusions. In T. F. Oltmanns & B. A. Maher (Eds.), *Delusional beliefs: Interdisciplinary perspectives* (pp. 66–109). New York: Wiley-Interscience.

Kihlstrom, J. F., & Nasby, W. (1981). Cognitive tasks in clinical assessment: An exercise in applied psychology. In P. C. Kendall & S. D. Hollon (Eds.), *Assessment strategies for cognitive-behavioral interventions* (pp. 287–317). New York: Academic Press.

Knight, R. A. (1984). Converging models of cognitive deficit in schizophrenia. In W. D. Spaulding & J. K. Cole (Eds.), *Nebraska Symposium on Motivation, 1983: Theories of schizophrenia and psychosis* (pp. 93–156). Lincoln, NE: University of Nebraska Press.

Knight, R. A., Elliott, D. S., & Freedman, E. G. (1985). Short-term visual memory in schizophrenics. *Journal of Abnormal Psychology*, *94*, 427–442.

Knight, R. A., & Sims-Knight, J. E. (1982). Evaluating pigeonholing as an explanatory construct for schizophrenics' cognitive deficiencies. *Behavioral and Brain Sciences*, *5*, 601–602.

Kraepelin, E. (1896). *Psychiatry* (5th ed.). Leipzig: Barth.

Kuiken, D. (1989). *Mood and memory: Theory, research, and applications.* Special issue of *Journal of Social Behavior and Personality*, *4*(2).

Lang, P. J. (1968). Fear reduction and fear behavior: Problems in treating a construct. In J. M. Shlein (Ed.), *Research in psychotherapy* (Vol. 3, pp. 90–103). Washington, DC: American Psychiatric Association.

Lindsley, O. R., & Skinner, B. F. (1954). A method for the experimental analysis of behavior of psychotic patients. *American Psychologist*, *9*, 419–420.

Magaro, P. A. (1980). *Cognition in schizophrenia and paranoia: The integration of cognitive processes.* Hillsdale, NJ: Lawrence Erlbaum Associates.

Maher, B. A. (1966). *Principles of psychopathology.* New York: McGraw-Hill.

Maher, B. A. (1972). The language of schizophrenia: A review and interpretation. *British Journal of Psychiatry*, *120*, 3–17.

Maher, B. (1988). Anomalous experience and delusional thinking: The logic of explanations. In T. F. Oltmanns & B. A. Maher (Eds.), *Delusional beliefs* (pp. 15–33). New York: Wiley-Interscience.

Maher, B. A., & Ross, J. S. (1984). Delusions. In H. E. Adams and P. B. Sutker (Eds.), *Comprehensive handbook of psychopathology* (pp. 383–409). New York: Plenum Press.

Mahoney, M. J. (1974). *Cognition and behavior modification.* Cambridge, MA: Ballinger.

Maier, N. R. F. (1949). *Frustration: The study of behavior without a goal.* New York: McGraw-Hill.

Maier, S. F., Seligman, M. E. P., & Solomon, R. (1969). Pavlovian fear conditioning and learned helplessness. In B. A. Campbell & R. M. Church (Eds.), *Punishment and aversive behavior* (pp. 299–342). New York: Appleton-Century-Crofts.

Malenka, R. C., Angel, R. W., Hampton, B., & Berger, P. A. (1982). Impaired central error-correcting behavior in schizophrenia. *Archives of General Psychiatry*, *39*, 101–107.

Marks, I. M. (1969). *Fears and phobias.* New York: Academic Press.

Marks, I. M. (1987). *Fears, phobias, and rituals: Panic, anxiety, and their disorders.* New York: Oxford University Press.

Marr, D. (1982). *Vision.* San Francisco: W H Freeman.

Maser, J. D., & Seligman, M. E. P. (1977). *Psychopathology: Experimental models.* San Francisco: W H Freeman.

Masserman, J. H. (1943). *Behavior and neurosis: An experimental psychoanalytic approach to psychobiologic principles.* Chicago: University of Chicago Press.

Matthysse, S., Spring, B. J., & Sugarman, J. (Eds.). (1979). *Attention and information processing in schizophrenia.* Oxford, England: Pergamon Press.

Mayer, J. D. (1986). How mood influences cognition. In N. E. Sharkey (Ed.), *Advances in cognitive science* (pp. 290–314). Chichester, England: Ellis Horwood.

McAndrews, M. P., Glisky, E. L., & Schacter, D. L. (1987). When priming persists: Long-lasting implicit memory for a single episode in amnesic patients. *Neuropsychologia*, *25*, 493–506.

McClelland, J. L., Rummelhart, D. E., & the PDP Research Group (1986). *Parallel distributed processing: Explorations in the microstructure of cognition. Vol. 2. Psychological and biological models.* Cambridge, MA: MIT Press.

McGhie, A., & Chapman, J. (1961). Disorders of attention and perception in early schizophrenia. *British Journal of Medical Psychology*, *34*, 103–116.

McGlynn, S. M., & Schacter, D. L. (1989). Unawareness of deficits in neuropsychological syndromes. *Journal of Clinical and Experimental Psychology, 11*, 143–205.

Meichenbaum, D. (1977). *Cognitive-behavior modification: An integrative approach.* New York: Plenum Publishing.

Metalsky, G. I., Halberstadt, L. J., & Abramson, L. Y. (1987). Vulnerability to depressive mood reactions: Toward a more powerful test of the diathesis-stress and causal mediation components of the reformulated theory of depression. *Journal of Personality and Social Psychology, 52*, 386–393.

Miller, W. R. (1975). Psychological deficit in depression. *Psychological Bulletin, 82*, 238–260.

Milner, B. (1962). Les troubles de la memoire accompagnant des lesions hippocampiques bilaterales. In *Physiologie de l'hippocampe.* Paris: Centre National de la Recherche Scientifique.

Milner, B., Corkin, S., & Teuber, H. L. (1968). Further analysis of the hippocampal amnesic syndrome: 14 year follow-up study of H. M. *Neuropsychologia, 6*, 215–234.

Mineka, S. (1982). Depression and helplessness in primates. In H. Fitzgerald, J. Mullins, & P. Gage (Eds.), *Primate behavior and child nurturance*, (pp. 197–242). New York: Plenum Publishing.

Mineka, S. (1985a). Animal models of anxiety based disorders: Their usefulness and limitations. In A. H. Tuma & J. D. Maser (Eds.), *Anxiety and anxiety disorders* (pp. 199–204). Hillsdale, NJ: Lawrence Erlbaum Associates.

Mineka, S. (1985b). The frightful complexity of the origins of fears. In J. B. Overmier & F. R. Brush (Eds.), *Affect, conditioning, and cognition: Essays on the determinants of behavior* (pp. 55–73). Hillsdale, NJ: Lawrence Erlbaum Associates.

Mineka, S. (1987). A primate model of phobic fears. In H. Eysenck & I. Martin (Eds.), *Theoretical foundations of behavior therapy* (pp. 81–111). New York: Plenum Publishing.

Mineka, S., & Kelly, K. A. (1989). The relationship between anxiety, lack of control and loss of control. In A. Steptoe & A. Appels (Eds.), *Stress, personal control, and worker health* (pp. 163–191). Brussels: John Wiley & Sons.

Mineka, S., & Kihlstrom, J. F. (1978). Unpredictable and uncontrollable events: A new perspective on experimental neurosis. *Journal of Abnormal Psychology, 87*, 256–271.

Moscovitch, M., & Umilta, C. (in press). Modularity and neuropsychology. In M. F. Schwartz (Ed.), *Modularity of dementia.* Cambridge, MA: Bradford Books.

Nasby, W., & Kihlstrom, J. F. (1986). Cognitive assessment of personality and psychopathology. In R. E. Ingram (Ed.), *Information processing approaches to clinical psychology* (pp. 219–239). Orlando, FL: Academic Press.

Neale, J. M., & Oltmanns, T. F. (1980). *Schizophrenia.* New York: John Wiley & Sons.

Neisser, U. (1967). *Cognitive psychology.* New York: Appleton-Century-Crofts.

Newell, A., & Simon, H. A. (1972). *Human problem solving.* Englewood Cliffs, NJ: Prentice-Hall.

Newman, J. P. (1987). Reaction to punishment in extraverts and psychopaths: Implications for the impulsive behavior of disinhibited individuals. *Journal of Research in Personality, 21*, 464–480.

Nisbett, R., & Ross, L. (1980). *Human inference: Strategies and shortcomings.* Englewood Cliffs, NJ: Prentice-Hall.

Nuechterlein, K. H., & Dawson, M. E. (1984). Information processing and attentional functioning in the developmental course of schizophrenic disorders. *Schizophrenia Bulletin, 10*, 160–203.

Oltmanns, T. F., & Neale, J. M. (1975). Schizophrenic performance when distractors are present: Attentional deficit or differential task difficulty? *Journal of Abnormal Psychology, 84*, 205–209.

Oltmanns, T. F., & Neale, J. M. (1982). Psychological deficits in schizophrenia: Information processing and communication problems. In M. Shepard (Ed.), *Handbook of psychiatry* (Vol. 3, pp. 55–61). Cambridge, England: Cambridge University Press.

Osmond, H., & Smithies, J. R. (1952). Schizophrenia: A new approach. *Journal of Mental Science, 98*, 309–315.

Patterson, C. M., & Newman, J. P. (1987). Reflectivity and learning from aversive events: Toward a psychological mechanism for the syndromes of disinhibition. Unpublished manuscript, University of Wisconsin.

Pavlov, I. P. (1927). *Conditioned reflexes: An investigation of the physiological activity of the cerebral cortex.* London: Oxford University Press.

Perry, C., & Laurence, J.-R. (1984). Mental processing outside of awareness: The contributions of Freud and Janet. In K. S. Bowers & D. Meichenbaum (Eds.), *The unconscious reconsidered* (pp. 9–48). New York: Wiley-Interscience.

Peterson, C., & Seligman, M. E. P. (1984). Causal explanations as a risk factor for depression: Theory and evidence. *Psychological Review, 91*, 347–374.

Pinker, S., & Mehler, J. (1988). Connections and symbols. *Cognition, 28.* Cambridge, MA: MIT Press.

Place, E. J. S., & Gilmore, G. C. (1980). Perceptual organization in schizophrenia. *Journal of Abnormal Psychology, 89*, 409–418.

Rachman, S. (1978). *Fear and courage.* San Francisco: W H Freeman.

Rachman, S., & Hodgson, R. J. (1980). *Obsessions and compulsions.* Englewood Cliffs, NJ: Prentice-Hall.

Reed, G. F. (1985). *Obsessional experience and compulsive behaviour: A cognitive-structural approach.* New York: Academic Press.

Ross, L. (1977). The intuitive psychologist and his shortcomings. In L. Berkowitz (Ed.), *Advances in Experimental Social Psychology* (Vol. 10, pp. 173–220). New York: Academic Press.

Rummelhart, D. E., McClelland, J. L., & the PDP Research Group (1986). *Parallel distributed processing: Explorations in the microstructure of cognition. Vol. 1. Foundations.* Cambridge, MA: MIT Press.

Saccuzzo, D. P. (1986). An information processing interpretation of theory and research in schizophrenia. In R. E. Ingram (Ed.), *Information processing approaches to clinical psychology* (pp. 195–214). Orlando, FL: Academic Press.

Saccuzzo, D. P., Hirt, M., & Spencer, T. J. (1974). Backward masking as a measure of attention in schizophrenia. *Journal of Abnormal Psychology, 83,* 512–522.

Sackeim, H. A., Nordlie, J. W., & Gur, R. C. (1979). A model of hysterical and hypnotic blindness: Cognition, motivation, and awareness. *Journal of Abnormal Psychology, 88,* 474–489.

Samelson, F. (1980). J. B. Watson's Little Albert, Cyril Burt's twins, and the need for a critical science. *American Psychologist, 35,* 619–625.

Sarbin, T. R., & Coe, W. C. (1979). Hypnosis and psychopathology: Replacing old myths with fresh metaphors. *Journal of Abnormal Psychology, 88,* 506–526.

Schacter, D. L. (1987). Implicit memory: History and current status. *Journal of Experimental Psychology: Learning, Memory, and Cognition, 13,* 501–518.

Schacter, D. L., & Graf, P. (1986a). Effects of elaborative processing on implicit and explicit memory for new associations. *Journal of Experimental Psychology; Learning, Memory, and Cognition, 12,* 432–444.

Schacter, D. L., & Graf, P. (1986b). Preserved learning in amnesic patients: Perspectives from research on direct priming. *Journal of Clinical and Experimental Neuropsychology, 8,* 727–743.

Schacter, D. L., McAndrews, M. P., & Moscovitch, M. (1988). Access to consciousness: Dissociations between implicit and explicit knowledge in neuropsychological syndromes. In L. Weiskrantz (Ed.), *Thought without language.* New York: Oxford University Press.

Schacter, D. L., & McGlynn, S. M. (1989). Implicit memory: Effects of elaboration depend on unitization. *American Journal of Psychology, 102,* 151–181.

Schacter, D. L., & Tulving, E. (1982). Memory, amnesia, and the episodic/semantic distinction. In R. L. Isaacson & N. E. Spear (Eds.), *The expression of knowledge* (pp. 33–65). New York: Plenum Publishing.

Schacter, S., & Singer, J. (1962). Cognitive, social, and physiological determinants of emotional state. *Psychological Review, 69,* 379–399.

Schwartz, M. F., Marin, O. S. M., & Saffran, E. M. (1979). Dissociations of language function in dementia: A case study. *Brain and Language, 7,* 277–306.

Schwartz, S. (1978). *Language and cognition in schizophrenia.* Hillsdale, NJ: Lawrence Erlbaum Associates.

Schwartz, S. (1982). Is there a schizophrenic language? *Behavioral and Brain Sciences, 5,* 579–626.

Seligman, M. E. P. (1971). Phobias and preparedness. *Behavior therapy, 2,* 307–320.

Seligman, M. E. P. (1975). *Helplessness: On depression, development, and death.* San Francisco: W H Freeman.

Singer, J. A., & Salovey, P. (1988). Mood and memory: Evaluating the network theory of affect. *Clinical Psychology Review, 8,* 211–251.

Smolensky, P. (1988). On the proper treatment of connectionism. With commentary. *Behavioral and Brain Sciences, 11,* 1–74.

Spaulding, W. D., & Cole, J. K. (1984). *Nebraska symposium on motivation. 1983: Theories of schizophrenia and psychosis.* Lincoln, NE: University of Nebraska Press.

Squire, L. R. (1986). Mechanisms of memory. *Science, 232,* 1612–1619.

Teasdale, J. D. (1974). Learning models of obsessional-compulsive disorder. In H. R. Beech (Ed.), *Obsessional states* (pp. 197–229). London: Methuen.

Thomas, E., & Dewald, L. (1977). Experimental neurosis. In J. D. Maser & M. E. P. Seligman (Eds.), *Psychopathology: Experimental models* (pp. 214–231). San Francisco: W H Freeman.

Tobias, B. A., Schacter, D. L., & Kihlstrom, J. F. (1990). Implicit and explicit aspects of emotion and memory. In S.-A. Christianson (Ed.), *Handbook of emotion and memory.* Hillsdale, NJ: Lawrence Erlbaum Associates.

Watson, J. B., & Rayner, R. (1920). Conditioned emotional reactions. *Journal of Experimental Psychology, 3,* 1–14.

Widlocher, D., & Hardy-Doyle, M.-C. (1989). Cognition and control of action in psychopathology. *European Bulletin of Cognitive Psychology, 9,* 1–33.

Wishner, J. (1955). The concept of efficiency in psychological health and psychopathology. *Psychological Review, 62,* 69–80.

Wolpe, J. (1958). *Psychotherapy by reciprocal inhibition.* Stanford, CA: Stanford University Press.

Yates, A. J. (1966). Psychological deficit. *Annual Review of Psychology, 17,* 111–144.

Yates, A. J. (1970). *Behavior therapy.* New York: John Wiley & Sons.

CHAPTER 15

PERSONALITY RESEARCH: THEORIES, ISSUES, AND METHODS

Norman S. Endler
James D. A. Parker

The study of personality is influenced by theories and models, existing methodologies, and sociopolitical factors. This chapter will examine how each of these factors influences personality research. We will also examine several issues in personality research and methodologies that continue to attract the attention of researchers. In particular, we will examine the consistency issue of human behavior. The chapter concludes with the examination of an interaction model of anxiety, stress, and coping and a brief summary of research that supports this interactional approach to the study of personality.

THEORIES OF PERSONALITY

In the personality area, as with science in general, a theory presents a framework for organizing empirical data, determining the priorities for research goals that should be given attention, and outlining the scope of subsequent research projects. Endler (1983) defined a theory as "a set of postulates from which we can derive testable hypotheses. The psychological theory aids us in explaining, understanding, predicting, controlling and measuring behavior" (p. 155). In the personality area, however, it may be more accurate to talk about personality models rather than personality theories. Endler (1983) noted that a model is "basically an analogical representation of a phenomena. It is less than a theory and is not meant to have as much explanatory value as a theory" (p. 157). While there are personality researchers who talk about different personality theories, the explanatory value of these theories is rather modest (Endler, 1983; Pervin, 1984). Instead of theories, personality researchers have actually developed personality models, which have varied greatly in the scope of the phenomena the researchers wish to understand.

The specific personality models that researchers have adopted have played a strong role in defining the basic concepts and issues to be addressed in the study

This paper was completed while the first author held a Killam Research Fellowship from the Canada Council and the second author held a Doctoral Fellowship from the Social Sciences and Humanities Research Council of Canada.
The authors wish to thank Brian J. Cox for his help with the survey of research trends in the personality literature.

of personality. Particular types of data collection and procedures for data analysis are associated with specific personality models. Reviewing a variety of different definitions of personality, Hall and Lindzey (1978) noted that the way researchers "define personality will depend completely upon their particular theoretical preference . . . *personality is defined by the particular empirical concepts that are a part of the theory of personality employed by the observers*" (p. 9).

Personality research has been directed by four major models (Endler, 1983; Endler & Magnusson, 1976): traits (the study of individual differences), psychodynamics, situationism, and interactionism. There are, of course, differing points of view within each of these models, just as one can find many similarities between them. In the following sections, however, we will focus on the major distinctions among the four models. In particular, we will focus on the differences among the four models in research strategies, methods and models of data collection, and the methods used to analyze this data. Table 15.1 presents a brief overview of the basic research strategies that are associated with the different personality models.

Trait (Individual Differences) Models

Throughout the history of the modern personality area, the trait or individual differences model has dominated research and theory (Endler, 1983; Hilgard, 1987). The primary determinants of behavior, according to the classic individual differences approach, were traits. This model has emphasized that stable and latent dispositions, or traits, played a dominant role in behavior. Traits function as a predispositional basis for response-response (R-R) consistencies of behavior in a variety of different situations (e.g., Cattell, 1957; Guilford, 1959).

Allport (1937), for example, conceptualized traits as tendencies or predispositions to respond in a particular fashion that were not linked to specific stimuli but were general and enduring. Cattell (1957, 1965) also conceived of traits as the basic units to be studied in personality. Although trait theorists such as Allport or Cattell frequently do not agree about the specific structure, number, and content of traits, they generally agree that traits are internal factors that account for the consistency in behavior across a variety of different situations.

Contrary to what has frequently been written by critics of the trait approach, those who advocate this model do not propose that persons behave exactly the same in different situations. However, an assumption is frequently made that the rank order of persons, for whatever the specified trait, would be the same across a variety of different situations (Edwards & Endler, 1983; Endler, 1983). As presented in Table 15.1, those advocating the trait model have sought R-R laws, encouraged the elaboration of formal test theory, and depended almost exclusively on correlational and factor-analytic techniques for data analysis.

Table 15.1. Four Basic Personality Models Compared on Basic Research Strategies

RESEARCH STRATEGY	MODEL			
	TRAIT	PSYCHODYNAMIC	SITUATIONISM	INTERACTIONISM
Method of data collection	Questionnaires, ratings, paper-and-pencil tests	Interviews, case histories, projective measures	Experiments, operant conditioning procedures	Observations, tests, questionnaires, and experiments
Types of data	Questionnaire scores, test scores, rating scores	Verbal descriptions	Experimental data, frequency counts, behavioral checklists	Test scores, questionnaire scores, experimental data
Treatment of data	Correlation, multiple regression, factor analysis	Interpretation of verbal descriptions	Analysis of variance, cumulative records	Analysis of variance, correlations, multiple regression, factor analysis, causal modeling
Populations of prime interest	Adults (normal and abnormal)	Adults and children (abnormal)	Adults, children, and animals (primarily normal, but also abnormal)	Adults and children (normal and abnormal)

Note. Adapted, revised, and modified from Endler and Magnusson, 1976, p. 959.

Much of the research conducted in the personality area, as recent reviewers have noted (Rorer & Widiger, 1983; Wiggins, 1980), continues to center on the study of individual personality traits. Wiggins (1980) pointed out that in much current personality research "the choice of which two constructs are to be related is not informed by theoretical considerations. Rather it appears to be determined by an author's reading of the zeitgeist in terms of the frequency with which the names of the two constructs have appeared in the titles of journal articles" (p. 286). A number of critics of contemporary trait research suggest that either psychologists abandon the use of trait concepts (Rorer & Widiger, 1983; Wiggins, 1979) or look beyond the study of single traits and focus attention on clusters and systems of related personality traits. Recently, several researchers have focused on establishing a taxonomy of core traits around which research should focus (Buss & Craik, 1985; Buss & Finn, 1987; Digman, 1989; McCrae & Costa, 1984; Wiggins, 1979).

Psychodynamic Models

Psychodynamic models of personality, such as psychoanalysis, share with the trait model an emphasis on the internal determinants of behavior. The psychodynamic model assumes that internal determinants (an essential core of personality) are the sources of behavior in different situations. In stressing the importance of these person factors, those advocating a psychodynamic model share an important feature with those advocating a trait model. The two models diverge, however, because psychodynamic theories are primarily concerned with personality structure, development, and dynamics (Freud, 1920, 1933).

For psychoanalysis, the issue of personality dynamics involves explaining the interaction of the core structures of id, ego, and superego (Freud, 1933). This interaction, or conflict among the various personality structures, creates anxiety, and the individual develops defense mechanisms for resolving this anxiety. Although the situation (environmental factors) played an important role in Freud's model—because the early experiences had an impact on the interaction of id, ego, and superego—it was primarily biological in nature.

Neo-Freudians, such as Horney (1945), Sullivan (1953), Fromm (1955), and Erikson (1963), minimized the role of the psychosexual stages of development and lessened the biological nature of Freud's model. These personality researchers emphasized psychosocial stages of development, thus giving situational factors more importance in their conception of personality. They placed greater emphasis on the ego, which mediates between the social reality and internal determinants of behavior.

The importance of the role of defenses and the unconscious in the psychodynamic model led to the development of assessment techniques designed specifically to explore underlying personality dynamics. Those conducting research in this area, as summarized in Table 15.1, have relied on interviews, case histories, and projective measures as the primary method of data collection. Research has tended to focus on abnormal groups. The free association test was one of the earliest assessment techniques used by advocates of this model, although more recently developed projective measures, such as the Rorschach and the Thematic Apperception Test (TAT), have been more widely used.

Situationism Models

While the trait and psychodynamic models focus on person factors, situationism (especially social learning theory) emphasizes situational factors as the major determinants of behavior. While some advocates of the situationist model have recognized the importance of individual differences, most have taken a stimulus-response (S-R) approach. Examples of classical social learning theory are Dewey and Humber (1951) and Dollard and Miller (1950). The assumptions of those advocating the situationist model, although emphasizing environmental factors, are certainly complex and do not represent a homogeneous set of propositions (Endler, 1983; Endler & Magnusson, 1976). Consider, for example, classical learning theorists such as Dollard and Miller (1950), who emphasized learning and situational factors yet also inferred organismic variables such as drives, motives, conflicts, and response-produced cues. Skinner (1938), on the other hand, did not infer internal drives, motives, or traits but focused his attention on an empirical analysis of the reinforcement conditions that shape behavior.

More recent social learning researchers, such as Bandura (1982), Mischel (1973), and Rotter (1975), although fundamentally concerned with the external factors shaping behavior, have given considerable attention to person factors in their models. Mischel's (1973) expectancy concept, like Bandura's (1977, 1982) concept of self-efficacy, can be viewed as a person variable (Endler, 1983). In recent reformulations of the social learning model, researchers like Bandura have begun to advocate a reciprocal interactional approach between persons and their environments. This approach has many features in common with the fourth personality model, interactionism. Bandura (1986) elaborated extensively on a model in which a person's behavior influences other individuals whose responses in turn influence the person— basically a transactional approach.

Since advocates of situationism have emphasized the role played by environmental factors on behavior, research has tended to focus on the effects of specific situational factors on particular behaviors. Researchers advocating situationism, as summarized in Table 15.1, have tended to use experimental procedures such as repeated measures or treatment groups— procedures associated with traditional experimental psychology (Cronbach, 1957). Since their goal is to make causal inferences about the effects of specific environmental factors on behavior, situationist researchers have advocated the use of data analysis procedures like analysis of variance, while looking with suspicion on procedures like correlations or factor analysis (Brigham, 1989).

Interactionism Models

In psychology, one of the first interactionist approaches was proposed by Kantor (1924, 1926), who suggested that "no biological fact may be considered as anything but the mutual interaction of the organism and the environment" (1926, p. 369). Kantor also suggested that the unit of analysis should be "the individual as he interacts with all of the various types of situations which constitute his behavior circumstances" (1924, p. 92). It was Lewin (1935), however, who offered the first explicit theoretical formulation of the person-situation interaction. He argued that the various elements within the person-situation relationship were mutually interdependent and not independent. Lewin focused on the reciprocal interaction between the person and his or her environment. An essential characteristic of Murray's (1938) approach to personality was the interaction between person and situational factors: "Since at every moment, an organism is within an environment which largely determines its behavior, and since the environment changes—sometimes with radical abruptness—the conduct of an individual cannot be formulated without a characterization of each confronting situation, physical and social" (Murray, 1938, p. 39). Murray used the construct of *presses* to refer to situational factors and *needs* to refer to person factors; the interaction of presses and needs was an explicit part of his model.

While theoretical interest in interaction is old, research on interactionism is a recent development. Despite early theoretical formulations of person-situ-

ation interactions, it was not until the late 1950s and early 1960s that empirical research on interactionism developed (Endler & Hunt, 1966; Endler, Hunt, & Rosenstein, 1962; Raush, Dittmann, & Taylor, 1959a). The controversy surrounding the cross-situational consistency or stability of behavior, which was intensified with the publication of Mischel's critique of the personality area (Mischel, 1968), generated renewed interest in the interactional model (Bowers, 1973; Ekehammar, 1974; Endler, 1976; Endler & Magnusson, 1976; Magnusson & Endler, 1977; Mischel, 1973).

According to the interactional model of personality proposed by Endler and Magnusson (1976) and Endler (1983), this approach

> postulates that behavior is a function of a continuous multidirectional process of person-by-situation interactions; cognitive, motivational and emotional factors have important determining roles on behavior, regarding the person side; and the perception or psychological meaning that the situation has for the person is an essential determining factor of behavior. (Endler, 1983, p. 160)

The major goals for the proponents of the interactional model, according to Endler (1983), "are (1) the description, classification and systematic analyses of stimuli, situations, and environments; and (2) the investigation of how persons and situations interact in evoking behavior, and the reciprocal interaction of persons and behavior, persons and situations, and situations and behavior" (1983, p. 160).

An important distinction in the interactionism literature is that between mechanistic and dynamic interactionism (Endler, 1983, 1988; Endler & Magnusson, 1976; Overton & Reese, 1973). Mechanistic interactionism refers to the interaction between independent variables (e.g., levels of a particular trait or different situations). This type of interaction model is concerned with unidirectional causality, and the primary technique for data analysis, as summarized in Table 15.1, is the analysis of variance (ANOVA). Research within the mechanistic model is concerned with the structure of the interaction between person and situation variables, rather than the process of this interaction. While the methodology used to study this model explicitly calls for the simultaneous assessment of person and situation variables, techniques like ANOVA are not particularly suited for the study of dynamic interactionism. Dynamic interaction implies reciprocal causation: "Not only do events affect the behavior of organisms, but the organism is also an active agent influencing environmental events"

(Endler & Magnusson, 1976, p. 969). Thus, dynamic interactionism suggests that the traditional distinction between dependent and independent variables may not be appropriate (Endler, 1983; Magnusson, 1988; Raush, 1977), especially if changes over time must be taken into account in understanding the interaction process. Researchers will need to explore research strategies like path analysis or causal modeling (Bentler, 1980; Bynner & Romney, 1985; Magnusson, 1988) to conduct the type of process-oriented research implied by the dynamic interactional model. Statistical procedures such as Linear Structural Relationships (LISREL) allow for the effects of numerous variables to be assessed simultaneously and allow for the reciprocal effects of variables to be identified (Bentler, 1980)—something that cannot be done with more traditional techniques like ANOVA or correlations. Procedures like LISREL are particularly suited for testing the type of complex models interactionists believe are necessary to explain human behavior.

In presenting this brief overview of the four models that have guided personality research, we have tried to emphasize the pervasive impact particular theoretical orientations can have on the type of research one conducts. Those researchers who emphasize the trait and psychodynamic model, and the primacy of person variables, have devised and elaborated on research procedures that measure and support the importance of internal factors. Situationists, on the other hand, depend on experimental techniques that allow them to measure the effects of manipulated environmental factors. The interactionists have attempted to utilize research techniques that allow the simultaneous assessment of person and situation variables, as well as the interaction between these variables.

METHODOLOGY AND PERSONALITY RESEARCH

Not only has the theoretical orientation of the researcher shaped the type of personality research that is conducted, but the popularity of particular methodologies has also played an important role. Craik (1986) examined personality research methods from a historical perspective and found several important trends. Overall, researchers have employed diverse research strategies to study personality. Craik (1986) identified seven basic types: (a) biographical or archival approaches, (b) field studies, (c) laboratory methods, (d) naturalistic observational assessment, (e) observer judgments, (f) personality scales and inventories (e.g., Minnesota Multiphasic Personality Inventory [MMPI]), and (g) projective techniques (e.g.,

Rorschach). Throughout this century, the use of particular research methods has changed considerably. Craik (1986) identified three basic patterns in the use of particular methods in the study of personality. (1) Since the beginning of this century there has been continuous interest in the use of observer judgments, personality scales and inventories, projective techniques, and laboratory methods. (2) The use of naturalistic observational assessment, on the other hand, which had been used by some personality researchers before World War II, has been neglected as a research method recently. (3) The use of archival or biographical approaches and field studies has waxed and waned over the years. Popular in the period before World War II, it is only in the last decade that active interest has again been generated in the use of archival or biographical material and field studies (Runyan, 1982). In the past decade, according to Craik (1986), researchers in the personality area would appear to be practicing a form of methodological pluralism that has not been practiced in the area since the first part of this century.

Regardless of the particular research methods used (whether in the laboratory or a field study), personality research involves the study of several basic categories of variables. In an early influential paper, Edwards and Cronbach (1952) categorized research into work involved with the study of response variables, stimulus variables, and organismic variables. Response variables are related to behaviors, while stimulus variables are related to situations. Organismic variables, by definition, imply that some feature or attribute of the individual may be inferred from the study of previous responses or from knowledge about the previous experience of the individual (Edwards & Endler, 1983).

With respect to personality research, Endler (1983), Edwards and Endler (1983), and Magnusson and Endler (1977) noted that an important distinction should be made between mediating variables (such as hypothetical constructs and intervening variables) and behavioral or response variables. There are at least three types of mediating variables that have played an important role in personality research: structural, content, and motivational variables. Examples of structural variables would be abilities, competencies, or cognitive styles. Bandura's (1977, 1986) concept of self-efficacy, or Lazarus and Folkman's (1984) concepts of problem-focused and emotion-focused coping style are recent examples of structural variables. Content variables are situationally determined, or they may be stored information, such as the contents of an aggression-arousing situation. Motivational variables are those factors that are actively involved in the arousal, direction, and maintenance of particular behaviors. Examples of motivational variables are attitudes, drives, and needs.

Mediating variables are not measured directly but are inferred from reaction variables. The responses of an individual that can be observed and measured are called reaction variables. Edwards and Endler (1983) and Magnusson and Endler (1977) classified four general categories for reaction variables: (a) overt behavior, (b) physiological reactions, (c) covert reactions, such as thoughts or feelings, and (d) artificial behavior, such as performance on paper-and-pencil tests, role-playing, or simulation behavior. There are at least four methods for assessing reaction variables—rating, self-reports, standardized tests, or objective measures—and a large literature distinguishing the type of personality data generated by these different methods (Block, 1977; Cattell, 1957, 1973; Endler, 1983, 1988; Magnusson & Endler, 1977; Snyder & Ickes, 1985). For those conducting personality research, the distinction between mediating variables and reaction variables, as well as the differentiation between measurement procedures and reaction variables, is an important one. Edwards and Endler (1983) noted that there is not necessarily a one-to-one relationship between mediating variables and reaction variables, and they used the mediating variable of anxiety as a good example of the relationship:

> Reaction variables that assess anxiety may differ for different individuals, in different situations, and at different times. Thus, being silent and withdrawn may indicate anxiety for an individual in a particular situation, whereas being talkative and gregarious may indicate anxiety for another individual or in a different situational context. In addition, objective measures may not agree with self-ratings of an individual regarding his or her degree of talkativeness. (Edwards & Endler, 1983, p. 228)

SOCIOCULTURAL CONTEXT OF PERSONALITY RESEARCH

The sociocultural context in which personality research is conducted also plays an important, and often overlooked, role in the development of psychological research (Buss, 1979; Craik, 1986; Edwards & Endler, 1983; Pervin, 1984). Pervin (1984) noted that "the general public and many scientists have the view of science as a purely objective pursuit and the view of scientists as purely rational individuals. Yet considerable evidence suggests that scientists are very much influenced by their personal histories and by the societal views of the time" (p. 289). Edwards and Endler (1983) and Endler (1982) pointed out that because of the ambiguous and personally relevant subject matter of personality research, the personal life history of the researcher may play an important role in the direction of research. In a series of studies that examine the life history of various personality researchers, Stolorow and Atwood (1979) made a strong case for the important role of life experiences on the subsequent development of particular personality theorists. In recent years, considerable attention has been directed at matching the biographical events and theoretical developments of a number of psychodynamic theorists (Carotenuto, 1984; Gay, 1988; Roazen, 1985).

Along with personal events, specific cultural or historical events have played an important role in shaping the development of the personality area. The origin of the personality area in American psychology was largely the result of psychologists responding to particular societal factors (Danziger, 1990; Parker, 1986). American psychologists of the early part of this century had been hard pressed to prove that their work had practical applications (Danziger, 1979, 1990). It was the development of intelligence tests in the early part of this century that produced the first sizeable group of consumers of psychological research in America. The mass testing of recruits by psychologists in World War I greatly accelerated research on intelligence tests (Samelson, 1979). At this time, the work with intelligence tests led many psychologists, as well as educational and business professionals, to conclude that psychology had produced a practical innovation (Danziger, 1990). However, shortly after World War I, there arose a number of voices, both from psychology and the consumers of psychological research, critical of the practical benefits of using intelligence test research. A growing number of reports began to comment on the poor prognostic value and overgeneralization of using intelligence tests with psychiatric patients, predicting success in school, or success on the job (Danziger, 1990; Parker, 1986). By implication, this critical literature challenged the psychologists' claim that psychological research had practical applications. Numerous psychologists responded by developing tests that assessed a variety of nonintellectual or personality traits (Parker, 1990). It was originally conceived that these tests would be used, along with intelligence tests, in a variety of applied contexts. Throughout the 1920s and early

1930s, the amount of work on these new tests increased substantially, with psychologists becoming interested in the study of personality traits for their own sake. The modern personality area was born.

More specific historical events have also played an important role in shaping personality research. World War II led to an increase in research on individual assessment. Henry Murray and his colleagues working for the Office of Strategic Service (OSS) were assigned the task of assessing and selecting men for intelligence work, as undercover agents, spies, and resistance leaders. Their task, outlined in the *Assessment of Men* (OSS Assessment Staff, 1948), was to determine which men would perform well in a variety of different military intelligence situations. The emergence of totalitarian regimes earlier in this century, and their promotion of anti-semitism, played an important role in stimulating interest in a research problem that led to the study of the authoritarian personality (Adorno, Frenkel-Brunswik, Levinson, & Sanford, 1950).

Larger sociocultural ideologies can also play an important role in determining what type of personality models will be developed and accepted, which research questions will be attempted, and which research methods will be used. Endler (1979) and Edwards and Endler (1983) noted that the trait-situation controversy is closely related to sociocultural events. Ichheiser (1943) suggested that the concern during the 1930s and 1940s with traits was the result of an overestimation of the importance of person factors and an underestimation of the importance of situational factors. This view was rooted in the existing social system and the ideology of 19th-century liberalism, which suggested that "our fate in social space depended exclusively, or at least predominantly, on our individual qualities—that we as individuals, and not by prevailing social conditions shape our lives" (Ichheiser, 1943, p. 152). Endler (1979) and Edwards and Endler (1983) suggested that the rise of situationism after the 1940s and 1950s may have been influenced by changing sociopolitical factors (e.g., World War II, the Cold War, Vietnam, the Civil Rights Movement), with a new interest in using social conditions to explain behavior. The 1980s, however, have seen a renewed interest in traits and the genetic study of personality (Endler, 1989; Loehlin, 1982; Scarr, Weber, Weinberg, & Wittig, 1981; and Tellegen et al., 1988). It is of some interest to point out that this interest has occurred at a time when most Western societies (e.g., Western Europe and North America) were moving, politically, toward the right.

CURRENT ISSUES IN PERSONALITY RESEARCH

Trends in Personality Research

In order to determine research trends in personality research in the late 1970s and early 1980s, Edwards and Endler (1983) surveyed three psychological journals for 1979, 1980, and 1981. To obtain a more current index of research trends, we surveyed the same three journals, namely the *Journal of Personality (JP)*, the *Journal of Research in Personality (JRP)*, the *Journal of Personality and Social Psychology (JPSP)* (section on *Personality Processes and Individual Differences*) for 1986, 1987, and 1988. For 1986 to 1988 there were 498 empirical papers and 74 theoretical and review papers in these three personality journals. (Since some of the papers included more than one study, sample, methodology, or type of statistical analysis the total number of methods of data collection, for example, added up to 620 rather than 498. The percentages reported here, however, are based on 498 papers. Because of multiple indices for some articles the percentages will add up to more than 100%.) For 1986 to 1988, with respect to methodology, 234 articles (or 47% of the 498 articles) used the nonexperimental classroom as the method of data collection; 186 articles (37.35%) used an experimental laboratory situation for data collection; 125 (25%) used a nonexperimental field setting, 67 (13.45%) used a nonexperimental laboratory setting (e.g., collecting questionnaires in the lab rather than the classroom), and less than 1% used an experimental field setting (four articles) or a classroom experiment (four articles). Only 9 of the 498 articles (1.8%) were cross-cultural.

With respect to the subjects or participants used in the studies, 376 articles (75.5%) used college students, 131 (26.3%) used adults, and 51 (10.24%) used children and adolescents. Of the 131 articles using adults, 20 (15%) used a clinical population, and 111 (85%) used a nonclinical population.

In terms of statistical analyses, 384 articles (77.1%) reported using analysis of variance of t tests, 350 (70.28%) used correlational analysis; 110 (22.09%) used multiple regression; 95 (19.08%) used factor analyses; 27 (5.42%) used causal modeling (LISREL, path analysis, etc.), and 92 (18.47%) used other types of analyses (e.g., chi-squared, discriminant analysis, or cluster analysis). There were three major methods used for the type of data collected: behavioral responses, 156 articles (31.32%); questionnaire, 409 articles (82.12%); and physiological responses, 22 articles (4.4%).

For 1986 to 1988 the classroom setting dominated the research methodology (47% of all articles). For 1979 to 1981 (see Edwards & Endler, 1983), the laboratory setting dominated the research methodology. Hence, there has been a shift from the laboratory to the classroom during the 1980s. The reasons for this are not readily apparent, other than noting that it is easier and less expensive (in terms of resources) to collect questionnaires in a classroom than to conduct experiments in the laboratory. This is probably the reason why college students are the most frequent participants (subjects) in the various studies (e.g., in 75.5% of the articles, or three out of every four studies). Once again, few cross-cultural studies appeared in the three journals surveyed. Questionnaire data were used in four out of every five studies; primarily a function of the ease of data collection.

With respect to statistical analyses, the analysis of variance (ANOVA) (and/or t tests) is the most common technique of data analysis (77.11% of the articles), with correlational analysis (70.28%) close behind. Only 1 out of every 20 articles used causal modeling as a technique for data analyses. Probably the ease of using the ANOVA and correlational techniques and the lack of familiarity with causal modeling techniques account for these trends.

For the three journals reviewed, no single content area predominated. This is comparable to what Edwards and Endler (1983) found for the journals earlier in the decade. It is possible that had we included two relatively new personality journals (*Personality and Individual Differences*, *PAID*, and the *European Journal of Personality*, *EJP*) the results might have been different. In order to make these results comparable to those reported by Edwards and Endler (1983) we only surveyed *JP*, *JRP*, and *JPSP*, for the present chapter. There were a number of popular topics that seemed to stand out in the literature: Type A behavior pattern, social cognition, coping, sex roles, and health psychology. Other recent reviewers have also suggested (Carson, 1989; Singer & Kolligian, 1987) that personality and health-related issues appear to be a large and growing research area. This would appear to be a recent development, one not detected when the literature was reviewed only a few years ago (Edwards & Endler, 1983).

Many of the criticisms that were made in the 1970s and early 1980s (e.g., Block, 1977; Carlson, 1971; Cronbach, 1975; Edwards & Endler, 1983; and Wiesenthal, Edwards, Endler, Koza, Walton, & Emmott,

1978) about the personality area are still relevant today. Personality research in the late 1980s appears to be dominated by questionnaire data collected on North American college students (a nonclinical population) with the data usually being analyzed by ANOVA or correlational techniques.

Person-Situation Debate: The Consistency or Specificity of Behavior

Over the past 2 decades, one of the most controversial issues in the personality area has been whether behavior is consistent across situations or is situation specific (Edwards & Endler, 1983; Endler, 1983; Kendrick & Funder, 1988). The recent literature on the person-situation debate is voluminous (see Kendrick & Funder, 1988 for a recent review. The *Journal of Personality* recently devoted a special issue to this topic; see West & Graziano, 1989), with ample evidence being offered for both sides of the issue. However, proponents have also confused the issue by painting inaccurate portraits of those in opposition. The question of the meaning of consistency is a case in point. There are at least three different meanings for consistency. The issue of absolute consistency assumes that an individual will manifest a particular behavioral trait (e.g., extraversion) to the same degree in all situations. No trait theorist has supported this position, although this is an image of the trait theorists that proponents of situationism have frequently presented. Those advocating the consistency of behavior have recognized that individuals change and alter their behavior depending on the situation (Endler, 1989). Relative consistency, which assumes that the rank-order of persons for a particular behavior (such as extraversion) is consistent across different situations for a specific group of people, is the type of consistency that advocates of the trait position have promoted (Endler, 1983; Kendrick & Funder, 1988). It is over this latter type of consistency that much of the person-situation debate has been fought. There is a third approach to consistency, one that has been offered by those advocating the interactionist model for the study of personality (Endler, 1977; 1983; 1988; Magnusson, 1976; Magnusson & Endler, 1977). Coherent consistency suggests that behavior is predictable but not necessarily consistent in an absolute or relative sense. From an interactionist position, the question of consistency is an emphasis on identifying the person's patterns of stable or changing behavior across a variety of situations—a pattern that is characteristic for the individual (Endler, 1983, 1988; Endler & Edwards, 1987; Magnusson & Endler, 1977).

There have been three major research strategies for investigating the consistency or inconsistency of behavior: (a) the correlational research strategy, (b) the multidimensional variance components strategy, and (c) the person-by-situation factorial experimental design (Endler, 1981, 1983; Endler & Magnusson, 1976). In the following three sections we will examine the nature of these approaches and review the major research findings.

Correlation Research Strategies

The correlational research strategy is the oldest approach that has been used to address the consistency issue. Following this approach, the question of consistent behavior can be examined either in terms of temporal (longitudinal) or situational (cross-situational) strategies. Another way of understanding these two approaches is to distinguish between consistency in similar and dissimilar situations (Edwards & Endler, 1983; Endler & Edwards, 1987; Magnusson & Endler, 1977). In general, those taking a cross-sectional approach have focused on studying behavior in similar situations over time.

One of the first important studies on the issue of consistency was Hartshorne and May's (1928) research on honesty. They reported cross-situational correlations for honesty of about + 0.30. Newcomb (1931) found that correlations for introversion–extraversion behaviors across different situations averaged approximately 0.30. Mischel (1968) reviewed a variety of personality studies and concluded that correlations of trait scores in different situations were seldom larger than 0.30. This review, in part, played a major role in fueling the recent person-situation debate. Subsequent researchers have argued that Mischel had lumped methodologically inferior and superior studies together (Block, 1977; Hogan, Desoto, & Solano, 1977). Epstein (1979, 1983) argued, for example, that higher correlations of 0.30 have been found when researchers have used aggregates of a particular behavior instead of single isolated behaviors.

With respect to the longitudinal study of consistency, an important early study was conducted by Newcomb, Koenig, Flacks, and Warwick (1967), who studied a group of Bennington college students for several decades. They found that these students became less conservative during their college years, and that this behavior was maintained for several decades after leaving college. Longitudinal studies by Block (1977), Epstein (1979), and Olweus (1979) have reported correlational data that supports the relative consistency of certain traits over time.

Multidimensional Variance Components Strategy

An important series of early studies (Raush, Dittmann, & Taylor, 1959a, 1959b; Raush, Farbman, & Llewellyn, 1960) examined the behavior of delinquent boys in a variety of situations. Conducting a multivariate analysis of the ratings of observed behavior in the different situations, Raush et al. (1959a, 1959b) and Raush et al. (1960) found that the person-by-situation interaction accounted for more variance in the prediction of behavior than either persons or situations. Endler and Hunt (1966, 1969) studied the contributions of person and situation variables, and the interaction of those variables, on self-reported levels of anxiety. Using a variance components technique for their analysis, they found that persons accounted for about 4% of the variance for males and approximately 8% for females. The person-by-situation interaction accounted for about 10% of the variance.

Anxiety has been the subject of a large body of research that has found the interaction of person and situation variables an important source of variation (Endler, 1975, 1983, 1988; Endler, Edwards, & Vitelli, 1990; Endler & Okada, 1975). However, research has also found support for the importance of person-by-situation interactions in the study of honesty (Nelson, Grinder, & Mutterer, 1969), social perception (Argyle & Little, 1972), conformity (Endler, 1966), aggression (Berkowitz, 1977), coping behavior (Cantor, Norem, Niedenthal, Langstonn, & Brower, 1987), and psychopathology (Magnusson & Ohman, 1987). Detailed reviews of this work can be found in Bowers (1973), Endler (1983, 1988), Endler and Magnusson (1976), and Ekehammar (1974).

Person-by-Treatment Experimental Designs

Although studies using a variance components strategy provide empirical evidence that person-by-situation interactions account for an important proportion of the variance in specific behaviors, they do not explain these interactions (Edwards & Endler, 1983; Sarason, Smith, & Diener, 1975). Early papers by Edwards and Cronbach (1952) and Cronbach (1957) proposed that factorial experimental designs could be used to understand how person and situational variables interact in eliciting particular types of behavior. Over the past 2 decades a number of researchers, studying diverse behaviors, have used person-by-treatment experimental designs. Domino (1971) found an interaction between situation (an instructor's teaching style) and the person variables of achievement via independence or achievement via conformance in a study of success in college. Berkowitz (1977) found an interaction of persons and situations in a study of aggressive behavior, while Fiedler (1971, 1977) found that situational variables interacted with the person variables of leadership style in influencing group effectiveness. Cantor et al. (1987) found support for a person-by-situation interaction model in a study of self-concepts and the use of particular cognitive strategies (coping behaviors) in different stressful situations. In a later section of this chapter we will examine a large program of research that has examined the interactional model of stress, anxiety, and coping.

Evaluation of the Consistency Issue

Over the past few decades the three research strategies reviewed here (correlational research, multidimensional variance components, and person-by-treatment experimental designs) have come under close critical scrutiny (Cronbach, 1975; Endler, 1983; Endler & Magnusson, 1976; Kenrick & Funder, 1988; Mischel & Peake, 1982). There is a general consensus, however, with respect to correlational research that while there is generally weak evidence for the cross-situational consistency of behavior, there is evidence for a moderate amount of consistency across similar situations (Block, 1971, 1977; Endler & Edwards, 1987; Magnusson, Gerzen, & Nyman, 1968). The variance components and person-by-treatment experimental approaches have found significant and theoretically meaningful interactions in the study of a diverse set of behaviors.

In general, the recent debate about the consistency of behavior has had a positive impact on the personality area. Kenrick and Funder (1988) pointed out that

> as with most controversies, the truth finally appears to lie not in the vivid black or white of either extreme, but somewhere in the less striking gray area. It would be a mistake, however, to claim that the interchange served only to bring out a number of 'straw man' positions that no one ever took seriously anyway, that the repetitive cycle of argument and reply produced no more than fatigue and deja vu, or that we are no closer to understanding personality traits than we were two decades ago. (p. 31)

An important development of the debate was the call for new research methodologies. Considerable interest has been generated in improving measurement techniques (Block, 1977; Epstein, 1979, 1983; Jackson & Paunonen, 1980). Epstein, for example, called for multiple measures of behavior to increase reliability (Epstein, 1979). The use of meta-analytic procedures has begun to appear with more frequency, as researchers attempt quantitatively to review a large body of empirical research on specific questions (cf. Booth-Kewley & Friedman, 1987; Friedman & Booth-Kewley, 1987). The development of research strategies that explored the interaction of person and situation variables was a direct result of an attempt to help resolve the person-situation debate (Endler, 1983). Proponents of an interactional model for the study of personality began to urge a systematic analysis of the dimensions of persons and situations that interact to affect behavior (Bowers, 1973; Endler, 1973, 1975, 1983; Endler & Magnusson, 1976). An important stage in the development of an interactional perspective of personality, they argued, was research techniques and strategies for a systematic analysis of situations.

THE SITUATION AS A VARIABLE IN PERSONALITY RESEARCH

Although psychologists advocating the situationist model have demonstrated the potential impact of the situation on behavior, and while interactionists argue that the situation is an integral variable for understanding behavior, there is still a basic need for a systematic study of situations (Edwards & Endler, 1983; Endler, 1983; Frederiksen, 1972). With respect to situational factors and personality, it is possible to distinguish among environments, situations, and stimuli. The environment is the general background within which behavior occurs. The situation, on the other hand, is the momentary background. Stimuli can be construed as being the elements within a situation (Endler, 1981). According to Pervin (1977), the terms *stimulus*, *situation*, and *environment* have been used interchangeably and have frequently been used without being defined. This has not always been the case. Experimental psychologists, notably perception psychologists, have focused on the stimulus; personality theorists, who have emphasized person-by-situation interactions, have been concerned with situations; and ecologists or environmental psychologists have emphasized the environment.

Another important issue in a systematic approach to the study of situations is whether we can define situations independently of the perceiver. Should the emphasis be on the subjective or objective characteristics of situations (cf. Endler, 1983)? The meaning or significance of a situation is an important determinant of behavior. Therefore, one should focus attention on the perception of situations when one is examining person-by-situation interactions. Two persons may perceive the same situation as stressful, but one individual may react by anxiously withdrawing and another individual may react by attacking. There is also a temporal factor in that persons may react differently at different times.

People not only react to situations, but they also affect the situations with which they interact. Bowers (1973) suggested that "situations are as much a function of the person as the person's behavior is a function of the situation" (p. 327). There is a constant and continuous interaction between people and situations, and it is necessary to examine this ongoing process (Endler, 1983; Endler & Magnusson, 1976). We frequently shop for and select the situations we encounter in our daily lives. Nevertheless, there are constraining conditions where situations are imposed on us. This is obviously a continuous and lifelong process. In studying these phenomena, however, we observe and study a cross-sectional slice of situations rather than examining situations longitudinally. It would be advantageous, however, to examine the ongoing and continuing process of situations. For the most part our daily routines are similar day to day: going to the same office, interacting with the same colleagues. We shop around and choose those people and situations that are rewarding and pleasurable, and avoid those situations that are unpleasant and painful. In addition to selecting situations, we also have situations imposed on us, such as work deadlines, salaries, supervisors. We both shape and are shaped by our environments; we both influence and are influenced by the people with whom we interact. However, the environmental influence is always mediated via actual situations (cf. Magnusson, 1974). Environmental stimulation affects behavior both in terms of current information that is being processed and also by interacting with previously stored information (Endler, 1983).

Levels of Analysis

Endler (1981, 1983) and Magnusson (1974) proposed the need for a differential psychology of situations. This would involve dimensionalizing situations in terms of impact, complexity, relevance, objectiveness, subjectiveness, and representativeness and would involve decisions about the appropriate units of analysis. It would also involve adequate and represen-

tative samplings of situations. However, there is an inherent danger in developing a taxonomy of situations, since different theorists may focus on different attributes and thereby develop different taxonomies. This has been one of the problems with trait models, since different trait researchers have developed different taxonomies or classifications of traits (Buss & Finn, 1987). Taxonomies of situations should be derived within the context of a theory and should not be developed primarily on an empirical basis. Obviously, the taxonomies need an empirical verification. These taxonomies should focus on the situations that persons experience and on perceptions and situations (Endler, 1983). Pervin (1977), for example, developed an ecological sampling of situations derived from the natural habitats that people encounter. He concluded that it may be important to emphasize the person-by-situation interaction as the unit of analysis. Personal projects may also be a basis for classification. All people have certain goals in life and certain projects that involve them (Endler, 1981). It may also be desirable to have people keep daily logs of their behavior and the situations they encounter.

Strategies for Situational Analyses

There have been few attempts to examine situations psychologically and few attempts to integrate personality research and ecological psychology (Endler, 1983). In terms of the environment, Craik (1973) and Moos (1973) provided early attempts at presenting a personality research paradigm for environmental psychology. Ekehammar (1974) described five major methods for investigating the problems of situational description and classification: "(1) a priori defined variables of *physical* and *social* character; (2) need concepts; (3) some *single reaction* elicited by the situations; (4) individuals *reaction patterns* elicited by the situations; and (5) individuals' *perceptions* of situations" (pp. 1041–1042). Two of these strategies (4 and 5) have special relevance for interactional research. Endler and Magnusson (1976) indicated that the psychological significance of the environment or situation can be assessed by both examining the perception of the situation and the reaction to the situation. Magnusson and his colleagues (Magnusson, 1971, 1974; Magnusson & Ekehammar, 1973) used an empirical psychophysical method for investigating the perception of situations. Situation reaction studies have also studied individuals' responses to situations (e.g., Endler et al., 1962; Frederiksen, 1972; Rotter, 1954).

INTERACTION MODEL OF ANXIETY, STRESS, AND COPING

The interaction model of anxiety, stress, and coping proposes that situation and person factors interact to determine how an individual responds, adapts, or copes with the experience of anxiety in stressful situations (Endler, 1988). This model is an extension of the interactional model of personality and of anxiety proposed by Endler (1983) and Endler and Magnusson (1976). An important conceptual distinction has been made in the interactional model between state and trait anxiety. State anxiety has been defined as a transitory emotional state of unpleasant feelings of tension and worry. These feelings are also associated with the activation of the autonomic nervous system (Endler, 1983; Spielberger, 1983). Trait anxiety refers to a predisposition to experience state anxiety (Endler, 1983; Spielberger, 1983). The state-trait distinction underscores the need to differentiate, conceptually and methodologically, the individual's predisposition and the actual responses in a specific situation.

The interactional model proposes that trait and state anxiety, as well as coping strategies, are all multidimensional constructs. Individual differences with respect to trait anxiety are specific to certain types of stressful situations. The dimensions of trait anxiety included in this model to date are social evaluation, physical danger, ambiguity, and daily routines (Endler, 1983; Endler et al., 1990). Other dimensions, such as loss and threat, are theoretically possible (Endler, 1983). Endler (1983), Endler, Edwards, Vitelli, and Parker (1989), and Sarason (1975) suggested that state anxiety is multidimensional and identified two basic components: autonomic-emotional state anxiety and cognitive-worry state anxiety. The autonomic-emotional component includes those symptoms associated with sympathetic nervous system arousal, such as sweaty hands, shortness of breath, or rapid heart rate. The cognitive-worry components are those cognitions focused on self-doubt and potential failure. To provide an adequate technique for assessing the multidimensional nature of state and trait anxiety, Endler and his colleagues developed the Endler Multidimensional Anxiety Scales (EMAS; Endler et al., 1990; Endler et al., 1989). With these scales, autonomic-emotional state anxiety is distinguished from cognitive-worry state anxiety. The EMAS also assesses four components of trait anxiety: social evaluation, physical danger, ambiguous, and daily routines. A third set of measures assesses the individual's perceptions of the particular stressful situation.

A recent study by Endler, Parker, Bagby, and Cox (in press) investigated the factor structure of the state and trait anxiety subscales of the EMAS. When items from the state and trait anxiety scales were factor analyzed together from a sample of approximately 2,000 college students, a five-factor solution was found with a separate factor for state anxiety, social evaluation trait anxiety, physical danger trait anxiety, ambiguous trait anxiety, and daily routines trait anxiety. When the 60 items of the EMAS trait anxiety scale were factor analyzed alone, with the same sample, four factors emerged: social evaluation, physical danger, ambiguous, and daily routines trait anxiety. When the EMAS state anxiety items were factor analyzed alone, with the same sample, two factors emerged: cognitive-worry and autonomic-emotional state anxiety. Similar results were found in a recent cross-cultural study of anxiety (Endler, Lobel, Parker, & Schmitz, in press). They found support for the multidimensional nature of state and trait anxiety in a study using the EMAS in samples of Canadian, American, German, and Israeli college students.

The interactional model of anxiety, stress, and coping also makes the assumption that coping is a multidimensional construct. There is a substantial literature supporting the multidimensional nature of coping (Billings & Moos, 1981, 1984; Carver, Scheier, & Weintraub, 1989; Endler & Parker, 1990a, 1990b; Folkman & Lazarus, 1985; Lazarus & Folkman, 1984; Pearlin & Schooler, 1978). An important distinction is made in this literature between two basic coping strategies: emotion-focused and problem-focused coping. Endler and Parker (1990a; 1990b) noted that problem-focused coping refers to a task orientation, while emotion-focused coping strategies refer to a person orientation. Person strategies might include emotional responses, self-preoccupation, and fantasizing reactions. Endler and Parker (1990b) identified a third basic coping strategy—avoidance (see also Krohne, 1988). This type of coping can include either person-oriented or task-oriented strategies. A person can avoid stressful situations by seeking out other people (seeking social support) or by engaging in another task than the one at hand (distraction activities). To provide an adequate technique for assessing the multidimensional nature of coping, Endler and Parker (1990a; 1990b developed the Coping Inventory of Stressful Situations (CISS). This 48-item scale is comprised of three scales that reliably assess task, emotion, and avoidance coping. The avoidance scale has two subscales: a seeking social support and a distraction scale. Endler and Parker (1990a; 1990b) factor analyzed a cross-section of coping with stressful situation items in a large sample of college students and a large sample of adults. In the analyses with both samples three identical factors emerged; task-oriented, emotion-oriented, and avoidance-oriented coping. A separate factor analysis of the items from the avoidance factor identified the same two subfactors in both samples: seeking social support and distraction.

At the core of the interactional model of anxiety, stress and coping are the differential hypotheses, which propose that state anxiety is a function of the interaction of a particular dimension of trait anxiety and the congruent situational threat. Thus, there will be a significantly greater increase in state anxiety in individuals who are high on a specific dimension of trait anxiety when they are in a congruent threatening situation than experienced by individuals who are low on that particular dimension of trait anxiety (see Figure 15.1). There is no interaction, however, when the situational stress and facet of trait anxiety are not congruent. For example, in a social evaluation situation, significantly greater increases in state anxiety would be predicted for those individuals who are high on social evaluation trait anxiety compared to those individuals who are lower.

Some of our results from a recent unpublished study, testing parts of the interactional model of anxiety, stress, and coping (see Figure 15.1), demonstrate the need for examining both person and situational variables in personality research. The study involved the prediction of state anxiety levels (EMAS-state anxiety) in two different situations in 185 college students: a stressful situation (10 minutes before a midterm examination) and a nonstressful situation (a classroom situation several weeks before the exam). The predictors were coping style (the coping subscales from the CISS) and trait anxiety (EMAS trait subscales). A regression analysis yielded a model with daily routines and emotion-oriented coping account-

ing for 23% of the variance with total state anxiety as the dependent variable. A regression analysis with total state anxiety from the stressful situation yielded a model with ambiguous trait anxiety and emotion-oriented coping accounting for 15% of the variance. Although emotion-oriented coping was a predictor of state anxiety regardless of the situation, only trait anxiety dimensions congruent with the situation (ambiguous trait anxiety for the ambiguous situation just before the exam, and daily routines for the regular classroom situation) were significant predictors.

A number of laboratory and field studies have provided empirical support for the differential hypotheses. The field studies have been conducted in such diverse settings as a classroom examination situation, track and field and karate situations, actors performing on stage, dental surgery situations, women undergoing a dilation and curettage or a laparoscopy, psychotherapy, and bankers in management positions in stressful on-the-job situations (cf. Endler, 1983; Endler et al., 1990). Out of 18 tests of the differential hypothesis conducted by Endler and his colleagues, this hypothesis was confirmed in 13 cases and not in five cases (a success rate of approximately 70%).

There are a number of implications of the interactional model of anxiety, stress, and coping for clinical and applied settings. Both environmental factors and individual vulnerabilities have been implicated in the development of psychopathology (Garmezy, 1981; Magnusson & Ohman, 1987; Sturgis, 1984). Individual vulnerabilities have been related to genetic factors (Loehlin, 1982), early experiences, physical disorders, and coping styles (Endler, 1988). The interactional model is a potentially useful guide of research that explores specific dimensions of individual differences in conjunction with specific environmental situations (cf. Magnusson & Ohman, 1987). In the treatment of particular psychological disorders, espe-

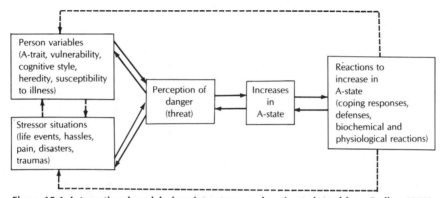

Figure 15.1 Interactional model of anxiety, stress, and coping (adapted from Endler, 1988).

cially anxiety, the interactional model suggests that researchers study interactions of person and treatment variables (Endler, 1983, 1988).

CONCLUSION

The present chapter has focused on describing the reciprocal relationships that exist among theories, methods, and the sociocultural context in shaping the direction of personality research. Throughout much of this century, personality research has tended to focus on either person or situation variables, with a preference for interest in the former. We have attempted to emphasize both the positive and negative aspects of research focusing on either type of variable. The present chapter also briefly examined recent trends in personality research. While the laboratory continues to be an important location for research, the classroom has now become the location of choice for personality research. This trend may explain why undergraduates continue to be the most frequently used group of subjects in personality research. Concerns expressed earlier in the decade about the need for conducting research with diverse populations (Pervin, 1984) are still relevant. Considerable attention has been devoted to describing the interactional model in this chapter—a view that explicitly advocates the study of person and situation variables and their interactions. Although most of the interactional research that has been done to date addresses mechanistic interactionism, we have briefly described the type of dynamic interactional research that future personality researchers may wish to pursue. We have briefly described a program of research on the interactional model of anxiety, stress, and coping. While primarily testing a mechanistic interactional model, this work may prove to be useful in studying anxiety, stress, and coping from a dynamic (process) perspective.

REFERENCES

Adorno, T. W., Frenkel-Brunswik, E., Levinson, D. J., & Sanford, R. N. (1950). *The authoritarian personality*. New York: Harper & Row.

Allport, G. W. (1937). *Personality: A psychological interpretation*. New York: Holt, Rinehart & Winston.

Argyle, M., & Little, B. R. (1972). Do personality traits apply to social behavior? *Journal of Theory and Social Behavior, 2*, 1–35.

Bandura, A. (1977). Self-efficacy: Toward a unifying theory of behavioral change. *Psychological Review, 84*, 191–215.

Bandura, A. (1982). Self-efficacy mechanism in human agency. *American Psychologist, 37*, 122–147.

Bandura, A. (1986). *Social foundations of thought and action: A social cognitive theory*. Englewood Cliffs, NJ: Prentice-Hall.

Bentler, P. M. (1980). Multivariate analysis with latent variables: Causal modeling. *Annual Review of Psychology, 31*, 419–456.

Berkowitz, L. (1977). Situational and personal conditions governing reaction to aggressive cues. In D. Magnusson & N. S. Endler (Eds.), *Personality at the crossroads: Current issues in interactional psychology* (pp. 165–171). Hillsdale, NJ: Lawrence Erlbaum Associates.

Billings, A. G., & Moos, R. H. (1981). The role of coping responses and social resources in attenuating the impact of stressful life events. *Journal of Behavioral Medicine, 4*, 139–157.

Billings, A. G., & Moos, R. H. (1984). Coping, stress, and social resources among adults with unipolar depression. *Journal of Personality and Social Psychology, 46*, 877–891.

Block, J. (1971). *Lives through time*. Berkeley, CA: Bancroft.

Block, J. (1977). Advancing the psychology of personality: Paradigmatic shift or improving the quality of research. In D. Magnusson & N. S. Endler (Eds.), *Personality at the crossroads: Current issues in interactional psychology* (pp. 37–63). Hillsdale, NJ: Lawrence Erlbaum Associates.

Booth-Kewley, S., & Friedman, H. S. (1987). Psychological predictors of heart disease: A quantitative review. *Psychological Bulletin, 101*, 343–362.

Bowers, K. S. (1973). Situationism in psychology: An analysis and a critique. *Psychological Review, 80*, 307–336.

Brigham, T. A. (1989). On the importance of recognizing the difference between experiments and correlational studies. *American Psychologist, 44*, 1077–1078.

Buss, A. (1979). *Psychology in social context*. New York: Irvington.

Buss, A. H., & Finn, S. E. (1987). Classification of personality traits. *Journal of Personality and Social Psychology, 52*, 432–444.

Buss, D. M., & Craik, K. H. (1985). Why not measure that trait? Alternative criteria for identifying important dispositions. *Journal of Personality and Social Psychology, 48*, 934–946.

Bynner, J. M., & Romney, D. M. (1985). LISREL for beginners. *Canadian Psychology, 26*, 43–49.

Cantor, N., Norem, J. K., Niedenthal, P. M., Langstonn, C. A., & Brower, A. M. (1987). Life tasks, self-concept ideals, and cognitive strategies in a life transition. *Journal of Personality and Social Psychology, 53*, 1178–1191.

Carlson, R. (1971). Where is the person in personality research? *Psychological Bulletin, 75*, 203–219.

Carotenuto, A. (1984). *A secret symmetry: Sabina Spielrein between Jung and Freud*. New York: Pantheon Books.

Carson, R. C. (1989). Personality. *Annual Review of Psychology, 40*, 227–248.

Carver, C. S., Scheier, M. F., & Weintraub, J. K. (1989). Assessing coping strategies: A theoretically based approach. *Journal of Personality and Social Psychology*, 56, 267–283.

Cattell, R. B. (1957). *Personality and motivation structure and measurement*. Yonkers, NY: World Book.

Cattell, R. B. (1965). *The scientific analysis of personality*. Chicago: Aldine de Gruyter.

Cattell, R. B. (1973). *Personality and mood by questionnaire*. San Francisco: Jossey-Bass.

Craik, K. H. (1973). Environmental psychology. *Annual Review of Psychology*, 24, 403–422.

Craik, K. H. (1986). Personality research methods: An historical perspective. *Journal of Personality*, 54, 18–51.

Cronbach, L. J. (1957). The two disciplines of scientific psychology. *American Psychologist*, 12, 671–684.

Cronbach, L. J. (1975). Beyond the two disciplines of scientific psychology. *American Psychologist*, 30, 116–127.

Danziger, K. (1979). The social origins of modern psychology. In A. Buss (Ed.), *Psychology in social context* (pp. 27–45). New York: Irvington.

Danziger, K. (1990). *Constructing the subject: Historical origins of psychological research*. New York: Cambridge University Press.

Dewey, R., & Humber, W. J. (1951). *The development of human behavior*. New York: MacMillan.

Digman, J. M. (1989). Five robust trait dimensions: Development, stability, and utility. *Journal of Personality*, 57, 195–214.

Dollard, J., & Miller, N. E. (1950). *Personality and psychotherapy: An analysis in terms of learning, thinking and culture*. New York: McGraw-Hill.

Domino, G. (1971). Interactive effects of achievement of orientation and teaching style on academic achievement. *Journal of Educational Psychology*, 62, 427–431.

Edwards, A. J., & Cronbach, L. J. (1952). Experimental design for research in psychotherapy. *Journal of Clinical Psychology*, 8, 51–59.

Edwards, J. M., & Endler, N. S. (1983). Personality research. In M. Hersen, A. E. Kazdin, & A. S. Bellack (Eds.), *The clinical psychology handbook* (1st ed., pp. 223–238). Elmsford, NY: Pergamon Press.

Ekehammar, B. (1974). Interactionism in personality from a historical perspective. *Psychological Bulletin*, 81, 1026–1048.

Endler, N. S. (1966). Conformity as a function of different reinforcement schedules. *Journal of Personality and Social Psychology*, 4, 175–180.

Endler, N. S. (1973). The person versus the situation—A pseudo issue? A response to Alker. *Journal of Personality*, 41, 287–303.

Endler, N. S. (1975). The case of person-situation interactions. *Canadian Psychological Review*, 16, 12–21.

Endler, N. S. (1976). Grand illusions: Traits or interactions? *Canadian Psychological Review*, 17, 174–181.

Endler, N. S. (1977). The role of person by situation interactions in personality theory. In I. C. Uzgiris & F. Weizman (Eds.), *The structuring of expering* (pp. 343–369), New York: Plenum Publishing.

Endler, N. S. (1979). Sociopolitical factors in theory construction. *Ontario Psychologist*, 11, 21–22.

Endler, N. S. (1981). Situational aspects of interactional psychology. In D. Magnusson (Ed.), *Toward a psychology of situations: An interactional perspective* (pp. 361–373). Hillsdale, NJ: Lawrence Erlbaum Associates.

Endler, N. S. (1982). Interactionism comes of age. In M. P. Zanna, E. T. Higgins, & C. P. Herman (Eds.), *Consistency in social behavior: The Ontario Symposium* (Vol. 2, pp. 209–249). Hillsdale, NJ: Lawrence Erlbaum Associates.

Endler, N. S. (1983). Interactionism: A personality model, but not yet a theory. In M. M. Page (Ed.), *Nebraska Symposium on Motivation 1982: Personality—Current theory and research* (pp. 155–200). Lincoln, NE: University of Nebraska Press.

Endler, N. S. (1988). Hassles, health and happiness. In M. P. Janisse (Ed.), *Individual differences, stress and health psychology* (pp. 24–56). New York: Springer.

Endler, N. S. (1989). The temperamental nature of personality. *European Journal of Personality*, 3, 151–165.

Endler, N. S., & Edwards, J. M. (1987). Variations on a theme. *European Journal of Personality*, 1, 17–20.

Endler, N. S., Edwards, J. M., & Vitelli, R. (1990). *Endler Multidimensional Anxiety Scales: Manual*. Los Angles, CA: Western Psychological Services.

Endler, N. S., Edwards, J. M., Vitelli, R., & Parker, J. D. A. (1989). Assessment of state and trait anxiety: Endler Multidimensional Anxiety Scales. *Anxiety Research: An International Journal*, 2, 1–14.

Endler, N. S., & Hunt, J. M. (1966). Sources of behavioral variance as measured by the S-R Inventory of Anxiousness. *Psychological Bulletin*, 65, 336–346.

Endler, N. S., & Hunt, J. M. (1969). Generalizability of contributions from sources of variance in the S-R Inventory of Anxiousness. *Journal of Personality*, 37, 1–24.

Endler, N. S., Hunt, J. M., & Rosenstein, A. J. (1962). An S-R Inventory of Anxiousness. *Psychological Monographs*, 76(17, Whole No. 536), 133.

Endler, N. S., Lobel, T., Parker, J. D. A., & Schmitz, P. (in press). Multidimensionality of state and trait anxiety: A cross-cultural study comparing U.S., Canadian, Israeli, and German young adults. *Anxiety Research: An International Journal*.

Endler, N. S., & Magnusson, D. (1976). Toward an interactional psychology of personality. *Psychological Bulletin*, 83, 956–974.

Endler, N. S., & Okada, M. (1975). A multidimensional measure of trait anxiety: The S-R inventory of general trait anxiousness. *Journal of Consulting and Clinical Psychology*, 43, 319–329.

Endler, N. S., & Parker, J. D. A. (1990a). *The coping inventory of stressful situations (CISS): Manual*. Toronto: Multi-Health Systems, Inc.

Endler, N. S., & Parker, J. D. A. (1990b). Multidimensional assessment of coping: A critical evaluation. *Journal of Personality and Social Psychology, 58*, 844–854.

Endler, N. S., Parker, J. D. A., Bagby, R. M., & Cox, B. J. (in press). The multidimensionality of state and trait anxiety: The factor structure of the Endler Multidimensional Anxiety Scales. *Journal of Personality and Social Psychology.*

Epstein, S. (1979). The stability of behavior: I. On predicting most of the people much of the time. *Journal of Personality and Social Psychology, 37*, 1097–1126.

Epstein, S. (1983). Aggregation and beyond: Some basic issues on the prediction of behavior. *Journal of Personality, 51*, 360–392.

Erikson, E. (1963). *Childhood and society* (2nd ed.). New York: W W Norton.

Fiedler, F. E. (1971). Validation and extension of the contingency model of leadership effectivensss: A review of empirical findings. *Psychological Bulletin, 76*, 128–148.

Fiedler, F. E. (1977). What triggers the person situation interaction in leadership? In D. Magnusson & N. S. Endler (Eds.), *Personality at the crossroads: Current issues in interactional psychology* (pp. 151–163). Hillsdale, NJ: Lawrence Erlbaum Associates.

Folkman, S., & Lazarus, R. S. (1985). If it changes it must be a process; A study of emotion and coping during three stages of a college examination. *Journal of Personality and Social Psychology, 48*, 150–170.

Frederiksen, N. (1972). Toward a taxonomy of situations. *American Psychologist, 27*, 114–123.

Freud, S. (1920). *A general introduction to psychoanalysis.* New York: Boni & Liveright.

Freud, S. (1933). *New introductory lectures on psychoanalysis.* New York: W W Norton.

Friedman, H. S., & Booth-Kewley, S. (1987). The disease-prone personality: A meta-analytic view of the construct. *American Psychologist, 42*, 539–555.

Fromm, E. (1955). *The sane society.* New York: Holt, Rinehart & Winston.

Garmezy, N. (1981). Children under stress: Perspectives on antecedents and correlates of vulnerability and resistance to psychopathology. In A. I. Rabin, L. Aronoff, A. M. Barclay, & R. A. Zucker (Eds.), *Further explorations in personality* (pp. 196–269). New York: John Wiley & Sons.

Gay, P. (1988). *Freud: A life for our time.* New York: W W Norton.

Guilford, J. P. (1959). *Personality.* New York: McGraw-Hill.

Hall, C. S., & Lindzey, G. (1978). *Theories of personality.* Toronto: John Wiley & Sons.

Hartshorne, H., & May, M. A. (1928). *Studies in the nature of character: 1. Studies in deceit.* New York: MacMillan.

Hilgard, E. R. (1987). *Psychology in America: An historical survey.* New York: Harcourt Brace Jovanovich.

Hogan, R., DeSoto, C. B., & Solano, C. (1977). Traits, tests and personality research. *American Psychologist, 32*, 255–264.

Horney, K. (1945). *Our inner conflicts.* New York: W W Norton.

Ichheiser, G. (1943). Misinterpretations of personality in everyday life and the psychologists's frame of reference. *Character and Personality, 12*, 145–160.

Jackson, D. N., & Paunonen, L. V. (1980). Personality structure and assessment. In M. R. Rosenzweig & L. W. Porter (Eds.), *Annual Review of Psychology, 31*, 503–552.

Kantor, J. R. (1924). *Principles of psychology* (Vol. 1). Bloomington, IL: Principia Press.

Kantor, J. R. (1926). *Principles of psychology* (Vol. 2). Bloomington, IL: Principia Press.

Kenrick, D. T., & Funder, D. C. (1988). Profiting from controversy: Lessons from the person-situation debate. *American Psychologist, 43*, 23–34.

Krohne, H. W. (1988). Coping research: Current theoretical and methodological developments. *The German Journal of Psychology, 12*, 1–30.

Lazarus, R. S., & Folkman, S. (1984). *Stress, appraisal and coping.* New York: Springer.

Lewin, K. (1935). *A dynamic theory of personality. Selected papers.* New York: McGraw Hill.

Loehlin, J. C. (1982). Are personality traits differentially heritable? *Behavior Genetics, 12*, 417–428.

Magnusson, D. (1971). An analysis of situational dimensions. *Perceptual and Motor Skills, 32*, 851–867.

Magnusson, D. (1974). The individual in the situation: Some studies on individuals' perception of situations. *Studia psychologica, 16*, 124–132.

Magnusson, D. (1976). The person and the situation in an interactional model of behavior. *Scandinavian Journal of Psychology, 17*, 253–271.

Magnusson, D. (1988). *Individual development from an interactional perspective: A longitudinal study.* Hillsdale, NJ: Lawrence Erlbaum Associates.

Magnusson, D., & Ekehammar, B. (1973). An analysis of situational dimensions: A replication. *Multivariate Behavioral Research, 8*, 331–339.

Magnusson, D., & Endler, N. S. (1977). Interactional psychology: Present status and future prospects. In D. Magnusson & N. S. Endler (Eds.), *Personality at the crossroads: Current issues in interactional psychology* (pp. 3–31). Hillsdale, NJ: Lawrence Erlbaum Associates.

Magnusson, D., Gerzen, M., & Nyman, B. (1968). The generality of behavioral data: I. Generalization from observation on one occasion. *Multivariate Behavioral Research, 3*, 295–520.

Magnusson, D., & Ohman, A. (1987). *Psychopathology: An interactional perspective.* New York: Academic Press.

McCrae, R. R., & Costa, P. T. (1984). *Emerging lives, enduring dispositions: Personality in adulthood.* Boston: Little Brown.

Mischel, W. (1968). *Personality and assessment*. New York: John Wiley & Sons.

Mischel, W. (1973). Toward a cognitive social learning reconceptualization of personality. *Psychological Review, 80*, 252–283.

Mischel, W., & Peake, P. K. (1982). Beyond deja vu in the search for cross-situational consistency. *Psychological Review, 89*, 730–755.

Moos, R. H. (1973). Conceptualizations of human environments. *American Psychologist, 28*, 652–665.

Murray, H. A. (1938). *Explorations in personality*. New York: Oxford University Press.

Nelson, E. A., Grinder, R. E., & Mutterer, M. L. (1969). Sources of variance in behavioral measures of honesty in temptation situations: Methodological analyses. *Developmental Psychology, 1*, 265–279.

Newcomb, T. M. (1931). An experiment designed to test the validity of a rating technique. *Journal of Educational Psychology, 22*, 279–289.

Newcomb, T. M., Koenig, K. E., Flacks, R., & Warwick, D. P. (1967). *Persistence and change: Bennington College and its students after twenty-five years*. New York: John Wiley & Sons.

Olweus, D. (1979). Stability of aggressive reaction patterns in males: A review. *Psychological Bulletin, 86*, 852–875.

OSS Assessment Staff. (1948). *Assessment of men*. New York: Holt, Rinehart & Winston.

Overton, W. F., & Reese, H. W. (1973). Models of development: Methodological implications. In J. R. Nesselroade & H. W. Reese (Eds.), *Life span developmental psychology: Methodological issues* (pp. 65–86). New York: Academic Press.

Parker, J. D. A. (1986). *From the intellectual to the nonintellectual traits: An historical framework for the development of American personality research*. Master's thesis, York University, Toronto.

Parker, J. D. A. (1990, June). From the intellectual to the non-intellectual traits: The origins of American personality research. Paper presented at the annual meeting of the Canadian Psychological Association, Ottawa, Ontario.

Pearlin, L. I., & Schooler, C. (1978). The structure of coping. *Journal of Health and Social Behavior, 19*, 2–21.

Pervin, L. A. (1977). The representative design of person-situation research. In D. Magnusson & N. S. Endler (Eds.), *Personality at the crossroads: Current issues in interactional psychology* (pp. 371–384). Hillsdale, NJ: Lawrence Erlbaum Associates.

Pervin, L. A. (1984). *Current controversies and issues in personality* (2nd ed.). New York: John Wiley & Sons.

Raush, H. L. (1977). Paradox, levels and junctures in person-situation systems. In D. Magnusson & N. S. Endler (Eds.), *Personality at the crossroads: Current issues in interactional psychology* (pp. 287–304). Hillsdale, NJ: Lawrence Erlbaum Associates.

Raush, H. L., Dittmann, A. T., & Taylor, T. J. (1959a). The interpersonal behavior of children in residential treatment. *Journal of Abnormal and Social Psychology, 58*, 9–26.

Raush, H. L., Dittmann, A. T., & Taylor, T. J. (1959b). Person, setting and change in social interaction. *Human Relations, 12*, 361–378.

Raush, H. L., Farbman, I., & Llewellyn, L. G. (1960). Person, setting and change in social interaction: II. A normal control study. *Human Relations, 13*, 305–333.

Roazen, P. (1985). *Helen Deutsch: A psychoanalyst's life*. New York: Anchor Press.

Rorer, L. G., & Widiger, T. A. (1983). Personality structure and assessment. *Annual Review of Psychology, 34*, 431–463.

Rotter, J. B. (1954). *Social learning and clinical psychology*. Englewood Cliffs, NJ: Prentice-Hall.

Rotter, J. B. (1975). Some problems and misconceptions related to the construct of internal versus external control of reinforcement. *Journal of Consulting and Clinical Psychology, 43*, 56–67.

Runyan, W. M. (1982). *Life histories and psychobiography: Explorations in theory and method*. New York: Oxford University Press.

Samelson, F. (1979). Putting psychology on the map: Ideology and intelligence testing. In A. Buss (Ed.), *Psychology in social context* (pp. 103–168). New York: Irvington.

Sarason, I. G. (1975). Test anxiety, attention and the general problem of anxiety. In C. D. Spielberger & I. G. Sarason (Eds.), *Stress and Anxiety* (Vol. 1, pp. 165–187). New York: Hemisphere.

Sarason, I. G., Smith, R. E., & Diener, E. (1975). Personality research: Components of variance attributable to the person and the situation. *Journal of Personality and Social Psychology, 32*, 199–204.

Scarr, S., Weber, P. L., Weinberg, R. A., & Wittig, M. A. (1981). Personality resemblance among adolescents and their parents in biologically related and adopted families. *Journal of Personality and Social Psychology, 40*, 885–898.

Singer, J. L., & Kolligian, J. (1987). Personality: Developments in the study of private experience. *Annual Review of Psychology, 38*, 533–574.

Skinner, B. F. (1938). *The behavior of organisms: An experimental analysis*. New York: Appleton-Century-Crofts.

Snyder, M., & Ickes, W. (1985). Personality and social behavior. In G. Lindzey & E. Aronson (Eds.), *Handbook of social psychology* (3rd ed., Vol. 2, pp. 883–948). Reading, MA: Addison-Wesley.

Spielberger, C. D. (1983). *Manual for the State-Trait Anxiety Inventory (Form V)*. Palo Alto, CA: Consulting Psychologists Press, Inc.

Stolorow, R. D., & Atwood, G. E. (1979). *Faces in a cloud: Subjectivity in personality theory*. New York: Jason Aaronson.

Sturgis, E. I. (1984). Anxiety disorders. In N. S. Endler & J.

McV. Hunt (Eds.), *Personality and the behavioral disorders*. (Vol. 2, 2nd ed., pp. 747–770). New York: John Wiley & Sons.

Sullivan, H. S. (1953). *The interpersonal theory of psychiatry*. New York: W W Norton.

Tellegen, A., Lykken, D. T., Bouchard, T. J., Wilcox, K. J., Segal, N. L., & Rich, S. (1988). Personality similarity in twins reared apart and together. *Journal of Personality and Social Psychology*, *54*, 1031–1039.

West, S. G., & Graziano, W. G. (1989). Long-term stability and change in personality: An introduction. *Journal of Personality*, *57*, 175–193.

Wiesenthal, D. L., Edwards, J., Endler, N. S., Koza, P., Walton, A., & Emmott, S. (1978). Trends in conformity research. *Canadian Psychological Review*, *19*, 41–58.

Wiggins, J. S. (1979). A psychological taxonomy of trait descriptive terms: I. The interpersonal domain. *Journal of Personality and Social Psychology*, *37*, 395–412.

Wiggins, J. S. (1980). Circumplex models of interpersonal behavior. In L. Wheeler (Ed.), *Review of Personality and Social Psychology* (Vol. 1, pp. 265–294). Beverly Hills, CA: Sage Publications.

CHAPTER 16

PSYCHOPATHOLOGY RESEARCH

Scott M. Monroe
John E. Roberts

Research on psychopathology, in its broad and varied forms, has expanded tremendously in the decades following World War II. The reasons for this increase are numerous, yet most accounts would include such explanations as increased academic interest in empirical research, expanded federal support for large-scale projects, greater public concern for the adverse effects of rapid technological development on the person and society, and the sense that psychopathology is becoming increasingly widespread (Gershon, Hamovit, Guroff, & Nurnberger, 1987; Klerman, 1988). A burgeoning research literature, too, has evolved in cognate areas of the life sciences (e.g., neurosciences and cognitive science). Findings from the latter have fueled further much enthusiasm for, and currently contribute to, many present-day research activities in psychopathology.

There are several consequences of this proliferation in study. First, the number of arenas for investigation has increased, while simultaneously the topics within these arenas have grown. For instance, new disciplines are emerging (e.g., psychoneuroendocrinol-

ogy), and there are new substantive divisions within traditional psychopathology groups (e.g., seasonal affective disorder in depression). Second, accompanying this broadening sweep of topic domains is the increasing sophistication of the technologies employed within the respective research areas. For example, novel methodologies for investigating genetic and biologic influences, cognitive processes, and socioenvironmental factors all have been improved and/or developed recently and have been employed extensively in furthering knowledge about the etiology and course of psychopathologic disturbances. With such large-scale increases in the relevant literatures, the associated methodologies, and the ever-present diversity of theoretical perspectives, the domain of psychopathology research has become exceedingly broad.

The scale of these developments defies summary descriptions of specific details, debates, and findings. There have been more general advances in perspectives and methods, however, that possess broad implications for understanding current research on psychopathology. The purpose of this chapter is selectively to

*This work was supported in part by National Institute of Mental Health grant MH-39139.

survey several of these advances. We have chosen two broad subjects for discussion. First, recent method developments hold considerable promise for increasing understanding of the etiology and pathophysiology of psychiatric disorders. In terms of technical details, it is important to have a general grasp of the nature of these procedures. Of equal importance is an appreciation of the conceptual context within which emerging findings that employ these procedures are embedded. In other words, what answers can we expect from such advances, and what new questions are raised in the quest? We attempt to shed some light on these concerns with respect to recent method developments in biological, cognitive, and socioenvironmental literatures.

Our second topic involves recent trends toward expanding conceptual perspectives on psychopathology. There are two ways in particular that investigators have begun to broaden the nature of this inquiry. The first has to do with expansion from the tradition of studying disorders in primarily patient samples to studying afflicted individuals—at all levels of intensity—in the nonpatient populations. Assisted by the advances of the last decade in operationalizing and standardizing diagnostic practices, investigators are no longer confined to the psychiatric hospital to study clinically relevant psychopathology. The second expansion in perspective involves the shift from a relative short-term focus on specific acute disorders to broader temporal perspectives on psychiatric functioning for individuals over more protracted periods of time. Such a shift has illuminated important concerns for understanding the longitudinal and lifetime course of psychopathology, and ultimately may raise intriguing questions concerning current classification procedures. We conclude the chapter by discussing the collective influence of these developments on the manner in which psychopathology may be conceptualized and investigated in the coming decade.

METHODOLOGICAL DEVELOPMENTS AND THEIR IMPLICATIONS

Progress in scientific understanding frequently develops through an informed interchange between advances in concepts and methods over time. Although concepts provide direction for the application of technological advances, the advances in methods often herald the ability to glean new insights into old problems. Psychopathology research, in particular, has been constrained historically by a lack of adequate techniques to investigate constructs embedded within

sophisticated theories. The need for a tighter correspondence between concept and method, then, places the potential contribution of recent method developments in an important position.

Basic Genetic and Biological Characteristics

Perhaps nowhere has progress been more spectacular or promising than in the realm of basic genetic and biologic characteristics involving the brain's activity. Although most work has been directed toward the understanding of normal biologic functioning, considerable interest and energy also have been focused on describing the implications of such work for pathological functioning. In particular, we outline two influential areas involving recent research in psychopathology: (a) genetic techniques, and (b) imaging techniques for probing central nervous system (CNS) structure and function.

Genetic Techniques

Although genetic contributions to the etiology of major mental disorders have long been recognized, conclusions were based primarily on indirect methods of genetic analysis (e.g., family and twin studies). Such evidence, while compelling, often yields information that is relatively distant from the action of the genes involved and is yet still vulnerable to various competing explanations (i.e., nongenetic factors such as shared environments).

The most dramatic recent research reports are those that link major psychiatric disorders to predisposition based on a single gene. These findings are made possible by current developments in the field of molecular genetics. DNA markers (technically, restriction fragment length polymorphisms [RFLPs]) are used as identification tags to trace the occurrence of abnormal genes through family pedigrees. The investigator attempts to link familial expression of the particular disorder under study with a specific marker RFLP. If such a linkage can be statistically demonstrated, firm evidence exists for the locus of the genetic susceptibility to the disease to lie in close proximity on the same chromosome (Gurling, 1985; Mullan & Murray, 1989). In other words, affirmative findings using such procedures not only document the genetic basis for the disorder; they provide important clues as to where in the genetic makeup of the person the anomaly resides. In such a manner, familial Alzheimer's disease has been linked to chromosome 21 (St. George-Hyslop et al., 1987); bipolar affective disorder (manic-depressive illness) has been linked both to the X chromosome (Baron et al., 1987) and to chromosome 11 (Egeland et al., 1987); and schizophrenia has been linked to chromosome 5 (Sherrington et al., 1988).

These findings hold strong promise for clarifying the heritable characteristics and underlying biological substrates for these disorders. The methods, though, are complex, and the information they yield must be understood in relation to a variety of considerations involving the disorder to which they are applied. At least three general points must be borne in mind to place such exciting work within an appropriate perspective. First, although the published findings represent compelling evidence for the genetic transmission of these disorders within these families, replication across families generally has not been successful. Indeed, two separate genetic loci have been implicated for bipolar disorder (X chromosome—Baron et al., 1987; chromosome 11—Egeland et al., 1987). For both bipolar disorder and schizophrenia, other investigations based on different family pedigrees have failed to find support for these specific genetic modes of transmission (for bipolar disorder, see Hodgkinson et al., 1987; for schizophrenia, see Kennedy et al., 1988).

The collective implication of these discrepant findings is that more than one etiologic subtype exists. In other words, there is genetic and/or genetic-environmental heterogeneity with respect to the etiology of these disorders. Furthermore, it appears that the specific genetic mechanisms that have been isolated may occur relatively infrequently within the population of afflicted individuals. Thus, the majority of cases of bipolar disorder probably do not arise from X-linked, or chromosome 11, abnormalities (Mullan & Murray, 1989). Clearly the groundwork for understanding the etiology and pathophysiology of these forms of psychopathology have been laid, yet the extent to which these foundations may generalize to, or shed light on, other phenotypically similar syndromes remains to be addressed.

A second point concerns the potency of such predisposition. Given the pathogenic genotype, what is the likelihood of eventual expression of the disorder (i.e., what is the penetrance of the genotype)? Although absolute values are unknown, it is strongly suspected that many—if not most—individuals with the genotype for these disorders do not develop the disorder. For example, Egeland et al. (1987) estimated a maximum penetrance of 63%: that is, at most 63% of those with the genotype will develop the disorder. Thus, for the genetic potential eventually to

be expressed, other permissive factors must be present.

Finally, another important issue is introduced by these findings from genetic linkage studies. It appears that not only is there convergence of different etiologies into a common phenotype (i.e., etiologic heterogeneity); there may also be "a divergence from a single genotype to several phenotypes" (Mullan & Murray, 1989, p. 594). These studies often assume a spectrum of psychopathologic disorders reflects expression of the underlying genotype. For example, the studies of Sherrington et al. (1988) found that schizophrenia may be associated with unipolar depression, alcoholism, and personality disorder. In a similar vein, the work of Egeland et al. (1987) indicates that unipolar depression and schizoaffective disorder may be alternative phenotypic expressions of the bipolar genotype (Mullan & Murray, 1989). Thus, while such work holds promise for clarifying the etiologic heterogeneity of major psychopathologic disorders, it may clash with the principle of phenotypic homogeneity that has tended to influence recent diagnostic systems. Put differently, these studies imply a possible reshuffling of classification groups, wherein future classification following from such findings could cut across contemporary nosologic boundaries.

Brain Imaging Techniques

Unlike other areas of medical inquiry wherein the biologic structures and associated tissues of interest are amenable to relatively direct assessment and manipulation, psychopathology research has always been constrained by the lack of suitable procedures for examining CNS characteristics and function in the living organism. The complexity of the brain's anatomy, the thoroughness of nature's protective coverings, and the vulnerability of the brain once the fortifications have been circumvented render direct examination of brain tissue and function most difficult. Previous research has consequently been confined to postmortem studies of humans and to observations or manipulations of animals using invasive techniques. Recently, however, in tandem with the progress of the neurosciences, more direct procedures have become available for exploring the anatomical and dynamic features of the living human brain.

Perhaps the most potentially informative of these developments are the brain imaging techniques.[1] Computerized tomography (CT) is a useful technique for generating two-dimensional images representing different cross-sections of the brain. Owing to difficulties in resolution capabilities, research employing this approach has commonly focused on crude anatomical characteristics of the brain that are amenable to measurement at this level. For example, studies of schizophrenia and mood disorders have compared volume sizes of cerebrospinal fluid spaces (e.g., the ventricles, cortical sulci) with other pathological groups and with normal controls. Although some recent reports have found differences between various pathological and control groups, it is important to note that adequate normative data on the standards for these brain characteristics are not yet available. Thus, without these normative data, many of the existing findings can be explained by anomalous values for the control groups (i.e., as opposed to the pathological groups; see Depue & Iaccono, 1989). Overall, CT provides a window into the gross structural features of the brain. Although this will undoubtedly be useful for probing the possibilities of relatively large-scale differences in brain anatomy and is of central importance for many medical purposes (e.g., space occupying lesions such as tumors), such information does not shed light on more subtle cortical differences or on dynamic processes that may be more the province of major psychiatric disturbances.

Positron emission tomography (PET) is a technique used to study the dynamic chemistry of the brain. This procedure allows for the study of brain function in relation to the brain's metabolic utilization of compounds labeled with positron emitters under natural, or alternatively under challenge, conditions. Thus, instead of quantifying structural differences as with CT, this technique assesses the dynamic function of the brain, potentially depicting brain activity under diverse environmental conditions. Because of the great expense of this procedure and its recent development, only limited applications to psychopathology research are yet evident. These findings are subject to qualification owing to an emerging awareness of the appropriate testing requirements and conditions. PET scanning, too, has serious limitations in terms of its resolution capacity for localization of anatomic sources for the observed dynamic functions. Perhaps most important is an underlying interpretational consideration. As emphasized by Depue and Iaccono (1989), the procedure is a psychophysiologic one: "An identified abnormality on a PET image could stem from a structural or physiological deficit or represent the biological substrate of a dysfunctional psychological process" (p. 479). In other words, while such methods are helpful for elucidating basic biologic processes, the origins of biologic differences that may be found between normal and pathologic groups could arise from differences in functioning at

any of several levels of analysis (e.g., biologic, psychological, or social differences).

Finally, magnetic resonance imaging (MRI) technology can be used to investigate aspects of CNS function that represent the combined capacities of CT and PET, such as assessing metabolism, tissue function, blood flow, as well as brain structure (Depue & Iaccono, 1989). Once again, owing to the great cost of such procedures and their recent implementation, few applications to psychopathological disorders have been performed. Yet it appears that this technology will be exploited in future studies, thereby increasing the investigator's ability to detect even more subtle deviations in structure or function of the human brain.

Collectively, these imaging techniques hold promise for delineating a variety of parameters along which pathologic groups may differ from normal individuals. Despite this apparent window into the soul of psychopathology, such techniques possess important limitations. Although weighing only about 3 pounds, the approximately 10,000 million neurons that constitute the human cerebrum have been described as "without any qualification the most highly organized and the most complexly organized matter in the universe" (Eccles, 1977, p. 1). These technologies afford better views into the structures and processes involved, but one still needs to know where to look, and if differences arise, the nature of the origins of such differences (e.g., psychological or physiologic). These techniques can be invaluable tools for probing such questions but alone may be incapable of answering the questions psychopathologists pose without the information gleaned from other levels of analysis (e.g., cognitive and social factors).

Cognitive Factors

The cognitive revolution has had a sweeping impact throughout psychology, reclaiming conceptual turf long abandoned by behaviorism. Within psychopathology, a multitude of cognitively oriented interventions and theoretical frameworks have emerged out of this resurgence of interest in thought processes (e.g., Abramson, Seligman, & Teasdale, 1978; Bandura, 1977; Beck, 1976; Ellis, 1962; Guidano & Liotti, 1983; Teasdale, 1983). Although most of these ideas were originally formulated within the clinical realm, recent developments in cognitive science are providing the basic tools and conceptual framework by which the role of cognition in psychopathology may be empirically investigated. After first sketching this conceptual framework, we review some of these more promising methodologies.

Conceptual Issues

Cognitively oriented clinicians postulate that at least some disorders arise from patients' idiosyncratic patterns of thinking and beliefs. Generally, they propose that maladaptive cognitive structures (schemata) make individuals vulnerable to particular disorders by influencing how these individuals see themselves and their worlds. Critical importance is ascribed to these internal, mental structures in determining how environmental input is processed for both normal and pathological functioning (e.g., Beck, 1976). Cognitive approaches have been predominantly applied to affective disorders, particularly depression and to a lesser extent anxiety, but also to eating disorders, sexual dysfunction, and anger control (Beck, 1967, 1976; Eysenck, MacLeod, & Mathews, 1987; Novaco, 1979; Schlesier-Carter, Hamilton, O'Neil, Lydiard, & Malcolm, 1989).

Within cognitive science, distinctions are made between cognitive products (e.g., conscious thoughts, attributions, etc.) and the factors that give rise to them (i.e., structures, content, processes) (Mandler, 1984, 1985; Marcel, 1983; Neisser, 1967). Such distinctions are beginning to be applied within clinical psychology (Ingram & Kendall, 1986; Ingram, Kendall, Smith, Donnell, & Ronan, 1987). Although cognitive schemata are defined in terms of cognitive content and an organized, well-integrated structure (Segal, 1988), until recently empirical evidence for distorted cognition in psychopathology came almost exclusively from investigations of cognitive products—the end result of the interaction between environmental input, cognitive structure, content, and processes. For example, paper-and-pencil tests have been used to assess attributional style (Peterson et al., 1982), automatic thoughts (Beck, Brown, Steer, Eidelson, & Riskind, 1987; Hollon & Kendall, 1980), dysfunctional beliefs (Weissman & Beck, 1978), and negative interpretations within Beck's cognitive triad (i.e., negative view of self, world, and future; Wilkinson & Blackburn, 1981). These methodologies generally find that various psychiatric groups endorse greater numbers of these thoughts (or cognitive products) than nonpsychiatric groups (e.g., Hollon, Kendall, & Lumry, 1986).

Such self-report evidence is weak support for the notion of the well-integrated cognitive structure or schema postulated by theory (see Segal, 1988). Further, such self-reports rely on introspection, which may be far removed from the actual structure, content, and operations of the cognitive system (Mandler, 1984, 1985; Nisbett & Wilson, 1977). Finally, when studied cross-sectionally these measures can be highly confounded with the disorder itself, making causal statements impossible (Blaney, 1977; Coyne & Gotlib, 1983). Although prospective studies are useful in disentangling this latter confound, such studies continue to be limited in terms of the first two criticisms.

More thorough and rigorous tests of cognitive models would come from closer examination of aspects of information processing other than simply cognitive products. Recent investigations have begun to employ creative methodologies developed within cognitive science to tap these more elusive constructs. These methodologies probe various aspects of memory, attention, and cognitive interpretation.

Memory biases. Biased memory was first investigated on normal individuals within a depth of processing paradigm. This methodology was based on the work of Craik and Tulving (1975), who found that meaningful encoding tasks (such as rating words semantically—e.g., "Does this word mean the same as x?") lead to stronger memory traces than less meaningful tasks (such as structural ratings—e.g., "Does this word have the same number of syllables as x?"). Other investigators have found that yes-rated adjectives on self-referent encoding tasks (e.g., "Does this word describe you?") lead to even stronger memory traces than semantic tasks, suggesting a strong self-schema (Rogers, Kuiper, & Kirker, 1977).

Within psychopathology models, various negative cognitive schemata have been postulated as operating (e.g., Beck, 1976), and investigators have begun to operationalize these schemata in terms of depth of processing memory tasks. For instance, Derry and Kuiper (1981) found that clinically depressed persons recalled more depressed content self-referent adjectives than nondepressed content self-referent adjectives, while nondepressed persons exhibited the opposite pattern. Some investigators have found additional support for this bias in depression (e.g., Greenberg & Beck, 1989; Ingram et al., 1987), whereas others have failed to replicate such findings (e.g., Dobson & Shaw, 1987). Further, measurement of reaction times in these ratings have shown that depressives' negative self-schemata are equally efficient in processing information as nondepressives' positive self-schemata but are not necessarily more efficient than their own positive schemata (Derry & Kuiper, 1981; Dobson & Shaw, 1987). Mixed results have been found in studies of anxiety: Some investigators find enhanced recall for anxiety-relevant content words (Greenberg & Beck, 1989; Ingram et al., 1987); others find a relatively diminished recall of such words (Mogg, Mathews, & Weinman, 1987).

Using a similar experimental paradigm, other investigators have examined the subjective organization imposed on self-referent adjectives during a multitrial free recall task (Davis, 1979; Davis & Unruh, 1981). If a well-organized cognitive schemata is involved in the processing of information, it would help structure that information within memory. Consistent clusterings of material during recall would be a sign of such a cognitive structure (Kihlstrom & Nasby, 1981). For example, Davis and colleagues found evidence for a developmental process in depressives' self-schemata with short-term depressives exhibiting weak, disorganized schemata relative to long-term depressives and normals (Davis, 1979; Davis & Unruh, 1981). Other investigators have studied the distinction between implicit memory (word completion) and explicit memory (cued recall), finding that anxiety patients demonstrate a bias toward threatening information only within implicit memory (i.e., automatic recall; Mathews, Mogg, May, & Eysenck, 1989).

Attentional processes. The role of attention in psychopathology has been investigated within several different research paradigms, including cognitive interference methodologies, such as Stroop tasks and dichotic listening, and distribution of visual attention. If hyperactive schemata are present, then it would be expected that they would direct one's attention toward schema-relevant information and thereby interfere with the processing of nonschema information.

In a recent example of this type of strategy, Gotlib and colleagues used a modified Stroop task to test this hypothesis. Subjects were timed as they read aloud the colors of ink of various content words. It was found that depressives were slower in reading the colors of negative content words (i.e., attention was differentially allocated to the meaning of the depressed words as opposed to the color of the nondepressed words; Gotlib & Cane, 1987; Gotlib & McCann, 1984). Such a method has the advantage of measuring automatic processing and is less susceptible to the effects of transient mood changes (Segal, 1988). Other investigators have found analogous results with threatening words in anxiety patients (Mathews & Macleod, 1985).

Dichotic listening tasks have been used to examine interference in the processing of attended to information due to the content of shadowed material. For instance, results from one study suggest that with anxiety patients threatening words automatically gain attention in the unattended to channel without conscious awareness (Mathews & MacLeod, 1986). Another study has employed a visual attention task to demonstrate that anxious patients shift their attention toward threatening information, while control groups tended to shift their attention away from such words (MacLeod, Mathews, & Tata, 1986).

Interpretation procedures. Cognitive interpretation has been examined recently in regard to homophones (i.e., words that sound alike but have different meanings). Subjects were asked to write the spelling of various words they heard. Some of these words were homophones that had a threatening meaning as one of their definitions. In this study, anxiety patients were found to use the more threatening spelling more frequently than controls, although both groups showed electrodermal reactions to the homophones (Mathews, Richards, & Eysenck, 1989).

Summary

As several authors have argued, self-report checklists are inadequate as the sole instruments for investigating the role of cognition in psychopathology (Coyne & Gotlib, 1983, 1986; Segal, 1988). Fortunately, methodologies now exist to probe aspects of information processing centering around memory, attention, and interpretation, avoiding some of the confounds and tautologies that have plagued the self-report literature. Nonetheless, future studies using these methodologies need to go beyond simple cross-sectional designs. Prospective and remission designs are required in order to establish whether biased information processing temporally precedes the disorder and exists after recovery, as theory would suggest, or acts more as a consequence of the disorder itself.

Socioenvironmental Factors

Clinical scientists have long been interested in the role of the individual's life context with respect to psychopathology (Rosen, 1959). It seems plausible that such disorders may arise at least in part owing to formidable life circumstances, or that these disturbances may be prone toward chronicity or repeated episodes when the daily pressures of life are extreme. Defining and measuring individual differences in socioenvironmental circumstances, however, proves to be a complicated affair. The basic problem concerns abstracting the major dimensions of importance associated with disorder from the background of life's ongoing changes and challenges (Monroe & Roberts, 1990). Two of the major domains that have emerged over the past several years are those of life stress and social support.

Life Stress

The concept of life stress is an appealing one for uniting the manifold adversities of existence under one common theme. In one form or another, the idea and its implications for psychopathology can be traced far back into the general history of medicine (Hinkle, 1977; Rees, 1976). Until relatively recent times, however, stress was mostly a concept in search of an appropriate methodology. Although a fertile and popular notion, stress often meant different things to different investigators. It was only with the advent of life events checklists in the late 1960s that the concept was given operational roots and an aura of scientific respectability (Holmes & Rahe, 1967). Once such relatively simple techniques were developed, their usage quickly spread into the operational void of many research literatures bearing on human disorder (Monroe, 1982c; Rabkin & Struening, 1976).

Although the initial wave of findings provided exciting suggestions concerning the role of life stress in relation to many varied forms of psychological and physical disturbances (Dohrenwend & Dohrenwend, 1974; Gunderson & Rahe, 1974), methodological and conceptual concerns eventually overcame the initial exploratory zeal (Monroe & Peterman, 1988). It was noted that self-report life event checklists suffered from poor reliability in reporting (Monroe, 1982a, 1982c; Sarason, de Monchaux, & Hunt, 1975). Further, it was found that many of the items included in these measures could be confounded directly with disorder. For example, items such as "A change in recreation," "Laid off from work," "Marital separation," and so on could all be seen as consequences of psychopathologic functioning rather than causes (Brown, 1974; Dohrenwend, 1974). This became especially problematic when it was recognized that many of the individuals included in such studies likely suffered from chronic, low-level forms of psychiatric disturbances (Depue & Monroe, 1986). Such reports cast strong doubt on the validity of the associations typically reported between life events and disorder.

Method advances were devised to control for such concerns. For example, only study participants were selected who did not initially evidence elevated symptom levels (Monroe, 1982b). Also, second generation life event checklists evolved that excluded, or controlled for, life events that could be a consequence of the disorder (e.g., Dohrenwend, Krasnoff, Askenasy, & Dohrenwend, 1978; Sarason, Johnson, & Siegel, 1978). Even with the implementation of these relatively conservative methods, life stress continued to predict a variety of pathological outcomes (Thoits, 1983).

Subsequent research, however, cast further and more penetrating doubts on the basic methodological approach that involves self-report checklists. Brown and Harris (1978, 1986) noted important discrepancies in the viewpoint of the investigator and the respondent with respect to the basic definition of what constitutes an event. Stated differently, respondents varied in their threshold for defining particular experiences as life events. For example, "A serious illness of a close family member" is ambiguous with respect to what constitutes serious and close; some individuals will interpret such adjectives broadly, and others more restrictively. The underlying concern is that if one wishes to assess individual differences in exposure to socioenvironmental events, there must be some common reference point across individuals for comparison. It is the responsibility of the investigator to ensure such standardization of measurement across individuals. Recent work by others substantiates the variability of experiences included under particular event labels when such decisions are left to the idiosyncratic interpretations of the respondent (Dohrenwend, Link, Kern, Shrout, & Markowitz, 1987).

In response to such concerns, interviewer-based methods have been developed for assessing life stress (see Brown & Harris, 1978, 1986; Dohrenwend et al., 1987; Monroe & Roberts, 1990; Paykel, 1982). These methods make more explicit the operational procedures for defining more precisely what constitutes an event. For example, the Bedford College Life Events and Difficulties Schedule (LEDS) has been developed by Brown and Harris over the past 20 years and includes an extensive interview protocol and highly detailed companion manuals. These manuals clearly specify the rules and criteria used to define and rate life events and ongoing chronic stressors, and include hundreds of examples for assisting in the complicated task of defining and rating these stressors (see Brown & Harris, 1978). Once such a standardized base is attained, investigators with different interests in particular dimensions of life stress or particular forms of pathology can build into the approach the particular qualities they desire (see Brown & Harris, 1989c).

Using such elaborate interview methods and manual-based rating procedures assures the measurement foundation adheres to the requirements of rigorous science. Studies of the psychometric properties of such approaches are typically favorable and are markedly more reliable than the typical self-report checklist (see Brown & Harris, 1989a). Investigators employing these procedures attain a common standard for comparison across time and diverse samples, the bedrock upon which programmatic inquiry is built. In addition, the flexibility of these procedures for examining particular dimensions of life stress that may be relatively specific to particular forms of pathology appears quite promising as well (see Brown & Harris, 1989c). The cost of such procedures is the far greater expenditure in time and effort to derive the information when compared to self-report checklist approaches. While some investigators continue to suggest that self-report measures may be developed that can address the problems currently endemic to them (Oei & Zwart, 1986; Zimmerman, Pfohl, & Stangl, 1986), the interview procedures at present are the most reliable measurement standard available.

These developments help to systematize individual differences in the surface characteristics of people's life situations and events. As they currently stand, however, they do not delve into the origins of such differences. Directly or indirectly, people are often the perpetrators of the fates they are forced to endure (Brown & Harris, 1989b; Monroe & Peterman, 1988; Rutter, 1986). For example, life stress may be generated in part owing to the biologic or cognitive predisposition a person possesses (Monroe & Simons, 1990). Once again, while these developments are of great use in clarifying processes within this level of study, they require information from other levels (i.e., genetic and biologic, cognitive) to understand the nature of the causal processes involved. Overall, though, the intuitive notions of the importance of life stress for psychopathology are being translated into appropriate methodologies for testing out the many facets of this important issue.

Social Support

Interest in the implications of social support in relation to health and well-being grew out of the observation that people who were more socially integrated appeared to be at reduced risk for incurring a variety of adverse mental and physical health outcomes (Cassel, 1976). Two general perspectives characterize the literature. On the one hand, social support is believed to moderate the effects of stress (i.e., only under stress does the protective impact of social support become manifest). Alternatively, social support is viewed as having a direct protective function (irrespective of stress) (Barrera, 1986; Brown & Harris, 1978; Cohen & Wills, 1985; House, Landis, & Umberson, 1988).

These interests have spawned a variety of measurement practices essaying to capture the important dimensions of social integration that confer such protective benefits. Such approaches can be divided into two generic categories. First are the measures that attempt

to describe features of the individual's social network (e.g., the number of persons in his or her social field, the frequency of contact with these individuals, interactions between separate network members, etc.) (House, Robbins, & Metzner, 1982). Second, and more commonly found in the recent psychopathology literature, are measures of the various qualities associated with the individual's interactions with important others. For instance, support may be elicited from others in modifying appraisals of threat, supplying emotional sustenance, providing tangible support, or maintaining self-esteem (Cohen & Hoberman, 1983; Cohen & McKay, 1984).

Various approaches have been developed to assess the many aspects of social ties and their associations with psychological functioning (for a recent extensive review of this literature, see Cohen & Wills, 1985). Further important distinctions have been made between perceived support and enacted support. With respect to the former, measures focus on the perceived quality support (or more specific support dimensions) that an individual believes he or she has available (e.g., perceived tangible, appraisal, self-esteem, and belonging support; Cohen & Hoberman, 1983). Measures of the latter distinction, support enactment, focus on the actual frequency of supportive transactions in the recent past (e.g., Barrera, Sandler, & Ramsay, 1981).

These systems rely on self-report procedures and as such are subject to some of the same caveats raised concerning the measurement of life stress. It is likely that the behaviors associated with psychopathology will result in alterations of the quality and quantity of social ties. For example, the social withdrawal and/or irritability so characteristic of clinical depressive episodes has clear implications for the receipt of support. Further, individuals under distress also may be more dependent and thereby more active in seeking out support. Finally, reporting of perceived support may be suspect, for individuals who are distressed may have different standards for defining support than individuals who are not distressed (e.g., Henderson, Byrne, & Duncan-Jones, 1981). Given the multiple interrelations between social support, psychopathology, and even personality, it becomes difficult to extract what components of the derived score are purely attributable to the hypothesized support versus alternative viable explanations (see Monroe & Steiner, 1986).

Only a few investigators have developed interview methods for standardizing definitions and measures of social support dimensions (e.g., Henderson et al., 1981; O'Connor & Brown, 1984). Early findings from these efforts suggest that felt attachment may obscure relations with psychiatric status that are found with investigator-based definitions of support (O'Connor & Brown, 1984). These measures, though, are still in the developmental phase, and appropriate procedures for disentangling the afore-mentioned interrelations with psychopathology and personality are needed (Henderson et al., 1981; Monroe & Steiner, 1986).

Overall, research on social support is moving toward the development of more refined measures of the constructs embedded within the global concept. Yet the measures do not appear to have progressed as far as the measures of life stress in terms of basic psychometric properties and the control over extraneous sources of measurement bias. Further, the difficulties in interpreting the origins of individual differences in social support parallel the problems raised previously for life stress, cognition, and genetic and biologic factors (Monroe & Steiner, 1986). The existing findings, however, suggest the potential importance of this domain of social functioning for a wide range of psychological and physical health effects (House et al., 1988).

Summary: Methodological Developments

At the three major levels of conceptualizing etiologic contributions of psychopathology (biologic, cognitive, social), new and improved methods are becoming available. While furthering specific understanding of the factors involved at these levels of resolution, these developments also begin to bring into focus larger theoretical considerations that have been previously obscured. Thus, along with the promise of such procedures comes a number of limitations, which we have highlighted throughout.

Although these developments provide a sense of optimism for clarifying important theoretical issues, their potential is bounded by other background conceptual forces that mold the manner in which they are used. There are several ways in which these conceptual boundaries are being pushed that may open the arena for even greater contributions from these developments. Two of these issues are discussed next.

EXPANDING PERSPECTIVES FOR INVESTIGATING PSYCHOPATHOLOGY

From the writings passed down from ancient medicine, recorded case histories of psychopathology have involved dramatic disorders that were clearly beyond the ken of normal psychological functioning (Jackson, 1986; Lewis, 1934). As medical specialties in diseases of the nervous system evolved in the latter half of the 19th century, prominent psychiatrists and neurologists in Germany, France, England, and America were those with primary appointments in the major psychiatric facilities of the day (e.g., Kraepelin, Pinel, Rush). These individuals were exposed predominantly to extreme groups of psychiatric deviance. Their explanations of such disorders, then, were based largely on the poor souls who, for a variety of reasons, found themselves trapped within the walls of the asylum.

Much of the conceptual heritage that has structured thought on psychopathology descends directly from the ideas of these forebears (Jackson, 1986). In fact, the recent developments in psychiatric classification are often referred to a Neo-Kraepelinean (Blashfield, 1984). (We do not wish to imply that other theorists did not develop their ideas on other individuals who were not confined to the psychiatric hospital. For example, the work of Freud generally dealt with less severely disturbed individuals. We simply wish to highlight the historical antecedents that provide the backdrop to current psychiatric thought and to provide the foundation from which the current developments derive.) However, theorizing derived from these extreme patient groups potentially leads to relatively parochial perspectives in at least two ways. First, it is not informed by the broader context of correlated conditions that, for one reason or another, do not enter into treatment. The psychiatric presentations and circumstances of patient samples could be unrepresentative of those that characterize the major mental miseries in the general population. Second, psychiatric inquiry also has been constrained in terms of the time perspective adopted for investigating the individual's psychological functioning. Patients, particularly in our age, tend to remain acutely distressed for a limited period of time. There has been little consideration of the true longitudinal course of disorder for such individuals. The lifetime course of psychological functioning provides considerable information for better understanding the nature of these disturbances and the factors that may influence their emergence, remission, and recurrence. We again have simplified the case somewhat. For example, Kraepelin (1921) was interested in both the wider range of psychiatric problems beyond the core severe groups (e.g., usually relatives of the severely disabled) and also observed the longitudinal course of many of his cases. Indeed, he strongly emphasized the importance of the clinical course and outcome for the classification of psychiatric disturbances. Nonetheless, these pioneering efforts were confined to a small segment of the population, probably a nonrepresentative segment of the population, and the longitudinal information was subject to many selection biases as well.

Recent trends in psychopathology research have begun to move beyond these limited perspectives in two important ways. A number of investigations have studied psychiatric disturbances and their correlates outside the confines of the psychiatric hospital. Further, interest in the clinical status of the person has expanded to address the lifetime course of psychopathology for the individual. Together, these efforts have begun to enlarge the scope of psychopathology research and again call into question some contemporary viewpoints on classification.

Community and Nonpatient Studies of Psychopathology

Although studies of psychological functioning in community samples have been common in the past, with checklist approaches to measuring symptoms (see Dohrenwend et al., 1980), such methods possess serious shortcomings when viewed within the context of psychiatric nomenclature and clinical conditions (Depue & Monroe, 1978). It is only relatively recently that formal interview schedules, employing operational criteria and standardized procedures, have been used to document the severity and duration of psychiatric problems in nonpatient populations (e.g., community or convenience samples not selected owing to patienthood; Depue & Monroe, 1983). Such work has been frequently directed toward epidemiologic estimates of incidence and prevalence, with an eye toward the public health implications (Klerman, 1986).

There are many theoretical implications of such work that have tended to be overlooked. For instance, individuals who meet full syndromal status but do not enter into contact with the mental health system may differ in several respects from their patient counterparts, some of which may be enlightening with respect to the nature of the disorder involved. A variety of person and social factors determine who seeks, is impelled into, or can find, treatment. Given estimates that most individuals who suffer from psychiatric disorders do not enter into treatment (Shapiro et al., 1984), patient samples may differ in important ways that bias the picture of the disorder under study and the remedies required for its amelioration. (For example, patients with clinical depression may deviate from their community counterparts with respect to person-

ality factors and suicidality; Brown, Craig, & Harris, 1985). Further, untreated community cases provide a better basis for studying the natural course of the disorder. Patient samples, in contrast, inevitably conflate the natural progression of the disorder with the effects of intervention. Finally, and perhaps most importantly, community samples provide the basis for studying the full span of psychiatric functioning. In contrast, by definition patient samples yield a truncated, albeit severe, end of the distribution. Questions concerning dimensionality (does the disorder represent a trait with a continuous distribution in the population?) versus typology (does the disorder represent qualitatively distinct states between the normal and abnormal?) can only be addressed when the full spectrum of the phenomenon is included within the purview of the project.

Several recent studies of community or nonpatient samples indicate that psychiatric problems beset a considerable number of individuals, many of whom do not seek formal treatment (Barrett & Rose, 1986; Brown & Harris, 1989a; Cooke, 1981; Depue, Krauss, Spoont, & Arbisi, 1989; Dohrenwend et al., 1980). The severity of these disturbances ranges from relatively mild psychological problems through significant subsyndromal disorders, with a significant proportion of full syndromal psychiatric cases often represented (Brown & Harris, 1986; Depue et al., 1989). Severity estimates for the latter suggest that these individuals suffer from degrees of disturbance at least comparable to typical individuals attending outpatient psychiatric facilities (see Brown & Harris, 1986; Dean, Surtees, & Sashidharan, 1983). It appears that severity alone, then, does not differentiate afflicted patients from afflicted nonpatients. The large numbers of the latter suggest a potentially important clinical mandate and also indicate a possible basis for deriving a better understanding of the nature of these disorders.

The differences and commonalities in psychiatric functioning between patients and disturbed nonpatients also opens other new areas for inquiry. For example, are the characteristics of an episode similar (e.g., length)? Do chronic or intermittent psychiatric problems tend to follow at a comparable rate? For nonpatient cases who do not seek formal treatment, what informal channels of help do they receive to cope with the crisis, and are there different outcomes associated with these informal treatments that they may have used (e.g., social support resources)? Such work raises the issue of the emerging importance of a more long-term longitudinal perspective on the life course of psychopathology, to which we now turn.

The Longitudinal Course
of Psychopathology

Although there has been considerable interest in the precipitants of psychopathology and the short-term course of these disorders, most information on more longitudinal characteristics has been based on clinical observations or on conventional wisdom. Only recently have efforts become more systematic in describing the broader temporal boundaries of psychiatric functioning in people with such disturbances. Although the vast literature on treatment outcome has clearly attempted to address the issue of individual differences in treatment response and maintenance of treatment gains, such work is directed more toward the clinical and theoretical concerns pertaining to the effects of treatment, rather than toward the implications for the course of the pathology per se. Two general topics are emerging in relation to this expanded focus: (a) remission, relapse, and recurrence; and (b) comorbidity.

Remission, Relapse, and Recurrence

It is the acute episodes of psychiatric disorders—the distinctive breaks with normal functioning—that have tended to capture the interest of investigators and have led to a preoccupation with how such dramatic psychobiologic alterations come about. In other words, how do relatively normal men and women move from one state of being to such a startlingly different one? In contrast, there has been relatively little effort expended to understand individual differences in eventual recovery following such vivid alterations (i.e., movement back to the premorbid condition), vulnerability to relapse (i.e., reemergence of symptoms shortly following recovery), or susceptibility to subsequent disorder (i.e., recurrence). Such issues not only merit such attention for their clinical import, but the findings may reflect back on issues that are germane for furthering understanding of the first causes of the disorder.

Recent research suggests that single episodes may be only a relatively small portion of the psychopathology that plays out over an individual's life. Once afflicted, most people are believed to be subsequently vulnerable. For example, it has been estimated that 40% to 50% of individuals with an episode of clinical depression will have at least another episode in their lifetime (Klerman, 1978). Yet not all individuals are destined to subsequent disability, suggesting that much is to be learned from such individual differences in long-term course and the factors associated with

good and poor prognoses. It is likely that separate social, psychological, and biologic factors come into play for determining recovery from an episode, maintenance of such gains, and vulnerability to subsequent episodes (Weiner, 1977). For example, particular environmental features predict relapse in patients with schizophrenia and depression (e.g., high levels of expressed emotion; Hooley, 1985; Leff & Vaughn, 1985). Other social factors, or personality characteristics, may predict recovery from depression (Brown & Harris, 1989a; Monroe & Depue, in press) or susceptibility to recurrence of the disorder (Frank, Kupfer, & Perel, 1989).

The emphasis on distinctive changes in psychiatric functioning (i.e., episodes) may also obscure the problems characterized by a more chronic course. It appears that a large portion of individuals who evidence symptoms at any point in time tend to display a chronic, albeit often fluctuating, clinical presentation over time. For instance, as noted previously, recent research on affective disorders suggests that many individuals display enduring, subsyndromal psychopathology (Akiskal, 1988; Depue et al., 1981; Keller, Lavori, Endicott, Coryell, Klerman, 1983). Although such symptomatology can be severe, it frequently does not reach full criteria for conventional syndromal definition of the disorder (Depue et al., 1981). Furthermore, these disturbances are linked to risk factors for full affective disease (e.g., family history; Klein, Depue, & Slater, 1985) and have been found to predict later full syndromal disorder (Depue et al., 1981; Keller et al., 1983). Given the chronicity of the underlying mood disorder within the groups characterized by "double-depressions" (Keller et al., 1983), one might question the degree to which a truly distinctive episode occurs as opposed to simply an exacerbation of the underlying condition. It may be that a large proportion of so-called episodes are better characterized as a drift across relatively arbitrary diagnostic boundaries, as opposed to a qualitative shift in psychobiologic status. Similar risk paradigms are under investigation with other disorders such as schizophrenia (Chapman & Chapman, 1985). Such findings raise intriguing possibilities for targeting relatively homogeneous risk groups and for studying the conditions that promote and retard the progression to full syndromal disorder.

From One Disorder to Another:
Comorbidity

Perhaps the most intriguing outgrowth of this concern for the lifetime course of psychological functioning is its implications for the boundaries that exist between conventional nosologic groups. For instance, with respect to anxiety and depression, it appears that over an afflicted individual's life there may be not only repeated episodes of depression but also episodes of anxiety disorders. Investigating the longitudinal course of psychiatric functioning highlights the frequent crossing over from one disorder to the other with the passage of time. As Tyrer (1985) indicated, these people "pass, chameleon-like, through different diagnostic hues depending upon the nature of the stresses they encounter" (p. 687).

Especially relevant are findings from recent research that indicate some individuals experience relatively severe episodes of depressive and anxiety disorders over extended periods of time (Breier, Charney, & Heninger, 1984, 1986). Individuals who display the features of one syndrome are at increased risk for the other, yet may exhibit intermorbid periods of relatively normal functioning. Importantly, these results are supported by research on family studies, wherein comorbidity of anxiety and depression of the proband predicts increased rates of lifetime major depression and anxiety disorders among family members (Leckman, Weissman, Merikangas, Pauls, & Prusoff, 1983; Van Valkenburg, Akiskal, Puzantian, & Rosenthal, 1984). Furthermore, recent genetic research suggests that while the propensity to experience psychiatric symptoms is under genetic influence, the qualities that determine the anxiety or depressive phenotype are likely to be under environmental control (Kendler, Heath, Martin, & Eaves, 1987; Monroe & Depue, in press). Finally, complementary results from the life stress literature exist. Life events that signified loss were found to occur more frequently before the onset of depression; life events that signified danger before the onset of anxiety disorders; and life events that signified both a loss and danger before the onset of mixed cases of anxiety and depression (e.g., Finlay-Jones & Brown, 1981). Preliminary findings suggest that the boundaries of other psychiatric categories reveal substantial overlap with one another when more longitudinal profiles are examined (Maser & Cloninger, 1990).

These findings raise important questions concerning the underlying etiology of these disorders and the utility of current classification systems. For instance, it has been hypothesized that the diverse presentations reflect a common underlying etiology (Breier et al., 1984, 1986). Alternatively, it has been suggested that incurring one form of disorder simply increases the susceptibility to other forms of psychiatric impairment, possibly either via sequelae associated with

biologic (Breier et al., 1984, 1986) or social (Monroe, 1990) mechanisms. Given the recent emergence of these concerns, there are few data on which to base firm conclusions. Yet such work may be of importance for altering our concepts of the fundamental characteristics of the disorders under study.

Summary

Such findings on studies involving nonpatient samples and the longitudinal course of psychopathology suggest that traditional ways of conceptualizing these disturbances may have been too strongly influenced by the cross-sectional psychiatric picture of patients with the predominance of clinical features expressed at one point in time. Expanding the perspective to more inclusive populations and enlarged time frames, the apparent nature of the psychopathology may take on different characteristics. While it is unlikely that such information will supplant current nosologic systems, it is conceivable that some reorganization of the traditional nomenclature based on such enlarged perspectives may occur.

Once again, however, the need for complementary method advances is worth mentioning. As investigators move into the community, and especially as they attempt to glean historical information on diverse aspects of prior psychiatric functioning, the limitations of current methodologies become apparent (e.g., Bromet, Dunn, Connell, Dew, & Schulberg, 1986; Zimmerman, & Coryell, 1986). For example, it is often a demanding task to characterize accurately recent psychiatric history of highly distressed individuals. When one inquires into previous periods of such distress, ranging from 1 to perhaps 40 years previously, current methods may be strained to the limit. In a sense, then, we have come full circle and find the limits of our ideas again bounded by the capabilities of our measures. Future work will require tandem development along these method lines.

CONCLUSION

We have attempted to survey major developments in methods and important trends in conceptual perspectives that will be prominent in the next decade of research in psychopathology. Owing to the vast scope of this topic, we have by necessity omitted other interesting developments and issues. No doubt other topics also will be influential in psychopathology research of the future (e.g., basic neurobiologic and neurochemical findings). We have tried to cover developments of a more general nature, though, that provide the reader with a background from which more specific concerns may be pursued.

The final issue to be addressed is in many ways the most promising, yet simultaneously the most vexing. This again pertains to enlarging the conceptual scope, but this time with respect to cutting across different levels of analysis. We refer here to the integration of different methods and levels of analysis into a more coherent picture of the integrated processes that lead to abnormal behavior. Multifactorial models have assumed a position of dominance in most literatures, and such thinking likely encapsulates the subtleties of the processes involved that eventuate in disorder. Yet such models are also vague in their specification and may serve more of a political and palliative function than a scientific one: "The kind of multifactorial theory that settles differences of opinion by a flat compromise, all-embracing and uninformative" (Dalén, 1969, p. 131). While developments in methods and conceptual perspectives at separate levels of the analysis certainly bring new levels of specific understanding, these developments alone will not lead to progress in developing more integrated and interactive models. As theories and methods must evolve symbiotically, so must different theories and methods at different levels of study evolve in a complementary manner to produce more inclusive, yet systematic models, of psychopathology (e.g., Abramson, Alloy, & Metalsky, 1988; Bebbington, 1987; Magnusson & Öhman, 1987; McGuffin, Katz, & Bebbington, 1988; Monroe & Simons, 1990).

We close with the concern with which we began: the tremendous surge in research on psychopathology over the past half century. With increased breadth of topics and greater depth of understanding within subjects, the task of integration—pulling diverse perspectives and procedures together into a coherent system of testable thought—is daunting. We may be moving toward the time when the separate methodological and conceptual tools are beginning to fall within our grasp. The challenge of the next decade, and on into the next century, is to understand how to use such information in a unified and concerted manner.

NOTES

1. We are indebted to the informative review by Depue and Iaccono (1989) for much of the information on brain imaging techniques presented in this chapter (see also Andreasen 1988).
2. It should be noted that recently published work based on expanded information from data reported by Egeland et

al. (1987) weakens the support for a major gene on chromosome 11 in the etiology of bipolar disorder (Kelsoe et al., 1989). Nonetheless, the general points raised remain of relevance for understanding the potential implications of advances in genetic techniques for psychopathology research.

REFERENCES

Abramson, L. Y., Alloy, L. B., & Metalsky, G. I. (1988). The cognitive diathesis-stress theories of depression: Toward an adequate evaluation of the theories' validities. In L. B. Alloy (Ed.), *Cognitive processes in depression* (pp. 3–30). New York: Guilford Press.

Abramson, L. Y., Seligman, M. E. P., & Teasdale, J. D. (1978). Learned helplessness in humans: Critique and reformulation. *Journal of Abnormal Psychology*, 87, 49–74.

Akiskal, H. S. (1988) Personality as a mediating variable in the pathogenesis of mood disorders: Implications for theory, research, and prevention. In T. Helgason & R. J. Daly (Eds.), *Depressive illness: Prediction of course and outcome* (pp. 131–146). New York: Springer-Verlag.

Andreasen, N. C. (1988). Brain imaging: Applications in psychiatry. *Science*, 239, 1381–1388.

Bandura, A. (1977). Self-efficacy: Toward a unifying theory of behavior change. *Psychological Review*, 84, 191–215.

Baron, M., Risch, N., Hamburger, R., Mandel, B., Kushner, S., Newman, D. D., & Belmaker, R. H. (1987). Genetic linkage between X-chromosome markers and bipolar affective illness. *Nature*, 326, 289–292.

Barrera, M., Jr. (1986). Distinctions between social support concepts, measures, and models. *American Journal of Community Psychology*, 14, 413–445.

Barrera, M., Jr., Sandler, I. N., & Ramsay, T. B. (1981). Preliminary development of a scale of social support: Studies on college students. *American Journal of Community Psychology*, 9, 435–447.

Barrett, J. E., & Rose, R. M. (1986). *Mental disorders in the community: Progress and challenge*. New York: Guilford Press.

Bebbington, P. (1987). Misery and beyond: The pursuit of disease theories of depression. *The International Journal of Social Psychiatry*, 33, 13–20.

Beck, A. T. (1967). *Depression: Clinical, experimental, and theoretical aspects*. New York: Harper & Row.

Beck, A. T. (1976). *Cognitive therapy and the emotional disorders*. New York: International Universities Press.

Beck, A. T., Brown, G., Steer, R. A., Eidelson, J. I., & Riskind, J. H. (1987). Differentiating anxiety and depression: A test of the cognitive content-specificity hypothesis. *Journal of Abnormal Psychology*, 96, 179–183.

Blaney, P. H. (1977). Contemporary theories of depression: Critique and comparison. *Journal of Abnormal Psychology*, 86, 203–223.

Blashfield, R. K. (1984). *The classification of psychopathology: Neo-Kraepelinian and quantitative approaches.* New York: Plenum Publishing.

Breier, A., Charney, D. S., & Heninger, G. R. (1984). Major depression in patients with agoraphobia and panic disorder. *Archives of General Psychiatry, 41,* 1129–1135.

Breier, A., Charney, D. S., & Heninger, G. R. (1986). Agoraphobia with panic attacks. *Archives of General Psychiatry, 1986, 43,* 1029–1036.

Bromet, E. J., Dunn, L. O., Connell, M. M., Dew, M. A., & Schulberg, H. C. (1986). Long-term reliability of diagnosing lifetime major depression in a community sample. *Archives of General Psychiatry, 43,* 435–440.

Brown, G. W. (1974). Meaning, measurement, and stress of life events. In B. S. Dohrenwend & B. P. Dohrenwend (Eds.), *Stressful life events: Their nature and effects* (pp. 217–243). New York: Wiley-Interscience.

Brown, G. W., Craig, T. K. J., & Harris, T. O. (1985). Depression: Disease or distress? Some epidemiologic considerations. *British Journal of Psychiatry, 147,* 612–622.

Brown, G. W., & Harris, T. O. (1978). *Social origins of depression: A study of psychiatric disorder in women.* New York: Free Press.

Brown, G. W., & Harris, T. O. (1986). Establishing causal links: The Bedford College studies of depression. In H. Katschnig (Ed.), *Life events and psychiatric disorders: Controversial issues* (pp. 107–187). Cambridge, England: Cambridge University Press.

Brown, G. W., & Harris, T. O. (1989a). Depression. In G. W. Brown & T. O. Harris (Eds.), *Life events and illness* (pp. 49–93). New York: Guilford Press.

Brown, G. W., & Harris, T. O. (1989b). Interlude: The origins of life events and difficulties. In G. W. Brown & T. O. Harris (Eds.), *Life events and illness* (pp. 363–383). New York: Guilford Press.

Brown, G. W., & Harris, T. O. (Eds.) (1989c). *Life events and illness.* New York: Guilford Press.

Cassel, J. (1976). The contribution of the social environment to host resistance. *American Journal of Epidemiology, 104,* 107–123.

Chapman, L. J., & Chapman, J. P. (1985). Psychosis proneness. In M. Alpert (Ed.), *Controversies in schizophrenia* (pp. 157–172). New York: Guilford Press.

Cohen, S., & Hoberman, H. (1983). Positive events and social supports as buffers of life change stress. *Journal of Applied Social Psychology, 13,* 99–125.

Cohen, S., & McKay, G. (1984). Social support, stress and the buffering hypothesis: A theoretical analysis. In A. Baum, J. E. Singer, & S. E. Taylor (Eds.), *Handbook of psychology and health* (Vol. 4, pp. 253–267). Hillsdale, NJ: Lawrence Erlbaum Associates.

Cohen, S., & Wills, T. A. (1985). Stress, social support, and the buffering hypothesis. *Psychological Bulletin, 98,* 310–357.

Cooke, D. J. (1981). Life events and syndrome of depression in the general population. *Social Psychiatry 1981, 16,* 181–186.

Coyne, J. C, & Gotlib, I. H. (1983). The role of cognition in depression: A critical appraisal. *Psychological Bulletin, 94,* 472–505.

Coyne, J. C., & Gotlib, I. H. (1986). Studying the role of cognition in depression: Well-trodden paths and cul-de-sacs. *Cognitive Therapy and Research, 10,* 695–705.

Craik, F. I. M., & Tulving, E. (1975). Depth of processing and the retention of words in episodic memory. *Journal of Experimental Psychology: General, 104,* 268–294.

Dalén, P. (1969). Causal explanations in psychiatry: A critique of some current concepts. *British Journal of Psychiatry, 115,* 129–137.

Davis, H. (1979). The self-schema and subjective organization of personal information in depression. *Cognitive Therapy and Research, 3,* 415–425.

Davis, H., & Unruh, W. R. (1981). The development of the self-schema in adult depression. *Journal of Abnormal Psychology, 90,* 125–133.

Dean, C., Surtees, P. G., & Sashidharan, S. D. (1983). Comparison of research diagnostic systems in an Edinburgh community sample. *British Journal of Psychiatry, 142,* 247–256.

Depue, R. A., & Iaccono, W. G. (1989). Neurobehavioral aspects of affective disorders. *Annual Review of Psychology, 40,* 457–492.

Depue, R. A., Krauss, S., Spoont, M. R., & Arbisi, P. (1989). General Behavior Inventory identification of unipolar and bipolar affective conditions in a nonclinical university population. *Journal of Abnormal Psychology, 98,* 117–126.

Depue, R. A., & Monroe, S. M. (1978). Learned helplessness in the perspective of the depressive disorders: Definitional and conceptual issues. *Journal of Abnormal Psychology, 87,* 3–20.

Depue, R. A., & Monroe, S. M. (1983). Psychopathology research. In M. Hersen, A. E. Kazdin, & A. S. Bellack (Eds.), *The clinical psychology handbook* (1st ed., pp. 239–264). Elmsford, NY: Pergamon Press.

Depue, R. A., & Monroe, S. M. (1986). Conceptualization and measurement of human disorder in life stress research: The problem of chronic disturbance: *Psychological Bulletin, 99,* 36–51.

Depue, R. A., Slater, J., Wolfstetter-Kausch, H., Klein, D., Goplerud, E., & Farr, D. (1981). A behavioral paradigm for identifying persons at risk for bipolar depressive disorder: A conceptual framework and five validation studies [Monograph]. *Journal of Abnormal Psychology, 90,* 381–437.

Derry, P. A., & Kuiper, N. A. (1981). Schematic processing and self-reference in clinical depression. *Journal of Abnormal Psychology, 90,* 286–297.

Dobson, K. S., & Shaw, B. F. (1987). Specificity and stability of self-referent encoding in clinical depression. *Journal of Abnormal Psychology, 96,* 34–40.

Dohrenwend, B. P. (1974). Problems in defining and sampling the relevant populations of stressful life events. In

B. S. Dohrenwend and B. P. Dohrenwend (Eds.), *Stress-ful life events: Their nature and effects* (pp. 275–310). New York: John Wiley & Sons.

Dohrenwend, B. S., & Dohrenwend, B. P. (Eds.) (1974). *Stressful life events: Their nature and effects*. New York: John Wiley & Sons.

Dohrenwend, B. P., Dohrenwend, B. S., Gould, M. S., Link, B. Neugebauer, R., & Wunsch-Hitzig, R. (1980). *Mental illness in the United States: Epidemiologic esti-mates*. New York: Praeger.

Dohrenwend, B. P., Krasnoff, L., Askenasy, A. R., & Dohrenwend, B. S. (1978). Exemplification of a method for scaling life events: The PERI life events scale. *Journal of Health and Social Behavior*, *19*, 205–229.

Dohrenwend, B. P., Link, B. G., Kern, R., Shrout, P. E., & Markowitz, J. (1987). Measuring life events: The prob-lem of variability within event categories. In B. Cooper (Ed.), *Psychiatric epidemiology: Progress and prospects* (pp. 103–119). London: Croom Helm.

Eccles, J. C. (1977). *The understanding of the brain* (2nd ed.). New York: McGraw-Hill.

Egeland, J. A., Gerhard, D. S., Pauls, D. L., Sussex, J. N., Kidd, K. K., Allen, C. R., Hostetter, A. M., & House-man, D. E. (1987). Bipolar affective disorder lined to DNA markers on chromosome 11. *Nature, 325*, 783–787.

Ellis, A. (1962). *Reason and emotion in psychotherapy*. New York: Lyle Stuart.

Eysenck, M. W., MacLeod, C., & Mathews, A. (1987). Cognitive functioning and anxiety. *Psychological Re-search*, *49*, 189–195.

Finlay-Jones, R., & Brown, G. W. (1981). Types of stress-ful life event and the onset of anxiety and depression disorders. *Psychological Medicine*, *11*, 803–805.

Frank, E., Kupfer, D. J., & Perel, J. M. (1989). Early recurrence in unipolar depression. *Archives of General Psychiatry*, *46*, 397–400.

Gershon, E. S., Hamovit, H. H., Guroff, J. J., & Nurn-berger, J. I. (1987). Birth-cohort changes in manic and depressive disorders in relatives of bipolar and schizoaf-fective patients. *Archives of General Psychiatry*, *44*, 314–319.

Gotlib, I. H., & Cane, D. B. (1987). Construct accessibility and clinical depression: A longitudinal investigation. *Journal of Abnormal Psychology*, *96*, 199–204.

Gotlib, I. H., and McCann, C. D. (1984). Construct acces-sibility and depression: An examination of cognitive and affective factors. *Journal of Personality and Social Psychology*, *47*, 427–439.

Greenberg, M. S., & Beck, A. T. (1989). Depression versus anxiety: A test of the content-specificity hypothesis. *Journal of Abnormal Psychology*, *98*, 9–13.

Guidano, V. F., & Liotti, G. (1983). *Cognitive processes and emotional disorders*. New York: Guilford Press.

Gunderson, E. K. E., & Rahe, R. H. (Eds.). (1974). *Life stress and illness*. Springfield, IL: Charles C Thomas.

Gurling, H. M. D. (1985). Application of molecular biology to mental illness. *Psychiatric Developments*, *3*, 257–273.

Henderson, A. S., Byrne, D. G., & Duncan-Jones, P. (1981). *Neurosis and the social environment*. New York: Academic Press.

Hinkle, L. E., Jr. (1977). The concept of "stress" in the biological and social sciences. In Z. J. Lipowski, D. R. Lipsitt, & P. C. Whybrow (Eds.), *Psychosomatic medi-cine: Current trends and clinical applications* (pp. 27–49). New York: Oxford University Press.

Hodgkinson, S., Sherrington, R., Gurling, H., Marchbanks, R., Reeders, S., Mallet, J., McInnis, M., Petursson, H., & Brynjolfsson, J. (1987). Molecular genetic evidence for heterogeneity in manic depression. *Nature, 325*, 805–808.

Hollon, S. D., & Kendall, P. C. (1980). Cognitive self-statements in depression: Development of an automatic thoughts questionnaire. *Cognitive Therapy and Re-search, 4*, 383–395.

Hollon, S. D., Kendall, P. C., & Lumry, A. (1986). Specificity of depressotypic cognitions in clinical depres-sion. *Journal of Abnormal Psychology*, *95*, 52–59.

Holmes, T. H., & Rahe, R. H. (1967). The Social Readjust-ment Rating Scale. *Journal of Psychosomatic Research*, *11*, 213–218.

Hooley, J. M. (1985). Expressed emotion: A review of the critical literature. *Clinical Psychology Review*, *5*, 119–139.

House, J. S., Landis, K. R., & Umberson, D. (1988). Social relationships and health. *Science, 241*, 540–545.

House, J. S., Robbins, C., & Metzner, H. L. (1982). The association of social relationships and activities with mortality: Prospective evidence from the Tecumseh Community Health Study. *American Journal of Epide-miology, 116*, 123–140.

Ingram, R. E., & Kendall, P. C. (1986). Cognitive clinical psychology: Implications of an information processing perspective. In R. E. Ingram (Ed.), *Information process-ing approaches to clinical psychology* (pp. 3–21). Or-lando, FL: Academic Press.

Ingram, R. E., Kendall, P. C., Smith, T. W., Donnell, C., & Ronan, K. (1987). Cognitive specificity in emotional distress. *Journal of Personality and Social Psychology*, *53*, 734–742.

Jackson, S. W. (1986). *Melancholia and depression*. New Haven: Yale University Press.

Keller, M. B., Lavori, P. W., Endicott, J., Coryell, W., & Klerman, G. L. (1983). "Double depression": Two-year follow-up. *American Journal of Psychiatry, 140*, 689–694.

Kelsoe, J. R., Ginns, E. I., Egeland, J. A., Gerhard, D. S., Goldstein, A. M., Bale, S. J., Pauls, D. L., Long, R. T., Kidd, K. K., Conte, G., Housman, D. E., & Paul. S. M. (1989). Re-evaluation of the linkage relationship be-tween chromosome 11p loci and the gene for bipolar affective disorder in the Old Order Amish. *Nature, 342*, 238–243.

Kendler, K. S., Heath, A. C, Martin, N. G., & Eaves, L. J. (1987). Symptoms of anxiety and symptoms of depres-sion: Same genes, different environments? *Archives of General Psychiatry, 44*, 451–457.

Kennedy, J. L., Guiffra, L. A., Moises, H. W., Cavalli-Sforza, L. L., Pakstis, A. J., Kidd, J. R., Castiglione, C. M., Sjogren, B., Wetterberg, L., & Kidd, K. J. (1988). Evidence against linkage of schizophrenia to markers on chromosome 5. *Nature, 336*, 167–169.

Kihlstrom, J. F., & Nasby, W. (1981). Cognitive tasks in clincial assessment: An exercise in applied psychology. In P. C. Kendall and S. D. Hollon (Eds.), *Assessment strategies for cognitive-behavioral interventions* (pp. 287–312). New York: Academic Press.

Klein, D. N., Depue, R. A., & Slater, J. (1985). Cyclothymia in the adolescent offspring of parents with bipolar affective disorder. *Journal of Abnormal Psychology, 94*, 115–127.

Klerman, G. L. (1978). Long-term treatment of affective disorders. In M. A. Lipton, A. DiMascio, & K. F. Killam (Eds.), *Psychopharmacology: A generation of progress* (pp. 1303–1311). New York: Raven Press.

Klerman, G. L. (1986). Scientific and public policy perspectives on the NIMH Epidemiologic Catchment Area (ECA) Program. In J. E. Barrett & R. M. Rose (Eds.), *Mental disorders in the community: Progress and challenge* (pp. 3–8). New York: Guilford Press.

Klerman, G. L. (1988). The current age of youthful melancholia: Evidence for increase in depression among adolescents and young adults. *British Journal of Psychiatry, 152*, 4–14.

Kraepelin, E. (1921). *Manic-depression insanity and paranoia*. Edinburgh: E. S. Livingstone.

Leckman, J. F., Weissman, M. M., Merikangas, K. R., Pauls, D. L., & Prusoff, B. A. (1983). Panic disorder and major depression: Increased risk of major depression, alcoholism, panic and phobic disorders in families with depressed probands with panic disorder. *Archives of General Psychiatry, 40*, 1055–1060.

Leff, J., & Vaughn, C. E. (1985). *Expressed emotion in families*. New York: Guilford Press.

Lewis, A. J. (1934). Melancholia: A historical review. *Journal of Mental Science, 80*, 1–42.

MacLeod, C., Mathews, A., & Tata, P. (1986). Attentional bias in emotional disorders. *Journal of Abnormal Psychology, 95*, 15–20.

Magnusson, D., & Öhman, A. (Eds.). (1987). *Psychopathology: An interactional perspective*. New York: Academic Press.

Mandler, G. (1984). *Mind and body*. New York: W W Norton.

Mandler, G. (1985). *Cognitive psychology*. Hillsdale NJ: Lawrence Erlbaum Associates.

Marcel, A. J. (1983). Conscious and unconscious perception: An approach to the relations between phenomenal experience and perceptual processes. *Cognitive Psychology, 15*, 238–300.

Maser, J. D., & Cloninger, C. R. (Eds.). (1990), *Comorbidity in anxiety and mood disorders*. Washington, DC: American Psychiatric Press, Inc.

Mathews, A., & MacLeod, C. (1985). Selective processing of threat cues in anxiety states. *Behavior Research and Therapy, 23*, 563–569.

Mathews, A., & MacLeod, C. (1986). Discrimination of threat cues without awareness in anxiety states. *Journal of Abnormal Psychology, 95*, 131–138.

Mathews, A., Mogg, K., May, J., & Eysenck, M. (1989). Implicit and explicit memory bias in anxiety. *Journal of Abnormal Psychology, 98*, 236–240.

Mathews, A., Richards, A., & Eysenck, M. (1989). Interpretation of homophones related to threat in anxiety states. *Journal of Abnormal Psychology, 98*, 31–34.

McGuffin, P., Katz, R., & Bebbington, P. (1988). The Camberwell Collaborative Depression Study III. Depression and adversity in the relatives of depressed probands. *British Journal of Psychiatry, 153*, 775–782.

Mogg, K., Mathews, A., & Weinman, J. (1987). Memory bias in clinical anxiety. *Journal of Abnormal Psychology, 96*, 94–98.

Monroe, S. M. (1982a). Assessment of life events: Retrospective versus concurrent strategies. *Archives of General Psychiatry, 39*, 606–610.

Monroe, S. M. (1982b). Life events and disorder: Event-symptom associations and the course of disorder. *Journal of Abnormal Psychology, 91*, 14–24.

Monroe, S. M. (1982c). Life events assessment: Current practices, emerging trends. *Clinical Psychology Review, 2*, 435–453.

Monroe, S. M. (1990). Psychosocial factors in anxiety and depression. In J. D. Maser & C. R. Cloninger (Eds.), *Comorbidity in anxiety and mood disorders* (pp. 463–497). Washington, DC: American Psychiatric Press, Inc.

Monroe, S. M., & Depue, R. A. (in press). Life stress and depression. In J. Becker, & A. Kleinman (Eds.), *Psychosocial aspects of mood disorders*. Hillsdale, NJ: Lawrence Erlbaum Associates.

Monroe, S. M., & Peterman, A. M. (1988). Life stress and psychopathology. In L. Cohen (Ed.), *Research on stressful life events: Theoretical and methodological issues* (pp. 31–63). New York: Sage Publications.

Monroe, S. M., & Roberts, J. E. (1990). Conceptualizing and measuring life stress: Problems, principles, procedures, progress. *Stress Medicine, 6*, 209–216.

Monroe, S. M., & Simons, A. D. (1990). Life stress in the context of diathesis-stress theories: Implications for the depressive disorders. Manuscript submitted for publication.

Monroe, S. M., & Steiner, S. C. (1986). Social support and psychopathology: Interrelations with preexisting disorder, stress, and personality. *Journal of Abnormal Psychology, 95*, 29–39.

Mullan, M. J., & Murray, R. M. (1989). The impact of molecular genetics on our understanding of the psychoses. *British Journal of Psychiatry, 154*, 591–595.

Neisser, U. (1967). *Cognitive psychology*. New York: Appleton-Century-Crofts.

Nisbett, R. E., & Wilson, T. D. (1977). Telling more than we can know: Verbal reports on mental processes. *Psychological Review, 84*, 231–259.

Novaco, R. W. (1979). The cognitive regulation of anger and stress. In P. C. Kendall & S. D. Hollon (Eds.),

Cognitive-behavioral interventions (pp. 241–278). New York: Academic Press.

O'Connor, P., & Brown, G. W. (1984). Supportive relationships: Fact or fancy? *Journal of Social and Personal Relationships, 1*, 159–175.

Oei, T. I. & Zwart, F. M. (1986). The assessment of life events: Self-administered questionnaire versus interview. *Journal of Affective Disorders, 10*, 185–190.

Panksepp, J. (1986). The neurochemistry of behavior. *Annual Review of Psychology, 37*, 77–107.

Paykel, E. S. (1982). Life events and early environment. In E. S. Paykel (Ed.), *Handbook of affective disorders* (pp. 146–161). New York: Guilford Press.

Peterson, C., Semmel, A., von Baeyer, C., Abramson, L. Y., Metalsky, G. I., & Seligman, M. E. P. (1982). The Attributional Style Questionnaire. *Cognitive Therapy and Research, 6*, 287–300.

Rabkin, J. G., & Struening, E. L. (1976). Life events, stress, and illness. *Science, 194*, 1013–1020.

Rees, W. L. (1976). Stress, distress, disease. *British Journal of Psychiatry, 128*, 3–18.

Rogers, T. B., Kuiper, N. A., & Kirker, W. S. (1977). Self-reference and the encoding of personal information. *Journal of Personality and Social Psychology, 35*, 677–688.

Rosen, G. (1959). Social stress and mental disease from the eighteenth century to the present: Some origins of social psychiatry. *Milbank Memorial Fund Quarterly, 37*, 5–32.

Rutter, M. (1986). Meyerian psychobiology, personality development, and the role of life experiences. *American Journal of Psychiatry, 143*, 1077–1087.

St. George-Hyslop, P. H., Tanzi, R. E., Polinsky, R. J., Haines, J. L., Nee, L., Watkins, P. C., Myers, R. H., Feldman, R. G., Pollen, D., Drachman, D., Growdon, J., Bruni, A., Foncia, J. F., Salmon, D., Frommelt, P., Amaducci, L., Sorbi, S., Piacentini, S., Stewart, C. D., Hobbs, W. J., Conneally, P. M., & Gusella, J. F. (1987). The genetic defect causing familial Alzheimer's disease maps on chromosome 21. *Science, 235*, 885–889.

Sarason, I. G., de Monchaux, C., & Hunt, T. (1975). Methodological issues in the assessment of life stress. In L. Levi (Ed.), *Emotions—Their parameters and measurement* (pp. 499–509). New York: Raven Press.

Sarason, I. G., Johnson, J. H., & Siegel, J. M. (1978). Assessing the impact of life changes: Development of the Life Experience Survey. *Journal of Consulting and Clinical Psychology, 46*, 932–946.

Schlesier-Carter, B., Hamilton, S. A., O'Neil, P. M., Lydiard, R. B., & Malcolm, R. (1989). Depression and bulimia: The link between depression and bulimic cognitions. *Journal of Abnormal Psychology, 98*, 322–325.

Segal, Z. V. (1988). Appraisal of the self-schema construct in cognitive models of depression. *Psychological Bulletin, 103*, 147–162.

Shapiro, S., Skinner, E. A., Kessler, L. G., Von Korff, M., German, P. S., Tischler, G. L., Leaf, P. J., Benham, L., Cottler, L., & Regier, D. A. (1984). Utilization of health and mental health services. *Archives of General Psychiatry, 41*, 971–978.

Sherrington, R., Brynjolfsson, J., Petursson, H., Potter, M., Dudleston, K., Barraclough, B., Wasmath, J., Dobbs, M., & Gurling, H. (1988). Localisation of a susceptibility locus for schizophrenia on chromosome 5. *Nature, 336*, 154–167.

Teasdale, J. D. (1983). Negative thinking in depression: Cause, effect, or reciprocal relationship? *Advances of Behavior Research and Therapy, 5*, 3–25.

Thoits, P. A. (1983). Dimensions of life events that influence psychological distress: An evaluation and synthesis of the literature. In H. B. Kaplan (Ed.), *Psychosocial stress: Trends in theory and research* (pp. 33–103). New York: Academic Press.

Tyrer, P. (1985). Neurosis divisible? *Lancet, 1*, 685–688.

Van Valkenburg, C., Akiskal, H. S., Puzantian, V., & Rosenthal, T. (1984). Anxious depressions: Clinical, family history, and naturalistic outcome—Comparisons with panic and major depressive disorders. *Journal of Affective Disorders, 6*, 67–82.

Weiner, H. M. (1977). *Psychobiology and human disease*. New York: Elsevier Science.

Weissman, A., & Beck, A. T. (1978). Development and validation of the Dysfunctional Attitude Scale: A preliminary investigation. Paper presented at the meeting of the American Educational Research Association, Toronto.

Wilkinson, I. M., & Blackburn, I. M. (1981). Cognitive style in depressed and recovered patients. *British Journal of Clinical Psychology, 20*, 283–292.

Zimmerman, M., & Coryell, W. (1986). Reliability of follow-up assessments of depressed inpatients. *Archives of General Psychiatry, 43*, 468–470.

Zimmerman, M., Pfohl, B., & Stangl, D. (1986). Life events assessment of depressed patients: A comparison of self-report and interview formats. *Journal of Human Stress, 11*, 13–19.

CHAPTER 17

TREATMENT RESEARCH: THE INVESTIGATION AND EVALUATION OF PSYCHOTHERAPY

Alan E. Kazdin

Psychotherapy research occupies a central role in clinical psychology. The area is one in which several conceptual, methodological, and applied issues converge. The overall goal stated in its most general way is to understand treatments and the means through which they operate. There are few, if any, areas related to understanding affect, cognition, and behavior that could be dismissed as irrelevant to psychotherapy. Human behavior in general can be understood from diverse perspectives and levels and types of influence. Add to this the diversity of clinical dysfunctions, the range of possible conceptual approaches, assessment strategies, and intervention techniques, and the domain becomes broad.

Interest and activity in psychotherapy research are great. Current work reflects new developments in the conceptualization of treatment and range of questions that are evaluated (see Goldfried, Greenberg, & Marmar, 1990; Kazdin, 1986b; VandenBos, 1986). Advances in methodology play an active role in fueling progress. Part of the progress is due to increased operationalization of facets critical to treatment evaluation. Three examples noted briefly convey the move toward description and operationalization and the benefits for treatment evaluation. First, the codification of treatment in the form of therapy manuals has proliferated in the last decade (Lambert & Ogles, 1988; Luborsky & DeRubeis, 1984). The manuals specify critical events and practices in treatment and guide the therapist through the treatment regimen. Many researchers lament that the manuals, including their own manuals, are incomplete and do not reflect the complexity of treatment and scope of the exchanges between therapist and patient. At the same time, the manuals facilitate research, spawn replication, and enhance the codification of accumulated clinical and empirical knowledge.

Second, developments in psychiatric diagnosis have enhanced treatment research. The focus on descriptive features of presenting symptoms (American Psychiatric Association, 1980, 1987) and the development of diagnostic instruments to assess these

Completion of this paper was facilitated by a Research Scientist Development Award (MH00353) and grants (MH35408) from the National Institute of Mental Health and The Robert Wood Johnson Foundation.

features have enhanced identification of homogeneous groups. There remain debates about psychiatric diagnosis and the existence, nature, and criteria of specific disorders. Nevertheless, specification of the criteria for many disorders has facilitated disorder-focused treatments and evaluations.

Third, the evaluation of critical treatment processes and events within the treatment session has accelerated by improvements in assessment (Beutler, 1990; Elliott et al., 1986). For example, evaluation of the immediate impact of therapist interpretations on patient functioning has been advanced by fine-grained evaluation of such interventions in terms of type (e.g., transference vs. nontransference) and appropriateness for the patient (e.g., Silberschatz, Fretter, & Curtis, 1986). In addition, developing alternative methods to code therapist and patient vocal patterns has permitted examination of within-session processes and their impact as well as common processes among alternative treatment modalities (e.g., Stiles, Shapiro, & Firth-Cozens, 1988; Wiseman & Rice, 1989). These and related advances in operationalizing treatment processes have facilitated research.

The task of therapy research is to draw valid inferences about treatment. The tasks of satisfying alternative criteria for drawing valid inferences (e.g., internal, external, construct, and statistical conclusion validity; Cook & Campbell, 1979) in any areas of research represent challenges, compromises, and limits to any conclusions that can be drawn. In psychotherapy research, the complexity of clinical dysfunction, the contextual factors that may bear on treatment (e.g., patient history, comorbidity, family dysfunction), emergent problems during treatment (e.g., attrition), and the potential variability among persons who deliver and receive treatment add to the methodological challenges. The purpose of the present chapter is to discuss critical methodological issues specific to the challenges of psychotherapy research. The chapter focuses on issues that relate directly to the conduct of individual studies. The overall purpose is to emphasize several specific design features to increase the quality of the empirical yield.

STRATEGIES FOR EVALUATING TREATMENT

A major task of psychotherapy research is to identify effective treatments and to understand the underlying bases of therapeutic change. At the general level, the tasks to which research is devoted have been framed as questions. Well known among these is what is sometimes viewed as the ultimate question of psychotherapy research, namely, "What treatment, by whom, is most effective for this individual with that specific problem, under which set of circumstances?" (Paul, 1967, p. 111). Developing effective treatments depends on understanding the nature and determinants of clinical disorders as well as the mechanisms of change that may address these determinants. The focus on dysfunction and mechanisms of change might be emphasized by a slightly different question, "For this clinical problem caused by these factors, what intervention produces what type of change process, which results in what type of outcome?" Understanding of psychopathology and psychotherapy is essential to identify what to change as well as the means through which these facets can be changed (Goldfried et al., 1990).

The focus on developing effective treatments and understanding the change process is evident in several specific treatment questions. These questions represent ways of dividing the overriding issues into manageable research strategies. Several treatment evaluation strategies that dominate contemporary research can be identified. Table 17.1 presents major strategies and the questions they are designed to address.

Treatment Package Strategy

Perhaps the most basic question is to ask whether a particular treatment or treatment package is effective for a particular clinical problem. This question is asked by the treatment package strategy, which evaluates the effects of a particular treatment as that treatment might be ordinarily used. The notion of a package emphasizes that treatment may be multifaceted and include several different components that could be delineated conceptually and operationally. The question addressed by this strategy is whether treatment produces therapeutic change. To rule out the influence of change as a function of historical events, maturation, spontaneous remission, repeated testing, and other threats to internal validity, a no-treatment or waiting-list control condition is usually included in the design.

Strictly speaking, evaluation of a treatment package only requires two groups; namely, one group that receives the intervention and the other group that does not. Random assignment of cases to groups and testing each group before and after treatment control the usual threats to internal validity. However, there has been considerable debate about the impact of nonspecific treatment factors and the effects they can exert on clinical dysfunction (e.g., Bowers & Clum, 1988; Horvath, 1988). These factors include attending

Table 17.1. Alternative Treatment Evaluation Strategies to Develop an Effective Intervention

TREATMENT STRATEGY	QUESTIONS ASKED	BASIC REQUIREMENTS
Treatment package	Does treatment produce therapeutic change?	Treatment versus no-treatment or waiting-list control
Dismantling strategy	What components are necessary, sufficient, and facilitative of therapeutic change?	Two or more treatment groups that vary in the components of treatment that are provided
Constructive strategy	What components or other treatments can be added to enhance therapeutic change?	Two or more treatment groups that vary in components
Parametric strategy	What changes can be made in the specific treatment to increase its effectiveness?	Two or more treatment groups that differ in one or more facets of the treatment
Comparative outcome strategy	Which treatment is the more or most effective for a particular problem and population?	Two or more different treatments for a given clinical problem
Client-therapist variation strategy	On what patient, family, or therapist characteristics does treatment depend for it to be effective?	Treatment as applied separately to different types of cases, therapists, and so on
Process strategy	What processes occur in treatment that affect within-session performance and that may contribute to treatment outcome?	Treatment groups in which patient and therapist interactions are evaluated within the sessions

sessions, meeting with a therapist, and, in general, engaging in procedures, whether or not designed to be therapeutic, that foster patient expectation of improvement. Although these elements are included in most forms of treatment, clinical researchers usually believe that the specific treatment they wish to evaluate is superior to the impact of the nonspecific factors associated with attending therapy. Consequently, treatment package research is likely to include a group that serves as an active control condition. In such groups, patients come to the treatment but do not receive an intervention designed to ameliorate the specific clinical dysfunction.

As an example, Longo, Clum, and Yeager (1988) evaluated a multifaceted psychosocial treatment package for adults with recurrent genital herpes. Herpes is a sexually transmitted viral disease with no known cure. Psychological treatment was considered to be appropriate because episodes of the disease are associated with and apparently fostered by stress and the experience of emotional distress. Individuals with recurrent herpes were assigned randomly to one of three groups. The psychosocial intervention package consisted of group meetings that provided training in stress management, relaxation, imagery, and planned exercises in these areas outside of the group treatment sessions. A second group was included in the design as an attention placebo control condition. Individuals also attended group treatment sessions; instead of specific training experiences, people in this group

discussed interpersonal conflicts. This intervention was not considered by the investigators to be a procedure likely to effect change. A final group consisted of a waiting-list (no-treatment) control condition.

The results indicated that episodes of herpes were fewer, less severe, and of a shorter duration for cases who received the intervention package, relative to each of the other groups. A similar pattern favoring the intervention group was evident for measures of depression, stress, and emotional distress. These results suggest that the package produced greater change than the passage of time and attending sessions that resemble treatment. Of course, the particular component(s) of the package that was responsible for change cannot be determined from the study. However, this is not a reasonable criticism given that the goal was to evaluate the impact of the overall package.

Dismantling Treatment Strategy

The dismantling treatment strategy consists of analyzing the components of a given treatment package. After a particular package has been shown to produce therapeutic change, research can begin to analyze the basis for change. To dismantle a treatment, individual components are eliminated or isolated from the treatment. Some clients may receive the entire treatment package, while other clients receive the package minus one or more components. Dismantling research can help identify the necessary and sufficient components of treatment.

As an illustration, Nezu and Perri (1989) evaluated social problem-solving therapy for the treatment of depressed adults. Problem-solving treatment included separate components: (a) a problem-solving orientation process that pertains to how individuals respond when presented with a problem or stressful situation, and (b) a set of skills or goal-directed tasks that enables people to solve a potential problem successfully. The investigators evaluated whether the full package of training was superior to an abbreviated version in which only the skills component was provided.

Clients were assigned to one of three groups that received either the full treatment, the skills component only, or served in a waiting-list control group. At posttreatment and a 6-month follow-up, clients who received the full package (orientation and skills training) were less depressed than those who received the abbreviated treatment (skills training). The findings suggest that the package offers more than skills training alone and that the orientation component provides a critical ingredient.

Constructive Treatment Strategy

The constructive treatment strategy refers to developing a treatment package by adding components to enhance outcome. In this sense, the constructive treatment approach is the opposite of the dismantling strategy. A constructive treatment study begins with a treatment that may consist of one or a few ingredients or a larger package. Various components are added to determine whether the outcome can be enhanced. The strategy asks the question, "What can be added to treatment to make it more effective?" A special feature of this strategy is the combination of individual treatments. Thus, studies may combine conceptually different treatments such as verbal psychotherapy and pharmacotherapy.

An illustration of the constructive strategy was provided by Alden (1989), who evaluated treatments for adults with avoidant personality disorder, a syndrome that consists of long-standing patterns of social withdrawal, sensitivity to social criticism, and low self-esteem. The study examined the incremental value of two treatments. The first treatment was social skills training, which develops specific social interaction skills. The second treatment was graduated exposure designed to assist in the management of anxiety by developing the use of relaxation skills and practicing exposure to interpersonal situations in a gradual fashion. Clients were assigned to either social skills,

graduated exposure, or their combination. A no-treatment control group was also included. After 10 weeks of treatment, clients in the three treated groups showed greater improvement on a variety of measures of social anxiety and functioning than the no-treatment control group. The three treatments were no different from each other at posttreatment or a 3-month follow-up. These results suggest that the components are largely equivalent and do not enhance treatment when combined. The combined treatment did not improve on the effects of the constituent treatments. This general finding is often found in treatment outcome research, a topic to which we will return in the discussion of power.

Parametric Treatment Strategy

The parametric treatment strategy refers to altering specific aspects of treatment to determine how to maximize therapeutic change. Dimensions or parameters are altered to find the optimal manner of administering the treatment. These dimensions are not new ingredients added to the treatment (e.g., as in the constructive strategy) but variations within the technique to maximize change. Increases in duration of treatment or variations in how material is presented are examples of the parametric strategy.

A basic parameter of treatment is duration. More treatment may not invariably lead to greater outcome (see Howard, Kopta, Krause, & Orlinsky, 1986). Yet, in cases in which treatment is only mildly effective or where effects are evident but short lived, duration or dose of treatment is a reasonable parameter to investigate. With this rationale in mind, Perri, Nezu, Patti, and McCann (1989) evaluated the effectiveness of behavior therapy in the treatment of obesity. Two versions of treatment were provided that varied in the number of weekly sessions (20 vs. 40). Both conditions included several components such as training in self-monitoring, stimulus control, self-reinforcement, cognitive modification, problem solving, and exercise, clearly a multifaceted package. At the end of 40 weeks, the group that had received the longer duration of treatment showed greater weight loss. The superiority of this group was evident at a follow-up approximately 8 months later. The results indicate that duration of treatment was an important parameter that contributed to outcome.

Comparative Treatment Strategy

The comparative treatment strategy, probably the most familiar approach, contrasts two or more treatments and addresses the question of which treatment is better (best) for a particular clinical problem. Comparative studies attract wide attention not only because they address an important clinical issue but also because they often contrast conceptually competing interventions. Among alternative treatment evaluation strategies, special difficulties often arise in comparative studies including obstacles in keeping the techniques distinct, in holding constant variables associated with treatment administration, and ensuring the integrity of the individual treatments. Nevertheless, comparative outcome studies have enjoyed widespread use (e.g., Heimberg & Becker, 1984; Kazdin, 1986a).

As an illustration, Szapocznik et al. (1989) compared structured family therapy and psychodynamic therapy to treat Hispanic boys (6 to 12 years old) referred for a variety of different problems (e.g., conduct disorder, anxiety disorder, adjustment disorders). In the family therapy condition, treatment with the family emphasized modifying maladaptive interactional patterns among family members. Psychodynamic therapy consisted of individual therapy with the child. Treatment focused on play, expression of feelings, transference interpretations, and insight. In general, the results indicated that both groups led to equivalent reductions in behavioral and emotional problems at posttreatment. Both groups were better at posttreatment than a control condition in which recreational activities were provided. Family therapy was superior to psychodynamic therapy on a measure of family functioning at a 1-year follow-up. However, there generally were no differences in child dysfunction at posttreatment and follow-up between treatment conditions.

Client and Therapist Variation Strategy

The previous strategies emphasize the technique as a major source of influence in treatment outcome. Researchers often focus on the techniques and their potential differences. In clinical practice, more weight is usually accorded characteristics of the client, therapist, and treatment process (Kazdin, Siegel & Bass, 1990). The effectiveness of treatments can vary widely as a function of characteristics of the patients and the therapists. The client and therapist variation strategy examines whether alternative attributes of the client (child, parent, family characteristics) or therapist contribute to outcome. The strategy is implemented by selecting clients and/or therapists on the basis of specific characteristics. When clients or therapists are classified according to a particular selection variable, the question is whether treatment is more or less effective with certain kinds of participants. For example, questions of this strategy might ask if treatment is more effective with younger versus older clients, or with certain subtypes of problems (e.g., depression) rather than with other subtypes.

An example of a client variation study was reported in the treatment of alcoholic patients (Kadden, Cooney, Getter, & Litt, 1989). The investigators evaluated two treatments: coping skills training and interactional group therapy. Three subject variables were investigated including sociopathy, overall psychopathology, and neuropsychological impairment, each of which has prognostic significance in relation to alcoholism. The authors reasoned that higher functioning patients (low on the three subject variables) would benefit from interactional experiences. Patients with greater impairment and relatively poorer prognosis would profit more from coping skills training that emphasized relapse prevention.

The results were complex due in part to different classification variables and outcome measures. In general, the findings indicated that patient characteristics interacted with type of treatment in the outcome results. Interaction-based treatment was more effective with higher functioning patients as reflected in days of drinking during the 6 months of treatment; coping skills were more effective for patients higher in sociopathy and psychopathology. Neuropsychological impairment as a subject variable did not clearly contribute to outcome.

Process Research Strategy

The previously noted strategies emphasize outcome questions or the impact of variations of the intervention on clients at the end of or subsequent to treatment. The process research strategy addresses questions pertaining to the mechanisms of change of therapy and what transpires between therapist and patient in the delivery of an intervention. Topics may focus on the transactions between therapist and client and the impact of intervening events on the moment-to-moment or interim changes during treatment. Many issues address questions of process including the sequence, stages, and progression of client or therapist affect, behavior, and cognition over the course of treatment or within individual sessions.

Treatment processes may also be examined in relation to clinical outcome. As an illustration, Rounsaville et al. (1986) examined the relation of alternative therapy processes in predicting outcome for the treatment of depression. Patients ($N = 35$) received interpersonal psychotherapy for depression. Therapists who provided treatment ($N = 11$) were evaluated by their supervisors, who observed tapes of several therapy sessions. Processes rated by the supervisors included therapist (exploration, warmth and friendliness, and negative attitude) and patient factors (participation, exploration, hostility, psychic distress), as measured by the Vanderbilt Psychotherapy Process Scale. Treatment outcome was assessed with measures of psychiatric symptoms, social functioning, and patient-evaluated change.

The results indicated that only one patient factor (hostility) was related to outcome on a measure of change completed by the patients. In contrast, therapist factors were much more strongly related to outcome. Therapist exploration was significantly and positively related to reductions in clinical evaluations of depression and patient-rated improvements. Therapist warmth and friendliness correlated significantly with improved social functioning and patient-rated improvements. These results convey the importance of specific therapist relationship characteristics in relation to treatment outcome.

Process research is critically important in understanding therapy (e.g., Beutler, 1990). As evident in the illustration, process can contribute to the understanding of outcome. Process research can test ways of altering potentially critical elements of treatment and evaluating their immediate impact. The changes may illuminate facets of treatment as well as the dysfunction.

General Comments

The strategies noted previously reflect questions frequently addressed in current treatment research. The questions posed by the strategies reflect a range of issues required to understand fully how a technique operates and can be applied to achieve optimal effects. The questions reflect a general progression. The treatment package strategy is an initial approach followed by the various analytic strategies based on dismantling, constructive, and parametric research. A high degree of operationalization is needed to investigate dismantling, constructive, and parametric questions. In each case, specific components or ingredients of therapy have to be sufficiently well specified to be withdrawn, added, or varied in an overall treatment package. In relatively few techniques are the critical procedures specified in operational terms to permit careful analytic investigation for dismantling these strategies. The comparative strategy probably warrants attention after prior work has not only indicated the efficacy of individual techniques but also has shown how the techniques can be administered to

optimize their efficacy. Comparative studies can and frequently are conducted early in the development of a treatment and possibly before the individual techniques have been well developed to warrant such a test.

METHODOLOGICAL AND DESIGN ISSUES

Alternative treatment strategies identify the specific type of questions that are asked. The question underlying a study is of course only the beginning of the research process. Several specific design issues can be identified pertaining to the quality of the investigation and the extent to which it contributes to the knowledge base. For example, in a treatment outcome study the manner in which patients are selected and the conceptualization underlying treatment not only affect the methodological quality of the experimental test but also the sophistication of the questions that are asked about treatment. These issues can greatly advance progress toward the ultimate question (i.e., what treatments work with what problems, under what circumstances, and so on).

Identification and Specification of Clinical Dysfunction

Interpretation of current treatment research and the accumulation of knowledge about treatment are greatly enhanced by careful specification of the clinical sample. In many cases, the sample is described in unclear terms. For example, cases are often referred to as informally as emotionally disturbed or socially withdrawn. Although such terms imply that the clients suffer impairment, the severity, duration, and scope of dysfunction are rarely discussed.

The use of general terms to define the subject samples tends to be idiosyncratic across studies. Thus, studies using the same term might be referring to different types of cases. The accumulation of information about a particular clinical problem in a consistent fashion across studies is difficult. The lack of specification of the sample also raises special issues in relation to the severity of the dysfunction. Across studies, operational criteria to define severity of the clinical problem may not be reported. The failure to use standard diagnostic criteria or widely used assessment devices makes it difficult to draw conclusions about the severity of dysfunction relative to other samples and to normal (nonreferred) peers.

An area of treatment research where clinical problems tend to be well specified is depression. Treatment studies routinely specify that the persons included in treatment met diagnostic criteria (e.g., *Diagnostic and Statistical Manual of Mental Disorders, Third Edition, Revised* [DSM-III-R], Research Diagnostic Criteria) for major depressive disorders or have met specific cutoff scores on standardized and widely used measures (e.g., Beck Depression Inventory (BDI), Hamilton Rating Scale for Depression). Studies are by no means uniform in how they used these criteria. For example, researchers using the BDI vary in their cutoff scores for defining a sample as depressed. However, this is a relatively minor point. Specification of level of severity on a standardized measure and the use of diagnostic criteria are exemplary on this point.

In general, critical to evaluation of treatment is careful delineation of the sample. The domains that are relevant may be broad, including various subject and demographic variables. However, the type, severity, and breadth of symptoms are central because these reflect facets of dysfunction presumably underlying the rationale for treatment. Performance on diagnostic interviews and multidimensional scales that are relatively standardized or commonly used (e.g., Symptom Checklist 90, Minnesota Multiphasic Personality Inventory [MMPI]) provide data that are likely to permit comparisons across studies. The absence of such information increases the difficulty in determining the persons for whom treatment in a given study was effective. The use of a standardized method of assessing symptoms is not intended to capture the unique features of the individual. The goal here is to clarify the nature of dysfunction in a way that permits cross-study integration.

Treatment Administration

Representativeness of Treatment

An initial issue in designing a treatment outcome study is ensuring that the treatment will be fairly and faithfully represented. This warrants consideration before the study begins to ensure that the test is not a unique or idiosyncratic application of the treatment that has little relation to the treatment as usually conceived or practiced. The need to address this issue before conducting the treatments has become especially clear in comparative outcome studies (e.g., DiLoreto, 1971; Paul, 1966; Sloane, Staples, Cristol, Yorkston, & Whipple, 1975; Willis, Faitler, & Snyder, 1987). The results of such studies are often discounted by critics after the fact because the specific

treatments, as tested, did not represent their usual application in practice (e.g., Boy, 1971; Collins & Thompson, 1988; Ellis, 1971; Heimberg & Becker, 1984; Rachman & Wilson, 1980; Roback, 1971).

There are, of course, many different reasons why treatments evaluated in research may not faithfully represent their counterparts in clinical practice (Parloff, 1984). Perhaps the main issue is that rarely is there a single agreed-on or standardized method that can be gleaned from prior research or clinical practice. Thus, investigators usually need to develop treatment guidelines and manuals and to make explicit those procedures that are poorly specified or highly variable in clinical work. Also, in clinical work the therapist has the luxury and obligation to vary critical dimensions of treatment (e.g., number of sessions, focus of content) in response to changes or lack of changes in the patient. Some of the departures in research are intentional to help standardize treatment or to evaluate treatment by itself without the addition of many accoutrements or other interventions that clinicians introduce.

Prior to the investigation, those features of treatment that might depart from standard practice to permit experimental investigation should be specified. Even more importantly, it is essential to ensure that treatment reflects or represents a reasonable variation or approximation of the treatment of interest. There currently are no standard ways to evaluate at the inception of a study whether the treatment faithfully represents the intervention(s) of interest. One alternative is to develop the treatment in manual form and to submit the manual to proponents and practitioners of the technique (Sechrest, West, Phillips, Redner, & Yeaton, 1979). The experts can examine whether specific procedures are faithfully represented and whether the strength and dose of treatment (e.g., duration, number of sessions) are reasonable. The information so gained might be useful to revise the manual to represent treatment better. It would be useful to have some assurance initially that the study provided a reasonable test of that treatment.

Specification and Integrity of Treatment

Whether a new or currently available treatment is to be investigated, several features deserve careful specification. To begin, the conceptual basis of treatment as applied to the specific clinical problem is critical. It is important to identify those factors in treatment that address the dysfunction and/or that explain how underlying processes (e.g., intrapsychic, familial, or social) contribute to the dysfunction. The conceptualization points to the specific treatment components or techniques that are likely to alter behavior and the processes through which they may operate. For example, in alternative family therapies, the functions of various behaviors, the roles of parents and children in relation to each other, and specific patterns of communication may be hypothesized to account for the problem behaviors evident in the child (as the identified patient). Specific structures and functions in the families should serve as the basis for the focus of treatment. The initial question would be to determine if the treatment produces greater changes than those associated with the passage of time (no-treatment or waiting-list control group). Early in the progression of research it is also important to measure the family processes considered to relate to the problem(s) and to show changes in these processes over the course of treatment.

It is also critical to specify what the treatment procedures are, to the extent possible, and to ensure that the treatment was conducted as intended. If possible, treatments should be delineated in manual form that includes written materials to guide the therapist in the procedures, techniques, topics, themes, therapeutic maneuvers, and activities that will attain the specific goals of treatment. Obviously, some treatments (e.g., systematic desensitization) are more easily specified in manual form than others (e.g., psychodynamically oriented psychotherapy).

The specification of treatment is not an end in itself but rather serves a larger purpose. An essential prerequisite of outcome research is to ensure the integrity of treatment—that the procedures are carried out as intended (Quay, 1977; Yeaton & Sechrest, 1981). Treatments can depart from the intended procedures in many ways. In perhaps the most dramatic examples where integrity has been sacrificed, none of the intended treatment sessions was actually held with the clients (see Sechrest, White, & Brown, 1979).

The breakdown of treatment integrity is one of the greatest dangers in outcome research. Interpretation of outcome assumes that the treatments were well tested and carried out as intended. Consider hypothetically a study in which two treatments are equally effective at posttreatment. The two treatments, if implemented as intended, may in fact be equally effective. However, a pattern of no difference might result from a failure to implement one or both of the treatments faithfully. Large variation in how individual treatments are carried out across patients within a given condition and failure to implement critical portions of treatments may also lead to no differences as between two or more treatment conditions. Even

when two treatments differ in the outcome they produce, it is important to rule out the possibility that the differences are due to variations of integrity with which each was conducted. One treatment, perhaps because of its complexity or novelty, may be more subject to procedural degradation and appear less effective because it was less faithfully rendered. Thus, integrity of treatment is relevant in any outcome study independently of the specific pattern of results.

There are several steps that can be performed to address treatment integrity. To begin with, the specific criteria, procedures, tasks, and therapist and patient characteristics that define the treatment can be well specified. Second, therapists can be trained to carry out the techniques. Training is usually defined by the number of cases the therapist has seen or amount of time (years of experience) in using the techniques, rather than proficiency in the constituent skills (see Kazdin, Kratochwill, & VandenBos, 1986). The training experience, however defined, obviously has important implications for how faithfully treatment is likely to be rendered. Third, and related, when treatment has begun, it may be valuable to provide continued case supervision. Listening to or viewing tapes of selected sessions, meeting regularly with therapists to provide feedback, and similar monitoring procedures may reduce therapist drift (departure) from the desired practices.

Whether treatment has been carried out as intended can only be evaluated definitively after the treatment has been completed. This evaluation requires measuring the implementation of treatment. Audio or video tapes of selected treatment sessions from each condition can be examined. Codes for therapist and/or patient behaviors or other specific facets of the sessions can operationalize important features of treatment and help decide whether treatment was conducted as intended (e.g., DeRubeis, Hollon, Evans, & Bemis, 1982).

Treatment integrity is not an all-or-none matter. Hence, it is useful to identify what a faithful rendition of each treatment is and what departures fall within an acceptable range. On some variables, decisions may be difficult to defend, but making them explicit facilitates interpretation of the results. For example, to consider a relatively simple characteristic, treatment may consist of 20 sessions of individual therapy. The investigator may specify that treatment is administered adequately (i.e., is reasonably tested) only if a client receives 15 (75%) or more of the sessions. For other variables, particularly those within-session procedures that distinguish alternative treatments, specification of criteria that define an acceptable range may be more difficult. In some cases, the presence of select processes (e.g., discarding irrational beliefs, improving one's self-concept) might be sufficient; in other cases, a particular level of various processes (e.g., exploration, transference) might be required to denote that treatment has been adequately provided.

Therapist Issues

Training

Treatment usually is administered by a therapist, trainer, or counselor. Although many substantive questions about therapist influences can be studied, there are manifold methodological considerations that must be addressed. It is important to make implausible the possibility that treatment outcome differences can be attributed to differences in therapist competence or other characteristics, unless evaluation of these differences reflects an objective of the study.

Different methodological issues emerge depending on the type of outcome study. If one treatment is being tested (e.g., treatment vs. no-treatment or waiting-list control condition), the major issue is ensuring that more than one therapist provides treatment in the study. With only one therapist, any intervention effects might really reflect an effect unique to that therapist. This amounts to a treatment × therapist interaction that cannot be detected by the design. If two or more therapists are utilized, then the effect of the therapist and therapist × treatment can be evaluated as part of the results.

In a study with two or more treatments, other issues emerge. Depending on many practical issues as well as the specific treatments that are studied, a decision needs to be made whether therapists as a factor should be crossed with or nested within treatment. When therapists are crossed with treatment, each therapist administers each of the treatment conditions in the investigation. Therapists can then be identified as a factor in the data analysis. Such analyses permit evaluation of the impact of therapists alone (as a main effect) and in combination (interaction) with treatment.

If therapists are nested within treatments, separate sets of therapists are used to administer the separate treatments. Thus, therapists only administer one of the treatments rather than all of the different treatments. The impact of therapists as a group cannot be separated from treatment effects. Any treatment difference can be reinterpreted as a difference in the therapists who provided the respective treatments. The alternative hypothesis of therapist effects cannot be treated lightly because different sorts of therapists might be attracted to different treatments. It is important to try to rule out the alternative hypothesis that therapist variables accounted for the results. To that end, such characteristics as age, gender, and professional experience should be similar across the sets of therapists administering alternative conditions. It may be difficult to match on other characteristics that in a given case might differentiate groups of therapists because the number of such therapists in any single outcome study typically is small (e.g., two or three therapists for each treatment condition). The small contingent of therapists may also preclude meaningful statistical evaluation of therapist attributes in relation to outcome.

Purely from the standpoint of experimental design, crossing therapists with treatment is preferable because that portion of patient change attributed to therapists (therapist variance) can be separated from the portion due to treatment technique (treatment variance). Yet in outcome studies, overriding reasons may dictate the nesting of therapists within treatments. An obvious advantage of nesting therapists is that therapists of a given technique can be selected for their background, skill level, commitment to, and enthusiasm for a specific technique. The alternative of having all therapists administer all techniques raises other problems such as the differential skill level and background for the different techniques within a given therapist and across therapists. Also, each therapy technique may require considerable training and experience. Consequently, it may be unreasonable to attempt to train novices to master each technique. Furthermore, it may not be feasible to conduct such training because professional therapists, unlike graduate student therapists, may have less time available or be less willing to learn multiple treatments for a research project.

Even when therapists are selected for their expertise or proficiency within a given technique, the multiple considerations related to treatment integrity should be addressed. Therapist training in the specific version that is to be tested should be provided, supervision should be ongoing to avoid drift from the treatment guidelines or manual, and selected sessions should be assessed to evaluate treatment integrity.

Therapist Characteristics

It seems obvious that there will be differences among people who administer treatment and that some of these differences will influence therapeutic change. Indeed, characteristics of therapists have been studied rather extensively (Beutler, Crago, & Arizmendi, 1986). A variety of therapist characteristics can play an important role in treatment outcome, such as level of empathic understanding, amount of experience, degree of openness, and directiveness, to mention a few (e.g., Feldman, Caplinger, & Wodarski, 1983; Kolvin et al., 1981; Lafferty, Beutler, & Crago, 1989).

Of interest here are the methodological considerations raised by the study of therapist characteristics. First, many different types of characteristics can be studied, and these may raise different sorts of problems. Subject and demographic characteristics (e.g., age, experience, treatment orientation) may be of interest. Alternatively, characteristics that emerge over the course of treatment (e.g., expressions of warmth, self-disclosure) can be evaluated as well. Selection of characteristics for study ideally rely on theory about the treatment, clinical problem, and youth to whom treatment is applied. Second, the study of therapist characteristics requires a sufficient number of therapists to evaluate different levels or degrees of the characteristic of interest. For example, evaluation of the impact of therapist warmth (high vs. low) is not well studied by utilizing two therapists to administer treatment. Several therapists are needed, and they may need to be carefully selected for their initial characteristics.

Many considerations that might be raised in studying patients are somewhat neglected when therapists in some way become the subjects. For example, the importance of sampling and sample size to provide statistically sensitive tests are obviously important. Typically, procuring therapists is much more difficult than procuring patients as subjects because of availability. The exception is analog research, where students are placed in quasi-therapist roles as part of a laboratory study designed to resemble a segment of treatment. The difficulties in obtaining large numbers of cases for the study of therapist characteristics has implications for the types of designs and tests that can be provided and the generality of effects beyond the specific characteristics of the sample that might be conveniently available. Also, with a relatively small number of therapists as subjects, analyses of the data to partial out potential influences (e.g., sex, race, experience, orientation) are difficult.

Assessment Issues

Selection of Outcome Measures

There is general consensus that outcome assessment needs to be multifaceted, involving different perspectives (e.g., patients, significant others, mental health practitioners), different facets of the individual (e.g., affect, cognitions, and behavior), and different methods of assessment (e.g., self-report, direct observation) (see Kazdin & Wilson, 1978; Lambert, Christensen, & DeJulio, 1983; Strupp & Hadley, 1977).

The diversity of measures relevant to evaluate outcome leads to multifaceted assessment batteries in individual outcome studies. The inevitable result often is the ambiguity in comparisons of treatments. Professionals and lay persons alike often wish to know whether treatment worked, which treatment was more successful, or how many people got better. Although one can sympathize with these questions, the answers depend on the specific outcome measure. Different conclusions are possible, if not likely, as a function of different outcome measures (e.g., Szapocznik et al., 1989; Webster-Stratton, Hollinsworth, & Kolpacoff, 1989).

The differences in measures are not inherently problematic. However, from the standpoint of the design of a study, it is useful to identify in advance the goals of treatment and the primacy of alternative outcome measures in relation to these goals. Specification of the goals and relations to specific measures will not reduce the ambiguity that different outcome measures may produce. However, these strategies will permit stronger conclusions about the extent to which well-specified goals are achieved by a given technique.

Reducing Symptoms and Increasing Prosocial Functioning

The impetus for seeking treatment usually is the presence of various symptoms, or maladaptive, disturbing, or disruptive behaviors. Naturally, the effects of treatment would be measured by the extent to which the problems identified at the outset are reduced when treatment is completed. Often assessment includes other symptom areas to see if treatment reduced dysfunction in other domains than those initially identified as problematic. The reduction of symptoms that impair performance is obviously central to the evaluation of outcome.

In addition to symptom reduction, it is important to assess prosocial functioning or positive experiences. Prosocial functioning refers to the presence of positive adaptive behaviors and experiences such as participation in social activities, social interaction, and making friends. Reducing symptoms no doubt can improve a person's functioning. Yet, the overlap of symptom reduction and positive prosocial functioning may not be great.

As might be expected, symptoms and prosocial behavior tend to be inversely related (e.g., Kazdin, 1989; Kazdin et al., 1989). However, the correlations tend to be in the low to moderate range and hence share little variance. In addition, in treatment changes in symptoms show little relation to changes in prosocial functioning. These findings suggest that prosocial functioning and symptom reduction are not equivalent. Prosocial functioning may be an important indicator for treatment evaluation in separate ways. It is possible that treatments that appear equally effective in reducing symptoms vary in the extent to which they promote and develop prosocial behaviors. In addition, for clients whose symptom reduction is similar, the prognosis may vary as a function of prosocial behaviors evident at treatment outcome. For these reasons, assessment of prosocial behavior is worth incorporating into treatment outcome.

Other Types of Measures

The emphasis of outcome measures overlooks many other types of measures that may contribute as much or more information about the relative utility and value of alternative treatments. One type of measure worth including pertains to the processes within the treatment sessions. The value of such measures is that they can shed light on the mechanisms of therapeutic change and serve as a partial test of the model that underlies treatment. Thus, it is valuable to show that changes in, say, cognitive processes occur during treatment when such processes are assumed to mediate change.

Another type of measure that is important to include in outcome studies might be referred to generally as client reactions to treatment. These measures may reflect dimensions that do not necessarily refer to the adjustment or dysfunction of the clients but still may distinguish alternative treatments. For example, attrition, untoward side effects, adherence to the prescribed regimen, attendance, and satisfaction with and acceptability of treatment might vary among treatments. Even if the outcomes of alternative treatments were identical, the treatment of choice might be determined by one or more of these other criteria. Indeed, these other criteria may be of such significance that one treatment slightly less effective than another might still be preferred because the loss in effectiveness is much less than the gain in other benefits. For example, a treatment that clients find acceptable and easy to comply with might be the treatment of choice over an alternative that is more effective but without these characteristics.

Finally, and related to the foregoing, measures concerning the administration of treatment can elaborate the yield from outcome studies. Such measures as cost of the treatments, requirements for training therapists, ease of application of procedures by paraprofessionals, resistance of treatment to violations of integrity, and other measures are relevant. Again, treatments similar in outcome may differ on these measures. In general, the extent to which treatment leads to improvements on outcome measures is obviously of central importance. Yet, the exclusive focus on outcome neglects many other significant measures that professionals and consumers consider as important distinctions among alternative treatments.

Timing of Follow-up Assessment

Assessment immediately after treatment is referred to as posttreatment assessment; any point beyond that ranging from weeks to years typically is referred to as *follow-up* assessment. Follow-up raises important issues for psychotherapy outcome research such as whether gains are maintained and whether conclusions can be reached at all given patient attrition.

Conclusions about the efficacy of a treatment or relative effectiveness of alternative treatments may vary depending on when assessments are conducted. For example, in one study, two of the interventions (group therapy, behavior modification) provided to maladjusted children showed different outcome effects depending on the point in time that assessment was completed (Kolvin et al., 1981). Immediately after treatment, few improvements were evident in the areas of neuroticism, antisocial behavior, and total symptom scores. These areas improved markedly over the course of follow-up approximately 18 months after treatment ended. The authors discussed a sleeper effect (i.e., improvements that are not evident immediately after treatment but emerged and/or increased over time).

Several other studies involving child and adult samples point to the significance of the timing of outcome assessments (e.g., Craighead, Stunkard, & O'Brien, 1981; Deffenbacher & Shelton, 1978; Heinicke & Ramsey-Klee, 1986; Jacobson, 1984; Kingsley & Wilson, 1977; Patterson, Levene, & Breger, 1977; Wright, Moelis, & Pollack, 1976). In these studies, conclusions about the effectiveness of a given treatment relative to a control condition or another treatment differed at posttreatment and follow-up. Thus, the treatment that appeared more or most effective at posttreatment did not retain this status at follow-up.

Not all studies find that the pattern of results and conclusions about a given treatment relative to another treatment or control condition vary from posttreatment to follow-up assessment. Indeed, a review of treatment studies has suggested that as a rule the pattern between treatments evident at posttreatment remains evident at follow-up (Nicholson & Berman, 1983). However, the number of clear exceptions suggests that the conclusions about a given treatment in any particular study might well depend on when the assessment is conducted. The occasional finding that treatment effects are delayed (e.g., Heinicke & Ramsey-Klee, 1986; Kolvin et al., 1981) and that changes at follow-up are often greater than those immediately after treatment (e.g., Wright et al., 1976) underscores the possibility that a given treatment may vary in outcomes at different assessment points.

Power to Detect Group Differences

A critical research issue is the extent to which an investigation can detect differences between groups when differences exist within the population. This notion is referred to as statistical power and reflects the probability that the test will lead to rejection of the null hypothesis. Power (1-beta) is the probability of rejecting the null hypothesis when it is false. Stated differently, power is the likelihood of finding differences between the treatments when in fact the treatments are truly different in their outcomes. Power is a function of the criterion for statistical significance (alpha), sample size (N), and the difference that exists between groups (effect size).

Although power is an issue in virtually all research, it raises special issues in studies where two or more conditions (groups) are not significantly different. The absence of significant differences can contribute to knowledge under a variety of circumstances. However, an essential precondition is that the investigation was sufficiently powerful to detect meaningful differences. In the vast majority of psychotherapy outcome studies that contrast two or more treatments, the power may be relatively weak due to small sample sizes.

There are many reasons to suspect that outcome studies as a general rule provide weak tests. Analyses of research in clinical psychology have revealed relatively weak power in detecting differences between groups. For example, Cohen (1962) examined clinical research published in the *Journal of Abnormal and Social Psychology* for a 1-year period (1960). Over 2,000 statistical tests were identified (from 70 articles) that were considered to reflect direct tests of the hypotheses. To evaluate power, Cohen examined different sizes (i.e., the magnitude of the differences

between alternative groups based on standard deviation units. Cohen distinguished three levels of effect sizes (small = .25; medium = .50; and large = 1.00) and evaluated the power of published studies to detect differences at these levels, assuming alpha = .05 and nondirectional (two-tailed) tests.

The results indicated that power was generally weak for detecting differences equivalent to small and medium effect sizes. For example, the mean power of studies to detect differences reflecting small and medium effect sizes was .18 and .48, respectively. This means that, on the average, studies had slightly less than a 1 in 5 chance to detect small effect sizes and less than a 1 in 2 chance to detect medium effect sizes. These levels are considerably below the recommended level of power = .80 (4 in 5 chance). The level of power that is adequate is not easily specified or justified mathematically. As with the level of confidence (alpha), the decision is based on convention about the margin of protection one should have against falsely accepting the null hypothesis (beta). Cohen (1965) recommended adoption of the convention that beta = .20 and hence power (1 − beta) = .80 when alpha = .05. This translates to the likelihood of 4 in 5 in detecting an effect when a difference exists in the population. Although power ≥ .80 is used as a criterion for discussion in the present chapter, a higher level (.90, .95) is often encouraged as the acceptable criterion (e.g., Friedman, Furberg, & DeMets, 1985). Cohen concluded that the power of the studies was weak and that sample sizes in future studies routinely should be increased (see also Cohen, 1977). A more recent analysis of the literature (Rossi, 1990) has revealed that the vast majority of studies continue to be quite weak with regard to detecting small and medium effects.

In psychotherapy research, issues of power might emerge as a function of the different types of comparisons that are made and the different effect sizes the comparisons are likely to generate. The comparison of treatment versus no treatment is likely to produce relatively large effect sizes. In contrast, comparisons of two or more active treatments or treatment variations (e.g., dismantling, parametric, comparative outcome strategies) are likely to produce smaller effect sizes. Thus, the power of a study to detect differences with a given sample size may vary depending on the type of study.

An evaluation of psychotherapy outcome research suggests that studies comparing treatment versus no-treatment generally are sufficiently powerful to detect such differences (Kazdin & Bass, 1989). Given the effect sizes usually reported in such comparisons (median effect size = .78), sample sizes need not be large to detect group differences (e.g., sample size of 27 cases per group for this effect size and power = .80). However, in studies where the investigator wishes to detect differences between alternative treatments or variations of treatments, effect sizes tend to be much smaller (median effect size = .47). A much larger sample would be needed to detect differences (e.g., sample size of approximately 70 cases per group for this effect size and power = .80). In fact, approximately 55% of treatment outcome studies examined over a 2-year period fail to meet power of $\geq$ .80 in their comparisons of groups at posttreatment; approximately 70% fail to meet the power criterion for comparisons at follow-up.

The claim that power of most studies is likely to be inadequate is too general to convey impact on interpretation of individual studies. Consider an example that is rather typical in the types of comparisons and conclusions that are drawn in studies of psychotherapy. Alexander, Neimeyer, Follette, Moore, and Harter (1989) compared two treatments and a waiting-list control condition on the adjustment of women who as children had been victims of sexual abuse. One treatment (interpersonal transaction) focused on discussion of experiences and feelings associated with abuse in the context of the group. The other treatment (process group format) focused primarily on processes within the group and styles of relating to others in the group. At posttreatment the results indicated treatments were not different from each other but superior to the wait-list condition in measures of fearfulness, depression, and social adjustment. Are the treatments different in their outcomes? We really do not know with this test given the likelihood of weak power. With a sample size of 65 (minus seven to attrition) divided among three groups, weak power to detect between-treatment differences remains plausible as an explanation of the pattern of results.

The weak power of therapy research is not a minor methodological annoyance. As illustrated in these examples, the neglect of power has major implications for interpreting research. Psychotherapy research is an area where the absence of differences (i.e., support for the null hypothesis) is often taken to be significant from conceptual and clinical perspectives (see Frank, 1982; Luborsky, Singer, & Luborsky, 1975; Stiles, Shapiro, & Elliott, 1986). It may well be the case that treatments are similar in the outcomes they produce, and "no difference" reflects the actual state of affairs. However, a plausible alternative is that the power of studies comparing alternative treatments is relatively weak. The neglect of power is not unique to psycho-

therapy research. Repeated lamentations of the weak power in several areas of psychological research have had little impact on research, a situation leading two reviewers to note that researchers "stubbornly neglect" the issue (Sedlmeier & Gigerenzer, 1989, p. 313).

Clinical Significance

Typically, conclusions about the relative effectiveness of alternative psychotherapies are based on statistical evaluation of treatment outcome. Statistically significant differences may be important when testing alternative theories or isolating and identifying variables that may have conceptual significance if they lead to different results. In clinical trials it is not only important to evaluate treatment differences but also to examine if there is some clear benefit of a more practical nature favoring one treatment over another.

Several different measures of clinical significance have been posed for the psychotherapy research including measurement of the extent to which treatment returns clients to normative levels of functioning, the degree to which change is perceptible to significant others in the clients' everyday lives, and elimination of the presenting problem (see Hugdahl & Ost, 1981; Jacobson, Follette, & Revenstorf, 1984; Jacobson & Revenstorf, 1988; Kazdin, 1977; Kendall & Norton-Ford, 1982; Yeaton & Sechrest, 1981). As yet, there is no standard or uniformly adopted procedure or measurement strategy to assess clinical significance.

Relatively few psychotherapy studies incorporate any of the measures designed to evaluate the clinical significance of change. Among those studies that do, one of the most frequently used measures is the extent to which treated patients are returned to normative levels of functioning (e.g., Forehand & Long, 1988; Kazdin et al., 1989; Webster-Stratton et al., 1989). To invoke this criterion, a comparison is made between treated patients and peers who are functioning well or without problems in everyday life. Prior to treatment, the patient sample presumably would depart considerably from their well-functioning peers in the area identified for treatment (e.g., anxiety, social withdrawal, aggression). One measure of the extent to which treatment produced clinically important changes would be the demonstration that at the end of treatment the patient sample was indistinguishable from or well within the range of a normative, well-functioning sample on the measures of interest. A main issue for invoking this criterion is determining the level or range that defines normal functioning.

As an illustration, in the study by Alden (1989) clients treated for avoidant personality disorder were

compared to normative samples on measures of shyness and self-esteem. Prior to treatment, clients departed significantly from normative sample on these
measures (greater shyness, lower self-esteem). After
treatment, treated cases improved significantly on the
measures (by approximately one standard deviation).
However, they still remained significantly different
from normative levels. These results are informative
and add greatly to the between-group differences.
Alternative treatments were effective and led to
marked changes, but none produced effects that
brought clients to within the normative range.

A related criterion for evaluating clinical significance is to examine the departure of treated cases from
a dysfunctional sample, the converse of comparison
with normative samples. A clinically significant
change is evident if treated cases depart markedly
from the level of dysfunction of untreated dysfunctional cases. As an illustration, Nezu and Perri (1989)
compared two variations of problem solving to treat
depression, as highlighted previously. In evaluating
the clinical significance of change, they examined the
proportion of cases in each group whose score on
measures of depression fell two or more standard
deviations below (i.e., less depressed) the mean of the
untreated sample. For example, on one measure (the
BDI), 85.7% of the cases who received the full
problem-solving condition achieved this level of
change. In contrast, 50% of the cases who received the
abbreviated problem-solving condition achieved this
level of change.

Although there are no standard measures of clinical
significance, there is general agreement that outcome
measures must move beyond those that reflect statistical significance alone. Measures of clinical significance are not without ambiguity and arbitrariness. For
example, magnitude of change used to define clinical
significance may be expressed in standard deviation
units. However, such units may not necessarily relate
to the phenomenological experience of the patient or
equally across all patients, or reflect actual impairment in everyday life. Nevertheless, the measures
provide important information about the impact of
treatment and the need to develop treatments further.
As such, clinical significance addresses questions
other than those raised by statistical significance
alone.

PLANNING, IMPLEMENTING,
AND EVALUATING AN
OUTCOME STUDY

The previous comments are directed to several
issues that relate to methodology of treatment evaluation. When discussed generally, they do not serve as a

sufficient guide for research. The issues are better
translated into practice by examining major questions
that warrant consideration in the design of a specific
treatment study. Several questions can be asked before the investigation is conducted. Ensuring that
these are answered at the outset can enhance the
quality of and yield from research. Table 17.2 presents a set of some of the major questions that would
be useful to address.

Sample Characteristics

Investigations could be improved by specifying the
criteria of clinical dysfunction that served as the basis
for selection of the sample. Frequently, investigators
allude to the fact that patients were referred for
treatment. However, this is of little use in terms of
understanding the problems the patients present.
Progress can be enhanced by specifying the inclusion
and exclusion criteria for patient selection. Use of a
specific diagnostic system such as DSM-III-R or
scores on a dimensional scale to describe or to select
patients would be helpful as well. It is unreasonable to
expect that different investigators will adopt the same
criteria for a given clinical problem. Yet, in any study
it is reasonable to demand that the criteria be specified
and operationalized.

Specification of the sample involves more than a
clarification of the clinical dysfunction and criteria for
selection. Subject and demographic variables, including age, sex, socioeconomic status, intelligence, and
achievement, are prime candidates. These characteristics are often related to clinical dysfunction and
adaptive functioning and may influence treatment
efficacy. They need to be specified so that it is clear to
others who was treated.

With respect to both the nature of the clinical
dysfunction and subject and demographic variables,
the investigator might be advised to consider whether
relatively homogeneous or heterogeneous samples
should be selected. A relatively homogeneous sample
in this context refers to the fact that subjects are
selected for their narrow range of variation with regard
to the clinical problem and/or subject and demographic characteristics. A heterogeneous sample
would include patients that varied more broadly with
regard to the clinical problem and/or subject and
demographic characteristics.

A homogeneous sample would be selected if the
investigator believes that the treatment is likely to be
effective with a specific type of problem or set of
patients or wishes to minimize variance due to inter-
subject differences. On the other hand, the investigator may believe or wish to test that the treatment is

Table 17.2. Selected Questions to Raise in Planning a Therapy Outcome Study

Sample Characteristics
1. By what criteria regarding dysfunction has the sample been chosen?
2. How were the criteria operationalized?
3. Can the selection procedure be replicated in principle and practice?
4. What are the subject and demographic characteristics of the sample?
5. Why were these cases selected or studied?
6. With regard to clinical dysfunction or subject and demographic characteristics, is this a relatively homogeneous or heterogeneous sample?

Therapists
1. Who are the therapists? What are their characteristics?
2. Why are these therapists suited to or appropriate for the study?
3. Can the influence of the therapist be evaluated in the design either as a factor (as in a factorial design), or can therapist effects be evaluated within a condition?
4. Are the therapists adequately trained? By what criteria?
5. Can the quantity and quality of their training and implementation of treatment be measured?

Treatment
1. What characteristics of the clinical problem make this particular treatment a reasonable approach?
2. Does the version of treatment represent the treatment as it is usually carried out?
3. Does the investigation provide a strong test of treatment? On what basis has one decided this is a strong test?
4. Has treatment been specified in manual form, or have explicit guidelines been provided?
5. Has the treatment been carried out as intended? (Integrity is examined during but evaluated after the study is completed.)
6. Can the degree of adherence of therapists to the treatment manual be codified?
7. What defines a complete case (e.g., completion of so many sessions)?

Assessment
1. If specific processes are hypothesized to change with treatment, are these to be assessed?
2. If therapy is having the intended effect on these processes, how would performance be evident on the measure? How would groups differ on this measure?
3. Are there additional processes in therapy that are essential or facilitative to this treatment, and are these being assessed?
4. Does the outcome assessment battery include a diverse range of measures to reflect different perspectives, methods, and domains of functioning?
5. Are treatment effects evident in measures of daily functioning (e.g., marital or work adjustment, other adaptive behaviors)?
6. Are outcomes being assessed at different points in time after treatment?

General
1. What is the status of contemporary research that makes this particular test worthwhile?
2. What is the likely effect size that will be found based on other treatment studies or meta-analyses?
3. Given the likely effect size, how large of a sample is needed to provide a strong (powerful) test of treatment (e.g., power > .85)?
4. What is the likely rate of attrition over the course of treatment and posttreatment and follow-up assessments?
5. With the anticipated loss of cases, is the test likely to be sufficiently powerful to demonstrate differences between groups if all cases complete treatment?

more effective with some problems rather than others (e.g., anxiety rather than eating disorders) or some types of cases (e.g., males vs. females, children vs. adolescents). In such cases, a more heterogeneous sample would be selected.

Homogeneity versus heterogeneity is always a matter of degree. An investigator invariably imposes some restrictions on the sample. Thus, cases of all ages (e.g., 12 to 70 years) or with all presenting problems (e.g., anxiety disorders, psychoses, personality disorders) are not likely to be entered into the study. However, the precise rationale for selecting patients and the characteristics that are or are not allowed to vary deserve careful planning.

Therapists/Trainers

The therapist questions in Table 17.2 refer to characteristics of the therapists and the rationale for their selection. The reason(s) why a particular set of therapists or trainers was selected are rarely stated. It is possible that the therapists were selected because of convenience or their availability to work on a project or because of a special therapeutic orientation. The selection for convenience (e.g., graduate student therapists) is not inherently undesirable. However, people available to serve as therapists might have special skills, orientations, or status that could influence the generality of the results. It is important to specify the characteristics that might be unique to those who were selected to serve as therapists, because selection usually cannot be assumed to reflect a representative or random sample from the population of persons who are therapists.

In general, it is valuable to specify characteristics of the therapists in a similar way to those that are identified for the patients. The relevant dimensions may vary but presumably include experience and level of training, age, and sex. Given the clinical focus, population, or technique, race and ethnicity may be essential to specify as well (e.g., Costantino, Malgady, & Rogler, 1986). An especially critical feature is the level of training. Specific criteria to define competence of therapists to administer the techniques in the study (e.g., successfully completed a particular course or training experience) would be important to note. It is valuable to describe as much as one can about the training experience therapists have received and, if possible, why this experience can be used to infer competence. In the usual study, therapists are described by referring to therapist experience, orientation, and professional degree. This is fine, but further information on skills in use of the technique(s) in the study would be helpful. The likelihood of replicating the findings of the study may be influenced by knowing the characteristics of the therapists and the details of their training.

An evaluation of the influence of therapists on outcome is worthwhile planning in the design if at all feasible. If each therapist administers each of the conditions, then the effects can be examined in a factorial design. A therapist × condition analysis at posttreatment will examine if therapists differed (main effect of therapist) or if some therapists were more (or less) effective with one or more of the treatments compared to other therapists (therapist × condition interaction).

It is often the case that different therapists administer the different treatment conditions. The reason is that each treatment may require special skills and one person has not been trained to conduct both. Thus, therapists A, B, and C administer Treatment 1 and therapists D, E, and F administer Treatment 2. For a given treatment, the investigator could evaluate the effects of therapists (A vs. B vs. C for Treatment 1). An evaluation of therapists is important to present even when a factorial design does not isolate the effects independently (i.e., statistically) of treatments.

Treatment

Questions regarding the treatment pertain to conceptualization of the clinical problem. The treatment implicitly embraces a particular conceptual view about processes related to the specific clinical dysfunction and the way in which these are to be addressed in treatment. The connections between means, ends, and intervening processes of treatment and the connection of the clinical problem and this particular treatment need to be explicitly stated. It is likely that the investigator will not be able to trace the connections between conceptualization of the clinical problem, treatment techniques, intervening processes that produce change, and improvements on the outcome measures. The importance of the process of specifying the connections stems from revealing those areas that are not clear. The gaps in the conceptual process generate thoughts and hypotheses about what may be needed in treatment and can accelerate the development of techniques.

Several questions about the specific version of treatment are important to raise including whether the version represents the treatment the investigator wishes to study, whether the version is a strong test, and whether the treatment could be followed and replicated by others. The use of treatment manuals facilitates training of therapists, replication of treatment by others, and evaluation of treatment integrity.

Assessment

It is helpful to specify and then to assess processes within treatment that are assumed to mediate therapeutic change. Assessment of such processes as attributions and beliefs or self-esteem, if these are central to the technique of interest, can provide valuable information. Apart from the evaluation of treatment outcome, the investigator can correlate changes in processes with changes in outcome. In effect, the study can become a test of the model of therapeutic change as well as a measure of outcome.

The processes through which treatment leads to change are critical to understand. Yet they may be relegated to a secondary importance in one sense. It is critical to demonstrate that the treatment produces reliable and clinically important changes. Once an effective treatment is in hand, an analysis of the process(es) is especially important.

It is arguable to state that understanding processes is important prior to even developing a treatment. Clearly, understanding the processes underlying the clinical problem is helpful to ensure that these are addressed in treatment. Once a treatment is developed, processes remain important. Yet, the clinical priority of developing an effective treatment must be the initial goal. This may need to be achieved before rather than after the study of process. It is difficult to defend an unvarying sequence in the study of processes and treatment outcomes because the study of process and outcome is intertwined.

Central assessment questions pertain to the outcome assessment battery and the administration of this battery over time. A great deal has been written about the assessment of therapeutic change (e.g., Lambert et al., 1983). There is incomplete agreement on measures but general consensus that multiple domains of functioning need to be selected that directly reflect the basis for clinical referral. Usually this refers to reductions of symptoms in specific areas of functioning. In addition, it is important to examine prosocial functioning. The ultimate adjustment of the case may not derive from the reduction of symptoms but rather, or in addition, the integration of the individual in his or her everyday life.

The timing of assessment is important, too. Administration of the assessment battery prior to treatment usually is desirable on clinical and methodological grounds. Initial pretest data identify the initial level and scope of dysfunction. Also, such data increase the power of the statistical analyses to identify treatment differences. Posttreatment assessment obviously is provided to evaluate the change after treatment. Follow-up assessment permits examination of the extent to which treatment effects are stable and/or change in relation to other treatment and control conditions within the study. Studies of diverse techniques cited earlier have shown that the conclusions drawn about the effects of a treatment or relative effectiveness of alternative treatments may vary greatly over time. Different assessment occasions (e.g., posttreatment, 1-year and 2-year follow-up assessments) are difficult to obtain but important to seek.

General Comments

There are additional questions listed in Table 17.2 that address general issues. These include the rationale for the particular study and where it fits in current theory, research, and practice. Careful evaluation of their contexts for the study are likely to influence concrete decisions (e.g., number and duration of sessions) of the study as well as more basic features such as selection of treatment and control conditions.

Other questions pertain to statistical power. The ability of the study to detect differences is obviously critical. The likely effects that a given treatment produces can be estimated in different ways. Meta-

analyses that report effect sizes for different types of treatment, clinical problems, and measures provide one source of guidelines. From this information, the sample size needed to detect differences, if differences exist, between (or among) conditions can be easily extracted (from Cohen, 1977; Kraemer & Thiemann, 1987). Alternatively, examination of effect sizes, sample sizes, and power from psychotherapy studies suggest guidelines based on the types of comparisons of interest (Kazdin & Bass, 1989).

Attention to these and to other questions in Table 17.2 will not yield uniform answers among clinical researchers. Different conceptualizations of treatments and research will yield great variability in methodological approaches. The advantage of the preceding questions is not in dictating answers but rather in increasing the explicitness of the research process. Attention to the questions would not only improve the yield of individual investigations but also facilitate replication in clinical practice and research.

CONCLUSIONS

The methodological rigor and quality of individual investigators are pivotal to any area of work. This is not merely a vacuous statement of the obvious. Within psychotherapy research, the importance of experimental validity and methodological quality has been challenged. For example, meta-analyses of psychotherapy have added to the evaluative armamentarium by quantitatively examining the effects of alternative treatments (see Brown, 1987). The evaluation of large bodies of evidence is occasionally extolled as a means of overcoming the shortcomings of individual investigations. Indeed, whether methodological features (e.g., random assignment, use of a control group) affect the conclusions reached about treatment outcome has been evaluated quantitatively (e.g., correlations with effect size) (e.g., Landman & Dawes, 1982; Shapiro & Shapiro, 1982; Smith & Glass, 1977; Smith, Glass, & Miller, 1980). Individual methodological features (e.g., random assignment, matching, experimental mortality) and overall evaluations of experimental methodology have shown little or no relation to effect sizes and hence the conclusions reached about treatment. This conclusion itself can be challenged (e.g., Wortman, 1983). Reasonable people might well disagree on the verdict. However, the mere discussion raises questions about the value of careful methodology.

A related issue pertains to the effectiveness of alternative forms of treatment. Quantitative (meta-analytic) and qualitative (narrative) evaluations of psychotherapy occasionally have reached the verdict that all treatments are generally similar in the outcomes they produce (e.g., Brown, 1987; Luborsky et al., 1975; Stiles et al., 1986). This conclusion, too, can be challenged, and indeed on methodological grounds (Kazdin & Bass, 1989). Yet, that is not the point. The conclusion suggests in yet another way that what we actually do in substance (specific form of treatment) or method (niceties of design) makes little difference. The present chapter began with an initial assumption, namely, that quality of design at the level of the individual study is critically important and makes a pivotal difference to the accumulation of knowledge. Psychotherapy trials are difficult to mount and usually costly in both time and money. A given investigator is not likely to conduct many research projects involving clinical treatments and samples given the complexity of individual projects and current life expectancies. Methodology is all the more critical. The cost of such studies lobbies for ensuring that the knowledge yield of individual projects is maximized. Methodological features related to implementation of individual studies are directed toward this goal.

REFERENCES

Alden, L. (1989). Short-term structured treatment for avoidant personality disorder. *Journal of Consulting and Clinical Psychology, 57*, 756–764.

Alexander, P. C., Neimeyer, R. A., Follette, V. M., Moore, M. K., & Harter, S. (1989). A comparison of group treatments of women sexually abused as children. *Journal of Consulting and Clinical Psychology, 57*, 479–483.

American Psychiatric Association. (1980). *Diagnostic and statistical manual of mental disorders* (3rd ed). Washington, DC: Author.

American Psychiatric Association. (1987). *Diagnostic and statistical manual of mental disorders* (3rd ed. Revised). Washington, DC: Author.

Beutler, L. E. (Ed.) (1990). Special series: Advances in psychotherapy process research. *Journal of Consulting and Clinical Psychology, 58*, 263–303.

Beutler, L. E., Crago, M., & Arizmendi, T. G. (1986). Therapist variables in psychotherapy process and outcome. In S. L. Garfield & A. E. Bergin (Eds.), *Handbook of psychotherapy and behavior change* (3rd ed., pp. 257–310). New York: John Wiley & Sons.

Bowers, T. G., & Clum, C. A. (1988). Relative contribution of specific and nonspecific treatment effects: Meta-analysis of placebo-controlled behavior therapy research. *Psychological Bulletin, 103*, 315–323.

Boy, A. V. (1971). A critique by Angelo V. Boy. In A. O. DiLoreto (Ed.), *Comparative psychotherapy: An experimental analysis* (pp. 233–245). Chicago: Aldine de Gruyter.

Brown, J. (1987). A review of meta-analyses conducted on psychotherapy outcome research. *Clinical Psychology Review, 7*, 1–23.

Cohen, J. (1962). The statistical power of abnormal-social psychological research: A review. *Journal of Abnormal and Social Psychology, 65*, 145–153.

Cohen, J. (1965). Some statistical issues in psychological research. In B. B. Wolman (Ed.), *Handbook of clinical psychology* (pp. 95–121). New York: McGraw-Hill.

Cohen, J. (1977). *Statistical power analysis for the behavioral sciences* (2nd ed.). New York: Academic Press.

Collins, F. L., Jr., & Thompson, J. K. (1988). On the use of symbolic labels in psychotherapy outcome research: Comment on Wills, Faitler, and Synder. *Journal of Consulting and Clinical Psychology, 56*, 932–933.

Cook, T. D., & Campbell, D. T. (Eds.). (1979). *Quasi-experimentation: Design and analysis issues for field settings*. Chicago: Rand McNally.

Costantino, G., Malgady, R. G., & Rogler, L. H. (1986). Cuento Therapy: A culturally sensitive modality for Puerto Rican children. *Journal of Consulting and Clinical Psychology, 54*, 639–645.

Craighead, L. W., Stunkard, A. J., & O'Brien, R. (1981). Behavior therapy and pharmacotherapy for obesity. *Archives of General Psychiatry, 38*, 763–768.

Cross, D. G., Sheehan, P. W., & Khan, J. A. (1982). Short- and long-term follow-up of clients receiving insight-oriented therapy and behavior therapy. *Journal of Consulting and Clinical Psychology, 50*, 103–112.

Deffenbacher, J. L., & Shelton, J. L. (1978). Comparison of anxiety management training and desensitization in reducing test and other anxieties. *Journal of Counseling Psychology, 25*, 277–282.

DeRubeis, R. J., Hollon, S. E., Evans, M. D., & Bemis, K. M. (1982). Can psychotherapies for depression be discriminated? A systematic investigation of cognitive therapy and interpersonal therapy. *Journal of Consulting and Clinical Psychology, 50*, 744–756.

DiLoreto, A. O. (1971). *Comparative psychotherapy: An experimental analysis*. Chicago: Aldine de Gruyter.

Elliott, R., Hill, C. E., Stiles, W. B., Friedlander, M. L., Maher, A. R., & Margison, F. R. (1986). Primary therapist response modes: Comparison of six rating systems. *Journal of Consulting and Clinical Psychology, 55*, 218–223.

Ellis, A. (1971). A critique by Albert Ellis. In A. O. DiLoreto (Ed.), *Comparative psychotherapy: An experimental analysis* (pp. 213–221). Chicago: Aldine de Gruyter.

Feldman, R. A., Caplinger, T. E., & Wodarski, J. S. (1983). *The St. Louis conundrum: The effective treatment of antisocial youths*. Englewood Cliffs, NJ: Prentice-Hall.

Forehand, R. L., & Long, N. (1988). Outpatient treatment of the acting out child: Procedures, long-term follow-up data, and clinical problems. *Advances in Behavior Research and Therapy, 10*, 129–177.

Frank, J. D. (1982). Therapeutic components shared by all psychotherapies. In J. H. Harvey & M. M. Parks (Eds.),

Psychotherapy research and behavior change (Vol. 1, pp. 5–37). Washington, DC: American Psychological Association.

Friedman, L. M., Furberg, C. D., & DeMets, D. L. (1985). *Fundamentals of clinical trials* (2nd ed.) Littleton, MA: PSG Publishing Company.

Goldfried, M. R., Greenberg, L. S., & Marmar, C. (1990). Individual psychotherapy: Process and outcome. *Annual Review of Psychology, 41*, 659–688.

Heimberg, R. G., & Becker, R. E. (1984). Comparative outcome research. In M. Hersen, L. Michelson, & A. S. Bellack (Eds.), *Issues in psychotherapy research* (pp. 251–283). New York: Plenum Publishing.

Heinicke, C. M., & Ramsey-Klee, D. M. (1986). Outcome of child psychotherapy as a function of frequency of session. *Journal of the American Academy of Child Psychiatry, 25*, 247–253.

Horvath, P. (1988). Placebos and common factors in two decades of psychotherapy research. *Psychological Bulletin, 104*, 214–225.

Howard, K. I., Kopta, S. M., Krause, M. S., & Orlinsky, D. E. (1986). The dose-effect relationship in psychotherapy. *American Psychologist, 41*, 159–164.

Hugdahl, K., & Ost, L. (1981). On the difference between statistical and clinical significance. *Behavioral Assessment, 3*, 289–295.

Jacobson, N. S. (1984). A component analysis of behavioral marital therapy: The relative effectiveness of behavior exchange and communication/problem-solving training. *Journal of Consulting and Clinical Psychology, 52*, 295–305.

Jacobson, N. S., Follette, W. C., & Revenstorf, D. (1984). Psychotherapy outcome research: Methods for reporting variability and evaluating clinical significance. *Behavior Therapy, 15*, 336–352.

Jacobson, N. S., & Revenstorf, D. (1988). Statistics for assessing the clinical significance of psychotherapy techniques: Issues, problems, and new developments. *Behavioral Assessment, 10*, 133–145.

Kadden, R. M., Cooney, N. L., Getter, H., & Litt, M. D. (1989). Matching alcoholics to coping skills or interactional therapies: Posttreatment results. *Journal of Consulting and Clinical Psychology, 57*, 698–704.

Kazdin, A. E. (1977). Assessing the clinical or applied importance of behavior change through social validation. *Behavior Modification, 1*, 427–452.

Kazdin, A. E. (1986a). Comparative outcome studies of psychotherapy: Methodological issues and strategies. *Journal of Consulting and Clinical Psychology, 54*, 95–105.

Kazdin, A. E. (1986b). Special issue: Psychotherapy research. *Journal of Consulting and Clinical Psychology, 54* (February, Whole No. 1).

Kazdin, A. E. (1989). Hospitalization of antisocial children: Clinical course, follow-up status, and predictors of outcome. *Advances in Behaviour Research and Therapy, 11*, 1–67.

Kazdin, A. E., & Bass, D. (1989). Power to detect differ-ences between alternative treatments in comparative psychotherapy outcome research. *Journal of Consulting and Clinical Psychology, 57*, 138–147.

Kazdin, A. E., Bass, D., Siegel, T., & Thomas, C. (1989). Cognitive-behavioral treatment and relationship therapy in the treatment of children referred for antisocial behavior. *Journal of Consulting and Clinical Psychology, 57*, 522–535.

Kazdin, A. E., Kratochwill, T. M., & VandenBos, G. R. (1986). Beyond clinical trials: Generalizing from research to practice. *Professional Psychology: Research and Practice, 17*, 391–398.

Kazdin, A. E., Siegel, T., & Bass, D. (1990). Drawing upon clinical practice to inform research on child and adolescent psychotherapy: A survey of practitioners. *Professional Psychology: Research and Practice, 21*, 189–198.

Kazdin, A. E., & Wilson, G. T. (1978). *Evaluation of behavior therapy: Issues, evidence, and research strategies.* Cambridge, MA: Ballinger.

Kendall, P. C., & Norton-Ford, J. D. (1982). Therapy outcome research methods. In P. C. Kendall & J. N Butcher (Eds.), *Handbook of research methods in clinical psychology* (pp. 429–460). New York: John Wiley & Sons.

Kingsley, R. G., & Wilson, G. T. (1977). Behavior therapy for obesity: A comparative investigation of long-term efficacy. *Journal of Consulting and Clinical Psychology, 45*, 288–298.

Kolvin, I., Garside, R. F., Nicol, A. R., MacMillan, A., Wolstenholme, F., & Leitch, I. M. (1981). *Help starts here: The maladjusted child in the ordinary school.* London: Tavistock.

Kraemer, H. C., & Thiemann, S. (1987). *How many subjects? Statistical power analysis in research.* Newbury Park, CA: Sage Publications.

Lafferty, P., Beutler, L. E., & Crago, M. (1989). Differences between more and less effective psychotherapists: A study of select therapist variables. *Journal of Consulting and Clinical Psychology, 57*, 76–80.

Lambert, M. J., Christensen, E. R., & DeJulio, S. S. (Eds.). (1983). *The assessment of psychotherapy outcome.* New York: John Wlley & Sons.

Lambert, M. J., & Ogles, B. M. (1988). Treatment manuals: Problems and promise. *Journal of Integrative and Eclectic Psychotherapy, 7*, 187–204.

Landman, J. T., & Dawes, R. M. (1982). Psychotherapy outcome: Smith and Glass' conclusions stand up under scrutiny. *American Psychologist, 37*, 504–516.

Longo, D. J., Clum, G. A., & Yeager, N. J. (1988). Psychosocial treatment of recurrent genital herpes. *Journal of Consulting and Clinical Psychology, 56*, 61–66.

Luborsky, L., & DeRubeis, R. J. (1984). The use of psychotherapy treatment manuals: A small revolution in psychotherapy research style. *Clinical Psychology Review, 4*, 5–14.

Luborsky, L., Singer, B., & Luborsky, L. (1975). Comparative studies of psychotherapies: Is it true that "everyone has won and all must have prizes"? *Archives of General Psychiatry, 32*, 995–1008.

Nezu, A. M., & Perri, M. G. (1989). Social problem-solving therapy for unipolar depression: An initial dismantling investigation. *Journal of Consulting and Clinical Psychology, 57*, 408–413.

Nicholson, R. A., & Berman, J. S. (1983). Is follow-up necessary in evaluating psychotherapy? *Psychological Bulletin, 93*, 555–565.

Parloff, M. B. (1984). Psychotherapy research and its incredible credibility crisis. *Clinical Psychology Review, 4*, 95–109.

Patterson, V., Levene, H., & Breger, L. (1977). A one-year follow-up of two forms of brief psychotherapy. *American Journal of Psychotherapy, 31*, 76–82.

Paul, G. L. (1966). *Insight versus desensitization in psychotherapy: An experiment in anxiety reduction*. Stanford, CA: Stanford University Press.

Paul, G. L. (1967). Outcome research in psychotherapy. *Journal of Consulting Psychology, 31*, 109–118.

Perri, M. G., Nezu, A. M., Patti, E. T., & McCann, K. L. (1989). Effect of length of treatment on weight loss. *Journal of Consulting and Clinical Psychology, 57*, 450–452.

Quay, H. C. (1977). The three faces of evaluation: What can be expected to work. *Criminal Justice and Behavior, 4*, 341–354.

Rachman, S. J., & Wilson, G. T. (1980). *The effects of psychological therapy* (2nd ed.). Elmsford, NY: Pergamon Press.

Roback, H. B. (1971). The comparative influence of insight and non-insight psychotherapies on therapeutic outcome: A review of experimental literature. *Psychotherapy: Theory, Research and Practice, 8*, 23–25.

Rossi, J. S. (1990). Statistical power of psychological research: What have we gained in 20 years? *Journal of Consulting and Clinical Psychology, 58*, 646–656.

Rounsaville, B. J., Chevron, E. S., Prusoff, B. A., Elkin, I., Imber, S., Sotsky, S., & Watkins, J. (1986). The relation between specific and general dimensions of the psychotherapy process in Interpersonal Psychotherapy of depression. *Journal of Consulting and Clinical Psychology, 55*, 379–384.

Sechrest, L., West, S. G., Phillips, M. A., Redner, R., & Yeaton, W. (1979). Some neglected problems in evaluation research: Strength and integrity of treatments. In L. Sechrest, S. G. West, M. A. Phillips, R. Redner, & W. Yeaton (Eds.), *Evaluation studies: Review annual* (Vol. 4, pp. 15–35). Beverly Hills, CA: Sage Publications.

Sechrest, L., White, S. O., & Brown, E. D. (Eds.). (1979). *The rehabilitation of criminal offenders: Problems and prospects*. Washington, DC: National Academy of Sciences.

Sedlmeier, P., & Gigerenzer, G. (1989). Do studies of statistical power have an effect on the power of studies. *Psychological Bulletin, 105*, 309–316.

Shapiro, D. A., & Shapiro, D. (1982). Meta-analysis of comparative therapy outcome research: A replication and refinement. *Psychological Bulletin, 92*, 581–604.

Silberschatz, G., Fretter, P. B., & Curtis, J. T. (1986). How do interpretations influence the process of psychotherapy? *Journal of Consulting and Clinical Psychology, 54*, 646–652.

Sloane, R. B., Staples, F. R., Cristol, A. H., Yorkston, N. J., & Whipple, K. (1975). *Psychotherapy versus behavior therapy*. Cambridge, MA: Harvard University Press.

Smith, M. L., & Glass, G. V. (1977). Meta-analysis of psychotherapy outcome studies. *American Psychologist, 32*, 752–760.

Smith, M. L., Glass, G. V., & Miller. T. I. (1980). *The benefits of psychotherapy*. Baltimore, MD: Johns Hopkins University Press.

Stiles, W. B., Shapiro, D. A., & Elliott, R. (1986). Are all psychotherapies equivalent? *American Psychologist, 41*, 165–180.

Stiles, W. B., Shapiro, D.A., & Firth-Cozens, J. A. (1988). Verbal response-mode use in contrasting psychotherapies: A within-subjects comparison. *Journal of Consulting and Clinical Psychology, 56*, 727–733.

Strupp, H. H., & Hadley, S. W. (1977). A tripartite model of mental health and therapeutic outcomes. *American Psychologist, 32*, 187–196.

Szapocznik, J., Rio, A., Murray, E., Cohen, R., Scopetta, M., Rivas-Vazquez, A., Hervis, O., Posada, V., & Kurtines, W. (1989). Structural family versus psychodynamic child therapy for problematic Hispanic boys. *Journal of Consulting and Clinical Psychology, 57*, 571–578.

VandenBos, G. (1986). Special Issue: Psychotherapy research. *Americal Psychologist, 41* (February, Whole No. 2).

Webster-Stratton, C., Hollinsworth, T., & Kolpacoff, M. (1989). The long-term effectiveness and clinical significance of three cost-effective training programs for families with conduct-problem children. *Journal of Consulting and Clinical Psychology, 57*, 550–553.

Willis, R. M., Faitler, S. L., & Snyder, D. K. (1987). Distinctiveness of behavioral versus insight-oriented marital therapy: An empirical analysis. *Journal of Consulting and Clinical Psychology, 55*, 685–690.

Wiseman, H., & Rice, L. N. (1989). Sequential analyses of therapist-client interaction during change events: A task-focused approach. *Journal of Consulting and Clinical Psychology, 57*, 281–286.

Wortman, P. M. (1983). Meta-analysis: A validity perspective. *Annual Review of Psychology, 34*, 223–260.

Wright, D. M., Moelis, I., & Pollack, L. J. (1976). The outcome of individual child psychotherapy: Increments at follow-up. *Journal of Child Psychology and Psychiatry, 17*, 275–285.

Yeaton, W. H., & Sechrest, L. (1981). Critical dimensions in the choice and maintenance of successful treatments: Strength, integrity, and effectiveness. *Journal of Consulting and Clinical Psychology, 49*, 156–167.

CHAPTER 18

STATISTICAL ISSUES IN CLINICAL RESEARCH

Bruce E. Wampold
Richard D. Freund

To a large extent, statistical methods are the basic tools of the clinical psychology researcher. Ordinarily, research in this area involves measuring various characteristics of units (typically, but not limited to, clients and therapists) and analyzing the resulting data by means of one or more statistical methods. If the research is well designed, the results will have important, although often indirect, implications for clinical psychology and specifically for the treatment of clients. However, if the research is flawed, at best the results will be uninformative and at worst they will be misleading.

Ideally, the design of a research project and the statistical analysis work together harmoniously to answer the research questions posed. In many respects, design and analysis are inextricably entwined. For example, decisions about the number of subjects needed for a design hinge on the degree of statistical power desired. Used properly and imaginatively, statistics can reveal beautiful patterns in the data that inform us about psychological processes that otherwise would be camouflaged from our view. Nevertheless, there is much more to research than statistical analysis; indeed, statistical concerns compose one of four areas necessary for the validity of research studies

(viz., statistical conclusion validity, internal validity, construct validity, and external validity; Cook & Campbell, 1979).

Although statistical theory is well developed, the applications of statistics to applied areas such as clinical psychology raise a number of issues. Failure to attend to statistical issues will attenuate the importance of the research. The purpose of this chapter is to discuss issues that appear frequently in clinical psychology research.

STATISTICAL POWER

Technically, the power of a statistical test is the probability of rejecting the null hypothesis when in fact the null hypothesis is false. In other words, power is the ability of the statistical test to detect an effect should it be present. Suppose, for example, that Treatment A truly is superior to Treatment B. If the statistical power of a test related to the relative efficacy of the two treatments is .80, then there is an 80% chance that the test will be statistically significant. That is, if the study were replicated many times, 80% of those studies will lead to the conclusion that Treatment A is superior to Treatment B. Of course, it

313

is desirable to conduct statistical tests with sufficient power. Before discussing sufficiency of power, several questions about the nature of power need to be discussed.

The first question is: What factors affect the power of a statistical test? For a given statistical test, power is dependent on the size of the effect to be detected, the sample size, the significance level (typically .05 or .01), and directionality of the test (i.e., one- or two-tailed test). Once each of these aspects (viz., effect size, sample size, significance level, and directionality) are stipulated, power can be calculated, although the process for doing so is mathematically complex. Fortunately, tables have been prepared so that power can be determined relatively easily. Cohen (1988) compiled tables for the commonly used statistical tests (including many varieties of the analysis of variance [ANOVA], correlation, and regression) and provided extensive instructions and many examples.

A second question is: How is effect size stipulated? Of all the components involved with power, effect size is the most troublesome. Typically, the null hypothesis stipulates an effect size of zero; when the null hypothesis is not true, there is a nonzero effect size. The degree to which Treatment A is superior to Treatment B is an effect size. Keep in mind that the effect size refers to the true, or population, state of affairs. In the two treatment example, the population effect size typically is measured in standard deviation units; that is, the effect size is given by $(\mu_A - \mu_B)/\sigma$, where μ_A refers to the population mean level of functioning under Treatment A, μ_B refers to the population mean level of functioning under Treatment B, and σ is the standard deviation of both populations (under the assumption of homogeneity of variance). Effect size is directly related to the difference between means and inversely related to the variability of the scores (i.e., the less the variability of the scores in the population, the larger the effect).

To calculate power (or alternatively sample size), as mentioned earlier, the size of the population effect must be stipulated. Of course, if the population effect size for a given problem were known, there would be no reason to conduct the study. In practice, the expected effect can be stipulated by examining prior research in the area or related areas, by conducting pilot studies, by determining the size of effect that is meaningful (e.g., clinically significant), or by using Cohen's (1988) taxonomy of effect size. Cohen classified effect sizes as small, medium, or large; to determine power (or sample size), the researcher stipulates which size effect he or she desires to detect. Although Cohen's taxonomy has been criticized as

being arbitrary (Glass, McGaw, & Smith, 1981), when there is insufficient information to stipulate the effect size in a power analysis, it provides a reasonable procedure.

When a power analysis is used, a third question is raised: How many subjects should be used in a study? A general rule is that there should be sufficient power to detect an effect size of interest to the investigator (Hays, 1988; Wampold & Drew, 1990). Power in the neighborhood of .80 is considered adequate (Cohen, 1988). If too few subjects are used in a study, power will be too low, and true effects that have clinical importance likely will not be discovered; that is, the statistical test probably will not yield significant results. However, in this case it would be incorrect to conclude that there was no effect, because there was insufficient power to detect the effect even if it had existed. On the other hand, the use of large numbers of subjects is problematic. Besides being uneconomical, small effects, which are possibly inconsequential, will have a good chance of being detected by studies with an excessive number of subjects (Hays, 1988; Wampold & Drew, 1990; Wampold, Furlong, & Atkinson, 1983). Nevertheless, if the effect to be detected has unusual clinical importance (e.g., cure for anorexia) and thus there is a high social cost of failure to detect this effect, then one should consider levels of power in excess of conventional levels.

Because the researcher typically wants to determine the sample size needed to obtain a given level of power, Cohen (1988) and Kraemer and Thiemann (1987) presented tables organized around sample size. To use these tables, the desired level of power as well as the effect size, significance level, and directionality of the test are stipulated and the number of subjects needed to obtain the stipulated level of power is found. Kraemer and Thiemann's (1987) instructions for using their tables are simplified by the use of approximations, which is not problematic because the degree of error involved in these approximations is negligible.

Another important means to increase statistical power for a given problem is to use a more powerful statistical test. Under certain conditions, various alternatives to traditionally used statistical tests will yield greater power, thus reducing the number of subjects needed to obtain a given level of power. For example, the analysis of covariance can be used to reduce the error variance under certain conditions where an analysis of variance would routinely be used (Elashoff, 1969; Hays, 1988; Huitema, 1980; Porter & Raudenbush, 1987). It is not uncommon to find that the use of analysis of covariance will require half as many subjects to achieve the same level of power as a traditional analysis of variance (Porter & Raudenbush, 1987). Procedures that tend to increase power are especially useful in clinical psychology where much of the variability of the dependent measures is attributable to sources other than the independent variable, such as nuisance factors and measurement error (Kraemer & Thiemann, 1989; Meehl, 1978). Variables such as age, socioeconomic status, family history, and intelligence are related to many dependent variables in clinical research, and the variance due to these variables can be removed from the dependent variable with the analysis of covariance, yielding more powerful tests of the hypotheses. Other procedures that are applicable to such data include paired *t* tests (Hays, 1988; Wampold & Drew, 1990), randomized block designs (Hays, 1988; Kirk, 1982; Wampold & Drew, 1990), repeated measures designs (Kirk, 1982; Winer, 1971; Kraemer & Thiemann, 1989), and Model II tests in hierarchical regression (Cohen & Cohen, 1983). A particularly promising approach for research in clinical trials is discussed by Kraemer and Thiemann (1989). However attractive these alternatives appear, there is a price to be paid in terms of additional assumptions, decreased power under certain conditions, and increased complexity of the tests. For the most part, however, these alternatives have not been used to their full advantage in clinical psychology research but should be considered by researchers in this area (Porter & Raudenbush, 1987).

ROLE OF ASSUMPTIONS IN STATISTICAL TESTS

The validity of statistical tests relies on various assumptions. For instance, the F statistic in ANOVA has an F distribution only if normality and homogeneity of variance assumptions are satisfied. When there are violations of the assumptions, the true significance levels may be different from those used to make decisions about the hypotheses. For example, $p < .05$ indicates that there are less than 5 chances out of 100 of being incorrect in deciding that there is a nonzero effect. However, if one or more assumptions are violated, the probability of making an incorrect statement may be considerably greater than .05, say .20 (or in certain cases less than .05). Violations of assumptions also may affect the power of the statistical test.

When the probability of making incorrect decisions about hypotheses is relatively unaffected by violations of the assumptions, the statistical test is said to be robust. Clearly, robustness is a desirable property and statisticians have attended extensively to this problem, although there remain differences in opinions with regard to the robustness of commonly used statistical tests. Consider the case of ANOVA. There is conclusive evidence that ANOVA is robust with respect to the normality assumption, especially for moderate to large samples, and with respect to the homogeneity of variance assumption, especially for equal sample sizes (Glass & Hopkins, 1984; Hays, 1988). Nevertheless, there is increasing evidence that ANOVA is not robust to violations of these two assumptions conjointly, especially for various types of distributions (Bradley, 1968, 1977; Wilcox, 1987). Opinions range from those who claim that traditional parametric tests are robust and can be used with impunity with most data collected in the social sciences (e.g., Cohen & Cohen, 1983) to those who claim alternative methods that do not rely on distribution assumptions (e.g., nonparametric tests) should typically be used (e.g., Bradley, 1968; Edgington, 1980b). A compromise position would be that if there are reasons to believe that violations of assumptions are present, precautions should be exercised.

Previous research, the nature of the construct being investigated, the characteristics of the instrument or the procedures of the study, nature of the measurements (e.g., proportions), and examination of the sample data provide clues about violations of assumptions. Some have advocated direct tests of assumptions, but often these tests themselves are not robust or have insufficient power (Keppel, 1982; Winer, 1971). Precautions often involve larger sample sizes, equal sample sizes, transformations of the data, or use of alternative tests (Bradley, 1968; Edgington, 1980b; Winer, 1971). Wilcox (1987) discussed this topic comprehensively in the context of ANOVA.

A problematic but ubiquitous assumption of most statistical tests is independence of observations. If observations are more similar or dissimilar than observations randomly selected from a population, the observations are not independent (Darlington & Carlson, 1987). This is the case for biased samples, for instance. Nonindependence also occurs in another troublesome and often ignored manner. Often, subjects are selected randomly but are affected by similar uncontrolled influences. This occurs when subjects are treated and/or tested collectively; some external influence, such as the sounding of a fire alarm, or some internal influence, such as a disruptive member of a therapy group, would affect all subjects in the collection. Interactions among subjects always create a dependence. The dependence might be minor, as would be the case where the treatment was didactic (e.g., parent education) and the interaction among the subjects minimal. On the other hand, observations of subjects in group therapy are dependent, as most conceptualizations of group therapy focus on the therapeutic nature of group process. Unfortunately, commonly used statistical tests are not robust with regard to the independence of observations assumption.

There are statistical tests that model dependent observations, but these tests are complex, and typically not enough is known about the dependencies to model them adequately. A viable alternative is to treat each collection of subjects as a unit of observation and statistically analyze a single index for each unit. For example, a study of group therapy for depression might involve six groups of five clients who receive cognitively oriented group therapy and six groups of five clients who receive dynamically oriented group therapy. One index for each group (for example, the mean of the six clients on the Beck Depression Inventory) would be analyzed, thus yielding six indexes for the cognitive therapy and six indexes for the dynamic therapy. Although it would appear that the reduction in number of observations using this strategy would attenuate power drastically, such is not the case. Because each group mean is more stable than a single observation (i.e., less variability in the scores), the attenuation of power is often negligible (Darlington & Carlson, 1987). Hopkins (1982) proposed a more comprehensive framework for analyzing dependent measures, where subjects are nested within the collection. This model allows using the collection as the unit of analysis but also is able to answer several other interesting questions.

CLINICAL VERSUS STATISTICAL SIGNIFICANCE

As mentioned previously, a statistically significant result may not be clinically relevant. Until recently, clinical significance was defined qualitatively; for example, as a large change, an improvement in everyday functioning, a change recognizable by peers and significant others, elimination of the presenting problem, and posttreatment functioning that is similar to functional peers (Jacobson, Follette, & Revenstorf, 1984; Kazdin, 1977). Jacobson, Follette, and Revenstorf (1984) attempted to develop statistical procedures to assess clinical significance. They classified a change as clinically significant when "the client moves from the dysfunctional to the functional range during the course of therapy" (p. 340) and proposed

three criteria for making this determination: (a) The level of functioning of the client after treatment is more than two standard deviations (in the direction of functionality) from the mean of the dysfunctional population, (b) the level of functioning of the client after treatment is not more than two standard deviations (in the direction of dysfunctionality) from the mean of the functional population, and (c) the level of functioning of the client after treatment is more likely given the functional distribution than the dysfunctional distribution (i.e., the posttest score would more readily lead to the conclusion that the subject is functional). Accordingly, application of one of the criteria (which should be chosen a priori by the researcher) will determine whether each subject has improved clinically. To determine whether a change is also reliable (i.e., was not due to chance), Jacobson, Follette, & Revenstorf (1984) proposed a reliable change index. Errors in the original reliable change index (Christensen & Mendoza, 1986) have led to some modifications (Jacobson & Revenstorf, 1988).

The criteria of clinical significance and the reliable change index provide methods to assess the clinical efficacy of treatments and can be used in several ways. First, they could be reported in conjunction with statistical significance in the results of treatments studies. This would provide the consumer with information about the clinical importance of the results as well as the statistical significance and would answer the important question often raised by these types of studies: What proportion of the subjects had clinical and reliable improvements? A second way that these indexes can be used is to assess the efficacy of particular treatments across many studies. Jacobson and his colleagues reanalyzed outcome data to examine the efficacy of behavioral marital therapy (Jacobson, Follette, Revenstorf, Baucom, Hahlweg, & Margolin, 1984) and exposure-based interventions for agoraphobia (Jacobson, Wilson, & Tupper, 1988).

Alternatives to the methods proposed by Jacobson and his colleagues involve comparing entire samples (Kendall & Grove, 1988; Kendall & Norton-Ford, 1982; Nietzel & Trull, 1988). These methods yield conclusions about the clinical significance of a particular treatment, whereas Jacobson et al.'s methods yield conclusions about the clinical significance for each subject. Nietzel and Trull (1988), following the lead of Kendall (1984), presented a meta-analytic approach that compares both the treated and the control group means to the mean of a functional group. This approach has been used to study the clinical significance of psychotherapy for unipolar depression (Nietzel, Russell, Hemmings, & Gretter,

1987) and for agoraphobia (Trull, Nietzel, & Main, 1988).

Statistical methods to assess clinical significance are not without their problems. All statistical approaches to this problem involve defining and identifying the functional population and its parameters, a task that has inherent pragmatic and epistemological difficulties (Hollon & Flick, 1988; Jacobson & Revenstorf, 1988; Kendall & Grove, 1988; Nietzel & Trull, 1988; Saunders, Howard, & Newman, 1988; Wampold & Jenson, 1986). Other problems include definition of the dysfunctional population, reliability of measures, criteria for clinical significance, and desire to accept the null hypothesis (viz., the mean of the treated population is equal to the mean of the functional population) rather than the alternative.

CAUSALITY

One frequent classification of research dichotomizes it into experimental and relational types. In the experimental paradigm, the researcher manipulates the independent variable with the goal of ascertaining the effect of the manipulation on the dependent variable. If the manipulation produces a change in the dependent variable, frequently an attribution of causation is made. For instance, if the mean anxiety level for treated individuals is significantly lower than that of untreated individuals and all other factors were comparable across the two samples (i.e., the study was internally valid), then the conclusion that the treatment was responsible for the reduction in anxiety is justified. In the relational paradigm, the researcher seeks to discover the relation between two or more variables of equal status (i.e., there is no independent and dependent variable). These designs are often referred to as correlational designs, and the phrase "correlation does not imply causation" has been used to describe their ability to infer causality. With regard to anxiety, the fact that gender (coded 0 for males and 1 for females) and anxiety are significantly correlated does not imply that gender causes anxiety, but only that they appear to covary.

Although the distinction between experimental and relational designs is relatively clear, there are a number of statistical issues raised by this distinction. The first and foremost point is that it is the nature of the design and not the statistical procedure that distinguishes experimental from relational research (Cohen, 1968). This point can be illustrated in a number of ways. In the aforementioned anxiety treatment study, typically a t test for independent samples would be used to test for equality of the means for the treatment and control groups; however, a test of correlation could be computed by assigning a zero to the control group and a one to the treatment group and computing a Pearson correlation coefficient. The significance level of the correlation coefficient would be identical to the significance level obtained with the t statistic. Similarly, the relation between gender and anxiety could be investigated using a t test to compare the mean anxiety levels of men and women. Regression analysis is often associated with relational designs, but classically regression is used in experimental designs where levels of the independent variable are quantitative (e.g., dosages of drugs) (Cohen & Cohen, 1983; Hays, 1988; Wampold & Drew, 1990). Cohen and Cohen (1983) popularized regression analysis for relational designs. Discussions about the relative merits of ANOVA and regression are superfluous because they are mathematically equivalent (Hays, 1988; Wampold & Drew, 1990). The statistical software package SAS has a procedure called GLM in which the user does not specify whether a regression or ANOVA is to be conducted.

Although attributions of causality are often restricted to experimental designs, this view is arguable (Cook & Campbell, 1979; Einhorn & Hograth, 1986). A conservative view states that causation is demonstrated only by the manipulation of the independent variable and observing concomitant changes in the dependent variable (and controlling for alternative explanations of those changes). One model of causality in this vein states that a variable that is not amenable to manipulation cannot be said to be a possible causal factor (Holland, 1986). For example, gender, which cannot be experimentally manipulated, could not be a causal factor of any other variable. Smoking, which could conceivably be manipulated, could be a causal factor. However, because smoking cannot be experimentally manipulated in humans for ethical reasons, experimental designs involving this variable are precluded.

A more liberal view of causality is that it can be plausibly established by nonexperimental designs under the proper circumstances. Criteria for causality vary; however, many scientists and philosophers would be willing to make an attribution of causation when concomitant change (e.g., correlation) exists provided the purported cause precedes the effect in time, there is a scientific explanation for the causal relationship, and other alternative explanations can be ruled out (Cook & Campbell, 1979). Most scientists are now willing to state that smoking is a causal factor of health in humans, even without experimental manipulation of the independent variable (Cook, 1980).

Statistical methods that are designed to establish causality in the context of relations between variables are becoming increasingly popular in the social sciences (Joreskog & Sorbom, 1988; Pedhazur, 1982). For example, path analysis and covariance structure analysis can be used to support causal inferences and have been used extensively to test theoretical models. Patterson (1986) relied heavily on these sophisticated and complex methods to test various models of antisocial behavior. It should be recognized that the logic behind these complex statistical methods for establishing causality is vastly different from that of experimental designs where the independent variable is manipulated, and the veridicality of these methods is not universally accepted (e.g., Cliff, 1983; Haertel & Thoresen, 1987; Pedhazur, 1982).

STATISTICAL ANALYSIS OF SINGLE-CASE DESIGNS

One of the major research designs in clinical psychology is the single-case experimental design (Barlow & Hersen, 1984). These designs are used to establish the functional relationship between various conditions and behavior in a single or a few individuals. The use of these designs avoids many problems inherent in group designs, including withholding treatment from subjects, the averaging of results across subjects in each condition, the necessity of a large number of subjects, and the obfuscation of idiosyncratic response patterns (Barlow & Hersen, 1984; Sidman, 1960). These designs have played an important role in psychology; for example, Skinner's (e.g., 1953) investigations of reinforcement schedules relied primarily on single-case designs. In clinical psychology, the research in applied behavior analysis and behavior modification predominantly has relied on single-case designs. The use of statistical methods to analyze the data generated by single-case experimental designs is controversial. Typically, for these types of designs, statistical analysis is eschewed in favor of plotting the raw data and making inferences from the graphed data, a process often referred to as visual analysis. According to many single-case methodologists and behavior analysts, visual analysis is the preferred method of analysis because it does not rely on summarizations and reductions of the data (such as means and test statistics), allows the consumer of the research to make his or her own inference from the data, and is designed to detect large and important effects and ignore small effects that might be detected by statistical analyses (Barlow & Hersen, 1984; Sidman, 1960). Nevertheless, a strong case for the use of statistical analyses in single-case designs can and has

been made. Because visual analysis is an imprecise and idiosyncratic process, visual analysis may be unreliable and systematically biased; indeed a number of studies have shown that this is so (DeProspero & Cohen, 1979; Furlong & Wampold, 1982; Jones, Weinrott, & Vaught, 1978; Knapp, 1983; Wampold & Furlong, 1981a). On the other hand, statistical tests, which rely on an explicit algorithm, produce the same inference each time they are applied to a given set of data. Furthermore, the statistical tests available for single-case designs are flexible enough to detect the myriad effects that can be displayed in graphed data. Finally, many small effects that may be detected by statistical analyses but not by visual inspection have theoretical if not clinical importance (Gottman & Glass, 1978). A discussion of statistical procedures proposed for single-case studies follows; however, it should be noted that statistical tests are infrequently used to analyze data derived from single-case research.

A variety of statistical tests have been proposed for single-case designs (see Kazdin, 1984, for an overview of available tests). The first tests proposed were traditional t and F tests in which it was suggested that phases were analogous to conditions (Gentile, Roden, & Klein, 1972). These tests were criticized because they assume independent observations, and it was thought that behavioral data is characterized by serial dependence (Hartmann, 1974; Toothaker, Banz, Camp, & Davis, 1983). Time series analysis, a statistical procedure that accounts for serial dependence, was touted as a viable alternative for single-case designs (Glass, Willson, & Gottman, 1974; Hartmann et al. 1980; Jones, Vaught, & Weinrott, 1977). Several recent developments have complicated the evaluation of the appropriateness of these two competing statistical paradigms: traditional t and F tests, which have dubious validity in the presence of serial dependence, and time-series analysis, which models the serial dependence. Time-series analysis has not been used frequently in the single-case domain because it is a complex procedure to use and to understand and because the requirements of the procedure were thought to be too stringent for single-case data typically collected (e.g., large number of data points in each phase; Glass, Willson, & Gottman, 1974). However, recent investigations suggest that time-series analysis is far less demanding to the researcher than was previously believed, although this issue remains controversial (Gottman, 1981; Sharpley & Alavosius, 1988; Velicer & McDonald, 1984). On the other hand, Huitema (1985, 1986, 1988) claimed that serial dependence in behavioral data is a myth. In a comprehensive analysis of behavioral data, he found that behavioral data are not characterized by serial dependence; although data from some studies may exhibit serial dependence (i.e., in that particular sample), on the whole (i.e., in the population) it does not appear to exist. If such is the case, then traditional tests that depend on independence of observations, such as t and F tests, could be appropriately used. Although having consequential implications for our understanding of behavior (Baer, 1988), Huitema's findings have been challenged on a number of statistical grounds (Busk & Marascuilo, 1988; Sharpley & Alavosius, 1988; Suen, 1987; Suen & Ary, 1987).

A set of procedures that avoid the serial dependence problem and are generally adaptive to single-case designs are randomization tests (Edgington, 1980a, 1980b, 1980c, 1982, 1987; Levin, Marascuilo, & Hubert, 1978; Revusky, 1976; Wampold & Furlong, 1981b; Wampold & Worsham, 1986). Randomization tests involve randomizing some aspect of the single-case design (e.g., the point at which the intervention is introduced) and comparing a statistic that is sensitive to the expected effect for the obtained data to the same statistic computed for all other possible combinations of the obtained data. If the obtained statistic demonstrates that the expected effect occurred to a greater extent in the obtained data vis-à-vis all other combinations, the conclusion is drawn that the experimental manipulation had the expected effect. However, the requirement of randomization decreases the researcher's freedom to introduce interventions at the most opportune time—one of the stated advantages of single-case designs (Kazdin, 1980a).

Graphical aids to visual inference that have statistical bases, such the split middle technique (White, 1974), and other related statistical tests, such as the binomial test (Kazdin, 1984; White, 1974) have been proposed. Although such procedures have some utility in applied settings (e.g., Shinn, Good & Stein, 1989), the validity of these methods has been challenged (Crosbie, 1987; Good & Shinn, 1990).

VARIETY OF METHODS

Several surveys of journal articles in psychology have found that the most frequently used statistical procedure is ANOVA (Edgington, 1974; Wampold, 1986). Reliance on one procedure is unnecessarily restricting, and the clinical researcher should be acquainted with a variety of methods so that when a research question suggests a particular procedure, it will be used (Wampold, 1987). In this section, a number of procedures will be discussed briefly.

Multiple regression is a method of studying the separate and collective contributions of one or more predictor variables to the variation of a single quantitative criterion variable. The predictor variables can be quantitative or qualitative, can be experimentally manipulated or represent attributes (i.e., status), and can be considered additively or interactively. Variations of multiple regression can accommodate unequal sample sizes, analyses of covariance, and repeated measures, among others. Although, as mentioned previously, multiple regression and ANOVA are mathematically equivalent, multiple regression provides a comprehensive and fairly easy framework to analyze data from a number of experimental and nonexperimental designs. For example, groups with unequal sample sizes present difficulties in the ANOVA context (especially for factorial designs) but are easily managed with a multiple regression approach (Cohen & Cohen, 1983). Many good references on this topic are available (Cohen, 1968; Cohen & Cohen, 1983; Kleinbaum, Kupper, & Muller, 1988; Pedhazur, 1982; Wampold & Freund, 1987).

One of the central tasks of clinicians historically has been to classify clients into diagnostic categories; a statistical procedure that is particularly suitable for this task is discriminant analysis. Discriminant analysis is similar to multiple regression with the exception that the criterion variable in a discrimant analysis is categorical. Rather than accounting for a percentage of the variance in the criterion variable, discriminant analysis involves classification of the cases into categories of the criterion variable. Discriminant analysis provides the percentage of cases correctly classified based on the optimal combination of the predictor variables, as well as discriminant functions, which reflect the relative importance for classification of the predictor variables. Discriminant analysis is a flexible strategy that can be used to understand differences between or among groups, to identify variables that best differentiate groups, to describe the dimensionality of group differences, to test theories involving taxonomies, and as a follow-up test for the multivariate ANOVA. Hare (1985) used discriminant analysis (along with other methods) to compare the efficacy of several clinical-behavioral and self-report measures to assess psychopathology. Most texts on multivariate methods contain discussions of discriminant analysis; more introductory discussions are available, however (e.g., Betz, 1987; Hair, Anderson, Tatham, & Grablowsky, 1984).

Frequently, it is recommended that multiple measures of responding be obtained in clinical studies (Barlow, Hayes, & Nelson, 1984; Kazdin, 1980b); accordingly treatment studies, as well as most other clinical studies, typically contain more than one dependent variable. For group designs that contain multiple dependent measures, multivariate ANOVA is most appropriate. Multivariate ANOVA is an extension of the ANOVA to those instances when there are two or more dependent variables. Multivariate ANOVA is preferable to multiple univariate ANOVAs (one for each dependent variable) because the multivariate procedure holds the rate of making false decisions about the null hypothesis to levels set by the researcher (e.g., .05 or .01) whereas multiple univariate tests allow this rate to escalate dramatically (Haase & Ellis, 1987). Furthermore, multivariate procedures allow examination of the dimensionality of the dependent variables (Bray & Maxwell, 1982).

Often, the clinical researcher is faced with many observed variables and is curious about the psychological constructs that may underlie this set of observed variables. Factor analysis is a procedure that reduces a set of interrelated observed variables to a smaller set of latent (unobserved) factors, which parsimoniously reflect the underlying structure of the observed variables. Suppose that a set of 10 variables can be reduced to three factors via a factor analysis. It is more parsimonious to refer to the three factors than 10 observed variables; more importantly, the three factors likely reflect psychological constructs to a greater extent than any of the 10 observed variables. The observed variables that contribute to (or technically "load on") each of the factors measure the same construct; taken together, these variables reflect the construct better than any single observed variable. Used in this way, factor analysis is often used to identify the constructs measured by an instrument or instruments (i.e., establish the construct validity) and to explore the nature of psychological constructs, such as intelligence. For example, Beck, Epstein, Brown, and Steer (1988) factor analyzed the Beck Anxiety Inventory to establish that the scale measured two constructs (somatic symptoms and subjective anxiety) and to establish that these constructs were different from depression. Gorsuch (1984) presented a thorough discussion of factor analysis; discussions of applications of factor analysis are found elsewhere (e.g., Comrey, 1988; Tinsley & Tinsley, 1987).

Recently, methods have been developed that combine factor analyses and regression analyses. These methods, which have been labeled as structural equation modeling, LISREL, or covariance structure analysis, test the interrelationships between latent variables. Essentially, these methods allow the researcher to perform a regression analysis on the factors obtained from a factor analysis. Typically, a model is proposed that posits the relation between or among constructs (i.e., the latent variables) and posits how the latent variables are measured (i.e., which observed variables in concert form the latent variable). The adequacy of this model is statistically tested; if the test is significant, the model is rejected in that it is not shown to be congruent to the data. Rejection can occur because the measurement component was inadequate (the observed variables did not adequately reflect the constructs) or because the structural component was inadequate (the posited relations among the constructs were not verified). When a model is not rejected, the fit of the model to the sample data is reasonably good; however, other models may fit the data as well as or better than the one proposed. Structural equation modeling can be used to test two competing models (see Kerlinger, 1980, for a good example). One of the disadvantages of structural equation modeling is the complexity of the method. Introductory discussions of this topic are available (Fassinger, 1987; James, Mulaik, & Brett, 1982; Joreskog & Sorbom, 1988; Long, 1983). Patterson (1986) used structural equation modeling to show how discipline and child coercion lead to antisocial behavior. In his model of antisocial behavior, each construct was measured with multiple observed variables; for example, antisocial behavior was based on parent reports, telephone interviews, teacher questionnaires, and peer nominations.

Frequently, the variables in clinical research are categorical. In such cases, the researcher is interested in frequency counts of various categories. Research involving diagnostic categories, attributes such as gender or ethnicity, and discrete treatment groups (and control groups) involve categorical variables. A common practice is to study categorial variables two at a time by forming the two-way contingency table and performing a chi-square test of association. Loglinear analysis is a methodology developed to investigate the multivariate relations between many categorical variables in a unified way. These methods can be used with several independent and dependent variables, to test hypotheses or build models, and to investigate main effects and interactions. Because categorical variables are ubiquitous in clinical research and because it is questionable whether traditional statistical tests should be used with data that are not measured on an interval scale (e.g., Townsend & Ashby, 1984), loglinear analysis is a propitious alternative. Tracey et al. (1984) used loglinear methods to explore the relationship of student characteristics and university counseling center descriptions to help seeking attitudes and behaviors. There are a number of helpful introductions to this topic (Agresti, 1984; Aldrich & Nelson, 1986; Fienberg, 1980; Knoke & Burke, 1980; Marascuilo & Busk, 1987).

There are a variety of other methods that, although not commonly used or discussed in introductory texts, could be instrumental in clinical psychology research. Cluster analysis refers to techniques for forming homogeneous groups of either subjects or variables (Aldenderfer & Blashfield, 1984; Blashfield, 1980; Borgen & Barnett, 1987). When applied to variables, clusters of homogeneous variables are formed; as such this procedure produces an alternative solution to factor analysis because the variables that load on a particular factor are also homogeneous (note, however, that there are some important differences—see Tinsley & Tinsley, 1987). Application of cluster analysis to subjects yields homogeneous clusters of subjects. This is a potentially useful application for clinical psychology research because the notion of diagnostic groups is based on the homogeneity of subjects within groups. For example, Turk and Rudy (1988) applied cluster analysis to the scores of chronic pain patients on the West Haven-Yale Multidimensional Pain Inventory and established three subgroups of patients—dysfunctional, interpersonally distressed, and minimizers and adaptive copers.

Clinicians often are interested in the manner in which people construe the world (i.e., the structure of their internal frames of reference). Multidimensional scaling is a technique to represent spatially the dimensions underlying a set of related stimuli, where the stimuli have some psychological relevance (Davison, 1983; Fitzgerald & Hubert, 1987; Kruskal & Wish, 1978; Schiffman, Reynolds, & Young, 1981). The relations between the stimuli are expressed as similarities (or dissimilarities) and may be correlations, similarity judgments, indexes of stimulus confusion, co-occurrences of sorted stimuli, and so on. Horowitz (1979) used multidimensional scaling to examine the structure of interpersonal problems and found three dimensions that underlaid these problems—psychological involvement, nature of the involvement (hostile vs. friendly), and interpersonal influence. When combined with cluster analysis, Horowitz produced five themes in interpersonal problems—intimacy, aggression, compliance, independence, and sociability.

Because behavior typically occurs in a social context, there has been increased reliance on techniques designed to understand social interactions. These methods, which have become known as sequential analyses, are used to study the probabalistic nature of the sequence of behaviors produced in a social interchange (Allison & Liker, 1982; Bakeman & Gottman, 1986; Russell & Trull, 1986; Sackett, 1979; Wampold, 1984; Wampold & Margolin, 1982). Essentially, the sequence of behaviors produced by interacting members of a system are observed, recorded, and analyzed to ascertain the dependence among the behaviors. In its simplest form, sequential analysis can determine whether the emission of a behavior by one member of the system increases (or decreases) the probability that a behavior will be emitted by another member of the system. Variations of sequential analysis are designed to investigate constructs such as reciprocity and dominance. Sequential analysis is applicable to a wide range of clinical areas including psychotherapy, marital interactions, supervisory relations, and mother and child interactions. For example, Margolin and Wampold (1981) found that distressed and nondistressed marital partners did not differ in their rate of negative responses in an interaction but found that distressed couples tended to reciprocate negative behaviors to a greater degree than did nondistressed couples.

ALTERNATIVE PARADIGMS

The traditional statistical strategy in psychology is to hypothesize a null effect and an alternative, set the rate at which one is willing to reject the null hypothesis when it is true (alpha level), collect evidence about the statistical hypotheses (typically derived from a sample), and make a decision whether to reject the null hypothesis based on the evidence at the given level of alpha. From a scientific standpoint, testing of statistical hypotheses should have implications for the theoretical understanding of psychology. However, this hypothesis testing strategy has been severely criticized, most notably by Meehl (1978), who stated that "the almost universal reliance on merely refuting the null hypothesis as the standard method for corroborating substantive theories is a terrible mistake, is basically unsound, poor scientific strategy, and one of the worst things that ever happened in the history of psychology" (p. 817). To illustrate the problem, consider the etiology of aggressive behavior in children. Possible factors include heredity, parental child-rearing styles, cultural and sociological influences, physiology, and environmental contingencies, among others. Each of these factors likely has some relation to aggressive behavior, and thus the null hypothesis that states that there is no (i.e., zero) relation between each factor and aggressive behavior is false. With sufficiently powerful statistical tests all null hypotheses will be rejected, leading to corroboration of all theories of aggressive behavior that are based on nonzero relations between the factor and aggression.

Essentially, the problem is this: In psychology, because of the complex interrelationships among constructs, it is unreasonable to believe that there will be literally no relation between variables or that populations (such as treated and untreated populations) will have literally the same means. Thus, the null hypothesis is always false, and given sufficiently powerful tests, the null hypothesis will always be rejected, leading to corroboration of many competing theories. That is to say, larger sample sizes and more reliable and valid measurements will lead to the proliferation of theoretical positions, just the opposite of what should take place (i.e., as measurements are improved, theories should be winnowed; Serlin & Lapsley, 1985). The issue here is similar to that of clinical significance: A small (nonzero) but unimportant effect, under the proper circumstances, will lead to rejection of the null hypothesis. In one sense, nonsignificant findings are the most informative because they suggest that there is no effect, thus disconfirming a theoretical position. However, nonsignificant effects can be due to a number of factors other than a true zero effect, such as low power, poor measurements, poor method, and poor design.

Various alternatives to the traditional hypothesis testing strategy have been proposed. At the most basic level, it has been suggested that confidence intervals and effect sizes be reported along with decisions to reject the null hypothesis thus providing additional information to the conclusion that there is a nonzero effect. However, standards by which to make decisions about these additional indexes do not exist and, in addition, there are problems with sample estimates of population effect sizes (Mitchell & Hartmann, 1981; Murray & Dosser, 1987; O'Grady, 1982).

Another alternative to the traditional hypothesis testing strategy is the Bayesian paradigm (Winkler, 1972). Performing a test of a statistical hypothesis based on a single sample ignores previous knowledge about the relation among variables. A Bayesian analysis provides a statistical method that takes into account prior knowledge and readjusts the prior knowledge on the basis of the new evidence. In this way, knowledge accumulates, and estimates of population values are adjusted as opposed to the historically blind approach of traditional hypothesis testing. Bayesian analysis is particularly well suited to the study of decision making and thus has applications to many areas of clinical psychology, such as diagnosis (see von Winterfeldt & Edwards, 1986, chapter 12).

Serlin (1987; Serlin & Lapsley, 1985) proposed the "good-enough principle" to test hypotheses. According to this principle, the researcher stipulates the magnitude of an effect that is good enough; the null hypothesis is that the population effect is greater than the stipulated effect. Thus, rejection of the null hypothesis leads to disconfirmation of the theory, a process that more closely follows the scientific tradition than does traditional statistical testing (Popper, 1968; Serlin & Lapsley, 1985).

Consideration of alternative paradigms bolsters the contention that statistical tests of null hypotheses are insufficient in most instances and issues such as power, effect size, clinical significance, and causality must be considered as well. Reliance solely on statistical tests can be misleading, and researchers are urged, whether alternative paradigms are used or not, to examine other aspects of their data.

SUMMARY

Phenomena of interest to clinical psychologists are complex. Although occasionally there are simple answers to complex questions, increasingly the clinical psychology researcher must rely on sophisticated tools. Fortunately, various statistical methods have been developed that can be used to explore the nature of psychological processes. As well, access to these methods has been facilitated by computer applications; sophisticated software packages are now available for personal computers. Nevertheless, recent developments have introduced increased complexity, and the potential for the misapplications of methods is troublesome. Although advice from experts is needed when a researcher's statistical footing is not firm, it is clear that researchers need adequate training to make appropriate decisions about their research.

From this chapter it should be abundantly clear that statistics involves more than the analysis of data. Many statistical decisions impinge on the design of the study. The most profound decision (and probably the one to which the least attention is given) is the choice of statistical paradigms. From there, decisions about statistical procedures, power and sample size, possible violations of assumptions, and clinical significance need to be considered during the design of the study and prior to the collection of the data. If all goes well, the resulting data analysis will move the field of clinical psychology forward.

REFERENCES

Agresti, A. (1984). *Analysis of ordinal categorical data.* New York: John Wiley & Sons.

Aldenderfer, M. S., & Blashfield, R. K. (1984). *Cluster analysis.* Beverly Hills, CA: Sage Publications.

Aldrich, J. H., & Nelson, F. D. (1986). Logit and probit

models for multivariate analysis with qualitative dependent variables. In W. D. Berry & M. S. Lewis-Beck (Eds.), *New tools for social scientists: Advances and applications in research methods* (pp. 115–155). Beverly Hills, CA: Sage Publications.

Allison, P. D., & Liker, J. K. (1982). Analyzing sequential categorical data on dyadic interaction: Comment on Gottman. *Psychological Bulletin, 91,* 393–403.

Baer, D. M. (1988). An autocorrelated commentary on the need for a different debate. *Behavioral Assessment, 10,* 295–297.

Bakeman, R., & Gottman, J. M. (1986). *Observing interaction: An introduction to sequential analysis.* New York: Cambridge University Press.

Barlow, D. H., Hayes, S. C., & Nelson, R. O. (1984). *The scientist practitioner: Research and accountability in clinical and educational settings.* Elmsford, NY: Pergamon Press.

Barlow, D. H., & Hersen, M. (1984). *Single case experimental designs: Strategies for studying behavior change* (2nd ed.). Elmsford, NY: Pergamon Press.

Beck, A. T., Epstein, N., Brown, G., & Steer, R. A. (1988). An inventory for measuring clinical anxiety: Psychometric properties. *Journal of Consulting and Clinical Psychology, 56,* 893–897.

Betz, N. E. (1987). Use of discriminant analysis in counseling psychology research. *Journal of Counseling Psychology, 34,* 393–403.

Blashfield, R. K. (1980). Propositions regarding the use of cluster analysis in clinical research. *Journal of Consulting and Clinical Psychology, 48,* 456–459.

Borgen, F. H., & Barnett, D. C. (1987). Applying cluster analysis in counseling psychology research. *Journal of Counseling Psychology, 34,* 456–468.

Bradley, J. V. (1968). *Distribution-free statistical tests.* Englewood Cliffs, NJ: Prentice-Hall.

Bradley, J. V. (1977). A common situation conducive to bizarre distribution shapes. *The American Statistician, 31,* 147–150.

Bray, J. H., & Maxwell, S. E. (1982). Analyzing and interpreting significant MANOVAS. *Review of Educational Research, 52,* 340–367.

Busk, P. L., & Marascuilo, L. A. (1988). Autocorrelation in single-subject research: A counterargument to the myth of no autocorrelation. *Behavioral Assessment, 10,* 229–242.

Christensen, L., & Mendoza, J. L. (1986). A method of assessing change in a single subject: An alteration of the RC index. *Behavior Therapy, 17,* 305–308.

Cliff, N. (1983). Some cautions concerning the application of causal modeling methods. *Multivariate Behavioral Research, 18,* 115–126.

Cohen, J. (1968). Multiple regression as a general data-analytic strategy. *Psychological Bulletin, 70,* 426–443.

Cohen, J. (1988). *Statistical power analysis for the behavioral sciences* (2nd ed). Hillsdale, NJ: Lawrence Erlbaum Associates.

Cohen, J., & Cohen, P. (1983). *Applied multiple regression/correlation analysis for the behavioral sciences* (2nd ed.). Hillsdale, NJ: Lawrence Erlbaum Associates.

Comrey, A. L. (1988). Factor-analytic methods of scale development in personality and clinical psychology. *Journal of Consulting and Clinical Psychology, 56,* 754–761.

Cook, R. D. (1980). Smoking and lung cancer. In S. Fienberg & D. Hinkley (Eds.), *R. A. Fisher: An appreciation* (pp. 182–191). New York: Springer-Verlag.

Cook, T. D., & Campbell, D. T. (1979). *Quasi-experimentation: Design & analysis issues for field settings.* Chicago: Rand McNally.

Crosbie, J. (1987). The inability of the binomial test to control Type I error with single-subject data. *Behavioral Assessment, 9,* 141–150.

Darlington, R. B., & Carlson, P. M. (1987). *Behavioral statistics: Logic and methods.* New York: Free Press.

Davison, M. L. (1983). *Multidimensional scaling.* New York: John Wiley & Sons.

DeProspero, A., & Cohen, S. (1979). Inconsistent visual analysis of intrasubject data. *Journal of Applied Behavior Analysis, 12,* 513–519.

Edgington, E. S. (1974). A new tabulation of statistical procedures used in APA journals. *American Psychologist, 29,* 25–26.

Edgington, E. S. (1980a). Random assignment and statistical tests for one-subject experiments. *Behavioral Assessment, 2,* 19–28.

Edgington, E. S. (1980b). *Randomization tests.* New York: Marcel Dekker.

Edgington, E. S. (1980c). Validity of randomization tests for one-subject experiments. *Journal of Educational Statistics, 5,* 235–251.

Edgington, E. S. (1982). Nonparametric tests for single-subject multiple schedule experiments. *Behavioral Assessment, 4,* 83–91.

Edgington, E. S. (1987). Randomized single-subject experiments and statistical tests. *Journal of Counseling Psychology, 34,* 437–442.

Einhorn, H. J., & Hograth, R. M. (1986). Judging probable cause. *Psychological Bulletin, 99,* 3–19.

Elashoff, J. D. (1969). Analysis of covariance: A delicate instrument. *American Educational Research Journal, 6,* 383–401.

Fassinger, R. E. (1987). Use of structural equation modeling in counseling psychology research. *Journal of Counseling Psychology, 34,* 425–436.

Fienberg, S. E. (1980). *The analysis of cross-classified data* (2nd ed.). Cambridge, MA: MIT Press.

Fitzgerald, L. F., & Hubert, L. J. (1987). Multidimensional scaling: Some possibilities for counseling psychology. *Journal of Counseling Psychology, 34,* 469–480.

Furlong, M. J., & Wampold, B. E. (1982). Intervention effects and relative variation as dimensions in experts' use of visual inference. *Journal of Applied Behavior Analysis, 15,* 415–421.

Gentile, J. R., Roden, A. H., & Klein, R. D. (1972). An analysis of variance model for the intrasubject replication design. *Journal of Applied Behavior Analysis, 5,* 193–198.

Glass, G. V., & Hopkins, K. D. (1984). *Statistical methods in education and psychology.* Englewood Cliffs, NJ: Prentice-Hall.

Glass, G. V., McGaw, B., & Smith, M. L. (1981). *Meta-analysis in social research.* Beverly Hills, CA: Sage Publications.

Glass, G. V., Willson, V. L., & Gottman, J. M. (1974). *Design and analysis of time-series experiments.* Boulder: Colorado Associated University Press.

Good, R. H., III, & Shinn, M. R. (1990). Forecasting accuracy of slope estimation for reading curriculum-based measurement: Empirical evidence. *Behavioral Assessment, 12,* 179–193.

Gorsuch, R. L. (1984). *Factor analysis.* Hillsdale, NJ: Lawrence Erlbaum Associates.

Gottman, J. M. (1981). *Time-series analysis.* New York: Cambridge University Press.

Gottman, J. M., & Glass, G. V. (1978). Analysis of interrupted time-series experiments. In T. R. Kratochwill (Ed.), *Single-subject research: Strategies for evaluating change* (pp. 197–237). New York: Academic Press.

Haase, R. F., & Ellis, M. V. (1987). Multivariate analysis of variance. *Journal of Counseling Psychology, 34,* 404–413.

Haertel, E. H., & Thoresen, C. E. (1987). Buyers beware: The deceptively high cost of LISREL. *The Counseling Psychologist, 15,* 316–319.

Hair, J. F., Jr., Anderson, R. E., Tatham, R. L., & Grablowsky, B. J. (1984). *Multivariate data analysis with readings.* New York: Macmillan.

Hare, R. D. (1985). Comparison of procedures for the assessment of psychopathology. *Journal of Consulting and Clinical Psychology, 53,* 7–16.

Hartmann, D. P. (1974). Forcing square pegs into round holes: Some comments on "An analysis-of-variance model for the intrasubject replication design." *Journal of Applied Behavior Analysis, 7,* 635–638.

Hartmann, D. P., Gottman, J. M., Jones, R. R., Gardner, W., Kazdin, A. E., & Vaught, R. S. (1980). Interrupted time-series analysis and its applications to behavioral data. *Journal of Applied Behavior Analysis, 13,* 543–559.

Hays, W. L. (1988). *Statistics* (4th ed.). New York: Holt, Rinehart, and Winston.

Holland, P. W. (1986). Statistics and causal inference. *Journal of the American Statistical Association, 81,* 945–960.

Hollon, S. D., & Flick, S. N. (1988). On the meaning and methods of clinical significance. *Behavioral Assessment, 10,* 197–206.

Hopkins, K. D. (1982). The unit of analysis: Group means versus individual classrooms. *American Educational Research Journal, 19,* 5–18.

Horowitz, L. M. (1979). On the cognitive structure of interpersonal problems treated in psychotherapy. *Journal of Consulting and Clinical Psychology, 47,* 5–15.

Huitema, B. E. (1980). *The analysis of covariance and alternatives.* New York: John Wiley & Sons.

Huitema, B. E. (1985). Autocorrelation in applied behavior analysis: A myth. *Behavioral Assessment, 7,* 107–118.

Huitema, B. E. (1986). Autocorrelation in behavior modification data: Wherefore art thou? In A. Pling & R. W. Fuqua (Eds.), *Research methods in applied behavior analysis: Issues and advances* (pp. 187–208). New York: Plenum Publishing.

Huitema, B. E. (1988). Autocorrelation: 10 years of confusion. *Behavioral Assessment, 10,* 253–294.

Jacobson, N. S., Follette, W. C., & Revenstorf, D. (1984). Psychotherapy outcome research: Methods for reporting variability and evaluating clinical significance. *Behavior Therapy, 17,* 336–352.

Jacobson, N. S., Follette, W. C., Revenstorf, D., Baucom, D. H., Hahlweg, K., & Margolin, G. (1984). Variability in outcome and clinical significance of behavioral marital therapy: A reanalysis of outcome data. *Journal of Consulting and Clinical Psychology, 52,* 497–504.

Jacobson, N. S., & Revenstorf, D. (1988). Statistics for assessing the clinical significance of psychotherapy techniques: Issues, problems, and new developments. *Behavioral Assessment,* 133–145.

Jacobson, N. S., Wilson, L., & Tupper, C. (1988). The clinical significance of treatment gains resulting from exposure based interventions for agoraphobia: A reanalysis of outcome data. *Behavioral Therapy, 19,* 539–554.

James, L. R., Mulaik, S. A., & Brett, J. M. (1982). *Causal analysis: Assumptions, models, and data.* Newbury Park, CA: Sage Publications.

Jones, R. R., Vaught, R. S., & Weinrott, M. R. (1977). Time-series analysis in operant research. *Journal of Applied Behavior Analysis, 10,* 151–167.

Jones, R. R., Weinrott, M. R., & Vaught, R. S. (1978). Effects of serial dependency on the agreement between visual and statistical inference. *Journal of Applied Behavior Analysis, 11,* 277–283.

Joreskog, K. G., & Sorbom, D. (1988). *LISREL VII: A guide to the program and applications.* Chicago: SPSS.

Kazdin, A. E. (1977). Assessing the clinical or applied importance of behavior change through social validation. *Behavior Modification, 54,* 95–105.

Kazdin, A. E. (1980a). Obstacles in using randomization tests in single-subject experimentation. *Journal of Educational Statistics, 5,* 253–260.

Kazdin, A. E. (1980b). *Research design in clinical psychology.* New York: Harper & Row.

Kazdin, A. E. (1984). Statistical analyses for single-case experimental designs. In D. H. Barlow & M. Hersen (Eds.), *Single case experimental designs: Strategies of studying behavior change* (pp. 285–324). Elmsford, NY: Pergamon Press.

Kendall, P. C. (1984). Behavioral assessment and methodology. In G. T. Wilson, C. M. Franks, K. D. Brownell, & P. C. Kendall (Eds.), *Annual review of behavior therapy* (Vol. 9, pp. 123–163). New York: Guilford Press.

Kendall, P. C., & Grove, W. M. (1988). Normative comparisons in therapy outcome. *Behavioral Assessment, 10,* 147–158.

Kendall, P. C., & Norton-Ford, J. D. (1982). Therapy outcome research methods. In P. C. Kendall & N. Butcher (Eds.), *Handbook of research methods in clinical psychology* (pp. 429–460). New York: John Wiley & Sons.

Keppel, G. (1982). *Design and analysis: A researcher's handbook* (2nd ed.). Englewood Cliffs, NJ: Prentice-Hall.

Kerlinger, F. N. (1980). Analysis of covariance structures tests of a criterial referents theory of attitudes. *Multivariate Behavioral Research, 15,* 403–422.

Kirk, R. E. (1982). *Experimental design: Procedures for the behavioral sciences* (2nd ed.). Monterey, CA: Brooks/Cole.

Kleinbaum, D. G., Kupper, L. L., & Muller, K. E. (1988). *Applied regression analysis and other multivariate methods* (2nd ed.). Boston: PWS-KENT.

Knapp, T. J. (1983). Behavior analysts' visual appraisal of behavior change in graphic display. *Behavioral Assessment, 5,* 155–164.

Knoke, D., & Burke, P. J. (1980). *Log-linear models.* Beverly Hills, CA: Sage Publications.

Kraemer, H. C., & Thiemann, S. (1987). *How many subjects: Statistical power analysis in research.* Newbury Park, CA: Sage Publications.

Kraemer, H. C., & Thiemann, S. (1989). A strategy to use soft data effectively in randomized controlled clinical trials. *Journal of Consulting and Clinical Psychology, 57,* 148–154.

Kruskal, J. B., & Wish, M. (1978). *Multidimensional scaling.* Beverly Hills, CA: Sage Publications.

Levin, J. R., Marascuilo, L. A., & Hubert, L. J. (1978). N = Nonparametric randomization tests. In T. R. Kratochwill (Ed.), *Single-subject research: Strategies for evaluating change* (pp. 167–196). New York: Academic Press.

Long, J. (1983). *Covariance structure models: An introduction to LISREL.* Beverly Hills, CA: Sage Publications.

Marascuilo, L. A., & Busk, P. L. (1987). Loglinear models: A way to study main effects and interactions for multidimensional contingency tables with categorical data. *Journal of Counseling Psychology, 34,* 443–455.

Margolin, G., & Wampold, B. E. (1981). Sequential analysis of conflict and accord in distressed and nondistressed marital partners. *Journal of Consulting and Clinical Psychology, 49,* 559–567.

Meehl, P. (1978). Theoretical risks and tabular asterisks: Sir Karl, Sir Ronald, and the slow progress in soft psychology. *Journal of Consulting and Clinical Psychology, 46,* 806–834.

Mitchell, C., & Hartmann, D. P. (1981). A cautionary note on the use of omega squared to evaluate the effectiveness of behavioral treatments. *Behavioral Assessment, 3,* 93–100.

Murray, L. W., & Dosser, D. A., Jr. (1987). How significant is a significant difference? Problems with the measurement of magnitude of effect. *Journal of Counseling Psychology, 34,* 68–72.

Nietzel, M. T., Russell, R. L., Hemmings, K. A., & Gretter, M. L. (1987). The clinical significance of psychotherapy for unipolar depression: A meta-analytic approach to social comparison. *Journal of Consulting and Clinical Psychology, 55,* 156–161.

Nietzel, M. T., & Trull, T. J. (1988). Meta-analytic approaches to social comparisons: A method for measuring clinical significance. *Behavioral Assessment, 10,* 159–169.

O'Grady, K. E. (1982). Measures of explained variance: Caution and limitations. *Psychological Bulletin, 92,* 766–777.

Patterson, G. R. (1986). Performance models for antisocial boys. *American Psychologist, 41,* 432–444.

Pedhazur, E. J. (1982). *Multiple regression in behavioral research* (2nd ed.). New York: Holt, Rinehart & Winston.

Popper, K. (1968). *Conjectures and refutations.* London: Routledge & Kegan Paul.

Porter, A. C., & Raudenbush, S. W. (1987). Analysis of covariance: Its model and use in psychological research. *Journal of Counseling Psychology, 4,* 383–392.

Revusky, S. H. (1976). Some statistical treatments compatible with individual organism methodology. *Journal of the Experimental Analysis of Behavior, 10,* 319–330.

Russell, R. L., & Trull, T. J. (1986). Sequential analyses of language variables in psychotherapy process research. *Journal of Consulting and Clinical Psychology, 54,* 16–21.

Sackett, G. P. (1979). The lag sequential analysis of contingency and cyclicity in behavioral interaction. In J. D. Osofsky (ed.), *Handbook of infant development* (pp. 623–649). New York: John Wiley & Sons.

Saunders, S. M., Howard, K. I., & Newman, F. L. (1988). Evaluating the clinical significance of treatment effects: Norms and normality. *Behavioral Assessment, 10,* 207–218.

Schiffman, S. S., Reynolds, M. L., & Young, F. W. (1981). *Introduction to multidimensional scaling.* New York: Academic Press.

Serlin, R. C. (1987). Hypothesis testing, theory building, and the philosophy of science. *Journal of Counseling Psychology, 34,* 365–371.

Serlin, R. C., & Lapsley, D. K. (1985). Rationality in psychological research: The good-enough principle. *American Psychologist, 40,* 73–83.

Sharpley, C. F., & Alavosius, M. P. (1988). Autocorrelation in behavioral data: An alternative perspective. *Behavioral Assessment, 10,* 243–251.

Shinn, M. R., Good, R. H., III, & Stein, S. (1989). Summarizing trend in student achievement: A comparison of methods. *School Psychology Review, 18,* 356–370.

Sidman, M. (1960). *Tactics of scientific research: Evaluating experimental data in psychology.* New York: Basic Books.

Skinner, B. F. (1953). *Science and human behavior*. New York: Macmillan.

Suen, H. K. (1987). On the epistemology of autocorrelation in applied behavior analysis. *Behavioral Assessment, 9*, 113–124.

Suen, H. K., & Ary, D. (1987). Autocorrelation in applied behavior analysis: Myth or reality? *Behavioral Assessment, 9*, 125–130.

Tinsley, H. E. A., & Tinsley, D. J. (1987). Uses of factor analysis in counseling psychology research. *Journal of Counseling Psychology, 34*, 414–424.

Toothaker, L. E., Banz, C., Camp, C., & Davis, D. (1983). N = 1 designs: The failure of ANOVA based tests. *Journal of Educational Statistics, 8*, 289–309.

Townsend, J. T., & Ashby, F. G. (1984). Measurement scales and statistics: The misconception misconceived. *Psychological Bulletin, 96*, 394–401.

Tracey, T. J., Sherry, P., Bauer, G. P., Robins, T. H., Todaro, L., & Briggs, S. (1984). Help seeking as a function of student characteristics and program description: A logit-loglinear analysis. *Journal of Counseling Psychology, 31*, 54–62.

Trull, T. J., Nietzel, M. T., & Main, A. (1988). The use of meta-analysis to assess the clinical significance of behavior therapy for agoraphobia. *Behavior Therapy, 19*, 527–538.

Turk, D. C., & Rudy, T. E. (1988). Toward an empirically derived taxonomy of chronic pain patients: Integration of psychological assessment data. *Journal of Consulting and Clinical Psychology, 56*, 233–238.

Velicer, W. F., & McDonald, R. P. (1984). Time-series analysis without model identification. *Multivariate Behavioral Research, 19*, 33–48.

Wampold, B. E. (1984). Tests of dominance in sequential categorical data. *Psychological Bulletin, 96*, 424–429.

Wampold, B. E. (1986). Toward quality research in counseling psychology: Curricular recommendations for design and analysis. *The Counseling Psychologist, 14*, 37–48.

Wampold, B. E. (1987). Guest editor's introduction. *Journal of Counseling Psychology, 34*, 364.

Wampold, B. E., & Drew, C. L. (1990). *Theory and application of statistics*. New York: Random House.

Wampold, B. E., & Freund, R. D. (1987). Use of multiple regression in counseling psychology research: A flexible data-analytic strategy. *Journal of Counseling Psychology, 34*, 372–382.

Wampold, B. E., & Furlong, M. J. (1981a). The heuristics of visual inference. *Behavioral Assessment, 3*, 79–82.

Wampold, B. E., & Furlong, M. J. (1981b). Randomization tests in single-subject designs: Illustrative examples. *Journal of Behavioral Assessment, 3*, 329–341.

Wampold, B. E., Furlong, M. J., & Atkinson, D. R. (1983). Statistical significance, power, and effect size: A response to the reexamination of reviewer bias. *Journal of Counseling Psychology, 30*, 459–463.

Wampold, B. E., & Jenson, W. R. (1986). Clinical significance revisited. *Behavior Therapy, 17*, 302–305.

Wampold, B. E., & Margolin, G. (1982). Nonparametric strategies to test the independence of behavioral states in sequential data. *Psychological Bulletin, 92*, 755–765.

Wampold, B. E., & Worsham, N. L. (1986). Randomization tests for multiple-baseline designs. *Behavioral Assessment, 8*, 135–143.

White, O. R. (1974). *The "split middle": A "quickie" method for trend estimation*. Seattle: University of Washington, Experimental Education Unit, Child Development and Mental Retardation Center.

Wilcox, R. R. (1987). New designs in analysis of variance. *Annual Review of Psychology, 38*, 29–60.

Winer, B. J. (1971). *Statistical principles in experimental design* (2nd ed.). New York: McGraw-Hill.

Winkler, R. L. (1972). *An introduction to Bayesian inference and decision*. New York: Holt, Rinehart and Winston.

von Winterfeldt, D., & Edwards, W. (1986). *Decision analysis and behavioral research*. Cambridge: Cambridge University Press.

PART IV

ASSESSMENT AND DIAGNOSIS

EDITOR'S COMMENTS

In the last decade, significant developments have emerged to improve our ability to assess and diagnose clinical dysfunction. These developments are pivotal to all facets of psychopathology including the study of epidemiology, etiology, treatment, prevention, and other areas. The emergence of the third edition of the *Diagnostic and Statistical Manual of Mental Disorders* (DSM-III) in 1980 and its revision in 1987 (DSM-III-R) is particularly important. The substantive gains in diagnostic categories and the clarity and nature of specific disorders continue to be matters of active debate and research. Noteworthy is the marked impact that these diagnostic systems have had on research. The empirical impact is felt in several interrelated areas including the development of assessment techniques designed to measure clinical dysfunction more reliably. Apart from diagnosis, assessment has continued to develop in diverse areas of clinical psychology. The present section considers several major types of assessment in clinical work and their recent developments.

In chapter 19, June Sprock and Roger K. Blashfield consider the development of classification including the evolution of the DSMs. They examine reliability of diagnosis, the empirical basis for alternative disorders, and the validity of diagnostic categories more generally. The chapter ends with a discussion of alternative models on which diagnosis can be based.

In chapter 20, Arthur N. Wiens relates diagnostic interviewing to current classification schemes. Interviewing is viewed as central to clinical decision making and accumulating important information about the patient. Among the salient topics in this chapter are clinical versus actuarial prediction, biological markers for diagnosis, and alternative types of interviews.

In chapter 21, Stephen E. Finn and James N. Butcher examine objective personality assessment and its special contribution to clinical work. Attention is accorded the Minnesota Multiphasic Personality Inventory (MMPI) and Millon Clinical Multiaxial Inventory (MCMI) as measures of psychopathology. Central topics to this chapter are administration and interpretation of objective tests. In addition, recent material on the revision of the MMPI-2 is provided.

In chapter 22, Robert L. Hale traces the history and current status of intelligence testing. In addition, he examines the current role of intelligence tests in clinical work. Current definitions of intelligence, the prediction of academic achievement, biases in testing, and the relations of alternative intelligence tests are presented.

In chapter 23, Barbara Pendleton Jones and Nelson Butters detail the historical and current developments in neuropsychological assessment. Descriptions of individual measures and assessment batteries are provided along with indications of their advantages and disadvantages. Major developments in the field, including neuropsychological rehabilitation, are also presented.

In chapter 24, Stephen N. Haynes documents the growth and development of behavioral assessment. Assessment options and their impact on clinical work and the relation of assessment and intervention are discussed. The chapter covers alternative assessment methods, reliability and validity, sources of error, and the clinical utility of various strategies.

In chapter 25, James M. Raczynski, William J. Ray, and Paul McCarthy discuss psychophysiological assessment. The history of psychophysiology, conceptual issues related to interpretation of alternative measures and measurement patterns, and assessment issues are discussed. Applications of psychological assessment are presented in relation to a variety of normal processes and activities including cognitive processes, personality, sleep, sexual arousal, and others and in relation to psychopathology as reflected in specific disorders.

In chapter 26, Anselm George presents the topic of medical assessment. Although this topic is often overlooked by clinical psychologists, the chapter conveys the importance of medical evaluation including history taking, physical exams, and laboratory work. Critical to the chapter is the material on the comorbidity of medical and psychological dysfunction and the role of medical issues in relation to specific clinical disorders.

In chapter 27, the final chapter in this section, Benjamin Kleinmuntz discusses the role of computers in clinical assessment. Computers have assumed multiple roles in assessment. The chapter highlights different roles and raises critical questions about the place of computerized assessment and clinical assessment in patient evaluation.

CHAPTER 19

CLASSIFICATION AND NOSOLOGY

June Sprock
Roger K. Blashfield

Classification refers to the process of forming groups of entities. Simpson (1961) divided the study of classification into three areas: (a) *taxonomy:* the theoretical study of classification without regard to content; (b) *classification:* the formation of groups or subsets from a large collection of entities; and (c) *identification:* the process of assigning particular entities or individuals to categories in an existing classification system. In the medical sciences, the preferred term for identification is *diagnosis*. Diagnosis means, literally, to distinguish or differentiate. In Simpson's terminology, the product of the process of classification is the classification system. A *nomenclature* is a specific set of terms used to identify categories. It includes both the names of the categories and technical terms to describe identified entities. A nomenclature is an approved list of terms that is independent of any underlying characteristics of the categories. A classification system of diseases is called a *nosology*.

There are a number of purposes served by the classification and diagnosis of psychopathology. For instance, Blashfield and Draguns (1976b) listed five important functions of a classification. First, a classification provides a nomenclature. Thus, a classification contains the nouns that are used by the profession-

als concerned with psychopathology. A second major purpose is the accumulation of clinical knowledge. A third purpose of classification is to describe important similarities and differences between patients. The fourth major purpose—prediction of outcome or prognosis—has been argued to be the most important function of classification, especially to clinicians (Panzetta, 1974; Zubin, 1967). The final purpose is to provide the concepts that will serve as the basis for theories of psychopathology. Other purposes of classification suggested by different writers include the formation of groups for administrative purposes such as insurance payments, the allocation of research funds, and the planning of treatment programs (Goldenberg, 1977).

Over the first half of the 20th century, psychiatric classification fell into increasing disfavor. Neither of the dominant perspectives in psychiatry (psychoanalysis) or clinical psychology (behaviorism) considered classification to be a topic worthy of major interest. In addition, a number of serious concerns had been raised about the negative consequence of diagnosis and classification to individuals and society. A diagnostic label might function as a stereotype (Allport, 1961) or perpetrate deviant behavior by being a self-fulfilling prophecy (Laing, 1967). In addition, a diagnosis is stigmatizing and emphasizes a person's weaknesses (Korchin, 1976). By the 1960s, the pejorative view of classification could best be summarized by a comment attributed to Szasz (1961): "Classifiers should be classified, not people."

In the last decade, the topic of classification has experienced renewed interest. Much of this renewed interest was stimulated by the formulation of the *Diagnostic and Statistical Manual of Mental Disorders, Third Edition, Revised* (DSM-III) (APA, 1980) and the research of the neo-Kraepelinians who created the DSM-III. This chapter will start with a historical review of psychiatric classification. However, most of the chapter will focus on the four editions of the DSM.

PRE-DSM CLASSIFICATION SYSTEMS

Ancient Nosologies

Mental disorders have been recognized and described since humans have kept written records. Some concepts, like depression (melancholia), mania, and hysteria, date back to as early as 2600 B.C. Psalm 102 contains a graphic portrayal of a person suffering from depression. Hippocrates (460 to 377 B.C.) was the first to introduce the concept of psychiatric illness to medicine. He divided mental disorders into acute mental disturbances with and without fever, chronic disturbances without fever (melancholia), hysteria, and scythian disease (transvestism). Before the Renaissance, all mental disorders were believed to have originated from a single pathological process. The famous British physician Sydenham (1624 to 1663), however, thought that there were multiple mental disorders, each with a specific course. Pinel (1745 to 1826), a French physician, organized mental disorders into four fundamental types—mania, melancholia, dementia, and idiotism—that resembled the Hippocratic categories. In his 1809 *Traite Medico-Philosophique Sur L' alienation Mental,* Pinel argued for the scientific study and categorizing of mental diseases, for the use of case records and life histories, and for the study of treatment methods. He also proposed that some psychiatric disorders may have psychogenic origins.

Nineteenth-Century European Classifications

Before the 20th century, most classifications of psychopathology only categorized forms of insanity (psychoses). Moreover, until the mid-1800s, most classification systems were developed by philosophers or general physicians, rather than by specialists in the mental disorders. During the middle of the 19th century, however, insane asylums were established that allowed observation of the course of the illness. In addition, the growth of insane asylums led to the need for specialized professionals to work with the inmates. Also, there was a growing interest in classification. The early systems were crude; the categories were overly broad; and the idiosyncratic terms had questionable validity.

The 19th-century view was that all disorders were manifestations of physical lesions. Griesinger (1818 to 1868), for example, said that all mental disorders are diseases of the brain. Morel (1809 to 1873) was the first to use the course of a disorder to classify mental disorders. A wide variety of classifications was proposed during this time. Hurd (1881) criticized the variation in classification systems among different insane asylums and called for the adoption of a uniform system. In 1852, Morel was appointed chairperson of the Congress of Mental Medicine to consider the existing classifications and derive a single system. This Congress agreed on the following 11 categories:

- Mania
- Melancholia
- Periodical insanity
- Progressive systematic insanity
- Dementia
- Organic and senile dementia
- General paralysis
- Insane neuroses
- Toxic insanity
- Moral and impulsive insanity
- Idiocy

Even though this system was different from contemporary classifications, most of these terms are still recognizable 100 years later.

Interest in classification in the 19th century culminated with the work of Emil Kraepelin (1856 to 1926). His organization of mental disorders served as a basis of modern nosologies. As a textbook author, Kraepelin wrote exceptionally clear case histories using behavioral observations. The chapters of these textbooks were organized around the major categories of mental disorders. What has become known as Kraepelin's classification systems was the table of contents for the various editions of his textbooks.

Kraepelin believed that mental disorders reflected an underlying organic etiology, but he was less enthralled by the medical model than were many of his contemporaries. He advocated a careful behavioral analysis of the patient and use of applied psychological research to improve the understanding of the mental disorders. The behavioral influence in Kraepelin's work was a result of his early studies with a famous early psychologist, Wundt. Kraepelin synthesized the clinical-descriptive approach of Wundt and somatic view of Griesinger with Morel's emphasis on the course of the disorder. Kraepelin believed that mental disorders could be classified according to symptom patterns, precipitating circumstances, course, and outcome. However, grouping by course was his major organizing principle. He realized that symptoms could be misleading and thought that it was important to differentiate symptoms that could not be used for diagnosis from those that consistently occurred in the course of the disorder.

The major work for which Kraepelin became known was the sixth edition of his *Clinical Psychiatry* (1899). Sixteen major categories of mental disorders were recognized in this book. Two of these categories stimulated a major international controversy over Kraepelin's de facto classification. The first of these controversial categories was manic-depressive insanity, which combined the historically recognized but independent categories of mania and melancholia. Kraepelin combined these concepts into one disorder because of his observations of a similar course in both, thereby suggesting that the two disorders were different phases of the same disorder. In his 1899 textbook, Kraepelin also introduced the category of dementia praecox, arguing that this disorder had three forms: hebephrenic, catatonic, and paranoid. The idea of an early (precocious = praecox) form of psychosis, which was chronic in its course but presumably did not lead to death, was revolutionary in its own right. Later, Bleuler (1857 to 1937) changed the name of dementia praecox to schizophrenia because the disorder represented a schism or split between the intellectual and emotional life of the patient. In contrast to Kraepelin, Bleuler integrated psychoanalytic views of the mental disorders with the more conventional medical views of the time.

AMERICAN CLASSIFICATIONS OF PSYCHOPATHOLOGY

The earliest American classification of mental disorders probably was proposed by Benjamin Rush (1745 to 1813). Rush was a prominent American physician who resided in Philadelphia and was one of the signatories to the Declaration of Independence. Rush was the first American psychiatrist and was interested in the forms of insanity. Rush published a book, *Medical Inquires and Observations upon the Diseases of the Mind* (1812/1962), that listed five major categories of mental disorder: hypochondriasis, amenomania, mania, manicula, and manalgia as well as a collection of lesser categories.

Another prominent 19th-century American physician interested in the mental disorders was William Hammond. He had served as the Surgeon General for the U.S. Army during the Civil War. In 1883, Hammond published a book, *A Treatise on Insanity in Its Medical Relations,* on psychopathology. In this work, Hammond divided the mind into four functions: perception, intellect, emotion, and will. His classification of mental disorders was organized according to these four mental functions:

1. Perceptual insanities (e.g., hallucinations)
2. Intellectual insanities (e.g., fixed delusions)
3. Emotional insanities (e.g., depression)
4. Volitional insanities (e.g., disorder of impulse control)
5. Compound insanities that affect more than one mental function (e.g., senile dementia)
6. Constitutional insanities (e.g., epileptic psychosis)

In 1917, the newly formed American Psychiatric Association (APA) proposed an official psychiatric classification that was structurally similar to Kraepelin's 1899 classification. A second official classification, the Standard Classified Nomenclature of Diseases, was proposed in 1933 (APA, 1933). This system had 24 major categories, 19 of which had been contained in Kraepelin's system. As a result, this classification was considered archaic by the dominant psychoanalytically oriented psychiatrists of the time and never gained widespread acceptance. By World War II, there were three dominant classification systems in American psychiatry: the Army had a system; the Navy had a system; and the Veterans Administration (VA) used yet another system. To reduce confusion after the war, the APA decided to create a task force that would generate a system acceptable to all American psychiatrists. The result was the *Diagnostic and Statistical Manual of Mental Disorders* (DSM-I) (APA, 1952). The DSM-I contained 108 categories and grew from the VA's classification system as revised by comments from members of the APA. The DSM-I did achieve its goal of being the consensual classification system in the United States and was used by virtually all American clinicians of the time.

Impressed by the success of American psychiatrists to create a consensual classification, the World Health

Organization (WHO) formed a series of committees to create an internationally accepted psychiatric classification. The result was published in 1967 as part of the eighth edition of the *International Classification of Diseases,* or ICD-8 (WHO, 1967). The American version of the ICD-8 was published in 1968 and was known as the DSM-II (APA, 1968). The DSM-II contained 185 categories organized under 10 major headings:

• Mental retardation
• Organic brain syndromes
• Functional psychoses
• Neuroses
• Personality disorders
• Psychophysiological disorders
• Special symptoms
• Transient situational disturbances
• Behavioral disorders of childhood
• Conditions without manifest psychiatric disorders

One major difference between the DSM-I and DSM-II was that the DSM-I had heavily used the concept of reaction to emphasize person-situation interactions in the formation of symptoms. For instance, the DSM-I used the term *schizophrenic reaction* while the DSM-II simply used the term *schizophrenia*. In addition, the DSM-II expanded the sections on mental disorders, behavioral disorders of childhood, and the functional psychoses relative to the DSM-I. Both systems used short prose definitions for the mental disorders, in contrast to the ICD-8, which was simply a nomenclature and contained no definitions of terms.

A number of criticisms were aimed at the DSM-II after its publication. One major criticism was that it was not based on a single organizing principle (Korchin, 1976). Instead, some disorders were defined by etiology (organic brain syndromes), some by the age of the patients (adjustment reaction of adolescence), some by behavioral symptoms (antisocial personality disorder), and others by life events (neurotic depression). Still other categories, such as sexual deviation, were based on apparently arbitrary and subjective decisions (Goldenberg, 1977). The DSM-II categories, despite being more numerous than the DSM-I categories, still did not achieve complete coverage and only broadly defined some categories (Korchin, 1976).

Another area of controversy concerned the way in which the different mental disorders were defined (Spitzer & Wilson, 1975). For instance, comparative international research studies in the early 1970s (Kendell et al., 1971; Kendell, 1975) showed that Americans were different from the rest of the world in the use of the concept of schizophrenia. American clinicians appeared to use the term *schizophrenia* to diagnose almost any psychotic patient, while clinicians from most other countries had a more precise meaning to the concept of schizophrenia.

Another important criticism of the DSM-II concerned reliability. Reliability is essential for a classification system to be used for communication among mental health professionals. If professionals do not agree on the meaning of the concepts they use, successful communication will be difficult. Agreement among clinicians is the major type of reliability that was studied regarding the DSM-I and DSM-II. Blashfield and Draguns (1976a) identified four factors that influenced interdiagnostician agreement: the specificity of the defining criteria, the training of the clinicians, the amount and nature of information used in making the diagnosis, and intraclinician consistency. The more specific, explicit, and precise the definition of a category, the less room there is for subjectivity, bias, and disagreement. The DSM-I and DSM-II definitions were criticized for being overly vague. The authors of the DSM-II tried to excuse their use of vague definitions by remarking that their system was only intended for use by trained professionals. Kendell (1973), however, found no relationship between length of experience in psychiatry and diagnostic accuracy.

Three influential reviews of reliability studies appeared that were of relevance to the DSM-I and DSM-II. The earliest was the most insightful by modern standards (Kreitman, 1961). Kreitman noted that many of the authors of reliability studies had concluded that the DSM-I had inadequate levels of reliability. However, Kreitman argued that the issue of reliability was being overemphasized in face of the need for validity studies and that the negative conclusions about the reliability of the DSM-I were overly skeptical.

The second important review was published by Zubin in 1967. Zubin reviewed all studies on diagnostic reliability published before 1965. He grouped the studies into three sets: (a) interclinician agreement studies, (b) studies of diagnostic consistency over time, and (c) studies comparing diagnostic frequencies. Zubin noted that distinctly different statistical measures of interclinician agreement were used in these reliability studies, and he showed how differences in the statistical measures alone could have led to variability in the conclusions of these studies.

The third review was by Spitzer and Fleiss (1974), who analyzed nine major studies of diagnostic reliability. They advocated the use of a statistic called kappa for assessing interclinician agreement. This statistic corrected for chance agreement and had a well-defined formula. Using kappa to reanalyze the results of previous reliability studies, Spitzer and Fleiss concluded that only three categories—mental deficiency, organic brain syndrome, and alcoholism—had satisfactory levels of reliability in the DSM-I and DSM-II systems. The reliability of schizophrenia and the psychoses was fair, but that of the neuroses, affective and personality disorders was inadequate. They agreed with a study by Ward, Beck, Mendelson, Mock, and Erbaugh (1962), in which diagnostic unreliability had been attributed to ambiguity in the DSM-I and DSM-II prose definitions of the disorders.

The Neo-Kraepelinian Movement

The development of the DSM-III was associated with the growth of a back-to-basics movement in psychiatry that espoused a biological approach to psychopathology and emphasized that psychiatry is a branch of medicine (as opposed to being a clinical branch of psychology). This approach to psychiatry, known as the neo-Kraepelinian movement (Klerman, 1978), was responsible for the growth of research on classification over the last 2 decades. The neo-Kraepelinian movement started with psychiatrists who worked with Eli Robins at Washington University in St. Louis and spread to the University of Iowa, the New York State Psychiatric Institute, the University of Minnesota, and Hillside Hospital in New York. Prominent psychiatrists in this movement were Guze, Klein, Spitzer, Winokur, Tsuang, Clayton, Cloninger, and Helzer. The movement was developed in reaction to the increasing dissatisfaction with psychiatric classification as embodied in the DSM-I and DSM-II and with the dominance of American psychiatry by the psychoanalytic perspective.

The neo-Kraepelinians focused on the need to develop a reliable classification largely because of their conclusions that reliability was a necessary precursor to validity, and because they believed that the reliability studies had shown the first two editions of the DSM to be deficient in this regard (Spitzer & Fleiss, 1974). As a result, they proposed the use of relatively behavioral diagnostic criteria that had clearly specified rules for when a given patient met or failed to meet a particular diagnosis. The first set of

diagnostic criteria was published in a seminal paper by Feighner et al. (1972). This paper contained explicit criteria for 15 mental disorders that the authors felt had demonstrable validity. Since the existing official classification, the DSM-II, contained 185 categories, they were implying that 170 of the DSM-II categories lacked adequate validity. They also proposed five phases to establish the validity of a psychiatric disorder, including: (a) clinical description, (b) laboratory studies, (c) differentiation from other disorders, (d) follow-up studies, and (e) family studies.

The Feighner paper was an influential journal article, garnering over 1,000 references in less than 10 years. A major reliability study using the Feighner criteria was performed by Helzer and associates (Helzer, Clayton, et al., 1977; Helzer, Robins et al., 1977). A standard interview was performed on 101 randomly selected admissions to a short-term inpatient unit. Three clinicians interviewed the patients on the first and second days after admission. Helzer et al. found significantly higher reliability values for the Feighner criteria than had been reported for the DSM-I and DSM-II.

Although the reliability of categories defined using the Feighner criteria was generally acceptable, other studies suggested that the coverage of categories defined using the Feighner criteria was a problem. For instance, Helzer, Robins, et al. (1977) found that the coverage for the Feighner definition of schizophrenia was overly restrictive, with only 3 of 101 inpatients receiving this diagnosis. Morrison, Clancy, Crowe, and Winokur (1972) found that only 31% of patients with a chart diagnosis of schizophrenia met the Feighner criteria for this disorder. Ries, Bokan, and Schuckit (1980) noted that 40% of a group of 254 patients were undiagnosed by the Feighner criteria. Brockington, Kendell, and Leff (1978) also presented data that led them to conclude the Feighner criteria for schizophrenia were overly restrictive.

Given the high reliability of the Feighner criteria, Eli Robins, who had been the second author on the Feighner paper, joined with Robert Spitzer and Jean Endicott to formulate the *Research Diagnostic Criteria* (RDC) (Spitzer, Endicott, & Robins, 1975). This classification primarily focused on the functional psychoses including the schizophrenic, the affective, and the paranoid disorders. Diagnostic criteria were offered for a number of subtypes of these disorders. The RDC became officially sanctioned by the National Institute of Mental Health (NIMH), and research studies funded by NIMH during the late 1970s were required to use the RDC to define patient groups.

The DSM-III

By the mid-1970s, Spitzer was the chairperson for another new classification. This classification system was the DSM-III (APA, 1980). The earliest versions of the DSM-III developed from the RDC. However, the authors of the DSM-III were concerned with proposing diagnostic criteria for all recognized mental disorders. In the final version of this classification, 265 different categories of mental disorders were recognized, virtually all of which were defined using diagnostic criteria.

There were four major differences between the DSM-III and its predecessors. The first of these differences was the emphasis in the DSM-III on being a scientifically viable classification. As noted earlier, the overriding goals of the DSM-I and DSM-II were consensus. Both were intended to be classifications that psychiatrists could live with. For DSM-I, the group of psychiatrists for whom the classification was aimed was American; for the DSM-II, the target group of psychiatrists was international. Nonetheless, both systems contained a number of compromises, and these compromises reflected the opinions of the target psychiatric audiences. In the DSM-III, consensus was less of an issue than was the scientific validity of the disorders. This emphasis led to a decidedly different classification of affective disorders, for instance. In the DSM-I and DSM-II, the primary distinction among the affective disorders concerned psychotic versus neurotic forms. The DSM-III dropped this distinction and instead used a bipolar versus unipolar distinction. The reason for the change was the genetic and biochemical studies that supported the bipolar versus unipolar distinction, while few research studies supported the psychotic versus neurotic dichotomy.

A second major difference between the DSM-III compared to earlier editions was its organization of categories. As noted earlier, the affective disorders were organized according to a bipolar versus unipolar distinction rather than psychotic versus neurotic. Within the category of schizophrenia, the number of subtypes was reduced from 14 in the DSM-II to five in the DSM-III in an attempt to narrow the concept of schizophrenia. This narrowing was a response to the research cited earlier (Kendell et al., 1971) showing that the American use of the concept of schizophrenia was much broader than the international use. Another area of major change was an increase in the number of subtypes of childhood disorders. These disorders were divided into five major categories: intellectual, behavioral, emotional, physical, and developmental. In ad-dition, these disorders were classified by their initial appearance in childhood or adolescence, rather than by the age of the patient, so that a patient of any age can receive these diagnoses.

A third major innovation was the use of a multiaxial system of diagnosis. The idea of using a multiaxial system was relatively new. Essen-Moller (1961) first suggested using two axes, one for the clinical syndrome and one for etiology, in order to prevent the confusion that occurs when these two different organizing principles are mixed. Gardner (1968) also suggested a three-axis multidimensional system than included type of disorder, level and course of disability, and basic pattern of adjustment. Mezzich (1978) concluded that three advantages could result from a multiaxial system. First, more information about a patient is represented in such a system that may assist in the treatment planning for a patient. Second, more and better information about mental disorders can be gathered using a multiaxial system. For instance, Rutter (Rutter et al., 1969; Rutter, Shaffer, & Shepherd, 1975) found that when clinicians are presented with an autistic, mentally retarded child who acts out, the clinicians typically will only assign one diagnosis (autism, mental retardation, or conduct disorder) rather than using multiple diagnoses. Finally, the multiaxial system has educational advantages in that it forces students to examine the patient's personality, medical problems, psychosocial environment, and previous level of functioning, instead of focusing exclusively on symptoms.

The fourth major difference between the DSM-II and DSM-III was that the DSM-III used diagnostic criteria to define its categories. Thus, the DSM-III continued the tradition started with the Feighner criteria in an attempt to improve the reliability of its categories. The result was much more detailed and clearer definitions of the disorders than had been presented in the DSM-I and DSM-II. As a corollary, the size of the DSM-III manual (494 pages) was greatly expanded over the DSM-II (134 pages).

Despite its innovations and generally positive acceptance by mental health professionals, a number of criticisms were leveled at the DSM-III. One focus of criticism concerned the diagnostic criteria. Despite the desire to make decisions regarding the classificatory categories on the basis of scientific evidence, most diagnostic criteria were developed intuitively by experts in the field, rather than using evidence from the research literature. In addition, even though the goal when formulating diagnostic criteria was to make them as behavioral and explicit as possible, not all criteria met this goal. Consider part of the DSM-III criteria for passive-aggressive personality disorder, for instance.

> Resistance expressed through two of the following:
> 1) procrastination
> 2) dawdling
> 3) stubbornness
> 4) intentional inefficiency
> 5) "forgetfulness"

Note that common language terms such as *dawdling* were highly subjective. In addition, the last two symptoms required the inference of motivations and reasons, rather than direct observation of behaviors.

A second major criticism of the DSM-III concerned the multiaxial system. First, diagnosing multiple axes required increased time and effort by clinicians, an exercise they were unlikely to do unless they were certain that the gain in information was significant. Second, the measurement of the axes in the DSM-III was criticized. In the DSM-III manual, almost 300 pages were devoted to defining the Axis I disorders, another 39 pages were spent on Axis II disorders, while only two pages each were devoted to Axes IV and V. Moreover, Axes I and II were assessed using diagnostic categories while Axes IV and V were measured using relatively crude, ordinal rating scales. Third, the particular axes were also criticized. For instance, Rutter (Rutter et al., 1969; Rutter, Shaffer, & Shepherd, 1975) had advocated the use of one axis for the clinical syndrome in childhood disorders with a second focusing on intellectual level. Instead, both clinical syndromes and mental retardation were Axis I disorders in the DSM-III. A group of psychoanalysts argued that defense mechanisms should have been included as a sixth axis, while psychiatric nurses advocated a sixth axis for a nursing diagnosis relevant to the level of care required by a patient.

A third major criticism of the DSM-III focused on the reorganization of the categories. For instance, many researchers were critical of the DSM-III subtypes of childhood disorders. When Cantwell, Russel, Mattison, and Will (1979) designed case histories representing different DSM-III childhood disorders, they found only 15% to 55% agreement with the diagnoses they were intended to represent. Rutter and Shaffer (1980) concluded that there was insufficient evidence of reliability and validity for many of the specific disorders of childhood included in the DSM-III, but they supported the division of disorders into the five general headings. Achenbach (1980) argued that there was a general association between the DSM-III categories for childhood disorders and those developed through factor analysis. However, some significant differences existed. For instance, the

DSM-III had no category for depressive disorder of childhood, yet Achenbach noted at least seven factor analytic studies that discovered a depressive syndrome in children.

The final group of criticisms of the DSM-III was political in nature. Although some psychologists applauded the DSM-III, others were concerned because this system had been created by psychiatrists, and its recognition implicitly asserted the dominance of psychiatry among the mental health professions (Schacht & Nathan, 1977). There was even a movement within the American Psychological Association to create a competing classification system for psychologists. Even within psychiatry, the political nature of classification became apparent. Psychoanalysts became upset with the exclusion of the concept of neurosis for the final draft versions of the DSM-III and threatened to have the classification rejected during a convention of the APA (Bayer & Spitzer, 1985). A last-minute compromise in which the term *neurosis* was included into the DSM-III, but only in parentheses, allowed the DSM-III to be published.

Despite the controversies and criticisms, the DSM-III was recognized as the most significant restructuring of psychiatric classification during the 20th century. The apparent improvement in reliability, the reorganization of categories to improve structural consistency, and the attempt to make classification responsive to contemporary research were all seen as significant advances.

DSM-III-R

Only 7 years later, a revision to the DSM-III was published. This version, known as the DSM-III-R (APA, 1987), was intended primarily to update diagnostic criteria in light of the research that had been stimulated by the DSM-III. It was called a revision because the changes were not significant enough to consider this a totally new edition, but some of the changes were substantial, especially to researchers within specific areas. Changes from the DSM-III to the DSM-III-R included renaming some categories (e.g., paranoid disorder was renamed delusional disorder), changes in specific criteria for disorders (e.g., the criteria for schizoaffective disorder), and reorganization of categories (e.g., panic disorder and agoraphobia were explicitly linked). In addition, six diagnostic categories originally in the DSM-III were deleted (e.g., ego-dystonic homosexuality and attention deficit disorder without hyperactivity) while a number of new specific disorders were added (e.g., body dysmorphic disorder and trichotillomania). As a result, the DSM-III-R contained 297 categories compared to the 264 categories in the DSM-III.

The most substantial revisions in the DSM-III-R occurred for the major psychotic disorders, affective disorders, personality disorders, and childhood disorders. Revisions in the major psychoses include changing the name of paranoid disorder to delusional disorder and elimination of its subtypes. These changes were based on the recognition that nonparanoid delusions (e.g., grandiose delusions) may occur in older individuals without a history of psychosis and that few cases of acute paranoid disorder occurred (i.e., this concept had low coverage). Shared paranoid disorder was retained, but its name was changed to induced paranoid disorder, and it was moved into the group of psychotic disorders not elsewhere classified. Another change under the major psychoses was the inclusion of diagnostic criteria for schizoaffective disorder. In the DSM-III, schizoaffective disorder was the only category with no diagnostic criteria. The DSM-III-R criteria for schizoaffective emphasized schizophrenic-like symptoms in conjunction with a transient mood disorder. The maximum duration of brief reactive psychosis was increased to 1 month, while the minimum duration of schizophreniform disorder was reduced to 1 week. Finally, the minimum duration of the active phase in a schizophrenic episode was clearly specified as 1 week to reduce possible confusion with personality disorders.

A number of changes occurred within the affective disorders. The DSM-III-R more appropriately called these "disorders of mood" based on the distinction between affect (temporary expression of emotions) and mood (underlying predominant emotion). Under the general heading of mood disorders, there were two major subtypes: depressive and bipolar disorders. Finally, there was a reorganization of the format of the criteria for major depression so that a different combination of symptoms was required in the DSM-III-R. On superficial examination, the changes in the definition of depression did not appear to be significant. However, Zimmerman (1988) found the revised criteria to be more restrictive with 10% to 15% of DSM-III major depressives failing to meet the new criteria. Another change in the disorders of mood was the provision for further specification of disorders as primary, secondary, early or late onset, or as a seasonal mood disturbance.

One of the major revisions concerned the criteria for the personality disorders. The classification of personality disorders was criticized in the DSM-III because the criteria were presented as vague, prose-like descriptions reminiscent of the DSM-II. The DSM-III-R attempted to provide more explicit, operational criteria for the personality disorders. Changes also occurred in the conceptualizations of some personality disorders. For example, the concept of paranoid personality disorder was narrowed to include only the core concept of suspiciousness while less central symptoms (e.g, inability to relax) were eliminated. The criteria for avoidant personality disorder were broadened to include not only avoidance of people, but also avoidance of new places and situations. Finally, the name of compulsive personality disorder was changed back to obsessive-compulsive personality disorder, the term used in the DSM-II. While overall the revision in the personality disorders appeared to be a significant improvement, these last two changes had the potential of causing confusion with the anxiety disorders (i.e., agoraphobia and obsessive-compulsive anxiety disorder).

Several significant changes were made for the childhood and adolescent disorders. Two categories previously under the psychosexual disorders, gender identity disorder of childhood and transsexualism, were added to the childhood disorders since these disorders first appear during childhood. The category attention deficit disorder without hyperactivity was eliminated due to low coverage. Two disorders, sleepwalking and sleep terror disorder, were moved to the new chapter on sleep disorders. Finally, consistent with Rutter et al.'s (1969, 1975) recommendation that deficits in intellectual functioning be diagnosed on Axis II, mental retardation as well as the "V code" of borderline intellectual functioning were coded on Axis II in the DSM-III-R. In addition, pervasive developmental disorders (autism) joined the specific developmental disorders as Axis II diagnoses.

Other changes associated with the DSM-III-R occurred in the general areas of the psychosexual disorders (now simply called sexual disorders), anxiety disorders, disorders of impulse control, organic mental disorders, and substance use disorders. A major change in the DSM-III-R was the deletion of ego-dystonic homosexuality—a concept that had been used to replace homosexuality after a major controversy in psychiatry during the 1970s. Within the anxiety disorders, the most substantial change was the explicit linking of panic disorder to agoraphobia based on research showing the frequent association of these two disorders and the finding that panic attacks frequently precipitate the onset of agoraphobia. Within the disorders of impulse control, isolated explosive disorder was eliminated due to low coverage, while a new category, trichotillomania (impulse to pull out one's own hair), was added. This latter category was said to be associated with intellectual impairment or high stress levels. Whether it proves to be a syndrome in its own right or a symptom of other disorders remains to be demonstrated.

A classification of sleep disorders was also added in the DSM-III-R. Actually, this classification had been planned for inclusion in the DSM-III, but the committee responsible for this area did not conclude their work in time for publication of the DSM-III. This new heading included two major groupings, dyssomnias or difficulties with the sleep pattern itself (e.g., insomnia and hypersomnia disorders) and parasomnias or abnormal events occurring during sleep (e.g., sleep terror and sleepwalking disorders).

Another significant revision in the DSM-III-R concerned Axis V. In the DSM-III, this axis was titled the "highest level of adaptive functioning" and was measured by a seven-point rating scale. In the DSM-III-R, this axis was replaced by the Global Assessment of Functioning (GAF) scale (Endicott, Spitzer, Fleiss, & Cohen, 1976). The GAF is a 90-point ordinal scale that had an extensive history of use in clinical research.

Associated with the DSM-III-R was the development of a major controversy that had political overtones. Among the changes proposed for the DSM-III-R was the addition of three new disorders: premenstrual dysphoric disorder, masochistic personality disorder, and paraphilic rapism. These additions raised the ire of a number of groups, especially feminists. Concerning premenstrual dysphoric disorder, feminists argued that the inclusion of this disorder into the DSM would be another instance of blaming women's emotions on their biology. If it were a disorder, they argued that it should be classified as a gynecological disorder rather than a psychiatric disorder. Masochistic personality disorder had been suggested for inclusion by modern psychoanalysts who noted the extensive literature during the 20th century on this category (under the name of moral masochism). Feminists, however, believed that this diagnosis would be assigned to repeatedly abused women, thereby blaming these women for their roles as victims when, in fact, they were often powerless to alter their life circumstances. Finally, paraphilic rapism was criticized because the feminists felt that this diagosis would allow chronic rapists to escape punishment for their crimes because their behaviors could be attributed to a mental disorder over which these men had no control.

In the ensuing controversy, another compromise was attempted. The authors of the DSM-III-R revised the names of the first two disorders to periluteal phase dysphoric disorder and self-defeating personality disorder while deleting paraphilic rapism. In addition, another disorder, sadistic personality disorder, was added presumably to blame the abuser and balance the potential antifeminine connotations of self-defeating and masochistic personality disorder. This compromise was not successful. As a result, the executive committee for the Amerian Psychiatric Association decided not to include these categories in the body of the DSM-III-R, but to place them in an appendix as disorders needing more research (Simons, 1987; Walker, 1987).

Apart from the controversial categories, the changes in the DSM-III-R have not received as much attention as was given to the DSM-III. Perhaps these changes were perceived as insignificant. This perception was suggested by the title of an article published by Williams in 1986, "*DSM-III-R:* What's all the fuss about?" Students and clinicians have complained that the revision has forced them to purchase another book and that they have had to learn a new system. At this time, some changes appear to be significant improvements (e.g., providing specific diagnostic criteria for the personality disorders and linking panic disorder to agoraphobia), while others appear to be detrimental (e.g., changing the name of compulsive personality disorder to obsessive-compulsive personality disorder). Some of the new categories (e.g., frotteurism and trichotillomania) may prove to have low coverage, thereby being eliminated in the next revision.

At the time of this writing, the DSM-IV is being developed. Given the steady increase in the number of categories across editions of the DSM from 108 in the DSM-I to 297 in the DSM-III-R, a linear extrapolation would suggest that the DSM-IV will have about 360 categories. The chairperson for the DSM-IV, Allen Frances, has stated that changes for the DSM-IV will be conservative. There have been criticisms of the DSM-III-R that rapid alterations in diagnostic criteria made performing research difficult. For instance, changes in criteria could have major effects when defining patient samples (Zimmerman, 1988).

Associated with the DSM-III and DSM-III-R were five broad developments in research about psychopathology: (a) the creation of new instruments to assess psychopathology, especially in the form of structured interviews; (b) research studies on the validity of diagnostic categories; (c) research on the prevalence of the mental disorders; (d) studies documenting the overlap (comorbidity) of mental disorders; and (e) the proposal of alternative taxonomic models for psychiatric classification. This chapter will end by discussing each of these developments.

New Instruments to Assess Psychopathology

Given the dramatic changes in classification associated with the DSM-III and DSM-III-R, the development of new instruments to assess mental disorders was not surprising. In particular, a series of structured interviews was created that became the standard in psychiatric research as the methods of ascertaining research diagnoses of patient samples. The oldest of the structured interviews was developed before the DSM-III. This interview was a British instrument created by Wing, Cooper, and Sartorius (1974) and was named *The Present State Examination* (PSE). The interview was designed to carefully describe a wide range of psychopathology, but it focused primarily on the psychotic disorders.

The next major structured interview was the *Schedule of Affective Disorders and Schizophrenia* (SADS) (Endicott & Spitzer, 1978), which was designed to elicit information from patients that could be used to arrive at a RDC diagnosis. Since the SADS was the measurement instrument for the RDC, it was the major structured interview used in research during the last half of the 1970s to assess psychopathology.

After the SADS and PSE, a number of other structured interviews for assessing psychopathology, both across a broad spectrum of disorders and for specific subheadings, have been developed and used (Goldstein & Hersen, 1984). Prominent in the list of these interviews were the *Diagnostic Interview Schedule* (DIS) (Helzer et al., 1985), which was used in the large-scale epidemiological studies of mental disorders in the United States; the *Structured Clinical Interview for DSM-III-R* (SCID) by Spitzer, Williams, and Gibbon (1987), which was designed to elicit information for assessing diagnostic criteria in the DSM-III-R; and the *Personality Disorder Examination* (PDE) by Loranger, Susman, Oldham, and Russakoff (1987) for measuring symptoms of the personality disorders.

A major reason for the use of structured interviews in psychiatric research was to improve the reliability by which the symptoms of various disorders were assessed. Clinical diagnoses have been recognized to vary markedly as a function of administrative needs and other issues of clinical settings; thus, differences in clinical diagnoses often failed to reflect differences in patients' psychopathology. Research diagnoses, independently assessed through structured interviews, were more likely to reflect patient symptomatology. The use of structured interviews was not without cost, however. Most of these interviews required 1 to 2

hours to administer. Virtually all of the interviews had branching decision points to streamline their administration, but nonetheless they were costly in terms of clinicians' time. Moreover, there was evidence (Helzer et al., 1985) that the results of these interviews were affected by the experience of the interviewers. For instance, lay interviewers tend to underdiagnose depression while overdiagnosing obsessive-compulsive disorder.

Validity of Diagnostic Categories

Another important advance regarding psychopathology that has been stimulated by the DSM-III and DSM-III-R was the performance of empirical studies to evaluate the validity of diagnostic categories. These validity studies took many forms. For instance, Zimmerman and Spitzer (1989) reviewed studies that analyzed the evidence for the validity of melancholia as a subtype of depression. Monroe, Thase, Hersen, Himmelhoh, and Bellack (1985) failed to note any association between the diagnosis of melancholia (endogenous depression) and stressors as measured through life events. Studies using electroconvulsive therapy (ECT) and antidepressant medications also failed to support the validity of this subtype of depression.

Another mental disorder that had attracted a number of validity studies was borderline personality disorder. Gunderson (1982), for instance, reviewed 11 different studies that demonstrated significant differences between borderlines and other diagnostic groups (e.g., schizophrenics and depressives) across a range of variables. Akiskal and his colleagues challenged the validity of borderline personality disorder in an article with an amusing title: "Borderline: An Adjective in Search of a Noun" (Akiskal et al., 1985). Akiskal et al. concluded that borderline personality was probably better classified as an atypical affective disorder rather than having a separate nosological status. Gunderson and Elliott (1985) responded by discussing alternative models for explaining the overlap between borderline personality disorder and affective disorder. Aronson (1985) presented a thought-provoking review of the controversies surrounding borderline personality disorder within the context of conflicting theoretical models in psychiatry.

A third disorder with a large research literature debating its validity was childhood depression. Factor analytic studies of behaviors in children who were referred to clinics consistently demonstrated the existence of a depressive factor in these children (Quay, 1986). Achenbach and Edelbrock (1978), for instance, found a factor in school-aged boys that contained items like "feels worthless," "feels unloved," "sad," "lonely," and "withdrawn." Despite the consistent findings of a depressive syndrome among children in descriptive studies, the DSM-III and DSM-III-R did not include the category of childhood depression. Instead, depression was listed under the adult disorders with a specific proviso that the diagnostic criteria for depression can be applied (slightly modified) to children. Part of the reason for not recognizing childhood depression as a separate category was the psychoanalytic view that depression results from an overly strong superego, and superego development is insufficient in children to lead to depression. Other criticisms of the concept of childhood depression can be found in Lefkowitz and Burton (1978).

Although the DSM-III and DSM-III-R stimulated a number of research studies, there was little empirical evidence about the validity of a number of disorders. One example was the category of passive-aggressive personality disorder. This diagnosis existed in all four editions of the DSM, a feat matched by only four other personality disorders (antisocial, dependent, obsessive-compulsive, and schizoid). Moreover, American psychiatrists have insisted on keeping this diagnosis in the DSM-II despite the fact that this concept was not recognized in the ICD-8. Despite this history in American classifications, there have been almost no empirical studies on this disorder (Parsons & Wicks, 1983). Perhaps forthcoming research (McCann, 1988) will allow some determination of the validity of this disorder.

Epidemiological Studies

A third major development in psychopathology made possible by the DSM-III and DSM-III-R was the performance of large-scale epidemiological studies on the prevalence of mental disorders in the general population. Historically, there were two major epidemiological studies of the mental disorders: the Midtown Manhattan study (Srole, Langner, Michael, Opler, & Rennie, 1962) and the Nova Scotia study (Leighton, Harding, Macklin, MacMillan, & Leighton, 1963). Although the methodologies of these early studies were often criticized, these studies have been repeatedly cited because they contained the major studies on the prevalence of mental disorders within the general population before the DSM-III (Dohrenwend & Dohrenwend, 1974).

With the publication of the DSM-III and the creation of the Diagnostic Interview Schedule (DIS) as a structured interview to assess DSM-III criteria, NIMH funded a large-scale epidemiological study to assess psychopathology in the general population. The assessments were performed in five sites: New Haven, Los Angeles, Durham, Baltimore, and St. Louis. The combined prevalence results (Robins et al., 1984) suggested that alcoholism, phobias, and depression were the most frequent disorders in urban areas of the U.S. Among males, alcohol abuse and antisocial personality were relatively more likely compared to women. For females, the relatively likely disorders were depression, agoraphobia, and simple phobia. New epidemiological studies allowed better estimates of the national prevalence rates for mental disorders than occurred with earlier studies (Karno, Golding, Sorenson, & Burnam, 1988).

Overlap

A fourth interesting development about the classification of mental disorders was the recent awareness of the degree of overlap that exists among mental disorders. With the use of structured interviews that allowed the independent assessment of symptoms that can be later combined to show multiple diagnoses, the evidence for significant overlap in a number of the mental disorders became striking. Stated somewhat more tersely, if a patient met the criteria for any one DSM-III-R mental disorder, more often than not the same patient met the criteria for at least one other mental disorder. Rates of overlap were estimated from 1.7 mental disorders per patient to 3.7 mental disorders (Boyd et al., 1984). Even within specific subheadings of the mental disorders, the overlap rates were substantial. For instance, among the personality disorders, rates of overlap had been estimated from 2.2 to 3.75 personality disorders per patient (Widiger, Frances, Warner, & Bluhm, 1986).

The discovery of high rates of overlap led to a growing literature on comorbidity (i.e., the cooccurrence of different mental disorders). The high rates of overlap led to questions about whether the overlapping mental disorders were simply different manifestations of the same underlying disorder, whether the overlap simply reflected the statistical correlation of certain symptom constellations, or if diagnostic overlap resulted from environmental factors that favor the mutual development of certain disorders.

Alternative Taxonomic Models

The final major development regarding the classification of psychopathology was the discussion of alternative taxonomic models. Generally, the implicit taxonomic model associated with psychiatric classification was the categorical model. Under the categorical model, diagnostic categories represent sets of patients with mental disorders. Each category in a classification is defined by reference to characteristics (diagnostic criteria) that can be used to differentiate members of the category from nonmembers. Within a category, patients who are members of the category are assumed to be relatively similar to each other. Moreover, patients in different categories should be relatively dissimilar. Restated, diagnostic categories are considered to consist of relatively homogeneous groups of patients.

A second taxonomic model that experienced a resurgence of interest was the dimensional model. The history of this model extended back to the 1950s and was associated with factor analytic approaches to psychopathology. Recently, however, the dimensional model was suggested as possibly useful in a number of new contexts. For instance, Cloninger (1987), Wiggins (1982), McLermore and Benjamin (1979), and Frances (1982) suggested different types of dimensional models as alternatives to the categorical model of personality disorders. Zimmerman and Spitzer (1989) discussed data that suggested a dimensional model of melancholia appeared more parsimonious than a categorical model. In contrast, Cloninger, Martin, Guze, and Clayton (1985) provided convincing data on the categorical nature of schizophrenia.

A third model of psychiatric classification was the disease model. This model often was assumed to be identical with the categorical model. However, Skinner (1986) suggested that the disease model, when analyzed carefully, could be seen as consistent with a special type of dimensional model. The important, and controversial, aspect of the disease model has been the definition of the concept of disease. Kendell (1986) provided the most exhaustive discussions of the meaning of disease and how this concept might or might not fit various aspects of psychopathology. Wing (1978) argued that the concept of disease has two essential parts: (a) A disease is associated with a clinical syndrome; and (b) there is an underlying biological disturbance. Viewed from Wing's perspective, most mental disorders recognized in the DSM-III and DSM-III-R have not been proven to be diseases. Some of these disorders, such as schizophrenia, were generally believed to be diseases, but until the etiology of schizophrenia (or of the schizophrenias) has been demonstrated, the disease model for schizophrenia will be unresolved. Moreover, there were other disorders, such as many of the personality disorders,

for which hardly anyone would suggest a disease model (contrast Akiskal et al., 1985). Blashfield (1984) argued that much of the discussion around the disease (medical) model was an intellectualized presentation of the politics of interprofessional rivalries that exist among the mental health professions.

The final alternative taxonomic model for psychiatric classification was the prototype model. The best way to explain the prototype model is by example. Consider, for instance, that a mother is attempting to teach a child what a bird is. What the mother does not do is to list the features of birds (e.g., have wings, feathers) for the child. Instead, what the mother is likely to do is point out the window at a robin and say, "bird." Later, the child may point at a cat and say, "bird." The mother would respond, "No, that is not a bird. That is a cat." Then she would point at a sparrow and say "bird" to the child. After the child had learned to associate the word with different instances of the concept, the child would be later able to abstract those features that separate instances of the concept from instances that do not fit the concept.

An important aspect of the prototype model is that not all members of a category are equally representative of the category. For instance, a sparrow is a good example of bird, while a penguin is not. In teaching a child about birds, taking the child to the zoo and pointing at a penguin while saying the word *bird* is more likely to be confusing than helpful. The variations in the prototypicality of different members of a category are accounted for by differences in the number and saliency of the defining features that members possess.

The prototype model stimulated a growing research literature on psychiatric classification (Cantor & Genero, 1986; Cantor, Smith, French, & Mezzich, 1980; Clarkin, Widiger, Frances, Hurst, & Gilmore, 1983; Horowitz, Post, French, Wallis, & Siegelman, 1981; Horowitz, Wright, Lowenstein, & Parad, 1981; Livesley, 1985a, 1985b; Livesley, Reiffer, Sheldon, & West, 1987; Sprock, 1988). Although the prototype model has only appeared in the last decade in the literature on psychopathology, the research methods associated with this model were used in a number of studies published before the DSM-III (Overall, 1963; Bartko, Strauss, & Carpenter, 1971; Spitzer, Williams, & Skodol, 1979; Strauss et al., 1979; Warner, 1978).

CONCLUSION

For readers who are interested in learning more about contemporary views of psychiatric classification, the classic book on the topic was written by

Kendell (1975). Although Kendell's book was written during the era of the DSM-II and ICD-8, his clarity and perceptiveness regarding such issues as the meaning of disease, the topics of reliability and validity, and the dimensional and categorical models are still unsurpassed. The second best resource on psychiatric classification was an edited volume by Millon and Klerman (1986). This volume contained a remarkable collection of chapters from authors such as Quay, Albee, Eysenck, Klerman, Frances, Lorr, Cantwell, and Kiesler. The volume was subtitled *Toward the DSM-IV*. Other recent books focusing on the issues of psychiatric classification were by Agassi (1981), Blashfield (1984), Colby and Spar (1983), Flach (1987), Freedman, Brotman, Silverman, and Hutson (1986), Last and Hersen (1987), Mezzich and von Cranach (1988), Robins and Barrett (1989), and Tichler (1987).

REFERENCES

Achenbach, T. M. (1980). *DSM-III* in light of empirical research on the classification of child psychopathology. *Journal of the American Academy of Child Psychiatry, 19,* 395–412.

Achenbach, T. M., & Edelbrock, C. S. (1978). The classification of child psychopathology: A review and analysis of empirical efforts. *Psychological Bulletin, 85,* 1275–1301.

Agassi, J. (Ed.). (1981). *Psychiatric diagnosis.* Philadelphia: Balabon International Science Services.

Akiskal, H. S., Chen, S. E., Davis, G. C., Puzantian, V. R., Kashgarian, M., & Bolinger, J. M. (1985). Borderline: An adjective in search of a noun. *Journal of Clinical Psychiatry, 46,* 41–48.

Allport, G. W. (1961). *Pattern and growth of personality.* New York: Holt, Rinehart & Winston.

American Psychiatric Association. (1933). Notes and comment: Revised classified nomenclature of mental disorders. *American Journal of Psychiatry, 90,* 1369–1376.

American Psychiatric Association. (1952). *Diagnostic and statistical manual of mental disorders.* Washington, DC: Author.

American Psychiatric Association. (1968). *Diagnostic and statistical manual of mental disorders* (2nd ed.). Washington, DC: Author.

American Psychiatric Association. (1980). *Diagnostic and statistical manual of mental disorders* (3rd ed.). Washington, DC: Author.

American Psychiatric Association. (1987). *Diagnostic and statistical manual of mental disorders* (3rd ed., revised). Washington, DC: Author.

Aronson, T. A. (1985). Historical perspectives on the borderline concept. *Psychiatry, 48,* 209–222.

Bartko, J. J., Strauss, J. S., & Carpenter, W. T. (1971). An evaluation of taxometric techniques for psychiatric data. *Classification Society Bulletin, 2,* 2–28.

Bayer, R., & Spitzer, R. L. (1985). Neurosis, psychodynamics and *DSM-III. Archives of General Psychiatry, 42,* 187–196.

Blashfield, R. K. (1984). *Classification of psychopathology.* New York: Plenum Publishing.

Blashfield, R. K., & Draguns, J. G. (1976a). Evaluative criteria for psychiatric classification. *Journal of Abnormal Psychology, 85,* 140–150.

Blashfield, R. K., & Draguns, J. G. (1976b). Towards a taxonomy of psychopathology: The purposes of psychiatric classification. *British Journal of Psychiatry, 129,* 574–583.

Boyd, J. H., Burke, J. D., Gruenberg, E., Holzer, C. E., Rae, D. S., George, L. K., Karno, M., Stoltzman, R., McEvoy, L., & Nestadt, G. (1984). Exclusion criteria of *DSM-III:* A study of co-occurrence of hierarchy-free syndromes. *Archives of General Psychiatry, 41,* 983–989.

Brockington, I. F., Kendell, R. E., & Leff, J. P. (1978). Definitions of schizophrenia: Concordance and prediction of outcome. *Psychological Medicine, 8,* 387–398.

Cantor, N., & Genero, N. (1986). Psychiatric diagnosis and a natural categorization: A close analogy. In T. Millon & G. Klerman (Eds.), *Contemporary directions in psychopathology: Towards the DSM-IV* (pp. 233–256). New York: Guilford Press.

Cantor, N., Smith, E. E., French, R., & Mezzich, J. (1980). Psychiatric diagnosis as prototype categorization. *Journal of Abnormal Psychology, 89,* 181–193.

Cantwell, D. P., Russel, A. T., Mattison, R., & Will, L. (1979). A comparison of *DSM-II* and *DSM-III* in the diagnosis of childhood psychiatric disorders. *Archives of General Psychiatry, 36,* 208–213.

Clarkin, J. F., Widiger, T. A., Frances, A., Hurst, S. W., & Gilmore, M. (1983). Prototypic typology and the borderline personality disorder. *Journal of Abnormal Psychology, 92,* 263–275.

Cloninger, C. R. (1987). A systematic method for clinical description and classification of personality variants. *Archives of General Psychiatry, 44,* 573–588.

Cloninger, C. R., Martin, R. L., Guze, S. B., & Clayton, P. (1985). Diagnosis and prognosis in schizophrenia. *Archives of General Psychiatry, 42,* 15–25.

Colby, K. M., & Spar, J. E. (1983). *The fundamental crisis in psychiatry.* Springfield, IL: Charles C Thomas.

Dohrenwend, B. P., & Dohrenwend, B. S. (1974). Social and cultural influences on psychopathology. *Annual Review of Psychology, 25,* 417–452.

Endicott, J., & Spitzer, R. L. (1978). A diagnostic interview: The Schedule for Affective Disorders and Schizophrenia. *American Journal of Psychiatry, 143,* 131–139.

Endicott, J., Spitzer, R. L., Fleiss, J., & Cohen, J. (1976). The Global Assessment Scale: A procedure for measuring overall severity of psychiatric disturbance. *Archives of General Psychiatry, 33,* 766–771.

Essen-Moller, E. (1961). On the classification of mental disorders. *Acta Psychatrica Scandinavia, 37,* 119–126.

Feighner, J. P., Robins, E., Guze, S., Woodruff, R. A., Winokur, G., & Munoz, R. (1972). Diagnostic criteria for use in psychiatric research. *Archives of General Psychiatry, 26,* 57–63.

Flach, F. (Ed.). (1987). *Diagnostics and psychopathology* (Vol. 1). New York: W W Norton.

Frances, A. (1982). Categorical and dimensional systems of personality disorder. *Comprehensive Psychiatry, 23,* 516–527.

Freedman, A. M., Brotman, R., Silverman, I., & Hutson, D. (Eds.). (1986). *Issues in psychiatric classification.* New York: Human Sciences Press.

Gardner, E. A. (1968). The role of the classification system in outpatient psychiatry. In M. M. Katz, J. O. Cole, & W. E. Barton (Eds.), *The role and methodology of classification in psychiatry and psychopathology.* Chevy Chase, MD: U.S. Department of Health, Education, and Welfare.

Goldenberg, H. (1977). *Abnormal psychology: A social/community approach.* Monterey, CA: Brooks/Cole.

Goldstein, G., & Hersen, M. (Eds.). (1984). *Handbook of psychological assessment.* Elmsford, NY: Pergamon Press.

Gunderson, J. G. (1982). Empirical studies of the borderline diagnosis. *American Psychiatric Association Annual Review, 11,* 414–437.

Gunderson, J. G., & Elliott, G. R. (1985). The interface between borderline personality disorder and affective disorder. *American Journal of Psychiatry, 142,* 277–288.

Hammond, W. A. (1883). *A treatise on insanity in its medical relations.* New York: Appleton-Century-Crofts.

Helzer, J. E., Clayton, P. J., Pambakian, R., Reich, T., Woodruff, R. A., & Reveley, M. A. (1977). Reliability of psychiatric diagnosis: II. The test/retest reliability of diagnostic classification. *Archives of General Psychiatry, 34,* 136–141.

Helzer, J. E., Robins, L. N., McEvoy, L. T., Spitznagel, E. L., Stoltzman, R. K., Farmer, A., & Brockington, I. F. (1985). A comparison of clinical and Diagnostic Interview Schedule diagnoses. *Archives of General Psychiatry, 42,* 657–666.

Helzer, J. E., Robins, L. N., Taibleson, M., Woodruff, R. A., Reich, T., & Wish, E. D. (1977). Reliability of psychiatric diagnosis: I. Methodological review. *Archives of General Psychiatry, 34,* 129–133.

Horowitz, L., Post, D., French, R., Wallis, K., & Siegelman, E. (1981). The prototype as a construct in abnormal psychology: 2. Clarifying disagreement in psychiatric judgments. *Journal of Abnormal Psychology, 90,* 575–585.

Horowitz, L., Wright, J., Lowenstein, E., & Parad, H. (1981). The prototype as a construct in abnormal psychology: 1. A method for deriving prototypes. *Journal of Abnormal Psychology, 90,* 568–574.

Hurd, H. M. (1881). A plea for systematic therapeutical, clinical and statistical study. *Journal of Insanity, 38,* 16–31.

Karno, M., Golding, J. M., Sorenson, S. B., & Burnam, A. (1988). The epidemiology of obsessive-compulsive dis-order in five U.S. communities. *Archives of General Psychiatry, 45,* 1094–1099.

Kendell, R. E. (1973). Psychiatric diagnoses: A study of how they are made. *British Journal of Psychiatry, 122,* 437–445.

Kendell, R. E. (1975). *The role of diagnosis in psychiatry.* Oxford: Blackwell Scientific Publications.

Kendell, R. E. (1986). What are mental disorders? In A. M. Freedman, R. Brotman, I. Silverman, & D. Hutson (Eds.), *Issues in psychiatric classification.* New York: Human Sciences Press.

Kendell, R. E., Cooper, J. E., Gourlay, A. J., Copeland, J. R. M., Sharpe, L., & Gurland, B. J. (1971). Diagnostic criteria of American and British psychiatrists. *Archives of General Psychiatry, 25,* 123–130.

Klerman, G. L. (1978). The evolution of a scientific nosology. In J. C. Shershow (Ed.), *Schizophrenia: Science and practice* (pp. 99–121). Cambridge, MA: Harvard University Press.

Korchin, S. J. (1976). *Modern clinical psychology.* New York: Basic Books.

Kraepelin, E. (1899). *Psychiatrie, ein lehrbuch fur studirende und aerzte* [Clinical psychiatry: A textbook for students and physicians] (6th ed., Vols. 1–2). Leipzig: Verlag von Johann Ambrosius Barth.

Kreitman, N. (1961). The reliability of psychiatric diagnosis. *Journal of Mental Science, 107,* 878–886.

Laing, R. D. (1967). *The politics of experience.* New York: Pantheon Books.

Last, C., & Hersen, M. (Eds.). (1987). *Issues in diagnostic research.* New York: Plenum Publishing.

Lefkowitz, M. M., & Burton, N. (1978). Childhood depression: A critique of the concept. *Psychological Bulletin, 85,* 716–726.

Leighton, D. C., Harding, J. S., Macklin, D. B., MacMillan, A. M., & Leighton, A. H. (1963). *The character of danger.* New York: Basic Books.

Livesley, W. J. (1985a). Classification of personality disorders: I. The choice of category concept. *Canadian Journal of Psychiatry, 30,* 353–358.

Livesley, W. J. (1985b). Classification of personality disorders: II. The problem of diagnostic criteria. *Canadian Journal of Psychiatry, 30,* 359–362.

Livesley, W. J., Reiffer, L. I., Sheldon, A. E. R., & West, M. (1987). Prototypicality ratings of *DSM-III* criteria of personality disorders. *Journal of Nervous and Mental Disease, 175,* 395–401.

Loranger, A. W., Susman, V. L., Oldham, J. M., & Russakoff, L. M. (1987). The Personality Disorder Examination: A preliminary report. *Journal of Personality Disorders, 1,* 1–13.

McCann, J. (1988). Passive-aggressive personality disorders: A review. *Journal of Personality Disorders, 2,* 170–187.

McLermore, C. W., & Benjamin, L. S. (1979). What happened to interpersonal diagnosis: A psychosocial alternative to *DSM-III. American Psychologist, 34,* 17–34.

Mezzich, J. E. (1978). Evaluating clustering methods for psychiatric diagnosis. *Biological Psychiatry, 13,* 265–281.

Mezzich, J. E., & von Cranach, M. (Eds). (1988). *International classification in psychiatry: Unity and diversity.* Cambridge: Cambridge University Press.

Millon, T., & Klerman, G. L. (Eds.). (1986). *Contemporary directions in psychopathology.* New York: Guilford Press.

Monroe, S. M., Thrase, M. E., Hersen, M., Himmelhoch, J. M., & Bellack, A. S. (1985). Life events and the endogenous-nonendogenous distinction in the treatment and posttreatment course of depression. *Comprehensive Psychiatry, 26,* 175–186.

Morrison, J., Clancy, J., Crowe, R., & Winokur, G. (1972). The Iowa 500: I. Diagnostic validity in mania, depression and schizophrenia. *Archives of General Psychiatry, 27,* 457–461.

Overall, J. E. (1963). A configural analysis of psychiatric diagnostic stereotypes. *Behavioral Science, 8,* 211–219.

Panzetta, A. F. (1974). Towards a scientific psychiatric nosology: Conceptual and pragmatic issues. *Archives of General Psychiatry, 30,* 154–161.

Parsons, R. D., & Wicks, R. J. (Eds.). (1983). *Passive-aggressiveness: Theory and practice.* New York: Brunner/Mazel.

Pinel, P. (1976). *Traite medico-philosophique sur l'alienation mental.* New York: Arno Press. (Original work published 1809)

Quay, H. C. (1986). A critical analysis of *DSM-III* as a taxonomy of psychopathology in childhood and adolescence. In T. Millon & G. L. Klerman (Eds.), *Contemporary directions in psychopathology* (pp. 151–165). New York: Guilford Press.

Ries, R., Bokan, J., & Schuckit, M. A. (1980). Modern diagnosis of schizophrenia in hospitalized psychiatric patients. *American Journal of Psychiatry, 137,* 1419–1421.

Robins, L. N., & Barrett, J. E. (1989). *The validity of psychiatric diagnosis.* New York: Raven Press.

Robins, L. N., Helzer, J. E., Weissman, M. M., Orvaschel, H., Gruenberf, E., Burke, J. D., & Reiger, D. A. (1984). Lifetime prevalence of specific psychiatric disorders in three sites. *Archives of General Psychiatry, 41,* 949–958.

Rush, B. (1962). *Medical inquires and observations upon the diseases of the mind.* New York: Hafner. (Original work published 1812)

Rutter, M., Lebovici, S., Eisenberg, L., Sneznevskij, A. V., Sadoun, R., Brooke, E., & Lin, T. Y. (1969). A tri-axial classification of mental disorders in childhood. *Journal of Child Psychology, Psychiatry and Related Disciplines, 10,* 41–61.

Rutter, M., & Shaffer, D. (1980). DSM-III: A step forward or back in terms of the classification of child psychiatric disorders? *Journal of the American Academy of Child Psychiatry, 19,* 371–394.

Rutter, M., Shaffer, D., & Shepherd, M. (1975). *A multi-axial classification of child psychiatric disorders.* Geneva: World Health Organization.

Schacht, T., & Nathan, P. E. (1977). But is it good for psychology? Appraisal and status of the *DSM-III. American Psychologist, 32,* 1017–1025.

Simons, R. C. (1987). Self-defeating and sadistic personality disorders: Needed additions to the diagnostic nomenclature. *Journal of Personality Disorders, 1,* 161–167.

Simpson, G. G. (1961). *Principles of animal taxonomy.* New York: Columbia University Press.

Skinner, H. A. (1986). Construct validation approach to psychiatric classification. In T. Millon & G. L. Klerman (Eds.), *Contemporary directions in psychopathology* (pp. 307–330). New York: Guilford Press.

Spitzer, R. L., Endicott, J., & Robins, E. (1975). *Research diagnostic criteria (RDC) for a selected group of functional disorders.* New York: New York State Psychiatric Institute.

Spitzer, R. L., & Fleiss, J. L. (1974). A re-analysis of the reliability of psychiatric diagnosis. *British Journal of Psychiatry, 125,* 341–347.

Spitzer, R. L., Williams, J. B. W., & Gibbon, M. (1987). *SCID: Structured clinical interview for DSM-III-R.* New York: New York State Psychiatric Institute.

Spitzer, R. L., Williams, J. B. W., & Skodol, A. E. (1979). *DSM-III:* A major achievement and an overview. *American Journal of Psychiatry, 137,* 151–164.

Spitzer, R. L., & Wilson, P. T. (1975). Nosology and the official psychiatric nomenclature. In A. Freedman, H. Kaplan, & B. Sadock (Eds.), *Comprehensive textbook of psychiatry.* Baltimore: Williams & Wilkins.

Sprock, J. (1988). Classification of schizoaffective disorder. *Comprehensive Psychiatry, 29,* 55–71.

Srole, L., Langner, T. S., Michael, S. T., Opler, M. K., & Rennie, T. A. (1962). *Mental health in the metropolis.* New York: McGraw-Hill.

Strauss, J. S., Gabriel, R. K., Kokes, R. F., Ritzler, B. A., VanOrd, A., & Tarana, E. (1979). Do psychiatric patients fit their diagnoses? Patterns of symptomatology as described with the biplot. *Journal of Nervous and Mental Disease, 167,* 105–113.

Szasz, T. S. (1961). *The myth of mental illness.* New York: Hoeber-Harper.

Tichler, G. L. (Ed.). (1987). *Diagnosis and classification in psychiatry: A critical appraisal of DSM-III.* Cambridge: Cambridge University Press.

Walker, L. E. (1987). Inadequacies of the masochistic personality disorder diagnosis for women. *Journal of Personality Disorders, 1,* 183–195.

Ward, C. H., Beck, A. T., Mendelson, M., Mock, J. E., & Erbaugh, J. K. (1962). The psychiatric nomenclature. *Archives of General Psychiatry, 7,* 198–205.

Warner, R. (1978). The diagnosis of antisocial and hysterical personality disorders: An example of sex bias. *Journal of Nervous and Mental Disease, 166,* 839–845.

Widiger, T. A., Frances, A., Warner, L., & Bluhm, C. (1986). Diagnostic criteria for the borderline and schizotypal personality disorders. *Journal of Abnormal Psychiatry, 95,* 43–51.

Wiggins, J. (1982). Circumplex models of interpersonal behavior in clinical psychology. In P. Kendell & J. N. Butcher (Eds.), *Handbook of research methods in clinical psychology* (pp. 183–221). New York: John Wiley & Sons.

Williams, J. B. W. (1986). *DSM-III-R:* What's all the fuss about? *Hospital and Community Psychiatry, 37,* 549–550.

Wing, T. K. (1978). *Reasoning about madness.* London: Oxford University Press.

Wing, J. K., Cooper, J. E., & Sartorius, N. (1974). *The description and classification of psychiatric symptoms: An instruction manual for the PSE and Catego System.* London: Cambridge University Press.

World Health Organization. (1967). *International classification of diseases* (8th ed.). Geneva: Author.

Zimmerman, M. (1988). Why are we rushing to publish *DSM-IV? Archives of General Psychiatry, 45,* 1135–1138.

Zimmerman, M., & Spitzer, R. L. (1989). Melancholia: From *DSM-III* to *DSM-III-R. American Journal of Psychiatry, 146,* 20–28.

Zubin, J. (1967). Classification of behavior disorders. *Annual Review of Psychology, 18,* 373–406.

CHAPTER 20

DIAGNOSTIC INTERVIEWING

Arthur N. Wiens

The lay definition of diagnosis is a careful investigation of the facts to determine the nature of a thing. Synonyms include terms like *distinguishing, discrimination,* and *discerning between.* The verb *diagnose* calls to mind terms like *estimate, forecast, gauge, predict,* and *project;* as well as terms like *analyze, assess, examine, probe, scope, solve, understand,* and *unravel.*

An important caveat to keep in mind when thinking about diagnosis in psychology and psychiatry is that in many respects we are still a long way from determining the nature of etiology, final classification, and predictive powers of various behaviors or mental illnesses. For these reasons, in many instances of diagnosis in psychiatry and psychology, the diagnoses presently in use are conventions to be adopted or discarded depending on whether they contribute usefully to functions of administration, treatment, research, or prevention. Like the term *disease,* or any other abstraction, a given diagnosis may not actually correspond to anything in nature; just as diseases have come and gone, the classification schemata called diagnoses that we presently use may not survive; more useful ones may emerge. Diagnostic nomenclatures represent current ways of thinking and communicating with each other. They should not be thought of as defining reality, which will continue to be increasingly approximated with future advances in scientific understanding.

Garfield (1986) made a similar point when he noted that during psychiatry's history, a number of designated mental illnesses have appeared in the various diagnostic classifications, only to recede later or to be replaced by new diseases or disorders. He noted that the most important mental disease when he was a graduate student, dementia praecox, has been replaced by schizophrenia. This does not necessarily mean that the disorder in question or the pathological behaviors have disappeared. Rather, it signifies a changed conceptualization and description of a segment or type of disordered behavior. He indicated that in some cases this is due to an increase in our knowledge of psychopathology. In others, it is due to changing theories or views.

EARLY HISTORY OF PSYCHIATRIC DIAGNOSIS

There is no better way to remind ourselves of the importance of and the evolving nature of diagnosis in psychology and psychiatry than to recall aspects of the history of psychiatric diagnosis. The word *diagnosis* is derived from the Greek preposition *dia* (apart) and *gnosis* (to perceive or to know). Thus, to know the nature of something requires at the same time distinguishing it from nonmembers of the class to which it belongs.

Diagnosis has a long history. As far back as 2600 B.C., what we now label melancholia and hysteria were described in Sumerian and Egyptian literature. The basic descriptions of a set of fairly global classifications appear to have changed little over several thousand years. These classifications include psychosis, epilepsy, alcoholism, senility, hysteria, and mental retardation (Wiens & Matarazzo, 1983).

The first official system for tabulating mental disorders in this country, used in the decennial census in 1840, contained only one category for all mental disorders and grouped together the idiotic and the insane. Much more diagnostic differentiation has followed. Since 1952, four editions of the *Diagnostic and Statistical Manual of Mental Disorders* (DSM) have been published. DSM-III included 18 major classifications and more than 200 specific disorders. DSM-III-R, published in 1987, was designed to provide further diagnostic criteria to improve the reliability of diagnostic judgments. The clinician's task is conceived to be to determine the presence or absence of specific clinical signs and symptoms and then to use the DSM-III-R criteria for making the diagnosis.

CLASSIFICATION AND DIAGNOSIS

Diagnostic systems abound. They are useful in communication purporting to reveal diseases in people, malfunctions in nuclear power plants, flaws in manufactured products, threatening activities of foreign enemies, collision courses of aircraft, and prior entries of burglars. Such undesirable conditions or events usually call for corrective action. Other diagnostic systems are used to make judicious selection among many units. They include the identification of job or school applicants who are likely to succeed, income tax returns that are fraudulent, oil deposits in the ground, criminal suspects who lie, and relevant documents in a library.

The aforementioned observations were made by John A. Swets (1988), who recognized that diagnostic systems are not perfectly accurate and suggested a methodology to measure their accuracy. Swets also called attention to efforts of scientists in many different fields of study, and application, to improve their diagnostic accuracy. Psychologists are in good com-

pany with their own such efforts. His paper also calls attention to the fact that the act of classification is basic to all science and to every other aspect of living. Accurate and reliable description that differentiates and predicts is the basis of hypothesis formation and testing in science (Wiens & Matarazzo, 1983). Classification makes it possible for us to discriminate days and nights, the seasons, edible and inedible foods, and so on; these are discriminations that we take for granted but that make survival possible. Diagnosis in clinical practice introduces order into the clinician's observations, with an attendant increase in meaningfulness and, ultimately, control (prevention and amelioration). Placing an object or organism or a set of behaviors into a certain class allows us to infer certain other characteristics of that same class without needing to demonstrate each characteristic *de novo*. Classification can also help to put individual observations into a different perspective or context, and stimulate new questions for better treatment, prevention, control, and future research (i.e., to help with theory building and thus better prediction and understanding).

Skinner (1986) noted that, in science, classifications generally evolve from the initial description of events to the formulation of underlying causal mechanisms or scientific theories. In the health sciences we may observe clinical syndromes and then try to explain them with causal mechanisms that are not observable (e.g., a virus). Such a process goes on in successive iterations until we reach an impasse beyond which we lack either the imagination or technical resources to go beyond.

Skinner noted that perhaps the best example of this stratification process is the periodic table of elements, which began with preliminary groupings (such as potassium and sodium) drawn from observations about their common characteristics. Mendeleyev formulated the periodic table, which was subsequently refined through understanding of atomic structure and chemical valency. Today, another stratum is being unveiled with evidence of subatomic particles.

In contrast to these impressive developments, progress has been much slower in the classification and understanding of psychiatric disorders. Skinner (1986) stated that there are three factors that should be emphasized in trying to understand why we have failed to penetrate lower strata in our understanding of psychiatric disorders. First, much of the theorizing in psychiatry and clinical psychology, such as psychoanalytic theory, is not couched in a form that is readily open to empirical evaluation and falsification. Secondly, there have been problems with the measurement or recognition of characteristic features of different disorders. In recent years, considerable effort has been directed toward upgrading the reliability of psychiatric diagnoses through the use of explicit operational definitions. Third, present diagnostic systems rely less on the presence of a known etiological agent (as in paresis caused by syphilis of the brain) and, instead, are largely based on consensual, operational features of individual disorders with much less emphasis on etiological concepts.

Sprock & Blashfield (1983) provided further conceptualization of the process of classification. Citing the work of Simpson (1961), they divided the study of classification into three areas. The first of these was taxonomy, by which they meant simply the theoretical study of classification without reference to particular content. The second was classification, which is the formation of groups or subsets from a larger collection of entities. The product of the process of classification is the classification system; a nomenclature is names of the categories and the technical terms to describe heuristically assumed entities. The list of terms in a nomenclature is independent of underlying characteristics of the categories or subsets. A classification system of diseases is called a *nosology*. The third area of study in a classification system is the process of identification, or assigning individuals or entities to categories in an existing classification system (i.e., diagnosis).

In further discussion of classification systems, Sprock & Blashfield (1983) noted that ideally categories are mutually exclusive and jointly exhaustive so that individuals fit into only one class, and defining features are either absent or present (monothetic). All real classification systems, however, are polythetic, meaning that defining features are present in partial form. In the study of diseases, nosologies may be complicated when a patient has more than one disease simultaneously, or recovers from one disease and subsequently has another.

Operational Definitions in Psychiatric Diagnosis

As Skinner noted (1986), classification in science generally begins with descriptions of events; this description precedes efforts to formulate underlying causal mechanisms or scientific theories. Empiricism in the mental health sciences is relatively recent, and the current era of operational definitions in psychiatric diagnosis probably began in the 1950s.

The current state of the art and science of differential diagnosis was discussed by Wiens and Matarazzo

(1983). Referring to the work of Spitzer and Williams (1980), they noted that these authors listed at least three purposes to be achieved in a classification of mental disorders. The first of these is communication. A classification schema must allow its users to communicate with each other about the disorders with which they deal. This is not too different from everyday thinking and communication, which is successful to the degree that we have some clear and firm definitions of words and word combinations. This is even more important in science because the material is more complex. The desired outcome of classification in clinical practice is to have terms that communicate a cluster of clinical features about a person without having to list each time all of the features that constitute a given diagnostic entity. In addition to a clear definition of terms, Spitzer and Williams pointed out that there must also be a high level of agreement among clinicians when the classification categories are actually applied to people.

A second purpose in classification is control in the service of the client. Ideally, the classification of a psychological dysfunction should include knowledge about how to prevent its occurrence or how to ameliorate it through treatment. As noted earlier, it has been difficult to derive therapeutic control or treatment implications from past diagnostic categories. Yet, when we look at the changes in diagnosis and treatment over a longer time span (e.g., 50 to 100 years), change and progress are indeed apparent.

The third purpose of classification is comprehension, which implies understanding the causes of mental disorders and the processes involved in their development and maintenance (Spitzer & Williams, 1980). It is recognized that treatment can often proceed effectively without knowledge of the cause of a particular disorder. However, comprehension is desired because it usually leads to better control of the disorder. The assertion that one does not need to know about diagnosis in order to treat carries the implicit assumption that there is no preferred treatment available. This assumption no longer appears tenable. Rather, the preferred assumption is that differential diagnosis does serve to identify patients with similar treatment responses and permits further search for meaningful relationships and differences among them.

There also are three assumptions that are often made when classification of mental disorders is conceptualized and are often thought to be necessary but are not (Spitzer & Williams, 1980). One of these assumptions is that there must be a biological abnormality or dysfunction within the organism to account fully for the condition. One can more reasonably assume that a mental disorder is the result of multiple factors. This assumption, incidentally, also holds true for most instances of physical illnesses. A second frequent, but unnecessary, assumption is that there is a discontinuity between a given mental disorder and other disorders, and between it and normality. There is obviously a continuum of severity for most disorders, and some conditions are defined as a disorder only after they reach a certain point (e.g., interpersonal or job impairment). A third frequent and unnecessary assumption is that there is homogeneity of psychopathology within each diagnostic category. Classification into any category only implies that persons in that category share certain characteristics used as defining features of that category. As Spitzer & Williams (1980) noted, Americans, Lithuanians, trees, and cats differ among themselves, yet within each group they share those features that qualify them for membership in those groups. This is equally true for persons falling within any one of our diagnostic categories. A person possesses some defining characteristic that allows classification into a given category, but may not possess other characteristics of that category or be exactly like another person similarly classified. In individual assessment and care, we obfuscate our thinking if we refer to a given patient as "the schizophrenic" rather than to "Mr. Jones, who had an acute schizophrenic episode following a job loss."

Reliability in Diagnosis

Reliable diagnosis in clinical practice and in the specific disorders of individual patients is not a simple matter. While global classifications of insanity have been recognized throughout all ages, the empiricism of the modern mental health sciences is much more recent. Because reliable diagnosis almost always must precede effective treatment, there is presently a great deal of interest in diagnostic classifications and interrater reliability and validity. A great deal of effort also went into the study of the reliability of DSM-III before it was introduced for general clinical use.

Spitzer and Williams (1980) reported that over 700 clinicians participated in several phases of the field trials using successive drafts of DSM-III. The last phase involved more than 500 clinicians participating in a formal field trial sponsored by the National Institute of Mental Health (NIMH). A large majority of these clinicians felt that DSM-III was an improvement over DSM-II, that the multiaxial system was a useful addition, that the diagnostic criteria are a major contribution, and that they agreed with the generally atheoretical approach taken in the description of the diagnostic categories.

In the phase-one reliability study, Spitzer, Forman, and Nee (1979) and Spitzer and Forman (1979) used volunteer clinicians from all parts of the country, including Hawaii. Each clinician was provided a working copy of DSM-III and was asked first to practice using it on 15 patients from his or her own patient population. Following this, the clinician, paired with another local clinician, was to carry out at least four reliability evaluations, with each clinician using each of the five axes in the evaluation. With few exceptions, the reliability interviews were conducted as part of the initial evaluation of a patient whom neither clinician had seen previously. As to format, the two clinicians could be present at the same evaluation, following which they independently recorded their judgments (joint interview method). If that was inconvenient, separate evaluations could be done, preferably within 1 day of the first interviewer's evaluation (test-retest interview method). Spitzer, Forman, and Nee (1979) reported that 40% of these test-retest interviews were done within 1 day of each other, whereas almost half had a test-retest interval of more than 3 days. In either format, both clinicians were instructed to make use of all the material available on the patient, such as case records, letters of referral, nursing notes, and family information.

In all, 274 clinicians, out of 365 recruited, participated in the phase-one field trial using the January 15, 1978, draft, and they collectively evaluated 281 adult patients in this first phase. A total of 71 children, under age 18, were evaluated in phase one. The overall kappa coefficient of agreement for Axis I diagnoses of 281 adult patients was .78 for joint interviews and .66 for diagnoses made after separate interviews. For Axis II, coefficients of agreement on the presence of a personality disorder were .61 (joint assessment) and .54 (test-retest). Spitzer, Forman, and Nee (1979) indicated that inasmuch as the kappa reliability coefficients are corrected for chance agreements, a reader may conclude that:

high kappa (generally .70 and above) indicates good agreement as to whether or not the patient has a disorder within that diagnostic class, even if there may be a disagreement about the specific disorder within the class. For example, diagnoses of paranoid schizophrenia by two clinicians would be considered agreement on schizophrenia. The overall kappa for the major classes of Axis I indicates the extent to which there is agreement across all diagnostic classes for all patients given an Axis I diagnosis by at least one of the clinicians and is thus an overall index of diagnostic agreement. (pp. 816–817)

In the companion article on the remaining data of this same phase-one study, Spitzer & Forman (1979) reported comparable data for Axis IV (stressors) and Axis V (adaptive functioning). Thus, for the same 281 patients interviewed by the same 274 clinicians, the kappa coefficient of agreement for Axis IV was .62 for joint interviews and .58 for separate test-retest interviews. Reliability for Axis V was even better: .80 for joint interviews and .69 for separate interviews. Importantly, for the acceptability of DSM-III among clinicians, Spitzer & Forman (1979) reported that 81% of the 274 clinicians participating "judged the multiaxial system to be a useful addition to traditional diagnostic evaluation, although many indicated that they had difficulty quantifying severity of psychosocial stressors" (p. 818).

As stated earlier, this phase-one study was followed by a phase-two study that employed a slightly improved version of DSM-III. The interested reader will find the kappa coefficients for the major and specific diagnostic categories that comprise Axes I and II, and the ratings that comprise Axes IV and V, in a sample utilizing adults and a second sample utilizing children and adolescents in three tables in an appendix to the 1980 manual (APA, 1980, pp. 467–472). These phase-two results are too numerous to discuss in summary fashion here. The following global statement may suffice, however, to indicate their magnitudes: "It is noteworthy that the reliability in general improved in Phase Two, perhaps due to refinements in the criteria used in Phase Two" (APA, 1980, p. 468).

In a thoughtful discussion on the reliability of psychiatric diagnosis, Garfield (1986) called attention to the problems of unreliability encountered in the past. Reflecting on his own experience, he noted that he participated in staff conferences in which the final diagnosis was conclusively settled by an eight-to-seven vote of the staff members present. He further observed that some staff had preferred diagnoses that have been offered with unusual frequency. Thus, when the incidence of diagnoses of patients in hospitals has differed from time to time, it has not been possible to know whether that reflected a change in the incidence of a particular illness or whether it reflected unreliability and variability in diagnostic performance. According to Garfield, the criteria for diagnoses in DSM-III are more clearly delineated and the rules more strictly set down than in DSM-II, but problems still remain.

Garfield (1986) noted that compared with DSM-I and DSM-II, DSM-III does appear to have higher reliability. The reliabilities secured by means of the kappa statistic for broad classifications such as schizophrenia or major affective disorders were generally good. However, the reliabilities for some other classifications were lower and much more variable. The reliability in the broad category of personality disorders was somewhat low (kappa = .56), and the kappas for specific personality disorders are low. In addition, the reliability of diagnosis of childhood disorder was not good. Garfield stated that in clinical diagnosis and practice the clinician usually wants to go beyond the diagnosis of broad classifications to specific disorders assuming that the more specific diagnosis carries implications for treatment and prognosis.

Garfield also raised another interesting issue: Namely, the more stringent the criteria for making a diagnosis, the more reliable the diagnosis should be; but the cost associated with this is that many patients may remain undiagnosed. He pointed out that whether this is a desirable outcome is a matter of value judgment (Garfield, 1986).

In the history of the development of DSM-III, reference is usually made to the earlier research-generated Feighner criteria (Feighner et al., 1972) and the Research Diagnostic Criteria (Spitzer, Endicott, & Robins, 1978). These research criteria were incorporated into the development of the DSM-III. Thus, Garfield (1986) noted that when diagnoses from the DSM-III system correlate highly with the Feighner criteria and the RDC systems, one should not be too surprised because they served as models for it. He called attention to the fact that there are other diagnostic systems extant (e.g., the Flexible System from the World Health Organization International Pilot Study of Schizophrenia and Schneider's first-rank symptoms), and when systems were compared with each other the intercorrelations ranged from −.21 to .89. Garfield observed that there are important differences between the diagnostic systems and that different numbers of patients will be diagnosed as cases of schizophrenia by the different criteria. He stated, "In the absence of a universally accepted definition or criteria of schizophrenia, it is impossible to decide which system is the most valid in diagnosing cases of schizophrenia" (Garfield, 1986, p. 105). He further observed that the range of symptomatology that is included within any given diagnostic category can be broad, and he wondered about the importance of the different symptomatic features. He stated that grouping together diverse groups of symptomatic behaviors has resulted in conflicting reports that have appeared in the research literature on diagnosis. An important area for future research is study of prognostic signs and specific subgroups appearing to have some uniqueness.

DIAGNOSIS (CLINICAL JUDGMENT) IN THE COURTROOM

Wiens and Matarazzo (1983) expressed concern that clinical psychologists and psychiatrists were disgracing themselves in the courtroom. They noted that experts from the mental health professions were routinely disagreeing with each other when they testified as expert witnesses in court trials. For example, almost without fail the expert called by the defense offered the opinion that the accused was legally insane, and the expert with similarly impressive credentials called by the prosecution offered the opinion that the accused was legally sane. In fact, they suggested that reliability and validity of psychological and psychiatric diagnoses in the past have been so poor that they have been of little value in legal proceedings. They felt that ambiguous diagnostic criteria probably were a major factor in discrepant expert testimony. With the more clearly defined 1980 DSM-III diagnostic criteria and attendant improvement in diagnostic reliability, both the pubic and the professional experts should be well served by more credible testimony.

Still, one should consider the cautionary statement included in the DSM-III-R manual, namely:

> The purpose of DSM-III-R is to provide clear descriptions of diagnostic categories in order to enable clinicians and investigators to diagnose, communicate about, study, and treat the various mental disorders. It is to be understood that inclusion here, for clinical and research purposes, of a diagnostic category such as Pathological Gambling or Pedophilia does not imply that the condition meets legal or other non-medical criteria for what constitutes mental disease, mental disorder, or mental disability. The clinical and scientific considerations involved in categorization of these conditions as mental disorders may not be wholly relevant to legal judgments, for example, that take into account such issues as individual responsibility, disability determination, and competency. (APA, 1987, p. xxix)

The insightfulness of this cautionary statement can be realized when reviewing the guidelines for the evaluation of mental impairments for disability determination for Social Security. First of all, there is explicit recognition that without the cooperation of psychiatrists and psychologists in the local communities, the disability program would be unable to give adequate service to those who seek a disability decision. Perhaps as many as 35 million people in the United States have some type of physical or mental disability; it is evident that this is an important practice arena.

Clinicians quickly learn, however, that impairment does not necessarily mean disability for Social Security purposes and that there is a system of concepts and procedures to learn to be an effective clinical consultant. Specific examination procedures are requested and specific impairment criteria are provided. There are even specific report requirements that have been set forth. The psychologist addresses questions of impairment and is not requested or allowed to make decisions about disability; that is a legal decision.

Despite the progress in arriving at more reliable diagnosis and the implementation of some guidelines for psychologists' participation in the legal arena, Ziskin and Faust (1988) and Faust and Ziskin (1988) concluded that studies show that professionals often fail to reach reliable or valid conclusions and that the accuracy of their judgment does not necessarily surpass that of laypersons, thus raising substantial doubt that psychologists or psychiatrists meet legal standards for expertise (Faust & Ziskin, 1988).

Their standards for expert status are twofold. First, the expert must be able to state opinions with reasonable medical certainty, which they interpret to mean "pretty likely accurate." Then they noted that psychiatry has been continuously plagued by difficulties in achieving reliable classification (i.e., diagnosis). Their second standard is that an expert should be able to help the judge, or jury, reach a more valid conclusion than would be possible without the expert's testimony. Their conclusion is that studies show that professional clinicians do not, in fact, make more accurate clinical judgments than lay persons.

The editor of *Science* (Koshland, 1988) noted increasing use of scientific evidence in the courtroom. On the one hand, evidence based on scientific data can often be decisive, as is the case with the new DNA fingerprinting procedures. On the other hand, the data can be controversial, as in cases in which psychiatrists argue over pleas of not guilty by reason of insanity. Koshland expressed concern over psychiatrists and others who serve as so-called expert witnesses, frequently appearing on opposite sides of a case and preparing contradictory interpretations with apparent confidence. He felt that a solution might lie in the development of a "scientific qualifying examination" (p. 993). For example, professional societies could help in calibrating the reliability and specificity of scientific evidence and identify areas in which the use of diagnostic procedures are appropriate, as well as those in which they are not. Psychologists might identify those areas of mental aberration in which conduct can be predicted and also be willing to expose those who claim certainty when the data indicate otherwise. Koshland (1988) noted,

> It is clear that not every biochemical test is accurate and every psychological test questionable. What is needed is to pinpoint areas in which reliable predictions can be made in each field. Otherwise, the misleading assertions of self-appointed experts will prejudice the use of scientific evidence when it could be helpful. (p. 993)

Other writers have offered additional criticisms of the Faust & Ziskin article in *Science*. Hoge and Grisso (1988), commenting on legal standards for the admissibility of expert testimony, noted that Faust and Ziskin concluded that there are two essentials to be considered in the admissibility of scientific testimony: (a) Opinions must be held to a reasonable medical certainty, which they take to mean "pretty likely accurate"; and (b) the testimony must help the court reach a more valid conclusion. Regarding the first point, legal analysis suggests that the court is interested in testimony that is deduced from a well-recognized scientific principle or discovery; namely, the thing from which the deduction is made must be sufficiently established to have gained general acceptance in the particular field in which it belongs. What must be generally accepted by the field is "the thing from which the deduction is made," not the deduction itself. Thus, "reasonable medical certainty" is ineptly paraphrased as "pretty likely accurate" by Faust and Ziskin (1988, p. 31), again suggesting that the goal is a high level of certainty that the expert's opinion is correct. "Reasonable medical certainty" has legally been consistently interpreted as referring to the degree of confidence the clinician places in his or her opinion, not to the underlying accuracy or scientific basis (Hoge & Grisso, 1988).

Professionals would wish not to foist unreliable opinions on the courts, but the judicial system often asks the mental health professional to go beyond the self-imposed limit of general acceptance and, for example, make predictions of future violence in the absence of conclusive research. Hoge and Grisso (1988) noted:

> The courts' desire to hear the opinions of professionals is especially apparent in testimony on forensic assessments, when professionals are asked to answer the ultimate legal question. Ultimate legal questions never correspond to clinical diagnoses and are related to issues of morality, justice, and social policy rather than science. While leaders in the field of forensic mental health generally agree that clinicians in pro-viding assistance to the legal system should stop short of answering the ultimate legal question (for example whether the defendant is criminally responsible), most courts not only permit but sometimes insist on experts answering it. Inevitably, this results in contamination of clinical opinion, which reflects special expertise, with value judgments which do not. (p. 2)

Faust and Ziskin suggested that clinical conditions (diagnoses) do not necessarily correspond to legal concepts such as competency to stand trial or lack of criminal responsibility. We think most clinicians would agree. Mental health experts' clinical opinions do not have to answer the legal questions of competence or criminal responsibility in order to provide valid assistance to courts. A useful and proper role is to acknowledge the reliability of such judgments and then to describe the relevant abilities, disabilities, symptoms, and diagnostic conditions in clinical and behavioral terms, leaving the court to weigh these observations against legal concepts and standards.

From a legal perspective, Faust and Ziskin hold mental health experts to a different standard than one imposed on other medical and nonmedical experts. They asserted that mental health testimony must be accurate, whereas legally what is required is the field's general acceptance of a theory, concept, test, or method before an expert can rely on it for arriving at an opinion entered into evidence.

Faust and Ziskin argued that mental health professionals' clinical diagnoses are too unreliable to be admitted as evidence at trial. In other words, diagnoses are so inaccurate that the field of mental health should not even be allowed to set its own threshold of general acceptance. These are serious charges, and the credibility of psychiatrists and psychologists as expert witnesses may suffer if they are left unanswered (Hoge & Grisso, 1988).

Russ Newman (1989), in commenting on Faust and Ziskin (1988), observed that testimony offered by mental health experts plays a useful role in the courtroom. Newman also drew a distinction between legal decisions and clinical observations and diagnoses. He acknowledged that precise predictability of behavior is not possible, but then he noted that that is not the determining factor in whether testimony by a mental health professional will be useful in the courtroom. He asserted that the more that the judge or jury can know or understand about the defendant's behavior, the better off they will be in making legal decisions. It would seem self-evident, Newman argued, that neither judges nor jurors have the degree of knowledge of an individual's mental functioning that mental health experts have.

Newman (1989) suggested a number of considerations to keep in mind. First, focusing on things like the reliability of diagnostic labels results in a myopic view of the courtroom process, which at best misses the point and at worst contributes to an unnecessary public discrediting of the mental health professions. Second, mental health professionals must take heed of the research that delineates their limitations and endeavor to stay within the limits of their expertise, while at the same time working to develop better techniques and skills to expand their limits. Third, the existence of limitations, which prevents experts from being 100% certain, does not rule out the usefulness of mental health expert testimony.

Faust and Ziskin (1988) did hold out some hope for help to the courtroom process through actuarial methods, which eliminate the human judge and base conclusions solely on empirically established frequencies and correlations. In their view, the expert would then simply advise the court whether an actuarial procedure is applicable to the particular examinee and question of interest. The expert's involvement should end in the explanation of the actuarial procedure.

CLINICAL VERSUS ACTUARIAL JUDGMENT

Paul Meehl (1954) introduced the issue of clinical versus actuarial judgment to a broad range of social scientists in 1954, and his lucid exposition stimulated a great deal of research on this topic. Dawes, Faust, and Meehl (1989) reviewed much of this research and concluded that research comparing these two approaches shows the actuarial method to be superior. Clinical diagnosticians must be aware of these research findings and face a significant challenge in planning how to incorporate them into their clinical practices.

Faust and Ziskin (1988) also addressed the topic of factors limiting clinical judgment. They noted, to begin with, that mental health practitioners are limited by the state of their science in that psychology lacks a formalized, general theory of human behavior that permits accurate prediction. One example that they cited is that there are dozens of personality theories and hundreds of approaches to psychotherapy. More specifically regarding limitations in clinical judgment, they suggested that clinicians often underuse information about the frequency of occurrence, or base rates. For example, if a suicide indicator occurs in 80% of true cases and 10% of negative cases, and if suicidal intent is present in 1 per 1,000 patients, the one patient will likely be identified correctly by such a

suicide indicator, but about 99 will be misidentified. Faust and Ziskin expressed concern that clinicians often overvalue supportive evidence and undervalue counterevidence. Clinicians expect to and typically find evidence of abnormality in individuals they examine, even normal persons. Faust and Ziskin also noted that clinicians often practice under conditions that do not promote experiential learning; that is, they often receive little or no outcome information or feedback about their judgments. With reference to psychotherapy outcome, it is usually the satisfied patients who may make follow-up contact with the clinician to express their satisfaction. Patients who were unhappy with the clinician's judgments may simply absent themselves from further contact.

Dawes et al. (1989) made clear that clinical judgment should not be equated with a clinical setting or a clinical practitioner. A clinician in psychiatry, psychology, or medicine may use the clinical or actuarial method. The definition of the clinical method is that the decision maker combines or processes information in his or her head. In the actuarial or statistical method, the human judge is eliminated and conclusions rest solely on empirically established relations between data and the condition or event of interest. According to Dawes et al.,

> the actuarial method should not be equated with automated decision rules alone. For example, computers can automate clinical judgments. The computer can be programmed to yield the description "dependency traits," just as the clinical judge would, whenever a certain response appears on a psychological test. To be truly actuarial, interpretations must be both automatic (that is, prespecified or routinized) and based on empirically established relations. (1989, p. 243)

Dawes et al. (1989) also stated that virtually any type of data is amenable to actuarial interpretation. Qualitative observations (e.g., patient appears withdrawn) can be coded quantitatively and incorporated into a predictive equation. Actuarial output statements can be written for virtually any prediction of human interest.

A well-known example of actuarial prediction is the Goldberg rule in differentiating neurosis from psychosis on the Minnesota Multiphasic Personality Inventory (MMPI). (The following research is noted with an important caveat to the reader: Namely, the research was done during the years when clinical diagnoses, as noted earlier, were not as reliably made as they are now. It would be of interest to know whether the same findings would obtain if the research were done with present-day clinical diagnostic procedures. Nonetheless, the Goldberg research is of considerable interest.) Goldberg (1965) showed that the most effective rule for distinguishing psychosis from neurosis is simple: Add scores from three scales and then subtract scores from two other scales. A cutting score was selected; if the sum falls below 45, the patients is diagnosed neurotic, and if above 45 the patient is diagnosed psychotic. The criterion diagnosis was the patient's discharge diagnosis. The decision rules were then applied to new cases and also compared with clinical judges. In each of seven different settings, the Goldberg rules performed as well as or better than clinical judges. In another study, judges were given training packets and even the outcome of the Goldberg rule for each MMPI and were free to use the rule when they wished. Judges generally made modest gains in performance, but none could match the rule's accuracy; every judge would have done better by always following the rule. In an interesting further elaboration of this research, Goldberg (1970) constructed mathematical models of the judges' decision making. In principle, if a judge weights variables with perfect consistency, the same data will always lead to the same decision and the model will always reproduce the judge's decision. Goldberg found that the judges were not always consistent, and in cases of disagreement the models were more often correct than the judges on whom they were based. Dawes et al. (1989) noted that the perfect reliability of the models likely explains their superior performance in this and related studies. After reviewing a sample of 100 studies that showed the superiority of actuarial decision making in almost every case, Dawes et al. (1989) concluded that the actuarial advantage is general and likely encompasses even judgment tasks not yet studied. They felt that there is no other body of research in psychology in which the findings are coming out as uniformly as they are in the studies of clinical versus actuarial prediction.

In thinking about factors underlying the superiority of actuarial methods, Dawes et al. (1989) noted, first, that actuarial procedures, unlike the human judge, always lead to the same conclusion for a given data set. Second, the mathematical features of actuarial methods ensure that variables contribute to conclusions based on their actual predictive power and relation to the criterion of interest. Individuals often have difficulty distinguishing valid and invalid variables and may develop false beliefs in association between variables. Clinicians often do not obtain immediate feedback on the validity of their diagnoses. Self-fulfilling prophecies may come into play as when prediction of an outcome leads to decisions that

influence or bias that outcome. The clinician may also be exposed to a limited or skewed sample of humanity and, without exposure to truly representative samples, may not be able to determine relationships among variables. One cannot determine whether a relation exists unless one also knows whether the sign occurs more frequently among those with, versus those without, the condition. As Dawes et al. (1989) pointed out, if 10% of brain-damaged individuals make a particular response on a psychological test and only 5% of normals, but 9 of 10 clinic patients are not brain damaged, most patients who show the feature will not be brain damaged.

Although surpassing clinical methods, actuarial procedures are also fallible and sometimes can achieve only modest results. They need to be periodically reevaluated, and they need to be established for each new setting. Reevaluation is aided by the fact that actuarial methods are explicit and can be subjected to informed criticism and be made freely available to other members of the scientific community who might wish to replicate or extend research. Clinician-researchers must lament with Dawes et al. (1989) that the research on clinical versus statistical judgment has had so little impact on everyday decision making, particularly within its field of origin, clinical psychology. Although of demonstrated value, actuarial interpretation of interviews is still rarely used. As relevant research findings accumulate, actuarial interpretation will be relied on more heavily in the future. When actuarial methods prove more accurate than clinical judgment, the benefits to individuals and society are apparent. Much would be gained, for example, by increased accuracy in the prediction of violent behavior and parole violation, the diagnosis of disorder, and the identification of effective treatment (Dawes et al., 1989). Even lacking any outcome information, it is possible to construct models of judges' decision making that will likely surpass their clinical judgment accuracy.

CLINICAL INTERVIEW

Despite the plea for a more actuarial approach to clinical decision making, it must be acknowledged that most clinicians still rely on the clinical interview in their assessment of patients. We now turn our attention to trying to understand why that might be the case.

Many clinicians have been heavily influenced by earlier psychoanalytic thought that placed considerable emphasis on the indirect techniques of interviewing and a free-flowing exchange between the clinician and patient. Generally, such unstructured interviews allow the clinician freedom to reword questions, to introduce new questions, to modify question order, and to follow patients' spontaneous sequence of ideas. It is often assumed that such spontaneous discussion allows patients to follow more nearly their natural train of thought and may allow them to bring out interview material that is more predictive of what they would say or do in real-life situations. The flexibility of the unstructured interview allows clinicians to adapt their techniques to patients' particular situations. In some cases the interviewer may omit topics that do not seem applicable, and in other cases he or she may introduce related topics not originally planned (e.g., that may be unique to that patient's history). Many readers may have watched skilled clinician-interviewers elicit previously hidden facts, using attention to conflicts, dysphoric affects, defenses used by the patient, and symptom origins.

Experienced clinicians often assume that they can maintain best rapport with patients by formulating questions in words that are familiar to patients and habitually used by them, and by pursuing topics when patients indicate a readiness and willingness to discuss them. It is usually assumed that the unstructured clinical interview gives more discretion to the clinician in formulating the wording and sequence of questions in this way, and accordingly it requires a higher level of experience, skill, and training than is required in following a more standardized interview format. Required in particular are an overall conceptual grasp of theoretical context and considerable prior knowledge of the subject matter of the interview.

While clinicians may have espoused a spontaneous interview style, most experienced clinicians have adopted a semistandardized interviewing style or format. If one listens to a clinician interviewing a series of patients, one soon discerns topic areas that he or she routinely introduces and questions that he or she asks in almost the same way of every patient.

Furthermore, the topics to be covered in an initial clinical interview are relatively consistent from one clinician to the next. The general objective is to obtain a careful history that can be the foundation for the diagnosis and treatment of the patient's disorder (Kaplan & Sadock, 1988). More specific objectives of the clinical interview are to understand the individual patient's personality characteristics, including both strengths and weaknesses; to obtain insight into the nature of their relationships with those closest to them, both past and present; and to obtain a reasonably comprehensive picture of the patient's development from the formative years until the present.

In preparing a written record of a clinical interview, most clinicians begin by presenting identifying information such as the patient's name, age, marital status, sex, occupation, race, place of residence and circumstances of living, history of prior clinical contacts, and referral and information sources. The chief complaint, or the problem for which the patient seeks professional help, is usually reviewed next and is stated in the patient's own words or in the words of the person supplying this information. The intensity and duration of the presenting problem is noted, specifically the length of time each symptom has existed and whether there have been changes in quality and quantity from a previous state. It is also useful to include a description of the patients's appearance and behavior. In reviewing present illness or presenting problem, the clinician looks for the earliest and most disabling behavior or symptoms and whether there were any precipitating factors leading to the chief complaint. Often the precipitating or stress factors associated with the onset of symptoms may be subtle and require the clinician to draw on knowledge of behavior and psychopathology to help with inquiry regarding relevant life change events. The clinician should also report on how the patient's problems have affected his or her life activities. It is important to review past health history for both physical and psychological problems; for example, physical illnesses that might be affecting the patient's emotional state. Prior episodes of emotional and mental disturbances should be described. The clinician also needs to inquire about and report prescribed and nonprescribed medication and alcohol and drug use. Possible organic mental syndromes must be noted. Personal and social history usually includes information about the patient's parents and other family members and any history of psychological or physical problems. The account of the patient's own childhood and developmental experiences may be detailed. Educational and occupational history is noted as well as social, marital, military, legal, and other experiences. The personal history should provide a comprehensive portrait of the patient independent of his or her illness (Siassi, 1984). The mental status examination is reviewed under the following headings: general appearance and behavior; mood, feelings, and affect; perception; speech and thought; sensorium and cognition; judgment; insight; and reliability. The section on initial impression or findings follows. This should include deductions made by the clinician from all sources available to this point regarding the patient's past history, description of the present problems, and results of the clinician's examination as determined from the mental status examination, results of psychological testing, contributions of family members and significant others, and so on. Finally, recommendations are presented about what kind of treatment the patient should receive for what problems and target symptoms.

Many chapters and books have been written on the clinical interview. Included are chapters by Wiens (1976, 1983) on assessment interviewing, a volume on diagnostic interviewing by Herson and Turner (1985), and an excellent volume on psychiatric interviewing by Shea (1988). The interested reader is encouraged to consult these sources and many others for information and guidelines on clinical assessment.

Topic areas to be covered are also relatively consistent among clinicians with different theoretical approaches. The interested reader may note commonalities between the description of the clinical interview and the assessment scheme that many behavioral interviewers refer back to (Kanfer & Saslow, 1969). These authors suggest examination of the following areas: analysis of the problem situation (including behavioral excesses, deficits, and assets); clarification of the problem situation that maintains the targeted behaviors; a motivational analysis; a developmental analysis (including biological, sociological, and behavioral spheres); a self-control analysis; an analysis of social relationships; and an analysis of the sociocultural-physical environment.

STRUCTURED INTERVIEWS

As reviewed in Wiens (1989), sources of diagnostic unreliability in diagnosis include criterion variance as well as information variance. With the publication of the Feighner diagnostic criteria and the Research Diagnostic Criteria (RDC), the issue of criterion variance was addressed.

Research efforts to reduce information variance (the second most important source of unreliability) led to the development of structured clinical interviews, which reduce that portion of the unreliability variance based on different interviewing styles and coverage. That is, the development of the RDC criteria did not assure that clinicians in other settings would know how to elicit the necessary information from a clinical interview to permit them to apply the interview information to the diagnostic criteria. Importantly, the RDC employs not only inclusion criteria that must be present (e.g., for depression the presence of sadness, poor appetite, sleep disturbances), but also exclusion criteria (e.g., the presence of specific kinds of delusions or hallucinations whose presence rules out the diagnosis of depression and helps rule in another

equally explicitly defined syndrome such as schizoaffective disorder, depressed subtype).

The development of both inclusive and exclusive criteria for the diagnosis of specific syndromes in the RDC criteria was an important development in the history of psychiatric and psychological classification. In following RDC, the clinician is required to use these criteria regardless of his or her own personal conception of the disorder and regardless of the type of interview being used to elicit the diagnostic information. However, this requirement presented a major methodological problem because the theoretical and clinical framework within which mental health clinicians elicited clinical information from the same patient varied so much from one clinician to another. That is, if clinicians of differing theoretical orientations (e.g., psychoanalytic, nondirective, pharmacobiological) each conducted the interview in their own idiosyncratic manner, there would be less likelihood that the resulting clinical information needed to apply a binary (yes-no) decision to one or another of the RDC criteria would have been elicited by each clinician from the same patient. To ensure that clinicians in the same or different settings would conduct interviews that would maximize the likelihood of obtaining necessary information to use the RDC criteria, it was necessary to develop an interview format that would structure or standardize the questions asked by each interviewer. The structured interview that was developed is only one of some 10 structured interview guides distributed through Biometric Research of Columbia University.

Siassi (1984) concluded that the structured psychiatric interview has already become the foundation of much modern clinical research and that the clinical psychiatric interview and mental status examinations, as used in the past, will likely be replaced in the future with the use of structured interview schedules for routine examinations. This shift is supported by trends toward the use of operational criteria for diagnosis, well-defined taxonomies, almost exclusive use of structured examinations in research settings, and the growing influence of clinician-researchers. Further, the demand for accountability has also forced a problem-oriented type of recordkeeping system in most institutions, with emphasis on branch-logic systems of psychiatric decision making, and progress notes that reflect resolution of symptom-syndromes and changes in problem status, rather than changes in psychodynamics. Finally, the impact of computers appears decisive in that they allow for efficient retrieval of information, unlike the clinician's specific narrative interviews. Computers can also be used to apply an algorithm to yield reliable diagnoses from raw data (Siassi, 1984).

The nature of a structured clinical interview is discussed by Edelbrock and Costello (1984), who noted that it is essentially a list of target behaviors, symptoms, and events to be covered and some guidelines or rules for conducting the interview and recording the data. Interview schedules vary in that some offer only general and flexible guidelines and others have strict and detailed rules (i.e., some are semistructured and others are highly structured. With the latter, wording and sequence of questions, recording responses, and rating responses are all specified and defined. The interviewer may be regarded as an interchangeable piece of the assessment machinery. Clinical judgment in eliciting and recording information is minimized and, given the same patient, and given the predetermined standardized set of questions asked, different interviewers of necessity obtain the same information.

However, clinical judgment and personal style play more of a role in the semistructured interview with more latitude about what is asked, how it is asked, and how it is recorded. Edelbrock and Costello (1984) suggested that both types of interviews have some advantages. Highly structured interviews reduce the role of clinical inference and interpretation in the assessment and diagnostic process, and they typically yield more objective and quantifiable raw data. Alternatively, semistructured interviews are less stilted and permit a more spontaneous interview that can be tailored to each patient's particular problem, including idiosyncratic material.

Edelbrock and Costello (1984) also concluded that structured interviews are here to stay, that they will become the standard assessment and diagnostic tools in clinical research and epidemiology, and that they will become more closely integrated into the training of mental health professionals and the delivery of service. They also predicted that the interview would continue to evolve along the lines of increasing specialization of purpose, coverage, age, range, degree of structure, and interviewer qualifications. As diagnostic taxonomies evolve and become more differentiated, structured interviews will necessarily change in terms of their content. We can also expect results obtained via structured interviews to precipitate change in the diagnostic systems. They noted another significant development: namely, the synergistic combination of structured interview data with data derived from other assessment methods such as checklists, rating scales, and self-report inventories. They expect multimethod assessment to yield a more com-

prehensive, reliable, and valid picture of the patient. Finally, they saw a significant trend toward computer-assisted diagnosis, especially the use of the computer to sift through numerous bits of data relevant to diagnostic decision making.

Computer-Assisted Interview

While psychological software has not kept pace with hardware development, the availability of new programs of interest to psychologists and other clinicians has been dramatic. Samuel E. Krug (1989) compiled a product listing that includes 451 programs designed to assess or modify human behavior. Of these listings, 44 are categorized as structured interviews. The products in this category almost always are designed to be self-administered.

One of the earliest proponents of automated computer interviewing, John H. Greist (1984), observed that clinician training, recent experience, immediate distractions, and foibles of memory are among the factors that may compromise our competence as diagnosticians. Further, he stated that in virtually every instance in which computer interviews and clinicians have been compared, the computer outperforms the clinician in terms of completeness and accuracy. Erdman, Klein, and Greist (1985) suggested that one appeal of computer interviewing is the ability of the computer to imitate, even if only to a limited degree, the intelligence of a human interviewer. Like a human interviewer, the computer can be programmed to ask follow-up questions for problems that the respondent reports and to skip follow-up questions in those areas of no problem. This branching capability leads to an interaction between computer and human (i.e., what happens in the interview depends on what the subject says). Thus, a computer interview can be tailored to the person using the program (e.g., not to ask a male subject about pregnancy). Of more interest, though, is the capacity to ask follow-up questions in the subject's own words and to compare responses from different points in the interview. While it has been asserted that computers cannot detect flat affect, Erdman et al. (1985) noted that it is possible to record simultaneously response latency and heart rate and use these variables to branch into questions and comments regarding emotional arousal. It does seem clear, however, that to date it has not been possible for the computer to report the many nonverbal cues that a human interviewer can observe and respond to. To balance the argument, however, it must be acknowledged that a human interviewer also remains oblivious to a great deal of information available in a two-person interaction.

Diagnostic Interview Schedule

Wiens (1989) reviewed a variety of structured interviewing and clinical data gathering procedures that are available to the present-day diagnostic clinician. The focus of this chapter is on only one of these procedures, the Diagnostic Interview Schedule (DIS).

The DIS (Robins, Helzer, Croughan, & Ratcliff, 1981) is a fully structured interview schedule designed to enable clinicians to make consistent and accurate DSM-III psychiatric diagnoses. It was designed to be administered by persons not professionally trained in clinical psychiatry or psychology, and all of the questions and the probes to be used are fully explained. It reminds interviewers not to omit critical questions and presents well-tested phrasing for symptoms that are difficult to explain or potentially embarrassing to patients. Questions about symptoms cover both their presence or absence and severity (e.g., taking medication for the symptoms, seeing a professional about the symptom, and having the symptom significantly interfere with one's life). In addition, the interview ascertains whether the symptom was explained entirely by physical illness or injury or as a complication of the use of medication, illicit drugs, or alcohol. The age at which a given diagnostic symptom first appeared is also determined along with the most recent experience of the symptom. These questions are designed to help determine whether a disorder is current (i.e., the last 2 weeks, the last month, the last 6 months, or the last year). Demographic information including age, sex, occupation, race, education, marital status, and history of treatment is also determined. Current functioning is evaluated by ability within the last 12 months to work or attend school, maintain an active social life, act as head or cohead of a household, and get along without professional care for physical or emotional problems.

Aside from a few open-ended questions at the start of the interview to allow the interviewee the opportunity to voice the chief complaint and to give the interviewer some background for understanding answers to close-ended questions, the interview is completely precoded. Symptoms assessed by the computer are precoded at five levels: (a) negative, the problem has never occurred; (b) present, but so minimal as to be of no diagnostic significance; (c) present and meets criteria for severity, but not relevant to the psychiatric diagnosis in question because every occurrence resulted from the direct or side effects of prescribed, over-the-counter, or illicit drugs or alcohol; (d) present and meets criteria for severity but not relevant to the psychiatric diagnosis in question because every occurrence resulted from medical illness or injury; and (e) present, meets criteria for severity, and is relevant to the psychiatric diagnosis under consideration.

The DIS has been translated into different languages, and its use is now underway, or planned, in about 20 different countries. Cross-national comparisons in psychiatric and psychological epidemiology are possible due to the growing number of population surveys in various countries that have used the DIS. Similarly, cross-cultural surveys of anxiety disorders and prevalence, and symptomatic expression and risk factors in alcoholism have been planned. Computerization of the DIS makes direct patient administration possible either in its entirety (18 sections) or one section at a time. The computer printout lists all DSM-III diagnoses for which the patient meets criteria. It also presents additional information about each diagnosis including the recency of symptoms, duration, and age of onset. In addition, the printout lists for the clinician what other diagnoses must be ruled out before this diagnosis can be assigned according to the DSM-III hierarchy.

BIOLOGICAL MARKERS IN DIAGNOSIS

Earlier in this chapter it was observed that, in science, diagnoses generally evolve from the initial description of events to the formulation of underlying causal mechanisms or scientific theories. We may observe clinical syndromes and then try to explain them with causal mechanisms that are not observable (e.g., a virus). Such a process goes on in each era until we reach an impasse beyond which a scientist lacks either the imagination or technical resources to go beyond. Progress has been quite slow both in the development of dependable classification systems in psychiatry and psychology as well as in establishing an understanding of causal mechanisms in the diagnoses that are agreed on. Clearly the initial effort has been on establishing reliability in diagnostic classification, and probably rightly so.

In a thought-provoking chapter, Meehl (1986) acknowledged that the careful delineation of the signs, symptoms, and course of a disorder so as to increase the reliability of classifying patients is desirable. However, he noted that there are instances in which changes in content or format that increase reliability may theoretically decrease validity. He cited an example of an effort to change the open-ended, unstructured format of Rorschach administration, which seemed to eliminate whatever slight validity the instrument has as usually administered. He noted that reliability and validity trade-offs can be somewhat complicated. Another example that he cited is that in a standard medical examination the general medical examination always includes blood pressure and not anthropometric determination of wrist width, despite the mediocre reliability of the former and $r = .98$ for the latter. He added,

> We simply say, "Blood pressure unreliably measured is a stronger indicator of more different and important conditions than wrist width reliably measured." Similarly, a psychotherapist who employs dream interpretation . . . would not seriously consider substituting reliably scorable multiple-choice inquiry for free association. (Meehl, 1986, p. 216)

Meehl (1986) further observed that organic diseases are defined by a conjunction of their etiology and pathology when these are known, and otherwise they remain simply as syndromes to be further researched to be medically understood. We must be careful not to make a literal identification of a disease entity with its currently accepted signs and symptoms.

Thinking in terms of underlying pathology correlates of personality structure, one might consider genetic dispositions such as anxiety conditionability, rage readiness, hedonic capacity, general intelligence, and the like and the learning history imposed on an organism whose varied behavior acquisition functions are characterized by inherited parameters. Meehl added, "Our problem in psychopathology of the so-called functional behavior disorders is obvious, to wit, that we do not possess an equivalent to the pathologist's and microbiologist's report telling us the right answer at the conclusion of a clinicopathological case conference" (1986, p. 222). Meehl stated,

> To a thoughtful clinician with philosophical sophistication, it is perfectly obvious that disease syndromes are inherently open concepts. . . . Nothing but dogmatism on the one hand, or confusion on the other, is produced by pretending to give operational definitions in which the disease entity is literally identified with the list of signs and symptoms. Such an operational definition is a fake. (Meehl, 1986, p. 222)

There are some situations in which the sequential model of diagnosis, treatment formulation, and finally etiology have been shown to function in synergistic fashion. Khouri and Akiskal (1986) pointed out that the nosological boundaries of manic-depressive illness have been considerably broadened in the past few years, in part due to the availability of a relatively specific pharmacological agent for its treatment. They suggested that recent research has shown that some conditions, previously subsumed under schizophrenic, neurotic, and personality disorder rubrics, represent variants of manic-depressive illness and that such findings have led to a formulation in which bipolar illness is viewed as a spectrum of disorders, from the temperamental to the psychotic (Khouri & Akiskal, 1986, p. 457). They stated that research evidence supports a partial return to Kraepelin's broad concept of manic-depressive illness and that there is genetic and neurobehavioral support for this formulation. They noted the following: (a) shared core phenomenological disturbances: In the bipolar spectrum, cyclical fluctuations in mood and circadian functions of sleep, libido, appetite, and psychomotor activity span a spectrum from the paranoid, disorganized manic to the episodically and intermittently depressed individual with pharmacologically mobilized hypomania; (b) overlapping family histories with increased risks of other spectral disorders for each discrete entity within the spectrum; (c) shared response to the same pharmacological agents; and (d) neurobiological abnormalities such as shortened rapid eye movement (REM) latency and cholinergic supersensitivity. These appear shared by almost all the phenotypes within the bipolar spectrum (Khouri & Akiskal, 1986). Using trait markers, they would hope to identify milder phenotypes of bipolar disorder for earlier treatment intervention with the ultimate purpose of halting their progression to more seriously disruptive mood swings.

Karson, Kleinman, and Wyatt (1986) observed that the notion that mental illness has its origin in neurochemical events has been embraced by leading neuropsychiatrists for over a century. The successful pharmacological treatment of mental illness has subsequently lent support to the hypothesized link between biochemistry and psychiatric illness. A noteworthy example that they cited is the dopamine hypothesis of schizophrenia, which is based, in part, on the antipsychotic and antidopaminergic properties of the neuroleptic medications. Their conclusion, however, is that although the pharmacological approach has yielded numerous hypotheses and therapeutic benefits, the integration of biochemistry and schizophrenia is a difficult endeavor perhaps because schizophrenia is a heterogeneous disorder, with some subgroups of patients that are biochemically deviant. It has been suggested that patients whose illness is characterized by positive symptoms are most likely to have dopaminergic hyperactivity, while patients with social and intellectual deterioration (negative symptoms or defect state) as the prominent clinical problems may have structural brain abnormalities. These authors concluded by noting that most of the neurochemicals of the human brain probably remain unknown. Perhaps the future rests with an approach that integrates biochemical, morphological, immunological, or viral concepts (Karson, Kleinman, & Wyatt, 1986).

Gold (1986) acknowledged that the DSM-III has enormous influence and that its diagnostic codes are used by all mental health providers whose services are reimbursable by insurance companies. However, he was concerned that it encourages its users to believe that behavioral symptoms necessarily mean something psychiatric and leads clinicians not to consider organic conditions that can mimic psychiatric illnesses. Further, he asserted that the DSM-III categories do not parallel the biological subtypes that are being revealed in laboratory research (as in biological differences among depressed people). In the case of depression, it is necessary to differentiate primary and secondary affective disorders and to recognize that systemic medical diseases, central nervous system (CNS) disorders, endocrine disorders, drug-induced disorders, and infections are major bases for secondary affective disorder. Gold suggested that at least 75 illnesses or conditions can cause symptoms of apparent mental disorder and, importantly, that psychiatric symptoms are often the first and only signs of a developing illness. In the diagnosis of cancer, he noted that many types of tumors throughout the body can exhibit mental symptoms, which may be the only symptoms to appear for weeks, months, or years. In fact, he asserted that anyone who has an abrupt personality change, depression without a history of mood disorders, or weight loss of greater than 20 pounds—or who is unresponsive to standard psychiatric treatment—should be evaluated for cancer or other mimickers (Gold, 1986). The most common mimickers of psychiatry, according to Gold (1986), are: (a) drug (illicit, prescribed, and over-the-counter) and alcohol reactions; (b) endocrine disorders; and (c) diseases of the CNS, infectious diseases, cancers, metabolic conditions, and nutritional and toxic disorders. Drugs, for example, must be considered in all psychiatric diagnoses, no matter how classically psychiatric the person may appear, because everyone takes them in one form or another. Since the brain is quicker to react than the rest of the body, mental and behavioral symptoms may outweigh organic signs as an indicator of reaction to environmental toxins. The generalization to be drawn for the construct of diagnosis, in the case of depression, is that no one can conclude that a patient is in the midst of a major depressive episode without first ruling out possible organic causes.

Related to this generalization is the obvious truism that symptoms, particularly emotional symptoms, are not specific. First, the patient report of something like depressive symptoms is colored by the emotion itself; and second, the depressive emotion may be related to infectious mononucleosis, a bad marriage, an enzyme deficiency, or other etiologies. Clearly, objective measures are needed to verify, or clarify, particular diagnoses. Laboratory tests have come to play a more important role in psychiatry in screening for medical illness, improving diagnostic reliability, monitoring treatment (especially through measurement of the blood levels of psychoactive drugs), and continuing research into mental illness. Kaplan and Sadock (1988) noted a number of neuroendocrine tests (used particularly in depression), tests for sexually transmitted diseases, tests to assess plasma levels of psychotropic drugs, electroencephalography, evoked potentials, radioisotope brain scanning, and tests of regional blood flow.

In a paper on brain imaging in psychiatry, Andreasen (1988, p. 1387) concluded that brain imaging offers a broad range of investigative techniques that fulfill the popular fantasy of being able to "read the mind," albeit in the form of "seeing the brain" both structurally and functionally. At present, brain imaging provides a modest amount of information that is useful in differential diagnosis, as in distinctions between depression and dementia. It has provided more information about possible pathophysiological mechanisms of major mental illnesses, including structural abnormalities in some forms of schizophrenia. Metabolic abnormalities, such as hypofrontality in schizophrenia or hyperfrontality in obsessional disorder, have also been observed. The long-term promise of brain imaging is substantial. It will permit the mapping of cerebral function in normal individuals so that we can achieve a better understanding of normal brain structure, physiology, chemistry, and functional organization. On the basis of this knowledge, the abnormalities underlying the major mental illness can also be mapped.

Andreasen's report gives further support to the hope that we are now at the threshold of important new knowledge of the relationships between neurochemical changes and behavior changes. The properties of behavior that are included in these new relationships may be different from those that form the content of current assessments.

Implications for Psychologists

Dale L. Johnson (1989) noted that there is a changing *zeitgeist* in the way the etiology of schizophrenia is viewed by mental health researchers in general. This change has come about because the evidence for a family environmental cause of schizophrenia has never been confirmed, whereas evidence for some form of brain dysfunction as an etiological agent has grown stronger in recent years. Theories of the origins of schizophrenia have adapted to technological advances. Obviously, it will be necessary to ascertain whether there are different forms of schizophrenia, or whether some forms of schizophrenia will show no brain dysfunction.

Johnson noted that psychoanalytic and social learning theories inadequately recognize the recent evidence regarding brain dysfunction. A simple medical model is also too limited because it does not deal adequately with the complex social and cognitive phenomena of schizophrenia. One must think in terms of a more comprehensive biopsychosocial model.

In terms of treatment, the implication for the schizophrenic patient is, in common with other patients who have impaired brain functions, that the patient is vulnerable to stress. Neuroleptic medication alone has its limitations, and therapies designed to resolve experience-based conflicts should be reserved for different groups of patients. The treatment of choice is to reduce environmental stress and to help the person develop coping abilities that will minimize the effects of stress. This will usually involve treatment settings that do not intensify stress and, instead, emphasize a high degree of predictability, order, and structure. In terms of assessment, using the Rorschach as an example, the focus is not on trying to identify underlying psychodynamic conflicts but rather whether the patient's responses reveal evidence of a thought disorder. Various behavioral assessment procedures might be predictive, and neuropsychological assessment should be routine.

The research in schizophrenia appears to be an example of the synergistic evolution of description of a phenomenon, the development of causal evidence or theory, and the further differentiation of the descriptive classification. Over time, such developments can be expected to take place with other diagnostic descriptors.

REFERENCES

American Psychiatric Association. (1980). *Diagnostic and statistical manual of mental disorders* (3rd ed.). Washington, DC: Author.

American Psychiatric Association. (1987). *Diagnostic and statistical manual of mental disorders* (3rd ed., revised). Washington, DC: Author.

Andreasen, N. C. (1988). Brain imaging: Applications in psychiatry. *Science, 239,* 1381–1388.

Dawes, R. M., Faust, D., & Meehl, P. E. (1989). Clinical versus actuarial judgment. *Science, 243,* 1668–1674.

Edelbrock, C., & Costello, A. J. (1984). Structured psychiatric interviews for children and adolescents. In G. Goldstein & M. Herson (Eds.), *Handbook of psychological assessment* (pp. 276–290). Elmsford, NY: Pergamon Press.

Erdman, H. P., Klein, M. H., & Greist, J. H. (1985). Direct patient computer interviewing. *Journal of Consulting and Clinical Psychology, 53,* 760–773.

Faust, D., & Ziskin, J. (1988). The expert witness in psychology and psychiatry. *Science, 241,* 31–35.

Feighner, J. P., Robins, E., Guze, S. B., Woodruff, R. A., Winokur, G., & Munoz, R. (1972). Diagnostic criteria for use in psychiatric research. *Archives of General Psychiatry, 26,* 57–63.

Garfield, S. L. (1986). Problems in diagnostic classification. In T. Millon & G. L. Klerman (Eds.), *Contemporary directions in psychopathology: Toward the DSM-IV* (pp. 99–114). New York: Guilford Press.

Gold, M. S. (1986). *The good news about depression.* New York: Bantam Books.

Goldberg, L. R. (Ed.). (1965). Diagnosticians vs. diagnostic signs: The diagnosis of psychosis vs. neurosis from the MMPI. *Psychological Monographs, 79*(9).

Goldberg, L. R. (1970). Man versus model of man: A rationale plus some evidence, for a method of improving on clinical inferences. *Psychological Bulletin, 73,* 422–432.

Greist, J. H. (1984). Conservative radicalism: An approach to computers in mental health. In M. D. Schwartz (Ed.), *Using computers in clinical practice: Psychotherapy and mental health applications* (pp. 191–194). New York: Haworth Press.

Hersen, M., & Turner, S. M. (1985). *Diagnostic interviewing.* New York: Plenum Publishing.

Hoge, S. K., & Grisso, T. (1988). Fryeing Faust and Ziskin. *Expert Opinion: A Newsletter of Forensic Mental Health Information for the Commonwealth, 2,* 1–7.

Johnson, D. L. (1989). Schizophrenia as a brain disease: Implications for psychologists and families. *American Psychologist, 44,* 553–555.

Kanfer, F. H., & Saslow, G. (1969). Behavioral diagnosis. In C. M. Franks (Ed.), *Behavior therapy: Appraisal and status* (pp. 417–444). New York: McGraw-Hill.

Kaplan, H. I., & Sadock, B. J. (1988). *Synopsis of psychiatry.* Baltimore: Williams & Wilkins.

Karson, C. N., Kleinman, J. E., & Wyatt, R. J. (1986). Biochemical concepts of schizophrenia. In T. Millon & G. L. Klerman (Eds.), *Contemporary directions in psychopathology: Toward DSM-IV* (pp. 495–518). New York: Guilford Press.

Khouri, P. J., & Akiskal, H. S. (1986). The bipolar spectrum reconsidered. In T. Millon & G. L. Klerman (Eds.), *Contemporary directions in psychopathology: Toward the DSM-IV* (pp. 457–471). New York: Guilford Press.

Koshland, D. E., Jr. (1988). A tale of two techniques. *Science, 242,* 993.

Krug, S. E. (1989). *Psychware sourcebook: 1988–1989.* Kansas City: Test Corporation of America.

Meehl, P. E. (1954). *Clinical versus statistical prediction: A theoretical analysis and a review of the evidence.* Minneapolis: University of Minnesota Press.

Meehl, P. E. (1986). Diagnostic taxa as open concepts: Metatheoretical and statistical questions about reliabiity and construct validity in the grand strategy of nosological revision. In T. Millon & G. L. Klerman (Eds.), *Contemporary directions in psychopathology: Toward the DSM-IV* (pp. 215–231). New York: Guilford Press.

Newman, R. (1989). Expert testimony in mental health useful in the courtroom. *Practitioner Focus, 3,* 12.

Robins, L. N., Helzer, J. E., Croughan, J., & Ratcliff, K. (1981). National Institute of Mental Health Diagnostic Interview Schedule. *Archives of General Psychiatry, 38,* 381–389.

Shea, S. C. (1988). *Psychiatric interviewing: The art of understanding.* Philadelphia: W B. Saunders.

Siassi, I. (1984). Psychiatric interview and mental status examination. In G. Goldstein & M. Hersen (Eds.), *Handbook of psychological assessment* (pp. 259–275). Elmsford, NY: Pergamon Press.

Simpson, G. G. (1961). *Principles of animal taxonomy.* New York: Columbia University Press.

Skinner, H. A. (1986). Construct validation approach to psychiatric classification. In T. Millon & G. L. Klerman (Eds.), *Contemporary directions in psychopathology: Toward the DSM-IV* (pp. 307–330). New York: Guilford Press.

Spitzer, R. L., Endicott, J., & Robins, E. (1978). Research diagnostic criteria. *Archives of General Psychiatry, 35,* 773–782.

Spitzer, R. L., & Forman, J. B. W. (1979). DSM-III field trials: II. Initial experience with the multiaxial system. *American Journal of Psychiatry, 136,* 818–820.

Spitzer, R. L., Forman, J. B. W., & Nee, J. (1979). DSM-III field trials: I. Initial interrater diagnostic reliability. *American Journal of Psychiatry, 136,* 815–817.

Spitzer, R. L., & Williams, J. B. W. (1980). Classification in psychiatry. In A. Kaplan, A. Friedman, & B. Sadock (Eds.), *Comprehensive textbook of psychiatry: III.* Baltimore: Williams & Wilkins.

Sprock, J., & Blashfield, R. K. (1983). Classification and nosology. In M. Hersen, A. E. Kazdin, & A. S. Bellack (Eds.), *The clinical psychology handbook* (1st ed., pp. 289–307). Elmsford, NY: Pergamon Press.

Swets, J. A. (1988). Measuring the accuracy of diagnostic systems. *Science, 240,* 1285–1293.

Wiens, A. N. (1976). The assessment interview. In I. Weiner (Ed.), *Clinical methods in psychology.* New York: John Wiley & Sons.

Wiens, A. N. (1983). The assessment interview. In I. B. Weiner (Ed.), *Clinical methods in psychology* (2nd ed., pp. 3–57). New York: John Wiley & Sons.

Wiens, A. N. (1989). Structured clinical interviews for adults. In G. Goldstein & M. Hersen (Eds.), *Handbook of psychological assessment* (2nd ed.). Elmsford, NY: Pergamon Press.

Wiens, A. N., & Matarazzo, J. D. (1983). Diagnostic interviewing. In M. Hersen, A. E. Kazdin, & A. S. Bellack (Eds.), *The clinical psychology handbook* (1st ed., pp. 309–328). Elmsford, NY: Pergamon Press.

Ziskin, J., & Faust, D. (1988). *Coping with psychiatric and psychological testimony* (Vols. 1–3). Venice, CA: Law and Psychology Press.

CHAPTER 21

CLINICAL OBJECTIVE PERSONALITY ASSESSMENT

Stephen E. Finn
James N. Butcher

Clinical objective personality assessment is clearly entering a new era. Since the publication of *The Clinical Psychology Handbook* in 1983, the Minnesota Multiphasic Personality Inventory (MMPI), the most widely used objective personality instrument, has been restandardized. Newer tests, such as the Millon Clinical Multiaxial Inventory (MCMI; Millon, 1983b), are now included in many clinical assessment batteries. In numerous settings, computers are now routinely used to administer, score, and even interpret objective personality tests. These and other changes may leave many psychologists confused and unsure in an area where they formerly felt secure and well versed. In this chapter we hope to reorient practicing psychologists to objective personality assessment by reviewing recent developments and evaluating their impact on clinical work.

USING OBJECTIVE PERSONALITY TESTS IN CLINICAL WORK

First the good news: The basics remain essentially the same. Let us start by reviewing the uses of objective personality tests with clinical populations.

While many of these points will be familiar and have been elaborated elsewhere (cf. Butcher & Finn, 1983), we offer new thoughts and illustrations from recent research. With this framework in place, we then consider recent trends in clinical objective personality assessment.

Assessing Psychiatric Diagnosis

Probably the most common reason for using objective personality tests in clinical work is to obtain information about psychiatric diagnosis or abnormal personality traits. Thus, a psychiatrist may request testing on a client to determine whether certain symptoms constitute schizophrenia or bipolar affective disorder. Or an alcohol treatment program may routinely screen clients with the MMPI for antisocial personality disorder because of the program's history of negative results with such clients. In such instances, the objective personality test is often viewed by the referring professional much as a blood test is in medical diagnosis: an independent source of information that infallibly indicates the real diagnosis.

Unfortunately, such a view may be misguided. As we have indicated elsewhere (Butcher & Finn, 1983), objective tests are best seen as a way of generating diagnostic and trait hypotheses about clients. These hypotheses are not infallible. However, they are useful because objective tests make different types of errors than do diagnostic interviews or other assessment procedures. Because objective personality tests are imperfect, their results must always be carefully confirmed or integrated with information from the diagnostic interview, family history, and other tests. When independent sources of information converge, a diagnostic inference may be made with confidence. When objective testing disagrees with other diagnostic procedures, the psychologist is challenged to integrate these conflicting results, taking into account the known biases and shortcomings of the various sources of information.

For example, a clinical psychologist is consulted to determine the level of disturbance of a patient involuntarily hospitalized in a psychiatric setting. By interview, the patient denies any serious symptomatology, and an MMPI is within normal range, with the exception of a slight elevation on the Depression scale. The Rorschach, however, suggests serious psychopathology, with prominent thought disturbance and suicidal tendencies. The most parsimonious explanation of these results is that this patient is managing to conceal serious pathology (with the exception of whatever incident led to his hospitalization).

At first glance, this may seem like an instance where objective personality assessment fails to make a valid diagnosis. Consider, however, the useful information that is gained from the normal MMPI results. The psychologist knows that this patient attempts to present himself as having dysthymic symptomatology, that he manages to hide more serious psychopathology in relatively structured situations requiring limited responses, and that he fails to hide it in less structured situations such as when responding to the Rorschach. Finally, the admission of some distress on the MMPI suggests an opening for the psychologist to begin discussing this man's problems with him.

This kind of multistep thinking is difficult to adopt; it seems a natural tendency is to ask, "Is this test result right or wrong?" rather than "How is this test result informative?" We often explain to consulting psychiatrists that the MMPI may be most useful when it suggests a different conclusion than they reached from an interview. After all, if objective tests always simply confirmed what was known by interview, there would be little purpose in using them.

Choosing an Appropriate Treatment Plan

Implicit in the search for diagnostic information is the goal of matching clients and appropriate treatments. Thus, objective personality testing may be requested to clarify whether a client is manifesting schizophrenia or bipolar affective disorder, with hopes of choosing between lithium or neuroleptic medication. Or clients showing signs of severe personality disorder on objective tests may be screened out of a treatment program offering short-term, insight-oriented psychotherapy.

Nevertheless, diagnosis and treatment planning are separate uses of objective personality tests, since treatment choice may be mediated by other information than psychiatric diagnoses. For example, Simons, Lustman, Wetzel, and Murphy (1985) found that the optimum treatment for depressed patients depended on their score on Rosenbaum's (1980) Self-Control Scale. Subjects scoring high on the Self-Control Scale had a better treatment response when randomly assigned to cognitive therapy. Subjects with low scores on the Self-Control Scale did better with a regimen of nortriptyline. Self-Control scores are not directly related to psychiatric diagnosis; however, they appear to predict treatment response.

Even when treatment response can be related to psychiatric diagnoses, it may be useful to predict it directly from objective personality test scores rather than to determine diagnosis first. For instance, over the years researchers have identified reliable subgroups of alcoholic patients using the MMPI (cf. Graham & Strenger, 1988, for a review). Sheppard, Smith, and Rosenbaum (1988) reported a relationship between three of these MMPI subgroups and continuance in a residential alcoholism treatment program. Patients in one cluster type were substantially more likely to drop out of residential treatment than were patients in the other subgroups. Sheppard et al. could have predicted treatment response just as well using *Diagnostic & Statistical Manual of Mental Disorders, Third Edition* (DSM-III) diagnoses. However, it may be more cost-effective to use the MMPI to predict continuance in this type of treatment.

We have found that the process of objective personality assessment can be as important as the content of test results in making treatment recommendations. A client who is resistant and noncooperative with objective personality testing is likely to be noncompliant with other aspects of treatment as well. A client who is threatened by even basic information offered in an

MMPI feedback session is probably not a good candidate for insight-oriented therapy. Objective personality tests may provide the clinical psychologist with a wealth of information relevant to choosing a treatment plan for a specific client.

Making a Therapeutic Impact

A little recognized aspect of objective personality assessment is that it may itself produce therapeutic change in a client or, at the least, set the stage for subsequent treatment. Although the therapeutic potential of assessment has long been recognized by practicing clinicians (Berg, 1985; Dana & Leech, 1974; Fischer, 1979, 1985; Leventhal, Slepian, Gluck, & Rosenblatt, 1962), little research has been done to document this aspect of objective personality assessment. Thus, we rely mainly on clinical experience to describe the sources of this therapeutic potential.

Building Rapport

When objective personality testing is performed in a collaborative atmosphere with the client—with attention to the client's goals and questions, full test feedback as to results, and post hoc explanations about the nature of the test—it can be a positive experience for the client. We have repeatedly found that clients who markedly distrust both assessment and therapy can increase their trust through participating in objective personality assessment. How does this come about?

First, one must recognize that both assessment and psychotherapy are experienced by clients as situations of vulnerability and power imbalance. The psychologist has information about them that they do not have in return, and most clients are aware, if only unconsciously, that such information could be used to their disadvantage—to coerce them, embarrass them, or attack them. If, instead, the clients are treated with respect and concern—with the psychologist sharing results and using privileged information only for their good—many are then willing to participate in further treatment.

Besides concerns about exploitation, clients also commonly experience feelings of shame when they are tested. The underlying fear in this instance is, "Once you know who I really am, you will despise me and reject me." Again, if the psychologist disproves this fear, by interacting with clients after testing and showing an appreciation for their life difficulties, increased trust and rapport is almost always the result.

Not surprisingly, many clients report an increase in self-esteem following an assessment.

Interestingly, the increased trust resulting from an objective personality assessment may extend beyond the person conducting the assessment. Many clients are more cooperative with the rest of a treatment team or more willing to follow through with an outside referral. An experience with objective personality assessment probably also influences whether clients will use mental health services in the future. Those with positive experiences may be more likely to entrust themselves to a psychologist's care again, should this become necessary. Those with negative experiences may shy away from seeking further help.

Naming the Client's Experience

One of the most beneficial aspects of objective personality testing, and indeed of all assessment, is that it helps clients to put words to, or name, their experiences. This may sound like a trivial matter, but its importance cannot be overestimated. By providing clients with a language and a context with which to discuss their experiences, an assessment reduces clients' isolation and gives them a medium to help deal with problems. By aiding clients in naming their experiences, the psychologist also communicates that these experiences, while unique, can be conceptualized and understood by others. Finally, the psychologist provides new labels for experiences that clients may have previously framed negatively: "Laziness" is renamed "the inertia that comes with depression," "weakness" becomes "interpersonal sensitivity," and "crazy thoughts" become "symptoms of thought disorder."

Notice here our underlying assumption in the test feedback process: We firmly believe that clients know, on some level, almost all that we tell them on the basis of an objective personality test. Our role is simply to rename, reframe, and validate the clients' experiences. When we are able to do this in our role as clinical psychologists, clients benefit therapeutically from participating in objective personality testing, even if those test results never go farther than their own ears.

Introducing Material into Therapy

Once an experience or feeling is named, it can be an open topic of discussion. Objective personality assessment is often a nonthreatening way to raise sensitive topics in therapy sessions and to return to those topics during the course of a psychotherapy. The beauty of using test results for this purpose is that if the client is threatened by or denies emotionally sensitive material, the therapist can always defer, placing responsibility for the interpretation on the objective personality test. Williams (1986) recommended just this approach in using the MMPI with adolescents, who are notoriously reluctant to discuss emotionally charged material in psychotherapy. Also, just because a test result has been denied once does not mean that it must be dropped for all time. A skilled therapist may reintroduce a previously contested result later in therapy, asking the client, "Is this an example of what the MMPI said, that we weren't sure was true for you?"

Documenting Therapeutic Change

Objective personality assessment may be helpful in recording changes in a client during the course of treatment. Some changes may be readily apparent to client and therapist—the client's depression has declined, disturbing thoughts are less frequent, or the client is less withdrawn. Other changes may only become evident through the process of the testing—although once they are named, they may be noticeable. Even if a repeat testing simply confirms what the therapist and client already know, it stimulates discussion of the client's experience and provides a context for reviewing the treatment and setting future goals.

One complication in performing pre- and posttreatment comparisons with objective personality tests is that some tests are more sensitive to state changes, which commonly occur in therapy, while others are dependent mainly on stable trait variance. Tests of the latter sort may be less useful in assessing therapeutic change. Hence, Butcher and Tellegen (1978) cautioned that some scales of the MMPI cannot reasonably be expected to change with intervention. The same is true of other objective personality tests. The practicing psychologist must be cautious in interpreting change or lack of change in objective personality test scores from pre- to posttreatment.

Advantages of Objective Tests over Other Assessment Methods

Many of the clinical goals just described may also be achieved through other assessment procedures (viz., the diagnostic interview or projective personality testing). Are there reasons to prefer objective personality assessment over these methods? We believe there are.

First, there is the issue of cost. Objective personality tests require little professional time for administration or scoring. Other things being equal, then, objective tests should always be more cost-efficient than the interview or time-consuming projective tests such as the Rorschach.

Of course, other considerations are not always equal; however, another important factor favors objective personality tests. Garb (1984) reviewed the literature on a number of assessment procedures in terms of their incremental validity (i.e., their relative validity contributions compared with other information). He found that when an MMPI was added to an interview, or vice versa, both procedures led to an increase in the validity of clinical judgments compared to either procedure used alone. However, the same could not be said for projective tests such as the Rorschach or Sentence Completions. In fact, in some studies, adding the Rorschach to an MMPI and an interview led to a decrease in the overall validity of clinical judgments.

One variable on which objective personality tests have not been compared with other procedures is that of therapeutic efficacy. Do objective tests lead to more or less rapport, insight, and treatment compliance than interviews or projective tests? The relevant studies remain to be performed. In a similar vein, Hayes, Nelson, and Jarrett (1987) proposed that assessment procedures be compared in terms of their contribution to treatment outcome or utility. Again, empirical information is lacking.

Remember, in general, we recommend a multistep clinical assessment procedure in which information from independent sources is weighed, contrasted, and integrated. However, available information suggests that objective personality assessment should play a prominent role in any clinical assessment battery.

RECENT DEVELOPMENTS IN CLINICAL OBJECTIVE PERSONALITY ASSESSMENT

Computerized Personality Assessment

Computers are in the process of revolutionizing psychological testing. Objective personality assessment is not immune from this trend, although it has been somewhat slower than other assessment areas to make use of the unique features of the computer. We will briefly review recent advances in computerized objective personality assessment. More detailed information is available in Butcher, Keller, and Bacon (1985) and Butcher (1987).

Computerized Scoring

Increasingly, psychologists in clinical settings are finding it expedient to have objective personality tests scored by computer. There are a number of advantages to computer scoring: (a) It is less time-consuming (for example, compare the 30 to 40 minutes required to hand score and plot a standard MMPI-2 profile with the 5 to 15 minutes needed to score it by computer); (b) computer scoring can produce a greater amount of information in less time. A computer-scored MMPI profile can easily include the Harris-Lingoes subscales, the MMPI-2 content scales, as well as a host of other scales and t score options. Obtaining comparable information by hand would be cumbersome, if not impossible, in most clinical settings; and (c) computer scoring is probably more accurate than hand scoring, in most cases.

A variety of options exist for computerized scoring of objective personality tests. Some testing services require answer sheets to be mailed in or teleprocessed from the local to the central facility. A scored profile is then mailed to the test user or printed out on a local terminal. For other tests, scoring packages are available for use with microcomputers in the local clinical facility. This is often the easiest and most cost-efficient method of computer scoring.

One caveat must be made about the superior accuracy of computer-scored personality tests: They are only as accurate as the particular program used to score them. The practicing clinician must be careful to verify the accuracy of any computer program purchased or written. For example, although there are several MMPI microcomputer scoring programs available, some do not generate accurate scores.

Computerized Administration

Objective personality tests are easily adapted for computer administration because of their standardized test stimuli and their limited, structured response options. The last 5 years have seen an increasing number of research projects examining the effects of computerized administration on objective personality testing.

In general, when test instructions are similar, computer-administered tests appear to yield scores that are equivalent to paper-and-pencil administrations for the Eysenck Personality Inventory (Katz & Dalby, 1981) and for the MMPI (Rozensky, Honor, Rasinski, & Tovian, 1986; Russell, Peace, & Mellsop, 1986; White, Clements, & Fowler, 1985). There is some evidence that subjects endorse more socially undesir-

able items with a computer (Moreland, 1987). However, few studies have been done with clinical populations. One exception is the study by Lambert, Andrews, Reagan, Rylee, and Skinner (1987), which showed the equivalence of computer and standard MMPI administrations among substance abusers.

Computer administration of objective personality tests may have distinct advantages over paper-and-pencil administration. Rozensky et al. (1986) reported that subjects found the computer-administered MMPI more interesting, less anxiety provoking, and more relaxing. White et al. (1985) found that computerized administration of the MMPI required substantially less time than did paper-and-pencil administration. Such benefits may be even more evident in clinical than normal populations. We suspect that disturbed subjects, especially those with disorders that affect concentration and attention, such as schizophrenia or organic brain syndrome, will find objective personality testing easier with the structure and guidance of computerized administration. Research on such questions remains to be completed.

Computerized Interpretation

While computer scoring and administration have had a major impact on clinical use of objective personality tests, nothing can compare with the excitement, interest, and controversy that have surrounded computerized interpretation of these tests. Since the early MMPI interpretive system developed by Rome and colleagues at the Mayo Clinic (Rome et al., 1962), computer interpretation of objective personality tests has become increasingly sophisticated and more common. Many clinical settings now rely heavily on computerized interpretations, and some inventories, such as the MCMI-II, are utilized almost exclusively via computer interpretive reports.

One obvious question about computerized interpretations is, "Are they valid?" There are a number of complexities in conducting research on this question (Moreland, 1985), and only a few objective personality instruments and interpretive systems have been subjected to empirical scrutiny. As Moreland (1985, 1987) noted, most research on the validity of computerized interpretations has centered on the MMPI, although one recent study examined Millon's interpretive report for the MCMI (Moreland & Onstad, 1987). Although it is difficult to generalize, research so far suggests that computerized interpretation of objective personality tests has great promise and that computer-generated reports are at least as good as average clinician-generated reports, "if those [interpretive] systems are developed to mimic expert interpretations of thoroughly researched instruments" (Moreland, 1987, p. 44). There are wide variations, however.

In a comprehensive study, Eyde, Kowal, and Fishburne (1987) and Fishburne, Eyde, and Kowal (1988) provided an objective evaluation of independent computer-based MMPI reports. MMPI answer sheets for six patients, three of whom were black, were submitted to seven commercially available computer reporting services. The computer-based reports on each patient were then compared for accuracy as follows: The reports were separated into their component statements and coded. The separate statements (with statements from the various reports intermixed) were then submitted to clinicians who were familiar with the case being studied. The clinicians were asked to rate whether the statement was accurate for the patient. Accuracy levels for the seven reports differed substantially, and a number of reports were considered too inaccurate for clinical use. The Minnesota Report (University of Minnesota Press, 1982) was consistently found to be the most accurate of the seven MMPI reports.

A separate but related issue involves how computerized interpretations are used by professionals. Matarazzo (1983, 1986) argued that computerized interpretations of personality tests seem more valid than they actually are, and that slick promoting on the part of marketing companies encourages clinicians to be overconfident about computerized interpretations. Both Matarazzo (1986) and Lanyon (1984) called for stricter federal regulation of computerized test interpretations. Fowler and Butcher (1986), in response to such concerns, pointed out that research suggests computerized interpretations are at least as good, and perhaps superior, to those of the average clinician. However, Fowler and Butcher also argued that "computer-based reports will never be a substitute for the clinician's skills and were never intended to be" (p. 95). Matarazzo (1986) and Fowler and Butcher (1986) all agreed that strict professional standards must be maintained in the use of automated personality tests.

Implications of Computerization for Clinical Work

How have advances in computerized objective personality assessment affected clinical work with these instruments? Apart from the aforementioned studies about client attitudes toward computerized test administration, little research has addressed this topic. Many intriguing questions remain.

Do professionals weigh diagnostic inferences from computerized interpretations more than those from clinician-generated interpretations? If so, it will be important to remind them that the multistep assessment process we outlined is still desirable, with computerized interpretations being integrated with other sources of information. In fact, the computer service with which we are most familiar, the Minnesota Clinical Interpretive Report for the MMPI (University of Minnesota Press, 1982), has the following disclaimer on the front page of all reports: "This MMPI interpretation can serve as a useful source of hypotheses about clients. . . . The personality descriptions, inferences, and recommendations contained herein need to be verified by other sources of clinical information since individual clients may not fully match the prototype." Indeed, such advice is worth remembering for all objective personality test interpretations, computer generated or not.

Another question is how computerized procedures affect rapport building and other therapeutic uses of objective personality assessment. Available information suggests that computerized administration does not aversely affect the clinician-client relationship; however, the advice of Moreland (1987) is sound: "If an individual expresses reluctance to interact with the computer, the test or interview should probably be administered in the conventional fashion" (p. 36). Are clients more accepting of interpretations generated from computer-administered or computer-interpreted tests? This has not been tested, to our knowledge.

Our clinical experience suggests that computerized interpretations can be particularly useful in introducing material from objective personality tests for discussion in psychotherapy. The advantage here seems to be the added objectivity apparent in computer-based, compared to clinician-generated, interpretations. We often treat the computer report as an outside expert that should be listened to but taken with a grain of salt. As we read selected excerpts from reports to clients (Note: Never simply read the entire report to clients), we invite their participation in confirming the interpretations. Clients seem more comfortable making denials with computerized interpretations, as there is less risk of the examiner losing face.

The MCMI

The MCMI (Millon, 1983b) and its successor, the MCMI-II (Millon, 1987), are objective personality instruments that were specifically designed for use in clinical settings. Given the rising popularity of these tests and the unfamiliarity of many clinicians with their major features, we present a short review. Because the MCMI-II is relatively new and there has been less empirical research using it, the comments in this section focus primarily on the MCMI. We will attempt to indicate where changes in the revised instrument are relevant to our comments.

Features

The MCMI and the MCMI-II are 175-item true–false inventories designed to measure psychopathology, with hopes of circumventing the shortcomings of the MMPI. Unlike the MMPI, the MCMI was based on a theoretical system, spelled out clearly in two books by Millon (1969, 1981). There is also a much closer correspondence between the MCMI and current diagnostic nosology, partly because of its recency and because of Millon's (1983a) ties to the American Psychiatric Association's Advisory Committee for the Personality Disorders. Finally, the MCMI is a much shorter inventory than the MMPI, because it contains a considerable degree of item overlap between scales.

The MCMI has a number of clinical scales, some designed specifically to measure DSM-III (Axis II) personality disorders, and others DSM-III (Axis I) clinical syndromes. There is a validity scale intended to detect careless, confused, or random responding, and the MCMI-II includes three measures of response set: disclosure, desirability, and debasement. Items for the clinical scales were selected to differentiate specific diagnostic groups from a general psychiatric patient population, rather than from normals, as with the MMPI. The MCMI was standardized on a large normative group, and it uses base rate scores rather than standard scores. In part because of these scoring complexities, when the MCMI was first marketed, users were required to purchase an expensive interpretive report for the test. Later, a computer-scored profile became available, and eventually, hand-scoring keys. At this time, no hand-scoring keys are sold for the MCMI-II.

Initial Reviews

Although the MCMI has been available since 1976, it received little attention initially. Recently, it has been the subject of several careful reviews; the reader is referred to these for more in-depth evaluation of the test (Hess, 1985; Lanyon, 1984; McCabe, 1987; Widiger, 1985). We will summarize major points here.

All reviewers seemed impressed by the care and rationale used in the construction of the MCMI. All lamented its lack of widespread use and the small number of research studies available to evaluate it. At the time of Widiger's (1985) review, he felt that the validity of the MCMI was oversold and that the much publicized correspondence between the MCMI and the DSM-III was less than claimed (Widiger, Williams, Spitzer, & Frances, 1985). Many reviewers expressed serious concerns about the high number of overlapping items between scales, which Hess (1985) described as playing "havoc with the statistical analyses" (p. 985). Several reviewers pointed out a major shortcoming of the system of base rate scores: "The cutoff scores . . . will not optimize accurate diagnosis when the local base rates differ from the base rates obtained in Millon's normative sample" (Widiger, 1985, p. 987). This difficulty could lead to high rates of overdiagnosis or underdiagnosis in certain clinical settings. Finally, several reviewers decried the unavailability of hand-scoring keys, now remedied for the MCMI but not for the MCMI-II.

Recent Research

Research on the MCMI has continued since these reviews were completed, although it has not kept pace with the increased clinical use of the MCMI. Nevertheless, more information is now available to evaluate adequacy of this objective personality instrument.

On the positive side, when the MCMI has been administered in conjunction with the MMPI, it has shown reasonable concurrent validity (Montag & Comrey, 1987; Smith, Carroll, & Fuller, 1988). The MCMI has also shown good correspondence with some DSM-III personality disorders, although the concordance is best for these disorders where the DSM-III and Millon's typology agree (Widiger & Sanderson, 1987). The MCMI has been shown to predict failure in Air Force basic training (Butters, Retzlaff, & Gibertini, 1986). Interpretive statements from the MCMI computerized report have been rated by clinicians as more accurate for specific clients than randomly generated interpretive statements (Moreland & Onstad, 1987).

On the negative side, a number of consistent problems have emerged concerning clinical use of the MCMI. First, independent studies have found that the test underestimates the diagnosis of depressive disorders among both inpatients (Patrick, 1988; Piersma, 1987) and outpatients (Goldberg, Shaw, & Segal, 1987). This consistent bias in the MCMI may be due to its neglect of vegetative symptoms of depression (Goldberg et al., 1987). Second, as the early reviewers predicted, factor analyses of the MCMI suggest that much of its meaningful variance is confounded due to item overlap, resulting in artifactual relationships between scales (Choca, Peterson, & Shanley, 1986; Flynn & McMahon, 1984; Montag & Comrey, 1987; Retzlaff & Gibertini, 1987). Finally, several studies have raised serious questions about the diagnostic accuracy of the MCMI for Axis II disorders. Consistent with our clinical experience with this instrument, it appears to overdiagnose personality disorders (Cantrell & Dana, 1987; Piersma, 1987). This latter difficulty may be more or less serious, depending on how local base rates differ from those Millon used in setting cutting scores.

Implications for Clinical Use

Our review of the literature suggests that the MCMI and the MCMI-II are mainly appropriate at this time as clinical research instruments, and that further empirical study is badly needed before these tests can be unequivocally recommended for applied use. Possibly, as part of a multistep clinical assessment battery, the MCMI helps to detect and distinguish between personality disorders. For example, Antoni, Levine, Tischer, Green, and Millon (1987) found that by using the MMPI and MCMI in conjunction, they were able to discriminate meaningful subgroups of the MMPI 78-87 code type, according to Axis II type characteristics. Currently, however, if the MCMI is to be used in clinical work, it should be given less weight than other instruments in determining Axis I diagnoses.

Interestingly, although Millon recommended the combined use of the MMPI and MCMI in clinical assessment, recent research has shown that diagnostic information in the MCMI on personality disorders is also well provided by the MMPI. Morey and Levine (1988), in a multitrait-multimethod examination of the MMPI and MCMI, reported that there was significant convergence between the two instruments for the assessment of personality disorders. Consequently, the clinician may find that the MCMI does not provide unique personality-based diagnostic information beyond what is available through the MMPI.

The MMPI-2

As this edition of *The Clinical Psychology Handbook* goes to press, the date is nearing for the publication of the Minnesota Multiphasic Personality Inventory-2 (MMPI-2), the restandardized version of the MMPI (University of Minnesota Press, in press). As a detailed description of the MMPI is provided in our previous article (Butcher & Finn, 1983), we concentrate here on the rationale of the restandardization and the major changes in the MMPI-2.

Reasons for the Restandardization

The MMPI was aging. Although still the most widely used psychological test in the U.S. (Lubin, Larsen, Matarazzo, & Seever, 1985), it was clearly in need of attention. In the 5 decades since the MMPI items were originally written by Hathaway and McKinley, changes in American culture made some of the items obscure, obsolete, or objectionable. Also, with the increased use of the MMPI for nonclinical purposes, such as personnel screening, items dealing with sexual adjustment, bodily functions, and excessive religiosity began to seem unnecessarily intrusive. Recent research showed that even apart from item difficulties, responses to the MMPI questions had changed in the time since the test was normed. Contemporary normal subjects admitted to more problems than did the original normative sample (Colligan, Osborne, Swenson, & Offord, 1984). Finally, it was increasingly recognized that the original normative sample was far from optimal. It was small ($N = 724$), had been used both for scale development and for norm generation, and had few subjects from different regional areas, cultural settings, or ethnic and racial groups. Although in many respects typical of the Minnesota population of the 1930s, the normative sample was certainly not representative of the contemporary U.S. population.

For these reasons, in the late 1970s, the University of Minnesota Press undertook a major revision and restandardization of the MMPI. The restandardization committee attempted to find ways to address the aforementioned difficulties with the test, while keeping the basic format of the test as close to the original as possible. This continuity would allow new and experienced users to continue to benefit from many years of research and clinical experience with the MMPI.

Major Changes in the MMPI-2

We will now briefly discuss the major features of the MMPI-2. Table 21.1 summarizes differences between the MMPI and MMPI-2.

Items. The MMPI-2 booklet is approximately the same length as the original booklet; however, duplicate, outmoded, and objectionable items were eliminated, some items were edited, and many new items

Table 21.1. Summary of Changes in the Restandardized MMPI (MMPI-2)

	OLD MMPI	MMPI-2
Items	566 items, including 16 duplicates and many outmoded or objectionable items	567 items; no duplicates; outmoded items eliminated; some items edited; items with new content added; basic scales in items 1–370
Norms	Based on a sample of $N = 724$ Minnesota adult hospital visitors; few minorities included	Based on a sample of $N = 2600$ adults recruited nationwide; more minorities included
t scores	Simple linear t scores; positively skewed, with different degrees of skewness across scales	Uniform t scores; positively skewed; uniform skewness produces essentially same distribution across scales
Validity scales	?, L, F, K used to determine profile validity	?, L, F, and K retained; three new validity scales added: F_B, VRIN, and TRIN
Clinical scales	10 basic scales, including 5 and 0	The 10 basic scales are retained; some are shortened
Research scales	A, R, Es, MAC, O-H, Do, Re, MT are commonly used	A, R, Es, O-H, Do, Re, and MT are retained; MAC is revised, replacing 4 items
Content scales	Wiggins and Harris-Lingoes scales are widely used; Serkownek scales used for 5 and 0	The Harris-Lingoes scales are kept; the Serkownek scales are not retained; a set of 15 new content scales replaces the Wiggins scales; 3 new subscales exist for scale 0

were added to address content areas not covered in the original MMPI. The item order was changed so that, similar to the previous Form R, all of the basic scales may be scored from the first 370 items of the test.

Norms. The most significant change in the MMPI-2 is the use of norms based on a national sample of $N = 2600$. Subjects were solicited via advertisements and special appeals in seven states. They ranged from 18 to 90 years of age, and the final sample was much more representative of the current U.S. population, although both Hispanic and Asian-American minorities remain underrepresented.

As expected, the raw-score means and standard deviations on the clinical scales were much larger for the current normative group compared to the original group. This produces a general lowering of t scores across the MMPI-2 profile, compared to t scores based on the original norms.

Uniform t *scores.* Another major change concerns the process used to calculate t scores from raw scores. The original MMPI t scores were developed using a simple linear transformation. This resulted in positively skewed t-score distributions among normals, with different degrees of skewness across scales. In the MMPI-2, t scores on each scale were transformed to produce the same degree of positive skewness. The

result is that the percentile rank for any t score is easily determined and is equivalent across the scales.

Validity scales. The standard validity scales remain essentially the same. Three new validity scales were added: Back F (F_B), Variable Response Inconsistency (VRIN), and True Response Inconsistency (TRIN). VRIN replaces Greene's (1978) carelessness (CS) scale. TRIN is a measure of acquiescence, based on the work of Tellegen (1982). F_B resembles the standard F scale, but is scored for items on the back of the answer sheet.

Clinical scales. The 10 basic clinical scales remain essentially unchanged in terms of item content. Several were shortened slightly due to the elimination of outmoded or objectionable items.

Research scales. Many of the commonly scored research scales from the MMPI may be scored on the MMPI-2. The popular MacAndrew Alcoholism Scale (MacAndrew, 1965) was revised.

Content scales. The Wiggins content scales were abolished and are replaced by a carefully developed set of 15 content scales (Butcher, Graham, Williams, and Ben-Porath, 1989). The Harris-Lingoes subscales may still be scored for the basic scales. The Serkownek subscales for scales 5 and 0 are no longer recommended. Three new content subscales were developed for scale 0.

Implications of the Changes for Clinical Work

There is little doubt that the changes incorporated in the MMPI-2 will greatly improve the clinical usefulness of this major objective personality instrument. Undoubtedly, there will be a period of transition, while experienced users of the MMPI become familiar with the MMPI-2. Initially, the most noticeable difference should be a general decrease in t-score elevations in clinical as well as normal samples. Clinical psychologists will need to become sensitive to the meaning of t scores in the 65 to 70 range, as well as those above the traditional point of clinical significance.

The uniform t scores should make it easier to explain the meaning of scale elevations to clients. However, they are likely to affect slightly the frequency of two-point codes in clinical populations. Some codes will become more common and others less so, due to the altered distributions of the clinical scales. While these changes are not expected to affect the validity of the standard code type interpretations, refinements in certain code type characteristics may eventually be needed.

The new content scales will gain meaning as they are used in research and clinical work. Luckily, there is general agreement that the interpretation of content scales is highly face valid; thus, clinicians can begin using these scales immediately.

Computerized scoring, administration, and interpretation of the MMPI-2 continues to be available, just as it was for the MMPI. Hand scoring remains available for psychologists who prefer this method.

CONCLUSION

Objective personality tests continue to be integral to the work of practicing clinical psychologists. These tests are widely used in diagnosis and treatment planning, in part because of their ease of use and their established incremental validity. By entering into a collaborative relationship with clients, the psychologist can use objective personality assessment to build rapport and facilitate treatment. Further research is greatly needed on the therapeutic aspects of clinical assessment.

Computerized scoring, administration, and interpretation of objective tests have proved an economical

time-saver for many clinical settings. Our review supports the use of computers in all phases of objective personality assessment. We agree with other writers, however, that computers will never replace the psychologist's need for interpersonal sensitivity, thoughtful integration of test findings, or respect for clients.

We reviewed two new objective personality instruments, the MCMI and the MMPI-2. While possessing many laudable features, the MCMI appears to be most appropriate at this time as a research instrument. Further study is needed before its suitability for clinical work can be determined. The MMPI-2 is the restandardized version of the MMPI. It retains many features of the MMPI, while introducing changes that should substantially enhance clinical use of the instrument.

It is difficult to predict what major developments are on the horizon for clinical objective personality assessment. Certainly, new tests will be constructed and modifications made in existing ones. Computers will continue to rise in their use and usefulness. In the midst of these changes it is useful to remind ourselves of a guiding principle put forth by Fischer (1985): "Assessment, even of the traditional sort, always affects the client—who inevitably finds the experience meaningful in one way or another. The human-science assessor acknowledges this and tries to make sure that the inevitable interventions are constructive" (p. 47).

REFERENCES

Antoni, M. H., Levine, J., Tischer, P., Green, C., & Millon, T. (1987). Refining personality assessment by combining MCMI high-point profiles and MMPI codes: V. MMPI code 78/87. *Journal of Personality Assessment, 51*, 375–387.

Berg, M. (1985). The feedback process in diagnostic psychological testing. *Bulletin of the Menninger Clinic, 49*, 52–69.

Butcher, J. N. (1987). (Ed.) *Computerized psychological assessment*. New York: Basic Books.

Butcher, J. N., & Finn, S. (1983). Objective personality assessment in clinical settings. In M. Hersen, A. E. Kazdin, & A. S. Bellack (Eds.), *The Clinical Psychology Handbook* (1st ed., pp. 329–344). Elmsford, NY: Pergamon Press.

Butcher, J.N., Graham, J. R., Williams, C. L., & Ben-Porath, Y. (1989). *Innovations in MMPI-2 interpretation: Development and use of the MMPI-2 content scales*. Minneapolis, MN: University of Minnesota Press.

Butcher, J. N., Keller, L. S., & Bacon, S. F. (1985). Current developments and future directions in computerized personality assessment. *Journal of Consulting and Clinical Psychology, 53,* 803–815.

Butcher, J. N., & Tellegen, A. (1978). Common methodological problems in MMPI research. *Journal of Consulting and Clinical Psychology, 46,* 620–628.

Butters, M., Retzlaff, P., & Gibertini, M. (1986). Nonadaptability to basic training and the Millon Clinical Multiaxial Inventory. *Military Medicine, 151,* 574–576.

Cantrell, J. D., & Dana, R. H. (1987). Use of the MCMI as a screening instrument at a community mental health center. *Journal of Clinical Psychology, 43,* 366–375.

Choca, J. P., Peterson, C. A., & Shanley, L. A. (1986). Factor analysis of the Millon Clinical Multiaxial Inventory. *Journal of Consulting and Clinical Psychology, 54,* 253–255.

Colligan, R. C., Osborne, D., Swenson, W. M., & Offord, K. P. (1984). The aging MMPI: Development of contemporary norms. *Mayo Clinic Proceedings, 59,* 377–390.

Dana, R. H., & Leech, S. (1974). Existential assessment. *Journal of Personality Assessment, 38,* 428–435.

Eyde, L., Kowal, D., & Fishburne, J. (1987, August). *Clinical implications of validity research on computer based test interpretations of the MMPI.* Paper presented at the annual meeting of the American Psychological Association, New York.

Fischer, C. T. (1979). Individualized assessment and phenomenological psychology. *Journal of Personality Assessment, 43,* 115–122.

Fischer, C. T. (1985). *Individualized psychological assessment.* Monterey, CA: Brooks/Cole.

Fishburne, J., Eyde, L., & Kowal, D. (1988, August). *Clinical implications of validity research on computer based test interpretations of the MMPI.* Paper presented at the Annual Meeting of the American Psychological Association, Atlanta, GA.

Flynn, P. M., & McMahon, R. C. (1984). An examination of the factor structure of the Millon Clinical Multiaxial Inventory. *Journal of Personality Assessment, 48,* 308–311.

Fowler, R. D., & Butcher, J. N. (1986). Critique of Matarazzo's views on computerized testing: All sigma and no mean. *American Psychologist, 41,* 94–96.

Garb, H. N. (1984). The incremental validity of information used in personality assessment. *Clinical Psychology Review, 4,* 641–655.

Goldberg, J. O., Shaw, B. F., & Segal, Z. F. (1987). Concurrent validity of the Millon Clinical Multiaxial Inventory depression scales. *Journal of Consulting and Clinical Psychology, 55,* 785–787.

Graham, J. R., & Strenger, V. E. (1988). MMPI characteristics of alcoholics: A review. *Journal of Consulting and Clinical Psychology, 56,* 197–205.

Greene, R. L. (1978). An empirically derived MMPI carelessness scale. *Journal of Clinical Psychology, 34,* 407–410.

Hayes, S. C., Nelson, R. O., & Jarrett, R. B. (1987). The treatment utility of assessment: A functional approach for evaluating assessment quality. *American Psychologist, 42,* 963–974.

Hess, A. K. (1985). Review of Millon Clinical Multiaxial Inventory. In J. V. Mitchell (Ed.), *The ninth mental measurements yearbook* (Vol. 1, pp. 984–986). Lincoln, NE: Buros Institute of Mental Measurements.

Katz, L., & Dalby, J. T. (1981). Computer and manual administration of the Eysenck Personality Inventory. *Journal of Clinical Psychology, 37,* 586–588.

Lambert, M. F., Andrews, R. H., Reagan, H., Rylee, K., & Skinner, J. R. (1987). Equivalence of computerized and traditional MMPI administration with substance abusers. *Computers in Human Behavior, 3,* 139–143.

Lanyon, R. (1984). Personality assessment. *Annual Review of Psychology, 35,* 667–701.

Leventhal, T., Slepian, H. J., Gluck, M. R., & Rosenblatt, B. P. (1962). The utilization of the psychologist-patient relationship in diagnostic testing. *Journal of Projective Techniques, 26,* 66–79.

Lubin, B., Larsen, R. M., Matarazzo, J. D., & Seever, M. (1985). Psychological test usage patterns in five professional settings. *American Psychologist, 40,* 857–861.

MacAndrew, C. (1965). The differentiation of male alcoholic outpatients from non-alcoholic psychiatric patients by means of the MMPI. *Quarterly Journal of Studies of Alcohol, 26,* 238–246.

Matarazzo, J. D. (1983). Computerized psychological testing. *Science, 221,* 323.

Matarazzo, J. D. (1986). Computerized clinical psychological test interpretations: Unvalidated plus all mean and no sigma. *American Psychologist, 41,* 14–24.

McCabe, S. P. (1987). Millon Clinical Multiaxial Inventory. In D. J. Keyser & R. C. Sweetland (Eds.), *Test critiques compendium* (pp. 304–315). Kansas City, MO: Westport Publishers, Inc.

Millon, T. (1969). *Modern psychopathology: A biosocial approach to maladaptive learning and functioning.* Philadelphia: W B Saunders.

Millon, T. (1981). *Disorders of personality: DSM-III, Axis II.* New York: John Wiley & Sons.

Millon, T. (1983a). The DSM-III: An insider's perspective. *American Psychologist, 38,* 804–814.

Millon, T. (1983b). *Millon Clinical Multiaxial Inventory manual* (3rd ed.). Minneapolis: Interpretive Scoring Systems.

Millon, T. (1987). *Manual for the Millon Clinical Multiaxial Inventory-II.* Minneapolis, MN: National Computer Systems.

Montag, I., & Comrey, A. L. (1987). Millon MCMI scales factor analyzed and correlated with MMPI and CPS scales. *Multivariate Behavioral Research, 22,* 401–413.

Moreland, K. L. (1985). Validation of computer-based interpretations: Problems and pitfalls. *Journal of Consulting and Clinical Psychology, 53,* 816–825.

Moreland, K. L. (1987). Computerized psychological assessment: What's available. In J. N. Butcher (Ed.),

Computerized psychological assessment (pp. 26–49). New York: Basic Books.

Moreland, K. L., & Onstad, J. A. (1987). Validity of Millon's computerized interpretation system for the MCMI: A controlled study. *Journal of Consulting and Clinical Psychology, 55,* 113–114.

Morey, L. C., & Levine, D. J. (1988). A multitrait-multimethod examination of Minnesota Multiphasic Personality Inventory (MMPI) and Millon Clinical Multiaxial Inventory (MCMI). *Journal of Psychopathology and Behavioral Assessment, 10,* 333–344.

Patrick, J. (1988). Concordance of the MCMI and the MMPI in the diagnosis of three DSM-III Axis I disorders. *Journal of Clinical Psychology, 44,* 186–190.

Piersma, H. L. (1987). Millon Clinical Multiaxial Inventory computer-generated diagnoses: How do they compare to clinician judgment? *Journal of Psychopathology and Behavioral Assessment, 9,* 305–312.

Retzlaff, P. D., & Gibertini, M. (1987). Factor structure of the MCMI basic personality scales and common-item artifact. *Journal of Personality Assessment, 51,* 588–594.

Rome, H. P., Swenson, W. M., Mataya, P., McCarthy, C. E., Pearson, J. S., Keating, F. R., & Hathaway, S. R. (1962). Symposium on automation techniques in personality assessment. *Proceedings of the Staff Meetings of the Mayo Clinic, 37,* 61–82.

Rosenbaum, M. (1980). A schedule for assessing self-control behaviors: Preliminary findings. *Behavior Therapy, 11,* 109–121.

Rozensky, R. H., Honor, L. F., Rasinski, K., & Tovian, S. (1986). Paper-and-pencil versus computer-administered MMPIs: A comparison of patients' attitudes. *Computers in Human Behavior, 2,* 111–116.

Russell, G. K., Peace, K. A., & Mellsop, G. W. (1986). The reliability of a micro-computer administration of the MMPI. *Journal of Clinical Psychology, 42,* 120–122.

Sheppard, D., Smith, G. T., & Rosenbaum, G. (1988). Use of MMPI subtypes in predicting completion of a residential alcoholism treatment program. *Journal of Consulting and Clinical Psychology, 56,* 590–596.

Simons, A. D., Lustman, P. J., Wetzel, R. D., & Murphy, G. E. (1985). Predicting response to cognitive therapy of depression: The role of learned resourcefulness. *Cognitive Therapy and Research, 9,* 79–90.

Smith, D., Carroll, J. L., & Fuller, G. B. (1988). The relationship between the Millon Clinical Multiaxial Inventory and the MMPI in a private outpatient mental health clinic population. *Journal of Clinical Psychology, 44,* 165–174.

Tellegen, A. (1982). *Brief manual for the Differential Personality Questionnaire.* Minneapolis, MN: University of Minnesota Press.

University of Minnesota Press. (1982). *User's guide for the Minnesota Report.* Minneapolis, MN: National Computer Systems.

University of Minnesota Press. (in press). *Manual for the restandardized Minnesota Multiphasic Personality Inventory: MMPI-2.* Minneapolis, MN: University of Minnesota Press.

White, D. M., Clements, C. R., & Fowler, R. D. (1985). A comparison of computer administration with standard administration of the MMPI. *Computers in Human Behavior, 1,* 153–167.

Widiger, T. (1985). Review of Millon Clinical Multiaxial Inventory. In J. V. Mitchell (Ed.) *The ninth mental measurements yearbook* (Vol. 1, pp. 986–988). Lincoln, NE: Buros Institute of Mental Measurements.

Widiger, T. A., & Sanderson, C. (1987): The convergent and discriminant validity of the MCMI as a measure of the DSM-III personality disorders. *Journal of Personality Assessment, 51,* 228–242.

Widiger, T., Williams, J., Spitzer, R., & Frances, A. (1985). The MCMI as a measure of DSM-III. *Journal of Personality Assessment, 49,* 366–378.

Williams, C. L. (1986). MMPI profiles from adolescents: Interpretive strategies and treatment considerations. *Journal of Child and Adolescent Psychotherapy, 3,* 179–193.

CHAPTER 22

INTELLECTUAL ASSESSMENT

Robert L. Hale

The IQ evolved from the interplay between disorder and direction; its natures determined by the problems immigration represented and the solutions education offered; its form and meaning determined by the needs of the society for which it provided solutions, explanations, and ultimately its own future problems. (Fass, 1980)

ASSESSMENT OF INTELLIGENCE

Two basic approaches have often been taken in discussion of the assessment of intelligence, and authors have often treated these approaches as if they were mutually incompatible. The first approach includes an analysis of the available instruments that purport to measure intelligence. The salient aspects of these tests were analyzed, and some direction concerning which test to use under various assessment circumstances is provided. Authors who use this approach assume that the assessment of intelligence is a legitimate enterprise and that intelligence is a concrete entity that psychologists can measure. They infrequently consider exactly what one is attempting to measure when using an intelligence test. They often completely fail to discuss the constructs underlying

intelligence. The second approach discusses intelligence as a hypothetical construct. Authors who use this approach frequently make little mention of the instruments that are currently used. In fact, it is assumed that the construct of intelligence is so complex that no existing test is capable of measuring it and therefore that the assessment of intelligence is an illegitimate activity. These two positions have recently come into sharp conflict. As Kaufman (1979) notes, "The intelligence testing scene is currently in turmoil, highlighted by litigation, legislation and outbursts by well-intentioned professionals. Advocates of both sides are polarized and many arguments are emotional and uncompromising" (p. xi).

In this chapter, an attempt is made to blend these two approaches. First, the historical development of current intelligence tests is reviewed. Then, the conceptual definitions of intelligence and the more practical uses of the tests are interwoven. Major areas of concern in relation to these current tests are discussed later. These concerns include: (a) heritability, (b) bias, (c) stability, (d) equivalence, and (e) reporting results. Finally, the future of intellectual assessment is discussed. Recent advances in neuropsychology and microcomputer usage are discussed along with the likelihood that the term *IQ* may be dropped altogether.

HISTORY OF INTELLIGENCE TESTS

European Influences

It is impossible to tease apart the history of intellectual assessment from the history of man. Homo sapiens have most likely informally measured each others' mental capabilities for as long as we have existed. Formal measurements of mental ability came much later. Sattler (1982) notes that Fitzherbert (1470–1538) proposed a formal method of measuring a person's mentality by requiring one to count 20 pence, tell one's age, and identify one's father. The fundamental history of intelligence testing, however, is basically confined to the United States of the 20th century. Like a child whose record begins at birth, but is dynamically influenced by events prior to its birth, so too was the development of intellectual assessment influenced by events prior to 1905 when the grandfather of modern intelligence tests, the Binet-Simon Scale, was developed. The more important of those early European events included the establishment of Galton's anthropometric laboratory at the International Health Exhibition in 1884, the development of the statistical techniques of correlation by Karl Pearson and Charles Spearman, the concern with precise measurement of various types of perceptual, memory, reading and conceptual differences in the laboratories in Germany, and the focus on higher mental functions in France. The influence of the researchers from England, Germany, and France on American psychologists, combined with the social–political environment in the United States during the early 20th century, provided the perfect nutritive substrata for the growth and development of intellectual assessment. The Europeans had initially concentrated on the gross measurement of physical attributes. The research then began to focus on processes that we would today agree are cognitive instead of physical. Finally they provided the statistical sophistication to evaluate the worth of the intellectual measures. The influence of the Europeans need not further concern us except that one should keep firmly in mind the fact that the 1905 Binet-Simon was given its impetus for construction by the Minister of Public Instruction in Paris 1 year earlier. The minister appointed a committee, of which Binet was a member, to find a way to separate mentally retarded from normal children in the schools (Sattler, 1982). Originally, modern mental test results were to be used to determine how well children should do in school.

Early Developments in the United States

In the United States the assessment of mental ability provided a way of organizing an American society, which by all accounts was chaotic. It is the social–political turmoil in the beginning of the 20th century that must be understood if we are to comprehend why the assessment of intelligence became so important in the United States. Fass (1980) and Marks (1976–77) discuss 10 factors that were part of the American experience in the early 20th century and that directly contributed to the growth of the mental measurement industry. The 10 influences are: (1) massive immigration with ethnic and racial diversity, (2) urbanization, (3) the growing influence of science, (4) the progressive educational movement, (5) World War I, (6) the supposed utility of the Army tests, (7) the putative empirical relation between race and IQ, (8) stricter school attendance laws, (9) the development of child labor legislation, and (10) the belief in a competitive meritocratic society. The men they list as most influential in the development of intellectual assessment in the United States are: (1) Lewis Terman, (2) H. H. Goddard, (3) Walter Lippman, (4) J. M. Cattell, (5) Robert Yerkes, (6) E. L. Thorndike, and (7) John Dewey. Arthur Otis, overlooked in most historical accounts of the development of mental tests, should definitely be included in this list of influential men.

As noted above, the early development of the mental test by Binet clearly stemmed from an expressed need to differentiate between those French children who could be successful in traditional educational programs and those who could not. Goddard, who first translated Binet's scales into English in 1910, used the test to distinguish among the "feebleminded" children attending the Vineland Training School in New Jersey. With some revisions and a change in the scoring of the test by incorporating the concept of the intelligence quotient developed by Stern in 1912 and later described in his book (Stern, 1914). Terman produced the Stanford revision in 1916. This revision was similarly used to differentiate "feebleminded" from normal children in California. Thus, the first modern intelligence test began with a perceived need to differentiate between children and continued to have as its primary purpose the detection of mental differences in people. As Marks (1976–77) points out, the decision to investigate individual differences or similarities is clearly arbitrary. One has to ask, "Why did it become so important to differentiate between people?" (Marks, 1976–77, p. 3). As stated previously, the sociopolitical situation in America was quite chaotic. This situation demanded the detection of individual differences so that those differences could be used to order an educational system in a rapidly changing society. This educational system was seen not only as a method by which America could educate its citizens, but also as a method of teaching cultural values (good citizenship).

Immigration into America during the early 20th century put tremendous stress on the educational system. Immigration into the United States has never been evenly distributed with regard to either time or ethnicity. In the early 20th century, there were both more immigrants and those that did arrive came from cultures that, because of their differences with respect to the dominant culture, required more time to adjust to American life. As Thomas Sowell (1981a) vividly demonstrates, the reasons for differential immigration are explained by the economics prevalent during the time period one is considering. Before the widespread use of passenger ships, it was simply less expensive to purchase a ticket to America on a cargo ship. During the era of sailing vessels, America sold large quantities of agricultural and forest products to northern and western Europe and in turn purchased manufactured goods from these countries. Thus, ships returning to the United States carried less bulk than when they left. On returning to America, the ship's extra space could inexpensively be sold to passengers. These northern and western Europeans fit easily into the current social environment. On the other hand, persons from southern and eastern Europe with whom the United States had limited trade would have to pay the full expense of passage on ships that did not carry cargo to the United States. The high cost of such transportation simply prohibited the development of immigration from these countries. After the development of the steamship, however, the cost of crossing the Atlantic was brought down to a point where formerly excluded southern and eastern Europeans could afford to purchase tickets to America. The upshot of this economic situation was that the major immigrations from Ireland and Germany were completed by the 1880s, whereas immigrants from Italy and Russia were just arriving in the early 1900s:

> The Anglo-Saxons, Germans, and Irish, etc. began their adjustment to American life generations before peoples of Italian, Polish, or eastern European Jewish ancestry. As of the early twentieth-century, the former groups—the "old" immigrants, as they were called—were as a group economically, educationally, and socially well in advance of the "newer" immigrant groups. (Sowell, 1981a, p. 54)

The impact of immigration early in the 20th century on the social fabric of America was enormous. In terms of sheer numbers, "Between 1901 and 1910 alone, nearly nine million people migrated to this country—more than the combined populations of the states of New York, Maryland, and New Hampshire in 1900" (Kownslar & Frizzle, 1967, pp. 600–601).

Another migration should be noted. African-Americans from the South, provoked by Jim Crow laws and the rise of the Klu Klux Klan and later reinforced by the availability of jobs during World War I, migrated in ever-increasing numbers to northern urban centers. They brought with them their unique cultural heritage formed during slavery, which resulted in their having little formal education. It was with this lack of education that both blacks and society at large would later be asked to grapple. The fact that intelligence tests indicated racial differences in favor of the older immigrants actually enhanced the acceptance of mental tests as a social organizing force (Gould, 1981). The meaning and effects of social and racial bias in intelligence tests will be taken up more fully later in the chapter.

This was also the end of the age of the robber barons and the beginning of a new social awakening in the United States. No longer was America going to tolerate the building of fortunes for a few on the backs of immigrant labor. In 1901 Theodore Roosevelt succeeded William McKinley as president. Roosevelt and the country took on two broad social aims concerning the immigrant. First, the immigrant was to be set free from the daily grind of work and poverty. Second, the immigrant was to be set free from the liabilities of his native tongue:

> Roosevelt's bravest mission was to try and see through social legislation and the new resources of education, that the immigrants should no longer be looked on as nationally identifiable pools of cheap labor. The country must stop talking about German-Americans and Italian–Americans and Polish–Americans: [As Roosevelt stated] "we have room but for one language here, and that is the English language, for we intend to see that the crucible turns our people out as Americans." There must be no more "hyphenated Americans." (Cooke, 1974, p. 299)

Other evidence of social reform can be noted in the passing of the Keating-Owen child labor act in 1916. Even though it was declared unconstitutional 2 years later by the Supreme Court, it heralded an age of concern for children. Other evidence of concern for youth and the educational process can be found in the fact that the last state to enact laws requiring child school attendance was Mississippi in 1918. This combination of child labor and compulsory attendance laws assured that most youngsters would be in school. The task of turning these children into competent Americans then fell to the public schools. It was not just a coincidence that Terman, who had served for many years as a public school administrator, completed the Stanford revision of the Binet test in 1916. Necessity, as usual, was the mother of "invention," or in this instance, revision. Intelligence tests were seen as a possible way to organize children within the schools. The stress put on the public schools through social reform might have in and of itself led to a rapid increase in the utilization of IQs within education. World War I, however, interrupted this reform movement. The perceived success of intelligence test results during the war, combined with the rejuvenated stresses on education, accelerated the use of IQ as an organizing factor after the war.

Influence of World War I

When the United States declared war on Germany on April 6, 1917, a major task faced America. The country quickly had to form an efficient military unit. Robert Yerkes, the president of the American Psychological Association, offered the services of psychologists to the military:

> In a remarkable short time of about one month, Lewis Terman, Edward Thorndike, Henry Goddard, Robert Yerkes and others designed tests of intelligence for the army. Their purpose was to classify men according to their intellectual ability and to assist in selecting the most competent for leadership positions as well as to eliminate the incompetents. (Marks, 1976–77, p. 5)

Over 1.7 million men were evaluated with the Army Alpha and Beta tests. It was the publicly assumed success of these intelligence tests in the face of a national emergency that contributed to the increased use of such assessment outside of the military.

It was also at this point that misunderstandings and misinterpretations of exactly what these mental tests could and could not do were first pointed out. For example, Goddard accepted the Stanford-Binet 16-year mental age norm as representing the average adult attainment level. He also defined the term *moron* as meaning an adult who could obtain a mental age of up to 12 years. Using the Army test results that indicated that on the Alpha and Beta tests the average mental age was approximately 13, Goddard argued

that the Army results established that half the persons in the United States were little better than morons. Walter Lippman correctly argued that Goddard's conclusion, stating that the average mental age of adult Americans was only 13 years, was neither correct nor incorrect but simply nonsense. "Nonsense because it would be equivalent to the assertion that the average intelligence of adults is below the average intelligence of adults" (Pastore, 1978, p. 323).

Gould (1981) reports that contrary to popular opinion, the Army tests were actually not useful. In fact, he reports that the Army never really used the scores. Tension between the psychologists and the commanding officers of the army camps became so intense that the Secretary of War asked the officers to give him their opinion of Yerkes's tests:

> He received one hundred replies, nearly all negative. They were, Yerkes admitted, "with few exceptions, unfavorable to psychological work, and have led to the conclusion on the part of various officers of the General Staff that this work has little, if any value to the army and should be discontinued." (Gould, 1981, p. 202)

Whether or not the Alpha and Beta were useful to the Army is debatable. However, the developments that led to these first group tests of mental ability were certainly significant for testing in general. Arthur Sinton Otis, a graduate student of Terman's prior to the war, developed several of the objective item-scoring formats so necessary for group paper-and-pencil tests. Most notable was his suggestion that instead of asking questions that required recalling answers, one might present a stimulus with several possible response alternatives. This innovation led directly to the multiple-choice item format. Terman introduced Otis's ideas to the committee developing the Army tests. Otis was asked to join this group. His methods of item construction proved to be both effective and economical. It was only a short time before the methods of group assessment found their way into schools, with publication of the *Otis Group Intelligence Scale* and the *National Intelligence Tests* by the World Book Company in 1918.

Before proceeding, a review of what the measures of intellectual functioning had been able to demonstrate is in order. First, on a limited basis, the tests were successful in demonstrating that they could differentiate between children who could be successful in academics and those who could not (the tests could predict academic achievement). This is not to say that the mental tests could predict standardized achievement test results. The first standardized achievement battery to evaluate the academic areas of reading, spelling, sentence meaning, and vocabulary appeared in the first volume of the *Journal of Educational Research* (Pressey, 1920). However, the Stanford-Binet had been able to differentiate between pupils judged by their teachers to be adequately and inadequately achieving (Sattler, 1974). Second, the public believed that the tests had demonstrated on a very large scale that they could differentiate leadership ability in Army inductees. Third, and perhaps most important, the Army report (Yerkes, 1921) brought to the public's attention the alleged differences in mental ability among blacks and whites as well as inductees from eastern Europe. These racial differences were based on inadequate statistical procedures and analyses. For a detailed discussion of the testing inadequacies during World War I, the interested reader is referred to Gould (1981). Suffice it to say that Gould has more than adequately demonstrated that the Army data were poorly collected and largely misinterpreted. Nevertheless, the racial interpretations given to the data ultimately captured the public's attention. The data fit nicely into the social prejudices then prevalent. This was unfortunate, because as Gould explains, if the data had been properly evaluated:

> The army mental tests could have provided an impetus for social reform, since they documented that environmental disadvantages were robbing from millions of people an opportunity to develop their intellectual skills. Again and again, the data pointed to strong correlations between test scores, and environment. Again and again, those who wrote and administered the test invented tortuous, ad hoc explanations to preserve their hereditarian prejudices. (p. 221)

Post-World War I Influences

After the war ended, America was able to turn its attention inward to its own pressing needs. As noted previously, the war interrupted the earlier social reform movement directed toward the European immigrant and the black migrant. After the war, things had changed. The new immigrants were viewed as an economic enemy. America had just fought a war supposedly to preserve democracy. In 1917, the Bolsheviks had taken over political control of Russia and the immigrants from Europe were considered a threat to democracy in this country. Shortly after the armistice, American soldiers were called upon to break up a socialist rally in New York. The next night sympathizers of the Russian Revolution were dispersed in a bloody battle.

African-Americans were also seen as threatening. They had moved north during the war and had remained there. The economy was slowing down and competition for a declining number of jobs became fierce. In 1919, 23 cities had race riots, and there were many local strikes accompanied by a national steel strike. The social mood in America was a strange mixture of racism combined with isolationism and the previously described self-improvement. As examples of the latter two characteristics of this mood, it can be noted that in 1920 the Senate: (a) rejected the Treaty of Versailles, (b) refused to allow the United States to join the League of Nations, and (c) passed prohibition. With these details about post–World War I America, some light can be shed on the frequent criticism that intelligence tests based on middle-class values prevented the entry of foreign-born minorities into the United States.

In 1924, Congress established quotas on the number of immigrants who could enter the United States. The English, Irish, and Germans received the largest quotas. Several scholars (i.e. Fass, 1980; Marks, 1976–77) have noted that the low IQs that they believed were "clearly discriminatory" in relation to the new immigrants, caused or contributed to the Immigration Act of 1924. Relatively few intelligence tests were given on Ellis Island. Goddard did, however, send two women to the island in 1913: "They were instructed to pick out the feebleminded by sight, a task Goddard preferred to assign to women, to whom he granted superior intuition" (Gould, 1981, p. 165). These women tested a small group of immigrants with Goddard's Binet scale. Goddard eventually concluded that the data indicated that 40% to 50% of the immigrants were "feebleminded." Later, however, it was shown that his version of the Binet scale yielded lower scores than Terman's revision (Gould, 1981). Even though Congressional debates concerning the Immigration Act constantly referred to the Army data to support eastern and southern European exclusion, it does not follow that the Immigration Act was a direct result of the low mental abilities reported for the foreign immigrants. Many social variables were stacked against the southern and eastern immigrants, the most notable one being the fact that they were perceived as advocates of socialism:

> Every misfortune that normally follows in the train of a great war—the closing of munitions factories, a cutback in the working week, a slump in the price of crops that for four years had poured into the granaries of the Allies—could be interpreted as tactical triumphs of the Communist strategy to overthrow the American republic. . . . The first law officer of the

United States, the Attorney General himself, had his house in Washington blown up. He was Mitchell Palmer. . . .

Palmer's name should be memorized in schools as the archetype of the paranoid witch hunter with which the Republic is regularly afflicted whenever an unpleasant turn of history . . . seems to be beyond the control of the government of the United States. He ordered or condoned raids on magazine offices, public halls, private houses, union headquarters, meetings big and small of anyone—socialists, liberals, atheists, freethinkers, social workers—who could be identified or accused as Bolsheviks. . . . Palmer's hysterical example led, among other horrors, to a drastic revision of the immigration laws. The flow of immigrants from eastern and southern Europe slowed to a dribble, and there was a time when more people were being deported from Ellis Island than were coming in. (Cooke, 1974, p. 310)

This is not to belittle the fact that when a person was suspected of being mentally deficient, an immigration official would chalk a circle with a cross in the middle on the immigrant's back. This symbol signified that the immigrant was thought to be feebleminded. It also meant certain deportation. If low IQs were not the direct cause of the Immigration Act, however, they unquestionably contributed indirectly to its passage. Nevertheless, as Paula Fass (1980) pointed out: "If immigration exclusion was one response to the alien presence, Americanization, remedial socialization, and vocational training, all of which were school centered, were others" (p. 448). Besides exclusion and deportation, the progressive educational movement (founded in 1919 and supported by John Dewey after he joined in 1927) promised educational reform, which would provide some answers to the immigration problem:

It would be unfair and meanspirited to argue that educators used IQs to cut across the problem and to exclude the newer immigrants from the lines of advancement which the schools now promised. It was never so simple. The schools continued to be theoretically and actually a force that facilitated immigrant access to society's rewards, both as an agency incorporating immigrant children into the mainlines of the culture and as a lever for social and occupational advancement for individuals. (Fass, 1980, pp. 448–449)

School Organization

Mental ages, or IQs, have never been the primary organizational metric used in schools. Intelligence test results were simply, albeit naively and often inappropriately, used to organize an educational system that had previously adopted chronological age as the primary method for school organization. The complete separation of children into separate "graded" classrooms, each with its own teacher, was reportedly accomplished first by John Philbrick, who organized the Quincy, Massachusetts, grammar school in 1847 (Potter, 1967). The Ohio State Commissioner of Education reported that between 1854 and 1855, nearly 150 towns had converted to age-graded schools. Intelligence quotients, which were first available with the 1916 Stanford-Binet, allowed the tracking of pupils within the broader age categories. The claim is often made that these special educational and vocational training programs effectively prevented the upward social mobility of the immigrant groups. The data provided by Thomas Sowell (1981b), however, does not support this conclusion. Jews, who initially scored low as a group on intelligence tests and who have faced centuries of anti-Semitism, currently have the highest family incomes in the United States. Their IQs had risen past the national average by 1920. And, according to Sowell, "Polish IQs which averaged eighty-five in the earlier studies—the same as that of blacks today—had risen to 109 by the 1970s. This twenty-four point rise is greater than the current black–white difference (fifteen points)" (1981b, p. 9). The current Polish family income is well above that of the typical Anglo-Saxon family. Even the traditional black–white income differences have disappeared in college-educated persons with similar family characteristics.

Obviously, the IQ has been misinterpreted; it is not an immutable measure of a person. Few would disagree with the contention that IQs have frequently been misused. Since IQs can change with a person's familiarization with what can broadly be termed the "American Culture," its use in the denial of education, or the provision of relatively poorer educational opportunities to persons not familiar with mainstream cultural standards was, and continues to be, a disservice to those persons. The use of IQs to deny a person's right to fail is always a misuse of the metric. Perhaps a case can be built for using gains in IQs as a measure of a minority's assimilation into the cultural mainstream. Certainly Sowell's data and Gould's reinterpretation of the Army data would support that position.

Early Attitudes

One of the unfortunate linkages in the history of intellectual assessment is the well-documented prejudicial attitudes of Terman and Goddard. It is really unnecessary to reiterate the racial slurs in their writings. Their Social Darwinistic attitudes did a great disservice to the IQ. Gould (1981) contends that Goddard's views were so myopic on the subject of preventing the "feebleminded" from having children (Goddard believed intelligence was almost exclusively inherited) that he disfigured photographs of the faces of the Kallikak family who were living in the Pine Barrens of New Jersey to make them "look evil and stupid" (Goddard, 1914). According to Gould, Goddard did not retouch Deborah Kallikak's photos, who lived at Goddard's Vineland Institution. Gould believes Goddard's reasons for altering the other family members' photographs become apparent when one reads the conclusions of his book:

> Feeble-mindedness is hereditary and transmitted as surely as any other character. We cannot successfully cope with these conditions until we recognize feeble-mindedness and its hereditary nature, recognize it early, and take care of it. In considering the question of care, segregation through colonization seems in the present state of our knowledge to be the ideal and perfectly satisfactory method. Sterilization may be accepted as a makeshift, as a help to solve this problem because the conditions have become so intolerable. But this must at present be regarded only as makeshift and temporary, for before it can be extensively practiced, a great deal must be learned about the effects of the operation and about the laws of human inheritance. (Goddard, 1914, p. 117)

However, other historians (Fancher, 1987; Glenn & Ellis, 1988; Kral, 1988; Zenderland, 1988) make convincing arguments that the photos were probably not retouched by Goddard. Perhaps they were retouched by the publisher because of the poor quality of the original photographs. In any case, retouching the photographs would have been counterproductive to Goddard's contention that feebleminded children most often looked quite normal. Even in these rebuttals to Gould's interpretations of photographic doctoring, the scholars who quote Goddard are faced with the singular fact that Goddard's own words provide evidence of his faulty thinking (see Zenderland, 1988).

   Through the influence of these men, the original intent of Binet (to identify and assist children who were in need of special educational services) was frequently changed to one of rank-ordering children. Children who scored exceedingly low were often denied any opportunity for an educational experience. This denial of service ended with the *P.A.R.C.* v. *Commonwealth of Pennsylvania* decision in 1972. This legal decision established the right of all children to an appropriate education. Because mentally re-

tarded children could not be denied educational programs, the decision put an end to one of the major misuses of the IQ.

   Although IQs have been, are, and will continue to be misused, they can also serve well. Intelligence test results can aid practitioners in the decision-making processes concerning certain socially significant criteria. Binet's proposed use of mental tests was noble. When used for like purposes today, the IQ is still a useful device for aiding both individuals and institutions in cooperative endeavors to make life better for themselves and others.

Development of Test Items

   One of the startling facts that quickly emerges when one explores the actual test questions over the history of mental measurement is that the items have changed so little. In *The Measurement of Intelligence,* Terman (1916) lists the tests as arranged by Binet in 1911 shortly before his death. Examples include: (a) at age 3 a child is supposed to point to nose, eyes, and mouth; (b) at age 6, distinguish between pictures of pretty and ugly faces; (c) at age 9, answer easy comprehension questions; (d) at age 12, compose one sentence given three words; and (e) at the adult level, give differences between pairs of abstract terms. These items as well as many others should be quite familiar to current Stanford-Binet users. Likewise, the interested observer can find many similarities between the 1981 Wechsler Adult Intelligence Scale-Revised (WAIS-R) and the 1939 Wechsler Bellevue.

   The reasons given for the stability of the subtests and items making up intelligence tests range from a lack of creativity in the test constructors to the statement that these items have withstood the test of time. The latter interpretation is probably the more correct as various attempts have been made to change the test items. Some attempts have been successful. For example, Wechsler added the new subtests Animal House, Geometric Design, and Sentences to several modified subtests from the Wechsler Intelligence Scale for Children (WISC; Wechsler, 1949) to produce the Wechsler Preschool and Primary Scale of Intelligence (WPPSI; Wechsler, 1967). Other attempts, however, have not been successful. Wechsler continued to experiment with new measures for his intelligence tests.

> Two new tests were tried out experimentally as possible additions to the WAIS-R. The first was a test of Level of Aspiration, which was studied as a possible means of broadening the coverage of the WAIS-R to include a measure of nonintellective

ability. It had a number of interesting features, but seemed to require further research before it could be added as a regular member of the battery. The second test was a new measure of spatial ability: Although this test also had a number of merits it was too highly correlated with block design to warrant inclusion in the revised scale. (Wechsler, 1981, p. 10)

In summary, however, it can be stated that the actual format of the major intelligence tests has changed little since their initial introductions.

DEFINITION OF INTELLIGENCE

It is noteworthy that thus far we have talked about the history and development of mental tests and have not yet tendered a definition of the construct those tests are intended to measure. Early in the development of intellectual assessment, the concepts of *individual* and *social worth* were tied into the definition of intelligence. Studies like Goddard's *The Kallikak Family* (1914), and *The Criminal Imbecile* (1915), Danielson and Davenport's *The Hill Folk* (1912), and Dugdale's *The Jukes* (1910) firmly implanted in both the professional's and the layperson's minds the concept that mental ability and individual worth were intimately related. This linking of intelligence and social worth is reflected in Terman's comment, "In other words, not all criminals are feeble-minded, but all feeble-minded are at least potential criminals" (1916, p. 11) and Goddard's statements that the most dangerous children in a community were those feeble-minded children who look entirely normal (Zenderland, 1988). Although these linkages have remained close to the surface in lay definitions of intelligence, they are not part of the professional use of the term.

In 1921, the *Journal of Educational Psychology* published the now famous piece that asked 17 of the leading experts to respond to the following questions: What is the definition of intelligence? What are the next important steps needed in intellectual assessment research? A review of the definitions given by the experts who replied shows little evidence of the linkage of "intelligence" with "individual worth." What is apparent, however, is a lack of general agreement on the definition of intelligence. In 1975, Wechsler, reflecting back on the fact that nearly as many definitions of intelligence were offered as contributors who replied, remarked: "Since 1921, there have been many symposia on intelligence and innumerable articles and books on the subject. A count of the views expressed in them would show no greater percentage of agreement today than it did two generations ago" (p. 135). An additional 14 years and many more scholarly publications have not changed the situation.

Sattler (1982) discusses nine major theorists who have differing views on the definition and measurement of intelligence. Even within the empirical factor-analytic camps (all of which use similar statistical procedures to develop models of intelligence), there remains a great deal of controversy concerning the structure and definition of intelligence. (See, e.g., Guilford, 1980; Kelderman, Mellenbergh, & Elshout, 1981). At present, there does not appear to be a movement toward a consolidated theory of intelligence. Most of the theorists, however, would agree that existing intelligence tests neither are capable of, nor attempt to deal with, most of the behaviors that might be subsumed under the word intelligence:

> When well defined, "intelligence" is too broad to be measured by any test available today. It is a mistake to think we are measuring the full meaning of intelligence with any one test or even several of them. Therefore, it is not only important for test authors to specify the content of their test but also for users to interpret the scores within the limitations of the scores derived and make other observations to fill in around the scores. (French, 1979, p. 756)

Intelligence is not a single entity but is composed of many complex facets. Just because there are numerous definitions, however, does not mean that the term is useless. As Wechsler (1975) stated:

> What is not admissible is the assertion that because there are so many views "nobody really knows what one is talking about" when one uses the term intelligence or the equally false assertion that it is all a matter of semantics. . . . An average adult and a normal 12-year-old will understand the word intelligent if it is used in a meaningful context. (p. 139)

If, however, one is talking about field-based problems where intelligence is actually being measured with a currently available test, one must emphatically make the distinction between the different definitions of intelligence on the one hand and the tests and scores that are designed to measure intelligence on the other. When Boring (1923) reacted to the seemingly hopeless efforts of others to agree on the definitions of intelligence by stating that it "must be defined as the capacity to do well on an intelligence test," he focused attention where it belonged—on the tests themselves. Practitioners use the tests to aid in their decision-making processes.

Intelligence tests and the scores they generate (IQs and subtest scores) are used in very practical applications. Although the tests may not measure all (perhaps not even any) of the constructs involved in various formal definitions of intelligence, in some situations, they allow the people who use them to make statements about individuals with more confidence in the truthfulness of those statements than they could if the mental test were not used. In other situations, intelligence test results are often used to make statements about individuals that research evidence clearly indicates are impossible. Practitioners must first determine to what purpose the mental test is to be put. The answer to this question defines the scores that need to be generated and simultaneously determines what kind of validity the test must generate in order to justify this usage. As with all tests, intelligence tests are not valid in a general sense; their validity can only be substantiated with regard to the purpose for which they are used.

USES OF INTELLIGENCE TESTS

Several uses of IQs that are currently in vogue in education will be taken up and discussed in turn. Some of these uses will be supported by the research evidence. Others must be interpreted as current abuses. Education and school practice was chosen as the field of IQ application because many of the recent controversies that surround usage of intelligence tests have been generated in this field. Educational environs are where the great bulk of intelligence tests are given. Currently 3% to 5% of public school children are referred for psychological evaluations by their teachers. Of those children, 92% are tested and 73% are placed in special education programs. Since the 1976–77 school year there has been a 16% increase in the number of children in special education programs and a 40% increase in the number of children classified as learning disabled. In 1988 there were approximately 4 million students in special education programs and 1.7 million (41%) of those children were classified as learning disabled (Graden, 1988). The methods of evaluation used in this chapter, however, would remain applicable whether the reader is interested in children and education or adults and psychopathology.

To Measure Intelligence

If one asks psychologists working in public schools why they give intelligence tests to children, a frequent answer (at least in the author's experience) is that they say they administer intelligence tests to measure the child's intelligence. This, of course, begs for a defi-nition of intelligence. The psychologist has responded that he or she uses the test to measure a construct. It therefore follows that the user should be able adequately to define the construct and support the use of the test in that manner by citing construct validity evidence.

Construct validity is not as precisely defined, from a statistical point of view, as predictive validity. In general, however, the construct validity of a test can be supported through three different approaches. Nunnally (1978) lists the following three aspects of construct validation:

> (1) specifying the domain of observables related to the construct; (2) from empirical research and statistical analyses, determining the extent to which the observables measure the same thing, several different things, or many different things; and (3) subsequently performing studies of individual differences and/or controlled experiments to determine the extent to which supposed measures of the construct produce results which are predictable from highly accepted theoretical hypotheses concerning the construct. (p. 98)

Although it is well beyond the scope of this chapter to discuss construct validation in any detail, a brief comment concerning each of these aspects with respect to the major individual intelligence tests is in order. First, under the aspect of specifying the domain of observable behaviors related to intelligence, there is still much debate. Wechsler believed that performance items were part of adult intellectual functioning and introduced them into his scales. As noted earlier, he continued to attempt to introduce what he termed *nonintellective* measures into his intelligence tests. He believed that other personality variables were important in the assessment of intelligence, but were not evaluated by present intelligence tests (Wechsler, 1950). Logically, Wechsler would have argued that present tests do not adequately cover the domain of observables that are related to intelligence. Present intelligence tests are narrowly composed of items that are mainly oriented toward scholastic achievements. Berger (1978) argues that intelligence tests measure a certain structure of modern consciousness that is something different from intelligence. Individual items from intelligence tests have also been criticized because some of them are thought to be unfair to minority groups. This topic will be discussed more fully under the topic of IQ bias.

The second aspect discussed by Nunnally—seeing whether the tests measure one or many things—is often approached through both reliability and factor-analytic studies. High internal consistency reliability estimates indicate the test items are measuring attributes that are similar enough to make adding up the results obtained over all of the items sensible. The reliability estimates for most of the major tests of cognitive functioning used with children are high enough so that the test items can be added together to obtain IQs or their equivalents.

Factor-analytic results of the Wechslers and the Stanford-Binet prior to the fourth edition have been quite consistent across different investigations. The number of factors found on the older Stanford-Binet depends upon the age of the subjects being investigated. At the upper age levels, this test was mainly measuring verbal fluency and reasoning, whereas at the lower age levels the factor composition was more complex (Sattler, 1982). However, Sattler (1982) reported that a single "general" factor appeared to carry most of the variance on the instrument. Factor analyses of the newer fourth edition of the Stanford-Binet provide a different structure. Keith, Cool, Novak, White, and Pottelbaum (1988) have summarized the information from the new Binet's technical manual (Thorndike, Hagen, & Sattler, 1986a), and have provided the following four points: (a) This test appears to continue to have a high "g" loading just like the previous Binets. (b) The underlying hypothesized factors of verbal reasoning, quantitative reasoning, abstract/visual reasoning, and short-term memory are supported in children above 6 years of age. (c) In children below 7 years of age, it was difficult to separate reasoning from memory. (d) When the scales are combined to measure crystallized versus fluid intelligence there is little supportive evidence for the model.

The Wechslers are primarily two-factor scales. Exploratory studies (Blaha & Vance, 1979; Carlson & Reynolds, 1981; Kaufman, 1975; Peterson & Hart, 1979; Reschly, 1978; Schooler, Beebe, & Koepke, 1978; Silverstein, 1969; Wallbrown, Blaha, & Wherry, 1974) have indicated that the tests show sometimes either a two- or three-factor structure. However, confirmatory analyses (Ramanaiah & Adams, 1979; Ramanaiah, O'Donnell, & Ribich, 1976) indicate that these tests have a two-factor structure. Research with the Wechsler Intelligence Scale for Children—Revised (WISC-R; Wechsler, 1974) indicates that this test's third factor (Freedom From Distractibility) does not meet the .90 reliability standards needed to make decisions about individuals (Gutkin, 1978). Thus, even when found in some exploratory investigations, the reliability of this factor is not high enough to make it useful for practitioners. In addition, the difficulty in interpreting the Freedom

From Distractibility factor as either a measure of the ability to concentrate or a measure of numerical ability has been previously noted by Sattler (1974).

Factor analysis has been the primary tool for studying the structure of intelligence. As a social science research tool, it continues to generate arguments about which techniques should be used. Factor analysis is not a single mathematical technique. The results one obtains concerning a test are dependent upon the factoring technique used. Because factor analysis generally developed within a social science context (Cattell, 1978) and specifically evolved in relation to intelligence tests, a brief description of the problems with respect to Spearman's general intelligence (g) is presented. The reader who is unfamiliar with factor analysis but who would like an extended discussion of the problems inherent in studying intelligence tests with factor-analytic techniques is referred to an excellent elementary discussion by Gould (1981). Spearman, an English psychologist, initially developed principal components analysis because he noted the positive correlations behind most measures of mental ability. He wondered if there was some simpler structure behind these correlations. Principal components without rotations of the axes assures that a g factor will be found. In the United States, Thurstone developed factor rotations that he termed *simple structure;* these rotations mathematically rotated out g. Thurstone felt that these rotated factors were more representative of the "real" world. Mathematically, both solutions are equivalent. Philosophically, there are large differences. If g exists, and is the most important attribute of an intelligence test, than a single number can be used to summarize the test. However, Thurstone continually found simple structures using his technique and therefore proclaimed that the tests measure a small number of "primary mental abilities." Both of the techniques discussed only find mathematically defined factors. Just because a statistical technique grinds out a solution does not assure that the factor(s) found have a necessary correspondence to reality. Several statements made by Gould (1981) about the major factor theorists capture the difficulty in using factor analytic results in interpreting intelligence tests. The first principal component:

> For Spearman it is to be cherished as a measure of innate general intelligence, for Thurstone, it is a meaningless average of an arbitrary battery of tests, devoid of psychological significance, and calculated only as an intermediary step in rotation to simple structure. (p. 301)
> For Cyril Burt, the group factors, although real and important in vocational guidance, were subsidiary to

a dominant and innate g. For Thurstone, the old group factors became primary mental abilities. They were the irreducible mental entities; g was a delusion. (p. 303)

The very fact that estimates for the number of primary abilities have ranged from Thurstone's seven or so to Guilford's 120 or more indicates that vectors of the mind may be figments of the mind. (p. 309)

Even though factor analysis has not determined the structure of intelligence, and indeed intelligence tests may be developed to conform to almost any a priori structure, factor analysis is a useful technique for studying current tests. The evaluation of developed tests through factor analysis will continue as long as the results continue to improve the efficiency of our predictions.

In an investigation that contrasted the efficacy of using WISC-R factor scores compared to the traditionally reported IQs, Hale (1981) indicated that by using factor scores, practitioners could account for appreciably more variance in the prediction of mathematics achievement. The WISC-R Performance IQ never aided in the prediction of academic achievement. Hale (1981) also noted that the Freedom From Distractibility factor was highly related to mathematics achievement. The factor scores obviously could be used by psychologists to improve their predictions. Test constructors might also use the information to support adding another number-related test so that the Freedom From Distractibility factor's reliability would be increased.

In any event, if the Stanford-Binet is primarily a single-factor test, and the Wechslers chiefly two-factor instruments, it is difficult to see how these particular intelligence tests correspond to the structural theories of Guilford or Thurstone. Our major tests do not measure as many things as are required by those theorists. As noted by Keith et al. (1988), the Stanford-Binet Fourth Edition does not conform to Cattell and Horn's theory of intelligence (Cattell, 1982; Horn & Cattell, 1966), which guided its development.

Many investigations have been conducted with reference to Nunnally's third aspect of construct validation: performing studies to verify hypotheses predictable from definitions of intelligence. Most of these investigations, however, are ex post facto due to the obvious ethical concerns of varying an independent variable powerful enough to change intelligence. Bereiter (1976–77) has effectively argued that the construct measured by intelligence tests is very important. He shows that a society run by low IQ elites is bound to collapse. This line of evidence, however, does not detract from the position that present intelligence tests measure an ability that greatly determines academic achievement. Modern societies require leaders who are efficient learners of academic material.

In summary, if one is using the intelligence test to measure the construct of intelligence, definitions of that construct should be offered. Present intelligence tests appear to measure only one or two factors adequately. These factors appear to be Verbal (Reasoning, Fluency, and/or Comprehension) and Perceptual Organization. It should be kept in mind that these factors may only be true in a mathematical sense and may not correspond to any psychological or physiological truth. The factors these tests measure are important, however, because of their relationship with the skills necessary for the successful performance of an individual in a modern technological society.

Subtest Analysis

Subtest analysis of intelligence tests has been mainly confined to the Wechsler series of tests for the obvious reason that the physical structure of the Wechslers simply lend themselves to subtest analysis. With the advent of the Stanford-Binet Fourth Edition, this may change. The literature on subtest analysis has always been quite controversial. Subtest analysis of the various Wechsler tests has been cyclical. Following the release of new or revised tests, another series of subtest investigations would be published. With both the WISC and the Wechsler Adult Intelligence Scale (WAIS; Wechsler, 1955), the conclusion has eventually been reached that subtest analysis was a relatively useless enterprise (Huelsman, 1970; Rabin, 1965). These results, however, never generalized from one test and its set of researchers to the next test, even though the psychometric properties of the test are similar. Even though Hirshoren and Kavale (1976) have shown that the relatively low reliabilities of the WISC-R subtests preclude accurate profile analyses, the importance of WISC-R profile analysis is still being debated. Both major texts currently being used by school psychology training programs for teaching WISC-R interpretation (Kaufman, 1979; Sattler, 1988) indicate that subtest analysis may be useful. Many pages of these texts are devoted to analyzing the strengths and weaknesses in a child's cognitive abilities that might be revealed by relatively high and low subtest scores. Although research results in this area are seen as inconsistent by the casual observer, a more intensive investigation will lead the observer to the realization that the literature is quite consistent. From a practical point of view, the literature can be broken down into two types of studies. First are those investigations that start with previously defined groups of children (e.g., reading disabled, conduct disordered, etc.) and ask if significant subtest differences can be found between these groups, or between a group and the standardization sample data. This is termed a *classical validity* study. The second set of investigations starts with the subtest scores and asks if knowledge of these subtest results can aid in the prediction or differentiation of a socially significant criterion. This criterion might be a child's academic achievement or handicapping condition. These studies are termed *clinical utility* studies. (For an in-depth discussion of the distinctions between classical validity and clinical utility, see Wiggins, 1973.) Miller (1980) contends that the inconsistency that is thought to exist in this body of research exists because, although investigators have found statistically significant WISC-R profiles to be characteristic of certain handicapped groups, there has been a failure to demonstrate that these profiles are distinctive enough to allow practitioners to differentiate between handicapped and normal children. In other words, he argues that significant patterns have been found using the classical validity research strategy, but the clinical research does not support the use of these results. My review of the literature supports this contention. In those studies starting with intact groups (Ackerman, Peters, & Dykman, 1971; Dean, 1977; Rugel, 1974; Smith, Coleman, Dokecki, & Davis, 1977; Vance, Wallbrown, & Blaha, 1978), significant subtest differences have been found between children classified as handicapped and those classified as normal. In those investigations that started with subtest results and attempted to classify children into diagnostic categories (Hale, 1979; Hale & Landino, 1981; Hale & Raymond, 1981) or those studies where reclassification could take place (Tabachnick, 1979; Thompson, 1980), high degrees of diagnostic error were encountered. In one investigation (Hale, 1979), a 100% error rate was found when classifying reading underachievers using a significant discriminant function identified in the same group of children. In another related investigation, Hale and Landino (1981) found, using significant WISC-R subtest differences to reclassify behaviorally disordered and normal boys, that the results obtained were no better than chance. Other investigations have found that patterns of subtest strengths and weaknesses on the WISC-R derived either through rules provided by Kaufman (1979) or sophisticated profile cluster schemes (Skinner & Lei, 1980) do not aid in the prediction of a child's academic achievement level (Hale & Raymond, 1981; Hale &

Saxe, 1983). Finally, Kavale and Forness (1984) in a recent meta-analysis of the available literature concluded that Wechsler patterns were in fact parodies.

In summary, these results suggest that knowledge of a child's subtest profile does not appreciably help the clinician in predicting either academic achievement levels or behavioral difficulties. There is increasing evidence that WISC-R subtest analysis lacks utility for making special education placement decisions (Hale, 1979; Hale & Landino, 1981; Kavale & Forness, 1984; Thompson, 1980; Vance, Singer, & Engin, 1980). In fairness to Sattler (1982 & 1988) and Kaufman (1979), it should be noted that these authors offer various cautions to profile analysis: "The hypotheses should be treated as tentative, formulated in relation to the child's absolute scaled scores, and not referred to as 'verifiable insights' " (Sattler, 1982, p. 201). If, however, as is presently the case, the procedure is supported as "only" a hypothesis-generating procedure, those hypotheses should be generated and tested. Otherwise, on the basis of these findings, the use of subtest analysis appears unconscionable.

Predicting Academic Achievement

The primary usage of intelligence tests in the public schools is to help in the determination of special education for children. Thus, the major convention today is the same as that for which Binet developed the test. The major question that school psychologists are still confronted with is, "How well can we expect this child to do in school?" (Hale, 1978). If IQs are employed in this fashion, a presumption is made that they are related to and can be used to predict academic achievement.

More formally, the definition of IQ under this usage might be stated: An IQ allows one to predict a youngster's academic achievement in a typical school environment if the child is left to his or her own devices and all things remain equal. The term "typical school environment" would exclude those academic environs where emphasis was not placed on traditional educational curricular materials. The term "left to his or her own devices" would exclude children from the prediction model if they were given support services (i.e., special education). "All things remain equal" would exclude children where traumatic events, like the death of a parent, might be expected to affect test scores. The prediction definition of intelligence assumes we are predicting in a culturally loaded environment. It also assumes that the IQ is changeable. Intelligence, in any practically meaningful sense of the word, can be increased by education and exposure to the mainstream culture; it is not a fixed, inborn quantity. Sowell's (1981a) earlier reported figures of group IQ changes and Yerkes's (1921) findings that the Army test scores were correlated with years of residence in the United States certainly corroborate allegations that scores improve with exposure to the American middle-class culture. The final assumption, that these cultural standards and methods of performance are the most appropriate standards on which to measure and train individuals, remains open to debate. Use of intelligence tests in this manner assumes that they can demonstrate adequate predictive validity.

Primary Predictive Validity Model

The correlation coefficient between a selected test of intelligence and a selected measure of academic achievement is a direct method of evaluating IQs in relation to the academic prediction model. Some tests would fare quite well under this model, and others, of course, would not. Again a discussion that included all of the tests available would deserve a chapter in itself. Therefore, the two major individual tests given to public school children who are deemed to have serious enough difficulties to warrant a psychological evaluation (Stanford-Binet & WISC-R; Wechsler, 1974) will be discussed in some detail.

Correlations between two variables can best be represented by a bivariate plot of their relationship. Figure 22.1 shows a hypothetical situation where there is no relation between intelligence (IQ) and achievement (Ach). The correlation (r_{Ach-IQ}) in such a circumstance would equal zero. If practitioners found themselves working in that situation and needed to predict a person's score on the criterion variable, knowledge of the person's score on the predictor would not aid the prediction process. The practitioner would be left with predicting the mean criterion score for everyone. The prediction equation would be:

$$\widehat{Ach} = \overline{Ach} \qquad (22.1)$$

Where $\widehat{Ach}$ = predicted criterion score and $\overline{Ach}$ = mean criterion score. To establish confidence intervals around this predicted value, one could add and subtract the standard deviation (SD) of the test:

$$\widehat{Ach} = \overline{Ach} \pm SD_{Ach} \qquad (22.2)$$

Equation 22.2 represents the predicted score of a person under the situation represented by Figure 22.1, with 68% confidence limits. This is the *base rate* of prediction. Anyone can predict with this level of accuracy knowing only the descriptive statistics of the criterion variable. This is exactly the situation that is assumed when one expects every child to achieve an average score on an achievement test. Any predictive test of value should allow its user to improve significantly upon the predictions offered by this situation.

Figure 22.2 represents a situation where perfect prediction is possible. Every data point falls exactly on a straight line. The more closely the data points can be represented by a straight line, the higher the correlation. Figure 22.2 shows a situation where $r_{Ach-IQ} = 1.0$. The equation for this straight line (the regression equation) would be:

$$\widehat{Ach} = b(IQ) + a \qquad (22.3)$$

where b is the slope of the line and a is the intercept (the point where the prediction line crosses the criterion axis when the predictor value is zero). In social science research, this situation never occurs. It might be called the "ideal psychometric" situation because there is absolutely no error in the predictions made. If we assume that IQ and achievement scores are distributed in exactly the same manner (i.e., means = 100, SD = 15), then slope of the equation would equal one. As the child's intelligence scores increased by one point, the achievement scores would also increase by a single point. Although no IQ measure yields scores of zero, if the prediction line were extrapolated to the point where, theoretically, the IQ would equal zero, the achievement score obtained from the prediction equation would also equal zero. Equation 22.4 represents this perfect prediction situation.

$$\widehat{Ach} = 1(IQ) + 0 \qquad (22.4)$$

Figure 22.3 represents the more typical situation in the social sciences. It was constructed from the data available from Hale (1978). This figure shows the relationship between the WISC-R Full Scale IQ (FSIQ) and the Wide Range Achievement Test (WRAT; Jastak & Jastak, 1976) Reading standard score. The solid line through the data points represents the best prediction line. This line, as noted above, is called the regression line. If one knows the descriptive statistics for both the predictor and the criterion variables as well as the correlation between them, the equation for the best prediction line is easily found using Equation 22.5.

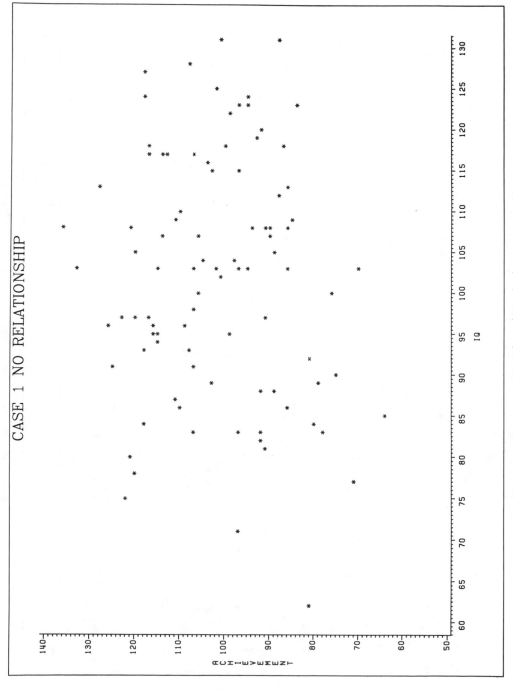

Figure 22.1. A representation of no relationship between 2 variables.

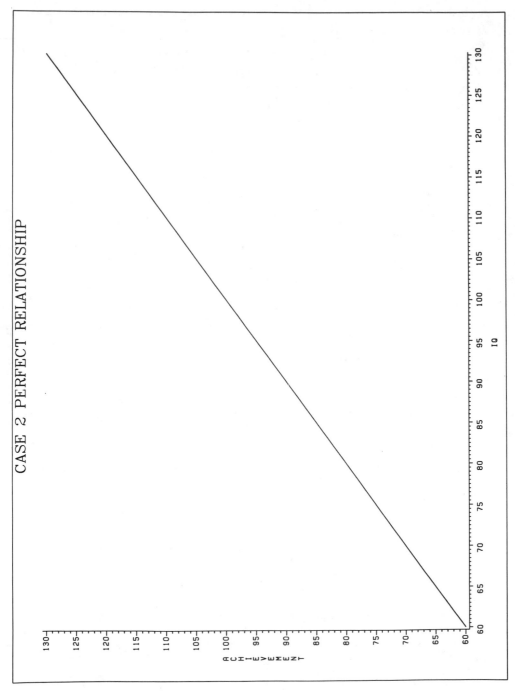

Figure 22.2. A representation of a perfect relationship between 2 variables.

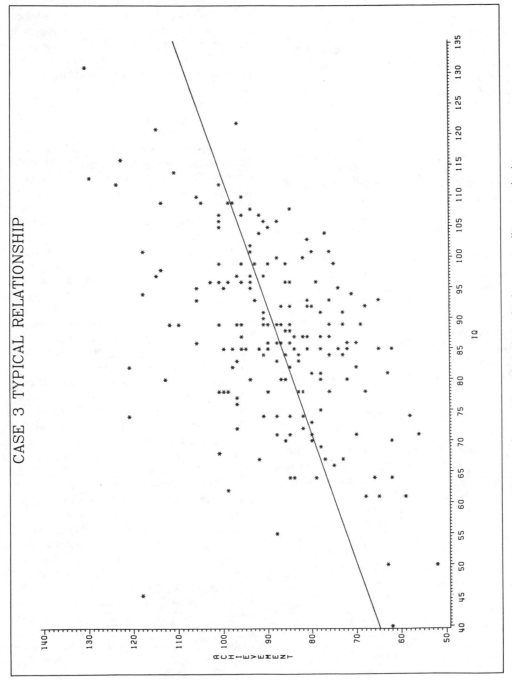

Figure 22.3. A representation of the typical relationship between intelligence and achievement.

$$\widehat{Ach} = \left\{ \left[r_{Ach-IQ} \frac{(SD_{Ach})}{(SD_{IQ})} (IQ - \overline{IQ}) \right] + \overline{Ach} \right\}$$

$$(22.5)$$

Sattler (1982) reports the median correlation between WISC-R FSIQ and WRAT Reading to be .60. Both WISC-R FSIQ and WRAT Reading standard scores are distributed with means equal to 100 and standard deviations (SD) equal to 15. These numbers can be substituted into Equation 22.5, resulting in the following:

$$\widehat{Ach} = \left\{ \left[.6 \frac{15}{15} (IQ - 100) \right] + 100 \right\} \quad (22.6)$$

By multiplying and collecting terms, Equation 22.6 can be simplified to:

$$\widehat{Ach} = .60(IQ) + 40 \quad (22.7)$$

Equation 22.7 is equivalent in form to Equation 22.3 where .60 is the slope and 40 is the intercept.

The amount of error in prediction in all three cases is given by the standard error of estimate (SEe). Assuming large sample sizes in the investigation, the SEe is given by multiplying the SD of the criterion by the square root of 1 minus the square of the correlation found between the predictor and criterion. With respect to IQ predicting achievement the equation would be:

$$SEe = SD_{Ach} \sqrt{1 - r^2_{Ach-IQ}} \quad (22.8)$$

Using the WISC-R FSIQ and the WRAT Reading standard score as the predictor and criterion variables, the SEe for the three cases can be calculated. For Case 1 where $r_{Ach-IQ} = 0$, SEe $= SD_{Ach}\sqrt{1-0}$ $= SD_{Ach} = 15$. For Case 2 where $r_{Ach-IQ} = 1$, the SEe $= SD_{Ach}\sqrt{1-1} = 0$. In this case, there is no error in prediction. For the achievement data in Case 3 where $r_{Ach-IQ} = .60$, SEe $= 15\sqrt{1-.36} = 12$. Thus, the entire equation, including 68% confidence intervals, can be written as follows:

$$\widehat{Ach} = \left\{ \left[r_{Ach-IQ} \frac{(SD_{Ach})}{(SD_{IQ})} (IQ - \overline{IQ}) \right] + \overline{Ach} \right\}$$
$$\pm SD_{Ach}\sqrt{1 - r^2_{Ach-IQ}} \quad (22.9)$$

using data where $r_{xy} = .60$:

$$\widehat{Ach} = .6(IQ) + 40 \pm 12 \quad (22.10)$$

The traditional method of evaluating the utility of the regression equation is to look at the coefficient of determination r^2_{x-y}. The coefficient of determination tells the investigator the proportion of variance in the criterion which is accounted for by knowledge of the client's score on the predictor variable. Returning to the baseline situation ($r_{Ach-IQ} = 0.0$), one sees that $15^2 = 225$ variance units are unaccounted for. This figure is simply the standard deviation of the test squared. When the prediction situation has changed by knowledge of a predictor score that correlates .60 with the criterion, one sees that $12^2 = 144$ variance units remain unaccounted for. This figure is simply the standard error of estimate squared. Thus in moving from $r_{Ach-IQ} = 0.0$ to $r_{Ach-IQ} = .60$, $225 - 144 = 81$ units of variance are accounted for (are removed from the standard error). Therefore $\frac{81}{225} = .36$ is the proportion of variance accounted for. Of course, this figure is more simply calculated by squaring the correlation coefficient ($.60^2 = .36$).

Comparing the standard error of prediction (estimate) where $r_{Ach-IQ} = 0.0$ (baseline condition) with the case where $r_{Ach-IQ} = .60$, one sees that at 68% confidence intervals the range of prediction has been reduced by six points. Of course, practitioners would probably not make predictions using 68% confidence intervals. More appropriate confidence intervals would be 85% or 95%. At the 95% confidence interval, the practitioner operating under the baseline condition would be adding and subtracting $1.96(15) = 29.4$ points to the predicted score of 100 for each child. The entire 95% confidence interval would then encompass a spread of 58.8 points. On the other hand, using an IQ that correlated .60 with the criterion, the point spread at 95% confidence is reduced to 47.04 points. The 11.04 point decrement represents a reduction of over three-fourths of a standard deviation on the test. Garrett (1966) gives a formula for calculating the efficiency rate of the regression equation over that available using baseline conditions. Garrett's efficiency statistic is: E $= 1 - \sqrt{1 - r^2_{x-y}}$. The regression situation encountered $r_{Ach-IQ} = .60$ is thus 20% efficient ($1 - \sqrt{1 - .6^2} = .20$). Both the WISC-R and the Stanford-Binet correlate with achievement tests (using school-aged children) at about the same level ($r_{Ach-IQ} = .60$). Both of these intelligence tests account for approximately 36% of the variance in achievement and are approximately 20% efficient in these prediction situations. With the older version of the Binet, predictions were less stable for those students at the upper end of the scale than for those scoring at the lower end. Also, when the older Binet was used with preschoolers (ages 2 to 4), the test did not predict future scholastic achievement as well as when the children were tested at older ages. With the new Binet, not enough data have been collected to make these pronouncements.

CURRENT ISSUES IN INTELLECTUAL ASSESSMENT

Heritability of IQs

A measure of the heritability of a trait is given by the correlation between the genetic constitutions of a group of individuals and the trait in which one is interested. Heritability estimates for intelligence are given by correlating IQs with different degrees of kinship within groups of people, such as monozygotic or dizygotic twins. Sattler (1982) reports that "Studies of European and North American Caucasian populations suggest that the heritability of intelligence varies from .40 to .80" (p. 49). The coefficient of determination (r^2_{xy}) would therefore indicate that somewhere between 16% and 64% of the variance in IQs is accounted for by genotype. This range of numbers in and of itself does not conflict with statements that the environment is important in the expression of intelligence or that supplementary environmental or educational programs can increase intelligence. Academic success or failure is more often the real criterion of interest for psychologists using intelligence tests. Remembering that correlations between intelligence and achievement are around .60, even if intelligence scores were 100% determined by genetics, it would not necessarily follow that achievement would also be perfectly determined. Much of the confusion begins when the words "inherited" and "inevitable" are thought of as being equivalent. Diabetes mellitus is inherited, but certainly its debilitating effects are mitigated by the environmental manipulation of insulin. The potential hazards of the disease are certainly not inevitable.

Gould (1981) and MacKenzie (1980) both point out a serious flaw in our statistical thinking about heritability. Both authors note that studies of heritability of IQ are all of the "within-group" type. That is, the investigations permit an estimate of heritability *within* a single, coherent population (white Americans, for example). The extension of this percentage figure derived from the *within-group* study to explain differences *between* groups (differences between blacks and whites) is simply unfounded. Gould (1981) gives the following example:

Human height has a higher heritability than any value ever proposed for IQ. Take two separate groups of males. The first, with an average height of 5 feet 10 inches, live in a prosperous American town. The second, with an average height of 5 feet 6 inches, are starving in a third-world village. Heritability is 95 percent or so in each place—meaning that relatively tall fathers tend to have tall sons and relatively short fathers short sons. This high within-group heritability argues neither for nor against the possibility that better nutrition in the next generation might raise the average height of third-world villagers above that of prosperous Americans. Likewise, IQ could be highly heritable within groups, and the average difference between whites and blacks in America might still only record the environmental disadvantages of blacks. (pp. 156–157)

Again, if we take the practitioner's point of view, the exact heritability index is not of great importance. Even extremely high heritability of IQ should not prevent the provision of environmental and educational support to those persons whose functioning may be enhanced by those social services.

Bias in Intelligence Testing

Recently, a great deal of renewed interest has been focused on the issue of test bias. Two recent events have promoted this renewed concern: (a) the enactment of Public Law 94-142, which requires that handicapped children be found and provided with appropriate educational programming using nonbiased assessment procedures and (b) the two court cases (*Larry P.* v. *Wilson Riles* and *PASE* v. *Hannon*) that are diametrically opposed in their findings as to the use of IQs in the determination of educable mental retardation (EMR) as a handicap with minority children. Concern about nonbiased assessment in relation to intelligence testing has been so piqued that major efforts have been expended in the psychology community to educate practitioners. With reference to individually administered intelligence tests, the two recent legal decisions will be briefly discussed. The empirical results concerning bias in relation to Wechsler's series of tests and the older version of the Stanford-Binet will then be presented. (The Stanford-Binet Intelligence Scale: Fourth Edition is too new for extensive information concerning its bias or lack thereof to have accumulated.)

In the *Larry P.* decision of 1979, Judge Peckham, upholding his earlier judgment, ruled that (a) California schools could not utilize, permit the use of, or approve the use of any standardized intelligence test for the identification of black EMR children or their placement into EMR classes without securing ap-

proval by his court; (b) the disproportionate representation of blacks in EMR classrooms was to be eliminated; and (c) the harm done to blacks misclassified as
EMRs was to be remedied and discrimination caused
by IQ usage could not be allowed to recur. Also, every
black child in EMR placement in California should be
reevaluated, but the evaluation was to exclude standardized intelligence tests. Intelligence tests were
found to be biased against blacks and the EMR classes
into which they were placed were characterized as
"stigmatizing" and "dead end."

Judge Grady, on the other hand, in *PASE* v. *Hannon,* found that the same tests were not biased with
respect to minority status within Chicago. He faulted
Judge Peckham for not looking at and evaluating all of
the individual test items himself. Obviously, both
judges cannot be correct. With neither decision on
appeal, and with the Chicago Board of Education
requiring that black children not be evaluated with
intelligence tests, a resolution with respect to this
judicial dilemma will not be forthcoming.

In any event, it is the author's opinion that both
judges failed to adequately distinguish between the
tests' ability to *discriminate* between groups and
individuals and whether the tests are *biased* against
those same groups and individuals. For a thorough
discussion of both court cases, interested readers are
strongly urged to read Elliott (1987). Intelligence tests
were designed to discriminate between children who
were able to be scholastically successful and those
who were not. If, as the current research suggests,
minority children are not as successful as majority-
status children in traditional school environments,
then IQs should reflect this. If intelligence tests are
doing their job, minority children should have lower
IQs as a group than majority children. If IQs are used
as a component of remedial educational placement,
then proportionally more minority children will be
found in specialized educational programs. Proportionally more minority students are experiencing difficulty in scholastic endeavors. If the definition of bias
adopted by the reader is that IQs are biased if there are
mean differences between ethnic groups or that an
intelligence test is biased if its utilization leads to
disproportional representation in specialized educational programs of minority groups, then intelligence
tests are indeed biased.

In the author's judgment, these definitions of bias
incorrectly presume that IQs are a measure of potential
and are for all intents and purposes stable characteristics of an individual or group. Those who adopt the
mean difference/proportional imbalance definition of
IQ bias often maintain that intelligence tests have been
improperly used to buttress the proposition that black
children have lower intelligence (less potential) than
whites (Madden, 1980). A position that is, however,
rarely contested is that black children are currently
achieving at lower levels in school subjects than are
white youngsters. These mean IQ differences can
certainly be measuring the relative environmental
disadvantages experienced by blacks for generations.
The reader is referred back to the same arguments
proposed above in the section on heritability. If these
differences did not exist, intelligence tests would
simply not discriminate between students who are
adequately achieving in school and those who are
not—the task for which the instrument was devised.
The test's ability to *discriminate* is thus a necessary
function. *Bias,* on the other hand, refers to the unequal
measurement in differing groups, and is detrimental to
proper test usage.

Bias in intelligence tests can be appraised by in-
specting the test's differential validity across groups.
In other words, if a test does not display the same
validity for different groups, it may be said to be
biased. Validity is primarily of three types: content,
construct, and criterion-related. An intelligence test
may be biased if differential validity can be demonstrated in any one of the three areas for or against one
or more groups (Cleary, Humphreys, Kendrick, &
Wesman, 1975). Excellent reviews of the methods of
bias detection under these psychometric definitions
may be found in Jensen (1980) and Reynolds (1982).
These authors find that, in general, there is very little
psychometric evidence for intelligence test bias. The
evidence that has indicated that IQs may be biased has
generally suggested that the tests are biased in favor of
minorities instead of against them. A brief review of
some of the research conducted using the Binet and
Wechslers is in order. In the following sections, no
attempt is made to provide a complete overview of the
pertinent research findings. Only a summary of the
findings is provided. The interested reader is strongly
urged to read the primary sources.

Content Bias

One of the charges in the *Larry P.* decision was that
items for intelligence tests are drawn from white
middle-class culture. These items are assumed to be
more difficult for black and other minority children
than they are for white children. If it is assumed for a
moment that it is responsible to group persons on some
color index, and that blacks should be grouped together and whites should be grouped together, and that
differences, if found, would be meaningful, one can

ask if the available evidence indicates that some of the test items are more difficult for blacks. As Reschly (1980) points out, there are two distinct methods of "evidence" concerning this hypothesis. The most common method has been subjective "expert" examination of the items. Subjective judgment involves gathering opinion on whether the items are biased. The item in the WISC-R that is frequently pointed to as being culturally biased is the "Fight" item. The Fight item asks what one should do if a same-sex child much younger than yourself starts to fight with you. The opinion of those who believe this item is biased (more difficult) for blacks assumes that urban black children are taught by parents and peers that it is appropriate to strike younger children who are bothering them. As Reschly (1980) notes: "It is doubtful whether such attitudes or behaviors are any more typical or acceptable in that situation than in white, middle class environments" (p. 127).

When these subjective impressions are put to empirical test, the statistical evidence suggests that expert judgments are both unreliable (Sandoval & Millie, 1980) and invalid (Sandoval, 1979). Empirical methods of item analysis simply do not support the subjective judgments.

Schmeiser and Ferguson (1978) evaluated the performance of black and white students and found that test content differing on the amount of material based on black and white cultures did not have a major effect on student performance. Item difficulties for the WISC and WISC-R in several recent studies (Miele, 1979; Oakland & Feigenbaum, 1979; Sandoval, 1979) show that the item difficulty levels are not ordered differently for blacks and whites. Lambert (1981) notes that, "The Race X Items interaction, although it is significant for some items at some age levels, accounts for only 1%–2% of the variance. The only data that supports item bias at present is judgmental" (p. 942).

Construct Bias

One way that construct bias can be empirically evaluated is through factor-analytic techniques. Recent investigations with the WISC-R have consistently shown equivalent factor structures (no construct bias) across race (Dean, 1980; Gutkin & Reynolds, 1980; Oakland & Feigenbaum, 1979; Reschly, 1978; Reynolds, 1982; Vance, Huelsman, & Wherry, 1976; Vance et al., 1978). Another concern, in fact a line of defense offered by the defendants in the PASE versus Hannon case, was that although IQs may not be biased against any of several racial groups, they might be biased against socially and economically disadvantaged groups, irrespective of race. It was proposed by the defendants that intelligence tests might be biased when used to evaluate minority children because a large proportion of these children are members of lower socioeconomic groups. Hale (1983) presents research evidence concerning the construct validity of the WISC-R in relation to this "poverty principle." The results suggest that under realistic testing conditions, the factor structure of the WISC-R is consistent with respect to socioeconomic status.

Criterion-Related Bias

Although we have discussed a variety of models and criteria for defining the presence of test bias, Reynolds (1982) has stated that criterion-related validity is the most crucial type in relation to test bias. As discussed under "Uses of Intelligence Tests," predictive validity (a type of criterion-related validity) refers to how well a test forecasts a criterion of interest. This definition of bias is especially relevant to evaluating IQs because their ultimate utility depends on their ability to predict academic achievement. The predictive definition of test bias states that bias exists if the regression equations for two separate groups are different. Bias in regression equations can be reflected in the slopes of the lines, the intercepts, or both slopes and intercepts. Figures 22.4, 22.5, and 22.6 demonstrate graphically what bias would look like under these three situations.

Most of the research has been directed toward investigating differences between the regression lines generated for blacks and whites. Recent research has indicated that WISC-R scores are not racially biased according to the predictive definition when only the slopes are considered (Reschly & Sabers, 1979; Reynolds & Hartledge, 1979). When the intercepts are included, the evidence is not consistent. When bias in intercepts is found, however, the evidence indicates that most aptitude tests, including the WISC-R, *overestimate* the achievement of blacks (Reschly & Sabers, 1979). This means that for children with identical IQs, the achievement of the black child is more often lower than what one would predict using a regression equation developed using only white children or one developed using both black and white children together. Figure 22.7 was constructed using data provided by Bossard, Reynolds, and Gutkin (1980). They found that the regression lines using Stanford-Binet IQs to predict WRAT achievement scores were not statistically distinct (no bias existed). In Figure 22.7, Stanford-Binet IQs were regressed on

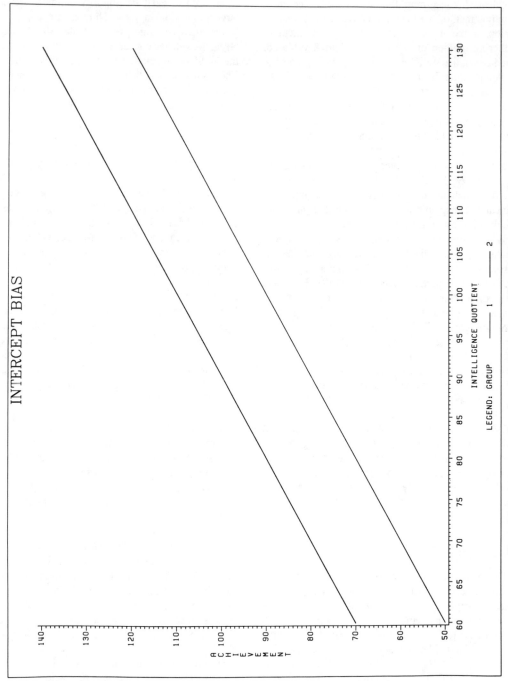

Figure 22.4. A representation of predictive bias due to differences in regression intercepts.

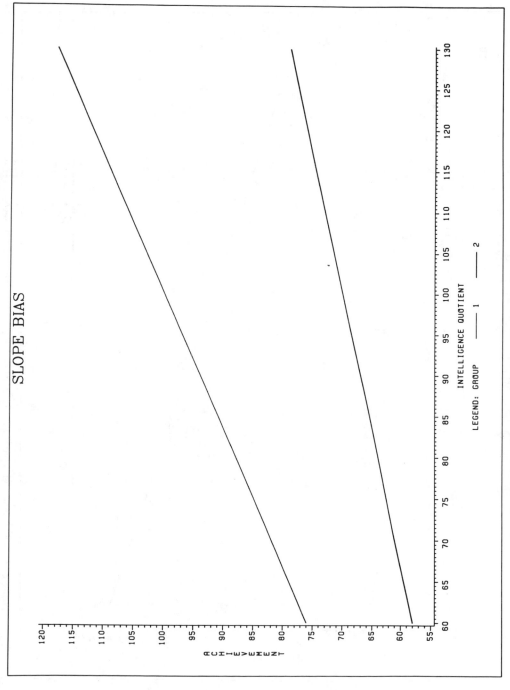

Figure 22.5. A representation of pred ctive bias due to differences in regression slopes.

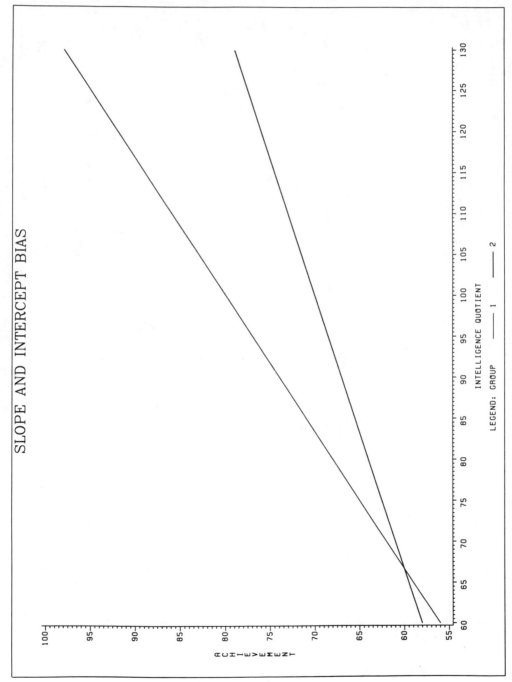

Figure 22.6. A representation of predictive bias due to a combination of differences in regression slopes and intercepts.

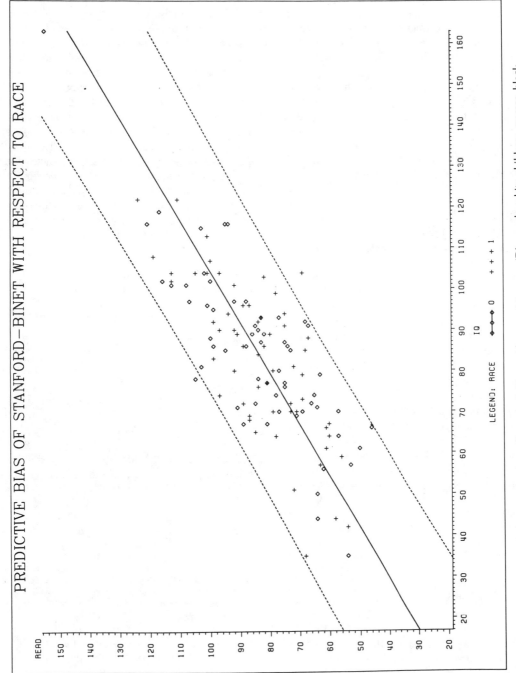

Figure 22.7. The predictive bias of Stanford–Binet with respect to race. (Diamonds–white children; crosses–black children.)

WRAT Reading achievement scores. White students are represented by diamonds, black students by crosses. By evaluating Figure 22.7, one can see the extensive overlap between black and white children in the bivariate space provided by Stanford-Binet and WRAT Reading. The solid line represents the common regression line. The broken lines define 95% confidence boundaries for individuals around the regression line.

Hale, Raymond, and Gajar (1982) have investigated WISC-R bias across socioeconomic status using the predictive bias criterion. Their study provides preliminary evidence that suggests that when bias is defined as significantly different regression lines, the WISC-R Verbal IQ is a nonbiased predictor of WRAT Reading with respect to socioeconomic status.

Stability of IQs

Throughout this chapter, emphasis has been placed on the fact that IQs are not immutable measures of individuals. Just how much they may be expected to change is a complex interaction between many factors such as: (a) the child's familiarization with mainstream cultural standards; (b) the age at which the initial test was administered; (c) the time interval between testing; (d) intervening environmental changes such as special education; and (e) whether the child is handicapped. In general, however, the following rules of thumb may be advanced. First, if a youngster is not familiar with the culture, his or her IQ would be expected to change with increasing familiarization. No current intelligence test is "culture-free." Second, infant intelligence tests measure perceptual skills to a greater degree than intelligence tests given to older children. Because more growth may be evidenced by younger children and the constructs being measured by intelligence tests actually change over certain ages, IQs are more stable if the scores are obtained after the child has attained at least 5 years of age (Sattler, 1982). Third, the longer the time interval between testing, the less stable the measurements tend to be. Fourth, environmental changes, such as special education, may be expected to change IQs (Morris & Clarizio, 1977). Fifth, retarded children tend to have more stable IQs than children with higher IQs. These influences might interact to produce many changes in IQs over a group of children. Hindley and Owen (1978), in a longitudinal study of British children between 6 months and 17 years of age, found that 50% of the children had IQ changes of 10 points or more.

It should certainly be stressed that intelligence tests are measures of current levels of functioning. Even though relatively high correlations are found for older children's intelligence test scores over repeated testing, it is necessary to have frequent and periodic evaluations of the individual child's level of functioning. This is especially important if the test scores are to be used to substantiate special educational placement decisions. An interesting point can be made with respect to the intelligence/achievement relationship. Each time one of the major intelligence tests has been renormed or revised, more raw score points have been required for a youngster to receive the same IQ. Intelligence as measured by the Stanford-Binet and Wechsler appears to have increased steadily. Over part of the same time period, academic achievement appears to have decreased. Anastasi (1982) notes that we have experienced a steady 14-year decline in Scholastic Achievement Test results. If the same trend continues, a youngster reevaluated on newer tests may be expected to obtain higher achievement scores and a lower IQ than those found on earlier testing.

Equivalence of Scores Across Different Intelligence Tests

A common misconception about intelligence tests is that they all measure the same thing and their scores are equivalent. Definitions of handicapping conditions, like mental retardation, often require measurement of intelligence (frequently the reporting of the IQ is required) but rarely is the instrument used to determine the score specified. State departments of education may formally circulate lists of approved tests (Lambert, 1981) but for the most part, psychologists are free to choose among the tests available. This freedom is necessary for professional flexibility, but the examiner should be aware that not all IQs are equal. As Sattler (1982) reports:

> An evaluation of the IQs provided by the WISC-R and other tests indicates that for group purposes, IQs on the Stanford-Binet and WISC-R are generally similar. The Slosson Intelligence Test, on the average, yields IQs that are about 5 points higher than those of the WISC-R. The McCarthy Scales of Children's Abilities, on the average, yields GCI's (General Cognitive Indexes) that are lower by about 6 points (p. 149)

Large differences between WISC and WISC-R IQs were noted by Schwarting (1976). Children also obtain higher WAIS than WISC-R IQs. Differences between the WAIS and WISC-R for Verbal, Performance, and Full Scale IQs were found to be 14, 9, and 13 points, respectively, in favor of the WAIS in a sample of mentally retarded children (Nagle & Lazarus, 1979). When the author was working in the public schools, it was common practice in his Educational Service Unit to tailor the intelligence test to the decision that was believed to be in the child's best interest. For example, although children were in school and believed to be in need of special educational services, WISC-R and Stanford-Binets were given as the intelligence measures of choice. These tests would most often qualify "borderline" children for placement into special education programs. The cost of those programs would then be partially reimbursed by state and federal funding. Just before these same youngsters graduated from school, they were often reevaluated with the WAIS. Their IQs would frequently increase dramatically and reports would then be written decertifying them as handicapped. The belief system was that once out of school, the children would no longer need special support services. After graduation, the handicapping label was perceived as detrimental, so an attempt was made to remove it. This author would be quite surprised if the same "ruse" could not be played with the WISC-R, WAIS-R, and Stanford-Binet Fourth Edition.

Another "trick of the trade" involved administering the WISC-R or Stanford-Binet in sequence if the child failed to meet the criteria for admittance to the "gifted" program on the first administration of one of the tests. For example, if a child was initially administered a WISC-R and obtained a higher Verbal IQ than Performance IQ and the Performance score was so low that the Full Scale score was pulled below the guidelines for admittance, a retest with the Binet (whose variance is more directly related to verbal abilities) often provided a second IQ above the cutoff. While professionals may argue that tailoring test usage to desired outcomes may be advantageous to some clients, it should be noted that it is just as easy to tailor the assessment to the institution's best interests. Flexibility in usage with the institution's best interests in the forefront may not be beneficial for the individual.

Reporting Intelligence Testing Results

Often the final product of a psychological evaluation is a written report. In many cases where the presenting problem is an academic learning difficulty, the IQ is recommended as the anchoring point for the report (Sattler, 1982, 1988). Because the IQ is used as a predictor of academic achievement, it provides an expectancy point to which observed achievement can be compared. The actual IQ itself, along with the predictions made from it, are only estimates. Several

references on report writing recommend that because IQs are estimates, point scores should not be reported (Kaufman, 1979; Salvia & Ysseldyke, 1978; Sattler, 1982). Instead these authors recommend that confidence intervals be reported. Some authors recommend reporting confidence intervals around obtained scores, whereas others recommend reporting confidence intervals around regressed scores (estimated true scores). The reasoning given for reporting confidence intervals is that the child's obtained score would change upon retesting, so the single score generated on a single test administration can be misleading. Confidence intervals represent an interval between which a child's "true" score will lie. The reporting of these confidence intervals is therefore seen as less misleading. Several problems are inherent in this line of reasoning. First, as Dudek (1979) points out, even the professionals often use confidence bands that are technically incorrect. Elementary assessment texts have recommended adding and subtracting standard errors of measurement for observed scores to regressed true scores and/or have misinterpreted the meaning of confidence intervals around observed scores. Second, reports are most often written for persons who are not statistically sophisticated. The belief that typical readers can interpret scores written in a confidence interval format with less ambiguity than point scores is, as far as the author knows, unsupported by empirical evidence. There is, however, another alternative: Simply report what the raw and standard scores mean and exclude the scores altogether. If one is clear about the meaning of the test results, then the actual score is only needed for administrative purposes. Not providing IQs in a psychological report is not the same as refusing to release them. Current legal action with respect to assessment practices makes any recommendations with respect to test scores problematic. The situation changes too rapidly for sound advice to be given. In the final analysis, however, it is not the IQ that is important. The important point is what the IQ allows one to say with some degree of certitude about the client. Again, in the author's opinion, a psychological report would be less confusing if the conclusions were stated without the use of standard scores. Problems, of course, arise when one has to substantiate that a client meets certain administrative or legal IQ criteria for service provision. With client permission, scores could be reported to agencies that require them without providing them in the psychological report. However, if the report is intended for other professionals, one can be somewhat assured that standard scores will be correctly interpreted. Historically, there is precedence for omitting IQs from reports not intended for other professionals. In the *Casebook on Ethical Standards of Psychologists* (American Psychological Association, 1967), Cases 14.B and 14.C point out the difficulties in providing clients with raw scores. In both cases clients were provided with test scores that were misinterpreted. In both cases, the American Psychological Association's Committee on Scientific and Professional Ethics and Conduct questioned the psychologists' judgment. Again, the reader is cautioned that these judgments are not immutable and were made considering the values of the times in which we live.

FUTURE DIRECTIONS

Much of *Intelligence* (1979) Volume 3 was devoted to predictions about the form and purposes of intelligence tests in the year 2000. Horn (1979) and Resnick (1979) suggest that realistically, tests very similar to the present ones will be needed. Indeed, in the two court trials noted above, antagonists of the current intelligence tests could not point to another measure to substitute for the present tests that were not clearly inappropriate (Elliott, 1987). In the near future there is no doubt that the traditional tests will be available. The Riverside Publishing Company has just recently revised the Stanford-Binet. Both Horn (1979) and Resnick (1979) along with Turnbull (1979) see future intelligence tests as being better able to measure distinct aptitudes and abilities in learners. Brown and French (1979) stress that the test's major function will continue to be prediction. They would like to see an increase in the predictive power of intelligence so that school failure can be accurately predicted prior to its occurrence. As Lambert (1981) notes, IQs presently are not the prime determinants of a child's eligibility for special educational support services—failure in school is. A child usually has a substantial history of school failure before he or she is ever given an individual intelligence test. As stressed throughout this chapter, academic prediction is a major function of IQs. To administer the predictor after the criterion of academic failure has been met is a serious underuse of intellectual measurement.

Incorporating Neuropsychology

There is increasing awareness among psychologists that the evaluation of neuropsychological functioning may lead to better understandings of children's educational needs (Gaddes, 1975; Hooper & Willis, 1988; Hynd & Obruzut, 1981; Rourke, 1975). Instrumentation available to psychologists to measure these strengths and weaknesses have been very limited. Instruments such as the Bender-Gestalt have been the measure of choice in measuring neuropsychological functioning (Hynd, Quackenbush, & Obruzut, 1980), even though the limitations of such tests as indicators of neurological strength and weakness are well documented in the literature. Kaufman and Kaufman (1983) have developed an assessment instrument based on neurological theory that will compete with present intelligence measures.

The Kaufmans' "intelligence scales" are composed of neuropsychological tasks, whereas the achievement scales are partially composed of items formerly included on verbal intelligence tests. There is some evidence that these neurological tasks may be equal to or better than the traditional intelligence tests in predicting academic achievement. Initial research evidence with another neurological assessment device—the Luria-Nebraska Neuropsychological Battery (Golden, Hammeke, & Purisch, 1980)—that was initially developed to isolate neurological strengths and weaknesses in adults, suggests that this instrument is able to predict academic achievement in children at a level above that afforded by the WISC-R (Hale & Foltz, 1982). In theory these new tests and others like them may allow investigators not only the ability to predict learning success and failure in children and adults but also to link the test results directly to remediational strategies.

Dropping the Term *Intelligence Quotient*

Sattler (1982) lists six misconceptions concerning intelligence tests: (a) IQs measure innate intelligence; (b) IQs are fixed and never change; (c) IQs are perfectly reliable; (d) intelligence tests tell us all we need to know about intelligence; (e) IQs from different tests are interchangeable; and (f) IQs are associated with the essential worth of a person. These misconceptions still exist in the minds of many, even though the evidence does not support these positions. Future assessment tools developed to compete with current intelligence tests will probably not call themselves intelligence tests and may drop the term *IQ*. Turnbull (1979) proposed that future tests would provide users with standard scores like IQs. However, he believed that the term IQ might disappear into educational and psychological history. Perhaps Turnbull was clairvoyant; this trend is already strongly evidenced by noting that the McCarthy Scale of Children's Abilities returns a General Cognitive Index, the Woodcock-

Johnson Psycho-Educational Battery (Woodcock, 1977) provides users with cluster scores, the Kaufman Assessment Battery for Children (K-ABC, Kaufman & Kaufman, 1983) provides sequential and simultaneous processing scores along with a mental processing composite score, and the newest intelligence test on the block, the Stanford-Binet Fourth Edition, reports Standard Age Scores and Composite scores. Indeed, in the manual for the new Binet and on the test protocol the term IQ cannot be found (Thorndike, Hagen, & Sattler, 1986a, 1986b).

Using Computers

The use of microcomputers in education is a rapidly developing field. Special emphasis is currently being placed on the needs of the handicapped learner. Efficacy studies of remedial programs have appeared in the literature for quite some time (Jamison, Suppes, & Wells, 1974; Vinsonhaler & Bass, 1972; Watkins & Webb, 1981) as well as assessment systems developed for actual test administration. With the use of microprocessors controlling videodisc equipment, it is only a matter of time before new tests are developed for use in evaluating both children and adults. Initially, these systems will be able to present tests in a manner very much like trained examiners—using both visual and auditory inputs. School psychologists, who currently report that they spend too much time in assessment (Barbanel & Hoffenberg-Rutman, 1974; Cook & Patterson, 1977; Fairchild, 1976; Giebink & Ringness, 1970; Keenan, 1964), will have more time to provide other services to education and children. Like all other applications of microprocessing, developments in measurement and assessment will initially provide the same services that currently are being provided through other methods. Eventually, the new developments in computer science and neuropsychological assessment may combine to provide psychologists with the more accurate predictive tests envisioned by Brown and French (1979). Later, new evaluation procedures we have not even considered will be developed. In the author's opinion, we may be on the leading edge of the first real changes in the measurement of intelligence since Binet was asked to identify those children who would not profit from academics.

CONCLUSION

Historically, one sees that the measurement of mental abilities received its impetus from concern about children who were unable to learn in school.

However, because of the sociopolitical climate in the United States in the early 20th century, intelligence test results were used not only to differentiate between children experiencing academic problems, but also as a measuring stick to organize an entire society. From the very beginning of the intellectual assessment movement, the results of these tests have been misused. Today, however, intelligence tests still provide practitioners with a method for predicting how well children should be expected to achieve in educational environs when left to their own devices and all other things remain equal.

Several popular conceptions concerning intelligence tests appear to be unfounded. First, even though the heritability of IQs may be high, the acceptance of these high heritability indexes does not preclude the possibility that the average difference of 15 IQ points between blacks and whites solely reflects environmental and educational disadvantages experienced by blacks. Second, if psychometric definitions of bias are used, little evidence of racial or socioeconomic bias can be found in the present measures of intelligence. When evidence of bias has been reported in the literature, it has usually been found to favor minority members. Third, IQs may not be highly stable for specific individuals. A set of rules of thumb was proposed to indicate the degree of stability one could expect to find in intellectual testing results. The reader was cautioned that even when the expectation was that the IQ would be stable for an individual, if the score was to be used in educational planning, frequent reevaluations should be conducted. Fourth, IQs from different tests are not the same. To understand fully the meaning of an IQ, understanding the test from which it was derived is also necessary.

An alternative method of reporting results from intellectual assessment was discussed. It was proposed that the reporting of standard IQs, even when accompanied by confidence intervals, is not preferential to simply reporting the conclusions that can be confidently arrived at by knowledge of the assessment results. One would expect that more than an intelligence test would be administered in all but the most superficial of psychological evaluations. The information from many sources will then need to be integrated with information from intelligence tests in order to arrive at a complete picture of the client. Breaking that picture back into isolated parts by focusing on individual test scores does not aid in the understanding of the whole client. Finally, future directions were considered. Perhaps, considering the bad press received by IQs, newly developed tests that measure mental or scholastic ability are simply abandoning the term. Most authorities, however, perceive a need for tests which can predict academic failure. Some standard score-generating instrument will no doubt exist in the years ahead. With the strong influences of neuropsychology and microcomputing power, it is hoped that we will be able to do an even better job of prediction in the future.

REFERENCES

Ackerman, P. T., Peters, J. E., & Dykman, R. A. (1971). Children with specific learning disabilities: WISC profiles. *Journal of Learning Disabilities, 4,* 33–49.

American Psychological Association. (1967). *Casebook on ethical standards of psychologists.* Washington, DC: Author.

Anastasi, A. (1982). *Psychological testing* (5th ed.) New York: Macmillan.

Barbanel, L., & Hoffenberg-Rutman, J. (1974). Attitudes toward job-responsibilities and training satisfaction of school psychologists: A comparative study. *Psychology in the Schools, 11,* 425–429.

Bereiter, C. (1976–77). IQ and elitism. *Interchange, 7,* 36–44.

Berger, B. (1978). A new interpretation of the IQ controversy. *Public Interest, 50,* 29–44.

Blaha, J., & Vance, H. B. (1979). The hierarchical factor structure of the WISC-R for learning disabled children. *Learning Disability Quarterly, 2,* 71–75.

Boring, E. G. (1923). Intelligence as the tests test it. *New Republic, 34,* 35–37.

Bossard, M. D., Reynolds, C. R., & Gutkin, T. B. (1980). A regression analysis of test bias on the Stanford-Binet intelligence scale. *Journal of Clinical Child Psychology, 9,* 52–54.

Brown, A. L., & French, L. (1979). The zone of potential development: Implications for intelligence testing in the year 2000. *Intelligence, 3,* 255–273.

Carlson, L., & Reynolds, C. R. (1981). Factor structure and specific variance of the WPPSI subtests at six age levels. *Psychology in the Schools, 18,* 48–54.

Cattell, R. B. (1978). *The scientific use of factor analysis in behavioral and life sciences.* New York: Plenum Publishing.

Cattell, R. B. (1982). *The inheritance of personality and ability: Research methods and findings.* New York: Academic Press.

Cleary, T. A., Humphreys, L. G., Kendrick, S. A., & Wesman, A. (1975). Educational uses of tests with disadvantaged students. *American Psychologist, 30,* 15–41.

Cook, V. J., & Patterson, J. G. (1977). Psychologists in the schools of Nebraska: Professional functions. *Psychology in the Schools, 14,* 371–376.

Cooke, A. (1974). *Allister Cooke's America.* New York: Alfred A Knopf.

Danielson, F. H., & Davenport, C. B. (1912). *The hill folk.* Cold Spring Harbor, Long Island, NY: Alfred A Knopf.

Dean, R. S. (1977). Patterns of emotional disturbance on the WISC-R. *Journal of Clinical Psychology, 33,* 486–490.

Dean, R. S. (1980). Factor structure of the WISC-R with Anglos and Mexican-Americans. *Journal of School Psychology, 18,* 234–239.

Dudek, F. J. (1979). The continuing misinterpretation of the standard error of measurement. *Psychological Bulletin, 86,* 335–337.

Dugdale, R. L. (1910). *The Jukes* (4th ed.). New York: G. P. Putman & Sons.

Elliott, R. (1987). *Litigating intelligence: IQ tests, special education, and social science in the courtroom.* Dover, MA: Auburn House Publishing Company.

Fairchild, T. N. (1976). School psychological services: An empirical comparison of two models. *Psychology in the Schools, 13,* 156–162.

Fass, P. S. (1980). The IQ: A cultural and historical framework. *American Journal of Education, 88,* 431–458.

Fancher, R. E. (1987). Henry Goddard and the Kallikak family photographs: "Conscious skulduggery" or "whig history"? *American Psychologist, 42,* 585–590.

French, J. L. (1979). Intelligence: Its measurement and its relevance for education. *Professional Psychology, 10,* 759.

Gaddes, W. H. (1975). Neurological implications for learning. In W. M. Cruikshank & D. P. Hallahan (Eds.), *Perceptual and learning disabilities in children:* Vol. 1. *Psychological practices* (pp. 148–194). Syracuse, NY: Syracuse University Press.

Garrett, H. E. (1966). *Statistics in psychology and education* (6th ed.). New York: Longmans.

Giehink, J. W., & Ringness, T. A. (1970). On the relevancy of training in school psychology. *Journal of School Psychology, 8,* 43–47.

Glenn, S. S., & Ellis, J. (1988). Do the Kallikaks look "menacing" or "retarded"? *American Psychologist, 43,* 742–743.

Goddard, H. H. (1914). *The Kallikak family: A study of the heredity of feeble-mindedness.* New York: Macmillan.

Goddard, H. H. (1915). *The criminal imbecile.* New York: Macmillan.

Golden, C. J., Hammeke, T. A., & Purisch, A. D. (1980). *The Luria-Nebraska Neuropsychological Battery.* Los Angeles: Western Psychological Services.

Gould, S. J. (1981). *The mismeasure of man.* New York: W W Norton.

Graden, J. (1988, October 19–20). *Alternative service: Implications for school psychology.* Robert G. Bernreuter Lecture. Twenty-second annual Pennsylvania School Psychologists Conference. University Park, PA.

Guilford, J. P. (1980). Fluid and crystallized intelligences: Two fanciful concepts. *Psychological Bulletin, 88,* 406–412.

Gutkin, T. B. (1978). Some useful statistics for the interpretation of the WISC-R. *Journal of Consulting and Clinical Psychology, 46,* 1561–1563.

Gutkin, T. B., & Reynolds, C. R. (1980). Factorial similarity of the WISC-R for Anglos and Chicanos referred for psychological services. *Journal of School Psychology, 18,* 34–39.

Hale, R. L. (1978). The WISC-R as a predictor of WRAT performance. *Psychology in the Schools, 15*, 172–175.

Hale, R. L. (1979). The utility of WISC-R subtest scores in discriminating among adequate and underachieving children. *Multivariate Behavioral Research, 14*, 245–253.

Hale, R. L. (1981). Concurrent validity of the WISC-R factor scores. *Journal of School Psychology, 19*, 274–278.

Hale, R. L. (1983). An examination for construct bias in the WISC-R across socioeconomic status. *Journal of School Psychology, 21*, 153–156.

Hale, R. L., & Foltz, S. G. (1982). Prediction of academic achievement in handicapped children using a modified form of the Luria-Nebraska Pathognomic Scale and WISC-R full scale IQ. *Clinical Neuropsychology, 4*, 99–103.

Hale, R. L., & Landino, S. A. (1981). The utility of WISC-R subtest analysis in discriminating among groups of conduct problem, withdrawn, mixed and nonproblem boys. *Journal of Consulting and Clinical Psychology, 49*, 91–95.

Hale, R. L., & Raymond, M. R. (1981). Wechsler Intelligence Scale for Children—Revised (WISC-R) patterns of strengths and weaknesses as predictors of the intelligence-achievement relationship. *Diagnostiqué, 6*, 35–42.

Hale, R. L., Raymond, M. R., & Gajar, A. H. (1982). Evaluating socioeconomic status bias in the WISC-R. *Journal of School Psychology, 20*, 145–149.

Hale, R. L., & Saxe, J. E. (1983). Profile analysis of the Wechsler Intelligence Scale for Children—Revised. *Journal of Psychoeducational Assessment, 1*, 155–161.

Hindley, C. B., & Owen, C. F. (1978). The extent of individual changes in IQ for ages between 6 months and 17 years in a British longitudinal sample. *Journal of Child Psychology and Psychiatry and Allied Disciplines, 19*, 329–350.

Hirshoren, A., & Kavale, K. (1976). Profile analysis of the WISC-R: A continuing malpractice. *The Exceptional Child, 23*, 83–87.

Hooper, S. R., & Willis, W. G. (1988). *Learning disability subtyping: Neuropsychological foundations, conceptual models, and issues in clinical differentiation.* New York: Springer-Verlag.

Horn, J. L. (1979). Trends in the measurement of intelligence. *Intelligence, 3*, 229–239.

Horn, J. L., & Cattell, R. B. (1966). Refinement and test of the theory of fluid and crystallized intelligence. *Journal of Educational Psychology, 57*, 253–270.

Huelsman, C. B., Jr. (1970). The WISC subtest syndrome for disabled readers. *Perceptual Motor Skills, 30*, 535–550.

Hynd, G. W., & Obruzut, J. E. (1981). School neuropsychology. *Journal of School Psychology, 19*, 45–49.

Hynd, G. W., Quackenbush, R., & Obruzut, J. E. (1980). Training school psychologists in neuropsychological assessment: Current practices and trends. *Journal of School Psychology, 18*, 148–153.

Jamison, D., Suppes, P., & Wells, S. (1974). The effectiveness of alternative instruction media: A survey. *Review of Educational Research, 44*, 1–67.

Jastak, J. F., & Jastak, S. R. (1976). *The Wide Range Achievement Test* (Manual, Rev. ed.). Wilmington, DE: Guidance Associates of Delaware.

Jensen, A. R. (1980). *Bias in mental testing.* New York: Free Press.

Kaufman, A. S. (1975). Factor structure of the WISC-R at 11 age levels between 6 1/2 and 16 1/2 years. *Journal of Consulting and Clinical Psychology, 43*, 133–147.

Kaufman, A. S. (1979). *Intelligent testing with the WISC-R.* New York: John Wiley & Sons.

Kaufman, A., & Kaufman, N. (1983). *Kaufman assessment battery for children, interpretive manual.* Circle Pines, MN: American Guidance Service.

Kavale, K., & Forness, S. (1984). A meta-analysis of the validity of Wechsler Scale profiles and recategorizations: Patterns or parodies? *Learning Disability Quarterly 7*, 136–156.

Keenan, L. (1964). A job analysis of school psychologists in the public schools of Massachusetts. *Psychology in the Schools, 1*, 185–186.

Keith, T. Z., Cool, V. A., Novak, C. G., White, L. J., & Pottelbaum, S. M. (1988). Confirmatory factor analysis of the Stanford-Binet Fourth Edition: Testing the theory-test match. *Journal of School Psychology, 26*, 253–274.

Kelderman, H., Mellenbergh, G. J., & Elshout, J. J. (1981). Guilford's facet theory of intelligence: An empirical comparison of models. *Multivariate Behavioral Research, 16*, 37–62.

Kownslar, A. O., & Frizzle, D. B. (1967). *Discovering American history.* New York: Holt, Rinehart & Winston.

Kral, M. J. (1988). More on Goddard and the Kallikak family photographs. *American Psychologist, 43*, 745–746.

Lambert, N. M. (1981). Psychological evidence in Larry P. versus Wilson Riles. *American Psychologist, 36*, 937–952.

MacKenzie, B. (1980). Hypothesized genetic racial differences in IQ: A criticism of three lines of evidence. *Behavior Genetics, 10*, 225–234.

Madden, P. B. (1980). Intelligence tests on trial. *The School Psychology Review, 9*, 149–153.

Marks, R. (1976–77). Providing for individual differences: A history of the intelligence testing movement in North America. *Interchange, 1*, 3–16.

Miele, F. (1979). Cultural bias in the WISC. *Intelligence, 3*, 149–164.

Miller, M. M. (1980). On the attempt to find WISC-R profiles for learning and reading disabilities (a response to Vance, Wallbrown, and Blaha). *Journal of Learning Disabilities, 13*, 338–340.

Morris, J. J., & Clarizio, S. (1977). Improvement in IQ of high risk, disadvantaged preschool children enrolled in a developmental program. *Psychological Reports, 41*, 1111–1114.

Nagle, R. J., & Lazarus, S. C. (1979). The comparability of the WISC-R and WAIS among 16-year-old EMR children. *Journal of School Psychology, 17*, 362–367.

Nunnally, J. C. (1978). *Psychometric theory* (2nd ed.). New York: McGraw-Hill.

Oakland, T., & Feigenbaum, D. (1979). Multiple sources of test bias on the WISC-R and the Bender Gestalt Test. *Journal of Consulting and Clinical Psychology, 47,* 968–974.

Pastore, N. (1978). The army intelligence tests and Walter Lippmann. *Journal of the History of the Behavioral Sciences, 14,* 316–327.

Peterson, C. R., & Hart, D. H. (1979). Factor structure of the WISC-R for a clinic referred population and specific subgroups. *Journal of Consulting and Clinical Psychology, 47,* 643–645.

Potter, R. E. (1967). *The stream of American education.* New York: Van Nostrand Reinhold.

Pressey, S. L. (1920). Scale of attainment No. 1: An examination of achievement in the second grade. *Journal of Educational Research, 1,* 572–581.

Rabin, A. I. (1965). Diagnostic use of intelligence tests. In B. B. Wolman (Ed.), *Handbook of clinical psychology.* (pp. 477–497). New York: McGraw-Hill.

Ramanaiah, N. V., & Adams, M. L. (1979). Confirmatory analysis of the WAIS and the WPPSI. *Psychological Reports, 45,* 351–355.

Ramanaiah, N. V., O'Donnell, J., & Ribich, F. (1976). Multiple group factor analysis of the Wechsler Intelligence Scale for Children. *Journal of Clinical Psychology, 32,* 329–330.

Reschly, D. J. (1978). WISC-R factor structures among Anglos, Blacks, Chicanos, and Native-American Papagos. *Journal of Consulting and Clinical Psychology, 46,* 417–422.

Reschly, D. J. (1980). Psychological evidence in the Larry P opinion: A case of right problem—wrong solution? *School Psychology Review, 9,* 123–135.

Reschly, D. J., & Sabers, D. (1979). Analysis of test bias in four groups with the regression definition. *Journal of Educational Measurement, 16,* 1–9.

Resnick, L. B. (1979). The future of IQ testing in education. *Intelligence, 3,* 241–253.

Reynolds, C. R. (1982). The problem of bias in psychological assessment. In C. R. Reynolds & T. B. Gutkin (Eds.), *A handbook for school psychology* (pp. 178–208). New York: John Wiley & Sons.

Reynolds, C. R., & Hartledge, L. C. (1979). Comparison of WISC and WISC-R regression lines for academic prediction with black and white children. *Journal of Consulting and Clinical Psychology, 47,* 589–591.

Rourke, B. P. (1975). Brain-behavior relationships in children with learning disabilities: A research program. *American Psychologist, 30,* 911–920.

Rugel, R. P. (1974). WISC subtest scores of disabled readers: A review with respect to Bannatyne's recategorization. *Journal of Learning Disabilities, 7,* 57–63.

Salvia, J., & Ysseldyke, J. E. (1978). *Assessment in special and remedial education.* Boston: Houghton-Mifflin.

Sandoval, J. (1979). The WISC-R and internal evidence of test bias with minority groups. *Journal of Consulting and Clinical Psychology, 47,* 919–927.

Sandoval, J., & Millie, M. (1980). Accuracy judgments of WISC-R item difficulties for minority groups. *Journal of Consulting and Clinical Psychology, 48,* 249–253.

Sattler, J. M. (1974). *Assessment of children's intelligence* (Rev. reprint). Philadelphia: W B Saunders.

Sattler, J. M. (1982). *Assessment of children's intelligence and special abilities.* Boston: Allyn & Bacon.

Sattler, J. M. (1988). *Assessment of children* (3rd ed.). San Diego: Sattler Publications.

Schmeiser, C. B., & Ferguson, R. L. (1978). Performance of black and white students on test materials containing content based on black and white cultures. *Journal of Educational Measurement, 15,* 293–300.

Schooler, D. L., Beebe, M. C., & Koepke, T. (1978). Factor analysis of WISC-R scores for children identified as learning disabled, educable mentally impaired, and emotionally impaired. *Psychology in the Schools, 15,* 478–485.

Schwarting, F. G. (1976). A comparison of the WISC and WISC-R. *Psychology in the Schools, 13,* 139–141.

Silverstein, A. B. (1969). An alternative factor analytic solution for Wechsler's intelligence scales. *Educational and Psychological Measurement, 29,* 763–767.

Skinner, H. A., & Lei, H. (1980). Modal profile analysis: A computer program for classification research. *Educational and Psychological Measurement, 40,* 769–772.

Smith, M. D., Coleman, J. M., Dokecki, P. R., & Davis, E. E. (1977). Recategorized WISC-R scores of learning disabled children. *Journal of Learning Disabilities, 10,* 437–443.

Sowell, T. (1981a). *Ethnic America.* New York: Basic Books.

Sowell, T. (1981b). *Markets and minorities.* New York: Basic Books.

Stern, W. (1914). *The psychological methods of testing intelligence.* Baltimore: Warwick & York.

Tabachnick, B. G. (1979). Test scatter on the WISC-R. *Journal of Learning Disabilities, 12,* 626–628.

Terman, L. M. (1916). *The measurement of intelligence.* Boston: Houghton Mifflin.

Thompson, R. J., Jr. (1980). The diagnostic utility of the WISC-R measures with children referred to a developmental evaluation center. *Journal of Consulting and Clinical Psychology, 48,* 440–447.

Thorndike, R. L., Hagen, E. P., & Sattler, J. M. (1986a). *Technical manual: Stanford-Binet Intelligence Scale* (Fourth ed.). Chicago: Riverside.

Thorndike, R. L., Hagen, E. P., & Sattler, J. M. (1986b). *Record booklet: Stanford-Binet Intelligence Scale* (Fourth ed.). Chicago: Riverside.

Turnbull, W. W. (1979). Intelligence testing in the year 2000. *Intelligence, 3,* 275–282.

Vance, H. B., Huelsman, C. B., & Wherry, R. J. (1976). The hierarchical factor structure of the Wechsler Intelligence Scale for Children as it relates to disadvantaged white and black children. *Journal of General Psychology, 95,* 287–293.

Vance, H. B., Singer, M. C., & Engin, A. W. (1980). WISC-R subtest differences for male and female LD children and youth. *Journal of Clinical Psychology, 36,* 953–957.

Vance, H. B., Wallbrown, F. H., & Blaha, J. (1978). Determining WISC-R profiles for reading disabled children. *Journal of Learning Disabilities, 11,* 656–661.

Vinsonhaler, J. F., & Bass, R. K. (1972). A summary of ten major studies of CAI drill and practice. *Educational Technology, 12,* 29–32.

Wallbrown, F. H., Blaha, J., & Wherry, R. J. (1974). The hierarchical factor structure of the Wechsler Adult Intelligence Scale. *British Journal of Educational Psychology, 44,* 47–56.

Watkins, M. W., & Webb, C. (1981, September–October). Computer assisted instruction with learning disabled students. *Educational Computer Magazine,* pp. 24–27.

Wechsler, D. (1949). *Manual for the Wechsler Intelligence Scale for Children.* New York: Psychological Corporation.

Wechsler, D. (1950). Cognitive, conative, and non-intellective intelligence. *American Psychologist, 30,* 78–83.

Wechsler, D. (1955). *Manual for the Wechsler Adult Intelligence Scale.* New York: Psychological Corporation.

Wechsler, D. (1967). *Manual for the Wechsler Preschool and Primary Scale of Intelligence.* New York: Psychological Corporation.

Wechsler, D. (1974). *Manual for the Wechsler Intelligence Scale for Children—Revised.* New York: Psychological Corporation.

Wechsler, D. (1975). Intelligence defined and undefined *American Psychologist, 30,* 135–139.

Wechsler, D. (1981). *Manual for the Wechsler Adult Intelligence Scale—Revised.* New York: Psychological Corporation.

Wiggins, J. S. (1973). *Personality and prediction: Principles of personality assessment.* Menlo Park, CA: Addison-Wesley.

Woodcock, R. W. (1977). *Woodcock-Johnson Psycho-Educational Battery: Technical report.* Boston: Teaching Resources.

Yerkes, R. M. (1921). Psychological examining in the United States army. In R. M. Yerkes (Ed.), *Memoirs of the National Academy of Sciences* (Vol. 15). Washington, DC: U.S. Government Printing Office.

Zenderland, L. (1988). On interpreting photographs, faces, and the past. *American Psychologist, 43,* 743–744.

CHAPTER 23

NEUROPSYCHOLOGICAL ASSESSMENT

Barbara Pendleton Jones
Nelson Butters

Neuropsychological assessment is a field with roots in a number of different areas, including clinical psychology, behavioral neurology, experimental neuropsychology (as applied both to animals and man), and aphasiology.[1] As a body of methods, neuropsychological assessment is used to evaluate the individual's higher nervous system functioning as reflected in a variety of tasks and to address some or all of the following questions. Does the subject of the assessment show evidence of higher nervous system dysfunction? If so, is the probable locus of dysfunction diffuse or focal, and if focal, affecting which hemisphere(s) and lobe(s)? How severe is the degree of functional impairment in the various areas of cognition, perception, sensorimotor functions, and personality? Is the etiology acute or slowly progressive in onset, and is the course likely to be progressive, static, or admitting of some recovery? What is the nature of the neuropathology (some neuropsychologists are willing to make more specific diagnoses than others)? What are the likely practical consequences of any

demonstrated neurological impairment for the individual's professional and interpersonal functioning and daily living activities? And finally, what are the recommendations for remediation? In some instances, neuropsychologists or clinical psychologists with neuropsychological training will become involved in the detailed planning of cognitive retraining and other remediation programs for neurologically impaired patients. And in some cases neuropsychological assessment may be performed at more than one point in time in order to monitor recovery or disease progression or to assess the effects of various treatment interventions.

Although the above outline of the scope of neuropsychological assessment has delineated its clinical application, the methods of neuropsychological assessment are also utilized in research on the behavioral correlates of brain damage, handedness, sex, age, and other variables. However, because the interests of the readers of the present volume are likely to be oriented toward clinical applications, the focus of this chapter

The preparation of this chapter was supported in part by funds from the Medical Research Service of the Veterans Administration.

will be strictly on clinical neuropsychological assessment.

Neuropsychological assessment cannot be competently or responsibly undertaken by the professional without some knowledge of neuroanatomy and neuropathology and the basic principles of the neurology of behavior. Although even a summary of these foundations is beyond the scope of this chapter, several authorities have attempted to construct reasonably comprehensive theories of brain-behavior relationships (Geschwind, 1974; Hecaen & Albert, 1978; Luria, 1980; Pribram, 1971). As outlined in a report by the Task Force on Education, Accreditation, and Credentialing of the International Neuropsychological Society (INS; Meier, 1981), the clinical neuropsychologist should also be knowledgeable in the following areas: central nervous system (CNS) effects of systemic disorders, developmental neuropsychology, the neuropsychology of aging, behavioral psychopharmacology, psychophysiology, sociocultural determinants of performance, personality assessment, and principles of test construction, administration, and interpretation. More recently, a joint task force of the INS and Division 40 (Clinical Neuropsychology) of the American Psychological Association (APA) has outlined detailed requirements for doctoral training programs, interns, and postdoctoral training in clinical neuropsychology (Reports of the INS, 1987).

This survey of the field of neuropsychological assessment begins with a brief history, proceeds to a presentation and critique of the major contemporary methods, and ends with a discussion of current and future trends.

HISTORY OF NEUROPSYCHOLOGICAL ASSESSMENT

Early Investigations in the East and West

If neuropsychological assessment is defined as the application of psychometric methods to the study of behavioral manifestations of neuropathological conditions, the field can be seen to have its origins in the first quarter of the twentieth century. In the West one might even trace its beginnings to Binet and Simon's testing of brain-damaged and retarded children in Paris in 1905. However, the first studies in the West to use psychological tests in the investigation of the behavioral effects of specified lesions seem to have appeared in the 1930s and 1940s. To cite only some of the better-known examples, there were studies of intellectual impairment in aphasia (Weisenburg &

McBride, 1935); the effects of frontal lobe lesions on intelligence and other higher functions (Columbia-Greystone Associates, 1949; Hebb, 1939, 1942; Rylander, 1940); visuospatial impairments in patients with right-hemisphere lesions (Paterson & Zangwill, 1944, 1945); the effects of brain lesions on abstraction abilities (Goldstein & Scheerer, 1941); and memory impairments in various amnesic syndromes (Zangwill, 1943). As is evident in the titles of these publications, these studies were for the most part ones in which psychometric methods were used to pursue a topic with a specific focus. In most cases, these early investigators were interested in studying particular functions and chose their tests accordingly; the concept of a neuropsychological battery was not pursued.

In Russia, interest in the behavioral concomitants of neuropathological changes was exemplified in the founding of the Psychoneurological Institute of Bekhterev in 1907. In the early 1930s, A. R. Luria began his neuropsychological studies under Vygotskii; Luria's contribution to clinical neuropsychology will be examined in several following sections.

Contribution of Ward Halstead

An important line of development in neuropsychological assessment began with the work of Ward C. Halstead. Halstead was a psychologist who was interested in studying the effects of brain damage on a broad range of cognitive, perceptual, and sensorimotor functions. Having established a neuropsychological laboratory at the University of Chicago in 1935, he began his work by carrying out field observational studies of brain-damaged subjects in both work and social settings in order to determine which behavioral characteristics should be measured through formal tests. He then assembled a battery of psychological tests (some modified revisions of existing measures and some newly developed tests), administered them to a number of brain-damaged subjects referred by neurosurgeons and other medical specialists, and subjected the results to factor analytic studies performed by both Holzinger and Thurstone. The results of these analyses led Halstead to the selection of seven tests (10 variables) for inclusion in his neuropsychological battery (1947): the Category Test, Tactual Performance Test, Speech Sounds Perception Test, Seashore Rhythm Test, Finger Oscillation Test, Critical Flicker Fusion Test, and Time Sense Test. (For a description of the tests retained in the current battery, see the section on the Halstead-Reitan Neuropsychological Test Batteries below.) It was also on the basis of these factor analytic studies that Halstead developed his four-factor theory of human performance (Halstead, 1947), which included a central integrative field factor C, representing the "organized experience of the individual" whose parameters were "probably reflected" in intelligence test measurements; an abstraction factor A; a power function P (later thought to be an indication of alertness or vigilance); and a directional factor D, specifying the sensory modality or motoric pathway involved.

In his work as a neuropsychologist, Halstead (1950, 1951) developed the concept of "biological intelligence," which subsumed the four factors enumerated above and denoted a basic capacity for controlled adaptability which he felt was not measured by traditional intelligence tests. He was particularly interested in the contributions of the frontal lobes to "biological intelligence," and collected data suggesting that a broad range of performances, which he thought to be reflective of "biological intelligence," was most impaired in patients with frontal lobe excisions (Halstead & Shure, 1954; Shure & Halstead, 1958). The concept of "biological intelligence" never found an enthusiastic audience among other neuropsychologists, probably because of its lack of specificity, and Halstead's overinsistence on it may have detracted from his contributions to the field. His work was of value in that he advocated sampling a wide range of behaviors in order to assess the effects of brain damage; he assembled a battery and performed systematic studies using groups of patients with focal brain lesions in order to observe the effects of lesions in various areas of the cortex; and he undertook to train other neuropsychologists.

Ralph Reitan and the Halstead-Reitan Battery

Halstead's work was continued and expanded by his former student Ralph M. Reitan, who established a neuropsychology laboratory at Indiana University Medical Center in 1951. Reitan (1955, 1966b, 1969, 1986) modified Halstead's original battery by deleting two tests (Critical Flicker Fusion and Time Sense Tests) and adding several others (Trail Making Test, Strength of Grip Test, Sensory-Perceptual Examination, Tactile Perception, and Modified Halstead-Wepman Aphasia Screening Test). In addition, a Wechsler-Bellevue Scale (Form 1) and Minnesota Multiphasic Personality Inventory (MMPI) now were routinely performed as part of the Halstead-Reitan Battery (HRB). During and after his modification of

Halstead's original battery, Reitan administered his set of tests to a large number of patients with focal and diffuse brain lesions. He also standardized his tests on a group of hospitalized control patients. As he worked with individual patients, he came to use four "methods of inference" to analyze his results. First, as Halstead had done, he looked at the overall level of performance as reflected in the "Impairment Index" (a function of how many scores fall below selected cutting scores). Second, he noted the presence of pathognomonic signs (e.g., inability to draw simple figures) which have a low rate of occurrence but, according to Reitan, are almost invariably associated with brain damage when they do occur. Third, he analyzed the pattern of performance, or the relative strengths and weaknesses in a subject's test scores, which frequently conveyed information about the locus and/or nature of the brain damage; such pattern analysis will be a familiar concept to clinicians accustomed to drawing inferences from the Wechsler Adult Intelligence Scale (WAIS) Verbal IQ/Performance IQ discrepancies and WAIS intertest scatter. And fourth, he compared scores on motor, sensory, and sensory-perceptual tasks involving the two sides of the body, as a means of helping to determine both the presence or absence of brain damage (the reasoning was that nonorganic causes of poor performance such as inadequate motivation or emotional disturbance are not likely to affect one side of the body more than the other) and the laterality of the lesions.

Since the late 1950s, Reitan and his collaborators have been using the HRB and related forms in human neuropsychological research (for reviews, see Farr, Greene, & Fisher-White, 1986; Klove, 1974; Reitan, 1966b). Most of their studies have involved localization (or the ability of the battery to specify the hemisphere and lobe of the lesion), process considerations (or the battery's discrimination of acute, relatively static, and chronic forms of brain damage), and diagnosis of type of brain damage (e.g., intrinsic tumor, extrinsic tumor, cerebrovascular lesion, etc.).

Reitan has had many students, who in turn have trained other psychologists in the Halstead-Reitan method. In 1980 the HRB was the commonly performed battery in the field (Hartlage, Chelune, & Tucker, 1980).

Postwar Growth of Experimental Neuropsychology and Its Impact on Clinical Assessment

Between the prewar and postwar decades there was a noteworthy increase in the number of neuropsychological studies performed, and a more remarkable leap occurred with the advent of the 1960s and the general acceleration of the pace of scientific research both in the United States and abroad. These studies were to prove influential in neuropsychology, not only for the advancement in the understanding of brain–behavior relationships that they provided, but also for their contribution to methodology. Although many very significant contributions were made to neuropsychological assessment during this period, those of a few groups stand out. .

Brenda Milner, Doreen Kimura, and the Montreal Neurological Institute–McGill University Group

From the late 1950s to the present, Brenda Milner and her colleagues at the Montreal Neurological Institute and McGill University have been engaged in a series of neuropsychological investigations of behavioral change in neurosurgical patients with focal lesions. Many of these patients came to surgery for the excision of epileptogenic tissue after other means of seizure control had failed. Both the effects of the preoperative focal lesions and those of the surgical excisions themselves have been studied in a remarkably fruitful and influential sequence of experiments. In their series of studies on the effects of temporal lobe lesions, for example, Milner and Kimura found evidence of impaired verbal learning in patients with left temporal lobe lesions and of impaired visual (nonverbal) perception and visual (nonverbal) learning in those with right temporal lobe lesions (Kimura, 1963; Milner, 1958, 1960, 1967, 1968, 1970; Milner & Kimura, 1964). Bilateral mesial temporal (hippocampal) lesions were found to be followed by severe and permanent anterograde amnesia with some degree of retrograde amnesia (Corkin, 1984; Milner, 1958, 1966, 1970; Scoville & Milner, 1957). The role of the temporal lobes in audition was also studied, with the finding of deficits in timbre discrimination and tonal memory after right temporal lobectomy (Milner, 1962) and impaired overall performance on a dichotic listening task (digits) after left temporal lobectomy (Kimura, 1961). Kimura (1961) also noted a right-ear advantage on dichotic digits testing in normal adults and normal children down to the age of 5 and hypothesized that this was due to left-hemisphere dominance for speech in the majority of subjects and the greater effectiveness of the contralateral auditory pathway under conditions of dichotic presentation.

Other important findings by this group have included those of impaired abstraction and set shifting on the Wisconsin Card Sorting Task by patients with either left or right frontal lobe excisions, decreased verbal fluency (on Thurstone's Word Fluency Test) in left frontal excision patients, and decreased nonverbal fluency (on a fluency for designs task) and spatial learning in patients with right frontal excisions (Jones-Gotman & Milner, 1977; Milner, 1964). From the perspective of neuroscience, Milner's greatest contribution may be her convincing demonstration that the material-specific memory deficits of her temporal lobe patients are correlated with the amount of hippocampal tissue excised during the operation (Milner, 1970, 1971). The linking of verbal and nonverbal memory deficits with the left and right hippocampi, respectively, remains the cornerstone of all current research on the neuropsychology of memory.

From these illuminating studies, several techniques either designed by Milner or her colleagues or first utilized by them in neuropsychological research have come into use for neuropsychological assessment purposes. These include Kimura's Recurring Figures Test, dichotic listening tests, the Thurstone type of verbal fluency test (Controlled Word Association Test), the Jones-Gotman Design Fluency Test, and the Wisconsin Card Sorting Test.

Hans-Lukas Teuber and His Colleagues

In the years following World War II, Hans-Lukas Teuber undertook a series of studies to investigate the effects of focal cerebral lesions on a variety of visual and spatial abilities. Working first at New York University College of Medicine and later at the Massachusetts Institute of Technology (MIT), he collaborated in these studies with Josephine Semmes, Sidney Weinstein, Lila Ghent, Mortimer Mishkin, William Battersby, Morris Bender, and others. The patient populations in these studies consisted of World War II veterans with penetrating missile wounds. Despite the limitations imposed by the nature of this population and available methods of lesion localization, these studies made significant contributions to human neuropsychology and were influential both in experimental and clinical settings. For example, in a summary discussion of these studies, Teuber (1972) related occipital lobe lesions to abnormalities in the "immediate presentation of visual space" as reflected in extensive studies of visual field defects (Teuber, Battersby, & Bender, 1960). Frontal lobe lesions, he concluded in the same review, were linked to impairment of the "mechanisms for compensation for changes in spatial order, under voluntary changes in posture." This conclusion was based on studies involving adjustment of a luminous line to the vertical under conditions of body tilt (Teuber & Mishkin, 1954) or adjustment to visual displacements induced by prismatic spectacles under conditions of self-produced movement (Held, 1961). Teuber related parietal lobe lesions to impairments in the representation of spatial relations as reflected in studies of route-finding ability (Semmes, Weinstein, Ghent, & Teuber, 1955). Teuber was particularly interested in the role of the frontal lobes and integrated a number of diverse findings in a theory of corollary discharge (Teuber, 1972).

The work of Teuber in human neuropsychology was particularly valuable in its attempt to integrate findings from human studies with the results of animal experiments and to articulate a theoretical basis for current and future research. Teuber was influential in infusing the field of neuropsychological assessment with a spirit of scientific inquiry at a time when it might well have proceeded to a set of repetitive diagnostic procedures lacking adequate conceptual bases. Some of the tests used by Teuber and his colleagues in their studies are still in current use (e.g., Thurstone's Version of Gottschaldt's Hidden Figures Test, optical illusions such as the Double Necker Cube, the Field of Search Test, the Personal Orientation Test, and the Extrapersonal Orientation Test [Lezak, 1983]).

Perhaps Teuber's most lasting gift to neuropsychology was the development of the psychology department at MIT. After assuming the chairmanship in the early 1960s, Teuber quickly organized the department into three sections: neuropsychology, basic neuroscience, and cognitive science. Between 1965 and 1978 such eminent scientists as Richard Held, Walle Nauta, Peter Schiller, Emilio Bizzi, Molly Potter, and Suzanne Corkin all established highly productive laboratories and research programs at MIT. Due to Teuber's encyclopedic knowledge of neuropsychology, anatomy, and physiology, and his ability to integrate these sometimes seemingly diverse fields, the psychology department at MIT became the standard that many other programs in psychobiology and neuroscience attempted to imitate. For neuropsychology, and psychology in general, Teuber's skills as a teacher and administrator assured that neuropsychology would be represented as an important facet of the still rapidly emerging field of neuroscience.

The Neuropsychology Unit of the Boston Veterans Administration Medical Center and the Boston University School of Medicine

Another active and prominent group of neuropsychologists assembled in the affiliated clinical and research programs of the Boston Veterans Administration (VA) Medical Center and the Boston University School of Medicine. Under the leadership of Harold Goodglass, Edith Kaplan, and Nelson Butters, this group carried out a large number of influential studies over a period of nearly 30 years and made important contributions to clinical neuropsychology in the areas of aphasia (e.g., Goodglass & Butters, 1988; Goodglass & Kaplan, 1963, 1972; Goodglass & Quadfasel, 1954; Goodglass, Quadfasel, & Timberlake, 1964), apraxia (Goodglass & Kaplan, 1963, 1979), amnesia (e.g., Albert, Butters, & Levin, 1979; Butters & Cermak, 1975, 1976, 1980, 1986; Cermak, 1985; Cermak & Butters, 1972; Oscar-Berman, 1973; Oscar-Berman & Samuels, 1977), general intelligence (Gardner, 1983), dementia (Albert, Butters, & Brandt, 1981; Butters, 1984; Butters, Sax, Montgomery, & Tarlow, 1978; Butters, Wolfe, & Granholm, 1986; Oscar-Berman & Zola-Morgan, 1980a, 1980b), aging (Albert & Kaplan, 1980; Albert & Moss, 1988), and the effects of brain damage on the chemical senses (Jones, Butters, Moskowitz, & Montgomery, 1978; Jones, Moskowitz, & Butters, 1975; Potter & Butters, 1980). Some of the tests developed by this group for research purposes have been widely adopted for general clinical neuropsychological assessment (e.g., the Boston Diagnostic Aphasia Examination [Goodglass & Kaplan, 1972] and the Boston Naming Test [Kaplan, Goodglass, and Weintraub, 1983]).

The research efforts of this group have consistently stressed two points with regard to neuropsychological assessment. First, aphasia, amnesia, and dementia are not unitary disorders each characterized by a single pattern of cognitive deficits. Rather, these neurological disorders are composed of numerous subtypes, each of which can be characterized by a specific neuropsychological profile. Thus, Goodglass and Kaplan's (1972) Boston Diagnostic Aphasia Examination allows the clinician to differentiate Broca's, Wernicke's, and conduction aphasias on the basis of a standardized battery of tasks of expressive language, comprehension, repetition, reading, and writing. Similarly, much of the clinical research of Butters and Cermak and of Oscar-Berman has successfully demonstrated that the anterograde and retrograde memory disorders of amnesic and demented patients can be differentiated along a number of qualitative and quantitative dimensions (for review, see Butters, 1984, 1986; Butters & Cermak, 1980; Oscar-Berman, 1980). Second, the Boston group has consistently stressed the importance of searching for the qualitative processes underlying a particular quantitative score. For example, patients with left- or right-hemisphere lesions may both earn poor quantitative scores on constructional and drawing tasks, but a close scrutiny of the patients' performances would show that the two patient groups are failing for quite different reasons. Patients with right-hemisphere lesions may be unable to grasp the overall contour or "gestalt" of a figure, whereas the patients with left-hemisphere damage may encounter difficulty in the analysis of the inner detail of the figure after successfully reproducing the external configuration. It is the contention of the Boston group that without such qualitative analyses of cognitive disorders much vital diagnostic and prognostic information would be lost (Albert & Kaplan, 1980; Butters, Miliotis, Albert, & Sax, 1984; Goodglass & Kaplan, 1972, 1979; Milberg, Hebben, & Kaplan, 1986).

It is important to note that as a result of the persistence with which the Boston group has applied its process-achievement approach to patient populations, numerous theoretical insights and discoveries concerning cerebral dominance (e.g., Butters & Barton, 1970; Gardner, 1975; Gardner, Ling, Flamm, & Silverman, 1975; Oscar-Berman, Goodglass, & Cherlow, 1973; Shai, Goodglass, & Barton, 1972; Wapner, Hamby, & Gardner, 1981; Winner & Gardner, 1977), the linguistic features of aphasia (e.g., Blumstein, Cooper, Goodglass, Statlander, & Gottlieb, 1980; Blumstein, Cooper, Zurif, & Caramazza, 1977; Caramazza & Zurif, 1976; Milberg & Blumstein, 1981; Zurif, 1980; Zurif & Caramazza, 1976), and the role of encoding in episodic and semantic memory (e.g., Cermak, 1982, 1985; Cermak & Butters, 1972, 1976; Cermak, Butters, & Moreines, 1974; Cermak & Reale, 1978) have had a major impact upon experimental as well as clinical neuropsychology. Their work best exemplifies the close interdependence of clinical and experimental psychology.

Arthur L. Benton

Beginning with the publication of the now widely used Benton Visual Retention Test in 1945 (Benton, 1945), A. L. Benton of the University of Iowa has made a valuable series of contributions to human neuropsychology. Among the problems that he has addressed in his experimental and clinical studies are visual memory deficits; the varieties of visuoconstructive disorders; impairments in facial recognition; deficits in right–left discrimination, finger localization, and number operations; the diagnosis and measurement of aphasic disorders; differential effects of frontal lobe disease; and the differential diagnosis of Alzheimer's disease. Although his contributions to the field are too numerous to list, some examples are illustrative. In studies of facial discrimination, Benton and Van Allen (1968, 1972) demonstrated that impairment of facial discrimination and prosopagnosia were separate clinical entities, and that the former occurred more than twice as often in patients with right-hemisphere lesions as in those with left-hemisphere lesions. In the area of constructional apraxia, Benton was able to demonstrate that whereas impairments in two-dimensional block construction (e.g., WAIS Block Design) were equally frequent in left-hemisphere and right-hemisphere lesion patients, defective three-dimensional block construction occurred more than twice as frequently in patients with right-hemisphere lesions as in those with left-hemisphere lesions. Interestingly, of those left-hemisphere lesion patients who did demonstrate impaired three-dimensional block construction, a high percentage showed a receptive aphasic impairment (Benton, 1967). In a study of differential behavioral effects of left, right, or bilateral frontal lobe lesions, differential impairments in three-dimensional block construction and design copying in patients with right frontal or bilateral frontal lobe disease, Benton (1968) was able to show differential impairments in verbal association fluency in patients with left, right, or bilateral frontal lobe lesions; differential impairments in three-dimensional block construction and design copying in patients with right frontal or bilateral frontal lobe lesions; and differential impairments in paired-associate learning and temporal orientation in bilateral frontal lobe patients.

Among the tests designed by Benton and his colleagues, a number have come into wide use in clinical neuropsychology: the Revised Visual Retention Test (Benton, 1974), the Neurosensory Center Comprehensive Examination for Aphasia (Spreen & Benton, 1969), the Test of Three-Dimensional Constructional Praxis (Benton, 1973), and the Test of Facial Recognition (Benton & Van Allen, 1968). Benton, Hamsher, Varney, and Spreen (1983) have described the most recently revised forms of, and storing criteria for, these various visuoperceptual, constructional, and memory tests. Benton has trained a number of prominent neuropsychologists (e.g., Otfried Spreen, Harvey Levin, and Kerry de S. Hamsher) and has been a distinguished leader in the field of neuropsychological assessment. Costa and Spreen's (1985) recently edited book of Benton's selected papers provides an unusually thorough review of his vast contributions to neuropsychology.

H. Enger Rosvold, Allan F. Mirsky, and the Study of Attention

The wartime experience of H. Enger Rosvold with brain-injured Canadian veterans led him to conjecture that there were deficits in some patients (particularly those with anterior lesions) which none of the available tests were measuring. In later work at McGill University, where he was a colleague of Donald Hebb, at Yale University, and at the National Institute of Mental Health (NIMH), Rosvold developed several procedures for assessing brain damage. An additional stimulus to his research was the widespread use in the 1940s and 1950s of psychosurgery (usually involving destruction of tissue of the prefrontal lobes) for both war-related and other (e.g., schizophrenic) psychiatric disorders. One of the fruits of Rosvold's efforts was a method for assessing what he called microsleeps or lapses in attention; with Allan F. Mirsky, Rosvold developed the Continuous Performance Test (CPT) (Rosvold, Mirsky, Sarason, Bransome, & Beck, 1956). This test required sustained concentration and key-press responses to letter targets in a visual display and seemed clearly sensitive to the effects of cerebral lesions, although not especially to anterior or frontal lobe lesions. Subsequent studies by Mirsky and colleagues at NIMH and Boston University showed that patients with petit mal epilepsy (but not necessarily other epileptic disorders) had significant deficits in CPT performance (Fedio & Mirsky, 1969; Lansdell & Mirsky, 1964; Mirsky, Primac, Ajmone Marsan, Rosvold, & Stevens, 1960). A considerable portion of Mirsky's research has been devoted to an analysis of the attentional deficit in petit mal (absence) epilepsy, with both behavioral and electrophysiological methods (Mirsky & Orren, 1977; Mirsky & Van Buren, 1965; Myslobodsky & Mirsky, 1988). In recent years, the CPT has proven useful in delineating a marker for schizophrenia—a trait, rather than a state, marker. These findings have served to bring into focus a concentration on attentional impairment. Mirsky and others (presaged by Kraepelin and Bleuler) had argued that attentional impairment might be the core deficit in schizophrenia.

Mirsky has sought to develop a comprehensive theory of what he has referred to as the "elements" of attention, as viewed from a neuropsychological perspective (Mirsky, 1987, 1989). This work seeks to integrate disparate findings and techniques in this area into a more systematic and rational approach based on factor analysis, clinical neuropsychological observations, and relevant behavioral–neuroanatomical studies. The work of Mirsky and his students and colleagues has stimulated interest in a critical but neglected area of clinical neuropsychology and seems important as well in helping to provide a link between the related disciplines of neuropsychology and neuropsychiatry. The CPT has come into wide use as one of the most sensitive neuropsychological measures of attention.

A. R. Luria and the Luria-Nebraska Neuropsychological Battery

The contributions of Soviet psychologists to the field of neuropsychology were not widely recognized in the West until the publication in 1966 of the English translation of *Higher Cortical Functions in Man* by A. R. Luria. As has been noted, Luria had begun his neuropsychological studies under Vygotskii in the 1930s and subsequently was associated with the Burdenko Neurosurgical Institute in Moscow for many years until his death in 1977. During his long career, Luria worked with a large number of head-injured war veterans as well as with other types of neurological and neurosurgical patients and developed an extensive repertoire of tests for neuropsychological assessment. Whereas the thrust of clinical neuropsychology in the West had been to measure the abilities reflective of the integrity of various cortical areas, Luria's emphasis was more on theory building. He articulated a theory of functional systems in the brain that avoided the worst excesses of both localizationism and holism, and he devised corresponding principles for the evaluation of brain functioning. For example, he advocated breaking complex functions down into the simplest testable components and examining these behavioral components separately in order to see what portions of a functional system were compromised. His methods more resembled those of the neurologist than the psychologist, in that his tests had generally not been standardized or subjected to reliability and validity studies; evaluation procedures were more qualitative than quantitative; and the selection of tests, methods of administration, and scoring criteria were tailored to the individual patient. Although these considerations and others limited the application of his methods in the West, his comprehensive theoretical model excited considerable interest. Goldberg and Costa (1986) and Goldberg's (1989) recently edited volumes document the pervasive influence Luria's views have had on all aspects of American and European neuropsychology.

In 1975, Anna-Lise Christensen, a Danish psychologist, published a detailed description of Luria's method of neuropsychological assessment along with a manual and a set of stimulus cards, without, however, actually attempting to standardize examination procedures (Christensen, 1975). She rather advocated the kind of flexibility that Luria preferred.

The currently much-publicized Luria-Nebraska Battery was developed in an attempt to standardize and validate Luria's procedures (Golden, 1981a, 1981b; Golden, Hammeke, & Purisch, 1978). Charles Golden and his colleagues began with the several hundred items presented by Christensen and administered them first to normal control subjects and later to neurological patients in addition to normal and psychiatric control subjects. After discarding items that failed to discriminate between normal and brain-damaged subjects, they were left with a battery of 269 items that could be administered in 2 to 3 hours. Subsequent studies have undertaken to establish the reliability and validity of the battery, as well as to demonstrate the utility of the battery in localizing lesions and in specifying the type of neurological disorder. The Luria-Nebraska Neuropsychological Battery receives further consideration below.

CONTEMPORARY METHODS IN NEUROPSYCHOLOGICAL ASSESSMENT

A major dichotomy in the field of neuropsychological assessment is characterized by the use of either a uniform battery for all patients or an individualized approach. Practitioners of an individualized approach usually administer a small, core group of tests to all patients, and then select further tests for the optimal elucidation of the referral questions and issues that may have been raised in the initial stage of testing.

Batteries undoubtedly have some advantages. These include relative comprehensiveness in the range of functions they sample. They greatly facilitate the combination of research with clinical objectives in that the same data base will automatically be compiled for all patients. They facilitate the use of technicians for the administration of tests, since no expertise is needed for the selection of appropriate assessment measures.

A serious disadvantage of batteries is that they may be providing redundancy of information in some areas of functioning while achieving insufficient exploration of other areas. For example, in the case of a patient who achieves a Verbal IQ of 120, it is hardly necessary to administer a complete aphasia screening battery (although some special language functions, such as word finding, should still be assessed). On the other hand, a patient with a true aphasia by no means will be properly evaluated with the use of an aphasia screening device contained in a battery. A further disadvantage of batteries that is related to the problem of redundancy of information is that of cost effectiveness. Some batteries are sufficiently time-consuming that it is becoming increasingly difficult to justify (and recover) the expense incurred in testing, even when

technicians are employed for administration and scoring.

A final disadvantage of batteries is that there is usually no opportunity to modify assessment procedures over time to reflect the now rapid advances in the field of human neuropsychology research. Batteries, therefore, tend to show an insufficient reflection of recent discoveries and concepts in neuropsychology.

The assets and liabilities of an individual approach to neuropsychological assessment tend to be the reverse of those noted for batteries. Among advantages of individualized approaches one may list efficiency: In areas where performance in the core group of tests demonstrates intact functioning, further tests need not be administered. By the same token, in-depth analyses of impairment may be achieved, as the test selection is tailored to this end. Currency is also an important attribute of the individual approach. That is, as research provides more precise instruments for demonstrating and measuring specific types of impairments associated with specific brain lesions, these new instruments can be incorporated into the neuropsychologist's repertoire. Finally, because test selection is not automatic but must be determined with sophisticated knowledge of brain–behavior relationships, and because there are no rules (much less automated systems) for interpretation of results, use of individualized approaches tends to require a higher level of training and experience in neuropsychological assessment.

Disadvantages of the individualized approach include the examiner's inability to rely on technicians for administration of all tests (some would see this as an advantage) and the length of time required for training in this method. With individualized approaches there is less ease in combining research with clinical objectives, since different patients will have been given different selections of tests.

Now that consideration has been given to some general characteristics of batteries and individualized approaches, the major batteries in current use are described, followed by a section outlining several well-known individual approaches. Obviously space limitations have necessitated the omission of some batteries and many individualized approaches.

Batteries

Halstead-Reitan Neuropsychological Test Batteries

Composition of the batteries. As recounted in the historical section, Ralph Reitan's (1969) modification of Ward Halstead's battery of tests (Reitan, 1955, 1966b, 1969) resulted in the now widely used HRB. This battery is applicable to individuals aged 15 and older. Also in use are the Halstead Neuropsychological Test Battery for Children (a revision of the adult battery used for children 9 to 14 years of age), and the Reitan-Indiana Test Battery for Children (used for 5- to 8-year-olds).

The complete version of the HRB now consists of the following tests (for a more complete description see Boll, 1981):

- *Halstead Category Test:* a nonverbal test requiring the formulation of abstract principles for categorizing stimulus displays of visual figures. According to Boll (1981), the test "taps current learning skill, abstract concept formulation and mental efficiency."
- *Tactual Performance Test:* a form-board test performed in a blindfolded condition with the preferred hand, nonpreferred hand, and both hands. The test is thought to assess "motor speed and the use of the tactile and kinesthetic cues to enhance psychomotor coordination, learning, response to the unfamiliar, and . . . (incidental memory)" (Boll, 1981).
- *Rhythm Test:* a rhythm discrimination test that taps "nonverbal auditory perception, attention, and sustained concentration" (Boll, 1981).
- *Speech Sounds Perception Test:* a test of the ability to identify auditorily presented nonsense words. It is thought to measure "auditory verbal perception, auditory-visual coordination of language processing, and sustained attention and concentration" (Boll, 1981).
- *Finger Oscillation Test:* a test of finger tapping speed, performed with each hand.
- *Trail Making Test:* a test requiring connection of consecutively numbered circles scattered on a page (Trails A) and connection in alternating sequence of numbered and lettered circles scattered on a page (Trails B). The test is thought to assess psychomotor speed, visual scanning, sequencing ability, and the ability to maintain and shift sets.
- *Strength of Grip Test:* a measure of grip strength taken on a hand dynamometer with each hand.
- *Sensory-Perceptual Examination* (Tactile, Auditory, and Visual): tests of the ability to perceive unilateral stimuli and double (bilateral) simultaneous stimuli to the right and left sides of the body in the tactile, auditory, and visual modalities.
- *Tactile Perception:* tests of tactile finger localization and graphesthesia (deciphering numbers traced on the subject's fingertips while his or her eyes are closed).

- *Modified Halstead-Wepman Aphasia Screening Test:* a brief screening device of both language and selected nonlanguage abilities.
- *Wechsler Adult Intelligence Scale*
- *Minnesota Multiphasic Personality Inventory*

In the Halstead Neuropsychological Test Battery for Children and the Reitan-Indiana Neuropsychological Test Battery for Children, some of these tests have been modified, some have been retained without alteration, and some have been omitted (for a more complete description, see Boll, 1981); a Wide Range Achievement Test is usually added to the children's batteries.

Methods of scoring and interpretation. Most commonly used is the method of scoring and interpretation developed by Reitan and described in the historical section above. To recapitulate, in using this method the evaluator examines the level of performance (reflected in the Impairment Index), the pattern of performance, the presence or absence of pathognomonic signs, and the right–left comparison (relative performances on measures of motor, sensory, and perceptual functioning involving the right and left sides of the body).

It is worth noting that this method of scoring and interpretation, as utilized by Reitan and many of its practitioners, contains a large element of subjective evaluation and is therefore in some measure dependent on the examiner's level of clinical experience and training. For example, the interpreter must make a judgment about what constitutes "pathognomonic signs," and similarly, the evaluation of the pattern of performance and the significance of the right–left comparisons is largely subjective. Reitan (1974) acknowledged that, despite an impressive record of diagnostic accuracy with regard to localization and lesion type when HRB results are qualitatively assessed by a trained evaluator, statistical analyses of test results on groups of brain-damaged patients with focal and diffuse lesions of differing etiologies have generally shown comparatively few significant differences.

In an attempt to objectify clinical inference in the analysis of HRB results, several researchers have developed semi-actuarial systems of interpretation (Adams, 1975; Finkelstein, 1977; Russell, Neuringer, & Goldstein, 1970). Russell et al. developed a neuropsychological key approach. Briefly, in a manner somewhat analogous to that employed by biologists to determine the class into which a species or individual fits (the taxonomic key), they constructed neuropsychological keys based on verbalized rules of inference used by neuropsychologists. Their key program included subroutines for identifying the presence or absence of brain damage, for lesion localization, and for specifying process (e.g., active, static, or congenital). These keys could be run via computer program when the data from the HRB (with some modifications) were entered. In a study comparing the diagnostic accuracy of the Russell et al. system with that of two trained clinicians (Heaton, Grant, Anthony, & Lehman, 1981), it was found that the clinicians were more accurate than the automated system in predicting presence and laterality of lesions but less accurate in predicting chronicity; neither clinicians nor automated procedure exceeded base-rate predictions on chronicity. Two other programs have been developed to simulate the activity of the clinician in interpreting HRB results—BRAIN I (Finkelstein, 1977), which utilizes Reitan's four methods of interpretation, and Adams's Revised Program (Adams, 1975), which includes steps having to do with the specification of psychological abilities based on analysis of test scores. In a comparison of the three major computer programs developed for the interpretation of HRB data, Adams and Brown (1986) concluded that although all three performed adequately at determining the presence or absence of cerebral dysfunction, none of the three fared very well at lateralization. In addition to these objective systems of HRB interpretation, alternative methods (e.g., Kiernan & Matthews, 1976; Swiercinsky & Warnock, 1977) have been proposed. Swiercinsky's (1978) SAINT program utilizes a geographic/geometric model of brain functioning along three major axes in which new cases are compared for "goodness of fit" to a three-dimensional ideal.

Advantages and disadvantages. In an assessment of the advantages and disadvantages of the Halstead-Reitan neuropsychological test batteries, it should first be pointed out that Reitan and his followers (e.g., Boll, 1981; Reitan, 1974, 1986) emphatically deny that the primary function of these methods is the neurodiagnostic function. Rather, they see these batteries primarily as techniques for research in evaluating brain–behavior relationships. For both purposes the batteries have the advantage of sampling a wide range of functions (intellectual and cognitive, visual-spatial, sensory-perceptual, motor, personality, etc.) by means of tests that have been standardized and normed. Studies have indicated that presence or absence of brain damage can be predicted on the basis of standard HRB summary indexes with 70% to 90% accuracy (Anthony, Heaton, & Lehman, 1980; Rus-

sell et al., 1970; Vega & Parsons, 1967; Wheeler, Burke, & Reitan, 1963).

Furthermore, when dealing with brain-damaged patients, trained HRB clinicians can make inferences as to lesion localization and chronicity with considerable success (for reviews, see Klove, 1974; Reitan, 1966a). Success in specifying localization and chronicity (process) requires extensive clinical experience and "intuitive" decisions, and attempts to use actuarial systems for such specifications have met with disappointing results (e.g., Anthony et al., 1980).

The HRB shares with most other neuropsychological approaches the disadvantage that its accuracy in detecting the presence of structural brain damage declines dramatically when it is applied to psychiatric patients. Heaton and his colleagues reviewed the literature concerning neuropsychological test performances in psychiatric patients (Heaton, Baade, & Johnson, 1978; Heaton & Crowley, 1981), and Malec (1978) has specifically reviewed neuropsychological assessment of schizophrenia versus structural brain damage. Briefly, although the HRB and many other neuropsychological tests perform acceptably in discriminating between the less severe and intractable forms of psychiatric illness and structural lesions, the HRB and related forms (again, like many other tests) perform at little better than a chance level in discriminating between chronic or process schizophrenics and subjects with structural lesions (Lacks, Colbert, Harrow, & Levine, 1970; Watson, Thomas, Anderson, & Felling, 1968). It is now widely accepted that a number of psychiatric disorders (e.g., schizophrenia, unipolar and bipolar affective disorders, panic disorder, and obsessive-compulsive disorder) are accompanied by cerebral dysfunction; the task for both the HRB and other neuropsychological approaches is to be able to distinguish among the neuropsychological profiles of these and other neuropsychiatric disorders (many of which are presumed to involve abnormalities in neurotransmitter systems rather than structural lesions) and other neuropathological entities.

Other disadvantages of the HRB include its length and costliness, the absence of measures for the assessment of memory, and, most importantly, the fact that it does not reflect a number of advances in neuropsychological assessment of the past 40 years. With regard to the time required for administration, Boll (1981) has recently stated that the adult battery "requires about 5 hours . . . but frequently as little as 4 hours for other than the most impaired 20% of the medical center population" (p. 37). Given that it is the most impaired individuals who will usually be referred for neuropsychological testing, one must anticipate frequent overruns of the 5-hour limit. Many experienced neuropsychologists will supplement the HRB measures with additional tests (especially tests of memory) in order to gain a more comprehensive data base; this approach, although serving the interests of the individual patient, may not be practicable in many settings because of time and cost limitations.

The Luria-Nebraska Neuropsychological Battery

Composition of the battery. As currently published, the Luria-Nebraska Neuropsychological Battery (LNNB; Golden, Purisch, & Hammeke, 1985) contains 269 items comprising 11 content scales. Two sensorimotor scales, a pathognomonic scale, and sets of localization and factor scales are also derived from the 269 items. As in the case of the MMPI, the number of scales that can be devised using the items is not limited to the original group, and research on experimental scales is proceeding. The 11 content scales are as follows:

- *Motor:* items assessing unilateral and bilateral motor speed and coordination, praxis, copying of hand and arm movements, motor alternation and inhibition, verbal control of motor movements, oral-motor movement, and drawing ability and speed.
- *Rhythm:* items evaluating rhythm discrimination and reproduction.
- *Tactile:* items assessing tactile and pain discrimination, tactile extinction, graphesthesia, position sense, and stereognosis.
- *Visual:* items measuring visual-perceptual skills and visual-spatial abilities.
- *Receptive Speech:* items assessing phonemic discrimination and comprehension of simple words and phrases and grammatically complex forms.
- *Expressive Speech:* items requiring repetition, object naming, automatic speech, spontaneous speech, etc.
- *Reading:* items measuring oral reading ability.
- *Writing:* items assessing writing to dictation, spontaneous writing, and other writing skills.
- *Arithmetic:* items relevant to number recognition, simple calculation, and more complex number operations.
- *Memory:* items assessing verbal and nonverbal short-term memory with and without interference.
- *Intellectual Processes (Intelligence):* items measuring various higher cognitive skills such as concept formation, the comprehension of thematic pictures and texts, complex mathematical reasoning, and so forth. The *Pathognomonic* scale consists of items

rarely missed by normal subjects and items rarely passed by brain-damaged patients. The *Left* and *Right Hemisphere* scales comprise the motor and tactile items performed by the right and left limbs, respectively.

In addition to the foregoing 14 scales, localization (McKay & Golden, 1979a) and lateralization (McKay & Golden, 1979b) scales were developed and were cross-validated by Golden, Moses, et al. (1981). "Factor scales" developed from factor analytic studies of the content scales have been described in McKay and Golden (1981).

An alternative version of the LNNB, Form II, has been developed in order to facilitate serial testing of patients. A version of the battery for children aged 8 to 12 years (the Luria-Nebraska Battery for Children) is also available.

Interpretation. The interpretive strategies for the LNNB are articulated in Golden, Hammeke, and Purisch (1980) and Moses, Golden, Ariel, and Gustavson (1983) and include use of a critical level for establishing the presence or absence of brain damage, pattern analysis of the clinical scales and localization scales, qualitative evaluation of item patterns and individual items, and the presence of specific pathognomonic signs. The authors note that full interpretation of the LNNB is dependent on a thorough knowledge of neuropsychological theory (especially Luria's theory) and on clinical neuropsychological training and experience.

Advantages and disadvantages. The LNNB in its present form offers the advantages of brevity and relative comprehensiveness in the screening of a number of areas of higher functioning. Furthermore, in accordance with Luria's approach, complex functions are broken into simpler components so that more information is gleaned about the precise nature of deficits. In early validation studies, the developers of the test reported hit rates in the region of 90% in discriminating between brain-injured and control subjects (Golden et al., 1978; Hammeke, Golden, & Purisch, 1978) and between brain-damaged and schizophrenic subjects (Purisch, Golden, & Hammeke, 1978). Several subsequent studies comparing the LNNB and the HRB have indicated that the two batteries are comparable in their ability to identify the presence or absence of brain damage (Golden, Kane, et al., 1981; Kane, Parsons, & Goldstein, 1985; Kane, Sweet, Golden, Parsons, & Moses, 1981; Shelly & Goldstein, 1982). On the other hand, a number of serious criticisms have been raised against the LNNB. Adams (1980a, 1980b), Spiers (1981, 1982), and Stambrook (1983) have criticized the construction of the test and flawed techniques in the standardization, validity, and reliability studies. Spiers presented a detailed critique of the composition of the various content scales of the LNNB, arguing that many items purporting to measure one neuropsychological function in reality reflect another, that items in a number of the scales are too limited in number or too superficial to assess comprehensively the function in question, and that Luria's original method of detailed qualitative analysis of responses is lost in the current LNNB system. Critiques by Crosson and Warren (1982) and Delis and Kaplan (1982, 1983) have focused on the problem of content validity of some of the clinical scales. A number of studies published between 1980 and 1988 attempted to correct problems in the standardization, validity, and reliability studies. (See Moses & Maruish, 1987a, for a comprehensive bibliography of the LNNB literature during this period.)

The most recent reviews of the LNNB literature (Moses & Maruish, 1987b, 1988a, 1988b) continue to leave some of the major criticisms unanswered. For example, in a review of the literature concerning the construct validity of the LNNB (Moses & Maruish, 1988a), the authors discuss four types of studies. They acknowledge that the early univariate interitem correlations were methodologically unsound; they cite a "latent trait analysis," which assesses internal consistency and, in the absence of data external to the test, gives little information about construct validity; they cite scalewise factor analyses with approval, although these studies merely demonstrated what factors seemed to be represented in each of the scales, and in some cases demonstrated reasons for *concern* about construct validity (e.g., the Visual scale was represented by complex visual analysis and by visual stimulus *naming*); and finally, the authors cite four factorial comparisons with other tests, two of which were methodologically unsound, one of which concerned only the Memory scale, and one of which concerned only the language-related scales, whose adequacy has been severely criticized elsewhere (Crosson & Warren, 1982).

A fundamental issue raised in virtually all discussions of the LNNB may be expressed in the form of a question: Is the method of neuropsychological assessment developed by A. R. Luria by its very nature one that cannot be operationalized as a fixed battery? Adams (1980b) stated that "the approach may not translate to a battery of tests, and Luria had made this point emphatically" (p. 523). He appears to suggest

that followers of Luria should not attempt a battery, which is not consistent with the approach, but should rather be content with a "neuropsychological investigation" as in Christensen's approach. If the LNNB proponents are going to continue to promulgate their battery, it is to be hoped that the major concerns outlined above will be addressed.

Individualized Approaches

Despite the widespread use of fixed batteries in neuropsychological assessment and the recent promotion of the LNNB, a number of influential neuropsychologists active in both training and research continue to prefer an individualized approach. Three such approaches are described in the following sections.

The Boston process approach. The Boston Process Approach (Goodglass, 1986; Milberg et al., 1986; Kaplan, Fine, Morris, & Delis, in press) is a flexible but comprehensive approach that aims at a qualitative analysis of the nature of patients' deficits in addition to the usual specifications as to the presence or absence of brain damage, probable lesion site, severity of deficit, probable etiology, and lesion status (e.g., acute, chronic, progressive, resolving). The three neuropsychologists most responsible for shaping the Boston approach have been Edith Kaplan, Harold Goodglass, and Nelson Butters. Impressed by the fruitfulness of Heinz Werner's (1937) distinction between process and achievement in the study of developmental psychology, the Boston group has applied similar principles to the understanding of compromised functioning in patients with brain damage. To this group of neuropsychologists, overemphasis on scores and score patterns without analysis of the *quality* of the patient's failures and successes, the strategies which the patient either employs or fails to employ, and the cognitive processes evident in the responses leads at best to the neglect of a rich mine of information and at worst to misconstrued diagnosis (e.g., Delis & Kaplan, 1982). The emphasis on process and strategy contributes to a more than usually detailed analysis of patients' deficits, with the recognition that superficially similar deficits can reflect quite distinctive underlying processes.

The Boston Process Approach uses a core selection of tests for most patients. Subsequently, the examiner will choose one or more sets of "satellite tests" to be given to the patient (Milberg et al., 1986); the selection of satellite tests is guided by the referral question and by hypotheses generated by the patient's complaints, observations of his or her behavior, and by his or her performances on the core set of tests. Attention to the strategies and processes involved in patients' failures and successes in test performance partially determines the selection of tests to be used in addition to those in the core group. Table 23.1 contains a listing of a representative sample of the tests used in the Boston Process Approach. In some cases the satellite tests will include tasks designed for the particular patient.

The discussion of featural versus contextual priority in a recent publication (Milberg et al., 1986) provides an example of the richness of the Boston Process Approach. The advantages of the Boston approach include comprehensiveness, especially in the areas of language functions and memory; its sensitivity; its usefulness in rehabilitation planning; and the emphasis on higher cortical functions. Disadvantages include incomplete standardization and validation of

some of the measures used. In recent years, the Boston group has progressed in the task of translating its insights into reproducible methods (e.g., Delis, Kramer, Kaplan, & Ober, 1987), in publishing norms (e.g., Butters, Salmon, Cullum, et al., 1988; Borod, Goodglass, & Kaplan, 1980), and in disseminating information about their methods through workshops and seminars.

Muriel D. Lezak

In her volume entitled *Neuropsychological Assessment* (1983), Muriel Lezak presents an insightful discussion of the use of batteries versus individualized approaches in clinical neuropsychology. According to Lezak, in order to be adequate, a test battery must be suitable, practicable, and useful. Her opinion is that no currently available neuropsychological battery ful-

Table 23.1. A Representative Sample of the Tests Used in the Boston Process Approach to Neuropsychological Assessment

INTELLECTUAL AND CONCEPTUAL FUNCTIONS	
Wechsler Intelligence Scale-Revised*	Wechsler, 1981
Standard Progressive Matrices	Raven, 1960
Shipley Institute of Living Scale	Shipley, 1940
Wisconsin Card Sorting Test	Grant and Berg, 1948
Proverbs Test	Gorham, 1956

MEMORY FUNCTIONS	
Wechsler Memory Scale*	Wechsler, 1945
Rey Auditory Verbal Learning Test*	Rey, 1964
Rey-Osterrieth Complex Figure	Osterrieth and Rey, 1944
Benton Visual Recognition Test (Multiple Choice Form)	Benton, 1950
Consonant Trigrams Test	Butters and Grady, 1977
Cowboy Story Reading Memory Test	Talland, 1965
Corsi Blocks	Milner, 1971

LANGUAGE FUNCTIONS	
Narrative Writing Sample	Goodglass and Kaplan, 1972
Tests of Verbal Fluency (Word List Generation)	Thurstone, 1938

VISUO-PERCEPTUAL FUNCTIONS	
Cow and Circle Experimental Test	Palmer and Kaplan, 1985
Automobile Puzzle	Wechsler, 1974
Parietal Lobe Battery	Goodglass and Kaplan, 1972
Hooper Visual Organization Test	Hooper, 1958

ACADEMIC SKILLS	
Wide Range Achievement Test	Jastak and Jastak, 1978

SELF-CONTROL AND MOTOR FUNCTIONS	
Porteus Maze Test	Porteus, 1965
Stroop Color-Word Interference Test	Stroop, 1935
Luria Three-Step Motor Program	Christensen, 1975
Finger Tapping	Halstead, 1947

Note. From "The Boston Process Approach to Neuropsychological Assessment" by W. P. Milberg, N. Hebben, and E. Kaplan, in *Neuropsychological Assessment of Neuropsychiatric Disorders* (p. 68) by I. Grant and K. M. Adams (Eds.). New York: Oxford University Press, 1986. Copyright 1986 by Oxford University Press. Reprinted by permission.
*These tests include procedural modifications.

fills all of these criteria, and she prefers an individualized approach. Her core battery of tests is composed of two portions: an individually administered part (nine subtests of the WAIS or WAIS-R and nine other measures, requiring a total of 2½ to 3 hours for administration), and a section of paper-and-pencil tests that may be given by clinical or nursing staff (six measures tapping a wide variety of areas requiring 3 to 6 hours for administration). Additional special tests will usually be selected in order to answer referral questions of a detailed nature (e.g., differential diagnosis, comprehensive description, and analysis of impaired function), or questions raised by the results of the core battery. For a complete discussion of this approach and its rationale, the reader is referred to Lezak (1983). Attention to the strategies and processes involved in patients' failures and successes in test performance partially determines the selection of tests to be used in addition to those in the core group.

Arthur L. Benton

Arthur L. Benton and his colleagues at the University of Iowa constitute another prominent school of neuropsychologists who advocate an individualized or patient-oriented approach to clinical neuropsychological assessment (Benton, Hamsher, Varney, & Spreen, 1983). They begin their assessment with a fixed set of tests of minimal length, consisting of a brief test of temporal orientation, two WAIS (or WAIS-R) Verbal subtests (usually Information and Arithmetic), and two WAIS (or WAIS-R) Performance subtests (usually Block Design and Picture Arrangement). The selection of additional tests is governed by the questions raised in the request for examination, by complaints mentioned by the patient during a preliminary interview, and by findings on the initial set of tests. The essential characteristic of their approach is that it is a sequential process leading to a diagnostic decision. They estimate that an experienced neuropsychologist utilizing their approach will complete testing in 60 to 90 minutes in 80% of cases, in less than 60 minutes in 10%, and in over 90 minutes in 10%. The armamentarium of tests that they draw from in completing their examinations follows:

- *Wechsler Adult Intelligence Scale (WAIS or WAIS-R)*
- *Tests of Orientation, Learning, and Memory*
  Temporal Orientation
  Presidents Test
  Galveston Orientation and Amnesia Test
  Paired-Associate Learning
  Benton Visual Retention Test
  Serial Digit Learning
  Selective Reminding Test
  Rey Auditory-Verbal Learning Test
- *Tests of Attention-Concentration and Speed of Information Processing*
  WAIS (WAIS-R) Digit Span
  WAIS (WAIS-R) Digit Symbol
  Paced Auditory Serial Addition Task
- *Tests of Abstract Reasoning*
  Abstractions from Shipley Institute of Living Scale
  Raven Progressive Matrices Wisconsin
  Card Sorting Test
- *Tests of Body Schema*
  Right–Left Orientation
  Finger Localization
- *Tests of Visual Performance*
  Test of Facial Recognition
  Judgment of Line Orientation
  Visual Form Discrimination
  Pantomime Recognition
  Dot Localization
- *Tests of Auditory Performance*
  Recognition of Environmental Sounds
  Phoneme Discrimination
- *Tests of Tactile Performance*
  Tactile Form Perception
  Tactile Naming
- *Tests of Constructional Praxis*
  Test of Three-Dimensional Construction Praxis
  Copying Designs
- *Tests of Verbal Functions*
  Controlled Word Association Test
  Vocabulary (WAIS or WAIS-R and Shipley)
  Token Test
  Reading Section for Wide Range Achievement Test
- *Tests of Psychomotor Performance*
  Purdue Pegboard
  Finger Praxis
  Motor Impersistence
  Rotary Pursuit Learning
- *Arithmetic Tests*
  Oral Arithmetic Calculation
  Written Arithmetic Calculation
  Arithmetic Reasoning
  Arithmetic Section From Wide Range Achievement Test
- *Tests of Lateral Neglect*
  Line Cancellation
  Bisection of Lines
  Geographic Orientation
  Constructional Praxis Tasks
  Double Simultaneous Stimulation
- *Aphasia Batteries*
  Neurosensory Center Comprehensive Examination for Aphasia (NCCEA)

Multilingual Aphasia Examination
• *Tests of Lateralization of Function*
Dichotic Listening
Tachistoscopic Visual Field Study
Somatosensory Threshold Determinations
NCCEA Handedness Inventory
• *Personality Assessment Tests*
MMPI
Rorschach

Single Tests

It is apparent from the discussion of individualized approaches that there are a large number of single tests available for the detailed examination of a variety of higher functions. Lezak's (1983) volume describes a number of the available tests under the following categories: tests of intellectual ability, verbal functions, perceptual functions, constructional functions, memory functions, conceptual functions, executive functions and motor performance, orientation and attention, and personal adjustment. Lezak's book remains the most comprehensive available listing of individual tests in use for neuropsychology assessment, but the reader also is referred to the *Journal of Clinical and Experimental Neuropsychology, Neuropsychologia, Archives of Clinical Neuropsychology,* and *The Clinical Neuropsychologist* for references concerning other commonly used measures.

Reitan (1974) criticized the use of single tests:

> Obviously, we will never develop a meaningful conceptualization of the extent and manner in which brain lesions alter ability structure in individual human beings if each group of subjects is studied with a different set of measurements and the measurements, in turn, are never put in a meaningful overall behavioral context. Thus the use of single tests can scarcely contribute very significantly to an overall understanding of the behavioral correlates of brain lesions nor can a single test, considering the complexity of brain functions, be expected to serve as an adequate diagnostic instrument. (p. 22)

One must emphatically agree with the last point. No responsible neuropsychologist would advocate the use of a single test as an "adequate diagnostic instrument." The field is no longer at the naive stage of thinking that any single measure can serve as a litmus test for the presence of organic dysfunction. However, a test originally devised and studied in isolation from other tasks can fruitfully be used as a part of a carefully chosen array of tests. The fact that one chooses to use a selection of independently developed tests does not mean that one sacrifices the ability to consider each

measurement in a "meaningful overall behavioral context." It is the selection of tests that is critical here. Indeed, the same methods of interpretation that Reitan advocates for the HRB are applicable to any well-chosen array of tests. Furthermore, one must always remain cognizant of the possibility that a single test may be shown to detect and/or localize focal lesions more accurately than any single test in a formal battery. For example, the Wisconsin Card Sorting Test has been shown to discriminate between frontal and nonfrontal lesions more successfully than any test in the HRB (Robinson, Heaton, Lehman, & Stilson, 1980). In this kind of situation, it is difficult to defend continued reliance on a battery alone, no matter how enshrined in tradition it may be.

CURRENT AND FUTURE TRENDS IN NEUROPSYCHOLOGICAL ASSESSMENT

In the first edition of this work (Jones & Butters, 1983), we predicted that no single battery was likely to dominate the field of clinical neuropsychological assessment, a prediction that has proven to be accurate. While the two major batteries, the HRB and the LNNB, enjoy continued popularity, the major individualized approaches have exerted increasing influence. As we had also predicted, there have been a number of experimental and theoretical papers published in which batteries, or diverse systems of interpretation for a single battery, have been compared (Anthony et al., 1980; Chelune, 1982; Golden, Kane, et al., 1981; Goldstein, 1986; Goldstein & Incagnoli, 1986; Heaton, et al., 1981; Kane, 1986; Kane, Parsons, & Goldstein, 1985; Kane, Parsons, Goldstein, & Moses, 1987; Swiercinsky & Warnock, 1977). It appears that the field has progressed beyond the stage in which advocates of a particular battery or individualized approach are still hoping to convert the infidels, to a stage in which there is more acceptance of diversity and a scientific interest in comparing diverse methodologies and in objectifying procedures involved in clinical interpretation.

As in many fields, the current decade has witnessed the burgeoning growth of computer applications in clinical neuropsychology (Adams & Brown, 1986). The number of new computer-administered neuropsychological tests (both new versions of old tests and entirely new measures) grows monthly. It is imperative that the originators of such tests adhere to American Psychological Association (APA, 1974) standards in test development, and also, in the case of computer-administered versions of old tests, that data comparing subject performance on both old and new forms are available. The use of computer programs for interpretation of neuropsychological data has been discussed in the section on the HRB; current programs perform adequately only in predicting the presence or absence of brain damage.

In addition to the traditional emphases on elucidating the behavioral correlates of such variables as structural brain lesions, handedness, sex, and age, there has been intensive activity during the past decade in exploring, via neuropsychological assessment, the biological bases of psychiatric disorders. In a number of neuropsychological studies researchers are beginning to delineate patterns of cerebral dysfunction in schizophrenia (for a review, see Goldstein, 1986), affective disorders (e.g., Caine, 1986; Jones, Henderson, & Welch, 1988; Weingartner, Cohen, Murphy, Martello, & Gerdt, 1981), dissociative states (Devinsky, Putnam, Grafman, Bromfield, & Theodore, 1989), multiple personality disorder (Grafman, Devinsky, Putnam, Nissen, & Schachter, in preparation), and eating disorders (e.g., Hamsher, Halmi, & Benton, 1981; Jones, Duncan, Brouwers, & Mirsky, in preparation; Small, Madero, Teagno, & Ebert, 1983). Given that many referrals to neuropsychologists involve psychiatric patients, the study of neuropsychological functioning in psychiatric syndromes is a most welcome trend.

In 1983 we noted the trend toward increasing involvement of neuropsychologists in rehabilitation planning for brain-damaged patients (Jones & Butters, 1983). We commented there that as a result of the emphasis on diagnosis and research that had characterized the early development of the field of clinical neuropsychology, the need for practical recommendations for treatment strategies had been all too often overlooked. Clinical neuropsychologists have made considerable contributions in the area of rehabilitation in the 6 years that have intervened, and this trend will undoubtedly continue. Before surveying some of the major developments in this area, however, we would offer a caveat. Some neuropsychologists seem to feel that, with the development of novel, powerful ancillary techniques in neurological diagnosis, the diagnostic role of neuropsychological assessment is becoming increasingly secondary. For example,

With the advent of new and sophisticated noninvasive methods such as the CT and PET scans and magnetic resonance techniques, the utility of clinical neuropsychology as a purely diagnostic discipline has been, and will continue to be, progressively diluted. (Hart & Hayden, 1986, p. 21)

The corollary of this view is that the neuropsychologist's role becomes increasingly that of rehabilitation planning. Although neuropsychologists need to be knowledgeable about the relationships between test data and functioning in the real world and need to be prepared either to be involved in, or to make appropriate referrals for, rehabilitation planning, we do not agree that neuropsychological assessment as a diagnostic discipline is becoming superfluous, obsolete, or "diluted." There are a number of neuropathological entities in which neuropsychological assessment may provide the earliest, the most sensitive, or even the only evidence of abnormality. Furthermore, even where ancillary techniques document cerebral lesions or other abnormalities in exquisite detail, neuropsychological assessment may provide the most complete diagnostic information about the resultant *cognitive deficit* (e.g., does the patient have aphasia as a result of a left posterior infarct, and if so, what type of aphasia?).

Among the major developments in the field of neuropsychological rehabilitation are the following: (a) a renewed interest in the recovery processes per se, with special attention to the neural mechanisms involved (e.g., Finger, 1978; Uzzell, 1986); (b) perceptual–cognitive retraining in stroke victims, with particular attention to the problems of left visual neglect and maintenance of arousal (e.g., Ben-Yishay & Diller, 1983; Diller & Weinberg, 1986; Weinberg, Piasetsky, Diller, & Gordon, 1982); (c) increased attention to the relationship between neuropsychological test scores and real life functioning (e.g., Acker, 1986; Hart & Hayden, 1986); (d) elaboration of approaches to the special problems in neuropsychological rehabilitation planning for patients with traumatic brain injuries, especially those with closed head injuries (e.g., Edelstein & Couture, 1984; Levin, Benton, & Grossman, 1982; Milton & Wertz, 1986); (e) increasing application of the individualized neuropsychological assessment approach to remediation (e.g., Christensen & Uzzell, 1987; Uzzell & Gross, 1986); (f) advances in memory rehabilitation (e.g., Grafman, 1984; O'Connor & Cermak, 1987; Salmon & Butters, 1987; Schacter & Glisky, 1986; Wilson & Moffat, 1983); and (g) integration of neuropsychological principles with behavioral techniques in rehabilitation strategies (e.g., Seron, 1987; Wood, 1987).

CONCLUSION

From its modest beginnings toward the early part of this century, the field of neuropsychological assessment has become one of the fastest growing subspecialties within psychology and has gained increasing recognition as a valuable and even necessary service in the diagnosis of and treatment planning for a significant subset of psychiatric, neurological, and neurosurgical patients.

There is considerable diversity among neuropsychological assessment procedures in current use. Although some neuropsychologists insist on the need for a fixed battery, others are equally convinced of the advantages of a flexible, individualized approach. Among those who favor batteries, opinion is divided as to the relative advantages of the Halstead-Reitan and Luria-Nebraska batteries, and neither seems likely to monopolize the field. Among the individualized approaches, the Boston Process Approach, the approach developed by A. L. Benton and his colleagues, and that of M. D. Lezak are perhaps most influential.

By all accounts, the "state of the art" in neuropsychological assessment is still somewhat primitive. Although many methodologies yield quite acceptable results in discriminating between brain-damaged subjects and normal control subjects, distinctions as to lateralization, localization, disease process or course, and differential diagnosis are more difficult and depend in large measure on subjective clinical inference. The clinician's skill in drawing inferences is a function of a sophisticated knowledge of brain–behavior relationships and clinical experience. A problem for most neuropsychological methodologies is the distinction between patients with structural brain lesions and patients with the more severe and intractable forms of psychiatric illness. However, recent work in delineating neuropsychological profiles in neuropsychiatric syndromes promises to enhance the contributions of clinical neuropsychologists in this area.

NOTE

1. Davison (1974) presents a useful discussion of the relation between clinical neuropsychology and allied fields, and of the differences between traditional clinical psychological and clinical neuropsychological approaches to the assessment of brain damage.

REFERENCES

Acker, M. B. (1986). Relationships between test scores and everyday life functioning. In B. P. Uzzell & Y. Gross (Eds.), *Clinical neuropsychology of intervention* (pp. 85–117). Boston: Martinus Nijhoff.

Adams, K.M. (1975). Automated clinical interpretation of the neuropsychological test battery: An ability-based approach (Doctoral dissertation, Wayne State University, 1974). *Dissertation Abstracts International, 35,* 6085B. (University Microfilms No. 75-13, 289)

Adams, K. M. (1980a). In search of Luria's battery: A false start. *Journal of Consulting and Clinical Psychology, 48,* 511–516.

Adams, K. M. (1980b). An end of innocence for behavioral neurology? Adams replies. *Journal of Consulting and Clinical Psychology, 48,* 522–524.

Adams, K. M., & Brown, G. C. (1986). The role of the computer in neuropsychological assessment. In I. Grant & K. M. Adams (Eds.), *Neuropsychological assessment of neuropsychiatric disorders* (pp. 87–99). New York: Oxford University Press.

Albert, M. S., Butters, N., & Brandt, J. (1981). Patterns of remote memory in amnesic and demented patients. *Archives of Neurology, 38,* 495–500.

Albert, M. S., Butters, N., & Levin, J. (1979). Temporal gradients in the retrograde amnesia of patients with alcoholic Korsakoff's disease. *Archives of Neurology, 36,* 211–216.

Albert, M. S., & Kaplan, E. (1980). Organic implications of neuropsychological deficits in the elderly. In L. W. Poon, J. L. Fozard, L. S. Cermak, D. Arenberg, & L. W. Thompson (Eds.), *New directions in memory and aging: Proceedings of the George A. Talland Memorial Conference* (pp. 403–432). Hillsdale, NJ: Lawrence Erlbaum Associates.

Albert, M. S., & Moss, M. B. (1988). *Geriatric neuropsychology.* New York: Guilford Press.

American Psychological Association. (1974). *Standards for educational and psychological tests.* Washington, DC: Author.

Anthony, W. Z., Heaton, R. K., & Lehman, R. A. (1980). An attempt to cross-validate two actuarial systems for neuropsychological test interpretation. *Journal of Consulting and Clinical Psychology, 48,* 317–326.

Benton, A. L. (1945). A visual retention test for clinical use. *Archives of Neurology and Psychiatry, 54,* 212–216.

Benton, A. L. (1950). A multiple-choice type of visual retention test. *Archives of Neurology and Psychiatry, 64,* 699–707.

Benton, A. L. (1967). Constructional apraxia and the minor hemisphere. *Confinia Neurologica, 29,* 1–16.

Benton, A. L. (1968). Differential behavioral effects in frontal lobe disease. *Neuropsychologia, 6,* 53–60.

Benton, A. L. (1973). *Test of three-dimensional constructional praxis manual.* (Publication No. 286). University of Iowa, Iowa City: Neurosensory Center.

Benton, A. L. (1974). *The Revised Visual Retention Test* (4th ed.). New York: Psychological Corporation.

Benton, A. L., Hamsher, K. de S., Varney, N., & Spreen, O. (1983). *Contributions to neuropsychologial assessment: A clinical manual.* New York: Oxford University Press.

Benton, A. L., & Van Allen, M. W. (1968). Impairment in facial recognition in patients with cerebral disease. *Cortex, 4,* 344–358.

Benton, A. L., & Van Allen, M. W. (1972). Prosopagnosia and facial discrimination. *Journal of Neurological Sciences, 15,* 167–172.

Ben-Yishay, Y., & Diller, L. (1983). Cognitive deficits. In M. Rosenthal, E. R. Griffith, M. R. Bond, & J. D. Miller (Eds.), *Rehabilitation of the head injured adult* (pp. 167–183). Philadelphia: F. A. Davis.

Blumstein, S. E., Cooper, W. E., Goodglass, H., Statlander, S., & Gottlieb, J. (1980). Production deficits in aphasia: A voice-onset time analysis. *Brain and Language, 9,* 153–170.

Blumstein, S. E., Cooper, W. E., Zurif, E. B., & Caramazza, A. (1977). The perception and production of voice-onset time in aphasia. *Neuropsychologia, 15,* 371–383.

Boll, T. J. (1981). The Halstead-Reitan Neuropsychology Battery. In S. B. Fisher & T. J. Boll (Eds.), *Handbook of clinical neuropsychology* (Vol. 1, pp. 577–607). New York: Wiley-Interscience.

Borod, J. C., Goodglass, H., & Kaplan, E. (1980). Normative data on the Boston Diagnostic Aphasia Examination, Parietal Lobe Battery and the Boston Naming Test. *Journal of Clinical Neuropsychology, 2,* 209–215.

Butters, N. (1984). The clinical aspects of memory disorders: Contributions from experimental studies of amnesia and dementia. *Journal of Clinical Neuropsychology, 6,* 17–36.

Butters, N. (1986). The clinical aspects of memory disorders: Contributions from experimental studies of amnesia and dementia. In T. Incagnoli, E. Goldstein, & C. Golden (Eds.), *Clinical application of neuropsychological test batteries* (pp. 361–382). New York: Plenum Press.

Butters, N., & Barton, M. (1970). Effect of parietal lobe damage on the performance of reversible operations in space. *Neuropsychologia, 8,* 205–214.

Butters, N., & Cermak, L. S. (1975). Some analyses of amnesic syndromes in brain-damaged patients. In R. Isaacson & K. Pribram (Eds.), *The hippocampus. Vol. 2: Neuropsychology and behavior* (pp. 377–409). New York: Plenum Press.

Butters, N., & Cermak, L. S. (1976). Neuropsychological studies of alcoholic Korsakoff patients. In G. Goldstein & C. Neuringer (Eds.), *Empirical studies of alcoholism* (pp. 153–192). Cambridge, MA: Ballinger Press.

Butters, N., & Cermak, L. S. (1980). *Alcoholic Korsakoff's Syndrome: An information-processing approach to amnesia.* New York: Academic Press.

Butters, N., & Cermak, L. S. (1986). A case study of the forgetting of autobiographical knowledge: Implications for the study of retrograde amnesia. In D. C. Rubin (Ed.), *Autobiographical memory* (pp. 253–272). New York: Cambridge University Press.

Butters, N., & Grady, M. (1977). Effect of predistractor delays on the short-term memory performance of patients with Korsakoff's and Huntington's disease. *Neuropsychologia, 15,* 701–706.

Butters, N., Miliotis, P., Albert, M. S., & Sax, D. (1984). Memory assessment: Evidence of the heterogeneity of amnesic symptoms. In G. Goldstein (Ed.), *Advances in clinical neuropsychology* (Vol. 1, pp. 127–159). New York: Plenum Press.

Butters, N., Sax, D., Montgomery, K., & Tarlow, S. (1978). Comparison of the neuropsychological deficits associated with early and advanced Huntington's disease. *Archives of Neurology, 35,* 585–589.

Butters, N., Salmon, D. P., Cullum, C. M., Cairns, P., Troster, A. I., Jacobs, D., Moss, M., & Cermak, L. S. (1988). Differentiation of amnesic and demented patients with the Wechsler Memory Scale—Revised. *The Clinical Neuropsychologist, 2,* 133–148.

Butters, N., Wolfe, J., & Granholm, E. (1986). An assessment of verbal recall, recognition and fluency abilities in patients with Huntington's disease. *Cortex, 22,* 11–32.

Caine, E. (1986). The neuropsychology of depression: The pseudodementia syndrome. In I. Grant & K. M. Adams (Eds.), *Neuropsychological assessment of neuropsychiatric disorders* (pp. 221–243). New York: Oxford University Press.

Caramazza, A., & Zurif, E. B. (1976). Dissociation of algorithmic and heuristic processes in language comprehension: Evidence from aphasia. *Brain and Language, 3,* 572–582.

Cermak, L. S. (1982). The long and short of it in amnesia. In L. S. Cermak (Ed.), *Human memory and amnesia* (pp. 43–59). Hillsdale, NJ: Lawrence Erlbaum Associates.

Cermak, L. S. (1985). The episodic-semantic distinction in amnesia. In L. R. Squire & N. Butters (Eds.), *Neuropsychology of memory* (pp. 55–62). New York: Guilford Press.

Cermak, L. S., & Butters, N. (1972). The role of interference and encoding in the short-term memory deficits of Korsakoff patients. *Neuropsychologia, 10,* 89–95.

Cermak, L. S., & Butters, N. (1976). The role of language in the memory disorders of brain-damaged patients. *Annals of the New York Academy of Sciences, 280,* 857–867.

Cermak, L. S., Butters, N., & Moreines, J. (1974). Some analyses of the verbal encoding deficit of alcoholic Korsakoff patients. *Brain and Language, 1,* 141–150.

Cermak, L. S., & Reale, L. (1978). Depth of processing and retention of words by alcoholic Korsakoff patients. *Journal of Experimental Psychology: Human Learning and Memory, 4,* 165–174.

Chelune, G. J. (1982). A reexamination of the relationship between the Luria-Nebraska and Halstead-Reitan batteries: Overlap with the WAIS. *Journal of Consulting and Clinical Psychology, 50,* 578–580.

Christensen, A. L. (1975). *Luria's neuropsychological investigation: Text, manual, and test cards.* New York: Spectrum.

Christensen, A.-L., & Uzzell, B. P. (Eds.). (1987). *Neuropsychological rehabilitation. Proceedings of the Conference on Rehabilitation of Brain Damaged People—Current Knowledge and Future Directions.* Meeting held in Copenhagen, June 15–16, 1987. Boston: Kluwer Academic.

Columbia-Greystone Associates. (1949). *Problems of the*

human brain: I. Selective partial ablation of the frontal cortex. New York: Hoeber.

Corkin, S. (1984). Lasting consequences of bilateral medial temporal lobectomy: Clinical course and experimental findings in H. M. *Seminar in Neurology, 6,* 249–259.

Costa, L., & Spreen, O. (1985). *Studies in neuropsychology: Selected papers of Arthur Benton.* New York: Oxford University Press.

Crosson, B., & Warren, R. L. (1982). Use of the Luria-Nebraska Neuropsychological battery in aphasia: A conceptual critique. *Journal of Consulting and Clinical Psychology, 50,* 22–31.

Davison, L. A. (1974). Introduction. In R. M. Reitan & L. A. Davison (Eds.), *Clinical neuropsychology: Current status and applications* (pp. 1–18). Washington, DC: V. H. Winston & Sons.

Delis, D. C., & Kaplan, E. (1982). The assessment of aphasia with the Luria-Nebraska Neuropsychological Battery: A case critique. *Journal of Consulting and Clinical Psychology, 50,* 32–39.

Delis, D. C., & Kaplan, E. (1983). Hazards of a standardized neuropsychological test with low content validity: Comment on the Luria-Nebraska Neuropsychological Battery. *Journal of Consulting and Clinical Psychology, 51,* 396–398.

Delis, D. C., Kramer, J., Kaplan, E., & Ober, B. A. (1987). *California Verbal Learning Test: Research edition.* New York: Psychological Corporation.

Devinsky, O., Putnam, F., Grafman, J., Bromfield, E., & Theodore, W. H. (1989). Dissociative states and epilepsy. *Neurology, 39,* 835–840.

Diller, L., & Weinberg, J. (1986). Learning from failures in perceptual cognitive retraining in stroke. In B. P. Uzzell & Y. Gross (Eds.), *Clinical neuropsychology of intervention* (pp. 283–293). Boston: Martinus Nijhoff.

Edelstein, B. A., & Couture, E. T. (1984). *Behavioral assessment and rehabilitation of the traumatically brain-damaged.* New York: Plenum Press.

Farr, S. P., Greene, R. L., & Fisher-White, S. P. (1986). Disease process, onset, and course and their relationship to neuropsychological performance. In S. B. Filskov & T. J. Boll (Eds.), *Handbook of clinical neuropsychology* (Vol. 2, pp. 213–253). New York: Wiley-Interscience.

Fedio, P., & Mirsky, A. F. (1969). Selective intellectual deficits in children with temporal lobe or centrencephalic epilepsy. *Neuropsychologia, 7,* 287–300.

Finger, S. (Ed.). (1978). *Recovery from brain damage: Research and theory.* New York: Plenum Press.

Finkelstein, J. N. (1977). BRAIN: A computer program for interpretation of the Halstead-Reitan Neuropsychological Test Battery (Doctoral dissertation, Columbia University, 1976). *Dissertation Abstracts International, 37,* 5349B. (University Microfilms No. 77-8, 8864)

Fox, C. F. (1981). Neuropsychological correlates of anorexia nervosa. *International Journal of Psychiatry and Medicine, 11,* 285–290.

Gardner, H. (1975). *The shattered mind: The person after brain damage.* New York: Knopf.

Gardner, H. (1983). *Frames of mind: The theory of multiple intelligences.* New York: Basic Books.

Gardner, H., Ling, P. K., Flamm, L., & Silverman, J. (1975). Comprehension and appreciation of humorous material after brain damage. *Brain, 98,* 399–412.

Geschwind, N. (1974). *Selected papers on language and the brain: Boston studies in the philosophy of science* (Vol. 16). Boston: Reidel.

Goldberg, E. (Ed.). (1989). *Contemporary Neuropsychology and the Legacy of Luria.* Hillsdale, NJ: Lawrence Erlbaum Associates.

Goldberg, E., & Costa, L. D. (1986). Qualitative indices in neuropsychological assessment: An extension of Luria's approach to executive deficit following prefrontal lesions. In I. Grant & K. Adams (Eds.), *Neuropsychological assessment of neuropsychiatric disorders* (pp. 48–64). New York: Oxford University Press.

Golden, C. J. (1981a). A standardized version of Luria's neuropsychological tests: A quantitative and qualitative approach to neuropsychological evaluation. In S. B. Filskov & T. J. Boll (Eds.), *Handbook of clinical neuropsychology* (Vol. 1, pp. 608–642). New York: Wiley-Interscience.

Golden, C. J. (1981b). The Luria-Nebraska Neuropsychological Battery: Theory and research. In P. McReynolds (Ed.), *Advances in psychological assessment* (Vol. 5, pp. 191–235). San Francisco, CA: Jossey-Bass.

Golden, C. J., Hammeke, T. A., & Purisch, A. D. (1978). Diagnostic validity of a standardized neuropsychological battery derived from Luria's neuropsychological tests. *Journal of Consulting and Clinical Psychology, 46,* 1258–1265.

Golden, C. J., Hammeke, T., & Purisch, A. (1980). *A manual for the administration and interpretation of the Luria-Nebraska Neuropsychological Battery.* Los Angeles: Western Psychological Services.

Golden, C. J., Kane, R., Sweet, J., Moses, J. A., Jr., Cardellino, J. P., Templeton, R., Vicente, P., & Graber, B. (1981). The relationship of the Halstead-Reitan Neuropsychological Battery to the Luria-Nebraska Neuropsychological Battery. *Journal of Consulting and Clinical Psychology, 49,* 410–417.

Golden, C. J., Moses, J. A., Jr., Fishburne, F. J., Engum, E., Lewis, G. P., Wisniewski, A. M., Conley, F. K., Berg, R. A., & Graber, B. (1981). Cross validation of the Luria-Nebraska Neuropsychological Battery for the presence, lateralization, and localization of brain damage. *Journal of Consulting and Clinical Psychology, 49,* 491–507.

Golden, C. J., Purisch, A. D., & Hammeke, T. A. (1985). *Luria-Nebraska Neuropsychological Battery: Forms I and II Manual.* Los Angeles: Western Psychological Services.

Goldstein, G. (1986). The neuropsychology of schizophrenia. In I. Grant & K. M. Adams (Eds.), *Neuropsychological assessment of neuropsychiatric disorders* (pp. 147–171). New York: Oxford University Press.

Goldstein, G., & Incagnoli, T. (1986). A comparison of the

Halstead-Reitan, Luria-Nebraska, and flexible batteries through case presentations. In T. Incagnoli, G. Goldstein, & C. J. Golden (Eds.), *Clinical application of neuropsychological test batteries* (pp. 303–327). New York: Plenum Press.

Goldstein, K., & Scheerer, M. (1941). Abstract and concrete behavior: An experimental study with special tests. *Psychological Monographs, 53*(2, Whole No. 239).

Goodglass, H. (1986). The flexible battery in neuropsychological assessment. In T. Incagnoli, G. Goldstein, & C. J. Golden (Eds.), *Clinical application of neuropsychological test batteries* (pp. 121–134). New York: Plenum Press.

Goodglass, H., & Butters, N. (1988). Psychobiology of cognitive processes. In R. Atkinson, R. J. Herrnstein, G. Lindzey, & R. D. Luce (Eds.), *Stevens' handbook of experimental psychology* (2nd ed., pp. 863–952). New York: John Wiley & Sons.

Goodglass, H., & Kaplan, E. (1963). Disturbance of gesture and pantomime in aphasia. *Brain, 86*, 703–720.

Goodglass, H., & Kaplan, E. (1972). *The assessment of aphasia and related disorders.* Philadelphia: Lea & Febiger.

Goodglass, H., & Kaplan, E. (1979). Assessment of cognitive deficit in the brain-injured patient. In M. Gazzaniga (Ed.), *Handbook of behavioral neurobiology: Vol. 2. Neuropsychology* (pp. 3–22). New York: Plenum Press.

Goodglass, H., & Quadfasel, F. A. (1954). Language laterality in left-handed aphasics. *Brain, 77*, 521–548.

Goodglass, H., Quadfasel, F. A., & Timberlake, W. H. (1964). Phrase length and the type and severity of aphasia. *Cortex, 1*, 133–153.

Gorham, D. R. (1956). *Proverbs test.* Missoula, MN: Psychological Test Specialists.

Grafman, J. (1984). Memory assessment and remediation in brain-injured patients: From theory to practice. In B. A. Edelstein & E. T. Couture (Eds.), *Behavioral assessment and rehabilitation of the traumatically brain-damaged* (pp. 151–189). New York: Plenum Press.

Grafman, J., Devinsky, O., Putnam, F., Nissen, M. J., & Schachter, D. (1989). *Observations on amnesia in multiple personality disorder.* Manuscript in preparation.

Grant, D. A., & Berg, E. A. (1948). A behavioral analysis of degree of reinforcement and ease of shifting to new responses in a Weigl-type card-sorting program. *Journal of Experimental Psychology, 38*, 404–411.

Halstead, W. C. (1947). *Brain and intelligence: A quantitative study of the frontal lobes.* Chicago: University of Chicago Press.

Halstead, W. C. (1950). Frontal lobe functions and intelligence. *Bulletin of the Los Angeles Neurological Society, 15*, 205–212.

Halstead, W. C. (1951). Biological intelligence. *Journal of Personality, 20*, 118–130.

Halstead, W. C., & Shure, G. (1954). Further evidence for a frontal lobe component in human biological intelligence. *Transactions of the American Neurological Association, 79*, 9–11.

Hammeke, T. A., Golden, C. J., & Purisch, A. D. (1978). A standardized, short, and comprehensive neuropsychological test battery based on the Luria neuropsychological evaluation. *International Journal of Neuroscience, 8*, 135–141.

Hamsher, K. de S., Halmi, K. A., & Benton, A. L. (1981). Prediction of outcome in anorexia nervosa from neuropsychological status. *Psychiatry Research, 4*, 79–88.

Hart, T., & Hayden, M. E. (1986). The ecological validity of neuropsychological assessment and remediation. In B. P. Uzzell & Y. Gross (Eds.), *Clinical neuropsychology of intervention* (pp. 21–50). Boston: Martinus Nijhoff.

Hartlage, L., Chelune, G., & Tucker, D. (1980). *Survey of professional issues in the practice of clinical neuropsychology.* Unpublished report from membership survey, Division 40, American Psychological Association. Washington, DC: American Psychological Association.

Heaton, R. K., Baade, L. E., & Johnson, K. L. (1978). Neuropsychological test results associated with psychiatric disorders in adults. *Psychological Bulletin, 85*, 141–162.

Heaton, R. K., & Crowley, T. J. (1981). Effects of psychiatric disorders and their somatic treatments on neuropsychological test results. In S. B. Filskov & T. J. Boll (Eds.), *Handbook of clinical neuropsychology* (Vol. 1, pp. 481–525). New York: Wiley-Interscience.

Heaton, R. K., Grant, I., Anthony, W. Z., & Lehman, R. A. (1981). A comparison of clinical and automated interpretation of the Halstead-Reitan Battery. *Clinical Neuropsychology, 3*, 121–141.

Hebb, D. O. (1939). Intelligence in man after large removals of cerebral tissue: Defects following right temporal lobectomy. *Journal of General Psychology, 21*, 437–446.

Hebb, D. O. (1942). The effect of early and late brain injury upon test scores, and the nature of normal adult intelligence. *Proceedings of the American Philosophical Society, 85*, 275–292.

Hecaen, H., & Albert, M. L. (1978). *Human neuropsychology.* New York: Wiley-Interscience.

Held, R. (1961). Exposure-history as a factor in maintaining stability of perception and coordination. *Journal of Nervous and Mental Disease, 132*, 26–32.

Hooper, H. E. (1958). *The Hooper Visual Organization Test Manual.* Los Angeles: Western Psychological Services.

Jastak, J. F., & Jastak, S. R. (1978). *The Wide Range Achievement Test Manual (Revised).* Los Angeles: Western Psychological Services.

Jones, B. P., Brouwers, P., Mirsky, A. F., & Duncan, C. C. (1989). *Cognition and personality in eating disorders.* Manuscript in preparation.

Jones, B. P., & Butters, N. (1983). Neuropsychological assessment. In M. Hersen, A. Kazdin, & A. Bellack (Eds.), *The clinical psychology handbook* (pp. 377–396). Elmsford, New York: Pergamon Press.

Jones, B. P., Butters, N., Moskowitz, H. R., & Montgomery, K. (1978). Olfactory and gustatory capacities of alcoholic Korsakoff patients. *Neuropsychologia, 16,* 323–337.

Jones, B. P., Henderson, M., & Welch, C. A. (1988). Executive functions in unipolar depression before and after electroconvulsive therapy. *International Journal of Neuroscience, 38,* 287–297.

Jones, B. P., Moskowitz, H. R., & Butters, N. (1975). Olfactory discrimination in alcoholic Korsakoff patients. *Neuropsychologia, 13,* 173–179.

Jones-Gotman, M., & Milner, B. (1977). Design fluency: The invention of nonsense drawings after focal cortical lesions. *Neuropsychologia, 15,* 653–674.

Kane, R. L. (1986). Comparison of Halstead-Reitan and Luria-Nebraska Neuropsychological Batteries: Research findings. In T. Incagnoli & G. Goldstein (Eds.), *Clinical application of neuropsychological test batteries* (pp. 277–301). New York: Plenum Press.

Kane, R. L., Parsons, O. A., & Goldstein, G. (1985). Statistical relationships and discriminative accuracy of the Halstead-Reitan, Luria-Nebraska, and Wechsler IQ scores in the identification of brain damage. *Journal of Clinical and Experimental Neuropsychology, 7,* 211–223.

Kane, R. L., Parsons, O. A., Goldstein, G., & Moses, J. A., Jr. (1987). Diagnostic accuracy of the Halstead-Reitan and Luria-Nebraska Neuropsychological Batteries: Performance of clinical raters. *Journal of Consulting and Clinical Psychology, 55,* 783–784.

Kane, R. L., Sweet, J. J., Golden, C. J., Parsons, O. A., & Moses, J. A., Jr. (1981). Comparative diagnostic accuracy of the Halstead-Reitan and Standardized Luria-Nebraska Neuropsychological Batteries in a mixed psychiatric and brain damaged population. *Journal of Consulting and Clinical Psychology, 49,* 484–485.

Kaplan, E., Fine, D., Morris, R., & Delis, D. C. (in press). *The WAIS-R as a neuropsychological instrument.* New York: New York Psychological Corporation.

Kaplan, E., Goodglass, H., & Weintraub, S. (1983). *Boston Naming Test.* Philadelphia: Lea & Febiger.

Kiernan, R. J., & Matthews, C. G. (1976). Impairment index versus *T*-score averaging in neuropsychological assessment. *Journal of Consulting and Clinical Psychology, 44,* 951–957.

Kimura, D. (1961). Some effects of temporal lobe damage on auditory perception. *Canadian Journal of Psychology, 15,* 156–165.

Kimura, D. (1963). Right temporal lobe damage. *Archives of Neurology, 8,* 264–271.

Klove, H. (1974). Validation studies in adult clinical neuropsychology. In R. M. Reitan & L. A. Davison (Eds.), *Clinical neuropsychology: Current status and applications* (pp. 211–235). Washington, DC: V. H. Winston & Sons.

Lacks, P., Colbert, J., Harrow, M., & Levine, J. (1970). Further evidence concerning the diagnostic accuracy of the Halstead Organic Test Battery. *Journal of Clinical Psychology, 26,* 480–481.

Lansdell, H., & Mirsky, A. F. (1964). Attention in focal and centrencephalic epilepsy. *Experimental Neurology, 9,* 463–469.

Levin, H. S., Benton, A. L., & Grossman, R. G. (1982). *Neurobehavioral consequences of closed head injury.* New York: Oxford University Press.

Lezak, M. D. (1983). *Neuropsychological assessment* (2nd ed.). New York: Oxford University Press.

Luria, A. R. (1980). *Higher cortical functions in man* (2nd ed.). New York: Basic Books.

Malec, J. (1978). Neuropsychological assessment of schizophrenia versus brain damage: A review. *Journal of Nervous and Mental Disease, 166,* 507–516.

McKay, S., & Golden, C. J. (1979a). Empirical derivation of experimental scales for localizing brain lesions using the Luria-Nebraska Neuropsychological Battery. *Clinical Neuropsychology, 1*(2), 19–23.

McKay, S., & Golden, C. J. (1979b). Empirical derivation of neuropsychological scales for the lateralization of brain damage using the Luria-Nebraska Neuropsychological Battery. *Clinical Neuropsychology, 1*(2), 1–5.

McKay, S. E., & Golden, C. J. (1981). The assessment of specific neuropsychological skills using scales derived from factor analysis of the Luria-Nebraska Neuropsychological Battery. *International Journal of Neuroscience, 14,* 189–204.

Meier, M. J. (1981). Report of the Task Force on Education, Accreditation and Credentialing of the International Neuropsychological Society. *The INS Bulletin,* September, pp. 5–10.

Milberg, W., & Blumstein, S. E. (1981). Lexical decisions and aphasia: Evidence for semantic processing. *Brain and Language, 14,* 371–385.

Milberg, W., Hebben, N., & Kaplan, E. (1986). The Boston Process Approach to neuropsychological assessment. In I. Grant & K. M. Adams (Eds.), *Neuropsychological assessment of neuropsychiatric disorders* (pp. 65–86). New York: Oxford University Press.

Milner, B. (1958). Psychological defects produced by temporal lobe excision. *Research Proceedings of the Association for Research in Nervous and Mental Disorders, 36,* 244–257.

Milner, B. (1960, February). *Impairment of visual recognition and recall after right temporal lobectomy in man.* Paper presented at the annual meeting of the Psychonomic Society, Chicago, IL.

Milner, B. (1962). Laterality effects in audition. In V. B. Mountcastle (Ed.), *Interhemispheric relations and cerebral dominance* (pp. 177–195). Baltimore: The Johns Hopkins University Press.

Milner, B. (1964). Some effects of frontal lobectomy in man. In J. M. Warren & K. Akert (Eds.), *The frontal granular cortex and behavior* (pp. 313–334). New York: McGraw-Hill.

Milner, B. (1966). Amnesia following operation on the temporal lobes. In C. W. M. Whitty & O. L. Zangwill (Eds.), *Amnesia* (pp. 109–133). London: Butterworths.

Milner, B. (1967). Brain mechanisms suggested by studies of temporal lobes. In C. H. Millikan & F. L. Darley

(Eds.), *Brain mechanisms underlying speech and language*. Proceedings of a conference held in Princeton, NJ, November 9–12, 1965 (pp. 122–145). New York: Grune & Stratton.

Milner, B. (1968). Visual recognition and recall after right temporal-lobe excision in man. *Neuropsychologia, 6*, 191–209.

Milner, B. (1970). Memory and the medial temporal regions of the brain. In K. H. Pribram & D. E. Broadbent (Eds.), *Biology of memory* (pp. 29–50). New York: Academic Press.

Milner, B. (1971). Interhemispheric differences in the localization of psychological processes in man. *British Medical Bulletin, 27*, 272–275.

Milner, B., & Kimura, D. (1964). *Dissociable visual learning defects after unilateral temporal lobectomy in man*. Paper presented at the annual meeting of the Eastern Psychological Association, Philadelphia.

Milton, S. B., & Wertz, R. T. (1986). Management of persisting communication deficits in patients with traumatic brain injury. In B. P. Uzzell & Y. Gross (Eds.), *Clinical neuropsychology of intervention* (pp. 223–256). Boston: Martinus Nijhoff.

Mirsky, A. F. (1987). Behavioral and psychophysiological markers of disordered attention. *Environmental Health Perspectives, 74*, 191–199.

Mirsky, A. F. (1989). The neuropsychology of attention: Elements of a complex behavior. In E. Perecman (Ed.), *Integrating theory and practice in clinical neuropsychology* (pp. 75–91). Hillsdale, NJ: Lawrence Erlbaum Associates.

Mirsky, A. F., & Orren, M. M. (1977). Attention. In L. H. Miller, A. J. Kastin, & C. A. Sandman (Eds.), *Neuropeptide influences on the brain and behavior* (pp. 233–267). New York: Raven Press.

Mirsky, A. F., Primac, D. W., Ajmone Marsan, C., Rosvold, H. E., & Stevens, J. A. (1960). A comparison of the psychological test performance of patients with focal and nonfocal epilepsy. *Experimental Neurology, 2*, 75–89.

Mirsky, A. F., & Van Buren, J. M. (1965). On the nature of the "absence" in centrencephalic epilepsy: A study of some behavioral, electroencephalographic and autonomic factors. *Electroencephalography and Clinical Neurophysiology, 18*, 334–348.

Moses, J. A., Golden, C. J., Ariel, R., & Gustavson, J. L. (1983). *Interpretation of the Luria-Nebraska Neuropsychological Battery* (Vol. 1). New York: Grune & Stratton.

Moses, J. A., Jr., & Maruish, M. E. (1987a). *A bibliography for the Luria-Nebraska Neuropsychological Battery: 1977–1986*. Madison, WI: Melnic Press.

Moses, J. A., Jr., & Maruish, M. E. (1987b). A critical review of the Luria-Nebraska Neuropsychological Battery literature: I. Reliability. *International Journal of Clinical Neuropsychology, 9*, 149–157.

Moses, J. A., Jr., & Maruish, M. E. (1988a). A critical review of the Luria-Nebraska Neuropsychological Bat-

tery literature: II. Construct validity. *International Journal of Clinical Neuropsychology, 10*, 5–11.

Moses, J. A., Jr., & Maruish, M. E. (1988b). A critical review of the Luria-Nebraska Neuropsychological Battery literature: III. Concurrent validity. *International Journal of Clinical Neuropsychology, 10*, 12–19.

Myslobodsky, M. S., & Mirsky, A. F. (Eds.). (1988). *Elements of petit mal epilepsy*. New York: Peter Lang.

O'Connor, M., & Cermak, L. S. (1987). Rehabilitation of organic memory disorders. In M. J. Meier, A. L. Benton, & L. Diller (Eds.), *Neuropsychological rehabilitation* (pp. 260–279). New York: Guilford Press.

Oscar-Berman, M. (1973). Hypothesis testing and focusing behavior during concept formation by amnesic Korsakoff patients. *Neuropsychologia, 11*, 191–198.

Oscar-Berman, M. (1980). Neuropsychological consequences of long-term chronic alcoholism. *American Scientist, 68*, 410–419.

Oscar-Berman, M., Goodglass, H., & Cherlow, D. G. (1973). Perceptual laterality and iconic recognition of visual materials by Korsakoff patients and normal adults. *Journal of Comparative and Physiological Psychology, 83*, 316–321.

Oscar-Berman, M., & Samuels, I. (1977). Stimulus-preference and memory factors in Korsakoff's syndrome. *Neuropsychologia, 15*, 99–106.

Oscar-Berman, M., & Zola-Morgan, S. M. (1980a). Comparative neuropsychology and Korsakoff's syndrome: I. Spatial and visual reversal learning. *Neuropsychologia, 18*, 499–512.

Oscar-Berman, M., & Zola-Morgan, S. M. (1980b). Comparative neuropsychology and Korsakoff's syndrome: II. Two-choice visual discrimination learning. *Neuropsychologia, 18*, 513–525.

Osterrieth, P., & Rey, A. (1944). Le test de copie d'une figure complexe. *Archives de Psychologie, 30*, 206–356.

Paterson, A., & Zangwill, O. L. (1944). Disorders of visual-space perception associated with lesions of the right cerebral hemisphere. *Brain, 6*, 331–358.

Paterson, A., & Zangwill, O. L. (1945). A case of topographical disorientation associated with a unilateral cerebral lesion. *Brain, 68*, 188–212.

Porteus, S. D. (1956). *Porteus Maze Test*. Palo Alto, CA: Pacific Books.

Potter, H., & Butters, N. (1980). Continuities in the olfactory deficits of chronic alcoholics and alcoholics with the Korsakoff syndrome. In M. Galanter (Ed.), *Currents in alcoholism* (Vol. 7, pp. 261–271). New York: Grune & Stratton.

Pribram, K. H. (1971). *Languages of the brain: Experimental paradoxes and principles in neuropsychology*. Englewood Cliffs, NJ: Prentice-Hall.

Purisch, A. D., Golden, C. J., & Hammeke, T. A. (1978). Discrimination between schizophrenic and brain-injured patients by a standardized version of Luria's neuropsychological tests. *Journal of Consulting and Clinical Psychology, 46*, 1266–1273.

Raven, J. C. (1960). *Guide to the standard progressive matrices*. London: H. K. Lewis.

Reitan, R. M. (1955). An investigation of the validity of Halstead's measure of biological intelligence. *Archives of Neurology and Psychiatry, 73*, 28–35.

Reitan, R. M. (1966a). Problems and prospects in studying the psychological correlates of brain lesions. *Cortex, 2*, 127–154.

Reitan, R. M. (1966b). A research program on the psychological effects of brain lesions in human beings. In N. R. Ellis (Ed.), *International review of research in mental retardation* (Vol. 1, pp. 153–218). New York: Academic Press.

Reitan, R. M. (1969). *Manual for administration of neuropsychological test batteries for adults and children*. Indianapolis: Privately published by the author.

Reitan, R. M. (1974). Methodological problems in clinical neuropsychology. In R. M. Reitan & L. A. Davison (Eds.), *Clinical neuropsychology: Current status and applications* (pp. 19–46). Washington, DC: V. H. Winston & Sons.

Reitan, R. M. (1986). Theoretical and methodological bases of the Halstead-Reitan Neuropsychological Test Battery. In I. Grant & K. Adams (Eds.), *Neuropsychological Assessment of Neuropsychiatric Disorders* (pp. 3–30). New York: Oxford University Press.

Reports of the INS—Division 40 Task Force on Education, Accreditation, and Credentialing. (1987). *The Clinical Neuropsychologist, 1*, 29–34.

Rey, A. (1964). *L'examen clinique en psychologie*. Paris: Presses Universitaires de Paris.

Robinson, A. L., Heaton, R. K., Lehman, R. A., & Stilson, D. W. (1980). The utility of the Wisconsin Card Sorting Test in detecting and localizing frontal lobe lesions. *Journal of Consulting and Clinical Psychology, 48*, 605–614.

Rosvold, H. E., Mirsky, A. F., Sarason, I., Bransome, E. D., Jr., & Beck, L. H. (1956). A continuous performance test of brain damage. *Journal of Consulting Psychology, 20*, 343–350.

Russell, E. W., Neuringer, C., & Goldstein, G. (1970). *Assessment of brain damage: A neuropsychological key approach*. New York: Wiley-Interscience.

Rylander, G. (1940). *Personality changes after operations on the frontal lobes*. Copenhagen: Munksgaard.

Salmon, D. P., & Butters, N. (1987). Recent developments in learning and memory: Implications for rehabilitation of the amnesic patient. In M. J. Meier, A. L. Benton, & L. Diller (Eds.), *Neuropsychological rehabilitation* (pp. 280–293). New York: Guilford Press.

Schacter, D. L., & Glisky, E. L. (1986). Memory remediation: Restoration, alleviation, and the acquisition of domain-specific knowledge. In B. P. Uzzell & Y. Gross (Eds.), *Clinical neuropsychology of intervention* (pp. 257–282). Boston: Martinus Nijhoff.

Scoville, W. B., & Milner, B. (1957). Loss of recent memory after bilateral hippocampal lesions. *Journal of Neurology, Neurosurgery and Psychiatry, 20*, 11–21.

Semmes, J., Weinstein, S., Ghent, L., & Teuber, H.-L. (1955). Spatial orientation in man after cerebral injury: I. Analyses by locus of lesion. *Journal of Psychology, 39*, 227–244.

Seron, X. (1987). Operant procedures and neuropsychological rehabilitation. In M. J. Meier, A. L. Benton, & L. Diller (Eds.), *Neuropsychological rehabilitation* (pp. 132–161). New York: Guilford Press.

Shai, A., Goodglass, H., & Barton, M. (1972). Recognition of tachistoscopically presented verbal and non-verbal stimuli after unilateral cerebral damage. *Neuropsychologia, 10*, 185–191.

Shelly, C., & Goldstein, G. (1982). Psychometric relations between the Luria-Nebraska and the Halstead-Reitan Neuropsychological Test Batteries in a neuropsychiatric setting. *Clinical Neuropsychology, 4*, 128–133.

Shipley, W. C. (1940). A self-administering scale for measuring intellectual impairment and deterioration. *Journal of Psychology, 9*, 371–377.

Shure, G., & Halstead, W. C. (1958). Cerebral localization of intellectual processes. *Psychological Monographs, 72*, No. 12 (Whole No. 465).

Small, A., Madero, J., Teagno, L., & Ebert, M. (1983). Intellect, perceptual characteristics, and weight gain in anorexia nervosa. *Journal of Clinical Psychology, 39*, 780–782.

Spiers, P. A. (1981). Have they come to praise Luria or to bury him? The Luria-Nebraska Battery controversy. *Journal of Consulting and Clinical Psychology, 49*, 331–341.

Spiers, P. A. (1982). The Luria-Nebraska Neuropsychological Battery revisited: A theory in practice or just practicing? *Journal of Clinical Psychology, 50*, 301–306.

Spreen, O., & Benton, A. L. (1969). *Neurosensory Center Comprehensive Examination for Aphasia*. Victoria, BC: Neuropsychology Laboratory, Department of Psychology, University of Victoria.

Stambrook, M. (1983). The Luria-Nebraska Neuropsychological Battery: A promise that may be partly fulfilled. *Journal of Clinical Neuropsychology, 5*, 247–269.

Stroop, J. R. (1935). Studies of interference in serial verbal reactions. *Journal of Experimental Psychology, 18*, 643–662.

Swiercinsky, D. (1978, August). *Computerized SAINT: System for analysis and interpretation of neuropsychological tests*. Paper presented at the annual meeting of the American Psychological Association, Toronto.

Swiercinsky, D. P., & Warnock, J. K. (1977). Comparison of the neuropsychological key and discriminant analysis approaches in predicting cerebral damage and localization. *Journal of Consulting and Clinical Psychology, 45*, 808–814.

Talland, G. A. (1965). *Deranged memory*. New York: Academic Press.

Teuber, H.-L. (1972). Unity and diversity of frontal lobe functions. *Acta Neurobiologica Experimentalis, 32*, 615–656.

Teuber, H.-L., Battersby, W. S., & Bender, M. B. (1960).

Visual field defects after penetrating missile wounds of the brain. Cambridge, MA: Harvard University Press.

Teuber, H.-L., & Mishkin, M. (1954). Judgment of visual and postural vertical after brain injury. *Journal of Psychology, 38*, 161–175.

Thurstone, L. L. (1938). *Primary mental abilities*. Chicago: University of Chicago Press.

Uzzell, B. P. (1986). Pathophysiology and behavioral recovery. In B. P. Uzzell & Y. Gross (Eds.), *Clinical neuropsychology of intervention* (pp. 3–18). Boston: Martinus Nijhoff.

Uzzell, B. P., & Gross, Y. (Eds.) (1986). *Clinical neuropsychology of intervention*. Boston: Martinus Nijhoff.

Vega, A., & Parsons, O. A. (1967). Cross-validation of the Halstead-Reitan tests for brain damage. *Journal of Consulting Psychology, 31*, 619–625.

Wapner, W., Hamby, S., & Gardner, H. (1981). The role of the right hemisphere in the apprehension of complex linguistic materials. *Brain and Language, 14*, 15–33.

Watson, C. G., Thomas, R. W., Anderson, D., & Felling, J. (1968). Differentiation of organics from schizophrenics at two chronicity levels by use of the Reitan-Halstead Organic Test Battery. *Journal of Consulting and Clinical Psychology, 32*, 679–684.

Wechsler, D. A. (1945). A standardized memory scale for clinical use. *Journal of Psychology, 19*, 87–95.

Wechsler, D. A. (1974). *Wechsler Intelligence Scale for Children—Revised*. New York: Psychological Corporation.

Wechsler, D. A. (1981). *Wechsler Adult Intelligence Scale—Revised*. New York: Psychological Corporation.

Weinberg, J., Piasetsky, E., Diller, L., & Gordon, W. (1982). Treating perceptual organization deficits in nonneglecting RBD stroke patients. *Journal of Clinical Neuropsychology, 4*, 59–75.

Weingartner, H., Cohen, R. M., Murphy, D. L., Martello, J., & Gerdt, C. (1981). Cognitive processes in depression. *Archives of General Psychiatry, 38*, 42–47.

Weisenberg, T. M., & McBride, K. E. (1935). *Aphasia: A clinical and psychological study*. New York: The Commonwealth Fund.

Werner, H. (1937). Process and achievement: A basic problem of education and developmental psychology. *Harvard Educational Review, 7*, 353–368.

Wheeler, L., Burke, C. J., & Reitan, R. M. (1963). An application of discriminant functions to the problem of predicting brain damage using behavioral variables. *Perceptual and Motor Skills, 16*, 417–440. (Monograph Supplement 3-VIb)

Wilson, B. A., & Moffat, N. (Eds.). (1983). *Clinical management of memory problems*. Rockville, MD: Aspen Systems.

Winner, E., & Gardner, H. (1977). The comprehension of metaphor in brain-damaged patients. *Brain, 100*, 717–729.

Wood, R. L. (1987). *Brain injury rehabilitation: A neurobehavioural approach*. Rockville, MD: Aspen Systems.

Zangwill, O. L. (1943). Clinical tests of memory impairment. *Proceedings of the Royal Society of Medicine, 36*, 576–580.

Zurif, E. B. (1980). Language mechanisms: A neuropsychological perspective. *American Scientist, 68*, 305–311.

Zurif, E. B., & Caramazza, A. (1976). Psycholinguistic structures in aphasia: Studies in syntax and semantics. In H. Whitaker & H. A. Whitaker (Eds.), *Studies in neurolinguistics* (Vol. 1, pp. 261–292). New York: Academic Press.

CHAPTER 24

BEHAVIORAL ASSESSMENT

Stephen N. Haynes

In clinical psychology, progress in the ability to predict behavior, to develop conceptual models of behavior disorders,[1] and to develop technologies for facilitating behavior change are highly dependent on advances in measurement methods, models, and theory (Haynes, 1978; Korchin, 1976; Weiner, 1976; Wolman, 1965). These measurement systems provide the means for testing hypotheses about the determinants of behavior disorders, the relationships among behaviors, and for evaluating intervention effects.

One conceptual and methodological basis for advancements in clinical psychology has been provided by behavioral assessment. It has significantly facilitated the identification and measurement of behavior and behavior problems. In addition, it has contributed to the conceptual framework within which behavior is viewed and to the development of more effective and efficient intervention programs.

The vitality of behavioral assessment becomes evident when published research, books, journals, and its incorporation across disciplines are surveyed over the past 15 years. Although prior to 1976 no general texts on behavioral assessment were published, a number were published in the late 1970s and early 1980s (e.g., Barlow, 1981; Ciminero, Calhoun, & Adams, 1977;

Cone & Hawkins, 1977; Haynes, 1978; Haynes & Wilson, 1979; Mash & Terdal, 1981). During the last part of the 1980s, the number of behavioral assessment books has continued to grow (e.g., Bellack & Hersen, 1988; Ciminero, Calhoun, & Adams, 1986; Mash & Terdal, 1988; Nelson & Hayes, 1987). In addition, it is now common for broadly focused books on clinical psychology, assessment, and psychopathology (e.g., Donovan & Marlatt, 1988; Frame & Matson, 1987; Goldstein & Hersen, 1990, 1989; Hersen, Kazdin, & Bellack, 1984; Karoly, 1988; Parks & Hollon, 1988; Rutter, Tuma, & Lann, 1988) to include coverage of behavioral assessment. Two journals, *Behavioral Assessment* and *Journal of Psychopathology and Behavioral Assessment*, both begun in 1979, focus primarily on methodological and conceptual advances in behavioral assessment. Additionally, many broadly focused journals (e.g., *Psychological Assessment: A Journal of Consulting and Clinical Psychology, Clinical Psychology Review*) publish numerous articles involving behavioral assessment. The *Dictionary of Behavioral Assessment Techniques*, published in 1988 (Hersen & Bellack, 1988), presents descriptive and psychometric data on hundreds of assessment instruments used in behavior therapy.

Advances in research design and in methods of statistical analysis such as time-series analyses and within-subject designs have also been associated with behavioral assessment (Barlow & Hersen, 1984; Barlow, Nelson, & Hayes, 1987; Busk & Marascuilo, 1988; Edgington, 1984; Glass, Wilson, & Gottman, 1975; Gorsuch, 1983; Kazdin, 1982a; Kratochwill & Brody, 1978; Kratochwill & Piersel, 1983) and have aided the incursion of scientific methods into the clinic.

Behavioral-assessment methods (e.g., naturalistic observation, analogue assessment, self-monitoring, behavioral interviews, behavioral questionnaires, and psychophysiological assessment) are also being incorporated in disciplines as diverse as social psychology (Lindgren & Harvey, 1971), ethology (Hutt & Hutt, 1970), education (Kratochwill & Roseby, 1988), community psychology (Nietzel, Winett, MacDonald, & Davidson, 1977), developmental disabilities (Castles & Glass, 1986; Sackett, 1978), behavioral medicine (Davidson & Davison, 1980), substance abuse (Donovan & Marlatt, 1988), and psychophysiology (Turpin, 1989). The growing applicability of behavioral assessment is further indicated by its applications to diverse personal and social problems such as learning disabilities (Lahey, Vosk, & Habif, 1981), sexual dysfunctions (Barlow, 1986), chronic pain (Chapman & Wyckoff, 1981), marital dissatisfaction (Gottman, 1979; Haynes & Chavez, 1983; Jacobson, Elwood, & Dallas, 1981), depression (Carson, 1986), headache (Adams, Sutker & Feuernstein, 1980), sleep disorders (Youkilis & Bootzin, 1981), and a wide range of other psychophysiological disorders (Blanchard, 1981; Haynes, Falkin, & Sexton-Radek, 1989), delinquency (Braukman & Fixen, 1975), neuropsychological disorders (Boll, 1981), eating disorders (Brownell, 1981), substance abuse (Correa & Sutker, 1986; Donovan & Marlatt, 1988), childhood pediatric problems (Beck & Smith, 1988; Eisenstein & Copeland, 1988), social skills (Becker & Heimberg, 1988; Conger & Conger, 1986), anxiety disorders (Bernstein, Borkovec, & Coles, 1986), and many others (see Bellack & Hersen, 1988; Ciminero et al., 1986; Mash & Terdal, 1988; Turner, Calhoun, & Adams, 1981). In summary, behavioral assessment has demonstrated a remarkable record of applicability, utility, and productivity.

The historical roots of specific behavioral-assessment procedures are quite diverse. Behavioral observation was used by early Pavlovian experimentalists (see review by Kazdin, 1978) and can be traced to the Hellenic and Egyptian eras (Alexander & Selesnick, 1966; Zilboorg & Henry, 1941). The more systematic methods of behavioral observation currently in use reflect the varied influences of operant psychology and other fields of experimental psychology (Kling & Riggs, 1971; Wolman, 1973), ethology (Hutt & Hutt, 1970), social psychology (Sellitz, Wrightsman, & Cook, 1976), developmental psychology (Wright, 1960), and comparative psychology (Kazdin, 1978). Other behavioral-assessment methods, such as questionnaires, interviews, and self-monitoring, were selectively borrowed or derived from traditionally used clinical, developmental, and social psychology assessment instruments (McReynolds, 1978; Wolman, 1978; Woody, 1980). Finally, the technological bases for psychophysiological methods in behavioral assessment were provided by the disciplines of electrophysiology and psychophysiology (Martin & Venables, 1980; Turpin, 1989) and more recently neurophysiology and neuroendocrinology (Asterita, 1985).

Perhaps the most powerful impetus for the development of behavioral assessment has been the phenomenal growth of the behavior therapies in the 1960s and 1970s (see Kazdin, 1978). The behavior therapies differ from the traditional non-behavioral therapies in the type of interventions and intervention designs that are employed, the underlying assumptions concerning the etiology of behavior, the behaviors targeted for modification, and in their empirical and theoretical bases (Bandura, 1969; Barlow & Hersen, 1984; Emmelkamp, 1986; Eysenck & Martin, 1987). During the proliferation of the behavioral therapies in the 1960s, many of the assessment instruments available were based upon unsuitable conceptual systems (Bandura, 1969; Kanfer & Phillips, 1970; Ullmann & Krasner, 1965). For example, most of the assessment instruments at that time measured higher order more inferential and less situationally sensitive personality "traits." In contrast, the behavior therapies focused on less inferential targets (e.g., observed behaviors) and emphasized the situational and environmental determinants of behavior.

The accelerating level of activity in the field of behavioral assessment has been occurring for less than 15 years and represents a belated response to the perceived need for assessment techniques and instruments that are more compatible with behavioral construct systems. Although occasional symposia, published articles, and book chapters focused on behavioral assessment throughout the 1950s and the 1960s (Bachrach, 1962; Bandura, 1969; Eysenck, 1960a; Rachman & Costello, 1961; Salter, 1961; Wolpe, 1958), it was not until the early and mid-1970s that behavioral assessment became the subject of more systematic investigation and conceptualization. The

1975 West Virginia Conference on Behavioral Assessment was both a reflection of and impetus to this new field of inquiry. The proceedings were later published as an edited book by Cone and Hawkins (1977). Subsequent to that conference, the number of books, published articles, symposia, and presentations at scientific meetings focusing on behavioral assessment burgeoned and continues to grow.

This chapter presents an overview of the foundations, methods, trends, and issues in behavioral assessment. The first section addresses the conceptual and epistemological assumptions underlying the methods and focus of behavioral assessment. The second section introduces dimensions for evaluating behavioral assessment methods; specific methods of assessment are then discussed. The last section addresses recent developments and issues in the field.

CONCEPTUAL FOUNDATIONS

Every behavioral, psychodynamic, or biological assessment system is based upon a set of underlying assumptions regarding behavior, its determinants, and methods of inquiry. These assumptions influence the types of assessment instruments utilized, the phenomena upon which they focus, and the populations to which they are applicable. Conceptual foundations also affect the types of data acquired, the inferences derived from their applications, the intervention programs based on these inferences, the methods of investigating intervention effects, and hypotheses about the determinants of behavior disorders.

The methods and focus of behavioral assessment are closely tied to behavioral construct systems and these conceptual foundations have been well articulated (Bandura, 1969; Eysenck & Martin, 1987; Haynes, 1978; Kanfer & Phillips, 1970; Nelson & Hayes, 1987; Rimm & Masters, 1987). In addition, conceptual and methodological differences between behavioral and traditional clinical assessment systems have been frequently noted (Barrios, 1988; Goldfried, 1977; Goldfried & Kent, 1972; Hartmann, Roper, & Bradford, 1979; Mash, 1979; Nelson & Hayes, 1979, 1986).

The purpose of this section is to examine the underlying assumptions of behavioral construct systems and the impact of these assumptions on behavioral-assessment methods and foci. Several assumptions will be highlighted: (a) a causal model of behavior disorders emphasizing social–environmental interactions, (b) reciprocal determinism, (c) the importance of temporally contiguous controlling variables, (d) situational control of behavior, (e) multiple

causality, (f) a focus on minimally inferential variables, (g) response fractionation, and (h) a cybernetic construct system.

A Social–Environmental Causal Model

Perhaps the assumptions that most strongly influence the methods and focus of an assessment system are those about the causes of behavior and behavior disorders. For example, an assumption that behavior can best be understood through reference to biological determinants necessitates an assessment focus on physiological events and the use of assessment procedures such as serum and urinalysis, CAT scans, or electroencephalograms (EEGs). Alternatively, assumptions that behavior can best be understood through reference to intrapsychic events necessitate a focus on hypothetical intrapsychic factors and the use of assessment procedures such as the Rorschach and Thematic Apperception Test (TAT) that are designed to "uncover" such factors.

Behavioral construct systems frequently, but not invariably, attribute the determinants of behavior disorders to social–environmental events, particularly phenomena that are consistent with a social-learning model of behavior disorders (Bandura, 1969). The determinants include social and nonsocial response contingencies, situational contexts, antecedent cues, and associative learning experiences. A fundamental assumption of most behavioral construct systems is that it is possible to account for a significant proportion of variance in the occurrence, or other parameters of behavior (e.g., duration, magnitude), through reference to antecedent and consequent social–environmental events. For example, it is presumed that marital distress can often result from dysfunctional dyadic communication between spouses or aversive dyadic exchanges (Gottman, 1979; Margolin, Michelli, & Jacobson, 1988), that paranoid behaviors can often be a function of exposure to particular social stressors in the absence of social supports (Haynes, 1986), that depression can often result from a reduced rate of social reinforcement (Carson, 1986; Clarkin & Glazer, 1981), that antisocial behavior can often be attributed to social and nonsocial reinforcement contingencies (Patterson, 1982), that muscle-contraction and migraine headaches can sometimes result from sustained life stressors or their termination (Adams, Feuerstein, & Fowler, 1980), and that childhood conduct problems can often be a function of unintended parental reinforcement contingencies (McMahon & Forehand, 1988; Patterson, 1982).

A social–environmentalist position does not preclude a significant etiological role for physiological, genetic, cognitive, or other nonenvironmental factors. There is little doubt, 'for example, that catecholamines and other neurotransmitters, intrauterine environments, and diet can have profound effects on behavior (Anisman & LaPierre, 1982; Asterita, 1985; Gannon, 1981; Turpin, 1989). There is also ample evidence that cognitive phenomena such as attention, ruminative thoughts, expectancies, and self-evaluative statements can exert strong effects on behavior (Eisenstein & Copeland, 1988; Kendall & Bemis, 1984; Kendall & Braswell, 1985; Merluzzi, Glass, & Genest, 1981).

While acknowledging these important alternative sources of behavior control, the emphasis of behavioral construct systems is clear and well supported—social–environmental factors often play a powerful causal role in behavior disorders, and assessment strategies should carefully evaluate the potential role of these factors.

The presumed causal role of environmental events has a profound impact upon the targets and methods of behavioral assessment. During interviews to assess bulimic episodes, for example, behavior analysts[2] carefully examine the potential causal role of environmental events occurring before, during, and after binging or purging, because such events have been shown to have triggering or reinforcing functions for some persons (Schlundt, Johnson, & Jarrell, 1986). Also, self-monitoring is often used to assess the environmental context of target behaviors such as studying, self-injury, or alcohol intake (Bornstein, Hamilton, & Bornstein, 1986). Most important, a focus on environmental determinants strengthens the emphasis in behavioral assessment on *direct observation* of target behaviors in their environmental contexts. Such procedures and foci in the assessment of behavior problems facilitate the identification of antecedent and consequent events that may serve to trigger or maintain their occurrence.

The mechanisms through which environmental events affect behavior often involve complex and multiple paths and are influenced by *mediating variables*. For example, the probability that exposure to a group of social drinkers will result in relapse in a treated alcoholic may be mediated by the person's self-efficacy and outcome expectancies and social supports for maintaining abstinence (Brownell, Marlatt, Lichtenstein, & Wilson, 1986). Consequently, behavior analysts attend closely to the assessment of variables that may mediate the direct impact of environmental variables. This example further underscores the assessment–treatment symbiosis in behavior therapy—intervention efforts often focus on variables, identified during assessment, that mediate the impact of environmental causal variables.

All attempts to identify causal relationships involve the identification, either subjectively or objectively, of *conditional probabilities* for behavior problems—the identification of those events that are statistically associated with the occurrence (or other parameter) of a behavior problem. For any event to serve as a causal variable[3] for a behavior problem, there must be a higher probability of occurrence for the behavior in its presence than in its absence. For example, performance-related distraction cannot be a cause of male sexual dysfunction (Barlow, 1986) unless the probability of sexual dysfunction is higher in its presence than in its absence.

Reciprocal Determinism: A Person–Environment Interaction Model

The concept of environmental determinism does not presume that individuals are passive recipients of environmental stimuli or that behavior can be treated simply as a dependent variable. Rather, behavioral construct systems strongly endorse a person–environment interaction model (Bandura, 1981; Beck & Smith, 1988; Depue, Slater, Wolfsetter-Kausch, Klein, Goplerud, & Farr, 1981; Kanter, 1985; Mash & Terdal, 1988; Parmalee, 1986) in which the behavior of each individual is presumed to affect his or her environment, which, in turn, affects how the individual thinks, feels, and behaves. Thus, individuals are viewed as both strongly influenced by and powerful shapers of their environment. For example, depression may result from loss of support from close associates but that loss may be precipitated or exacerbated by the behaviors of the depressed person (Billings & Moos, 1981; Carson, 1986). Person–environment interaction models have been advanced for a number of behavior disorders including depression, insomnia, marital distress, psychosomatic disorders, child behavior and family problems, ingestive disorders, and learning disorders (see reviews in Adams & Sutker, 1984; Bellack & Hersen, 1988; Ciminero et al., 1986; Frame & Matson, 1987; Mash & Terdal, 1988).

The mechanisms through which behavior–environment interactions operate are multiple and complex. For example, an individual can affect the social reinforcement rate from the environment by differentially consequating the social behaviors of others. He or she can also provide discriminative stimuli or prompts for the behavior of others, can affect the degree of exposure to environmental stressors, or determine the environmental contexts within which to operate.

A presumption of reciprocal determinism mandates a careful assessment, not only of relevant social–environmental variables, but also of the way in which persons interact with their environment and particularly the *behavioral skills* of persons. For example, behavior analysts carefully assess basic social skills of isolated or depressed individuals, social and sexual intimacy skills of lonely or sexually dysfunctional persons, time-management and study skills of students, parenting skills in cases of conduct disorder, communication skills for persons with distressed marriages, and the contingency management skills of teachers and institutional staff. Focused interviews, observation in natural and analogue environments, participant observation, and self-monitoring are particularly well suited for these purposes.

Temporal Contiguity of Determinants

In contrast to most nonbehavioral construct systems, behavioral construct systems emphasize the importance of determinants in close temporal proximity to the targeted behavior. It is assumed that a greater proportion of the variance in behavior can be accounted for through reference to current, rather than to historical, behavior–environment interactions. The de-emphasis of historical determinants is based as much on pragmatic as on empirical considerations. It reflects the assumption that currently occurring causal variables are more amenable to assessment and modification, as well as being more important determinants of behavior problems. Thus, although the importance of early learning experiences (e.g., abusive parent–child interactions, physically traumatic experiences, early illnesses) in the development of later behavior disorders such as marital distress, depression, anxiety disorders, learning disabilities, and addictive disorders is acknowledged, the current behavior–environment interactions that may be serving to maintain these behavior problems remain the primary focus of assessment. Support for this assumption also derives from the thousands of published studies that demonstrate that clinically meaningful behavior change can result from changes in contemporaneous behaviors, environmental variables, and cognitions.

The de-emphasis of historical determinants in behavioral assessment is consistent with the products of self-monitoring, participant monitoring, behavioral observation, and psychophysiological assessment—assessment methods whose focus is limited to current behaviors and presumed determinants. Although some authors (Lazarus, 1986; Wolpe, 1982) recommend a fairly exhaustive, historically based assessment, the relative emphasis on more immediate determinants is apparent in most behavioral interviews (Haynes & Chavez, 1983; Haynes & Jensen, 1979; Morganstern, 1988; Turkat, 1986) and questionnaires (Galassi & Galassi, 1980; Jensen & Haynes, 1986).

The temporal relationships between causal events and behavior problems are quite complex and reservations concerning an exclusive emphasis on temporally contiguous causal events have been frequently expressed (e.g., Russo, Bird, & Masek, 1980). For example, the latency between causal variables and their effects may vary considerably, the apparent strength of causal relationships may be affected by how they are sampled in time, the effects of particular causal variables may vary across developmental stages, there may be *critical periods* for the impact of causal variables, and causal variables differ in the duration of their effects.

These observations suggest that an exclusive focus on contemporaneous phenomena and relationships may limit the validity and applicability of behavioral construct systems. For example, most direct observation procedures are currently used to detect determinants that occur within several minutes of the target behavior. Obviously, powerful causal factors may occur well beyond that time frame and a number of authors (Gottman, 1979; Margolin, 1981; Russo et al., 1980) have recommended extending the interval of temporal analysis. Increasing attention to historical and temporally noncontiguous factors and complex relationships might facilitate the development of prevention programs, reduce recidivism by identifying potential triggers, and enhance the predictive validity of the behavioral construct system.

Situationally Determined Behavior Variance

Closely associated with assumptions of reciprocal environmental determinism is the assumption that a significant proportion of the variance in the occurrence or characteristics of behavior can be accounted for by reference to antecedent situational factors (Eisler, Hersen, Miller, & Blanchard, 1975; Mash & Terdal, 1988).[4] Antecedent environmental stimuli are presumed to operate as eliciting stimuli (conditional or unconditional stimuli in a classical conditioning paradigm), or as discriminative stimuli (stimuli associated with differential probabilities of contingencies for particular behaviors in an operant conditioning paradigm; Kazdin, 1979). For example, sleep disturbances may occur in some sleep environments but not others; a child's headaches may occur at school but not at home; deficits in the assertive skills of an elderly person may be evident with some people but not others. This model suggests that the conditional probability of behavior may vary significantly across settings.

Despite the importance of situational determinants of behavior, it is illogical to assume that individuals are passive responders to transient environmental stimuli; it is more reasonable to assume that variance in behavior can be accounted for through reference to both situations and persons and that behavior patterns can generalize across situations for some persons, behaviors, and situations.

Cross-situational variance in the conditional probabilities of behavior has important implications for assessment methods, the identification of etiological factors, and planning and evaluating interventions. For example, differences in the rate at which a child emits aggressive behaviors in the presence of each parent suggest the operation of different eliciting or contingency operations. These differential behavior patterns must be carefully assessed and the outcome of assessment is likely to suggest potential targets of intervention. Such situational differences also suggest caution in presuming the generalizability of treatment outcome across settings. Behavior analysts, therefore, attempt to carefully assess the degree and determinants of cross-situational variance in behavior, both before and after intervention (Foster & Cone, 1986; Galassi & Galassi, 1980; McFall, 1982).

Multiple Causality and Individual Differences

Assumptions that a particular behavioral syndrome can be attributed to univariate causes (e.g., presuming that either neurotransmitter dysfunctions or negative cognitions are *the* causes of depression) are common in clinical psychology. Such causal models minimize the necessity for preintervention assessment beyond that necessary for diagnosis (Bandura, 1981; Haynes, 1987; Hersen, 1981; Karoly, 1988; Russo, Hamada, & Marques, 1988). However, behavior analysts have often emphasized the concept of *multiple causality of behavior:* That any behavior or behavior problem is usually affected by multiple and interacting causal variables. The assumption, which is not universally supported by behavior analysts (see Baer, 1977), that

it is difficult to account satisfactorily for behavioral variance within univariate causal models, suggests that additive and interactive causal models involving multiple factors are necessary to satisfactorily account for behavioral variance (Haynes & O'Brien, 1988).

A corollary to the assumption of multiple determinants of behavior is that there are significant *individual differences* in the determinants of behavior, in the variables that mediate treatment effects, and in responses to specific treatments. Furthermore, individual differences in causality are assumed to occur both between and within syndromes. For example, the determinants of depression are presumed to differ from the determinants of other behavior disorders, and the determinants are presumed to vary among individuals labeled as depressed.

An emphasis on multiple and idiosyncratic causality promotes *broad-spectrum, multimodal, behavioral assessment:* The use of multiple assessment methods and a focus on multiple modes (e.g., cognitive and overt behavioral modes; Conger & Keane, 1981; Nelson & Hayes, 1986). A behavior problem, such as a child's social isolation, may be the result of various interacting combinations of determinants, including inadequate parental modeling of social behaviors, insufficient exposure to social-learning experiences, reinforcement of inappropriate social-interaction behaviors, interference with social behaviors by elevated "anxiety" responses (conditioned emotional responses), expectancies, or punishment of social interactions. Most important, behavior assessment is necessary to identify which of these potential factors are the most salient for a particular child.

An assumption of multiple causality diminishes the clinical utility of diagnosis for intervention systems that attack the determinants of behavior problems. Intervention programs cannot be based solely on a diagnostic or classification category such as "depression," "substance abuse," "hyperactivity," or "hypertension," because such topographically based diagnoses do not identify which of many possible determinants are operational for a particular person. An extensive evaluation of the behavior problem and the etiological role of various possible determinants, using multiple assessment methods, is necessary to design appropriate interventions and to identify appropriate targets for intervention (Hawkins, 1987; Haynes, 1987; Hersen, 1981).

The assumptions of multiple and varying causality within and between behavior disorders do not preclude the development of treatment protocols for individuals manifesting the same disorder. Examples of successful application of such treatments are widespread. It does imply, however, that the probability and magnitude of effective treatment can be significantly enhanced if treatments are tailored to fit the idiosyncratic determinants identified in pretreatment behavioral assessment.

The primary importance ascribed to the individuality of people also influences measurement procedures. Because behavior analysts are often concerned with the problem behaviors and goals of individual clients, an *idiographic* rather than *nomothetic* set is more often assumed (Cone, 1988). Behavior analysts are more likely to develop goals and apply measurement strategies that do not involve normative comparisons, and to use within-subject, rather than between-subject, research designs (see following section on "cybernetic" qualities).

Minimizing Inferential Qualities

One factor that stimulated the early development of behavioral construct systems was the perceived stagnation of traditional clinical psychology. Many investigators (Eysenck, 1952, 1960b; Ullmann & Krasner, 1965; Wolpe, 1958; see review by Kazdin, 1978) believed that the effectiveness of interventions in clinical psychology, the degree of predictive power of the favored variables, and the utility and applicability of traditional clinical conceptual models had improved little in the preceding three decades. This lack of development was attributed, in part, to conceptual and epistemological deficiencies, including a reliance on highly inferential constructs, assessment systems, and intervention targets. The causes of behavior disorders were attributed to hypothetical, mentalistic, mediating, and intervening variables (e.g., intrapsychic conflicts, urges) that were difficult to operationalize and measure. As a result, these traditional causal models and treatment procedures were not amenable to empirical investigation or refutation—a process necessary for the conceptual and technical development of any construct system and discipline.

In partial reaction to these epistemological impediments, behavioral construct systems attempt to minimize the inferential qualities of constructs by focusing on lower-level, well-specified, measurable behaviors in the natural environment. This has strongly affected the method and focus of behavioral assessment. For example, the emphasis on direct observation of public events is attributable, in part, to the desirability of deriving verifiable and minimally inferential indexes of specified targeted behaviors. Also, behavioral, compared to nonbehavioral, assessment interviews are more often focused on what persons do in their natural environment and involve more specification of client[5] reports of phemomena such as "anxiety," "guilt," or "behaving responsibly." Behavior analysts are also less likely to ascribe determinants of behavior to internal, nonpublic variables, although the importance of subjective feelings, physiological events, attitudes, expectancies, and other cognitions as mediating or dependent variables is recognized.

The avoidance of inferential variables, although facilitating the development of behavioral construct systems, has led to some methodological deficiencies and frictions within the discipline. For example, because of the inferential nature of data derived from interviews and other subjective self-report instruments, they have been applied with greater reticence and have been subjected to less empirical investigation than have other behavioral assessment instruments (Haynes & Chavez, 1983; Haynes & Jensen, 1979; Morganstern, 1988; Turkat, 1986). Also, the recent incorporation of cognitive variables within behavioral construct systems (Kendall & Hollon, 1981; Parks & Hollon, 1988) has been accompanied by reasonable objections that it represents a regression to older models of an excessively inferential, nonparsimonious, nonproductive, and value-laden discipline (Sampson, 1981). It is too early, however, to determine if such movements within the behavioral construct system serve to enhance its conceptual validity or merely decrease the parsimony of the system without a concomitant enhancement of validity.

Response Fractionation

Response fractionation (sometimes referred to as response *desynchronization* or *discordance*) refers to the assumption that behavior problems, such as "aggression," "sexual dysfunction," or "attention deficits," are composed of multiple elements that frequently demonstrate low levels of covariation (Gannon & Haynes, 1987). For example, anxiety and fear responses may involve specific cognitions, avoidance behaviors, subjective perceptions of discomfort, and elevated levels of autonomically mediated arousal; importantly, these components may not demonstrate a high level of covariation across or within persons (Barlow, 1985; Bernstein et al., 1986; Nietzel, Bernstein, & Russell, 1988). Response fractionation may occur between different measures of the same mode (such as low correlations between skin conductance and skin potential responses), as well as between modes (May, 1977; Schwartz, 1977).

As Gannon and Haynes (1987), Kaloupek and Levis (1980), and Hartmann et al. (1979) noted, the degree of response covariance or discordance varies across individuals, disorders, and response systems and is strongly influenced by the methods of measurement. Gannon and Haynes suggested that discordance among response systems may even serve as a causal factor for the development of behavior disorders.

Variables likely to influence the apparent degree of response fractionation include: (a) the sources of error uniquely associated with each measurement instrument; (b) the degree to which the content of the instruments converge (Kaloupek & Levis, 1980); (c) sources of measurement variance (such as variance in situational stimuli, sampling procedures, duration of samples, and the time frame of comparisons); (d) the degree of similarity in determinants of targeted behaviors (Mischel, 1968); and (e) the variability or intensity of the target variables (Patterson & Bechtel, 1977). Cone (1979) noted that most studies examining response covariation have confounded methods of assessment with the content area, and he recommended using a multicontent-multimethod-multibehavior matrix to evaluate the covariation among multiple response systems more validly.

The assumption of response fractionation suggests that no single target or measure is a valid representation of all components of a complex behavior disorder. In most cases, a multimodal focus is necessary to adequately define a behavior disorder and to adequately monitor the effects of intervention.

Importance of an Empirically Based, Cybernetic Construct System

The most important criteria for evaluating the viability of a psychological construct system is its rate of theoretical and technical evolution—the rate of increase in the proportion of variance in behavior that can be accounted for (predictive validity) and the rate of increase in the effectiveness and applicability of intervention strategies based upon the construct system. Most psychological construct systems have been developed through rationally and experientially based, rather than empirically based, processes. Their assumptions about behavior tend to be stable over time, and most cease to evolve to a significant degree following their initial development. For example, classical psychoanalysis, person-centered therapy, Gestalt therapy, and rational-emotive therapy, despite numerous derivatives and branches (themselves a product of experientially based dissatisfaction with a particular construct system) retain most of their original concepts, and their intervention strategies remain basically unchanged since their original formulation.

Unless one adopts the indefensible position that a particular construct system can account for most of the variance in human behavior and can be used as the sole basis of effective treatments, the nonevolutionary nature of a construct system is a strong indictment against its viability.

The most important characteristic of a behavioral construct system is its emphasis upon empiricism as the primary method of conceptual and technological development—hypotheses about the characteristics, causes, and treatment of behavior disorders are developed, specified, empirically tested, and refined (Barlow & Hersen, 1984; Barlow, Nelson, & Hayes, 1987). Thus, behavioral construct systems emphasize *methods of inquiry* rather than fixed concepts of etiology and treatment—a necessary component of a cybernetic behavioral construct system that emphasizes self-assessment and self-correction and, consequently, enhanced viability over time.

The importance of methodological empiricism affects behavioral assessment concepts and procedures in many ways. In addition to minimizing the use of inferential concepts, there is a strong emphasis on quantification. Although qualitative (descriptive) information about clients and behavior is important, behavior analysts also seek data on the rate, duration, intensity, frequency, latency, cyclicity, and conditional probability of behavior. Quantitative information is useful in selecting target behaviors, designing intervention programs, testing causal models, and evaluating program effectiveness. The importance of quantification is apparent, not only in the efforts to obtain data through direct observation, self-monitoring, participant monitoring, and psychophysiological assessment, but also in interviews where behavior analysts are likely to seek quantitative indexes of behavior problems, associated behaviors, and potentially relevant environmental factors.

An empirical orientation is also reflected in the *ongoing assessment of intervention effects* and in the application of *single-case or time-series clinical research designs* in clinical situations (Barlow & Hersen, 1984; Kazdin, 1982a; Kratochwill, 1978). The purpose of behavioral assessment is not simply to select target behaviors and facilitate the development of intervention plans, it is also to provide a mechanism for ongoing evaluation of intervention effects, to provide information for changing intervention strategies during treatment, and to facilitate the derivation of inferences about what factors are responsible for observed effects. For example, the assessment of a family with an aggressive child might include daily parent reports of multiple child and parent behaviors throughout the course of intervention, as well as weekly home or clinic observations of parent–child interactions. These data would help the behavior analyst to track the effects of his or her interventions and to institute program changes when needed.

Summary

There are a number of assumptions in a behavioral construct system that affect the methods, applications, and focus of behavioral assessment. These assumptions emphasize the importance of social–environmental determinants of behavior disorders, reciprocal determinism, contiguous controlling variables, situational control of behavior, and person by environment interactions, multiple and idiosyncratic causality, minimally inferential variables, response fractionation, and a cybernetic construct system.

These assumptions underscore the essential role of assessment in behavioral intervention and in the continued vitality of the behavioral construct system. The selection of target behaviors, the identification of controlling variables, the interventions designed, and the probability of successful intervention are contingent upon the outcome of valid assessment procedures that are, in turn, determined by the assumptions reviewed in this section. They also affect the purposes and methods of assessment. The following sections will examine the purposes of behavioral assessment, methods of behavioral assessment, and a number of evaluative dimensions.

PURPOSES OF BEHAVIORAL ASSESSMENT

Assessment systems vary in the functions or purposes for which they are applied. Behavioral assessment has several purposes (e.g., the identification of causal variables that are congruent with those of traditional assessment systems (Haynes, 1989). The differences between behavioral and nonbehavioral assessment systems in these goals are primarily in their level. That is, behavioral assessment results in the identification of more specific and operationalized behavior problems and causal variables. For example, specific verbal communication deficits or self-instructions, rather than "low frustration tolerance" or an "identity crisis," are more likely to be identified as causal variables in behavioral assessment. Similarly, behavioral assessment may result in recommendations for specific intervention strategies, such as a specific family contingency management program for developmentally disabled individuals or adolescents with conduct disorders (Patterson, 1982). Treatment rec-

ommendations at this level of specificity are not usually products of traditional assessments.

Other functions of behavioral assessment are more idiosyncratically aligned with its conceptual foundations. For example, behavioral assessment is often used to identify specific target behaviors, identify functional response classes, identify alternative behaviors, generate functional analyses of behavior problems, and design intervention programs. These functions are considered in more detail below.

The *selection of target behaviors* is an important and deceptively complex function of behavioral assessment (Hawkins, 1987). Clients often seek psychological services with poorly defined problems (e.g., feeling "unloved" and "taken for granted," not showing a "sense of responsibility"), which require considerable effort to specify. The instability of target behaviors further complicates specification—what is identified as a problem with a client tends to change over the course of assessment and therapy. Furthermore, clients almost always present with *multiple target problems*. For example, seldom do we work with a client who is experiencing marital distress without some permutation of additional problems such as negative self-evaluations, sleep or substance-abuse disorders, or communication skills deficits.

Given the specification of multiple target problems and the impossibility of concomitantly treating all of them, one principle that dictates the selection of target behaviors for intervention is that of *shared* variance. That is, the functional relationships between target behaviors, causal and mediating variables are estimated; that behavior whose modification is expected to result in the greatest degree of improvement in the greatest number of life problems is often selected as the initial target. Other factors also affect target behavior selection (e.g., salience, frequency, amenability to intervention, social acceptability) and these have been outlined in greater detail by Barrios (1988), Evans (1985), Hawkins (1987), Kanfer (1985), and Kratochwill (1985).

Another function of behavioral assessment is to identify *functional response class*—groups of behaviors that tend to or are expected to covary. Often, functional response classes include behaviors that differ in form but are under the control of similar antecedent, consequent, or cognitive variables. For example, for some individuals, exercise and substance abuse may be part of the same response class because both involve opioid receptor stimulation (endogenous or exogenous; Verebey, 1982). Cooperative play and "showing off" may be part of the same response class for a child if both serve to increase peer attention.

The concept of functional response classes are infrequently invoked in behavioral assessment but are important because intervention programs often attempt to substitute a more adaptive member of a response class for one that is less adaptive. For example, relaxation exercises may be substituted for substance abuse, if both function to reduce levels of physiological arousal.

In other cases, functional response classes are useful because the assessment of high-rate behaviors in a class can be used to estimate the rate of low-rate behaviors. If an adolescent's frequent verbal complaints or whining covaries with less frequent instances of stealing or lying, changes in the rate of verbal noncompliance as a function of family behavior therapy may provide an estimate of the treatment effects on stealing and lying.

Despite their importance and potential clinical utility, little is known about which behaviors tend to covary together, the degree of covariance among behaviors in the same response class, the generality of response classes across people, or the factors that control covariation among behaviors.

The identification of alternative behaviors and the *design of intervention programs* are other important functions of behavioral assessment (Hawkins, 1987; Kanfer, 1985). In many cases, behavior analysts attend less to identifying problem behaviors than to identifying positive treatment goals—behavioral skills that may be positive alternatives to problem behaviors. Thus, we may attempt to identify the behavioral skills that are necessary for a diabetic adolescent to gain control over his or her blood glucose level, cognitive strategies that may help a client alleviate paranoid ideation, or social skills necessary for a socially anxious person to achieve comfortable and rewarding social interactions.

A focus on positive goals in behavioral assessment has several advantages: (a) it often arouses less discomfort for clients than does a focus on deficiencies or problem behaviors, (b) it is often more acceptable to social agents such as parents, staff, and teachers, (c) it encourages the use of positive rather than punitive intervention procedures, (d) it reduces the importance of assessing low-frequency behaviors, and (e) it alleviates some validity problems associated with assessment of behavior problems (e.g., trying to attribute "responsibility" for marital arguments). However, at times negative behaviors (e.g., physical violence, verbal abuse of a spouse, negative ruminations) are so pervasive, salient, or intervention-hindering that their targeting for intervention is unavoidable.

Perhaps the most complex and clinically significant goal of behavioral assessment is the integration of the assessment data into a comprehensive and valid *functional analysis* of a client: an integrated conceptualization of targeted behaviors, determinants, mediational variables, and the form and strength of their relationships (Haynes & O'Brien, 1989). For example, a functional analysis of a family with an aggressive child might include qualitative and quantitative information on the specific types of aggressive behaviors emitted, conditional probabilities of aggressive behavior being emitted across various situations (school versus home; presence of father vs. mother), chains of behavioral and environmental events that precede aggressive behaviors, differential contingencies associated with aggressive behaviors, contingencies placed on alternative social behaviors, avoidance or escape functions of aggressive behavior, and other behaviors that covary with aggressive behaviors. A more extensive functional analysis might also include information on causal attributions of the child and his or her parents, economic conditions, other cognitive antecedent or consequent factors, level of intellectual functioning, the presence or absence of learning disabilities or other academic deficits, the possible contribution of the parents' marital relationship, possible models for aggressive behaviors, and the consequent and eliciting effects of peer behaviors.

Because the functional analysis involves an integrated conceptualization of the target individual(s), the validity of the data upon which those conceptualizations are based is of paramount importance. Consequently, psychometric characteristics of the assessment instruments have a significant impact on the validity and utility of the functional analysis. However, valid data do not ensure a valid functional analysis.

Despite its central role in the conceptualization and treatment of behavior disorders, the derivation of the functional analysis is one of the least investigated and most subjective functions of behavioral assessment (Curran & Wessberg, 1981; Felton & Nelson, 1984; Nelson, 1987). More data are needed on: (a) the reliability of functional analyses across behavior analysts based on a particular data set, (b) the degree to which the quality and quantity of data affect treatment decisions and/or treatment outcome, (c) the type of data that are most useful for deriving functional analyses, (d) the relative treatment efficacy (Nelson & Hayes, 1987) of functional analyses versus conceptualizations based upon traditional clinical assessment, and (e) the decision-making process involved in deriving functional analyses. Haynes and O'Brien (1989) have outlined a conceptual basis and provided recommendations for generating functional analyses.

Other purposes of behavioral assessment are also

important. Because behavioral assessment stresses the importance of an empirically based, hypothesis-testing approach to assessment and intervention, assessment continues throughout intervention in order to *evaluate the effects of intervention* and to provide the data necessary for the *modification of intervention programs*. This is best pursued through the application of behavioral assessment instruments within carefully controlled time-series, multiple-baseline, or replication/reversal treatment designs (Barlow & Hersen, 1984; Kazdin, 1982a). Comprehensive evaluation of treatment effects should also include the evaluation of *side (unintentioned) effects* (e.g., the effects of a smoking program on cardiac functioning or weight; the effects of psychotropic medications on motor behavior, the effects of a time-out program in the classroom on peer interactions).

Finally, the assessment process must provide a reinforcing and facilitative interpersonal ambience for both the client and behavior analyst. Failure to generate a positive relationship will decrease the chance of continued assessment and therapy and impede client compliance with the between-session assignments that are frequently a part of behavioral interventions. These variables have only just recently been subjected to investigation.

In summary, behavioral assessment has multiple functions that are aligned with its conceptual foundations. These include the identification of problem behaviors, the identification of causal variables, the design of intervention programs, the identification of functional response classes, the identification of alternative behaviors, the generation of functional analyses of behavior problems, the design intervention programs, and the creation of a positive therapeutic ambience. Behavioral assessment methods differ in the degree to which they address these various functions. Although some of these functions overlap with the functions of nonbehavioral assessment methods, behavioral methods tend to have a more precise and molecular focus.

DIMENSIONS OF EVALUATION

The examination of any assessment method necessitates reference to several interdependent dimensions of evaluation. Assessment methods may be evaluated on applicability and utility, cost-efficiency, validity, reliability, and sensitivity. These dimensions are outlined below and are then used to provide the context for examining specific behavioral assessment methods.

Despite the importance of psychometric and qualitative considerations, clinical psychologists, especially behavior analysts, often develop or apply assessment instruments and interpret results from instruments without carefully considering their relevant psychometric and qualitative properties. Inferences derived from the application of inadequately developed or evaluated assessment instruments must be viewed with extreme caution because the validity of the obtained measures are questionable.

Although evaluative considerations are important in all assessment endeavors (Achenbach & McConaughy, 1987), they are particularly important in behavioral assessment for several reasons: (1) The results of preintervention assessment have a strong impact on the development of intervention strategies. (b) The evolution of behavioral construct systems and intervention strategies are dependent upon data derived from behavioral assessment. And (c) some of the assumptions inherent in behavioral construct systems differ from those upon which traditional psychometric principles are based.

Psychometric evaluation of behavioral assessment has been an issue of contention among behavioral theorists (e.g., Cone, 1981, 1988; Suen, 1988). The bases of these disagreements include conflicting definitions of terms (e.g., *accuracy* vs. *validity*) and disagreements about the degree to which traditional psychometric concepts can be applied to an assessment system that often assumes an inherent validity in "observed behavior," true variance in behavior across time and situations, and an idiographic, rather than nomothetic, focus. However, behavioral assessment methods must be subject to strict standards of evaluation; they have important sources of error that can render resultant data uninterpretable, and an intrinsic validity of nomothetically focused assessment methods cannot be presumed.

Psychometric dimensions of evaluation are briefly outlined below. More extensive discussions of qualitative and psychometric aspects of assessment instruments may be found in Anastasia (1986), Berk (1984), Hartmann and Wood (1982), Haynes (1978), Jones and Applebaum (1989), Kerlinger (1972), Linn (1988), Maloney and Ward (1976), Mischel (1968), Nunnally (1967), Sellitz, Wrightsman, and Cook (1976), and Wainer and Braun (1988).

Applicability and Utility

Applicability and utility refer to the amenability of particular methods or instruments for the assessment of particular populations, behaviors, environments, or purposes. The applicability and utility of each instrument and method vary across these dimensions. Thus, naturalistic observation may be very applicable with high-rate child conduct problems occurring in the classroom but less applicable with low-rate adolescent antisocial behaviors, such as substance abuse, that occur in the community.

The applicability and utility of an assessment instrument vary with the *purpose of its application*. Gottman (1979) developed a method of analyzing power and reciprocity factors in marital interaction from samples of verbal interaction between the spouses. This time-series analysis of behavior codes derived from dyadic interaction is very useful for research purposes but, because of the extensive time required, is less applicable for clinical assessment purposes. Hayes, Nelson, and Jarret (1987) recommended that assessment instruments be evaluated on their degree of *treatment utility*—the degree to which information derived from them is useful for selecting the most efficacious interventions.

The applicability and utility of an instrument are also influenced by *cost-benefit* or *cost-efficiency ratios*—the amount and utility of information gained per unit of assessment time, effort, or expense. Some behavioral-assessment instruments, such as naturalistic observation, provide very useful data but are frequently time-consuming and expensive (although Reid, Baldwin, Patterson, & Dishion, 1987, reported that their home family observation package cost less than a battery of personality tests). Others, such as self-monitoring or behavioral questionnaires are less costly but more susceptible to unknown sources of error. The clinical psychologist must decide if the type and amount of information gained warrant the use of a particular instrument. This decision is based, in turn, upon the availability of alternative, less costly instruments and the potential significance of the obtained information. Cost factors are frequently weighted more heavily in clinical applications and benefit factors are frequently weighted more heavily in research applications.

A cost-benefit analysis also influences the duration and/or extent of assessment. Although behavioral assessment is a continuous process occurring before, during, and following intervention, there is a point at which additional assessment (more questionnaires, more hours of observation) is not warranted by the amount of new information gained. Assessment efforts should be parsimonious, and there is a negatively accelerating relationship between the amount of assessment and the amount of new information gained. Initial assessment efforts have a greater impact on our inferences than subsequent efforts.

A number of other factors influence the applicability of an assessment instrument. These include communicability (the degree to which assessment proce-

dures can be understood by the individuals being assessed); social acceptability or social validity (the acceptability of the assessment procedures or goals to the individuals being assessed); reactivity (the degree to which the assessment process modifies the behavior of individuals being assessed); and other sources of measurement error (response biases, time-sampling errors, technical difficulties; Foster & Cone, 1986; Haynes & Horn, 1982; Jacobson, 1985).

Although generic evaluations of multicomponent assessment systems must be carefully tempered, behavioral-assessment methods, overall, demonstrate a remarkable degree of research applicability and utility and a lesser but growing degree of clinical applicability (Russo, Hamada, & Marques, 1988). Methods such as self-monitoring, participant observation, and naturalistic observation can be used in diverse environments, across diverse populations, and with diverse behavior problems (Bellack & Hersen, 1988; Ciminero et al., 1986; Haynes & Wilson, 1979). No other assessment system has approximated this degree of applicability and utility while yielding valid quantitative data.

Validity

Perhaps the most important dimension for evaluating an assessment instrument, but one that is also a source of debate (Cone, 1988), is the degree to which it measures the construct it is intended to measure. Data derived from an assessment instrument are used to derive causal hypotheses, to make diagnostic and treatment decisions, and to evaluate intervention outcome. If the data are not valid representations of the targeted construct, erroneous inferences and decisions are likely and the probability of intervention success is significantly diminished. Examples of validity dimensions include the extent to which data derived from home observation of family interaction are representative of the typical family interaction, the degree to which data derived from self-monitoring of cigarette smoking accurately represents the number of cigarettes usually smoked, and the degree to which a questionnaire measure of heterosocial anxiety accurately predicts social behaviors and/or feelings of distress in heterosocial situations.

Validity is a complex multicomponent construct that is often difficult to estimate. Aspects of validity include criterion-referenced validity (including internal, external, concurrent, and predictive validity), content validity, and construct validity.

One type of validity is *criterion-referenced validity*—the degree to which data from an assessment instrument correlate with data from another assessment instrument presumed to measure the same or a similar construct. Examples of criterion-referenced validity evaluation include correlating two questionnaire measures of marital satisfaction or comparing data derived from self-monitoring and participant monitoring of a child's headaches.

Criterion-referenced validity may be either internal, external, concurrent, or predictive. Internal validity is closely related to the concept of accuracy, whereas external validity is closely related to the concept of situational generalizability (Barrios, 1988; Coates & Thoresen, 1978; Cronbach, Gleser, Nanda, & Fajaratman, 1972; Tunnell, 1977). For example, the internal validity, or accuracy, of data from observing mother–child interactions in a clinic playroom can be assessed by adding a second observer (resulting in coefficients of interobserver agreement). The external validity of the same assessment instrument can be assessed by examining the degree to which the data derived from the clinic playroom predict mother–child interactions in the home. The degree to which data from one assessment instrument are correlated with data from another instrument administered contiguously is a measure of *concurrent validity*. The degree to which the data are correlated with data from another instrument administered at a later time is a measure of *predictive validity*.

One method of deriving an estimate of validity is through assessing the *reliability* of data derived from an instrument. Reliability refers to the degree of *temporal consistency* (external reliability) or *homogeneity* (internal reliability) of an instrument: the degree to which data obtained from serial administration of the same instrument correlate (test–retest reliability; external reliability), or the degree of correlation among elements within an assessment instrument (such as homogeneity coefficients; internal reliability).

The implications of low coefficients of reliability and validity vary as a function of the assumptions underlying the assessment instrument and target. For constructs that are assumed to be relatively stable across situations and time (such as intelligence, height, defensiveness), low reliability and criterion validity coefficients suggest that at least one instrument does not validly measure the targeted construct. For constructs that are assumed to vary across time or situations (such as social initiation responses or blood pressure), low coefficients of reliability can be attributed to real variance in the targeted construct and/or measurement error (Hartmann & Wood, 1982).

Because behavioral, compared to traditional, construct systems assume a greater degree of temporal and situational variability in targeted behaviors, separating observed variance into error and true sources of variability is difficult (Cone, 1988; Hartmann & Wood, 1982). The concept of criterion-referenced validity is based upon traditional psychometric assumptions of cross-situation stability, homogeneous and stable behavioral syndromes, the measurement of higher level constructs, and a high degree of response covariation. This foundation in traditional psychometric assumptions presents challenging conceptual and methodological problems for behavioral assessment. Because of assumptions of situationally controlled behavioral variance and response fractionation, presumed measurement variance would be expected to be greater and "validity" coefficients lower. As in the case of reliability, low indexes of criterion-referenced validity may suggest errors in the assessment instrument but may also reflect true behavioral variance, variance in situational factors, or variance in the components of the construct being sampled. For example, behavioral observation of marital interactions and subjective reports of marital distress may both be valid, but they may demonstrate low levels of correlation.

Regardless of the sources of variance, psychometric considerations affect our interpretation of assessment data. Low validity or reliability coefficients suggest restrictions in presumptions of the data's generalizability across situations, time, modes of behavior (e.g., subjective, overt behavioral), and/or people. Thus, validity inferences must be placed in the context of the *intent* of the assessment. If observations of parent–child interactions in the clinic are designed to provide an estimate of those interactions in the home, the degree to which data from the clinic correlate with data from the home is a measure of the validity of that assessment, *for that purpose*. However, if the intent of the clinic assessment is only to measure parent–child interactions in the clinic situation (e.g., as a test of a new intervention strategy), low correlations with data from the home do not invalidate the assessment instrument.

Another form of validity is *content validity*—the degree to which the product of an assessment instrument reflects the relevant dimensions of the targeted construct. A content-valid questionnaire on depression should reflect behavioral conceptualizations of that construct and should include not only items monitoring mood and affect (as in traditional depression inventories), but items focusing on social initiation behaviors, reinforcement decrements, expectancies and beliefs, perceptions of control or helplessness, aversive life events, and social consequences for depressive behaviors (Lewinsohn, 1975; Seligman, Klein, & Miller, 1976). Although content validity is a qualitatively inferred attribute of an assessment instrument, it is also reflected in coefficients of criterion-referenced validity in that an instrument with a low level of content validity would not normally correlate highly with more valid measures (Nunnally, 1967).

The degree of content validity of an assessment instrument is influenced primarily by its method of development. Most behavioral, as well as nonbehavioral, instruments are derived solely by induction and, consequently, have questionable content validity. However, other methods of selecting elements for an instrument, such as contrasted groups comparisons (e.g., selecting observation codes based on behaviors that discriminate between satisfied and dissatisfied marital couples), drawing from previously validated assessment instruments, and samples from the populations of interest, can enhance the content validity of an instrument (e.g., Kelley & Carper, 1988).

Because the behavioral construct system is evolving and conceptualizations of the targeted constructs continue to be refined, the content validity of assessment instruments is never stable. When our conceptual models of behavioral syndromes, such as anxiety disorders (Barlow, 1985), learning disabilities (Lahey et al., 1981), or social skills (Becker & Heimberg, 1988; McFall, 1982) became more sophisticated through the inclusion of additional topographical, mediating, or causal factors, assessment instruments must also change.

In content- and criterion-referenced validity we are concerned with the degree to which the assessment instrument measures the validity of the construct it is designed to measure and, concurrently, whether the construct itself is useful—its *construct validity* (Kerlinger, 1972; Maloney & Ward, 1976; Messick, 1981; Nunnally, 1967; Sellitz et al., 1976). Constructs are higher-order concepts that help summarize observed relationships and provide the basis for theoretical elaboration (Messick, 1981). Constructs, and the instruments that are designed to measure them also vary in the degree to which they fulfill these functions. For example, the individual codes as well as sampling procedures in behavioral observation systems for syndromes such as child aggression (Patterson, 1982), social behaviors (Glass & Arnkoff, 1989), hyperactivity (Abikoff, Gittelman-Klein, & Klein, 1977), and marital distress (Markman, Floyd, Stanley, & Storaasli, 1988) are based upon conceptualizations of these syndromes and their determinants. The validity of these coding systems cannot exceed the validity of

the constructs upon which they were based, and it is important to evaluate the degree to which the instrument measures these constructs.

Construct validity can be evaluated in terms of the proportion of variance in behavior that can be accounted for by the construct (concurrent and predictive validity), the degree to which the data derived are in agreement with data derived from similarly focused instruments, and the proportion of variance in behavior accounted for by the construct in comparison to alternative constructs. A particularly important means of construct validation in behavioral assessment is intervention validity (or treatment validity, Nelson & Hayes, 1979)—that is, the effectiveness of intervention based upon assessment procedures derived from the construct.

Sensitivity

Another dimension upon which assessment instruments can be evaluated is their sensitivity—the degree to which they reflect actual changes in the various components of a construct. Sensitivity is related to content- and criterion-referenced validity and may vary among the components of a construct tapped by an instrument. For example, a questionnaire on social anxiety may be sensitive to changes in subjective discomfort in social situations but not to changes in the frequency with which an individual initiates social contact. Similarly, an observation system for family interaction may be sensitive to changes in parent-delivered contingencies but not to changes in child- or sibling-delivered contingencies.

Instruments may also vary in temporal sensitivity. For example, classroom observation by external observers may show decreases in the rate of classroom aggressive behaviors or activity level before such changes are reflected in data derived from teacher questionnaires. In this example, observation was more sensitive than questionnaires in measuring aggressive behaviors.

Sources of Error

Sources of measurement error vary widely among assessment methods and instruments. They include observer bias and drift, procedures for assessing observer accuracy, errors in the content validity or construction of an instrument, reactive effects of the assessment process, errors in time, behavior, or situation sampling; the social influence process of the assessment situation, and technical misapplication of assessment instruments. Sources of measurement error directly affect the validity of inferences derived from an assessment instrument and will be considered in greater detail when specific assessment methods are addressed. It is important to emphasize that because sources of error vary across instruments, expected levels of correlation among instruments are reduced, and multimethod assessment is recommended to increase our confidence in the resulting inferences.

Summary

Because the outcome of behavioral assessment has a significant impact on the design and evaluation of intervention programs and on the growth and refinement of the behavioral construct systems, behavioral assessment instruments should be carefully evaluated on several psychometric dimensions, including applicability and utility, cost-efficiency, validity, reliability, and sensitivity. The next section examines specific assessment methods in the context of these dimensions and also considers their idiosyncratic sources of error.

METHODS OF BEHAVIORAL ASSESSMENT

As noted by several authors (Barrett, Johnston, & Pennypacker, 1986; Bellack & Hersen, 1988), the boundaries between behavioral and nonbehavioral assessment methods are increasingly diffuse, primarily because behavior analysts are becoming increasingly inclusive in the assessment instruments used in their clinical and research activities. The most visible example of this inclusiveness is the *Dictionary of Behavioral Assessment Techniques* by Hersen and Bellack (1988). The authors edited a comprehensive catalog of the assessment instruments used in published behavior therapy research; each entry includes a description of the instrument, its psychometric characteristics, clinical utility, and future directions. Although many instruments were well constructed, well validated, and congruent with the conceptual foundations of behavioral construct systems, many others (e.g., Minnesota Multiphasic Personality Inventory, [MMPI], Beck Depression Inventory [BDI], Mental Competence to Stand Trial, Type A Personality, Coping Strategies Scales) violate numerous tenets of behavioral construct systems.

There appear to be several reasons for use of "nonbehavioral" assessment instruments by behavior analysts. First, behavior analysts often address behavior problems (e.g., depression) for which no appropriate measurement instruments exist. The choice then becomes whether to measure poorly or not at all.

Second, behavior analysts are expanding their modes of assessment to include cognitive, subjective, and physiological variables that sometimes necessitate the use of measures with greater inferential qualities and less situational specificity. Third, the selection of specific measures is often influenced by the politics of publication and grant acquisition.

Of most concern is that many behavior analysts seem unaware of the basic tenets of the construct systems within which they operate, the degree to which the assessment instruments they use are congruent with that construct system, or basic psychometric principles. For example, many behavior analysts fail to note (a) that presumptions of unwarranted situational generalizability often accompany their instruments, (b) that an overall score from an instrument may not be meaningful if there are several "factors" in the instrument, (c) that many resulting coefficients are actually sums across multiple response modes (e.g., sums of physiological, cognitive, and subjective measures of depressions) that may not actually covary, (d) that for many purposes norm-based instruments may not be optimally useful for assessing a particular individual, (e) that highly inferential constructs result from their assessment instrument, and (f) that their instruments may not be empirically constructed or psychometrically evaluated for the population to which it is applied.

Although it acknowledges difficulties in defining which methods and instruments are "behavioral," the following survey of behavioral assessment methods is limited to those which are congruent with behavioral construct systems. A reader interested in examining the breadth of instruments used, both appropriately and inappropriately, by behavior analysts may consult Hersen and Bellack (1988).

Naturalistic Observation

Naturalistic observation is the systematic monitoring and recording of behavior in the natural environment, usually by trained observers who are not typically part of the natural environment (Foster, Bell-Dolan, & Burge, 1988; Hartmann & Wood, 1982). The frequent use of naturalistic observation in behavioral assessment reflects the emphasis on minimizing the inferential nature of assessment. It also reflects the importance of acquiring quantitative indexes of target behaviors and behavior–environment interactions as they occur in the natural environment.

Methods of naturalistic observation vary widely but most often involve *time sampling*, in which a number of circumscribed observation sessions (e.g., three half-hour sessions per week) are divided into brief intervals (e.g., 15-second segments). Trained observers (at least two are required to derive observer accuracy estimates) then record the occurrence of preselected and predefined behaviors within each interval. Behaviors can be recorded in the form of frequency tallies, response chains, or sequences involving a number of social interactions, real-time durations, observer ratings (e.g., of social skills), or contingency matrixes of antecedent-behavior or behavior-consequent chains (Faraone & Hurtig, 1985; Foster et al., 1988; Kratochwill & Roseby, 1988). Recording and coding of behavior can sometimes be facilitated with the use of audio or video recordings (Cuvo, Leaf, & Borakove, 1978), electromechanical multiple-event recorders (Gardner, Pearson, Berocovici, & Bricker, 1968), automated data-acquisition systems (Fitzpatrick, 1977), electronic devices for the direct monitoring of behavior (Schulman, Stevens, & Kupst, 1977), and lap-top computers for real-time recordings.

Naturalistic observation can provide data on behavior frequencies and/or durations, social interactions, and conditional probabilities, and is a particularly powerful tool for evaluating treatment effects. It is the least inferential, most sensitive method of acquiring information about behavior in the natural environment.

Naturalistic observation has been used with a broad range of target behaviors, populations, and settings, including parent–child interaction in the home (Mash & Barkley, 1986) and in hospital environments (Bakeman & Brown, 1977); stuttering (James, 1981); interactions of depressed adults and children (Hops, Biglan, Sherman, Arthur, Friedman, & Osteen, 1987; Kazdin, 1988); social anxiety (Glass & Arnkoff, 1989); childhood fears and anxieties (Mash & Terdal, 1988); social and institutional behaviors of psychiatric patients in inpatient and day-treatment settings (Alevizos, DeRizi, Liberman, Eckman, & Callaghan, 1978; Matson & Stephens, 1977); children's interactions at a summer day camp (Barret & Yarrow, 1977); alcohol ingestion (Correa & Sutker, 1986); assertion skills (St. Lawrence, 1987); academic and conduct behaviors in the classroom (Kratochwill & Roseby, 1988); and marital interaction in the home (Haynes, Follingstad, & Sullivan, 1979).

There are several sources of error associated with naturalistic observation. Some of these sources of error can be attributed to the use of external observers: (a) observers may be insufficiently trained, (b) observer characteristics or behavior may influence the behavior of target individuals, (c) observers are susceptible to bias and drift, (d) the method of assess-

ing interobserver agreement may affect coefficients of interobserver agreement, and (e) the coding system may be complex. The data derived from naturalistic observation are also influenced by the sampling parameters used within sessions, the schedule of sessions over time, the method of collecting data, and the environmental contexts in which observation occurs (Boykin & Nelson, 1981; Haynes & Horn, 1982; Sackett, 1978; Suen, 1988; Wasik & Loven, 1980).

One potential source of error in all assessment methods that is particularly relevant in naturalistic observation is *reactivity*—the process in which behavior is affected by its assessment. Although observer errors are associated with threats to the internal validity of observation, reactivity is associated with threats to its external validity—the degree to which the data acquired are representative of the targeted phenomena in the absence of the observers. If the process of observing behavior modifies its characteristics or rate, it is impossible to assume that the derived data validly represent behavior when it is not being observed. Three articles (Baum, Forehand, & Zegiob, 1979; Haynes & Horn, 1982; Kazdin, 1982b) have reviewed research on reactive effects in behavioral observation. Both noted strong evidence for reactive effects with some observation procedures and populations, and both identified a number of variables that may affect the occurrence, degree, or direction of reactive effects. The conceptual paradigms offered included stimulus control, novelty, habituation, and obtrusiveness.

Although it is a threat to generalizability, it should be noted that reactivity does not necessarily diminish utility or other forms of validity. For example, functional and dysfunctional families may still behave significantly differently when being observed, even though their behaviors are affected by the observation process. As noted by Haynes and Horn (1982), however, reactive effects may be so great in some cases (e.g., sexual interaction, antisocial behavior) as to preclude the use of naturalistic observation.

Cost-efficiency factors are also important when considering the use of naturalistic observation (Reid et al., 1987). Despite the utility and the importance of observing behavior in the natural environment, it can be time-consuming and expensive and difficult to implement in a systematic manner outside of clinical research centers.

Analogue Assessment

Analogue assessment involves the measurement of behavior in environments that are structured to increase the efficiency of observation situations (Nay,

1986). This is accomplished by arranging the measurement situation in such a way that the behaviors of interest are more likely to occur. It is particularly useful for observing low-rate behaviors that would be difficult to observe in the natural environment (such as discussion of a problem topic by a distressed marital couple or the responses of an unassertive person to a situation requiring assertion) or the behaviors that may never occur (such as a heterosexually anxious person initiating conversation with a member of the opposite sex).

Analogue observation can involve a variety of populations, settings, and behaviors such as imposed restrictions on the location of family members during the observation of marital and family interaction at home (Patterson, 1982); observations of marital and family interactions in structured clinic situations (Jacobson, 1977; Markman et al., 1988; O'Leary & Turkewitz, 1978); the observation of behaviors of children with conduct disorders in structured playrooms (Mash & Terdal, 1988); the measurement of subjective distress, overt behavior, and psychological responses during behavioral avoidance tests with phobic individuals (Taylor & Agras, 1981); the assessment of social skills and social fears in role-playing situations for adults (Conger & Conger, 1986; Curran et al., 1980; Glass & Arnkoff, 1989; Merluzzi & Biever, 1987) and children (Beck & Smith, 1988); the observation and self-report of pain behaviors during exercise (Turner & Clancy, 1988); the measurement of reinforcer preferences (Pace, Ivancic, Edwards, Iwata, & Page, 1985; Sisson, Van Hasselt, Hersen, & Aurand, 1988); or the assessment of drinking behaviors in artificially structured bars (Correa & Sutker, 1986).

Analogue assessment may involve a range of structures: (a) *Situation analogues*, in which the individual is assessed in an artificial situation such as a simulated bar or playroom that resembles the natural environment (Frisch, 1977; Sobel, Schafer, & Mills, 1972); (b) *Stimulus analogues*, in which artificial stimuli are provided, such as in role-played situations involving tape-recorded assertion stimuli (Edinberg, Karoly, & Gleser, 1977; Greenwald, 1977); and (c) *Behavior analogues*, in which observed behaviors are assumed to be part of the same functional response class as the behaviors of primary interest, such as bar pressing of psychotics (Lindsley, 1960) or marble dropping by children (Patterson, Littman, & Hinsey, 1964).

The measurement methods used in analogue situations are similar to those used in naturalistic situations. Typically, the observation session is divided into short time samples; the occurrence of specific,

predefined behaviors or sequences of behaviors within those intervals is recorded by trained observers or taped for later recording. Other dependent variables, such as the distance to a feared object, subjective ratings of discomfort, physiological responses or observer ratings of anxiety or skill may also be derived (Bellack, 1979; Curran et al., 1980; Nay, 1986). In other analogue assessments (e.g., Pace et al., 1985; Sisson et al., 1988), the occurrence or nonoccurrence of predefined behaviors is measured and time-sampling procedures are unnecessary.

Some sources of variance and error in analogue assessment are similar to those of naturalistic observation, and include factors associated with the use of observers, instructions to subjects, the specific situation in which observation occurs, and temporal parameters of the sampling (Bellack, Hersen, & Lamparski, 1979; Forehand & Atkeson, 1977; Hughes & Haynes, 1978; Nay, 1986). The primary psychometric concern with analogue assessment is the degree of situational generalizability or external validity of the derived data. Because behavior often varies as a function of situational factors, the process of observing behavior in a highly structured and novel clinical/laboratory environment would be expected to affect behavior, perhaps to the extent that it is no longer a valid representation of the targeted constructs.

The external validity of analogue assessment has been examined by a number of researchers (see reviews by Bellack & Hensen, 1988; Haynes & Wilson, 1979; Nay, 1986). Some have suggested that measures of behavior emitted in analogue situations may not be predictive of behavior in the natural environment. Others have noted a satisfactory degree of criterion-referenced validity. As Foster and Cone (1986) noted, there can be little doubt that threats to generalizability of data *can* occur. Thus, the most appropriate research strategy is to identify the variables (behavior problems, situations, instructions) that affect the occurrence or degree of generalizability.

Although it is important to acknowledge that problems with the situational generalizability of analogue assessment may arise, it remains an extremely powerful, efficient, and clinically useful method of assessment. It can be a useful assessment method for identifying problem behaviors, measuring treatment effects, and generating causal hypotheses.

Participant Monitoring

Another method of decreasing the expense, and possibly the reactivity, associated with naturalistic observation is through participant monitoring—the use of observers who are part of the targeted individual's natural environment. In participant monitoring, a person (such as a parent, spouse, teacher, or peer) in the target individual's natural environment monitors and records selected behaviors emitted by that individual, usually within specified times during the day. For example, a parent may monitor the number of his or her child's nighttime asthma attacks, or a client may monitor the number of pleasing events emitted by a spouse each day.

Participant monitoring has been a frequently used assessment method. Examples include the observation of partners' sleeping behaviors (Bootzin & Engle-Friedman, 1981), parents monitoring the conduct behaviors of their children (Karoly, 1981), and teachers monitoring the academic behaviors of their students (Nunes, Murphy, & Reprecht, 1977). As with analogue observation, participant monitoring is particularly useful in the assessment of low-rate behaviors (such as marital fights, seizures, stealing) or behaviors that might be highly reactive to the presence of external observers (such as sexual interaction, antisocial behaviors, some ingestive and substance abuse behaviors).

Although participant monitoring is a cost-efficient method of gathering both qualitative and quantitative data on behaviors in the natural environment (Foster et al., 1988), it is also subject to numerous sources of error. In addition to the sources of error that are applicable to the use of any observers in the natural environment, participant monitoring may be more susceptible to *observer bias*. Sources of observer bias in participant monitoring include: (a) the history of interaction between the target individual and the observer, (b) labels placed on the target individual by the observer, and (c) the potential use or impact of acquired data.

Because participant monitoring introduces a new dimension into the social relationship between the observer and target, care must be exercised to preclude disruption of that relationship. In most cases, it is preferable for the monitored person to provide informed consent and to understand the rationale and methods. The methods of monitoring, confidentiality of acquired data, and the use of the data must be carefully established to guarantee confidentiality and preclude abuse by the observer.

Another major source of error, and also a threat to external validity, is reactivity. Hay, Hay, and Nelson (1977), for example, noted that participant observation of students by teachers was associated with significant modifications in the behavior of both students and teachers. In contrast, a number of studies (e.g., Broden, Beasley, & Hall, 1971; Reid & Hurlbut, 1977) have found a satisfactory degree of criterion-referenced validity (both internal and external) for participant monitoring. There is little doubt, however, that reactivity and bias can occur, and caution should be exercised in assuming external validity of the data acquired through participant monitoring. Additional study of factors influencing the occurrence and direction of these sources of error is needed. The presumed sensitivity of participant monitoring to observer bias and reactivity probably accounts for the fact that participant observation is most often used as supplementary, rather than as a primary outcome measure in behavior therapy research.

Self-Monitoring

Self-monitoring is another method of efficiently acquiring qualitative and quantitative data on the behavior of target individuals and behavior–environment interactions in the natural environment (Bornstein et al., 1986). With this method, individuals record the occurrence or other characteristics of their own target behaviors either continuously or within a time-sampling framework. Targets may include overt behaviors (e.g., eating, social initiations), thoughts (positive self-evaluative statements), subjective states (e.g., dysphoric mood), and physiological variables (e.g., blood pressure) and can also involve behavior–environment interactions (e.g., thoughts occurring following aversive interactions at work). (See reviews in Bellack & Hersen, 1988.)

Self-monitoring has been used with a wide range of behaviors and environments such as children's classroom activities (Kratochwill & Roseby, 1988), smoking (Glasgow, Kleges, Godding, & Gegelman, 1983), alcohol consumption (Dericco & Garlington, 1977), social skills and interactions (Dodge, Heimberg, Nyman, & O'Brien, 1987; Glass & Arnkoff, 1989; Merluzzi & Biever, 1987), headaches (Feuerstein & Adams, 1977), sleep patterns (Lick & Heffler, 1977; Youkilis & Bootzin, 1981), fuel consumption (Foxx & Hake, 1977), blood pressure (Beiman, Graham, & Ciminero, 1978), parent responses to their children (Mash & Terdal, 1988), obsessive ruminations (Emmelkamp & Kwee, 1977), eating patterns (Brownell, 1981; Schlundt et al., 1986), and alcohol and drug ingestion (Alden, 1988; Donovon & Marlatt, 1988). It has also been applied to a wide range of populations including mentally retarded children and adults, outpatient adults, children in classrooms, psychiatric inpatients, families, and institutions (Haynes & Wilson, 1979).

Perhaps the most important threat to the validity of self-monitoring is reactivity. The reactive effects of self-monitoring can be so powerful that self-monitoring is frequently used as an intervention method (Leitenberg, Agras, Thompson, & Wright, 1968; Kilmann, Wagner, & Sotile, 1977). The reactive effects sometimes associated with self-monitoring are a threat to the external validity of the acquired data in that they may not be valid reflections of the individual's behavior when he or she is not self-monitoring. However, reactive effects appear inconsistently within and between subjects, and the factors that control the occurrence and direction of reactive effects require additional study (Bornstein et al., 1986).

A number of factors that contribute to the reactive effects of self-monitoring and to its utility as an assessment device have been identified (Kratochwill & Roseby, 1988; Nelson, 1977). These include the number, valence, and complexity of behaviors monitored, the temporal relationship between the behavior occurrence and its recording, the method of recording (e.g., wrist counter, paper-pencil), whether the behavior or product of that behavior is being monitored, the effort required to monitor, awareness of accuracy assessment, whether occurrences or nonoccurrences of the behavior are recorded, training in self-monitoring, the complexity of the situation in which monitoring occurs, and social and self-delivered contingencies associated with self-monitoring.

An additional concern with self-monitoring is that of accuracy (Nelson, 1977): the degree to which data derived from self-monitoring reflect the rate or characteristics of targeted behavior during the self-monitoring interval. A number of investigators have addressed this issue. Most studies have found satisfactory levels of agreement between self-monitored data and data derived concurrently from other assessment procedures, when monitoring conditions and instructions are carefully controlled. Despite its clinical utility, inaccuracy and reactivity remain potential threats to the level of confidence that can be placed in data derived from self-monitoring, and behavior analysts should carefully attend to the variables that affect its accuracy.

Behavioral Assessment Interviews

The interview is the most frequently employed but one of the least frequently researched behavioral assessment methods (Bierman & Schwartz, 1986; Emmelkamp, 1981; Haynes & Chavez, 1983; Haynes

& Jensen, 1979; Morganstern, 1988; Turkat, 1986; Wiens, 1981). Because of its multiple functions, it is an indispensable element of almost all assessment-intervention packages. The assessment interview and data derived from it are used to select additional assessment procedures, identify target behaviors, provide informed consent to clients about the assessment-intervention process, survey historical events that may be relevant to a particular client, identify potential causal and mediating variables for behavior disorders, assess mediation potential, develop a functional analysis, design intervention programs, motivate the client for behavior change, and evaluate intervention effects. Until recently, however, the behavioral assessment interview has been infrequently subjected to empirical and conceptual attention (Bierman & Schwartz, 1986; Brown, Kratochwill, & Bergan, 1982; Edelbrock & Costello, 1984; Hay et al., 1979; Haynes et al., 1981).

Although interviews are used in all intervention systems, behavioral and nonbehavioral interviews differ in focus, function, and process, reflecting differences in their underlying assumptions and functions. The behavioral interview, compared to the nonbehavioral interview, is more likely to focus on current behavior and its determinants, the role of behavior-environmental interactions, to solicit quantitative indexes of specific behavioral and environmental events, and to be used in a structured fashion prior to intervention (Barlow, 1985; Edelbrock & Costello, 1984).

There are multiple sources of error in behavioral interviews. Major threats to the validity of data derived from an interview include the subjective and retrospective quality of the data acquired, the susceptibility to client bias in information derived from an interview, and demand factors and other social influences of the client by the interviewer (Linehan, 1977).

Because of a distrust of subjective data, behavior analysts have erroneously presumed that discrepancies in data derived from interviews and from less subjectively based assessment methods are an indictment against the validity of the interview. However, there is currently a growing awareness that each assessment method has independent sources of measurement error, and different determinants and referents.

One of the major advances in behavioral assessment interviewing is in the development and evaluation of structured interviews. For example, structured interviews have been developed for anxiety disorders (Barlow, 1985) and alcohol intake (Marlatt & Miller, 1988). Structured compared to unstructured interviews facilitate the identification of sources of error, the evaluation of psychometric dimensions of the interview, and comparisons of data acquired across time and people.

Other Self-Report Methods

There are a number of other self-report methods used in behavioral assessment, including questionnaires, checklists, rating scales, and computer-assisted assessment (Barkley, 1987; Bellack & Hersen, 1988; Jensen & Haynes, 1986). These instruments cover virtually every target behavior and construct addressed in the behavior therapies.

Although many are directly borrowed from other areas of psychology, behavioral self-report instruments are frequently derivatives of traditional clinical assessment instruments that have been modified to be more congruent with a behavioral construct system. Compared to nonbehavioral self-report instruments, they tend to be more specifically worded, narrowly focused, to include more situational factors, to focus to a greater extent on overt motor behaviors and behavior-environment interactions, to provide less inferential indexes, and to have a higher degree of face validity.

The benefits, applicability and utility, threats to validity, and other psychometric dimensions of self-report instruments have been reviewed extensively (e.g., Anastasi, 1986; Berk, 1984; Maloney & Ward, 1976; Mischel, 1968; Wainer & Braun, 1988). Particular attention should be drawn to psychometric evaluation of behavioral self-report instruments. Behavior analysts rely, more extensively than do traditional test constructionists, on the face validity of questionnaires. Consequently, there is a proliferation of instruments developed in an unsystematic fashion that measure unspecified constructs with an unknown degree of validity.

Computer-assisted assessment may increase the efficiency of both behavioral and traditional self-report assessment. Computers have been used in an interactive manner to administer interview and questionnaire items and to store and provide evaluative summaries of client responses (Angle, 1981; Angle, Ellinwood, Hay, Johnson, & Hay, 1977; Angle, Hay, Hay, & Willinwood, 1977; Butcher, 1987; Eyde, 1987; Forehand, 1986; Romanczyk, 1986). The interactive format is fairly consistent across applications: A client sits in front of a computer screen upon which queries are presented. The client enters responses on a keyboard and additional queries are then presented, sometimes as a function of the client's responses.

Following completion of the administration, a printout is provided that summarizes the client's responses on dimensions of interest. Although promising, the effects of computer assessment on the other functions of behavioral assessment (e.g., client-assessor relationship, social validity) and unique sources of variance have yet to be sufficiently investigated.

Psychophysiological Assessment

Psychophysiological assessment is frequently used in behavioral assessment (Blanchard, 1981; Haynes, Falkin, & Sexton-Radek, 1989; Kallman & Feuerstein, 1986; Williamson, McKenzie, & Duchmann, 1988). As indicated in Haynes (1989), this increasing utilization can be attributed to four phenomena. First, there is a growing recognition that physiological events are important components in many behavior problems. In behavior disorders such as childhood fears (Barrios & Hartmann, 1988), social phobias (Glass & Arnkoff, 1989), children's somatic disorders (Beck & Smith, 1988), and addictive disorders (Donovan & Marlatt, 1988), physiological responses can function as important dependent variables, causal variables, or mediators.

Second, behavior analysts increasingly treat medical-psychological behavior disorders such as hypertension and other cardiovascular disorders, sexual dysfunctions, headaches, diabetes, sleep disorders, and pain (Davidson & Davison, 1980; Haynes & Gannon, 1981; Krasnegor, Arasteh, & Cataldo, 1986; Keefe & Blumenthal, 1982; Melamed & Siegel, 1980). These disorders are defined or characterized primarily by dysfunctions in physiological systems. Consequently, a comprehensive, multimodal assessment of these disorders necessitates a focus on physiological as well as behavioral, environmental, and cognitive variables.

Third, there is an increasing use of intervention procedures, such as biofeedback, relaxation training, and covert conditioning, which, incidentally or intentionally, affect psychophysiological responses. Any comprehensive assessment of the effects of these intervention procedures must include their physiological effects.

Fourth, advances in measurement technology have facilitated the cost-efficiency and applicability of psychophysiological assessment. For example, improvements have occurred in computer-aided data collection, reduction, and analysis and ambulatory monitoring of psychophysiological responses in the natural environment (Haynes et al., 1989; Kallman & Feuerstein, 1986; Williamson et al., 1988). These improvements have made it easier for behavior analysts to collect and interpret psychophysiological data for a wider range of subjects and environments.

Psychophysiological methods are very congruent with the assumptions of a behavioral construct system because they provide specific, quantifiable data with minimally inferential qualities. Specific measures can include the electromyogram, respiration, heart rate and wave formation, penile erections, brain waves, skin conductance, peripheral blood flow, blood pressure, and a variety of serum and urine tests for endocrine and neurotransmitter substances and metabolites.

There are numerous sources of error and threats to the internal and external validity of these measures including filtering, electrode placement and conductive media, method of data integration, the ambient environment of the assessment, posture, and movement artifact. These have been reviewed extensively in a number of books (Greenfield & Sternbach, 1972; Martin & Venables, 1980; Turpin, 1989).

Additional Assessment Methods

There arc several less frequently used but promising behavioral assessment methods: (a) product-of-behavior measures, (b) critical-event sampling, and (c) manipulation. *Product-of-behavior measures* minimize the reactivity and cost sometimes associated with naturalistic observation and allow assessment of behavior by measuring its permanent or transient product. Examples include weight as a measure of eating behavior and caloric intake (Foreyt & Goodrick, 1988; Foreyt & McGavin, 1988), serum or urine glucose tests as measures of fluid and food intake for patients undergoing dialysis (Magrab & Papadopolou, 1977) or of drug ingestion (Stitzer, Bigtelow, Liebson, & Hawthorne, 1982), and workbook performance as a measure of academic behaviors in the classroom (Hay, Nelson, & Hay, 1977).

Product-of-behavior measures have the advantages of being fairly cost-efficient, relatively permanent, available, quantifiable, amendable to psychometric evaluation, and unobtrusive (with the exception of serum and urinalyses). However, there can be significant problems with the internal validity of these measures because it is difficult to attribute the measured product to specific behaviors. For example, weight change may reflect changes in caloric intake, caloric expenditure, fluid intake, purging, or the intake of diuretics.

Critical-event sampling is very promising but infrequently used and evaluated method of efficiently acquiring data on behavior–environment relationships. In critical-event sampling, an audio or video record is made, in the natural environment, during time periods or situations in which there is a high probability that targeted behaviors will be emitted. Examples include audio recordings of family interactions during suppertime, parent–child interactions at bedtime, marital interaction during disagreements at home, or social interactions on dates. Although this method offers a potentially inexpensive and efficient method of acquiring data on target behaviors and behavior–environmental interactions in the natural environment, issues of external validity or generalizability, sensitivity, and other sources of error have yet to be addressed. Reactivity is a particularly probable source of error (e.g., the potential reactive effects of activating a tape recorder during a heated marital disagreement).

Manipulation is one of the most powerful methods of assessing hypothesized controlling variables. We tend to assume a causal relationship between two variables when the systematic manipulation of one is consistently associated with changes in the other.

Manipulation can be used to test for the effects of both antecedent and consequent stimuli. For example, the degree to which social interaction can operate as reinforcers for autistic children can be evaluated through response-contingent systematic presentation and withdrawal of these stimuli; the etiological role of stimulus-control factors in insomnia can be evaluated through systematic manipulation of presleep environmental stimuli; the relative discriminative stimulus properties of mothers and fathers can be evaluated through systematically exposing a child to each parent under similar conditions; the degree to which headaches are a function of stressors can be evaluated through careful exposure to stressful and nonstressful laboratory situations. As indicated by these examples, systematic manipulation of hypothesized controlling variables can strengthen or weaken our etiological hypotheses and, consequently, aid in intervention decisions.

Although manipulations are normally part of the intervention process (behavior analysts usually attempt to modify hypothesized controlling variables), are important components of the methodologies of many behavioral and nonbehavioral sciences (e.g., neurophysiology, chemistry), and are used frequently to test hypotheses in controlled experimental contexts (see examples in the *Journal of Applied Behavior Analysis* and the *Journal of the Experimental Analysis of Behavior*), they are infrequently used in preintervention behavioral assessment. However, they are particularly well-suited for studying the effects of low-frequency events and effects, are amenable to multimodal measurement, and warrant increased attention.

RECENT DEVELOPMENTS AND ISSUES IN BEHAVIORAL ASSESSMENT

There are a number of recent conceptual and methodological developments in behavioral assessment that reflect its vitality, early developmental stage, and cybernetic self-correcting quality. These include (a) the epistemology of behavioral assessment—methodological issues such as research design, statistics, and psychometric principles—and (b) clinical utility.

Epistemology

Because behavioral construct systems emphasize empiricism, several issues relating to methods of empirical inquiry have recently been the focus of discussion. First, behavioral assessment methods have often been "validated," and sources of error studied, on analogue subjects in analogue environments (e.g., examining variables that affect clinical intake interviews using nonclinical college student volunteers). Although analogue studies can contribute to the early developmental stages of assessment methods, psychometric characteristics (e.g., validity coefficients) are not generalizable across samples and situations. Consequently, analogue studies cannot be used to evaluate the psychometric characteristics of an assessment method or instrument in the clinical context in which it would most likely be used. Therefore, the clinical utility of analogue studies is limited (Glass & Arnkoff, 1989). Fortunately, the necessity of psychometric evaluation of assessment instruments in clinical settings and with clinical populations is more frequently recognized (see reviews in Ciminero et al., 1986; Mash & Terdal, 1988).

Second, as indicated in "Dimensions or Evaluation" psychometric principles and sources of error in behavioral assessment are receiving increasing attention (e.g., Fagot & Hagan, 1988). Behavior analysts are more often conducting discriminant function analyses, criterion-referenced validity examinations, utilizing appropriate content validity instrument-development procedures, assessing reliability and internal homogeneity, and examining the construct validity of assessment instruments (Barrios, 1988; Dodge et al., 1987; Garfield, 1984; Kelley & Carper, 1988).

In the early stages of the behavior therapy movement, behavior analysts developed and applied many assessment instruments that were derived intuitively rather than empirically and were not subjected to psychometric evaluation. This disregard for psychometric principles was probably based on five factors: (a) the necessity of applying assessment instruments at a time when empirically validated, behaviorally oriented instruments were not available; (b) an assumption that the applicability of psychometric principles was limited to instruments developed within traditional trait construct systems; (c) an excessive reliance on face validity of behavioral-assessment instruments; (d) a lack of training of behavior analysts in psychometric principles and procedures, and (e) a rejection of most assessment instruments associated with traditional clinical paradigms.

Behavior analysts were particularly lax in evaluating the content validity of assessment instruments. Individual behavior codes in observation systems, items on questionnaires, and situations used in analogue observation or role-play assessments have typically been intuitively selected by the instrument's developers. There were few attempts to apply empirical methods of content derivation or to determine the extent to which an instrument's content reflected the targeted constructs. As a result, many behavioral assessment instruments are representative of the developer's personal conceptualizations, which may or may not validly reflect the construct being evaluated.

Although there are disagreements as to the conceptual basis, appropriateness, and applicability of traditional psychometric concepts (e.g., Cone, 1988), a psychometric emphasis is necessary if behavioral assessment methods are to gain in acceptance and utility and their results are to be accurately and confidently interpreted.

Third, the epistemology of any construct system is facilitated by the adoption of a consistent nomenclature and the terminology of behavioral assessment is undergoing a period of refinement and specification. For example, the definition of terms such as *accuracy, reliability, agreement,* and *validity,* as pertaining to behavioral observation, was discussed by Suen (1988). Such terminology refinements facilitate the communication among behavior analysts and between behavioral analysts and other scientist-practitioners.

Fourth, the data derived from behavioral assessment often involve repeated measures, of several target events, for one or a few clients, over a substantial period of time, within one or two conditions (e.g., baseline, intervention). This research paradigm is a very powerful method of deriving inferences about causal relationships and about the effects of intervention. However, the analysis of these data can be complicated by temporal autocorrelation of the data (see special issue on autocorrelation, *Behavioral Assessment*, 1988, Vol. 10, no. 3). Inferences from time-series designs are being facilitated by advances in statistical methods, particularly *time-series analysis* (Huitema, 1985; Kratochwill & Piersel, 1983; Notarius, Krokoff, & Markham, 1981; Sackett, 1982; Sharpley & Alavosius, 1988; Suen, 1988). Time-series designs allow inferences to be derived about the relationships among serially collected and autocorrelated variables and the impact of interventions instituted within such data collection procedures.

Other advances in the application of statistical procedures include attention to magnitude-of-effect analyses as adjuncts to typical analyses of variance, the use of multiple regression to identify proportions of variance in independent variables accounted for by dependent variables, multivariate analysis of variance to correct for inappropriate confidence levels when using multiple dependent measures, calculation of conditional probabilities to identify possible causal or covariance relationships, the use of nonparametric statistics, statistical analyses for inferring the clinical significance of treatment effects, the application of generalizability theory, and calculation of interobserver agreement using formulas that more accurately control for chance agreement (Cronbach et al., 1972; Coates & Thoresen, 1978; Curran et al., 1980; Edgington, 1982, 1984; Foster & Cone, 1980; Jacobson & Revenstorf, 1988; Marascuilo & Busk, 1988; Trull, Nietzel, & Main, 1988).

It should be noted that the adoption of statistical procedures to the analysis of "single-subject" time-series designs has not been universally applauded (Baer, 1977; Johnston & Pennypacker, 1980; Michael, 1974; Sidman, 1960). There are two primary concerns: (a) statistics allow error variance to be "partialed out," which reduces the impetus to reduce it through more rigorously controlled assessment situations, and (b) an inappropriate emphasis may be placed on variables that are clinically unimportant but statistically significant.

Proponents of the use of statistical inference note many advantages: (a) many important determinants of behavior have relatively "weak" effects that may be identified through statistics, (b) variability may be a true state of behavior rather than a reflection of uncontrolled sources of error, (c) relationships among variables that are often not readily apparent from visual inspection of data may be identified, and (d) statistics can enhance confidence in the interpretation of observed effects.

Finally, even within a criterion-based approach to assessment (the use of assessment data for within- rather than across-subject inferences), the development of *norms* helps the behavior analyst interpret the outcome of assessment (Achenbach & McConaughy, 1987). Furthermore, the development of such norms, as well as the development of more valid assessment instruments, can be facilitated through the standardization of assessment procedures.

Clinical Utility and Applicability

Behavioral assessment is a very powerful research tool: It facilitates the acquisition of specific and valid data across a variety of individuals, behaviors, and settings and is an important component in etiological and treatment evaluation research. As such, it has been instrumental in the development of powerful conceptual systems and intervention strategies. However, behavioral assessment has often proved to be a less powerful clinical tool (Barlow, 1980; Emmelkamp, 1981; Keefe, Kopel, & Gordon, 1978; Mash, 1979; Mash & Terdal, 1981; Swan & MacDonald, 1979; Wade, Baker, & Hartmann, 1979; Wicramesekera, 1981).

The restricted clinical utility of behavioral assessment seems to be a function of cost-effectiveness considerations, contingencies operating in applied settings and deficiencies in the methodologies and underlying conceptual models of behavioral assessment. For example, behavioral coding systems for marital or family interaction (Gottman, 1979; Margolin et al., 1988; Markman et al., 1988; Wahler, House, & Stambaugh, 1976) can provide useful and valid data on social interaction among family members and, therefore, are powerful research tools. However, the use of observation-coding systems typically requires many hours for observer training and for data collection, reduction, and analysis. Although these demands do not preclude the use of behavioral observation in clinical settings, in many cases they render it prohibitively costly.

Another powerful factor accounting for the infrequent application of behavioral-assessment methods in clinical settings is the contingency systems that frequently operate in those settings. For agencies and individuals in private practice, the development, application, and interpretation of behavioral-assessment instruments, and their continued administration during intervention, are typically unreimbursed by clients or third party payers.

Despite these time and financial limitations, the clinical utility of behavioral assessment is clearly expanding in two areas: (a) a focus on more complex behavior–environment interactions and (b) an increasingly multimodal approach.

Congruent with causal assumptions associated with an operant paradigm, behavioral assessment efforts have traditionally focused on the relationship between two variables in close temporal proximity (e.g., immediate teacher and peer contingencies as controlling variables for classroom out-of-seat behavior), and interactions between a target individual and those in his or her immediate environmental (e.g., marital communication patterns as a controlling variable for marital satisfaction). Although such foci have been heuristic (e.g., Notarius et al., 1981) behavioral assessment foci have recently expanded to include the examination of *noncontemporaneous relationships* and interactions in *extended social systems*. For example, it may be helpful to examine events that are separated from the target behavior by hours, days, or longer in order to identify factors that influence marital distress (Gottman, 1979), the stressors that precipitate migraine headache or ulcers (Haynes & Gannon, 1981), or the stimuli that influence the aggressive behavior of a child (Patterson, 1982). Behavior analysts are also now more likely to examine the effects of parent–child interactions on classroom performance of the child and the effects of the social support system of parents on parent–child interactions or on parental responses to intervention (Dunst & Trivette, 1986; Mash & Terdal, 1988).

This represents a growing acceptance of a *systems* view of persons and behavior disorders (Beck & Smith, 1988; Karoly, 1988; O'Leary, 1984; Rodick, Henggeler, & Hanson, 1986; Russo, Hamada, & Marques, 1988; Schwartz, 1982), particularly in family assessment and therapy. A systems model presumes an extended number of interdependent causal paths, all of which may have an influence on the behaviors of individuals in it and all of which may be affected by changes in the behavior of one person within the system (Cromwell & Peterson, 1981). This expanded focus is likely to assist in the identification of important sources of variance in behavior disorders and, therefore, enhance the effectiveness of the resulting intervention programs.

An enhanced analysis of complex interactions is also evident in the sequential analyses of behavioral observation data. An increasing number of studies are examining complex *reciprocal and bidirectional interactions, interrelationships among multiple behaviors*, and *behavior chains* that are often associated with behavior problems (e.g., Gottman, 1980; Russo et al., 1988). Time-series analyses are very useful for these purposes.

These conceptual and methodological expansions

significantly advance the construct validity of behavioral construct systems, and the implications for the theoretical bases and methods of behavioral assessment are far reaching. Reliable demonstrations of such complex behavioral interrelationships would suggest that (a) it is difficult to account satisfactorily for behavioral variance through reference only to contemporaneous situational or consequent factors, (b) multimethod/multisituation/multitarget assessment is needed for a comprehensive functional analysis and for a comprehensive evaluation of treatment effects, and (c) examination of response chains and hierarchies may facilitate the derivation of valid and useful functional analyses and treatment plans.

Behavioral interrelationships must be considered a dependent variable that is under the control of other variables. It is apparent that some responses covary whereas others do not, that hierarchies may be reliable or unreliable, that functional interrelationships may vary across developmental stages, situations, responses, and individuals.

A *multimodal* approach is evidenced by a growing assessment interest in neurophysiological and psychophysiological variables (Blanchard, 1981; Haynes et al., 1989; Haynes & Gannon, 1981; Kallman & Feuerstein, 1986), cognitive variables (Eisenstein & Copeland, 1988; Karoly, 1988; Parks & Hollon, 1988; Russo et al., 1988; Schwartz, 1982), affective variables (Glass & Arnkoff, 1989; Schlundt et al., 1986), and community and ecological targets (Carr, Schnell, & Kirchner, 1980). Additionally, these assessment modalities are measured on a growing domain of targets (see Bellack & Hersen, 1988; Mash & Terdal, 1988).

The assessment of cognitive variables is becoming increasingly prominent in behavioral construct systems. Cognitive variables are presumed to function as precipitating factors (such as catastrophic thoughts preceding social interactions), as triggered or mediating variables (such as thoughts of helplessness triggered by social rejection), as contingencies (such as self-punitive thoughts following failure experiences), as primary target behaviors (such as ruminative or obsessive thoughts or nightmares), and as variables mediating treatment outcomes (such as attributions of causality, expectancies, or perceived credibility of treatment).

The clinical, social, ecological, or personal validity of assessment and treatment have also become frequent targets of evaluation. For example, several authors (Garfield, 1984; Kazdin, 1977; Lebow, 1982; Runco & Schreibman, 1988; Wolfe, 1978) have emphasized the importance of evaluating the significance and acceptability of assessment and intervention programs and their outcome—their *social validity*. The concept of social validity implies that, sometimes, consultation with target individuals, and others in the natural environment of the target (e.g., peers, parents), regarding their perceptions of desirable target behaviors, attributions of causation, expected intervention methods, and outcome of intervention can aid in the evaluation of behavior therapy. These perceptions should be considered not only as major dependent variables but as mediators of intervention outcome. They also help maintain client rights and informed consent.

As reviewed in Haynes (1989) additional variables have been targeted by behavior analysts. These include mediators of intervention outcome (Blanchard, 1981; Cooke & Meyers, 1980), treatment compliance, and side effects of treatment. Again, the idiographic emphasis in behavioral assessment is evident (Wolpe, 1986).

In a related development, a number of authors (Christensen & Mendoza, 1986; Himadi, Boice, & Barlow, 1986; Hoge & Andrews, 1986; Jacobson & Revenstorf, 1988; Jacobson, Follette, & Revenstorf, 1986; Mavissakalian, 1986; Nietzel, Russell, Hemmings, & Gretter, 1987; Trull et al., 1988; Wampold & Jensen, 1986) have discussed statistical methods of estimating the clinical significance of intervention effects. Most of the discussions resolve around the feasibility and desirability of evaluating the posttreatment functioning or status of clients relative to those of a "normal" population or the application of "effect size" estimates.

Although the inclusion of a wider range of variables into behavioral construct systems is appropriate and desirable, it has not always been pursued with an optimal degree of conceptual and methodological rigor. Thus, concepts such as "emotionality" and "internal dialogue" (Eisenstein & Copeland, 1988) and a large array of cognitive variables are too frequently invoked without precise definition and operationalization. Without definitional precision, careful operationalization, and empirical rigor, behavioral construct systems will regress to the conceptually muddled, unscientific state characterizing many non-behavioral systems.

Behavioral Assessment and *The Diagnostic and Statistical Manual of Mental Disorders, Third Edition, Revised* (DSM-III-R)

The DSM-III-R is a multiaxial system for the classification of behavior disorders, primarily on the basis of their form or topography (American Psychi-

atric Association, 1987). Because in the United States it is the dominant system for classifying behavior disorders and is incongruent with aspects of behavioral construct systems that emphasize functional or causal relationships, it has been the topic of extensive discussion among behavior analysts (see Mini-Series "Behavioral Assessment and DSM-III-R" in *Behavioral Assessment*, 1988, *10*, 43–121).

The DSM-III-R, compared to its predecessors, has been applauded for greater operationalization of decision-making rules, a more inclusive categorization of behavior disorders, and a more consistent organizational scheme. However, several concerns among behavior analysts remain. First, many classes of behavior disorders were determined by rational rather than logical procedures. Consequently, there is considerable across-class variance in the degree to which behavioral components of the classes actually covary. Second, some categories illustrate political influences in the decision-making process, and some categories also have political/social repercussions for the treatment of women (see review in Haynes & O'Brien, 1988). Third, the degree to which the specific categories point to causal variables and, therefore, to treatment programs is undetermined.

SUMMARY

In the past 15 years, behavioral assessment has grown dramatically in applicability, utility, psychometric and conceptual sophistication, and research productivity. The major impetuses for this growth have come from the expanding application of behavior therapies and dissatisfaction with the constructs and assessment methods of traditional clinical psychology.

A number of assumptions have affected the goals and methods of behavioral assessment. These include emphases on social–environmental causal models of behavior disorders, multiple causality and reciprocal determinism, individual differences in the determinants of behavior disorders, temporally contiguous controlling variables, situational control of behavior, minimally inferential variables, response fractionation, and the empirical evaluation of hypotheses. Because of this empirical emphasis, behavioral assessment is more a methodological than a conceptual system and will, therefore, continue to demonstrate increasing levels of validity, applicability, and utility.

Behavioral assessment has several functions: the identification of target behaviors, the design of intervention programs, the identification of functional response classes, the identification of treatment goals or alternative behaviors, and the reinforcement of both the client and therapist. Perhaps the most important function is to provide information for the development of a functional analysis—an integrated conceptualization of targeted behaviors, determinants, mediational variables, and the form and strength of their relationships.

There are several dimensions upon which behavioral assessment can be evaluated. These include applicability and utility, cost-efficiency, validity, reliability, and sensitivity. Because behavioral construct systems presume a significant degree of situationally controlled behavioral variance and stress minimally inferential constructs, issues of reliability and validity have been a particular focus of debate. Many behavioral assessment instruments are expensive to apply, but the cost/efficiency ratio for clinical purposes has been improving. There are also numerous sources of error, both common and idiosyncratic, in behavioral assessment. Reactivity is a special concern.

The methods of behavioral assessment are diverse and include naturalistic observation, analogue observation, participant monitoring, self-monitoring, interviews, psychophysiological measurement, critical event sampling, product-of-behavior measures, questionnaires, rating scales, and computer-assisted assessment. These methods are derived from various disciplines but all reflect the concepts and assumptions underlying a behavioral construct system. In addition, each has been the subject of an accelerating amount of psychometric investigation.

Behavioral assessment is an evolving conceptual and methodological system and there have been a number of recent developments within it. These include an increased attention to psychometric principles and statistics, particularly time-series designs and analyses, a move away from analogue studies, and a refinement of nomenclature.

There is also an expansion in the clinical applicability of behavioral assessment. Some behavioral assessment methods are becoming more cost-efficient, and behavioral conceptual systems are addressing more complex functional and causal relationships. A focus on a wider range of variables, adoption of a "systems" perspective, a multimethod/multimodal approach, and a concern with ecological and clinical validity contribute to the growing clinical utility of behavioral assessment.

NOTES

1. *Behavior disorder* is a term of convenience used to refer to commonly labeled behavior problems. It does not denote a qualitative difference between disordered and nondisordered behaviors or persons.

2. The term *behavior analyst* is used generically to refer to a professional involved in behavior therapy and/or behavioral assessment. Its use is not limited to someone who functions within an operant paradigm.

3. A *causal* variable is one whose modification leads to a change in the probability, rate, severity, duration, or recidivism of a behavior disorder. Causal variables may be original or maintaining and need not be necessary, sufficient, or exclusive. A *causal model* refers to a conceptualization of the determinants or controlling variables and relationships, operating on and interacting with a specific target behavior or syndrome (Haynes & O'Brien, 1988).

4. Achenbach & McConaughy (1987) and Pervin (1985) provide good discussions of cross-situational variance from nonbehavioral perspectives.

5. The term *client* refers to any object of assessment. Thus, a client may include an outpatient adult, classroom, police department, family, dyadic relationship, or institution.

REFERENCES

Abikoff, H., Gittelman-Klein, R., & Klein, D. F. (1977). Validation of a classroom observation code for hyperactive children. *Journal of Consulting and Clinical Psychology, 84*, 460–476.

Achenbach, T. M., & McConaughy, S. H. (1987). *Empirically based assessment of child and adolescent psychopathology*. New York: Sage.

Adams, A. E., & Sutker, P. B. (1984). *Comprehensive handbook of psychopathology*. New York: Plenum Press.

Adams, H. E., Feuerstein, M., & Fowler, J. L. (1980). Migraine headache: Review of parameters, etiology and intervention. *Psychological Bulletin, 87*, 217–237.

Alden, L. E. (1988). Behavioral self-management controlled drinking strategies in a context of secondary prevention. *Journal of Consulting and Clinical Psychology, 56*, 280–286.

Alevizos, P., DeRisi, W., Liberman, R., Eckman, T., & Callaghan, E. (1978). The behavior observation instrument: A method of direct observation for program evaluation. *Journal of Applied Behavior Analysis, 11*, 243–257.

Alexander, F. G., & Selesnick, S. T. (1966). *The history of psychiatry: An evaluation of psychiatric thought and practice from prehistoric times to the present*. New York: Harper & Row.

American Psychiatric Association. (1987). *Diagnostic and statistical manual of mental disorders* (3rd ed. rev.) Washington, DC: Author.

Anastasi, A. (1986). Evolving concepts of test validation. *Annual Review of Psychology, 37*, 1–16.

Angle, H. V. (1981). The interviewing computer: A technology for gathering comprehensive treatment information. *Behavior Research Methods and Instrumentation, 13*, 607–612.

Angle, H. V., Ellinwood, E. H., Hay, W. M., Johnson, T.,

& Hay, L. R. (1977). Computer-aided interviewing in comprehensive behavioral assessment. *Behavior Therapy, 8*, 747–754.

Angle, H. V., Hay, L. R., Hay, W. M., & Willinwood, E. H. (1977). Computer assisted behavioral assessment. In J. D. Cone & R. P. Hawkins (Eds.), *Behavioral assessment: New directions in clinical psychology*. New York: Brunner/Mazel.

Anisman, H., & LaPierre, Y. (1982). Neurochemical aspects of stress and depression: Formulations and caveats. In R. W. J. Neufeld (Ed.), *Psychological stress and psychopathology* (pp. 172–197). New York: McGraw-Hill.

Asterita, M. F. (1985). *The physiology of stress*. New York: Human Sciences Press.

Bachrach, A. J. (Ed.). (1962). *Experimental foundations of clinical psychology*. New York: Basic Books.

Baer, D. M. (1977). Perhaps it is better not to know. *Journal of Applied Behavior Analysis, 10*, 167–172.

Bakeman, R., & Brown, J. V. (1977). Behavioral dialogues: An approach to the assessment of mother-infant interactions. *Child Development, 48*, 195–203.

Bandura, A. (1969). *Principles of behavior modification*. New York: Holt, Rinehart & Winston.

Bandura, A. (1981). In search of pure unidirectional determinants. *Behavior Therapy, 12*, 315–328.

Barkley, R. A. (1987). A review of child behavior rating scales and checklists for research in child psychopathology. In M. Rutter, H. Tuma, & I. Lann (Eds.), *Assessment and diagnosis in child psychopathology* (pp. 113–155). New York: Guilford Press.

Barlow, D. H. (1980). Behavior therapy: The next decade. *Behavior Therapy, 11*, 315–328.

Barlow, D. H. (Ed.). (1981). *Behavioral assessment of adult disorders*. New York: Guilford Press.

Barlow, D. H. (1985). The dimensions of anxiety disorders. In A. H. Tuma & J. D. Maser (Eds.), *Anxiety and the anxiety disorders* (pp. 479–500). Hillsdale, NJ: Lawrence Erlbaum Associates.

Barlow, D. H. (1986). Causes of sexual dysfunction: The role of anxiety and cognitive interference. *Journal of Consulting and Clinical Psychology, 54*, 140–148.

Barlow, D. H., & Hersen, M. (1984). *Single case experimental designs: Strategies for studying behavior change* (2nd ed). Elmsford, NY: Pergamon Press.

Barret, D. E., & Yarrow, M. R. (1977). Prosocial behavior, social inferential ability, and assertiveness in children. *Child Development, 48*, 475–481.

Barrett, B. H., Johnston, J. M., & Pennypacker, H. S. (1986). Behavior: Its units, dimensions, and measurement. In R. O. Nelson & S. C. Hayes (Eds.), *Conceptual foundations of behavioral assessment* (pp. 156–200). New York: Guilford Press.

Barrios, B. A. (1988). On the changing nature of behavioral assessment. In A. S. Bellack & M. Hersen (Eds.), *Behavioral assessment: A practical handbook* (pp. 3–41). Elmsford, NY: Pergamon Press.

Barrios, B. A., & Hartmann, D. P. (1988). Fears and anxieties. In E. J. Mash & L. G. Terdal (Eds.), *Behavioral assessment of childhood disorders* (pp. 196–262). New York: Guilford Press.

Baum, C. G., Forehand, R., & Zegoib, L. E. (1979). A review of observer reactivity in adult–child interactions. *Journal of Behavioral Assessment, 1*, 167–177.

Beck, S., & Smith, L. K. (1988). Personality and social skills assessment of children, with special reference to somatic disorders. In P. Karoly (Ed.), *Handbook of child health assessment* (pp. 149–172). New York: John Wiley & Sons.

Becker, R. E., & Heimberg, R. G. (1988). Behavioral assessment of social skills. In M. Hersen & A. S. Bellack (Eds.), *Behavioral assessment: A practical handbook* (3rd ed.) (pp. 365–395). Elmsford, NY: Pergamon Press.

Beiman, J., Graham, L. E., & Ciminero, A. R. (1978). Self-control progressive relaxation training as an alternative nonpharmacological treatment for essential hypertension: Therapeutic effects in the natural environment. *Behavior Research and Therapy, 16*, 371–375.

Bellack, A. S. (1979). A critical appraisal of strategies for assessing social skill. *Behavioral Assessment, 1*, 157–176.

Bellack, A. S., & Hersen, M. (1988). Future directions of behavioral assessment. In A. S. Bellack, & M. Hersen (Eds.), *Behavioral assessment: A practical handbook* (pp. 610–615). Elmsford, NY: Pergamon Press.

Bellack, A. S., & Hersen, M. (1988). *Behavioral assessment: A practical handbook*. Elmsford, NY: Pergamon Press.

Bellack, A. S., Hersen, M., & Lamparski, D. (1979). Role-play tests for assessing social skill: Are they valid? Are they useful? *Journal of Consulting and Clinical Psychology, 47*, 335–342.

Berk, R. A. (1984). *A guide to criterion-referenced test construction*. Baltimore: Johns Hopkins University Press.

Bernstein, D. A., Borkovec, T. D., & Coles, M. G. H. (1986). Assessment of anxiety. In A. R. Ciminero, C. S. Calhoun, & H. E. Adams (Eds.), *Handbook of behavioral assessment* (pp. 353–403). New York: John Wiley & Sons.

Bierman, K. L., & Schwartz, L. A. (1986). Clinical child interviews: Approaches and developmental considerations. *Journal of Child and Adolescent Psychotherapy, 3*, 267–268.

Billings, A. G., & Moos, R. H. (1981). The role of coping responses and social resources in attenuating the impact of stressful life events. *Journal of Behavioral Medicine, 4*, 139–157.

Blanchard, E. B. (1981). Behavioral assessment of psychophysiologic disorders. In D. H. Barlow (Ed.), *Behavioral assessment of adult disorders*. New York: Guilford Press.

Boll, T. J. (1981). Assessment of neuropsychological disorders. In D. H. Barlow (Ed.), *Behavioral assessment of adult disorders* (pp. 45–86). New York: Guilford Press.

Bootzin, R. R., & Engle-Friedman, M. (1981). The assessment of insomnia. *Behavioral Assessment, 3*, 107–126.

Bornstein, P. H., Hamilton, S. B., & Bornstein, M. T. (1986). Self-monitoring procedures. In A. R. Ciminero, C. S. Calhoun, & H. E. Adams (Eds.), *Handbook of behavioral assessment* (pp. 176–222). New York: John Wiley & Sons.

Boykin, R. A., & Nelson, R. O. (1981). The effects of instructions and calculation procedures on observers' accuracy, agreement, and calculation correctness. *Journal of Applied Behavior Analysis, 14*, 479–489.

Braukmann, C. J., & Fixen, D. L. (1975). Behavior modification with delinquents. In M. Hersen, R. M. Eisler, & P. M. Miller (Eds.), *Progress in behavior modification* (Vol. 1, pp. 191–232). New York: Academic Press.

Broden, M., Beasley, A., Hall, R. F., & Mitts, B. (1971). The effect of self-recording on the classroom behavior of two eighth-grade students. *Journal of Applied Behavior Analysis, 4*, 191–199.

Brown, D. K., Kratochwill, T. R., & Bergan, J. R. (1982). Teaching interview skills for problem identification: An analogue study. *Behavioral Assessment, 4*, 63–73.

Brownell, K. D. (1981). Assessment of eating disorders. In D. H. Barlow (Ed.), *Behavioral assessment of adult disorders* (pp. 329–404). New York: Guilford Press.

Brownell, K., Marlatt, R., Lichtenstein, E., & Wilson, G. T. (1986). Understanding and preventing relapse. *American Psychologist, 41*, 765–782.

Busk, P. L., & Marascuilo, L. A. (1988). Autocorrelation in single subject research: A counterargument to the myth of no autocorrelation. *Behavioral Assessment, 10*, 229–242.

Butcher, J. N. (Ed.). (1987). *Computerized psychological assessment: A practitioner's guide*. New York: Basic Books.

Carr, A. F., Schnell, J. F., & Kirchner, R. E., Jr. (1980). Police crackdowns and slowdowns: A naturalistic evaluation of changes in police traffic enforcement. *Behavioral Assessment, 2*, 33–41.

Carson, T. P. (1986). Assessment of depression. In A. R. Ciminero, K. S. Calhoun, & H. E. Adams (Eds.), *Handbook of behavioral assessment* (pp. 404–445). New York: John Wiley & Sons.

Castles, E. E., & Glass, C. R. (1986). Empirical generation of measures of social competence for mentally retarded adults. *Behavioral Assessment, 8*, 319–330.

Chapman, C. R., & Wyckoff, M. (1981). The problem of pain: A psychobiological perspective. In S. N. Haynes & L. R. Gannon (Eds.), *Psychosomatic disorders: A psychophysiological approach to etiology and treatment*. New York: Praeger.

Christensen, L., & Mendoza, J. L. (1986). A method of assessing changes in a single subject: An alteration of the RC index. *Behavior Therapy, 17*, 305–308.

Ciminero, A. R., Calhoun, K. S., & Adams, H. E. (Eds.). (1977). *Handbook of behavioral assessment*. New York: John Wiley & Sons.

Ciminero, A. R., Calhoun, K. S., & Adams, H. E. (Eds.). (1986). *Handbook of behavioral assessment* (2nd ed.). New York: John Wiley & Sons.

Clarkin, J. F., & Glazer, H. I. (1981). *Depression: Behavioral and directive intervention strategies*. New York: Garland Press.

Coates, T. J., & Thoresen, C. E. (1978). Using generalizability theory in behavioral observation. *Behavior Therapy, 9*, 157–162.

Cone, J. D. (1979). Confounded comparisons in triple response mode assessment research. *Behavioral Assessment, 1*, 85–95.

Cone, J. D. (1981). Psychometric considerations. In M. Hersen & A. S. Bellack (Eds.), *Behavioral assessment: A practical handbook* (2nd ed.). Elmsford, NY: Pergamon Press.

Cone, J. D. (1988). Psychometric considerations and the multiple models of behavioral assessment. In A. S. Bellack & M. Hersen (Eds.), *Behavioral assessment: A practical handbook* (pp. 42–66). Elmsford, NY: Pergamon Press.

Cone, J. D., & Hawkins, R. P. (Eds.). (1977). *Behavioral assessment: New directions in clinical psychology*. New York: Brunner/Mazel.

Conger, J. C., & Conger, A. J. (1986). Assessment of social skills. In A. R. Ciminero, K. S. Calhoun, & H. E. Adams (Eds.), *Handbook of behavioral assessment* (2nd ed., pp. 526–560). New York: John Wiley & Sons.

Conger, J. C., & Keane, S. P. (1981). Social skills intervention in the treatment of isolated or withdrawn children. *Psychological Bulletin, 90*, 478–495.

Cooke, C. J., & Meyers, A. (1980). The role of predictor variables in the behavioral treatment of obesity. *Behavioral Assessment, 2*, 59–69.

Correa, E. I., & Sutker, P. B. (1986). Assessment of alcohol and drug behaviors. In A. R. Ciminero, K. S. Calhoun, & H. E. Adams (Eds.), *Handbook of behavioral assessment* (pp. 446–495). New York: John Wiley & Sons.

Cromwell, R. E., & Peterson, G. W. (1981). Multisystem-multimethod assessment: A framework. In E. E. Filsinger & R. A. Lewis (Eds.), *Assessing marriage: New behavioral approaches* (pp. 38–54). Beverly Hills, CA: Sage Publications.

Cronbach, L. J., Gleser, C. C., Nanda, H., & Fajaratman, N. (1972). *The dependability of behavioral measurements: Theory of generalizability for scores and profiles*. New York: John Wiley & Sons.

Curran, J. P., Monti, P. M., Corriveau, D. P., Hay, L. R., Hagerman, S., Zwick, W. R., & Farrell, A. D. (1980). The generalizability of a procedure for assessing social skills and social anxiety in a psychiatric population. *Behavioral Assessment, 2*, 389–401.

Curran, J. P., & Wessberg, H. W. (1981). Assessment of social inadequacy. In D. H. Barlow (Ed.), *Behavioral assessment of adult disorders* (pp. 405–438). New York: Guilford Press.

Cuvo, A. J., Leaf, R. B., & Borakove, L. A. (1978). Teaching janitorial skills to the mentally retarded: Acquisition, generalization, and maintenance. *Journal of Applied Behavior Analysis, 11*, 345–355.

Davidson, P. O., & Davison, S. M. (1980). *Behavioral medicine: Changing health lifestyles.* New York: Brunner/Mazel.

Depue, R. A., Slater, J. F., Wolfsetter-Kausch, H., Klein, D., Goplerud, E., & Farr, D. (1981). A behavioral paradigm for identifying persons at risk for bipolar depressive disorder: A conceptual framework and five validation studies. *Journal of Abnormal Psychology* (Monograph), *90*, 381–437.

Dericco, D. A., & Garlington, W. K. (1977). An operant treatment procedure for alcoholics. *Behaviour Research and Therapy, 15*, 497–499.

Dodge, C. S., Heimberg, R. G., Nyman, D., & O'Brien, G. T. (1987). Daily heterosocial interactions of high and low socially anxious college students: A diary study. *Behavior Therapy, 18*, 90–96.

Donovan, D. M., & Marlatt, G. A. (1988). *Assessment of addictive disorders.* New York: Guilford Press.

Dunst, C. J., & Trivette, C. M. (1986). Looking beyond the parent–child dyad for the determinants of maternal styles of interaction. *Infant Mental Health Journal, 7*, 69–80.

Edelbrock, C., & Costello, A. J. (1984). Structured psychiatric interviews for children and adolescents. In G. Goldstein & M. Hersen (Eds.), *Handbook of psychological assessment* (pp. 276–304). Elmsford, NY: Pergamon Press.

Edgington, E. S. (1984). Statistics and single case analysis. In M. Hersen, R. M. Eisler, & P. M. Miller (Eds.), *Progress in behavior modification* (Vol. 16, pp. 83–120). New York: Academic Press.

Edgington, E. S. (1982). Nonparametric tests for single-subject multiple schedule experiments. *Behavioral Assessment, 4*, 83–91.

Edinberg, M. A., Karoly, P., & Glesser, G. C. (1977). Assessing assertion in the elderly: An application of the behavioral-analytic model of competence. *Journal of Clinical Psychology, 33*, 869–874.

Eisenstein, J. L., & Copeland, A. P. (1988). Cognitive-behavioral assessment of children in health settings. In P. Karoly (Ed.), *Handbook of child health assessment* (pp. 128–148). New York: John Wiley & Sons.

Eisler, R. M., Hersen, M., Miller, P. N., & Blanchard, E. B. (1975). Situational determinants of assertive behavior. *Journal of Consulting and Clinical Psychology, 43*, 330–340.

Emmelkamp, P. M. G. (1981). The current and future status of clinical research. *Behavior Assessment, 3*, 249–253.

Emmelkamp, P. M. G. (1986). Behavior therapy with adults. In S. L. Garfield & A. E. Bergin (Eds.), *Handbook of psychotherapy and behavior change* (3rd ed., pp. 166–203). New York: John Wiley & Sons.

Emmelkamp, P. M. G., & Kwee, K. C. (1977). Obsessional ruminations: A comparison between thought stopping and prolonged exposure in imagination. *Behaviour Research and Therapy, 15*, 441–444.

Evans, I. M. (1985). Building systems models as a strategy for target behavior selection in clinical assessment. *Behavioral Assessment, 7*, 21–32.

Eyde, L. D. (Ed.). (1987). Computerized psychological testing (special issue). *Applied Psychology, 36*, 3–4.

Eysenck, H. J. (1952). The effects of psychotherapy: An evaluation. *Journal of Consulting Psychology, 16*, 319–324.

Eysenck, H. J. (1960a). The effects of psychotherapy. In H. J. Eysenck (Ed.), *Handbook of abnormal psychology: An experimental approach* (pp. 76–111). London: Pitman Medical Publishing.

Eysenck, H. J. (1960b). Personality and behavior therapy. *Proceedings of the Royal Society of Medicine, 53*, 504–508.

Eysenck, H. J., & Martin, I. (1987). *Theoretical foundations of behavior therapy.* New York: Plenum Press.

Fagot, B., & Hagan, R. (1988). Is what we see what we get? Comparisons of taped and live observations. *Behavioral Assessment, 10*, 367–374.

Faraone, S. V., & Hurtig, R. R. (1985). An examination of social skill, verbal productivity, and Gottman's model of interaction using observational methods and sequential analysis. *Behavioral Assessment, 7*, 349–366.

Felton, J. L., & Nelson, R. O. (1984). Inter-assessor agreement on hypothesized controlling variables and treatment proposals. *Behavioral Assessment, 6*, 199–208.

Feuerstein, M., & Adams, H. E. (1977). Cephalic vasomotor feedback in the modification of migraine headache. *Biofeedback and Self-Regulation, 3*, 241–254.

Fitzpatrick, L. J. (1977). Automated data collection for observed events. *Behavior Research Methods and Instrumentation, 9*, 447–451.

Forehand, G. A. (1986). *Computerized diagnostic testing.* ETS Research Memorandum 86-2. Princeton: Educational Testing Service.

Forehand, R., & Atkeson, B. M. (1977). Generality of treatment effects with parents as therapists: A review of assessment and implementation procedures. *Behavior Therapy, 8*, 575–593.

Foreyt, J. P., & Goodrick, G. K. (1988). Childhood obesity. In E. J. Mash & L. G. Terdal (Eds.), *Behavioral assessment of childhood disorders* (pp. 528–551). New York: Guilford Press.

Foreyt, J. P., & McGavin, J. K. (1988). Anorexia nervosa and bulimia. In E. J. Mash & L. G. Terdal (Eds.), *Behavioral assessment of childhood disorders* (pp. 776–805). New York: Guilford Press.

Foster, S. L., Bell-Dolan, D. J., & Burge, D. A. (1988). Behavioral observation. In A. S. Bellack & M. Hersen (Eds.), *Behavioral assessment: A practical handbook* (pp. 119–160). Elmsford, NY: Pergamon Press.

Foster, S. L., & Cone, J. D. (1980). Current issues in direct observation. *Behavioral Assessment, 2*, 313–338.

Foster, S. L., & Cone, J. D. (1986). Design and use of direct observation systems. In A. R. Ciminero, C. S. Calhoun, & H. E. Adams (Eds.), *Handbook of behavioral assessment* (pp. 253–324). New York: John Wiley & Sons.

Foxx, R. M., & Hake, D. R. (1977). Gasoline conservation: A procedure for measuring and reducing the driving of college students. *Journal of Applied Behavior Analysis, 10*, 61–74.

Frame, C. L., & Matson, J. L. (1987). *Handbook of assessment in childhood psychopathology: Applied issues in differential diagnosis and treatment.* New York: Plenum Press.

Frisch, H. L. (1977). Sex stereotypes in adult–infant play. *Child Development, 48*, 1671–1675.

Galassi, M. D., & Galassi, J. P. (1980). Similarities and differences between two assertion measures: Factor analysis of college self-expression scale and the Rathus Assertiveness Inventory. *Behavioral Assessment, 2*, 43–57.

Gannon, L. (1981). The psychophysiology of psychosomatic disorders. In S. N. Haynes & L. Gannon (Eds.), *Psychosomatic disorders: A psychophysiological approach to etiology and treatment* (pp. 1–31). New York: Praeger.

Gannon, L. R., & Haynes, S. N. (1987). Cognitive–physiological discordance as an etiological factor in psychophysiologic disorders. *Advances in Behavior Research and Therapy, 8*, 223–236.

Gardner, J. E., Pearson, D. T., Berocovici, A. N., & Bricker, D. C. (1968). Measurement, evaluation and modification of selected social interactions between a schizophrenic child, his parents and his therapist. *Journal of Consulting and Clinical Psychology, 32*, 537–542.

Garfield, S. L. (1984). Methodological problems in clinical diagnosis. In H.E. Adams & P.E. Sutker (Eds.), *Comprehensive handbook of psychopathology* (pp. 27–46). New York: Plenum Press.

Glasglow, R. E., Klesges, R. C., Godding, P. R., & Gegelman, R. (1983). Controlled smoking, with or without carbon monoxide feedback, as an alternative for chronic smokers. *Behavior Therapy, 14*, 386–397.

Glass, C. R., & Arnkoff, D. B. (1989). Behavioral assessment of social phobia. *Clinical Psychology Review, 9*, 75–90.

Glass, G. V., Wilson, V., & Gottman, J. M. (1975). *Design and analysis of time-series experiments.* Boulder, CO: Colorado Associated University Press.

Goldfried, M. R. (1977). Behavioral assessment in perspective. In J. D. Cone & R. P. Hawkins (Eds.), *Behavioral assessment: New directions in clinical psychology* (pp. 3–22). New York: Brunner/Mazel.

Goldfried, M. R., & Kent, R. N. (1972). Traditional versus behavioral assessment: A comparison of methodological and theoretical assumptions. *Psychological Bulletin, 77*, 409–420.

Goldstein, M., & Hersen, M. (Eds.). (1990). *Handbook of psychological assessment.* New York: Pergamon Press.

Gorsuch, R. L. (1983). Three methods for analyzing limited time series (N of 1) data. *Behavioral Assessment, 5*, 141–145.

Gottman, J. M. (1979). *Marital interaction: Experimental investigation.* New York: Academic Press.

Gottman, J. M. (1980). Analyzing for sequential connection and assessing interobserver reliability for the sequential analysis of observational data. *Behavioral Assessment, 2*, 361–368.

Greenfield, N. S., & Sternbach, R. A. (1972). *Handbook of psychophysiology.* New York: Holt, Rinehart & Winston.

Greenwald, D. P. (1977). The behavioral assessment of differences in social skill and social anxiety for female college students. *Behavior Therapy, 8*, 925–937.

Hartmann, D. P., Roper, B. L., & Bradford, D. C. (1979). Some relationships between behavioral and traditional assessment. *Journal of Behavior Assessment, 1*, 3–21.

Hartmann, D. P., & Wood, D. D. (1982). Observation methods. In A. S. Bellack, A. E. Kazdin, & M. Hersen (Eds.), *International handbook of behavior modification and therapy* (109–138). New York: Plenum Press.

Hawkins, R. P. (1987). Selection of target behaviors. In R. O. Nelson & S. C. Hayes (Eds.), *Conceptual foundations of behavioral assessment* (pp. 311–385). New York: Guilford Press.

Hay, L. R., Nelson, R. O., & Hay, W. M. (1977). The use of teachers as behavioral observers. *Journal of Applied Behavior Analysis, 10*, 345–348.

Hay, W. M., Hay, L. R., Angle, H. V., & Nelson, R. O. (1979). The reliability of problem identification in the behavioral interview. *Behavioral Assessment, 1*, 107–118.

Hay, W. M., Hay, L. R., & Nelson, R. O. (1977). Direct and collateral changes in on-task and academic behavior resulting from on-task versus academic contingencies. *Behavior Therapy, 8*, 431–441.

Hayes, S. C., Nelson, R. O., & Jarret, R. B. (1987). The treatment utility of assessment: A functional approach to evaluate assessment quality. *American Psychologist, 42*, 963–974.

Haynes, S. N. (1978). *Principles of Behavioral Assessment.* New York: Gardner Press.

Haynes, S. N. (1986). A behavioral model of paranoid behaviors. *Behavior Therapy, 17*, 266–287.

Haynes, S. N. (1987). Behavioral assessment in the design of intervention programs. In R. O. Nelson & S. Haynes (Eds.), *Conceptual foundations of behavioral assessment.* New York: Guilford Press.

Haynes, S. N. (1990). Behavioral assessment of adults. In G. Goldstein & M. Hersen (Eds.), *Handbook of psychological assessment* (pp. 423–463). Elmsford, NY: Pergamon Press.

Haynes, S. N., & Chavez, R. (1983). The interview in the assessment of marital distress. In E. E. Filsinger (Ed.), *A sourcebook of marriage and family assessment* (pp. 260–291). Beverly Hills, CA: Sage Publications.

Haynes, S. N., Falkin, S., & Sexton-Radek, K. (1989). Psychophysiological measurement in behavior therapy. In G. Turpin (Ed.), *Handbook of clinical psychophysiology.* London: John Wiley & Sons.

Haynes, S. N., Follingstad, D. R., & Sullivan, J. C. (1979). Assessment of marital satisfaction and interaction. *Journal of Consulting and Clinical Psychology, 47*, 789–791.

Haynes, S. N., & Gannon, L. R. (1981). *Psychosomatic*

disorders: A psychophysiological approach to etiology and treatment. New York: Praeger.

Haynes, S. N., & Horn, W. F. (1982). Reactive effects of behavioral observation. Behavioral Assessment, 4, 369–385.

Haynes, S. N., & Jensen, B. J. (1979). The interview as a behavioral assessment instrument. Behavioral Assessment, 1, 97–106.

Haynes, S. N., & O'Brien, W. (1988). The Gordian knot of DSM III-R use: Integrating principles of behavior classification and complex causal models. Behavioral Assessment, 10, 95–105.

Haynes, S. N., & O'Brien, W. O. (1989). The functional analysis in behavioral assessment. Unpublished manuscript.

Haynes, S. N., & Wilson, C. C. (1979). Behavioral assessment: Recent advances in methods and concepts. San Francisco: Jossey-Bass.

Hersen, M. (1981). Complex problems require complex solutions. Behavior Therapy, 12, 15–29.

Hersen, M., & Bellack, A. S. (1988). DSM-III and behavioral assessment. In A.S. Bellack & M. Hersen (Eds.), Behavioral assessment: A practical handbook (pp. 67–84). Elmsford: NY: Pergamon Press.

Hersen, M., Kazdin, A. E., & Bellack, A. S. (Eds.). (1984). The clinical psychology handbook. Elmsford, NY: Pergamon Press.

Himadi, W. G., Boice, R., & Barlow, D. H. (1986). Assessment of agoraphobia: Measurement of clinical change. Behaviour Research and Therapy, 24, 321–332.

Hoge, R. D., & Andrews, D. A. (1986). A model for conceptualizing interventions in social service agencies. Canadian Psychology, 27, 332–341.

Hops, H., Biglan, A., Sherman, L., Arthur, J., Friedman, L., & Osteen, V. (1987). Home observations of family interactions of depressed women. Journal of Consulting and Clinical Psychology, 55, 341–346.

Hughes, H. M., & Haynes, S. N. (1978). Structured laboratory observation in the behavioral assessment of parent–child interactions: A methodological critique. Behavior Therapy, 9, 428–447.

Huitema, B. E. (1985). Autocorrelation in applied behavior analysis: A myth. Behavioral Assessment, 7, 107–118.

Hutt, S. J., & Hutt, C. (1970). Direct observation and measurement of behavior. Springfield, IL: Charles C Thomas.

Jacobson, N. S. (1985). The uses versus abuses of observational measures. Behavioral Assessment, 7, 323–330.

Jacobson, N. S. (1977). Problem solving and contingency contracting in the treatment of marital discord. Journal of Consulting and Clinical Psychology, 45, 92–100.

Jacobson, N. S., Elwood, R. W., & Dallas, M. (1981). Assessment of marital dysfunction. In D. H. Barlow (Ed.), Behavioral assessment of adult disorders (pp. 439–479). New York: Guilford Press.

Jacobson, N. S., Follette, W. C., & Revenstorf, D. (1986). Toward a standard definition of clinically significant change. Behavior Therapy, 17, 308–311.

Jacobson, N. S., & Revenstorf, D. (1988). Statistics for

assessing the clinical significance of psychotherapy techniques: Issues, problems and new developments. Behavioral Assessment, 10, 133–145.

James, J. E. (1981). Behavioral self-control of stuttering using time-out from speaking. Journal of Applied Behavior Analysis, 14, 25–37.

Jensen, B. J., & Haynes, S. N. (1986). Self-report questionnaires. In A. R. Ciminero, C. S. Calhoun, & H. E. Adams (Eds.), Handbook of behavioral assessment (pp. 150–175). New York: John Wiley & Sons.

Johnston, J. M., & Pennypacker, H. S. (1980). Strategies and tactics of human behavioral research. Hillsdale, NJ: Lawrence Erlbaum Associates.

Jones, L. V., & Applebaum, M. I. (1989). Psychometric methods. In M. R. Rosenzweig & L. M. Porter (Eds.), Annual review of psychology (Vol. 40, pp. 23–43).

Kallman, W. M., & Feuerstein, M. J. (1986). Psychophysiological procedures. In A. R. Ciminero, C. S. Calhoun, & H. E. Adams (Eds.), Handbook of behavioral assessment (pp. 325–350). New York: John Wiley & Sons.

Kaloupek, D. G., & Levis, D. J. (1980). The relationship between stimulus specificity and self-report indices in assessing fear of heterosexual social interaction: A test of unitary response hypothesis. Behavioral Assessment, 2, 267–281.

Kanfer, F. H. (1985). Target selection for clinical change programs. Behavioral Assessment, 7, 7–20.

Kanfer, F., & Phillips, J. S. (1970). Learning foundations of behavior therapy. New York: John Wiley & Sons.

Karoly, P. (1981). Self-management problems in children. In E. J. Mash & L. G. Terdal (Eds.), Behavioral assessment of childhood disorders (pp. 79–126). New York: Guilford Press.

Karoly, P. (1988). Handbook of child health assessment. New York: John Wiley & Sons.

Karoly, P. (1988). Child health assessment: Toward a biopsychosocial frame. In P. Karoly (Ed.), Handbook of child health assessment (pp. 3–10). New York: John Wiley & Sons.

Kazdin, A. E. (1977). Assessing the clinical and applied importance of behavior change through social validation. Behavior Modification, 1, 427–452.

Kazdin, A. E. (1978). History of behavior modification. Baltimore: University Park Press.

Kazdin, A. E. (1979). Situational specificity: The two-edged word of behavioral assessment. Behavioral Assessment, 1, 57–75.

Kazdin, A. E. (1982a). Single-case research designs: Methods for clinical and applied settings. New York: Oxford University Press.

Kazdin, A. E. (1982b). Observation effects: Reactivity of direct observation. In D. P. Hartman (Ed.), Using observation to study behavior (pp. 5–20). San Francisco: Jossey Bass.

Kazdin, A. E. (1988). Childhood depression. In E. J. Mash & L. G. Terdal (Eds.), Behavioral assessment of childhood disorders (pp. 157–195). New York: Guilford Press.

Keefe, F. J., & Blumenthal, J. A. (1982). Assessment

strategies in behavioral medicine. New York: Grune & Stratton.

Keefe, F. J., Kopel, S. A., & Gordon, S. B. (1978). *A practical guide to behavioral assessment*. New York: Academic Press.

Kelley, M. L., & Carper, L. B. (1988). The Mother's Activity Checklist: An instrument for assessing pleasant and unpleasant events. *Behavioral Assessment, 10*, 331–341.

Kendall, P. C., & Bemis, K. M. (1984). Thought and action in psychotherapy: The cognitive-behavioral approaches. In M. Hersen, A. E. Kazdin, & A. S. Bellack (Eds.), *The clinical psychology handbook* (pp. 565–592). Elmsford, NY: Pergamon Press.

Kendall, P. C., & Braswell, L. (1985). *Cognitive-behavioral therapy for impulsive children*. New York: Guilford Press.

Kendall, P. C., & Hollon, S. D. (Eds.). (1981). *Assessment strategies for cognitive-behavioral intervention*. New York: Academic Press.

Kerlinger, F. N. (1972). *Foundations of behavioral research* (2nd ed.) New York: Holt, Rinehart & Winston.

Kilmann, P. R., Wagner, M. K., & Sotile, W. M. (1977). The differential impact of self-monitoring on smoking behavior: An explanatory study. *Journal of Clinical Psychology, 33*, 912–914.

Kling, J. W., & Riggs, L. A. (1971). *Experimental psychology*. New York: Holt, Rinehart & Winston.

Korchin, S. J. (1976). *Modern clinical psychology*. New York: Basic Books.

Krasnegor, N. A., Arasteh, J. D., & Cataldo, M. F. (Eds.). (1986). *Child health behavior: A behavioral pediatrics perspective*. New York: John Wiley & Sons.

Kratochwill, T. R. (Ed.). (1978). *Single subject research: Strategies for evaluating change*. New York: Academic Press.

Kratochwill, T. R. (1985). Selection of target behaviors: Issues and directions. *Behavioral Assessment, 7*, 3–5.

Kratochwill, T. R., & Brody, G. H. (1978). Single-subject designs: A perspective on the controversy over implying statistical inference and implications for research and training in behavior modification. *Behavior Modification, 2*, 291–307.

Kratochwill, T. R., & Piersel, W. C. (1983). Time-series research: Contributions to empirical clinical practice. *Behavioral Assessment, 5*, 165–176.

Kratochwill, T. R., & Roseby, V. (1988). Psychoeducational assessment. In P. Karoly (Ed.), *Handbook of child health assessment* (pp. 173–226). New York: John Wiley & Sons.

Lahey, B. B., Vosk, B. N., & Habif, V. L. (1981). Behavioral assessment of learning disabled children: A rationale and strategy. *Behavioral Assessment, 3*, 3–14.

Lazarus, A. A. (1976). *Multimodal behavior therapy*. New York: Springer.

Lebow, J. (1982). Consumer satisfaction with mental health treatment. *Psychological Bulletin, 91*, 244–259.

Leitenberg, H., Agras, W. S., Thompson, L. E., & Wright, D. E. (1968). Feedback in behavior modification: An experimental analysis in two phobic cases. *Journal of Abnormal Psychology, 1*, 131–137.

Lewinsohn, P. M. (1975). The behavioral study and treatment of depression. In M. Hersen, R. M. Eisler, & P. M. Miller (Eds.), *Progress in behavior modification* (Vol. 1, pp. 19–65). New York: Academic Press.

Lick, J. R., & Heffler, D. (1977). Relaxation training and attention placebo in the treatment of severe insomnia. *Journal of Consulting and Clinical Psychology, 45*, 153–161.

Lindgren, H. C. & Harvey, J. H. (1971). *An introduction to social psychology*. St. Louis: CV Mosby.

Lindsley, O. R. (1960). Characteristics of the behavior of chronic psychotics as revealed by free-operant conditioning methods. *Diseases of the Nervous System, 21*, 66–78.

Linehan, M. M. (1977). Issues in behavioral interviewing. In J. D. Cone & R. P. Hawkins (Eds.), *Behavioral assessment: New directions in clinical psychology*, (pp. 30–51). New York: Brunner/Mazel.

Linn, R. L. (1988). *Educational measurement*. (3rd ed.) New York: American Council on Education/Macmillan.

Magrab, P. R., & Papadopolou, Z. L. (1977). The effect of a token economy on dietary compliance for children on hemodialysis. *Journal of Applied Behavior Analysis, 10*, 573–578.

Maloney, M. P., & Ward, M. P. (1976). *Psychological assessment: A conceptual approach*. New York: Oxford University Press.

Marascuilo, L. A., & Busk, P. L. (1988). Combining statistics for multiple-baseline AB replicated ABAB designs across subjects. *Behavioral Assessment, 10*, 1–28.

Margolin, G. (1981). Practical applications of behavioral marital assessment. In F. F. Filsinger & R. A. Lewis (Eds.), *Assessing marriage: New behavioral approaches* (pp. 90–111). Beverly Hills, CA: Sage Publications.

Margolin, G., Michelli, J., & Jacobson, N. (1988). Assessment of marital dysfunction. In A. S. Bellack & M. Hersen (Eds.), *Behavioral assessment: A practical handbook* (pp. 441–489). Elmsford, NY: Pergamon Press.

Markman, H. J., Floyd, F. J., Stanley, S. M., & Storaasli, R. D. (1988). Prevention of marital distress: A longitudinal investigation. *Journal of Consulting and Clinical Psychology, 56*, 210–217.

Marlatt, G. A., & Miller, W. R. (1988). Comprehensive drinker profile. In M. Hersen & A. S. Bellack (Eds.), *Dictionary of behavioral assessment techniques* (pp. 144–146). Elmsford, NY: Pergamon Press.

Martin, I., & Venables, P. H. (Eds.). (1980). *Techniques in psychopathology*. New York: John Wiley & Sons.

Mash, E. J., (1979). What is behavioral assessment? *Behavioral assessment of childhood disorders*. New York: Guilford Press.

Mash, E. J., & Barkley, R. A. (1986). Assessment of family interaction with the response-class matrix. In R. J. Prinz (Ed.), *Advances in the behavioral assessment of children and families* (pp. 29–67). Greenwich, CT: JAI Press.

Mash, E. J., & Terdal, L. G. (1981). *Behavioral assessment of childhood disorders*. New York: Guilford Press.

Mash, E. J., & Terdal, L. G. (1988). Behavioral assessment of child and family disturbance. In E. J. Mash & L. G. Terdal, *Behavioral assessment of childhood disorders* (pp. 3–65). New York: Guilford Press.

Matson, J. L., & Stephens, R. M. (1977). Overcorrection of aggressive behavior in a chronic psychiatric patient. *Behavior Modification, 1*, 559–564.

Mavissakalian, M. (1986). Clinically significant improvements in agoraphobia research. *Behaviour Research and Therapy, 24*, 369–370.

May, J. R. (1977). Psychophysiology of self-regulated phobic thoughts. *Behavior Therapy, 8*, 849–861.

McFall, R. M. (1982). A review and reformulation of the concept of social skills. *Behavioral Assessment, 4*, 1–33.

McMahon, R. J., & Forehand, R. (1988). Conduct problems. In E. J. Mash & L. G. Terdal (Eds.), *Behavioral assessment of childhood disorders* (pp. 105–156). New York: Guilford Press.

McReynolds, P. (Ed.). (1978). *Advances in psychological assessment*. San Francisco, CA: Jossey-Bass.

Melamed, B. G., & Siegel, L. J. (1980). *Behavioral medicine: Practical applications in health care*. New York: Springer.

Merluzzi, T. V., & Biever, J. (1987). Role-playing procedures for the behavioral assessment of social skill: A validity study. *Behavioral Assessment, 9*, 361–377.

Merluzzi, T. V., Glass, C. R., & Genest, M. (1981). *Cognitive assessment*. New York: Guilford Press.

Messick, S. (1981). Constructs and their vicissitudes in educational and psychological measurement. *Psychological Bulletin, 89*, 575–588.

Michael, J. (1974). Statistical inference for individual organism research: Some reactions to a suggestion by Gentile, Roden, and Klein. *Journal of Applied Behavior Analysis, 7*, 627–628.

Mischel, W. (1968). *Personality and assessment*. New York: John Wiley & Sons.

Morganstern, K. P. (1988). Behavioral interviewing. In A. S. Bellack & M. Hersen (Eds.), *Behavioral assessment: A practical handbook* (pp. 86–118). Elmsford, NY: Pergamon Press.

Nay, W. R. (1986). Analogue measures. In A. R. Ciminero, C. S. Calhoun, & H. E. Adams (Eds.), *Handbook of behavioral assessment* (pp. 223–252). New York: John Wiley & Sons.

Nelson, R. O. (1977). Assessment and therapeutic functions in self-monitoring. In M. Hersen, R. M. Eisler, & P. M. Miller (Eds.), *Progress in behavior and modification* (Vol. 5, pp. 264–309). New York: Academic Press.

Nelson, R. O. (1987). Relationship between assessment and treatment within a behavioral perspective. *Journal of Psychopathology and Behavioral Assessment, 10*, 159–170.

Nelson, R. O., & Hayes, S. C. (1979). Some current dimensions of behavioral assessment. *Behavioral Assessment, 1*, 1–16.

Nelson, R. O., & Hayes, S. C. (1986). *Conceptual foundations of behavioral assessment*. New York: Guilford Press.

Nelson, R. O., & Hayes, S. C. (1987). The nature of behavioral assessment. In R. O. Nelson & S. C. Hayes (Eds.), Conceptual foundations of behavioral assessment (pp. 3–41). New York: Guilford Press.

Nietzel, M. T., Bernstein, D. A., & Russell, R. L. (1988). Assessment of anxiety and fear. In A. S. Bellack & M. Hersen (Eds.), *Behavioral assessment: A practical handbook* (pp. 280–312). Elmsford, NY: Pergamon Press.

Nietzel, M. T., Russell, R. L., Hemmings, K. A., & Gretter, M. L. (1987). The clinical significance of psychotherapy for unipolar depression: A meta-analytic approach to social comparison. *Journal of Consulting and Clinical Psychology, 55*, 196–202.

Nietzel, M. T., Winett, R. A., MacDonald, M. L., & Davidson, W. S. (1977). *Behavioral approaches to community psychology*. Elmsford, NY: Pergamon Press.

Notarius, C. I., Krokoff, L. J., & Markham, H. J. (1981). Analysis of observational data. In E. E. Filsinger & R. A. Lewis (Eds.), *Assessing marriage: New behavioral approaches*. Beverly Hills, CA: Sage Publications.

Nunes, D. L., Murphy, R. J., & Ruprecht, M. L. (1977). Reducing self-injurious behavior of severely retarded individuals through withdrawal of reinforcement procedures. *Behavior Modification, 1*, 499–516.

Nunnally, J. (1967). *Psychometric theory*. New York: McGraw-Hill.

O'Leary, K. D. (1984). Marital discord and children: Problems, strategies, methodologies, and results. In A. Doyle, D. Gold, & D. S. Moskowitz (Eds.), *Children in families under stress* (pp. 35–46). San Francisco, CA: Jossey-Bass.

O'Leary, K. D., & Turkewitz, H. (1978). Methodological errors in marital and child treatment research. *Journal of Consulting and Clinical Psychology, 46*, 747–758.

Pace, G. M., Ivancic, M. T., Edwards, G. L., Iwata, B. A., & Page, T. J. (1985). Assessment of stimulus preference and reinforcer value with profoundly retarded individuals. *Journal of Applied Behavior Analysis, 18*, 249–255.

Parks, C. W., Jr., & Hollon, S. D. (1988). Cognitive assessment. In A. S. Bellack & M. Hersen (Eds.), *Behavioral assessment: A practical handbook* (pp. 161–211). Elmsford, NY: Pergamon Press.

Parmalee, A. H. (1986). Children's illnesses: Their beneficial effects on behavioral development. *Child Development, 57*, 1–10.

Patterson, G. R. (1982). *Coercive family processes*. Eugene, OR: Castalia.

Patterson, G. R., & Bechtel, C. G. (1977). Formulating the situational environment in relation to states and traits. In R. B. Cattell & P. M. Greger (Eds.), *Handbook of modern personality therapy* (pp. 83–111). Washington, DC: Halstead.

Patterson, G. R., Littman, R. E., & Hinsey, W. C. (1964). Parental effectiveness as reinforcers in the laboratory and its relation to child-rearing practices and child adjustment in the classroom. *Journal of Personality, 32*, 180–199.

Pervin, L. A. (1985). Personality: Current controversies, issues and directions. *Annual Review of Psychology, 36*, 83–114.

Rachman, S., & Costello, C. G. (1961). The aetiology and treatment of children's phobias: A review. *American Journal of Psychiatry, 118*, 97–105.

Reid, D. H., & Hurlbut, B. (1977). Teaching nonvocal communication skills to multi-handicapped retarded adults. *Journal of Applied Behavior Analysis, 10*, 591–603.

Reid, J. B., Baldwin, D. V., Patterson, G. R., & Dishion, T. J. (1987). Some problems relating to the assessment of childhood disorders: A role for observational data. In M. Rutter, A. H. Tuma, & I. Lann (Eds.), *Assessment and diagnosis in child psychopathology* (pp. 46–73). New York: Guilford Press.

Rimm, D. C., & Masters, J. C. (1987). *Behavior therapy, techniques, and empirical findings*. New York: Academic Press.

Rodick, J. D., Henggeler, S. W., & Hanson, C. L. (1986). An evaluation of the Family Adaptability and Cohesion Evaluation Scales and the Circumplex Model. *Journal of Abnormal Child Psychology, 14*, 77–87.

Romanczyk, R. G. (1986). *Clinical utilization of microcomputer technology*. Elmsford, NY: Pergamon Press.

Runco, M. A. & Schreibman, L. (1988). Children's judgments of autism and social validation of behavior therapy efficacy. *Behavior Therapy, 19*, 565–576.

Russo, D. C., Bird, B. L., & Masek, B. J. (1980). Assessment issues in behavioral medicine. *Behavioral Assessment, 2*, 1–18.

Russo, D. C., Hamada, R. S., & Marques, D. (1988). Linking assessment and treatment in pediatric health psychology. In P. Karoly (Ed.), *Handbook of child health assessment* (pp. 30–50). New York: John Wiley & Sons.

Rutter, M., Tuma, A. H., & Lann, I. S. (Eds.). (1988). *Assessment and diagnosis in child psychopathology*. New York: Guilford Press.

Sackett, G. P. (1978). *Observing behavior: Vol. 1. Theory and applications in mental retardation*. Baltimore: University Park Press.

Sackett, G. P. (1982). Data analysis: Methods and problems. In D. P. Hartmann (Ed.), *Using observers to study behavior* (pp. 81–100). San Francisco, CA: Jossey-Bass.

Salter, A. (1961). *Conditioned reflex therapy*. New York: Putnam.

Sampson, E. E. (1981). Cognitive psychology as ideology. *American Psychologist, 36*, 730–743.

Schlundt, D. G., Johnson, W. G., & Jarrell, M. P. (1986). A sequential analysis of environmental, behavioral, and affective variables predictive of vomiting in bulimia nervosa. *Behavioral Assessment, 8*, 253–269.

Schulman, J. L., Stevens, T. M., & Kupst, M. J. (1977). The biomotometer: A new device for the measurement

and remediation of hyperactivity. *Child Development, 48*, 1152–1154.

Schwartz, G. E. (1977). Biofeedback and patterning of autonomic and central processes: CNS-cardiovascular interactions. In G. E. Schwartz & J. Beatty (Eds.), *Biofeedback: Theory and research* (pp. 38–72). New York: Academic Press.

Schwartz, G. E. (1982). Testing the biopsychosocial model: The ultimate challenge facing behavioral medicine? *Journal of Consulting and Clinical Psychology, 50*, 1040–1053.

Seligman, M. E., Klein, D. C., & Miller, M. R. (1976). In H. Leitenberg (Ed.), *Handbook of behavior modification and behavior therapy* (pp. 168–210). New York: Appleton-Century-Crofts.

Sellitz, C., Wrightsman, L. S., & Cook, S. W. (1976). *Research methods in social relations*. New York: Holtz.

Sharpley, C. F., & Alavosius, M. P. (1988). Autocorrelation in behavioral data: An alternative perspective. *Behavioral Assessment, 10*, 243–251.

Sidman, M. (1960). *Tactics of scientific research*. New York: Basic Books.

Sisson, L. A., Van Hasselt, V. B., Hersen, M., & Aurand, J. C. (1988). Tripartite behavioral intervention to reduce stereotypic and disruptive behaviors in young multihandicapped children. *Behavior Therapy, 19*, 503–526.

Sobell, M. B., Schafer, H. H., & Mills, K. C. (1972). Differences in baseline drinking behavior between alcoholics and normal drinkers. *Behaviour Research and Therapy, 10*, 257–267.

St. Lawrence, J. S. (1987). Assessment of assertion. In M. Hersen, R. M. Eisler, & P. M. Miller (Eds.). *Progress in behavior modification* (Vol. 21, pp. 152–190). Newbury Park, CA: Sage Publications.

Stitzer, M. L., Bigtelow, G. E., Liebson, I. A., & Hawthorne, J. W. (1982). Contingent reinforcement for benzodiazepine-free urine: Evaluation of a drug abuse treatment intervention. *Journal of Applied Behavior Analysis, 15*, 493–503.

Suen, H. K. (1988). Agreement, reliability, accuracy and validity: Toward a clarification. *Behavioral Assessment, 10*, 343–366.

Swan, G. E., & MacDonald, M. L. (1979). Behavior therapy in practice: A national survey of behavior therapists. *Behavior Therapy, 9*, 799–807.

Taylor, C. B., & Agras, S. (1981). Assessment of phobia. In D. H. Barlow (Ed.), *Behavioral assessment of adult disorders* (pp. 181–208). New York: Guilford Press.

Trull, T. J., Nietzel, M. T., & Main, A. (1988). The use of meta-analysis to assess the clinical significance of behavior therapy with agoraphobia. *Behavior Therapy, 19*, 527–538.

Tunnell, G. B. (1977). Three dimensions of naturalness: An expanded definition of field research. *Psychological Bulletin, 84*, 425–437.

Turkat, I. (1986). The behavioral interview. In A. Ciminero, K. S. Calhoun, & H. E. Adams (Eds.), *Handbook of* behavioral assessment (pp. 109–149). New York: John Wiley & Sons.

Turner, J. A., & Clancy, S. (1988). Comparison of operant behavioral and cognitive-behavioral group treatment for chronic low back pain. Journal of Consulting and Clinical Psychology, 56, 261–266.

Turner, S. M., Calhoun, K. S., & Adams, H. E. (1981). Handbook of clinical behavior therapy. New York: John Wiley & Sons.

Turpin, G. (Ed.) (1989). Handbook of clinical psychophysiology. London: John Wiley & Sons.

Ullmann, L. P., & Krasner, L. (1965). Case studies in behavior modification. New York: Holt, Rinehart & Winston.

Verebey, K. (Ed.). (1982). Opioids in mental illness. New York: New York Academy of Science.

Wade, T. C., Baker, T. B., & Hartmann, D. P. (1979). Behavior therapists' self-reported views and practices. The Behavior Therapist, 2, 3–6.

Wahler, R. B., House, A. E., & Stambaugh, E. E. (1976). Ecological assessment of child problem behavior: A clinical package of home, school, and institutional settings. Elmsford, NY: Pergamon Press.

Wainer, H., & Braun, H. I. (1988). Test validity. Hillsdale, NJ: Lawrence Erlbaum Associates.

Wampold, B. E., & Jensen, W. R. (1986). Clinical significance revisited. Behavior Therapy, 17, 302–305.

Wasik, B. H., & Loven, M. D. (1980). Classroom observation data: Sources of inaccuracy and proposed solutions. Behavioral Assessment, 2, 211–277.

Weiner, E. B. (1976). Clinical methods in psychology. New York: John Wiley & Sons.

Wicramesckera, I. E. (1981). Clinical research in a behavioral medicine private practice. Behavioral Assessment, 3, 265–271.

Wiens, A. N. (1981). The assessment interview. In I. B.

Wiener (Ed.), Clinical methods in psychology (pp. 3–60). New York: John Wiley & Sons.

Williamson, D. A., McKenzie, S. J., & Duchmann, E. G. (1988). Psychophysiological assessment. In P. Karoly (Ed.), Handbook of child health assessment (pp. 64–83). New York: John Wiley & Sons.

Wolfe, M. M. (1978). Social validity: The case of subjective measurement or how applied behavior analysis is finding its heart. Journal of Applied Behavior Analysis, 11, 203–214.

Wolman, B. B. (Ed.). (1965). Handbook of clinical psychology. New York: McGraw-Hill.

Wolman, B. B. (1973). Handbook of general psychology. Englewood Cliffs, NJ: Prentice-Hall.

Wolman, B. B. (1978). Clinical diagnosis of mental disorders. New York: Plenum Press.

Wolpe, J. (1958). Psychotherapy by reciprocal inhibition. Stanford, CA: Stanford University Press.

Wolpe, J. (1982). Behavior therapy. Elmsford, NY: Pergamon Press.

Wolpe, J. (1986). Individualization: The categorical imperative of behavior therapy practice. Journal of Behavior Therapy and Experimental Psychiatry, 17, 145–153.

Woody, R. H. (1980). Encyclopedia of clinical assessment. San Francisco, CA: Jossey-Bass.

Wright, H. D. (1960). Observation child study. In P. Mussen (Ed.), Handbook of research methods in child development (pp. 241–266). New York: John Wiley & Sons.

Youkilis, H. D., & Bootzin, R. R. (1981). A psychophysiological perspective of the etiology and treatment of insomnia. In S. N. Haynes & L. R. Gannon (Eds.), Psychosomatic disorders: A psychophysiological approach to etiology and treatment (pp. 179–221). New York: Praeger.

Zilboorg, G., & Henry, G. W. (1941). A history of medical psychology. New York: WW Norton.

CHAPTER 25

PSYCHOPHYSIOLOGICAL ASSESSMENT

James M. Raczynski
William J. Ray
Paul McCarthy

It is commonly agreed that the use of psychophysiological measures in understanding human functioning is increasing in popularity among clinical psychologists (e.g., Arena, Blanchard, Andrasik, Cotch, & Myers, 1983; Feuerstein & Schwartz, 1977). The primary uses of psychophysiological assessment procedures have been in two clinical areas, behavioral medicine and anxiety-based disorders (Arena et al., 1983). However, an increasing number of clinical areas are being investigated with psychophysiological measures, and the use of psychophysiological assessment expands beyond clinical psychology into research areas involving cognitive psychology, social psychology, and marketing research. Although somewhat dated, a survey of directors of the American Psychological Association (APA)-approved clinical psychology programs suggests strong interest in psychophysiology, with 86% of those surveyed indicating the availability of psychophysiological training or the interest in developing psychophysiological training (Feuerstein & Schwartz, 1977).

Not only is the interest in psychophysiological assessment expanding, but also the availability of other physiological assessment methodologies is changing the scope of psychophysiological assessment. With the growth of medical technology, sophisticated methodologies are now available to psychophysiologists. Among these are regional cerebral blood flow (RCBF; e.g., Larsen, Skinhoj, & Larsen, 1978), brain electrical activity mapping (BEAM) of electroencephalographic (EEG) parameters (e.g., Duffy, 1982; Duffy, McAnulty, & Shachter, 1984), positron emission tomography (PET; e.g., Phelps & Mazziotta, 1985), magnetic resonance imaging (MRI; e.g., Price & Mesulam, 1987), metabolic activity assessment (e.g., Sims, Carroll, Turner, & Hewitt, 1988), intraocular pressure assessment methods (e.g., Silvia, Raczynski, & Kleinstein, 1984), blood assays of a variety of biochemical indexes such as catecholamine and cortisol levels (e.g., Bassett, Marshall, & Spillane, 1987), lymphocyte alterations (e.g., Zautra, Okun, Robinson, Lee, Roth, & Emmanual, 1989), blood glucose changes (e.g., Diamond, Massey, & Covey, 1989), and blood lipid levels (e.g., Jorgensen, Nash, Lasser, Hymowitz, & Langer, 1988). These methodologies have expanded tremendously the scope of physiological variables available to researchers since the days in which psychophysiological research was commonly limited to noninvasive polygraph measures of physiological function. In most cases, these complex methodologies have expanded the inferences that researchers can make about physiological functioning and about psychological and physiological relations, that is, psychophysiological functioning.

For the clinician, however, complex physiological assessment methodologies may seem irrelevant to common clinical practice. However, these complex methodologies are revealing conceptually relevant data about psychophysiological relations, data which are important for the scientist-practitioner. Furthermore, the same technological advances that have resulted in complex physiological assessment methodologies have also resulted in the miniaturization of polygraph-like instrumentation and reductions in unit prices, enabling clinicians to incorporate cost-effective physiological measures into assessment and treatment. Finally, it becomes important for clinicians to be aware of psychophysiological relations in order to communicate with medical professionals. With the changes occurring in the medical care system, such as the proliferation of health maintenance organizations (HMOs) in which a primary care physician commonly is the gatekeeper for both medical and psychological services, it may become increasingly important for clinicians to be able to communicate knowledgeably about psychophysiological relations.

With the broad scope of psychophysiology, in a chapter that relates psychophysiological measures to clinical process, we are faced with a number of difficulties. One initial difficulty involves the manner in which both areas are structured. Psychophysiology traditionally has been structured around measures, such as heart rate, EEG activity, electromyographic (EMG) activity, and so forth, whereas clinical processes have been structured more around diagnostic classifications. In psychophysiological tradition, these measures are bound together by theoretical and conceptual issues. Thus, it is often difficult to find a review of interest to the clinician or clinical researcher because of this organizational difference between clinical psychology and psychophysiology. So that the clinician may better understand the psychophysiological perspective, the present chapter starts with a brief overview of psychophysiological history and speculates about the current state and future of psychophysiology. To enable the clinician to better utilize physiological data, the chapter next discusses basic theoretical and conceptual issues of psychophysiology. Finally, the remainder of the chapter is organized around psychological processes and attempts to provide sufficient examples of various psychophysiological measures to be of use to the clinician, realizing, of course, that an exhaustive review is not possible. The present chapter does not emphasize how the psychophysiological measures are to be recorded and the technical questions that arise with these procedures. The interested reader should consult either an introductory text (e.g., Stern, Ray, & Davis, 1980), a more advanced series of readings (e.g., Brown, 1967; Cacioppo & Tassinary, 1989; Martin & Venables, 1980) emphasizing recording technique, or published guidelines for recording specific psychophysiological measures such as those available for heart rate (Jennings, Berg, Hutcheson, Obrist, Porges, & Turpin, 1981) and electrodermal activity (Fowles, Christie, Edelberg, Grings, Lykken, & Venables, 1981).

HISTORY OF PSYCHOPHYSIOLOGY

The earliest reports of psychophysiological assessment date back to the beginnings of recorded time. However, psychophysiology, as a field, did not develop until the 1940s and 1950s as two conditions were met: (a) equipment became available to record and to quantify physiological activity; and (b) researchers interested in the relationship between physiological and psychological processes emerged. Psychophysiological assessment was first introduced by these early researchers, but the area did not expand rapidly with clinical populations until clinical psychologists developed the conceptual models that fostered multiaxial assessment, including assessment of physiological function.

Early History

Some of the earliest reports, relating psychological and physiological processes, date back to the clinical cases of Erasistratos in the third century B.C. and Galen in the second century A.D. (Mesulam & Perry, 1972). Galen, a physician who is considered the father of modern physiology, reported a case in which he was called to treat a woman suffering from insomnia. Observing the woman to be restless and reluctant to answer questions about her condition, Galen looked to the possibility of an emotional problem underlying the insomnia. By chance, one day when Galen was examining the woman, a person returned from the theater and mentioned the name of a particular male dancer. Galen reported that, "at that instant, her expression and the color of her face were greatly altered . . . I observed her pulse was irregular . . . which points to a troubled mind." Not wanting to jump to conclusions, Galen had a colleague mention the names of various dancers as Galen was examining the woman over the next few days. There was no physiological reaction to any of the dancers except one. From this reaction, Galen suggested that the woman was in love with one particular dancer, a love which was the source of her insomnia and which was confirmed over the next few days according to Galen.

There have been numerous other examples of observations of relations between physiological and psychological processes over the centuries. However, the roots of modern-day psychophysiology took hold with the development of devices capable of recording physiological responses precisely enough so that systematic relations could be discerned.

Evolution of Psychophysiology

Despite the early history, psychophysiology was not capable of significantly advancing until instrumentation was available for the recording of bioelectric responses. Early instruments capable of providing a continuous record of bioelectric events emerged in the 1870s (Geddes & Baker, 1968). Later instruments were refined until polygraphs, capable of measuring and recording bioelectric responses, were developed during the 1950s. The history of psychophysiology as a discipline did not formally begin until the 1950s when researchers formed an informal group; this group evolved into the Society for Psychophysiological Research in 1960, and the discipline was formally recognized with the publication of the journal *Psychophysiology* in 1964 (Venables, 1975a).

Modern Psychophysiology

Modern psychophysiology is not a well-organized discipline. Work in the area spans many journals from those which deal with fairly traditional polygraph measures to those which involve behavioral assessment and specialized assessment methodologies. However, in terms of basic principles that have evolved from early work dealing mainly with polygraph measures, psychophysiology is still organized well in the principles that apply to the discipline and the scientific methods that allow relations between psychological and physiological processes to be examined.

Conceptual Basis for Psychophysiological Assessment

Psychophysiological assessment has grown with the general field of psychophysiology, starting with early descriptions of psychophysiological responding (e.g., Lacey, 1950; Lacey, Bateman, & Van Lehn, 1953). The interest in psychophysiological assessment with anxiety-based disorders, however, has grown, at least in part, out of the use of multiple response systems to measure anxiety (Lang, 1969, 1977; Paul, 1966), suggesting that physiological responding be considered as but one of several response systems. It is interesting to note that a psychophysiologist, John Lacey, first argued for a tripartite assessment of emotion (Lacey, 1967). In considering the concept of arousal, Lacey viewed a unidimensional conceptualization as too simple and one that ignored the complexity of the phenomenon. He suggested that in order to understand the construct of arousal, one must determine whether one is discussing cortical, autonomic, or behavioral arousal.

Early views of tripartite assessment have evolved into the general behavioral perspective of physiological responding representing a response modality that, when incorporated with other modalities in behavioral assessment, yields a more complete view of the target problem than when only isolated modalities are assessed (Kazdin, 1982). This view of psychophysiological assessment by clinical psychologists, as but one component of a more complete behavioral assessment of response modalities, has resulted in increased attention to physiological responding in other disorders than the anxiety-based ones, such as depression (Craighead, Kennedy, Raczynski, & Dow, 1984).

In addition, this tripartite perspective has led to observations by researchers such as Borkovec (1976) and Davidson and Schwartz (1976) that it is possible to show arousal in one area (e.g., cognitive) and not in another (e.g., somatic). Lacey (1967) further suggested that even among autonomic variables it is possible to have a patterning that is inconsistent with a unidirectional arousal continuum. That is to say, it is quite possible to find a situation that produces an increase in skin conductance and muscle tension but a decrease in heart rate and respiration rate (Lacey, Kagan, Lacey, & Moss, 1963).

The conceptual evolution of psychophysiological assessment in behavioral medicine is fairly straightforward. Psychophysiological measures have long been used in assessing disorders that have a strong physiological component. However, this assessment has resulted in apparent relations that are not straightforward, such as in the area of headache research (Philips, 1978). The traditional hypothesized relationships between headache activity and muscular and vascular mechanisms do not appear to be well substantiated by critical psychophysiological data.

THEORETICAL/CONCEPTUAL ISSUES IN PSYCHOPHYSIOLOGY

General Organization of the Nervous System

Both sides of psychological/physiological relations require a focus on assessment and quantification of activity. On the physiological side, the heart of physiological assessment is the measurement of nervous system activity. The nervous system is composed of the central nervous system (CNS) and the peripheral nervous system. The CNS consists of all cells within the bony enclosures of the spinal cord and skull, whereas the peripheral nervous system is composed of those neurons that are outside of these structures. The CNS is subdivided into the brain and the spinal cord, each of which is further divided along anatomical lines. The peripheral nervous system is also divided into two main parts: the somatic system and the autonomic nervous system (ANS). The somatic system is concerned with adjustment between the external world and the organism, and the ANS deals with the organism's internal regulation. The ANS is further divided into two parts, depending upon where the neurons originate along the spinal cord: The sympathetic nervous system (SNS) is contained within the thoracic and lumbar sections of the spinal cord, whereas the parasympathetic nervous system (PNS) originates in the cranial and sacral regions.

The ANS and its interaction with the CNS has been of particular interest to psychologists because of its important role in the experience of emotion. In general, the sympathetic division activates the body, whereas the parasympathetic division conserves the resources of the body and helps to return physiological functioning to a state of equilibrium. For example, increases in heart rate, sweating, vasoconstriction of the peripheral blood vessels, and stimulation of the sphincters (bladder and intestine) are all controlled in part by the SNS. The PNS, on the other hand, decreases heart rate, controls erection of the genitalia, stimulates the peristalsis of the gastrointestinal tract, and increases tearing and salivation but has little effect on the peripheral vasculature. In general, the SNS acts more diffusely, whereas the PNS is capable of independent actions in each of its parts.

As a *general* formulation, the SNS facilitates activity that aids muscular activity and inhibits activity that would restrict it. The PNS, on the other hand, tends to conserve and to store energy. This general view of the nervous system has led some to postulate prematurely an opposing role for the SNS and PNS. Furthermore, many have related this view of opposing sympathetic and parasympathetic systems to Cannon's (1939) "fight or flight" notion. This manner of characterizing the opposing influences of the SNS and PNS is too simplistic, however. In some cases, parasympathetic activity actually increases activity, such as the activity of the stomach and intestine walls as well as in the glands of the stomach. Thus, for certain stomach problems, procedures such as relaxation training (which one might view as decreasing sympathetic activity) may actually exacerbate the problem. Reducing stress to the body may not always be equal to decreasing sympathetic activity. As we also discuss later, there are also situations in which increasing arousal may actually be accompanied by a *decrease* in heart rate rather than the increase in heart rate that one might assume from viewing arousal as a simple process of increasing SNS activity. Rather than simply viewing the SNS and PNS as opposing systems, these systems might be better viewed as complementary rather than antagonistic to one another.

Concepts Related to the Interpretation of Psychophysiological Processes

As the field of psychophysiology developed, a number of basic descriptive and theoretical principles have evolved. Although most of this work has evolved out of researchers' work with polygraph measures of physiological functioning, the principles also pertain to the many nonpolygraph physiological measures that are today being used during psychophysiological assessment. Given that psychophysiology is a relatively recent science devoted to very old questions, many of the concepts presented are incomplete and are still being developed and refined.

Stimulus Response Specificity

Beginning with the work of Ax (1953), Lacey and colleagues (Lacey et al., 1953; Lacey et al., 1963), and Engel (1972) among others, it has been observed that certain patterns of physiological responses may occur across individuals in response to particular situations. Ax (1953) first noted that participants showed greater increases in respiration rate and palmar sweat gland activity when placed in a situation that elicited fear than during an anger-provoking situation; however, anger resulted in greater increases in muscle activity and diastolic blood pressure and decreases in heart rate than did fear. Lacey et al. (1963) later showed that situations that required subjects to process cognitive tasks, such as performing mental arithmetic problems, resulted in increases in both heart rate and palmar sweat gland activity; however, situations that necessitated that subjects attend to the environment resulted in decreases in heart rate but increases in palmar sweat gland activity. As a more recent example, Ray and Cole (1985) reported that cognitive and emotional tasks that required attention to the environment resulted in differential EEG activity in comparison to those that were more internal in focus.

Individual Response Stereotypy

The concept of individual response stereotypy refers to the consistency of an individual's pattern of physiological responses either over time or across stimulus conditions. In an early report, Malmo and Shagass (1949) reported that psychiatric patients with a history of either cardiovascular problems or complaints of head and neck pain showed heart rate and head muscle activity responses that were consistent with their complaints in response to stimulation. That is, the patients with cardiovascular problems showed greater heart rate increases than the patients with head and neck complaints, and those with head and neck complaints showed greater muscle activity responses than those with the cardiac symptoms. Lacey and colleagues (Lacey et al., 1953) later demonstrated the consistency of some subjects' responses across cold pressor, mental arithmetic, letter association, and hyperventilation conditions. As we will discuss later, these early reports have direct bearing on psychophysiological assessment in determining the reliability of these assessment methods.

The Law of Initial Values

The law of initial values is not really a law, per se, but is a concept that reflects differential changes in physiological activity based on baseline levels. First identified and named by Wilder (1967), these differential changes that occur with different baseline levels reflect physiological limits in certain systems. For example, someone with a heart rate of 180 beats per minute, a level that may be close to their maximum heart rate, will tend to show less of an increase in heart rate to a fearful stimulus than someone with a resting heart rate of 70 beats per minute. However, if the stimulus resulted in a decrease in heart rate, our participant with a heart rate of 180 would be expected to show a much greater response or decrease in heart rate than our person with a heart rate of 70. More

formally, the law of initial values states that the psychophysiological response to particular stimulation is related to the prestimulus level of the response being measured. Although the relationship was first thought to apply to all autonomic responses, exceptions (such as skin conductance) are reported in the literature that do not follow the suggested relationship. From a practical standpoint, the law of initial values requires that someone interested in assessment take into account prestimulus levels when utilizing psychophysiological measures.

Homeostasis

Homeostasis is best understood as part of general systems theory. The homeostatic state is a state of equilibrium that is maintained through a negative feedback loop. For example, when a thermostat is set at 65°, the heating system will be cut off once the temperature rises above this setting. The body has also been conceptualized in this manner as can be illustrated through sweating. As the temperature of the body is increased, negative feedback mechanisms produce perspiration until the temperature is returned to a homeostatic state. Likewise, it has been suggested that there is a normal return to equilibrium after an anxiety-producing event.

A variety of homeostatic mechanisms are contained within the body to maintain equilibrium in physiological functioning. Cardiac activity alone involves a number of intrinsic control mechanisms. The heart itself exhibits a strong tendency to maintain adequate function, termed *autoregulation*. Furthermore, two broad groups of receptors function to maintain homeostatic control of the heart. Baroreceptors are stretch receptors, sensitive to changes in pressure within the cardiovascular system, which result in stretch of the arterial walls, whereas chemoreceptors respond to changes in carbon dioxide and oxygen in the blood. Both of these homeostatic mechanisms act reflexively on systems in the body that affect cardiovascular activity (Siddle & Turpin, 1980).

Habituation

Habituation is the process by which physiological responses diminish with continued presentation of stimuli. Although most physiological responses appear to habituate, Pribram has pointed out that there is little evidence showing habituation of such responses as EEG (Pribram, 1981). Generally, habituation will be slower the greater the intensity of stimulation, the more unique the stimulus, and the more complex the stimulus (cf. Graham, 1973). With extremely intense stimulation, habituation may be very minimal across repeated presentations (Lynn, 1966).

Orienting and Defensive Responses

Pavlov (1927) noticed that animals demonstrated physiological responses in the presence of novel stimuli. This process is now called the orienting response (OR). Lynn (1966) has summarized the OR as follows: (a) an increase in sensitivity of sense organs, (b) body orientation toward sound (turning head, etc.), (c) increase in muscle tone with decrease in irrelevant motor activity, (d) pattern of EEG activation (faster frequency, lower amplitude), (e) vasoconstriction in the periphery (limbs) and vasodilation in the head, (f) skin conductance increase, (g) after initial delay, respiration shows amplitude increase and frequency decrease, and (h) slowing of heart rate. Understanding the orienting response prevents a researcher from confusing initial OR reactions, as might be displayed to the first few stimuli in a series, from the physiological response to the stimuli themselves. Because it is often difficult to differentiate which psychophysiological responses result from stimuli themselves and which represent ORs, the beginning stimuli are often disregarded in psychophysiological research.

Whereas the OR represents attention to novel stimuli, the defensive response (DR) is thought to represent a turning away from painful or intense stimuli. The psychophysiological responses of the OR and DR are similar except that vasomotor activity in the head shows constriction in a DR, whereas heart rate increases during a DR (Sokolov, 1963, 1965). The DR also habituates to repeated stimulus presentations much slower than the OR.

The distinction between OR and DR has found particular relevance for the clinical psychologist among the anxiety-based disorders. For example, Hare (1973) reported heart rate responses to spider slides consistent with an OR among nonphobic participants and with a DR among spider-phobic subjects.

Uses of Psychophysiological Assessment Procedures

The uses of psychophysiological procedures must take into consideration the basic principles of psychophysiology. Furthermore, as with any assessment procedure, the utility of the method depends upon having a reliable set of procedures. Finally, issues concerning the validity of the methods must be considered.

Application of Basic Principles to Psychophysiological Assessment

Any application of psychophysiology must involve consideration of psychophysiological principles that impact upon design, analysis, and interpretation. Stimulus response specificity suggests that psychophysiological assessment designs involve multiple stimuli if implications about general response patterns are desired. If the goal of psychophysiological assessment is to determine individual response stereotypy, as is the case with most examinations with psychophysiological assessment, then multiple stimuli must be presented so that a pattern across stimuli may be determined. If the goal is to assess general patterns of activation, then multiple responses must be assessed so that general patterns may be determined. The law of initial values must be considered so that differences in response magnitudes between or within individuals at different baseline levels are not inappropriately ascribed to factors other than baseline differences. Some knowledge of the negative feedback mechanisms involved in maintaining bodily homeostasis must be retained in considering all psychophysiological responses. The phenomenon of habituation needs to be remembered so that processes other than habituation are not proposed to account for diminished responding over time. Knowledge of orienting and defensive responses allows the psychologist to differentiate between responses to novel or painful stimuli from responses to other characteristics of stimuli. It is the knowledge and application of these basic principles that enables the psychologist to conduct appropriate psychophysiological assessments and to interpret better psychophysiological data.

Reliability of Psychophysiological Assessment

Early work reported good test–retest reliability across several days of psychophysiological responses for frontalis and forearm flexor muscle measures (Martin, 1956, 1958). Lacey and Lacey (1962) found good reliability over a longer period of time. More recently, several researchers (Giordani, Manuck, & Farmer, 1981; Manuck & Garland, 1980; Manuck & Schaeffer, 1978; McKinney et al., 1985) have noted good reliability in measures of cardiovascular reactivity. Across multiple measures, however, Arena and colleagues (Arena, Blanchard, Andrasik, Cotch, & Myers, 1983) reported relatively low reliability in a small sample of 15 subjects. Faulstich and colleagues (Faulstich, Williamson, McKenzie, Duchmann,

Hutchinson, & Blouin, 1986) suggested that the degree of reliability is related to the method of quantifying the psychophysiological measure; baseline values were reliable across a 2-week period among several measures of physiological activity, but difference scores, subtracting levels obtained during stimuli from baseline values, generally revealed low reliability. Although these reports appear to question the value of psychophysiological assessment, there is a suggestion that clinical populations, such as those with psychological or physiological disorders, may show individual response stereotypy (Engel, 1972). These individual response stereotypy patterns may reveal greater test–retest reliability than found with less stereotyped patterns. Issues of reliability in psychophysiological measures need to be addressed in future research.

Validity of Psychophysiological Assessment

Recording valid psychophysiological measures requires utilizing adequate instruments and adequate attention to psychophysiological methods and procedures. These procedures and methods can be somewhat involved, such as the use of particular types of conductive gel, particular types of electrodes, and special care and application procedures for the electrodes used in electrodermal recording (cf. Fowles et al., 1981). However, provided that adequate instruments are used and appropriate methods and procedures are followed, psychophysiological measures themselves are generally valid measures of physiological function. The difficulty arises from the validity of inferring relations between physiological and psychological processes. Confidence in the validity of psychophysiological inferences can be increased by attention to basic psychophysiological principles. Confidence in the validity of inferences can also be increased by replicating findings across measures and across studies. This view argues for examining psychophysiological response patterns across measures instead of considering single measures or results in isolation in much the same manner that a multiaxial assessment provides a better assessment view than assessment of a single response modality. The activity of a single response should not be inferred as representing activity of the system. A comprehensive assessment approach thus necessitates not only measurement of cognitive, behavioral, and physiological components but also multiple types of physiological activity.

PSYCHOPHYSIOLOGICAL ASSESSMENT APPLICATIONS

Applications With the Assessment of Normal Variations in Activity

Psychophysiological assessment has been employed to characterize a variety of types of normal activity, including: cognitive processes, personality factors, emotionality, sleep, sexual arousal, deception, aging, and a variety of other organismic and environmental influences.

Cognitive Processes

The effects of such cognitive processes as intelligence, attention, arousal, information processing, performance, motivation, achievement, and learning have been the focus of several literature reviews, the majority of which have stressed electrocortical measures such as evoked potentials and contingent negative variations. Several reviews exist that have examined the relation between cognitive processes and electrocortical activity (e.g., Donchin, 1979; John, 1967; Naatanen, 1975; Tecce, 1972). In regard to intelligence, Shagass (1972) has suggested that EEG correlates of intelligence are very weak at best. Studies of specific cognitive processes, however, have suggested specific relations with EEG activity. Ritter (1979), for example, has reviewed the literature on attention and indicated that an event-related potential (i.e., a specific change in brain waves associated with a particular stimulus and only seen when background noise is averaged out over repeated presentations of the stimulus), N100, was associated with active attention. Similarly, Pritchard (1981) has reviewed the relationships of another evoked potential, the P300, with a host of stimulus and subject variables, including such things as information delivery and stimulus salience.

Among noncortical measures of autonomic activity, a few relations between cognitive activity and ANS have emerged, such as those suggested by Shapiro and Schwartz (1970). Ax, Lloyd, Gorham, Lootens, and Robinson (1978) similarly review ANS activity relations with motivation.

Personality Factors

For at least 2,000 years, a connection has been suggested between physiological processes and personality/temperament. The four-humor theory of Hippocrates and Galen in which black bile, yellow bile, blood, and phlegm form the basic elements of understanding personality was one such example. Pavlov reformulated this classic presentation and discussed the strength of the nervous system as a personality determinate (Teplov, 1964). In modern psychology, the work of Hans Eysenck and his study of introversion and extraversion have contributed a basic underlying theory to the study of psychophysiology and personality (Eysenck, 1968). In general, this work led to a variety of studies in which electrocortical measures of personality were compared between extraverts and introverts. Little of this research has brought forth consistent results (cf. Gale, 1983) or answers which would be of use in psychophysiological assessments. For an introduction to the area of psychophysiology and personality, Gale and Edwards (1983) and Strelau, Farley, and Gale (1985) offer excellent overviews of a variety of current research activities.

Investigations of personality relations to EEG activity are limited in number. Greater amounts of alpha have been associated with passive, dependent individuals, and low levels of alpha activity have been associated with consistent and well-directed individuals. These relations may not be surprising, given that alpha activity is indicative of a calm and relaxed state, suggesting that passive people are engaged in lower amounts of cognitive processing, whereas well-directed individuals are engaged in more cognitive processing. The correlations between psychological tests, such as the Rorschach and the Minnesota Multiphasic Personality Inventory (MMPI), and EEG measures have been either negative or highly inconsistent from one study to the next.

The relationships between various personality factors and electrodermal activity have been inconclusively reviewed by Edelberg (1972). The personality trait of introversion–extroversion has been assessed by psychophysiological means; the ANS measures of electrodermal activity and heart rate suggest greater arousal among introverts than among extroverts (Stern & Janes, 1973). Other reviews have dealt with the development of specific psychosomatic disturbances (Graham, 1962, 1972), introversion and extraversion (Gray, 1970, 1972; Shagass & Canter, 1972), ego strength (Roessler, 1973), and the area of personal development and relationship enhancement (Kiritz & Moos, 1974). Zuckerman, Buchsbaum, and Murphy (1980) present data suggesting that the trait of sensation seeking may be identified by electrodermal ORs and auditory-evoked potentials. Although some of this literature has been criticized for attempting to predict overt behavior on the basis of assessing hypo-thetical constructs (Goldfried & Kent, 1972), there is support for the notion that differences exist in psychophysiological responsivity among individuals on whom self-report and behavioral measures vary.

Emotion

Psychophysiological differentiation of emotions has been discussed in a number of reviews (Lang, Rice, & Sternback, 1972; Pribram, 1967; Schacter, 1971; Schwartz, 1978). Although the literature regarding the psychophysiological aspects of affective disorders is extensive, investigations focused on the psychophysiology of emotionality are less often encountered. Ekman, Levenson, and Friesen (1983) reported that generating emotional expressions resulted in differential ANS activity reflected in heart rate and skin temperature. However, the EEG literature suggests that high anxiety may engage the left hemisphere, whereas high mood might arouse the right hemisphere (Tucker, 1981). Data concerning more general relations between positive and negative moods and brain hemisphere lateralization have been ambiguous. Some studies have suggested a relation between negative emotions and the right hemisphere and positive emotions and the left hemisphere (e.g., Schwartz, Ahern, & Brown, 1979; Tucker, 1981), whereas other investigations have suggested the opposite relations between general mood and hemispheric activation (Erlichman & Weiner, 1980; Harman & Ray, 1977). More recently, Ray and Cole (1985) reported differential EEG beta activity in the temporal areas of the cortex for positive and negative emotionally valenced stimuli. In attempting to integrate neuropsychological, physiological, and psychophysiological data, Pribram (1981) probably correctly suggested that the cortical contribution to emotionality is a complex interaction involving many processes, such as a concept of self, organized and enhanced by parietal areas, selectively inhibited by frontal areas, and affectively regulated by the right hemisphere.

Sleep

Psychophysiological changes that occur with sleep have been examined thoroughly and well described in both general reviews (e.g., Johnson 1970, 1975; Snyder & Scott, 1972) and reviews of specific measures, such as electrocortical activity (Feinberg & Evarts, 1969), electrodermal activity (Edelberg, 1972), and electromyographic activity (Goldstein, 1972). The effects of sleep deprivation have also been summarized by Naitoh (1975), and the effects seen during the hypnagogic state have been reviewed by Schacter (1976).

Sexual Arousal

The psychophysiological effects of normal sexual responsivity to erotic stimuli and during coital activity (and masturbation to orgasm) have been the topic of several reviews, beginning with the pioneering efforts by Masters and Johnson (1966), and have more recently included a number of reviews (Bancroft, 1971; Heiman, 1977; Stern, Farr, & Ray, 1975; Zuckerman, 1971, 1972). Direct assessment measures of genital activity have been reviewed for both males (Barlow, 1977; Wincze & Lange, 1981) and females (Barlow, 1977; Heiman, 1978; Wincze & Lange, 1981)

Detection of Deception

The use of psychophysiological measures to assist in the determination of whether or not an individual is telling the truth has a long history dating back to Munsterberg (1908). Recently, the detection of deception literature has been reviewed in the areas of laboratory studies by Podlesney and Raskin (1977) and field investigations by Raskin, Barland, and Podlesney (1977). The consensus of opinions supports the continued use of physiological measures to detect deception (Andreassi, 1980; Barland & Raskin, 1973; Lykken, 1974; Orne, Thackray, & Poskewitz, 1972). However, more recent critical reviews of field uses of lie detection methods suggest the need for strong cautions in the use of psychophysiological assessment in this manner (Gale, 1988).

Aging

Psychophysiological effects of aging have been considered in several reviews (Marsh & Thompson, 1977; Woodruff, 1978). Significant changes with aging have been reported both in brain-evoked potentials (Dustman, Snyder, Callner, & Beck, 1979; Perry & Childers, 1969; Shagass, 1972; Tecce, 1971) and more generalized brain activity (Shagass, 1972) with increasing age. Electrocortical measures taken during sleep have also noted substantial changes with advancing age (Feinberg & Evarts, 1969). Changes in ANS measures also suggest changes with aging, such as with the electrodermal changes that occur not only during later years but across the life span (Edelberg, 1972).

Health Behaviors

Aside from dealing with medical disorders, clinical psychologists involved in behavioral medicine have become very involved in promoting health through behavior change. This has necessitated a focus on such issues as psychophysiological changes that occur with unhealthy behaviors, such as caffeine ingestion (e.g., Greenberg & Shapiro, 1987; Lane & Williams, 1987), smoking (MacDougall, Musante, Castillo, & Acevedo, 1988), and unhealthy eating patterns (e.g., Jorgensen et al., 1988). In addition, the beneficial effects of other health behaviors has also been a focus of research, such as with the decreased psychophysiological reactivity that occurs with exercise (e.g., Light, Obrist, James, & Strogatz, 1987).

Other Organismic Variations

A variety of other organismic variables have been examined and covered in reviews, including literature on sexual differences (Edelberg, 1972; Perry & Childers, 1969; Shagass, 1972), the menstrual cycle (Bell, Christie, & Venables, 1975), sociocultural differences (Shapiro & Schwartz, 1970), racial and ethnic differences (Christie & Todd, 1975), and circadian rhythm effects (Mefferd, 1975).

Environmental Influences

In addition to all of the sources of variance reviewed thus far, there remains the interaction between the environment and psychophysiological assessment findings. Mefferd (1975) has reviewed the relationships between physiological assessment and environmental variables such as temperature, humidity, barometric pressure, weather fronts, wind speed, amount of sunshine, and geomagnetic activity. In addition, the time of year and day of week have been investigated by Christie (1975), and the time within the academic cycle for students has been implicated as another potential confound by Fisher and Winkel (1979).

Psychopathological Applications

Although psychophysiological assessment has generally been conducted more with anxiety-based disorders and disorders in which there is a presumed underlying pathophysiology, that is, behavioral medicine disorders, psychophysiological measures are increasingly being used with a variety of disorders for which the presumed pathology is psychologically based. A comprehensive review of the use of psychophysiological measures with all disorders is beyond the scope of a single chapter. However, what we now present is a brief overview of psychophysiological assessment with disorders classified according to DSM-III-R (APA, 1987) criteria.

Disorders Usually First Evident in Infancy, Childhood, and Adolescence

Most of the psychophysiological assessment literature with children has focused on four diagnostic areas: (a) attention-deficit and hyperactivity disorder (ADHD), (b) academic skills disorder, (c) mental retardation categories, and (d) the identification of children at risk for developing schizophrenia. Unfortunately, the differential diagnosis in older studies between the first of these two categories appears somewhat questionable by today's standards. We have thus elected to combine reports of the first two categories.

ADHD and academic skills disorders. As reviewed by Satterfield, Cantwell, and Satterfield (1974), and more recently by Hastings and Barkley (1978), several interesting relationships have emerged between ADHD and psychophysiological measures, including underarousal of resting cortical activity among hyperactive children, no differences in basal levels of autonomic arousal between normal and ADHD children, some indication that some children are autonomically underreactive or "underarousable" to environmental stimuli, and a suggestion that stimulant drugs have been found to increase the environmental reactivity or "underarousability" among ADHD children.

On the electrocortical level, Hall and his colleagues (Hall, Griffin, Moyer, Hopkins, & Rappoport, 1976) and Halliday, Rosenthal, Naylor, and Callaway (1976) have suggested that event-related potentials may be related to the degree of hyperactivity reduction during treatment with dextroamphetamine and Ritalin, respectively. Among academic skills disorders, there also appears to be some value in a psychophysiological approach. Preston (1979), for example, reviewed the literature concerning event-related EEG potentials and reading disabilities and concluded that differences exist between normal and reading-disabled individuals, particularly when recording from parietal areas and when using linguistic stimuli.

Mental retardation. Stern and Janes (1973) have reviewed ANS functions among retarded persons, and Russo and Kedesdy (1989) have provided a recent overview of this area. Investigations that have examined electrodermal level and specific aspects of electrodermal responses, such as duration and latency, habituation, and conditioning, have yielded data that are inconclusive and often contradictory. Looking at autonomic responses to a signaled reaction time task, Krupski (1975) has demonstrated significantly lower levels of heart rate, slower reaction time scores, and lower heart rate deceleration prior to reaction signal onset among retarded males than is found in nonretarded males. With electocortical activity, marked hemisphere asymmetry in event-related potentials have been found in mentally retarded subjects when compared to nonmentally retarded individuals (Galbraith, Squires, Altair, & Gliddon, 1979).

Prediction of schizophrenia and major psychiatric disorders. A number of other investigations have examined possible relations between psychophysiological measures and the prediction of psychiatric disorders. Venables (1977) reviewed these data (primarily electrodermal activity), attempting to identify those children for whom there exists a relatively high risk of psychiatric breakdown. With electrocortical activity, Friedman, Frosch, and Erlenmeyer-Kimling (1979) presented auditory-evoked potential (AEP) data in an attempt to establish some criteria to identify children with high risk for schizophrenia. Unfortunately, their data do not suggest a methodology for predicting these children.

Organic Mental Disorders

Electrocortical measures have often been employed in the neurological and even the psychophysiological assessment of various brain disorders. The literature has been reviewed for the assessment of electroencephalographic (EEG) activity during sleep by Feinberg and Evarts (1969), indicating that frequent awakenings and a decrease in total sleep time, as well as rapid eye movement (REM) periods, often accompany neurological disorders. Data concerning contingent negative variation have been reviewed by Tecce (1971), suggesting a decrement in contingent negative variation (CNV) amplitude, especially on the side of the cortex that was lesioned. Visual-evoked potentials (VEPs) have been reviewed by Cracco (1979) and have been found to be useful in identifying patients with visual loss due to optic nerve lesions and in patients with multiple sclerosis when there is no accompanying evidence of visual disturbance. AEPs have been found to provide accurate information in the evaluation of cochlear function and peripheral hearing deficits. Somato sensory-evoked potentials have been found to add little to information acquired through clinical evaluation or EEG assessment. Pace, Molfese, Schmidt, Mikula, and Ciano (1979) have suggested that AEP data may be successful in the differential assessment of aphasic and non-aphasic disorders.

Autonomic measures have been less commonly examined among neurological patients than electrocortical activity. Stern and Jones (1973), in their review, suggested conflicting and inconclusive findings regarding autonomic measures of brain-damaged patients.

Psychoactive Substance Use Disorders

Stroebel (1972) has reviewed the utility of psychophysiological assessment in evaluating pharmacological effects, while recent investigations have examined the psychophysiological effects of such drugs as marijuana (e.g., Naliboff, Rickles, Cohen, & Naimante, 1976). The psychophysiological reactivity of drug abusers has been reviewed by Prystav (1975). Ex-drug addicts matched for sex and age with controls demonstrated activity in a number of psychophysiological assessment measures that suggest decreased autonomic activity in drug-dependent individuals as compared to controls (Prystav, 1975).

Miller (1977) reviewed the articles pertaining to the use of psychophysiological measures to assess changes as a function of treatment. This preliminary review of the literature provided inconclusive data to suggest the value of psychophysiological activity in evaluating the effects of drug and alcohol treatment. The value of VEPs, however, was demonstrated in differentiating between alcoholics and young and elderly non-alcoholics (Dustman et al., 1979). In another study of alcoholics, Porjesz and Begleiter (1979) investigated VEPs among normal subjects and chronic alcoholics and reported that brain functioning impaired by acute doses of alcohol is more permanent among the chronic alcoholics. They have also reported that alcoholics exhibited increased early and decreased late components in addition to delayed latencies, all of which parallel changes seen among elderly normal individuals.

Several recent studies have utilized ANS measures to evaluate anxiety levels among substance abusers. Nirenberg, Ersner-Hershfield, Sobell, and Sobell (1981) reviewed the use of electromyographic and electrodermal assessments in determining anxiety levels of alcoholics. In a similar manner, Raczyński, Weibe, Milby, and Gurwitch (1988) used a variety of autonomic measures as one component of a multiple response system assessment approach to assess narcotic detoxification fear among a subgroup of addicts.

Finally, with respect to the area of tobacco dependence, the electrocortical activity of smokers has been investigated by Knott and Venables (1977). These authors have reported slower dominant alpha frequency in deprived smokers relative to nonsmokers and nondeprived smokers in presmoking assessment and postsmoking assessment, with postsmoking increases in the dominant alpha frequency of deprived smokers to a level comparable to nonsmokers and nondeprived smokers. Gilbert and colleagues (Gilbert, Robinson, Chamberlin, & Speilberger, 1989) have also reported relationships between smoking, anxiety, heart rate, and EEG lateralization during a stressor. Pomerleau (1980) has called for an examination of psychophysiological activity to study the manner in which physiological activities are perceived by smokers as well as to determine the influences of physiological responding on smoking behaviors.

Schizophrenia

Next to anxiety-based disorders and behavioral medicine problems, schizophrenia has probably received the greatest amount of attention within the literature on psychophysiological assessment. Because schizophrenia is characterized as a thought disorder, most investigations of psychophysiological activity with schizophrenics have focused on a variety of measures of cerebral activity, including: general waking EEG activity (e.g., Itil, 1977), general EEG activity taken during sleep (e.g., Feinberg & Evarts, 1969), measures of lateralized brain functioning (Flor-Henry & Gruzelier, 1983), event-related activity (e.g., Shagass, 1977a, 1977b, 1979), a specialized measure of brain response known as contingent negative variation waves (e.g., McCallum & Abraham, 1973), and other more complex measures of cerebral functioning such as measures of cerebral circulation (e.g., Buchsbaum, 1977; Franzen & Ingvar, 1975).

In reviewing generalized brain measures, Itil (1977) concluded that the most important finding in the electrocortical research is that schizophrenic patients seemed to have less well-organized alpha activity and demonstrated considerably greater amounts of beta activity than normal persons. In a more recent investigation, Karson, Coppola, Daniel, and Weinberger (1988) compared the EEG of chronic schizophrenic patients to normal control subjects. Patients, as compared to control subjects, showed increased generalized delta activity in the EEG, increased activity in faster frequencies (fast beta) in the left hemisphere, suggesting increased activation of the left hemisphere, and overall reduced alpha activity in 7 of 16 patients, suggesting generalized activation of the brain. Their findings indicated that the EEG is sensitive to neurophysiological changes that accompany schizophrenia.

Event-related EEG potentials have suggested that these measures may yield important information to differentiate brain functioning among schizophrenics and normal subjects. Shagass (1977a, 1977b, 1979) reviewed evoked responses to auditory and visual stimuli and suggested that these data appear to point to some differences in evoked potentials between schizophrenic subgroups and normal subjects. More recent work has suggested that a particular component of evoked potentials, the amplitude of the P300 wave of event-related activity, is reduced among schizophrenic patients (cf. Duncan, 1988). Duncan, Morihisa, Fawcett, and Kirch (1987) have even examined the state versus trait aspects of this P300 component. Improved clinical state was highly correlated with increased visual P300 but not with auditory P300. They interpreted these results as indicating that the visually elicited P300 has the characteristic of a state marker of schizophrenia. Furthermore, auditory P300 may be a vulnerability trait marker for schizophrenia. They proposed that the core deficit in this disorder may involve the auditory information-processing system, whereas fluctuations in the clinical state may be reflected in the visual system. These data, along with other specific measures of brain activity such as contingent negative variation waves (McCallum & Abraham, 1973) and cerebral circulation (Buchsbaum, 1977; Franzen & Ingvar, 1975), strongly suggest that specific measures of brain functioning differentiate schizophrenic from normal persons. The impact of this work may have specific relevance for differential diagnosis, prediction of treatment response, early identification of individuals at risk, as well as the theoretical understanding of schizophrenia.

Although the main focus of psychophysiological assessment studies with schizophrenic persons has been on measures of brain functioning, ANS measures have also been extensively examined and may reveal information that may be of great importance. A variety of autonomic measures have been investigated and reviewed, including electrodermal activity (Depue & Fowles, 1973; Jordan, 1974; Stern & Janes, 1973; Zahn, 1977; Venables, 1975b), electromyographic activity (Goode, Meltzer, Crayton, & Mazura, 1977), skeletal muscle hemodynamics (Buchs-

baum, 1977), eye movement activity (Holzman & Levy, 1977), and skin temperature data (Buchsbaum, 1977). Venables's (1975b) early review suggested that data on tonic level, referring to the average level over time, and phasic activity, referring to the number and characteristics of responses, for skin conductance measures were inconsistent. Higher levels of spontaneous activity were reported among schizophrenics as compared to normal subjects, yet no differences were reported between normal individuals and schizophrenics on measures of tonic skin potential levels. In another early review, Spohn and Patterson (1979) examined ANS measures among schizophrenic people, including an examination of electrodermal activity, cardiovascular activity, smooth pursuit eye movements, electrocortical activity, and evoked potentials. Contrary to the findings of Venables (1975b), Spohn and Patterson (1979) concluded that schizophrenics are far less responsive in electrodermal measures than normal subjects, although agreement emerged over the rapid habituation of skin conductance orienting responses seen in schizophrenics when compared to normal subjects. Their review of cardiovascular activity suggested that schizophrenics' cardiovascular responses to orienting stimuli may differ from normal individuals. To add to the confusion found among automatic measures among schizophrenics, other studies have suggested that, when compared to normal control subjects, unmedicated schizophrenic patients have been found to show high baseline levels of electrodermal activity and heart rate, slow rates of habituation to novel stimuli, and attenuated autonomic reactivity to task-relevant stimuli (e.g., Zahn, 1975; Zahn, Carpenter, & McGlashan, 1981; Zahn, Schooler, & Kammen, 1985).

Most recently, Ohman, Nordby, and D'Elia (1989) compared measures of bilateral skin conductance, finger pulse volume, and heart rate in schizophrenic patients to normal control subjects in response to neutral stimuli. Subjects were further separated into high- and low-responsive groups by splitting on the common median in skin conductance responding to constant intensity tones. High-responsive patients showed larger skin conductance response amplitudes and shorter rise and recovery times. Also, high skin conductance responsive subjects showed more heart rate deceleration, and patients had a greater number of deceleratory responses. Finger pulse volume responses recorded from the left hand were smaller in the patient group, possibly suggesting some relationship between bilateral responding and lateralized brain functioning.

Contradictory ANS findings among schizophrenics, although possibly resulting in loss of enthusiasm for ANS psychophysiological assessment procedures with schizophrenics, may on the other hand strongly suggest that ANS activity will prove to be of major value with this complex disorder. Although much of this variance in ANS findings may relate to medication and a variety of other organismic and environmental effects, ANS measures may provide enough variance related to potentially important theoretical constructs to be of value in assisting us to understand schizophrenia better.

Mood Disorders

Although the physiological symptoms of depression have been well articulated (cf. Craighead, Kennedy, Raczynski, & Dow, 1984), psychophysiological assessment of depression has been less aggressively pursued than with anxiety-based disorders and schizophrenia. As with schizophrenia, probably more studies exist that have examined brain activity among depressed persons than ANS measures. Early investigations dealing with the electrocortical activity of depressives have been reviewed by Feinberg and Evarts (1969), Mendels and Chernik (1975), and Lader (1975). As Lader (1975) summarized, the examination of global EEG activity has generally yielded inconclusive findings.

Given the apparent relationship between lateralized brain functioning and emotion (e.g., Tucker, 1981), more recent investigations of affective disorders have often examined lateralized brain activity. Flor-Henry and Koles (1980), for example, examined the EEG of unipolar and bipolar depressed patients, finding that affective disorder was generally associated with reduced alpha power, suggesting increased activation in the right parietal region. Davidson and colleagues (Davidson, Schaffer, & Saron, 1985) reported similar reductions in right hemisphere alpha activity in subjects with depressed mood. However, these alpha differences were found in the frontal region. Using a somewhat different type of EEG analysis, Perris (1975, 1980) reported data from depressed inpatients that indicated that a ratio (left/right) of the mean integrated amplitude of the EEG correlated negatively with ratings of severity of depressive symptomatology. Furthermore, interhemispheric differences were notably diminished following successful electroshock treatment.

Many studies of event-related potentials (ERPs) of depressed patients have also been conducted, and most have found that the amplitude of early components are reduced significantly for unipolar depres-

sives (e.g., Buchsbaum, Goodwin, Murphy, & Borge, 1971; Levit, Sutton, & Zubin, 1973; Perris, 1974; Shagass, 1981). However, results regarding the latency of these early components have been inconsistent. Studies examining the P300 ERP component in depressed patients have yielded results parallel in form to those found for early components (i.e., reduced amplitude) but without reaching significance.

Some investigators have claimed that depression involves an unstable state of hyperexcitability within the organism (Akiskal & McKinney, 1975; Whybrow & Mendels, 1969). Therefore, ANS measures have been examined in a effort to investigate this notion. Some early support for the hyperexcitability concept was derived from investigations that revealed greater electromyographic activity in depressed patients and subsequent decrements in electromyographic activity following electroconvulsive treatment (Whatmore & Ellis, 1959, 1962). However, Lader and Wing (1969) found significant differences between what were characterized as agitated and retarded groups of depressed patients during their examination of skin conductance, pulse rate, and forearm extensor muscle activity to auditory stimuli. Agitated patients had greater spontaneous skin conductance fluctuations, no skin conductance habituation, and slight pulse rate increases compared to nonagitated depressed patients, whereas the control group values fell between the two groups of patients. These findings have been interpreted as contradictory to the excitability model.

Given the strong theoretical and empirical interest in cerebral lateralization, several investigators have focused on lateralization of peripheral activity as an indicator of lateralized brain activity. Gruzelier and Venables (1974), for example, have investigated the notion of hemispheric dominance in depressed patients by examining skin conductance response characteristics including orienting, habituation, amplitude, latency, recovery time, spontaneous fluctuations, and average skin conductance levels among schizophrenics, depressed patients, and "personality disorder" patients of both inpatient and outpatient status. Their results led them to classify depression as an affective disorder of right-hemisphere dominance, whereas schizophrenia was classified as a thought disorder of left-hemisphere dominance. These findings correspond well with the research of Flor-Henry (1976) in which manic-depressive syndromes were found to reflect "disorganization of the nondominant anterior limbic structures" (p. 792).

Facial electromyographic studies have reported that patterns of facial muscle activity discriminated depressed from nondepressed subjects (e.g., Greden,

Genero, Price, Feinberg, & Levine, 1986; Schwartz, Fair, Salt, Mandel, & Klerman, 1976). Furthermore, a change in facial muscle patterns toward that seen among nondepressed persons has been demonstrated as subjects clinically improved in their depression (Schwartz, Fair, Mandel, Salt, Mieske, & Klerman, 1978). These data, as well as those obtained from nondepressed subjects in whom mood changes were induced (e.g., Sirota, Schwartz, & Kristeller, 1987), strongly suggest that facial muscle patterns show consistent patterns during depression and even during depressed moods.

Anxiety Disorders

Psychophysiological assessment was utilized early in the evaluation of treatment effects with systematic desensitization (Paul, 1966), leading to the early discussion of the benefits of psychophysiological measures in the study of process and outcome psychotherapy (Mathews, 1971). Psychophysiological measures have also proven of value in differentiating anxiety disorder types. For example, Davidson (1978) has reported being able to distinguish cognitive from somatic anxiety on the basis of psychophysiological specificity. Cognitive anxiety was associated with increased skin conductance responses relative to somatic anxiety, whereas somatic anxiety was associated with higher heart rate and electromyographic activity than was found with cognitive anxiety.

Within the broad class of anxiety disorders, psychophysiological methods have been employed in numerous studies to understand better mechanisms active in various anxiety disorders. However, many papers that have reviewed such studies have treated anxiety as a unitary phenomenon, summarizing anxiety studies by the dependent physiological measure(s) recorded, rather than by the specific type of anxiety disorder evaluated. Our review highlights, by anxiety disorder, some of the most notable studies using psychophysiological measures.

Social phobia. Social phobics have shown psychophysiological response patterns similar to simple phobics when confronted with social interactions, indicating heightened physiological activity during the interactions relative to a baseline period. For example, Borkovec, Stone, O'Brien, and Kaloupek (1974) found significantly elevated heart rate during a brief social interaction for heterosocially anxious males as compared to nonanxious control subjects. More re-

cently, Beidel, Turner, and Dancu (1985) examined the heart rate and blood pressure of socially anxious and nonanxious subjects during a brief speech and same- and opposite-sex role plays. Greater systolic blood pressure differentiated socially anxious and non-anxious subjects during the speech condition, while anxious subjects showed greater systolic blood pressure and heart rate during opposite-sex role plays. Equivalent physiological responding was found for both groups during the same-sex role play.

Simple phobia. Since the early work of Paul (1966), numerous studies have utilized psychophysiological measures to study monosymptomatic phobias. In general, a consistent pattern of increased autonomic activity coincident with exposure to feared stimuli has been reported (cf. Lader, 1967, 1980; Mathews, 1971). Also, a number of studies have reported finding this autonomic arousal was diminished following successful treatment. In one such study, Lang, Melamed, and Hart (1970) examined measures of respiration, heart rate, and skin conductance level for snake phobic subjects during conditions of relaxation and concurrent with desensitization treatment. Phobic subjects showed greater autonomic activity for all measures with visualized exposure to snakes and reduced autonomic responding with repeated visualization of these feared stimuli. Furthermore, progressive exposures to more threatening stimuli produced autonomic gradients that varied with fear content and reported clarity of visualization.

The concepts of orienting and defensive responses have been found useful in conceptualizing simple phobias. For example, using groups of spider phobics and nonfearful control subjects, Hare and colleagues (Hare, 1973; Hare & Blevings, 1975) found a DR (forehead vasoconstriction and heart rate acceleration) to spider pictures and an OR (forehead vasodilation and heart rate deceleration) to neutral stimuli among the spider phobics. Nonphobic subjects, however, were found to show a pattern indicating orienting responses during presentation of both neutral pictures and the spider pictures. Similar findings have been reported in other phobic groups (e.g., Klorman, Weissberg, & Wiesenfeld, 1977).

Post-traumatic stress disorder (PTSD). An early study which examined psychophysiological responding in subjects with PTSD was conducted by Dobbs and Wilson (1960). Physiological measures, including EEG alpha activity, heart rate, and respiratory rate, were recorded during exposure to combat sounds for three groups: veterans experiencing "combat neurosis," veterans with equivalent combat experience, but without the disorder; and nonveteran control subjects. Veterans with combat neurosis were distinguished from control subjects by significantly higher heart and respiration rates during exposure to combat sounds. More recently, investigations have found generally greater physiological activation of PTSD patients during exposure to combat sounds (Blanchard, Kolb, Pallmeyer, & Gerardi, 1982) and in comparison to other non-PTSD groups during videotaped combat scenes (Malloy, Fairbank, & Keane, 1983), tapes of combat sounds (Pallmeyer, Blanchard, & Kolb, 1986), and even combat-related words (McNally, Luedke, Besyner, Peterson, Bohm, & Lips, 1987). Most recently, parallel findings have been reported in individuals experiencing PTSD following rape (e.g., Kozak, McCarthy, Foa, Rothbaum, & Murdock, 1988). These findings clearly support the concept of hyperarousal of PTSD subjects specific to trauma-relevant stimuli.

Obsessive compulsive disorder (OCD). Although not extensively investigated, cardiac and electrodermal activity have been used to isolate possible psychophysiological response patterns characteristic of OCD. During early reports, Rachman and colleagues (Hodgson & Rachman, 1972; Roper & Rachman, 1976; Roper, Rachman, & Hodgson, 1973) found increased heart rate among OCD participants during exposure to feared stimuli and reduced heart rate with exposure to neutral stimuli. More recent reports have demonstrated similar findings (e.g., Boulougouis, Rabavilas, & Stefanis, 1977; Grayson, Nutter, & Mavissakalian, 1980). Treatment gains have also been reported to be associated with reductions in physiological activity upon exposure to feared stimuli (Boulougouis et al., 1977; Kozak, Foa, & Steketee, 1988).

A few studies have examined patterns of electrocortical activity in OCD. Flor-Henry, Yeudall, Koles, and Howarth (1979) found that the eyes-closed baseline EEGs of OCs differed from normal subjects. Most recently, McCarthy, Ray, and Foa (1989) examined OCD patients, anxious control subjects, and normal control subjects using a spectral analysis of the EEG recorded during various attentional tasks. Both at rest and during cognitive tasks, differences in brain activity were found between groups. These authors interpreted these findings as indicating some frontal lobe dysfunction during information processing in OCD patients. ERPs have also been used to examine OCD patients. ERP data (Beech, Ceiseilski, & Gordon, 1983; Ceiseilski, Beech, & Gordon, 1981) appear to suggest that OCD patients demonstrated shorter latency and lower amplitude ERPs than did normal subjects only during more complex information processing.

Generalized anxiety disorder (GAD) and panic disorder. Several studies have evaluated the physiological responding of GAD patients. In one such study, Barlow, Cohen, Waddell, Vermilyea, Klosko, Blanchard, and DiNardo (1984) compared the heart rate and muscle activity for patients with GAD to panic-disordered patients during a baseline relaxation period and during mental and physical stressor tasks. Subjects with panic disorder showed higher heart rate and integrated electromyographic levels for all conditions as compared to GAD patients. Similarly, Rapee (1985) has reported cardiac data indicating greater heart rate for panic patients as compared to GADs.

In an interesting recent study, MacLeod, Hoehn-Saric, and Stefan (1986) compared self-report ratings of various bodily sensations (sweating, palpitations, muscle tension, trembling) to actual physiological recordings of skin conductance, interbeat heart rate intervals, and electromyographic activity during conditions of relaxation and psychological stress for a group of 20 GAD patients. The relationship between self-report estimates of physiological activity and actual recordings was poor while patients were relaxed. However, parallel directional changes occurred between self-report and psychophysiological measures during stress. The authors interpreted their findings as indicating that GAD patients are sensitive to the direction, but not the degree, of changes in physical symptoms of anxiety.

Several reports have appeared of psychophysiological activity during panic attacks. In an early report, Lader and Mathews (1970) found substantial increases in heart rate and electrodermal activity during spontaneous panic attacks. Several studies have examined panic induced with sodium lactate challenge, a potentially useful diagnostic test for proneness to panic attacks (e.g., Klein, 1981), and found greater increases in psychophysiological index among panic disorder patients than normal control subjects with the challenge (e.g., Ehlers, Margraf, & Roth, 1986; Freedman, Ianni, Ettedgui, Pohl, & Rainey, 1984; Taylor et al., 1986).

Somatoform and Factitious Disorders

These disorders include those for which there are symptoms that suggest a physical disorder but for which there are no demonstrable physical findings or known physiological mechanism to account for the symptoms (APA, 1987). The essential difference between these categories is, of course, that factitious disorders are viewed as under voluntary control, whereas somatoform disorders are seen as not being under voluntary control. Factitious disorders also may consist of either physical or psychological symptoms, whereas somatoform disorders are viewed as consisting of physical symptoms. Although clinical psychologists obviously must use physiological data, usually from medical evaluations, in making clinical decisions about clients with these diagnoses, we know of no systematic psychophysiological data approaching these categories.

Dissociative Disorders

Few psychophysiological assessment investigations have been conducted with dissociative disorders. However, Mesulam (1981) has reported on the electrocortical data of 12 cases with a clinical picture reminiscent of multiple personality disorder and concluded that dissociative phenomena may be more likely to occur in patients with EEG abnormalities located in the right temporal lobe.

Sexual Disorders

Peripheral autonomic measures have been examined among those with psychosexual disorders. However, as noted by reviewers, measures of nongenital activity do not appear to differentiate sexual stimuli well, including: measures of electrodermal activity (Tollison & Adams, 1979); measures of cardiovascular activity (Bernick, Kling, & Borowitz, 1986) including heart rate, facial temperature, and finger pulse volume; pupillary responses (e.g., Chapman, Chapman, & Brelje, 1969); and respiratory activity (e.g., Bancroft & Mathews, 1971). Although blood pressure has been reported to increase with increasingly arousing stimuli, lack of discriminative validity has been noted with this measure (Bernick et al., 1986). The use of direct genital measures has been supported in the assessment of male dysfunctions, such as with the use of nocturnal penile tumescence (NPT) assessment, usually recorded in conjunction with the EEG as a measure of brain activity and the electrooculogram as a measure of eye movement, as a diagnostic procedure for male erectile problems (Freund & Blanchard, 1981; Karacan, Salis, & Williams, 1978). The use of direct genital measures, as well as possibly electrocortical measures, has also been suggested as promising with paraphilias, such as pedophilia (Freund, 1981).

Sleep Disorders

Clinical evaluation of sleep disorders usually involves the collection of psychophysiological data through a polysomnographic evaluation in which EEG, respiration, and muscle activity measures are commonly recorded. However, most behavioral research has relied almost exclusively on self-report data (Morin & Kwentus, 1988). Disorders of initiating and maintaining sleep (DIMS) are the most common of sleep disorders with reported prevalence rates up to 32% (U.S. Department of Health, Education and Welfare, 1970). The disorders are defined by complaints of nonrestorative sleep or lack of sleep. Although polysomnographic recordings appear to contribute to making the differential diagnosis, these methods do not usually appear helpful in determining the severity of the disorder or even in confirming the presence or absence of a disorder (Nino-Murcia & Keenan, 1988). Particularly when polysomnographic methods have been combined with self-report data, the theoretical and therapeutic value of psychophysiological assessment methods have been realized with sleep disorders (e.g., Borkovec, 1979).

Psychological Factors Affecting Physical Condition

These diagnoses include those in which psychological factors contribute to the initiation or exacerbation of a physical condition (APA, 1987). This diagnostic category includes the bulk of the data addressing psychophysiological assessment with medical problems such as headache, chronic pain, hypertension, and heart disease. The literature in these areas are too voluminous to address in this chapter, but the reader interested in the psychophysiologic assessment of these disorders is referred to more extensive works in the area (e.g., Keefe & Blumenthal, 1982; Tryon, 1985). However, it is important to note that literature with these diagnostic categories strongly suggests the utility of psychophysiological assessment methods beyond merely integrating medical data into a psychophysiological perspective.

For example, Williams, Thompson, Haber, and Raczynski (1986) examined traditional psychometric data (MMPI) along with physiological data and behavioral information for a group of headache sufferers. Despite comparable medical classification and behavioral self-report of these patients, the pattern of psychophysiological and psychological data differentiated individual patients. Some patients were found to be high in psychological distress and low in physiological indexes of arousal, whereas others showed the reverse pattern. What is perhaps most interesting is that treatment response appeared to be related to the assessment, suggesting the importance of client-treatment matching and psychophysiological assessment strategies.

In other pain disorders, such as back pain, psychophysiological data have also been thought to contribute both conceptually and clinically. Dolce and Raczynski (1985) summarized the psychological and biomechanical models that may contribute to chronic back pain and the contribution that psychophysiological assessment may make in clarifying psychological and physiological involvement in these pain disorders. Although the medical care system endeavors to manage the estimated seven million Americans who are incapacitated with back pain (LaFreniere, 1979), 20% to 85% of all back pain cases have been described as having no discernible physiological basis (White & Gordon, 1982). Assessment of the psychophysiological component of pain disorders in combination with a broader multidimensional assessment holds promise for understanding these disorders better (Karoly & Jensen, 1987).

Personality Disorders

A number of review articles have been concerned with personality disorders, including Schacter (1971), Schacter and Latane (1964), and Stern and Janes (1973). Psychophysiological investigations with personality disorders have dealt almost exclusively with antisocial personality disorders or sociopaths.

In terms of resting levels of electrodermal activity, Stern and Janes (1973) suggested that those with antisocial personality disorders are either not significantly different from normal individuals in terms of resting levels of skin conductance or have significantly lower resting levels on this measure. Hare (1975a) similarly reported that the tonic skin conductance levels of sociopathic inmates are significantly lower than those of other inmates and noncriminal control subjects (e.g., Shalling, Lindberg, Levander, & Dahlin, 1973).

Psychophysiological responses to stimuli have been the major focus with sociopathic subjects since degree of psychophysiological response may relate to concepts such as classical conditioning (Eysenck, 1977), passive avoidance learning (Siddle & Trasler, 1981), and sensation-seeking (Quay, 1965). A number of studies have reported autonomic measures that conform to these theoretical formulations, although there is debate about which aspect of electrodermal activity is the most adequate test of the hypoarousal hypothesis (cf. Raine, 1987).

The hypoarousal hypothesis has also encountered difficulties when responses to different types of stimuli and from multiple systems have been examined. Stern and Janes (1973) reported that significantly fewer nonspecific responses were observed among people with antisocial personality disorders when compared to normal people but that the two groups do not differ with respect to ORs to simple stimuli. Hare (1975b) suggested that sociopaths are poor electrodermal conditioners but good cardiovascular conditioners. Hare (1975a) also reported that sociopaths exhibit fewer spontaneous fluctuations in skin conductance than do normal subjects and that most investigations have failed to find any significant relationship between sociopathy and tonic heart rate (e.g., Hare & Craigen, 1974).

Overall, the autonomic data appear to be more complex for sociopaths than suggested by simple hypoarousal hypotheses. Electrodermal data suggest that sociopaths may be hyporesponsive to intense stimuli that are ordinarily considered stressful. Small cardiac ORs suggest that psychopaths are less responsive and/or sensitive to changes in environmental stimuli than are normal individuals. Hare (1975b) has suggested that electrodermal responses of sociopaths preceding aversive stimuli reflect absence of fear or arousal, whereas anticipatory heart rate activity is a protective response that serves to decrease the emotional impact of the situation. Fowles (1980) similarly suggested that sociopaths have a deficient behavioral inhibition system, reflecting normal approach and active avoidance in heart rate activity but demonstrating poor passive avoidance and extinction with reduced electrodermal response to threatening stimuli.

Electrocortical investigations reviewed by Hare (1975b) indicated that approximately 30% to 60% of sociopaths exhibited EEG abnormalities, generally widespread slow wave activity (e.g., Aurthers & Cahoon, 1964). McCallum and Abraham (1973) and Tecce (1971) have reported reduced contingent negative variation, a specific type of evoked response, among psychopaths compared to normal subjects. In an interesting study, Paty, Benezech, Eschapasse, and Noel (1978) recorded several types of evoked responses from two groups of psychopaths, one having a double-Y chromosomal abnormality and the other consisting of Klinefelter sociopaths, and a group of normal subjects. The two groups of sociopaths differed significantly in VEPs and AEPs but were alike on contingent negative variation measures. The contingent negative variation measure also differentiated the two groups of sociopaths from normal subjects. This work may provide the basis for differential diagnosis of psychopathic types. The pattern seen in contingent negative variation activity may, however, also be present in other disorders, such as schizophrenia, autism, and depressive psychoses, and, therefore, may not be a good indicator of psychopathy per se.

V Codes

The DSM-III-R classification scheme has established this category to account for conditions that are not attributable to a mental disorder that are a focus of attention or treatment. Within this category exists an area referred to as noncompliance with treatment. Frederiksen, Martin, and Webster (1979) have suggested that this phenomenon be considered with psychophysiological assessment as a component of the inquiry, although a paucity of research addresses psychophysiological approaches with these disorders.

THE FUTURE OF PSYCHOPHYSIOLOGICAL ASSESSMENT

Psychophysiological assessment applications are expanding rapidly. Future investigations may see psychophysiological assessment used more often in an increased number of target areas to allow us to conduct a more thorough assessment. For example, as suggested by others (e.g., Wells, 1981), psychophysiological measures with children have only infrequently been used, although they promise a very useful addition to behavioral assessment with children's disorders. Similarly, others (e.g., Pomerleau, 1980) have suggested that psychophysiological measures may be important in understanding better the relations between physiological responses and smoking behavior.

Psychophysiological relations may also enable us to examine surrogate measures for disorders. For example, cardiovascular reactivity, if shown to be highly predictive of hypertension or heart disease, may enable us to examine etiological or predictive relations in cross-sectional designs or short-term longitudinal research rather than waiting for the slow development of hypertension in long-term longitudinal studies.

Technological advances will also undoubtedly continue to make advances in measures that are already being taken and even to make new measurement methods available to clinical psychologists. For example, newer ambulatory blood pressure monitoring instruments that include technological refinements may better enable us to record automated blood pressure and to assess other measures in combination with blood pressure (such as ECG components for determining silent ischemia). The increased focus on behavioral medicine research, promoting collaborative efforts between medical personnel and psychologists, should aid in greater access in the future by psychologists to sophisticated medical technologies. Infrared temperature measurements from the body, Doppler measures of cardiac and vascular functioning, computerized axial tomography (CAT) scanning methods, positron emission tomography (PET), and nuclear magnetic resonance (NMR) are all examples of methods which psychophysiologists are beginning to use.

SUMMARY

Psychophysiological assessment is a complex area, spanning work that appears in many different areas of the literature and from many different disciplines. Adding to the complexity, for many clinical psychologists is a lack of familiarity with physiology and the underlying neurophysiology of central and peripheral nervous system activity. Furthermore, the instrumentation used in psychophysiological assessment often appears intimidating. Although psychophysiological assessment methods require knowledge, appropriate use of principles, and attention to methodological details necessary to obtain and to analyze physiological data appropriately, the area is not as intimidating as those not familiar with the area might expect. In addition, for both the researcher and the practicing clinician, the use of psychophysiological assessment, that is, combining physiological data with cognitive and behavioral assessment information, provides a more complete view of the target area than available without physiological data.

REFERENCES

Akiskal, H.S., & McKinney, W.T. (1975). Overview of recent research in depression: Integration of ten conceptual models into a comprehensive clinical frame. *Archives of General Psychiatry, 32*, 285–305.

American Psychiatric Association. (1987). *Diagnostic and statistical manual of mental disorders—Revised* (3rd ed.), Washington, DC: Author.

Andreassi, J.L. (1980). *Psychophysiology: Human behavior and physiological responses*. New York: Oxford University Press.

Arena, J., Blanchard, E., Andrasik, F., Cotch, P., & Myers, P. (1983). Reliability of psychophysiological assessment. *Behaviour Research and Therapy, 21*, 447–460.

Aurthers, R.G., & Cahoon, E.B. (1964). A clinical and electroencepalographic survey of psychopathic personality. *American Journal of Psychiatry, 120*, 875–882.

Ax, A. (1953). The physiological differentiation between fear and anger in humans. *Psychosomatic Medicine, 15*, 433–442.

Ax, A.F., Lloyd, R., Gorham, J.C., Lootens, A.M., & Robinson, R. (1978). Autonomic learning: A measure of motivation. *Motivation and Emotion, 2*, 213–242.

Bancroft, J. (1971). The application of psychophysiological measures to the assessment-modification of sexual behavior. *Behaviour Research and Therapy, 8*, 119–130.

Bancroft, J., & Mathews, A. (1971). Autonomic correlates of penile erection. *Journal of Psychosomatic Research, 15*, 159–167.

Barland, G.H., & Raskin, D.C. (1973). Detection of deception. In W.F. Prokasy & D.C. Raskin (Eds.), *Electrodermal activity in psychological research* (pp. 417–477). New York: Academic Press.

Barlow, D.H. (1977). Assessment of sexual behavior. In A.R. Ciminero, K.S. Calhoun, & H.E. Adams (Eds.), *Handbook of behavioral assessment* (pp. 461–462). New York: John Wiley & Sons.

Barlow, D., Cohen, A., Waddell, M., Vermilyea, J., Klosko, J., Blanchard, E., & DiNardo, P. (1984). Panic and generalized anxiety disorder: Nature and treatment. *Behavior Therapy, 15*, 431–449.

Bassett, J.R., Marshall, P.M., & Spillane, R. (1987). The physiological measurement of acute stress (public speaking) in bank employees. *International Journal of Psychophysiology, 5*, 265–273.

Beech, H.R., Ceiseilski, K.T., & Gordon, P.K. (1983). Further observations of evoked potentials in obsessional patients. *British Journal of Psychiatry, 142*, 605–609.

Beidel, D.C., Turner, S.M., & Dancu, C.V. (1985). Physiological, cognitive, and behavioral aspects of social anxiety. *Behaviour Research and Therapy, 23*, 109–117.

Bell, B., Christie, M.J., & Venables, P.H. (1975). Psychophysiology of the menstrual cycle. In P.H. Venables & M.J. Christie (Eds.), *Research in psychophysiology* (pp. 181–207). New York: John Wiley & Sons.

Bernick, N., Kling, A., & Borowitz, G. (1986). Physiological differentiating, sexual arousal, and anxiety. *Psychosomatic Medicine, 65*, 427–433.

Blanchard, E.B., Kolb, L.C., Pallmeyer, D., & Gerardi, S. (1982). A psychophysiological study of posttraumatic stress disorder in Vietnam veterans. *Psychiatric Quarterly, 54*, 220–229.

Borkovec, T.D. (1976). Physiological and cognitive process in the regulation of anxiety. In G.E. Schwartz & D. Shapiro (Eds.), *Consciousness and self-regulation* (Vol. 1, pp. 261–312). New York: Plenum Press.

Borkovec, T.D. (1979). Pseudo (experiential)-insomnia and idiopathic (objective) insomnia: Theoretical and therapeutic issues. *Advances in Behaviour Research and Therapy, 2*, 27–55.

Borkovec, T.D., Stone, N.M., O'Brien, G.T., & Kaloupek, D.G. (1974). Evaluation of a clinically relevant target behavior for analog outcome research. *Behaviour Research and Therapy, 5*, 503–513.

Boulougouis, J.C., Rabavilas, A.D., & Stefanis, C. (1977). Psychophysiological responses in obsessive-compulsive patients. *Behaviour Research and Therapy, 15*, 221–230.

Brown, C.C. (1967). *Methods in psychophysiology*. Baltimore: Williams & Wilkins.

Buchsbaum, M.S. (1977). Psychophysiology and schizophrenia. *Schizophrenia Bulletin, 3*, 7–14.

Buchsbaum, M., Goodwin, F., Murphy, D., & Borge, G. (1971). AER in affective disorders. *American Journal of Psychiatry, 128*, 19–25.

Cacioppo, J.T., & Tassinary, L.G. (Eds.). (1989). *Principles of psychophysiology: Physical, social and inferential elements*. Cambridge: Cambridge University Press.

Cannon, W.B. (1939). *The wisdom of the body* (2nd ed.). New York: WW Norton.

Ceiseilski, K.T., Beech, H.R., & Gordon, P.K. (1981). Some electrophysiological observations in obsessional states. *British Journal of Psychiatry, 138*, 479–484.

Chapman, L.J., Chapman, J.P., & Brelje, T. (1969). Influence of the experimental or pupillary dilation to sexually provocative pictures. *Journal of Abnormal Psychology, 74*, 396–400.

Christie, M.J. (1975). The psychosocial environment and precursors of disease. In P.H. Venables & M.J. Christie (Eds.), *Research in psychophysiology* (pp. 234–257). New York: John Wiley & Sons.

Christie, M.J., & Todd, J.L. (1975). Experimenter-subject-situational interactions. In P.H. Venables & M.J. Christie (Eds.), *Research in psychophysiology* (pp. 50–70). New York: John Wiley & Sons.

Cracco, R.Q. (1979). Evoked potentials in patients with neurological disorders. In H. Begleiter (Ed.), *Evoked brain potentials and behavior* (pp. 365–384). New York: Plenum Press.

Craighead, W.E., Kennedy, R.E., Raczynski, J.M., & Dow, M.G. (1984). Affective disorders—Unipolar. In S.M. Turner & M. Hersen (Eds.), *Adult psychopathology: A behavioral perspective* (pp. 184–244). New York: John Wiley & Sons.

Davidson, R.J. (1978). Specificity and patterning in biobehavioral systems. *American Psychologist, 33*, 430–436.

Davidson, R.J., Schaffer, C.E., & Saron, C. (1985). Effects of lateralized presentations of faces on self-reports of emotion and EEG asymmetry in depressed and non-depressed subjects. *Psychophysiology, 22*, 353–364.

Davidson, R.J., & Schwartz, G.E. (1976). The psychobiology of relaxation and relaxed states: A multiprocess theory. In D.I. Mostofsky (Ed.), *Behavior control and modification of physiological activity* (pp. 399–442). Englewood Cliffs, NJ: Prentice-Hall.

Depue, R.A., & Fowles, D.C. (1973). Electrodermal activity as an index of arousal in schizophrenics. *Psychological Bulletin, 79*, 233–238.

Diamond, E.L., Massey, K.L., & Covey, D. (1989). Symptom awareness and blood glucose estimation in diabetic adults. *Health Psychology, 8*, 15–26.

Dobbs, D., & Wilson, W.P. (1960). Observations on persistence of war neurosis. *Diseases of the Nervous System, 21*, 40–46.

Dolce, J.J., & Raczynski, J.M. (1985). Neuromuscular activity and electromyography in painful backs. *Psychological Bulletin, 97*, 502–520.

Donchin, E. (1979). Event-related brain potentials: A tool in the study of human information processing. In H. Begleiter (Ed.), *Evoked brain potentials and behavior* (pp. 3–88). New York: Plenum Press.

Duffy, F. (1982). Topographic display of evoked potentials: Clinical applications of brain activity mapping (BEAM). *Annals of the New York Academy of Sciences, 388,* 183–196.

Duffy, F., McAnulty, G., & Schachter, S. (1984). Brain electrical activity mapping. In N. Geschwind & A. Galaburda (Eds.), *Cerebral dominance* (pp. 53–74). Cambridge, MA: Harvard University Press.

Duncan, C.C. (1988). Event-related brain potentials: A window on information processing in schizophrenia. *Schizophrenia Bulletin, 14,* 199–203.

Duncan, C.C., Morihisa, J.M., Fawcett, R.W., & Kirch, D.G. (1987). P300 in schizophrenia: State or trait marker? *Psychopharmacology Bulletin, 23,* 497–501.

Dustman, R.E., Snyder, W.E., Callner, D.A., & Beck, E.C. (1979). The evoked response as a measure of cerebral dysfunction. In H. Begleiter (Ed.), *Evoked brain potentials and behavior* (pp. 321–364). New York: Plenum Press.

Edelberg, R. (1972). Electrical activity of the skin. In N.S. Greenfield & R.A. Sternbach (Eds.), *Handbook of psychophysiology* (pp. 367–418). New York: Holt, Rinehart & Winston.

Ehlers, A., Margraf, J., & Roth, W.T. (1986). Experimental induction of panic attacks. In I. Hand & H.U. Wittchen (Eds.), *Panic and phobias* (pp. 53–66). Berlin: Springer.

Ekman, P., Levenson, R., & Friesen, W. (1983). Autonomic nervous sytem activity distinguishes among emotions. *Science, 221,* 1208–1210.

Engel, B.T. (1972). Response specificity. In N.S. Greenfield & R.A. Sternbach (Eds.), *Handbook of psychophysiology* (pp. 571–576). New York: Holt, Rinehart & Winston.

Erlichman, H., & Weiner, M.A. (1980). EEG asymmetry during covert mental activity. *Psychophysiology, 17,* 228–235.

Eysenck, H.J. (1968). *The biological basis of personality.* Springfield, IL: CC Thomas.

Eysenck, H.J. (1977). *Crime and personality* (3rd ed.). St. Albins: Paladin.

Faulstich, M.E., Williamson, D.A., McKenzie, S.J., Duchmann, E.G., Hutchinson, K.M., & Blouin, D.C. (1986). Temporal stability of psychophysiological responding: A comparative analysis of mental and physical stressors. *International Journal of Neuroscience, 30,* 65–72.

Feinberg, I., & Evarts, E.V. (1969). Some implications of sleep research for psychiatry. In J. Zubin & C. Shagass (Eds.), *Neurobiological aspects of psychopathology.* New York: Grune & Stratton.

Feuerstein, M., & Schwartz, G.E. (1977). Training in clinical psychophysiology: Present trends and future goals. *American Psychologist, 32,* 560–567.

Fisher, L.E., & Winkel, M.H. (1979). Time of quarter effect: An uncontrolled variable in electrodermal research. *Psychophysiology, 16,* 158–163.

Flor-Henry, P. (1976). Lateralized temporal-limbic dysfunction and psychopathology. *Annals of the New York Academy of Sciences, 280,* 777–795.

Flor-Henry, P., & Gruzelier, J. (Ed.). (1983). *Laterality and psychopathology.* New York: Elsevier Science Publishers.

Flor-Henry, P., & Koles, Z. (1980). EEG studies in depression, mania, and normals: Evidence for parietal shifts of laterality in the affective psychoses. *Advances in Biological Psychiatry, 4,* 21–43.

Flor-Henry, P., Yeudall, L.T., Koles, Z.J., & Howarth, B.G. (1979). Neuropsychological and power spectral EEG investigations of the obsessive-compulsive syndrome. *Biological Psychiatry, 14,* 119–130.

Fowles, D.C. (1980). The three arousal model: Implications of Gray's two-factor learning theory for heart rate, electrodermal activity, and psychopathy. *Psychophysiology, 17,* 87–104.

Fowles, D.C., Christie, M.J., Edelberg, R., Grings, W.W., Lykken, D.T., & Venables, P.H. (1981). Publication recommendations for electrodermal measurements. *Psychophysiology, 18,* 232–239.

Franzen, G., & Ingvar, D.H. (1975). Abnormal distribution of cerebral activity in chronic schizophrenia. *Journal of Psychiatric Research, 12,* 199–214.

Frederiksen, L.W., Martin, J.E., & Webster, J.S. (1979). Assessment of smoking behavior. *Journal of Applied Behavior Analysis, 12,* 653–664.

Freedman, R.R., Ianni, P., Ettedgui, E., Pohl, R., & Rainey, J.M. (1984). Psychophysiological factors in panic disorder. *Psychopathology, 17(Suppl. 1),* 66–73.

Freund, K. (1981). Assessment of pedophilia. In M. Cook & K. Howells (Eds.), *Adult sexual interest in children.* London: Academic Press.

Freund, K., & Blanchard, R. (1981). Assessment of sexual dysfunction and deviation. In M. Hersen & A.S. Bellack (Eds.), *Behavioral assessment: A practical handbook* (2nd ed., pp. 427–455.) New York: Pergamon Press.

Friedman, D., Frosch, A., & Erlenmeyer-Kimling, L. (1979). Auditory evoked potentials in children at high risk for schizophrenia. In H. Begleiter (Ed.), *Evoked brain potentials and behavior* (pp. 385–400). New York: Plenum Press.

Galbraith, G.C., Squires, N., Altair, D., & Gliddon, J.B. (1979). Electro-physiological assessments in mentally retarded individuals: From brainstem to cortex. In H. Begleiter (Ed.), *Evoked brain potentials and behavior* (pp. 229–246). New York: Plenum Press.

Gale, A. (1983). Electroencephalographic studies of extraversion–introversion: A case study in the psychophysiology of individual differences. *Personality and Individual Differences, 4,* 371–380.

Gale, A. (Ed.). (1988). *The polygraph test.* London: Sage Publications.

Gale, A., & Edwards, J. (Eds.). (1983). *Physiological correlates of human behavior.* London: Academic Press.

Geddes, L.A., & Baker, L.E. (1968). *Principles of applied biomedical instrumentation.* New York: Wiley.

Gilbert, D., Robinson, J., Chamberlin, C., & Speilberger,

C. (1989). Effects of smoking/nicotine on anxiety, heart rate, and lateralization of EEG during a stressful movie. *Psychophysiology, 26,* 311–320.

Giordani, B., Manuck, S., & Farmer, J. (1981). Stability of behaviorally-induced heart rate changes in children after one week. *Child Development, 52,* 533–537.

Goldfried, M.R., & Kent, R.N. (1972). Traditional versus behavioral assessment: A comparison of methodological and theoretical assumptions. *Psychological Bulletin, 77,* 409–420.

Goldstein, I.B. (1972). Electromyography. In N.S. Greenfield & R.A. Sternbach (Eds.), *Handbook of psychophysiology* (pp. 329–365). New York: Holt, Rinehart & Winston.

Goode, D.J., Meltzer, H.Y., Crayton, J.W., & Mazura, T.A. (1977). Physiologic abnormalities of the neuromuscular system in schizophrenia. *Schizophrenia Bulletin, 3,* 121–139.

Graham, D.T. (1962). Some research in psychophysiologic specificity and its relation to psychosomatic disease. In R. Roessler & N.S. Greenfield (Eds.), *Physiological correlates of physiological disorder* (pp. 221–238). Madison: University of Wisconsin Press.

Graham, D.T. (1972). Psychosomatic medicine. In N.S. Greenfield & R.A. Sternbach (Eds.), *Handbook of psychophysiology* (pp. 839–924). New York: Holt, Rinehart & Winston.

Graham, F.K. (1973). Habituation and distribution of responses innervated by the autonomic nervous system. In H.V.S. Peek & M.J. Herz (Eds.), *Habituation. Vol. 1. Behavioral studies* (pp. 163–218). New York: Academic Press.

Gray, J.A. (1970). The psychophysiological basis of introversion–extraversion. *Behavior Research and Therapy, 8,* 249–266.

Gray, J.A. (1972). The psychophysiological nature of introversion–extraversion: A modification of Eysenck's theory. In V.D. Nebylitsyn & J.A. Gray (Eds.), *Biological bases of individual behavior* (pp. 182–205). New York: Academic Press.

Grayson, J.B., Nutter, D., & Mavissakalian, M. (1980). Psychophysiological assessment of imagery in obsessive–compulsives: A pilot study. *Behaviour Research and Therapy, 18,* 580–593.

Greden, J.F., Genero, N., Price, H.L., Feinberg, M., & Levine, S. (1986). Facial electromyography in depression. *Archives of General Psychiatry, 43,* 269–274.

Greenberg, W., & Shapiro, D. (1987). The effects of caffeine and stress on blood pressure in individuals with and without a family history of hypertension. *Psychophysiology, 24,* 151–156.

Gruzelier, J., & Venables, P. (1974). Bimodality and lateral asymmetry of skin conductance orienting activity in schizophrenics: Replication and evidence of lateral asymmetry in patients with depression and disorders of personality. *Biological Psychiatry, 8,* 55–73.

Hall, R.A., Griffin, R.B., Moyer, D.L., Hopkins, K.H., & Rappoport, M. (1976). Evoked potential, stimulus intensity, and drug treatment in hyperkinesis. *Psychophysiology, 13,* 405–415.

Halliday, R., Rosenthal, J.H., Naylor, H., & Callaway, E. (1976). Averaged evoked potential predictors of clinical improvement in hyperactive children treated with methylphenidate: An initial study and replication. *Psychophysiology, 13,* 429–440.

Hare, R.D. (1973). Orienting and defensive responses to visual stimuli. *Psychophysiology, 10,* 453–464.

Hare, R.D. (1975a). Psychopathy. In P.R. Venables & M.J. Christie (Eds.), *Research in psychophysiology* (pp. 325–348). New York: John Wiley & Sons.

Hare, R.D. (1975b). Psychophysiological studies of psychopathology. In D.C. Fowles (Ed.), *Clinical applications of psychophysiology* (pp. 77–105). New York: Columbia University Press.

Hare, R.D., & Blevings, G. (1975). Defensive responses to phobic stimuli. *Biological Psychology, 3,* 1–13.

Hare, R.D., & Craigen, D. (1974). Psychopathology and physiological activity in a mixed-motive game situation. *Psychophysiology, 11,* 197–206.

Harman, D.W., & Ray, W.J. (1977). Hemispheric activity during affective verbal stimuli: An EEG study. *Neuropsychologia, 15,* 457–460.

Hastings, J.E., & Barkley, R.A. (1978). A review of psychophysiological research with hyperkinetic children. *Journal of Abnormal Child Psychology, 6,* 413–447.

Heiman, J.R. (1977). A psychophysiological exploration of sexual arousal patterns in females and males. *Psychophysiology, 14,* 266–274.

Heiman, J.R. (1978). Uses of psychophysiology in the assessment and treatment of sexual dysfunction. In J. LoPiccolo & L. LoPiccolo (Eds.), *Handbook of sex therapy* (pp. 123–135). New York: Plenum Press.

Holzman, P.S., & Levy, D.L. (1977). Smooth pursuit eye movements and functional psychoses: A review. *Schizophrenia Bulletin, 3,* 15–27.

Hodgson, R.J., & Rachman, S. (1972). The effects of contamination and washing in obsessional patients. *Behaviour Research and Therapy, 10,* 111–117.

Itil, T.M. (1977). Qualitative and quantitative EEG findings in schizophrenia. *Schizophrenia Bulletin, 3,* 61–79.

Jennings, J.R., Berg, W.K., Hutcheson, J.S., Obrist, P., Porges, S., & Turpin, G. (1981). Publication guidelines for heart rate studies in man. *Psychophysiology, 18,* 226–231.

John, E.R. (1967). *Mechanisms of memory.* New York: Academic Press.

Johnson, L.C. (1970). A psychophysiology for all states. *Psychophysiology, 6,* 501–516.

Johnson, L.C. (1975). Sleep. In P.H. Venables & M.J. Christie (Eds.), *Research in psychophysiology* (pp. 125–152). New York: John Wiley & Sons.

Jordan, L.S. (1974). Electrodermal activity in schizophrenics: Further considerations. *Psychological Bulletin, 81,* 85–91.

Jorgensen, R.S., Nash, J.K., Lasser, N.L., Hymowitz, N., & Langer, A.W. (1988). Heart rate acceleration and its relationship to total serum cholesterol, triglycerides, and blood pressure reactivity in men with mild hypertension. *Psychophysiology, 25*, 39–44.

Karacan, I., Salis, P.J., & Williams, R.L. (1978). The role of the sleep laboratory in diagnosis and treatment of impotence. In R. Williams & I. Karacan (Eds.), *Sleep disorders: Diagnosis and treatment* (pp. 353–382). New York: John Wiley & Sons.

Karoly, P., & Jensen, M.P. (1987). *Multimethod assessment of chronic pain*. Elmsford, NY: Pergamon Press.

Karson, C.N., Coppola, R., Daniel, D.G., & Weinberger, D.R. (1988). Computerized EEG in schizophrenia. *Schizophrenia Bulletin, 14*, 193–197.

Kazdin, A.E. (1982). History of behavior modification. In Bellack, A.E., Hersen, M., & Kazdin, A.E. (Eds.), *International handbook of behavior modification and therapy* (pp. 3–32). New York: Plenum Press.

Keefe, F.J., & Blumenthal, J.A. (1982). *Assessment strategies in behavioral medicine*. New York: Grune & Stratton.

Kiritz, S., & Moos, R.H. (1974). Physiological effects of social environments. *Psychosomatic Medicine, 36*, 96–114.

Klein, D. (1981). Anxiety reconceptualized. In D. Klein & J. Rabkin (Eds.), *Anxiety: New research and changing concepts* (pp. 235–264). New York: Raven Press.

Klorman, R., Weissberg, R.P., & Wiesenfeld, A.R. (1977). Individual differences in fear and autonomic reactions to affective stimulation. *Psychophysiology, 12*, 553–560.

Knott, V.J., & Venables, P.H. (1977). EEG alpha correlates of non-smokers, smokers, and smoking deprivation. *Psychophysiology, 14*, 150–156.

Kozak, M.J., Foa, E.B., & Steketee, G. (1988). Process and outcome of exposure treatment with obsessive–compulsives: Psychophysiological indicators of emotional processing. *Behavior Therapy, 19*, 157–169.

Kozak, M.J., McCarthy, P.R., Foa, E.B., Rothbaum, B.O., & Murdock, T.B. (1988, November). *Rape survivors with post-traumatic stress disorder: Autonomic responding to simple auditory tones*. Paper presented at the annual meeting of the Association for the Advancement of Behavior Therapy, New York.

Krupski, A. (1975). Heart rate changes during a fixed reaction time task in normal and retarded adult males. *Psychophysiology, 12*, 262–267.

Lacey, J.I. (1950). Individual differences in somatic response patterns. *Journal of Comparative and Physiological Psychology, 43*, 338–350.

Lacey, J.I. (1967). Somatic response patterning and stress: Some revisions of activation theory. In M.H. Appley & R. Trumbull (Eds.), *Psychological stress* (pp. 14–42). New York: Appleton-Century-Crofts.

Lacey, J.I., Bateman, D.E., & Van Lehn, R. (1953). Autonomic response specificity: An experimental study. *Psychosomatic Medicine, 15*, 8–21.

Lacey, J.I., Kagan, J., Lacey, B.C., & Moss, H.A. (1963). The visceral level: Situational determinant and behav-

ioral correlates of autonomic response patterns. In P.H. Knapp (Ed.), *Expression of the emotions in man* (pp. 161–196). New York: International University Press.

Lacey, J., & Lacey, B. (1962). The law of initial value and the longitudinal study of autonomic constitution: Reproduceability of autonomic responses and response patterns over a four-year interval. *Annals of the New York Academy of Sciences, 98*, 1257–1290.

Lader, M.H. (1967). Palmar conductance measures in anxiety and phobic states. *Journal of Psychosomatic Research, 11*, 271–281.

Lader, M.H. (1975). The psychophysiology of anxious and depressed patients. In D.C. Fowles (Ed.), *Clinical applications of psychophysiology* (pp. 12–41). New York: Columbia University Press.

Lader, M.H. (1980). The psychophysiology of anxiety. In H.M. Van Pragg (Ed.), *Handbook of biological psychiatry* (Vol. 5, pp. 225–248). New York: Marcel Dekker.

Lader, M.H., & Mathews, A.M. (1970). Physiological changes during spontaneous panic attacks. *Journal of Psychosomatic Research, 14*, 377–382.

Lader, M.H., & Wing, L. (1969). Physiological measures in agitated and retarded depressed patients. *Journal of Psychiatric Research, 7*, 89–100.

LaFreniere, J.G. (1979). *The low back patient*. New York: Mason.

Lane, J.D., & Williams, R.B. (1987). Cardiovascular effects of caffeine and stress on blood pressure in individuals with and without a family history of hypertension. *Psychophysiology, 24*, 157–164.

Lang, P.J. (1969). The mechanisms of desensitization and the laboratory study of fear. In C.M. Franks (Ed.), *Behavior therapy: Appraisal and status* (pp. 160–191). New York: McGraw-Hill.

Lang, P.J. (1977). Physiological assessment of anxiety and fear. In J.D. Cone & R.P. Hawkins (Eds.), *Behavioral assessment: New directions in clinical psychology* (pp. 178–195). New York: Brunner/Mazel.

Lang, P.J., Melamed, B.G., & Hart, J.D. (1970). A psychophysiological analysis of fear modification using an automated desensitization procedure. *Journal of Abnormal Psychology, 31*, 220–234.

Lang, P.J., Rice, D.G., & Sternbach, R.A. (1972). The psychophysiology of emotion. In N.S. Greenfield & R.A. Sternbach (Eds.), *Handbook of psychophysiology*, (pp. 623–643). New York: Holt, Rinehart & Winston.

Larsen, B., Skinhoj, E., & Larsen, N. (1978). Variations in regional cortical blood flow in the right and left hemispheres during automatic speech. *Brain, 101*, 193–209.

Levit, R.A., Sutton, S., & Zubin, J. (1973). Evoked-potential correlates of information processing in psychiatric patients. *Psychological Medicine, 3*, 487–494.

Light, K.C., Obrist, P.A., James, S.A., & Strogatz, D.S. (1987). Cardiovascular responses to stress: II. Relationships to aerobic exercise patterns. *Psychophysiology, 24*, 79–86.

Lykken, D.T. (1974). Psychology and the lie detection industry. *American Psychologist, 29*, 725–739.

Lynn, R. (1966). *Attention, arousal and the orientation reaction*. Oxford, England: Pergamon Press.

MacDougall, J.M., Musante, L., Castillo, S., & Acevedo, M.C. (1988). Smoking, caffeine, and stress: Effects on blood pressure and heart rate in male and female college students. *Psychophysiology, 7*, 461–478.

MacLeod, D.R., Hoehn-Saric, R., & Stefen, R.L. (1986). Somatic symptoms of anxiety: Comparison of self-report and physiological measures. *Biological Psychiatry, 21*, 301–310.

Malloy, P.F., Fairbank, J.A., & Keane, T.M. (1983). Validation of a multimethod assessment of posttraumatic stress disorders in Vietnam veterans. *Journal of Consulting and Clinical Psychology, 51*, 488–494.

Malmo, R.B., & Shagass, C. (1949) Physiologic study of symptom mechanisms in psychiatric patients under stress. *Psychosomatic Medicine, 11*, 25–29.

Manuck, S.B., & Garland, F.N. (1980). Stability of individual differences in cardiovascular reactivity: A thirteen-month follow-up. *Physiology and Behavior, 24*, 621–624.

Manuck, S.B., & Schaeffer, D.C. (1978). Stability of individual differences in cardiovascular reactivity. *Physiology and Behavior, 21*, 675–678.

Marsh, G.R., & Thompson, L.W. (1977). Psychophysiology of aging. In J.E. Birren & K.W. Schaie (Eds.), *Handbook of the psychology of aging* (pp. 219–248). New York: Van Nostrand Reinhold.

Martin, I. (1956). Levels of muscle activity in psychiatric patients. *Acta Psychologica, 12*, 326–341.

Martin, I. (1958). Blink rate and muscle tension. *Journal of Mental Science, 104*, 123–132.

Martin, I., & Venables, P.H. (Eds.). (1980). *Techniques in psychophysiology*. New York: John Wiley & Sons.

Masters, W.H., & Johnson, V.E. (1966). *Human sexual response*. Boston: Little, Brown.

Mathews, A.M. (1971). Psychophysiological approaches to the investigation of desensitization and related procedures. *Psychological Bulletin, 76*, 73–91.

McCallum, W.C., & Abraham, P. (1973). The contingent negative variation in psychosis. *Electroencephalography and Clinical Neurophysiology, 33*, 329–335.

McCarthy, P.R., Ray, W.J., & Foa, E.B. (1989). *Cognitive influences on autonomic and central nervous system activity in obsessive-compulsive disorder*. Unpublished manuscript.

McKinney, M.E., Miner, M.H., Ruddel, H., McIlvain, H.E., Witte, H., Buell, J.C., Eliot, R.S., & Grant, L.B. (1985). The standardized mental stress test protocol: Test–retest reliability and comparison with ambulatory blood pressure monitoring. *Psychophysiology, 22*, 453–463.

McNally, R.J., Luedke, D.L., Besyner, J.K., Peterson, R.A., Bohm, K., & Lips, O.J. (1987). Sensitivity to stress relevant stimuli post-traumatic stress disorder. *Journal of Anxiety Disorders, 1*, 105–116.

Mefferd, R.B. (1975). Some experimental implications of change. In P.H. Venables & M.J. Christie (Eds.), *Re-search in psychophysiology* (pp. 16–49). New York: John Wiley & Sons.

Mendels, J., & Chernik, D.A. (1975). Psychophysiological studies of sleep in depressed patients: An overview. In D.C. Fowles (Ed.), *Clinical applications of psychophysiology* (pp. 42–76). New York: Columbia University Press.

Mesulam, M.M. (1981). Dissociative states with abnormal temporal lobe EEG: Multiple personality and the illusion of possession. *Archives of Neurology, 38*, 176–181.

Mesulam, M., & Perry, J. (1972). The diagnosis of love-sickness: Experimental psychophysiology without the polygraph. *Psychophysiology, 9*, 546–551.

Miller, P.M. (1977). Assessment of addictive behaviors. In A.R. Ciminero, K.S. Calhoun, & H.E. Adams (Eds.), *Handbook of behavioral assessment* (pp. 429–459). New York: John Wiley & Sons.

Morin, C.M., & Kwentus, J.A. (1988). Behavioral and pharmacological treatments for insomnia. *Annals of Behavioral Medicine, 10*, 91–100.

Munsterberg, H. (1908). *On the witness stand*. New York: Doubleday, Page.

Naatanen, R. (1975). Selective attention and evoked potentials in humans—A critical review. *Biological Psychology, 2*, 237–307.

Naitoh, P. (1975). Sleep deprivation in humans. In P.H. Venables & M.J. Christie (Eds.), *Research in psychophysiology* (pp. 153–180). New York: John Wiley & Sons.

Naliboff, B.D., Rickles, W.H., Cohen, M.J., & Naimante, R.S. (1976). Interactions of marijuana and induced stress: Forearm blood flow, heart rate, and skin conductance. *Psychophysiology, 13*, 517–522.

Nino-Murcia, G., & Keenan, S. (1988). A multicomponent approach to the management of insomnia. *Annals of Behavioral Medicine, 10*, 101–106.

Nirenberg, T.D., Ersner-Hershfield, S., Sobell, L.C., & Sobell, M.B. (1981). Behavioral treatment of alcohol problems. In C.K. Prokop & L.A. Bradley (Eds.), *Medical psychology: Contributions to behavioral medicine* (pp. 267–290). New York: Academic Press.

Ohman, A., Nordby, H., & D'Elia, G. (1989). Orienting in schizophrenia: Habituation to auditory stimuli of constant and varying intensity in patients high and low in skin conductance responsivity. *Psychophysiology, 26*, 48–61.

Orne, M.T., Thackray, R.I., & Poskewitz, D.A. (1972). On the detection of deception. In N.S. Greenfield & R.A. Sternbach (Eds.), *Handbook of psychophysiology* (pp. 743–785). New York: Holt, Rinehart & Winston.

Pace, S.A., Molfese, D.L., Schmidt, A.L., Mikula, W., & Ciano, C. (1979). Relationships between behavioral and electrocortical responses of aphasic and non-aphasic brain-damaged adults to semantic materials. In H. Begleiter (Ed.), *Evoked brain potentials and behavior* (pp. 303–320). New York: Plenum Press.

Pallmeyer, T.P., Blanchard, E.B., & Kolb, L.C. (1986). The psychophysiology of combat-induced post-traumatic stress disorder in Vietnam veterans. *Behaviour Research and Therapy, 24*, 645–652.

Paty, J., Benezech, M., Eschapasse, P., & Noel, B. (1978). Neurophysiological study of 47,XYY and 47,XXY psychopaths: Contingent negative variation, evoked potentials and motor nerve conduction. *Neuropsychobiology, 4*, 321–327.

Paul, G.L. (1966). *Insight vs. desensitization in psychotherapy: An experiment in anxiety reduction*. Stanford, CA: Stanford University Press.

Pavlov, I.P. (1927). *Conditional reflexes: An investigation of the cerebral cortex*. London: Oxford University Press.

Perris, C. (1974). Averaged evoked responses in patients with affective disorders. A pilot study of possible hemispheric differences in depressed patients. *Acta Psychiatrica Scandinavia (Supplement), 255*, 89–98.

Perris, C. (1975). EEG techniques in the measurement of the severity of depressive syndromes. *Neuropsychobiology, 1*, 16–25.

Perris, C. (1980). Central measures of depression. In H.M. Van Pragg, M.H. Lader, O.J. Rafaelson, & E.J. Sachar (Eds.), *Handbook of biological psychiatry, Part II* (pp. 183–224). New York: Marcel Dekker.

Perry, N.W., & Childers, D.G. (1969). *The human visual evoked response: Methods and theory*. Springfield, IL: Charles C. Thomas.

Phelps, M., & Mazziotta, J. (1985). Positron emission tomography: Human brain function and biochemistry. *Science, 135*, 156–162.

Philips, C. (1978). Tension headache: Theoretical problems. *Behavior, Research and Therapy, 16*, 249–261.

Podlesney, J.A., & Raskin, D.C. (1977). Physiological measures and the detection of deception. *Psychological Bulletin, 84*, 782–799.

Pomerleau, O.F. (1980). Why people smoke: Current psychobiological models. In P.O. Davidson & S.M. Davidson (Eds.), *Behavioral medicine: Changing health lifestyles* (pp. 94–115). New York: Brunner/Mazel.

Porjesz, B., & Begleiter, H. (1979). Visual evoked potentials and brain dysfunction in chronic alcoholics. In H. Begleiter (Ed.), *Evoked brain potentials and behavior* (pp. 247–268). New York: Plenum Press.

Preston, M.S. (1979). The use of evoked response procedures in studies of reading disability. In H. Begleiter (Ed.), *Evoked brain potentials and behavior* (pp. 277–302). New York: Plenum Press.

Price, B.H., & Mesulam, M.M. (1987). Behavioral manifestations of central pontine syelinolysis. *Archives of Neurology, 44*, 671–673.

Pribram, K.H. (1967). The new neurology and the biology of emotion: A structural approach. *American Psychologist, 22*, 830–838.

Pribram, K.H. (1981). Emotions. In S. Filskov & T. Boll (Eds.), *Handbook of clinical neuropsychology* (pp. 102–134). New York: John Wiley & Sons.

Pritchard, W.S. (1981). Psychophysiology of P300. *Psychological Bulletin, 89*, 506–540.

Prystav, G.H. (1975). Autonomic responsivity to sensory

stimulation in drug addicts. *Psychophysiology, 12*, 170–178.

Quay, H.C. (1965). Psychopathic personality as pathological stimulation-seeking. *American Journal of Psychiatry, 122*, 180–183.

Raczynski, J.M., Weibe, D., Milby, J., & Gurwitch, R. (1988). Behavioral assessment of narcotic detoxification fear. *Addictive Behaviors, 13*, 165–169.

Raine, A. (1987). Effect of early environment on electrodermal and cognitive correlates of schizotypy and psychopathy in criminals. *International Journal of psychophysiology, 4*, 277–287.

Rapee, R.M. (1985). A distinction between panic disorder and generalized anxiety disorder: Clinical presentation. *Australian and New Zealand Journal of Psychiatry, 19*, 227–232.

Raskin, D.C., Barland, G.H., & Podlesney, J.A. (1977). Validity and reliability of detection of deception. *Polygraph, 6*, 1–39.

Ray, W.J., & Cole, H. (1985). EEG alpha reflects attentional demands, and beta activity reflects emotional and cognitive processes. *Science, 228*, 750–752.

Ritter, W. (1979). Cognition and the brain. In H. Begleiter (Ed.), *Evoked brain potentials and behavior* (pp. 197–228). New York: Plenum Press.

Roessler, R. (1973). Personality, psychophysiology, and performance. *Psychophysiology, 10*, 315–325.

Roper, G., & Rachmun, S. (1976). Obsessional-compulsive checking: Experimental replication and development. *Behaviour Research and Therapy, 14*, 25–32.

Roper, G., Rachman, S., & Hodgson, R.J. (1973). An experiment of obsessional checking. *Behaviour Research and Therapy, 11*, 271–277.

Russo, D., & Kedesdy, J. (1989). *Behavioral medicine with the developmentally disabled*. New York: Plenum Press.

Satterfield, J.H., Cantwell, D.P., & Satterfield, B.T. (1974). Psychophysiology of the hyperactive child syndrome. *Archives of Child Psychiatry, 31*, 839–844.

Schacter, S. (1971). *Emotion, obesity, and crime*. New York: Academic Press.

Schacter, D.L. (1976). The hypnagogic state: A critical review of the literature. *Psychological Bulletin, 83*, 452–481.

Schacter, S., & Latane, B. (1964). Crime, cognition and the autonomic nervous system. In M.R. Jones (Ed.), *Nebraska symposium on motivation*. Lincoln: University of Nebraska Press.

Schwartz, G.E. (1978). Psychobiological foundations of psychotherapy and behavior change. In S.L. Garfield & A.E. Bergin (Eds.), *Handbook of psychotherapy and behavior change: An empirical analysis* (2nd ed., pp. 63–99). New York: John Wiley & Sons.

Schwartz, G.E., Ahern, G.L., & Brown, S.L. (1979). Lateralized facial muscle response to positive and negative emotional stimuli. *Psychophysiology, 16*, 561–571.

Schwartz, G.E., Fair, P.L., Mandel, M.R., Salt, P., Mieske, M., & Klerman, G.L. (1978). Facial electromyography in the assessment of improvement of depression. *Psychosomatic Medicine, 40*, 355–360.

Schwartz, G.E., Fair, P.L., Salt, P., Mandel, M.R., & Klerman, G.L. (1976). Facial muscle patterning to affective imagery in depressed and nondepressed subjects. *Science, 192*, 489–491.

Shagass, C. (1972). Electrical activity of the brain. In N.S. Greenfield & R.A. Sternbach (Eds.), *Handbook of psychophysiology* (pp. 263–328). New York: Holt, Rinehart & Winston.

Shagass, C. (1977a). Early evoked potentials. *Schizophrenia Bulletin, 3*, 89–92.

Shagass, C. (1977b). Twisted thoughts, twisted brain waves? In C. Shagass, S. Gershon, & A.J. Friedhoff (Eds.), *Psychopathology and brain dysfunction* (pp. 353–378). New York: Raven Press.

Shagass, C. (1979). Early evoked potentials in psychosis. In H. Begleiter (Ed.), *Evoked brain potentials and behavior* (pp. 467–498). New York: Plenum Press.

Shagass, C. (1981). Neurophysiological evidence for different types of depression. *Journal of Behavioral Therapy and Experimental Psychiatry, 12*, 99–111.

Shagass, C., & Canter, A. (1972). Cerebral evoked responses and personality. In V.D. Nebylitsyn & J.A. Gray (Eds.), *Biological bases of individual behavior* (pp. 111–127). New York: Academic Press.

Shalling, D., Lindberg, L., Levander, S., & Dahlin, Y. (1973). Spontaneous activity as related to psychopathy. *Biological Psychology, 1*, 83–98.

Shapiro, D., & Schwartz, G.E. (1970). Psychophysiological contributions to social psychology. *Annual Review of Psychology, 21*, 87–112.

Siddle, D.A.T., & Trasler, G. (1981). The psychophysiology of psychopathic behavior. In M.J. Christie & P.G. Mellett (Eds.), *Foundations of psychosomatics* (pp. 283–303). London: John Wiley & Sons.

Siddle, D.A.T., & Turpin, G. (1980). Measurement, quantification, and analysis of cardiac activity. In I. Martin & P.H. Venables (Eds.), *Techniques in psychophysiology* (pp. 139–246). New York: John Wiley & Sons.

Silvia, E.S.M., Raczynski, J.M., & Kleinstein, R.N. (1984). Self-regulated facial muscle tension effects on intraocular pressure. *Psychophysiology, 21*, 79–82.

Sims, J., Carroll, D., Turner, J.R., & Hewitt, J.K. (1988). Cardiac and metabolic activity in mild hypertensive and normotensive subjects. *Psychophysiology, 25*, 172–178.

Sirota, A.D., Schwartz, G.E., & Kristeller, J.L. (1987). Facial muscle activity during induced mood states: Differential growth and carry-over of elated versus depressed moods. *Psychophysiology, 24*, 691–699.

Snyder, F., & Scott, J. (1972). The psychophysiology of sleep. In N.S. Greenfield & R.A. Sternbach (Eds.), *Handbook of psychophysiology* (pp. 645–708). New York: Holt, Rinehart & Winston.

Sokolov, E.N. (1963). *Perception and the conditioned reflex*. New York: MacMillan.

Sokolov, E.N. (1965). The orienting reflex, its structure and mechanisms. In L.G. Veronin, A.N. Leontrev, A.R. Luria, E.N. Sokolov, & O.S. Vinogradova (Eds.), *Orienting reflex and exploratory behaviour* (pp. 141–151). Washington, DC: American Institute of Biological Sciences.

Spohn, H.E., & Patterson, T. (1979). Recent studies of psychophysiology in schizophrenia. *Schizophrenia Bulletin, 5*, 581–611.

Stern, R.M., Farr, J.H., & Ray, W.J. (1975). Pleasure. In P.H. Venables & M.J. Christie (Eds.), *Research in psychophysiology* (pp. 208–233). New York: John Wiley & Sons.

Stern, J.A., & Janes, C.L. (1973). Personality and psychopathology. In W.F. Prokasy & D.C. Raskin (Eds.), *Electrodermal activity in psychological research* (pp. 248–346). New York: Academic Press.

Stern, R.M., Ray, W.J., & Davis, C.M. (1980). *Psychophysiological recording*. New York: Oxford University Press.

Strelau, J., Farley, F., & Gale, A. (Eds.). (1985). *The biological bases of personality and behavior*. Washington, DC: Hemisphere.

Stroebel, C.F. (1972). Psychophysiological pharmacology. In N.S. Greenfield & R.A. Sternbach (Eds.), *Handbook of psychophysiology* (pp. 787–834). New York: Holt, Rinehart & Winston.

Taylor, C.B., Sheikh, J., Agras, S., Roth, W.T., Margraf, J., Ehlers, A., Maddock, R.J., & Gossard, D. (1986). Ambulatory heart rate changes in patients with panic attacks. *American Journal of Psychiatry, 143*, 478–482.

Tecce, J.J. (1971). Contingent negative variation and individual differences. *Archives of General Psychiatry, 24*, 1–16.

Tecce, J.J. (1972). Contingent negative variation (CNV) and psychological processes in man. *Psychological Bulletin, 77*, 73–108.

Teplov, B.M. (1964). Problems in the study of general types of higher nervous activity in man and animals. In J.A. Gray (Ed.), *Pavlov's typology* (pp. 3–136). New York: MacMillan.

Tollison, C.D., & Adams, H.E. (1979). *Sexual disorders: Treatment, theory, and research*. New York: Academic Press.

Tucker, D.M. (1981). Lateral brain function, emotion, and conceptualization. *Psychological Bulletin, 89*, 19–46.

Tryon, W.W. (Ed.). (1985). *Behavioral assessment in behavioral medicine*. New York: Springer.

U.S. Department of Health, Education and Welfare. (1970). *Selected symptoms of psychological distress*. Rockville, MD: Author.

Venables, P.H. (1975a). Progress in psychophysiology: Some applications in a field of abnormal psychology. In P.H. Venables & M.J. Christie (Eds.), *Research in psychophysiology* (pp. 418–437). New York: John Wiley & Sons.

Venables, P.H. (1975b). Psychophysiological studies of schizophrenic pathology. In P.H. Venables & M.J. Christie (Eds.), *Research in psychophysiology* (pp. 282–324). New York: John Wiley & Sons.

Venables, P.H. (1977). The electrodermal psychophysiology of schizophrenics and children at risk for schizophrenia: Controversies and developments. *Schizophrenia Bulletin*, *3*, 28–48.

Wells, K.C. (1981). Assessment of children in outpatient settings. In M. Hersen & A.S. Bellack (Eds.), *Behavioral assessment: A practical handbook* (2nd ed., pp. 484–533). Elmsford, NY: Pergamon Press.

Whatmore, G.B., & Ellis, R.M. (1959). Some neurophysiologic aspects of depressed states: An electromyographic study. *Archives of General Psychiatry*, *1*, 70–80.

Whatmore, G.B., & Ellis, R.M. (1962). Further neurophysiologic aspects of depressed states: An electromyographic study. *Archives of General Psychiatry*, *6*, 243–253.

White, A.A., & Gordon, S.L. (1982). Synopsis: Workshop on idiographic low-back pain. *Spine*, *7*, 141–149.

Whybrow, P.C., & Mendels, J. (1969). Toward a biology of depression: Some suggestions from neurophysiology. *American Journal of Psychiatry*, *125*, 1491–1500.

Wilder, J. (1967). *Stimulus and response: The law of initial value*. Bristol: Wright.

Williams, D.E., Thompson, J.K., Haber, J.D., & Raczynski, J.M. (1986). MMPI and headache: A review of the literature with special focus on differential diagnosis, prediction of outcome, and client-treatment matching. *Pain*, *24*, 143–158.

Wincze, J.P., & Lange, J.D. (1981). Assessment of sexual behavior. In D. Barlow (Ed.), *Behavioral assessment of adult disorders* (pp. 301–328). New York: Guilford Press.

Woodruff, D.A. (1978). Brain electrical activity and behavior relationships over the life span. In P. Baltes (Ed.), *Life span development and behavior* (Vol. 1, pp. 112–181). New York: Academic Press.

Zahn, T. (1975). Psychophysiological concomitants of task performance in schizophrenia. In M. Kietzman, S. Sutton, & J. Zubin (Eds.), *Experimental approaches to psychopathology* (pp. 109–131). New York: Academic Press.

Zahn, T. (1977). Autonomic nervous system characteristics possibly related to a genetic predisposition to schizophrenia. *Schizophrenia Bulletin*, *3*, 49–60.

Zahn, T., Carpenter, W.T., & McGlashan, T.H. (1981). Autonomic nervous system responsivity in acute schizophrenia. *Archives of General Psychiatry*, *38*, 251–266.

Zahn, T., Schooler, C., & Kammen, D.P. (1985). Autonomic activity in unmedicated schizophrenics during task performance. *Psychophysiology*, *22*, 619–620.

Zautra, A.J., Okun, M.A., Robinson, S.E., Lee, D., Roth, S.H., & Emmanual, J. (1989). Life stress and lymphocyte alterations among patients with rheumatoid arthritis. *Health Psychology*, *8*, 1–14.

Zubin, J., & Shagass, C. (Eds.). (1969). *Neurobiological aspects of psychopathology*. New York: Grune & Stratton.

Zuckerman, M. (1971). Physiological measures of sexual arousal in the human. *Psychological Bulletin*, *75*, 297–329.

Zuckerman, M. (1972). Physiological measures of sexual arousal in the human. In N.S. Greenfield & T.A. Sternbach (Eds.), *Handbook of psychophysiology* (pp. 709–742). New York: Holt, Rinehart & Winston.

Zuckerman, M., Buchsbaum, M.S., & Murphy, D.L. (1980). Sensation seeking and its biological correlates. *Psychological Bulletin*, *88*, 187–214.

CHAPTER 26

MEDICAL ASSESSMENT

Anselm George

THE CLINICAL PROBLEM

The need for a medical evaluation of persons seeking treatment for various psychological symptoms may first be illuminated by the following case vignette from my clinical practice.

    T.F. was a 36-year-old white single Jewish woman who presented to the psychiatric emergency room with complaints of depression and thoughts of suicide. The patient said that she felt more desperate and worried after she had been hospitalized for chest pain a month ago, and was discharged with a diagnosis of costochondritis. The patient was known to have adult onset diabetes mellitus (Type 2) and was controlled on insulin.
    The patient related that she had always had low self-esteem and was shy as a teenager. When she was 17 years old her mother died. Subsequently, the patient was involuntarily hospitalized for depression, treated with electroconvulsive therapy (ECT), and spent more than a year in a state hospital. After discharge, she obtained a high school equivalency diploma and worked in several secretarial positions. Because of several recent health problems, she lost her job and had returned to live with her elderly father. Her social contacts outside the home dwindled.
    The patient was diagnosed in the emergency room with a major depressive disorder and referred for outpatient therapy. She was encouraged to get medical follow-up by her private doctor, but since she lost her insurance and owed a considerable amount of money she hesitated to see him. Since the patient's general health seemed to decline, she was finally urged to be evaluated at the medical clinic associated with our psychiatric hospital. Her diabetes was found to be in poor control and an enlarged thyroid gland together with tremor and elevated thyroid function tests were discovered. Work-up and conservative therapy for Graves's disease was initiated, but her thyroid functions and her diabetes remained poorly controlled. Psychiatrically, she continued to complain of depression and anxiety. Her tremor was becoming more and more noticeable. Because of increasing suicidal ideation, hospitalization was discussed but she adamantly refused, citing her past traumatic experience as a reason. The patient also refused radioactive iodine treatment of her hyperthyroidism, which is normally performed on an outpatient basis. At this point, the treating psychiatrist as well as the internists were gravely concerned about the patient. T.F. was finally admitted to the medical hospital with thyrotoxicosis and thyroid storm. She was put on suicide precautions and followed by the psychiatric consultation liaison service. She underwent a successful uncomplicated subtotal thyroidectomy with rapid improvement in her general health. The patient now agreed to a voluntary transfer to the psychiatric hospital where she was treated with the antidepressant phenelzine, a monoamine oxidase in-

hibitor (MAOI). Her mood improved, suicidal ideation diminished and her diabetes could now be easily
controlled with oral hypoglycemic medications. After 2 weeks, the patient was discharged and continued
in outpatient follow-up for her medical as well as
psychiatric problems.

Two months after her hospitalization, an attempt to
withdraw her antidepressant medication had to be
aborted because of increased anxiety, depression,
and sleeplessness. T.F. did quite well, moved out of
her father's house, found a rewarding interpersonal
relationship, and engaged in vocational rehabilitation
with plans to improve her education.

This case illustrates that etiology is often multifactorial. It seems fair to conclude that physical conditions, psychiatric symptoms, and social factors all
exerted a powerful influence on this patient's treatment. The interdependence of joint assessment and
treatment of psychiatric and medical problems is
clearly evident and fundamental to the successful
outcome of this case.

CONCEPTUAL ISSUES

The task of finding medical explanations for psychological symptoms is traditionally predicated on a
dichotomy between psychological disorders and medical illnesses, or organic versus functional disorders.
Such a distinction has always been logically unsatis-
factory and may be unnecessary for the task of medical
evaluation. Most medical illnesses have psychological symptoms, and patients with psychological disturbances may complain of somatic symptoms. Biological psychiatry, which has enjoyed increased popularity recently, contributes to the blurring of the
functional versus organic dichotomy by suggesting
that biological abnormalities are responsible for functional disorders. At the same time the distinction
between psychobiological research and medical evaluation becomes unclear. For example, the Dexamethasone Suppression Test can be used for the
diagnosis of Cushing's disease in medical assessment,
and a slightly refined version of the same test has been
suggested as a research tool to evaluate melancholia.

However, we think that the goals of medical evaluation and psychobiological research are different and
would suggest the following distinction: The goal of
biological research is the elucidation of previously
unknown biological factors that are thought to be of
etiological significance for a given psychiatric disorder. In contrast, the goal of the medical assessment is
the diagnosis of *established medical disorders* in
psychiatric patients (i.e., comorbidity) regardless of
etiological significance. All too often, research tools

have been prematurely introduced in the arena of
standard medical evaluation.

As an alternative to evaluating the medical versus
psychological dichotomy, we would suggest viewing
all disorders in question along the following continuum: On one end are disorders with known etiology
and pathogenesis for which specific and effective
treatments are available; on the other end are syndromes with unknown etiology, pathogenesis, and
unspecific, ineffective treatments. We can now reframe our task as follows: The goal of medical evaluation is to find the disorders with the best known
etiology and the most specific treatment that could
explain the patient's problems. Because most psychological problems are still unspecific syndromes, such
an investigation may lead to the more specific medical
illnesses. However, this is not necessarily true. As
more becomes known about psychiatric disorders and
their treatment, a psychological diagnosis may form a
better basis for treatment planning than some medical
diagnoses. A clinician faced with a differential diagnosis of multiple sclerosis versus major depressive
disorder, for example, may choose to treat the latter on
the basis of a better known etiology, more effective
treatment, and better prognosis without endangering
the patient. For the nonmedically trained reader, it is
also important to point out that medicine is not free of
nebulous (and sometimes fashionable) entities that
convey few insights into etiology and treatment. Examples of these disorders are discussed later. Such
entities should have no precedence in diagnosis over
well-founded psychiatric disorders.

The greatest mistakes in medical evaluation are
made if a serious, even life-threatening illness is
overlooked for which specific treatment would be
available, and the patient is subjected to a lengthy,
costly, and less effective psychological treatment.

Medical evaluation also serves the purpose of decreasing the morbidity and mortality of patients with
chronic *unrelated* psychopathology. Chronic psychiatric patients often receive inferior medical care with
detrimental consequences.

When investigating the coexistence of medical
disorders with psychological syndromes these two
areas may have the following etiological relationships
with each other (Dietch & Zetin, 1983):

1. Patients may present with a "medical" complaint
   but are subsequently found to have a "functional"
   psychological disorder; for example, a patient
   complains of palpitations, shortness of breath, or
   stomach upset and is diagnosed with an anxiety
   disorder.

2. Patients may present with psychological complaints but are diagnosed with a medical "organic" disorder; for example, complaints of low mood, loss of energy, and weight loss are found to be secondary to an occult cancer.

3. Psychological symptoms may occur as "normal" reactions to the awareness of a serious medical illness or the associated impairment; for example, anxiety after a heart attack or depression in the end stages of a malignant disease.

4. The psychological disorder and the medical condition may be independent and/or occurring together.

As long as the etiologies of most psychological disturbances are unclear and the diagnoses are established using an assortment of unspecific symptoms, it is difficult or impossible to decide which of these relationships are operating in a given case.

Because of the overlap in symptomatology between medical and psychological disorders, we can predict that psychological complaints will be spuriously increased in patient samples with defined medical diagnoses. However, if we start by defining a psychiatric patient population and search for medical disorders, this effect would not be as important because specific (laboratory) techniques could be used for the diagnosis of the medical illness. We will later discuss specific examples of this phenomenon. These studies show that medical patients have a high psychiatric comorbidity, whereas psychiatric diagnostic groups do not yield comparable levels of medical comorbidity.

COMORBIDITY BETWEEN MEDICAL AND PSYCHOLOGICAL SYNDROMES

To what degree, then, can we demonstrate more specific diagnostic entities in relatively unselected patients presenting with psychological symptoms? The answer depends on the patient population, the practice setting, and on the methods used to make these diagnoses. Table 26.1 gives an overview of the literature dealing with relatively unselected psychiatric patients. We can conclude the following:

1. Approximately 30% to 80% of these patients have significant medical problems. Five to 40% have specific medical problems considered to have etiological significance for the presenting psychological complaint.

2. Although the percentages vary among different studies, the numbers are clearly greater than the prevalence of medical disorders in the population at large.

3. It is not sufficiently clear whether the medical disorders seen in a psychiatric population differ significantly from the groups and classes of medical problems seen in comparable primary care medical settings.

4. Because of this large degree of comorbidity, it is from the public health standpoint advisable and cost-effective to provide easy access, primary medical care to psychiatric patients. This is particularly necessary for patients from lower socioeconomic status backgrounds (Hall, Beresford, Gardner, & Popkin, 1982).

MEDICAL CONSIDERATIONS IN SPECIFIC PSYCHOLOGICAL SYNDROMES

It can be generally stated that every psychiatric symptom can occasionally be caused by a well-established medical condition and conversely that a large number of diseases can present with psychological symptoms. This chapter cannot present an exhaustive account of all these interactions. The reader is referred to several more comprehensive books on this subject (Hall, 1980; Koranyi, 1982; Lishman, 1987; Stoudemire & Fogel, 1987). Nevertheless, the clinician needs to know the most common examples of overlap so that he or she can request a full-scale medical evaluation when appropriate. We will start with prevalent psychological complaints and discuss briefly the major medical correlates.

Anxiety

Anxiety is a very common complaint known by several different names (cardiac neurosis, effort syndrome, irritable heart, hyperdynamic beta adrenergic circulating state (Frohlich, Tarazi, & Dustan, 1969). From the earliest descriptions (DaCosta, 1871) a disordered function of the heart was a central feature of anxiety. Overlap with cardiovascular and respiratory conditions remains a prominent feature today. If an organic etiology of anxiety has been established, the condition is diagnosed according to *The Diagnostic and Statistical Manual of Mental Disorders. Third Edition Revised* (DSM-III-R, APA, 1987) as an organic anxiety disorder on Axis I. The associated physical disorder is listed on Axis III.

Table 26.1. Studies of the Comorbidity Between Medical and Psychological Syndromes

AUTHOR	YEAR	POPULATION STUDIED	METHOD	% OF PATIENTS WITH MEDICAL ILLNESS	% OF PATIENTS WITH ILLNESSES CONSIDERED CAUSATIVE
Comroe	1936	100 Medical outpatients "neurotic"	2 year follow-up	24%	11% Causative or contributory
Phillips	1937	164 Inpatients	?	45% Serious	
Marshall	1949	175 Inpatients	?	44% Needing treatment	22% Contributory
Herridge	1960	209 Inpatients	Chart review	50% (21% "Concomitant")	5% Causative
Davis	1965	72 Outpatients	?	51%	36% Related
Johnson	1968	250 Inpatients	Physical	—	12% Causative
Maguire & Granville-Grossman	1968	200 Inpatients	?	33.5%	23.5% "Severe"
Hall et al.	1978	658 Outpatients	History, physical, biochemical screening	—	9.1% Causative
Hall et al.	1980	100 Inpatients	History, physical, biochemical screening CBC, etc.	80% Needing treatment	46% Causative or exacerbating
Maricle et al.	1987	43 Outpatients	History, physical, biochemical screening CBC, etc.	88% (46% Required follow-up)	3.5% Causal 19% Exacerbating
Lima & Pai	1987	427 Outpatients	Chart review	32% Major	—

Coronary Insufficiency

Patients with sudden anxiety attacks are frequently admitted to emergency rooms for fear of a "heart attack." Although in classical presentations of angina pectoris and myocardial infarction severe chest pain is the most prominent symptom, this pain can at times be less pronounced (described as "tightness" or "pressure") or localized elsewhere (back, neck, jaw, left arm, and the gastric area). These symptoms are typically provoked by exercise and sometimes associated with dyspnea, nausea, or diaphoresis. A whole spectrum of diagnostic tests is available ranging from simple electrocardiograms to cardiac catheterization. With the use of selected Thallium Stress tests, a 90% sensitivity and specificity for detecting significant coronary artery disease in a noninvasive manner has been achieved (Willerson, 1988).

Paroxysmal Supraventrical Tachycardia

Among the cardiac arrhythmias the paroxysmal supraventricular tachycardia most frequently gives rise to complaints of anxiety. These attacks start abruptly and end abruptly compared to the waxing and waning course of panic attacks. During the attacks, the heart rate is in the range of 150 to 220 beats per minute, which is associated with the sensation of fear and palpitation (Bigger, 1988). In contrast, the heart rate during anxiety attacks rarely exceeds 140 beats per minute (Lader, 1972). Patients with paroxysmal supraventricular tachycardia sometimes learn certain maneuvers (coughing, valsalva maneuver) that interrupt the attack. The diagnosis is usually made by recording the electrocardiogram during the attack. Paroxysmal supraventricular tachycardia is, in uncomplicated cases, a benign disorder requiring little more treatment than reassurance. As with all cardiac arrhythmias, an ambulatory 24-hour ECG recording (Holter monitor) may be required to detect and quantify these problems.

Mitral Valve Prolapse

This condition has been found to be associated with panic anxiety and is caused by defective valve leaflets that protrude into the left atrium of the heart during the systole and emit a characteristic click. The definitive diagnosis is made by echocardiography (Rackley, 1988). If treatment is necessary, beta-blocking drugs are advocated. These are also effective against other manifestations of anxiety disorders, reducing the therapeutic consequences of the diagnosis of mitral valve prolapse. The nature and extent of the association between the anatomical abnormality, impaired function of the mitral valve, associated symptoms, and anxiety remains unclear. The mitral valve prolapse syndrome and panic attacks both share symptoms such as lightheadedness, fainting, chest discomfort, and palpitations. Both conditions occur in approximately 5% of the general population and predominantly in women (Dager et al., 1986). Current data make it unlikely that the anatomical defect of the mitral valve causes anxiety attacks. It is more likely that hemodynamic changes related to beta adrenergic hyperactivity as seen in anxiety states unmask the cardiac dysfunction and account for the statistical association in the literature (Crowe, 1985; Davies et al., 1987). Most authors do not recommend routine echocardiograms for every patient with panic or anxiety symptoms because of the limited therapeutic consequences resulting from a diagnosis of mitral valve prolapse. Telling a somatically preoccupied anxious patient that he or she has a defective heart valve may also be counterproductive from a psychotherapeutic point of view (Klein & Gorman, 1984).

Hypoglycemia

This is another frequently quoted medical condition associated with anxiety. Although it is true that anxiety, tachycardia, tremor, and lightheadedness occur during the hypoglycemic attacks experienced by diabetics, more severe forms of panic anxiety are unusual during these episodes (Raj & Sheehan, 1988). Patients who suffer from panic disorder can distinguish artificially induced hypoglycemia from their usual panic attacks (Uhde, Vittone, & Post, 1984). Although there are several serious medical conditions marked by hypoglycemia, the diagnosis of reactive (postprandial) hypoglycemia as an explanation for anxiety symptoms is vastly overused. The reliance on the standard oral glucose tolerance test for the diagnosis of this condition is fraught with several problems that are well documented (Service, 1988). Work-up for hypoglycemia should be considered if anxiety symptoms occur after meals, if they are accompanied by hunger or if the patient has a history of gastric surgery (Raj & Sheehan, 1987). The cornerstone of the medical work-up is the demonstration that a blood glucose below 40 mg/dl is associated with symptoms and that these symptoms are relieved by the correction of hypoglycemia.

Hyperthyroidism

As our initial example highlights, *hyperthyroidism* is frequently associated with anxiety. Emotional lability, fine tremor of the extremities, weight loss with increased appetite, palpitations, heat intolerance, and muscle weakness are other common symptoms. The physical examination reveals tachycardia, enlargement of the thyroid gland, warm smooth skin and the classical bulging eyes of Graves's ophthalmopathy. The most valuable laboratory screening test is the determination of the free T_4 Index, which is almost always elevated (Larsen, 1988). Examining 13 patients with untreated hyperthyroidism (Graves's disease; Trzepacz et al., 1988) demonstrated that 8 out of 13 patients met the diagnosis of generalized anxiety disorder using standardized criteria. These authors commented that the severity of psychiatric symptoms could easily result in an inappropriate referral to a psychiatrist prior to the diagnosis of hyperthyroidism. Determining the thyroid status of patients with DSM-III anxiety disorders has yielded the following results: 9.2% of phobic patients (Lindemann, Zitrin, & Klein, 1984) and 8% of patients with panic disorder (Lesser et al., 1987) reported some form of thyroid dysfunction. Both papers concluded that this exceeded the expectation of thyroid problems in the general population. Lack of a control group and retrospective analysis of patient reports weakened these conclusions. Other reports based on laboratory evidence (Fishman, Sheehan, & Carr, 1985; Lesser et al., 1987; Munjack & Palmer, 1988; Pariser et al., 1979; Stein & Uhde, 1988, 1989) found no difference in thyroid function of patients with panic disorders and other anxiety disorders compared to controls. We would conclude from these data that patients who complain of unusual anxiety features (e.g., heat intolerance, restlessness, increased appetite), need a laboratory screening for thyroid abnormalities.

The evaluation of thyroid function tests is not without potential sources of confusion. For example, patients hospitalized for acute psychiatric disorders have a high incidence of elevated T_4 hormone (Spratt et al., 1982). This abnormality returns to normal a few weeks after hospitalization (transient hyperthyroxinemia) and must be distinguished from thyrotoxicosis (Borst, Eil, & Burman, 1983). We will discuss hypothyroidism in the section on depression.

Drug-Induced Syndromes

Among the other medical causes of anxiety listed in Table 26.2, the long list of drug-related anxiety syndromes needs to be specially emphasized. Alcohol abuse/dependence and phobias are among the most prevalent psychiatric disorders (Myers et al., 1984; Robins et al., 1984). In addition, the risk of alcohol-

Table 26.2. Medical Disorders Associated with Anxiety

Cardiovascular—Respiratory
  Cardiac arrhythmias
  Coronary insufficiency
  Congestive heart failure
  Mitral valve prolapse
  Asthma
  Chronic obstructive pulmonary disease
  Hyperventilation syndrome

Endocrine
  Thyroid dysfunction
  Parathyroid dysfunction
  Hypoglycemia
  Pheochromocytoma
  Carcinoid
  Adrenal cortical dysfunctions

Neurological
  Epilepsy (complex partial seizure)
  Organic brain syndromes (delirium, dementia, etc.)
  Post-concussion syndrome
  Post-encephalitis syndrome
  Huntington's chorea
  Hepatolenticular degeneration (Wilson's disease)
  Vestibular dysfunction

Drug-Induced Syndromes
  Intoxications
    Caffeine
    Cocaine
    Hallucinogens
    Stimulants, etc.

  Withdrawal
    Alcohol
    Opioids
    Sedative hypnotics

Miscellaneous Conditions
  Collagen vascular disease
  Chronic infections
  Malignancies

ism in persons with phobias of any type is about 2.5 times higher than in the general population (Weissman, 1988). Because alcohol and drug abuse are frequently kept secret by patients, these conditions are probably the most frequently overlooked "medical" causes of anxiety. A careful inquiry into substance use patterns is a mandatory part of the evaluation of anxious patients. This can be augmented if necessary by urine drug testing.

Medical Conditions Associated With Mood Disorders

The comorbidity between depression and physical illness has recently been reviewed (Schulberg, McClelland, & Burns, 1987). Table 26.3 gives an overview of conditions frequently associated with mood disorders. These conditions are diagnosed according to DSM-III-R (APA, 1987) as organic mood disorder on Axis I. The predominant mood is specified as manic, depressed, or mixed. The associated physical disorder is listed on Axis III. Of these disorders, depression is by far the most common and also the most likely to be confused with medical conditions.

Cancer

The relationship between various cancers and depression is a multifaceted one and has recently been reviewed by Noyes and Kathol (1986). There is no doubt that depression is a frequent complication of neoplastic disease. Approximately 50% of the psychiatric consultations on cancer patients receive the diagnosis of depression (Levine, Silberfarb, & Lipowski, 1978). Even reports using defined criteria for various depressive disorders yield a wide range of results depending on the severity of the medical condition. Some of the difficulties result from the overlap in symptomatology between the depressive disorder and the neoplasm (e.g., weight loss, loss of energy, or fatigue) which we discussed earlier.

Studies of depression in cancer patients lead to the conclusion that this form of depression is less severe than in psychiatric populations as indicated by fewer of the following indicators: psychotic symptoms, melancholia, guilt feelings, low self-esteem, and suicidal ideation. This would lead to the possibility that much of the observed depression in cancer patients is due to the psychological response to a serious disease or its treatment.

Biological mechanisms, however, may also be important. The most frequently quoted example is the carcinoma of the pancreas in which depression is frequently an early symptom preceding physical manifestations by an average of 6 months (Fras, Litin, & Pearson, 1967). Seventy-six percent of the patient group with carcinoma of the pancreas had psychiatric symptoms. The most characteristic depressive complaint was loss of ambition. Feelings of guilt and worthlessness were rare. A control group of patients with colon cancer showed a low incidence of psychiatric symptoms. In spite of great advances in the diagnosis of pancreatic cancer, patients are still coming to medical attention so late that the tumor has frequently already spread to other organs. It may well be that a growing tumor of considerable size leads (via unclear mechanisms) initially to unspecific symptoms, such as loss of ambition, which are followed only after a considerable lag time by more specific abdominal complaints. This would argue for mecha-

nisms shared to varying degrees by other malignancies (Jacobsson & Ottosson, 1971) and maybe by other catastrophic illnesses.

Chronic Epstein-Barr Virus Infection

Recently, the association of a syndrome of chronic fatigue and malaise with chronic Epstein-Barr virus (EBV) infection (the chronic form of infectious mononucleosis) has received considerable attention in the professional (Jones, Ray, & Minnich, 1985; Straus et al., 1985) and lay (Hartley, 1985) literature. In addition to fatigue, the syndrome is characterized by such symptoms as headaches, muscle and joint pain, fever, sore throat, painful lymph nodes, weight loss, sleep disturbance, and so forth. It is known by various names such as chronic mononucleosis, yuppie-flu, chronic fatigue syndrome, and chronic Epstein-Barr virus syndrome. Because fatigue is often a symptom of depression, a number of difficult diagnostic issues have to be answered. Most recently, this research has concentrated on the definition of a chronic fatigue syndrome (Holmes et al., 1988) independent of assumed etiology. The association of this syndrome with laboratory evidence for viral diseases on one hand and depressive disorder on the other can then be evaluated. Fatigue is one of the most common complaints in primary medical care (Koch, 1978) occasionally causing serious disability (Kroenke et al., 1988). Furthermore, more than 90% of adults have been infected with EBV (Kieff, 1988). A majority of chronic fatigue patients meet criteria for one or more psychiatric diagnoses, chiefly depression and anxiety disorders (Kroenke et al., 1988; Manu, Lane, & Matthews, 1988). There is little evidence that the chronic fatigue syndrome is causally related to the EBV (Buchwald, Sullivan, & Komaroff, 1987; Hellinger et al., 1988; Holmes et al., 1987).

When patients were selected on the basis of a depressive disorder, no significant differences between patients and control subjects were found in three studies (Amsterdam et al., 1986; DeLisi et al., 1986; Miller et al., 1986). One uncontrolled study of 12 patients claimed a causal relationship between depression and EBV infection (Allen & Tilkian, 1986). These data would indicate that patients complaining of chronic fatigue may have several and often unknown disorders. EBV may play only a minor etiological role, and psychiatric syndromes need to be primarily considered. The therapy of chronic fatigue syndromes is in its infancy. Patients with major depressive disorder are not likely to suffer from chronic EBV syndrome and the clinical determination of antibody profiles is not recommended for most depressed patients.

Hypothyroidism

Psychological consequences of hypothyroidism (myxedema) have been clearly described in the previous century. Whereas in these early accounts psychotic manifestations were prominent ("myxedematous madness" [Ascher, 1949]), today depression and impaired cognitive functions are more common mental sequelae of hypothyroidism because of earlier detection. Since sophisticated assays for all hormones of the hypothalamic pituitary thyroid axis have become available, three stages of primary hypothyroidism are generally recognized. The subclinical and mild stage do not involve consistently reduced thyroid hormone levels or overt signs of myxedema. Using this classification, investigators (Gold, Pottash, & Extein, 1981) found that 20 of 250 patients with depression or anergia had some form of hypothyroidism. Only two patients had the overt disorder; the remainder was mild or subclinical. At present, it is unclear which of these disorders requires hormone replacement, and how such a treatment may influence the course of a depressive episode (Brent & Hershman, 1986).

A considerable amount of research has been conducted on the function of the hypothalamic pituitary thyroid axis in affective disorders (Prange, Garbutt, & Loosen, 1987). This research has yielded important results. For example, the thyrotropin-releasing hormone (TRH) stimulation test has been found to be abnormally blunted in approximately 25% of depressed patients (Loosen & Prange, 1982). Another result is the possible potentiation of antidepressant effects by thyroid hormones in patients not responding to standard pharmacotherapy (Goodwin et al., 1982). Nevertheless, as discussed before, it would be premature to make the TRH stimulation test part of a routine medical evaluation. Even more misguided would be to label patients with abnormal endocrine responses as suffering from clinical thyroid disease rather than depressive disorders.

More has also been learned about conditions that produce falsely low thyroid hormone levels in the absence of thyroid disease. The "euthyroid sick syndrome" (Wartofsky & Burman, 1982) is characterized by low T_3 levels in normal or slightly reduced T_4 and normal TSH levels. This pattern is due to impaired conversion of T_4 to T_3 and occurs in a wide range of serious illnesses, in starvation, and in some psychiatric patients (Chopra et al., 1979; Linnoila et al., 1982).

From the preceding discussion, it is quite clear that the evaluation of abnormal thyroid tests in psychiatric patients requires the expert judgment of a skilled endocrinologist.

Cushings Syndrome

This group of disorders is characterized by an excess of glucocorticoid hormones (principally cortisol). The most frequent clinical features are truncal obesity, facial hair growth (in women), hypertension, and muscle weakness. This syndrome is commonly seen in patients receiving steroid therapy. The rare spontaneous cases are often caused by pituitary tumors secreting increased amounts of adrenocorticotrophic hormone (ACTH). This disorder affects predominantly women between 20 and 40 years of age (Tyrrell & Baxter, 1988).

Psychological symptoms occur in a variety of forms and severities in approximately 50% of the cases. These symptoms include depression as well as mania and delusional syndromes and are summarized adequately in the older literature (Sachar, 1975).

The diagnostic work-up for Cushings syndrome includes measurement of urinary free cortisol levels and the dexamethasone suppression test.

This last test has generated an enormous literature based on the initial finding that 67% of melancholic patients had abnormal test results (Carroll et al., 1981). These data are reviewed elsewhere (Arana & Baldessarini, 1987). It appears that hopes of finding a simple laboratory test for melancholia have faded somewhat recently, but that an increasingly complicated knowledge base regarding hypothalamic-pituitary-adrenal feedback mechanisms has been generated. These data make simple distinctions between depression and endocrine disease difficult and increase the need for consultations between medical disciplines.

Secondary Mania

Manic symptoms are usually regarded as indicative of a bipolar disorder ("primary mania"). However, numerous reports have appeared in the literature describing manic symptoms related to a variety of medical conditions. These "secondary" manias are generally rare and the associated illnesses are listed in Table 26.3. Nevertheless, it is important for the clinician to realize that medical evaluation is necessary in even classic manic presentations. The drug-induced cases were recently reviewed (Sultzer & Cummings, 1989). Anabolic steroids, as used by athletes to increase muscle strength, present a consid-

Table 26.3. Medical Conditions Associated with Mood Disorders

Drug Induced Syndromes
Steroids: M,D
Dopamingergic Agents: M
(CNS) Stimulants, Appetite Suppressants: M
Sedatives, Anxiolytics: D
Thyroid Hormones: M
Hallucinogens: M
Antihypertensives: D

Endocrine
Cushing's Syndrome: D,M
Hypothyroidism: D
Diabetes Mellitus: D
Menopause, Postparum Disorders: D

Neurological
Cerebral Infarction: D,M
Brain Tumors: D
Epilepsy: D
Infections, e.g., EBV or HIV: D
Degenerative diseases of the CNS: D
Head Injury: D

Miscellaneous Conditions
Malignancies: D
Nutritional Disorders: D
Collagen Vascular Diseases: D

D = primarily depression
M = primarily mania

erable risk for serious manic symptoms. Fourteen out of 41 subjects interviewed (Pope & Katz, 1988) experienced these problems during periods of steroid use and 5 developed withdrawal depression. Cases of encephalitis or brain injury are also often reported (Krauthammer & Klerman, 1978). It appears in the latter group that an interaction between location of the injury in the right hemisphere and genetic factors contribute to the development of mania (Robinson, et al., 1988).

Hallucinosis And Delusional Syndrome

These syndromes are often collectively referred to as *organic psychosis* (Cummings, 1988). They are diagnosed when persistent hallucinations or delusions occur in the presence of a clear sensorium, that is, without further symptoms indicating a delirium. According to DSM-III-R, Organic Delusional Disorder or Organic Hallucinosis is specified on Axis I and the associated medical condition is indicated on Axis III (APA, 1987). If the organic psychosis is characterized equally by delusions and hallucinations, both conditions should be diagnosed.

There is general agreement that the first onset of an acute psychotic disorder requires an extensive medical evaluation. Therefore, the discussion of these conditions can remain brief. Again, a whole host of medical conditions needs to be considered. Some of them are temporal lobe epilepsy, degenerative diseases of the Central Nervous System (CNS), brain tumors, cerebral infarction, amphetamine intoxication, viral encephalitis (Torrey, 1986), and so forth. The importance of these conditions lies in the fact that they can, at times, be indistinguishable from schizophrenia with respect to formal thought disorder and Schneiderian first rank symptoms (Lishman, 1987).

To confuse the issues further, certain psychoses are sometimes called "organic" on the basis of certain symptoms such as disorientation, disturbance of memory, and visual hallucinations rather than on the basis of their etiology (Hays, 1985). However, it would be dangerous to limit medical evaluation only to those disorders with "organic" features. A recent comparison of the phenomenology of psychoses secondary to medical disorders versus patients meeting criteria for schizophrenia, mania, and depression found few significant differences between these groups and considerable overlap (Johnstone et al., 1988).

AIDS-Related Problems

Issues related to infection with the human immunodeficiency virus (HIV) are of such importance for the medical evaluation that a few principles should be summarized here. A more comprehensive review can be found elsewhere (Ostrow, Grant & Atkinson, 1988; Perry, 1990a). The clinician will start to suspect acquired immunodeficiency syndrome (AIDS) related problems when he or she identifies one of the following risk factors: (a) men engaging in homosexual activity, (b) intravenous drug users, (c) people receiving blood or blood products between 1978 and 1985, and, (d) sexual partners of the above three groups. In connection with the AIDS epidemic, a whole spectrum of psychological problems have occurred which follow the principles discussed earlier.

Even before infection has taken place, high risk behaviors may be accompanied by overwhelming anxiety and guilt. Misinformation about routes of transmission may lead to emotional reactions far out of proportion to the actual medical risk. Some patients have the hypochondriacal preoccupation that they have symptoms of AIDS in spite of repeated negative HIV tests. This group has been given the misleading name "worried well" (Faulstich, 1987).

Transient adjustment reactions also occur surrounding HIV testing. Testing should therefore be done only with extensive pre- and posttest counseling. In the pretest session, the following areas should be covered: (a) education about the nature of the HIV infection and routes of transmission; (b) explanation of the meaning of the test; (c) discussion of the impact of the test results on the patient's lifestyle, behaviors, employment, insurance, and social supports; (d) confidentiality of the test results; and (e) exploration of potential sources of exposure. Informed consent should be obtained during this session. During the posttest session, the results of the HIV test are explained and, if positive, the following areas are discussed: ways to prevent HIV transmission to others; the need that the patient notify others who might have been exposed; and requirements for continuing medical care. During this session, the patient should be given ample opportunity to express his emotions regarding the impact of the test result on his future health and his daily life.

Later in the course of HIV infection more serious "functional" psychiatric disorders may develop (Miller & Riccio, 1990), chiefly major depressive disorder but also delusional syndromes and hypomania. At the present state of our knowledge, it is not sufficiently clear whether these disturbances represent early symptoms of an HIV-related organic mental disorder or are mediated by changes in psychosocial status which occur when the first signs of the disease become manifest. The clinician needs to be aware of an increased risk of suicide at this stage (Marzuk, Tierney, & Tardiff, 1988). Further, pre-existing psychiatric disorders in the homosexual high risk group are quite significant (Atkinson et al., 1988).

The HIV also affects the CNS directly. Early in the course of infection it can be cultured in the spinal fluid of affected individuals. Symptoms of an organic mental disorder are very likely to occur at some time during the course of this disease. However, it remains unclear to what extent the virus causes impaired cognitive functioning in otherwise symptom-free individuals. Early mental changes in the form of altered personality, apathy, mental slowing, and social withdrawal may easily be attributed to psychological causes (Ostrow et al., 1988; Perry, 1990b). Recent studies have not been able to guide the clinician in providing reliable and practical methods for diagnosing these early mental changes. Numerous preliminary data are reviewed by Perry (1990). In the absence of a "gold standard," combined use of the mental status examination, more extensive neuropsychological testing, neurological examination, electroencephalogram, and sophisticated imaging studies such as magnetic resonance imaging (MRI) or single photon emission computed tomography (SPECT) may lead to an informed clinical judgment. Antiviral treatment with zidovudine (AZT) may result in mea-

surable psychological improvement (Schmitt et al., 1988).

PRACTICAL CONSIDERATIONS OF MEDICAL ASSESSMENT

Referral Patterns

The clinician evaluating patients with primarily psychological complaints needs to decide which of these patients need medical evaluations and how to obtain these consultations. As we have seen, patients with the three syndromes of anxiety, mood disorders, and psychosis need special attention.

Patient complaints have been divided in three areas (Hollender & Wells, 1980): those involving (a) the body (e.g., headaches, weakness, and palpitations), (b) the mind (e.g., depression, anxiety, hallucinations, and delusions), and (c) social interactions (e.g., difficulties with teachers, parents, or spouses). These authors suggest that when problems are limited to the social sphere, medical assessment is not necessary.

Clinical psychologists practice in very different settings, and this will have an impact on the need for medical assessment and the availability of medical consultation. Clinicians practicing in clinics catering to lower income and geriatric populations will see more medical problems than those seeing primarily affluent or adolescent groups. In medical settings, good consultations may be more readily available than in a solo private practice.

The source of the referral also needs to be considered. If patients are referred from a *primary care physician*, the first information about the patient's medical status should usually be obtained from that source. However, the patient may have presented to this physician with a specific complaint, and the medical evaluation may have been limited to that problem. In this situation, the patient should be sent back to the physician with a request for a comprehensive assessment highlighting specific areas of concern. Such an assessment can be considered a reliable baseline, but it does not rule out pathology with certainty. If new somatic symptoms surface during treatment, additional tests should be ordered or a consultation with a medical specialist requested. It is important that the possibility of a medical disorder not be prematurely dismissed.

In a *self-referred patient*, who complains of symptoms suggestive of a medical disorder, obtaining a medical consultation may be more problematic. Although some authorities advocate that psychiatrists are the appropriate specialty for such consultations, psychiatrists rarely maintain their skills in physical examination at a level that can be expected from a full-time general practitioner. On the other hand, a family physician may not be comfortable enough with psychological disturbances to put the complaints into perspective and avoid premature judgments. Obviously, the skill and interests of psychiatrists as well as family practitioners vary. A clinical psychologist in private practice is, therefore, well advised to develop and nurture a working relationship with at least one physician in his or her area. Knowing a particular physician and his or her strengths and weaknesses will go a long way in obtaining maximum benefit from the consultation reports.

A psychiatrist who can keep medical considerations in mind during treatment and can coordinate medical and psychological investigations is a valuable resource for certain cases. For example, he or she can treat patients in whom neither the primary care physician nor the clinical psychologist can arrive at a diagnosis with reasonable certainty. In addition, patients who have both medical and psychological disorders that need attention are probably best treated by such an individual.

Medical Assessment

Medical History

The medical assessment is not confined to a physical examination. In general medical practice most clues are developed from a complete history. In psychiatric patients who cannot always give a reliable history, the physical examination may become relatively more important, but the medical history is still a valuable predictor of psychiatric outcome (Chandler & Gerndt, 1988). Although only a person familiar with the specific symptoms of a suspected disease can elicit the history in the optimal way, every evaluation by a clinical psychologist should include general health questions. A review of past illnesses, their treatment, and outcome should be included as well as current health problems, current medications, and illicit drug use. The latter cannot be emphasized enough because patients seldom volunteer this information or they minimize its significance. Information on health habits, sexual practices, and occupational hazards may prove valuable. With the patient's permission, information from collateral sources, such as relatives and old records, should be sought.

Physical Examination

The physical examination is usually the next step in medical assessment. The referring clinician needs to keep in mind that this benign procedure is, nevertheless, quite anxiety-provoking for some patients. In general, a simple explanation that a physical examination is needed as part of a comprehensive evaluation may be sufficient. In some situations, it may be wise to defer a complete physical examination. Examples' are: the acutely agitated psychotic individual, or the paranoid patient who has specific delusions pertaining to the physical examination or the physician. Under these circumstances, symptomatic psychiatric treatment has to render the patient more amenable to the physical examination. In these cases, the medical evaluation can be dispensed with in the beginning of treatment, but medical and psychiatric evaluation as well as medical and psychiatric treatment have to go hand in hand as tolerated by the patient.

Laboratory Tests

The last step in the medical assessment is laboratory testing. In psychiatric patients it may be justified to deviate from the usual medical practice of ordering specific tests to evaluate diagnostic possibilities formed during the history and physical. Instead, it may be more cost-effective to order a basic test battery that can, in part, be provided by an automated biochemical profile. The tests may include a complete blood count, urinalysis, electrolytes, glucose, hepatic, renal, and thyroid function tests, VDRL test for syphilis, urine drug screen, ECG, chest x-ray, PPD skin test for tuberculosis, EEG, CAT scan (Hall & Beresford, 1984) and if indicated, HIV testing. This list should be modified depending on which particular diseases are suspected. See Table 26.4 for clues that raise the level of suspicion. If abnormal test results are discovered, more specialized diagnostic procedures can be ordered for a final diagnosis.

Disadvantages of a Medical Orientation

Although this chapter emphasizes the need to "think medically" (Dietch & Zetin, 1983) about some patients with psychological disorders, we cannot deny considerable risks and pitfalls of this orientation.

Psychological Problems In Primary Medical Care

Mental health practitioners need to be reminded to "think medically," but primary medical caregivers need to "think more psychologically." Because the majority of treatment for mental illness takes place in the primary medical care sector, the second rule may

Table 26.4. Indicators of Increased Risk for Medical Problems as Revealed During the Psychological Evaluation

Demographic Information
Advanced age
First episode of psychological problem

Time Course Of Psychological Disorder
Concomitant with medical illness
Onset while taking drugs known to cause psychological symptoms
Acute onset of a serious mental disorder

History
Absence of apparently stressful life events
Alcohol and drug abuse
Known major medical illness

Family History
Inheritable brain diseases
Inheritable metabolic diseases

Mental Status Examination
Decreased level of consciousness
Cognitive impairment
Disorientation
Fluctuating mental status findings
Visual and tactile hallucinations

Note. This table is modified from Hoffman & Koran, 1984.

be applicable to a larger part of the population. This has been convincingly documented for depressive disorders (Schulberg et al., 1985).

Hypochondriasis and Conversion Disorder

Patients with somatic symptoms present primarily to the medical sector. Medical caregivers are trained to regard psychological disturbances primarily as diagnoses of exclusion. Therefore, patients are frequently submitted to a lengthy and sometimes dangerous series of tests. This can lead to iatrogenic morbidity, for example, adhesions after exploratory surgery. Instead of trying to disprove medical disorders quickly with a series of more and more invasive tests, we prefer sometimes an attitude of open-minded observation ordering noninvasive tests repeatedly as needed.

CONCLUSION

Considerable conceptual difficulties exist in understanding the nature of comorbidity between medical and psychological problems. The proper scope of the medical assessment can also be questioned on theoretical as well as practical grounds. Nevertheless, it is well established that medical illnesses and psychological disorders can be confused with each other. The

lack of medical assessment in patients presenting for psychological intervention can have life-threatening consequences and needs to be carefully avoided. Some of the medical disorders masquerading as psychological syndromes have been discussed and diagnostic approaches suggested. It is hoped that this information, in conjunction with clinical experience, can lead to a more comprehensive treatment for our patients and to an improved therapeutic outcome.

REFERENCES

Allen, A.D., & Tilkian, S.M. (1986). Depression correlated with cellular immunity in systemic immunodeficient Epstein-Barr virus syndrome (SIDES). *Journal of Clinical Psychiatry, 47*, 133–135.

American Psychiatric Association (1987). *Diagnostic and statistical manual of mental disorders—Revised* (3rd ed.). Washington DC: Author.

Amsterdam, J.D., Henle, W., Winokur, A., Wolkowitz, O.M., Pickar, D., & Paul, S.M. (1986). Serum antibodies to Epstein-Barr virus in patients with major depressive disorder. *American Journal of Psychiatry, 143*, 1593–1596.

Arana, G.W., & Baldessarini, R.J. (1987). Clinical use of the dexamethasone suppression test in psychiatry. In H.Y. Meltzer (Ed.), *Psychopharmacology: The third generation of progress* (pp. 609–615). New York: Raven Press.

Ascher, R. (1949). Myxedematous madness. *British Medical Journal, 2*, 555.

Atkinson, J.H., Grant, I., Kennedy, C.J., Richman, D.D., Spector, S.A., & McCutchan, J.A. (1988). Prevalence of psychiatric disorders among men infected with human immunodeficiency virus. *Archives of General Psychiatry, 45*, 859–864.

Bigger, Jr., J.T. (1988). Cardiac arrhythmias. In J.B. Wyngaarden & L.S. Smith, Jr. (Eds.), *Cecil textbook of medicine* (18th ed, pp. 250–274). Philadelphia: WB Saunders Company.

Borst, G.C., Eil, C., & Burman, K.D. (1983). Euthyroid hyperthyroxinemia. *Annals of Internal Medicine, 98*, 366–378.

Brent, G.A., & Hershman, J.M. (1986). Thyroxine therapy in patients with severe nonthyroidal illnesses and low serum thyroxine concentration. *Journal of Clinical Endocrinology and Metabolism, 63*, 1–8.

Buchwald, D., Sullivan, J.L., & Komaroff, A.L. (1987). Frequency of chronic active Epstein-Barr virus infection in a general medical practice. *Journal of the American Medical Association, 257*, 2303–2307.

Carroll, B.J., Feinberg, M., Greden, J.F., Tarika, J., Albala, A.A., & Haskett, R.F. (1981). A specific laboratory test for the diagnosis of melancholia. *Archives of General Psychiatry, 38*, 15–22.

Chandler, J.D., & Gerndt, J.E. (1988). The role of the

medical evaluation in psychiatric inpatients. *Psychosomatics*, *29*, 410–416.

Chopra, I.J., Solomon, D.H., Hepner, G.W., & Morgenstein, A.A. (1979). Misleadingly low free thyroxine index and usefulness of reverse triiodothyronine measurement in nonthyroidal illnesses. *Annals of Internal Medicine*, *90*, 905–912.

Comroe, B.I. (1936). Follow-up study of 100 patients diagnosed as neurotic. *Journal of Nervous and Mental Disease*, *83*, 679–684.

Crowe, R.R. (1985). Mitral valve prolapse and panic disorder. *Psychiatric Clinics of North America*, *8*, 63–71.

Cummings, J.L. (1988). Organic psychosis. *Psychosomatics*, *29*, 16–26.

DaCosta, J.M. (1871). On irritable heart: A clinical study of a form of functional cardiac disorder and its consequences. *American Journal of the Medical Sciences*, *61*, 17.

Dager, S.R., Comess, K.A., Saal, A.K., & Dunner, D.L. (1986). Mitral valve prolapse in a psychiatric setting. *Integrative Psychiatry*, *4*, 211–223.

Davies, A.O., Mares, A., Pool, J.L., & Taylor, A.A. (1987). Mitral valve prolapse with symptoms of beta-adrenergic hypersensitivity. *American Journal of Medicine*, *82*, 193–201.

Davis, D.W. (1965). Physical illness in psychiatric outpatients. *British Journal of Psychiatry*, *111*, 27–33.

DeLisi, L.E., Nurnberger, J.I., Goldin, L.R., Simmons-Alling, S., & Gershon, E.S. (1986). Epstein-Barr virus and depression. *Archives of General Psychiatry*, *43*, 815–816.

Dietch, J.T., & Zetin, M. (1983). Diagnosis of organic depressive disorders. *Psychosomatics*, *24*, 971–979.

Faulstich, M.E. (1987). Psychiatric aspects of AIDS. *American Journal of Psychiatry*, *144*, 551–556.

Fishman, S.M., Sheehan, D.V., & Carr, D.B. (1985). Thyroid indices in panic disorder. *Journal of Clinical Psychiatry*, *46*, 432–433.

Fras, I., Litin, E.M., & Pearson, J.S. (1967). Comparison of psychiatric symptoms in carcinoma of the pancreas with those in some other intra-abdominal neoplasms. *American Journal of Psychiatry*, *123*, 1553–1562.

Frohlich, E.D., Tarazi, R.C., & Dustan, H.P. (1969). Hyperdynamic beta-adrenergic circulatory state. *Archives of Internal Medicine*, *123*, 1–7.

Gold, M.S., Pottash, A.L.C., & Extein, I. (1981). Hypothyroidism and depression. *Journal of the American Medical Association*, *245*, 1919–1922.

Goodwin, F.K., Prange, A.J., Post, R.M., Muscettola, G., & Lipton, M.A. (1982). Potentiation of antidepressant effects by L-Triiodothyronine in tricyclic nonresponders. *American Journal of Psychiatry*, *139*, 34–38.

Hall, R.C.W. (1980). *Psychiatric presentation of mental illness: Somatopsychic disorders*. New York: SP Medical & Scientific Books.

Hall, R.C.W., & Beresford, T.P. (1984). Laboratory evaluation of newly admitted psychiatric patients. In R.C.W. Hall & T.P. Beresford (Eds.), *Handbook of psychiatric diagnostic procedures* (pp. 255–314). New York, Spectrum Publications.

Hall, R.C.W., Beresford, T.P., Gardner, E.R., & Popkin, M.K. (1982). The medical care of psychiatric patients. *Hospital and Community Psychiatry*, *33*, 25–34.

Hall, R.C.W., Gardner, E.R., Stickney, S.K., LeCann, A.F., & Popkin, M.K. (1980). Physical illness manifesting as psychiatric disease. *Archives of General Psychiatry*, *37*, 989–995.

Hall, R.C.W., Popkin, M.K., Devaul, R.A., Faillace, L.A., & Stickney, S.K. (1978). Physical illness presenting as psychiatric disease. *Archives of General Psychiatry*, *35*, 1315–1320.

Hartley, J. (1985). Virus linked to depression. *Moody news: Newsletter of the Manic-Depressive Association of Dallas*.

Hays, P. (1985). Implications of the distinction between organic and functional psychoses. *Acta Psychiatrica Scandinavica (Supplement)*, *71*, 620–625.

Hellinger, W.C., Smith, T.F., Van Scoy, R.E., Spitzer, P.G., Forgacs, P., & Edson, R.S. (1988). Chronic fatigue syndrome and the diagnostic utility of antibody to Epstein-Barr virus early antigen. *Journal of the American Medical Association*, *260*, 971–973.

Herridge, C.F. (1960). Physical disorders in psychiatric illness. *Lancet*, *2*, 949–951.

Hoffman, R.S., & Koran, L.M. (1984). Detecting physical illness in patients with mental disorders. *Psychosomatics*, *25*, 654–660.

Hollender, M.H., & Wells, C.E. (1980). Medical assessment in psychiatric practice. In H.I. Kaplan, A.M. Freedman, & B.J. Sadock (Eds.), *Comprehensive textbook of psychiatry III*. (3rd ed, pp. 981–989). Baltimore: Williams & Wilkins.

Holmes, G.P., Kaplan, J.E., Gantz, N.M., Komaroff, A.L., Schonberger, L.B., & Straus, S.E. (1988). Chronic fatigue syndrome: a working case definition. *Annals of Internal Medicine*, *108*, 387–389.

Holmes, G.P., Kaplan, J.E., Stewart, J.A., Hunt, B., Pinsky, P.F., & Schonberger, L.B. (1987). A cluster of patients with a chronic mononucleosis-like syndrome. *Journal of the American Medical Association*, *257*, 2297–2302.

Jacobsson, L., & Ottosson, J.O. (1971). Initial mental disorders in carcinoma of pancreas and stomach. *Acta Psychiatrica Scandinavica (Supplement)*, *221*, 120–127.

Johnson, D.A.W. (1968). The evaluation of routine physical examination in psychiatric cases. *Practitioner*, *200*, 686–691.

Johnstone, E.C., Cooling, M.J., Frith, C.D., Crow, T.J., & Owens, D.G.C. (1988). Phenomenology of organic and functional psychoses and the overlap between them. *British Journal of Psychiatry*, *153*, 770–776.

Jones, J.F., Ray, G., & Minnich, L.L. (1985). Evidence for active Epstein-Barr virus infection in patients with persistent, unexplained illnesses: Elevated anti-early antigen antibodies. *Annals of Internal Medicine*, *102*, 1–7.

Kieff, E. (1988). Infectious mononucleosis: Epstein-Barr

virus infection. In J. B. Wyngaarden & L.H. Smith, Jr. (Eds.), *Cecil textbook of medicine* (18th ed, pp. 1786–1788). Philadelphia: WB Saunders.

Klein, D.F., & Gorman, J.M. (1984). Panic disorders and mitral valve prolapse. *Journal of Clinical Psychiatry Monograph, 2*, 14–16.

Koch, H.K. (1978). *The national ambulatory medical care survey: 1975 summary.* U.S. Dept. of Health and Human Services Publication (PHS), pp. 78–84.

Koranyi, E.K. (1979). Morbidity and rate of undiagnosed physical illnesses in a psychiatric clinic population. *Archives of General Psychiatry, 36*, 414–419.

Koranyi, E.K. (1982). *Physical illness in the psychiatric patient.* Springfield, IL: Charles C Thomas.

Krauthammer, C., & Klerman, G.L. (1978). Secondary mania: Manic syndromes associated with antecedent physical illness or drugs. *Archives of General Psychiatry, 35*, 1333–1339.

Kroenke, K., Wood, D.R., Mangelsdorff, A.D., Meier, N.J., & Powell, J.B. (1988). Chronic fatigue in primary care: Prevalence, patient characteristics, and outcome. *Journal of the American Medical Association, 260*, 929–934.

Lader, M.H. (1972). The nature of anxiety. *British Journal of Psychiatry, 121*, 481.

Larsen, P.R. (1988). The thyroid. In J.B. Wyngaarden & L.H. Smith, Jr. (Eds.), *Cecil textbook of medicine* (18th ed, pp. 1315–1340). Philadelphia: WB Saunders Company.

Lesser, I.M., Rubin, R.T., Lydiard, R.B., Swinson, R., & Pecknold, J. (1987). Past and current thyroid function in subjects with panic disorder. *Journal of Clinical Psychiatry, 48*, 473–476.

Levine, P.M., Silberfarb, P.M., & Lipowski, Z.J. (1978). Mental disorders in cancer patients: A study of 100 psychiatric referrals. *Cancer, 42*, 1385–1391.

Lima, B.R., & Pai, S. (1987). Concurrent medical and psychiatric disorders among schizophrenic and neurotic outpatients. *Community Mental Health Journal, 23*, 30–39.

Lindemann, C.G., Zitrin, C.M., & Klein, D.F. (1984). Thyroid dysfunction in phobic patients. *Psychosomatics, 25*, 603–606.

Linnoila, M., Lamberg, B.A., Potter, W.Z., Gold, P.W., & Goodwin, F.K. (1982). High reverse T3 levels in manic and unipolar depressed women. *Psychiatry Research, 6*, 271–276.

Lishman, W.A. (1987). *Organic psychiatry: The psychological consequences of cerebral disorder* (2nd ed.). Oxford: Blackwell Scientific Publications.

Loosen, P.T., & Prange, A.J. (1982). Serum thyrotropin response to thyrotropin-releasing hormone in psychiatric patients: A review. *American Journal of Psychiatry, 139*, 405–416.

Maguire, G.P., & Granville-Grossman, K.L. (1968). Physical illness in psychiatric patients. *British Journal of Psychiatry, 115*, 1365–1369.

Manu, P., Lane, T.J., & Matthews, D.A. (1988). The frequency of the chronic fatigue syndrome in patients with symptoms of persistent fatigue. *Annals of Internal Medicine, 109*, 554–556.

Maricle, R.A., Hoffman, W.F., Bloom, J.D., Faulkner, L.R., & Keepers, G.A. (1987). The prevalence and significance of medical illness among chronically mentally ill outpatients. *Community Mental Health Journal, 23*, 81–90.

Marshall, H.E.S. (1949). Incidence of physical disorders among psychiatric inpatients. *British Medical Journal, 2*, 468–470.

Marzuk, P.M., Tierney, H., & Tardiff, K. (1988). Increased risk of suicide in persons with AIDS. *Journal of the American Medical Association, 259*, 1333–1337.

Miller, A.H., Silberstein, C., Asnis, G.M., Munk, G., Rubinson, E., & Spigland, I. (1986). Epstein-Barr virus infection and depression. *Journal of Clinical Psychiatry, 47*, 529.

Miller, D., & Riccio, M. (1990). Non-organic psychiatric and psychosocial syndromes associated with HIV-1 infection and disease. *AIDS, 4*, 381–388.

Munjack, D.J., & Palmer, R. (1988). Thyroid hormones in panic disorder, panic disorder with agoraphobia, and generalized anxiety disorder. *Journal of Clinical Psychiatry, 49*, 229–231.

Myers, J.K., Weissman, M.M., Tischler, G.L., Holzer, C.E. III, Leaf, P.J., & Orvaschel, H. (1984). Six-month prevalence of psychiatric disorders in three communities. *Archives of General Psychiatry, 41*, 959–967.

Noyes, R., Jr., & Kathol, R.G. (1986). Depression and cancer. *Psychiatric Developments, 2*, 77–100.

Ostrow, D., Grant, I., & Atkinson, H. (1988). Assessment and management of the AIDS patient with neuropsychiatric disturbances. *Journal of Clinical Psychiatry, 49*, 14–22.

Pariser, S.F., Jones, B.A., Pinta, E.R., Young, E.A., & Fontana, M.E. (1979). Panic attacks: Diagnostic evaluations of 17 patients. *American Journal of Psychiatry, 136*, 105–106.

Perry, S.W. (1990a). AIDS and psychiatry. In R. Michels, A.M. Cooper, S.B. Guze, L.L. Judd, G.L. Klerman, A.J. Solnit, A.J. Stunkard, & P.J. Wilner (Eds.), *Psychiatry* (pp. 1–21). New York: JB Lippincott.

Perry, S.W. (1990b). Organic mental disorders caused by HIV: Update on early diagnosis and treatment. *American Journal of Psychiatry, 147*, 696–710.

Phillips, R.J. (1937). Physical disorder in 164 consecutive admissions to a mental hospital. *British Medical Journal, 2*, 781–786.

Pope, H.G., Jr., & Katz, D.L. (1988). Affective and psychotic symptoms associated with anabolic steroid use. *American Journal of Psychiatry, 145*, 487–490.

Prange, A.J., Jr., Garbutt, J.C., & Loosen, P.T. (1987). The hypothalamic-pituitary-thyroid axis in affective disorders. In H.Y. Meltzer (Ed.), *Psychopharmacology: The third generation of progress* (pp. 629–636). New York: Raven Press.

Rackley, C.E. (1988). Valvular heart disease. In J.B. Wyngaarden & L.H. Smith, Jr. (Eds.), *Cecil textbook of medicine* (18th ed, pp. 340–352). Philadelphia: WB Saunders Company.

Raj, A.B., & Sheehan, D.V. (1987). Medical evaluation of panic attacks. *Journal of Clinical Psychiatry, 48*, 309–313.

Raj, A.B., & Sheehan, D.V. (1988). Medical evaluation of the anxious patient. *Psychiatric Annals, 18*, 176–181.

Robins, L.N., Helzer, J.E., Weissman, M.M., Orvaschel, H., Gruenberg, E., & Burke, J.D. Jr. (1984). Lifetime prevalence of specific psychiatric disorders in three sites. *Archives of General Psychiatry, 41*, 949–958.

Robinson, R.G., Boston, J.D., Starkstein, S.E., & Price, T.R. (1988). Comparison of mania and depression after brain injury: Causal factors. *American Journal of Psychiatry, 145*, 172–178.

Sachar, E.J. (1975). Psychiatric disturbances associated with endocrine disorders. In M.F. Reiser (Ed.), *American handbook of psychiatry* (2nd ed, vol. 4, pp. 299–313). New York: Basic Books.

Schmitt, F.A., Bigley, J.W., & McKinnis, R. (1988). Neuropsychological outcome of zidovudine (AZT) treatment of patients with AIDS and AIDS-related complex. *New England Journal of Medicine, 319*, 1573–1578.

Schulberg, H.C., McClelland, M., & Burns, B.J. (1987). Depression and physical illness: The prevalence, causation, and diagnosis of comorbidity. *Clinical Psychology Review, 7*, 145–167.

Schulberg, H.C., Saul, M., McClelland, M., Ganguli, M., Christy, W., & Frank, R. (1985). Assessing depression in primary medical and psychiatric practices. *Archives of General Psychiatry, 42*, 1164–1170.

Service, F.J. (1988). Hypoglycemic disorders. In J.B. Wyngaarden & L.H. Smith, Jr. (Eds.), *Cecil textbook of medicine* (18th ed, pp. 1381–1387). Philadelphia: WB Saunders Company.

Spratt, D.I., Pont, A., Miller, M.B., McDougall, I.R., & Bayer, M.F. (1982). Hyperthyroxinemia in patients with acute psychiatric disorders. *American Journal of Medicine, 73*, 41–48.

Stein, M.B., & Uhde, T.W. (1988). Thyroid indices in panic disorder. *American Journal of Psychiatry, 145*, 745–747.

Stein, M.B., & Uhde, T.W. (1989). Autoimmune thyroiditis and panic disorder. *American Journal of Psychiatry, 146*, 259–260.

Stoudemire, A., & Fogel, B.S. (1987). *Principles of medical psychiatry*. Orlando, FL: Grune & Stratton.

Straus, S.E., Tosato, G., Armstrong, G., Lawley, T., Preble, O.T., & Henle, W. (1985). Persisting illness and fatigue in adults with evidence of Epstein-Barr virus infection. *Annals of Internal Medicine, 102*, 7–16.

Sultzer, D.L., & Cummings, J.L. (1989). Drug-induced mania—causative agents, clinical characteristics and management. *Medical Toxicology and Adverse Drug Experience, 4*, 127–143.

Torrey, E.F. (1986). Functional psychoses and viral encephalitis. *Integrative Psychiatry, 4*, 224–236.

Trzepacz, P.T., McCue, M., Klein, I., Levey, G.S., & Greenhouse, J. (1988). A psychiatric and neuropsychological study of patients with untreated Graves' disease. *General Hospital Psychiatry, 10*, 49–55.

Tyrrell, J.B., & Baxter, J.D. (1988). Disorders of the adrenal cortex. In J.B. Wyngaarden & L.H. Smith, Jr. (Eds.), *Cecil textbook of medicine* (18th ed., pp. 1340–1360). Philadelphia: WB Saunders.

Uhde, T.W., Vittone, B.J., & Post, R.M. (1984). Glucose tolerance testing in panic disorder. *American Journal of Psychiatry, 141*, 1461–1463.

Wartofsky, L., & Burman, K.E. (1982). Alterations in thyroid function in patients with systemic illness: The "euthyroid sick syndrome." *Endocrine Reviews, 3*, 164–216.

Weissman, M. (1988). Anxiety and alcoholism. *Journal of Clinical Psychiatry, 49*, 17–19.

Willerson, J.T. (1988). Disorders of coronary arteries: Angina pectoris. In J.B. Wyngaarden & L.H. Smith, Jr. (Eds.), *Cecil textbook of medicine* (18th ed., p. 323). Philadelphia: WB Saunders.

CHAPTER 27

CAN COMPUTERS BE CLINICIANS? THEORY AND DESIGN OF A DIAGNOSTIC SYSTEM

Benjamin Kleinmuntz

In the paper, "A Portrait of the Computer as a Young Clinician" (Kleinmuntz, 1963a), I held out high hopes that computers would soon fulfill the esteemed role of clinical psychologist. That was more than a quarter of a century ago. Some 5 years later, in a similarly enthusiastic vein, I wrote in "The Processing of Clinical Information by Man and Machine" (Kleinmuntz, 1968) that we were quickly approaching the day when we could count on machines to replace human clinicians, both in clinical psychology and medicine. Now, some 25 years after the initial article—except for several unvalidated automated cookbook uses in clinical psychology (Matarazzo, 1983, 1985; Meehl, 1986) and more ambitious, but equally unsuccessful uses in medicine (Kleinmuntz & Elstein, 1987)—I pose the question more modestly: Can computers be clinicians?

The question is intentionally ambiguous. The word *clinicians* refers to a group of professionals who earn their livelihood by offering predictions about people's well-being in addition to treating them, *and* to the process of arriving at these decisions by subjective rather than mechanical modes of information processing. The two, although similar, are distinct. The present chapter's focus is on the second meaning of *clinician*. Thus, the initial question can be reformulated as: Can computers process data like human clinicians?

The reformulation invites discussion of how clinicians process data; that is, it requests an answer to the problem of what sorts of cognitive activities would computers have to simulate. But since there is limited information available about these activities—except, perhaps, in statistical policy capturing studies within limited clinical and nonclinical spheres (e.g., Einhorn, Kleinmuntz & Kleinmuntz, 1979; Hammond, 1955; Hammond, Hursch, & Todd, 1964; Hoffman, 1960; Kleinmuntz, & Elstein, 1987), all of which would take us too far afield from our intended purpose—I propose to design a hypothetical computer system that can perform two cognitive functions of clinicians: diagnosis and treatment. Although I deal

The preparation and writing of this chapter were supported in part by the National Library of Medicine (Grant No. 1R01 LM 05483-02), to whom I am grateful. I acknowledge also the help of Don N. Kleinmuntz, who provided many of the formalisms that appear in the chapter.

mainly with the broader terms of diagnosis and treatment that apply to clinical activities generally, my intent is to communicate that the proposed system can be applied equally as well to psychodiagnosis and psychotherapy (e.g., see B. Kleinmuntz & D.N. Kleinmuntz, 1981; see also Kleinmuntz, 1985; D.N. Kleinmuntz & B. Kleinmuntz, 1981).

BACKGROUND AND RATIONALE

My prior writing on the use of computers in clinical psychology includes discussions of their empirical use as computational and noncomputational devices (Kleinmuntz, 1982) and as information processors in personality test interpretation (Kleinmuntz, 1963b, 1968), interviewing (Brooks & Kleinmuntz, 1974; Kleinmuntz & McLean, 1968), and, more generally, their future as neuropsychological assessors (B. Kleinmuntz, 1987) and clinicians (Kleinmuntz, 1975, 1990). All of these writings had as their main focus the practical possibility of laying the groundwork for applications in mental health or medicine. This chapter has no such practical objective. Rather, it is concerned with the design of a model that lends itself to future experimentation with the process of clinical judgment; an attempt at the design of a cognitive wind tunnel, as it were.

Consequently, in its practical aspirations, this chapter is on a par with a seemingly inane question that Boring (1946), in a little-known paper, once posed: "What properties would a potato have to have in order to be conscious?" (p. 192). The rationale for such a question is hardly silly, however, for it forces one to be precise about both cognition and the environment in which such activity occurs. In a similar advocacy of this approach, Simon (1956) held forth on permissible survival strategies for developing a hypothetical creature in an artificial microcosm in which it has to find solutions for survival. And, following up on this idea, Toda (1962; see also Toda, 1980) constructed "fungus-eating" robots whose job was to mine uranium in an artificial environment while eating fungi as their source of sustenance. Such analyses highlight the design requirements needed by organisms to survive in strange environments and force the designer to think about the tradeoffs between problem solution strategies and survival. Or put more elegantly, as Simon (1969) tells us, "the computer becomes an obvious device for exploring the consequences of alternative organizational assumptions for human behavior" (p. 22).

Simon and his associates (e.g., Kotovsky, Hayes,

& Simon, 1985; Laird, Newell, & Rosenbloom, 1987; Newell, Shaw, & Simon, 1958; Newell & Simon, 1972; Simon, 1979) have pursued this tack by means of the "program first" method, which I adopt here. This approach works as follows: Given the problem of analyzing a judgmental task, the idea is to write a computer program that performs the task in a way that fits currently available data about human behavior. The difference between pursuing this strategy and doing artificial intelligence or AI research, and its applied branch, expert systems development, is one of intent.

AI's so-called knowledge engineer wants to discover the best procedure for accomplishing a given task and to construct the most efficient program for decision support. The program-first strategist, by comparison, wants to explore the processes of human cognition in all its facets, in addition to evaluating their modeling capabilities. The latter method is useful for the following reasons: (a) It can suggest and promote the development of formal models of human behavior. (b) It can be used to explore alternate assumptions in those models, via simulation. And (c) these models provide strong predictions about human performance in the same tasks, which can subsequently be tested. Similar forays into model building are discussed elsewhere (e.g., B. Kleinmuntz & D.N. Kleinmuntz, 1981; Kleinmuntz, 1985; D.N. Kleinmuntz & B. Kleinmuntz, 1981; see also Kleinmuntz & Elstein, 1987, for a discussion of computer modeling in medicine); and here I shall design a hypothetical computer clinician that (who?) will be asked to diagnose and treat disorders in a simulated environment.

DESIGN OF A SIMULATED PSYCHODIAGNOSTIC SYSTEM AND TREATMENT DECISIONS

To demonstrate the possibilities inherent in this approach, I shall construct a simulated psychodiagnostic environmental task that can be input to the computer, along with several diagnostic and treatment strategies that can be used by a programmed clinician. The hypothetical problem space can contain such diagnostic symptoms and signs as put forth in the latest American Psychiatric Association's *Diagnostic and Statistical Manual of Mental Disorders, Third Edition, Revised* ([DSM-III-R], 1987), although no advocacy of such a taxonomic system is intended here, or it can be constituted by problem behaviors and their remediation. I shall use the terms *symptoms, signs,* and *disorders* simply because an earlier version of the model was intended for use in medical problem solving.

The psychodiagnostic task environment can be constructed by assigning symptoms and signs to disorders—the precise numbers of these to be determined by the complexity of the environment intended for any particular problem. Each symptom has assigned to it a probability of association to a disorder. Configurations of symptoms in various combinations are also given probabilities that change as a function of given prior probability or base rate data. Base rates, or priors, refer to the distribution of a disorder in a population and are adjustable values that may be subject to normative or regional changes.

Case history data and information obtained from observations, interviews, and tests can then have varying diagnostic values that can be adjusted according to the complexity of the problem desired. Each datum and each test have prescribed reliabilities, predictive validities, and cutting scores assigned to it, as well as a diagnostic specificity and sensitivity.

Treatments for particular disorders can be stipulated, and these have diagnostic and therapeutic values attributed to them. If the treatment is somatic rather than psychological, risk factors associated with its administration and withholding are also assigned, depending on the treatment's past and potential harm to patients. Important criteria of a good case history, test, and treatment are that they result in a correct diagnosis and lead to proper treatment. Incorrect diagnoses and improper treatments move the patient further away from good mental health. The latter is defined by a scale ranging from 0 (*very good mental health*, i.e., no symptoms of disorder) to 100 (*very poor mental health*). Deterioration and improvement in a patient's condition are measurable in terms of quantitative movements toward and away from very good mental health, repectively. Some patients deteriorate if left undiagnosed and untreated; others show spontaneous remission if they are left alone. Precisely which result occurs under what circumstances is varied by the experimenter, depending on the prespecified parameters of a particular computer problem.

Values are also assigned to improvements in the quality of a patient's life, and these quality-of-life considerations are traded off with the probability of risking death or discomfort in the case of somatic treatment, or monetary and time and effort costs in the case of psychotherapy.

Inasmuch as we are also interested in clinicians as decision makers, their design is equally critical. The clinicians can use decision rules of three types: (a) expected utility Bayesian rules, (b) heuristic search

strategies, and (c) generate-and-test strategies. Only the latter two types of decision strategies will be considered here. The expected utility Bayesian rules require more computation and derivation of equations than are necessary for our purposes of illustration, have been computed elsewhere (e.g., D.N. Kleinmuntz & B. Kleinmuntz, 1981), and were shown to be a slight improvement over the other two strategies, but were not found to be worth the extra computational effort necessary.

The *generate-and-test* treatment strategy makes minimal demands on the decision maker, regardless of whether this is a computer or a human. It requires negligible knowledge and very little in the way of cognitive effort. A treatment is generated at random and is tested as long as the results are favorable. If the observed effectiveness of a treatment falls below a minimal level, a new treatment is selected. This continues, with the treatment being kept as long as it seems to be effective. The symptoms of the patient are ignored, and no attempt is made to diagnose. This is in sharp contrast to the expected utility Bayesian and heuristic strategies, which require extensive computational or human effort to diagnose a disorder before assigning a treatment. The generate-and-test treatment strategy is a very simple example of trial-and-error learning and is comparable to how a novice clinical psychologist may go about treating a patient without any diagnostic or other understanding of what may be the patient's problem.

A somewhat more demanding strategy—at least from a designer's perspective—is the *heuristic* decision strategy, which views people as *satisficers* (see Simon, 1957), who indulge in a limited amount of search until a satisfactory rather than a optimal solution is reached. Satisficers are closest to clinical qua clinical intuiters who place little faith in formal clinical information processing. They tend to have great self-confidence in their own expertise (e.g., see Arkes, Dawes, & Christensen, 1986) but are often poorly calibrated after a tally is taken of their predictive accuracy.

More formally, now, so as to demonstrate how the heuristic strategy works, I must create "cases," and for each case, the computer-programmed clinician is confronted with a hypothetical patient complaining of, let us say, three symptoms, S1, S2, and S3, from among a finite set of symptoms, and is afflicted with a particular disorder, labeled Di, also selected from a finite set of possible disorders. Furthermore, for the general population of patients, there is a base rate probability for each Di, denoted as P(Di). Each patient is represented as a vector of symptoms, each of which can be either positive (present) or negative (absent). Given that the patient has Di, I denote the conditional probability of Symptom j, or S_j, being positive by $P\{S_j + \mid Di\}$. The complementary probability of S_j being negative is $P\{S_j - \mid Di\} = 1 - P\{S_j + \mid Di\}$. Also, I assume that any two symptoms are conditionally independent of the disease category (i.e., $P\{S_j + \mid Di, S_j+\} = P\{S_j + \mid Di\}$, for all i, and j = k). This is a considerable simplification, since it ignores configurations such as syndromes, where the presence of one symptom can increase the likelihood of certain others.

Next, the patient's health condition is represented by a variable Ct, which changes over time (Ct denotes the condition in time period t). Ct is measured on a 0–100 scale, corresponding to "percent of full mental health." In particular, as Ct increases, the patient is said to be healthier, whereas a value of Ct at or below zero indicates severe personality decompensation. Clearly, the computer-programmed clinician's task is to prevent the latter and improve the patient's condition as much as possible. Factors that influence the patient's health are: (a) the severity of the disorder, (b) the effect of specific treatments given to the patient, and (c) the cost to the patient's health of diagnostic tests, particularly physiologically based tests. These will be explained in turn.

The disorder generally causes the patient to get progressively closer to severe personality decompensation. This is represented by a linear trend, with random variation. Thus, in each period, Ct decreases by an amount d + e, where e is a normally distributed random variable, with zero mean, and d is a positive constant. Because of random variation, in any single period the patient may improve. However, on average, his or her condition will deteriorate.

The computer program as clinician has a number of treatments available, and in any one period may select one treatment (T_k) to apply to the patient. The treatment effectiveness is denoted by random variable $\mu[k,i]$, with a normal distribution whose parameters depend on which T_k was selected, as well as which Di the patient has. The same treatment will have vastly different effectiveness depending on Di, so treatments may have positive or negative effects, with a large range of variation (caused by the variance of $\mu[k,i]$).

The patient's symptoms are initially unknown to the computer-programmed clinician. However, once each period, just before selecting a T_k, it is possible to test for the presence or absence of a single S_j. The tests provide reliable results (an assumption that can be relaxed), but also have a detrimental effect on the patient's health, called p. As a simplification, the cost

will be assumed uniform over all the possible tests, and also, p will be relatively small. The clinician (i.e., computer program) need not test for a symptom every period, but rather, only as necessary.

The sequence of events is as follows: The patient is presented to the computer clinician with an unknown disorder, complaining of three symptoms. In addition, the clinician is informed of the patient's initial condition, CO. Then, during each time period, t, the clinician may do two things. First, he or she may request a test for some S_j. Because test reports are reliable, S_j will always be some symptom that has not previously been observed. Once the test results are received (with no time lag), a treatment T_k is selected. The clinician then receives immediate feedback about the change in the patient's condition following treatment. However, no information is provided about the extent to which results are due to chance events as opposed to treatment effects. This concluded period t. The clinician then starts the next period (t + 1), requesting a test, and so on. Generally, the process continues until either (a) the patient deteriorates severely (Ct $\leq$ 0), (b) the patient is "cured" (Ct $\geq$ 100), or (c) some arbitrary stopping point is reached (in this case t = 60).

Heuristic Decision Strategy

Having now put in place the computer-programmed clinician and the decision environment, I can proceed with outlining the more demanding of the two programs, the *heuristic decision* strategy. In particular, assume that the decision maker has knowledge of the following: $P\{S_j + \mid Di\}$, a measure of the extent to which the presence of Symptom j, S_j+, is diagnostic of Di (measured on a 0–1 scale); $E[\mu(k, i)]$, the average *effectiveness* of T_k given Di; and $E[\mu(k,i)]-2V[\mu(k,i)]^{1/2}$, a measure of the "worst case" outcome of applying T_k to a patient with Di.

The general procedure is to develop a hypothesis about the patient's disorder, Dh, and to try to confirm that hypothesis. The type of evidence that is most salient is symptoms that are strongly diagnostic if present, and are, in fact, present. Although the absence of undiagnosed symptoms might be equally strong support for Dh, it is assumed that only positive evidence is sought. This is a bias in favor of data that will confirm the current hypothesis, a bias that has been observed in human subjects (Bruner, Goodnow, & Austin, 1956; Mynatt, Doherty, & Tweney, 1977; Wason & Johnson-Laird, 1972).

The criterion for selecting a test is that, if positive, the symptom will provide reasonably strong confirmation of Dh, the hypothesized disorder. Thus, if $P\{S_j + | Dh\}$ is above some threshold level (or level of aspiration), then that symptom, S_j, will be tested. Furthermore, if the body of positive evidence is strong (as represented by the sum of the $P\{S_j + | Dh\}$ for all symptoms observed present), no further testing is done. If the resulting test for S_j is positive, this merely reinforces the current Dh. If the evidence is disconfirming (negative result), then a new hypothesis must be adopted. The Di with the largest sum of $P\{S_j + | Di\}$, over observed symptoms, becomes the new Dh. Note that it is possible for the Dh to remain the same if no better candidate exists.

Selection is made randomly from those treatments that meet the following criteria: (a) $E[\mu(k,h)]$, the *expected effectiveness* of T_k given Dh, exceeds a minimal level, (b) the "worst case" outcome of T_k, given Dh, exceeds a minimal level, and (c) previous applications of T_k to this patient have not been negative. This last condition prevents the decision maker from making the same mistakes over and over at the risk of prematurely rejecting a good treatment.

If the selected treatment works well according to prespecified criteria (e.g., has the patient improved, on average, using this treatment?), it is kept, and applied in later periods. When the results for any treatment are observed to be unfavorable, then a new T_k is selected, and possibly, a new Dh formulated. The minimal levels of the treatment selection criteria are lowered as needed, so some treatment can always be found. The principal advantage to this strategy is that it uses simple rules, and further decision-making activity is halted as long as treatment results are satisfactory. Figure 27.1 presents this strategy as a flow chart.

Generate-and-Test Treatment Strategy

The generate-and-test treatment strategy, as indicated earlier, makes minimal demands on the decision maker. It requires negligible knowledge, and little in the way of cognitive effort. It will be recalled that a treatment is generated at random and it is tested for favorable results. Figure 27.2 shows this strategy in flow-chart form.

Note that in both Figures 27.1 and 27.2, the term *death* is used as a terminal program alternative to *cured* and *time expired*. For our purposes, this can be translated to read *severe personality decomposition*. *Death* is intended for use of this system in clinical decision making in medicine, which has several other computational complexities not included here.

SIMULATION RESULTS

Each of the two strategies were simulated for 100 computer-simulated cases. The diseases were observed in proportion to their base rates, and symptoms randomly assigned according to their likelihoods. The results are summarized in Table 27.1. The comparison point taken was C60, the patient's condition after 60 minutes of treatment. In cases where the patient decompensated earlier, C60 was assumed to be zero. In cases where the patient was cured earlier (i.e., condition greater than or equal to 100 at some period), C60 was assumed to be 100. Table 27.1 presents the median, mean, and standard deviation of C60 for each strategy and for each disease.

Generally, the heuristic strategy does slightly better than the generate-and-test strategy. These results only weakly support the contention that the more complex rules are superior. The generate-and-test strategy is inferior, but to a lesser extent than one might expect from such an unsophisticated and random decision rule procedure.

The notable exception to the above generalization is the result for Disorder 2 (D2). In this case, the generate-and-test strategy has a higher median and mean level of performance than the heuristic strategy.

Table 27.1. Summary of Simulation Results

	STRATEGY	
DISORDER	GENERATE AND TEST	HEURISTIC
D1	77.8*	100*
n = 35	72.89**	90.21**
	20.83s	16.24s
D2	41.7	24.7
n = 25	43.41	30.90
	42.10	22.92
D3	100	100
n = 20	98.50	96.92
	4.16	13.77
D4	100	100
n = 15	95.86	100
	16.03	0
D5	100	100
n = 5	81.60	93.82
	26.11	13.82
Total	89.7	100
n = 100	74.52	78.37
	32.85	32.14

Note. * Median; ** mean; s = standard deviation. The same pattern occurs for each disorder in each of the two strategies.

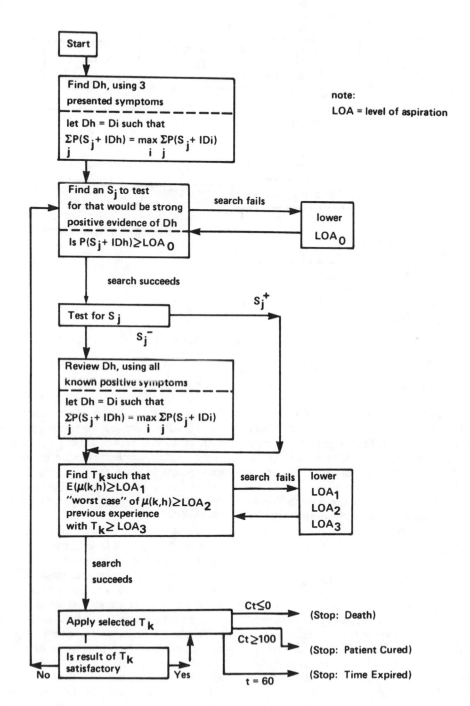

Figure 27.1. Heuristic decision strategy.

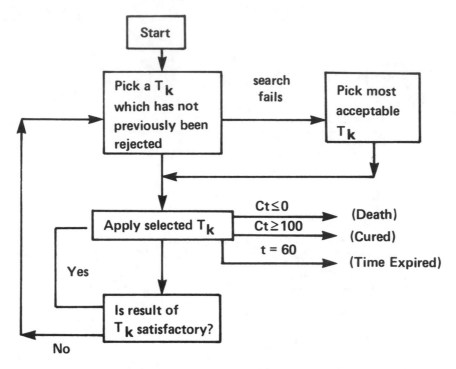

Figure 27.2. Generate-and-test strategy.

In addition, the random strategy produced much greater variation in results than the other two (SD of 42.1 vs. 22.9 or 17.3). This is a reflection of the fact that the generate-and-test strategy managed to both deteriorate (originally, kill) more patients and cure more patients suffering from D2 than either of the other strategies, which only achieved a uniformly mediocre level of performance.

One other feature of the simulation is worth observing. The generate-and-test and heuristic strategies required an average of .25 and .30 seconds of computer time per case (not shown in Table 27.1).

Teaching Problems and Solutions To Humans

So that a comparison can be made of humans with computers in solving hypothetical problems, I must first teach humans the features and the solutions to problems such as those described above. I can do this in one of two ways: by means of the deductive or inductive method. Learning by deduction requires that inferences be made on what the data imply as well as what information the data contain; learning by induction involves reasoning from the particulars of the data to the general. The latter involves the process of discovery by observing instances and features of the data. Teaching a computer or a human by induction rather than deduction suits our research purposes quite well, because it permits these problem solvers to extract information from specific examples of the environment in much the same way that problem solvers form connections from characteristics of the task environment to solution methods (see Newell & Simon, 1972).

My view is that a problem solver learns by constructing elements of a table of connections between features of the task environment and solution methods. When enough data have been assembled in such a table, the problem solver induces rules that specify which situations are present and which solutions are good in each instance of the situation. The induction of these rules based on the data in the table of connections could be accomplished by an induction process that maps classes of stimulus values into utilities for solution methods. Huesmann and Cheng (1973) stated this more formally as follows: "To induce a rule for solving a problem one must find a function $f(X_1, X_2, \ldots X_p)$, such that if $X_1, X_2, \ldots X_p$ are stimulus variables and y is a variable representing the utility of a particular solution method, then $f(X_1, X_2, \ldots X_p) = y$ for all observed instances of $X_1, X_2, \ldots X_p, y)$" (p. 126).

Less formally, Simon and Lea (1974, pp. 109–110) have expressed this procedure as follows: "(1) There is a problem space whose elements are knowledge states. (2) There are one or more generative processes (operators) that take a knowledge state as input and produce a new knowledge state as output. (3) There are one or more test processes for comparing a knowledge state with specification of the problem state and for comparing pairs of knowledge states and producing differences between them. (4) There are processes for selecting which of these generators and tests to employ, on the basis of information contained in the knowledge states."

Still less formally, it can be stated that, given that the machine or human problem solver has already encountered a number of features in the problem space, he or she can determine the direction in which to continue to search by two kinds of decisions: (a) selection of a knowledge state from among those already encountered, and (b) selection of an inference rule to apply at a particular juncture in order to reach a new knowledge state.

Translating this into a rule-induction system that learns a hypothetical mental health decision environment such as one represented earlier, we refer the reader to the inductive discovery system developed by Langley, Simon, Bradshaw, and Zytkow (1986) for scientific discovery that asks the user (computer program or human) a number of questions about the task the system is to solve and about the solution. Our system, which would work somewhat like Langley et al.'s, would use the following methods to teach the human the elements of the mental health decision problem:

1. Gathering symptom, disorder, and other similar data: A set of productions (see Newell & Simon, 1972, pp. 32–34), or if/then computer subroutines, asks the user (computer display) a number of questions about the task the system is to solve. As the data are gathered, the system constructs a set of more specific productions to carry out the experiment. Simultaneously with the gathering of the problem features, then, the system can collect connections data for the problem solutions.

2. Detecting regularities: A second set of productions are responsible for discovering regularities in the data collected by the first set. The system's regularity detectors can be divided into a set of constancy detectors and a set of trend detectors. These can deal with nominal and numerical data, respectively, and lead to the postulation of generalizations about the connections between the problem features and solutions.

3. Computing higher-level values: Another set of productions is used to compute the values of new attributes that the system presents. Included in this set are productions that discover and compute independent and dependent values that may, in turn, generalize to still higher level values.

4. Testing hypotheses: A final set of productions need to be developed that are responsible for testing generalizations that emerge from the prior subroutines. When a generalization is first made, a set of preexisting test productions will be set in motion to compare the known data with the generalization. When the problem space is deterministic, the test productions will require a perfect comparison. In an uncertain, probabilistic task, the generalization can be less perfect.

The next step following devising a system for inductive rule learning is to display the problem task features to humans on a computer terminal. The environmental features can be displayed in manageable chunks, and the problem solver interacts with the system and can ask for more information about other features of the environment.

The initial givens to the subject and the complexity of the problems to be solved are raised along several dimensions of complexity. For example, the initial number of symptoms, disorders, differential tests, and treatments can be made more or less complex, depending on what probabilities are assigned to their covariations, and likewise, the seriousness of the consequences of misdiagnosis can be adjusted according to prespecified values. Approximately 10 problems can be presented to each of five subjects.

While the problem solving is underway, verbal protocols can be obtained, as well as the solution times of the participating subjects. The idea of obtaining "thinking-aloud" protocols as well as other records of subjects' modes of proceeding (i.e., pointing at various displayed task features with a light pen) is to construct models about human problem solving. These models are in the form of simulation programs that produce two types of output that can be compared with the solutions humans generate: (a) The program prints a protocol of its solution process, and (b) it computes the simulated time needed to reach any point in the solution process. To test whether these models produce human performance, humans and computers need to be compared in their learning of problem spaces and solutions.

CONCLUSION

What do the preceding considerations tell us about human performance and decision making in mental health settings? The main insight to be gained from our prescribed use of the computer in the foregoing novel ways is the knowledge that computers can be used as cognitive "wind-tunnels," as it were, for simulating a variety of mental health and other clinical environments. Second, we gain knowledge about apparent tradeoffs between computational and cognitive efforts in reaching certain decisions and about the adaptability of both computers and humans to new problem environments. The extent to which our approach provides useful information for specific environments, of course, depends on how well our problem tasks share features with real-world environments.

Our approach should also provide insights about "optimality" in non-mental health decision-making spheres. There has been a growing realization among decision scientists (see Einhorn et al., 1979; March, 1978) that real-world decision problems should not be considered exclusively in terms of mathematical optimality. It may be more interesting to give a good description of the problem and its solution than to compute what constitutes rigorous or correct solutions.

Clearly, the potential for elaboration of types of strategies and extrapolation to other decision tasks is immense. The general approach of devising artificial environments that simulate real-world tasks and a variety of cognitive strategies could be a powerful one, and it should be useful in generating interesting hypotheses about human judgment. As these are developed and investigated, perhaps we obtain and provide some insights into the cognitive processes that underlie decision making in problem spaces that resemble a variety of demanding and dynamic decision environments.

Finally, this type of research should lend itself to restructuring existing real-world environments such as DSM-III-R, and perhaps even to modifying these and other flawed taxonomic systems. Thus, although we deal mainly with hypothetical symptoms, signs, disorders, treatments, and so on, our system can be used quite readily to discover what taxonomic features of the current diagnostic nomenclature should be modified or elaborated in order to create a more scientifically sound nomenclature and one that will facilitate better decision making. A bit ambitious? Perhaps. But not out of reach, given the increased sophistication of computer software capabilities. For example, work currently coming out of the Carnegie-Mellon information processing group, which is focusing on a unified theory of cognition (e.g., see Laird et al., 1987; Waldrop, 1988), dwarfs the modest proposal of the present chapter. Their computer program system, Soar, is now poised, or at least so they write, to display intelligent learning abilities in a vast area of problem solving, planning, and diagnosis, and is ready to apply this intelligence to most cognitive situations currently facing humans.

REFERENCES

American Psychiatric Association (1987). *Diagnostic and statistical manual of mental disorders* (3rd ed., Rev.). Washington, DC: Author.

Arkes, H.R., Dawes, R.M., & Christensen, C. (1986). Factors influencing the use of a decision rule in a probabilistic task. *Organizational Behavior and Human Decision Processes, 37*, 93–110.

Boring, E.G. (1946). Mind and mechanism. *The American Journal of Psychology, 59*, 173–192.

Brooks, R., & Kleinmuntz, B. (1974). Design of an intelligent interviewer. *Behavioral Science, 19*, 16–20.

Bruner, J.S., Goodnow, J.J., & Austin, G.A. (1956). *A study of thinking.* New York: John Wiley & Sons.

Einhorn, H.J., Kleinmuntz, D.N., & Kleinmuntz, B. (1979). Linear regression *and* process-tracing models of judgment. *Psychological Review, 86*, 465–485.

Hammond, K.R. (1955). Probabilistic functioning and the clinical method. *Psychological Review, 62*, 255–262.

Hammond, K.R., Hursch, C.J., & Todd, F.J. (1964). Analyzing the components of clinical inference. *Psychological Review, 71*, 438–456.

Hoffman, P.J. (1960). The paramorphic representation of clinical judgment. *Psychological Bulletin, 57*, 116–131.

Huesmann, L.R., & Cheng, C.A. (1973). A theory for the induction of mathematical functions. *Psychological Review, 80*, 126–138.

Kleinmuntz, B. (1963a). A portrait of the computer as a young clinician. *Behavioral Science, 8*, 154–156.

Kleinmuntz, B. (1963b). Personality test interpretation by digital computer. *Science, 139*, 416–418.

Kleinmuntz, B. (1968). The processing of clinical information by man and machine. In B. Kleinmuntz (Ed.), *Formal representation of human judgment* (pp. 149–186). New York: John Wiley & Sons.

Kleinmuntz, B. (1975). The computer as clinician. *American Psychologist, 30*, 379–387.

Kleinmuntz, B. (1982). Computational and noncomputational clinical information processing by computer. *Behavioral Science, 27*, 164–175.

Kleinmuntz, B. (1987). Automated interpretation of neuropsychological test data: Comments on Adams and Heaton. *Journal of Consulting and Clinical Psychology, 55*, 266–267.

Kleinmuntz, B. (1990). Why we still use our heads instead of formulas. *Psychological Bulletin, 107*, 296–310.

Kleinmuntz, B., & Elstein, A.S. (1987). Computer modeling of clinical judgment. *Critical Reviews of Medical Informatics, 1*, 209–228.

Kleinmuntz, B., & Kleinmuntz, D.N. (1981). Psychodiagnosis in hypothetical problem spaces. *Behavior Research Methods and Instrumentation, 13*, 417–420.

Kleinmuntz, B., & McLean, R.S. (1968). Diagnostic interviewing by digital computer. *Behavioral Science, 13*, 75–80.

Kleinmuntz, D.N. (1985). Cognitive heuristics and feedback in a dynamic decision environment. *Management Science, 31*, 650–702.

Kleinmuntz, D.N., & Kleinmuntz, B. (1981). Decision strategies in simulated environments. *Behavioral Science, 26*, 294–305.

Kotovsky, K., Hayes, J.R., & Simon, H.A. (1985). Why are some problems hard? Evidence from Tower of Hanoi. *Cognitive Psychology, 17*, 248–294.

Laird, J.E., Newell, A., & Rosenbloom, P.S. (1987). Soar: An architecture for general intelligence. *Artificial Intelligence, 33*, 1–64.

Langley, P., Simon, H.A., Bradshaw, G.L., & Zytkow, J.M. (1986). *Scientific discovery*. Cambridge, MA: MIT Press.

March, J. (1978). Bounded rationality, ambiguity, and the engineering of choice. *Bell Journal of Economics, 9*, 587–608.

Matarazzo, J.D. (1983). Computerized psychological testing. (Editorial). *Science, 221*, 323.

Matarazzo, J.D. (1985). Clinical psychological test interpretations by computer: Hardware outpaces software. *Computers in Human Behavior, 1*, 235–253.

Meehl, P.E. (1986). Causes and effects of my disturbing little book. *Journal of Personality Assessment, 50*, 370–375.

Mynatt, C.R., Doherty, M.E., & Tweney, R.D. Confirmation bias in a simulated research environment: An experimental study of scientific inference. *Quarterly Journal of Experimental Psychology, 29*, 85–95.

Newell, A., Shaw, J.C., & Simon, H.A. (1958). Elements of theory of human problem solving. *Psychological Review, 65*, 151–166.

Newell, A., & Simon, H.A. (1972). *Human problem solving*. Englewood Cliffs, NJ: Prentice-Hall.

Simon, H.A. (1956). Rational choice and the structure of the environment. *Psychological Review, 63*, 129–138.

Simon, H.A. (1957). *Administrative behavior* (2nd ed.). New York: Macmillan.

Simon, H.A. (1969). *The sciences of the artificial*. Cambridge, MA: MIT Press.

Simon, H.A. (1979). Information processing models of cognition. *Annual Review of Psychology, 30*, 363–396.

Simon, H.A., & Lea, G. (1974). Problem solving and rule induction: A unified view. In L.W. Gregg (Ed.), *Knowledge and cognition* (pp. 105–127). Hillsdale, NJ: Lawrence Erlbaum Associates.

Toda, M. (1962). The design of a fungus-eater: A model of human behavior in an unsophisticated environment. *Behavioral Science, 7*, 164–186.

Toda, M. (1980). What happens at the moment of decision? Meta decisions, emotions, and volitions. In J. Sjoberg, T. Tyszka, & J.A. Wise (Eds.), *Human decision making* (Vol. 2). Sweden: Doxa.

Waldrop, M.M. (1988). Soar: A unified theory of cognition? *Science, 241*, 296–298.

Wason, P.C., & Johnson-Laird, P.N. (1972). *Psychology of reasoning: Structure and content*. Cambridge, MA: Harvard University Press.

PART V

TREATMENT

EDITORS' COMMENTS

It is fitting that this section, Treatment, is the largest in the book. From a small beginning as ancillary personnel, clinical psychologists have assumed a vital role in the delivery of treatment services, the development of new procedures, and the scientific study of treatment programs. The scientific contributions of psychologists to this arena have been well known for decades. In fact, psychologists, notably Carl Rogers and Hans Eysenck, were primarily responsible for stimulating the scientific study of psychotherapy. Public acceptance of psychologists as treaters has increased gradually during this period, and is now broad based. Legal and financial equality with physicians has come belatedly, highlighted by the recent inclusion of psychologists as Medicare providers.

This section of the volume highlights the diverse interests and contributions of psychologists to the treatment of psychological and behavioral dysfunction. The chapters describe the predominant models, provide an overview of procedures, summarize relevant research, and point to future directions for the field. In chapter 28, Butler and Strupp review recent developments in psychodynamic psychotherapy, including the increasing emphasis on object relations and transactional processes. They also highlight the increased interest on research, including the manualization of dynamic procedures. Chapter 29, by Fischer, deals with phenomenological therapy. She first explains basic terms and concepts in phenomenology and existentialism, and then describes therapeutic procedures. As in the previous chapter, the increasing emphasis on research is highlighted in the concluding section.

Chapters 30 and 31 focus on behavior therapy with adults and children, respectively. Franks and Barbrack provide an update on behavior therapy with adults in chapter 30. This chapter focuses on "meta-issues," including history, definition, role of learning theory and conditioning, public image, and so on. In contrast to psychodynamic and phenomenological treatments, the empirical basis of behavioral procedures is well established, but theory and definition lag behind. Franks and Barbrack argue for more critical thought in how behavior therapists conceptualize what they do. Harris, Alessandri, and Nathan have opted to describe the most widely used behavioral techniques for some of the common disorders of childhood, including: anxiety disorders, enuresis, Attention-deficit hyperactivity disorder (ADHD), mental retardation and autism, and conduct disorder. Their chapter underscores the creativity of behavior therapists and the broad range of available techniques.

The diversity within psychology is well illustrated in the contrast between chapters 31 and 32, which deal with psychoanalytic approaches with children. Whereas 31 is technique oriented and empirical, 32 reflects the more philosophical and phenomenological orientation of child analysts. O'Connor and Lee first discuss the relationship of child analysis to adult analysis, and then describe recent trends and developments, including the increased role afforded to parents. They then identify new approaches for special populations, including children with medical illnesses and children who have been adopted.

Chapter 33 covers what may be the fastest-growing therapeutic approach: cognitive-behavior therapy (CBT). As described by Kendall, Vitousek, and Kane, CBT reflects something of a middle ground between traditional behavioral approaches and dynamic-phenomenological approaches. The various cognitive strategies maintain the contemporary, objective, and empirical orientation of behavior therapy but venture inside the "black box" to deal with thought and feeling. This chapter reviews representative cognitive-behavioral strategies. The authors take an empirical stance and describe limitations and unanswered questions, as well as areas of success.

As reflected in chapters 28, 29, and 30, individual treatment has traditionally been the predominant modality regardless of theoretical orientation. This pattern has been gradually changing. Due to theoretical and/or empirical developments and to economics, there now is increasing emphasis on group, marital, and family treatments. These approaches are reviewed in chapters 34 by Rose (group therapy), and 35 by Fruzetti and Jacobson (marital and family therapy). Both chapters begin with historical overviews of the respective domains and describe basic concepts. Each chapter then reviews predominant approaches, including human growth, psychodynamic, systems, and behavioral strategies.

The final three chapters in this section deal with issues whose relevance to clinical psychologists has only recently become apparent. Alford and Bishop provide a lucid review of basic issues in psychopharmacology in chapter 36. This chapter is an excellent primer for the nonphysician. It describes relevant concepts and terminology and reviews the uses, side effects, and mechanisms of action of the major psychopharmacologic drug classes. The increasing collaboration between psychologists and biological psychiatrists in both research and clinical practice makes this chapter particularly important. Chapter 37, by Carmody and Matarazzo, deals with health psychology. This area has experienced meteoric growth in the last decade and is rapidly becoming a distinct subspecialty. Following a brief historical overview, Carmody and Matarazzo describe applications in behavioral health and behavioral medicine. The former involves preventive programs and health habits in such areas as obesity, cigarette smoking, alcohol abuse, and stress. The latter deals with physical illnesses, such as chronic pain, cardiovascular disease, and neurological disorders. The chapter concludes with a discussion of a broad range of professional issues, including training, specialty status, and new areas of application.

In the final chapter in this section, Minorities (chapter 38), Jenkins and Ramsey discuss the importance of ethnic and sociocultural differences in the practice of clinical psychology. Psychology has a tradition of concern for minority groups, but Jenkins and Ramsey point out that the field has not been sensitive enough. The first section of the chapter poignantly highlights some of the socioeconomic handicaps faced by minorities in the United States. The authors next provide a brief historical perspective on how minority issues have been addressed by psychology and psychiatry. The remainder of the chapter deals with clinical issues, including prevalent and potential biases in assessment and treatment. The authors' focus throughout is not so much on critique of majority group clinicians, as on the need for *all* professionals to be attuned to the potential for bias and the need to modify techniques to meet the needs of a multicultural society. This chapter is *must* reading for anyone serving a heterogeneous population.

CHAPTER 28

PSYCHODYNAMIC PSYCHOTHERAPY

Stephen F. Butler
Hans H. Strupp

The birth of modern psychotherapy is commonly traced to Josef Breuer's famous patient Anna O., who gained relief from her hysterical difficulties by means of the "talking cure." Sigmund Freud, Breuer's young colleague, built on Breuer's early insights, and his subsequent discoveries of psychological dynamics ushered in a revolution that continues to have profound effects on contemporary clinical thinking and practice.

The method and theory of therapy pioneered by Freud and Breuer, and later developed by Freud into psychoanalysis, has branched into a variety of approaches, all of which are subsumed under the rubric of psychodynamic or psychoanalytic psychotherapy. There is perhaps no single way to view this evolution in psychoanalytic theory, nor is it clear that psychodynamic thinkers would agree on which modifications of the initial theory represent genuine theoretical and therapeutic advances. In this chapter, we will present a particular perspective on the development of theory and practice in psychodynamic psychotherapy that reflects a progression of thinking leading, in our opinion, from quasibiological concepts of internal drives to a potentially more empirical and systematic interpersonal approach to psychotherapy. This devel-

opment involves changes in the fundamental view of personality development and organization, which, in turn, has direct implications for therapeutic concepts, especially *transference* and *countertransference*. As the nature of these concepts has changed, so has the ability of researchers to empirically study psychodynamic psychotherapy. Recent findings of psychodynamic research will be summarized along with a discussion of methodological issues in the scientific study of psychodynamic psychotherapies, including current efforts to "manualize" the psychodynamic therapies. Implications of these theoretical and research advances for future research and training in psychodynamic psychotherapy will also be presented.

FUNDAMENTAL THEORETICAL DEVELOPMENTS SINCE FREUD

Freud's Impulse Theory

Although psychoanalysis is generally regarded as a theory of mental events, recent authors (e.g., Eagle, 1984; Sulloway, 1983) have underscored Freud's original interest in relating psychological events to physiological processes. In the latter part of the 19th century, when Freud studied medicine and neurology, Western thinking was rapidly assimilating the powerful ideas of Charles Darwin (1859, 1871). The young Freud, heavily influenced by the then burgeoning revolution in biology and physiology, completed his medical education under Ernst Brücke, a renowned Viennese physiologist and materialist.[1] As Sulloway (1983) persuasively argued, the biological bent evident in Freud's early medical career was never fully abandoned. Indeed, a cornerstone concept of psychoanalytic theory ties Freud's thinking to biological processes, namely the concept of instinct or drive.

This concept of *drive* is central to Freud's emphasis on instincts as the human being's evolutionary heritage. For Freud, these instincts are ultimately physiological (biochemical) energies. In psychoanalytic theory, these physiological energies were represented psychologically as *wishes*, the psychological counterpart to the instinctual energy or *libido*. Consistent with the Darwinian emphasis on individual and species survival, Freud envisioned these primitive, uncivilized wishes as reflecting survival needs such as thirst, hunger, elimination, and reproduction. He eventually subsumed these under the general category of "sexual" or sensual impulses. Equally important for survival were the aggressive impulses. Both classes of impulses, and their corresponding wishes, play major roles in personality development. Freudian metapsychology—for example, the theories of anxiety, defense, repression—rests on the assumption that individuals experience a continual press to discharge the libidinal energy, obtaining pleasure through tension release when libidinal impulses are gratified.

An important theoretical question emerges at this point. Freud's description of these basic instincts implies the presence of an *object* toward which the instincts are to be directed. The idea of object embodies the notion of the human being in interaction with other human beings. Clearly, sexual gratification and aggression typically are manifested in interactions with people. The theoretical question relates to whether the primary psychological forces in personality development are other people/objects, or whether such primacy belongs to the libidinal impulse. In Freud's view, the object's importance is only as a target for the libidinal drive. From this perspective, an object can be anything, human or animal, animate or inanimate. It can be a "part-object," such as a breast or penis; in short, anything that can be used to discharge energy. As such, the object is only important in terms of its potential for discharging energy. Discussing this view, Eagle (1984) pointed out, "Were drive gratifi-

cation possible without objects . . . one would develop neither an interest in objects nor object relations" (p. 8). Interpersonal attachments are, therefore, developed simply as a means of obtaining instinctual gratification; "love has its origins in attachment to the satisfied need for nourishment" (Freud, 1940, p. 188). Thus, in Freudian terms, interpersonal and social needs are secondary concerns of the personality, necessary only in that drive gratification is impossible without commerce with other human beings. Freud never swayed from the emphasis on gratification of the libidinal (biologically based) impulse as the primary motivation of human behavior.

Object Relations and Sullivan's Interpersonal Theory

Although much of Freud's metapsychology involves the early, psychosexual development of the child, these formulations were constructed almost entirely out of the childhood reminiscences of his adult patients. Freud never directly treated a child. Among the first psychoanalytic observations of children were those made by Melanie Klein (1952), who applied psychoanalytic techniques in her therapies with children. Klein's observations, made in an effort to clarify the connections between childhood experiences and adult personality, conflicted with the expectations of Freudian theory. Instead of trying to control libidinal impulses, children devoted the greatest amount of energy to constructing their interpersonal worlds. Thus, children were not so much driven by the need to control erotic impulses as by the need to control feelings directed at significant figures in their lives. As Cashdan (1988) pointed out, Klein discovered "the inner world of the child was a world of human relationships" (p. 5).

Observations by Klein and others paved the way for subsequent theories leading away from Freud's drive theory. Several object relations theories were developed by the "British School" of object relations, including Klein, W.R.D. Fairbairn (1954), and Margaret Mahler (1952; Mahler, Pine, & Bergman, 1975). Later theories were contributed by two American theorists, Kernberg (1975, 1976, 1984) and Kohut (1971, 1977). Although each of these theorists presents a different view of the specific developmental phases of object relations, the importance of the movement can best be appreciated by reflecting on the commonalities these approaches share.

Of foremost concern to object relations theorists is the role that human relationships play in personality development. From this perspective, the best way to view the infant is not as *pleasure seeking*, as Freud would have it, but rather, as *object seeking*. Because the child's first encounter with another human being is typically the mother, these authors focus on this relationship as the setting for a drama with profound effects on the child's developing sense of "self." Although the role of the self is most unequivocally articulated in Kohut's writings, the development of the self is directly or indirectly addressed by all object relations theorists.

According to these theories, the child interacts with the mother through a variety of stages (depending on the particular theory[2]). Consonant with Freudian theory, the goal of these mother-child interactions is often viewed as the gratification of basic needs. However, in object relations theory, the child internalizes or "introjects" aspects of the objects with whom he or she interacts. The child initially divides or *splits* these internalized perceptions of others into essentially gratifying objects ("the good breast," "the good [rewarding] mother") and bad or frustrating objects ("the bad or empty breast," "the bad [punishing] mother"). These rudimentary divisions of the world constitute the beginnings of discriminations from which the child will develop a sense of self in relation to other people. An important aspect of splitting is the assumption that in early development, the child's experience of objects is "either/or." That is, if the good object is present, the bad object does not exist, and vice versa. Further maturation brings with it some extraordinarily difficult tasks as the child becomes increasingly aware that the same object can be both "good" and "bad" and begins to construct an internal world of objects (internalized or introjected aspects of people) whose relations to the child literally define his or her sense of self. Simply stated, in the normal course of events, the process of establishing clear boundaries between the "other" and the "I" or "me" continues as the child's sense of self solidifies into a separate, organized, and essentially positive self-system capable of giving and receiving love and sustaining a sense of identity. When the mother-child interactions are tinged with too many negative, frustrating experiences, difficulties in developing an independent, organized sense of self can occur, giving rise to psychopathology in the object relations view.

There is disagreement in psychoanalytic circles regarding the degree to which an object relations model of personality development is consistent with, that is, an extension of instinct theory, or whether these approaches are in direct contrast. Many of the object relations theorists themselves uphold an essential compatibility with instinct theory (e.g., Kernberg,

1976), whereas other authors suggest a modification of the original instinct theory (e.g., Eagle, 1984), and still others (e.g., Greenberg & Mitchell, 1983) see the two approaches as epistemologically incompatible.

Whatever may be the ultimate resolution of this dispute, there is increasing evidence that interpersonal/object needs are not merely "secondary drives," derived from more primary, biologically based drives. Probably the most compelling evidence comes from Harlow's (1958) famous studies of infant monkeys and surrogate mothers. In these studies, the infant monkeys were observed to attach to a soft, terrycloth surrogate mother, even when a wire surrogate providing satisfaction of the so-called primary drives of hunger and thirst was available. As Eagle (1984) pointed out, Harlow's investigations "showed rather decisively that the infant monkey's attachment to its surrogate mother was not derived from or secondary to the latter's association with reduction of so-called primary drives (i.e., hunger, thirst)" (p. 10). Interestingly, from a Darwinian perspective, such animal studies support the notion that our evolutionary heritage need not be conceptualized only in physiochemical terms.

Although object relations theory emphasizes the role of interpersonal relations, the interpersonal perspective of Harry Stack Sullivan and his followers is usually considered separately, and the relationship between interpersonal theory and object relations is unclear. Some authors consider Sullivan to be an American counterpart of the British object relations theorists. Although there is obvious overlap between these approaches, Sullivan's interpersonal stance is more clearly differentiated from the original Freudian position on instincts. Like object relations theory, Sullivan (1953) focuses on the earliest interactions between mother and child, but his model of personality development includes important stages into late adolescence. For instance, his discussion of the critical importance for the child to establish a preadolescent relationship with a peer or "chum" clearly proposes that such a relationship can, under some circumstances, salvage the effects of earlier, problematic interactions with others. And, although Sullivan does postulate the existence of needs, tensions, "energy transformations," and "biological disequilibration," even these quasibiological concepts are viewed in inherently interpersonal terms. For instance, Sullivan writes, *"The observed activity of the infant arising from the tension of needs induces tension in the mothering one, which tension is experienced as tenderness and as an impulse to activities toward the relief of the infant's needs"* (1953; p. 39), and *"The tension of anxiety, when present in the mothering one, induces anxiety in the infant*" (p. 41, original italics). The implications of this view cannot be underestimated. Even the earliest physiological experiences are experienced by the infant as inextricably embedded in a context of interpersonal interactions. Sullivan's point makes clear that it is inconceivable to conceptualize the individual apart from a context of other persons and that personality is *only* manifest in interpersonal situations. From this perspective Swensen (1973) noted, "Literally to exist as a person, to have a self, to be a personality, one must have others to interact with. If there is no one around to interact with, no self, no personality, no human being, as we usually think of the concept, can exist" (p.6). Indeed, for Sullivan, an important step in the development of the self is the "personification of the self." This refers to the formation of an internalized image of the self that has characteristics (e.g., the "good me," the "bad me," and the "not me") and can be *the object of self–self interactions* (e.g., self-love, self-hate, self-control, etc.). In this view, the self is developed entirely out of interactions with others that are internalized (or introjected). Although similar to the object relations view, rather than introjecting aspects of the other, the child introjects his or her *interactions* with the other. It should be recognized that this dichotomy between Sullivan's theory and object relations theory may be more accurately stated as a relative emphasis. Object relations theorists would maintain that interaction with the object is necessary for introjection to take place. It may be unwise to postulate too clear a distinction between one's experience of an object and interaction with that object. "What we think of ourselves is inextricably interwoven with what we think others think of us" (i.e., as inferred from how others treat us; Kiesler, 1982, p. 6).

Again, the importance of conceptualizing human personality in this way has profound implications. The theoretical focus on interpersonal interactions directs the attention of the therapist and researcher to social *transactions* and interpersonal communication. These phenomena, that is, social transactions, are intrinsically observable and, therefore, are more susceptible to empirical investigation than the vicissitudes of internal drives. Furthermore, social transactions can be shown to follow general "laws" governing the oscillating sequences of each participant's contribution to the ongoing interaction (Anchin & Kiesler, 1982).

Interpersonal theorists are aware, for instance, that interpersonal transactions are inherently circular, that "human social behavior is embedded in a feedback network wherein the 'effect' influences or alters the 'cause'" (Kiesler, 1982, p. 9). This circularity can be further characterized as *complementary*, in that the cause and effect sequences in interpersonal communication are predictable. Hence, a person's interpersonal actions tend to invite, evoke, or "pull" for predictable responses from the other. In one sense, the universal predictability of interpersonal interactions, based on learning in previous interactions, permits comprehensible and efficient social intercourse. If, however, one's previous interpersonal interactions have been marred by trauma, neglect, or other painful experience, distorted and overly rigid expectations of others' responses can result. When this happens the individual attempts to constrain the other's reaction, creating a "pull" for the other to respond in a way that is congruent with the rigid expectations. At the same time, the individual is unaware of the nature of his or her communications, and there is a tendency to deny the inflexible, controlling aspects of these communications. The result is duplicitous or mixed messages. When the recipient responds to the unacknowledged "pull" in such messages, a kind of self-fulfilling prophecy takes place, sometimes referred to as maladaptive or vicious cycles (Butler & Binder, 1987; Schacht, Binder, & Strupp, 1984; Wachtel, 1977). These interpersonal sequences can be relatively precisely operationalized (e.g., Benjamin, 1982; Kiesler, 1986; Leary, 1957), and the laws of complementarity allow the specification of classes of behaviors that should be engaged in or avoided by the therapist (see discussion on research below).

THERAPEUTIC ISSUES IN DYNAMIC PSYCHOTHERAPY

The perspectives on personality development proposed by the various schools of psychodynamic psychotherapy are essentially maps for guiding the therapist's formulation of a patient's diagnosis (i.e., a conception of what is "wrong") and for guiding interventions. All dynamic therapies, however, follow the same basic outline for conceptualizing the therapeutic endeavor. As Freud observed earlier, despite the patient's conscious endorsement of the therapeutic aim of release from symptoms, the therapist meets with "a violent and tenacious resistance, which persists throughout the whole length of treatment" (Freud, 1920/1966, p. 286). In dynamic therapy, however, the existence of this *resistance* represents the essence of the patient's psychological problems. When resistance is manifested toward the therapist, it is known as *transference*. Analysis of this reaction to the therapist, that is, analysis of the transference, is the sine qua non of dynamic therapy. All dynamic therapies assume that, in some manner or other, the patient *repeats*, with the therapist, attitudes and emotional reactions from earlier relationships. This repetition in the therapeutic relationship of earlier relationship problems permits the therapist to facilitate changes in the present of emotional problems that originated in the past. As such, dynamic therapy is an in vivo therapy.

Transference

For Freud, psychopathology was the result of an unconscious conflict between the socialized ego and the threatened expression of unsocialized, libidinal (sexual and aggressive) impulses. The neurotic conflict can be abolished by teaching the ego to accept, tolerate, and modify the subjectively threatening impulse. In the Freudian view, the patient's entire psychological system resists conscious awareness of the libidinal impulses, as well as awareness of or memory of the original conflict. Repression (literally: forgetting) of the conflict has two results: one is maintenance of the status quo, the other is a tendency to "act out" or repeat attitudes and emotions relevant to the conflict rather than consciously remembering it. The patient's compulsion to repeat with the therapist the essence of the early conflict is the transference. According to Freud, this repetition occurs because of a so-called "regressive instinct" that attempts to restore the organism to an earlier psychical state (Freud, 1920). Thus, Freud explained the concept of transference (i.e., repetition), ultimately, in terms of an instinct, that is, an instinct to repeat. In this way, the fundamentally interpersonal phenomenon of transference was seen as the manifestation of the more primary intrapsychic instincts.

For the object relations theorists, the patient's inner world is composed of the internalized and fantasized, good and bad experiences with past objects. These objects are *projected* onto the therapist and distort the "real" relationship with the therapist (Greenberg & Mitchell, 1983; Guntrip, 1973). These distorted perceptions of the therapist, based on early object relations, constitute the transference. Some object relations theorists have included the experience of the therapist (or other object of the projection) in the concept of *projective identification*. This refers to "patterns of interpersonal behavior in which a person induces others to behave or respond in a circumscribed fashion" (Cashdan, 1988, p. 55). In this view, one person is more or less manipulated into behaving in a

manner that reflects an identification with a disowned, or split-off, aspect of the person doing the projecting.

This projection process is similar to the transactional conception of transference held by interpersonal theorists, whose theoretical approach is quite compatible with an object relations view (Strupp & Binder, 1984). However, rather than projection, the interpersonal conception of transference emphasizes the circular, transactional quality of human social relations. As previously described, a history of problematic interpersonal experiences culminates in overly rigid styles of interacting, designed to reduce threats to the self. The circular, complementary nature of human interactions stipulates that an overly rigid style of interacting will tend to constrict the other's possible responses, leading to predictable outcomes. *Evoking style* (Anchin & Kiesler, 1982; Strupp & Binder, 1984) is the term used to describe characteristic patterns of interacting with people that pull for a more or less specific counterresponse from the other person. When this occurs with the therapist, the evoking style can be viewed as a transference phenomenon, in that its origin is traced to experiences with significant others in the past, and its purpose is to recreate old, familiar (predictable) interpersonal scenarios. Quite literally, the interpersonal problems that brought the patient into therapy emerge within the therapeutic relationship itself. This is the concept of transference in interpersonal terms.

Countertransference

In classical psychoanalysis, countertransference is the therapist's version of transference; accordingly, the patient comes to represent an object of the therapist's past onto whom feelings and wishes derived from unresolved conflicts are projected. The orthodox position, then, conceives of countertransference as a breach of the therapist's objectivity and neutrality. The introduction of such subjectivity into the therapist's observations is an impediment to the therapy that must be overcome, usually via the therapist's personal analysis. The goal is to achieve and maintain an objective point of view.

This orthodox view of countertransference began to yield to an emerging perspective that viewed the therapist's personal reactions to the patient as useful information for understanding the patient. In a radical paper titled, "Hate in the Countertransference," Winnicott (1949) distinguished "objective countertransference" from other types of therapist reactions. Briefly, this term refers to "the analyst's love and hate in reaction to the actual personality and behavior of the patient based on objective observation" (p. 70). Because certain behavior naturally engenders certain reactions, the therapist can use his or her own reactions in the therapy to better understand the patient's conflicts. To experience, tolerate, and not act out the "objective" hate one might experience with a given patient is an essential part of treatment for Winnicott. The patient must receive realistic feedback concerning his or her impact on others as a condition for psychological growth.

Since Winnicott's work, the idea that countertransference reactions can be useful in assessment and treatment has gained increasing acceptance. For instance, considerable attention has been given to countertransference reactions commonly encountered with certain types of patients, such as those with borderline and narcissistic disorders (e.g., Giovacchini, 1979; Kernberg, 1975), because these patients tend to elicit from therapists a more or less predictable set of responses. Indeed, the utility of countertransference responses for enhancing a therapist's understanding of patients has become a generally accepted tenet of psychoanalytic thinking (e.g., Epstein, 1979; Langs, 1976; Menninger & Holzman, 1973).

Again, the interpersonal view of countertransference is very similar to the psychoanalytic one, although certain important philosophical differences remain (e.g., Binder, Strupp, & Schacht, 1983; Butler, Flasher, & Strupp, in press). For the interpersonal theorist, countertransference refers to the therapist's inevitable interpersonal involvement with the patient and cannot be minimized or eliminated. Indeed, the therapist is a participant observer who cannot avoid being "hooked" by the patient (Kiesler, 1982). The interpersonal theorist's emphasis on interpersonal/social reality underscores the idea that there is no objective reality independent of the social interpretations consciously and unconsciously (automatically) generated by the participants. Both members of the therapeutic dyad are responding to "real" aspects of the current situation, and both participants bring with them knowledge, expectations, and styles of behavior based on experiences with significant others in the past. In psychopathology, early interpersonal deprivations, traumatic experiences and the like leave patients with unrealistic expectations of themselves and others and contribute to an inability to achieve sufficient gratifications from contemporary interactions with significant others. These rigid and maladaptive expectations fuel the evoking style, which comprises the patient's transference. In turn, these evocative maneuvers "pull" more or less specific responses from significant others that will confirm the patient's rigid,

maladaptive expectations. This process results in the vicious cycles of self-defeating interpersonal sequences (Butler & Binder, 1987; Carson, 1982) mentioned earlier. Within this conceptual scheme, countertransference is seen as the therapist's experience of the "pull" to respond to the patient's evoking style.

Modern Dynamic Psychotherapy

In the wake of these various descriptions of dynamic theories of personality and therapeutic concepts, one might reasonably ask: What precisely is dynamic therapy? In general, it can be stated that all dynamic approaches involve an acceptance of the idea that problematic behavior involves actions (Schafer, 1976) and attitudes about which the patient is unaware; or, stated differently, dynamic therapies emphasize unconscious determinants of behavior. Although some psychodynamic theorists postulate a distinction between "exploratory" or "uncovering" techniques and "supportive" techniques that involve such tactics as encouragement and advice (e.g., Luborsky, 1984; Menninger & Holzman, 1973), probably the therapeutic approach most widely accepted by dynamic theorists involves some form of analysis of the transference (Anchin & Kiesler, 1982; Gill, 1982; Strupp & Binder, 1984).

From our perspective, neurotic and characterological problems are seen as the result of disturbed interpersonal patterns that interfere with the person's adaptive functioning. Symptoms, such as anxiety, depression, somatic complaints, and so on, accompany the sense of helplessness, frustration, and dissatisfaction that result from self-defeating attempts to manage or cope with interpersonal situations. Rather than symptoms, dynamic therapies address the interpersonal *patterns* that give rise to the symptoms. The patient is viewed as someone who has a history of difficulty achieving satisfying and rewarding relationships. Examination of the patient's history reveals the nature of his or her maladaptive patterns. Usually learned in childhood as a response to certain familial situations, these patterns of relating typically reflect problems of intimacy and autonomy. When the patient enters therapy, he or she experiences essentially the same form of impediments to the success of *this* relationship (i.e., a successful therapy). As a result, the impediments or resistances to the therapeutic work represent the patient's difficulty establishing a meaningful, collaborative, and successful relationship with the therapist. The form these problems take with the therapist is not fundamentally different from the patient's problems establishing satisfying relationships outside of therapy. The therapeutic situation is structured in such a way as to cast the patient's difficulties with interpersonal relationships in bas-relief, making it an ideal setting for eliciting, observing, and working through issues of autonomy and intimacy.

Dynamic psychotherapies can also be defined in contrast to other models of psychological treatment, especially behavioral, cognitive-behavioral, or medical (pharmacological) approaches. Unlike these modalities, dynamic therapists view themselves as treating underlying "problems in living" (Anchin & Kiesler, 1982; Strupp & Binder, 1984) rather than symptoms or a disease. In addition, the behavioral approaches see people as basically rational, logical, and aware of their motivations. Thus, behavioral therapists tend to accept at face value the patient's stated desire to change. Dynamic therapists, on the other hand, assume that patients both desire to change and, unconsciously, resist and fear the changes that treatment may bring (see, e.g., the debate in Wachtel, 1982). Patients come to us in pain, seeking relief, yet by their actions and attitudes they continually resist efforts of the therapist to help. If asked straight away, "Do you want help to change?" patients uniformly answer in the affirmative. But the tenacity with which they hold onto maladaptive beliefs, perceptions, and behaviors points toward an irrational, nonlogical process that works to resist beneficial change. Emphasis on this clinical observation constitutes one of the main schisms between the dynamic and nondynamic camps. Despite recent developments in the thinking of some cognitive-behavioral theorists (e.g., Meichenbaum & Gilmore, 1984), who propose the theoretical recognition of unconscious or "automatic" thoughts, it is psychodynamic theory that takes most seriously the primacy of unconscious involvement in the emotional and interpersonal processes underlying psychopathology.

RESEARCH AND PSYCHODYNAMIC PSYCHOTHERAPY

In 1952, Hans Eysenck challenged the field, which at that time was dominated by psychoanalysis, when he purported to show that response rates to psychotherapy were no greater than would be expected with the passage of time, that is, the "spontaneous remission" concept. Nearly 35 years later, Lambert, Shapiro, and Bergin (1986), in their review of the psychotherapy research literature, draw the following conclusion:

Psychotherapy outcome research shows that some control patients improve with the passage of time, that a variety of "placebo" control procedures produce gains that exceed those in no-treatment controls, and that psychotherapies produce gains that exceed those obtained through the use of "placebo" controls. Psychotherapists are more than placebologists. (p. 163).

In addition, these authors also document that the gains made in psychotherapy tend to be lasting. However, despite these optimistic conclusions, psychotherapy research has failed to identify any particular theory or set of techniques as clearly superior to any other (e.g., DiLoreto, 1971; Elkin, Shea, Watkins, & Collins, 1986; Kernberg et al., 1972; Klein, Zitrin, Woerner, & Ross, 1983; Miller & Berman, 1983; Pilkonis, Imber, Lewis, & Rubinsky, 1984; Sloane, Staples, Cristol, Yorkston, & Whipple, 1975; Smith, Glass, & Miller, 1980; Strupp & Hadley, 1979). Luborsky, Singer, and Luborsky (1975) evoked the "Alice in Wonderland" quality of this predicament by quoting the dodo bird's ruling, "everybody has won and all must have prizes." This inability to differentiate specific effects for the various treatments has resulted in a methodological and assessment crisis in psychotherapy research, which can be seen in negative terms (e.g., Prioleau, Murdock, & Brody, 1983) or as a challenge to reconceptualize our theories of psychotherapy and the methods used to investigate them.

In light of these findings, the question arises as to the contribution that research can be expected to make to the understanding of psychotherapy in general and dynamic psychotherapy in particular. We now turn our attention to a brief discussion of methodological and assessment issues that are relevant to the scientific study of psychotherapy.

Problem of Psychotherapy Outcome

The single most important problem, overshadowing all others and placing them in perspective, is the issue of psychotherapeutic effectiveness. Despite the preponderance of evidence cited above, further understanding of the effectiveness of psychodynamic psychotherapy is hampered by the fact that researchers and practitioners alike have difficulty adequately conceptualizing and defining the notion of "outcome." This lack of clarity is problematic for both psychotherapy researchers and for those charged with policy decisions regarding psychotherapy (Strupp, 1986). To scientifically study psychotherapy, currently accepted experimental designs typically require a particular patient's response to psychotherapy to be distilled into an easily manipulatable number that can be statistically analyzed. The resulting oversimplification of the phenomenon appears to render the "scientific" findings questionable at best and often irrelevant. Concern with such oversimplification is an important reason why the majority of psychotherapy practitioners continue to report low usage rates of psychotherapy research (Cohen, Sargent, & Sechrest, 1986; Morrow-Bradley & Elliott, 1986).

The problem of defining psychotherapy outcome touches on many facets of human life. Conceptions of mental health and illness cannot be considered apart from the problems of philosophy, ethics, religion, and public policy. Inescapably, we deal with human existence and the person's place in the world, and ultimately, any adequate conception of outcome must confront questions of *value* (Strupp & Hadley, 1977). Someone must make a judgment whether a person's concern with duty is a virtue or a symptom of compulsiveness; whether a decrement of 10 *T*-score points on the Depression Scale of the Minnesota Multiphasic Personality Inventory (MMPI) in the 90 to 100 range is a greater or a lesser "improvement" than a like change between 50 and 60; whether in one case we accept a patient's judgment that he or she feels "better," whereas in another we set it aside, calling it "flight into health," "reaction formation," "delusional," and so forth. These decisions can only be made by reference to the values society assigns to feelings, attitudes, and actions. These values are inherent in conceptions of mental health and illness as well as in clinical judgments. As Strupp and Hadley (1977) have shown, few therapists or researchers have taken seriously the implications of this complex view of outcome. Therapists continue to assess treatment outcomes on the basis of global clinical impressions, whereas researchers persist in the assumption that quantitative indexes can be interpreted as if they were thermometer readings. In reality, values influence and suffuse every judgment of outcome.

An additional dilemma for scientific considerations of outcome relates to the "uniformity myth" (Kiesler, 1966) inherent in the assumptions of most psychotherapy research. Psychotherapy is not a unitary process, applied by interchangeable therapists to unitary problems. Yet, questions regarding the "effectiveness" of a given psychotherapeutic approach assume such uniformity exists; otherwise it makes little sense to conclude that a particular therapy is effective. In actuality, as we shall discuss in greater detail below, the effectiveness of any particular therapy depends entirely on the persons involved, the patient qualities, therapist skills, and other factors that render any conclusion about the "effectiveness" of a given ther-

apy or technique per se virtually meaningless (Butler & Strupp, 1986).

A special problem exists for dynamic psychotherapy when one considers outcome issues. Psychodynamic therapists specifically do *not* regard symptom measures as the ultimate gauge of change. Although improvements in this domain are clearly expected, symptoms are neither the target of psychodynamic interventions nor is change conceptualized along this dimension. Indeed, it is entirely possible within a dynamic framework for a decrease in symptomatology to mask the continuing persistence of maladaptive patterns, whereas a temporary worsening of symptoms might herald genuine changes. Rather than symptom change, dynamic therapy postulates change in intrapsychic and/or interpersonal functioning, which is most likely manifest in changes in patterns of relating to other people. For example, the depressed married woman who comes to realize that her patterns of self-doubt and submission have kept her in a destructive marital situation may experience increased dysphoria as she faces the difficult choices (e.g., divorce) that accompany real change in longstanding, habitual patterns. Symptomatic assessment at this point in the treatment could conceivably yield data that would characterize the therapy as "unsuccessful"! Although such illustrations may be convincing, the methodological dilemma places the burden squarely on the shoulders of dynamic theorists and researchers to develop measures and assessment methodologies that would adequately measure these outcomes.

There have been some promising, though largely untested, attempts to evolve more satisfactory outcome measures. As one might expect, however, these are more cumbersome than simple symptom checklists. One notion involves the idea of "micro-outcomes" (Orlinsky & Howard, 1986). Micro-outcomes refer to the idea that the "effectiveness" of a given therapist's action is most productively observed in the more or less immediate response of the patient. If changes in interactions with others is the goal, then the initial changes ought to be observed in the patient's interactions with the therapist. Thus, if a therapist's comment is followed by increased sharing and exploration (increased intimacy) with the therapist, then a beneficial effect is presumed to have occurred. On the other hand, increased defensiveness and withdrawal is expected in those instances where the intervention has a negative effect. Silberschatz, Fretter, and Curtis (1986), for example, successfully used this methodology to assess the effectiveness of various types of interpretations. Of course, this methodology assumes that these momentary outcomes eventually culminate in larger outcomes, an assumption for which there is some evidence (e.g., Gomes-Schwartz, 1978). Yet, it may be too simplistic to assume that the effectiveness of a given intervention should always be followed by immediate relaxation of defenses. It may be that truly effective therapist actions are initially followed by some defensiveness, precisely because they somehow "hit home" to the patient. Another effort, largely explored by Luborsky and his colleagues (Luborsky, Crits-Christoph, Mintz, & Auerbach, 1988), involves efforts to measure change in patients' core conflictual relationship themes (CCRT). Such methods require large investments of researchers' time and are, therefore, usually restricted to investigations of only a small number of cases. Indeed, it is likely that intensive studies of a small number of cases will turn out to be the best use of the psychotherapy researcher's time. Another approach to measuring psychodynamic change has been attempted by members of our research team who have explored the use of Benjamin's (1982) system for measuring patients' introjects (based on the interpersonal idea that we internalize how others see us). This system, known as Structural Analysis of Social Behavior (SASB) permits the detection of changes in how an individual treats him- or herself. Such changes do correlate positively with symptomatic changes (Pearson rs in the range of .30 to .44), and have been successfully related to therapy process variables (Henry, 1986). The definitive utility of any of these new methods awaits replication and further development. Without the adoption of more useful and ecologically valid assessment measures, further strides in the scientific understanding of psychotherapy will be limited.

Problems in Measuring Patient and Therapist Variables

Although there are problems measuring the dependent variable in psychotherapy research (i.e., outcome), there are no fewer problems in measuring and conceptualizing the independent variables, namely, patient characteristics and therapist qualitites, actions, or techniques. Patient characteristics have often been studied by focusing on static, demographic variables such as age, sex, social class, education, intelligence, income, degree of psychopathology, and the like. The findings of such studies tend to find contradictory or weak relationships between such variables and outcome (Garfield, 1986). More promising are studies of patients' willingness and ability to engage in verbal psychotherapies, which tend to show significantly positive association with outcome (Orlinsky &

Howard, 1986). However, as we found using measures of patient suitability (Butler, Thackrey, & Strupp, 1987), such significant relationships tend to be in the range of Pearson rs of about .33 to .52, which account for only about 9% to 25% of the variance. Although such findings are relevant to the scientific understanding of psychotherapy, the use of such measures to predict whether a particular patient will or will not be able to make use of psychotherapy is premature at best. Nevertheless, evidence is mounting that patients who become actively involved in their therapy tend to do better than those who remain hostile or aloof (Gomes-Schwartz, 1978; Orlinsky & Howard, 1986). Rather than attempting probabilistic predictions of patient response, such research may make a greater contribution by helping to identify patients likely to present specific difficulties and by helping therapists learn to deal more productively with them.

Investigation of the therapist's contribution to psychotherapy outcome has been fraught with enormous difficulties. As previously discussed, the initial expectation that a particular theory or set of techniques could be identified as "correct" has proven to be a "dead end" (Strupp, 1986). The traditional paradigms used to compare the various approaches reflect a linear model where the therapist does something that is assumed to have a unidirectional effect on the patient. The failure of these paradigms highlights a fundamental inappropriateness of linear models for understanding psychotherapy. There may be greater promise in adopting the model of circular causality. Consider the studies by Strupp (1980a, 1980b, 1980c, 1980d), Henry, Schacht, and Strupp (1986), and Henry (1986). In these investigations, patient communications defined as hostile, withdrawn, or otherwise provocative tended to be met with complementary responses by the therapist. Thus, the therapists' actions in poor outcome cases are not applications of procedure directed toward the patient in a linear fashion, but rather, are influenced by the ongoing interactions with patients. These therapist reactions, in turn, appear to negatively affect the patient, perhaps by confirming the patient's maladaptive expectations. Such results do not imply that that technique is irrelevant. Rather, they argue against the idea of technique as something the therapist does to the patient and in favor of a view of technique as involving principles and strategies for managing the therapeutic relationship. In this sense, technical considerations are not independent of the context of the interpersonal relationship (Butler & Strupp, 1986). Specification of the relationship between technical and interpersonal *skill* has been greatly furthered by the advent of therapy manuals, to which we now turn.

Psychodynamic Therapy Manuals

Investigations of and training in dynamic psychotherapy have been hampered from the beginning by unsystematic and global descriptions of therapeutic technique. Very early investigations of psychoanalysts (Glover, 1955) showed that therapists who identified themselves as practicing psychoanalysis were actually behaving quite differently in sessions. Not until the 1980s, however, were there serious efforts to define precisely the actions expected of the therapist. Klerman, Rounsaville, Chevron, Neu, and Weissman (1984) introduced a manual describing an interpersonal therapy (IPT) for depression,[3] and Luborsky (1984) authored the first manual on psychoanalytic psychotherapy. These efforts were followed by Strupp and Binder (1984), who published a manual on time-limited dynamic psychotherapy (TLDP). This latter work was based on the idea that therapists could benefit from specialized training to improve awareness of and attention to the transference and countertransference problems that can derail a therapy.

The purpose of these manuals, as far as psychotherapy research is concerned, is to achieve a reasonable degree of uniform quality and consistency of therapist performance, and thereby exert greater control over the treatment variable in psychotherapy studics. The ability of current therapy manuals to accomplish this goal has yet to be established. The results of recent major psychotherapy research programs involving manualized therapies (Elkin, Parloff, Hadley, & Autry, 1985; Elkin, Shea, Watkins, et al., 1989; Luborsky, McLellan, Woody, O'Brien, & Auerbach, 1985; Strupp, Butler, & Henry, 1986) suggest that controlling the treatment variable may be more complex than originally assumed.

A major advantage of manualization is the ability to specify the activities expected of the therapist conducting a particular type of therapy. This has fostered the creation of so-called *adherence scales* (Butler & Strupp, in press; Butler, Strupp, & Lane, 1987; Luborsky, 1984; O'Malley et al., 1988; Rounsaville, O'Malley, Foley, & Weissman, 1988). Early results, however, have failed to support the notion that adherence to manual prescriptions (technical adherence) per se is related to superior outcomes. Although Luborsky et al. (1985) reported a relation between "purity" of adherence and outcome, the more general finding is a lack of correlation between adherence and outcome (Butler, Lane, & Strupp, 1988; Rounsaville et al.,

1988). Somewhat separate from considerations of adherence is the question of therapist skill. O'Malley et al. (1988) found that patient-reported change and lower termination levels of apathy and anxiety/depression were related to supervisors' ratings of "skill." Rounsaville et al. (1988) found that therapists who deviated from the manual guidelines in an attempt to work with more difficult patients were judged by supervisors to be more skillful. Although preliminary, our data also suggest that a therapist's skill is more critical than adherence to particular techniques.

This emphasis on therapeutic skill represents a growing area of interest in psychotherapy research. In their exhaustive review of the literature, Orlinsky and Howard (1986) concluded that, although specific interventions were not consistently associated with outcome, therapist "skillfulness" was shown to be consistently associated with outcome. Such conclusions tend to be based on judges' global impressions of skill. Further efforts to operationalize skill have proven difficult.

An additional dimension of skill was highlighted by Luborsky et al.'s (1985) finding that therapists' ability to establish a "helping alliance" far outweighed the contribution of technical adherence. Traditionally, the therapist's ability to establish a collaborative relationship was discussed with respect to the personal characteristics of the therapist, such as warmth, genuineness, positive regard, and so forth (cf. Rogers's, 1956, facilitative factors). Although measures of these therapist qualities rarely yield negative relations to outcome (Beutler, Crago, & Arizmendi, 1986; Orlinsky & Howard, 1986), such terms have only been loosely defined and tend to be considered separate from technical matters.

In our view, the quality of the therapist–patient interactions represents more than simply an "alliance" to be established before the "therapy" can begin. Rather, the creation and maintenance of a collaborative relationship can be viewed as the heart of the therapy itself. Sharp distinctions between the technical and personal influence of the therapist are rejected in favor of a position that recognizes the essential totality of the therapist's skillful performance.

Viewing therapist skill in this way has important implications for the use of manuals in research and training. Although the dynamic therapy manuals to date have attempted to specify the therapeutic interventions prescribed by dynamic theory, they have assumed an adequate level of interpersonal skill. Early reports of studies designed to evaluate the effectiveness of manuals to enhance the quality and consistency of therapists' performance have shown that adherence to prescribed techniques can be taught (Butler et al., 1988; Dobson & Shaw, 1988; Rounsaville et al., 1988; Shaw & Dobson, 1988). However, only a weak relationship has been demonstrated between such technical adherence and independently rated competent performance (Dobson & Shaw, 1988; Rounsaville et al., 1988; Schaffer, 1982, 1983). It seems evident that psychotherapy manuals have not yet been shown to produce more effective therapists; nor have they yielded greater consistency and skill.

To further illustrate this problem, consider the following example taken from a therapy conducted as part of our research program. After training to deal directly with interpersonal problems that arise in the patient–therapist relationship, one therapist was observed to discuss with the patient how he (the patient) had given up a pattern of submissively deferring to the therapist's views. On the surface, this reflects adherence to the technical recommendations prescribed by the manual (Strupp & Binder, 1984). Yet, clinical judges rated the therapist's comments in that transaction as highly controlling and the patient's response as highly submissive, suggesting that their conversation represented a reenactment of the very maladaptive interpersonal pattern under discussion.

Such observations reveal a discrepancy between therapists' conceptual knowledge of therapeutic principles and procedures on the one hand and their ability to translate that knowledge into consistently skillful performance on the other. Having identified this discrepancy, the task is now to further delineate the constituent elements of skillful performance. As the evidence cited above suggests, the most productive direction for further investigation of skill involves the study of interpersonal skills. Indeed, such skills are likely to underlie the effectiveness of technical adherence in any form of therapy (including the nondynamic therapies). Thus, we believe that efforts to manualize dynamic therapy must move to a new *level*, designed specifically to describe and teach these underlying interpersonal skills.[4]

Conclusions: Looking Toward the Future

Freud and Breuer's discoveries led to the realization that talking could help people who suffered from serious, debilitating symptoms. Despite early reliance on quasibiological and mechanistic formulations, these ideas laid the groundwork for an appreciation of the power of communication in human affairs, for good or ill. As the theory and practice of psychodynamic psychotherapy developed and matured, the role of interpersonal communication has taken center stage. This development has led to efforts by interpersonal theorists to describe the laws that govern communications between people. Furthermore, the emphasis on communication has reflected an increasing recognition of the importance of viewing causal relationships in circular rather than linear terms. Circular causality and the principles of feedback, mutual influence, and complementarity have proven to be extremely powerful ideas, both in the clinical and research domains. Recent dissatisfactions with traditional experimental designs and clinical trial methodologies used to study psychotherapy have led to calls for the development of new and creative methodologies for investigating psychotherapy (Butler, 1988; Greenberg, 1986; Strupp, 1986). In particular, we believe that the place to begin is to study the interactions/communications occurring between two people when one of them is in distress and seeks help from the other. Greenberg (1986) has stressed the necessity for basic descriptive work along these lines with the goal of creating a "shared descriptive framework" or descriptive language for therapeutic phenomena. This may require, for instance, observations of the same therapy session(s) by researchers in different settings. Without such a shared language, based on direct observations of the same therapies, psychotherapy researchers will have difficulties communicating with each other, let alone arriving at a consensus on the nature of communications between patient and therapist. The problems inherent in such an undertaking are legion. Take, for example, the fact that our perception of language is intrinsically context-dependent (e.g., Bransford & Franks, 1971; Neisser, 1976). This means that the same words have different meanings depending on the unique characteristics of a given situation. How to account for such contextual differences from therapy to therapy, even from session to session, is the foremost scientific hurdle for psychotherapy research; it may also represent *the* scientific and methodological frontier for the foreseeable future (Butler & Strupp, 1986; Rice & Greenberg, 1984; Stiles, 1988).

Furthermore, we believe that the impact of these research advances may become most prominent in the area of training therapists. Accordingly, we hope that the recent push toward defining therapeutic "competence" in empirical terms (Strupp, Butler, & Rosser, 1988) will ultimately result in an improved ability to stipulate what is expected of a competent therapist and methods for evaluating a particular therapist's competence. We are confident that it is now possible to define competent performance in terms of how the therapeutic process is managed. As these issues are clarified, they will affect the manner in which therapists are trained. In contrast to the traditional model of focusing on the teaching of techniques, we have shown that much greater attention must be given to therapists' basic interpersonal skills.

Although these notions arise from within a dynamic/interpersonal model, the issues they address are characteristic of all therapeutic disciplines. Such training issues as definitions of competent performance, the relationship between adherence and skill, problems with difficult patients, establishing a workable interpersonal climate, and personal qualities of the therapist are universal concerns for therapists and researchers of all theoretical persuasions. Perhaps, as Wachtel (1982) has suggested, a "spirit of détente" might emerge between the various approaches around these mutual problems. By focusing the meager fiscal resources available for psychotherapy research on the resolution of these fundamental issues, we might all profit from a greater understanding of the science and art of psychotherapy.

NOTES

1. Brücke belonged to a group of physiologists who had a major impact on the study of physiology in the latter half of the 19th century. This group, referred to as the "Helmholtz school of medicine," proposed that all activity within an organism could be reduced to physical–chemical forces.
2. Exposition of the various object relations theories and their differences is beyond the scope of this chapter. The interested reader is referred to the original sources referenced here or to the excellent summary by Cashdan (1988).
3. The manual by Klerman et al. is routinely included in discussions of dynamic psychotherapy; however, it is not, strictly speaking, a dynamic therapy. Although focusing on interpersonal conflicts as the basis for depression, this form of therapy is more educational than exploratory and expressly avoids analysis of transference themes.
4. We wish to acknowledge the seminal contributions of Dr. Thomas Schacht, Dr. William Henry, and Dr. Jeffrey Binder in the development of these ideas.

REFERENCES

Anchin, J.C., & Kiesler, D.J. (1982). *Handbook of interpersonal psychotherapy*. Elmsford, NY: Pergamon Press.

Benjamin, L.S. (1982). Use of structural analysis of social behavior (SASB) to guide intervention in psychotherapy. In J.C. Anchin & D.J. Kiesler (Eds.), *Handbook of interpersonal psychotherapy* (pp. 190–212). Elmsford, NY: Pergamon Press.

Beutler, L.E., Crago, M., & Arizmendi, T.G. (1986). Research on therapist variables in psychotherapy. In S.L. Garfield & A.E. Bergin (Eds.), *Handbook of psychotherapy and behavior change* (Vol. 3, pp. 257–310). New York: John Wiley & Sons.

Binder, J.L., Strupp, H.H., & Schacht, T.E. (1983). Countertransference in time-limited dynamic psychotherapy: Further extending the range of treatable patients. *Contemporary Psychoanalysis, 19*, 605–623.

Bransford, J.D., & Franks, J.J. (1971). The abstraction of linguistic ideas. *Cognitive Psychology, 2*, 331–350.

Butler, S.F. (1988). *On psychotherapy research and clinical practice*. Invited paper presented at the annual meeting of the Society for Psychotherapy Research, Santa Fe, NM.

Butler, S.F., & Binder, J.L. (1987). Cyclical psychodynamics and the triangle of insight: An integration. *Psychiatry, 50*, 218–231.

Butler, S.F., Flasher, L.V., & Strupp, H.H. (in press). Countertransference and qualities of the psychotherapist. In N.E. Miller, L. Luborsky, J.P. Barber, & J. Docherty, (Eds.), *Handbook of dynamic psychotherapy research and practice*. New York: Basic Books.

Butler, S.F., Lane, T.W., & Strupp, H.H. (June, 1988). *Patterns of therapeutic skill acquisition as a result of training in time-limited dynamic psychotherapy*. Paper presented at the meeting of the Society for Psychotherapy Research, Santa Fe, NM.

Butler, S.F., & Strupp, H.H. (1986). "Specific" and "nonspecific" factors in psychotherapy: A problematic paradigm for psychotherapy research. *Psychotherapy, 23*, 30–40.

Butler, S.F. & Strupp, H.H. (in press). The effects of training psychoanalytically oriented therapists to use a manual. In N.E. Miller, L. Luborsky, J.P. Barber, & J. Docherty (Eds.), *Handbook of dynamic psychotherapy research and practice*. New York: Basic Books.

Butler, S.F., Strupp, H.H., & Lane, T.W. (1987). *The time-limited dynamic psychotherapy therapeutic strategies scale: Development of an adherence measure*. Paper presented at the annual meeting of the Society for Psychotherapy Research in Ulm, Germany.

Butler, S.F., Thackrey, M., & Strupp, H.H. (June, 1987). *Capacity for Dynamic Process Scale (CDPS): Relation to patient variables, process and outcome*. Paper presented at the annual meeting of the Society for Psychotherapy Research, Ulm, Germany.

Carson, R.C. (1982). Self-fulfilling prophecy, maladaptive behavior, and psychotherapy. In J.C. Anchin & D.J. Kiesler (Eds.), *Handbook of interpersonal psychotherapy* (pp. 64–77). Elmsford, NY: Pergamon Press.

Cashdan, S. (1988). *Object relations therapy*. New York: WW Norton.

Cohen, L.H., Sargent, M.M., & Sechrest, L.B. (1986). Use of psychotherapy research by professional psychologists. *American Psychologist, 41*, 198–206.

Darwin, C.R. (1859). *On the origin of species by means of natural selection, or, The preservation of favoured races in the struggle for life*. London: John Murray.

Darwin, C.R. (1871). *The descent of man, and selection in relation to sex* (Vol. 2). London: John Murray.

DiLoreto, A.O. (1971). *Comparative psychotherapy: An experimental analysis.* Chicago: Aldine-Atherton.

Dobson, K.S., & Shaw, B.F. (1988). Use of treatment manuals in cognitive therapy: Experience and issues. *Journal of Consulting and Clinical Psychology, 56,* 673–680.

Eagle, M.N. (1984). *Recent developments in psychoanalysis: A critical evaluation.* New York: McGraw-Hill.

Elkin, I., Parloff, M.B., Hadley, S.W., & Autry, J.H. (1985). NIMH treatment of depression collaborative research program: Background and research plan. *Archives of General Psychiatry, 42,* 305–316.

Elkin, I., Shea, M.T., Watkins, J.T., Imber, S.D., Sotsky, S.M., Collins, J.F., Glass, D.R., Pilkonis, P.A., Leber, W.R., Docherty, J.P., Fiester, S.J., & Parloff, M.B. (1989). National Institute of Mental Health treatment of depression collaborative research program. *Archives of General Psychiatry, 46,* 971–982.

Epstein, L. (1979). The therapeutic function of hate in the countertransference. In L. Epstein & A.H. Feiner (Eds.), *Countertransference: The therapist's contribution to the therapeutic situation* (pp. 213–234). New York: Jason Aronson.

Eysenck, H.J. (1952). The effects of psychotherapy: An evaluation. *Journal of Consulting Psychology, 16,* 319–324.

Fairbairn, W.R.D. (1954). *An object relations theory of the personality.* New York: Basic Books.

Freud, S. (1920). Beyond the pleasure principle. *Standard edition* (Vol. 18). London: Hogarth.

Freud, S. (1940). An outline of psychoanalysis. *Standard edition* (Vol. 23). London: Hogarth.

Freud, S. (1966). Resistance and repression. *Introductory lectures on psychoanalysis* (pp. 286–302). New York: WW Norton. (Original work published 1920)

Garfield, S.L. (1986). Research on client variables in psychotherapy. In S.L. Garfield & A.E. Bergin (Eds.), *Handbook of psychotherapy and behavior change* (3rd ed., pp. 213–256). New York: John Wiley & Sons.

Gill, M.M. (1982). *Analysis of transference: Theory and technique.* New York: International Universities Press.

Giovacchini, P.L. (1979). Countertransference with primitive mental states. In L. Epstein & A.H. Feiner (Eds.), *Countertransference: The therapist's contribution to the therapeutic situation* (pp. 235–265). New York: Jason Aronson.

Glover, E. (1955). *The technique of psychoanalysis.* New York: International Universities Press.

Gomes-Schwartz, B. (1978). Effective ingredients in psychotherapy: Predictions of outcome from process variables. *Journal of Consulting and Clinical Psychology, 46,* 1023–1035.

Greenberg, J.R., & Mitchell, S.A. (1983). *Object relations in psychoanalytic theory.* New York: Basic Books.

Greenberg, L.S. (1986). Research strategies. In L.S. Greenberg & W.M. Pinsof (Eds.), *The psychotherapeutic process: A research handbook.* New York: Guilford Press.

Guntrip, H. (1973). *Psychoanalytic theory, therapy, and the self.* New York: Basic Books.

Harlow, H.F. (1958). The nature of love. *American Psychologist, 13,* 673–685.

Henry, W.P. (1986). *Interpersonal process in psychotherapy.* Unpublished doctoral thesis, Vanderbilt University.

Henry, W.P., Schacht, T.E., & Strupp, H.H. (1986). Structural analysis of social behavior: Application to a study of interpersonal process of differential therapeutic outcome. *Journal of Consulting and Clinical Psychology, 54,* 27–31.

Kernberg, O.F. (1975). *Borderline conditions and pathological narcissism.* New York: Jason Aronson.

Kernberg, O.F. (1976). *Object relations theory and clinical psychoanalysis.* New York: Jason Aronson.

Kernberg, O.F. (1984). *Severe personality disorders: Psychotherapeutic strategies.* New Haven, CT: Yale University Press.

Kernberg, O.F., Bernstein, E.D., Coyne, L., Appelbaum, A., Horowitz, L., & Voth, H. (1972). Psychotherapy and psychoanalysis: Final report of the Menninger Foundation's psychotherapy research project. *Bulletin of the Menninger Clinic, 36,* 1–276.

Kiesler, D.J. (1966). Some myths of psychotherapy research and the search for a paradigm. *Psychological Bulletin, 65,* 110–136.

Kiesler, D.J. (1982). Interpersonal theory for personality and psychotherapy. In J.C. Anchin & D.J. Kiesler (Eds.), *Handbook of interpersonal psychotherapy* (pp. 3–24). Elmsford, NY: Pergamon Press.

Kiesler, D.J. (1986). Interpersonal methods of diagnosis and treatment. In A.M. Cooper, A.J. Frances, & M.H. Sacks (Eds.), *The personality disorders and neuroses* (pp. 53–75). New York: Basic Books.

Klein, M. (1952). Some theoretical conclusions regarding the emotional life of the infant. In M. Klein (Ed.) *Envy and gratitude and other works, 1946–1963* (pp. 61–93). New York: Delta.

Klein, D.F., Zitrin, C.M., Woerner, M.G., & Ross, D.C. (1983). Treatment of phobias: II. Behavior therapy and supportive psychotherapy: Are there any specific ingredients? *Archives of General Psychiatry, 40,* 139–145.

Klerman, G.L., Rounsaville, B.J., Chevron, E., Neu, C., & Weissman, M.M. (1984). *Interpersonal psychotherapy of depression (IPT).* New York: Basic Books.

Kohut, H. (1971). *The analysis of the self.* New York: International Universities Press.

Kohut, H. (1977). *The restoration of the self.* New York: International Universities Press.

Lambert, M.J., Shapiro, D.A., & Bergin, A.E. (1986). The effectiveness of psychotherapy. In S.L. Garfield & A.E. Bergin (Eds.), *Handbook of psychotherapy and behavior change* (Vol. 3, pp. 157–211). New York: John Wiley & Sons.

Langs, R. (1976). *The bipersonal field.* New York: Jason Aronson.

Leary, T. (1957). *Interpersonal diagnosis of personality*. New York: Ronald Press.

Luborsky, L. (1984). *Principles of psychoanalytic psychotherapy: A manual for supportive-expressive treatment*. New York: Basic Books.

Luborsky, L., Crits-Christoph, P., Mintz, J., & Auerbach, A. (1988). *Who will benefit from psychotherapy? Predicting therapeutic outcomes*. New York: Basic Books.

Luborsky, L., McLellan, A.T., Woody, G.E., O'Brien, C.P., & Auerbach, A. (1985). Therapist success and its determinants. *Archives of General Psychiatry, 42*, 602–611.

Luborsky, L., Singer, B., & Luborsky, L. (1975). Comparative studies of psychotherapy. *Archives of General Psychiatry, 32*, 995–1008.

Mahler, M (1952). On child psychosis and schizophrenia: Autistic and symbiotic infantile psychoses. *Psychoanalytic Study of the Child, 7*, 206–305.

Mahler, M., Pine, R., & Bergman, A. (1975). *The psychological birth of the human infant*. New York: Basic Books.

Meichenbaum, D., & Gilmore, J.E. (1984). The nature of unconscious processes: A cognitive-behavioral perspective. In K. Bowers & D. Meichenbaum (Eds.), *The unconscious reconsidered*. New York: John Wiley & Sons.

Menninger, K.A., & Holzman, P.S. (1973). *Theory of psychoanalytic technique* (Vol. 2). New York: Basic Books.

Miller, R.C., & Berman, J.S. (1983). The efficacy of cognitive behavior therapies: A quantitative review of the research evidence. *Psychological Bulletin, 94*, 39–53.

Morrow-Bradley, C., & Elliott, R. (1986). Utilization of psychotherapy research by practicing psychotherapists. *American Psychologist, 41*, 188–197.

Neisser, U. (1976). *Cognition and reality*. San Francisco: WH Freeman.

O'Malley, S.S., Foley, S.H., Rounsaville, B.J., Watkins, J.R., Stosky, S.M., Imber, S.D., & Elkin, I. (1988). Therapist competence and patient outcome in interpersonal psychotherapy of depression. *Journal of Consulting and Clinical Psychology, 56*, 496–501.

Orlinsky, D.E., & Howard, K.I. (1986). Process and outcome in psychotherapy. In S.L. Garfield & A.E. Bergin (Eds.), *Handbook of psychotherapy and behavior change* (3rd ed., pp. 311–381). New York: John Wiley & Sons.

Pilkonis, P.A., Imber, S.D., Lewis, P., & Rubinsky, P. (1984). A comparative outcome study of individual, group, and conjoint psychotherapy. *Archives of General Psychiatry, 41*, 431–437.

Prioleau, L., Murdock, M., & Brody, N. (1983). An analysis of psychotherapy versus placebo studies. *Behavioral and Brain Sciences, 6*, 275–310.

Rice, L.N., & Greenberg, L.S. (1984). *Patterns of change*. New York: Guilford Press.

Rogers, C.R. (1956). The necessary and sufficient conditions of therapeutic personality change. *Journal of Consulting Psychology, 21*, 95–103.

Rounsaville, B.J., O'Malley, S., Foley, S., & Weissman, M.M. (1988). The role of manual-guided training in the conduct and efficacy of interpersonal psychotherapy for depression. *Journal of Consulting and Clinical Psychology, 56*, 681–688.

Schacht, T.E., Binder, J.L., & Strupp, H.H. (1984). The dynamic focus. In H.H. Strupp & J.L. Binder (Eds.), *Psychotherapy in a new key* (pp. 65–109). New York: Basic Books.

Schafer, R. (1976). *A new language for psychoanalysis*. New Haven, CT: Yale University Press.

Schaffer, N.D. (1982). Multidimensional measures of therapist behavior as predictors of outcome. *Psychological Bulletin, 92*, 670–681.

Schaffer, N.D. (1983). The utility of measuring the skillfulness of therapeutic techniques. *Psychotherapy: Theory, Research and Practice, 20*, 330–336.

Shaw, B.E., & Dobson, K.S. (1988). Competency judgments in the training and evaluation of psychotherapists. *Journal of Consulting and Clinical Psychology, 56*, 666–672.

Silberschatz, G., Fretter, P.B., & Curtis, J.T. (1986). How do interpretations influence the process of psychotherapy? *Journal of Consulting and Clinical Psychology, 54*, 646–652.

Sloane, R.B., Staples, F.R., Cristol, A.H., Yorkston, N.J., & Whipple, K. (1975). *Psychotherapy versus behavior therapy*. Cambridge, MA: Harvard University Press.

Smith, M.L., Glass, G.V., & Miller, T.I. (1980). *The benefits of psychotherapy*. Baltimore, MD: Johns Hopkins University Press.

Stiles, W.B. (1988). Psychotherapy process–outcome correlations may be misleading. *Psychotherapy, 25*, 27–35.

Strupp, H.H. (1980a). Success and failure in time-limited psychotherapy: A systematic comparison of two cases. *Archives of General Psychiatry, 37*, 595–603.

Strupp, H.H. (1980b). Success and failure in time-limited psychotherapy: A systematic comparison of two cases. *Archives of General Psychiatry, 37*, 708–716.

Strupp, H.H. (1980c). Success and failure in time-limited psychotherapy: A systematic comparison of two cases. *Archives of General Psychiatry, 37*, 831–841.

Strupp, H.H. (1980d). Success and failure in time-limited psychotherapy: A systematic comparison of two cases. *Archives of General Psychiatry, 37*, 947–954.

Strupp, H.H. (1986). Psychotherapy: Research, practice, and public policy (How to avoid dead ends). *American Psychologist, 41*, 120–130.

Strupp, H.H., & Binder, J.L. (1984). *Psychotherapy in a new key: A guide to time-limited dynamic psychotherapy*. New York: Basic Books.

Strupp, H.H., Butler, S.F., & Henry W.P. (June, 1986). *The Vanderbilt II study: A progress report*. Paper presented at the meeting of the Society for Psychotherapy Research, Wellesley, MA.

Strupp, H.H., Butler, S.F., & Rosser, C.L. (1988). Training in psychodynamic therapy. *Journal of Consulting and Clinical Psychology, 56*, 689–695.

Strupp, H.H., & Hadley, S.W. (1977). A tripartite model of

mental health and therapeutic outcomes: With special reference to negative effects in psychotherapy. *American Psychologist, 32*, 187–196.

Strupp, H.H., & Hadley, S.W. (1979). Specific versus nonspecific factors in psychotherapy: A controlled study of outcome. *Archives of General Psychiatry, 36*, 1125–1136.

Sullivan, H.S. (1953). *The interpersonal theory of psychiatry*. New York: WW Norton.

Sulloway, F.J. (1983). *Freud, biologist of the mind: Beyond the psychoanalytic legend*. New York: Basic Books.

Swensen, C.H. (1973). *Introduction to interpersonal relations*. Glenview, IL: Scott Foresman.

Wachtel, P.L. (1977). *Psychoanalysis and behavior therapy: Toward integration*. New York: Basic Books.

Wachtel, P.L. (1982). Vicious circles: The self and the rhetoric of emerging and unfolding. *Contemporary Psychoanalysis, 18*, 259–272.

Winnicott, D.W. (1949). Hate in the coountertransference. *International Journal of Psychoanalysis, 30*, 69–74.

CHAPTER 29

PHENOMENOLOGICAL-EXISTENTIAL PSYCHOTHERAPY

Constance T. Fischer

This is the first clinical psychology handbook to include a full chapter on phenomenological psychotherapy. The approach is still relatively young, with its founding clinical publications in North America dating back just 30 years (e.g., Lyons, 1963; May, Angel, & Ellenberger, 1958, 1964; Strasser & May, 1963; Straus, 1963, 1966; Van den Berg, 1955; Van Kaam, 1959, 1966a, 1966b). Its theoreticians and its practitioner-spokespersons are still few. Therefore, in writing this chapter I have opted for broad coverage of foundational, consensual themes rather than for detailed presentation of representative therapists' understandings of their work. (See Valle & King, 1978, chapter 14, for succinct summaries of Binswanger, Boss, Frankl, May, and Van den Berg; and see Yalom, 1980, for an overview of existential therapy.) I also have chosen to orient this chapter not toward a new characterization of this therapy, but toward undoing the prevailing misunderstandings of phenomenological-existential psychotherapy.

The first section presents a series of clarifications of the phenomenological-existential approach. Because it is philosophy rather than techniques that characterizes this psychotherapy, the major section of the chapter describes the philosophy of science and the philosophical anthropology that undergird all phenomenological-existential approaches. A relatively short section then addresses the therapeutic relationship that necessarily flows from that undergirding. Several representative therapeutic interventions are described. The next section addresses the qualitative, empirical research approach that marks phenomenological-existential psychology's development from a philosophically based discipline to a science, especially as it has evolved at Duquesne University. The general research approach and the circumstances under which it is useful are reviewed. Examples of basic and clinical research are provided. The chapter concludes by summarizing the status of phenomenological-existential psychotherapy.

PRELIMINARY CLARIFICATIONS

The following two notions of phenomenology, although legitimate in their own contexts, are *not* the topic of this chapter. The first is the medical meaning

---

William F. Fischer was second author of the 1983 version of this chapter.

of the term *phenomenology*, namely, the outward appearance or visible symptoms of a disease or disorder, in contrast to its etiology. For example, one may speak of the phenomenology of schizophrenia, referring to the presence of hallucinations, loose associations, and perceptual distortion, and then go on to say that there may be different courses of development for those apparently similar symptoms, such as dopamine abnormalities, stimulus deprivation during infancy, or double-bind family communications. The second meaning of phenomenology also refers to appearances, in this case in terms of an individual's own experience and perceptions. Here, "the phenomenology of schizophrenia" would refer to what it is like to be schizophrenic. Both meanings hearken back to Kant's distinction between *phenomena* (things as they appear to us) and *noumena* (things as they really are). This second meaning of phenomenology is the one assumed by North American humanistic psychology, which until recently has not been inclined to go beyond attending to an individual's experience in its own right.

In contrast, *philosophical* phenomenology begins with phenomenal events, but it studies them to gain understandings of the ways we humans participate in what "appears" to us. This study is in pursuit of the nature of human knowing and of human knowledge, as well as of ontological "Being." Phenomenological *psychology* empirically studies sampled experiences to identify patterns of construing and relating to one's world, for example, brain-damaged (Dunn, 1974; Jubala, 1988) and drugged ways of relating (Deegan, 1984). It also studies everyday moments of construing and relating to one's world, such as when one is angry (Stevick, 1971), anxious (W. Fischer, 1974, 1982), learning (Colaizzi, 1969), jealous (Ramm, 1980), or mourning (Brice, 1988). As will be seen later, psychologists who identify with this orientation are grounded in a philosophy of science, in a method for attending to phenomena, and in a qualitative research tradition. It is this grounding that is referred to by the term *phenomenology*, the first half of this chapter's hyphenated title. But of course the clinician, while practicing psychotherapy, neither philosophizes nor conducts formal research. Psychotherapy addresses individual lives; the person's phenomenal world is attended to in terms of its significance for the individual's life and choices. The therapist's concerns and dealings thus are necessarily existential—hence the second half of the hyphenated title. The order of the terms, however, is a matter of choice. They easily could be reversed to give priority to existence as the subject matter of phenomenology. Moreover, some

theories of existence predate the Husserlian and Heideggerian historical foundations of contemporary phenomenology. Finally, many existential psychologists base their practices on existential philosophy without concerning themselves with phenomenology.

Although some practitioners have drawn on partial aspects of existential notions, particularly Sartrean ones, those who have developed a thorough going theoretical approach do not agree with the typical survey textbook's representation of existential theory. The following points correct misrepresentations: (a) It is true that our lives are not totally determined by natural events; we shape as well as are shaped by circumstances as we act in accordance with our understanding of them. However, "free will" is a misnomer. We are constrained by our biological, biographical, and environmental situations. (b) We cannot help but give meaning to circumstances, and hence bear responsibility for subsequent action. However, Sartrean emphasis on this "condemnation" to choice, and to concomitant angst, dread, and the like is not essential to, or even typical of, existential theory or therapeutic practice. (c) The much-referenced "here and now" is indeed the place where therapeutic intervention occurs. Regardless of how a person arrived at a current crossroad, it is his or her present values, perceptions, habits, and so on, that constrain choice. Nevertheless, phenomenologically grounded therapists, no less than others, find that exploration of the past enriches and clarifies the present. This exploration can assist the client to see that his or her present is understandable given that past, and that alternative courses can now be undertaken.

No particular techniques are essential for phenomenological-existential psychotherapy, although therapists have contributed diverse techniques such as Frankl's (1962) paradoxical intention and Rogers's (1942) mirroring. However, there are no essential or even prevailing exercises akin to free association in psychoanalysis or to reinforcement in behavior modification. Like these therapies, the methodological approach of this one too is characterized by its philosophical anthropology—its prepsychological understanding of the nature of being human. Its therapeutic relationship and its interventional techniques have to do with being open to uniquely human realities. Within that disciplined openness, phenomenological-existential therapists are methodologically eclectic and theoretically pluralistic. The therapist may make use, for example, of desensitization procedures, values clarification exercises, or free association. Likewise, the therapist may draw on the developmental insights of Freud, Vygotsky, Sullivan, Kohut, and others, as well as on contemporary social science research findings.

Like all theorists of therapy, it is in terms of their own theory that phenomenological-existential authors understand how other therapies actually work. Barton (1974) created a particularly plausible description of the same (fictitious) woman going through three therapies—Freudian, Jungian, and Rogerian, each therapy portrayed sympathetically. Barton shows that each approach works, even as it contributes to the way both therapist and patient give shape to and cope with the presenting problems. Like most phenomenologically grounded therapists, Barton gives credence to the techniques and insights of alternative theories, but is wary of possible inclinations to reduce human affairs to mechanisms, whether biological, environmental, or interactionist. Barton and other phenomenologically oriented therapists are equally wary of leftover "sixties" self-help optimism.

Any reader who feels that the first wariness is based on a false image of psychology perhaps should be reminded that phenomenology and existentialism arose as reactions against early and mid-twentieth century physicalism, and in particular that the social sciences were modeling themselves after the physical sciences. Today, psychology in general and psychoanalysis and behavior modification in particular have broadened their language and practices to the point that most psychologists, especially clinicians, do not regard themselves as absolute determinists. Nevertheless, mainstream psychology has not developed a philosophy of science that explicitly and systematically takes into account humans' differences from other objects of nature. Likewise, many of humanistic psychology's attitudes have been absorbed into practice without explicit revision and integration at theoretical levels. Phenomenology does provide a viable foundation for such goals.

PHENOMENOLOGY AND EXISTENTIALISM

Psychoanalysis and early behavior modification were both grounded in prepsychological conceptions of being human. These conceptions were of people as homo natura—things of nature, explicable in terms of, and reproducible to, the laws of physical and chemical bodies. Homo natura required no principles of understanding beyond those required for any object. Reactions against these conceptions arose independently in Europe and North America. Reactive authors, whether individually or in groups, were often unaware of each other's works, at least initially. Further, the specific themes of the revolt—that is, the particular features of the natural scientific philosophies that were rejected—varied from theorist to theorist. For example, precursors of North American phenomenology such as Rogers (1942) rejected the analyst's exclusive preoccupation with the patient's past and questioned the assumption that human life is comprehensible as a constant struggle to control one's animal nature. Twenty or so years later, the humanistic psychology movement in North America, through its multiple spokespersons (e.g., Bugental, 1965; Severin, 1965), protested not so much psychoanalysis as American academic empiricism, especially its emphasis in both theory and practice on quantification, classification, and explanation solely in terms of antecedent events. In Europe, psychiatrists, such as Binswanger (1938–43/1963), although accepting Freud's interest in unconscious dynamics and in associative methods of exploring them, explicitly rejected his natural scientific philosophical anthropology (philosophy of the nature of being human).

The sources of inspiration for these various reactions, which were to become known collectively as Third-Force psychology (after psychoanalysis and behaviorism), differed significantly. Rogers's thought seems to have been an expression of his commitments to "Protestant individualism" and "democratic humanism" (Barton, 1974). The European psychiatrists, Boss (1957/1963), Minkowski (1933/1970), and Straus (1935/1963, 1930–62/1966) were profoundly influenced by the philosopher Husserl's (1913/1969, 1954/1970) phenomenological method of reflection and findings. The closely related work of Binswanger was influenced by the existential analyses authored by the phenomenological philosopher, Heidegger (1927/1968). A third group, best exemplified by the German psychiatrist Frankl (1946/1962, 1946/1966), was inspired by existential thinkers such as Kierkegaard (1843, 1849/1954), Buber (1926–39/1965), and Marcel (1949/1965), all of whom were concerned with the spiritual as well as the psychological dimensions of existence. By now the products of these varying early reactions are fairly well homogenized in the thought and work of phenomenological-existential therapists. Of course most psychologists of this orientation do have preferred resource authors, such as the French philosopher Ricoeur (1949–57/1966) or the French psychologist-philosopher Merleau-Ponty (1945/1962, 1942/1963) for foundational matters, and psychotherapists such as the Americans Bugental (1965), Farber (1966), May (1979), and Yallom (1980, 1989) for discussions of existential issues pertinent to therapy.

Two further preliminary clarifications are in order before finally addressing the Husserlian philosophy and the existential anthropology that ground existential therapy. First, some practitioners characterize their orientation as phenomenological and/or existential, but have merely borrowed a few notions or practices. This is akin to practitioners who refer to themselves as behavior modifiers, even though they have not studied how their borrowed practices are based in a behavioral theory or in empirical research. Second, the majority of practitioners who participated in humanistic psychology's heyday were what we might call phenomenalists rather than phenomenologists. That is, they were interested in an individual's immediate experience, usually on the assumption that its expression would lead to growth. Except for a very few researchers (e.g., Severin, 1965), there was little interest in studying phenomenal worlds to build a systematic body of knowledge. Nevertheless, humanistic psychology's protests bear much responsibility for mainstream psychology's broadening its purview to include consciousness and purposiveness. Today's cognitive therapy probably would have been regarded as unscientific 20 years ago.

Husserl and Phenomenological Psychology

Edmund Husserl (1859–1938) is the founder of phenomenology and the philosopher upon whose shoulders most existential philosophers, as well as psychologists, stand. Perhaps the best way of describing phenomenological-existential psychotherapy is to characterize Husserl's contribution, at least as it has been taken up by psychologists. The reader who wishes to go beyond the following highly schematic remarks, and to pursue Husserl's broader interests, may want to see *Husserl: An Analysis of His Phenomenology* (Ricoeur, 1967). It is through consciousness that a person is present to his or her world. To study consciousness is to study how humans differ from other studiable objects. It is also to explore the nature of how humans participate in what they know of their world. Husserl, himself an expert in mathematics, was particularly concerned that the natural sciences had ignored the fact that we do not just go around discovering scientific truths that are independent of our questions. Furthermore, there is no humanly experienceable or knowable world apart from human ways of relating to that world. Hence, Husserl argued that an adequate science required a preliminary study of consciousness. Between 1900 and 1938 Husserl undertook a systematic investigation of consciousness

in most, if not all, of its different modalities, such as perception and judgment. In the course of his researches, he demonstrated the fundamentally relational character of human consciousness, and in that process developed the guiding principles of the phenomenological method of investigation.

We could say that consciousness is modes (e.g., perceiving, remembering, anticipating, thinking) and types (e.g., anxious, joyful, angry) of being in touch with the world. Of course, "modes and types" always occur in unity, as in anxiously perceiving. Those pervasive hyphens in existential-phenomenological writing ("person-in-the-world," etc.) are an effort to capture the unity and relational character of consciousness. Much of the awkwardness of phenomenological writing similarly is due to efforts to evoke that relational unity. People are both separate from and yet already incorporate their worlds. Existential literature sometimes refers to a person's "lived world" as a way of describing this relation that is not merely interactive. *Intentionality* is the philosophical term that points to this nature of consciousness as always consciousness *of* something, something that, for finite humans, can never be known except through human ways of relating. (The term *intentionality* only indirectly implies purposiveness; we necessarily relate to our worlds in terms of our projects.)

Consciousness is not necessarily self-reflective, that is, conscious of being in relation to something. In fact, consciousness is typically unreflective. For example, as we go about our day, we most often are not focally conscious *of* being present to people, environments, or situations. However, consciousness is not adequately characterized as a trait, such as IQ or dependency. Neither is it a sorting machine or information processor. Above all, consciousness is not a container that could be said to have contents, as a piggy bank has pennies.

Husserl's major effort at clarifying the character of consciousness, however, was addressed to the pervasive inclination of his contemporaries to engage in what came to be known as "psychologism." Husserl's contemporaries were claiming that all presences to objects, others, and the world were mediated by mental representations located somewhere within the mind. They then claimed that without direct access to the world, all knowledge, judgments, and so on, of consciousness were "merely psychological"—subjectivistic and dubious. Husserl pointed out that since his contemporaries, by their own argument, could not have direct access to the posited "mediations," their position that the knowledge of consciousness is dubious was itself vulnerable to their own condemnation.

An incisive characterization of Husserl's critique of psychologism may be found in Zaner's (1970) *The Way of Phenomenology* (pp. 51–62).

In the process of critiquing psychologism, Husserl realized that it was necessary to undertake a systematic study of experience, that is, of consciousness and of how the world appears to it. The method that he developed for this enterprise is known as the phenomenological method. Phenomenology *is* this method and the resulting studies. Of course, Husserl's followers have adapted his method to the phenomena that have been of interest to them. Still, we can delineate in simplified form the core themes that are present in most, if not all, of the method's variations.

First, a phenomenological method is employed when one seeks to describe the essence of some phenomenon, that is, the interrelated features without which it would not be what it is. For example, the phenomenon of remembering is re-presenting a past event, as past, from the perspective of the present. If one did not recognize the past event as past, as something one has experienced before and is not experiencing now for the first time, one would not be remembering.

Second, the method is used when one seeks to understand rather than to demonstrate, explain, or assume; one attempts to suspend preconceptions concerning the phenomenon. This suspension is known as "bracketing." For example, a phenomenologically oriented researcher who wants to understand what being anxious is does not presume in advance that "being anxious" is really a mental event or a physical/physiological event, or fundamentally quantitatively a measurable event. Instead, the researcher begins with detailed descriptions of his or her own and others' moments of being anxious. Every effort is made to allow the phenomenon, in ths case "being anxious," to become evident in its own right, as it was actually lived and experienced by the subject. In this way, its constituent meanings, whether they be affective, perceptual, bodily, behavioral, or whatever, can be characterized in their interrelationships, their structural unity. The phenomenon as a whole is described; because all described aspects are essential for the phenomenon to be whatever it is, no aspect is regarded as explanatory of the others.

Of course, researchers will not discover in their own or in their subjects' descriptions features that are not either known about, experienced, or lived out by these persons. Such features might be the neurophysiology of anxiety, or infantile events that are available now only prototaxically. Subjects are not aware of which aspects of their own reports will turn out to be fundamental to all accounts of the phenomenon. More will be said about research method later; for now it should be noted that the phenomenological method is devised for exploration of what Merleau-Ponty (1963) referred to as the human order. At other times we wish to know about the physical and biological orders, but they are not more real than the human world. Of course, whether or not our research subjects are aware of it, other orders are taken up within and are part of our lived worlds.

Third, practitioners of the phenomenological method recognize the fundamentally perspectival character of people's presences to phenomena. Traditional experimental research also is perspectival, but it downplays or ignores this fact. All research tools provide only partial, interest-laden, technique-bound access to events. The researcher is present to the phenomenon through only certain of its profiles, depending upon which of several modes of access to a phenomenon he or she utilizes. Similarly, research subjects provide only perspectival accounts. For example, being anxious appears somewhat differently to (a) someone who is concerned with the possibility of becoming anxious, (b) someone who is reflectively living through it, (c) someone who can still vividly recall having been anxious in a situation, and (d) someone who is or has just been in the presence of an anxious person.

No mode of access or revealed profile is a priori the best; no single mode of access offers "the real meaning" of being anxious. Furthermore, no particular profile of being anxious is exclusive of the others. The researcher asks: "What is revealed that is essential to being anxious in each of these profiles, through each of these modes of access?" Almost needless to say, standard content analysis is inappropriate for this endeavor. Yes, the written results of the phenomenological method vary with the researcher, much as different authors of psychological assessment reports may write differently even while they agree about their findings. Again, not unlike an assessment, repetitions of the method and discussion among researchers do not exhaust what could be said. Because our access to phenomena is always perspectival, reality always remains partially ambiguous. This is not due to deficiency in method, but to the nature of human perception and knowledge.

The above discussion stressed notions derived from Husserl because phenomenological-existential philosophy and psychology, at least in their present form, would not have been possible without Husserl's thought. The method provides a framework for a social science explicitly designed for humans, so that we need not rely totally on the framework designed by natural scientists. Phenomenology also provides a foundation for clinicians, one that is consistent with the existential anthropology of phenomenological-existential therapists.

Existential Anthropology

The following characterizations of human nature are found in, or are consistent with, the writings of the previously mentioned philosophers and psychiatrists, as well as with the writings and practices of contemporary North American existential psychotherapists. These perspectives on human nature were developed by their authors through bracketing prior conceptions about human functioning and describing what was then evident.

First, the meanings of one's existence are never settled once and for all. Understandings of oneself, others, and the world emerge in the context of particular situations and one's current projects. One continually re-creates those projects in light of the possibilities as well as the givens of one's existence (a particular body, parents, aging, etc.). To be a person means that one is engaged in a never to be completed task of discovering, positing, and making sense of one's existence. To be a person means that, in actions if not in words, one questions and is questioned by self, others, and the world. Although the questions vary across developmental stages and from relationship to relationship (Am I a good child, student, spouse, parent, etc.?), the fundamental themes do not vary. They are lived, implicitly if not explicitly, as: What is the world about? Who am I? Who are you? Who have I been? Who might I become?

Second, to be human means that one has no choice but to act and to find meanings in one's actions. But options are restricted by circumstances and are undertaken without either complete self-awareness or complete knowledge of the consequences. There are no guarantees of success—not even that one will continue to value earlier goals. Yet one recognizes at some level that one is inevitably engaged in a lifelong task for which one is irrevocably responsible.

Third, to be a person is to be in relation to others whether or not they are physically present. Not only does one shape one's life under the influence of others, especially during formative years, one also comes to know oneself only in relation to others. One never exists first as an absolutely separate individual who subsequently comes to have relations with others. From birth until death we are embedded in and know ourselves in terms of a variety of relationships, with

their multiple themes of love, fear, competition, cooperation, and the like. I discover the other person's significance, as well as my own, in the ways that he or she calls or allows or demands me to be. For example, it is the child who in being a child calls the mother to be a mother. Relationships are not simple juxtapositions of discrete individuals; a marriage is not a man plus a woman. Rather, one's relation to the other is mutually and reciprocally implicative. Each way of being requires the other's and makes sense only in relation to it. It is for these reasons that the existentialist asks: "Who does one call the other to be? Who does one demand that the other be? Who does one allow the other to be? How is one co-creating oneself in calling forth or demanding or allowing the other to be in those particular ways?"

Fourth, to be a person is to be an embodied subject, a *unity* that cannot be adequately comprehended or conceptualized as the parallelistic, interactionistic, or epiphenomenalistic union of two substances, mental and physical. The living human body is a subject; it is a system of projects through which the meanings of situations are co-created. Could there be near or far if the human body were not self-moving? Could there be tall or short, high or low, if the human body were not statured, a being that attains perspective by raising itself from the ground and standing on its feet? Could there be hot or cold, backward or forward, if the human body were not temperatured and coronally asymmetrical? In short, the possible modes of being and the dimensions of the human world are co-created by that world and the human body. Hence, a psychologically relevant description of the body cannot be given in terms of physiology alone. Likewise, a physiological account ought to at least intimate how the body affords, delimits, and participates in the possibilities of experiencing and acting. It is true that we can objectify a person's body and treat it as a thing, just as we can objectify a person's styles of approaching problematic situations and treat them as traits over which the person has no control. But doing either falsely denies that people are active subjects as well as objects.

Phenomenological-Existential Approach to Psychopathology

All psychopathology involves disordered, restricted existence. The forms and aspects of psychopathology that have been of most interest to existential therapists are those that the person has participated in bringing about. The four characteristics of such pathology that are described below are found in the writings of all phenomenological-existential authors, either explicitly in their theory or implicitly in their therapeutic practices. Halling and Nill (1989) provide consonant clinical examples of "Demystifying Psychopathology: Understanding Disturbed Persons," enroute illustrating the roles of embodiment and context. There are, of course, disagreements within the field, mostly about the nature of specific disorders such as schizophrenia, mania, and depression. I will not review the literature on particular psychopathologies because of their complexities and because of space limitations.

The principles of phenomenology and existentialism are useful for understanding and helping people with the everyday difficulties that we all face, as well as for understanding and helping people faced with restricted existences that they were not responsible for bringing about, such as their brain damage or mental retardation, or the loss of a loved one. The following features of psychopathology are those for which the individual bears at least partial responsibility, even though these features may be constituents of any classification, from personality disorder to affective disorder, and so on.

First, a psychopathologically disordered person is stuck or is at an impasse in regard to developing ways of being that allow questioning of who he or she is and of what the world is about. On the basis of certain childhood experiences and relationships with significant others, the person has become committed to his or her life projects in ways that are not easily open for discussion, reflection, or modification, even in the face of changing circumstances (Boss, 1963; Gendlin, 1978; Van Kaam, 1966a). For example, efforts to be pure by being clean, to be strong by being all-knowing, and so on, are lived as though they always must be kept true. Circumstances that might contradict or undermine these efforts, such as being impure by having "dirty thoughts," are concurrently lived as something that must never be true. In short, one has fled from, or at least placed severe restrictions upon, openly discovering, shaping, and making sense of one's existence. Of particular interest to existential therapists are the self-deceptions through which one flees from and restricts one's life (W. Fischer, 1985; Sartre, 1956).

Second, being stuck or stopped takes on the character of self-imprisonment as the person continues to live in terms of musts and must-nots, including a necessity of not recognizing that these are one's own terms. The person has turned away from his or her freedom to find and develop alternatives. Occasionally, through anxious or frantic outbursts of activity, the person attempts to will life's meanings rather than

to discover them (Farber, 1966). Still, life is frequently experienced as superficial, as lacking richness and depth, because the person is unable to find positive meaning in activities and relationships. There is a horizontal but occasionally intrusive, oppressive, sense of emptiness and sham (Frankl, 1962). The individual frequently experiences despair and anxiousness over the senselessness of his or her life, but these experiences are fled from rather than explored (Frankl, 1962; Keen, 1970).

Third, the self-imprisoned person turns away from his or her body's revelations of unwanted meanings. In particular, the anxious body is turned away from; being anxious is a bodily recognition that one is faced with the possibility of feeling guilty, ashamed, inadequate, or some other "must-not" condition. By heeding instead only what he or she knows with clarity, the person beclouds and evades personal truth (W. Fischer, 1985; Keen, 1970). At the same time, the individual self-deceptively struggles to reaffirm the truncated world and projects to which he or she is already committed. These projects are buttressed and maintained as being unambiguous and unchanging.

Fourth, the person's psychopathological relationships with others, both past and present, are dominated by a past. He or she continues to live in terms of identities and scenarios that are no longer appropriate, that should have been surpassed, and that now preclude ways of being that he or she occasionally longs for but cannot actualize. The unfolding of an I–Other dialectic has been arrested. Instead, the person remains who he or she was with the significant others with whom he or she became "the child," "the rebel," and the like. In their effort to continue being what they "must" and to avoid being what they "must not," such people find themselves increasingly alienated and lonely (Van den Berg, 1971).

To repeat, the above four features of psychopathology are those for which there is broadest agreement among existential therapists. These features emphasize the person's participation in the evolution of his or her restricted existence. Other approaches to psychopathology and psychotherapy are by now much more open to these notions. Nevertheless, they have yet to be formally or thoroughly integrated into mainstream theories. Cognitive therapy, of course, has made room for clients' cognitions and has characterized them as actively shaping clients' lives. But thus far in both literature and practice, these cognitions have been dealt with in isolation from the clients' broader life course and projects. Moreover, as Mahoney pointed out in 1977, cognitive therapy is advancing rapidly without conceptual, theoretical clarity about what "cognitive" means. Phenomenological-existential theory in general, and its characterization of pathology in particular, may be helpful in that regard. Moreover, as North American psychiatry continues its biologizing movement, and a new generation of psychiatrists learns pathology primarily in terms of the behavioral symptoms approach of the American Psychiatric Association's (e.g., 1987) *Diagnostic and Statistical Manual(s)*, the above existential themes offer an increasingly pertinent counterpoint.

In their emphasis on client responsibility, however, existential writers have not attended systematically to the roles of neurophysiology, genetic predisposition, or social environments in psychopathology. Phenomenology, as a philosophical foundation, definitely could ground such an effort. For example, Moss (1989) "utilizes the topic of body image to introduce current concepts in a phenomenologically informed psychology of the body" (p. 80). Human-science psychology, which is addressed in the section of this chapter titled "Research," specifically proposes an approach for psychology that integrates the physical, biological, and human orders. In addition, researchers are gradually building a phenomenological human-science content base, for example, differentiating depression (Carter, 1988; Linn, 1985) from despair (Goldsmith, 1987), embarrassment from shame (Vallelonga, 1986), and shame from guilt (Lindsay-Hartz, 1984). In the meantime, in actual practice, existential therapists have their own individual ways of understanding how the givens of a person's life (constitutional make up, family history, responsiveness to neuroleptics, etc.) are taken up by that person, and how they may be part of psychopathology. This circumstance is the other side of the prevailing one in North American psychology, where practitioners' schooling had dealt with the givens but has left them to find their own ways of taking into account the above existential characteristics of restricted existence.

PSYCHOTHERAPY

As mentioned earlier, most phenomenological-existential therapists are eclectic in their methods. Many existential psychiatrists, for example, were trained in and still practice psychoanalysis. It is the above framework—phenomenology, existential anthropology, and understanding of pathology—that characterizes how existential therapy is different from others.

Psychotherapeutic Relationship

The invariant theme that appears in existential understandings of the psychotherapeutic relationship is that of respect. This respect is not just a "nice guy" social presence, nor is it an approval of who the client is or of what he or she may have done (C. Fischer 1969, 1985). Rather, it is a respect for clients' potential to cope authentically with how they have been part of the trouble they are in, and for their potential to discover viable adaptations of earlier projects and styles. However, this respect is also for the reality that many clients, even more than the rest of us, are severely limited in their options. Those limitations include who the person is trying to be, and his or her present ways of being. The word *ways,* refers not just to habitual actions, but also to the world as it is experienced and shaped through those actions. In the popular language of our time, to be effective, a therapist must "reach" clients "where they are" and in terms of where they are "coming from" and "what they are up to."

Both aspects of this respect foster a relationship in which personal truths may be discovered, faced, and explored. Even when clients are childlike, compulsive, negativistic, seductive, or whatever, they are understood and addressed in terms of their own worlds, because that is the location of whatever freedom they have. Although therapists from other theoretical orientations may affirm the above statements, it is the existential therapists' radical commitment to them that renders these practitioners least likely to revert to thinking of a client in terms of forces that are out of equilibrium, of sickness, or of needing to be made better, made more adaptive, or made free from defenses.

The psychotherapeutic relationship as the existentialist understands it likewise cannot be grasped in terms of transference of feelings and attitudes that really belong to another relationship, such as the relationship of the client to his or her parents. Feelings and attitudes are not entities or forces that a psyche can direct and displace. It is more to the point to say that if the client is, for example, still living in the mode of the child, ambivalently struggling with the question of how to be or how to express himself or herself in relation to authority figures, then he or she will be particularly attuned to the parent or authority possibilities of the therapist. If the client comes to feel love or hate for the therapist, this cannot be dismissed as merely a transference reaction. The love or hate (or whatever) is indeed an expression of a person who is struggling at a certain developmental level, and in learned ways, with personal issues. It is *also* occurring now in relation to this particular practitioner's way of being present (and absent) to the person.

"Transference" is continuance (C. Fischer, 1987). Van Kaam (1966a) has characterized the meeting of the existential psychotherapist with his or her client as an encounter, a meeting in which the psychotherapist, while being a disciplined professional in the usual ways, extends to clients "trust," "a defenseless presence," "a commitment to [the clients'] autonomous development," and an invitation to be who they would or can be. Clients do differ greatly in the degree to which they can respond to this invitation. Sometimes, for example with institutional patients, the invitation is offered within a case-management context. Nevertheless, the encounter and the invitation characterize the relationship.

Friedman (1985), while explicating the implications of Buber's work for psychotherapy, emphasized "healing through meeting," wherein each person responds out of his or her uniqueness but also through shared "touchstones of reality." Through this dialogic encounter, both participants find the courage to respond to the other's difference, and both change. Yalom's (1989) lively accounts of his therapeutic work illustrate the challenge, drama, and altogether human character of what Friedman calls the "interhuman sphere."

Psychotherapeutic Interventions

Existential psychotherapy usually takes the form of typical "talk" sessions, where the therapist assists clients in their efforts to understand how they, along with circumstances, have gotten themselves into their present, truncated lives. The goal is for clients to discover, through reflection and action, that they can continue their lives and identities without remaining committed to earlier, no longer useful, assumptions, goals, and patterns. The additional goal, of course, is for clients both within and beyond sessions, to begin developing more freely chosen ways of being.

There is certainly nothing startling about the preceding paragraph. Many nonexistential psychotherapists share the same goals. The difference is that the therapist whose practices are consistent with an existential anthropology does not think in terms of altering hypothetical psychic apparati, maladaptive habit family hierarchies, or even cognitive distortions as such. The changes sought are in clients' lived worlds, not in any other level of presumed causal order.

It will be recalled that the words "lived world" refer simultaneously to what one apprehends of the world "out there," and to the fact that whatever one apprehends occurs through a believing, feeling, behaving, reflecting, and so on, relation with that world. "Lived world" points to a structural unity, respect for which disallows reductive explanations in terms only of parts. Surely standard psychoanalysis, strict behavior modification, rational-emotive therapy, and so on all occasion positive results. Existential therapists, however, understand those results as changes in lived worlds. Medication, life experiences (e.g., camping, art classes), and behavior modification exercises could all be suggested within the existential framework. That is, these interventions could all be undertaken in the service of broadening clients' lived worlds, both directly and through occasioning questions about the necessity of prior assumptions.

Just as what is changed via therapy is nonreducible to some substrate reality, so too the change is not understood as occurring just within the client. Nor is it an abstract "world" that changes. Rather, the client is always a very particular existence, changing in the company of a particular therapeutic person. Who that person is varies in each instance, of course, but who he or she is, and what he or she comprehends of that other person are critical aspects of the therapeutic process. The therapist cannot be assumed as a constant.

As mentioned several times, there is no specific intervention that is essential to existential therapy. There are numerous ways to interrupt the client's persistence in evading recognition of past and present (partial) self-determination, and hence of not seeing alternatives as personally viable. The truism "timing is all" also applies here. Any intervention, to be effective, must be one that the client is ready to follow to self-discoveries. Therapists differ among themselves as to whether the discoveries must involve reflective insight or just adaptations of action or mood or the like.

The phenomenological-existentially oriented therapist typically has been trained pluralistically, and draws on, for example, psychoanalytic self-theory, cultural critiques by deconstructionists and feminists, research on infant development (especially Stern, 1985), and on diverse techniques such as family sessions, hypnosis, dream analysis, behavior tracking, and journal reflections. The therapist uses these diverse contributions within a phenomenological-existential framework and hence is less likely than many practitioners of other orientations to fall into the technological stance of applying a method or technique as though it were adequate to induce and account for change. Below are three interventions that grew specifically out of an existential-philosophical anthropology. None of these interventions is seen by its author as "the" method of therapy.

Frankl (1962) developed "paradoxical intention." In a spirit of humor and irony, the therapist invites the client to imagine, think about, or engage in an activity that he or she has typically experienced in an anxious, fearful, guilty, or shamed manner. A woman who complains that she is embarrassed by blushing, for example, is playfully invited to practice blushing until she is really good at it. The suggestion is not primarily aimed at extinguishing the symptom or even at uncovering its etiology. Rather, client and therapist become attuned to the activity's personal significance—what it reveals to the client about himself or herself as a person. The playfulness of the exercise tells clients that the therapist will not reject them for their activity, that it is speakable, and that it can be safely explored. During this exploration, clients discover that they can themselves take different attitudes toward the activity. In that process they also discover that the activity and its past meanings did not "just happen," but that there were previously unreflected upon reasons for the activity and for its earlier personal meanings. Choices become possible as clients realize that those reasons and meanings served their purposes and are no longer salient.

Boss (1963), who was trained as a psychoanalyst, found that Freud's method "aims at enabling the patient to unveil himself and to unfold into his utmost openness" (p. 62). In regard to suffering unwanted psychological states, Boss, however, asserted that rather than ask the patient "Why," the existential psychotherapist should pose the question, "Why not?" In his discussion of this intervention, Boss suggested that, for the most part, patients live in anxiously constricted worlds. Many possibilities—ways of desiring, thinking, imagining, feeling, acting, and so on—are lived as closed off, as taboo. If the possibilities were instead to be appropriated as their own, patients would be anxious about their participation in bringing about what they would see as a shameful, guilty, or embarrassing world, one where they could no longer understand themselves as worthy. In asking "Why not?" the therapist encourages patients "to even greater tests of daring" (Boss, 1963, p. 248). Not only does this question invite patients to take up possibilities as their own, it also opens opportunities to explore the lived prohibitions that constrict their worlds. Furthermore, if patients take up such exploration, they are more likely to discover that the prohibitions do not arise from the world alone, but rather, are actively co-created by themselves. Patients thus can be helped to experience themselves as co-determining agents of their existence, as people who can enact alternative decisions.

Boss also suggested that existential therapists should not be satisfied with patients' expositions, no matter how detailed and candid, of past experiences.

The danger is that the therapy may readily become an endless, sterile, and stereotyped series of accusations and recriminations. Instead, existential psychotherapists can ask: Granted that you understand who others *were* for you and who you *were* for them, why not abandon these understandings in your present relations and involvements? Why not exercise your freedom to experience or relate to others as well as yourself differently? Aren't there other possibilities?

Gendlin, one of Carl Rogers's original collaborators, has integrated themes from Heidegger's existential philosophical anthropology with client-centered therapy. He accepts Heidegger's claim that persons' moods—their pervasive yet inarticulately lived and typically ignored modes of being affected—express their felt sense of how they are faring in their life projects. Gendlin accepts Rogers's assertion that above all the therapist should be oriented toward the client's feelings and should help the client explicate and own them.

Gendlin describes neurotic individuals as being rigidly committed to their life projects, but as impeded, if not altogether blocked, in their efforts to actualize them. These persons are generally disinclined toward exploration and articulation of their projects and of the ways in which they co-create the moods that oppress them.

To help these clients surpass the impasse that they have participated in bringing about, Gendlin (1978) developed "focusing" as an intervention, which he sees as consistent with the client-centered attitude. Gendlin suggests that clients should be invited to dwell with, rather than dismiss or flee from, their various moods. Clients should be encouraged to feel these moods bodily and thereby come to grips with the reality of being mooded in this or that manner. Finally, Gendlin proposes that clients be invited to explore and articulate the various significations of their moods. What do moods suggest about the meaning of situations in which clients find themselves, and what do these moods and meanings reveal to clients about their life projects?

As clients take up this style of dwelling with, feeling, exploring, and articulating the significations of their moods, they abandon generalizations and rationalizations and turn concretely to their specific situations. Self-discovery and self-exploration facilitate letting go of rigid commitments to impossible projects.

CURRENT STATUS

Today, practitioners of all persuasions tend to speak beyond their own theories of pathology and therapy to address the person's actual life—his or her lived world. There has been a general broadening of theories that acknowledge this realm, and many if not most practitioners refer to themselves as eclectic. Hence, some readers regard existential writings as superfluous. Other readers reject the phenomenological-existential approach because its earlier reactions against absolute determinism frequently were cast in extreme terms, ones that did not give adequate acknowledgment to the contingencies of existence. However, phenomenological-existential theorists and practitioners alike, when not stressing their differences from mainstream pathology, have always acknowledged that freedom is limited to the attitudes with which we take up the conditions in which we find ourselves. The potential power of phenomenological-existential psychology lies in its readiness to contribute to an integrated social science, one that acknowledges that even scientific findings are human formulations, and that the boundaries separating our realms of study are permeable, just as the areas themselves are mutually influenceable. A psychologically traumatized or depressed person may gradually become neurophysiologically depressed; a determined person may enhance his or her immune system's defense against cancer. Social science can become integrated through an existential-phenomenological philosophy that allows researchers and practitioners in specialized areas to share their work.

Unfortunately for this effort, phenomenological academicians are usually lone representatives located in a university's department of philosophy, sociology, or psychology. Systematic coordination has been difficult. There are, however, several centers of such activity. At Duquesne University, the Philosophy Department has one of the strongest phenomenology and existentialism sections in the country. The Psychology Department's graduate program is totally devoted to development of psychology as a human science (Giorgi, 1970). For 25 years the department has developed phenomenology's implications for a science that would integrate "consciousness" (those bodily, affective, behavioral, reflective, and so on, relations through which the rest of the world is "lived") with the data of physiology, physics, and other realms of natural sciences. The work of the philosopher-psychologist Merleau-Ponty (1962, 1963), emphasizing the bodily character of human functioning, has been important for this project. Beyond philosophical foundations, the department has developed an empirical qualitative research tradition, stressing both method and the concomitant building of a body of findings. Finally, faculty members teach

theory, research, and practice of phenomenologically oriented psychological assessment (C. Fischer, 1979, 1985), psychotherapy (Barton, 1974; Smith, 1979), and developmental psychology (Knowles, 1986). Breadth and diversity within its philosophical orientation are a hallmark of Duquesne's efforts. Representative writings from the above areas may be found in the series of *Duquesne Studies in Phenomenological Psychology* (Giorgi, Barton, & Maes, 1983; Giorgi, Fischer, & Murray, 1975; Giorgi, Fischer, & von Eckartsberg, 1971; Giorgi, Knowles, & Smith, 1979). The Simon Silverman Phenomenology Center at Duquesne's library is the most extensive resource in North America. It is one of six official branches of the Husserl Archives at Leuven, Belgium, housing copies of the transcribed shorthand notes of Husserl's unpublished papers. The Center also contains copies of Heidegger's unpublished Marburg lectures and the donated personal libraries of several of the leading early European philosophers and psychiatrists, such as Jan Bauman, F. J. J. Buytendijk, Aron Gurwisch, Stephen Strasser, and Erwin Straus.

Other psychology departments with a strong emphasis on the development of a phenomenologically grounded psychology include those at Saybrook Institute, Seattle University, the University of Dallas, and West Georgia College. Among psychologists who are working individually at systematic development, including empirical qualitative research, are Keen (1970, 1975) at Bucknell University, de Rivera (1981) at Clark University, and Wertz (1983) at Fordham University. Giorgi (1970, 1985) is now at the University of Quebec at Montreal. Journals to which psychologists across North America contribute include *Human Studies, The Humanistic Psychologist, Journal of Phenomenological Psychology, International Journal of Qualitative Studies in Education, Methods, Phenomenology + Pedagogy, Review of Existential Psychology and Psychiatry, Theoretical and Philosophical Psychology*, and similar specialized philosophy journals. Phenomenologically oriented psychologists, in addition to being involved in such American Psychological Association divisions as Clinical, Psychotherapy, and Independent Practice, are among the most active members of the Division of Theoretical and Philosophical Psychology and the Division of Humanistic Psychology, as well as of the International Human-Science Research Conference, the Society for Phenomenology and the Human Sciences, and the Southern Society for Philosophy and Psychology.

While these effects are underway, what difference does the present state of phenomenological-existential psychology make for the practice of psychotherapy? It allows therapists to systematically take into account their clients' full humanness. In particular, this orientation encourages six practices:

1. The therapist repeatedly brackets prior theoretical and practical assumptions about clients, therein listening more carefully to clients in terms of their own lives rather than in terms of formulations.

2. The therapist, in being open to, indeed attuned to, the uniquely human characteristic of co-creating one's world through one's relations with it, attends to "process" and "dynamics" in a way that allows so-called "inner" and "external" realities to be addressed in their unity. Even when focused upon separately, these constituents are regarded as mutually implicatory.

3. Any active interventions are not directed only to behaviors or to internal dynamics, but to both at once. They are addressed simultaneously in terms of clients' living of their worlds.

4. The therapist does not impose artificial clarity, but instead respects the ambiguity inherent in human reality's always being perspectival—that is, dependent on historical, personal, technological access. This is not to say that everything is merely relative, however. Although subject to varying expression, and never apprehended once and for all, humanly known reality has its own orderliness. Through joint respect for both ambiguity and orderliness, the therapist encourages clients to respect the complexities of their lives and to be open to conflicting motives.

5. Many conflicts are identified as existential—as choices reflecting one's values and authoring of one's own life even in the face of circumstantial limitations. Many existential therapists also look to phenomenological human-science research for guidance in regard to what options are structurally possible from where the client is at that point.

6. The therapist recognizes that his or her relationship with the client is powerful in its own right, that it affects both participants, and that when it might be helpful to the client it is spoken of openly.

Since the publication of this handbook's first edition, *postmodernism* has become an often cited term in both social science and popular publications. It points to the passing of the "modern" belief that pure rationality and positivistic empiricism would discover *the* truths of nature, that with enough such data accumulated through precise objective experiment and measurement, truth in itself would stand out clearly. With that passing, publishers have become increasingly receptive to printing accounts of the social construc-

tion of reality (Gergen, 1985; Kitzinger, 1987; Szekely, 1988).

As phenomenological and human-science psychology have advanced in the midst of expanding discussion of postmodernism, deconstructionism, and hermeneutics, so too have kindred efforts in education, sociology, and nursing. Perhaps soon we will develop in two critical areas: (a) interdisciplinary integration, and (b) broadening focus from the individual to that person within a political-economic-cultural context. Both of these developments would provide stimulating frames for the new developments in self-psychology and cognitive psychology, all of which will enhance psychotherapy.

EMPIRICAL QUALITATIVE RESEARCH

There is no published compilation research literature on phenomenological-existential psychotherapy. Psychologists of that orientation have, however, developed an empirical research approach and a beginning content base that is described below. The approach clearly is suitable for development of basic research on human experience, on pathological modes of being, and on the therapeutic process.

Existential psychotherapy may, of course, be practiced in accordance with its philosophical anthropology without concern for development of systematized research findings or for a philosophy of science grounding that research. Existential psychotherapy, however, will reach its fullest potential if it looks to Husserl's philosophy and method as a foundation for the development of psychology as a human science (Giorgi, 1970). That foundation is, in large part, an explicit acknowledgment that all knowledge, including scientific knowledge, is inescapably co-determined by the knower and the object. Because the knower can never exhaust perspectives on an object, knowledge is necessarily incomplete. When the object (subject matter) is human perception, experience, action, or the like, its radically relational structure leads phenomenologically grounded researchers to respect its essential ambiguity. "Either-or" and "once and for all" findings are the result of imposed clarity.

With these understandings, faculty and graduate students, especially those from the above-mentioned universities, have been developing methods for studying phenomena in their own right, prior to imposition of measurement schemas. For example, at Duquesne University, Giorgi and his students, following the initial lead of Van Kaam (1959), have systematically developed empirical phenomenological procedures and have also specialized in the content areas of learning and perception; W. Fischer and his students have focused on affective and emotional states; von Eckartsberg and his students have developed dialogal methods and have focused on social psychology topics; Smith and his students have addressed alcoholism; and Barton and Knowles and their students are among those who have directly addressed the process of psychotherapy.

Before looking at the general procedures of empirical research, the reader may wish to see an example of findings. I studied moments of being in privacy as a means of understanding how assessment and therapy can be intimate and interventional and yet not be experienced as invasions of privacy. The essence of being in privacy turned out to be the following:

> Privacy is, when: The watching self and world fade away, along with geometric space, clock time, and other contingencies, leaving an intensified relationship with the subject of consciousness lived in a flowing Now. The relationship is toned by a sense of at-homeness or familiarity, and its style is one of relative openness to or wonder at the object's variable nature. (C. Fischer, 1975)

The above example illustrates four points. First, research results are in the form of descriptive structures of the world as lived. The results do not address either a world in itself or internal events, but rather that unity mentioned above. Second, such structures disrupt preconceptions. Here, for example, it turned out that what society usually protects when it attempts to "protect privacy" is secrecy. A structural characterization of moments of disrupted privacy indicated that such disruptions are indeed intrusive, but not so much into a secret life as into reverie, insight, and so on. Indeed, in effective assessment and psychotherapy, the parties often are in *shared* privacy, looking together in openness and wonder at the unfolding and varying nature of the client's life. Third, the results of phenomenological research typically strike one, upon reflection, as familiar, as something we already knew. But we did not know it thematically, and hence we could not make use of it. Both our everyday and our trained ways of thinking about things often cover over unreflective understandings with various cause–effect forms of reasoning. Fourth, phenomenological research is appropropriate when we want to know the essence of a phenomenon, that is, its essential features as people live them. In contrast, our traditional natural-science research methods are appropriate when we want to know about physical and biological events at these levels, and when we want to know "how much" or "how many" behaviors occur in various conditions.

In very brief form, the following are the general steps of empirical, qualitative research as they have been developed at Duquesne University. (See also Fischer & Wertz, 1979; von Eckartsberg, 1986; Wertz, 1985.) There are, of course, many variations and alternatives (e.g., de Rivera, 1981). See Aanstoos (1987), Polkinghorne (1989), and Tesch (1990) for characterizations of human-science research methods developed beyond Duquesne. As mentioned in the section on variations on Husserl's method, a first step is to collect verbatim descriptions from subjects of some actual event (e.g., moments of being anxious, being in privacy, feeling understood by a therapist). For workability, transcriptions are demarcated into segments in accordance with shifts in what is being described. The researcher then strives to bracket (shelve, put away for the time being) prior conceptions; implicit conceptions crop up and are also noted and shelved. Segment by segment, the researcher asks: "What is the person saying here that is essential to 'being anxious' (or to whatever the phenomenon is)? In this regard, what is apparent in this segment about the person's lived relations with self, environment, and others?" The researcher writes out the answers to these questions, next to the transcript, sticking as closely as possible to the subject's original language. After finishing the transcript, the researcher writes a synopsis, tying together the segment analyses while also capturing the temporal unfolding of the described event. These steps are repeated for other subjects (anywhere from several to 50 in research to date). Then the synopses are asked the same question: "What is essential to being anxious (for example) that appears in all these instances?" Again, the language of the subjects is respected, but the resulting structure is necessarily more abstract because it must characterize what is true across all subjects.

Different researchers might word the structure differently, and researchers do vary in the scope of what becomes apparent to them. The research is empirical, however, in two respects. First, its focus throughout is the reported experience—the original referent for the term *empirical*. The focus is not transferred to secondary, derived data such as test scores or behavior tallies. Second, the researcher's procedures and analyses are available for other researchers' inspection and replication. (See C. Fischer & Wertz, 1979, for a discussion of how this qualitative research is empirical, of various forms of description the results may take, and for excerpts from different steps of analysis. The exemplar phenomenon in this case was the experience of being criminally victimized.)

Thus far, the bulk of empirical phenomenological research has been carried out in the form of over 135 doctoral dissertations at Duquesne University. The following are representative areas and topics. Among the studies of affective and emotional states are those by Schur (1979) and Daehn (1988) on being disappointed, Mruk (1981) on being pleased with oneself, Sadowsky (1985) on being resentful, and Frankel (1985) on being angry. Representative studies in established content areas are those by McConville (1975) on perception of horizontal space, Wertz (1982) on a critique of the New Look's conception of perception, and DeVries (1986) on prospective remembering. Studies of restricted existence include Dunn's (1974) on "a brain-damaged existence," Mitchell's (1976) on alcohol addiction, Murphy's (1978; Murphy & Fischer, 1983) on low back pain syndromes, and Carter's (1989) on unipolar depression. Among dissertations on different forms of therapy are Hofrichter's (1976) on trying out a different comportment through psychodrama, Sheridan's (1978) on psychoanalysts' perception during initial interviews, and Ward's (1978) on clients' experience during the imagining phase of systematic desensitization. Duquesne dissertations addressing therapy process include Fessler's (1978) on the client's and therapist's experience of interpretation, Carney's (1984) on the meanings of therapeutic psychological change, and Orbison's (1986) on confessing to another. Duquesne dissertations on contemporary social problems include Keairns's (1980) on the decision to have an abortion, Capone's (1986) on becoming addicted to heroin, and Lambert's (1989) on child abuse experienced as nondeliberate.

To give the reader a further sense of the results of the above research, the findings from two of them follow. Fessler (1978) found that the therapist and client experience an interpretation differently and do not fully understand the other's experience, despite shared speech. Much of what takes place during interpretation is outside both parties' reflective awareness. Nevertheless, success of the interpretation depends upon its closeness to the client's experience. Ward (1978) found that what happens for the client during systematic desensitization is best characterized as "the from-which, through-which, and to-which of a transformation of self-in-world." This transformation is a "restructurational process in which the subject maintains an engaged presence to the fearsome, thereby allowing familization with, differentiation of, and delimitation of the fearsome. Control of images and of behavior develops as [personally] viable responses are discovered, tried out, practiced, and mastered."

It is no accident that this research does not yet include "outcome" studies. Phenomenological researchers strongly believe that we must first conduct what have traditionally been called "process" studies in order to discover what clients *and* therapists experience during various moments and phases of therapy. Outcome could then be studied in relation to what went on during therapy. This approach would be much more precise than studies that compare ratings and scores of experimental groups without regard for what transpired among their participants. Similarly, studies of what happens in therapy for persons with particular difficulties would add precision to both process and outcome research. Finally, preliminary qualitative (phenomenological) study could identify which dimensions of the therapeutic process might most profitably be measured in large-scale quantitative studies.

SUMMARY

This chapter reviewed existential psychotherapy's grounding in both phenomenology and existential philosophy. It also reviewed the understandings, of both psychopathology and the psychotherapeutic relationship, that are most widely agreed upon by practitioners who refer to themselves as existential. The point was made that it is a philosophical stance that most characterizes this approach rather than specific techniques. There are no subschools or internal controversies, although both language analysis and revisions within psychoanalysis may later prove to be points of departure. At present, despite ever-increasing interest in a phenomenological-existential approach to therapy, and despite a broadening of other theories to accommodate many of its aspects, as Smith (1979) has said, phenomenological psychology offers not so much a school of therapy as a framework for understanding what is unique about human experience, action, and knowledge, as well as a methodology for conducting research into precisely these usually unstudied phenomena.

What is required next, if phenomenological-existential psychotherapy is to grow and to contribute maximally, is an agenda of studies designed systematically to evolve a body of knowledge on usual and restricted ways of being, on growth phenomena, and on what happens during psychotherapy.

REFERENCES

Aanstoos, C. M. (1987). A comparative survey of human science psychologies. *Methods, 1,* 1–36.
American Psychiatric Association. (1981). *Diagnostic and statistical manual of mental disorders* (3rd. ed., Revised). Washington, DC: Author.
Barton, A. (1974). *Three worlds of therapy: Freud, Jung, Rogers.* Palo Alto, CA: National Press Books.

Binswanger, L. (1963). *Being-in-the-world: Selected papers of Ludwig Binswanger* (J. Needleman, Trans.). New York: Basic Books. (Original work published 1938–1943)

Boss, M. (1963). *Psychoanalysis and daseinsanalysis*. New York: Basic Books. (Original work published 1957)

Boss, M. (1967). Anxiety, guilt and psychotherapeutic liberation. *Review of Existential Psychology and Psychiatry, 2*, 173–195.

Brice, C. (1988). What forever means: An empirical existential-phenomenological investigation of the maternal mourning of a child lost through death (Doctoral dissertation, Duquesne University, 1987). *Dissertation Abstracts International, 49*, 234B.

Buber, M. (1965). *Between man and man* (R. G. Smith, Trans.). New York: Macmillan. (Original work published 1926–1939)

Bugental, J. F. T. (1965). *The search for authenticity: An existential-analytic approach to psychotherapy*. New York: Holt, Rinehart & Winston.

Capone, M. (1986). Becoming addicted to heroin: An empirical phenomenological approach (Doctoral dissertation, Duquesne University, 1986). *Dissertation Abstracts International, 42*, 780B.

Carney, C. (1984). The meanings of therapeutic psychological change as revealed in short-term psychotherapy: A phenomenological inquiry (Doctoral dissertation, Duquesne University, 1984). *Dissertation Abstracts International, 45*, 1007B.

Carter, S. (1989). Unipolar clinical depression: An empirical-phenomenological study. (Doctoral dissertation. Duquesne University, 1988). *Dissertation Abstracts International, 50*, 4765B.

Colaizzi, P. F. (1969). The descriptive methods and the types of subject-matter of a phenomenological-based psychology: Exemplified by the phenomenon of learning (Doctoral dissertation, Duquesne University, 1969). *Dissertation Abstracts International, 30*, 2889B.

Daehn, M. P. (1988). Being disappointed: A phenomenological psychological analysis (Doctoral dissertation, Duquesne University, 1988). *Dissertation Abstracts International, 49*, 1929B.

Deegan, P. E. (1984). The use of diazepam in an effort to transform being anxious: An empirical phenomenological investigation (Doctoral dissertation, Duquesne University, 1983). *Dissertation Abstracts International, 45*, 666B.

de Rivera, J. (Ed.). (1981). *Conceptual encounter: A method for the exploration of human experience*. Lanham, MD: University Press of America.

DeVries, M. J. (1986). Remembering to perform actions: An empirical phenomenological study of prospective remembering (Doctoral dissertation, Duquesne University, 1986). *Dissertation Abstracts International, 47*, 1718B.

Dunn, M. J. (1974). An ideographic reflective analysis of a brain-injured existence (Doctoral dissertation, Duquesne University, 1974). *Dissertation Abstracts International, 35*, 1403B.

Farber, L. (1966). *The ways of the will*. New York: Basic Books.

Fessler, R. K. (1978). A phenomenological investigation of psychotherapeutic interpretation (Doctoral dissertation, Duquesne University, 1978). *Dissertation Abstracts International, 39*, 2981B.

Fischer, C. T. (1969). Rapport as mutual respect. *Personnel and Guidance Journal, 48*, 201–204.

Fischer, C. T. (1975). Privacy as a profile of authentic consciousness. *Humanitas, 11*, 27–43.

Fischer, C. T. (1979). Individualized assessment and phenomenological psychology. *Journal of Personality Assessment, 43*, 115–122.

Fischer, C. T. (1985). *Individualizing psychological assessment*. Monterey, CA: Brooks/Cole.

Fischer, C. T. (1987). Beyond transference. *Person-Centered Review, 2*, 157–164.

Fischer, C. T., & Wertz, F. J. (1979). Empirical phenomenological analyses of being criminally victimized. In A. Giorgi, R. Knowles, & D. L. Smith (Eds.), *Duquesne studies in phenomenological psychology* (Vol. 3, pp. 135–158). Pittsburgh: Duquesne University Press.

Fischer, W. F. (1974). On the phenomenological mode of researching being-anxious. *Journal of Phenomenological Psychology, 4*, 405–423.

Fischer, W. F. (1982). An empirical-phenomenological approach to the psychology of anxiety. In A. de Koning & F. Jenner (Eds.), *Phenomenology and psychiatry* (pp. 63–84). London: Academic Press.

Fischer, W. F. (1985). Self-deception: An empirical-phenomenological enquiry into its essential meanings. In A. Giorgi (Ed.), *Phenomenology and psychological research* (pp. 118–154). Pittsburgh: Duquesne University Press.

Frankel, C. A. (1985). The phenomenology of being angry: An empirical study approached from the perspective of self and other (Doctoral dissertation, Duquesne University, 1985). *Dissertation Abstracts International, 46*, 959B.

Frankl, V. E. (1962). *Man's search for meaning*. (I. Lasch, Trans.). Boston: Beacon Press. (Original work published 1946)

Frankl, V. E. (1966). *The doctor and the soul: From psychotherapy to logotherapy*. (R. and C. Winston, Trans.) (2nd ed.). New York: Vintage Books. (Original work published 1946)

Friedman, M. (1985). *The healing dialogue in psychotherapy*. New York: Jason Aronson.

Gendlin, E. T. (1978). *Focusing*. New York: Everest House.

Gergen, K. J. (1985). The social constructionist movement in modern psychology. *American Psychologist, 40*, 266–275.

Giorgi, A. (1970). *Psychology as a human science: A phenomenological approach*. New York: Harper & Row.

Giorgi, A. (Ed.). (1985). *Phenomenology and psychological research*. Pittsburgh: Duquesne University Press.

Giorgi, A., Barton, A., & Maes, C. (Eds.). (1983). *Du-*

quesne studies in phenomenological psychology (Vol. 4). Pittsburgh: Duquesne University Press.

Giorgi, A., Fischer, C. T., & Murray, E. (Eds.). (1975). *Duquesne studies in phenomenological psychology* (Vol. 2). Pittsburgh: Duquesne University Press.

Giorgi, A., Fischer, W. F., & von Eckartsberg, R. (Eds.). (1971). *Duquesne studies in phenomenological psychology* (Vol. 1). Pittsburgh: Duquesne University Press.

Giorgi, A., Knowles, R., & Smith, D. L. (Eds.). (1979). *Duquesne studies in phenomenological psychology* (Vol. 3). Pittsburgh: Duquesne University Press.

Goldsmith, M. M. (1987). Despair: An empirical phenomenological study (Doctoral dissertation, Duquesne University, 1987). *Dissertation Abstracts International, 48*, 1808B.

Halling, S., & Nill, J. D. (1989). Demystifying psychopathology: Understanding disturbed persons. In R. S. Valle & S. Halling (Eds.), *Existential-phenomenological perspectives in psychology* (pp. 179–192). New York: Plenum Press.

Heidegger, M. (1968). *Being and time* (J. Macquarrie & E. Robinson, Trans.). New York: Harper & Row. (Original work published 1927)

Hofrichter, D. A. (1976). Trying out a different comportment through psychodrama: The process of the possible becoming viable (Doctoral dissertation, Duquesne University, 1976). *Dissertation Abstracts International, 37*, 1902B.

Husserl, E. (1969). *Ideas: General introduction to pure phenomenology* (W. R. B. Gibson, Trans.). London: Allen & Unwin. (Original work published 1913)

Husserl, E. (1970). *The crisis of European sciences and transcendental phenomenology: An introduction to phenomenological philosophy* (D. Carr, Trans.). Evanston, IL: Northwestern University Press. (Original work published posthumously 1954)

Jubala, J. (1988). Right hemisphere cerebrovascular accident: A phenomenological study of the living through the first three months poststroke (Doctoral dissertation, Duquesne University, 1988). *Dissertation Abstracts International, 49*, 5520B.

Keairns, Y. E. (1980). Reflective decision-making: An empirical-phenomenological study of the decision to have an abortion (Doctoral Dissertation, Duquesne University, 1980). *Dissertation Abstracts International, 41*, 1892B.

Keen, E. (1970). *Three faces of being: Toward an existential clinical psychology*. New York: Appleton-Century-Crofts.

Keen, E. (1975). *A primer in phenomenological psychology*. New York: Holt, Rinehart & Winston.

Kierkegaard, S. (1954). *Fear and trembling and the sickness unto death* (W. Lowrie, Trans.). New York: Doubleday. (Original work published separately in 1843 & 1849)

Kitzinger, C. (1987). *The social construction of lesbianism*. London: Sage Publications.

Knowles, R. (1986). *Human development and human possibility: Erikson in the light of Heidegger*. Lanham, MD: University Press of America.

Lambert, J. (1989). Child abuse which is experienced by the abuser as nondeliberate: An empirical phenomenological investigation into a problem of will (Doctoral dissertation, Duquesne University, 1988). *Dissertation Abstracts International, 50*, 5523B.

Lindsay-Hartz, J. (1984). Contrasting experiences of shame and guilt. *American Behavioral Scientist, 27*, 689–704.

Linn, S. L. (1985). A systematic existential phenomenological investigation of the unfolding meaning of being depressed (Doctoral dissertation, Duquesne University, 1985). *Dissertation Abstracts International, 46*, 2070B.

Lyons, J. (1963). *Psychology and the measure of man*. New York: Free Press.

Mahoney, M. J. (1977). Reflections on the cognitive-learning trend in psychotherapy. *American Psychologist, 32*, 5–13.

Marcel, G. (1965). *Being and having: An existential diary*. New York: Harper & Row. (Original work published in 1949)

May, R. (1964). On the phenomenological bases of psychotherapy. *Review of Existential Psychology and Psychiatry, 4*, 22–36.

May, R. (1979). *Psychology and the human dilemma*. New York: WW Norton.

May, R., Angel, E., & Ellenberger, H. (Eds.). (1958). *Existence: A new dimension in psychiatry and psychology*. New York: Basic Books.

McConville, M. G. (1975). Perception of the horizontal dimension of space: An empirical phenomenological study (Doctoral dissertation, Duquesne University, 1974). *Dissertation Abstracts International, 36*, 476B.

Merleau-Ponty, M. (1962). *Phenomenology of perception* (C. Smith, Trans.). New York: Humanities Press. (Original work published 1945)

Merleau-Ponty, M. (1963). *The structure of behavior* (A. Fischer, Trans.). Boston: Beacon Press. (Original work published in 1942)

Minkowski, E. (1970). *Lived time: Phenomenological and psychopathological studies* (N. Metzel, Trans.). Evanston, IL: Northwestern University Press. (Original work published 1933)

Mitchell, R. M. (1976). An existential-phenomenological study of the structure of addiction with alcohol as revealed through the significant life-historical drinking situations or alcohol related situations of one self-confirmed alcoholic male (Doctoral dissertation, Duquesne University, 1975). *Dissertation Abstracts International, 36*, 6392B.

Moss, D. (1989). Brain, body, and world: Body image and the psychology of the body. In R. S. Valle & S. Halling (Eds.), *Existential-phenomenological perspectives in psychology* (pp. 63–82). New York: Plenum Press.

Mruk, C. (1981). Being pleased with oneself in a biographically critical way: An existential-phenomenological investigation (Doctoral dissertation, Duquesne University, 1981). *Dissertation Abstracts International, 42*, 4937B).

Murphy, M. A., & Fischer, C. T. (1983). Styles of living with low back injury: The continuity dimension. *Social Sciences and Medicine, 17*, 291–297.

Murphy, M. A. (1978). The living of low back pain after injury: A phenomenological investigation. (Doctoral dissertation, Duquesne University, 1978). *Dissertation Abstracts International, 39*, 1964B.

Orbison, D. (1986). Confessing to another: A phenomenological investigation. (Doctoral dissertation, Duquesne University, 1986). *Dissertation Abstracts International, 47*, 4659B.

Polkinghorne, D. E. (1989). Phenomenological research methods. In R. S. Valle & S. Halling (Eds.), *Existential-phenomenological perspectives in psychology* (pp. 41–60). New York: Plenum Press.

Ramm, D. R. (1980). A phenomenological investigation of jealousy (Doctoral dissertation, Duquesne University, 1979). *Dissertation Abstracts International, 40*, 5828B.

Ricoeur, P. (1966). *Freedom and nature: The voluntary and the involuntary* (E. V. Kohak, Trans.). Evanston, IL: Northwestern University Press. (Originally published in 1950)

Ricouer, P. (1967). *Husserl: An analysis of his phenomenology* (E. G. Ballard & L. E. Embree, Trans.). Evanston, IL: Northwestern University Press. (Original work published 1949 to 1957)

Rogers, C. (1942). *Counseling and psychotherapy*. Boston: Houghton Mifflin.

Sadowsky, S. (1985). An empirical phenomenological investigation of being resentful (Doctoral dissertation, Duquesne University, 1984). *Dissertation Abstracts International, 46*, 703B.

Sartre, J. P. (1956). *Being and nothingness* (H. Barnes, Trans.). New York: Philosophical Library. (Original work published 1943)

Schur, M. M. (1979). An empirical-phenomenological study of situations of being disappointed (Doctoral dissertation, Duquesne University, 1978). *Dissertation Abstracts International, 39*, 5584B.

Severin, F. T. (1965). *Humanistic viewpoints in psychology*. New York: McGraw-Hill.

Sheridan, T. W. (1978). An existential phenomenological study of perception's life in dialogue as exemplified by two psychoanalysts' conduct during interviews (Doctoral dissertation, Duquesne University, 1977). *Dissertation Abstracts International, 38*, 5594B.

Smith, D. L. (1979). Phenomenological psychotherapy: A why and a how. In A. Giorgi, R. Knowles, & D. L. Smith (Eds.). *Duquesne studies in phenomenological psychology* (Vol. 3, pp. 32–48). Pittsburgh: Duquesne University Press.

Stern, D. N. (1985). *The interpersonal world of the infant: A view from psychoanalysis and developmental psychology*. New York: Basic Books.

Stevick, E. L. (1971). An empirical investigation of the experience of anger. In A. Giorgi, W. F. Fischer, & R. von Eckartsberg (Eds.), *Duquesne studies in phenomenological psychology* (Vol. 1, pp. 132–148). Pittsburgh: Duquesne University Press.

Strasser, S. (1963). *Phenomenology and the human sciences*. Pittsburgh: Duquesne University Press.

Straus, E. (1963). *The primary world of the senses*. (J. Needleman, Trans.). Glencoe, IL: Free Press. (Original work published 1935)

Straus, E. (1966). *Phenomenological psychology: Selected papers* (E. Eng, Trans.). New York: Basic Books. (Original work published 1930 to 1962)

Szekely, E. (1988). *Never too thin*. Toronto: The Women's Press.

Tesch, R. (1990). *Qualitative research: Analysis types and software tools*. New York: Falmer Press.

Valle, R. S., & King, M. (1978). *Existential-phenomenological alternatives for psychology*. New York: Oxford University Press.

Vallelonga, D. S. (1986). The lived structure of being embarrassed and being ashamed-of-oneself: An empirical phenomenological study (Doctoral dissertation, Duquesne University, 1986). *Dissertation Abstracts International, 47*, 2217B.

Van den Berg, J. H. (1955). *The phenomenological approach to psychiatry*. Springfield, IL: CC Thomas.

Van den Berg, J. H. (1971). What is psychotherapy? *Humanitas, 7*, 321–370.

Van Kaam, A. L. (1959). Phenomenal analyses: Exemplified by a study of the experience of "really feeling understood." *Journal of Individual Psychology, 15*, 66–72.

Van Kaam, A. L. (1966a). *The art of existential counseling: A new perspective in psychotherapy*. Wilkes-Barre, PA: Dimension.

Van Kaam, A. L. (1966b). *Existential foundations of psychology*. Pittsburgh: Duquesne University Press.

von Eckartsberg, R. (1986). *Life-world experience: Existential-phenomenological research approaches in psychology*. Washington, DC: Center for Advanced Research in Phenomenology and University Press of America.

Ward, W. F. (1978). Transformation of self-in-world through the imagining phase of systematic desensitization. (Doctoral dissertation, Duquesne University, 1977). *Dissertation Abstracts International, 38*, 5600B.

Wertz, F. J. (1982). A dialogue with the New Look: A historical critique and a descriptive approach to everyday perceptual process. Unpublished doctoral dissertation, Duquesne University, Pittsburgh.

Wertz, F. J. (1983). From everyday to psychological description: Analyzing the moments of a qualitative data analysis. *Journal of Phenomenological Psychology, 14*, 197–241.

Wertz, F. J. (1985). Method and findings in a phenomenological psychology study of a complex life event. In A. Giorgi (Ed.), *Phenomenology and psychological research* (pp. 155–216). Pittsburgh: Duquesne University Press.

Yalom, I. (1980). *Existential psychotherapy*. New York: Basic Books.

Yalom, I. D. (1989). *Love's executioner and other tales of psychotherapy*. New York: Basic Books.

Zaner, R. (1970). *The way of phenomenology*. New York: Pegasus Press.

CHAPTER 30

BEHAVIOR THERAPY WITH ADULTS: AN INTEGRATIVE PERSPECTIVE FOR THE NINETIES

Cyril M. Franks
Christopher R. Barbrack

HISTORICAL AND CONCEPTUAL FOUNDATION

In 1983, an introductory footnote made the point that the presence of separate chapters devoted to behavioral assessment, behavior therapy with children, and behavior therapy with adults, respectively, reflected organizational rather than conceptual differentiation. As far as we were concerned, behavior therapy was and is an across-the-board approach, an interwoven mosaic of assessment and intervention that applies regardless of content. This approach is characterized by the application of behavioral science principles within a broadly conceived learning theory framework offering guiding principles rather than rigid adherence to overarching postulates. Current strategy is to be continually reappraised in the light of incoming data. Thus, the hallmarks of contemporary behavior therapy include accountability, openness to alternatives, and appeal to data rather than authority.

Preparation of this revision serves to strengthen our conviction that this is what behavior therapy is about. Once again, we begin with the suggestion that readers seeking further guidance consult the following sources: (a) *An Introduction to the Principles of Behavior Therapy* (Wilson & O'Leary, 1980); (b) *The History of Behavior Therapy* (Kazdin, 1978c); and (c) the *Review of Behavior Therapy*, an ongoing chronicle of developments in behavior therapy (Franks & Wilson, 1973–). Once again, we offer a discussion of historical and conceptual foundations, the characteristics of contemporary behavior therapy, prevailing misconceptions and unresolved issues, and finally, a brief review of current status and future directions. And once again, we offer a reading list of recent practice-oriented texts to make up for the fact that this chapter is neither a how-to manual nor a compendium of techniques.

Behavior therapy began in the late 1950s as an antimentalistic, somewhat blinkered alternative to the prevailing disease-oriented model of psychodynamic psychotherapy. But conceptually, its roots go back much farther, to the development of exact, quantifiable, and objective ways of thinking about human behavior. It was not until psychology had abandoned the nonexperimental speculations of the philosopher and initiated the precise methodology of the experimental laboratory that the ground was ready for behavior therapy to take root.

The names of Pavlov, Thorndike, and Skinner come readily to mind as the precursors of behavior therapy. Each worked with single subjects and each used primarily inductive models of human behavior. Each made signal contributions to the developments of behavior therapy. But the implications and translation into practice of their work had to await two developments: the accumulation of sufficient empirical laboratory data and the emergence of the scientist–practitioner model in clinical psychology. It was not until the late 1950s that it was possible to incorporate the early foundations in conditioning and learning established by Pavlov, Thorndike, Watson, Skinner, Hull, and other stimulus-response (S-R) learning theorists into a methodological framework of behavioral science. Other contributing factors included the burgeoning postwar need for mental-health care, the lack of trained psychiatrists, the limited availability of effective pharmacological therapy, the growing dissatisfaction with the prevailing psychodynamic model—applicable primarily to the more verbal, intact, and better-educated patient—and the increased funds available, at least in the United States, for the training of clinical psychologists.

If the times were ripe for the genesis of behavior therapy, it did not emerge without birth pangs and often frank hostility from a variety of sectors: from psychiatrists for reasons both professional and economic, from traditional clinical psychology, for reasons to be discussed, and from certain segments of the general community. For obvious reasons, most behavior therapists were and still are to be found among the ranks of psychologists rather than psychiatrists or social workers, and this served to create further divisiveness. Parenthetically, it might be noted that the first "breakthrough," a viable alternative to either psychodynamic therapies or drugs that could be readily applied to the literate, intact patient, was developed by a psychiatrist, Wolpe. Prior to this launching of systemic desensitization, a technique allegedly based on the physiological principles of Sherrington and the classical conditioning of Pavlov, conditioning, in 1958, was something to be applied to the white rat and the hospitalized vegetative idiot but never to the literate adult. It might also be noted that at first desensitization was used largely for the treatment of specific fears. It was only later, as behavior therapy became more sophisticated, that the procedure was adapted to accommodate an increasingly complex range of situations (Kazdin, 1978a, 1978c).

Early attempts to establish a learning-theory basis for clinical phenomena (e.g., Dollard & Miller, 1950) were essentially exercises in translation. The implicit assumption was that the psychodynamic model was psychological "truth" but that certain elements could be better appreciated and utilized if translated into S-R

terminology. It was not until the advent of systematic desensitization in 1958 and the use of operant techniques to condition socially appropriate behavior in chronic schizophrenics (Ayllon & Michael, 1959), followed a decade later by the design of a token economy for institutional application (Ayllon & Azrin, 1968), that behavior therapy as we know it today began to emerge.

Concurrent with these developments were the formation in 1966 of the Association for Advancement of Behavior Therapy (AABT) in the United States and the emergence of several journals devoted exclusively to behavior therapy in the United Kingdom and this country. Today, there are over 50 behavior therapy journals scattered throughout the world, perhaps as many national and regional behavior therapy associations, and a world association in the process of formation.

The term *behavior therapy* seems to have been introduced independently by three groups of researchers. In 1953, Lindsley, Skinner, and Solomon referred to their use of operant conditioning principles with hospitalized psychotic patients as behavior therapy. In 1959, Eysenck used the term in written material to refer to a new approach to therapy. Eysenck viewed behavior therapy as the application of "modern learning theory" to the treatment of psychological disorders. Whereas Lindsley and his colleagues (1953) conceptualized behavior therapy exclusively in terms of Skinnerian operant conditioning, Eysenck adopted a broader perspective. For Eysenck, behavior therapy encompassed operant conditioning, classical conditioning, and, later, modeling, with increasing acknowledgments to Pavlov, Mowrer, and such neobehaviorists as Hull, Spence, and (with certain qualifications) Bandura. In 1958, Lazarus independently coined the term *behavior therapy* to refer to the addition of objective laboratory procedures to traditional psychotherapeutic methods. In this respect, Lazarus (then as now) felt that behavior therapy is but one part of a multimodal totality that could include certain elements of traditional psychotherapy and psychiatry, together with validated techniques from any source (Lazarus, 1981).

The roots of behavior therapy or *behavior modification*, to use a term we employ interchangeably with behavior therapy, can be traced back to many schools of thought, to contrasting methodologies, to diverse philosophical systems, to different countries, and to various pioneers. Some individuals stress classical conditioning and its translation into practice by way of such techniques as aversion therapy and systematic desensitization. Others rely upon the Skinnerian legacy of operant conditioning and the experimental analysis of behavior. Yet others focus on the data of experimental psychology as a whole rather than exclusively rely on conditioning theory per se (Wilson & Franks, 1982). Sometimes behavior therapy takes on peculiarly idiosyncratic aspects, as for example with Yates's (1970) emphasis on the single case as the conceptual sine qua non of behavior therapy. The general trend is toward increasing complexity.

DEFINITION OF CONTEMPORARY BEHAVIOR THERAPY

For Kazdin (1978a), those who call themselves behavior therapists share the following characteristics: (a) a focus on current rather than historical determinants of behavior; (b) an emphasis on overt behavior change as the main criterion by which treatment is to be evaluated; (c) specification of treatment in objective terms so as to make replication possible; (d) a reliance upon basic research in psychology to generate both general hypotheses about treatment and specific therapeutic techniques; and (e) specificity in definition and accountability, treatment, and measurement.

Within the above context, most definitions of behavior therapy fall into one of two classes: doctrinal or epistemological. Doctrinal definitions attempt to link behavior therapy to doctrines, theories, laws, or principles of learning. Epistemological definitions tend to characterize behavior therapy in terms of the various ways of studying clinical phenomena. By and large, doctrinal definitions tend to be narrow and fail to accommodate all of behavior therapy, whereas epistemological definitions tend to be excessively accommodating and hence potentially applicable to many nonbehavioral therapies (Erwin, 1978; Franks & Wilson, 1973–1979). The definition of behavior therapy currently endorsed by the AABT attempts to combine the best elements of both:

> Behavior therapy involves primarily the application of principles derived from research in experimental and social psychology for the alleviation of human suffering and the enhancement of human functioning. Behavior therapy emphasizes a systematic evaluation of the effectiveness of these applications. Behavior therapy involves environmental change and social interaction rather than the direct alteration of bodily processes by biological procedures. The aim is primarily educational. The techniques facilitate improved self-control. In the conduct of behavior therapy, a contractual agreement is negotiated, in which mutually agreeable goals and procedures are specified. Responsible practitioners using behavioral ap-

proaches are guided by generally accepted ethical principles. (Franks & Wilson, 1975, p. 1)

The more flexible and comprehensive the definition, the greater the potential for overlap with nonbehavioral systems, and it may be as Erwin suggests, that a definition of behavior therapy that is acceptable to the majority of behavior therapists is not possible at this time. Perhaps for this reason, rather than attempt a definition, Davison and Stuart (1975) simply list "several important unifying characteristics." Erwin's (1978) characterization of behavior therapy as "a nonbiological form of therapy that developed largely out of learning theory research and that is normally applied directly, incrementally and experimentally in the treatment of specific maladaptive patterns" (p. 44) is consistent with this position.

CHARACTERISTICS OF CONTEMPORARY BEHAVIOR THERAPY

Contemporary behavior therapy is further characterized by doing as well as talking, by a variety of multidimensional methods, by a growing focus on client responsibility, by an emphasis on current rather than historical determinants, by accountability, outcome evaluation, and a healthy but critical respect for data, by objectivity and specificity in defining, treating, and measuring the target problems, and by a readiness to go beyond the confining straits of traditional conditioning or S-R learning theory for its data base. Above all, in behavior therapy a theory is a servant that is useful only until a better theory and a better type of therapy come along.

Modern behavior therapy is methodology rather than technique oriented. A clinician versed only in the techniques of behavior therapy is not a behavior therapist. To be a behavior therapist, concept and methodology must be primary, and specific techniques secondary or derived. Nevertheless, it is techniques that bring about change, and behavior therapy has many effective techniques to its credit. Of these, the most well known include systematic desensitization, behavioral rehearsal, contracting, assertion training, token reinforcement systems, numerous cognitive procedures, and the teaching of coping skills and self-control. Biofeedback, behavioral medicine, environmental psychology, ecology, and systems theory are increasingly part of the behavior therapy scene. No longer is treatment used primarily with people of limited sophistication or those with specific phobias; behavior therapy as a way of approaching a problem is applicable to all types of disorders, individuals, situations, or settings.

Modern behavior therapy is able to contain considerable diversity within its conceptual borders. There are those who accept trait theories as consistent with a behavioral position and those who avoid them like the plague. There are those for whom physiological and constitutional factors are paramount and those for whom the environment is all-encompassing. There are those for whom self-control is a delusion because they believe there is no such thing as the self, and there are those for whom self-control is a meaningful reality. There are those for whom the guiding framework is that of radical behaviorism and there are those whose only allegiance is to a behavioral methodology and not to any form of philosophical creed at all. For some, the principles of classical and operant conditioning, perhaps with the addition of modeling, are sufficient. For others, conditioning as a primary force in behavior therapy has had its day. For some, data are sufficient and theory is of no consequence. For others—and we belong in this category—theory is essential to the advancement of behavior therapy (Barbrack, 1985; Barbrack & Franks, 1986; Franks, 1969, 1984b, 1987a, 1987b).

Contemporary behavior therapy is thus characterized by both unity and diversity. In its formative years, behavior therapists focused on overt responses and avoided the "stigma" of mentalism by ignoring completely any form of cognitive process. This is no longer so. Similarly, in part because the necessary technology did not as yet exist, early behavior therapists directed their attention toward the individual rather than the group and toward specific responses rather than complex systems. Subtle and not so subtle influences of society, community, and system went largely unrecognized. This, too, is no longer so. The present day spectrum ranges from the inner space of "cognition," "awareness," and "self," at one extreme, to "community," "system," and "interaction" at the other. Whether this implies increased cohesiveness or the onset of disintegration within behavior therapy only the future can decide (Franks, 1981).

Bijou and Redd (1975) identified several theoretical models of behavior modification: applied behavioral analysis, predicated on Skinnerian operant conditioning; Pavlovian-based learning or conditioning therapies, as filtered through the vision of such neobehaviorists as Hull and Spence (we would add Eysenck, Rachman, and Wolpe); and social learning theory, with Bandura (1969) as its foremost spokesperson. Later, Redd, Porterfield, and Anderson (1979) appropriately added another model: cognitive behavior modification.

These seemingly disparate frameworks share a similar behavioral methodology, a limited rejection of the medical model, and a commitment to empirical validation and accountability. Whether this is enough to establish a unique identity for behavior therapy at large remains to be seen, as does the extent to which the practice of behavior therapy conforms to the principles.

If the first decade of behavior therapy was a matter of ideology and polemics and the second the era of consolidation, the third is characterized by sophisticated methodology, innovative conceptual models, and a search for new horizons. In the late 1970s, the "cognitive revolution" swept into behavior therapy as it swept into the rest of psychology. New frontiers with medicine, psychopharmacology, ecology, and systems theory were established. The 1980s was thus the era of biofeedback, behavioral medicine, and the community. If the principles of conditioning and modeling are still of significance, and we believe that they are, contemporary behavior therapy is also free to draw upon other branches of psychology and other disciplines. Private events, the cognitive mediators of behavior, are no longer beyond the psychological pale and a major role is now attributed to vicarious and symbolic learning processes. All of this is a far cry from the simplistic beginnings of little more than two decades ago.

MISCONCEPTIONS ABOUT CONTEMPORARY BEHAVIOR THERAPY

There are two kinds of major misconceptions in the realm of behavior therapy: those of the world outside and those held by behavior therapists themselves. It is still believed in certain lay and professional circles that behavior therapists reject interpersonal relationships, that behavior therapy cannot encompass the complexities of human behavior, that behavior therapy is a naive treatment of "symptoms" that must inevitably recur, that behavior therapists are not interested in insight, and that behavior therapy is limited in its applicability. Another misconception is that behavior therapy is simple to do and does not require any profound training, care, sophistication, or attention to detail (Walker, Hedburg, Clement, & Wright, 1981). Most of these faulty perceptions are based on inadequate knowledge of behavior therapy as currently practiced. In its beginnings, behavior therapy was simplistic and some of the misconceptions were valid at the time, but this is no longer so. Further confusion among the general public is engendered by the popular tendency to apply the terms *behavior therapy* and *behavior modification* to all techniques for changing behavior. Regrettably, these can include psychosurgery, drugs, torture, and coercion.

The misconceptions about behavior therapy that many behavior therapists themselves entertain are more subtle and less easily corrected. These include the fiction that behavior therapy consistently rests upon theory derived from experimental psychology, that behavior therapy in practice is invariably empirically based. Would that this were true! (For a more extended discussion of these matters, see Fishman, Rotgers, & Franks, 1988; Franks, 1981, 1982, 1987a; Franks & Rosenbaum, 1983; Kazdin, 1979; Mahoney & Kazdin, 1979.)

CURRENT ISSUES IN BEHAVIOR THERAPY

Role of S-R Learning Theory and Conditioning

To what extent is behavior therapy based on theories and principles of learning? Which learning theories or principles? What is the evidential status of these theories and principles? Is there an alternative scientific foundation for behavior therapy? Do the principles of learning, and in particular those of classical and operant conditioning, apply to covert, inner-directed processes, and are they sufficient to account for the data? Should we broaden the foundation of behavior therapy to include principles and knowledge drawn from social psychology, physiology, and sociology? (Kanfer & Grimm, 1980). We can do little more here than draw attention to the these issues and refer the reader elsewhere (e.g., Franks, 1982).

Conditioning is a word devoid of any precise meaning. It can refer to an experimental procedure, to the effectiveness of this procedure, or to the process believed to account for these effects. Many difficulties arise when one tries to extrapolate data derived from animal experiments to human patients, not least of which stem from confusion attached to the conditioning model. The precise relationships between classical and operant conditioning remain equivocal and some would doubt whether conditioning as generally envisaged exists at all.

The relationships between conditioning in the laboratory, conditioning in the clinic, and conditioning in daily life are complex and open to many interpretations. We speak liberally of a general factor of conditionability although no such factor has been demonstrated. Neither classical conditioning, operant conditioning, nor applied behavioral analysis accounts adequately for the many complexities of contemporary neuroses. Sophisticated explanations such as Mowrer's (1960) two-factor theory of avoidance behavior or Eysenck's (1982) more recent incubation conditioning explanation of the neuroses fare little better. Attempts to update conditioning theory in terms of cognition (Hillner, 1979), subjective experience (Martin & Levey, 1978), or interaction response patterns (Henton & Iverson, 1978) obscure rather than clarify. The evidence with respect to the utility of concepts of conditioning and their relationships to contemporary behavior therapy is best summed up in terms of the ancient Scottish verdict, "not proven."

The Behaviorism in Behavior Therapy

Closely related to the role of conditioning in contemporary behavior therapy is that of the nature of the behaviorism upon which much of conditioning theory and behavior therapy are predicated. Behaviorism is far from a monolithic concept and has to be understood both within a historic context and in terms of specific individuals and their writing (Franks, 1980). At least two major kinds of behaviorism can be identified. First, there is methodological behaviorism, whose proponents insist that behavior can be validly investigated and explained without direct examination of mental states. Methodological behaviorism is mediational, often mentalistic and inferential, and usually employs hypothetico-deductive methodology. It is possible to be a methodological behaviorist and espouse such notions as free will, self-control, and reciprocal determinism. Then there is metaphysical or radical behaviorism in which, by contrast, the existence of mental states as useful postulates is denied: it is nonmediational, antimentalistic, never inferential, and favors induction over hypothesis testing. Individuals such as Watson were metaphysical behaviorists. In contrast, Hull, Spence, Eysenck, and virtually all contemporary behavior therapists can more appropriately be viewed as methodological behaviorists. For such individuals, methodology is of more importance than any philosophical implications. Be that as it may, the debate about the behaviorism in behavior therapy remains lively and will doubtless continue to be so (see Franks, 1980, 1982; Tryon, Ferster, Franks, Kazdin, Levis, & Tryon, 1980).

Relationship Between Research and Clinical Practice in Behavior Therapy

In principle, one distinctive feature of behavior therapy is a reliance on the development and use of clinical procedures on knowledge derived from experimental psychology (Franks, 1984b, 1987b). The investigation of the treatment of agoraphobia by Barlow, Mavissakalian, and Schofield (1980) exemplifies the kind of relationship between research and practice most behavior therapists endorse. Unfortunately, ideals are not always followed in practice and much of behavior therapy is not based on legitimate scientific evidence at all (Farkas, 1980; Hayes & Nelson, 1981; Kendall, Plous, & Kratochwill, 1981; Swan & MacDonald, 1978). It may be that, even if behavior therapy is more than technology, there is no known set of learning-theory principles that can serve as a viable foundation for what behavior therapists actually do (as contrasted with that about which they write and talk). Practitioners are thus only partly culpable with respect to the widening gap between research and practice.

Clinical research has, can, and should lead to the development and improvement of clinical practice. At least publicly, behavior therapists continue to endorse the value of research–practice interaction even though most schools of professional psychology have abandoned the scientist-as-practitioner model in favor of the professional as a consumer of research carried out by others (Peterson, 1976). Which and to what extent either of these models would diminish the gap between research and practice is an empirical question yet to be addressed. Most active researchers report being trained under the scientist–practitioner model (Kendall et al., 1981): The extent to which these researchers implement their own findings or those of others has not been investigated.

Cognitive Behavior Therapy

The ongoing "cognitive revolution," endorsed with enthusiasm by many behavior therapists, departs significantly from radical behaviorism and, as such, has provoked many criticisms. For example, Ledwidge (1978) contended that cognitions are no more than hypothetical constructs used to account for relationships between environmental events and behaviors. Thus, cognitions are not behaviors and cognitive behavior therapy is not behavior therapy. These and other views expressed by Ledwidge are critically analyzed and partly rebutted by Rachman and Wilson (1980). Acknowledging the popularity and promise of cognitive behavior therapy, on the one hand, and the continuing controversy over its place in contemporary behavior therapy, on the other, Franks (1982) urged that the pertinent issues be moved from the theater of debate to the arena of empirical investigation. Prerequisites, still far on the behavioral horizon, would seem to include consensus on the definition of cognitive behavior therapy, precise technical specifications of the methods it employs, and compliance with these methods by behavior therapists (Rachman & Wilson, 1980).

Cognitive behavior therapy has got off to an auspicious (some would say suspicious) start. Because its position is consonant with contemporary behavior therapy, systematic research could enhance behavior therapy in general. As Mahoney and Kazdin (1979) argued, all therapies are simultaneously cognitive and behavioral to greater or lesser extents. The quality of clinical research in cognitive behavior therapy in the coming decade may be decisive in determining the nature of behavior therapy.

Reciprocal Determinism and Social-Learning Theory

Perhaps the most complete, clinically useful, and theoretically sophisticated model within contemporary behavior therapy is that of social-learning theory (Bandura, 1977a, 1977b). Social-learning theory in its most advanced form is interdisciplinary and multimodal. Although cognitions are important, it is performance that is paramount. Behaviorists ignore the role of cognition and cognitive therapists tend to minimize the importance of performance. Classical conditioning focuses upon external stimulus events; operant conditioning stresses reinforcement contingencies. Self-efficacy theory, now an essential component of social-learning theory, would seem to provide the necessary means of elucidating the interdependence between cognitive and behavioral changes, thereby integrating the three regulatory systems of antecedent, consequent, and mediational influences into a single comprehensive framework (Bandura, 1977a, 1977b, 1978a, 1978b). Although detailed investigation remains to be carried out, the theory is so formulated that it lends itself readily to experimental scrutiny. For example, according to Bandura (1982), self-efficacy influences thought patterns, actions, and emotional arousal across a variety of levels of human experience ranging from the physiology of the individual to the collective effort. At most levels, it is possible, at least in principle, to generate testable predictions, design appropriate investigative studies, and develop crucial experiments to differentiate among alternative models.

Causal processes are conceptualized by Bandura in terms of what he calls "reciprocal determinism." Viewed from this perspective, psychological functioning involves a continuous, reciprocal interaction among behavioral, cognitive, and environmental influences, and it is here that difficulties arise. Bandura's argument is cleverly conceived in that it creates the appearance of human freedom without either endorsing free will or abandoning the concept of determinism. In a nutshell, Bandura contends that, not unlike human behavior, environments have causes; in other words, the interplay between human behavior and environment is reciprocal. Human actions influence the nature of environmental events that, in turn, influence human actions, and so on.

The notion of reciprocal determinism is particularly enticing to clinicians seeking to reframe behavior therapy in terms that appeal to those who resent the popular comparison of behavior therapy to coercive manipulation, wholesale promotion of social conformity, and the curtailing of freedom of choice. But the use of reciprocal determinism to eliminate or at least diminish the appearance of external control can be troublesome. Adverse reactions to determinism can stem from opposing legal, philosophical, and theological conceptions of human nature (e.g., a belief in some sort of free will). Others do not deny the existence of some kind of determinism but believe that methods capitalizing on the fact of this belief (e.g., reinforcement schedules) should not be used in psychotherapy. It is unclear how reciprocal determinism resolves these objectives.

Furthermore, it is not clear how the theory of reciprocal determinism changes the nature of determinism as originally conceived. How does reciprocal determinism account for the manner in which human actions affect the environment? Specifically, are the principles that govern this process different from those governing the influence of environment on behavior? If the answer is no, then it is not clear how reciprocal determinism adds to human freedom. If the answer is that these influences are different, then it remains to be seen what additional principles govern the behavior–environment interaction. It could be that reciprocal determinism creates more of an illusion of human freedom than freedom itself. But then, perhaps, it is too much to expect anyone to resolve by experiment a dilemma that is fundamentally philosophic in nature.

Integration of Behavior Therapy and Psychoanalysis

Historically, renunciation of psychoanalytic theory or psychodynamic therapies played a central role in the development of behavior therapy and contributed to polarization between the two. Conclusions drawn by Luborsky, Singer, and Luborsky (1975), among others, to the effect that each type of therapeutic intervention has merit, conveniently suggested that questions regarding the relative superiority of one approach would probably never be resolved on the basis of empirical evidence alone. Resignation to this state of affairs led to entrenchment and superficial easing of tensions between behavior therapists and psychoanalysists. Factors external to psychology, including questions about psychologists receiving third party payments and demands that clinicians be held accountable for and demonstrate the efficacy of the therapeutic interventions, created a vexing predicament. On the one hand, it was apparent that questions about comparative effectiveness were complex and not readily amenable to resolution by experiment. On the other hand, external agencies were increasing their demands for scientific evidence that psychotherapy is effective. Neither faction could comfortably endure these pressures, yet there was no apparent way to resolve the dilemma. Integration of behavior therapy and psychoanalysis seemed to offer a solution. Agreement on the utility of shared concepts, the effectiveness of selected interventions, and the value of certain outcomes would at least allow therapists from each camp to join forces against an external threat.

Arguing from a perspective that assumed the basic truth of psychodynamic theory, Wachtel (1977) nevertheless endorsed the adjunctive use of behavioral techniques to break neurotic cycles. Arguing from a behavioral perspective, Franks (1984a) holds that behavior therapy and psychoanalysis are fundamentally incompatible in terms of theory and concept and only appear to be compatible in terms of clinical application. Behavior therapists and psychoanalysts adhere to different paradigms, understand and formulate psychological problems differently, rely on different methods of verification, and accept different "facts" as legitimate data. Proponents of either position can be consistent within the assumptions and constraints of their respective paradigms and thereby reach contradictory, possibly irreconcilable, conclusions.

For psychodynamicists Messer and Winokur (1980, 1984), the incompatibility of behavior therapy and psychoanalysis stems from their essentially irreconcilable visions of reality. Behavior therapy emphasizes the possibility of "non-ambiguous happy endings leading to security and gratification through direct action and removal of situational obstacles," whereas psychoanalysis emphasizes the tragic "inevitability and ubiquity of human conflicts and the limits placed by the individual's early history on the extent of possible change." Nevertheless, in spite of their persuasive rationale, Messer and Winokur refuse to close tight the door to integration. It is suggested that therapists strive to maintain a "dual focus between subjectivity governed by the ground rules of hermeneutics and objectivity governed by the traditional methods of science." In our view, this is more akin to sophistry than solution because it requires a simultaneous set of conditions that cannot coexist.

Methodological Issues in Behavior Therapy

Use of Analogue Studies

Analogue studies usually enlist volunteer, nonclinical subjects and expose them to therapeutic interventions of short duration under laboratory conditions. In exchange for the enticing advantages of control over dependent and independent variables, analogue studies suffer from several limitations, the most important of which is probably the extent to which the finding can be generalized to clinical populations (Emmelkamp, 1981; Kazdin, 1978b; Rachman & Wilson, 1980; Rakover, 1980). Until systematic study of the factors influencing the generalizability of analogue research findings is completed, questions regarding the utility of the ensuing data will persist.

Maintenance of Therapeutic Change

Most analogue research does not provide follow-up evaluation. In fact, surprisingly few follow-up studies of any kind exist in behavior therapy. Evidence bearing on effective maintenance strategies is sparse and equivocal (Rachman & Wilson, 1980). For example, periodic booster sessions for obesity control is logically appealing but the evidence suggests that they do not promote maintenance, whereas there is some evidence that involvement of family members in therapy is at least one component of an effective maintenance strategy (Wilson & O'Leary, 1980). Developing effective maintenance strategies is on the cutting edge of behavior therapy research, and issues involving the maintenance of initial therapeutic change are likely to receive considerable attention in the coming decade.

Single-Subject Experimental Designs

Traditional designs typically involve the random assignments of relatively large numbers of subjects to various treatment conditions. Independent variables are controlled and manipulated by the experimenter and the significance of their effects is determined by parametric statistical analyses. The excessive time and expense of this approach, together with the limited values of group outcomes that are merely statistically significant, led to the development of strategies geared specifically to the study of the single subject (Hersen & Barlow, 1976; Kazdin, 1978b; Kratochwill, 1978). Single-subject designs, ranging from the simple to the complex, are technically capable of controlling for most threats to internal and external validity at least as well as their more traditional counterparts. Single-subject approaches are meant to be used in conjunction with rather than replace traditional large-scale experimental designs.

Problems arise when replication is attempted and the ensuing results are less than clear-cut (see Franks & Wilson, 1978, pp. 176ff for a more extended discussion of the salient issues involved). By and large, single-case experimental studies are best viewed as guides for creative application rather than research strategies for direct clinical use.

Behavior Therapy in Institution and Community

Behavior therapy is now firmly entrenched in institution, community, and society at large. And in all of these domains, although accomplishments and advances are relatively easy to document, limitations and special problems are less evident. For example, institutional token economies, once relatively straightforward in both concept and application, now present formidable problems. Court rulings tax the ingenuity of the behavior therapist in the development of clinically effective yet legally sanctioned reinforcers. Problems of maintenance and generalization are compounded by the growing recognition that token economies are part of a more total socioeconomic, political, and environmental context (Franks, 1982; Winkler, 1983).

At one end of the spectrum there are concerted attempts to deal with complex issues, such as the energy crisis, in terms of behavioral principles (e.g., Winnett, 1981). At the other end, there are the ubiquitous studies of less pressing social problems such as litter control (e.g., Bacon-Prue, Blount, Pickering, & Drabman, 1980). But as behavior therapy marches boldly into the home, school, and community, doubts begin to arise. Too many unresolved issues are beginning to crop up in the transition from laboratory to the outside world. For example, Schneider, Lesko, and Garrett (1980) found that the hypothesized inhibitory effects of hot and cold temperatures on health behavior that emerged very clearly in the laboratory did not appear in real-life situations. Models and strategies that are effective within the laboratory or even within the natural environment on a small scale are not necessarily appropriate to larger settings (Franks, 1982).

In contrast to the (by now) familiar and relatively straightforward functional behavioral analysis of the individual, community behavior therapy is much more complex, and a variety of models to contend with these issues are beginning to emerge (e.g., Glenwick & Jason, 1980; Hutchinson & Fawcett, 1981). Although no one single approach dominates, certain common trends are apparent. First, to their credit, community behavior therapy research, program development, and outcome evaluation all rest firmly upon behavioral foundations. Second, considerable attention is now paid to the ecological intricacies of behavior–environment interactions, with the aim of designing environmental settings that will promote adaptive behavior. Third, the practice and process of community behavior therapy stresses the active involvement of community members. Fourth, the knowledge base for community behavior therapy is drawn from a variety of sources and disciplines. Fifth, there is a growing appreciation of the tremendous potential of mass media as vehicles for the delivery of behavioral interventions to large segments of society (e.g., Maccoby & Alexander, 1980). Sixth, community behavior therapists espouse a preventive approach.

Training in Behavior Therapy

In principle, behavior therapy belongs to no one discipline. In practice, at least in the United States, most formal, comprehensive training of behavior therapists (as contrasted with short-term specialized programs or with the training of behavioral aides and paraprofessionals) currently takes place within the orbit of some 4- or, preferably, 5-year scientist–practitioner doctoral program in clinical psychology. Such training usually stresses but is not confined to: a conceptual and methodological approach rather than primary adherence to technique and procedure (although the importance of both is recognized); behavioral assessment and intervention as an ongoing, integrated process; a thorough knowledge of the basic structure of the principles of psychology as a data-based behavioral science, predicated upon firm grounding in undergraduate and graduate core courses in general psychology; a comprehensive grasp of the principles and practice of clinical psychology through

a cross-section of applied courses across a diversity of orientations; a monitored appreciation of contributions from developmental psychology, systems theory, cognitive psychology, and ecology from an interdisciplinary perspective; the application of this knowledge in real-life settings in a clinically sophisticated and societally meaningfully fashion; and an appreciation of professional and related issues (e.g., human rights and minority concerns) as they impinge on clinical psychology and related disciplines. The student is introduced to a growing armamentarium of behavioral or behaviorally related procedures in which closely monitored initial supervision leads eventually to more functional autonomy. Throughout, the cultivation of empathy and interpersonal sensitivity is considered to be most important.

As noted, most behavior therapists are currently clinical psychologists and this trend is likely to continue in the foreseeable future. But if behavior therapy is to become interdisciplinary, it will need to feature more prominently in the training of psychiatrists and social workers. Training for paraprofessionals, continuing education, and short-term specialized training programs for nonbehavioral professionals also is of importance provided that such technique-oriented training not be regarded as qualification for the appellation "behavior therapist," per se.

Current shortcomings in the training of behavior therapists fall into four general areas. First, most behavior therapists are not being trained to do clinical research (Barlow, 1981). Second, behavior therapists are rarely given a thorough understanding of psychopathology (even in behavioral terms) and are not adequately trained in the practice of differential diagnosis (Hersen, 1981). Third, behavior therapists may not be prepared to deal constructively with negative client reactions (Kazdin & Cole, 1981). Fourth, somewhat related, behavior therapists are still not being taught how to enhance client–therapist relationships (Swan, 1979).

With respect to psychopathology and differential diagnosis, behavior therapists seem to be in an uncertain state of transition. Traditionally, these areas involve the medical model, nosological classification, and norm-referenced psychometric assessment, which are all emphases rejected by the pioneers of behavior therapy. To the extent that newer conceptions of psychopathology and assessment are connected with the selection of better and more multifacted interventions, the future training of behavior therapists may well reflect these changes. Training behavior therapists to anticipate and deal constructively with failures and negative reactions will probably occur incrementally as the factors that contribute to this phenomenon are isolated and clarified (see Kazdin & Cole, 1981; Mays & Franks, 1985).

Not all behavioral training programs practice what they teach. Performance criteria in the determination of goal attainment are available (e.g., Thomas & Murphy, 1981) but rarely used. Thus, when Heinrich (1980) developed a competency-based curriculum for training first-year psychiatry residents in behavior therapy, a favorable reception from students and faculty did not lead to enthusiasm for continuation. Perhaps the effort involved in such endeavors outweighs perceived benefits.

Licensing, Certification, and Guidelines for Behavior Therapists

Licensing is generally mandatory, broad-based, and geared toward minimum standards. Certification tends to be voluntary, focused on subspecialties, and goes beyond minimum standards. Some see the licensing process as a procedure for public protection (Shimberg, 1981). A more negative view suggests that licensing is largely self-serving, designed to allow certain therapists to receive third party payments and to keep others from so doing (Danish & Smyer, 1981). In either case, few believe that existing licensing procedures establish competency or improve the services offered. Be this as it may, licensing is a fact of life and it is futile to debate its merits. Certification is another matter. Certification of behavior therapists would require specification of competencies in clearly defined areas. Criteria by which such competencies could be judged would have to be empirically established, as would methods for evaluation and review. The resources required would be enormous, and there is no indication either that behavior therapists are currently prepared to undertake this endeavor or that behavior therapy is ready for this eventuality.

Short of formal certification procedures, behavior therapists have tended to resort to guidelines to govern some aspects of the practice of behavior therapy and to establish some basis for accountability. Franks (1982) reviewed the extensive discussion of guidelines in the recent literature and concluded that currently, the cons may outweigh the pros. By and large, it is our contention that, at this time, there should be no licensing or certification of behavior therapists as such. What is important is that all behavior therapists become fully accredited in terms of practice requirements set forth by law and the parent mental health profession with which they are identified. Within this context, informal or unofficial guidelines might be helpful.

Ethical and Legal Issues in Behavior Therapy

The ethics of behavior therapy are no different from those of any other mental-health profession. It is the emphasis on total accountability, openness, objectivity, and sensitivity to both societal and inner-directed determinants of behavior that makes behavior therapy unique. Interestingly enough, the mental-health community at large is beginning to follow suit. Witness, for example, the burgeoning interest in accountability and demonstrable validity as one criterion in the reimbursement of clinicians by insurance companies. This, of course, does not imply that behavior therapists are above suspicion. With good reason, and sometimes with no good reason, the value systems of certain behavior therapists have been assailed from within and without. Behavior therapists who are able to modify the behavior of others must be prepared to modify their own behavior if and as need be. House cleaning, like charity, begins at home (Franks, 1982).

Early in the development of behavior therapy, Bandura (1969) distinguished between values and science. Values, argued Bandura, contribute to the selection of the goal, whereas science governs the selection of procedures. In making this distinction, Bandura side stepped the implicit ethical issues that emerge in both instances, an omission that contributed to Franks and Wilson's (1973) contention that behavior therapy is independent of ethical considerations. Two years later, Franks and Wilson (1975) revised their opinions and concluded that ethical considerations could not be avoided in the application of behavioral technology, a statement now widely endorsed by clinical psychologists in general (Holt, 1978) as well as behavior therapists (Farkas, 1980; Kanfer & Grimm, 1980).

Kitchener (1980) argued that value judgments must be justified and pointed out serious flaws in the ethical relativism position of Skinner (1971), in which positive reinforcement is equated with that which is morally good or right. From another perspective, Kitchener attacked the so-called "evolutionary ethic" that equates moral goodness with those behaviors that, immediately and ultimately, contribute to the survival of a culture of species. Houts and Krasner (1980) attempted to refute Kitchener's arguments, but they begged the question by citing clinical examples in which client and therapist agree on treatment goals, thereby obscuring the values applied by the therapist in the goal-selection process. One is left to speculate whether the therapist's decision to pursue these goals is normally justified because the client agrees, because therapist and client agree, or because of other considerations (see also Ward, 1980).

If behavior therapists accept that the application of any technology is value-laden and that scientific and strictly logical paradigms cannot be applied to the resolution of issues pertaining to values, then they must step outside the scientific/technological domain in the search for an ethical paradigm to detect, understand, and resolve the ethical issues that frequently arise in the course and conduct of behavior therapy. In the interim, it is important for behavior therapists to continue to debate these issues. Individual practitioners might also do well to keep in mind Houts and Krasner's (1980) distinction between science and values. Values need to be made explicit (Bergin, 1980) and treatment goals negotiated with clients beforehand (Kanfer & Grimm, 1980; Turkat & Forehand, 1980) without obfuscation and pretense of appeal to science and technology alone.

Mental-health legislation, designed to protect the rights of clients, inadvertently creates problems by its use of vague terminology, conflicting aspirations, and a tendency to make assumptions about intrapsychic activity, responsibility, and free will that many behavior therapists find unacceptable (Franks & Wilson, 1979; Martin, 1979; Shah, 1978). The fact that some laws create problems for behavior therapists need not inevitably lead to the conclusion that legal restraints should be abandoned. Given sufficient ingenuity, most behavioral interventions can be accommodated to comply with current laws (e.g., Finesmith, 1979).

Image of Behavior Therapy

The public tends to view behavior therapy as a series of strong, potentially harmful techniques used to promote conformity and thereby control human behavior with little regard for the rights and feelings of others. This view has been promulgated in the press (Turkat & Feuerstein, 1978), in popular books about prisons (Mitford, 1973) and psychotherapy (Ehrenberg & Ehrenberg, 1977), and elsewhere.

These widespread negative reactions alarmed behavior therapists not only because they were distasteful and based on misrepresentation, but also because of their potential impact on the public's willingness to consider behavior therapy as a treatment option and the possible negative effects on treatment outcome (Mays & Franks, 1985). These concerns gave rise to several studies designed to shed light on the factors contributing to the negative public appraisal (e.g., Barling & Wainstein, 1979; Woolfolk & Woolfolk, 1979). One conclusion at that time was that the label "behavior modification" was an important contributor to the prevailing negative image. Consideration was even given to reviving an earlier, largely discarded proposal for relabeling behavioral procedures (Repucci & Saunders, 1974). The wisdom of this remedy is called into question by Kazdin and Cole's (1981) limited-sample demonstration that behavior modification procedures per se are inclined to be evaluated negatively regardless of how they are labeled. Clearly, further research is indicated.

On the basis of available information, what could be done to improve the public image of behavior therapy? Investigations might be undertaken to determine under what circumstances behavior therapy has a negative public image and how to make both individual and packaged behavioral treatments more acceptable. We also need to know more about the complex parameters involved in the negative attitudes toward behavior therapy sometimes observed in our nonbehavioral mental-health colleagues. If this involves putting our own house in order as part of the solution, then so be it.

Finally, there is that vexing question of terminology and the medical model. By maintaining the terminology of the medical model, behavior therapy is less likely to be construed as something malevolent. This must be weighed against the advantages of a thoroughgoing departure from the medical model. If a person's psychological problems are construed as signs of illness, it becomes difficult to think in terms of changing specific problem behaviors. If the behavioral alternative is pursued to the hilt, a different vocabulary will need to be devised and, more to the point, used. As the name indicates, behavior therapists are still inclined to use medical terminology and to refer to patients, cures, and treatments. Whether it is possible to modify this state of affairs and whether it is desirable at this stage is open to debate.

Present Status of Behavior Therapy

The prevailing mood in the early 1990s is best described as one of cautious optimism based upon solid accomplishments coupled with, on the one hand, a growing recognition of the need to return to the concept- and theory-based rigor that characterized our inception and, on the other hand, a forward-looking expansion into new intellectual and methodological horizons. Until very recently, the only behavior therapy text devoted exclusively to conceptual and philosophical issues was written by a philosopher (Erwin, 1978). Too many behavior therapists continued to think in linear, concrete terms, and the simplistic formulations of the 1960s.

At last there are signs of change. Within the AABT, the formation of a special interest group devoted exclusively to philosophical and theoretical concerns is gaining steady momentum (Franks, 1987b), and Erwin's text no longer stands alone. In these respects, two edited volumes merit attention. Eysenck and Martin (1987) reaffirm the notion that behavior therapy can be a conceptual unity rooted in rigor, theory, and data without loss of amenability to new ideas and expanding horizons. And Fishman, Rotgers, and Franks (1988) systematically articulate, probably for the first time in any one text, the basic assumptions underlying contemporary behavior therapy within a philosophy of science context.

Of perhaps equal, and somewhat related, significance is the current thrust toward a nonlinear approach that strives to take into account new horizons in the advancement of behavior therapy. Some three decades ago, it was sufficient to think in terms of discrete stimulus-response relationships studied within a traditional and rigidly delineated behavioral science methodology. This worked well when the subject matter was restricted primarily to specific problem areas such as spider phobias or token economies in the classroom. As behavior therapy evolved, the problems addressed became vastly more complex and less cut-and-dried. Interactionism, systems thinking, and ecology became the new buzzwords, and notions such as "cognition," "relationships," "life span," "nonlinear," and "empathy" part of the behavior therapist's evolving conceptual framework (e.g., see Delprato, 1989; Franks, 1988; Goldiamond, 1984; Locke, 1986; Ruben & Delprato, 1987; Russo & Budd, 1987; Wahler & Hann, 1986). This new behavior therapy is a logical progression from its beginnings. The original emphasis upon accountability, rigorous thinking, scientific method, and learning theory remains the same. What has changed is the complexity of the problems addressed and, with this, the need to adopt a multidimensional, interdisciplinary perspective that takes into account data, formulations, and even methodologies derived from disciplines once considered to be totally outside the traditional behavior therapist's bailiwick. The major task confronting behavior therapy today is how to take these developments into account while retaining the scientific integrity that brought behavior therapy into being in the first place. It is the combination of these forward-looking innovations with a return to theory, concept, and philosophical considerations that characterizes both the best of modern-day behavior therapy and the challenge for the future (Franks, 1987).

FUTURE DIRECTIONS

Behavior therapy is now an established part of the mental-health scene. It has been demonstrated that interdisciplinary, nonlinear formations can coexist with precise thinking, behavioral methodology, and a respect for both theory and data. Whether any one behavior therapist is able to span the technological/conceptual spectrum and incorporate these diverse areas of interest, personal inclinations, and expertise into his or her personal weltanschauung is a matter only the future can decide. It may be that such an integration is impossible at the personal level and that division of efforts is inevitable.

If the trend of the 1980s continues in the coming decade, and we have every reason to believe that it will, technological advances will go hand-in-hand with theory and concept. In so doing, individual, one-to-one intervention strategies will be deemphasized—but not disavowed—in favor of multifaceted community, societal, and systems-oriented modalities. Increased emphasis will be given to training for both professionals and paraprofessionals, each with its own modus operandi.

CONCLUSIONS

Within less than three decades, an unknown and initially simplistic application of conditioning principles to the treatment of specific problems has become a sophisticated and accepted approach to a broad spectrum of individual disorders and societal concerns (Barlow, 1980). If it has not become the solitary wave of the future that was predicted in a surge of initial enthusiasm, neither has it suffered the early demise in the murky depths that the prophets of doom foretold.

The appeal of modern behavior therapy is to those who prefer a coherent conceptual framework rather than a mélange of intuition, ancedotal evidence, and personal preference. Whether this will evolve into a meaningful model of humankind remains to be seen. If behavior therapy is to retain its unique identity, its advocates will need to effect some working compromise between conceptual and technical expansiveness, on the one hand, and its more narrow but rigorous historical foundations, on the other.

Despite certain weaknesses common to behavior therapy at large, such as a narrowness of vision, a still excessive reliance upon the medical model, and a reluctance to develop alternative models of service delivery, cognitively oriented social-learning theory seems to offer the most promise for advancement at this time (Rachman & Wilson, 1980). Behavior therapy still is at a vulnerable stage in its short but intensive history. When behavior therapists were busy challenging the traditional dogmas of psychotherapy it was relatively easy to be innovative. Now that behavior therapy is part of the establishment, many behavior therapists tend to be more cautious, more conservative, and even to recapitulate some of the tactical errors of their predecessors. For a time it looked as if behavior therapy was becoming an action science, a methodological link between fundamental research and clinical practice. The danger of losing this interface is now with us.

By way of conclusion, however, it must be remembered that behavior therapy is still a young psychological discipline and that learning theory itself is not very old. To expect unifying theories in such a relatively new field when physics and chemistry have failed to do so after 2,000 years seems unreasonable. In many respects, behavior therapy, like much of psychology, is still in a preparadigmatic stage. Problems remain, both in theory and in application, and it may be that, at least for the foreseeable future, microtheories and circumscribed resolution will be the order of the day rather than any grand solution. This, of course, need not negate an integrative balance between technology and theory that cuts across behavioral, physiological, and cognitive systems. When all is said, and sometimes even done, it seems appropriate to conclude that, despite theoretical controversies, occasional clinical insufficiencies, confrontations from within, and challenges from without, behavior therapy remains alive, well, and in accord with its founding mandate (Franks, 1982; Wilson, 1982).

A CLINICIAN'S READING LIST: SOME RECENT TEXTS

Becker, R.E., Heinberg, R.G., & Bellack, A.J. (1987). *Social skills training treatment for depression*. Elmsford, NY: Pergamon Press.

Barlow, D., & Cerny, J.N. (1988). *Psychological treatment of panic*. New York: Guilford Press.

Bellack, A.S., & Hersen, M. (Eds.). (1988). *Behavioral assessment: A practical handbook* (3rd. ed.). Elmsford, NY: Pergamon Press.

Blechman, E.A., & Brownell, K.D. (Eds.). (1988). *Handbook of behavioral medicine for women*. Elmsford, NY: Pergamon Press.

Ciminero, A.R., Calhoun, K.S., & Adams, H.E. (Eds.). (1986). *Handbook of behavioral assessment*. New York: John Wiley & Sons.

Dryden, W., & Golden, W.L. (Eds.). (1987). *Cognitive-behavioral approaches to psychotherapy*. Cambridge, England: Hemisphere/Harper & Row.

Ellis, A. (1985). *Overcoming resistance: Rational-emotive therapy with difficult clients*. New York: Springer Publishing Company.

Falloon, I.R.H. (Ed.). (1988). *Handbook of behavioral family therapy*. New York: Guilford Press.

Franks, C.M. (Ed.). (1984). *New developments in behavior therapy: From research to clinical application*. New York: Haworth Press.

Fensterheim, H., & Glaser, H.I. (Eds.). (1983). *Behavioral psychotherapy: Basic principles and case studies in an integrative clinical model*. New York: Brunner/Mazel.

Goldstein, A., & Stainback, B. (1987). *Overcoming agoraphobia: Conquering fear of the outside world*. New York: Viking.

Hatch, J.P., Fisher, J.B., & Rugh, J.D. (Eds.). (1987). *Biofeedback: Studies in clinical efficacy*. New York: Plenum Press.

Hersen, M., & Last, C.G. (1983). *Behavior therapy casebook*. New York: Springer Publishing Company.

Kanfer, F.H., & Schefft, B.K. (1988). *Guiding the process of therapeutic change*. Champaign, IL: Research Press.

Kaplin, S.J. (1986). *The private practice of behavior therapy: A guide for behavioral practitioners*. New York: Plenum Press.

Kelly, J.A. (1982). *Social-skills training: A practical guide for intervention*. New York: Springer Publishing Company.

Levant, R.F. (Ed.). (1986). *Psychoeducational approaches to family therapy and counseling*. New York: Springer Publishing Company.

Lichstein, K.L. (1988). *Clinical relaxation strategies*. New York: John Wiley & Sons.

Marks, I.M. (1987). *Fears, phobias, and rituals: Panic, anxiety, and their disorders*. New York: Oxford University Press.

McMullin, R.E. (1986). *Handbook of cognitive therapy techniques*. New York: WW Norton.

Meichenbaum, D. (1985). *Stress innoculation training*. Elmsford, NY: Pergamon Press.

Rosen, R.C., & Beck, J.S. (1988). *Patterns of sexual arousal: Psychophysiological processes and clinical applications*. New York: Guilford Press.

Sank, L.I., & Shaffer, C.S. (1984). *A therapist's manual for cognitive behavior therapy in groups*. New York: Plenum Press.

Stumphauzer, J.S. (1986). *Helping delinquents change: A treatment manual of social learning approaches*. New York: Haworth Press.

Teri, L., & Lewinsohn, P.M. (Eds.). (1986). *Geropsychological assessment and treatment: Selected topics*. New York: Springer Publishing Company.

Walker, C.E., Hedburg, A., Clement, P.W., & Wright, L. (1981). *Clinical procedures for behavior therapy*. Englewood Cliffs, NJ: Prentice-Hall.

Wolpe, J., & Wolpe, D. (1988). *Life without fear*. Oakland, CA: New Harbinger.

REFERENCES

Ayllon, T., & Azrin, N.H. (1968). *The token economy: A motivational system for therapy and rehabilitation*. New York: Appleton-Century-Crofts.

Ayllon, T., & Michael, J. (1959). The psychiatric nurse as a behavioral engineer. *Journal of the Experimental Analysis of Behavior, 2,* 323–336.

Bacon-Prue, A., Blount, R., Pickering, D., & Drabman, R.

(1980). An evaluation of the three litter control procedures—trash receptacles, paid workers, and the marked item technique. *Journal of Applied Behavioral Analysis, 13*, 165–170.

Bandura, A. (1969). *Principles of behavior modification*. New York: Holt, Rinehart & Winston.

Bandura, A. (1977a). Self-efficacy: Toward a unifying theory of behavioral change. *Psychological Review, 84*, 191–215.

Bandura, A. (1977b). *Social learning theory*. Englewood Cliffs, NJ: Prentice-Hall.

Bandura, A. (1978a). Reflections on self-efficacy. *Advances in Behaviour Research and Therapy, 1*, 237–269.

Bandura, A. (1978b). The self system in reciprocal determinism. *American Psychologist, 33*, 346–358.

Bandura, A. (1982). A self-efficacy mechanism in human agency. *American Psychologist, 37*, 122–147.

Barbrack, C.R. (1985). Negative outcome in behavior therapy. In D.T. Mays & C.M. Franks (Eds.), *Negative outcome in psychotherapy and what to do about it* (pp. 76–105). New York: Springer Publishing Company.

Barbrack, C.R., & Franks, C.M. (1986). Contemporary behavior therapy and the unique contribution of H.J. Eysenck: Anachronistic or visionary? In S. Modgil & C. Modgil (Eds.), *Hans Eysenck: Consensus and controversy* (pp. 233–246). Philadelphia: Falmer Press.

Barling, J., & Wainstein, T. (1979). Attitudes, labeling bias, and behavior modification in work organizations. *Behavior Therapy, 10*, 129–136.

Barlow, D. (1980). Behavior therapy: The next decade. *Behavior Therapy, 11*, 315–328.

Barlow, D.H. (1981). On the relationship of clinical research to clinical practice: Current issues, new directions. *Journal of Clinical and Consulting Psychology, 49*, 147–155.

Barlow, D.H., Mavissakalian, M., & Schofield, L. (1980). Patterns of desynchrony in agoraphobia. *Behaviour Research and Therapy, 18*, 441–448.

Bergin, A.E. (1980). Behavior therapy and ethical relativism: Time for clarity. *Journal of Consulting and Clinical Psychology, 48*, 11–13.

Bijou, J.W., & Redd, W.H. (1975). Behavior therapy for children. In D.X. Freedman & J.E. Dyrud (Eds.), *American handbook of psychiatry* (Vol. 5). New York: Basic Books.

Danish, S.J., & Smyer, M.A. (1981). Unintended consequences of requiring a license to help people. *American Psychologist, 36*, 13–21.

Davison, G.C., & Stuart, R.B. (1975). Behavior therapy and civil liberties. *American Psychologist, 30*, 755–763.

Delprato, D.J. (1989). Developmental interactionism: An emerging integrative framework for behavior therapy. *Advances in Behaviour Research and Therapy, 9*, 173–205.

Dollard, J., & Miller, N.D. (1950). *Personality and psychotherapy*. New York: McGraw-Hill.

Ehrenberg, O., & Ehrenberg, M. (1977). *The psychotherapy maze*. New York: Holt, Rinehart & Wilson.

Emmelkamp, P.M.G. (1981). The current and future status of clinical research. *Behavioral Assessment, 3*, 249–254.

Erwin, E. (1978). *Behavioral therapy: Scientific, philosophical, and moral foundations*. Cambridge, England: Cambridge University Press.

Eysenck, H.J. (1959). Learning theory and behavior therapy. *Journal of Mental Science, 105*, 61–75.

Eysenck, H.J. (1982). Neo-behavioristic (S-R) theory of behavioral therapy. In G.T. Wilson & C.M. Franks (Eds.), *Contemporary behavior therapy: Conceptual foundation of clinical practice* (pp. 205–276). New York: Guilford Press.

Eysenck, H.J., & Martin, I. (Eds.). (1987). *Theoretical foundations of behavior therapy*. New York: Plenum Press.

Farkas, G.M. (1980). An ontological analysis of behavior therapy. *American Psychologist, 35*, 364–374.

Finesmith, B.K. (1979). An historic and systematic overview of behavior management guidelines. *The Behavior Therapist, 2*, 2–6.

Fishman, D.L., Rotgers, F., & Franks, C.M. (Eds.). (1988). *Paradigms in behavior therapy: Present and promise*. New York: Springer Publishing Company.

Franks, C.M. (1969). Behavior therapy and its Pavlovian origins: Review and perspectives. In C.M. Franks (Ed.), *Behavior therapy: Appraisal and status* (pp. 1–26). New York: McGraw-Hill.

Franks, C.M. (1980). On behaviorism and behaviour therapy—Not necessarily synonymous and becoming less so. *Australian Behaviour Therapist, 7*, 14–23.

Franks, C.M. (1981). 2081: Will we be many or one—Or none? *Behavioural Psychotherapy, 9*, 287–290.

Franks, C.M. (1982). Behavior therapy: An overview. In C.M. Franks, G.T. Wilson, P. Kendall, & K.D. Brownell (Eds.), *Annual review of behavior therapy: Theory and practice* (Vol. 8, pp. 1–33). New York: Guilford Press.

Franks, C.M. (1984a). On conceptual and technical integrity in psychoanalysis and behavior therapy: Two fundamentally incompatable systems. In H. Arkowitz & S.B. Messer (Eds.), *Psychoanalytic and behavior therapy: Is integration possible?* (pp. 223–247). New York: Plenum Press.

Franks, C.M. (1984b). The place of theory and concept in a world of practice and doing: A clinician's guide to the behavioral galaxy. In C.M. Franks (Ed.), *New developments in behavior therapy: From research to clinical application* (pp. 1–19). New York: Haworth Press.

Franks, C.M. (1987a). Behavior therapy: An overview. In G.T. Wilson, C.M. Franks, P.C. Kendall, & J.P. Foreyt (Eds.), *Review of behavior therapy: Theory and practice* (Vol. 2, pp. 1–39). New York: Guilford Press.

Franks, C.M. (1987b). Behavior therapy and AABT: Personal recollections, conceptions, and misconceptions. *The Behavior Therapist, 10*, 171–174.

Franks, C.M. (1988). Foreward to M.D. Powers (Ed.), *Expanding systems of service delivery for persons with developmental difficulties*. Baltimore: Paul H Brookes.

Franks, C.M., & Rosenbaum, M. (1983). Behavior therapy: Overview and personal reflections. In M. Rosenbaum, C.M. Franks, & Y. Jaffe (Eds.), *Perspectives on behav-*

ior therapy in the eighties (pp. 3–14). New York: Springer.

Franks, C.M., & Wilson, G.T. (1973–1979) (Eds.), *Annual review of behavior therapy: Theory and practice* (Vol. 1–7). New York: Brunner/Mazel.

Glenwick, D., & Jason, L. (Eds.). (1980). *Behavioral community psychology: Program and prospects*. New York: Praeger.

Goldiamond, I. (1984). Training parent trainers and ethicists in nonlinear analysis of behavior. In R.F. Dangel & R.A. Polster (Eds.), *Parent training: Foundations of research and practice* (pp. 504–540). New York: Guilford Press.

Hayes, S.C., & Nelson, R.O. (1981). Clinically relevant research: Requirements, problems, and solutions. *Behavioral Assessment, 3*, 209–216.

Heinrich, R. (1980). Personal communication.

Henton, W.W., & Iversen, I.H. (1978). *Classical conditioning and operant conditioning: A response pattern analysis*. New York: Springer-Verlag.

Hersen, M. (1981). Complex problems require complex solutions. *Behavior Therapy, 12*, 15–29.

Hersen, M., & Barlow, D. (1976). *Single case experimental designs: Strategies for studying behavior change*. Elmsford, NY: Pergamon Press.

Hillner, K.P. (1979). *Conditioning in contemporary perspective*. New York: Springer Publishing Company.

Holt, R.R. (1978). *Methods in clinical psychology: Volume 2. Prediction and research*. New York: Plenum Press.

Houts, A.C., & Krasner, L. (1980). Slicing the ethical Gordian Knot: A response to Ketchener. *Journal of Clinical and Consulting Psychology, 48*, 8–10.

Hutchinson, W.R., & Fawcett, S.B. (1981). Issues in defining the field of behavioral community psychology and certifying (or not certifying) its members. *The Behavior Therapist, 4*, 5–8.

Kanfer, F.H., & Grimm, L.G. (1980). Managing clinical change. *Behavior Modification, 4*, 419–444.

Kazdin, A.E. (1978a). Behavior therapy: Evolution and expansion. *The Counseling Psychologist, 7*, 34–37.

Kazdin, A.E. (1978b). Evaluating the generality of findings in analogue therapy research. *Journal of Consulting and Clinical Psychology, 46*, 673–686.

Kazdin, A.E. (1978c). *History of behavior modification: Experimental foundations of contemporary research*. Baltimore: University Park Press.

Kazdin, A.E. (1979). Fictions, factions, and functions of behavior therapy. *Behavior Therapy, 10*, 629–656.

Kazdin, A.E., & Cole, P.E. (1981). Attitudes and labeling biases toward behavior modification: The effects of labels, content and jargon. *Behavior Therapy, 12*, 56–68.

Kendall, P.C., Plous, S., & Kratochwill, T.R. (1981). Science and behavior therapy: A survey of research in the 1970's. *Behaviour Research and Therapy, 19*, 517–524.

Kitchener, R.F. (1980). Ethical relativism and behavior therapy. *Journal of Clinical and Consulting Psychology, 48*, 1–7.

Kratochwill, T.R. (Ed.). (1978). *Single-subject research:*

Strategies for evaluating change. New York: Academic Press.

Lazarus, A.A. (1958). New methods of psychotherapy: A case study. *South African Medical Journal, 32*, 660–663.

Lazarus, A.A. (1981). *The practice of multimodal therapy*. New York: McGraw-Hill.

Ledwidge, B. (1978). Cognitive behavior modification: A step in the wrong direction. *Psychological Bulletin, 85*, 353–375.

Lindsley, O.R., Skinner, B.F., & Solomon, H.D. (1953). *Studies in behavior therapy: Status Report 1*. Waltham, MA: Metropolitan State Hospital.

Locke, E.A. (Ed.). (1986). *Generalizing from laboratory to field setting: Research findings from industrial psychology, organizational behavior, and human resource management*. Lexington, MA: Lexington Books.

Luborsky, L., Singer, B., & Luborsky, L. (1975). Comparative studies of psychotherapies: Is it true that everyone has won and all must have prizes? *Archives of General Psychiatry, 32*, 995–1008.

Maccoby, N., & Alexander, J. (1980). Use of media in life style programs. In P.O. Davidson & S.M. Davison (Eds.), *Behavioral medicine: Changing health life styles* (pp. 151–219). New York: Brunner/Mazel.

Mahoney, M.J., & Kazdin, A.E. (1979). Cognitive behavior modification: Misconceptions and premature evaluation. *Psychological Bulletin, 86*, 1044–1049.

Martin, I., & Levey, A.B. (1978). Evaluative conditioning. *Advances in Behaviour Research and Therapy, 1*, 57–102.

Martin, R. (1979). Comments on the "Wisconsin Experience." *The Behavior Therapist, 2*, 7.

Mays, D.T., & Franks, C.M. (Eds.). (1985). *Negative outcome in psychotherapy and what to do about it*. New York: Springer Publishing Company.

Messer, S.B., & Winokur, M. (1980). Some limits to the integration of psychoanalytic and behavior therapy. *American Psychologist, 35*, 818–827.

Messer, S.B., & Winokur, M. (1984). Ways of knowing and visions of reality in psychoanalytic and behavior therapy. In H. Arkowitz & S.B. Messer (Eds.), *Psychoanalytic and behavior therapy: Is integration possible?* (pp. 63–100). New York: Plenum Press.

Mitford, J. (1973). *Kind and usual punishment: The prison business*. New York: Alfred A. Knopf.

Mowrer, O.H. (1960). *Learning theory and behavior*. New York: John Wiley & Sons.

Peterson, D.R. (1976). Is psychology a profession? *American Psychologist, 31*, 572–581.

Rachman, S., & Wilson, G.T. (1980). *The effects of psychological therapy*. Elmsford, NY: Pergamon Press.

Rakover, S.S. (1980). Generalization from analogue therapy to the clinical situation: The paradox and the dilemma of generality. *Journal of Consulting and Clinical Psychology, 48*, 770–771.

Redd, W.H., Porterfield, A.L., & Anderson, B.L. (1979). *Behavior modification: Behavioral approaches to human problems*. New York: Random House.

Repucci, N., & Saunders, J. (1974). Social psychology of behavior modification: Problems of implementation in natural settings. *American Psychologist, 29,* 649–660.

Ruben, D.H., & Delprato, D.J. (Eds.). (1987). *New ideas in therapy: Introduction to an interdisciplinary approach.* Westport, CT: Greenwood Press.

Russo, D.C., & Budd, K.S. (1987). Limitations of operant practice in the study of disease. *Behavior Modification, 11,* 264–285.

Schneider, T.W., Lesko, W.A., & Garrett, W.A. (1980). Helping behavior in hot, comfortable and cold temperatures. *Environment and Behavior, 12,* 231–240.

Shah, S.A. (1978). Dangerousness: A paradigm for exploring some issues in law and psychiatry. *American Psychologist, 33,* 224–236.

Shimberg, B. (1981). Testing for licensure and certification. *American Psychologist, 36,* 138–141, 146.

Skinner, B.F. (1971). *Beyond freedom and dignity.* New York: Alfred A Knopf.

Swan, G.E. (1979). On the structure of eclecticism: Cluster analysis of eclectic behavior therapists. *Professional Psychology, 10,* 732–739.

Swan, G.E., & MacDonald, M.L. (1978). Behavior therapy in practice: A national survey of behavior therapists. *Behavior Therapy, 9,* 799–807.

Thomas, D.R., & Murphy, R.J. (1981). Practitioner competencies needed for implementing behavior management guidelines. *The Behavior Therapist, 4,* 7–10.

Tryon, W.W., Ferster, C.B., Franks, C.M., Kazdin, A.E., Levis, D.J., & Tryon, G.S. (1980). On the role of behaviorism in clinical psychology. *Pavlovian Journal of Biological Science, 15,* 12–20.

Turkat, I.D., & Feuerstein, M (1978). Behavior modification and the public misconception. *American Psychologist, 33,* 194.

Turkat, I.D., & Forehand, R. (1980). The future of behavior therapy. In M. Hersen, R.M. Eisler, & P.M. Miller (Eds.), *Progress in behavior modification* (Vol. 9, pp. 106–146). New York: Academic Press.

Wachtel, P.L. (1977). *Psychoanalysis and behavior therapy.* New York: Basic Books.

Wahler, R.S., & Hann, D.M. (1986). A behavioral systems perspective in childhood psychopathology: Expanding the three-term operant contingency. In N.A. Krasnegor, J.D. Arasteh, & M.F. Cataldo (Eds.), *Child health behavior: A behavioral pediatrics perspective* (pp. 146–167). New York: John Wiley & Sons.

Walker, C.E., Hedberg, A., Clement, P.W., & Wright, L. (1981). *Clinical procedures for behavior therapy.* Englewood Cliffs, NJ: Prentice-Hall.

Ward, L.C. (1980). Behavior therapy and ethics: A response to Kitchener. *Journal of Clinical and Consulting Psychology, 48,* 646–648.

Wilson, G.T. (1982). Psychotherapy process and procedure: The behavioral mandate. *Behavior Therapy, 13,* 291–312.

Wilson, G.T., & Franks, C.M. (1982). Introduction. In G.T. Wilson & C.M. Franks (Eds.), *Contemporary behavior therapy: Conceptual foundation of clinical practice* (pp. 1–7). New York: Guilford Press.

Wilson, G.T., & O'Leary, K.D. (1980). *Principles of behavior therapy.* Englewood Cliffs, NJ: Prentice-Hall.

Winnett, R.A. (1981). Behavioral community psychology: Integrations and commitments. *The Behavior Therapist, 5,* 5–8.

Winkler, R.C. (1983). The contribution of behavioral economics to behavior modification. In C.M. Franks, M. Rosenbaum, & Y. Jaffee (Eds.), *Perspectives on behavior therapy in the eighties* (pp. 397–415). New York: Springer Publishing Company.

Wolpe, J. (1958). *Psychotherapy by reciprocal inhibition.* Stanford, CA: Stanford University Press.

Woolfolk, A.E., & Woolfolk, R.L. (1979). Modifying the effect of the behavior modification label. *Behavior Therapy, 10,* 575–578.

Yates, A.J. (1970). *Behavior Therapy.* New York: John Wiley & Sons.

CHAPTER 31

BEHAVIOR THERAPY WITH CHILDREN

Sandra L. Harris
Michael Alessandri
Anne M. Nathan

To the endless perplexity, frustration, and enduring joy of most of us, children are very different from adults. As the research of developmental psychologists has documented, they construe the world differently than we do; these affective, social, and cognitive developmental differences dictate that we adapt our therapy techniques to meet their special needs. Behavior therapists, like their dynamically oriented peers, have evolved a distinctive field of child therapy with a variety of techniques, some of which are largely confined to application with children.

Because this chapter is for readers from diverse theoretical orientations, we have organized it around the various diagnostic categories of the *Diagnostic and Statistical Manual of Mental Disorders*—Third Edition, Revised (DSM-IIIR, American Psychiatric Association [APA], 1987). We have selected diagnostic categories that we view as representative of the child behavior therapy literature in general: Anxiety Disorders, Functional Enuresis, Attention-Deficit Hyperactivity Disorder, Mental Retardation and Autistic Disorder, and Conduct Disorder. Specific techniques of child behavior therapy, such as parent training, family therapy, cognitive-behavioral methods, and modeling, are examined.

ANXIETY DISORDERS

Although the effectiveness of behavioral techniques for modifying adult fears is well documented, there is considerably less research on behavioral approaches to the treatment of fears and phobias in children (Graziano, De Giovanni, & Garcia, 1979). This relative neglect may reflect the belief that children's fears are common and transient. Although there is empirical support for the expectation that fears diminish in frequency and intensity as children grow older (Graziano et al., 1979), there is a group of youngsters for whom intense and distressing anxiety persists through childhood. The APA's DSM-III-R (1987) includes a classification for "Anxiety Disorders of Childhood or Adolescence." In two of the categories, Separation Anxiety Disorder and Avoidant Disorder of Childhood or Adolescence, the anxiety is focused on specific situations; in the third category, Overanxious Disorder, anxiety is generalized to a variety of situations.

The behavioral treatment of children's fears generally consists either of direct exposure to feared stimuli or altering verbal or coping skills related to the fearful situation (Sheslow, Bondy, & Nelson, 1982). We will review here the use of systematic desensitization, modeling, and cognitive techniques for modification of children's fears.

Systematic Desensitization

Systematic desensitization, the most widely used approach to treating anxiety in children (Ollendick & Cerny, 1981), consists of gradual exposure to the fear-evoking stimulus while the child engages in an activity incompatible with fear. Typically, the child is trained in deep-muscle relaxation as an anxiety-inhibiting response, although other responses such as eating or assertiveness have been used, and special relaxation training scripts employing fantasy, simple language, and special wording have been developed to enhance the child's understanding and interest (Ollendick, 1979; Ollendick & Cerny, 1981).

In addition to rigorous case studies demonstrating the value of desensitization with phobic children (e.g., Van Hasselt, Hersen, Bellack, Rosenbloom, & Lamparski, 1979), several controlled studies have evaluated the effectiveness of the procedures with mildly fearful nonclinic children. Ollendick's (1979) review found that three out of four of these studies reported positive outcomes with systematic desensitization. Ultee, Griffioen, and Schellekens (1982) reported in vivo desensitization to be more effective than imaginal desensitization or no treatment.

Modeling

Modeling (Bandura, 1969) has been applied to the treatment of fear by having children observe child or adult models approach the feared object or engage in the anxiety-producing behavior (Strauss, 1987). This technique has been used to reduce common fears such as those of water (Bentler, 1962) or dogs (Bandura, Grusec, & Menlove, 1967), as well as intense, situation-specific fears, such as anticipation of surgery or dental procedures (e.g., Melamed & Siegel, 1975).

Research on the efficacy of modeling consists primarily of studies of nonclinic children with relatively mild specific fears (Ollendick, 1979); there are no controlled studies using clinic children with phobias (Strauss, 1987). Ollendick's (1979) review of 11 analogue studies of children with fears of animals, water, and heights showed that several versions of modeling were superior to "no treatment" in reducing these fears. Participant modeling has frequently been found to be superior to modeling alone (Ollendick, 1979). Similarly, exposure to models who interact fearlessly with the stimulus has sometimes, but not always, been found to be less effective than fearful models who "cope" with their fears (Ginther & Roberts, 1982).

Cognitive-Behavioral Approaches

Cognitive-behavioral approaches to children's fears include (a) directly training the child to recite statements of self-competence, (b) stress inoculation training, and (c) covert modeling. In the first approach, the child is taught to rehearse statements emphasizing competence in handling the feared situation; for example, Nocella and Kaplan (1982) had young dental patients recite coping verbalizations (e.g., "I'm doing terrific"). In a study of children with moderate to high dental anxiety, McMurray, Bell, Fusillo, Morgan, and Wright (1986) found a coping statement condition more effective than a placebo in reducing self-reported anxiety. Graziano and Mooney (1982) noted that fear reduction achieved through the recitation of brave self-statements was maintained as long as 3 years later.

Some studies have failed to support the use of coping self-statements (e.g., Fox & Houston, 1981; Sheslow et al., 1982). Significantly, the studies that found no benefits involved younger children (Sheslow et al., 1982), used an anxiety-provoking situation requiring task performance rather than passive endurance (Fox & Houston, 1981), and employed self-statements negating unpleasant aspects of the situation instead of emphasizing positive features.

Stress inoculation techniques have been used (e.g., Meichenbaum & Turk, 1976) to reduce dental phobia in young patients. Here, the child rehearses coping self-statements prior to exposure to lessen anxiety associated with various aspects of the dental visit. In addition, he or she uses positive self-statements following effective use of the cognitive strategies (e.g., "I did it"). In a study of covert modeling, Chertock and Bornstein (1979) asked children to visualize a hierarchy of increasingly anxiety-provoking scenes related to dental visits and to imagine a model coping with these scenes without actually observing live or filmed models.

Research and Clinical Issues

Several problems are evident in the literature on anxiety disorders in children. Most of the clinical data base is limited to case reports and studies with small samples; more rigorous studies are primarily with subjects having only mild-to-moderate fears and were done in laboratory rather than applied settings. Some of the research has been confounded by the use of treatment packages that combine several components, thus making it impossible to identify the effects of a specific intervention.

We must be wary of the assumption that our knowledge of children's anxiety disorders can be built upon the body of research concerning adults. An appreciation of cognitive and affective development may be crucial to the identification of effective treatments for children's clinical fears. Careful assessment seems crucial in this domain; some anxiety disorders may require the elimination of the fear and anxiety per se, whereas others may demand attention to the child's skill deficits. A child may be afraid to go to school because of poor academic performance, fear of separation from home, or fear of physical violence in school. Each of these requires a different intervention.

FUNCTIONAL ENURESIS

A clear example of the role of developmental factors in treatment is found in functional enuresis because this diagnosis hinges upon the child's chronological (and mental) age. Babies are in a perpetual state of wet diapers; adolescents are never expected to wet the bed. Although there is no precise age beyond which bed-wetting ceases to be simply an inconvenience and becomes a clinical problem, there are normative data that can guide the clinician in making a decision about when to intervene.

The prevalence of enuresis declines steadily throughout childhood and there is very little nocturnal wetting after 10 years of age. Somewhere around school age many parents become concerned if their child is wetting the bed with regularity and may seek help to stop the behavior. Any definition of functional enuresis must, of course, rule out children who suffer from a neurological or urological disorder that precludes their developing or maintaining bladder control. It is also important to take mental age as well as chronological age into account when making the decision to intervene. The child who is cognitively impaired may need special adaptations of training procedures. Traditionally, researchers have made a distinction between primary enuresis (no history of dryness) and secondary enuresis (dryness once established but now lost), but Doleys (1977) notes that this distinction has not been shown to have prognostic significance.

Our discussion briefly examines three major behavioral techniques for treating enuresis: the urine alarm, dry bed training, and retention control training.

Urine Alarm

The essentials of the enuresis treatment described by Mowrer and Mowrer (1938) remain in effect today. When using the urine alarm, the child sleeps in his or her own bed with a special pad beneath the sheet. When urine soaks through the sheet and makes contact with the pad, this completes an electric circuit and triggers an alarm that wakes the child. After waking, the child is expected to void in the toilet. Parents are advised to get up with their child to ensure the bed is remade and the alarm reset before the child goes back to sleep.

Doleys (1977) summarized 12 studies that met reasonable standards of experimental design in their evaluation of the efficacy of the urine alarm. He identified an overall success rate of 75% across this set of studies with the mean length of training running from 5 to 12 weeks; for those studies that provide follow-up data, there was a relapse rate of 41%. Among those relapsed subjects who were re-treated, there was a 68% success rate. Success with the bell and pad is greater with an immediate rather than a delayed alarm (Doleys, 1977), with an intermittent schedule of conditioning (Doleys, 1977), and with overlearning procedures in which liquid intake is increased once conditioning has occurred (e.g., Taylor & Turner, 1975).

Research on subjects who fail to respond to the bell and pad reveals that the most common reason for failure was lack of parental cooperation. Other difficulties include poor sleeping conditions in which to conduct treatment, the child's failure to wake to the alarm, the child's fear of the equipment, and incorrect use of the equipment (Doleys, 1977).

Dry Bed Training

In order to address some of the reasons for treatment failure, most current research on the treatment of enuresis includes a multicomponent package rather than the bell and pad alone. The best known of these packages is dry bed training (Azrin, Sneed, & Foxx, 1974).

Dry bed training requires the child repeatedly to practice the steps necessary to keep his or her bed dry at night. The youngster practices getting out of bed, walking to the toilet, and so on in the sequence one might use if waking at night with a full bladder. The parents have a major role to play, including reinforcing good behavior and reprimanding wetting. Most research has used the bell and pad as a component of dry bed training; the alarm is used to wake the child if wetting occurs and the child is required to clean up upon waking. The dry bed procedure is an intensive one that ensures that everyone is well trained, but it also demands a great deal from parents and child; it is not surprising that parents who used the bell and pad alone rated it more favorably than those who used dry bed training (Fincham & Spettell, 1984).

Studies of dry bed training report good success rates (e.g., Azrin et al., 1974; Doleys, Ciminero, Tollison, Williams, & Wells, 1977), although ongoing replication has led to more variability of outcome than was initially observed (e.g., Breit, Kaplan, Gauthier, & Weinhold, 1984). Repeated awakening of the child to void in the toilet is a standard component of the dry bed procedure. Several studies (e.g., Rolider & Van Houten, 1986) suggest that a systematic procedure of gradually fading the time of awakening is more important than the number of awakenings, and that this procedure may be an important component of treatment.

Houts and his colleagues (e.g., Houts, Whelan, & Peterson, 1987) developed a comprehensive treatment package for efficient delivery to families. In a 1-hour group session they describe the bell and pad, cleanliness training, retention control, and overlearning procedures. This package has a slightly better success rate than the bell and pad alone.

Retention Control Training

Retention control training is based on the notion that the bladder of the enuretic child has a smaller capacity than the nonenuretic child. Therefore, the child is taught to retain increasingly large amounts of fluid by inhibiting urination and thereby increasing functional bladder capacity (Kimmel & Kimmel, 1970). Doleys (1977) indicated that research has not shown the superiority of this approach to other treatments.

Research and Clinical Issues

Although the search continues for the essential ingredients to deliver the most efficient and effective behavioral treatment for enuresis, we already have some potent interventions for routine application. This satisfying level of success has brought the field to the point of employing relatively sophisticated research designs to dismantle the treatment packages. Follow-up data are essential in these studies because of the frequent high relapse rates.

Clinically, it is satisfying to have available treatment procedures of proven efficacy. Nonetheless, one must do an assessment of the context in which treatment is to be applied, and organic causes for enuresis must be ruled out. Although an extensive, uncomfortable urological examination may not be indicated before undertaking the relatively benign and short-term interventions described here, one would want the assurance of the child's physician that there was no indication of infection or gross pathology.

If the child fails to respond to initial treatment with a multicomponent package the clinician will want to explore a number of questions including the extent to which parents and child were able to apply the procedures, whether the wetting serves any reinforcing functions for members of the family, and whether there may be a physical basis for difficulty in achieving control. It is of interest to note that the presence of serious psychopathology need not rule out the use of the standard behavioral procedures to achieve dryness in children. Kolko (1987) described the effective use of a program similar to dry bed training on an inpatient psychiatric unit.

ATTENTION-DEFICIT HYPERACTIVITY DISORDER

Attention-deficit hyperactivity disorder (ADHD) is characterized by developmentally inappropriate degrees of inattention, impulsivity, and hyperactivity, which tend to worsen in situations requiring sustained attention. In the sections that follow we will examine the use of behavior modification, biofeedback, and relaxation procedures as well as cognitive-behavioral interventions to decrease hyperactivity and/or enhance attention.

Behavior Modification Procedures

Home- and school-based interventions consisting of training parents and teachers in behavior modification principles have been successful in treating hyperactive behavior (e.g., O'Leary, Pelham, Rosenbaum, & Price, 1976). For example, Dubey, O'Leary, and Kaufman (1983) implemented a behavioral parent training program in which parents of hyperactive children were trained to assess target behaviors, as well as design and carry out appropriate interventions in the home. Parents who received this training rated their hyperactive children as more improved than did parents assigned to a communication control group.

Similarly, classroom intervention consisting of systematically rewarding academic production and appropriate classroom behaviors leads to improved behavior (e.g., Dubey & Kaufman, 1978). For example,

O'Leary et al. (1976) deviscd a classroom intervention for hyperactive children that incorporated setting daily goals, praising appropriate behavior, ignoring inappropriate behavior, and completing daily report cards. Following treatment the children were significantly improved according to teacher ratings of behavior and activity level.

Home- and school-based behavioral interventions, although useful, may not always be cost-effective. The training and implementation of such procedures requires considerable energy and motivation. These methods are also of limited utility with adolescents (Abikoff & Gittelman, 1984), who can become more difficult to manage using behavior modification procedures.

Relaxation Procedures

An alternative approach to the treatment of ADHD is relaxation training in the form of biofeedback or progressive muscle relaxation to reduce a child's level of activity and arousal (Wahler & Fox, 1981).

The widespread popularity of biofeedback procedures for adult somatic complaints led to the exploration of these procedures for the treatment of hyperactive and impulsive behavior in children. In their review, Cobb & Evans (1981) identified 24 studies of biofeedback with hyperactive children. Overall, these studies indicate that young children do have the capacity to learn the necessary muscular control. Unfortunately, methodological flaws make it impossible to draw definitive conclusions about the clinical efficacy of the procedures.

To address the problem of accuracy in assessing a state of relaxation, behavioral relaxation training (BRT), consisting of 10 overt postures and behaviors taught by modeling, prompting, and feedback, was developed for use with hyperactive children (Raymer & Poppen, 1985). In general, assessments of BRT using objective measures of muscle tension and relaxation are encouraging (Raymer & Poppen, 1985). Parent ratings of changes in their child's hyperactive behavior, however, are less conclusive (Raymer & Poppen, 1985). Data are therefore needed to determine whether these procedures, once mastered, can reduce hyperactive behavior and/or increase attention span.

Cognitive-Behavioral Strategies

Consistent with the general trend in the child behavior therapy literature, there has been increasing interest in cognitive-behavioral techniques to help children with ADHD focus their attention and gain increased self-control. Typically, these strategies teach children to stop and think before they act (Kendall & Braswell, 1985). Methods have included self-instructional training in which a child is taught statements to rehearse actively while problem solving (e.g., "If I keep working I will be a good boy"; e.g., Whalen, Henker, & Hinshaw, 1985) and strategic problem-solving training in which a child is given a direct description of the necessary behavior (e.g., "Look and think before answering"; e.g., Whalen et al., 1985).

The impact of cognitive-behavioral approaches on inattentive or impulsive behavior has been inconsistent (Borden, Brown, Wynne, & Schleser, 1987). Some studies support the notion that this is a valuable and effective means of treating hyperactivity (e.g., Kendall & Braswell, 1982). Others find no empirical support for the clinical efficacy of such training (e.g., Brown, Borden, Schleser, Clingerman, & Orenczuk, 1985).

A notable problem in this literature is a lack of consideration of the role of cognitive development. Young, cognitively immature children may not be able to process and utilize cognitive therapy techniques appropriately and independently (Cohen, Sullivan, Minde, Novak, & Helwig, 1981). Interestingly, ADHD children seem to lag significantly behind their normal peers on basic conservation tasks (Brown, 1987) and to display cognitive deficits (Douglas, 1983). This developmental lag may help explain some of the disappointing results of cognitive training with young children (Cohen et al., 1981) as well as older children who appear cognitively delayed.

Pharmacotherapy Versus Nonpharmacological Approaches

There is considerable controversy over the use of pharmacological versus nonpharmacological treatments for hyperactive children (Ross & Ross, 1982). Some studies support the use of drugs rather than behavior therapy and/or cognitive behavior therapy (e.g., Brown et al., 1985); others lend support to the use of behavior therapy and/or cognitive-behavior therapy rather than psychostimulants (e.g., Hinshaw, Henker, & Whalen, 1984b); whereas others argue for a combination of psychostimulants with either behavior or cognitive-behavior therapy (e.g., Hinshaw, Henker, & Whalen, 1984a).

A major point of this debate concerns the effects of treatment on learning and academic achievement. To date, there is no conclusive evidence that stimulants enhance learning in an educationally meaningful way (e.g., Barkley & Cunningham, 1978; O'Leary, 1980). By contrast, behavior therapy has been found effective in increasing academic performance (Dubey & Kaufman, 1978), and several studies suggest that cognitive-behavioral approaches yield academic gains (e.g., Barkley, Copeland, & Sivage, 1980; Kendall & Braswell, 1982).

Research and Clinical Issues

Although medication has been the treatment of choice for many years, there are few data suggesting that this approach is superior to behavioral interventions with ADHD. To the contrary, a behavioral approach appears to have substantial advantages in terms of academic achievement. There are, however, some family or school settings where behavioral approaches may not be feasible and some individual children for whom the response to medication appears quite positive. Group studies cannot substitute for data-based judgments about individual clients.

There remain many inconsistencies in the ADHD treatment literature. Resolving these inconsistencies is quite complex because the studies vary along many dimensions, including IQ, social class, diagnosis, setting (i.e., home, school, or laboratory), skill level of the therapist, dosage of medication, assessment measures employed, treatment goals, and age of the subjects.

MENTAL RETARDATION AND AUTISTIC DISORDER

Child behavior therapy has had a substantial impact on the treatment of mental retardation and autistic disorder. After early translations of Skinnerian concepts of operant conditioning into direct application with autistic children (Ferster, 1961) there followed a series of successful efforts to use behavioral techniques with these youngsters (Lovaas, Berberich, Perloff, & Schaeffer, 1966).

Behavior Reduction

In dealing with mentally retarded and autistic youngsters one is often confronted by behaviors such as self-injury, temper tantrums, self-stimulation, and aggression. At the very least such behaviors reduce the accessibility of the child for learning; at worst they may threaten his or her life. Work with this population has therefore led to considerable research concerning the suppression of disruptive behavior and encourage-

ment of alternative responses. The question of the role of punishment in the management of disruptive behavior has become a controversial topic in both the professional and lay press—often with more passion than data underlying the debate.

Researchers in the past 20 years have done a great deal of work on the value of aversive procedures to deal with life-threatening behaviors (Harris & Ersner-Hershfield, 1978). Although important work continues to be done in this area, there has also emerged in recent years an examination of nonaversive alternatives to treating these problems. This research suggests that target behaviors once addressed primarily with aversive procedures sometimes can be treated with sophisticated nonaversive or mildly aversive alternatives.

Examples of mildly to moderately intrusive treatment procedures to treat self-injury, aggression, or self-stimulation include overcorrection (Foxx & Azrin, 1972) in which the client is required to engage in vigorous compensatory activity (e.g., Johnson, Baumeister, Penland, & Inwald, 1982), the use of contingent physical exercise such as jogging (e.g., Gordon, Handleman, & Harris, 1986), and brief, contingent physical restraint (Dorsey, Iwata, Reid, & Davis, 1982).

Those who oppose the use of even mild aversive procedures focus on the importance of modifying the instructional context and changing the environment to control unwanted behaviors. For example, task complexity can have an impact on eruption of aberrant behavior (e.g., Carr, Newsom, & Binkoff, 1976). Teaching a child to ask for help (Carr & Durand, 1985), and reinforcing appropriate play (Eason, White, & Newsom, 1982) can reduce troublesome behavior. Such findings provide support for a continued search for creative ways to cope with the seriously disruptive behaviors of autistic and mentally retarded youngsters. Unfortunately, to date these techniques have not been shown to have widely generalized efficacy in dealing with the most severe behavior problems.

Acquisition of New Skills

Although the use of aversive procedures has generated the most publicity in the past decade, it is in the area of acquisition of new skills where some of the most important progress has been made. Positive reinforcement, physical and verbal prompts, shaping techniques, and chaining of small behaviors into complex sequences are the kinds of techniques most commonly used to teach new skills. Many tasks once thought too difficult to be mastered by the mentally retarded or autistic person are teachable when broken into their component parts and taught systematically.

Teaching speech and language are high priorities in work with most developmentally disabled clients. Among the most interesting developments in this regard has been an increasing reliance on incidental teaching procedures to work with the developmentally disabled. These techniques create a stimulating environment and capitalize on the individual's attraction to naturally occurring events as training opportunities (e.g., McGee, Krantz, & McClannahan, 1985).

The use of normal peer models and tutors, particularly for very young children with autism has considerable promise as an intervention technique (e.g., Odom & Strain, 1986; Sainato, Strain, Lefebvre, & Rapp, 1987). The treatment of children who are mentally retarded or autistic is also an area where parent training techniques are well developed and integral to good progress (e.g., Harris, 1983; Koegel, Schreibman, Johnson, O'Neill, & Dunlap, 1984).

Research and Clinical Issues

The two most important papers on the behavioral treatment of autism were written by Ivar Lovaas. In 1966 he reported his initial success treating previously untreatable psychotic children with operant procedures (Lovaas et al., 1966). In 1987 he published a follow-up study of autistic preschoolers who were treated in a comprehensive behavioral program (Lovaas, 1987). His data suggest that an intensive treatment program begun at an early age offers the possibility that some children with autistic behavior will appear normal in mid-childhood. This very promising outcome, although not yet replicated, argues persuasively for the importance of early intervention.

Researchers and clinicians need to be acutely aware of the problem of generalization that may arise with these very handicapped children. It becomes the responsibility of the researcher to demonstrate that a behavior learned in one context is generalized to other settings.

CONDUCT DISORDER

Children and adolescents are diagnosed as exhibiting a conduct disorder when there is a consistent pattern of violating other people's rights or breaking social rules or norms. Many of these youths are the people whom we call predelinquents or delinquents. There is another group of youngsters, sometimes called oppositional or aggressive, whose behaviors may be less disruptive than the delinquent youth or who are younger and have not committed socially intrusive offenses, but whose behavior appears to be on a continuum with their more antisocial peers. Child behavior therapists have tried to modify these troublesome and antisocial behaviors in many settings including the youth's own home, community-based group homes, and more restrictive residential settings. Behavioral techniques have included direct reinforcement and punishment of targeted behaviors, token economies, and cognitive-behavioral techniques. Kazdin (1987) has reviewed this treatment literature in detail. We focus here on community-based, family-based, and child-focused cognitive-behavioral techniques.

Residential Treatment

The most important residential programs of recent years have been in community-based group homes. These home-like settings approximate the conditions one might find in a good family. The best known of these models is Achievement Place, a program for predelinquent youth below 16 years of age. These homes are the result of years of empirical work and are managed with a token economy.

Several important discussions of the Achievement Place model have appeared in recent years. In an evaluation of the original Achievement Place program and 12 replications of the program, along with 9 comparison group homes operated according to other models, it was noted that during treatment the Achievement Place model generated superior outcome in terms of rate of alleged criminal offenses, percentage of youths involved in these offenses, and consumer evaluations. Nonetheless, at posttreatment there were no significant differences between the two groups of programs (Kirigin, Braukmann, Atwater, & Wolf, 1982).

These sobering findings of difficulty maintaining changes led Wolf, Braukmann, and Ramp (1987) to consider alternative models to address the long-term needs of these young people. They noted that although we can create important changes in the behavior of predelinquent youth, we must develop a model that ensures that these gains are maintained over time. They suggest shifting from the search for a short-term "cure" to the development of long-term supportive intervention. They argue for a supportive family treatment in which a surrogate family provides a reinforcing relationship to the extent that the biological family is unable to do so.

Family Treatment

Even with the provision of effective out-of-home placements, many parents, judges, and clinicians prefer to keep a young person in his or her home and make changes in that home rather than remove the child. There have been two important family-based models of intervention and these models may be gradually converging in focus. One approach, often with younger children, has focused on parent management training, whereas the other, often with adolescents, has involved parents and adolescents in a process of family change.

Gerald Patterson's extraordinary series of studies on young, aggressive children in the home has provided the model for much of the parent training literature (e.g., Patterson, Chamberlain, & Reid, 1982; Patterson, Reid, Jones, & Conger, 1975). This work has demonstrated consistently that training parents in behavioral management techniques alters patterns of parent–child interaction, reducing the rates of deviant child behaviors. Significantly, these authors acknowledge that parent training alone is not sufficient for many families. "Consistent outcome success requires the use of both a parent training technology, and a set of skills for dealing with client resistance, marital conflict, and familial crises" (Patterson et al., 1982, p. 648).

Studies of parents of noncompliant children have revealed important data about parents who have difficulty sustaining change. Dumas (1984) noted that unsuccessful mother–child dyads tend to be from lower socioeconomic status backgrounds, that unsuccessful mothers emit more aversive responses and show more indiscriminate use of aversive behavior than do the successful mothers, and that the unsuccessful children emit more aversive behaviors than do the successful children. Webster-Stratton (1985) likewise reported that coming from a single-parent family or a socially disadvantaged or isolated family are predictors of lack of success in a parent training program.

These observations are bolstered by Dumas and Wahler's (1985) report that mothers in a less supportive social context are less likely to sustain their management efforts with their child than are mothers in a supportive network. The isolated mothers, whom they describe as "insular," probably require interventions aimed at improving their relationships with extended family, neighbors, and community services as well as their ability to manage their child.

Research on the variety of family stressors that can undermine the efficacy of parent training led Griest

and Wells (1983) to urge that child behavior therapy be expanded to a behavioral family therapy model. They note that parents do not always perceive their child's behavior accurately and that parental psychopathology and marital discord may be related to dysfunctional child behavior, although the causal relationship among these variables is not yet firmly established.

One group of researchers who attempted to do more broadly family-oriented intervention with conduct disordered youth is Alexander and his colleagues (e.g., Alexander & Parsons, 1982). In describing their techniques Alexander, Barton, Schiavo, and Parsons (1976) stated, "The focus was not on 'delinquent' target behaviors per se but on the family system functions served by the delinquency, such as maintaining adolescent–parent distance and independence and maintaining parental role relationships" (p. 658).

Cognitive-Behavioral Techniques

There is an important literature on cognitive behavioral techniques for altering conduct disorder problems (e.g., Kazdin, Esveldt-Dawson, French, & Unis, 1987; Lochman, Burch, Curry, & Lampron, 1984) that provides support for the efficacy of these methods. Nonetheless, Kazdin et al. (1987) caution that although improved on follow-up, these youngsters are still outside of the normative range of deviant behaviors.

Little and Kendall (1979) identified three specific areas of potential deficit for the delinquent: (a) lack of skills in interpersonal transactions (problem solving), (b) difficulty in assuming another person's point of view (role taking), and (c) inability to inhibit one's impulses (self-control). They suggest that a cognitive-behavioral approach to these deficits can be integrated into residential and family-based treatment programs (Little & Kendall, 1979). For example, one can teach problem-solving skills within a family context (similar to the work of Alexander and his colleagues cited above), although one could also use the techniques with the delinquent youth alone.

Research and Clinical Issues

The behavioral approach to conduct disordered, oppositional, and noncompliant behavior is becoming increasingly sophisticated. As we confront our short-term "success" and long-term "failure" with residential, parent training, and child-focused cognitive-behavioral treatments we are forced to recognize the complexity of these problems and look to multilevel solutions rather than to our earlier unidirectional approach. This shift is producing more careful inspection of the family as a unit and the broader social context in which it functions.

In a review of research on naturalistic observation of conduct-disordered children, McIntyre et al. (1983) urged that we pursue the question of the clinical significance of behavior change in these young people. Failure to bring deviant behaviors within the normative range calls into question the value of treatments that create statistical but not clinically meaningful changes. One way to assess change is to compare the behavior of the conduct-disordered youth with normative data from their normal peers, a model applied by Kazdin and his colleagues (1987).

Of all of the disorders reviewed in the present chapter, none points more pressingly to the need for a comprehensive evaluation of the total environment than does conduct disorder. The clinician has good reason to anticipate problems in enrolling parental cooperation with many of these families; the clinician may have to work slowly, one step at a time, in order to bring some semblance of organization to a chaotic family situation.

SUMMARY

Early behavioral interventions with children were typically based on simple operant or classical conditioning paradigms that worked well for a variety of clearly defined problems, including uncomplicated fears or wetting the bed. Nevertheless, the more complex the clinical picture presented by the child, the less satisfactory these early solutions appeared. As one moves into the realm of increasingly complex interpersonal problems it becomes necessary to develop more sophisticated tools of assessment and intervention. Fortunately, such techniques are evolving to work with families and their social ecology. There is also a growing sensitivity to developmental issues in assessment and treatment in general and cognitive-behavioral techniques in particular.

Initially, child behavior therapists focused on the notion that parents could be therapists to their own children. This approach was effective and continues to be one of the most popular forms of behavioral work with younger children. The data indicate that parent training is an effective way to change disrupted patterns of parent–child interaction and reduce aversive child behaviors (e.g., Patterson et al., 1982). Nonetheless, traditional parent training programs have assumed good will and unhindered motivation of parents in their interaction with their child; clinical

experience and a growing pool of data teach us this is not always possible.

Behavior therapists are writing more about assessing the child in his or her social-familial context. Although some simple behavior problems may be addressed with a primary child focus, we are increasingly moving to include the parent–child dyad, marital relationship, nuclear family, extended family, and community as potential targets of assessment and intervention. Data concerning the role of interparental conflict in disruptive child behavior (Emery, 1982), and particularly the difficulties encountered in working with multistressed, insular mothers (e.g., Dumas, 1984; Wahler & Dumas, 1986), have highlighted the need for a detailed, careful assessment of the child's life context.

In looking at the family's social context we are urged to consider the importance of race, ethnicity, and social class as variables of potential importance in treatment (Rios & Gutierrez, 1985/86). Although race has thus far been shown to have little impact on parental preference for various forms of behavioral intervention (e.g., Heffer & Kelley, 1987; Kazdin, 1984), social class is an important predictor both of treatment preference (Heffer & Kelley, 1987) and more importantly, of long-term prognosis (Dumas, 1984; Webster-Stratton, 1985).

One cannot assume that family or marital issues are inevitably important in working with a child; neither can one afford to ignore these factors in a behavioral assessment. The behavior therapist who is unable to intervene with marital, familial, or community issues will be unable to meet the needs of some of his or her child clients.

Yet another theme that emerged as we examined the child behavior therapy literature is recognition of the importance of developmental factors in assessment and treatment planning for children (Harris & Ferrari, 1983).

As Kendall (1985) noted even children of the same age may not be at the same developmental level. No single cognitive-behavioral procedure is best for all disorders. For example, Kendall observes that self-talk, a useful procedure for inhibiting action, is probably not going to be useful for children who are depressed, school phobic, or socially withdrawn—problems that do not involve a deficit in planful mental activity. Not only do we need to be sensitive to variation in developmental abilities, we also need to include this material in parent training curricula to help parents form realistic expectations of their child's behavior (Kendall, 1985).

Finally, as we examined the empirical basis for

child behavior therapy, we noted the uneven quality of the data. There are some areas, such as the treatment of enuresis and phobias, where the questions being asked and the designs being used are relatively sophisticated and the effects of treatment are quite gratifying and enduring. Other areas, such as the treatment of conduct disorders and pervasive developmental disorders, although topics of vigorous and important research, are still sorely limited in terms of data supporting maintenance of change. There are many domains in child behavior therapy where treatment decisions depend more on clinical judgment than on a well-established data base. Although some of the guiding principles for decision making are increasingly clear, there remain a great many questions to address.

REFERENCES

Abikoff, H., & Gittelman, R. (1984). Does behavior therapy normalize the classroom behavior of hyperactive children? *Archives of General Psychiatry, 41,* 449–454.

Alexander, J.F., Barton, C., Schiavo, R.S., & Parsons, B.V. (1976). Systems-behavioral intervention with families of delinquents: Therapist characteristics, family behavior, and outcome. *Journal of Consulting and Clinical Psychology, 44,* 656–664.

Alexander, J.F., & Parsons, B.V. (1982). *Functional family therapy.* Monterey, CA: Brooks/Cole.

American Psychiatric Association. (1987). *Diagnostic and statistical manual of mental disorders* (3rd. ed., Rev.). Washington, DC: Author.

Azrin, N.H., Sneed, T.J., & Foxx, R.M. (1974). Dry bed: Rapid elimination of childhood enuresis. *Behaviour Research and Therapy, 12,* 147–156.

Bandura, A. (1969). *Principles of behavior modification.* New York: Holt, Rinehart & Winston.

Bandura, A., Grusec, J., & Menlove, F. (1967). Vicarious extinction of avoidance behavior. *Journal of Personality and Social Psychology, 5,* 16–23.

Barkley, R.A., Copeland, A.P., & Sivage, C. (1980). A self-control classroom for hyperactive children. *Journal of Autism and Developmental Disorders, 10,* 75–89.

Barkley, R.A., & Cunningham, C.E. (1978). Do stimulant drugs improve the academic performance of hyperkinetic children? *Clinical Pediatrics, 17,* 85–92.

Bentler, P.M. (1962). An infant's phobia treated with reciprocal inhibition therapy. *Journal of Child Psychology and Psychiatry, 3,* 185–189.

Borden, K.A., Brown, R.T., Wynne, M.E., & Schleser, R. (1987). Piagetian conservation and response to cognitive therapy in attention deficit disordered children. *Journal of Child Psychology and Psychiatry and Allied Disciplines, 28,* 755–764.

Breit, M., Kaplan, S.L., Gauthier, B., & Weinhold, C. (1984). The dry-bed method for the treatment of enuresis: A failure to duplicate previous reports. *Child and Family Behavior Therapy, 6,* 17–23.

Brown, R.T. (1987). Attention deficit disorders. In C. Reynolds & H. Mann (Eds.), *Encyclopedia of special education* (pp. 145–148). New York: John Wiley & Sons.

Brown, R.T., Borden, K.A., Schleser, R., Clingerman, S.R., & Orenczuk, S. (1985). The performance of attention deficit disordered and normal children on conservation tasks. *Journal of Genetic Psychology, 146,* 535–540.

Carr, E.G., & Durand, V.M. (1985). Reducing behavior problems through functional communication training. *Journal of Applied Behavior Analysis, 18,* 111–126.

Carr, E.G., Newsom, C.D., & Binkoff, J.A. (1976). Escape as a factor in the aggressive behavior of two retarded children. *Journal of Applied Behavior Analysis, 13,* 101–117.

Chertock, S.L., & Bornstein, P.H. (1979). Covert modeling treatment of children's dental fears. *Child Behavior Therapy, 1,* 249–255.

Cobb, D.E., & Evans, J.R. (1981). The use of biofeedback techniques with school-aged children exhibiting behavioral and/or learning problems. *Journal of Abnormal Child Psychology, 9,* 251–281.

Cohen, N.J., Sullivan, J., Minde, K., Novak, C., & Helwig, C. (1981). Evaluation of the relative effectiveness of methylphenidate and cognitive behavior modification in the treatment of kindergarten-aged hyperactive children. *Journal of Abnormal Child Psychology, 9,* 43–54.

Doleys, D.M. (1977). Behavioral treatments for nocturnal enuresis in children: A review of the recent literature. *Psychological Bulletin, 84,* 30–54.

Doleys, D.M., Ciminero, A.R., Tollison, J.W., Williams, C.L., & Wells, K.C. (1977). Dry-bed training and retention control training: A comparison. *Behavior Therapy, 8,* 541–548.

Dorsey, M.F., Iwata, B.A., Reid, D.H., & Davis, P.A. (1982). Protective equipment: Continuous and contingent application in the treatment of self-injurious behavior. *Journal of Applied Behavior Analysis, 15,* 217–230.

Douglas, V.I. (1983). Attentional and cognitive problems. In M. Rutter (Ed.), *Developmental neuropsychiatry* (pp. 280–329). New York: Guilford Press.

Dubey, D.R., & Kaufman, K.F. (1978). Home management of hyperkinetic children. *Journal of Pediatrics, 93,* 141–146.

Dubey, D.R., O'Leary, S.G., & Kaufman, K.F. (1983). Training parents of hyperactive children in child management: A comparative outcome study. *Journal of Abnormal Child Psychology, 11,* 229–246.

Dumas, J.E. (1984). Interactional correlates of treatment outcome in behavioral parent training. *Journal of Consulting and Clinical Psychology, 52,* 946–954.

Dumas, J.E., & Wahler, R.G. (1985). Indiscriminate mothering as a contextual factor in aggressive-oppositional child behavior: "Damned if you do and damned if you don't." *Journal of Abnormal Child Psychology, 13,* 1–17.

Eason, L.J., White, M.J., & Newsom, C. (1982). Generalized reduction of self-stimulatory behavior: An effect of teaching appropriate play to autistic children. *Analysis and Intervention in Developmental Disabilities, 2*, 157–169.

Emery, R.E. (1982). Interparental conflict and the children of discord and divorce. *Psychological Bulletin, 92*, 310–330.

Ferster, C.B. (1961). Positive reinforcement and behavioral deficits of autistic children. *Child Development, 32*, 437–456.

Fincham, F.D., & Spettell, C. (1984). The acceptability of dry bed training and urine alarm training as treatments of nocturnal enuresis. *Behavior Therapy, 15*, 388–394.

Fox, J.E., & Houston, B.K. (1981). Efficacy of self-instructional training for reducing children's anxiety in an evaluative situation. *Behaviour Research and Therapy, 19*, 509–515.

Foxx, R.M., & Azrin, N.H. (1972). Restitution: A method of eliminating aggressive-disruptive behavior of retarded and brain damaged patients. *Behaviour Research and Therapy, 10*, 15–27.

Ginther, L.J., & Roberts, M.C. (1982). A test of mastery versus coping modeling in the reduction of children's dental fears. *Child and Family Behavior Therapy, 4*, 41–51.

Gordon, R., Handleman, J.S., & Harris, S.L. (1986). The effects of contingent versus noncontingent running on the out-of-seat behavior of an autistic boy. *Child and Family Behavior Therapy, 8*, 337–344.

Graziano, A.M., De Giovanni, I.S., & Garcia, K.A. (1979). Behavioral treatment of children's fears: A review. *Psychological Bulletin, 86*, 804–830.

Graziano, A.M., & Mooney, K.C. (1982). Behavioral treatment of "night fears" in children: Maintenance of improvement at 2-1/2- to 3-year follow-up. *Journal of Consulting and Clinical Psychology, 50*, 598–599.

Griest, D.L., & Wells, K.C. (1983). Behavioral family therapy with conduct disorders in children. *Behavior Therapy, 14*, 37–53.

Harris, S.L. (1983). *Families of the developmentally disabled: A guide to behavioral intervention*. Elmsford, NY: Pergamon Press.

Harris, S.L., & Ersner-Hershfield, R. (1978). The behavioral suppression of seriously disruptive behavior in psychotic and retarded patients: A review of punishment and its alternatives. *Psychological Bulletin, 85*, 1352–1375.

Harris, S.L., & Ferrari, M. (1983). Developmental factors in child behavior therapy. *Behavior Therapy, 14*, 54–72.

Heffer, R.W., & Kelley, M.L. (1987). Mothers' acceptance of behavioral interventions for children: The influence of parent race and income. *Behavior Therapy, 18*, 153–163.

Hinshaw, S.P., Henker, B., & Whalen, C.K. (1984a). Cognitive-behavioral and pharmacologic interventions for hyperactive boys: Comparative and combined effects. *Journal of Consulting and Clinical Psychology, 52*, 739–749.

Hinshaw, S.P., Henker, B., & Whalen, C.K. (1984b). Self-control in hyperactive boys in anger-inducing situations: Effects of cognitive-behavioral training and of methylphenidate. *Journal of Abnormal Child Psychology, 12*, 55–77.

Houts, A.C., Whelan, J.P., & Peterson, J.K. (1987). Filmed versus live delivery of full-spectrum home training for primary enuresis: Presenting the information is not enough. *Journal of Consulting and Clinical Psychology, 55*, 902–906.

Johnson, W.L., Baumeister, A.A., Penland, M.J., & Inwald, C. (1982). Experimental analysis of self-injurious, stereotypic, and collateral behavior of retarded persons: Effects of overcorrection and reinforcement of alternative responding. *Analysis and Intervention in Developmental Disabilities, 2*, 41–66.

Kazdin, A.E. (1984). Acceptability of aversive procedures and medication as treatment alternatives for deviant child behavior. *Journal of Abnormal Child Psychology, 12*, 289–302.

Kazdin, A.E. (1987). *Conduct disorders in childhood and adolescence*. Newbury Park, CA: Sage Publications.

Kazdin, A.E., Esveldt-Dawson, K., French, N.H., & Unis, A.S. (1987). Problem-solving skills training and relationship therapy in the treatment of antisocial child behavior. *Journal of Consulting and Clinical Psychology, 55*, 76–85.

Kendall, P.C. (1985). Toward a cognitive-behavioral model of child psychopathology and a critique of related interventions. *Journal of Abnormal Child Psychology, 13*, 357–372.

Kendall, P.C., & Braswell, L. (1982). Cognitive-behavioral self-control therapy for children: A components analysis. *Journal of Consulting and Clinical Psychology, 50*, 672–689.

Kendall, P.C., & Braswell, L. (1985). *Cognitive behavioral therapy with impulsive children*. New York: Guilford Press.

Kimmel, H.D., & Kimmel, E.C. (1970). An instrumental conditioning method for the treatment of enuresis. *Journal of Behavior Therapy and Experimental Psychiatry, 1*, 121–123.

Kirigin, K.A., Braukmann, C.J., Atwater, J.D., & Wolf, M.M. (1982). An evaluation of teaching-family (Achievement Place) group homes for juvenile offenders. *Journal of Applied Behavior Analysis, 15*, 1–16.

Koegel, R.L., Schreibman, L., Johnson, J., O'Neill, R.E., & Dunlap, G. (1984). Collateral effects of parent training on families with autistic children. In R.F. Dangel & R.A. Polster (Eds.), *Parent training: Foundations of research and practice* (pp. 358–378). New York: Guilford Press.

Kolko, D.J. (1987). Simplified inpatient treatment of nocturnal enuresis in psychiatrically disturbed children. *Behavior Therapy, 18*, 99–112.

Little, V.L., & Kendall, P.C. (1979). Cognitive-behavioral interventions with delinquents: Problem solving, role-taking and self-control. In P.C. Kendall & S.D. Hollon (Eds.), *Cognitive-behavioral interventions* (pp. 81–116). New York: Academic Press.

Lochman, J.E., Burch, P.R., Curry, J.F., & Lampron, L.B. (1984). Treatment and generalization effects of cognitive-behavioral and goal-setting interventions with aggressive boys. *Journal of Consulting and Clinical Psychology, 52,* 915–916.

Lovaas, O.I. (1987). Behavioral treatment and normal educational and intellectual functioning in young autistic children. *Journal of Consulting and Clinical Psychology, 55,* 3–9.

Lovaas, O.I., Berberich, J.P., Perloff, B.F., & Schaeffer, B. (1966). Acquisition of imitative speech by schizophrenic children. *Science, 151,* 705–707.

McGee, G.G., Krantz, P.J., & McClannahan, L.E. (1985). The facilitative effects of incidental teaching on preposition use by autistic children. *Journal of Applied Behavior Analysis, 18,* 17–31.

McIntyre, T.J., Bornstein, P.H., Isaacs, C.D., Woody, D.J., Bornstein, M.T., Clucas, T.J., & Long, G. (1983). Naturalistic observation of conduct-disordered children: An archival analysis. *Behavior Therapy, 14,* 375–385.

McMurray, N.E., Bell, R.J., Fusillo, A.D., Morgan, M., & Wright, F.A. (1986). Relationship between locus of control and effects of coping strategies and dental stress in children. *Child and Family Behavior Therapy, 8,* 1–17.

Meichenbaum, D., & Turk, D. (1976). *The cognitive-behavioral management of anxiety, depression, and pain.* New York: Brunner/Mazel.

Melamed, B.G., & Siegel, L.J. (1975). Reduction of anxiety in children facing surgery by modeling. *Journal of Consulting and Clinical Psychology, 43,* 511–521.

Mowrer, O.H., & Mowrer, W. (1938). Enuresis: A method for its study and treatment. *American Journal of Orthopsychiatry, 8,* 436–447.

Nocella, J., & Kaplan, R. (1982). Training children to cope with dental treatment. *Journal of Pediatric Psychology, 7,* 175–178.

Odom, S.L., & Strain, P.S. (1986). A comparison of peer-initiation and teacher-antecedent interventions for promoting reciprocal social interactions of autistic preschoolers. *Journal of Applied Behavior Analysis, 19,* 59–71.

O'Leary, K.D. (1980). Pills or skills for hyperactive children. *Journal of Applied Behavior Analysis, 13,* 191–204.

O'Leary, K.D., Pelham, W.E., Rosenbaum, A., & Price, G.H. (1976). Behavioral treatment of hyperkinetic children: An experimental evaluation of its usefulness. *Clinical Pediatrics, 15,* 510–515.

Ollendick, T.H. (1979). Fear reduction techniques with children. In M. Hersen, R.M. Eisler, & P.M. Miller (Eds.), *Progress in behavior modification* (Vol. 8, pp. 127–168). New York: Academic Press.

Ollendick, T.H., & Cerney, J.A. (1981). *Clinical behavior therapy with children.* New York: Plenum Press.

Patterson, G.R., Chamberlain, P., & Reid, J.B. (1982). A comparative evaluation of a parent-training program. *Behavior Therapy, 13,* 638–650.

Patterson, G.R., Reid, J.B., Jones, R.R., & Conger, R.E. (1975). *A social learning approach to family intervention: Vol. 1. Families with aggressive children.* Eugene, OR: Castilia.

Raymer, R., & Poppen, R. (1985). Behavioral relaxation training with hyperactive children. *Journal of Behavior Therapy and Experimental Psychiatry, 16,* 309–316.

Rios, J.D., & Gutierrez, J.M. (1985/86). Parent training with non-traditional families: An unresolved issue. *Child and Family Behavior Therapy, 7,* 33–45.

Rolider, A., & Van Houten, R. (1986). Effects of degree of awakening and the criterion for advancing awakening on the treatment of bed wetting. *Education and Treatment of Children, 9,* 135–141.

Ross, D.M., & Ross, S.A. (1982). *Hyperactivity.* New York: John Wiley & Sons.

Sainato, D.M., Strain, P.S., Lefebvre, D., & Rapp, N. (1987). Facilitating transition times with handicapped preschool children: A comparison between peer-mediated and antecedent prompt procedures. *Journal of Applied Behavior Analysis, 20,* 285–291.

Sheslow, P.V., Bondy, A.S., & Nelson, R.O. (1982). Comparison of graduated exposure, verbal coping skills, and their combination in the treatment of children's fear of the dark. *Child and Family Behavior Therapy, 4,* 33–45.

Strauss, C.C. (1987). Anxiety. In M. Hersen & V. Van Hasselt (Eds.), *Behavior therapy with children and adolescents: A clinical approach* (pp. 109–136). New York: John Wiley & Sons.

Taylor, P.D., & Turner, R.K. (1975). A clinical trial of continuous, intermittent, and overlearning "bell and pad" treatments for nocturnal enuresis. *Behaviour Research and Therapy, 13,* 281–293.

Ultee, C.A., Griffioen, D., & Schellekens, J. (1982). The reduction of anxiety in children: A comparison of the effects of "systematic desensitization in vitro" and "systematic desensitization in vivo." *Behaviour Research and Therapy, 20,* 61–67.

Van Hasselt, V.B., Hersen, M., Bellack, A.S., Rosenbloom, N.D., & Lamparski, D. (1979). Tripartite assessment of the effects of systematic desensitization in a multiphobic child: An experimental analysis. *Journal of Behavior Therapy and Experimental Psychiatry, 10,* 51–55.

Wahler, R.G., & Dumas, J.E. (1986). Maintenance factors in coercive mother–child interactions: The compliance and predictibility hypotheses. *Journal of Applied Behavior Analysis, 19,* 13–22.

Wahler, R.G., & Fox, J.J. (1981). Setting events in applied behavior analysis: Toward a conceptual and methodological expansion. *Journal of Applied Behavior Analysis, 14,* 327–338.

Webster-Stratton, C. (1985). Predictors of treatment outcome in parent training for conduct disordered children. *Behavior Therapy, 16,* 223–243.

Whalen, C.K., Henker, B., & Hinshaw, S.P. (1985). Cognitive-behavioral therapies for hyperactive children: Premises, problems, and prospects. *Journal of Abnormal Child Psychology, 13*, 391–410.

Wolf, M.M., Braukmann, C.J., & Ramp, K.A. (1987). Serious delinquent behavior as part of a significantly handicapping condition: Cures and supportive environments. *Journal of Applied Behavior Analysis, 20*, 347–359.

CHAPTER 32

ADVANCES IN PSYCHOANALYTIC PSYCHOTHERAPY WITH CHILDREN

Kevin O'Connor
Anna C. Lee

Psychoanalytic treatment of children, originally rooted in the psychoanalysis of adults, has truly come into its own since its inception with Freud's analysis of Little Hans (1905). It has acquired its own tenets, an accumulation of theories and techniques, and a body of knowledge that extends beyond its traditionally unidimensional framework to include advances in related scientific disciplines, including developmental and social psychology, pediatrics, and the neurosciences (Chess, 1988). Within the past decade, and since the initial review offered by the present authors, advances in child analytic therapy have burgeoned. This chapter reviews the major changes that have occurred during the past decade within the field of child analytic therapy. Chief among the concerns of the present authors is the relevance of advances made in four areas: (a) the interaction of child analysis with related disciplines—specifically, the contributions of child analysis to general analytic theory and practice and, in turn, the contribution of infant studies to the theory and practice of child analysis, (b) the debates and issues that remain unresolved within the field of child analysis, (c) the adaptations of the analytic parameters and technical advances that have been proposed, and (d) the treatment of children with

special needs, that is, those presenting emotional compromise resulting from either innate deficits or unique external circumstances (e.g., trauma, adoption, abuse, etc.). These children, manifesting disorders different from the neurotic disorders for which analysis was originally conceptualized, form the nucleus of subjects for the widening scope of child analytic therapy.

INTERACTION OF CHILD ANALYSIS WITH OTHER DISCIPLINES

We begin by reviewing the contributions of child analysis to psychoanalysis in general, as seen by current writers in the field and its notable differences from adult psychoanalysis. We direct our focus to child analysis because it presents the most organized and coherent body of theory and practice that underpins all other modalities of child analytic therapy. All the while we recognize that, underlying all modes of treatment with children, is the central goal of assisting the child in resolving conflicts that result in developmental fixation, regression, and so forth toward the resumption of normative development.

Contributions of Child Analysis to General Analysis

Though child analysis originated, unexpectedly, from the treatment of Little Hans by his father, as supervised by Freud, it rapidly came to maturity as a discipline, such that by 1933 its contributions to adult psychoanalysis were pronounced. Several schools of child analysis have evolved since its inception, including the classical, Freudian school following the teachings of Anna Freud, the Kleinian school, and, more recently, the British object relations school as expounded by Winnicott and others. We shall highlight more closely, however, the writings of Anna Freud because, of the three, she has been the most influential theoretician in the United States. The reason for this historical trend seems to lie in the objections raised by child analysts in the U.S. to the Kleinian focus on *verbalizing* oedipal and preoedipal interpretations to the young child in what seems, objectively, to be premature at best and verbally assaultive at worst (Harley, 1986).

In summarizing the historical beginnings and contributions of child analysis, E. J. Anthony (1986) noted that while Freud happened on child analysis quite by accident and was initially skeptical of its efficacy, he came to appreciate its eventual role in psychoanalysis in general. Indeed, Freud (1905) noted that (a) its contributions would become even more important as time went on; (b) theoretically, it had become invaluable in giving unequivocal information on problems that remained unresolved in the analyses of adults and alerted the adult analyst to possible errors in his or her work; (c) it permitted us to observe neurosis in the making when the picture was still relatively uncontaminated by subsequent psychological developments; (d) it could be applied to children who had no clear-cut neurotic symptoms but were moody, refractory, inattentive, nervous, anorexic, or sleepless—indications that went well beyond the simple phobia that had initiated the whole child analytic movement; and, lastly, (e) of even greater importance was the fact that if children with incipient neuroses were treated analytically, adult analysis might become unnecessary. A child analysis could then become "an excellent method of prophylaxis" (Anthony, 1986, p. 69).

In writing about the benefits of child analysis, Chused (1988) reminded us of the following:

> Analysis is not the only form of child psychotherapy; criteria of analyzability and whether or not one can or should analyze children with major ego deviations remain important issues for child analysts. Analysis

is quite a specific treatment for individuals whose development and functions are handicapped primarily by unconscious internal conflicts, not only by environmental interferences or by structural deficits, except when the latter are the results of fixations secondary to retreat from conflict. Neurotic individuals also can be helped by new ways of dealing with conflicts. However, if the therapy is aimed at the resolution of conflict (with an underlying assumption that with conflict resolution, development will resume of its own accord), then, to that end, there is nothing so effective as the development of a transference neurosis within the analytic setting. And if an analyst believes that intense transference (or a transference neurosis) is essential for a successful analysis, he needs to learn what interferes with its emergence and what promotes its development. (Chused, 1988, pp. 62–63)

With regard to differences between child and adult analysis, the reader is advised to keep in mind the initial resistance of classical adult analysts, including Freud and Anna Freud, to viewing the child as a suitable candidate for analysis. Indeed, the child seems unaware of his or her suffering, is ill prepared and unmotivated to get better, hardly able to delay gratification, not yet independent of his or her parents, unable to sustain a therapeutic alliance, nonintrospective, incapable of forming free associations, inept at working through or working with dreams, and scarcely able to experience a transference neurosis that can be systematically interpreted. Furthermore, the child shows anaclitically off-putting tendencies such as eschewing the couch, maintaining face-to-face contact, keeping on the go, and making predominant use of nonverbal communications (Anthony, 1986). Eventually, however, Freud became convinced that not only do children become more successful analysands than adults but that the child's unconscious urge to complete development represented a stronger therapeutic factor than the conscious motivation of the adult patient to get well. Indeed, the success of child analysis in treating the apparently unanalyzable has contributed, in large measure, to the success of analytic treatment with other patients hitherto considered unanalyzable such as delinquents, borderlines, psychotics, and those with predominantly narcissistic character pathology. That such endeavors have required the use of "parameters" of the basic treatment model forms the basis for much debate about whether or not these adaptations are genuine psychoanalysis or psychoanalytically oriented psychotherapy.

Abrams (1988, pp. 260–261) succinctly underscores a major difference between adult and child analysis when he noted that the adult uses the experiences of the analysis to revive the past, whereas children also use the experience of the analysis to establish structures that will prepare them for the future and enable them to deal with their pathogenic past more effectively. Because children also use the analytic setting for new experiences in the service of emerging developmental organizations, this can often cause bewildering cross-currents, forward and backward.

Child analysis's unique contributions to general psychoanalysis is summarized by Anthony (1986) in a number of excellent points:

1.   There is the area of the "real" relationship in the analytic situation which is an acceptable and workable phenomenon in child analysis when, from time to time, the analyst, as the child perceives him, seems to step out of his transference role to become a real person, belonging to a real world, and obviously functioning in a real manner. . . Child analysis, through Winnicott, has demonstrated that there is not only an internal analyst and an external analyst, but, in some intermediate area, a transitional analyst who can mediate between inside and outside, between fantasy and reality, and, in the situation of mutual play, can help the child patient to deal with his conflictual situation more creatively. (Anthony, 1986, p. 73)

2.   Recognizing the role of the "real" environment of the child (i.e., that of his or her family) is crucial to the work of the child analyst even if he or she has subscribed wholeheartedly to the encapsulation of the analytic situation. Indeed, child analysts span the spectrum from those who almost totally exclude the environment from the intimacy of the treatment to those who include it, even within some sessions. Anthony argued that those analysts who include the environment are able to learn something of the complex interplay between the home situation and the analytic situation, and this knowledge makes it easier to understand the child's behavior in analysis given the fact that children habitually externalize their intrapsychic conflicts. In fact, children often have a limited capacity for internalization while possessing an inordinate capacity for externalization; however, there are many adults who present in a similar fashion, notably those borderline cases where it may be equally important to take into account not only internal fantasies but current life conflicts and upsets. Child analysis can aid in the understanding of the process of working analytically while keeping an eye on the "real" environment in which the patient lives.

3.   The role of free association, an integral part of the analytic situation, shows a wide variability among adult patients, with some falling into it readily, others learning to do so during the course of treatment, and others never acquiring it at all. The child patient, on the other hand, makes use of both verbal and nonverbal activities to communicate his or her internal reality, moving from imaginary doll play to drawing, acting, and so on, all the while expressing free associations through these different media. The discerning therapist can thereby follow the chain of ideas within a given session. Thus, the nonverbal activities of the adult patient on the couch can continue a train of associations even as the verbal communication has ceased. Therefore, the child analyst may be in a unique position to help train adult analysts to observe this significant form of nonverbal communication that they often overlook while attending to their client's verbalization (Anthony, 1977).

4.   Aspects of transference have also been examined uniquely by child analysts, according to Anthony, inasmuch as development dictates for the child his or her need for the actual parents and, by extension, his or her capacity to develop transference neurosis and/or transferential reactions. Thus, it appears that although the child experiences the greatest need for the actual parent during the earliest years, this trend shifts during the school years and adolescence. The gradient for transference seems to be the opposite of this: As the actual parents become less essential to the daily life of the child, the psychic recreation on the parent in the transference is increased. This suggests that transference is not entirely a function of the repressed unconscious operating at the culmination of the nuclear complex: The availability of the actual parents and their necessity to the child also play important roles. The transference from deeply buried oedipal parents to the contemporary parents and then onto the person of the analyst is also well investigated by child analysts, providing potentially fresh insights applicable to adult cases.

5.   Lastly, the appearance of true insight, as in the understanding of causality and holding some sense of responsibility for one's inner life, is not expectable in the analysis of children, given their limited capacity for operational thinking. Though they may manifest a diffuse mixture of knowing and not knowing affectively, they do not recognize it cognitively, and therein lies a major difference between the analysis of child and adult patients. But as Anthony pointed out, "in both child and adult analysis, the analyst's insights into himself and into his patient are helpful to the ongoing analytic process even when the patient has failed to acquire any insights for himself" (Anthony, 1986, p. 78).

Contribution of Related Disciplines to Child Analysis

Child analysis has continued to grow and develop by incorporating information from other disciplines. In recent years, the burgeoning of related fields of psychotherapy, that is, family and marital therapy, has also exerted some influence on widening the scope of the field of inquiry when working with children. The choice to include data about the child's behavior within the family constellation and elsewhere (as in school or in other arenas) continues to remain an issue of debate that varies according to the strictness with which analysts abide by the rule of abstinence. As it is beyond the scope of this review to explore these areas at length, suffice it to state that the child analyst today would do well to be aware of the usefulness of other modes of psychotherapy that might serve as useful adjuncts to his or her own analysis of the child.

The findings of observational studies of infant development, especially those examining the area of the development of the child's emotional reactions from his or her earliest days of life, have also contributed significantly to child analysis. Of particular interest to the present authors were those studies focusing on the innate capacities of infants to engage in affective communication with their caretakers, for engagement with their social and inanimate environments (including interacting with others and maintaining proximity to them, engaging in interactions with caretakers that result in mutual delight, and acting upon objects), and in satisfaction of internal goals (e.g., maintaining homeostasis, establishing a feeling of security, experiencing positive emotions, and controlling negative emotions). Their accomplishment of the latter goals arouses different emotional states, depending on their success or failure, which include delight, anger, frustration, and withdrawal. Infants, moreover, are now seen as active agents in mutual affective exchange with their environment during the process of accomplishing these goals, often drawing upon the emotional expression of the other, that is, his or her mother, to form an appreciation of the event and using such to guide his or her action. Although much of the work is still speculative, an accumulating body of knowledge demarcates ways in which infants attempt, in quite active ways, to engage in self-directed or other-directed regulatory behaviors to cope with the internal states stimulated by interactive exchanges with their caretakers.

In his excellent summary of recent research findings of the development of emotional responsiveness in infants, Tronick (1989), citing the work of other notable infant researchers (Emde, 1983; Lewis, 1987; Stern, 1985) as well as his own, stressed the importance of early exchanges within infant–mother dyads that can have long-lasting consequences for the infant's emotional responsiveness, later defensive styles, and possible psychopathology in later childhood and/or adulthood. In discussing whether or not an infant's regulatory style of affective reparation can have lifelong implications, Tronick asserted, "Given the transformational nature of development, it would be foolish to assert that the infant's regulatory style and representations determine those of the adult, but it would be equally foolish to assert that they are without long-term influence. Certainly the way in which the adult-as-child regulated and represented the circumstances and the emotions he or she experienced accrue to the adult" (Tronick, 1989, p. 118).

More directly related to psychoanalytic metapsychology, Lichtenberg (1981) reviewed neonatal studies in light of existing theories, including drive theory, ego psychology, affect theory, and object relations theory. He then draws upon the findings of these studies to critically reevaluate four factors that have been previously suggested as important in the development of self and other. These include: (a) the existence of genetically endowed schemata that enable the infant to organize his or her experience gradually into units that have elements of self and other, affect, and cognition; (b) in his or her experience of the other, the individual shifts from a tendency to generalize to a tendency to particularize; (c) each human being experiences his- or herself in a context that includes an object, an affect, and elements of perception and cognition that develop in an interrelated way; and (d) crucial in the development of self and other is the polarity between schematic formalism and richness of experience, a continuum that can be used to distinguish between psychopathology and health. Although all human beings probably pass through an inborn schemata or developmental pathway, the full potential experience involves far more richness, complexity, and subtlety than a mere ritual of passage.

ONGOING DEBATES AND ISSUES IN CHILD ANALYSIS

Having reviewed the contributions of child analysis to related disciplines and the equally significant contributions of those disciplines to child analysis, we now examine the changes that have taken place in child analysis and psychotherapy in the recent decade and find several consistent trends. Chief among these are departures from the classical views about the nature of the working alliance, involving the parents in the treatment, as well as what constitutes true transference neurosis and transferential reactions in children. Harley (1986), for instance, clarified some changes that have occurred in several still debated issues, including the following: the child's capacity for working within the analytic frame of abstinence, the necessity of maintaining a positive transference between analyst and child at the risk of excessive gratifications, the tendency among some child analysts to extend the term *transference* to habitual modes of relating, that is, to character traits, and the extension of the term *transference* into the analytic situation of the child's current relationships to the primary objects.

Throughout the 1960s and 1970s, for example, lively debates occurred between child analysts about the child's capacity for developing classical transferences inasmuch as the child's parents, the original objects with whom the child's infantile relationships were formed, around whom his or her infantile relationships were woven, were still an integral part of the child's life. These concerns were first addressed by Anna Freud who prevailed as the dominant influence on child analysis in the United States. She later modified her position (A. Freud, 1965) to observe that a transference neurosis can develop in children, but not to the same extent as the transference neurosis does in the adult. Today, child analysts continue to discuss its too infrequent appearance with varying degrees of agreement (Chused, 1988; Sandler, Kennedy, & Tyson, 1980; Harley, 1986; Tyson & Tyson, 1986). Chused, for one, very clearly suggested the possibility of transferences occurring in children although they do differ in some respects from adult transferences. As he pointed out,

> In children, as in adults, Oedipal conflicts are a significant feature of the transference neurosis, with these conflicts reflecting not only pathogenic experiences during the Oedipal period but also organizing pathology derived from earlier preoedipal phases. When the developmental level of the child's ego functions, including cognitive development, affect tolerance, narcissistic vulnerability, and maturity of defenses are taken into account, as well as the nature of the child's attachment to this current object [R.L. Tyson & P. Tyson, 1986], a thoughtful analytic procedure, with strict attention to the analysis of resistance and to countertransference interferences, can lead to a full-blown transference neurosis in the child patient. (Chused, 1988, pp. 55–56)

It appears that the transference can and does develop regardless of the developmental phase the child is negotiating and/or the focus of the child's libidinal energies. It is true, however, that with advancing age the child develops a greater ability to internalize and that this, in turn, facilitates the development of a transference neurosis. The greater the child's ability to internalize, the more flexible the analyst can be in interpreting the child's aggressive strivings and fantasies. The more active the interpretive process, the more likely the child will be to develop a transference reaction.

The child's cognitive advancement seems, in some ways, more important to the child's development of a transference neurosis than does the child's independence from primary objects. After all, children do not come to analysis seeking to find gratifying objects (Chused, 1988). "Potentially gratifying objects are frequently available in our patients' lives; the problem is the patient's inability to be gratified" (Chused, 1988, p. 75). The child does not seek to replace the parents through the analysis; rather, the child must learn how to overcome unconscious conflicts over gratification which originate in past experiences and are now incorporated into the child's psychic structure. Thus the child may remain dependent on his or her parents while developing a transference relationship with the analyst through which the past experiences and related unconscious conflicts can be examined.

Related to the issue of transference is that of countertransference, a technical aspect of the treatment that is less discussed among child analysts but no less important. Thus, child analysis follows the trend of adult analysis in regarding the reactions of the analyst as less central to the work, although Freud described countertransference as an unfavorable contaminant in the understanding or development of the transference proper. With child analysands the reactions of the analyst are likely to be be even more intense and absorbing than those experienced in adult analysis, given the heightened resistance many children are likely to experience to the analytic process. Their refractoriness thereby renders more heated the interaction with the analyst. This is particularly evident when one considers the child's very active need to treat the analyst as a new, real object rather than one of transference. Marcus (1980) offered several helpful comments in understanding countertransferences as they inevitably occur in the analysis of children. He noted, for instance, that they may occur in specifically different ways depending on the child's developmental phase; that is, preoedipal and oedipal children may arouse different reactions in the analyst. Furthermore, countertransferences are likely to differ depending on the phase of the analysis as well as the child's unique reaction to each. He concluded with a rejoinder that countertransference "may be viewed the same way as all unconscious mechanisms: overdetermined in origin, uncontrollable at the source, but useful when the information is integrated by a receptive ego" (Marcus, 1980, p. 297).

More recently, Bernstein and Glenn (1988) distinguished between the various emotional responses of the analyst to his or her patient and the parents, urging the limiting of the term *countertransference* to the analyst's transference reactions to the transferences of his or her patients or their parents. Furthermore, they distinguished countertransferences from transference, identification, narcissistic attachment and responses, including empathy, to patients or parents as real people. The latter also included signal reactions or more intense responses to the behavior of patients or their parents, and failure to understand the patient due to differences in the developmental level of the patient and analyst.

Child analysts continue to debate the belief that the gender of the analyst plays an important role in the development of transference phenomena. Traditionally, many contend that, like adult analysis, the analyst's gender should make little difference in the appearance of the transference neurosis in the technically correct analysis, one where strict neutrality is adhered to. Tyson (1980) clearly articulated the opposing view, reminding us that the analyst's gender "may influence the content of nontransference configurations such as the use of the analyst as a figure for displacement or as a real object to accomplish a developmental step. Second, the gender of the analyst may contribute to an evolution of transference and countertransference manifestations, and this influence may be felt more at some phases of the analysis than at others. Third, the gender of the analyst may assume more importance for the child at certain developmental stages than it does at others, which may then be reflected in the transference" (Tyson, 1980, p. 321). Given the child's proclivity for using the real aspects of the analytic situation, he or she will likely use the analyst for expression and gratification of transferences as well as developmental and real needs. Indeed, he or she may use the gender of the analyst to fulfill a developmental need that may be inadequately fulfilled elsewhere, a need that may be more important at some developmental stages than at others. Dealing with the real factors of the person of the analyst, be it gender, age, race or other physical features, may affect the child's initial reaction to the analyst. With the development of the transference neurosis, how-

ever, the increasing stress on the revival of past conflicts with concomitant need to rework them will eventually render less important the issue of the analyst's gender. Instead, conflicts experienced vis-à-vis all prior levels of development, along with those related to both parents, will find eventual expression in the transference. In this regard, preoedipal and oedipal configurations are likely to pull for different reactions in child analysands and can often be complicated by the gender of the analyst. Some preference is likely to be given to those conflicts with the parent of the same gender as the analyst. Tyson reiterated, however, that all this notwithstanding, "the primary motivating force behind the content and evolution of transference manifestations stems from the pressure of the child's intrapsychic world. These manifestations are not necessarily influenced by the analyst's gender, but when this becomes a factor, this influence may result either in an attenuation of some aspect of the transference, or in an enhancement of it" (Tyson, 1980, p. 337).

Still another aspect of the analytic situation that causes continued debate among child analysts is the value of reconstruction in child analysis. Kennedy (1971), for instance, reiterated the child's greater concern for solving his or her problems in the here and now rather than for examining the past. Harley (1986) countered this observation, however, with a greater need to help the child understand his or her conflicts and work them through. She highlights the indispensable value of reconstruction of the affective components as well as proposing three particular useful concepts about reconstruction in child analysis:

> The first is the fact that not only is the integrative function essential to the patient's understanding of reconstruction, but reconstruction itself contributes to the development of the integrative function through the linkages thus made, something of special consideration in terms of fostering the child's development. [Secondly], . . . while it is the analytic process that makes possible the reconstruction, the latter, in turn, promotes the analytic process, thus enabling us to amplify the reconstruction. And [thirdly] . . . reconstruction may entail the near or even immediate past, especially so in children for whom time subjectively proceeds at a much slower pace, and who are more prone to quick denials and repressions. (Harley, 1986, p. 143)

Like transference and its associated therapeutic alliance, reconstruction is useful if maintained and promoted because all three interact, have connotations for the theory of analytic technique, and have been subjected repeatedly to scrutiny from many different perspectives. Given this new understanding of the child's cognitive and developmental capacities (Rees, 1978; Zelman, Samuels, & Abrams, 1985) and the strength of the therapeutic alliance to withstand the negative transference, the analyst is afforded greater freedom to interpret the positive transference resistance when indicated.

PARAMETER ADAPTATIONS AND TECHNICAL ADVANCES

Parameter Adaptations

The debates among child analysts extend beyond the theoretical to include adaptations and modifications of the so-called "parameters" of the psychoanalytic model that have been utilized in the treatment of child analysands. As Harley (1986) pointed out, Marianne Kris distinguishes between those adaptations of technique that were designed to attain compatibility with the basic analytic model and modifications of the technique that, depending on their nature and degree, might even bring out disruption of the analytic process.

Chief among these modifications would be those efforts on the part of the analyst aimed at changing the external environment of the child, including advice to parents, educational measures intended to correct the child's misconceptions or sexual confusions before the underlying fantasies have been explored and sufficiently analyzed, and providing undue gratifications (Harley, 1986, p. 130). The handling of the parents and their need to know poses a particular dilemma with regard to the wish to maintain analytic neutrality and encapsulation of the analysis. As already suggested, analysts disagree about the extent and degree of the involvement of the parents (Bernstein & Glenn, 1988; Chused, 1988; Harley, 1986), with some falling clearly on the side of inclusion of the parents in analytic efforts. This is predicated on the observation that a child's parents, especially if he or she is still negotiating preoedipal and oedipal issues, are so central to his or her life that it would be tantamount to ignoring basic aspects of development to exclude them from the treatment in a focused, organized way. They play a vital role in supporting the treatment and can often sabotage analytic efforts in their own unconscious struggles to prove themselves the more successful parent in competition with the analyst. However consciously endorsing they may be of their child's analysis, parents may even compete unconsciously with their own child for the analyst's attention. Single parents in this day and age are often needy

themselves of direction and guidance in their child-rearing efforts, and may seek the counsel of the analyst accordingly. Marcus (1980) discussed these issues persuasively when he wrote:

> The child analyst must rely on the parents' motivation and insight to support both the initial phase and the carrying through of the analysis to a satisfactory termination. The parents must serve as the auxiliary ego for the child, not only initially, but also in maintaining support for a therapeutic alliance, especially when the hostile elements of the transference appear and the child's ego is entangled in resistance. The parents' help is the sine qua non for child and adolescent analysis. If parents side with the child's resistance, an abrupt interruption is inevitable.
>
> In later stages of the analysis, parental understanding of the changing attitude in the child is necessary to avoid the parents' sabotaging the analysis when the young patient develops a strong positive (affectionate) transference to the analyst. If parents feel competitiveness or respond to the taunting rejection by the child of one or both of them, the analysis may be discontinued. The child or adolescent often acts out of a wish for developmental separation and a defensive independence. Parents under this form of attack may aggravate the patient's loyalty conflicts between parents and analyst. (Marcus, 1980, p. 294)

Formulation, Organization, and Delivery of Interpretations

Interpretation is the cornerstone of the analytic process. For this reason the authors have chosen to dedicate a large portion of this chapter to reviewing the state of the art relative to the formulation and delivery of interpretations within child analysis. The model presented here is but one of the models available to the practicing child analyst.

Interpretation is generally defined as "the analyst's explanation to the patient of the unconscious meaning of the neurotic manifestations as they contribute to the gain of insight and ultimately, to the reintegration of the patient's personality" (Eidelberg, 1968, p. 202). In most traditional psychoanalytic literature the use of the term *interpretation* is limited to labeling statements more specifically referred to as genetic interpretations, or those that provide the patient with the opportunity to connect current behavior with past experience or recall (Lewis, 1974). For the purposes of the discussion herein the term *interpretation* will be used to refer to any statement made by the analyst which adds to the child analysand's awareness of his or her internal processes or behavior.

The ultimate goal of analytic work, and interpretation in particular, is the revision of psychic structures and functions in order to foster optimum development

(O'Connor, Lee, & Schaefer, 1983). This revision is accomplished via the gradual working through of various intrapsychic issues. Working through is, in turn, accomplished when the child can elaborate and expand relevant interpretations across contexts allowing him or her to move to, and remain at, the next level of development (Sandler et al., 1980). Working through, as facilitated by interpretation, also promotes the child's move from insight to behavioral change.

There continues to be debate as to what, exactly, the child analyst should interpret. Due to the traditional foundations of child analysis there is a tendency to focus on verbal material. Anna Freud (1928) suggested that the analyst use the child's play as a way of developing a therapeutic alliance with the child analysand; however, once the alliance is formed the analyst should proceed to focus on verbal interactions. Undoubtedly, the child's verbalization of real or fantasied events, thoughts, and feelings lend themselves to interpretation most readily. Similarly, the child's behavior both in and out of the analytic session might be considered interpretable.

The specific analysis of a child's play behavior continues to be subject to theoretical and technical dispute. The two most extreme views can be characterized by the work of Klein and Bornstein. Melanie Klein (1932) emphasized the importance of analyzing the content of the child's play directly. For Klein the child's play was the equivalent of verbalizations and, therefore, equally amenable to interpretation. Klein advocated extensive interpretation of the unconscious meaning of the play. Bornstein (1945), on the other hand, felt that the child's play should not be directly interpreted because the material would manifest itself in other more obvious ways, the power of the interpretation might disrupt the child's play, and there is the risk of oversexualizing the child's material. Further complicating the discussion is the fact that, in the treatment of children, material may be available from other sources such as the parents or the child's teacher. Traditional analysts would certainly have considered such material a source of potential contamination of the transference that the child can barely maintain under the best of circumstances. On the other hand, the ability of the analyst to connect the child's behavior within sessions to events and circumstances outside the session may be critical to the development of an accurate interpretation. For the purposes of this discussion the term *material* will be used to refer to any content brought to the session. Material, therefore, includes the following: all of the child's verbalizations whether based in reality or fantasy, and all of the child's nonverbal behavior and play as well as any information gathered by the analyst from other sources.

In offering the interpretation the analyst must take external influences, including the person of the analyst, into account. Interpretations of conflictual material should be timely and offered in an empathic, human way that respects the patient's affect. This is especially true in communicating with children and, therefore, interpretations made to children should preclude heavy, ponderous comments that are seldom effectively received, much less understood (O'Connor et al., 1983).

Erikson (1940) describes three steps that lead to the formulation of an interpretation. First, the analyst observes and thinks about the child's play and this leads him or her to various "interpretive hints." The child's play may, for example, metaphorically reflect an avoided person, object, or idea, or it may represent the effort of the child to psychologically rearrange an experienced or expected danger. Second, the analyst continues to observe the actions of the child that may lead him or her to a reflection of the child's dynamic configuration of his or her inner and outer history. Finally, the analyst offers a therapeutic interpretation that conveys these reconstructions to the child at the appropriate time.

In relatively traditional analysis interpretations, the primary instrument of therapeutic change is generally made in an orderly and systematic way (Harley & Sabot, 1980). Typically, defenses are interpreted before drives, and surface material before deeper, unconscious material. In order to enhance the likelihood that the child will understand and effectively receive an interpretation the analyst should prepare the child by making comments that show the child that more than one meaning exists for his or her material. The analyst should also relate the defense to the unconscious material being defended against. By sharing this knowledge with the patient, the analyst helps the child to participate in the analytic process and renders the pathological configuration of psychic structures less ego syntonic (Kramer & Byerly, 1978).

Lowenstein (1957) and Lewis (1974) each developed models of interpretation organized by the level or depth of the analyst's verbalizations vis-à-vis the analysand's material. The purpose of these models is to facilitate the analyst's presentation of interpretations to the analysand in an orderly and systematic way. Each author noted the importance of preceding interpretations of very deep or core material with interpretations of more surface material.

Lowenstein (1957) incorporated concepts developed by himself and others in the creation of a model with four levels of interpretation: (a) *Preparation* (Lowenstein, 1951) involves the analyst pointing out commonalities in both the content of the material the analysand presents in session and the analysand's behavior; (b) *Confrontation* (Devereux, 1951) is simply another name for defense interpretations that draw on either past or present material; (c) *Clarification* (Bibring, 1954) is the process by which the analysand is prepared for the deepest level of interpretation, the: (d) *Interpretation proper* in which core unconscious material is presented.

Lewis' (1974) model of interpretation has six levels:

1. Setting statements create the structure of therapeutic interaction or context. The analyst's statements about the playroom rules and the length or content of the sessions would all be included here.

2. Attention statements include the analyst's attempts to verbalize labels for the child's behavior, cognitions, and feelings. These statements allow for the secondary processing of material and the consolidation of child's gains.

3. Reductive statements are those that the analyst delivers in order to make the child aware of patterns of emotion or behavior amidst material that the child has heretofore perceived as unrelated.

4. Situational statements provide the context in which the patterns identified by the reductive statements occurred.

5. Transference interpretations serve two functions. They clarify for the child the differences between the child's relationship with the analyst and his or her relationships with other people in the environment. They also facilitate the child's development and use of a transference neurosis even if it is unstable and imperfect.

6. Etiological statements, like genetic interpretations, create the link between the child's thoughts, feelings, and behavior in the here and now and events and responses in the past.

Glenn (1978) also proposed a model which includes five rules governing the analyst's timing and delivery of interpretation.

1. Defenses are interpreted before drives.

2. The interpretation of deep unconscious material must be preceded by the interpretation of surface material, particularly the analysand's anxiety and affects.

3. The delivery of any interpretation must take into consideration the status of the analysand's external environment.

4. Conflicts which the analysand is experiencing must be interpreted consistently so that he or she can maintain a balanced view of the self.

5. The analyst must present interpretations in an empathic manner.

Unlike the models proposed by Lewis and Lowenstein presented above, Glenn's rules are not limited to issues of organization and timing.

The model of interpretation presented in the following pages incorporates elements of these three models into a model with five hierarchically arranged levels representing the order in which the material should be presented to the child.

First level interpretations are called *reflections* and are similar to attention statements (Lewis, 1974). In this context the reflections are not used to simply mirror the child's behavior in the way which some Rogerian therapists use reflection. Rather, analytic reflections are statements the analyst makes in order to label the child's affect or motivation either as it pertains to the material the child is presenting verbally or behaviorally. Perhaps a child starts a family drawing while talking about her father who has just moved out in anticipation of a divorce and as the child talks she becomes teary. The child stops drawing and moves to the sand box and begins to pretend that there is a funeral going on amongst the figures. The analyst would not say, "Oh, you were drawing and now you're pretending to have a funeral." Rather, a series of analytic reflections on the same behavior might be, "You seemed happy when you started your picture of your family;" "It looked like you got to thinking about your dad leaving and it made you sad;" "Now you sure do look sad, and I'll bet the people at the funeral are very sad." If the child then asks to go to the bathroom just as the pretend funeral goers are about to bury their loved one the analyst might reflect the child's desire to avoid the saddest part of the funeral even if it means leaving the playroom. The analyst would, of course, continue to reflect the child's sadness as it is manifested in any other behaviors over the course of the session.

Reflections serve to expand child analysands' affective vocabulary. Many children have difficulty labeling affects other than happiness, anger, and sadness, which limits their appreciation of the complexity of both their own internal experience and the interpretive process. Second, reflections provide children with verbal labels for their behavior, cognitions, and feelings, allowing them to engage in secondary processing of their experience both during and after the treatment. Third, reflections reinforce the child's view that his or her affect plays an important part in the analytic process. The analysand comes to see that the analyst attends to the revelation of affect in a special way. Lastly, reflections allow the analyst to verify his or her hypotheses about the child's affects or motivations.

Present pattern interpretations, although considered second level, are made concomitantly with reflections but tend not to start until after the analyst has become somewhat familiar with the child. Present pattern interpretations require the analyst to identify and verbalize patterns in the child's material within sessions. This might include a statement building from the reflections the analyst has made in which those affects or motives which have arisen several times during the session are noted. The analyst might identify for the child mentioned above that sad topics or feelings have come up four or five times during a particular session. No attempt is made at this level to give meaning to the pattern; the goal is simply to identify it. Instead of identifying affects over time the analyst might simply point out behavioral patterns such as noting that the child started a drawing and then stopped, started to pretend that some figures were holding a funeral and stopped, and then started to talk about feeling sad before stopping by leaving for the bathroom. At first the analyst should take care to base his or her interpretations solely on information gathered in a single session so as to increase the likelihood that the child will be able to see the pattern. Later in the treatment patterns across sessions should be identified and interpreted. The goal of present pattern interpretation is to focus the child on the fact that behavior is consistent over time, that it is repetitious, and that the repetitions are of import in the analytic process.

The analyst uses third-level or *simple dynamic interpretations* to draw connections between the child's affects and motives as identified in previous reflections and the child's behavior as labeled in previous pattern interpretations. The analyst might identify for the child mentioned above, whose father has left the family, that the feelings of sadness are so intense that they make the child want to get away from the things which make her sad. Since the child has had her affect continually reflected and the patterns of her behavior identified, the connection between the two should prove relatively easy for her to accept. The child can now see, using examples from her own material, how her affects and behaviors are related.

As with present pattern interpretations, initial simple dynamic interpretations should be based solely on material from within a single session so as to ensure

that the child has access to all of the material to which the analyst is referring. Once the child becomes accustomed to such in-session interpretations, the analyst can go on to interpret the child's behavior across sessions. Some of the easiest simple dynamic interpretations which the analyst can offer very early in the child's treatment are those which identify the child's rituals for beginning and ending sessions, as most children develop certain patterns of behavior which they use to focus the anxiety they experience in transitioning from the world to the playroom and back again.

As with pattern interpretations the goal of simple dynamic interpretations is to help the child see the continuity of affects, motives, and behaviors over time even when the manifestations may not be exactly the same in each case. This creates the base upon which the analyst can build the child's understanding of the relationship between past experience and present behavior. Again, because all of the information upon which these interpretations are based has been observed by the analyst and previously labeled for the child, defense against the content tends to be minimal.

The analyst now uses the fourth level of interpretation, the *generalized dynamic interpretation,* to draw the same connections between the child's out-of-session affects and behaviors as those noted in previous simple dynamic interpretations of in-session behavior. This step in the interpretive process greatly facilitates the generalization of changes in the child's behavior beyond the playroom.

If the child has appeared to integrate interpretations presented at each of the previous levels he or she should finally be prepared for what many consider the only true form of interpretation: the *genetic interpretation.* At this fifth level the pattern of the child's behavior both in and out of session is related to a specific historic event or issue and/or its unconscious origins. A genetic interpretation identifies the source of a given behavior, the original stimulus, thereby allowing for true insight. With this information the child can examine the reality of his or her history as it applies to the present and decide how to behave in the future.

The transition from reflections to genetic interpretations will be illustrated using a case example.

Michael, age 6, had been in therapy for several months attempting to cope with the fallout of a particularly messy parental divorce and subsequent custody battle. The analyst developed the hypothesis that Michael could not express his anger about the situation directly, in part, because he was sure that his anger would destroy others and leave him totally alone. This belief was rooted in Michael's having witnessed extreme violence perpetrated by his father against his mother.

Over the course of many sessions Michael invented various games which involved him shooting a dart gun at objects in the playroom. Initially, he used this as a way of identifying when he was sad, afraid, or happy, by shooting at one of three pictures he had drawn. Each picture was of something which made him experience one of these three feelings. The analyst consistently reflected the obvious feelings including the fact that Michael looked angry as he shot the gun. The analyst also used a pattern interpretation to note that Michael engaged in this behavior twenty or thirty times each session and for four sessions in a row.

Eventually, Michael had a session where he added an angry picture to the series and continued the shooting. The analyst now used a simple dynamic interpretation to note that this picture seemed to match Michael's behavior. Now he looked angry, was talking about being angry, and was engaging in an angry behavior. Michael continued to play this game for a while and then asked the analyst to make a paper airplane and fly it across the room so that he (Michael) could shoot it down. At first the analyst simply reflected the fear of the passengers on the paper airplane as they were being targeted. Then the analyst made a generalized dynamic interpretation noting that the people on the plane were probably even more scared than Michael was when he had to go on a plane to visit his father. Although Michael had previously related his fear of flying, this time he added that he was not a passenger on this particular paper airplane; rather, it was his father who was the passenger. At this the analyst made a reflection noting Michael's apparent joy at being able to pretend to shoot down his father's plane, and then made a generalized dynamic interpretation noting how angry Michael was that he had to go on a plane at all and how he viewed it as a problem caused by his father.

As well-timed interpretations often do, the analyst's interpretation of Michael's anger induced Michael to describe his internal experience in more detail. He said he was pretending that this particular plane was flying over water since people died faster if their plane crashed into the ocean. The analyst offered one last generalized dynamic interpretation to prepare Michael for a genetic interpretation. The analyst noted how Michael always seemed to express his anger indirectly both in session and to his father, using Michael's history with the picture shooting game and his failure to talk to his father about his fear of flying as examples.

Having laid the groundwork, the analyst followed with a genetic interpretation in which a connection was made between Michael's fear of expressing anger in the present to his having witnessed episodes of violence between his parents in the past.

In this example the analyst built on simple reflections of the analysand's behavior until both had enough information to allow for the elucidation of the origins of one of the child's most disabling behaviors. In this case the historical events which had precipitated the behavior were both real and traumatic, greatly contributing to the child's fear of emotional expression in any setting. The genetic interpretation allowed him to focus on first learning to express his affect to others and later to attempt better communication with his father.

One can also note in the case example that the analyst chose to modify the impact of some of the interpretations by not offering them to the child directly. This can be done by interpreting within the play, or by using "as if" interpretations. Each of these strategies allows the analyst to reduce the impact of new or particularly powerful material so as to foster the child's acceptance of the interpretation.

To interpret within the child's play the analyst merely frames and delivers the interpretation relative to the characters or objects the child is using in his or her pretend play. In the case example, the analyst reflected the fear of the pretend passengers on the paper airplane before reflecting Michael's fear of flying directly. It is possible to rehearse the entire range of interpretive levels in the context of the child's play prior to offering any of the material to the child directly.

Similarly, "as if" interpretations allow the patient some distance from painful interpretive material by placing it in the context of normative behavior or experience. That is, the analyst does not talk about what the patient is feeling or thinking; rather, the interpretive material is framed in terms of what most people would feel in the situation the patient is describing. For example, the analyst might say, "You know, most kids are very scared the first time they spend the night at a friend's house" as a way of reflecting the feelings of a 10-year-old boy who is denying being afraid in this situation in spite of the fact that he was also reporting several nightmares. The similarity between the analysand and the normative group mentioned can be highlighted or diminished to further adjust the impact of the interpretation.

Direct and specific association of the child's play to the interpretation is cautioned because it often leads to constriction of the child's play behavior (O'Connor et al., 1983). Furthermore, the impact of interpretation must be adjusted whenever the patient is perceived to have limited ego strength. The limitations may be due to pathology or age. Adolescents are generally viewed to be in need of modified interpretation due to the ego fragility created by their attempts at separation and individuation from the parents.

Analysis of the defense and what it defends against should be undertaken simultaneously. The ultimate goal is to make clear that something is being warded off, and why. Observation of verbal and nonverbal behavior will lead to inference of the defenses and reasons for them. One should interpret the current behavior before dealing with the transference and making genetic interpretations. Analysis of the defense should not remove nor entirely destroy the defense. The patient is not forced to yield defenses. Rather, there is a modification and increased appropriateness of defenses (Settlage, 1974).

ADAPTATIONS OF CHILD ANALYSIS FOR SPECIAL POPULATIONS

Our previous review (O'Connor et al., 1983) documented a wide range of disorders in children for whom the analytic technique has been applied but who did not fit the original criteria for child psychoanalysis. Among this wide spectrum could be found children with gross developmental disturbances (including psychotic and borderline conditions), those with specific reality issues (handicapped, traumatized, and adopted children), those from toxic environments (abused or deprived children), and those with disorders of impulse control. This chapter does not attempt the exhaustive review hitherto undertaken. Instead, we focus on the recent application of child analytic technique to special groups where analysis has been successful. Where appropriate, the special parameters and modifications of technique employed are discussed.

Common to most of the literature surveyed is a deepening awareness and understanding of borderline and narcissistic pathology with a concomitant impact on child analysis (Kernberg, 1975; Kohut, 1971; Mahler, Pine, & Bergman, 1975). The close scrutiny of preoedipal factors that may adversely affect normal development has influenced not only metapsychology, but it has also reformed the technical aspects, as noted in earlier remarks on technique. Nowhere is this issue more notable than in the treatment of children with ego deficits rather than conflicts, or in children who are suffering character transformations due to chronic, repeated trauma within their environment.

Medically Ill Children

Children with chronic illness, physical disability, and mental retardation have come to the attention of child analysis of late as analysts become more flexible with regard to extending classical technique to address the emotional disturbances suffered by these youngsters. In so doing, however, there is greater recognition of the necessity of acknowledging these children's environmental realities. Often, this requires helping their caretakers, primary and secondary, to deal with the emotional needs of the children, a task often requiring more than the caretaker's resources can bear.

Asthmatic children are typical examples of children whose illness may profoundly affect their personality development. Bitz (1981) described the sense of falling apart, cracking open, and being hurt in a hypersensitive, asthmatic child with corresponding fears of damaging others. This child's need to preserve the illusion of perfect closeness and harmony, emotional and physical, to fight the terrors of feeling himself separate and vulnerable, echoes a theme prominent in many asthmatic children. More recently, Deutsch (1987) reviewed the analyses of several asthmatic children and offered very relevant and helpful comments. His remarks, though made specifically with regard to asthmatic children, apply aptly to other psychosomatic conditions. He stressed the issue of joint management of the patient by the psychoanalyst and another doctor, an internist, for example. Additionally, if medication is to be used, it should be a parameter of the treatment to be considered. Deutsch also pointed out that when the somatic manifestations of the illness subside, the most common neurotic symptom complex left is phobia. Interestingly, this is felt to be prognostically favorable for analysis. Indeed, the psychosomatic illness itself can be considered a phobic equivalent. He also stressed the importance of those doing psychotherapy or analysis with asthmatic patients being aware of the physiological pathways of the illness and of the medical management based on such understanding. Likewise, those involved in the medical management should be familiar with psychological issues of the disease.

The analysis of diabetic children demonstrates all too clearly the profound effect of the disease on the entire personality organization, affecting the balance of ego defense, superego structuralization, and object relations (Moran, 1984). Although biological growth and development can be adversely affected, psychologically the child's body image and self-representations may also be distorted by way of the illness and the treatment regimen as it impinges on the child. The emotional adaptations are enormous. Thus, there is a great interaction and interweaving between physiopathology and psychopathology that underlies effective treatment of chronic diabetic imbalance in children. As Moran noted, "The psychoanalytic approach underlies the value of attempting to distinguish between the child's psychological disturbance in its own right and those aspects of the disturbance which are associated with diabetes. When we consider psychological intervention with the more extreme cases of labile diabetic control in disturbed children, it may be useful, at least initially, to undertake the work in the protective environment of the pediatric ward which is carefully organized to cater to the highly specific and complex needs of these children" (Moran, 1984, p. 445).

Children with physical disabilities struggle with the visible evidence of a damaged body, and such injury, whether traumatic or congenital, can be experienced as damaging to one's internalized objects and their capacity to protect the integrity of the "self" from attack, or even worse, from disintegration (Dale, 1983). Often there is terror of falling into a void, an inner nothingness from which there is no escape or hope, especially when the child allows himself or herself to acknowledge the inescapable fact of his or her body. The fear of having something monstrous inside the body seems to be corroborated by external reality. Dale emphasized that therapists working with these children must first and foremost provide a safe setting—a psychic shell or skin within which previously intolerable experiences can be examined, reexperienced, and hopefully having been modified, can be transformed by the analytic experience, reintrojected into a more acceptable form. He also noted that crucial for these children is finding an object who can hold the pain for them, who is not destroyed or turned bad by their attacks, who does not retaliate, and who does not reject them. The therapist must act as the focus for the projections and later the introjections that are the necessary preconditions for any real change to take place (Dale, 1983, p. 45).

In addition to the psychosomatic disorders, child analysis and psychotherapy have also addressed such diverse questions as the emotional disturbance of children with stuttering (Ablon, 1988) and mental retardation (Symington, 1988). Although obviously different in many aspects, these single case studies served to highlight the effective application of psychoanalysis to resolve conflicts for both types of disorders in order to allow these children to return to progressive development, their deficits and conflicts notwithstanding.

Adopted Children

Adopted children have recently been studied at length through child analysis (Blum, 1983; Brinich, 1980; Hodges, Berger, Melzak, Oldeschultz, Rabb, & Salo, 1984; Weider, 1978). A central issue in their psychology is their coming to terms with the fact that they were born to, and relinquished by, their biological parents. The subject of adoption as a whole is very difficult for the child and his or her adoptive parents, and often there is great reluctance for all concerned to discuss this issue. Thus, as with their theories about sex and childbirth, these children arrive at their own version of events—bizarre to adults perhaps but wholly sensible to them (Bitz, 1981). They must contend with two crucial questions regarding their adoption: Who were my first parents? Why did they give me up? Adopted children are faced with the task of constructing an internal representation of their biological parents when there is no contact with the parents, no organized experience, and no memory upon which to draw. The child can only wish for this mental representation. So the representation of the biological parents is very largely a focus for feelings and fantasies, which are not modified by everyday reality experiences. There always looms large the very potent danger of disloyalty, of attack on the adoptive parents if anyone asserts that they are not the real parents. The family romance fantasy has come true for these children; unfortunately, they were also abandoned in reality by their first parents. The child's search for his or her identity is often at stake here as that individual attempts to discover who he or she truly is. Thus, adoptive children often desire to resemble someone else, and it is in this arena that transferences to the analyst take the form of resembling and identifying with the analyst. In examining the question Why was I given up? such children often manifest poor feelings of self-worth and self-esteem. They fear being given up again by later parents. The child often experiences aggressive wishes toward the biological parents and consequent fear of the latter being dead. "The self-representations of these children and their sense of themselves as being precious and valued, is damaged; damaged for reasons individual to the child but organized in terms of the adoption fantasy. One task of the child during development is to modify this, integrating the knowledge of having been given up and adopted, while yet maintaining adequate self-esteem" (Bitz, 1981, p. 56).

Jacobs (1988) described a related problem, that of psychopathology in the siblings of adopted children. He discussed, for example, their special place in the family by dint of their being the biological and, therefore, more desired children, with feelings of omnipotence and entitlement characterizing their self-concepts. There exists also extraordinarily strong oedipal conflicts that were most apparent in the special quality of the mother–son bond, especially since these children were the long awaited biological children, which their adopted siblings were not. Notable in these children was the uncertainty about their parentage, which also contributed to the clinical picture, as did fantasies that eliminated differences in origin between their adopted siblings and themselves.

Abused Children

For the analyst who will be treating sexually abused children, knowledge of some of the facts and dynamics of this problem are essential. In terms of precipitants of sexual abuse, emotional deprivation makes the child more vulnerable to seduction. However, one must be careful not to diminish the abuser's total responsibility for failing to maintain appropriate adult–child boundaries. Those analysts who choose to work with this population must also recognize that an unconscious conspiracy of silence about the abuse tends to exist, apparently to insulate adult society against the terrifying discovery that large numbers of children are molested, exploited, and raped. The analyst should also have a fundamental knowledge of the practices of abusers and what they might represent to the child in order to deal most effectively with the effects of sexual abuse.

In addressing the emotional disturbance of sexually abused children, Kato Van Leeuwen (1988) noted that there is a dearth of published analytic material about this group of children. The far-reaching effects of keeping guilty secrets seem inherent in all of the children seen in psychoanalytic therapy, but sexually abused children are too afraid of the consequences to tell or stick to the truth. They are also inclined to alter their stories. Fearful of consequences, they show a tendency to adapt themselves to living with the awful truth, maintaining equilibrium, and protecting family life. In addition, they experience enormous guilt about their own participation and the compulsion to repeat the trauma. Identification with the aggressor can lead the sexually abused children to do the same with other children, and often the perpetrators lead the child into these acts. Molesters in many instances see to it that the child repeats the act with someone else to make them coconspirators. A case study of a sexually abused 6-year-old girl demonstrated the seemingly bizarre and sometimes strange secret language used by some of these children. Most remarkable was the extraordinary suddenness of the nonverbal revelations. The deleterious effects on family ties are profound: The parental role ends and generational boundaries so important to family life are violated (Adams, 1986).

Van Leeuwen (1988) suggested that areas warranting further psychoanalytic study include the effects of sexual abuse at different stages of development and the comparison of analyses of instances where sexual abuse has actually taken place with those where seduction was fantasized.

Lastly, we come to the subject of physically abused children. Flynn (1988) suggested that the buildup of intolerable sexual tension between adult and child may be one possible cause of abuse that then results, largely to prevent an incestuous act. Regardless of the cause of the abuse the emotional sequelae of the psychic as well as physical trauma experienced by physically abused children are extensive. Fear of the fantasies of going out of control, as they have witnessed in the parent or caretaker, is frequent. In the analyses of abused children it is noted that the child who has not negotiated a loving relationship with the parent of the opposite sex may be restricted to a kind of deficiency state in which only two objects exist, the individual and his primary object, usually his mother. Flynn asserted that it is during these attempts to overcome this deficiency state, that is, in developing relationships further, that child and parents alike may face the most challenging emotional tasks within the family, that is, to make reparation for the damage suffered. Trauma suffered by the abused child can also result in a loss of the capacity to think and feel, that is, in ego synthetic functions. Massive isolation of feeling with confusion and denial is preferred; what is happening is so terrible that it cannot be registered. Soul-murder (Shengold, 1979) leads to mind-splitting, and the child must keep in one part of his or her mind the delusion of having good parents. This child is likely to provoke the parental abuse to test whether the next time the contact will bring love rather than hate. The child can have the utmost difficulty in seeing the parents as bad in any way, or even allowing himself or herself to have ambivalent feelings about the parents, thereby making it impossible to get over the trauma of the abuse, and hindering normal development (Flynn, 1988).

Cohen (1988) described the dilemmas posed by the abused child for their caretakers in residential treatment centers during various stages of the treatment process. He highlighted a phase after initial placement when disappointment and despair set in, noticeably affected by the child's disappointment that the placement cannot meet the expectations of a "golden fantasy" wherein all of the child's needs will be passively gratified. Cohen suggested ways in which staff members could grapple with the problem before its occurrence to preclude the child's premature discharge. Primary among the reasons for the phenomenon is the unconscious identification of the staff members with the abusing parent, often in reaction to the negativistic expressions of the abused child.

SUMMARY

In summary, the foregoing highlights some of the major shifts and trends in child analysis and, by extension, child psychoanalytic therapy that have been addressed in the literature of the past 5 years. The innovations are subtle but powerful, influencing all aspects of the ways in which child analysis formulates theory and technique. Chief among these are the interaction of child analysis with other fields, debates about transference and maintaining analytic neutrality, technical advances, and the unique application of analytic technique to children for whom it was not originally intended. Nonetheless, the child analysands appear to profit well from the effort of their analysts, corroborating once again the robustness of the human psyche, which, despite many obstacles and deviations, is in an ever progressive push to complete development.

REFERENCES

Ablon, S. L. (1988). Psychoanalysis of a stuttering boy. *International Review of Psycho-Analysis, 15,* 83–91.

Abrams, S. (1988). The psychoanalytic process in adults and children. *Psychoanalytic Study of the Child, 43,* 245–261.

Adams, P. (1986). Father-daughter incest: Impact on family subsystems. *The Psychiatric Times, 3,* 16.

Anthony, E. J. (1977). Nonverbal and verbal systems of communication. *Psychoanalytic Study of the Child, 32,* 307–325.

Anthony, E. J. (1986). The contributions of child psychoanalysis to psychoanalysis. *Psychoanalytic Study of the Child, 41,* 61–87.

Bernstein, I., & Glenn, J. (1988). The child and adolescent analyst's emotional reactions to his patients and their parents. *International Review of Psycho-Analysis, 15,* 225–241.

Bibring, E. (1954). Psychoanalysis and the dynamic psychotherapies. *Journal of the American Psychiatric Association, (2),* 745–770.

Bitz, E. J. (1981). When there were monsters: Asthma, anxiety and health in a three-year old boy. *Journal of Child Psychotherapy, 7,* 33–46.

Blum, H. P. (1983). Adoptive parents: Generative conflict and generational continuity. *Psychoanalytic Study of the Child, 38,* 141–163.

Bornstein, B. (1945). Clinical notes on child analysis. *Psychoanalytic Study of the Child, 1,* 151–166.

Brinich, P. M. (1980). Some potential effects of adoption on self and object representations. *Psychoanalytic Study of the Child, 35,* 107–133.

Chess, S. (1988). Child and adolescent psychiatry come of age: A fifty year perspective. *Journal of Child and Adolescent Psychiatry, 27,* 1–7.

Chused, J. F. (1988) The transference neurosis in child analysis. *Psychoanalytic Study of the Child, 43,* 51–81.

Cohen, Y. (1988). The "golden fantasy" and countertransference: Residential treatment of the abused child. *Psychoanalytic Study of the Child, 43,* 337–350.

Dale, F. (1983). The body as bondage: Work with two children with physical handicap. *Journal of Child Psychotherapy, 9,* 33–45.

Deutsch, L. (1987). Reflections on the psychoanalytic treatment of patients with bronchial asthma. *Psychoanalytic Study of the Child, 42,* 239–261.

Devereux, G. (1951). Some criteria for the timing of confrontations and interpretations. *International Journal of Psychoanalysis, 32,* 19–24.

Eidelberg, L. (1968). *Encyclopedia of psychoanalysis.* New York: Free Press.

Emde, R. (1983). The pre-representational self and its affective core. *Psychoanalytic Study of the Child, 38,* 165–192.

Erikson, A, (1940). Studies in the interpretation of play: Clinical observation of play disruption in young children. *Genetic Psychology Monographs, 22,* 557–671.

Flynn, D. (1988). The assessment and psychotherapy of a physically disabled girl during in-patient family treatment. *Journal of Child Psychotherapy, 14,* 61–78.

Freud, A. (1928). *Introduction to the technique of child analysis* (Trans. by L. P. Clark). New York: Nervous and Mental Disease Publishing.

Freud, A. (1965). *Normality and pathology in childhood.* New York: International University Press.

Freud, S. (1905). Analysis of a phobia in a five-year old boy. In J. Strachey (Ed.), *The complete works of Sigmund Freud* (Vol. 10, pp. 5–149). London: Hogarth Press.

Furman, E. (1984). *The seduction hypothesis.* Panel presentation at the annual meeting of the American Psychoanalytic Association, New York.

Glenn, J. (1978). General principles of child analysis. In J. Glenn (Ed.), *Child analysis and therapy* (pp. 29–64). New York: Jason Aronson.

Harley, M. (1986). Child analysis, 1947–1984: A retrospective. *Psychoanalytic Study of the Child, 4,* 129–153.

Harley, M., & Sabot, L. (1980). Conceptualizing the nature of the therapeutic action of child analysis. Scientific proceedings: Panel reports. *Journal of the American Psychoanalytic Association, 28,* 161–179.

Hodges, J., Berger, M., Melzak, S., Oldeschultz, R., Rabb, S., & Salo, F. (1984). Two crucial questions: Adopted children in psychoanalytic treatment. *Journal of Child Psychotherapy, 10,* 47–56.

Jacobs, T. J. (1988). On having an adopted sibling: Some psychoanalytic observations. *International Review of Psycho-Analysis, 15,* 25–35.

Kernberg, O. F. (1975). *Borderline conditions and pathological narcissism.* New York: Jason Aronson.

Klein, M. (1932). *The psychoanalysis of children.* London: Hogarth.

Kohut, H. (1971). *The analysis of the self.* New York: International University Press.

Kramer, S., & Byerly, L. (1978). Technique of psychoanalysis of the latency age child. In J. Glenn (Ed.), *Child analysis and therapy* (pp. 205–236). New York: Jason Aronson.

Lewis, M. (1974). Interpretation in child analysis: Developmental considerations. *Journal of the American Academy of Child Psychiatry, 13,* 32–53.

Lewis, M. (1987). Social development in infancy and early childhood. In J. D. Osofsky (Ed.), *Handbook of infant development* (2nd ed., pp. 419–555). New York: John Wiley & Sons.

Lichtenberg, J. D. (1981). Implications for psychoanalytic theory of research on the neonate. *International Review of Psycho-Analysis, 8,* 35–52.

Lowenstein, R. (1951). The problem of interpretation. *Psychoanalytic Quarterly, 20,* 1–14.

Lowenstein, R. (1957). Some thoughts on interpretation in the theory and practice of psychoanalysis. *Psychoanalytic Study of the Child, 12,* 127–150.

Mahler, M., Pine, F., & Bergman, A. (1975). *The psychological birth of the human infant.* New York: Basic Books.

Marcus, I. M. (1980). Countertransference and the negative psychoanalytic process in children and adolescents. *Psychoanalytic Study of the Child, 35,* 285–298.

Moran, G. (1984). Analytic treatment of diabetic children. *Psychoanalytic Study of the Child, 39,* 407–445.

O'Connor, K., Lee, A., & Schaefer, C. E. (1983). Psychoanalytic psychotherapy with children. In M. Hersen, A. E. Kazdin, & A. S. Bellack (Eds.), *The clinical psychology handbook* (pp. 543–564). Elmsford, NY: Pergamon Press.

Rees, K. (1978). The child's understanding of his past. *Psychoanalytic Study of the Child, 33,* 237–259.

Sandler, J., Kennedy, H., & Tyson, R. L. (1980). *The technique of child analysis.* Cambridge, MA: Harvard University Press.

Settlage, C. (1974). The technique of defense analysis in the psychoanalysis of the early adolescent. In M. Harley (Ed.), *The analyst and the adolescent at work* (pp. 3–39). New York: Quadrangle.

Shengold, L. L. (1979). Child abuse and deprivation: Soul murder. *Journal of the American Psychoanalytic Association, 27,* 533–559.

Stern, D. N. (1977). *The first relationship.* Cambridge, MA: Harvard University Press.

Stern, D. N. (1985). *The interpersonal world of the infant: A view from psychoanalysis and developmental psychology.* New York: Basic Books.

Symington, J. (1988). The analysis of a mentally-handicapped youth. *International Review of Psycho-Analysis, 15,* 243–250.

Tronick, E. F. (1989). Emotions and emotional communication in infants. *American Psychologist, 44,* 112–119.

Tyson, P. (1980). The gender of the analyst: In relation to transference and countertransference in prelatency children. *Psychoanalytic Study of the Child, 35,* 321–338.

Tyson, R. L., & Tyson, P. (1986). The concept of transference in child psychoanalysis. *Journal of the American Academy of Child Psychiatry, 25,* 30–39.

Van Leeuwen, K. (1988). Resistance in the treatment of a sexually molested six-year-old girl. *International Review of Psycho-Analysis, 15,* 149–156.

Weider, H. (1978). Special problems in the psychoanalysis of adopted children. In J. Glenn (Ed.), *Child analysis and child therapy* (pp. 557–580). New York: Jason Aronson.

Zelman, A. B., Samuels, S., & Abrams, D. (1985). I.Q. changes in young children following intensive long-term psychotherapy. *American Journal of Psychotherapy, 39,* 215–227.

CHAPTER 33

THOUGHT AND ACTION IN PSYCHOTHERAPY: COGNITIVE-BEHAVIORAL APPROACHES

Philip C. Kendall
Kelly Bemis Vitousek
Martha Kane

Despite the recency of their emergence, reviews of cognitive-behavioral processes and procedures (e.g., Kendall, 1985, 1987, 1990) have documented their remarkable influence on clinical research and practice (see also Beck, 1970; Kendall & Hollon, 1979; Mahoney & Arnkoff, 1978; Meichenbaum, 1977). In fact, in a survey of clinical and counseling psychologists (American Psychological Association members), Smith (1982) reported that of 13 theoretical orientations offered the respondents, cognitive-behavioral was the second most dominant theoretical orientation (behind eclecticism and, in terms of endorsement, not different from psychodynamic).

The parameters of the cognitive-behavioral approach are not as yet firmly established, and the relationship between the various cognitive-behavioral approaches remains unclear. This state of affairs is not altogether displeasing, for one aspect of cognitive-behavioral therapy that may be its most distinctive feature is "collaborative empiricism," in which client and therapist work together to evaluate problems and generate solutions. Although the cognitive-behavioral therapist's conceptual orientation guides the search for determinants and intervention tactics, the range of potentially useful strategies is not limited to a circum-

scribed set of techniques that may be said to comprise cognitive-behavioral treatment. There appear to be a number of principles that parsimoniously capture the basic tenets of cognitive-behavioral interventions. The following points are adapted from Kendall and Hollon (1979), Mahoney (1977), and Mahoney and Arnkoff (1978):

1. The human organism responds primarily to cognitive representations of its environments rather than to these environments per se.
2. Most human learning is cognitively mediated.
3. Thoughts, feelings, and behaviors are causally interrelated.
4. Expectancies, attributions, self-talk, and other cognitive activities are central to producing, predicting, and understanding psychopathological behavior and the effects of therapeutic interventions.
5. Cognitive processes can be cast into testable formulations that are integrated with behavioral paradigms, and it is possible *and* desirable to combine cognitive treatment strategies with enactive techniques and behavioral contingency management.

6. The task of the cognitive-behavioral therapist is to act as a diagnostician, educator, and consultant who assesses maladaptive cognitive processes and works with the client to design learning experiences that may remediate these dysfunctional cognitions and the behavioral and affective patterns with which they correlate (see also Kendall, 1991).

The multitude of constructs proposed within a cognitive-behavioral framework requires some organization. One system (e.g., Kendall & Ingram, 1987) distinguishes between cognitive structure, cognitive content, cognitive operations (processes), and cognitive products. Cognitive structures are seen as the internal organization of information, whereas cognitive content is used to refer to the actual content that is stored. Cognitive processes are the operations or manner of operation by which the system inputs, stores, transforms, and governs the output of information. Cognitive products are the results of the manipulation of the cognitive system. This organization provides one vantage point from which the various cognitive functions can be considered in relation to etiology, maintenance, and modification of dysfunctional processing of information.

A further differentiation of cognitive pathology has been suggested (e.g., Kendall, 1985, 1991). This model distinguishes between cognitive *distortions* and cognitive *deficiencies*. Cognitive deficiencies entail an insufficient amount of cognitive activity (e.g., a lack of thinking or problem solving) in situations wherein more forethought would be beneficial. Distortions, on the other hand, refer to dysfunctional thinking processes. To differentiate between these two concepts, consider this example. Impulsivity and aggressive behavior have as cognitive correlates a tendency toward failure to employ verbal mediation and a lack of self-control. The undercontrolled person demonstrates a cognitive deficiency—he or she does not seem to follow through on optimal goal-directed cognitive processing, and generates less-than-optimal cognitive products. In contrast, anxious or depressed individuals tend toward misperception of the demands of the environment, self-criticism, and underappraisal of personal abilities. These individuals are overcontrolled, and this overcontrol is characteristic of cognitive distortion. In aggression, both cognitive distortions and cognitive deficiencies have been identified.

Within the boundaries of these fundamental principles, there is room for variability in the actual implementation of cognitive-behavioral interventions. The commonalities and differences among cognitive-

behavioral therapies are examined through a review of rational-emotive therapy (RET), Beck's cognitive therapy, cognitive therapies for anxiety, self-instructional training, and cognitive assessment.

RET

Theory

One of the early examples of the cognitive-behavioral approach was articulated more than 25 years ago by Ellis. Departing from a psychoanalytic background, Ellis (1962) advanced the premise that psychological disturbances result from cognitive distortions that are labeled irrational beliefs. He contended that human beings habitually filter their perceptions through the distorted ideas they hold about themselves and the world, rather than reacting in an objective manner to external events. This basic postulate is expressed in Ellis's A-B-C model in which private beliefs (B) about particular activating events or situations (A) determine the emotional consequences (C) that are experienced. Although individuals are generally acutely aware of their affective responses at point C, they frequently fail to attend to the beliefs that mediate and determine them. When these silent assumptions are inaccurate and are framed in absolute or imperative terms, psychological maladjustment is likely to result. The primary goal of the RET Ellis developed is to teach clients to identify and change the irrational notions that underlie their distressing symptoms.

The clinician's task is to ferret out the particular irrational beliefs endorsed by a given client; this is simplified by the consistency of pathogenic beliefs across all clients. In various sources, Ellis cataloged 10 to 13 of such "basic" beliefs, including "the idea that one must have love or approval from all the people one finds significant" and "the idea that one must prove thoroughly competent, adequate, and achieving" (Ellis & Harper, 1975). Ellis maintains that such beliefs, and the misery they create in the lives of many people, do not derive solely from their lack of empirical validity but from their "demanding, commanding" nature, which he characterizes as "masturbatory ideology" (Ellis, 1977a).

Although Ellis's unidirectional A-B-C model has been considered simplistic, if clinically useful (Arnkoff & Glass, 1982; Meichenbaum, 1978), some of the basic tenets of his theory are endorsed by other cognitive-behavioral theorists and have received a degree of empirical support. The evidence indicates a correlation between a variety of psychiatric symptoms and disorders and the tendency to endorse irrational beliefs on paper-and-pencil inventories (e.g., Alden & Safran, 1978; Goldfried & Sobocinski, 1975). However, investigations of the more specific RET hypothesis that acceptance of irrational beliefs is associated with an increased likelihood of emotional arousal in negatively toned situations have yielded equivocal results (e.g., Craighead, Kimball, & Rehak, 1979; Goldfried & Sobocinski, 1975; Sutton-Simon & Goldfried, 1979).

What may be one of the more promising features of RET *today* is the fact that Ellis has made several revisions to his formulations—revisions based on the theoretical and empirical advances made by others—that can be found in Ellis's 1989 chapter, "Comments on My Critics." Perhaps the revised and/or refined version of RET will promote the research effort that the theory deserves.

Therapy

Until the mid to late 1970s, few details about specific *procedures* for optimal implementation of RET were available (Goldfried, 1979; Goldfried, Decenteceo, & Weinberg, 1974). Goldfried and his colleagues sought to remedy this situation by delineating specific techniques for the modification of irrational beliefs. The publication of *A Practitioner's Guide to Rational-Emotive Therapy* (Walen, DiGiuseppe, & Wessler, 1980) provided more counsel to therapists wishing to learn about the "orthodox" conduct of RET. In 1989, Bernard and DiGiuseppe edited a volume that offers a critical appraisal of the theory and therapy developed by Albert Ellis.

RET is a structured, directive intervention strategy that tends to focus on pervasive patterns of irrational thinking rather than on target symptoms. Although increasing emphasis has been placed on the incorporation of emotive and enactive techniques into standard RET treatment, it remains for the most part a semantic therapy that "largely consists of the use of the logico-empirical method of scientific questioning, challenging, and debating" (Ellis, 1977a, p. 20). Clients are trained to replace maladaptive thoughts such as "I can't *stand* it" or "It *shouldn't* happen" with more rational responses such as "it is unpleasant, but I can tolerate it," or "I wish it hadn't happened" (Lipsky, Kassinove, & Miller, 1980). The goal of this undertaking is to promote a "new philosophy" that will enable the client to view him- or herself and others in a more sensible, rational manner. In addition to such discussion and disputation, RET may also in-

clude the following techniques: rational role reversal, in which the patient guides the therapist through a problem using the A-B-C analysis; rational emotive imagery, in which patients engage in imaginal practice or rational thinking, feeling, and acting; shame-attacking exercises, in which clients are encouraged to perform embarrassing activities deliberately, in order to challenge their need for conventionality and to demonstrate that the consequences of carrying out socially prohibited acts are rarely catastrophic; and a variety of behavioral assignments such as in vivo desensitization and flooding. Bibliotherapy is routinely recommended as a supplement to office sessions and may draw on an extensive library of self-help manuals written by Ellis and his colleagues (e.g., *A New Guide to Rational Living*, Ellis & Harper, 1975; *Help Yourself to Happiness*, Maultsby, 1975; *Sex Without Guilt*, Ellis, 1977c; *A Guide to Successful Marriage*, Ellis & Harper, 1973).

Research

The earliest attempt to demonstrate the utility of RET was provided by Ellis's (1957) review of his own effectiveness as a therapist during three periods in his professional career when he was conducting therapy in orthodox psychoanalytic, directive psychodynamic, and RET models. His review of patient records indicated to him that the improvement rate of clients in his care increased after each shift in orientation, at the same time as the course of therapy became shorter. This review was admittedly deficient in experimental controls and highly vulnerable to methodological flaws such as differential enthusiasm about the three techniques, incremental development of general therapeutic skills, and the use of subjective and shifting criteria of improvement (Roper, 1976).

Initial experimental support was provided by Meichenbaum, Gilmore, and Fedoravicius (1971) who compared eight sessions of a group "insight" therapy "derived principally from Ellis's RET" to group desensitization, a combined insight-desensitization program, a speech-discussion placebo group, and a waiting-list control group. The results indicated that the insight and desensitization treatments were comparably effective for their speech-anxious subjects, with both producing greater reduction of anxiety on behavioral, cognitive, and self-report measures than did the control conditions. The most intriguing finding of the study was that different types of clients received differential benefit from the two effective treatment programs, with insight therapy proving most valuable for clients with high rather than low levels of social distress. Although the Meichenbaum et al. (1971) study is frequently cited as supportive of RET, it is evident from reading the published description of the "insight" therapy employed that it departed from the practice of RET prescribed by Ellis. The insight treatment used in this study appears at least as similar to the self-instructional training mode subsequently delineated by Meichenbaum as it was to Ellis's RET and might be more appropriately cited as providing early support of the former, cognitive-behavioral approach.

DiLoreto (1971) compared RET, client-centered therapy, and systematic desensitization to attention-placebo and noncontact groups in a 9-week treatment program for 100 college students with interpersonal anxiety. Posttest measures indicated that all three treatments produced more change than either control condition, with systematic desensitization achieving the greatest amount of symptom reduction. RET proved differentially effective with introverted clients, whereas client-centered therapy did better with extroverts. A 3-month follow-up indicated that students who had participated in the RET group demonstrated more generalization of treatment gains to interpersonal situations than did subjects in any other cell. The evaluation of this carefully conducted study must be tempered by several criticisms: the minimal level of symptomatic disturbance of the subjects included (out of a class of 600 undergraduates, no fewer than 100 qualified as socially anxious), and qualitative differences in therapist effectiveness between treatment types (DiGiuseppe & Miller, 1977; Goldfried, 1979; Roper, 1976). Other early studies providing some support for the effectiveness of RET include Karst and Trexler (1970) and Trexler and Karst (1972) with speech anxiety; Thompson (1974) with test anxiety; Maultsby and Graham (1974) with anxiety; and Keller, Crooke, and Brookings (1975) with irrational thinking in a geriatric population. Less positive results were obtained by Tiegerman (1975) with interpersonal anxiety.

It is surprising that it was not until 1980 that a study using a *clinical* population to compare the efficacy of RET to alternative treatments was published. Lipsky et al. (1980) reported on a study carried out with 50 outpatients at a community mental-health center who received diagnoses of "adjustment reaction of adulthood" or "neurosis." Subjects were randomly assigned to one of three RET conditions (RET cognitive restructuring alone, RET plus rational role reversal, RET plus rational-emotive imagery), and attention-alternative treatment control (a combination of supportive therapy and relaxation training), or no-contact control. Individual treatment sessions were held once a week over a 12-week period. Posttreatments results indicated that RET, either alone or in combination with rational role reversal or rational-emotive imagery, was superior to the control conditions on each of the self-report measures used. Both "extra" RET components seemed to add significantly to the basic RET strategy, with rational role reversal in particular proving to be a useful adjunct for alleviating symptoms of depression, trait anxiety, and neuroticism. The Lipsky et al. study provides support for the utility of RET as a relatively short-term intervention program for adult outpatient neurotics. However, the conclusions that may be drawn from the study are limited by the exclusively self-report outcome measures used and the absence of a follow-up phase (Kendall, 1982). For other reviews of the outcome literature on RET, the reader is referred to DiGiuseppe and Miller (1977), Haaga and Davison (1989), Kendall (1990), and Zettle and Hayes (1980).

Issues and Problems

Although the central tenet of RET theory—that thinking influences affect and behavior—has an empirical basis, specific theoretical extrapolations from this premise have been questioned philosophically and experimentally (see Bernard & DiGiuseppe, 1989; R. Lazarus, 1989; Mahoney, Lyddon, & Alford, 1989; Rorer, 1989). Ellis's own review of the evidence bearing on RET's conceptual propositions drew very favorable conclusions about their validity (Ellis, 1977b); the strategy he followed in surveying the literature, however, was somewhat unconventional. Ellis began by identifying a series of hypotheses purportedly bearing on RET theory, then listed as supportive of each postulate a broad range of studies, most of which were not designed to test RET constructs. He rarely offered any commentary on the methodological adequacy of these studies or their precise implications for RET hypotheses, and he frequently neglected to include even a brief synopsis of the findings obtained.

Conceptual criticisms of RET theory include questions about Ellis's identification of a set of "basic" irrational beliefs and his tendency to equate rationality and adaptiveness (Arnkoff & Glass, 1982; Beck, 1976; Kendall & Hollon, 1981b; Mahoney & Arnkoff, 1978; Smith, 1989; Zettle & Hayes, 1980). Although Ellis suggested that the therapist "can easily put almost all [the] thousands of ideas [expressed by clients] into a few general categories" (Ellis, 1977a, p. 5), Arnkoff and Glass (1982) argued that "there is no 'correct' list of irrational beliefs that can be decided on for all people on an *a priori* basis." They suggest that the conceptual distinction between the lists of 3, 12, or 259 beliefs to which Ellis refers is not clear-cut, and maintain that there can be no theoretical basis for favoring one hierarchical system of irrational belief classification over another. Arnkoff and Glass (1982) and Beck, Rush, Shaw, and Emery (1978) also expressed a preference for the characterization of beliefs as "maladaptive" or "dysfunctional" rather than "irrational." They contend that a functional view of "rationality" must take the *utility* of each client's beliefs into account, recognizing that "irrational" ideas can sometimes be effective and desirable, whereas "rational" ones may prove maladaptive in specific situations.

In RET, negative emotional reactions are viewed as problems—such distress is dysfunctional and in need of rational reevaluation. Authors such as Mahoney, Lyddon, and Alford (1989) have begun to describe adaptive roles for negative emotions. It is not that negative emotions should be eliminated, but that they are to serve as cues for the adaptive use of skills that would otherwise be overtaken by emotional distress. For instance, when an individual's adjustment is being challenged, as cued by the presence of negative arousal, it is a reminder for the use of coping skills. Negative emotions are important in the management of emotional equilibrium. Elsewhere, I have suggested that heightened emotional states, be they positive or negative, are important for the eventual generalization of newly acquired coping skills (Kendall, 1991).

Another area that needs to be addressed more adequately in the RET literature is the lack of attention to diagnostic issues and the failure to provide comprehensive RET analyses of and therapeutic strategies specifically designed for the different forms of psychopathology. Although a number of articles discussing the application of RET to particular disorders are available, few of these include specific prescriptions for tailoring therapeutic strategies to the target problems.

Until quite recently, the most serious indictment of the RET literature has been the high ratio of enthusiastic claims for its clinical efficacy to empirical evidence capable of supporting them. Although RET has generated a voluminous amount of written material, most of it has been in the form of self-help manuals, case reports, and noncomparative treatment studies. The few controlled trials that have been carried out have often included analogue subject populations treated by inexperienced therapists using poorly specified and unmeasured intervention techniques, with outcome judged on the basis of inadequate dependent variables and no provision made for follow-up assessment (see review by Haaga & Davison, 1989). The situation did appear to be changing in 1980 with the positive results obtained in the Lipsky et al. (1980) study, but other investigators still need to give RET the serious evaluation it merits.

BECK'S COGNITIVE THERAPY

Theory

From its inception (Beck, 1963), the cognitive model of psychopathology and psychotherapy has been closely identified with the affective disorders. As a function of this historical emphasis, the approach is often alluded to as "Beck's cognitive therapy for depression." It is apparent, however, when reading Beck's work that he views his cognitive model as a comprehensive framework of psychopathology and treatment and traces its origins to experience with a wide range of psychiatric conditions. Because the approach remains most fully elaborated and intensively studied with respect to the affective disorders, the present review concentrates on its empirical status with this population. More recent extensions of the approach to other disorders are discussed briefly in a subsequent section.

According to Beck (1967, 1970, 1976), psychological problems "are not necessarily the product of mysterious, impenetrable forces but may result from commonplace processes such as faulty learning, making incorrect inferences on the basis of inadequate or incorrect information, and/or not distinguishing adequately between imagination and reality" (Kovacs & Beck, 1978, pp. 19–20). Beck postulates that early in the developmental period individuals may begin to formulate rules that are overly rigid and absolutistic, and ones that are based on erroneous premises. Schemata, or complex patterns determining how objects or ideas will be perceived and conceptualized, develop out of such beliefs and begin to channel thought processes even in the absence of environmental data. A schema also comes to act as a kind of Procrustean mold, shaping the incoming data that are received to fit and reinforce preconceived notions (Beck & Emery, 1979). This distortion of experience is said to be maintained through the operation of characteristic errors in information processing. Beck (1970, 1976; Hollon & Beck, 1979) has postulated that the following kinds of fallacious thinking contribute to the feedback loops that maintain psychological disorders: *arbitrary inference* (or drawing conclusions when evidence is lacking or is contrary); *overgeneralization* (or making unjustified generalizations on the basis of single event); *magnification* and *minimization* (or exaggerating/downplaying the meaning or significance of selected incidents); *personalization* (or egocentric interpretation); and *polarized* or *all-or-none thinking* (or the tendency to think in extremes in situations that impinge on sensitive areas). Beck hypothesized that the form of psychiatric illness is related to the distinctive content of the predominant, aberrant ideation associated with it (Beck, 1970, 1976).

The thought content in depression is said to center on the experience of significant loss, the anticipation of negative outcomes, and the sense of being inadequate. Depressed individuals are characterized as possessing a "negative cognitive triad" (Beck, 1967; Beck et al., 1978; Hollon & Beck, 1979): "they regard *themselves* as deprived, defeated, or diseased, *their worlds* as full of roadblocks to their obtaining even minimal satisfaction, and *their futures* as devoid of any hope of gratification and promising only pain and frustration" (Hollon & Beck, 1979, p. 154). Depressed patients are said to have a limitation in the number, content, and formal qualities of cognitive response categories and to hold schemata that are global, rigid, and negatively toned (Hollon & Beck, 1979).

A variety of experimental tests have yielded some support for several of the major tenets of cognitive theory (see also Ingram, 1984). Studies have identified differences in the predicted direction between depressives and nondepressives in dysfunctional thoughts, irrational beliefs, expectancy and attribution measures, dream content, endorsement of distorted interpretations of hypothetical situations, and memory for negative events. Cognitive induction techniques have been shown to depress mood states, and associations have been found between negative thoughts and physiological changes.

Therapy

Beck's cognitive therapy (CT) is an active, structured, and usually time-limited approach to treatment. In the following discussion, the acronym CT is used to refer to the specific "cognitive therapy" approach delineated by Beck, as distinct from the much broader category of cognitive-based intervention strategies. It should be noted that *cognitive-behavioral therapy* would be a more accurate characterization of the method Beck advocates, as behavioral components figure prominently in the therapeutic program; however, to avoid confusion, Beck's own designation (CT) is followed here. CT includes seven phases, which are generally emphasized in the following sequence but which are not considered temporally or conceptually discrete:

- Provision of a cognitive rationale for depression and its remediation;
- Training in self-monitoring of mood and activities;
- Behavioral activation strategies;
- Training in the identification of automatic thoughts (which are defined as accessible ruminations that often exist on a "back channel" of the stream-of-consciousness);
- Evaluation of beliefs;
- Exploration of underlying assumptions (which are defined as higher-order beliefs inferred from consistencies in individual's thoughts, emotions, and behavior); and
- Preparation for termination and relapses.

The basic strategy of treatment is *collaborative empiricism*, in which the client and therapist work together as active collaborators in the identification of problems, the design and execution of tests of specific hypotheses, and the reanalysis of beliefs. In the ideal practice of CT, the data generated by the client himself or herself in unbiased experiments, rather than therapist credibility, persuasiveness, or authenticity, are seen as the instigators of adaptive change (Hollon & Beck, 1979). In contrast to RET, CT emphasizes inductive strategies for the modification of beliefs, operating from "the working assumption . . . that an actual demonstration of a belief's invalidity will go further to change a belief than will a discussion with the therapist" (Piasecki & Hollon, 1987, p. 123).

The specific strategies used in CT are an admixture of behavioral and cognitive techniques. Inactive and verbal-symbolic components are always viewed as complementary and interdependent, rather than as separate elements; behavioral procedures are implemented to collect cognitive data and to enhance the potential for disconfirmation of dysfunctional beliefs, rather than simply to get inactive clients moving or desensitizing clients to phobic situations (Hollon & Beck, 1979). Predominantly behavioral techniques include daily self-monitoring of activities and mood levels, activity scheduling, graded task assignment and chunking, and role-playing exercises. More cognitive procedures include extensive self-monitoring of cognitions and related affect on a structured data form, examination and reality testing of cognitions, and reattribution and decentering techniques. "Prospective hypothesis testing" is considered one of the most important components: the strategy involves helping clients (a) formulate specific predictions relevant to their dysfunctional beliefs, (b) design and carry out extra-therapy experiments that bear on these predictions, and (c) reevaluate their original hypotheses with respect to the data that are obtained.

Research

As recently as the early 1970s, there was no published evidence that any form of psychotherapy could approximate the results obtained with tricyclic antidepressants in the treatment of unipolar depression (Hollon & Beck, 1979). Because of the disappointing performance of psychological interventions when compared to pharmacotherapy, the first positive findings obtained with CT were received with considerable interest. Rush, Beck, Kovacs, and Hollon (1977) reported on the efficacy of individual CT versus imipramine; a clinical sample of 41 depressed outpatients was employed. After 12 weeks of treatment, both groups improved significantly, with CT subjects showing greater relief on both self-report and clinician-rated scales. Moreover, a significantly higher proportion of CT patients responded favorably to treatment (78.9% vs. 22.7%), and fewer dropped out over the course of therapy. Follow-up assessments at 6 and 12 months indicated maintenance of treatment gains and a continuation of between-group differences (Kovacs, Rush, Beck, & Hollon, 1981).

The promising results secured by Rush et al. (1977) stimulated other trials designed to replicate and refine knowledge of the clinical utility of CT. Without exception, subsequent tests have affirmed that CT equals or surpasses pharmacotherapy in the short-term treatment of unipolar depression and may offer superior benefit in reducing the risk of subsequent relapse (DeRubeis & Beck, 1988; Hollon & Beck, 1986).

A study by British investigators (Blackburn, Bishop, Glen, Whalley, & Christie, 1981) was one of the first to verify the efficacy of individual CT when applied outside the Philadelphia center in which it was developed. Patients who met criteria for primary major affective disorder were drawn from two populations, a hospital outpatient psychiatry department and general medical practice, and were randomly assigned to "drug of choice" pharmacotherapy, CT, or combined conditions. After a maximum of 20 weeks of active treatment, it was determined that for the hospital outpatient group, the combination condition was superior to either treatment alone, with little difference between the pharmacotherapy and CT-alone cells. For the group of general practice patients, the combined and CT-alone conditions both outperformed the drug-alone condition and were not significantly different from one another. A 2-year follow-up study determined that patients initially treated with CT or combined therapy were less likely to relapse than the pharmacologically treated subjects (Blackburn, Enson, & Bishop, 1986). A second British study (Teasdale, Fennell, Hibbert, & Amies, 1984) also drew subjects from a general practice population to examine the effects of adding CT to treatment-as-usual (which included the administration of antidepressants). CT produced a significant increment over treatment-as-usual by the end of the active treatment phase, but the conditions were not statistically discriminable 3 months later due to continuing improvement in subjects who had received conventional treatment.

The major studies conducted in the United States over the past decade have consistently demonstrated equivalence between drugs and CT in the short-term reduction of depressive symptomatology. Murphy, Simons, Wetzel, and Lustman (1984) compared CT-alone and medication-alone with combinations of CT-medication and CT-placebo and found all treatments equally effective. At 1-year follow-up, it was determined that the three cells incorporating CT yielded lower rates of relapse than the drug-alone condition (Simons, Murphy, Levine, & Wetzel, 1986). A second investigation by the Philadelphia group (Beck, Hollon, Young, Bedrosian, & Budenz, 1985) concluded that the addition of medication to CT produced no discernible benefit over that obtained by CT alone—in fact, there was a trend toward greater improvement among subjects who did not receive drugs. The combination of CT and pharmacotherapy *did* appear to enhance therapeutic response in a separate study (Hollon, DeRubeis, Evans, Tuason, Weimer, & Garvey, 1986), with a CT-drug condition outperforming drugs-alone on most outcome measures, and showing a trend toward superiority over CT-alone on some. A comparison of the three single-modality cells (CT-alone, drugs-alone, and drugs-alone with an extended medication maintenance period) included in the Hollon et al. (1986) study revealed approximate equivalence of these conditions, with a trend favoring CT when the two medication groups were pooled. A 2-year follow-up determined that drug-alone subjects who were withdrawn from medication after 3 months of treatment were more likely to relapse than subjects who were maintained on medication for 12 months or subjects who received CT with or without medication (Evans,

Hollon, DeRubeis, Piasccki, Tuason, & Vye, 1985). With a population of severely depressed inpatients, the addition of CT or social skills training to standard medication and milieu treatment has been found to produce greater improvement (Miller, Norman, Keitner, Bishop, & Dow, 1989); this improvement tended to continue through a 1-year follow-up (Miller, Norman, & Keitner, 1989).

The most ambitious comparative outcome study incorporating CT is the multicenter National Institute of Mental Health (NIMH) Treatment of Depression Collaborative Research Program (Elkin, Shea, Watkins, & Collins, 1986). Partial results from this 6-year project indicate that all three of the active treatments (CT, interpersonal therapy, and imipramine) proved more effective than a placebo control condition and were generally equivalent to each other, although there was a trend toward superiority for interpersonal therapy or medication with a subgroup of the most severely depressed participants.

Group applications of CT have also been studied extensively and have been reported to be superior to traditional group therapy (Covi, Lipman, Roth, Pattison, Smith, & Lasseter, 1984) or to alprazolam or placebo (Beutler et al., 1987), and superior to psychodynamic group therapy on self-rated measures but equivalent on clinician-rated measures (Steuer et al., 1986). The latter two studies targeted the special population of geriatric depressed clients, who have also been found to be responsive to individual CT. Gallagher and Thompson (1982) reported equivalence between CT and relational/insight therapy in the short-term, with CT maintaining improvement better at 1-year follow-up; Thompson, Gallagher, and Breckenridge (1987) found CT, behavior therapy, and brief psychodynamic therapy equally effective in obtaining immediate symptom remission.

A recent meta-analysis (Dobson, 1989) of all studies using CT published between 1976 and 1987 confirmed the favorable impression of its efficacy derived from the earlier reviews of the literature. A comparison of end-of-treatment scores on the Beck Depression Inventory indicated that average CT-treated subject did better than 98% of subjects in control conditions, 67% of subjects receiving behavior therapy, and 70% of subjects assigned to pharmacotherapy or to other forms of psychotherapy.

Issues and Problems

There is now little doubt that CT provides a competitive alternative to antipressant medication in the treatment of unipolar depression. Moreover, CT appears to possess prophylactic properties in reducing the risk of recurrence of depressive symptomatology, consistent with the theoretical model on which it is based (DeRubeis & Beck, 1988; Williams, 1984). One set of findings suggests that tricyclics may offer similar protection if, rather than being withdrawn soon after symptom suppression, they are continued past the expected duration of a depressive episode *not* interrupted pharmacologically (Evans et al., 1985). If this conclusion is borne out by further research, the appropriate comparison to make when weighing the professional, personal, and financial costs of effective treatment for depression would seem to be 1 year of medication versus 3 months of psychotherapy, given that both appear to offer equal benefit.

In spite of CT's rather impressive showing in clinical trials, a number of questions remain to be resolved concerning its applicability, relative potency, optimal delivery, and mode of action. CT has been tested almost exclusively on "rarefied" samples of single diagnosis, nonpsychotic, nonbipolar depressed patients, so that its effectiveness with the compound cases that populate inpatient and outpatient treatment centers has yet to be ascertained (Hollon, 1984). Although CT initially gained prominence as the only equipotent therapeutic alternative to pharmacotherapy, it now appears that several other focused, short-term therapies for depression may be efficacious. Comparative psychotherapy trials are needed to determine the strength and prophylactic effects of each and to identify responsive and resistant subpopulations. Risk–benefit ratios for combining CT and medication must also be calculated (see also Kendall & Lipman, 1991) after the accumulation of additional data, because there are currently some studies of the short-term effects of treatment that favor combined modalities (Blackburn et al., 1981; Hollon et al., 1986), some that find no incremental benefit (Blackburn et al., 1981; Covi et al., 1984; Murphy et al., 1984), and one that detected a trend for superiority for CT alone (Beck et al., 1985).

One of the most challenging questions for the next decade of research concerns the mechanisms of action through which CT exerts its effects. In theory, CT should operate by modifying the thinking processes and beliefs hypothesized to maintain symptomatology and should reduce the risk of subsequent relapse to the extent that it alters an underlying cognitive vulnerability to depression or teaches compensatory skills for fending off the recurrence of a full-blown episode. It might then be expected that (a) indexes of cognitive distortion would be selectively lowered (and lowered *before* symptom change) in patients receiving CT but not in patients receiving alternative forms of treatment, and that (b) measures of the presumed stable cognitive predisposition to affective disorder would remain elevated in the formerly depressed even during depression-free intervals, at least in untreated or non-CT treated individuals.

Currently available evidence provides minimal support for either of these propositions. It has been determined that noncognitive treatments, including both pharmacotherapy and other forms of psychotherapy, do produce cognitive changes equivalent in time course and magnitude to those produced by CT (Blackburn & Bishop, 1983; Imber, Pilkonis, Sotsky, & Elkin, 1986; Simons, Garfield, & Murphy, 1984; Zeiss, Lewinsohn, & Munoz, 1979; see reviews by Barnett & Gotlib, 1988; Beckham & Watkins, 1989; Coyne, 1989). A few investigators have found treatment-specific changes on some cognitive inventories (Hollon, 1987; Rush, Beck, Kovacs, Weissenburger, & Hollon, 1982); however, in one of these instances, the temporal sequence of change ruled out a mediational role for the selectively affected cognitive variable, because its reduction in CT-treated patients *followed* improvements in depressive symptomatology (Hollon, 1987).

Other studies have failed to detect any traces of the postulated cognitive vulnerability to depression during periods of remission (Dohr, Rush, & Bernstein, 1989; Hamilton & Abramson, 1983; Silverman, Silverman, & Eardley, 1984). By testing a large community sample twice, 8 months apart, Lewinsohn, Steinmetz, Larson, and Franklin (1981) ascertained that cognitive differences were neither detectable prior to the emergence of depressed mood nor durable after its resolution. Hollon, Kendall, and Lumry (1986) found that scores on cognitive inventories, which powerfully discriminate depressed and nondepressed individuals during the active phase of illness, had fully normalized in remitted subjects—even though a high percentage of these must be considered at risk for future depressive episodes because of the cyclical nature of the affective disorders (Belsher & Costello, 1988). The few studies reporting persistent cognitive abnormalities in the formerly depressed (Dobson & Shaw, 1986; Eaves & Rush, 1984) have employed samples that were "just-barely-formerly" depressed, leading to speculation that some cognitive variables have brief residual effects that eventually resolve spontaneously (Eaves & Rush, 1984; Hollon et al., 1986).

Although it does appear warranted to conclude that the cognitive factors tested to date behave more like "state" than "trait" variables, covarying with the emergence and disappearance of affective and somatic symptoms, it would be premature on the basis of this evidence to rule out a possible causal role for cognitive processes in initiating or maintaining depression—or moderating it through the operation of CT. Hollon, DeRubeis, and Evans (1987) presented an elegant critique of the fallacy of equating lack of differential treatment effects on a purported mediator with the disproof of any causal role for that mediator. They argued that the most plausible model would invoke both *causal specificity* (CT and perhaps other psychotherapies work *through* cognitive mechanisms) and *consequential nonspecificity* (all treatments that alleviate depression also produce consequent changes in the cognitive elements *of* depression). Alternative explanations for the absence of any cognitive residue after a depressive episode can also be entertained, including the possibility of methodological insensitivity and the possibility that any persistent cognitive predisposition to depression remains inaccessible until primed by life events (Barnett & Gotlib, 1988; Hollon et al., 1986). One recent study supportive of the latter interpretation determined that previously depressed subjects obtained high scores on a measure of dysfunctional attitudes only after negative mood induction procedures, whereas individuals without such a history scored low whether or not negative mood had been induced (Miranda & Persons, 1988).

Research With Other Psychiatric Populations

Beck's basic cognitive model of psychopathology and psychotherapy has been extended to analyses of anxiety disorders (Beck, 1976; Beck & Emery, 1985; Burns & Beck, 1978; Clark, 1986; Clark & Beck, 1988; Coleman, 1981; Emery & Tracy, 1987; Heimberg, Dodge, & Beck, 1987; Ingram & Kendall, 1987), paranoid states (Colby, Faught, & Parkison, 1979), substance abuse (Beck & Emery, 1977; Emery & Fox, 1981; Glantz, 1987; Harrison, 1981; Herman, 1981; McCarthy, 1989), personality disorders (Beck & Freeman, 1990; Freeman & Leaf, 1989; Paetzer & Fleming, 1989; Young & Swift, 1988a, 1988b), and eating disorders (Fairburn, 1985; Garner & Bemis, 1982, 1985). All of these analyses draw on Beck's thesis that distorted underlying assumptions and errors in information processing serve to maintain emotional disturbance. The conceptual models vary widely in their sophistication and comprehensiveness; only recently have any begun to accumulate empirical evidence for the validity of theoretical propositions or the efficacy of therapeutic techniques.

Beck postulated that in the anxiety disorders cognitions related to themes of threat and danger should predominate, increasing the personal salience of environmental cues that signal risk. A series of experiential psychopathology studies by Mathews and his colleagues has affirmed the hypotheses that anxious individuals allocate processing resources selectively to threatening stimuli and consider themselves particularly at risk (Butler & Mathews, 1983; Eysenck, MacLeod, & Mathews, 1987; MacLeod, Mathews, & Tata, 1986; Mathews & MacLeod, 1985; Mathews, Mogg, May, & Eysenck, 1989; Mathews, Richards, & Eysenck, 1989; Mogg, Mathews, & Weinman, 1987).

Although the differential attention to threat cues and overestimation of personal vulnerability demonstrated in this research appear to provide a solid conceptual basis for the therapeutic hypothesis-testing strategies Beck has delineated, representations of related approaches to treatment have been conspicuously absent from the anxiety literature (Hollon & Beck, 1986). Most comparative trials have contrasted exposure-based behavioral techniques with more purely cognitive modalities that stress rational restructuring, self-instructional training, or paradoxical intention, but have failed to test the effectiveness of therapies *integrating* cognitive and behavioral elements as specified by Beck (Beckham & Watkins, 1989; Hollon & Beck, 1986).

Quite recently, CT strategies consistent with Beck's approach have been found beneficial in the treatment of generalized anxiety (Borkovec & Mathews, 1988; Borkovec, Mathews, Chambers, Ebrahimi, Lytle, & Nelson, 1987; Durham & Turvey, 1987; Lindsay, Gamsu, McLaughlin, Hood, & Espie, 1987) and social phobia (Heimberg, 1989). Preliminary work with panic disorder has yielded encouraging results from a treatment program (Clark, 1986; DeRubeis & Beck, 1988) based on CT (Clark & Beck, 1988; Clark, Salkovskis, & Chalkley, 1985; Salkovskis, Jones, & Clark, 1986).

Some have suggested that the credibility of CT may be in jeopardy if it is detached from its origins in the affective disorders and applied to the treatment of other conditions. However, a review of the CT model delineated by Beck indicates that it was not conceptualized as a disorder-specific theory or treatment strategy. As a theme rather than a finite set of procedures, the CT model could guide the selection and application of fairly uniform *strategies*, such as collaborative empiricism and prospective hypothesis testing, to arrive at very different *conclusions* about the important issues within each of the emotional disorders. Although there is no reason to assume a priori that the

use of CT should be restricted to depressed patients, it is clear that speculation concerning its applicability must be supplanted by empirical data on effectiveness with other specific populations.

COGNITIVE THERAPIES FOR ANXIETY

Two cognitive-behavioral therapies for anxiety are reviewed in this section: systematic rational restructuring as articulated by Goldfried and colleagues (Goldfried et al., 1974) and stress inoculation training developed by Meichenbaum (1975b, 1985). Both therapies have been proposed as effective with several disorders, but over the last decade, each has demonstrated particular efficacy in the treatment of anxiety disorders.

SYSTEMATIC RATIONAL RESTRUCTURING

Theory

Although the terms *systematic rational restructuring* (SRR) and *cognitive restructuring* are used interchangeably in the following discussion, it should be clarified from the outset that the present section is concerned with the specific intervention strategy (SRR) developed by Goldfried and his colleagues. The term *cognitive restructuring* has a generic meaning covering all therapeutic approaches that employ strategies similar to those endorsed by Ellis, Beck, Meichenbaum, and Goldfried; only the more restricted denotation of the term is intended here. SRR developed out of Goldfried's dissatisfaction with the degree of procedural specification of RET, and a desire to fit RET within a self-control learning framework. The theoretical structure of SRR is not clearly distinguishable from that supporting RET, although the rationale for specific SRR techniques may draw on other cognitive-behavioral concepts. Goldfried's SRR places slightly more emphasis than RET does on the functionality of beliefs than on their rationality, and on conscious self-statements than on higher-order irrational beliefs. However, the primary distinction between the two approaches appears to be procedural rather than conceptual.

Therapy

Implementation of SRR is divided into a series of discrete stages (Goldfried et al., 1974; Goldfried, 1988).

1. *Presentation of assumption that thoughts mediate emotions*: The therapist explains the cognitive premise that many distressing feelings result from the expectations, assumptions, and labels people apply to situations rather than from the situations themselves. Clients are made aware that these thoughts may be easily identified or may be tacit, automatic constructions of experience. General rather than problem- or client-specific examples are preferred initially.

2. *Eliciting a realistic perspective from the client*: The therapist presents irrational beliefs, such as those identified by Ellis, in an extreme or exaggerated form, with the goal of getting the client to recognize the irrationality of those beliefs on his or her own. The therapist avoids debates about the logic of these beliefs, encouraging the client to provide his or her own counterarguments instead.

3. *Identifying the unrealistic assumptions mediating the client's anxiety*: The therapist and client then begin to analyze the specific situations with which the latter's problematic affect or behavior has been associated. The therapist attempts to help the client realize that his or her distress is mediated by unrealistic expectations or erroneous beliefs, however tacit or implicit these may be. An examination of the irrationality of the client's self-statements includes a review of both the *likelihood* that the client is interpreting the situation correctly and the *implications* of the way the client views events.

4. *Helping clients to reevaluate unrealistic beliefs*: At this stage the client should be prepared to take what he or she has learned in theory and begin to put it into practice in anxiety-generating situations using the experience of anxiety as a *signal* or *cue* to initiate the process of cognitive reanalysis. The process of training clients to examine their beliefs in anxiety-provoking situations is facilitated by the use of behavioral rehearsal. Through role-play or in imagination, clients practice rational reanalysis of thoughts in a hierarchically ordered series of relevant situations. The therapist may serve as a model who demonstrates by "thinking aloud" how to cope with unpleasant affect.

Research

In the paper outlining the model for SRR, Goldfried et al. (1974) reported on the treatment of four speech-anxious subjects using a modified form of the newly developed therapeutic program. Despite the brief duration of treatment (2 or 3 weeks), the absence of ongoing therapist contact, and a small sample, the results were suggestive of the potential therapeutic benefits. Kanter (1975) compared groups of socially anxious volunteers in one of four treatment conditions: SRR, systematic desensitization, SRR plus desensitization, or waiting list control. Subjects in all three treatment groups improved significantly more than the control subjects on a variety of measures, with the SRR-alone treatment proving more effective than the combined or desensitization programs. The gains evident at posttest were maintained on self-report measures after a 9-week follow-up period.

A study by Hammen, Jacobs, Mayol, and Cochran (1980) compared cognitive restructuring and skills-training programs for nonassertive subjects to a waiting-list control condition. The results indicated that the two forms of therapy were equally effective in the modification of difficulties with assertion. Clients with low levels of dysfunctional attitudes tended to improve most, but no interaction was obtained between level of dysfunctional attitudes and type of treatment.

Additional early studies that have obtained favorable results with SRR are Linehan, Goldfried, and Goldfried (1979) and Safran, Alden, and Davidson (1980) with assertiveness training; Glogower, Fremouw, and McCroskey (1978) with speech anxiety; Hamberger and Lohr (1980) with anger control; and Jenni and Wollersheim (1979) with Type A behavior. Mixed results were obtained by Woodward and Jones (1980) with an anxious outpatient population, and Biran, Augusto, and Wilson (1981) reported no effect of SRR with scriptophobia (fear of writing). For a more complete review of studies employing SRR in the treatment of anxiety, see Goldfried (1979, 1988).

Since the early 1980s, few studies have compared the effectiveness of SRR over other types of treatment with different disorders. Wise and Haynes (1983) compared SRR to attentional training in the treatment of test anxiety. Test anxious subjects were assigned to either a rational restructuring treatment condition, an attentional training treatment condition or wait-list control condition. The treatment groups received five 1-hour weekly sessions, differing only in the conceptualization of test anxiety and the specific coping strategies. In the SRR treatment condition, test anxiety was presented as being determined by irrational beliefs, whereas in the attentional training groups, it was conceptualized as resulting from ruminations elicited by the testing situation that interfered with performance. Both treatment groups improved relative to the control group but the treatments were not differentially effective. The authors suggest that the reductions in test anxiety were associated with nonspecific effects of the treatment. Subjects may incorporate a cognitive coping strategy that becomes generalized, influencing the fundamental belief system and reducing negative self-ruminations. Goldfried (1988) concurred, indicating that the effective component may be the inherent emphasis on coping with the anxiety rather than the specific intervention.

Additional support for this possibility comes from a study of the relative efficacy of cognitive versus relaxation coping skills interventions for anger reduction (Hazaleus & Deffenbacher, 1986). The two treatment conditions were equally effective in reducing anger across measures, but the cognitive coping skills training was significantly more effective in reducing general anxiety, a nontarget behavior. This was the case despite the emphasis on modifying cognitions associated with anger rather than anxiety, suggesting again that there may be a nonspecific effect of cognitive coping skills training that is useful in managing general levels of anxiety. Additional research is needed to clarify the nature of this effect and the implications of such a finding on the conceptualization of anxiety disorders.

STRESS INOCULATION TRAINING

Theory

In its earliest theoretical formulations stress inoculation training (Meichenbaum, 1975b; Meichenbaum & Cameron, 1974) was conceptualized as a therapeutic strategy designed to help clients develop and employ a repertoire of skills that would enable them to cope with a variety of stressful situations. The rationale for the training approach was to engender a sense of learned resourcefulness in clients undergoing stress (Meichenbaum & Turk, 1976), by providing success experiences in coping with manageable levels of stress and building a prospective defense composed of skills and positive expectations that will help clients tolerate more aversive situations. In an analogy to medical treatment, this approach was said to build "psychological antibodies" and enhance resistance through exposure to stimuli strong enough to arouse defenses but not powerful enough to overcome them (Meichenbaum & Cameron, 1974; Meichenbaum & Turk, 1976). Over time, Meichenbaum has continued to develop and articulate various aspects of his treatment, including his conceptualization of the nature of stress and the aspects of cognition that are important in treating stress-related disorders.

Additional research and analysis have led Meichenbaum to elaborate on the nature of stress and its impact on the individual. He defines stress as a cognitively mediated relational concept, the product of the dynamic relationship between the individual and his or her environment. The individual perceives the environment as threatening and views his or her resources for coping as inadequate. Based on this appraisal the individual may then engage in behaviors that inadvertently lead others to react in ways that maintain or intensify the maladaptive stress responses. As Meichenbaum (1985) stated, "The transactional model emphasizes the cognitive interpersonal context of stress" (p. 4). He argues that it is important for the client to conceptualize stress in this way before he or she will be able to analyze and reevaluate the cognitive aspects of his or her own distress.

Meichenbaum has also expanded his conceptualization of the cognitive change component. In the early descriptions of stress inoculation training, cognitive change was focused on the reframing of cognitive events. The goal was to help the client develop coping self-statements and images that were incompatible with the negative internal dialogue associated with anxiety disorders. However, more recently, Meichenbaum (1985; Meichenbaum & Deffenbacher, 1988) has further articulated the cognitive change component to include cognitive process and structures in addition to cognitive events (see also Kendall & Ingram, 1989). Cognitive processes refer to the automatic ways people process information, including the processes by which information is searched, stored, retrieved, and inferred. Cognitive structures are described as the "assumptions, beliefs, commitments, and meaning systems that influence the way the world and the individual are construed" (Meichenbaum & Deffenbacher, 1988, p. 72). Cognitive processes and structures have been included as elements of the cognitive change component because of the significant implications for generalization and maintenance of treatment effects as well as resistance to treatment.

It is perhaps most meaningful to discuss the conceptual basis for the application of stress inoculation with reference to the specifics of an anxiety disorder. Anxious people tend to respond to threat by becoming preoccupied with cognitions that tend to be negative, worrisome ruminations concerned with social disapproval, bodily sensations, performance expectancies, consequences of events, and feelings of inadequacy or self-doubt (Deffenbacher, 1978; Richardson, 1973, as cited in Meichenbaum & Deffenbacher, 1988). As Wine (1980) reported, when anxious individuals are absorbed in self-preoccupation, they tend to process information selectively so as to confirm their current cognitive structures. These cognitive structures may have a limited number of themes, largely centered on issues of control, danger, and social disapproval (Meichenbaum & Deffenbacher, 1988). Meichenbaum (1985) suggested that the stress inoculation training program concentrate on teaching clients the transactional nature of stress and coping, training them to monitor the negative internal dialogue and restructure the cognitive aspects of anxiety, and teach them problem solving and self-regulation techniques.

Therapy

In its earliest theoretical formulations stress inoculation training is divided into three distinct stages. A thorough explanation of each therapeutic phase is provided by Meichenbaum (1985).

Conceptualization Phase

The principal aim is to establish a warm and collaborative relationship with the client so as to facilitate progress through the other phases. In addition, the trainer completes a situational analysis of the client's problems and symptoms by collaborating with the client in the data-gathering process. An emphasis is placed on the transactional nature of stress and coping as the conceptual framework for interpreting the client's stress reactions is developed. The particular explanatory scheme selected may vary as a function of the client's presenting problems or the preference of the therapist. For example, Meichenbaum recommends the use of Schachter's two-component theory of emotion to teach anxious clients that reactions to stress involve both heightened arousal and negative self-statements, and Melzack and Wall's (1965) gate-control model of pain has been employed with subjects who must cope with laboratory-induced pain (Horan, Hackett, Buchanan, Stone, & Demchik-Stone, 1977; Klepac, Hauge, Dowling, & McDonald, 1981; Turk, 1975). Meichenbaum also suggests that it is helpful to describe the stress response as a series of phases (preparing for a stressor, confronting a stressor, possibly being overwhelmed by the stressor, and reinforcing oneself for having coped) rather than a single panic reaction, to build the expectation that it is possible to intervene at various points in the sequence (Meichenbaum & Turk, 1976). There has been some question as to whether or not this conceptualization and/or education phase has an independent contribution to the demonstrated effectiveness of stress inoculation training. Recently, Moses and Hollandsworth (1985) evaluated the contribution of the education phase toward reducing anxiety and increasing compliance in a group of dental phobics. They found that this

phase made no independent contribution; neither the self-report nor behavioral measures evidenced any increase in effectiveness over the coping skills training. Conversely, West, Horan, and Games (1984) found that it was difficult to institute the skills training phase without a conceptualization phase. The articulation of the aims of this initial phase has changed over time and as Meichenbaum (1985) noted, it is important that researchers agree on the nomenclature and aims of each phase before adequate component analyses can be conducted.

Skills Acquisition and Rehearsal Phase

During the next phase, clients are taught interpersonal and intrapersonal coping skills for the management of stress. A wide variety of techniques have been included within and across different stress inoculation treatment packages. Meichenbaum (1985) grouped the array into four categories: relaxation training, cognitive restructuring procedures, problem-solving procedures, and self-instructional training. Physical coping strategies such as muscle relaxation, mental relaxation, and deep breathing are routinely incorporated into most stress inoculation programs.

Application and Follow-Through Phase

In the final stage of stress inoculation training, clients are given the opportunity to practice newly acquired coping skills in stressful situations. This may be accomplished through role-playing exercises, imaginal or in vivo presentation of hierarchically ordered situations, or training coping skills to other clients. Planning for relapse prevention and follow-through of the treatment are also included in this phase. As with earlier phases, Jaremko (1979) noted that the implementation of this phase differs considerably across studies, with little information available about the optimal type or duration of exposure to practice stressors.

Research

An interesting study by Klepac et al. (1981) evaluated the contribution of several different components of stress inoculation training to pain tolerance: (a) the presence or absence of relaxation training, (b) instruction in cognitive coping skill, and (c) exposure to a stressor. Seventy-two subjects with a fear of dentists were assigned to one of eight treatment conditions, each representing a combination of the three components under investigation. "Untreated" subjects received only the education phase of stress inoculation training, in which a modified version of the gate-control theory of pain was offered as an explanation of the pain experience; other subjects also received between two and six therapy sessions, depending on the number of components administered in the cells to which they were assigned. Subjects whose training programs included exposure to stressors were given practice sessions involving shock to the forearm. Dependent measures included tolerance levels for arm and tooth shock and self-reported anxiety. The results on the measure of arm-shock tolerance indicated that each of the treatment components increased the subjects' ability to cope with pain, but none generalized to the tooth-shock stressor that had not been available to any subjects during the training phase. Klepac et al. concluded that because treatment effects were found for the training stressor but not the generalization stressor, it would be preferable to use the exact stressor for which increased tolerance is desired in the clinical application of stress inoculation procedures.

Other early investigators who obtained positive results using stress inoculation training with a variety of populations include Novaco (1975) with chronic anger problems; Horan et al. (1977) with laboratory-induced pain; Holcomb (1979) with hospitalized patients suffering from severe stress reactions; Hussian and Lawrence (1978) with test anxiety; Fremouw and Zitter (1978) with speech anxiety; Kendall, Williams, Pechacek, Graham, Shisslak, & Herzoff (1979) with the stress associated with undergoing cardiac catheterization; and Denicola and Sandler (1980) with lack of anger control associated with child abuse.

Since 1980, numerous studies of the efficacy of stress inoculation training have been conducted with mostly positive results. The focus is typically anxious or stressed populations. For example, stress inoculation training has been useful in reducing levels of stress with teachers (Forman, 1982; Sharp & Forman, 1985) and with adults suffering chronic, intermittent stress (Long, 1984, 1985). It has been demonstrated to be effective in reducing test anxiety (Deffenbacher & Hahnloser, 1981), interpersonal anxiety (Butler, Cullington, Munby, Amies, & Gelder, 1984), and performance anxiety (Sweeney & Horan, 1982). It has also been useful in the treatment of dental phobia (Moses & Hollandsworth, 1985), stress stemming from medical procedures (Wells, Howard, Nowlin, & Vargas, 1986), and tension headaches (Anderson, Lawrence, & Olson, 1981).

Recent research has continued to demonstrate the effectiveness of stress inoculation training, but an interesting trend has developed. Increasingly, re-searchers have assessed the efficacy of matching the type of anxiety response, cognitive or somatic, to a particular type of treatment that seems best suited for the response style. For example, Long (1984, 1985) compared the effectiveness of stress inoculation training versus aerobic conditioning with chronically stressed adults. She described her subjects as either cognitive or somatic responders and expected cognitive responders to benefit more from stress inoculation training and somatic responders to benefit more from the aerobic conditioning. She found that both groups evidence significant decreases in state and trait anxiety, but the groups did not respond differentially as a function of the type of treatment they received. However, she found that cognitive responders showed significant improvement relative to somatic responders regardless of type of treatment. In addition, subjects who received the stress inoculation training rated their self-statements as significantly more positive from pre- to posttreatment, regardless of the response style.

Haug, Brenne, Johnson, Berntzen, Gotestam, and Hugdahl (1987) reported similar results with a group of airline phobics. The subjects were divided into two groups by anxiety response style, either cognitive or somatic. Two treatments, stress inoculation training and applied relaxation, were compared for effectiveness across the two response styles. Stress inoculation training was considered to be consonant with the cognitive response style and applied relaxation consonant with the somatic response style. The results indicated that both treatments were effective in reducing physiological arousal and subjective reports of anxiety. However, there were no differences of consonant versus nonconsonant treatment for either physiological arousal or subjective anxiety. Taken together, these studies suggest that different response styles do not necessarily respond to a treatment program focused on the most salient symptoms, and selecting the most appropriate treatment strategy may not be a matter of matching symptoms to treatment components. There may be an as yet unidentified or nonspecific component to the treatments that accounts for the variability. These studies also raise the possibility that the particular anxiety response style may be more important than the type of treatment in predicting treatment outcome.

Issues and Problems

Both systematic rational restructuring and stress inoculation training have come to be primarily associated with the treatment of anxiety, and it is apparent that there is some overlap between the two therapies. Because each has been demonstrated to be efficacious with anxiety disorders, it is difficult to determine which therapy is most likely to be useful for an individual client. Systematic rational restructuring is a more circumscribed form of therapy, focusing primarily on analyzing and reorganizing the cognitive components of the disorder. It has been suggested that it may be most effective with phobic or anxious clients who have easily recognized dysfunctional cognitions without significant physiological arousal (Deffenbacher, 1978).

Stress inoculation training appears to be the more inclusive form of cognitive-behavioral therapy surveyed and may be useful with clients suffering a range of anxiety symptoms. What sometimes appears to be a haphazard, scattered approach to treatment in fact reflects a deliberate plan with a plausible underlying rationale: that the best way to match particular clients and problems to the techniques that will be most beneficial for them is to present a range of strategies from among which the most appealing and efficacious ones can be selected. In this way the client can serve as a collaborator in helping to generate an individually tailored coping package suited to his or her own needs and experiences (Turk, 1975). As discussed previously, attempts to match treatment strategies to the most salient anxiety symptom have not proved differentially effective (Haug et al., 1987; Long, 1984, 1985). As long as it remains unclear which elements of the treatment packages are effective, it is perhaps best to provide a variety of treatments and enlist the client's help in designing a package that proves most useful to him or her.

Although this cafeteria-style approach has some intuitive appeal and may well prove clinically advantageous, it also has some disadvantages in both clinical application and research. First, some stress inoculation programs appear to present more alternatives than can be assimilated in the amount of time allotted to the skills training phase. Second, the failure to evaluate the differential contribution of various techniques to treatment outcome may result in the retention of inactive components that unnecessarily clutter the treatment program and may dilute the effects of more potent procedures. Finally, the absence of assessments to determine which technique among the many presented to the clients is actually used makes it impossible to understand how successful stress inoculation programs work.

Additional comments about the current status of these cognitive therapies for anxiety reiterate familiar themes from the review of other cognitive-behavioral approaches: There is a continuing need for more research with clinically anxious populations to clarify the cognitive aspects of the disorder, to determine the effectiveness of various treatment components under various circumstances, and to determine how various symptomatic response styles interact with treatment strategies to impact on treatment effectiveness. There also continues to be a need for more studied efforts to promote treatment generalization. As with self-instructional training, one of the theoretical benefits of stress inoculation, inherent in the very name of the therapeutic approach, is that treatment generalization is "built into the therapy package" (Meichenbaum & Turk, 1976). Jaremko (1979) pointed out, however, that research has not overwhelmingly supported the ability of such training actually to inoculate clients against future stress; clearly, empirical investigations must demonstrate the utility of stress inoculation for such a purpose before claims to the effect can be accepted.

SELF-INSTRUCTIONAL TRAINING

Theory

The development of self-instructional training can be traced to Meichenbaum (Meichenbaum, 1975a, 1977). Self-instructional training is an intervention *strategy*; although the application of self-instructional training to the specific population with which it is most often used does have a clear conceptual basis, the general model is not associated with a comprehensive theoretical system. Self-instructional training is at present the most widely studied cognitive-behavioral strategy employed with impulsive, hyperactive, and behavior-problem children (see Kendall, 1991). As a therapeutic technique, it has also been used to treat other populations with different and less elaborate theoretical justifications. Although several of these applications are alluded to in the course of this discussion, only the well-developed theoretical rationale for the treatment of impulsive, attention-deficit, and low self-control disorders in children are reviewed in detail.

One major impetus to the work on self-instructional training with children has been the developmental theory and research of Luria (1961) and Vygotsky (1962; Meichenbaum & Asarnow, 1979). These investigators studied the manner in which language comes to acquire a self-regulatory function over the behavior of young children, suggesting that the internalization of verbal commands from others is a critical step in development. In an extrapolation from this postulate, it has been proposed that impulsive children may have failed to accomplish the transfer from external to internal control. A series of studies of children with self-control deficits has suggested that they do lack appropriate verbal mediation (see Kendall, 1977; Meichenbaum & Asarnow, 1979, for reviews). In contrast to the populations most often treated with cognitive-behavioral interventions (depressed), impulsive children do not appear to have problems with maladaptive or dysfunctional cognitions, but with a *lack* of task-facilitating cognitions in situations where such thinking behavior would be useful (Kendall, 1985, 1991). Therefore, a different sort of cognitive-behavioral intervention would seem indicated—one that tries to prevent automatic behavior and to interpolate thought between stimulus and response.

The original self-instructional training program was designed to replicate the developmental sequence through which the overt verbalizations of an adult gradually become internalized in the child's own covert verbal control of his or her nonverbal behavior (Meichenbaum & Goodman, 1971). More recently, self-instructional training has become one component of a more fully integrated cognitive-behavioral strategy for modifying impulsive child/adolescent behavior (Hinshaw & Erhardt, 1991) in which the more general emphasis is usually on training social problem-solving skills (Kazdin, Esveldt-Dawson, French, & Unis, 1987; Kendall, Reber, McLeer, Epps, & Ronan, 1990).

Therapy

The conduct of self-instructional training involves a series of sessions in which the therapist and subject work on a variety of training tasks, which may include impersonal-cognitive and/or interpersonal problem-solving exercises. At the beginning of the intervention sequence, the therapist verbalizes a variety of task-relevant self-statements out loud. These verbalizations are intended to *model* a variety of performance skills, including problem definition ("What do I need to do?"); problem approach ("I'm supposed to plan ahead and figure out how large I should make this first part"); coping statements and error-correcting options ("I did that part wrong—I can erase that and start again more carefully"); and self-reinforcement ("I finished it—and I did a pretty good job!"; Kendall, 1977; Meichenbaum & Asarnow, 1979). To facilitate the learning of the self-instruction problem-solving skills, Kendall and his colleagues have developed the *Stop and Think Workbook* (Kendall, 1980)—a program

with 16 sets of exercises for learning self-control skills.

The self-instructional treatment package employed in the research program of Kendall and his colleagues, for example, places a special emphasis on modeling and behavioral contingencies in addition to self-instruction. In this approach, the therapist models each form of self-instruction in turn (whispering, covert self-instruction) before asking the subject to employ it. The therapist also models instructional problem solving while carrying out his or her own tasks in the training situation. Response-cost contingencies are utilized as an adjunct procedure to help maintain interest in the training procedure and to prevent random guessing. In addition, social reward in the form of praise is given for appropriate behavior and correct responses.

Homework assignments, self-evaluation tasks, and practice of the skills under conditions of affective arousal are also a part of the training regimen. Several cognitive and behavioral techniques may be more effective with impulsive children than either alone (see Kendall, 1982, for a review).

Research

In the original paper in which they presented the rationale and procedures for self-instructional training, Meichenbaum and Goodman (1971) reported on two separate studies of its effectiveness in modifying the behavior of impulsive children. In the first investigation, 15 second-graders from a remedial class were assigned to self-instructional, attention-control, or no-treatment control conditions. After four half-hour individual sessions, it was determined that children in the self-instructional group attained higher scores on a variety of nonsocial problem tasks than did subjects in the other groups. However, no generalization of treatment effects to the classroom was obtained on a teacher questionnaire or through a time-sampling observational technique assessing behavior in the classroom. The second study assigned 15 children identified as impulsive on the basis of scores on the Matching Familiar Figures (MFF) test (Kagan, 1966) to cognitive modeling alone, cognitive modeling plus self-instructional training, or attention-control groups. The results indicated that although both active treatments were associated with increased response latencies on dependent measures, only the addition of explicit self-instructional training served to decrease error rates.

Kendall and Braswell (1982b) evaluated the contribution of the cognitive component of self-instructional training to the total cognitive-behavioral treatment program by comparing a self-instruction plus contingency management condition to a purely behavioral intervention. Cognitive strategies were not examined in isolation, because of the authors' belief in the fundamental importance of behavioral techniques in the management of impulsive disorders. Twenty-seven children with low self-control were randomly assigned to one of the two treatment cells or to an attention-control condition. All subjects received 12 sessions of individual therapist contact focusing on psychoeducational, play, and interpersonal tasks and situations. The behavioral condition involved the institution of response-cost contingencies and thera-pist modeling of task-appropriate behavior; the cognitive-behavioral condition added cognitive mod-eling and training in verbal self-instruction. At the end of the treatment period, both active treatments were associated with improvements on teachers' blind rat-ings of hyperactivity and on such performance mea-sures as cognitive style and academic achievement; however, only the self-instructional plus contingency management condition yielded improvements in teacher ratings of self-control or on self-report mea-sures of self-concept. Naturalistic observation in the classroom setting evidenced variability, but measures of off-task verbal and off-task physical behavior indi-cated treatment efficacy. In neither condition did parent ratings of children's behavior at home indicate desired gains. A 10-week follow-up provided addi-tional support for the efficacy of the cognitive-behavioral treatment, whereas 1-year follow-up did not show significant differences across conditions. The authors concluded that although the posttest and short-term follow-up data provided support for the efficacy of cognitive-behavioral treatment and the specific advantage of a combined program over a solely behavioral procedures, the interpretation of these results must be tempered by the lack of long-term maintenance of treatment gains and the absence of generalization to the home setting. Kendall and Braswell speculate that longer treatment periods with a greater focus on home situations and more in-class interventions may be required before truly satisfactory results can be anticipated.

Braswell, Kendall, Braith, Carey, and Vye (1983) conducted a process analysis of the audiotapes of the treatment reported in Kendall and Braswell (1982b). Among other findings, multiple regression analyses demonstrated that the frequencies of coded incidents of behavior labeled "involvement" were associated with improvement and maintenance of therapy gains.

The literature on self-instructional training with children includes studies supporting to some degree the utility of the intervention strategy in the modifica-tion of impulsivity and hyperactivity, although in almost every instance a variable pattern of results across dependent measures has been obtained (see Barabash, 1978; Cameron & Robinson, 1980; Dou-glas, Parry, Marston, & Garson, 1976; Kendall & Finch, 1978; Kendall & Wilcox, 1980; Kendall & Zupan, 1981; Parrish & Erickson, 1981; Varni & Henker, 1979; see also Braswell & Kendall, 1987; Hinshaw & Erhardt, 1991; Hughes, 1988). Positive but uneven results have also been obtained through the use of self-instructional training with aggressive chil-dren (Camp, Blom, Herbert, & van Doorinck, 1977), institutionalized adolescents (Snyder & White, 1979), retarded children (Burgio, Whitman, & Johnson, 1980), poor readers (Malamuth, 1979), and adoles-cents with low mathematics achievement scores (Gen-shaft & Hirt, 1980).

Recent applications of the integrated cognitive-behavioral (self-instructional) program have tackled the difficult problem of conduct disorder in youth. Two separate studies have provided limited evidence of the benefits of the treatment: that is, the effective-ness has been demonstrated, but the treatment does not so much cure the disorder as it provides for new prosocial behaviors that, eventually, will work to the advantage of the socialization of the conduct-disordered youth. In the Kazdin et al. study (1987) cognitive-behavioral problem-solving training was provided to inpatient antisocial children, with favor-able effects. The training led to significantly greater changes than a relationship treatment or a therapist-contact control—the improvements were especially marked for the prosocial behaviors. In another study, Kendall et al. (1990) also provided a cognitive-behavioral treatment for inpatient youth—these sub-jects were diagnosed as conduct-disordered. The re-sults of the Kendall et al. application indicated that the treated cases, compared to those receiving the stan-dard hospital program (supportive, psychodynamic treatment), showed significant improvements on teachers' ratings of self-control and teachers' ratings of appropriate/adaptive functioning. Although these outcomes are positive, and one can therefore consider the treatment to be active in the production of behav-ioral improvements, the effects were limited and an intervention that is more program-wide, involving school and family contexts, and of longer duration, may be necessary to produce truly durable improve-ments in such difficult cases.

Issues and Problems

Because the conceptual rationale for self-instructional training involves developing verbally mediated self-control, generalization was an expected as well as a desirable outcome of the treatment approach. However, a number of self-instructional studies have not found evidence that such a process has occurred as a consequence of treatment (see Burgio et al., 1980; Douglas et al., 1976; Meichenbaum & Goodman, 1971). In contrast, generalization to at least some tasks and situations has been obtained by Cameron and Robinson (1980), Kendall and Braswell (1982b), Kendall and Finch (1978), Kendall and Wilcox (1980), and Kendall and Zupan (1981). Kendall (1977) has commented that generalization may be affected by the use of incentive contingencies, particular training materials and settings, predetermined versus individualized self-instructions, and concrete versus conceptual verbalizations. It is noteworthy that the series of studies by Kendall and his colleagues that do show some evidence of generalization have involved somewhat longer training, modeling, response-cost, and role-playing strategies in addition to basic self-instructional procedures. As noted above, further increments in generalization may require even more extensive training with a greater emphasis on involving teachers and families in the treatment process (see Braswell, 1991).

Additional areas within self-instructional training that require further research include the identification of active-treatment components dismantling procedures and a more careful examination of the applicability of self-instructional training to other clinical populations. Although verbal self-instruction procedures are readily modifiable for other behavior problems, consideration of the rationale for such extensions as well as careful assessment and design must precede the decision to implement the approach with novel populations.

SORTING OR SPLITTING HAIRS? DIFFERENTIATING COGNITIVE-BEHAVIORAL APPROACHES

Many writers have commented on the essential theoretical and procedural similarity of the cognitive learning therapies that have been reviewed in this chapter. Cognitive-behavioral approaches share the assumption that disturbances in mediational processes give rise to maladaptive emotional states and behavior patterns, and the goal of correcting presumed dysfunctional relationships between external events and cognitions (Sutton-Simon & Goldfried, 1979). This common perspective naturally gives rise to an advocacy of similar techniques and treatment strategies. Proponents often tacitly acknowledge their kinship by citing the empirical findings of other schools as supportive of their own tenets. It is generally recognized, however, that there are differences between these approaches in their theoretical parentage, emphases, specific procedures, and the kinds of target problems for which they are usually deemed most appropriate (Dobson, 1988; Goldfried, 1979; Hollon & Kendall, 1979; Mahoney & Arnkoff, 1978). A number of writers have cautioned against extending the "uniformity myth" identified by Kiesler (1966) to cognitive-behavioral therapy by assuming that all conceptions of cognitive disturbances are equivalent and that all types of cognitive-behavioral treatment are equally appropriate in a given case (Meichenbaum, 1978; Sutton-Simon & Goldfried, 1979).

At present there are few systems for distinguishing among the variety of cognitive-behavioral therapies conceptually or procedurally. Kendall and Kriss (1983) have offered guidelines for characterizing cognitive learning approaches along five dimensions: the theoretical orientation of the therapy and its associated target of change; the nature of the therapeutic relationship; the presumed principal cognitive change agent; the source of evidence on which cognitive reappraisals are based; and the degree of emphasis on self-control. According to this system of classification, rational-emotive therapy, systematic rational restructuring, cognitive therapy, and stress inoculation each have different profiles and evidence degrees of relationship to one another that do not always accord with their historical derivation or stated affiliations. For example, systematic rational restructuring differs from stress inoculation and cognitive therapy on only one dimension; cognitive therapy and rational-emotive therapy emerge as highly discrepant from one another (differing on four of the five dimensions), although they are frequently viewed as closely related.

It is evident that it is possible to distinguish "textbook" or "theoretically specified" implementations of the cognitive-behavioral therapies along a number of dimensions. However, although there are clear differences in what the founders of the respective cognitive schools say *ought* to be done in the conduct of their various brands of treatment, it is not clear that what the practitioners of such therapies actually *do* is as readily discriminable. Even when methods are labeled by different names and acknowledge different sources of inspiration, the practice of therapy in an individual case may be virtually identical across schools (e.g., Beck's cognitive therapy, Goldfried's systematic rational restructuring, Meichenbaum's stress inoculation, and Mahoney's personal science). Such confusion in schools is compounded by the semantic dilemma described by Kendall (Kendall, 1982; Kendall & Kriss, 1983). The names given to different intervention programs are often inconsistent, with the label "cognitive" sometimes meaning "cognitive-behavioral," whereas "cognitive-behavioral" sometimes means solely "cognitive" and sometimes principally "behavioral," and "cognitive restructuring" may mean anything at all. Moreover, many recent intervention programs profess a deliberate cognitive eclecticism, incorporating elements from a number of relatively independent cognitive-behavioral schools. Without observational data and/or detailed specification of treatment procedures, it is not possible to determine which widely recognized approaches such therapies resemble most closely.

The consequence of this theoretical, terminological, and procedural confusion was clearly apparent in the process of scanning the cognitive-behavioral literature for the purposes of the present review. For example, in a paper outlining a cognitive-behavioral treatment program for the modification of obsessive-compulsive disorders, McFall and Wollersheim (1979) described an allegiance to RET; yet, along the contrasting dimensions identified earlier, the principles and procedures they advocate seem to conform at least as closely to those associated with Beck's CT. Most strikingly, a cognitive-behavioral intervention program employed by Holroyd (1976) for the reduction of test anxiety has been variously cited as exemplifying RET (DiGiuseppe & Miller, 1977; Roper, 1976), self-instructional training (Mahoney & Arnkoff, 1978), and stress inoculation (Jaremko, 1979; Kendall & Kriss, 1983). A form of therapy used with obsessive-compulsive patients in a study by Emmelkamp, van der Helm, van Zantan, and Plochg (1980) has been cited as an instance of systematic rational restructuring (Biran et al., 1981) and self-instructional training (Kendall & Kriss, 1983). It is by no means implied that research or treatment programs ought to conform to the specifications of any one cognitive-behavioral approach. However, it is suggested that unless or until the discipline concedes the essential equivalence of most cognitive-behavioral models, more care should be taken by researchers to label treatment programs accurately and identify the precise components included, and by reviewers to

evaluate the specific relevance of data obtained in each study to the status of the particular cognitive-behavioral model under review.

At the same time there is a pressing need for several kinds of research programs to disentangle the somewhat confusing array of cognitive-behavioral approaches. First, on the theoretical level, more studies such as those undertaken by Sutton-Simon and Goldfried (1979) and Gormally, Sipps, Raphael, Edwin, and Varvil-Weld (1981) are needed to investigate the involvement of different forms of faulty thinking (such as irrational beliefs, negative self-statements, and distorted information processing) in various psychological disorders. Second, process research into the procedures and styles employed by therapists who espouse different cognitive-behavioral models will be required to determine what is actually involved in the implementation of these forms of treatment. The need for this kind of investigation has been underscored in several reports (DeRubeis, Hollon, Evans, & Bemis, 1982; Kendall, 1982; Kiesler, 1980; Mahoney & Arnkoff, 1978). In addition to furnishing information about how closely the cognitive-behavioral treatments resemble one another in practice as well as in theory, such data could be used for therapist training and calibration of the skill with which psychotherapy is executed (DeRubeis & Beck, 1988; Kendall & Hollon, 1983; Shaw & Dobson, 1988). Finally, comparative outcome studies are needed to gauge the relative efficacy of competing cognitive-behavioral approaches with particular disorders (e.g., RET versus SRR versus CT versus stress inoculation for the treatment of interpersonal anxiety). A number of recent studies have incorporated multiple cells of cognitive-behavioral therapy for comparison purposes (e.g., Emmelkamp, Brilman, Kuiper, & Mersch, 1986, with agoraphobia; Arnkoff, 1986, with test anxiety); others have used a dismantling strategy to examine the contribution of elements differentially emphasized in cognitive-behavioral variants (e.g., Jarrett & Nelson, 1987; Zettle, 1987). When combined with outcome assessments, process data can also be applied to an analysis of the "active" components in each treatment modality (DeRubeis et al., 1982; Kiesler, 1980).

A related point concerns the need to match particular kinds of cognitive-behavioral strategies to specific types of psychological disorders. In many instances, a logical as well as historical affinity can be identified between specific cognitive-behavioral approaches and particular kinds of disorders; for example, SRR and anxiety, CT and depression, and self-instructional training and impulsivity/hyperactivity. The confounding of treatment type by disorder makes it difficult—and often inappropriate—to test the relative potency of different cognitive-behavioral interventions (Hollon & Beck, 1986). However, a trend is evident in the present review for the proponents of various cognitive-behavioral models to claim an "expanded terrain" of suitable patient populations. For further discussion, see Kendall and Bemis (1984).

COGNITIVE ASSESSMENT

It is beyond the scope of this chapter to offer more than an abbreviated survey of a few active issues in cognitive assessment. For a more complete discussion, the reader is referred to recent reviews by Arnkoff and Glass (1989), Clark (1988), Goldberg and Shaw (1989), Kendall and Ingram (1987), Martzke, Andersen, & Caccioppo (1987), Merluzzi and Boltwood (1989), and Segal and Shaw (1988).

An extraordinary variety of cognitive assessment strategies and instruments have been devised in the attempt to facilitate access to the essentially private subject matter of interest to cognitive researchers. Techniques include the recording of spontaneous speech, "think-aloud" instructions, thought reconstruction, thought listing, self-monitoring, random sampling, imagery, thought and belief inventories, multidimensional scaling, and a diverse range of experimental tasks designed to reveal cognitive structures and operations. These assessment tactics can be classified on a number of different dimensions, according to whether cognitive products are provided by the examiner (endorsement methods) or the subject (production methods), whether assessment occurs retrospectively or concurrently, whether subjects are keyed into a specific situation or instructed to average across situations, whether the content is disorder-specific or generic, and whether the data are taken as a sample of cognitive activity or a sign of inferred higher-order processes (Goldberg & Shaw, 1989; Glass & Arnkoff, 1982; Hollon & Bemis, 1981; Kendall & Hollon, 1981a).

Unfortunately, the ingenuity and resourcefulness that cognitive researchers have shown in the creation of assessment techniques has rarely been followed through with systematic examinations of their measurement properties. Little is known about interrelationships among the varied techniques, though there are some indications that method variance is considerable, with think-aloud procedures retrieving a different set of cognitions from thought listing (Blackwell, Galassi, Galassi, & Watson, 1985; Last, Barlow, & O'Brien, 1985), and self-statement inventories producing a different pattern of responses from thought listing, thought sampling, or postperformance videotape reconstruction (see discussions in Arnkoff & Glass, 1989; Hurlburt & Melancon, 1987; Schwartz & Garamoni, 1986). Few researchers have responded to the call for a multimethod–multitrait assessment strategy (Glass & Arnkoff, 1982) that could minimize' the hazards of depending on a single, incompletely understood device or technique while permitting greater confidence in convergent findings (Segal & Shaw, 1988).

In particular, there has been an overreliance on endorsement methods of cognitive assessment (Clark, 1988). Questionnaires that provide subjects with a checkoff inventory of cognitions (typically rated for frequency or degree of belief) have proliferated so rapidly in recent years that at least several alternatives are available for every common diagnostic category, with more than a dozen in circulation for depression. Such measures have a number of inherent advantages both for the test designers who construct them and the clinician-researchers who use them, because they can be readily compiled, standardized, administered, and scored. However, endorsement devices also carry a variety of potential disadvantages (Clark, 1988; Coyne, 1989; Glass & Arnkoff, 1982; Hollon & Bemis, 1981; Kendall & Hollon, 1981b; Segal & Shaw, 1988). The provision of a fixed set of response options delimits and almost certainly distorts the material collected, increasing demand characteristics, preventing the elicitation of idiosyncratic cognitions, and requiring subjects to make a series of unexamined decisions about the correspondence between the items listed and their private experience. Rating tasks that involve the estimation of frequency imply that subjects can count the occurrence of discrete cognitions; those that inquire about degree of belief ignore the temporal and situational instability of this complex judgment. The retrospective nature of assessment compounds the risk of forgetting and distortion, and the absence of contextual cues may decrease the accessibility of situation-specific beliefs.

A few cognitive inventories have established good track records for reliability and validity for depression; (e.g., the Automatic Thoughts Questionnaire [ATQ; Hollon & Kendall, 1980], and its revised form, the ATQ-R [Kendall, Howard, & Hays, 1989]), but many others flourish more on the strength of face validity, primacy, or the assiduous publication habits of their authors rather than proven conceptual or clinical utility. Many were initially developed by correlating items with symptom questionnaires in normal samples and remain unsupported by sufficient information on specificity, sensitivity, accuracy, and predictive validity (Clark, 1988; Goldberg & Shaw, 1989). Although most of the instruments were intended to assess disorder-specific cognitions, such as depressotypic beliefs or phobic expectancies, some appear to tap more general phenomena, such as neuroticism or low self-esteem (Clark, 1988; Hollon, Kendall, & Lumry, 1986); for example, the Dysfunctional Attitudes Scale (Weissman & Beck, 1978) fails to discriminate between the depressed population for which it was designed and a variety of other psychopathological groups (Dobson & Shaw, 1986; Hollon, Kendall, & Lumry, 1986).

Over the past decade, the burgeoning interest in schematic and information-processing models within clinical psychology (e.g., Goldfried & Robins, 1983; Hollon & Kriss, 1984; Ingram, 1986; Kendall & Ingram, 1987; Turk & Salovey, 1985) has deepened dissatisfaction with paper-and-pencil measures of cognitive phenomena. Researchers who are attempting to examine the knowledge structures and biases associated with different forms of psychopathology are particularly interested in capturing *automatic* processing rather than the more reflective, deliberate operations presumably assessed by self-report inventories. This shift in emphasis has prompted the development of a variety of assessment strategies—many inspired by the laboratory studies of cognitive science—that are designed to explore the encoding, retrieval, and organization of disorder specific material in diagnostic categories (Kihlstrom & Nasby, 1981; Landau & Goldfried, 1981; Mathews & MacLeod, 1985; Rudy & Merluzzi, 1984; Segal, 1988).

QUESTIONING THE PLACE OF DYNAMIC CONSTRUCTS IN COGNITIVE-BEHAVIORAL THERAPY

Question: "Do You Believe in the Unconscious?" Answer: "Not That I'm Aware of."

The popularity of cognitive-behavioral therapy has been attributed in part to its joint emphasis on enactive and verbal intervention strategies, and the ease with which a wide variety of techniques can be integrated into the basic model (Arnkoff, 1981; Glass & Arnkoff, 1982). Although the common meaning of the term *eclectic* does not aptly characterize an approach with a clear and relatively consistent framework for interpreting and modifying psychopathology, the cognitive-behavioral model is an "ideological hybrid" (Mahoney, 1977) that has been influenced by, and continues to express, disparate traditions.

If cognitive-behavioral therapy may be said to owe allegiance to both the cognitive and the behavioral models, the influence of the latter is clearly predominant in its current practice. Although it is by no means suggested that the commitment to methodological behaviorism or endorsement of enactive techniques should be moderated, it may be that the development of the cognitive-behavioral model would be enhanced by a closer attention to several issues traditionally considered the exclusive province of psychodynamic approaches. Several papers have explored the possibility of incorporating more dynamic material into the practice of cognitive-behavioral therapy while retaining the empirical emphasis of its behavioral heritage.

One of the concepts associated with this trend is that of *resistance*. The psychodynamic understanding of resistance invokes unconscious processes that actively oppose attempts to explore symptoms that presumably serve a defensive function. The term has been virtually absent from the behavioral and cognitive-behavioral literature, where the prevailing view is that "the notion that some internal process is responsible for most or many treatment failures is simply an unfortunate though convenient evasion of one's clinical responsibilities" (Lazarus & Fay, 1981, pp. 115–116). Recently a number of cognitive-behaviorists, conceding the importance of attending to related issues in the conduct of therapy, have offered alternative definitions of resistance that are consistent with a cognitive model and have proposed a variety of strategies for dealing with its occurrence. Wachtel (1981a) provided a forum for comparing and contrasting the cognitive-behavioral perspective on resistance with the traditional dynamic view.

An analysis of these position papers reveals characteristic differences in how resistance is conceptualized within the two orientations. Although psychoanalytic writers are likely to view resistance as a function of the patient's conflicts about change, cognitive-behavioral therapists tend to consider a broad range of variables before making attributions about the cause of resistance or lack of improvement (Glass & Arnkoff, 1982; Goldfried, 1981a, 1981b; Lazarus & Fay, 1981). In cognitive-behavioral approaches, the focus is shifted from active intrapsychic processes hypothesized to underlie noncompliance to the noncompliance itself; patient variables are considered a small subset of the factors that may be responsible for failures to adhere to the treatment program. Cognitive-behaviorists (e.g., Meichenbaum & Turk, 1988) focus on the application and evaluation of strategies that can influence treatment adherence. Treatment adherence is considered to be most strongly influenced by clients' beliefs concerning the therapeutic process. Private monologues about the progress of therapy, the attitudes of the therapist, the feasibility of change, and the meaning of setbacks may all lead to treatment impasses that appear to reflect a vested interest on the client's part in remaining distressed (Cameron, 1978; Lazarus & Fay, 1981; Meichenbaum & Gilmore, 1981; Meichenbaum & Turk, 1985).

Cognitive-behavioral therapists are more likely than their dynamic counterparts to focus on specific procedures for preventing the occurrence of resistance and modifying its effects. Recommended strategies for forestalling client resistance include offering a clear rationale for treatment procedures, emphasizing the gradual nature of change, using Socratic dialogue and hypothesis-testing techniques, and conducting thorough task analyses of the patient's problems, skills, and goals that can guide the therapist in the selection of appropriate procedures and homework assignments. When resistance does occur, it is treated as an opportunity for engaging in the same kind of cognitive analysis that is applied to other material; like anomalous data for the scientist, it can provide additional occasions for exploring the nature of the client's thoughts, feelings, and behavior (Meichenbaum & Gilmore, 1981).

Other traditionally "dynamic" concepts such as insight and the influence of early experience also deserve increased attention from cognitive behavioral therapists. It has been suggested that insight, defined as a heightened capacity for recognizing and expressing problems through the conceptual system taught in psychotherapy, may contribute significantly to the gains achieved with cognitive-behavioral interventions. Accurate assessment of the processes and mechanisms supporting such cognitive shifts during the course of treatment might prove to be of theoretical and practical benefit (Kendall, 1982). It may also be hypothesized that the "present tense," essentially ahistorical focus of cognitive-behavioral therapy has led to a neglect of variables such as interaction patterns within the family of origin that could furnish important data bearing on the development of irrational belief systems and distorted styles of information processing.

We are not endorsing a return to a psychodynamic perspective. Rather, we applaud the pivotal gains in the practice of psychotherapy that have resulted from the behavioral and cognitive influences and urge a continued alliance with action-oriented therapy. Nevertheless, members of the field must continue to broaden and deepen their understanding of all the variables involved in the process of intervention.

REFERENCES

Alden, L., & Safran, J. (1978). Irrational beliefs and nonassertive behavior. *Cognitive Therapy and Research*, *2*, 357–364.

Anderson, N. B., Lawrence, P. S., & Olson, T. W. (1981). Within-subject analysis of autogenic training and cognitive training in the treatment of headache pain. *Journal of Behavior Therapy and Experimental Psychiatry*, *12*, 219–223.

Arnkoff, D. B. (1981). Flexibility in practicing cognitive therapy. In G. Emery, S. Hollon & R. Bedrosian (Eds.), *New directions in cognitive therapy* (pp. 203–223). New York: Guilford Press.

Arnkoff, D. B. (1986). A comparison of the coping and restructuring components of cognitive restructuring. *Cognitive Therapy and Research*, *10*, 147–158.

Arnkoff, D. B., & Glass, C. R. (1982). Clinical cognitive constructs: Examination, evaluation, elaboration. In P. C. Kendall (Ed.), *Advances in cognitive-behavioral research and therapy* (Vol. 1, pp. 2–35). New York: Academic Press.

Arnkoff, D. B., & Glass, C. R. (1989). Cognitive assessment in social anxiety and social phobia. *Clinical Psychology Review*, *9*, 61–74.

Barabash, C. (1978). *A comparison of self-instruction training, token fading procedures, and a combined self-instruction/token fading treatment in modifying children's impulsive behavior.* Unpublished doctoral dissertation, New York University.

Barnett, P. A., & Gotlib, I. H. (1988). Psychosocial functioning and depression: Distinguishing among antecedents, concomitants, and consequences. *Psychological Bulletin*, *104*, 97–126.

Beck, A. T. (1963). Thinking and depression. *Archives of General Psychiatry*, *9*, 324–333.

Beck, A. T. (1967). *Depression: Clinical, experimental, and theoretical aspects.* New York: Harper & Row.

Beck, A. T. (1970). Cognitive therapy: Nature and relation to behavior therapy. *Behavior Therapy*, *1*, 184–200.

Beck, A. T. (1976). *Cognitive therapy and the emotional disorders.* New York: International Universities Press.

Beck, A. T., & Emery, G. (1977). *Cognitive therapy of substance abuse.* Philadelphia: Center for Cognitive Therapy.

Beck, A. T., & Emery, G. (1979). *Cognitive therapy of anxiety and phobic disorders.* Philadelphia: Center for Cognitive Therapy.

Beck, A. T., & Emery, G. (1985). *Anxiety disorders and phobias: A cognitive perspective.* New York: Basic Books.

Beck, A. T., & Freeman, A. (1990). *Cognitive therapy of the personality disorders.* New York: Guilford Press.

Beck, A. T., Hollon, S. D., Young, J., Bedrosian, R., & Budenz, D. (1985). Treatment of depression with cognitive therapy and amitriptyline. *Archives of General Psychiatry*, *42*, 142–148.

Beck, A. T., Rush, A. J., Shaw, B. F., & Emery, G. (1978).

Cognitive therapy of depression: A treatment manual. Philadelphia: Center for Cognitive Therapy.

Beckham, E. E., & Watkins, J. T. (1989). Process and outcome in cognitive therapy. In A. Freeman, K. M. Simon, C. E. Beutler, & H. Arkowitz (Eds.), *Comprehensive handbook of cognitive therapy* (pp. 61–81). New York: Plenum Press.

Belsher, G., & Costello, C. G. (1988). Relapse after recovery from unipolar depression: A critical review. *Psychological Bulletin, 104*, 84–96.

Bernard, M. E., & DeGiuseppe, R. (Eds.). (1989). *Inside rational-emotive therapy: A critical appraisal of the theory and therapy of Albert Ellis.* San Diego: Academic Press.

Beutler, L. E., Scogin, F., Kirkish, P., Schretlen, D., Corbishley, A., Hamblin, D., Meredith, K., Potter, R., Bamford, C. R., & Levenson, A. I. (1987). Group cognitive therapy and alprazolam in the treatment of depression in older adults. *Journal of Consulting and Clinical Psychology, 55*, 550–556.

Biran, M., Augusto, F., & Wilson, G. T. (1981). *In vivo* exposure vs. cognitive restructuring in the treatment of scriptophobia. *Behaviour Research and Therapy, 19*, 525–532.

Blackburn, I. M., & Bishop, S. (1983). Changes in cognition with pharmacotherapy and cognitive therapy. *British Journal of Psychiatry, 143*, 609–617.

Blackburn, I. M., Bishop, S., Glen, A. I. M., Whalley, L. J., & Christie, J. E. (1981). The efficacy of cognitive therapy in depression: A treatment trial using cognitive therapy and pharmacotherapy, each alone and in combination. *British Journal of Psychiatry, 139*, 181–189.

Blackburn, I. M., Enson, K. M., & Bishop, S. (1986). A two-year naturalistic follow-up of depressed patients treated with cognitive therapy, pharmacotherapy, and a combination of both. *Journal of Affective Disorders, 10*, 67–75.

Blackwell, R. T., Galassi, J. P., Galassi, M. D., & Watson, T. E. (1985). Are cognitive assessment methods equal? A comparison of think aloud and thought listing. *Cognitive Therapy and Research, 9*, 399–413.

Borkovec, T. D., & Mathews, A. M. (1988). Treatment of nonphobic anxiety disorders: A comparison of nondirective, cognitive, and coping desensitization therapy. *Journal of Consulting and Clinical Psychology, 56*, 877–884.

Borkovec, T. D., Mathews, A. M., Chambers, A., Ebrahimi, S., Lytle, R., & Nelson, R. (1987). The effects of relaxation training with cognitive therapy or nondirective therapy and the role of relaxation-induced anxiety in the treatment of generalized anxiety. *Journal of Consulting and Clinical Psychology, 55*, 883–888.

Braswell, L. (1991). Involving parents in cognitive-behavioral therapy with children and adolescents. In P. C. Kendall (Ed.) *Children and adolescent therapy: Cognitive-behavioral procedures.* New York: Guilford Press.

Braswell, L., & Kendall, P. C. (1987). Treating impulsive children via cognitive-behavioral therapy. In N. Jacob-

son (Ed.) *Psychotherapists in clinical practice: Cognitive and behavioral perspectives* (pp. 153–189). New York: Guilford Press.

Braswell, L., Kendall, P. C., Braith, J., Carey, M. P., & Vye, L. S. (1983). *"Involvement" in cognitive-behavioral therapy with children: Process and its relationship to outcome.* Manuscript submitted for publication, University of Minnesota.

Burgio, L. D., Whitman, T. L., & Johnson, M. R. (1980). A self-instructional package for increasing attending behavior in educable mentally retarded children. *Journal of Applied Behavior Analysis, 13*, 443–460.

Burns, D. D., & Beck, A. T. (1978). Cognitive behavior modification of mood disorders. In J. P. Foreyt & D. P. Rathjen (Eds.), *Cognitive behavior therapy: Research and application.* New York: Plenum Press.

Butler, G., Cullington, A., Munby, M., Amies, P., & Gelder, M. (1984). Exposure and anxiety management in the treatment of social phobia. *Journal of Consulting and Clinical Psychology, 52*, 642–650.

Butler, G., & Mathews, A. (1983). Cognitive processes in anxiety. *Advances in Behaviour Research and Therapy, 5*, 51–62.

Cameron, R. (1978). The clinical implementation of behavior change techniques: A cognitively oriented conceptualization of therapeutic "compliance" and "resistance." In J. P. Foreyt & D. P. Rathjen (Eds.), *Cognitive behavior therapy: Research and application.* New York: Plenum Press.

Cameron, M. I., & Robinson, V. M. J. (1980). Effects of cognitive training on academic and on-task behavior of hyperactive children. *Journal of Abnormal Child Psychology, 8*, 405–419.

Camp, B., Blom, G., Herbert, F., & van Doorninck, W. (1977). "Think aloud": A program for developing self-control in young aggressive boys. *Journal of Abnormal Child Psychology, 5*, 157–169.

Clark, D. M. (1986). A cognitive approach to panic. *Behaviour Research and Therapy, 24*, 461–470.

Clark, D. A. (1988). The validity of measures of cognition: A review of the literature. *Cognitive Therapy and Research, 12*, 1–20.

Clark, D. M., & Beck, A. T. (1988). Cognitive approaches. In C. G. Last & M. Hersen (Eds.), *Handbook of anxiety disorder* (pp. 362–385). Elmsford, NY: Pergamon Press.

Clark, D. M., Salkovskis, P. M., & Chalkley, A. J. (1985). Respiratory control as a treatment for panic attacks. *Journal of Behavior Therapy and Experimental Psychiatry, 16*, 23–30.

Colby, K. M., Faught, W. S., & Parkison, R. C. (1979). Cognitive therapy of paranoid conditions: Heuristic suggestions based on a computer simulation model. *Cognitive Therapy and Research, 3*, 55–60.

Coleman, R. E. (1981). Agoraphobia: Cognitive–behavioral treatment. In G. Emery, S. Hollon, & R. Bedrosian (Eds.), *New directions in cognitive therapy: A clinical casebook* (pp. 101–119). New York: Guilford Press.

Covi, L., Lipman, R. S., Roth, D., Pattison, J. H., Smith, J.

E., & Lasseter, V. K. (1984, May). *Cognitive group psychotherapy in depression*. Paper presented at the annual meeting of the American Psychiatric Association, Los Angeles.

Coyne, J. C. (1989). Thinking postcognitively about depression. In A. Freeman, K. M. Simon, C. F. Beutler, & H. Arkowitz (Eds.), *Comprehensive handbook of cognitive therapy* (pp. 227–244). New York: Plenum Press.

Craighead, W. E., Kimball, W. H., & Rehak, P. J. (1979). Mood changes, physiological responses, and self-statements during social rejection imagery. *Journal of Consulting and Clinical Psychology, 47*, 385–396.

Deffenbacher, J. L. (1978). Worry, emotionality and task generated interference in test anxiety: An empirical test of attentional theory. *Journal of Educational Psychology, 70*, 248–254.

Deffenbacher, J. L., & Hahnloser, R. M. (1981). Cognitive and relaxation coping skills in stress inoculation. *Cognitive Therapy and Research, 5*, 211–215.

Denicola, J., & Sandler, J. (1980). Training abusive parents in child management and self-control skills. *Behavior Therapy, 11*, 263–270.

DeRubeis, R. J., & Beck, A. T. (1988). Cognitive therapy. In K. S. Dobson (Ed.), *Handbook of cognitive–behavioral therapies* (pp. 273–306). New York: Guilford Press.

DeRubeis, R., Hollon, S., Evans, M., & Benis, K. M. (1982). Can psychotherapies be discriminated? A systematic investigation of cognitive therapy and interpersonal therapy. *Journal of Consulting and Clinical Psychology, 50*, 744–756.

Diament, C., & Wilson, G. T. (1975). An experimental investigation of the effects of covert sensitization in an analogue eating situation. *Behavior Therapy, 6*, 499–509.

DiGuiseppe, R. A., & Miller, N. J. (1977). A review of the outcome studies on rational-emotive therapy. In A. Ellis & R. Grieger (Eds.), *Handbook of rational-emotive therapy*. New York: Springer.

DiLoreto, A.O. (1971). *Comparative psychotherapy*. Chicago: Aldine-Atherton.

Dobson, K. S. (1988). The present and future of the cognitive–behavioral therapies. In K. S. Dobson (Ed.), *Handbook of cognitive–behavioral therapies* (pp. 387–404). New York: Guilford Press.

Dobson, K. S. (1989). A meta-analysis of the efficacy of cognitive therapy for depression. *Journal of Consulting and Clinical Psychology, 57*, 414–419.

Dobson, K. S., & Shaw, F. F. (1986). Cognitive assessment of major depressive disorders. *Cognitive Therapy and Research, 10*, 13–29.

Dohr, K. B., Rush, A. J., & Bernstein, I. H. (1989). Cognitive biases and depression. *Journal of Abnormal Psychology, 98*, 263–267.

Douglas, V. I., Parry, P., Marston, P., & Garson, C. (1976). Assessment of a cognitive training program for hyperactive children. *Journal of Abnormal Child Psychology, 4*, 389–410.

Durham, R. C., & Turvey, A. A. (1987). Cognitive therapy versus behaviour therapy in the treatment of chronic general anxiety. *Behaviour Research and Therapy, 25*, 229–234.

Eaves, C., & Rush, A. (1984). Cognitive patterns in symptomatic and remitted major depression. *Journal of Abnormal Psychology, 93*, 31–40.

Elkin, I., Shea, T., Watkins, J., & Collins, J. (1986, May). *NIMH Treatment of depression collaborative research program: Comparative treatment outcome findings*. Paper presented at the annual meeting of the American Psychiatric Association, Washington, DC.

Ellis, A. (1957). Outcome of employing three techniques of psychotherapy. *Journal of Clinical Psychology, 13*, 344–350.

Ellis, A. (1962). *Reason and emotion in psychotherapy*. New York: Stuart.

Ellis, A. (1977a). The basic clinical theory of rational-emotive therapy. In A. Ellis & G. Grieger (Eds.), *Handbook of rational-emotive therapy*. New York: Springer.

Ellis, A. (1977b). Research data supporting the clinical and personality hypotheses of RET and other cognitive-behavioral therapies. In A. Ellis & R. Grieger (Eds.), *Handbook of rational-emotive therapy*. New York: Springer.

Ellis, A. (1977c). *Sex without guilt*. Hollywood, CA: Wilshire.

Ellis, A. (1989). Comments on my critics. In M. E. Bernard & R. DiGiuseppe (Eds.), *Inside rational-emotive therapy: A critical appraisal of the theory and therapy of Albert Ellis* (pp. 199–233). New York: Academic Press.

Ellis, A., & Harper, R. A. (1973). *A guide to successful marriage*. Hollywood, CA: Wilshire.

Ellis, A., & Harper, R. A. (1975). *A new guide to rational living*. Hollywood, CA: Wilshire.

Emery, G., & Fox, S. (1981). Cognitive therapy of alcohol dependency. In G. Emery, S. Hollon, & R. Bedrosian (Eds.), *New directions in cognitive therapy: A clinical casebook* (pp. 181–200). New York: Guilford Press.

Emery, G., & Tracy, N. L. (1987). Theoretical issues in the cognitive-behavioral treatment of anxiety disorders. In L. Michelson & L. M. Ascher (Ed.), *Anxiety and stress disorders: Cognitive-behavioral assessment and treatment* (pp. 3–38). New York: Guilford Press.

Emmelkamp, P. M. G., Brilman, E., Kuiper, H., & Mersch, P. (1986). The treatment of agoraphobia: A comparison of self-instructional training, rational-emotive therapy, and exposure in vivo. *Behavior Therapy, 10*, 37–53.

Emmelkamp, P. M. G., van der Helm, M., van Zantan, B. L., & Plochg, I. (1980). Treatment of obsessive-compulsive patients: The contributions of self-instructional training to the effectiveness of exposure. *Behaviour Research and Therapy, 18*, 61–66.

Evans, M. D., Hollon, S. D., DeRubeis, R. J., Piasecki, J., Tuason, V. B., & Vye, C. (1985, November). *Accounting for relapse in a treatment outcome study of depression*. Paper presented at the annual meeting of the

Association for the Advancement of Behavior Therapy, Houston.

Eysenck, M. H., MacLeod, C., & Mathews, A. (1987). Cognitive functioning and anxiety. *Psychological Research*, *49*, 189–195.

Fairburn, C. C. (1985). Cognitive-behavioral treatment for bulimia. In D. M. Garner & P. E. Garfinkel (Eds.), *Handbook of psychotherapy for anorexia nervosa and bulimia* (pp. 160–192). New York: Guilford Press.

Foreyt, J. P., & Hagen, R. L. (1973). Covert sensitization: Conditioning or suggestion? *Journal of Abnormal Psychology*, *82*, 17–23.

Forman, S. G. (1982). Stress management for teachers: A cognitive-behavioral program. *Journal of School Psychology*, *20*, 180–187.

Freeman, A., & Leaf, R. C. (1989). Cognitive therapy applied to personality disorders. In A. Freeman, K. M. Simon, C. E. Beutler, & H. Arkowitz (Eds.), *Comprehensive handbook of cognitive therapy* (pp. 403–433). New York: Plenum Press.

Fremouw, W. J., & Zitter, R. E. (1978). A comparison of skills training and cognitive restructuring-relaxation for the treatment of speech anxiety. *Behavior Therapy*, *9*, 248–259.

Gallagher, D., & Thompson, L. W. (1982). Differential effectiveness of psychotherapies for the treatment of major depressive disorder in older adult patients. *Psychotherapy: Theory, Research and Practice*, *19*, 482–490.

Garner, D. M., & Bemis, K. M. (1982). A cognitive-behavioral approach to anorexia nervosa. *Cognitive Therapy and Research*, *6*, 123–150.

Garner, D. M., & Bemis, K. M. (1985). Cognitive therapy for anorexia nervosa. In D. M. Garner & P. E. Garfinkel (Eds.), *Handbook of psychotherapy for anorexia nervosa and bulimia* (pp. 107–146). New York: Guilford Press.

Genshaft, J. L., & Hirt, M. L. (1980). The effectiveness of self-instructional training to enhance math achievement in women. *Cognitive Therapy and Research, 4,* 91–97.

Glantz, M. D. (1987). Day hospital treatment of alcoholics. In A. Freeman & V. Greenwood (Eds.), *Cognitive therapy: Applications in psychiatric and medical settings* (pp. 51–68). New York: Human Sciences Press.

Glass, C. R., & Arnkoff, D. B. (1982). Thinking it through: Selected issues in cognitive assessment and therapy. In P. C. Kendall (Ed.), *Advances in cognitive-behavioral research and therapy* (Vol. 1, pp. 36–75). New York: Academic Press.

Glogower, F. D., Fremouw, W. J., & McCroskey, J. C. (1978). A component analysis of cognitive restructuring. *Cognitive Therapy and Research*, *2*, 209–223.

Goldberg, J. O., & Shaw, B. F. (1989). The measurement of cognition in psychopathology: Clinical and research applications. In A. Freeman, K. M. Simon, C. E. Beutler, & H. Arkowitz (Eds.), *Comprehensive handbook of cognitive therapy* (pp. 37–59). New York: Plenum Press.

Goldfried, M. R. (1979). Anxiety reduction through cognitive-behavioral intervention. In P. C. Kendall & S.

D. Hollon (Eds.), *Cognitive-behavioral interventions: Theory, research, and procedures* (pp. 117–152). New York: Academic Press.

Goldfried, M. R. (1981a). Resistance and clinical behavioral therapy. In P. L. Wachtel (Ed.), *Resistance: Psychodynamic and behavioral approaches*. New York: Plenum Press.

Goldfried, M. R. (1981b). Thoughts on the resistance chapters. In P. L. Wachtel (Ed.), *Resistance: Psychodynamic and behavioral approaches*. New York: Plenum Press.

Goldfried, M. R. (1988). Application of rational restructuring to anxiety disorders. *The Counseling Psychologist*, *16*, 50–68.

Goldfried, M. R., Decenteceo, E. T., & Weinberg, L. (1974). Systematic rational restructuring as a self-control technique. *Behavior Therapy*, *5*, 247–254.

Goldfried, M. R., & Robins, C. (1983). Self-schema, cognitive bias, and the processing of therapeutic experiences. In P. C. Kendall (Ed.), *Advances in cognitive-behavioral research and therapy*. New York: Academic Press.

Goldfried, M., & Sobocinski, D. (1975). Effect of irrational beliefs on emotional arousal. *Journal of Consulting and Clinical Psychology*, *43*, 504–510.

Gormally, J., Sipps, G., Raphael, R., Edwin, D., & Varvil-Weld, D. (1981). The relationship between maladaptive cognitions and social anxiety. *Journal of Consulting and Clinical Psychology*, *49*, 300–301.

Haaga, D. A. F., & Davison, G. C. (1989). Slow progress in rational-emotive therapy outcome research: Etiology and treatment. *Cognitive Therapy and Research*, *13*, 493–508.

Hamberger, K., & Lohr, J. M. (1980). Rational restructuring for anger control: A quasi-experimental case study. *Cognitive Therapy and Research*, *4*, 99–102.

Hamilton, E. W., & Abramson, L. Y. (1983). Cognitive patterns and major depressive disorder: A longitudinal study in a hospital setting. *Journal of Abnormal Psychology*, *92*, 173–184.

Hammen, C. L., Jacobs, M., Mayol, A., & Cochran, S. D. (1980). Dysfunctional cognitions and the effectiveness of skills and cognitive-behavioral assertion training. *Journal of Consulting and Clinical Psychology*, *48*, 685–695.

Harrison, R. (1981, November). *Cognitive therapy of substance abuse*. Paper presented at the annual meeting of the Association for Advancement of Behavior Therapy, Toronto.

Haug, T., Brenne, L., Johnson, B. H., Berntzen, D., Gotestam, K., & Hugdahl, K. (1987). A three-systems analysis of fear of flying: A comparison of a consonant vs. a non-consonant treatment method. *Behavior Research and Therapy*, *25*, 187–194.

Hazaleus, S. L., & Deffenbacher, J. L. (1986). Relaxation and cognitive treatments of anger. *Journal of Consulting and Clinical Psychology*, *54*, 222–226.

Heimberg, H. C. (1989). Cognitive and behavioral treatments for social phobia: A critical analysis. *Clinical Psychology Review*, *9*, 107–108.

Heimberg, R. C., Dodge, C. S., & Beck, R. E. (1987). Social phobia. In L. Michelson & L. M. Ascher (Eds.), *Anxiety and stress disorders: Cognitive-behavioral assessment and treatment* (pp. 280–309). New York: Guilford Press.

Herman, I. (1981, August). *Cognitive-behavioral therapy for substance abuse.* Paper presented at the annual meeting of the American Psychological Association, Los Angeles.

Hinshaw, S. P., & Erhardt, D. (1991). Attention deficit-hyperactivity disorder. In P. C. Kendall (Ed.), *Child and adolescent therapy: Cognitive-behavioral procedures* (pp. 98–128). New York: Guilford Press.

Holcomb, W. (1979). *Coping with severe stress: A clinical application of stress inoculation therapy.* Unpublished doctoral dissertation, University of Missouri, Columbia.

Hollon, S. D. (1984). Cognitive therapy for depression: Translating research into practice. *Behavior Therapist, 7,* 125–127.

Hollon, S. D. (1987, August). *Cognitive therapy and the prevention of relapse/recurrence in depression: Mechanisms and implications.* Paper presented at the annual meeting of the American Psychological Association, New York.

Hollon, S. D., & Beck, A. T. (1979). Cognitive therapy of depression. In P. Kendall & S. Hollon (Eds.), *Cognitive-behavioral interventions: Theory, research, and procedures.* New York: Academic Press.

Hollon, S. D., & Beck, A. T. (1986). Cognitive and cognitive-behavioral therapies. In S. L. Garfield & A. E. Bergin (Eds.), *Handbook of psychotherapy and behavior change* (3rd ed., pp. 443–489). New York: John Wiley & Sons.

Hollon, S. D., & Bemis, K. M. (1981). Self-report and the assessment of cognitive functions. In M. Hersen & A. S. Bellack (Eds.), *Behavioral assessment: A practical handbook.* (2nd ed.). Elmsford, NY: Pergamon Press.

Hollon, S. D., DeRubeis, R. J., & Evans, M. D. (1987). Causal mediation of change in treatment for depression: Discriminating between nonspecificity and noncausality. *Psychological Bulletin, 102,* 139–149.

Hollon, S. D., DeRubeis, R. J., Evans, M. D., Tuason, V. B., Weimer, M. J., & Garvey, M. J. (1986). *Cognitive therapy, pharmacotherapy, and combined cognitive-pharmacotherapy in the treatment of depression: Differential outcome.* Unpublished manuscript, University of Minnesota and the St. Paul–Ramsey Medical Center, Minneapolis–St. Paul, Minnesota.

Hollon, S. D., & Kendall, P. C. (1979). Cognitive-behavioral interventions: Theory and procedure. In P. Kendall & S. Hollon (Eds.), *Cognitive-behavioral interventions: Theory, research, and procedures* (pp. 445–453). New York: Academic Press.

Hollon, S. D., & Kendall, P. C. (1980). Cognitive self-statements in depression: Development of an automatic thoughts questionnaire. *Cognitive Therapy and Research, 4,* 383–395.

Hollon, S. D., Kendall, P. C., & Lumry, A. (1986). Specificity of depresso-typic cognitions in clinical depression. *Journal of Abnormal Psychology, 95,* 52–59.

Hollon, S. D., & Kriss, M. R. (1984). Cognitive factors in clinical research and practice. *Clinical Psychology Review, 4,* 35–76.

Holroyd, D. A. (1976). Cognition and desensitization in the group treatment of text anxiety. *Journal of Consulting and Clinical Psychology, 44,* 991–1001.

Horan, J., Hackett, G., Buchanan, J., & Stone, D. (1977). Coping with pain: A component analysis. *Cognitive Therapy and Research, 1,* 211–221.

Hughes, J. (1988). *Cognitive-behavioral therapy with children in schools.* Elmsford, NY: Pergamon Press.

Hurlburt, R. T., & Melancon, S. M. (1987). How are questionnaire data similar to, and different from, thought sampling data? Five studies manipulating retrospectiveness, single-moment focus, and indeterminacy. *Cognitive Therapy, 11,* 681–704.

Hussian, R. A., & Lawrence, P. S. (1978). The reduction of test, state, and trait anxiety by test-specific and generalized stress inoculation training. *Cognitive Therapy and Research, 2,* 25–37.

Imber, S.D., Pilkonis, P., Sotsky, S., & Elkin, I. (1986, May). *NIMH Treatment of depression collaborative research program; Differential treatment effects.* Paper presented at the annual meeting of the American Psychiatric Association, Washington, DC.

Ingram, R. E. (1984). Toward an information processing analysis of depression. *Cognitive Therapy and Research, 8,* 443–478.

Ingram, R. E. (Ed.). (1986). *Information-processing approaches to clinical psychology.* New York: Academic Press.

Ingram, R. E., & Kendall, P. C. (1987). The cognitive side of anxiety. *Cognitive Therapy and Research, 11,* 523–536.

Jaremko, M. E. (1979). A component analysis of stress inoculation: Review and prospectus. *Cognitive Therapy and Research, 3,* 35–48.

Jarrett, R. B., & Nelson, R. O. (1987). Mechanisms of change in cognitive therapy of depression. *Behavior Therapy, 18,* 227–241.

Jenni, M. A., & Wollersheim, J. P. (1979). Cognitive therapy, stress management training, and the type A behavior pattern. *Cognitive Therapy and Research, 3,* 61–73.

Kagan, J. (1966). Reflection-impulsivity: The generality and dynamics of conceptual tempo. *Journal of Abnormal Psychology, 71,* 17–24.

Kanter, N. J. (1975). *A comparison of self-control desensitization and systematic rational restructuring for the reduction of interpersonal anxiety.* Unpublished doctoral dissertation, State University of New York at Stony Brook.

Karst, T. O., & Trexler, L. D. (1970). Initial study using fixed-role and rational-emotive therapy in treating public-speaking anxiety. *Journal of Consulting and Counseling Psychology, 34,* 360–366.

Kazdin, A. E., Esveldt-Dawson, K., French, N., & Unis, A.

(1987). Problem-solving skills training and relationship therapy in the treatment of antisocial child behavior. *Journal of Consulting and Clinical Psychology*, *55*, 76–85.

Keller, J., Crooke, J., & Brookings, J. (1975). Effects of a program in rational thinking on anxiety in older persons. *Journal of Counseling Psychology*, *22*, 54–57.

Kendall, P. C. (1977). On the efficacious use of self-instructional procedures with children. *Cognitive Therapy and Research*, *1*, 331–341.

Kendall, P. C. (1982). Cognitive processes and procedures in behavior-therapy. In C. M. Franks, G. T. Wilson, P. C. Kendall, & K. Brownell (Eds.), *Annual review of behavior therapy* (Vol. 8, pp. 120–155). New York: Guilford Press.

Kendall, P. C. (1985). Cognitive processes and procedures in behavior therapy. In C. M. Franks, G. T. Wilson, P. C. Kendall, & K. D. Brownell. *Annual review of behavior therapy: Theory and practice* (Vol. 10, pp. 123–163). New York: Guilford Press.

Kendall, P. C. (1987). Cognitive processes and procedures in behavior therapy. In G. T. Wilson, C. M. Franks, P. C. Kendall & E. J. Foreyt. *Review of behavior therapy: Theory and practice* (Vol. 11, pp. 114–153). New York: Guilford Press.

Kendall, P. C. (1989). *Stop and think workbook*. (Available from the author, 238 Meeting House Lane, Merion Station, PA 19066.)

Kendall, P. C. (1990). Cognitive processes and procedures in behavior therapy. In C. M. Franks, G. T. Wilson, P. C. Kendall, & J. Foreyt, *Review of behavior therapy: Theory and practice* (Vol. 12, pp. 103–137). New York: Guilford Press.

Kendall, P. C. (1991). (Ed.). *Child and adolescent therapy: Cognitive-behavioral procedures*. New York: Guilford Press.

Kendall, P. C. (1991). Guiding theory for treating children and adolescents. In P. C. Kendall (Ed.), *Child and adolescent therapy: Cognitive-behavioral procedures* (pp. 3–24). New York: Guilford Press.

Kendall, P. C., & Bemis, K. M. (1984). Cognitive-behavioral interventions: Principles and procedures. In N. S. Endler & J. McV. Hunt (Eds.), *Personality and the behavioral disorders* (2nd ed., pp. 1069–1109). New York: John Wiley & Sons.

Kendall, P. C., & Braswell, L. (1982b). Cognitive-behavioral self-control therapy for children: A components analysis. *Journal of Consulting and Clinical Psychology*, *50*, 672–690.

Kendall, P. C., & Finch, A. J., Jr. (1978). A cognitive-behavioral treatment for impulsivity: A group comparison study. *Journal of Consulting and Clinical Psychology*, *46*, 110–118.

Kendall, P. C., & Hollon, S. D. (1979). Cognitive-behavioral interventions: Overview and current status. In P. C. Kendall & S. D. Hollon (Eds.), *Cognitive-behavioral interventions: Theory, research, and procedures* (pp. 1–9). New York: Academic Press.

Kendall, P. C., & Hollon, S. D. (1981a). *Assessment strategies for cognitive-behavioral interventions*. New York: Academic Press.

Kendall, P. C., & Hollon, S. D. (1981b). Assessing self-referent speech: Methods in the measurement of self-statements. In P. C. Kendall & S. D. Hollon (Eds.), *Assessment strategies for cognitive-behavioral interventions* (pp. 85–118). New York: Academic Press.

Kendall, P. C., Howard, B., & Hays, R. (1989). Self-referent speech and psychopathology: The balance of positive and negative thinking. *Cognitive Therapy and Research*, *13*, 583–598.

Kendall, P. C., & Ingram, R. E. (1987). The future of cognitive assessment of anxiety: Let's get specific. In L. Michelson & M. Ascher (Eds.), *Anxiety and stress disorders: Cognitive-behavioral assessment and treatment* (pp. 89–104). New York: Guilford Press.

Kendall, P. C., & Ingram, R. E. (1989). Cognitive-behavioral perspectives: Theory and research on anxiety and depression. In P. C. Kendall and D. Watson (Eds.) *Anxiety and depression: Distinctive and overlapping features*. New York: Academic Press.

Kendall, P. C., & Korgeski, G. P. (1979). Assessment and cognitive-behavioral interventions. *Cognitive Therapy and Research*, *3*, 1–21.

Kendall, P. C., & Kriss, M. R. (1983). Cognitive-behavioral interventions. In C. E. Walker (Ed.), *Handbook of clinical psychology*. Homewood, IL: Dow Jones-Irwin.

Kendall, P. C., & Lipman, A. (1991). Psychological and pharmacological therapy: Methods and modes for comparative outcome research. *Journal of Consulting and Clinical Psychology*, *59*, 78–87.

Kendall, P. C., Reber, M., McLeer, S., Epps, J., & Ronan, K. (1990). Cognitive-behavioral treatment of conduct-disordered children. *Cognitive Therapy and Research*, *14*, 279–298.

Kendall, P. C., & Wilcox, L. F. (1980). A cognitive-behavioral treatment for impulsivity: Concrete versus conceptual training non-controlled problem children. *Journal of Consulting and Clinical Psychology*, *48*, 80–91.

Kendall, P. C., Williams, L., Pechacek, T. F., Graham, L., Shisslak, C., & Herzoff, N. (1979). Cognitive-behavioral and patient education interventions in cardiac catheterization procedures. The Palo Alto medical psychology project. *Journal of Consulting and Clinical Psychology*, *47*, 49–58.

Kendall, P. C., & Zupan, B. A. (1981). Individual versus group application of cognitive-behavioral self-control procedures with children. *Behavior Therapy*, *12*, 344–359.

Kiesler, D. J. (1966). Some myths of psychotherapy research and the search for a paradigm. *Psychological Bulletin*, *65*, 110–136.

Kiesler, D. J. (1980). Psychotherapy process research; Viability and directions in the 1980's. In W. DeMoor & H. R. Nijingaarden (Eds.), *Psychotherapy: Research and training*. Amsterdam: Elsevier/North Holland Biomedical Press.

Kihlstrom, J. R., & Nasby, W. (1981). Cognitive tasks in clinical assessment: An exercise in applied psychology. In P. C. Kendall & S. D. Hollon (Eds.), *Assessment strategies for cognitive-behavioral interventions*. New York: Academic Press.

Kirsch, I. (1982). Efficacy expectations or response predictions: The meaning of efficacy ratings as a function of task characteristics. *Journal of Personality and Social Psychology*, *42*, 132–136.

Klepac, R. K., Hauge, G., Dowling, J., & McDonald, M. (1981). Direct and generalized effects of three components of stress inoculation for increased pain tolerance. *Behavior Therapy*, *12*, 417–424.

Kovacs, M., & Beck, S. T. (1978). Maladaptive cognitive structures in depression. *American Journal of Psychiatry*, *135*, 525–533.

Kovacs, M., Rush, A. J., Beck, A. T., & Hollon, S. D. (1981). Depressed outpatients treated with cognitive therapy or pharmacotherapy: A one-year follow-up. *Archives of General Psychiatry*, *38*, 33–39.

Landau, R. J., & Goldfried, M. R. (1981). The assessment of schemata: A unifying framework for cognitive, behavioral, and traditional assessment. In P. C. Kendall & S. D. Hollon (Eds.), *Assessment strategies for cognitive-behavioral interventions* (pp. 363–399). New York: Academic Press.

Last, C. G., Barlow, D. H., & O'Brien, G. T. (1985). Assessing cognitive aspects of anxiety: Stability over time and agreement between several methods. *Behavior Modification*, *9*, 72–93.

Lazarus, A. A., & Fay, A. (1981). Resistance or rationalization? A cognitive-behavioral perspective. In P. L. Wachtel (Ed.), *Resistance: Psychodynamic and behavioral approaches*. New York: Plenum Press.

Lazarus, R. S. (1989). Cognition and emotion from the RET viewpoint. In M. E. Bernard & R. DiGiuseppe (Eds.), *Inside rational-emotive therapy: A critical appraisal of the theory and therapy of Albert Ellis* (pp. 47–68). New York: Academic Press.

Leon, G. R. (1979). Cognitive-behavior therapy for eating disturbances. In P. C. Kendall & S. D. Hollon (Eds.), *Cognitive-behavioral interventions: Theory, research, and procedures* (pp. 357–388). New York: Academic Press.

Lewinsohn, P. M., Steinmetz, J. L., Larson, D. W., & Franklin, J. (1981). Depression-related cognitions antecedent or consequence? *Journal of Abnormal Psychology*, *90*, 213–219.

Lindsay, W. R., Gamsu, C. V., McLaughlin, E., Hood, E. M., & Espie, C. A. (1987). A controlled trial of treatments for generalized anxiety. *British Journal of Clinical Psychology*, *26*, 3–15.

Linehan, M. H., Goldfried, M. R., & Goldfried, A. P. (1979). Assertion therapy: Skill training or cognitive restructuring? *Behavior Therapy*, *10*, 372–388.

Lipsky, M. J., Kassinove, H., & Miller, N. J. (1980).

Effects of rational-emotive therapy, rational role reversal, and rational-emotive imagery on the emotional adjustment of community mental health center patients. *Journal of Consulting and Clinical Psychology*, *18*, 366–374.

Long, B. C. (1984). Aerobic conditioning and stress inoculation: A comparison of stress management interventions. *Cognitive Therapy and Research*, *8*, 517–542.

Long, B. C. (1985). Stress-management interventions: A 15-month follow-up of aerobic conditioning and stress inoculation training. *Cognitive Therapy and Research*, *9*, 471–478.

Luria, A. (1961). *The role of speech in the regulation of normal and abnormal behaviors*. New York: Liveright.

MacLeod, C., Mathews, A., & Tata, P. (1986). Attentional bias in anxiety states. *Journal of Abnormal Psychology*, *95*, 15–20.

Mahoney, M. J. (1977). Reflections on the cognitive-learning trend in psychotherapy. *American Psychologist*, *32*, 5–13.

Mahoney, M. J., & Arnkoff, D. B. (1978). Cognitive and self-control therapies. In S. L. Garfield & A. E. Bergin (Eds.), *Handbook of psychotherapy and behavior change* (2nd ed.) New York: John Wiley & Sons.

Mahoney, M. J., Lyddon, W. J., & Alford, D. J. (1989). An evaluation of the rational-emotive theory of psychotherapy. In M. E. Bernard & R. DiGiuseppe (Eds.), *Inside rational-emotive therapy: A critical appraisal of the theory and therapy of Albert Ellis* (pp. 69–94). New York: Academic Press.

Malamuth, Z. N. (1979). Self-management training for children with reading problems: Effects on reading performance and sustained attention. *Cognitive Therapy and Research*, *3*, 279–289.

Martzke, J. S., Andersen, B. L., & Caccioppo, J. T. (1987). Cognitive assessment of anxiety disorders. In L. Michelson & L. M. Ascher (Eds.), *Anxiety and stress disorders: Cognitive-behavioral assessment and treatment* (pp. 62–88). New York: Guilford Press.

Mathews, A., & MacLeod, C. (1985). Selective processing of threat cues in anxiety states. *Behavioral Research and Therapy*, *23*, 563–569.

Mathews, A., Mogg, K., May, J., & Eysenck, M. (1989). Implicit and explicit memory bias in anxiety. *Journal of Abnormal Psychology*, *98*, 236–240.

Mathews, A., Richards, A., & Eysenck, M. (1989). Interpretation of homophones related to threat in anxiety states. *Journal of Abnormal Psychology*, *98*, 31–34.

Maultsby, M. C., Jr. (1975). *Help yourself to happiness*. New York: Institute for Rational Living.

Maultsby, M., & Graham, D. (1974). Controlled study of the effect of psychotherapy on self-reported maladaptive traits, anxiety scores, and psychosomatic disease attitudes. *Journal of Psychiatric Research*, *10*, 121–132.

McCarthy, B. (1989). A cognitive-behavioral approach to sex therapy. In A. Freeman, K. M. Simon, C. E. Beutler, & H. Arkowitz (Eds.), *Comprehensive handbook of cognitive therapy* (pp. 435–447). New York: Plenum Press.

McFall, M. E., & Wollersheim, J. P. (1979). Obsessive-compulsive neurosis: A cognitive-behavioral formulation and approach to treatment. *Cognitive Therapy and Research, 3*, 333–348.

Meichenbaum, D. (1975a). Self-instructional methods. In F. Kanfer & A. Goldstein (Eds.), *Helping people change* (pp. 357–391). Elmsford, NY: Pergamon Press.

Meichenbaum, D. (1975b). A self-instructional approach to stress management: A proposal for stress inoculation training. In I. Sarason & C. D. Spielberger (Eds.), *Stress and anxiety*. New York: John Wiley & Sons.

Meichenbaum, D. (1977). *Cognitive-behavior modification: An integrative approach*. New York: Plenum Press.

Meichenbaum, D. (1978). Introduction to applied cognitive-behavior therapy. In D. Meichenbaum (Ed), *Cognitive behavior therapy: A practitioner's guide*. New York: BMA Audio Publications.

Meichenbaum, D. (1985). *Stress inoculation training*. Elmsford, NY: Pergamon Press.

Meichenbaum, D., & Asarnow, J. (1979). Cognitive-behavior modification and metacognitive development: Implications for the classroom. In P. C. Kendall & S. D. Hollon (Eds.), *Cognitive-behavioral intervention: Theory, research and procedures* (pp. 11–35). New York: Academic Press.

Meichenbaum, D. H., & Cameron, R. (1974). The clinical potential of modifying what clients say to themselves. *Psychotherapy: Theory, Research, and Practice, 11*, 103–117.

Meichenbaum, D. H., & Deffenbacher, J. L. (1988). Stress inoculation training. *The Counseling Psychologist, 16*, 69–90.

Meichenbaum, D. H., & Gilmore, J. B. (1981). Resistance: From a cognitive-behavioral perspective. In P. L. Wachtel (Ed.), *Resistance: Psychodynamic and behavioral approaches* (pp. 133–156). New York: Plenum Press.

Meichenbaum, D. H., Gilmore, J. B., & Fedoravicius, A. (1971). Group insight versus group desensitization in treating speech anxiety. *Journal of Consulting and Clinical Psychology, 36*, 410–421.

Meichenbaum, D. H., & Goodman, J. (1971). Training impulsive children to talk to themselves: A means of developing self-control. *Journal of Abnormal Psychology, 77*, 115–126.

Meichenbaum, D. H., & Turk, D. (1976). The cognitive-behavioral management of anxiety, anger and pain. In P. Davidson (Ed.), *Behavioral management of anxiety, depression and pain*. New York: Brunner/Mazel.

Melzack, R., & Wall, P. (1965). Pain mechanisms: A new theory. *Science, 150*, 971.

Merluzzi, T. V., & Boltwood, M. D. (1989). Cognitive assessment. In A. Freeman, K. M. Simon, C. E. Beutler, & H. Arkowitz (Eds.), *Comprehensive handbook of cognitive therapy* (pp. 249–266). New York: Plenum Press.

Miller, I. W., Norman, W. H., & Keitner, G. I. (1989). Cognitive-behavioral treatment of depressed inpatients:

Six- and twelve-month follow-up. *American Journal of Psychiatry, 146*, 1274–1279.

Miller, I. W., Norman, W. H., Keitner, G. I., Bishop, S. D., & Dow, M. G. (1989). Cognitive-behavioral treatment of depressed inpatients. *Behavior Therapy, 20*, 25–47.

Miranda, J., & Persons, J. B. (1988). Dysfunctional attitudes are mood-state dependent. *Journal of Abnormal Psychology, 97*, 76–79.

Mogg, K., Mathews, A., & Weinman, J. (1987). Memory bias in clinical anxiety. *Journal of Abnormal Psychology, 96*, 94–98.

Moses, A. N., & Hollandsworth, J. G. (1985). Relative effectiveness of education alone versus stress inoculation training in the treatment of dental phobia. *Behavior Therapy, 16*, 531–537.

Murphy, G., Simons, A. D., Wetzel, R. D., & Lustman, P. J. (1984). Cognitive therapy and pharmacotherapy, singly and together in the treatment of depression. *Archives of General Psychiatry, 41*, 33–41.

Novaco, R. W. (1975). *Anger control: The development and evaluation of an experimental treatment*. Lexington, MA: Heath.

Paetzer, J., & Fleming, B. (1989). Cognitive-behavioral treatment of personality disorders. *Behavior Therapist, 12*, 105–109.

Parrish, J. M., & Erickson, M. T. (1981). A comparison of cognitive strategies in modifying the cognitive style of impulsive third grade children. *Cognitive Therapy and Research, 5*, 71–84.

Piasecki, J., & Hollon, S. D. (1987). Cognitive therapy for depression: Unexplicated schemata and scripts. In N. S. Jacobson (Ed.), *Psychotherapists in clinical practice: Cognitive and behavioral perspectives* (pp. 121–152). New York: Guilford Press.

Roper, V. C. (1976). *Rational-emotive therapy: A critical review of the research*. Unpublished manuscript.

Rorer, L. G. (1989). Rational-emotive therapy: I. An integrated psychological and philosophical basis. *Cognitive Therapy and Research, 13*, 475–492.

Rudy, T. E., & Merluzzi, T. V. (1984). Recovering social-cognitive schemata: Descriptions and applications of multidimensional scaling for clinical research. In P. C. Kendall (Ed.), *Advances in cognitive-behavioral research and therapy* (Vol. 3, pp. 61–102). New York: Academic Press.

Rush, A. J., Beck, A. T., Kovacs, M., & Hollon, S. D. (1977). Comparative efficacy of cognitive therapy and pharmacotherapy in the treatment of depressed outpatients. *Cognitive Therapy and Research, 1*, 17–37.

Rush, A. J., Beck, A. T., Kovacs, M., Weissenburger, J., & Hollon, S. D. (1982). Comparison of the effects of cognitive therapy and pharmacotherapy on hopelessness and self-concept. *American Journal of Psychiatry, 139*, 862–866.

Safran, J. D., Alden, L. E., & Davidson, P. O. (1980). Client anxiety level as a moderator variable in assertion training. *Cognitive Therapy and Research, 4*, 189–200.

Salkovskis, P. M., Jones, D. R., & Clark, D. M. (1986).

Respiratory control in the treatment of panic attacks: Replication and extension with concurrent measurement of behavior and CO_2. *British Journal of Psychiatry, 148*, 526–532.

Schwartz, R. M., & Garamoni, G. L. (1986). Cognitive assessment: A multibehavior-multimethod-multiperspective approach. *Journal of Psychopathology and Behavioral Assessment, 8*, 185–197.

Segal, Z. V. (1988). Appraisal of the self-schema construct in cognitive models of depression. *Psychological Bulletin, 103*, 147–162.

Segal, Z. V., & Shaw, B. F. (1988). Cognitive assessment: Issues and methods. In K. Dobson (Ed.), *Handbook of cognitive-behavioral therapies* (pp. 39–81). New York: Guilford Press.

Sharp, J. J., & Forman, S. G. (1985). A comparison of two approaches to anxiety management for teachers. *Behavior Therapy, 16*, 370–383.

Shaw, B. F., & Dobson, K. S. (1988). Competency judgments in the training and evaluation of psychotherapists. *Journal of Consulting and Clinical Psychology, 56*, 666–672.

Silverman, J. S., Silverman, J. A., & Eardley, D. A. (1984). Do maladaptive attitudes cause depression? *Archives of General Psychiatry, 41*, 28–30.

Simons, A. D., Garfield, S. L., & Murphy, G. (1984). The process of change in cognitive therapy and pharmacotherapy for depression: Changes in mood and cognition. *Archives of General Psychiatry, 41*, 45–51.

Simons, A. D., Murphy, G., Levine, J. L., & Wetzel, R. D. (1986). Cognitive therapy and pharmacotherapy for depression: Sustained improvement over one year. *Archives of General Psychiatry, 43*, 43–48.

Smith, D. (1982). Trends in counseling and psychotherapy. *American Psychologist, 37*, 802–809.

Smith, T. W. (1989). Assessment in rational-emotive therapy: Empirical access to the ABCD model. In M. E. Bernard & R. DiGiuseppe (Eds.), *Inside rational-emotive therapy: A critical appraisal of the theory and therapy of Albert Ellis* (pp. 135–154). New York: Academic Press.

Snyder, J. J., & White, M. J. (1979). The use of cognitive self-instruction in the treatment of behaviorally disturbed adolescents. *Behavior Therapy, 10*, 227–235.

Steuer, J. L., Mintz, J., Hammen, C. L., Hill, M. A., Jarvik, L. F., McCarley, T., Motoike, P., & Rosen, R. (1986). Cognitive-behavioral and psychodynamic group psychotherapy in treatment of geriatric depression. *Journal of Consulting and Clinical Psychology, 52*, 180–189.

Sutton-Simon, K., & Goldfried, M. R. (1979). Faulty thinking patterns in two types of anxiety. *Cognitive Therapy and Research, 3*, 193–203.

Sweeney, G. A., & Horan, J. J. (1982). Separate and combined effects of cue-controlled relaxation and cognitive restructuring in the treatment of musical performance anxiety. *Journal of Counseling Psychology, 29*, 486–497.

Teasdale, J. D., Fennell, M. J. V., Hibbert, G. A., & Amies, P. L. (1984). Cognitive therapy for major depressive disorder in primary care. *British Journal of Psychiatry, 144*, 400–406.

Thompson, L. W., Gallagher, D., & Breckenridge, J. S. (1987). Comparative effectiveness of psychotherapies for depressed elderlies. *Journal of Consulting and Clinical Psychology, 55*, 385–390.

Thompson, S. (1974). *The relative efficacy of desensitization, desensitization with coping imagery, cognitive modification, and rational-emotive therapy with test-anxious college students.* Unpublished doctoral dissertation, University of Arkansas.

Tiegerman, S. (1975). *Effects of assertive training and cognitive components of rational therapy on the promotion of assertive behavior and the reduction of interpersonal anxiety.* Unpublished doctoral dissertation, Hofstra University.

Trexler, L. D., & Karst, T. O. (1972). Rational-emotive, placebo, and no treatment effects on public speaking anxiety. *Journal of Abnormal Psychology, 79*, 60–67.

Turk, D. (1975). *Cognitive control of pain: A skills training approach.* Unpublished manuscript, University of Waterloo.

Turk, D. C., & Salovey, P. (1985). Cognitive structures, cognitive processes, and cognitive-behavior modification: I. Client issues. *Cognitive Therapy and Research, 9*, 1–17.

Varni, J. W., & Henker, B. (1979). A self-regulatory approach to the treatment of three hyperactive boys. *Child Behavior Therapy, 1*, 171–192.

Vygotsky, L. S. (1962). *Thought and language.* Cambridge, MA: MIT Press.

Wachtel, P. L. (Ed). (1981a). *Resistance: Psychodynamic and behavioral approaches.* New York: Plenum Press.

Wachtel, P. L. (1981b). Resistance and the process of therapeutic change. In P. L. Wachtel (Ed.), *Resistance: Psychodynamic and behavioral approaches.* New York: Plenum Press.

Walen, S. R., DiGiuseppe, R., & Wessler, R. L. (1980). *A practitioner's guide to rational-emotive therapy.* New York: Oxford University Press.

Waskow, I. E., Hadley, S. W., Parloff, M. B., & Autrey, J. H. (1979). *Psychotherapy of depression collaborative research program.* Unpublished manuscript, National Institute of Mental Health, Rockville, MD.

Watkins, J. T. (1977). The rational emotive dynamics of impulsive disorders. In A. Ellis & R. Grieger (Eds.), *Handbook of rational emotive therapy.* New York: Springer.

Weissman, A. N., & Beck, A. T. (1978, April). *Development and validation of the Dysfunctional Attitudes Scale: A preliminary investigation.* Paper presented at the annual meeting of the American Educational Research Association, Toronto, Canada.

Wells, J. K., Howard, G. S., Nowlin, W. F., & Vargas, M. J. (1986). Presurgical anxiety and post surgical pain and adjustment: Effects of a stress inoculation procedure. *Journal of Consulting and Clinical Psychology, 54*, 831–835.

West, D., Horan, J., & Games, P. (1984). Component analysis of occupational stress inoculation applied to registered nurses in an acute care hospital setting. *Journal of Counseling Psychology*, *31*, 209–218.

Williams, J. M. G. (1984). Cognitive-behavior therapy for depression: Problems and perspectives. *British Journal of Psychiatry*, *145*, 254–262.

Wine, J. D. (1980). Cognitive-attentional theory of test anxiety. In I. G. Sarason (Ed.), *Test anxiety: Theory, research, and applications*. Hillsdale, NJ: Lawrence Erlbaum Associates.

Wise, E. H., & Haynes, S. N. (1983). Cognitive treatment of test anxiety: Rational restructuring versus attentional training. *Cognitive Therapy and Research*, *7*, 69–78.

Woodward, R., & Jones, R. B. (1980). Cognitive restructuring treatment: A controlled trial with anxious patients. *Behaviour Research and Therapy*, *18*, 401–407.

Young, J., & Swift, W. (1988a). Schema-focused cognitive therapy for personality disorders: Part I. *International Cognitive Therapy Newsletter*, *4*, pp. 5, 13–14.

Young, J., & Swift, W. (1988b). Schema-focused cognitive therapy for personality disorders: Part II. *International Cognitive Therapy Newsletter*, *4*, pp. 4–6.

Zeiss, A. M., Lewinsohn, P. M., & Munoz, R. F. (1979). Nonspecific improvement effects in depression using interpersonal skills training, pleasant activity schedules, or cognitive training. *Journal of Consulting and Clinical Psychology*, *47*, 427–439.

Zettle, R. D. (1987). Component and process analysis of cognitive therapy. *Psychological Reports*, *61*, 939–953.

Zettle, R. D., & Hayes, S. C. (1980). Conceptual and empirical status of rational-emotive therapy. In M. Hersen, R. M. Eisler, & P. M. Miller (Eds.), *Progress in behavior modification* (Vol. 9, pp. 125–166). New York: Academic Press.

CHAPTER 34

THE DEVELOPMENT AND PRACTICE OF GROUP TREATMENT

Sheldon D. Rose

THEORY AND PRACTICE OF GROUP TREATMENT

Society has long been organized into small groups: the family, the work group, the sports groups, and social friendship groups. In recent years the group has been used extensively for therapeutic and socioeducational purposes under many diverse theoretical frameworks. In the classical meta-analysis of outcome research by Smith, Glass, and Miller (1980), about half of the 475 studies they discovered were carried out within the context of the small group. Many clinical psychologists, and others in the helping professions, report that working with groups is a major part of their treatment practice. In a study by Rose, Siemons, and O'Bryan (1979), we reported that almost 50% of the practicing clinicians in the Association for the Advancement of Behavior Therapy claim that they were either working with groups or that they had recently been working with clients in groups.

Group therapy and counseling, according to its proponents, are used extensively because of its many advantages, most of which have been only clinically documented. In groups a client must learn to deal with the idiosyncrasies of other individuals. She or he must acquire skills in offering critical feedback and advice in a constructive and tactful manner. By helping others, clients are likely to practice a set of strategies for helping themselves and extend what they have learned about helping to others outside of the group. In this way they are likely to improve their extra-group relationships. Also among these advantages are the multiple roles that members are able to play in the group. They can be the helper of others or cotherapist, as well as client and target of change. In this capacity it is likely that they feel in greater charge of their lives than in the dyadic therapy situation, in which they are usually in a one-down position.

Groups provide frequent and varied opportunity for mutual reinforcement and support, which for clients is often far more powerful than reinforcement and support by the therapist alone. Reinforcement is a highly valued skill in our society; there is good reason to believe that as a client learns to reinforce others, she or he is reciprocally reinforced by others, and mutual liking also increases (Lott & Lott, 1965).

In the process of interaction in therapy groups, norms (informal agreements among members as to preferred modes of action and interaction in the group) often arise, which serve to influence the behavior of individual members. If these norms are introduced and effectively maintained by the group therapist they serve as powerful therapeutic tools. The group pressures deviant members to conform to such norms as open self-disclosure, attending regularly, reinforcing peers who do well), analyzing problems appropriately, and assisting peers with their problems.

More accurate assessment and diagnosis may also be a major contribution of therapy in groups. Clients can be observed in their typical reactions to peers as well as to authority figures. For the psychoanalyst, the group provides a prototype of the original family and hence greater opportunities for working through transference conflicts; moreover, the group provides the client with multiple opportunities and encouragement for catharsis.

Finally, in a review of the research of group versus individual treatment, Toseland and Siporin (1986) found that group approaches, with some exceptions, are just as or more effective than individual approaches; moreover, in most cases the group was more efficient than individual treatment.

Of course, the group is not without major disadvantages as well. Foremost is the negative expectations by many clients for group therapy. A survey of 206 clinical and nonclinical subjects reflected three categories of expectations: (a) group therapy is unpredictable, (b) group therapy is not as effective as individual therapy, and (c) group therapy can be detrimental to participants (Slocum, 1987). Many persons with extremely negative perceptions of the group or who are extremely shy may not able to use the group as a context of therapy.

Antitherapeutic norms can arise and be maintained if the therapist does not deal with such norms with the group members. Moreover, such group phenomena as group contagion and aggression can get out of hand more readily in groups than in the dyad, with the group members forming powerful coalitions against the group therapist (see Bion, 1961). In spite of such complications effective strategies for dealing with such group phenomena are available, and some authors (e.g., Bion, 1961; Rose, 1989; Yalom, 1985) claim to make use of these group phenomena to facilitate treatment. Finally, individualization of the client's problems is more difficult in groups than in individual treatment, though not impossible to carry out, and confidentiality is more difficult to maintain.

A BRIEF HISTORY

In spite of the advantages noted above (or because of the disadvantages), it was not until 1905 that Joseph Pratt, an internist working in Boston, organized one of the first groups for therapeutic purposes. The "class," as he called it, was composed entirely of tuberculosis patients, suffering from severe physical debilitation and despondency and who for the most part were rejected by the community. The group met once or twice weekly with 20 to 30 patients, with Pratt providing informational lectures about the disease and method of cure, as well as support and encouragement. Patients who had conquered their illness would describe to the group the ways in which they had been cured. Resistance to attending the group sessions resulted in 8 to 12 hours a day of bed rest, supervised by a nurse (Hadden, 1975).

As early as 1910 in Europe Jacob L. Moreno (1953) introduced psychodrama, the acting out of problem situations to achieve awareness of the internal conflict and its potential resolution. He introduced his methods to the U.S. in 1925. In psychodrama the therapist, known as the director, encourages each patient to act out situations from his or her past or current life. The other group members, the audience, may comment or see their own problems manifested in the role play. Many of these procedures are still used today, and the psychodrama as a group therapeutic approach seems to be thriving.

In 1919, a psychiatrist and minister, L. Cody Marsh, began to apply a method similar to that of Pratt with institutionalized mental patients. His program, too, was organized much like a class insofar as there were lectures, patients were expected to take notes, outside readings were assigned, and patients who "failed" were often required to take the "class" again.

At the same time, a psychiatrist, E.W. Lazell, also using lectures with schizophrenics, noted the effect of intermember discussion, and suggested that this sharing of information, comparing of symptoms, and general interaction might account for therapeutic progress (Hadden, 1975).

Although Freud did not do group therapy, his work with a study group in 1909, which included a number of prominent pioneers of psychoanalysis, and his treatises on group psychology originally published in 1921 (Freud, 1953) contributed to group psychotherapy in general. The ideas of Alfred Adler were integrated into group therapy to promulgate social and cultural adaptation. Adler emphasized, for the first time, the social atmosphere of equality and the encouragement and support that patients offer each other in group psychotherapy. He saw emotional disorders as "failures in life" or erroneous ways of living. The implication was that the group should be a place to teach members a life-style or approach to life that can realize their social interests. Moreover, rather than emphasizing early childhood experiences, Adler stressed the significance of the way we perceived those events. The approach is basically optimistic insofar as the group can help change the perception. This basically positive approach with a focus on improved life-style and changing distorted perceptions is also found in some of the current encounter group and group behavioral approaches.

The main impetus in America in the early 1920s for working with groups with neurotic outpatients came from Trigant Burrow, a psychiatrist, who had received his analysis from Jung. He used the group for the first time as a means for psychoanalytic treatment (Sadock & Kaplan, 1983). The class-like atmosphere was somewhat reduced, as patients were encouraged to share their thoughts and feelings (a crucial dimension of almost all current group therapy). One of his major contributions to the development of group psychotherapy occurred in 1920 when Jung brought a group of 20 people of diverse roles and social status together in an isolated rural setting so that they could examine distortions and facades due to this diversity. This program was a forerunner of the human potential or encounter group movement.

In the 1930s two other psychiatrists stand out in the history of group psychotherapy: Louis Wender and Paul Schilder, both of whom viewed the group as an opportunity to recreate the basic family. However, both continued to lecture their patients in the first part of the meeting. Wender advocated combined individual and group treatment. Schilder emphasized the commonality of feelings to be shared by all group members. Both men began to deal with problems of transference and countertransference in the groups and helped patients to work though their early conflicts (Sadock & Kaplan, 1983).

At the same time, Samuel Slavson (1951), originally an engineer, proposed activity group therapy. For the most part he ignored the group and encouraged members to perform spontaneously in order to act out their conflicts, which then could be more readily examined. In other ways he was loyal to psychoanalytic theory. As the organizer of the American Group Psychotherapy Association in 1948, and because of his theories and practical applications, Slavson played a major role in the development of the field.

Discovering Group Phenomena

Although it was Freud (1953) who first wrote about the leaderless group and the processes it engendered, it remained for an English psychiatrist, Wilfred Bion in the 1950s, to introduce group phenomena to group psychotherapy and use the group itself as a treatment procedure. Bion (1961) postulated three assumptions that interfere with the mature functioning of the group. The first is that members look for a leader on whom they can depend for emotional support; the second assumption is that in the absence of this support, members pair off with each other; and finally, not finding what they are looking for in each other, members either stay to fight each other and the leader or withdraw physically or psychologically from the group. The focus of the therapist is to lead the group through timely interpretations to a maturer state of functioning. The focus was on insight and working though one's conflict via the group. Determining or even considering success of the therapeutic endeavor was still ignored. Moreover, the role of therapist is highly restricted. He or she remains impersonal, passive, and limits activity to impersonal group interpretation.

Introducing Social Psychology to Group Therapy

Kurt Lewin (1951) went much further in the late 1930s in considering the group as a social phenomenon in its own right. Drawing from social psychology, he viewed the group as an entity having its own unique characteristics, which he called *group dynamics*. Lewin saw the individual's performance as being in response to this "field of forces" rather than individual psychodynamics. He introduced such concepts as group pressure, the influence of the group on the individual to conform to group standards, and group goals. By introducing social psychological concepts and the group to group therapists Lewin introduced a new stream of thought into group therapy. Another contribution of Lewin was his attempt to incorporate research into therapeutic action. Lewin's work stimulated a new branch of group therapy.

One of the direct results of his work was T-groups or training groups (which focused on organizational change). The T-group is a relatively unstructured group in which the participant functions as learner rather than patient. The trainer serves as a resource rather than leader of the group. The focus of interaction is on the here-and-now rather than on the then-and-there. Members learn through confrontation by other members of the group about the in-group behavior of each and its effects on others. New concepts were developed for the T-groups, such as feedback, unfreezing, phases of group development, and observer participation. These concepts were also incorporated into group therapy and still more into the encounter group movement. A whole new field of applied research was launched, group dynamics.

SOME CURRENT APPROACHES TO WORKING WITH GROUPS

Human Growth Groups: The Normal Person's Psychotherapy

Many people feel alienated from the world about them or have personal blocks to spontaneity or "real" contact with other people. Many of these people also feel they have no problem serious enough to warrant therapy and as a result they have turned to encounter growth groups (in contrast to therapy) as a means of gaining greater personal fulfillment. In response to this interest many types of encounter groups evolved in the 1950s. Most of these groups were time limited and many met in protected settings away from the stresses of everyday life, such as Esalen in Big Sur, California. Members in this type of group are encouraged to express their real feelings about each other and all aspects of life. They are encouraged to seek an "encounter" with another that would free them from their sense of isolation. Members are strongly urged to be open and honest with each other and, above all, with themselves. Often group exercises are used, such as fantasizing that the group is on an isolated island, in which each participant expresses whatever comes into his or her mind. Such exercises are used to enhance the discussion and to provide new experiences and insight into the shifting levels of awareness. In addition, touching, massage, meditation, and sensory awakening exercises are included. A great deal of attention is paid to the group process, for example, by building a group climate of trust or intense group cohesion. The basic difference between the encounter group and the therapy group, according to Yalom (1985, p. 514), is that patients in therapy groups have "different goals, more deeply disrupted intra- and interpersonal relationships and a closed and survival-based orientation to learning. These factors result in process and procedural differences both in the early stages and in the late working-through stages of the group."

Self-Help Movement

One characteristic of the encounter group movement is that therapists came from many different backgrounds and were not restricted to psychiatry and psychology. Many people had earlier become discouraged with the professional as therapist. In this period of rapidly expanding numbers of groups an indication of further rejection of the professional psychiatrist, social worker, or psychologist could be found in the self-help movement, which advocated total separation from professional organizations and professional practitioners.

Self-help groups are designed to help clients deal with critical life events or specific chronic problem situations. Because of the perceived failure of professionals who have never experienced the problem facing the group, clients band together according to their specific problem, such as recovering alcoholics, weight losers, former mental patients, cancer patients, recovering compulsive gamblers, the recently divorced, and parents who have lost a child. In many cases these groups have become social movements. These self-help groups generally provide mutual support and understanding for their members, which the members assume are best provided by people who have the same or similar problem. The self-help group provides an opportunity for persons with a common source of pain to grieve together. They do not usually aim at changing individuals' personality functioning, nor do they delve deeply into personal psychodynamics. Many self-help groups make use of public commitment to a course of action; they also provide an opportunity for an exchange of coping strategies. These groups appear to be helpful to a large number of people. Even professional therapists refer their clients to such groups to supplement individual therapy or as strategy for maintaining change. Self-help groups do run the risk of a leader arising out of the membership whose psychological needs are such that he or she controls or disrupts the group. Even well-motivated leaders without training have difficulty in handling the myriad of group problems that often arise in such groups. Some of these groups have turned to the use of professionals as consultants to rectify some of these problems.

Research Findings

Although the findings of at least one major retrospective study are available on the process of self-help groups and consumer satisfaction (Lieberman & Borman, 1979), there is little outcome research on the effectiveness of such groups. In at least one comparative outcome study of caregivers (in this case people who took care of aging parents) support groups (Toseland, Rossiter, & Labrecque, 1988) it was found that support groups were significantly more effective than a wait-list control whether or not they had a professional therapist. However, there was no difference between the professionally led and nonprofessionally led support groups. A similar finding in terms of member outcomes was obtained by Toro et al. (1988). They also found that the presence of professionals changed the general climate of the group to what the authors believed was to the detriment of the group. On the other hand, Lieberman and Bliwise (1985) found that professionally led groups had a greater impact on improvement of mental health indexes compared to the peer-led groups of elderly persons living in the community. In spite of only limited research, there are a growing number of different kinds of self-help groups being developed, many with a professional as consultant and a social agency as a sponsor.

Group-Oriented Group Psychotherapy

Although in recent years many outstanding group psychotherapists have described their work in detail and have many followers, Yalom stands out because of the clarity of his model, his active research program and reliance on research findings, and his articulation of the group as a major source of change in the group.

Yalom represents the integration of the psychodynamic and small group theoretical developments of the last 60 years and is open to new behavioral considerations as well. In the following section we present some of the major assumptions governing his model.

Group Curative Factors

Yalom, as do many of his colleagues, assumes that major therapeutic factors in group therapy are its potential for the corrective recapitulation of the primary family, the opportunity for catharsis, working through the transference conflict, as well as such group phenomena as group cohesion and interpersonal learning. He draws upon the behavioral theories that suggest that modeling is especially effective in group therapy in learning new and more effective interpersonal behavior.

Yalom also sees the group as an efficient means of imparting knowledge, as did the early group psychotherapists and current behaviorists and educationalists. In addition, he assumes that the group instills hope, helps develop socializing techniques, and encourages altruism. He labels these as curative factors. Some of these are passive group effects. Other must be promulgated by the actions of the therapist (Yalom, 1985, p. 4). Furthermore, he points to great differences among clients as to which combination of these factors has the greatest impact on positive outcomes. In general, he and his colleagues have determined the most valued factors by asking the consumers of therapy. The research support for these factors is limited to examining what clients perceive to be the most important factors in their therapy. Nevertheless, these factors provide a working framework for the therapist and point to a number of multivariate hypotheses waiting to be tested.

Therapist Tasks

Yalom gives as the primary task of the group therapist the creation and maintenance of the group. This therapist is responsible for developing a superindividual entity, the group, and to find ways of enhancing and protecting a high level of group cohesiveness that is, as stated above, in itself one of the assumed curative factors.

But encouraging high cohesion is not enough. The group must be shaped into a viable therapeutic social system. Desirable norms are established, for it is the members together who provide support and opportunities for altruism, instill hope in one another, provide an opportunity to universalize, and give significant advice. Thus, in Yalom's model the group is the major agent of change.

Because of the centrality of the group, Yalom sees the therapist, in his or her role of technical expert, as assisting the group in establishing norms, monitoring itself, increasing self-disclosure and mutual support, and facilitating certain procedural practices such as free interaction. He does not eschew using operant procedures, for which he cites research support, to achieve his goals, such as ignoring some behaviors and giving attention to others he wishes to increase. And, he gives careful attention to the mutual modeling effect of being in the group.

A third function of the leader is to keep the interaction in the here-and-now. Members are encouraged to experience each other as they react in the present. These here-and-now feelings become the basis of most of the discourse in the group. By staying in the here-and-now, feedback, catharsis, meaningful self-disclosure, and acquisition of socializing techniques are more readily facilitated. The fourth function is described as process illumination, which refers to the steps taken to help the group understand what is happening in the here-and-now among the members at the feeling level.

Organization for Group Therapy

Like most other group therapists, Yalom recommends a group size of 7 to 8 members, with his groups varying from 5 to 10 members. He recommends that meetings be of a duration of 80 to 90 minutes so as not to wear out clients. He does not appear to advocate time-extended or marathon groups because the latter does not favorably affect the communication patterns in the group following the marathon. He recommends a frequency of meeting at least twice a week or even more as a way of increasing the intensity of interaction in the group, but because of practicality, accepts a frequency of group meetings of no more than once a week. He supports the use of any setting with privacy and freedom from distraction. His groups tend to be open or closed depending on the stability of the environment. Most of the groups described by Yalom seem to have durations of 6 months or more.

Eclectic Theoretical Foundation

The Yalom model of group therapy attempts to integrate group and classical psychotherapeutic procedures with operant strategies and social learning procedures. It draws upon the assumptions of the human development groups and some of its techniques to enhance the well-being of the clients. It is one of the best described and illustrated models of group therapy, but its complexity and multitheoretical assumptions seem to make it difficult to carry out.

Research Support

Research is highly valued by Yalom, in contrast to many other group psychotherapy theoreticians. However, in spite of some interesting process research within the framework of group therapy, there is little outcome research to support its efficacy. Outcome research seems to fall primarily to the behavioral and cognitive-behavioral group therapy practitioners and scholars.

A major research project evaluating diverse approaches to group psychotherapy carried out by Lieberman, Yalom, and Miles (1973) indicated few differences in either outcome of actual leader activities among the various psychodynamic and encounter approaches. Because of this project's importance, we shall outline it in detail. The authors selected experienced and expert leaders from 10 schools of group psychotherapy: traditional National Training Laboratory (T-groups), encounter groups (personal growth group), gestalt groups, sensory awareness groups (Esalen group), transactional analytic groups, psychodrama group, Synanon, psychoanalytically oriented experiential groups, marathon groups, and encounter-tapes groups.

There were a total of 18 groups. Of the 210

subjects, all college undergraduates, who started, 40 dropped out before attending at least half of the meetings, and 170 finished the 30-hour group experience. One third of the participants at the termination of the group and at the 6 months follow-up had undergone moderate or considerable positive change. Maintenance of change was high for those who changed positively, and 75% maintained their change for at least 6 months. Approximately two-thirds found it an unrewarding experience (either dropout, casualty, negative change, or unchanged). Eight percent of the 210 suffered severe psychological upset that persisted for at least 6 months.

The results varied between groups but not between treatments. In some groups almost every member underwent some positive change with no one suffering injury; in other groups, not a single member benefitted, and a participant was fortunate to remain unchanged.

The ideological school to which a therapist belonged revealed little about the actual behavior of that therapist. The most successful therapist was one who was moderate in degree of emotional stimulation (challenging, confronting, overly active, intrusively modeling by personal risk-taking, and displaying high self-disclosure) and in expression of executive function (setting limits, rules, norms, goals; managing time; pacing, stopping, interceding, suggesting procedures). The successful therapist was also high in caring (offering support, affection, praise, protection, warmth, acceptance, genuineness, concern) and meaning attribution (explaining, clarifying, interpreting, providing a cognitive framework for change; translating feelings and experiences into ideas). Both caring and meaning attribution seemed necessary; neither alone was sufficient to ensure success.

In summary, one cannot conclude that group therapy or group encounters as practiced with college students is generally helpful. In fact, for some students, at least, it can be somewhat risky. However, the study has methodological weaknesses that prevent generalizing to all approaches and all populations.

In a well-designed control group outcome study Piper, Debbane, and Garant (1977) evaluated a group therapy program for 48 psychiatric outpatients. Matched on gender and certain selection criteria and then randomly assigned to one of four treatment groups, the subjects met weekly for 3 months. The subjects in dynamic interactional treatment groups improved significantly more than did the delayed treatment control on general psychiatric symptomatology and interpersonal functioning but not on patient ratings of improvement.

Short-term Psychotherapy in Groups

Although in the research studies mentioned above the groups lasted only for 3 months, Yalom's groups and those of most psychotherapists meet for upwards of 6 months. However, a new trend in group psychotherapy is short-term treatment, often only 6 to 14 weeks in duration. There are several reasons for this development. It is partially a result of research that indicates that short-term therapy is equally effective and less harmful than long-term therapy (see Reid & Shyne, 1969). Other reasons include the rising costs of therapy, the unwillingness of insurance companies to pay for extended treatment for which there is no empirical support, and the influence of short-term encounter groups and cognitive-behavioral groups, discussed below.

Short-term group psychotherapy tends to be a highly focused therapy that goes rapidly to a target problem. The group therapist, in contrast with other therapies, must be quite directive, informative, highly interpretive, and usually problem oriented. One of the most directive of short-term group therapies is the behavioral group therapy models.

Behaviorism and Group Therapy

Behaviorists discovered in the late 1960s that the group, for the most part, was a more efficient way of treating a common problem. In most of these studies, groups tend to be time-limited (6–18 sessions), meeting weekly with one or two therapists for 1 to 2 hours, with specific behaviors or cognitions as the target of change. Institutional and open-ended outpatient groups using behavioral methods are becoming more common (see, e.g., Flowers & Schwartz, 1985). Interventions are derived from social learning, operant, and cognitive theories. Groups are primarily used because many people can be treated at the same time in the same way and, thus, reduce the cost. Among the behaviorists only a few researchers today make explicit use of the group or even describe its attributes in their experiments. Group interventions are rarely made explicit in most of these descriptions, although it is probable that mutual reinforcement, the stimulation of high cohesion, mutual modeling, and group feedback occur in most of them. In most studies, the group phenomenon is confounded with intervention strategy. I shall discuss in detail one model of behavioral group treatment, variations of which are commonly seen in practice today: the group cognitive-behavioral method. Later I shall discuss a number of variations of this method or other behavioral methods.

Cognitive-Behavioral Group Therapy

The most common behavioral group approach to the treatment of adults is cognitive-behavioral group therapy. It is used for the treatment of a wide variety of complaints and is organized in much the same way as the groups mentioned above. Models of cognitive-behavioral group therapy vary considerably from each other, but most share the use of modeling, cognitive restructuring, problem solving, reinforcement, and relaxation. Let us look at one of these cognitive-behavioral models in more detail (for further elaboration on this approach with children see Rose & Edleson, 1987, and with adults see Rose, 1989).

Organization for Cognitive-Behavioral Group Therapy

Behavioral and cognitive-behavioral group therapy is usually time-limited treatment. Usually groups consists of 6 to 10 group members who share similar problems such as anger management, stress management or anxiety control, alcohol and drug abuse, pain management, phobic disorders, or depression. In many groups, models who have had the same problem but have demonstrated some skill in mastering it are included in the composition of the group. In most groups a treatment contract is employed as one means of orienting members to the group, to the procedures to be used, and to the mutual expectations for member and therapist behavior.

Assessment

Assessment is a concept central to all empirical approaches. The purpose of assessment is to determine the specific targets of interventions, the specific coping skills to be learned, formulated in such a way as to make them amenable to intervention. It has the additional purpose of determining whether the given group or another type of therapy might be the most appropriate setting for each potential client.

To answer all of these questions, data are usually collected before, during, immediately following, and at some time after therapy. Initial data are often collected in a pregroup interview. The most important tool in assessment is the group discussion of the types of situations clients find difficult or stressful to encounter, because the clients' responses to these situations are the major targets of change. For each client a list of such situations is ascertained. A situation is characterized by being recent, and specifies the time, place, who was involved, and what happened. The client describes the affective and behavioral responses with which she or he is dissatisfied. The question "why" is not asked. Clients interview each other until these criteria are met. As these situations evolve a number of interventions adapted from individual treatment or group procedures are selected to prepare the client to deal with these events. These interventions include reinforcement, cognitive and modeling procedures, relaxation, and homework.

Reinforcement

The use of high frequency of reinforcement in the initial phases of treatment has been demonstrated to increase the group cohesion (Goldstein, Heller, & Sechrest, 1966). Differential reinforcement is also used to increase certain group behaviors such as wide distribution of participation or, cooperative behaviors so as to create desirable group states. In addition, reinforcement is used for the completion of home tasks for which clients prepare themselves in the group. The frequency of reinforcement is often faded and the schedule of reinforcement becomes more intermittent as members approach termination in order to increase the likelihood of maintenance of the behaviors when the group has ended.

Modeling Interventions

Modeling interventions, though originally designed as individual treatment procedures, are uniquely suited to use in the group because of the ready availability of multiple models and multiple sources of feedback. The modeling sequence is used to train clients in those interpersonal skills needed to relate more effectively to significant people in their environment. The modeling sequence consists of role-played demonstrations, role-played practice by the client with the problem, feedback from the other clients, and homework to try out in the real world what was learned in the group.

Cognitive Interventions

These interventions are used to reduce stress and anxiety and to teach more effective cognitive coping skills for dealing with stress, anxiety, pain, or anger-inducing situations. Cognitive interventions in groups have been used to address a wide variety of other presenting problems as well.

When the goal is to ameliorate cognitive distortions that may be preventing effective problem solving or

other action, the coping skills to be learned are more appropriate cognitive evaluation and self-talk. Among the interventions introduced by group therapists to achieve these goals are cognitive restructuring, self-instructional training (Meichenbaum, 1986), and re-framing. (For a description of all of these, see Cormier & Cormier, 1985.) Cognitive restructuring can become a group procedure through the introduction of exercises in which the members evaluate as a group stressful situations and each other's self-defeating statements within those situational contexts and then suggest ways of rephrasing the statements. In addition, the members recommend to each other potential coping statements to be used in the above situations. Members help each other to identify self-defeating statements each manifests in the group. The group may use covert modeling to demonstrate to each other how these new coping statements should be carried out and covert rehearsal in which clients try out the new cognitions in front of the group under simulated conditions.

Systematic Problem Solving

Systematic problem solving is a central procedure in cognitive-behavioral group therapy insofar as clients bring problems of concern to the group and the group, under the guidance of the therapist, attempts to help them find solutions to those problems. These solutions often involve the development of coping skills. The basic assumptions of problem-solving theory are that problems constitute a normal part of one's life, one should identify troublesome situations and label them as such, and one should not act on impulse but rather in a systematic way to solve problems (Heppner, 1978). It is a systematic approach insofar as the members follow (or deviate by plan from) specified steps. These steps that are characteristic of the problem-solving process include orienting the members to the basic assumptions of problem solving, defining the problem, generating alternative solutions, selecting the best set of solutions, preparing for implementation, implementing the solution, and evaluating the outcome. These steps are a modification of those suggested by D'Zurilla and Goldfried (1971).

Problem solving is not only a general paradigm. It can be identified as a set of coping skills to be learned in its own right to replace more impetuous problem approaches. A review of research on the effectiveness of problem-solving training is found in Heppner (1978).

Relaxation Training

When the ability to relax in the face of stress-inducing situations is the goal, relaxation training is an appropriate intervention (Everly & Rosenfeld, 1981). The relaxation training program consists primarily of a brief lecture, a few questions answered by the therapist, a demonstration to the group, and practice by the members. One can convert relaxation training to an intensely interactive strategy by having the members work with each other in pairs—first, one member relaxes the other and each provides the other with feedback about the effectiveness of his or her respective roles, and then the roles are reversed. Instead of or in addition to relaxation, some group therapists teach meditation and/or deep breathing.

Extra-Group Tasks (Homework)

Another important but basically individual intervention strategy that facilitates generalization is the use of extra-group tasks. If the intervention is designed to bring about change in the real world, structured tasks performed in the real world appear to be the best way of achieving it. The in-group interventions must be viewed as a means of training people to perform and to monitor the performance of the extra-group task once it has occurred. Homework is used across all of the thematic groups already mentioned. Research to support the relevance of this intervention is described in Shelton and Levy (1981) for a variety of different types of individual settings. They also provide a theoretical foundation and criteria to increase the probability of extra-group task completion.

Extra-group tasks can be converted into a group procedure by having clients, in pairs, design tasks with each other. The assignment is then presented by the given member to the entire group, who give feedback to the member on the appropriateness of the extra-group task. The group members also monitor each other in terms of the quality of the extra-group work accomplished.

Group Procedures

Although all individual procedures must be adapted to use in the group, some procedures can be designated as group procedures because it is only in a group that they can be utilized. One of these procedures is the "buddy system," which is designed to achieve both common and group goals. In the buddy system members are paired to work together outside of the group.

The work entails monitoring each other, reinforcing each other for small achievements, and performing role plays carried out at least once in the group. Theory suggests that cohesion (Peteroy, 1983) begins with attraction to one or two persons in the group.

Group Problem Resolution

This process can actually occur at any time in the history of the group, although it is most likely to occur after the intervention phase begins. The threat of actually having to face the feared event in the natural environment will often trigger such group problems as interpersonal comparisons (mentioned above), lowering of cohesion, mutual disagreement with all plans, shared criticism of the therapist, a common failure to do homework, absenteeism, pairing off in the group meetings, off-task, and/or disruptive behavior in the group meeting. Usually a statement of what the group therapist perceives is happening plus encouragement to move on with the program is sufficient to handle the problem. If not, discussion of the therapist's observations followed by systematic problem solving provides the group with an opportunity to resolve the problem and to have a common experience in systematic problem solving.

Generalization

The purpose of most treatment is not only to achieve change but to transfer what has been learned in the clinical setting to the real world and to maintain what has been learned long after treatment has terminated. One of the major ways of transferring what is learned in the group is the use of homework to try out in the real world what one has learned in the group.

An important principle of maintaining change is preparation for setbacks. Mathews, Gelder, and Johnston (1981) made use of an individualized setback list for each patient. Such a list contained instructions as to what to do in case of a setback. The principles outlined were to go back to the anxiety-producing situation as soon as possible, to take one step back in practice and rehearse that step often, to brush up on coping instructions, and to remind oneself of previous gains.

Another procedure used in maintaining gains obtained in the group treatment of agoraphobics was the use of self-help groups following the more structured treatment (Sinnott, Jones, Scott-Fordham, & Woodward, 1981). Although increasing dependence on some external source of support, the self-help group reduces the dependency on the group worker and other professional staff. For those further along in treatment, social, recreational, or educational groups may be used.

Another principle of generalization is that the clients be maximally involved in their own treatment. Clients who make decisions about what happens to them in treatment appear to better maintain what they have done than those who are told what to do. Clients can be involved in a number of ways. First, each person decides for him- or herself the primary specific targets of change. Second, homework to be carried out is decided on by the clients. Third, they are involved in the evaluation of weekly programs and in providing suggestions for adaptations.

Rather than prepare people for the trauma of termination, clients are prepared to function independently of the group. However, in order to avoid abrupt termination, booster sessions are often held at 1-month, 2-month, and 6-month intervals. During this period the clients are asked to self-monitor their activities in the real world. At the sessions they report their successes and failures, and plans are made for how to deal with setbacks and prepare for the next booster session.

Research Support

Research for the most part indicates that behavioral and cognitive-behavioral procedures used in a group context are more effective than control groups in the treatment of stress (e.g., Tallant, Tolman, & Rose, 1989), pain (e.g., Puder, 1988; Subramanian & Rose, 1988; Turner & Clancy, 1988), social skill deficiencies, and self-control; however, when compared to other types of treatment, they are not significantly more effective.

In comparing behavioral and cognitive-behavioral treatment of depression in groups, Taylor and Marshall (1977) and Wilson, Goldin, and Charbonneau-Powis (1983) found that both were more effective than a control group in reducing depression and reducing negative self-talk. Shaw (1977) found that the cognitive-behavioral group approach was the more significant of the two in reducing depressive symptoms. However, cognitive-behavioral group therapy did not prove superior to the interpersonal group treatment approach (a group nondirective discussion method). Cognitive-behavioral treatment seems to be more effective at follow-up. Graff, Whitehead, and LeCompte (1986) studied long-term effects of the group treatment of divorced women. He found that though cognitive-behavioral and supportive-insight were

both more effective than a control group at the end of 12 sessions, at a 4-month follow-up cognitive-behavioral continued to be beneficial, whereas the supportive insight approach was consistently less effective.

Telch and Telch (1986) found that a support group for cancer patients showed little improvement, whereas cognitive-behavioral group treatment was consistently superior to both the support group as well as the control group.

When groups are compared to individual treatment, Shaffer, Shapiro, Sank, and Cohlan (1981) reported that cognitive behavior therapy in a group format is as effective as individual cognitive-behavior therapy in reducing symptoms of depression and anxiety and in enhancing assertiveness. Oei and Jackson (1980) found that group social skills training scored consistently better than individual social skills training on alcohol intake and personality measures throughout the 12-month treatment period. In the treatment of depression using a social learning approach, Teri and Lewinsohn (1985) found no significant differences between group treatment and individual treatment of major and minor depressive disorders on a number of outcome measures, although both resulted in significant pre–post change. Moreover, the group was more efficient in achieving the goals. On the other hand, Rush and Watkins (1981), in a nonrandom assignment study in which medication was confounded with individual therapy have found group treatment to be less effective than individual therapy using Beck's (1976) approach to cognitive-behavioral therapy.

Self-Control Groups

Self-control groups teach clients to use cognitive procedures to modify their evaluations of the environment and behavioral procedures to modify the environment itself in order to control a given behavior. The behavioral literature is replete with descriptions of weight control groups, eating disorders groups, alcohol and drug control groups, and sexual dysfunction groups that aim at increasing the clients' ability to achieve control of self and environment. Interventions rely largely on the provision of information to correct cognitive distortions, self-monitoring, self-reinforcement, positive self-talk, and self-instructions. However, increasing use seems to be made of social skill training based on the assumption that many self-control problems are correlated with social skill deficiencies. Most of these articles are descriptive or without control groups. One comparative study, Thomas, Petry, and Goldman's (1987), in comparing 12-hour (six session) self-control training with cognitive-behavior therapy in groups, found that both programs were followed by significant reductions in depression. These improvements remained stable at the follow-up, 6 months following termination.

Parent Training Groups

Another model that draws heavily on the cognitive-behavioral model is parent training. Parents are taught the essential parenting skills as a means of helping them to deal with their children's behavioral problems. The most common goals that parents have noted in these groups have been control of children's anger and other impulsive behavior, improving peer relationships and reducing social isolation, remediating self-control problems such as excessive eating, smoking, use of drugs and alcohol, and improving study habits. Of equal concern has been the parents' feeling of inadequacy in working with other professionals. Group discussion, modeling, didactic instruction, group exercises, and cognitive restructuring have all been combined into the parent package. Homework to try out newly learned procedures has been emphasized. In most case these procedures are used to help each parent with her or his own specific goals. Other parenting models have been far more didactic and of less duration. Parents are taught how to set limits, how to reinforce, and/or how to enter into problem solving with their child.

Research Support

Although research support is meager, some authors have found interesting comparisons between parent training in groups and contrast groups or wait-list controls. Using a similar package over a 9-week period, Adesso and Lipson (1981) found it more effective than no treatment control regardless of whether parents were seen individually or as a pair. Bernal, Klinnert, and Schultz (1980) studied the relative effectiveness of parent training in reducing conduct problems in children in comparison to client-centered parent counseling and compared both to a wait-listed group. Parent reports and paper-and-pencil tests of child deviance and parent satisfaction showed a superior outcome for behavioral over the client-centered and wait-listed control groups and no differences between the latter two groups. These differences were maintained at follow-up. Home observation data showed no advantage of behavioral over client-centered treatment, and neither of the treatment groups improved significantly more than the wait-listed control group. Webster-Stratton, Kolpa-

coff, and Hollinsworth (1988) compared four groups: an individually administered videotape modeling treatment (IVM), a group discussion videotape modeling treatment (GDVM), a group discussion treatment (GD), and a waiting-list control group. All three treatment groups of mothers reported significantly fewer child behavior problems, more prosocial behaviors, and less spanking than the control group. Fathers in the GDVM and IVM conditions and teachers of children whose parents were in the GDVM and GD conditions also reported significant reductions in behavior problems compared with control subjects. Home visit data indicated that all treatment groups of mothers, fathers, and children exhibited significant behavioral changes. There were relatively few differences between treatment groups on most outcome measures, although the differences found consistently favored the GDVM treatment.

Group Exposure for Agoraphobics

The exposure method, first reported on as a group approach by Watson, Mullett, and Pillay (1973) and Hand, LaMontagne, and Marks (1974), is an in vivo procedure in which the agoraphobic clients are treated in groups by means of confrontations in the real world with prolonged exposure to the objects of their fear. The clients not only discuss with the others the experience of going into various public places such as the streets, markets, and crowded buses, but they actually draw up a plan of action together and then carry it out as a group.

Group exposure interventions consist of (a) preparation for exposure, (b) group exposure, (c) evaluation of the exposure experience, and (d) homework in which exposure is carried out by the client as an extra-group assignment. During the preparation clients are trained in anxiety management procedures by means of modeling, simulated practice, and group discussion of any spontaneous accomplishments that occurred since the last session. In addition, the group members discuss the homework they have completed during the week. The major focus in the preparation part of the meeting is on the particular exposure exercise they will be performing at the given session. Often after a discussion of the exercise, the members will cognitively rehearse step-by-step what they will be doing shortly in the real world. In the extra-group exposure period, the group members leave the meeting room and go in the real world together to face the anxiety-producing situations.

Generally, a graduated program—from activities that are mildly anxiety producing to those that are highly anxiety producing—is used initially so as not to provoke an anxiety attack. Examples of high anxiety-producing events commonly used are shopping in a crowded supermarket, riding in a filled elevator, and taking a crowded bus.

In this model the group is used for mutual support when approaching the feared object and in trying out new behaviors. The group together can be used to determine a hierarchy of events, leading to the most fear-inducing ones.

Research Support

As compared with individual exposure, group approaches to the treatment of agoraphobia seem to be at least as effective and thus far more efficient in achieving the same level of goals (Emmelkamp & Emmelkamp-Benner, 1975). Some authors noted a consistent trend that patients treated individually tended to improve slightly less than those treated in a group (e.g., Hafner & Marks, 1976). Emmelkamp and van der Hout (1983) reported that some agoraphobics would not join a group, claiming that it was unsuitable to their problem. On the other hand, it is usually easier to convince clients in groups to try out the exposure exercises than clients in individual treatment, probably because of the mutual modeling and group reinforcement effect.

All of the behavioral models described above overlap considerably, which may be the reason that comparisons among behavioral models reveal few outcome differences. Most of the models seem to show improvement from pre- to posttesting and pre- to follow-up, and most seem to be significantly more effective than nontreatment controls.

SOME REMAINING ISSUES

Group Process Issues

A major limitation of all models of group behavioral therapy may be the fact that only a few authors seem to take advantage of the group as a source of intervention strategies or even as a source of error (see Rose, Tolman, & Tallant, 1985, for a review of research supporting this statement). Four exceptions have been Antonnucio, Lewinsohn, and Steinmetz (1982), Hand et al. (1974), Hoberman, Lewinsohn, and Tilson (1988), and Whitney and Rose (1989). Hand and his associates found that cohesive groups were more effective than less cohesive groups in achieving treatment goals. Antonnucio et al. (1982) found that there were large differences among leaders

but that these differences had little import for outcome in the group treatment of depression. In the Hoberman et al. (1988) study, it was noted that the outcome in the behavioral treatment of depression could in part be explained by the perception of cohesion at the earlier sessions. The Whitney and Rose (1989) findings suggest that groups using group process appear to be more effective in reducing perceived stress than groups that do not consider group process, whether or not behavioral procedures are used. For these reasons, the more common practice of not considering group process in studies in which the group is used as the context of treatment may be an important omission.

Integrating Behavioral and Nonbehavioral Methods

In some cases behavioral procedures have been integrated into nonbehavioral methods. For example, in some women's consciousness raising groups after consciousness is raised, the group has been refocused by using assertive training and cognitive restructuring to help the women determine what they should say when they are imposed upon and to reconceptualize how they view their rights.

Other examples can be found in those self-help groups where loss is the major theme, such as divorce groups or parents who have recently lost a child. Behavioral procedures, in my experience, could not be used until the members had had an opportunity to grieve. This shared grieving lends itself to mutual support and catharsis. However, at some point the clients want to return to a state of adequate functioning in their families, their jobs, and their other relationships. At this point in time behavioral interventions such as cognitive restructuring can help the clients deal with their newly changed world. As mentioned earlier, self-help groups have been used to maintain gains obtained in the group treatment of agoraphobics following the more structured treatment (Sinnott et al., 1981).

In groups in which resistance is high and motivation low, such as groups of men who batter, when new members say that they are different group confrontation may first be used to increase motivation and decrease resistance. It is at that point that more typical cognitive-behavioral methods can be introduced.

Many of the cognitive-behavioral groups with which I am familiar are not indisposed to using supportive methods along with behavioral methods, even though the former are often not reported in the research reports. These supportive endeavors may have a confounding effect on the results.

Yalom advises that group therapists use operant procedures such as extinction and verbal reinforcement to modify behaviors that disrupt or enhance the group process. For the most part therapists must be trained in both psychodynamic and behavioral procedures to integrate the methods. Before the reader becomes too enthusiastic about integration, it should be emphasized that there appears to be little research either to recommend or to rule out the practice. However, based on their experience, clinicians are moving toward an integrative practice from both behavioral and psychodynamic ends of the continuum.

Gender and Racial Issues

There are a number of gender issues that are rarely covered in the research on group outcome. For example, considering the gender composition of the group, what should be the gender of the therapist? Most therapy groups consist largely of women clients. The man as therapist provides a poor role model according to social learning and feminist theories. But the male therapist simulates more nearly the protagonist in the real world. If there are two therapists, a male and female, the problem may not be resolved, because often the male assumes the dominant role. We have some evidence that in assertive training groups of both genders men are more active than women and tend to assume leadership functions. Moreover, in groups messages to men are considered more acceptable than those to women (Wilson & Gallois, 1985). Similar questions must be raised in the area of racial composition, leadership differences, and so forth (Davis, 1984).

Training Issues

Most practitioners, including those belonging to the American Group Psychotherapy Association (AGPA), agree that at the very least the training of group therapists should include a set of seminars in theory and technique with emphasis on group procedures and group attributes in therapy, and a supervised clinical group experience as therapist or cotherapist; while leading groups, participation in a continuous case seminar on groups would also be helpful. Finally, training should include participation in a group as member or patient. Although these criteria do not establish quality control of content, only a small percentage of those serving groups have met even several of these criteria. In our survey mentioned earlier (Rose et al., 1979), we found that most behaviorists practicing group therapy had little training in

group therapy. Most obtained their training in brief workshops or by participating in an experiential group. A few had courses during their psychology training, but usually in a modality they were not using at the time of the survey. There is usually no supervised practice component in most training programs. Skill in individual therapeutic methods is necessary but not sufficient for most of those questioned. Although there is some literature on training it is generally didactic. Literature and research on training for group leadership need to be further integrated into curricula. If we look at the psychological damage to clients attributed to poor leaders in the Lieberman et al. (1973) study, we must give far greater attention to the training of good leaders.

CONCLUSION

The group as the context of treatment is probably here to stay. Not only is the group in common usage in clinical practice, it is a common context of treatment research. Practitioners will testify that the group can contribute to or prevent positive outcomes in clients. Summaries of research show that groups are consistently more effective than no treatment at all but not consistently more effective than other (i.e., individual) approaches. However, it is more efficient. There appears to be a growing together of different types of group approaches. Self-help groups are making greater use of professionals as consultants. Behavioral groups are more extensively drawing on the expertise of their members as models and in orienting new members and in performing other leadership functions. Group therapy too seems to be finding a greater balance between therapist control and client participation in leadership roles.

Although many groups are of long duration (6 months or longer), there is a growing number of short-term groups (6 to 14 weeks) designed to meet limited goals. This may be, in part, a function of insurance limitations as much as in the cognitive-behavioral developments, which are more focused than other therapies. Also, most of the research has been carried out on short-term groups.

Although without firm research support, there appears to be a growing interest in integration of various theoretical positions. Behaviorists are beginning to look again at relational skills and the drawing of behavioral patterns for clients, and the psychotherapeutic therapists are increasingly using operant, modeling, cognitive, relaxation procedures, and other coping strategies to supplement their interpretative methods. It remains to be determined whether this trend is beneficial to clients and for which clients it might be especially helpful.

Although training programs exist throughout the country, few have been systematically evaluated, and many therapists appear to be leading groups without benefit of much training of any sort. Such a condition must be given important consideration in the next decade to protect clients and to enhance the effectiveness of group training methods.

In spite of the problems mentioned above for the practice of group treatment the use of the group as a context of treatment seems to be expanding and branching into new areas. Workshops are being attended in great numbers by group practitioners who seek much needed training. Agencies are giving high priority to their group programs. At least six journals exist that are devoted to theory, practice, and occasionally research on group work, group therapy, and group counseling. These include: *International Journal of Group Psychotherapy*, *Journal of Specialists in Group Work*, *Social Work with Groups*, *Small Groups*, *The Group*, *Groupwork*, and *Empirical Group Work and Group Therapy: A Newsletter*. Many other journals in psychology, social work, and other clinical professions carry articles on group work and group therapy.

Unfortunately, the research has not kept pace with practice developments. Little research looks at both process and outcome. Although there have been many studies on groups, most have major methodological flaws. Most of the experiments have extremely small samples. The power in many cases is often too low to demonstrate the significance of small differences. Comparative programs tend to have overlapping conditions in the various treatment modalities. This overlap may wash out possibilities of finding differential outcomes. The individual is almost always used as the unit of analysis, when in fact the group should be the unit of analysis because of the dependency of clients interacting with each other. In some cases subjects are not randomly assigned or matched for the various conditions. The group leaders are often graduate students rather than experienced practitioners. As a result of these and other methodological deficiencies and the limited research carried out, there remain many unanswered questions. If group therapy is to become more than a weakly substantiated art, greater attention to research on clinical and evaluation practices is required.

REFERENCES

Adesso, V. J., & Lipson, J. W. (1981). Group training of parents as therapists for their children. *Behavior Therapy*, *12*, 625–633.

Antonuccio, D. O., Lewinsohn, P. M., & Steinmetz, J. L. (1982). Indentification of therapist differences in a group treatment for depression. *Journal of Consulting and Clinical Psychology*, *50*, 411–435.

Beck, A. T. (1976). *Cognitive therapy and emotional disorders*. New York: International Universities Press.

Bernal, M. E., Klinnert, M. D., & Schultz, L. A. (1980). Outcome evaluation of behavioral parent training and client-centered parent counseling for children with conduct problems. *Journal of Applied Behavior Analysis*, *13*, 677–692.

Bion, W. R. (1961). *Experiences in groups*. London: Tavistock Publications.

Cormier, W. H., & Cormier, L. S. (1985). *Interviewing strategies for helpers: Fundamental skills and cognitive behavioral interventions* (2nd Ed.). Monterey, CA: Brooks/Cole.

Davis, L. E. (1984). The essential components of group work with black Americans. *Social Work with Groups*, *7*, 97–109.

D'Zurilla, T. J., & Goldfried, M. R. (1971). Problem solving and behavior modification. *Journal of Abnormal Psychology*, *78*, 107–126.

Emmelkamp, P. M. G., & Emmelkamp-Benner, A. (1975). Effects of historically portrayed modeling and group treatment on self-observation: A comparison with agoraphobics. *Behavior Research and Therapy*, *13*, 135–139.

Emmelkamp, P. M. G., & van der Hout, A. (1983). Failure in treating agoraphobia. In E. B. Foa & P. M. G. Emmelkamp (Eds.), *Failures in behavior therapy*. New York: John Wiley & Sons.

Everly, G., & Rosenfeld, R. (1981). *The nature and treatment of the stress response: A practical guide for clinicians*. New York: Plenum Scientific and Medical Publications, pp. 89–112.

Flowers, J. V., & Schwartz, B. (1985). Behavior group therapy with heterogeneous clients. In D. Upper & S.M. Ross (Eds.), *Handbook of behavioral group therapy*. New York: Plenum Publishing.

Freud, S. (1953). *Group psychology and the analysis of the ego*. London: Hogarth Press.

Goldstein, A. P., Heller, K., & Sechrest, L. B. (1966). *Psychotherapy and the psychology of behavior change*. New York: John Wiley & Sons.

Graff, R. W., Whitehead, G. I., & LeCompte, M. (1986). Group treatment with divorced women using cognitive-behavioral support-insight methods. *Journal of Counseling Psychology*, *33*, 276–281.

Hadden, S. B. (1975). A glimpse of pioneers in group psychotherapy. *International Journal of Group Psychotherapy*, *25*, 271–289.

Hafner, I., & Marks, I. M. (1976). Exposure in vivo of agoraphobics: Contributions of diazepam, group exposure, and anxiety evocation. *Psychological Medicine*, *6*, 71–88.

Hand, I., LaMontagne, Y., & Marks, I. (1974). Group exposure (flooding) in vivo for agoraphobics. *British Journal of Psychiatry*, *124*, 588–602.

Heppner, P. P. (1978). A review of the problem-solving

literature and its relationship to the counseling process. *Journal of Counseling Psychology*, 25, 366–375.

Hoberman, H. M., Lewinsohn, P. M., & Tilson, M. (1988). Group treatment of depression: Individual predictors of outcome. *Journal of Consulting and Clinical Psychology*, 56, 393–398.

Lewin, K. (1951). *Field theory in social science*. New York: Harper & Brothers.

Lieberman, M. A., & Bliwise, N. G. (1985). Comparisons among peer and professionally directed groups for the elderly: Implications for the development of self-help groups. *International Journal of Group Psychotherapy*, 35, 155–175.

Lieberman, M. A., & Borman, L. D. (1979). *Self-help groups for coping with crisis*. San Francisco: Jossey-Bass.

Lieberman, M., Yalom, I., & Miles, M. (1973). *Encounter groups: First facts*. New York: Basic Books.

Lott, A. J., & Lott, B. E. (1965). Group cohesiveness as interpersonal attraction: A review of relationships with antecedent and consequent variables. *Psychological Bulletin*, 64, 259–309.

Mathews, A. M., Gelder, M. G., & Johnston, D. W. (1981). *Agoraphobia: Nature and treatment*. New York: Guilford Press.

Meichenbaum, D. (1986). Self-instructional methods. In F. Kanfer & A. Goldstein (Eds.), *Helping people change* (pp. 346–380.). Elmsford, NY: Pergamon Press.

Moreno, J. (1953). *Who shall survive?* New York: Beacon House.

Oei, T. P. S., & Jackson, P. R. (1980). Long-term effects of group and individual social skills training with alcoholics. *Addictive Behavior*, 5, 129–136.

Peteroy, E. T. (1983). Cohesiveness development in an ongoing therapy group: An exploratory study. *Small Group Behavior*, 14, 269–272.

Piper, W. E., Debbane, E. G., & Garant, J. (1977). An outcome study of group therapy. *Archives of General Psychiatry*, 34, 1027–1032.

Puder, R. S. (1988). Age analysis of cognitive-behavioral group therapy for chronic pain outpatients. *Psychology and Aging*, 3, 204–207.

Reid, W. J., & Shyne, A. (1969). *Brief and extended casework*. New York: Columbia University Press.

Rose, S. D. (1989). *Working with adults in groups: Integrating cognitive-behavioral and small group strategies*. San Francisco: Jossey-Bass.

Rose, S. D., & Edleson, J. (1987). *Working with children and adolescents in groups*. San Francisco: Jossey-Bass.

Rose, S. D., Tolman, R., Tallant, S. M., & Subramanian, K. A. (1987). Multimethod group approach: Program development research. *Social Work With Groups*, 9, 71–88.

Rose, S. D., Tolman, R. M., & Tallant, S. (1985). Group process in cognitive-behavioral therapy. *The Behavior Therapist*, 8, 71–75.

Rose, S. D., Siemons, J., & O'Bryan, K. (1979). The use of groups in therapy by members of AABT. *The Behavior Therapist*, 2, 23–24.

Rush, A. J., & Watkins, J. T. (1981). Group versus individual cognitive therapy: A pilot study. *Cognitive Therapy and Research*, 5, 95–104.

Sadock, B. J., & Kaplan, H. I. (1983). History of group psychotherapy. In B. J. Sadock and H. I. Kaplan (Eds.), *Comprehesive group psychotherapy* (pp. 1–8). Baltimore: Williams & Wilkins.

Shaffer, C. S., Shapiro, J., Sank, L. I., & Cohlan, D. J. (1981). Positive changes in depression, anxiety, and assertion following individual and group cognitive behavior therapy intervention. *Cognitive Therapy and Research*, 5, 149–157.

Shelton, J. L., & Levy, R. L. (1981). *Behavioral assignments and treatment compliance: A handbook of clinical strategies*. Champaign, IL: Research Press.

Shaw, B. F. (1977). Comparison of cognitive therapy and behavior therapy in the treatment of depression. *Journal of Consulting and Clinical Psychology*, 45, 543–551.

Sinnott, A., Jones, R. B., Scott-Fordham, A., & Woodward, R. (1981). Augmentation of in vivo exposure treatment for agoraphobia by the formation of neighbourhood self-help groups. *Behavior Research and Therapy*, 19, 339–347.

Slavson, S. R. (1951). *The practice of group therapy*. New York: International Universities Press.

Slocum, Y. S. (1987). A survey of expectations about group therapy among clinical and nonclinical populations. *International Journal of Group Psychotherapy*, 37, 39–54.

Smith, M., Glass, G., & Miller, T. (1980). *The benefits of psychotherapy*. Baltimore, MD: John Hopkins University Press.

Subramanian, K., & Rose, S. D. (1988). Group training for the management of chronic pain in interpersonal situations. *Health and Social Work*, 21, 29–30.

Tallant, S., Rose, S. D., & Tolman, R. (1989). Recent support for stress management training in groups. *Behavior Modification*, 13, 431–446.

Taylor, F. G., & Marshall, W. L. (1977). Experimental analysis of a cognitive or behavioural therapy for depression. *Cognitive Therapy and Research*, 1, 59–72.

Telch, C. F., & Telch, M. J. (1986). Training and supportive group therapy for enhancing cancer patients. *Journal of Consulting and Clinical Psychology*, 54, 802–808.

Teri, L., & Lewinsohn, P. M. (1985). Group intervention for unipolar depression. *The Behavior Therapist*, 8, 109–111.

Thomas, J., Petry, R. A., & Goldman, J. R. (1987). Comparison of cognitive and behavioral self-control treatments of depression. *Psychological Reports*, 60, 975–982.

Toro, P. A., Reischl, T. M., Zimmerman, M. A., Rappaport, J., Seidman, E., Luke, D. A., & Roberts, L. J. (1988). Professionals in mutual help groups: Impact on social climate and members' behavior. *Journal of Consulting and Clinical Psychology*, 56, 631–632.

Toseland, R. W., & Siporin, M. (1986). When to recommend group treatment: A review of the clinical and the research literature. *International Journal of Group Psychotherapy*, 36, 172–201.

Toseland, R. W., Rossiter, C. M., & Labrecque, M. A. (1988). *The effectiveness of two kinds of support groups for caregivers*. Albany, NY: SUNY School of Social Welfare.

Turner, J. A., & Clancy, S. (1988). Comparison of operant behavioral and cognitive-behavioral group treatment of chronic low back pain. *Journal of Consulting and Clinical Psychology*, *56*, 261–266.

Watson, J. P., Mullett, G. E., & Pillay, H. (1973). The effects of prolonged exposure to phobic situations upon agoraphobic patients treated in groups. *Behaviour Research and Therapy*, *11*, 531–545.

Webster-Stratton, C., Kolpacoff, M., & Hollinsworth, T. (1988). Self-administered videotape therapy for families with conduct-problem children: Comparison with two cost-effective treatments and a control group. *Journal of Consulting and Clinical Psychology*, *56*, 558–566.

Whitney, D., & Rose, S. D. (1989). The effect of process and structural content on outcome in stress management groups. *Social Service Research*, *3*, 120–128.

Wilson, L. K., & Gallois, C. (1985). Perception of assertive behavior: Sex combination: Role appropriateness, and message type. *Sex Roles*, *12*, 125–141.

Wilson, P. H., Goldin, J. C., & Charbonneau-Powis, M. (1983). Comparative efficacy of behavioural and cognitive treatments of depression. *Cognitive Therapy and Research*, *7*, 111–124.

Yalom, I. D. (1985). *The theory and practice of group psychotherapy*. New York: Basic Books.

CHAPTER 35

MARITAL AND FAMILY THERAPY

Alan E. Fruzzetti
Neil S. Jacobson

Although individual treatment has predominated for much of the history of psychotherapy, marital and family therapies have grown and flourished in the last 25 years. The shift to acceptability for marital and family therapy did not come easily, however, as therapists' preference for individual psychotherapy was slow to change, and research establishing the efficacy of marital and family therapies was meager for many years. Today, however, there exist many theoretical schools of marital and family therapy, with large followings and often with a substantial body of research supporting their effectiveness in treating a variety of problems.

This chapter first presents a brief history of marital and family therapy, two distinct, albeit related, disciplines. The historical roots of these two movements inform our current conceptualizations and allow us to understand better the similarities and differences between the various movements. We then present a broad overview of the theoretical and philosophical aspects of the major schools of marital and family therapy, as well as a description of the consequent therapies and their various applications. Following is a review of the efficacy of the therapies to the extent that data are available. Finally, we conclude with a

brief discussion about the present state of marital and family therapy and some comments concerning current issues.

HISTORY OF MARITAL AND FAMILY THERAPY

Context for the Emergence of Marital and Family Therapies

The origins of family therapy may be found in the social work movement of the 19th century (Broderick & Schrader, 1981; Rich, 1956), a time when working with the entire family unit was often standard practice for social workers. The absence of a substantive literature, however, and the subsequent dominance of the social work profession by psychiatry beginning in the 1920s prevented the early family focus of the social work movement from exerting any major influence on the early development of the practice of psychotherapy (see Spiegel, Block, & Bell, 1959).

Precursors to the development of marital and family therapy can also be found in the writings of neoanalytic theorists such as Sullivan (1953), Horney (1939), and Fromm (1941), who emphasized the interpersonal nature of psychiatric disorders; in the contributions of early sexologists such as Ellis (1936) and Hirschfield (see Broderick & Schrader, 1981), who counseled sexually dissatisfied individuals in the 1920s and 1930s; and in the Family Life Education Movement, whose educational program in universities during the 1930s constituted the first systematic efforts at preventative family counseling. However, these early efforts at marital and family work were the exception: The period during which marital and family therapy has significantly influenced the practice of psychotherapy has been quite brief.

The early history of psychotherapy, dominated by psychoanalytic theories, precluded engaging multiple family members in therapy sessions (Gurman, 1978). Inclusion of family members was considered a violation of the therapist–client relationship, even after theoretical notions about the underlying causes of psychopathology (e.g., the influence of the family environment) broadened. In the 1950s, major challenges to psychoanalytic dominance, such as client-centered therapy (Rogers, 1951) and behavior therapy (Wolpe, 1958), opened the door for the emergence of marital and family therapy as a viable alternative to individual psychotherapy for certain problems. During this same period psychodynamic theorists began to write about the role of marital relationships in perpetuating neuroses (Dicks, 1967; Eisenstein, 1956), and analytically trained clinicians began to acknowledge the desirability of simultaneous (although still *separate*) therapy with both spouses (Sager, 1966). These changes within the psychoanalytic community facilitated the development and acceptability of conjoint therapies. Thus, although the roots of marital and family therapy are quite old, only in the last few decades have these approaches found professional acceptability and widespread application.

Although marital and family therapies are often linked together as one movement, in reality they developed and matured in relative theoretical and practical isolation from each other. Marital therapy resulted largely as a response to a need for effective remediation of marital discord or relationship problems. Family therapy began as a treatment for certain individual problems, which were viewed as representing a family system deficit. Today, both approaches are employed effectively for a broad spectrum of individual, couple, and family problems. Although developed over somewhat similar time periods, only in relatively recent years have these two movements begun to communicate, and even to merge (Gurman & Kniskern, 1981). Yet marital therapy and family therapy remain considerably separate and distinct movements, each with its own history, pioneers, jargon, and adherents.

Marital Therapy

Marital therapy (or, marital counseling as it has been called through much of its history) began as a largely pragmatic response of professionals from several disciplines to their clients' marital problems. Thus, physicians, lawyers, and social workers found themselves in the role of marriage counselor by necessity rather than because of a firm commitment to marital counseling per se. The first three institutions primarily devoted to marriage counseling were started by physicians (see Mudd, 1951): the American Institute of Family Relations, founded by Paul Popenoe in Los Angeles in 1930; a clinic in New York City begun at approximately the same time by Abraham and Hannah Stone; and the Marriage Council in Philadelphia, started by Emily Hartshorne Mudd in 1932. These and other pioneers formed the American Associations of Marriage Counselors (AAMC) in 1945. Parallel developments occurred in England, spearheaded by David Mace.

The growth of marriage counseling into a distinct discipline was slow and difficult. For example, as recently as 1960, in the overwhelming majority of cases of marriage counseling, each spouse was seen individually rather than in the conjoint format that predominates today (see Gurman & Kniskern, 1978). As of 1965, 75% of AAMC members identified primarily with a discipline other than marriage counseling, and more recently the majority of major writers in the combined fields of marital and family therapy identified themselves primarily as psychologists, whereas only 33% identified themselves primarily as marital or family practitioners (Thomas & McKenzie, 1986). Prior to 1960, fewer than 100 articles on marriage counseling had been published in professional journals (Gurman, 1973), and most contained no research, few scientific citations, and were written as if the various authors were unaware of one another (Broderick & Schrader, 1981).

In contrast to the hundred years prior to the 1960s, the growth of marital therapy in the last 25 years has been remarkable. In addition to the expansion of psychodynamic theories into the analysis and treatment of distressed relationships, whole new approaches derived from alternative theoretical perspectives have flourished and now exert considerable influence. Today, the most prominent approaches are behavioral (Jacobson & Margolin, 1979; Stuart, 1980; Weiss, Hops, & Patterson, 1973); cognitive (Baucom & Epstein, 1989; Waring, 1988); affect- or emotion-focused (Greenberg & Johnson, 1988; Wile, 1981); prevention (Markman, Floyd, Stanley, & Lewis, 1986); relationship enhancement (Dinkmeyer & Carlson, 1986; Guerney, 1977); sex therapy (Heiman, 1986; Kaplan, 1974; LoPiccolo & Friedman, 1985); and the use of marital therapy as treatment for individual psychopathology (Beach & O'Leary, 1986; Jacobson, Dobson, Fruzzetti, Schmaling, & Salusky, 1990); or as an adjunct to other treatments (Dadds, Schwartz, & Sanders, 1987). These contemporary approaches are described below.

Family Therapy

The emergence of family therapy as a bona fide discipline grew from the work of several maverick psychiatrists and social scientists in the 1950s who reconceptualized several forms of individual psychopathology as reflective of dysfunctional family systems. Although many thinkers contributed to this reformulation, they worked independently and apparently without awareness of others' similar work. Although most of the pioneers in family therapy were trained in the psychoanalytic tradition, the broad theoretical framework that they developed diverged considerably from their roots in the psychoanalytic model. Instead of emphasizing the unconscious, intrapsychic determinants of the maladaptive behavior, the vanguard of family therapists and systems thinkers viewed psychiatric disorders as reflections of maladaptive family systems. It followed logically that the treatment of choice for individual problems would be therapy involving the entire family. From this perspective, the identified patient is viewed merely as a *scapegoat* or messenger, who announces to others that all is not well in her or his family.

Ackerman (1958) was a leader in the family therapy revolution. Trained as a child psychiatrist in orthodox psychoanalytic style, Ackerman gradually developed a model of problems in living as a function of factors in the immediate family environment. He was a true pioneer not only in the reconceptualization of children's problems in familiar terms, but also as an important early advocate of conjoint family therapy as treatment for problem children.

Like Ackerman, Murray Bowen (1978) trained in the traditional psychoanalytic mode as a psychiatrist. Bowen worked with schizophrenic patients at the National Institute of Mental Health in the 1950s,

where he experimented with the hospitalization of the patient and his or her entire family. This work convinced Bowen that family therapy was the treatment of choice for schizophrenia, and he developed a family systems theory to explain it. His model of theory and therapy has been broadened to incorporate other types of dysfunctional behavior, and his work has had an important impact on the field.

Perhaps the most influential group of early family systems theorists and therapists originated from Palo Alto, California, in the 1950s. Gregory Bateson, the eminent social scientist, organized this group, which included Donald Jackson, Jay Haley, and John Weakland, and later Paul Watzlawick, Virginia Satir, and others. This group has had an enormous influence on the theory and practice of family therapy. First, as a result of their work with schizophrenics and their families they developed the influential *double bind* theory of schizophrenia (Bateson, Jackson, Haley, & Weakland, 1956), which postulates that schizophrenia develops from persistent exposure to inconsistent and/or contradictory communication from parents, especially mothers. Although this theory of schizophrenia no longer exerts any major influence on the theories and treatments of schizophrenia, the notion that paradoxical or inconsistent parental messages can lead to psychopathology has endured as a major cornerstone of the family therapy movement. Second, Jay Haley and his associates adapted the work of the influential hypnotherapist, Milton Erickson, to a model of brief psychotherapy that is called *strategic* therapy (Bodin, 1981, Haley, 1963, 1987; Stanton, 1981). More than any other group, these creative clinicians and researchers from Palo Alto have fostered the family therapy revolution (Helay, 1963, 1987; Jackson, 1959; Satir, 1964; Watzlawick, Beavin, & Jackson, 1967).

More recently, there has been both division and development within the field of family therapy. The *structural* family therapy of Salvador Minuchin (e.g., Minuchin & Fishman, 1981; Minuchin, 1974; Aponte & Van Deusen, 1981) represents another contemporary approach to family therapy. Also, a group of clinicians and researchers centered in Milan, Italy, have developed their own subsystem of family therapy, *Milan* systemic family therapy (e.g., Boscolo, Cecchin, Hoffman, & Penn, 1987; Selvini Palazzoli, Boscolo, Cecchin, & Prata, 1978; Tomm, 1984a, 1984b). Finally, *feminist* family therapy (e.g., Bograd, 1986; Goldner, 1985; Hare-Mustin, 1980) has criticized some of the assumptions of systems theory and methods of mainstream family therapy, exerting a major influence in reformulating the field.

THEORY AND PRACTICE

Psychodynamic Models of Marital Distress

Through much of this century, psychoanalysis and its derivations have been the dominant theoretical models and the treatment of choice among psychotherapists (Broderick & Schrader, 1981; Gurman, 1978). From a psychodynamic perspective, understanding each spouse's unresolved intrapsychic conflicts from early childhood is essential to any understanding of mate selection and marital dysfunction. Accordingly, this view holds that each spouse evolves into adulthood only after surviving a series of developmental crises in childhood (Bowen, 1978; Meissner, 1978; Scharff & Scharff, 1987). Each developmental stage in childhood and adolescence is seen as a step toward individuation and separation from parental figures.

Adult intimate relationships are adversely affected when these developmental crises are incompletely resolved. For example, if the child's quest toward autonomy and independence is thwarted (e.g., by an overprotective mother), the child may grow up with a need to form interpersonal relationships based on helplessness and dependency. A fragile or incomplete sense of self may lead such a person to draw on the spouse to maintain her or his precarious identity (Erikson, 1959; Meisner, 1978).

When children grow up without an autonomous sense of self, they look for spouses who will help them feel whole or complete. A central concept of psychodynamic models is that people unconsciously choose mates who will complement them. This complementarity may take many forms. A woman with strong, unresolved dependency needs may choose a man whom she unconsciously views as having resolved such needs. Her unconscious wish would be that he will take care of her and meet her dependency needs. Another important part of the process is that the emergent adult has unconscious needs in addition to resolving the residues of childhood conflicts. Avoiding these conflicts and preventing them from reaching awareness is often an important motivating force in mate selection. The anxiety inherent in the conscious experience of these conflicts may prevail over the healthier, more mature strivings toward their resolution. To defend against awareness, adults often develop distorted perceptions of themselves, which then need to be confirmed by the marital partner. Therefore, one of the motivating factors in the choice of a mate is the desire to find a mate who will perceive him or her as he or she perceives him- or herself, and thereby allow the distortions in self-image to be maintained. For example, consider a hypothetical case of a man who "defends" himself against low self-esteem and feelings of underlying inferiority by consciously experiencing himself as confident and assertive, which might include the adoption of a life-style based on achievement, ambition, and aggressive dominance. Such a man, in order to maintain this defense, would choose a mate who idealizes him and validates his overcompensated view of himself.

The process of choosing mates who confirm each other's sense of self is a dyadic one, where mutual complementarity is sought. That is, both partners actively and simultaneously choose each other according to their unconscious needs. The psychodynamic position is that this unconscious choice is paralleled by an unspoken, unconscious contract between the spouses stipulating that each will protect the other from the anxiety inherent in exposing those self-distortions. This unconscious contract is called *collusion* (Dicks, 1967; Gurman, 1978).

The marital relationship thus may be viewed fundamentally as a surrogate of the parent–child relationship. Through the marital relationship, each spouse continues the life struggles begun in early childhood. Marital distress, then, may be the result of or intensified by the distortions in each spouse's perception of the other. Spouses choose each other based on perceptions that the other will be a certain kind of person. But to the extent that these perceptions are based on the perceiver's own unresolved conflicts rather than the love object's actual qualities, eventually the discrepancy will become apparent. Alternatively, if one spouse resolves his or her conflicts, the balance of unconscious needs may shift, rendering aspects of the partner's character no longer complementary to her or his own. Marital conflict occurs in the form of disappointment, hostility, or withdrawal when the spouses find their needs unmet, or, when formerly important needs are met or resolved, and new needs become important and unmet as the couple's balance shifts.

Psychodynamic Treatment Strategies

In traditional psychoanalysis, transference is essential to treatment success: When prior experiences with family members are projected onto the analyst, he or she becomes the surrogate parent. The patient's past is then reexperienced through the therapist–client relationship, a process through which unresolved conflicts are uncovered, exposed, and hopefully resolved. The client, freed from repeating past developmental failures, can then resume a more mature adult life with current love objects.

Although psychoanalysts once frowned on concurrent therapy of both spouses by the same analyst or conjoint therapy with both spouses, conjoint therapy is common and accepted today (Framo, 1981; Gurman, 1978; Sager, 1976). This change in approach is predicated on using an *existing*, powerful, transference relationship (that between spouses) rather than having to develop such a relationship between client and therapist (Meisner, 1978; Whitaker & Keith, 1981). The therapists can utilize marital transference to identify and point out concurrent perceptual distortions stemming from intrapsychic conflicts of each spouse, clarify lines of communication, and expose both unrealistic expectations and unconscious, collusive contracts between spouses (Sager, 1976).

Treatment goals include both interpersonal and intrapsychic restructuring. The latter is accomplished by making conscious the perceptual distortions and the transference occurring in the relationship. The methods used to do this seem to vary greatly among psychodynamic practitioners. Intrapsychic change in traditional psychoanalysis is thought to require long-term therapy emphasizing the therapist–client transference, strategies for which are well delineated. But the application to conjoint, brief, marital work is sometimes unclear because conjoint therapy presents conditions formerly thought to contradict the essentials for meaningful therapy. Most marital therapists are more active and directive than psychoanalysts and so the techniques used by psychodynamic marital therapists often bear little resemblance to classical analysis. Some "traditional" interventions, such as interpretation, are used. In addition, sometimes spouses' families of origin are included (Framo, 1981) in order to increase understanding and resolution of early conflicts. Typically, however, techniques in psychodynamic marital therapy include contracting between spouses, direct behavior exchange, and communication work, all strategies used by behavioral practitioners, and structural or strategic interventions borrowed from systems therapists. Thus, although the psychodynamic model informs the assessment of the couple or family, the psychodynamic marital therapist typically utilizes techniques derived from other theoretical frameworks. As a result, most of the prominent psychodynamic theorists are notably eclectic in their practice of marital and family therapy.

Family Systems Theories and Therapies

There are more therapies derived from a systemic view of the family than can be discussed here due to space limitations. However, there are many factors that unite various systemic applications and help provide the necessary framework for understanding both a systems theoretical perspective and much of its application to family therapy. Therefore, we focus on the unifying themes of family therapy and present the major contemporary schools based on this perspective.

A Model of Individual Psychopathology Based on Family Dysfunction

The fundamental tenet of a systems-theory application to psychotherapy is that problems in living and even major psychiatric disorders such as schizophrenia, depression, substance abuse, anxiety disorders, and so forth, are best understood as manifestations of dysfunction in the family (Haley, 1987; Minuchin, 1974; Minuchin, Rosman, & Baker, 1978; Stanton, 1981; Watzlawick, Weakland, & Fisch, 1974). The family member with the symptoms is little more than the messenger or family scapegoat; his or her symptoms are important allies in the cover-up of family dysfunction. Thus, from this perspective an identified patient's symptoms serve a necessary function for the family as a system despite the individual's level of personal distress suffered as a consequence of the systemic problem. For example, a disruptive or delinquent child may consume an inordinate amount of attention from other family members and thereby prevent her or his parents from quarreling about other issues (e.g., their own lack of intimacy). As long as the child continues to engage in delinquent behavior the parents are protected from having to focus on their marital relationship, which could in turn disrupt and threaten the entire family system. The functional value of the child's problem behavior may often be beyond the awareness of some or all family members.

The notion that symptoms of one family member are functional within the whole system reflects a view of families as complex interpersonal systems whose behavior patterns are generally considered to be repetitive and tend to occur in particular identifiable sequences. Consider the following example (Stanton, 1981):

> Spouse A is driving and Spouse B is in a hurry to get to their destination (and conveys this before the trip).

A accelerates through a yellow light, B grasps a dashboard handle and criticizes A, who retorts and steps on the gas. B protests more loudly, A shouts back and the child, C, starts to cry. At this point the argument stops while B attends to C and A slows down. (p. 364)

This example typifies one repetitive dysfunctional family process, where the child's behavior directs attention from the conflict between spouses.

Another important construct is that of *reciprocal causality*, wherein problems that family members have are viewed in an interdependent way, as opposed to a more tradional *linear* view of causality. Thus, the family system is viewed as relatively stable, having achieved some *homeostatic balance*, which maintains the status quo. Behavior among family members follows implicit rules about their interrelationships with one another designed to maintain that homeostasis, feeding back through interconnected and interdependent loops. The idea here is that the family is inherently motivated to maintain homeostatis and will therefore resist any effort on the part of outside forces (including a therapist) to modify the symptomatic behavior of the identified patient and that of other family members. This reluctance to shift behavior within the family in order to maintain homestatis is often referred to as *resistance*. The term *resistance* is borrowed from psychoanalytic thinking, but in family therapy is used to reflect the power of homeostasis (see, e.g., Anderson & Stewart, 1983). Resistance to change can make the tasks of a family therapist quite difficult.

Many prominent family theorists identify *triangles* within the family (e.g., mother–father–son) as the basic unit of family transactions (Bowen, 1978; Haley, 1987; Zuk, 1971). A third person (usually a family member) functions to stabilize a dyad (perhaps reducing or redirecting conflict), thereby creating a triadic unit. According to Haley (1987), most behavior problems in children are brought about by a cross-generational alliance between the child and the overinvolved parent (usually the mother). The third party in the triangle is the absent parent (usually the father). It is safe to assume, according to Haley, that symptomatic behavior on the part of the child is maintained by both parents, with the child serving as a buffer between the parents and saving them from more direct conflict.

Family Therapy

From a systemic view of the family where symptoms of an individual serve to stabilize the family and maintain homeostasis, the individual cannot be expected to change unless fundamental changes occur in the family system. It follows that the family will *resist* efforts to change behavior of the identified patient or other family members.

Strategic therapy was developed to combat family resistance. Haley, who has been a major force behind strategic therapy, defines strategic therapy (Haley, 1973) as an approach in which the therapist initiates and directs the therapeutic transactions and designs a particular approach, or set of interventions, for each problem. In this approach the therapist is quite active and attempts to influence people to change directly as a result of therapeutic interactions and the therapist's own power.

Although strategic therapy is certainly not the only type of family therapy to follow from systems theory, certain treatment interventions associated with strategic therapy are often equated with the systems model. This approach assumes that important changes in individual behavior will only occur when they are associated with systemic family changes. The target of change is always the family system, whether the therapist works with one, two, three, or more family members simultaneously. Inherent in the concept of resistance is the notion that family members will try to sabotage (although not necessarily intentionally) attempts by the therapist to alter the structure and/or function of the family system. Therefore, in order to counteract resistance to therapeutic change, the strategic therapist must maneuver the family by using subtle and sometimes covert interventions. Strategic therapy is thus as much a framework within which to conduct therapy as a set of specific techniques or interventions.

Certain types of interventions have been developed within the strategic tradition and are most associated with it. *Paradoxical* directives are perhaps the hallmark of the strategic approach and also may present one of its most controversial aspects. Paradoxical techniques involve tasks prescribed by the therapist that *appear* to contradict the stated goals of therapy. Most often these prescriptions are variations on the directive, "Don't change!" For example, in a family where the identified patient is an adolescent who habitually steals, the therapist might instruct the adolescent to go home and steal money from her or his mother. At times, the directive may be implicit in the therapist's expression of discouragement or hopelessness concerning the possibility of making changes in therapy (Haley, 1987; Watzlawick et al., 1974). Alternatively, the therapist might instruct the identified patient to exaggerate or pay more attention to his or her symptoms.

Paradoxical directives are based on the belief that family members will resist the therapist's direct attempts to influence their system. Because resistance is hypothesized to be out of family members' awareness, the therapist is able to capitalize on this strong reaction. Thus, when the therapist instructs the family to continue or even to *increase* their problem behavior, the only way for them to resist this strong apparent attempt to influence is to change in the opposite direction, toward less problematic behavior. In fact, advocates of paradoxical directives argue that once such a directive is delivered the therapist has improved her or his position regardless of how the family responds. In order to resist the therapist's attempts to influence, the family must improve. If they "obey" the directive, they are following the therapist's instructions and therefore the therapist has gained control of the problematic behavior. Once the family has surrendered this control, it is believed that significant improvement will likely follow.

The use of paradoxical directives is sometimes risky and therefore often controversial. Clients often do what their therapist tells them to do; if paradoxical directives are followed, the family deteriorates (at least temporarily) in some way. Haley (1987) and others have tried to specify the proper context in which such interventions are delivered in order to maximize their benefits and minimize the risks. Unfortunately, the stipulations are by necessity vague (many different variables affect the wise choice of paradox) and leave considerable room for interpretation and even misuse. The risks are more easily justified to the extent that the overall efficacy of paradox has been clearly established. As will be discussed later, there has been little experimental work evaluating the use of paradoxical directives, despite their use over many years. Direct, less risky, strategies may be just as or more effective. This controversy persists even among family systems therapists (e.g., Papp, 1979).

Reframing interventions are also common in strategic therapy, and involve attempts by the therapist to offer benign or even positive interpretations to behaviors labeled as negative by family members themselves. For example, an uninvolved father and husband might be described by the therapist as "feeling too inadequate and caring too much about the family to step in and mess things up." Or, a wife who neglects to tell her husband about a major debt might be described to the husband by the therapist as "caring about your opinion so much that she was afraid to tell

you." The essence of reframing involves casting behaviors that are viewed by family members as malevolent or blameworthy in a way that reduces the negative emotion associated with them, perhaps by emphasizing the well-intentioned but ineffectual aspects of the behavior. By averting the tendency to criticize and blame each other, family members can spend more energy and attention on change and less on defending themselves. Therefore, reframing is also another strategy to counter resistance. It is largely irrelevant whether the therapist actually believes the more benign interpretation, since from this perspective there is always a positive dimension to even apparently major problems (Haley, 1987; Minuchin, 1974; Stanton, 1981).

Structural family therapy is a popular addition or alternative to strategic therapy that is also based on systems theories. Developed by Salvador Minuchin (1974; Minuchin & Fishman, 1981), structural family therapy shares many theoretical and practical aspects of strategic therapy. Yet, structural family therapy emphasizes somewhat different aspects of systems theory and looks different in practice. Structural family therapy is often referred to as less a theory of change than a theory of the family (Stanton, 1981). The structural approach shares the systemic model of individual psychopathology and has as a cornerstone the assumption that significant and permanent changes in individual functioning can only result from changes in the family structure.

The emphasis in the structural approach is on changing the relationships between individuals within the family (called "family subsystems"). Efforts in structural family therapy are aimed toward *differentiating*, or distancing, *enmeshed* (excessively close) relationships while increasing involvement of pairs that are *disengaged* (Minuchin, 1974; Minuchin & Fishman, 1981; Stanton, 1981). For example, if the structure of the family consists of an enmeshed relationship between mother and son, whereas the father is detached and uninvolved, a structural intervention might involve directing the father henceforth to make all decisions regarding child discipline, and to take over exclusive responsibility for helping the son with homework. The goal for the structural family therapist here is to help the father become more involved and the mother less engaged with the child, which are viewed as interdependent issues. Because the presenting problem is viewed in terms of a dysfunctional family structure, the theory suggests that the problem will be solved if the therapist can succeed in altering the structure toward more balanced relationships.

Although structural family therapists sometimes utilize symptom-focused strategic interventions (Minuchin, 1981; Aponte & Van Deusen, 1981), they also employ additional interventions with a particular structural component. Because the goals of therapy are structural changes, the therapist may immerse himself or herself into the family and utilize their style of communicating (*joining* the family). The therapist may begin to use spatial relationships, such as seating arrangement, to assess and alter structural patterns. For example, the therapist may help to "separate" an enmeshed dyad by placing herself or himself between the two clients in the session, and may issue directives to further facilitate restructuring, such as instructing a disengaged pair to communicate directly, without an intermediary. Structural family therapists put considerable emphasis on change occurring in the session itself, rather than on outside tasks or indirect maneuvers.

Milan systemic family therapy is yet another brand of family therapy with its foundations rooted in systems theory. The theoretical framework of the Milan group extends to more recent thinking in the area of second-order cybernetic systems (Hoffman, 1985), also based on the work of Gregory Bateson (1979, 1972). In the Milan approach, the therapist is viewed as an integral part of the system itself (Boscolo et al., 1987). Thus, rather than viewing the family as the system to address, the Milan group looks toward the "treatment unit" (in which the therapist is a contributor) as the appropriate system of analysis (Boscolo et al., 1987). They maintain that the observer (therapist) and the observed (the family) only exist in context and are simply created units and must be analyzed critically as such. Thus, they employ a team approach to family therapy to help the therapist examine her or his own role, as well as family members', in the system.

The process of therapy of the Milan group differs from other systemic approaches in several important ways. The Milan method relies less on paradox and creating therapist power than does strategic therapy. The Milan group puts a premium on the family itself discovering a solution to their problems. This is presumed to create less resistance and be more lasting, largely because it is more freely chosen. Consistent with this view, the Milan group views behavior against the therapeutic initiative not as resistance per se but more as a window on how the family functions. Any resistance is simply considered an opportunity to understand the family better and to make changes in response to this new information.

Therapist neutrality is a central element in the Milan approach. Neutrality implies a respect and acceptance for the family system; precludes forming alliances with any individual or subgroup within the family; limits searching for any actual "truth" in an analysis of the family but seeing each individual's perspective; and involves taking a less directive, yet still active position within the treatment unit. The Milan approach uses *hypothesizing* about the family's functioning (Cecchin, 1987; Selvini Palazolli, Boscolo, Cecchin, & Prata, 1980) to help generate a new understanding of the dynamics of the family and to help maintain neutrality. With hypothesizing, the therapist verbally entertains new possible explanations and understandings of events and relationships. The Milan group puts a premium on *positive*, or *logical, connotation* (Selvini Palazzoli et al., 1980) of family members' behavior, which is as much designed to alter the therapist's consciousness as the family's. With positive connotation, as opposed to reframing, the behavior of *both* the identified patient and the rest of the family is viewed more positively by the therapist and the family. The goal is not to trick the family into a change but, as a treatment unit, to begin to view the family situation differently, and as a functional whole.

The Milan group views change as a result of new information given to the family that they then incorporate into new relationships and functions. Thus, considerable attention is paid to the process of interviewing the family, which is the main intervention tool of the Milan method. In the interview process the Milan group emphasizes the use of *circular questioning* (Cecchin, 1987; Penn, 1982; Tomm, 1987, 1988) in which the therapist exposed the pattern of family dysfunction through repeated questioning that often *seems* to cover similar ground but leads to uncovering new information. This is most often accomplished by the use of hypothesizing; "difference" questions (differences between family members' behavior, responses, values, beliefs, relationships, etc.); behavioral effect questions; and *triadic* questions (in which the therapist often asks one family member about the relationship between two others (Tomm, 1984b). The interview process helps to develop a family history from each member's perspective, which openly validates or invalidates hypotheses that the family or therapist might have. Moreover, the interview releases new information to the family, such as new connections between events, individuals' interpretations or meanings for behaviors, and so on. Thus, questions are informed by a growing understanding of the complexity of the situation and uncover new material for the whole family to see. For example, the family may cling to some beliefs about their presenting problem that, through circular questioning, turn out to be misleading or untrue. They may appreciate the greater complexity of their situation or begin to realize some family-perpetuated myth in this process.

Another important intervention most associated with the Milan group is the use of family *rituals*, which are often prescribed between sessions. In this process the therapist explains the newly discovered "rules" of interaction in the family, or how the family seems to function. The therapist simply prescribes these rules for the family in a neutral fashion, with no directive to change. Using rituals helps to explicate the binds of the family in a nonblaming, neutral, and almost dialectic way. Over time, this new information is expected to help the family to better understand their dilemma and thus to help to find their own solution. For example, in an intimacy paradox or bind (where one spouse seeks increasing closeness, the other more distance), the couple might be instructed to maintain the discrepancy by alternating days of increasing intimacy and then increasing independence. This obviates the suggestion that there might be a "correct" level of intimacy and that one spouse is at fault, helping to "unbind" the couple and provide a means for both to have their needs met.

Feminist family therapy is less a set of interventions than an approach, or overlay, that may be applied to any type of family therapy. However, most applications of the feminist perspective have come from the systems-oriented family therapists. Feminist family therapists have critiqued many theoretical and practical implications of family therapy as being insensitive to women's issues and perpetuating the power differential between men and women in relationships and in society. For example, many feminist family therapists have suggested that most family therapies promote a traditional family structure in which woman are less powerful (Goldner, 1985; Hare-Mustin, 1980). Moreover, they contend, most family therapists tacitly support "male" family models of "health" that may in fact be biased against women.

Feminist critics point out that even the jargon of family therapy (e.g., structural hierarchy, boundaries) may be quite biased. Women are more often described as emotional, enmeshed, or overinvolved, terms used to describe unhealthy relationships. A feminist perspective might relabel these traits as relationship skills if the context suggested it were appropriate. Thus, "female" qualities may be redefined in more positive, rather than pejorative, terms.

In general, the feminist family therapy movement seeks to provide what it considers to be most often missing from theories about family functioning: the woman's perspective. For example, systemic formulations of incest, battering, or children's behavior problems often implicitly blame the woman for the problem while absolving the man (Bogard, 1986).

The major contribution of feminist thinkers has been to help elucidate the inherent biases in so much of marital and family therapy (and how this reflects biases in society as a whole) and to suggest ways to incorporate women's concerns in a more balanced manner.

Behavioral and Cognitive Approaches to Marital and Family Therapy

Parent Training

Beginning with the seminal work of Gerald Patterson and his associates in the 1960s and early 1970s (Patterson, 1971, 1974; Patterson, Cobb, & Ray, 1972; Patterson & Fleischman, 1979; Patterson, Reid, Jones, & Conger, 1975), principles of learning theory have been applied increasingly to the analysis and treatment of disordered children (Allen & Harris, 1966; Berkowitz & Graziano, 1972; Forehand, 1977; Forehand & McMahon, 1981; Johnson & Lobitz, 1974; O'Dell, 1974; Wahler, 1969). Learning theory principles have led to a method of analyzing family interaction, a theory of child behavior disorders, and a comprehensive treatment focused on training parents in behavior modification techniques.

The behavioral approach to parent training, sometimes broadly referred to as *behavioral family therapy*, is based on the premise that disordered behavior in children is learned, just like any other type of behavior. This is in contrast to the psychodynamic model, which views problem behavior as an outward manifestation of intrapsychic conflict. From the behavioral perspective, it is assumed that parents have inadvertently prompted, shaped, and/or *reinforced* (made more likely) children's dysfunctional behavior, while having *punished* (decreasing the occurrence) and/or *extinguished* (failed to reinforce) more desired behavior. For example, children who are physically aggressive, verbally abusive, or simply noncompliant have somehow not been effectively punished for this behavior, whereas more prosocial behaviors (some of which would supersede the negative behaviors) went inadequately rewarded. In short, parents, although well-intentioned, may have failed to apply learning principles effectively to increase their childrens' desirable behavior.

An integral component of this theory is that parents themselves are shaped into their behavior vis-à-vis their children. Patterson (1982) has identified *coercive family processes*, wherein a cycle of coercion and negative behavior is reciprocated between parents and children. A child throwing a tantrum in public provides a common example. In order to avoid embarrassment the parent may give in to the child, thereby *positively reinforcing* her or his tantrum. But at the same time, the child stops screaming, *negatively reinforcing* (via the cessation of the aversive screaming) the parent's giving in. Thus, both parent and child play integral roles in maintaining this negative cycle.

As in other applications of behavioral principles, the therapist must first conduct a *functional analysis* of the presenting problems to identify the contingencies in the family that maintain the problem and to determine the pattern of interaction that inhibits more desirable behaviors from taking over on their own. A treatment plan is then established to restructure the environment and/or the patterns of interaction in such a way that problem behaviors are not reinforced and are therefore eliminated, while more desirable behaviors are strengthened and become more predominant.

The parent training rationale is simple: Parents exert considerable control over the contingencies affecting their children, yet they often lack skills in the application of learning principles. Thus, parents are instructed in the effective use of rewards and punishments. Training programs have varied from an emphasis on specific instruction to modify a particular behavior to the teaching of general strategies that can be applied to future, as well as current, problems. An example of the former approach would be teaching parents to *ignore*, rather than attend to, the child's temper tantrum described earlier. This would lead to *extinction* (diminished recurrence), and thus is quite different from the reinforcing attention usually paid to the tantrums. Another common strategy is *time out*, in which children are removed from a reinforcing environment for a specified period of time (usually brief), contingent upon the occurrence of a specific undesirable behavior. However, the emphasis in parent training is almost always on positive control, in which rewards are used to strengthen positive behaviors (such as complying with parental requests, doing homework, or solving conflicts with siblings in a socially desirable manner), which in turn replace problematic negative behaviors.

Behavioral Marital Therapy (BMT)

Like parent training, BMT involves the application of learning principles originally derived from the laboratory of experimental psychologists (e.g., Skinner, 1953, 1969) to the problems of distressed marital relationships. In addition, social psychological exchange theories (Thibaut & Kelley, 1959) have influenced the development of BMT. The behavioral approach to marital therapy, like other behavior therapies, tends to focus on current rather than on historical determinants of behavior, emphasizes overt behavior change, specifies treatment procedures in order to make replication possible, and carefully specifies treatment goals so that the efficacy of the treatment may be evaluated in a rigorous manner.

According to the behavioral principles on which BMT is founded, marital satisfaction for each spouse is a function of the ratio of rewards derived to costs incurred from the marriage. Several factors influence this ratio, including constitutional/genetic factors and each spouse's own learning history. Behavioral research on marital interaction has elucidated a number of parameters that differentiate happy from unhappy couples (Birchler, Weiss, & Vincent, 1975; Gottman, 1979; Gottman & Krokoff, 1989; Jacobson & Moore, 1981; Jacobson, Waldron, & Moore, 1980; Margolin & Wampold, 1981; Schaap, 1984; Wills, Weiss, & Patterson, 1974). All of these research findings, along with many others, have contributed to an empirically informed and tested model of marital distress and to the development of the BMT treatment model. These studies have shown that distressed couples reward each other less frequently, are more likely to reciprocate negative and punishing behavior, are more emotionally sensitive to immediate relationship events, exhibit greater deficiencies in their ability to deal with conflict, and disagree significantly more often in their description of what happens and how in their relationship, than do their nondistressed counterparts. Often, distressed couples are deficient in several skills necessary for effective relationship functioning. These deficits are most common and striking in the areas of conflict resolution and communication. Thus, helping couples develop these skills is an important part of BMT. BMT also focuses on the content of spouses' presenting complaints. The BMT model suggests that marital distress results not just from skill deficits but also because spouses are unable or unwilling to meet their spouses' needs in a variety of ways. Also, spouses may engage in interaction patterns that inhibit or preclude more positive or meaningful interactions. BMT therapists perform a functional analysis of these sequences in order to find ways to alter them and develop more reciprocating, positive interaction cycles.

Thus, BMT emphasizes both the *content* (meeting each others' specific needs with adequate levels of rewarding exchanges) and the *process* (rerouting negative interaction patterns to foster communication and problem-solving skills) necessary to establish and maintain a mutually satisfying relationship. Although this dual focus is generally characteristic of work with distressed couples, its particular application and the interventions chosen depend on the functional analysis of any given couple. The overriding therapy goal is *collaboration* between spouses toward improving their relationship, with a concomitant diminution of attacks, blaming, and "tit for tat" exchanges.

Few issues are assumed to be related a priori to marital conflict. More than in other theoretical frameworks, BMT therapists base intervention strategies on individualized assessment conducted through therapist observation in-session, self-reports given by spouses, or any other means of information-gathering available. Treatment plans are created to capitalize on current strengths while eliminating weaknesses, all from the perspective of modifying the antecedents (*stimulus control*) and altering the consequences (*contingency management*) of current behaviors. The treatment goals and plan are discussed and modified with the couple's agreement. Typically, following a detailed assessment and beginning functional analysis, BMT includes most or all of the following intervention strategies: behavior exchange, communication and problem-solving training, and the modification of deleterious patterns of interaction (Jacobson & Margolin, 1979; Schmaling, Fruzzetti, & Jacobson, 1989; Stuart, 1980; Weiss et al., 1973). BMT is typically performed conjointly but has also been employed in a group format (Wilson, Bornstein, & Wilson, 1988).

Behavior exchange is designed to increase the occurrence of positive behaviors by both spouses. BMT therapists help spouses learn to be more effective in providing their partners with what they want and need in order to become more satisfied with their relationship. Initially, spouses are asked to focus on changing their own behavior irrespective of what their partners do, with a goal of making the other spouse more satisfied. This helps to curtail a quid pro quo of negative exchanges that often characterizes distressed couples. This arrangement in which spouses initiate positive behaviors without necessarily being *immediately* reciprocated is similar to the pattern found among satisfied couples (Gottman, 1979; Jacobson et al., 1980). It is important for spouses to be able to choose freely which behaviors they would like to perform and not to do things that they might resent or that might require reciprocity. This helps minimize resistance to therapeutic directives. Moreover, the receiver therefore understands that anything his or her spouse does comes about from choice, not because of the therapist's directive. Behavior exchanges can be initiated early in treatment, later, or be used throughout marital therapy, depending on the specific needs of the couple.

Another important BMT intervention rests on *communication and problem-solving training*, in which couples develop and refine these skills in their relationship. One important difference between distressed and nondistressed couples is in their ability to manage conflict effectively (Gottman, 1979). Although deficiencies among distressed couples may not "cause" their marital distress (Markman, 1979), developing effective communication and problem-solving repertoires is thought to be essential for most couples to achieve and maintain marital satisfaction. Several strategies are employed to facilitate the development of these skills. Through practice, feedback, modeling, and instruction from the therapist, couples learn proficiency in the skills most associated with effective conflict resolution and prevention, and generally positive communication: how to express complaints within a context of support and appreciation; clear expression of feelings; defining problems specifically and in behavioral terms without blaming; accepting responsibility for one's role in the development and maintenance of problems; and active listening skills. Often an instructional manual for spouses is used to facilitate this process, and couples practice on smaller problems in their relationship before tackling major issues and more central relationship problems.

Cognitive interventions are widely employed within BMT, as well as within other approaches to marital and family therapy. With the rise in popularity of cognitive therapy for individual disorders (e.g., Beck & Emery, 1985; Beck, Rush, Shaw, & Emery, 1979), it is no surprise that cognitive techniques have been applied to the treatment of marital discord as well (Baucom & Epstein, 1989; Epstein, 1982; Waring, 1988). Cognitive interventions are usually employed in the context of behavioral marital therapy rather than as a complete marital therapy. Based on the work of Aaron Beck (1963, 1964) and Albert Ellis (1962), cognitive interventions include *relabeling* negative attributions made about partners, *modifying unrealistic expectations* about relationships in general or the particular spouse, and creating positive *expectancies* for change.

Cognitive techniques are usually employed as needed and can complement most other intervention strategies. Such techniques may be employed any time beliefs or expectancies seem to interfere with relationship functioning or the tasks of therapy. For example, it may be necessary to relabel a spouse's behavior in order to facilitate communication or problem solving designed to alter it. Relabeling differs somewhat in its conceptualization from reframing (see "Family Therapy") but is similar in practice. With reframing, an alternate meaning is attached to some behavior, and the therapist intends for the family to adopt this new meaning. In contrast, relabeling usually is meant simply as *another* explanation for one partner, perhaps equally true, but not intended necessarily to supplant the original attribution. More important is that consideration of the new label or alternate attribution diminishes negative emotions associated with the behavior in question, much like the "Negative Thought Record" is used in Beck's therapy for depression (Beck et al., 1979).

Similarly, a BMT therapist monitors expectancies for positive change throughout the course of therapy and constantly attempts to provide a therapeutic environment that maximizes spouses' positive, albeit realistic, expectancies. This may take the form of predicting expected relapses in order to diminish their negative impact and possible hopelessness; cheerleading and being enthusiastic about the potential for change while at the same time offering a sober account of the work necessary for change; engaging the couple with enthusiasm about the treatment model itself; perhaps using humor; and avoiding extreme statements or interpretations. Thus, by modifying negative cognitions about the spouse or the relationship in general and creating an environment of balanced optimism regarding outcome, the BMT therapist can facilitate important relationship changes throughout therapy.

In the course of assessing and exploring couples' relationship problems, facilitating behavior exchange, instructing the couple in communication and problem-solving skills, or working on cognitive restructuring, the therapist may also seek to *modify interaction patterns* or themes that are problematic for a couple. Affective exploration (see "Emotion-Focused Marital Therapy") may be employed in order to understand these patterns, expose them, and rework them into more positive ones. For example, couples often engage in destructive interactions around the issue of intimacy (Fruzzetti & Jacobson, 1990; Wile, 1981). In such a pattern, one spouse may seek greater closeness whereas the other avoids it. When one spouse demands more intimacy the other often responds by withdrawing more. Her or his withdrawal leads to greater demands, and the increased demands lead to further withdrawal. A careful explication of

this pattern to the couple is the first step toward changing it. This may include attention to underlying meanings within the interaction along with suggestions for steps to alter the pattern. The goal is to allow the couple to share intimacy at a mutually satisfying level. As a side benefit the couple may learn how to analyze their own interactions and make changes on their own.

In BMT couples not only solve current problems but learn skills to both prevent future problems and work through new ones on their own. Collaboration and mutual responsibility is emphasized throughout therapy while the therapist attempts to foster positive exchanges, increased intimacy, and the couple's own ability to analyze and work through difficulties without the need for a therapist.

In addition to its widespread use in the treatment of marital discord, BMT has recently been employed as a treatment for depression (Beach & O'Leary, 1986; Jacobson et al., 1990), and as an adjunct to parent training (Dadds et al., 1987).

Relationship Enhancement and the Prevention of Relationship Problems

In recent years several approaches have been developed and tested for the prevention of marital discord and/or to enhance relationship quality. This section describes a few of the most common approaches in this area.

Relationship Enhancement

Guerney (1977) was a leader in the development and testing of an *enrichment*, rather than remediation, approach to relationship counseling. He developed a group approach to communication skills training designed to foster direct and open communication between spouses. In this approach communication is broken into distinct modes and spouses work on them one at a time. Modes include direct expression of thoughts and feelings; listening skills; and skills in conflict resolution. Derived largely from Carl Rogers's (1951) client-centered model of therapy, the communication skills intervention package emphasizes unconditional acceptance of and respect for the feelings of others. However, the process of skill acquisition is quite similar to behavior therapy, utilizing modeling and behavior rehearsal. This model has been influential in the development of other approaches to relationship enhancement (e.g., O'Leary & Turkewitz, 1978).

By far the most utilized approach to marital enrichment is the *marriage encounter* program, a 44-hour enrichment weekend program developed by Gabriel Calvo, a Roman Catholic priest, and based on a religious interpretation of marriage (Calvo, 1975; Gallagher, 1975). In this approach, couples are taught a *dialogue* technique designed to heal the "spiritual divorce" that occurs when the illusion, or honeymoon phase, of the relationship turns to disillusion. The focus is on affective, as opposed to problem-solving, dialogue aimed toward marital unity (in the biblical sense), and the intensive weekend retreat culminates in a ceremonial renewal of marriage vows. Often, follow-up meetings are held to facilitate continued dialogue.

Another systematic approach to marital enrichment, developed by Dinkmeyer and Carlson (1984), is an Adlerian approach called the Training in Marriage Enrichment (TIME) program. TIME typically involves 10 structured sessions but has also been employed in the "retreat" or weekend mode. TIME follows a psychoeducational model designed to teach communication skills and help partners recommit to each other.

Finally, the Premarital Relationship Enhancement Program (PREP) developed by Howard Markman (Markman et al., 1986) is a short-term, largely behavioral program for unmarried couples. It differs from marital therapy in that it is *future oriented*, designed to capitalize on existing high levels of satisfaction and functioning and to prevent, rather than remediate, problems. Typically, PREP consists of five 3-hour group sessions that include three to six couples and are led by a consultant trained in PREP. Each session is devoted to one or two main topics (communication or problem-solving skills; clarification of expectations in marriage; sensual/sexual education; and relationship enhancement) and the format includes some teaching, practicing, homework, and exercises from *A Couple's Guide to Communication* (Gottman, Notarius, Gonso, & Markman, 1976).

Emotionally Focused Couples Therapy

In the last decade there has been an increasing focus on the role of affect in couple interactions, marital satisfaction, and marital therapy (Gottman & Krokoff, 1989; Greenberg & Johnson, 1986; Margolin & Weinstein, 1983; Wile, 1981). Although attention to spouses' affective arousal and affective communication has begun to inform many marital and family therapies, perhaps the most well-delineated therapy that considers affect as primary is emotion-focused marital therapy (EFT) developed by Leslie Greenberg and Susan Johnson (1988).

EFT blends cognitive, experiential, and systemic perspectives into a therapy whose goal is the *reprocessing* of the emotions underlying each spouse's role in their interactions. It is believed that such reprocessing of affect will lead to a shift toward diminished emotional rigidity and greater responsiveness. This approach is based on a network theory of emotion (e.g., Bower, 1981) in which emotional processing is viewed as a confluence of emotional memory, expressive motor, and cognitive mechanisms (Greenberg & Johnson, 1986). It is believed that emotional responses in relationships are not volitional, so they must be evoked in this manner.

In EFT the therapist emphasizes the spouses' interpersonal context and each partner's own "internal" experience, focusing on *current* issues and problems in the relationship. The basic intervention involves helping spouses to reenact interactions in the therapy session. In this process the therapist actively evokes the underlying emotional meanings of the roles each spouse plays by accessing, intensifying, exploring, and sharing these responses. The legitimacy of each partner's emotional experiences is assumed, so the therapist actively validates these feelings and facilitates acceptance by the other partner. The therapist thus attempts to restructure partners' subjective experiences along with the form of their interactions.

The basic procedures in EFT designed to reconstruct spouses' meaning systems and interaction patterns include the following: problem definitions; identification of negative patterns or cycles of interactions; exploring and facilitating partners' accessing their own emotions that underlie these negative cycles; redefinition of the problem in interactional and emotional terms; helping partners accept their own newly found emotions via *enactment* (e.g., employing gestalt techniques); helping each person to understand and accept her or his partner's emotional experience and meaning; helping to develop good communication between partners concerning the emergent definitions of their relationship issues, including a new understanding or *emotional synthesis* of their interactions; facilitating the development of new solutions to the newly defined problem areas; and helping partners to understand their new roles, perspectives of themselves and each other, and to express themselves in a new mode of communication (Greenberg & Johnson, 1988; Johnson & Greenberg, 1987). This process helps to consolidate their new positions and modes of interaction.

Sex Therapy

Although the techniques of sex therapy are employed by therapists from most schools of marital and family therapy, and vice versa, journal articles, research, and therapy books are largely published separately. Also, many techniques in sex therapy do not require both partners but are employed individually. Thus, we will also present the interventions of sex therapy separately.

Unlike the bulk of marital and family therapy, sex therapy is almost entirely empirically based and practiced in a relatively consistent manner regardless of the theoretical orientation of the therapist with respect to the etiology of marital, sexual, or family problems (Heiman, LoPiccolo, & LoPiccolo, 1981; LoPiccolo & LoPiccolo, 1978; Kaplan, 1974, 1979; Masters & Johnson, 1970). The relative homogeneity of clinical practice in sex therapy is a result of the pioneering work of Masters and Johnson (1970), who essentially created the field of sex therapy, and on whose work most other sex therapy has been based.

Much of the therapy and research has focused on sexual dysfunctions, the most common of which are (a) *erectile dysfunctions* in men, which are defined as the inability to obtain or sustain an erection long enough for the successful completion of the sexual act, (b) *premature ejaculation* in men, which is ejaculation that occurs too quickly to satisfy his partner, and (c) *orgasmic dysfunction* in women, which is the inability to have an orgasm in the desired sexual situation.

Although there is considerable theoretical speculation regarding the causes of these problems, little empirical work has been conducted to shed light on the questions of etiology. The most accepted view is that adequate and satisfying sexual performance is a natural biological concomitant of human functioning, and that it is inhibited only with negative learning experiences and/or when anxiety interferes. Thus, most sex therapy interventions are based on the assumption that learning certain sexual skills and eliminating anxiety will lead to "normal" sexual functioning.

Although sex therapy may have many goals, usually the target complaints of the couple (or individual) are addressed first, before looking for larger problems of which the sexual dysfunction might be a symptom (Heiman et al., 1981). Other common goals in sex therapy that are considered important to establishing and maintaining sexual satisfaction include the reduction of performance anxiety, provision of sex education, communication skills, and helping couples learn to share, understand, and accept partner preferences.

The basic model of sex therapy (Masters & Johnson, 1970) is based on anxiety reduction and is similar to the behavior therapy technique known as in vivo desensitization (e.g., Wolpe, 1958). Couples are first instructed to cease engaging in sexual behaviors that lead to anxiety. Then, sexual interaction is very gradually reintroduced in small, rudimentary steps. Early stages included *sensate focus*, in which partners engage in nonsexual physical stimulation with each other (e.g., nongenital touching). This helps couples to experience their physicality in a more relaxed context without performance tension, and it allows partners to practice communicating about what they like and don't like. Then, sexual stimulation is eased back into the relationship, but only when couples are able to tolerate the previous level of activity *without* anxiety. Each successive level of sexual activity is reintroduced in this manner until the couple is able to engage in satisfying sexual interactions.

Recently, there have been efforts to reintegrate sex therapy with marital and family therapy (e.g., Weeks & Hof, 1987; Heiman, 1986). With integration, a variety of common problems (in addition to specific sexual dysfunctions) such as marital discord, low or inhibited sexual desire, extramarital sexual relationships, infertility, or previous sexual abuse of one (or both) partners can be addressed in a comprehensive manner. Thus, the sexual aspects of these problems, their consequences on the marriage or family, and implications for individual functioning may be addressed in the same forum with just one therapist.

Similarities and Differences Among Marital and Family Therapies

In addition to the therapies described above there are many other approaches as well as variations on those already presented. Some intervention strategies are shared by several schools of marital and family therapy, yet they are applied from quite different theoretical perspectives. The number of alternative approaches alone can be quite confusing for both student and practitioner. Many former guidelines, such as "marital therapy is employed when the presenting problem is relationship distress, whereas family therapy is utilized when a family member's individual problem is the target symptom (e.g., depression, schizophrenia)" are simply no longer true. Fortunately, there are a few dimensions that serve to highlight differences among the approaches and several overriding commonalities that help to clarify the field. First we present some organizing similarities, then some important organizing differences among the marital and family therapies.

The first similarity is that most of the major models of marital and family therapy focus on *current*, rather than historical, determinants of marital and family functioning. Thus, emphasis is placed on current dysfunctional interaction patterns, and the goals include changing these modes of interaction in the couple or family. Although several schools might acknowledge the role of earlier factors in current distress, only in the more purely psychoanalytic paradigm are present problems conceptualized as having been caused by distal events in the developmental periods of individual family members.

Second, in most marital and family therapies the therapist plays an *active, often directive, role*. This is generally true across all of the major schools, although the types of directives and mode of activity may vary greatly.

Another similarity across therapies is the view that poor or *dysfunctional communication* is an integral part of the overall marital or family problem(s), and most approaches address this communication deficit. However, treatment approaches differ substantially in the explicitness with which treatment is focused on modifying communication. In general, direct communication training of some sort is used by behavioral, prevention, enrichment, sex, emotion-focused, and many psychoanalytic therapists. Systems therapists often use more indirect approaches, but they still often seek to modify communication in the family.

A final similarity worth noting is that marital and family therapies are typically *brief*, at least relative to many individual therapies. Marital and family therapy generally ranges from just a few sessions to 15 or 20 sessions, although there are some exceptions.

One major difference in the practice of therapists from different schools is the degree of *explicitness and overt structure* provided during therapy sessions. Behavioral, sex therapy, prevention, and relationship enhancement approaches generally call for somewhat structured therapy sessions in which the work of therapy is specified and explained to the clients, rendering the content teachable and replicable in different settings. Obviously, with more skill training or educational focus therapy becomes more structured. In contrast, psychodynamic and systems applications deemphasize skill training and *direct* education with couples or families, and are in general less explicit and specific (sometimes even overtly misleading, e.g., with paradoxical directives) with clients about their methods.

Another important difference among approaches is the definition or conceptualization of what constitutes meaningful change. All approaches acknowledge the necessity of alleviating or eliminating the couple's or family's presenting complaints. However, for behavioral, emotion focused, and sex therapists the elimination of presenting problems is often an end in itself, whereas for systems therapists this may depend on the subschool of therapy employed. For example, in strategic therapy the focus on presenting problems is viewed as a means by which to change the family system. In structural family therapy the focus is less on presenting problems and more on restructuring the relationships within the family.

EMPIRICAL STATUS OF MARITAL AND FAMILY THERAPIES

There has been an enormous increase in research investigating the efficacy of marital and family therapies over the past 15 years. However, the only general conclusion that seems safe to draw is that marital or family therapy is better, in most cases, than no therapy. Trying to draw more definitive conclusions, such as which therapies are most effective for what problems, is yet impossible. Unfortunately, there are no uniform methods but rather widespread differences among the various schools as to what constitute appropriate research strategies and definitions of change.

Psychodynamic therapists tend to prefer to use case studies to communicate treatment effectiveness; experimental evidence concerning the effectiveness of psychodynamic marital and family therapy has generally not been conducted (Gurman, Kniskern, & Pinsoff, 1986).

Some systemic proponents (e.g., Colapinto, 1983; Tomm, 1983) have rejected traditional research designs as inappropriate for evaluating reciprocal causality and the wholistic, interactional changes that they believe indicate systemic changes (although this view has been challenged; see Gurman, 1983). Many of the family therapy studies performed do not specify the particular approach or interventions used, or they do not randomly assign families to treatment conditions. From a researcher's perspective, too few methodologically rigorous, controlled trials have investigated the majority of the therapies described. Moreover, even those studies that have been attempted have often been plagued by methodological flaws such as inadequate measurement of treatment effects, an insufficient number of clients, lack of randomization, the absence of appropriate control groups or comparison treatments, and often nebulous or poorly specified treatment procedures. Thus, it is with caution that we present some research findings and draw some often tentative conclusions regarding the efficacy of marital and family therapy. We will present this overview in an order paralleling the presentation of therapies in the previous section and will focus mainly on controlled and methodologically sound research studies.

Family Systems Therapies

Given the large number of therapies based on systemic models there have been relatively few controlled attempts to investigate their efficacy. Irrespective of subtype, several prominent reviewers have concluded that family therapy from a systems perspective is at least as effective as individual therapies or approaches to family therapy from other perspectives (Hazelrigg, Cooper, & Borduin, 1987; Gurman et al., 1986). However, several approaches within the family systems domain (such as Bowen's family systems therapy and strategic family therapy) have not been subjected to controlled tests, so their efficacy has not been definitively established. Research conclusions in this area are further confused by the plethora of systemic approaches used in research programs in addition to those already described (e.g., Alexander & Parsons, 1973; Epstein & Bishop, 1981; Stanton, 1981; Zuk, 1971).

However, several studies have shown promising, but inconclusive, results for systemic family therapies. For example, in a series of well-designed studies conducted by James Alexander and associates (Alexander, Barton, Schiavo, & Parsons, 1976; Alexander & Parsons, 1973; Parsons & Alexander, 1973), interventions with families of delinquent adolescents were found to be particularly effective, even compared to psychodynamic and Rogerian alternatives. The interventions produced changes in family functioning, target delinquency behaviors, and recidivism rates. However, their basic approach, called *Functional Family Therapy* (Alexander & Parsons, 1982; Barton & Alexander, 1981), integrates behavioral and cognitive intervention strategies within the systemic structure of the treatment; therefore, conclusions cannot be drawn regarding the importance of the systemic aspects of the treatment per se.

Several studies investigating the effectiveness of structural family therapy have suggested a high level of treatment success; however, these studies do not include control groups or comparison treatments. For example, Minuchin's work with families of anorexics (Minuchin et al., 1978) resulted in high rates of improvement and reduced rehospitalization; impressive results have been reported with families whose constellation included adolescents with diabetes mellitus or chronic asthma (Minuchin, Baker, Rosman, Liebman, Milman, & Todd, 1975), elective mutism (Rosenberg & Lindblad, 1978), and psychogenic pain (Berger, Honig, & Liebman, 1977; Liebman, Honig, & Berger, 1976); in none of these studies were comparisons made with alternative treatments (or no treatment).

Structural-strategic therapy has been evaluated as a treatment for drug abuse. Stanton and associates (Stanton, 1979; Stanton & Todd, 1979; Stanton et al., 1982) found their structural-strategic interventions superior to control treatments on most outcome measurements but not on employment or school enrollment. Ziegler-Driscoll (1977, 1979) did not find improved treatment effects for family therapy over the control group.

More recently the Milan approach was investigated in a study that randomly assigned families to either standard treatment or Milan-style team consultation plus standard treatment (Green & Herget, 1989a). Families in the Milan condition showed significantly more improvement on several measures of outcome including a composite of several goal-attainment scales, client ratings of change, and therapist ratings of change. At a 3-year follow-up the Milan treatment still showed significantly better goal attainment than did the standard treatment group (Green & Herget, 1989b).

Overall, research suggests that at least some approaches to systemic family therapy can be effective treatments for a variety of problems. However, better designed studies need to be performed in order to define more clearly the presenting problems and family structures with which systemic approaches might be indicated.

Behavioral and Cognitive Approaches

Parent Training

Literally hundreds of studies have investigated the efficacy of parent training in the remediation of conduct-disordered behavior in children and adolescents across a variety of settings. Perhaps alone among psychotherapies, there is a general consensus that treatments based on Patterson's model (Patterson, 1982) are the most effective treatments (e.g., Gurman et al., 1986; Kazdin, 1984). Studies suggest that (a) changes in the targeted child's behavior lead to generalized positive changes in the family (Arnold, Levine,

& Patterson, 1975; Karoly & Rosenthal, 1977), (b) treatment gains are generally maintained, especially if occasional "booster" sessions are held (Fleischman, 1981; Fleischman & Szykula, 1981; Patterson & Fleischman, 1979), and (c) in addition to changes in the targeted child's behavior, treatment effects seem to generalize to sibling behavior (Arnold et al., 1975; Humphreys, Forehand, McMahon, & Roberts, 1978; Patterson, 1974). However, there is evidence that modification of child behavior problems at home may not generalize as well to the school setting (Breiner & Forehand, 1981; Forehand, Sturgis, McMahon, Aguar, Green, Wells, & Breiner, 1979).

Behavioral Marital Therapy

Like parent training, BMT has been subjected to numerous investigations. According to Gurman, Kniskern, and Pinsof (1986), "in terms of both the number and quality of this body of research, BMT has no peer in the marital sphere" (p. 585). Indeed, in the treatment of marital discord, BMT has been shown to be as effective, or more effective, than any other treatment approach. In a recent meta-analysis, Hahlweg and Markman (1988) found the average effect size to be 0.95 for the 17 studies included, which indicates (see also Smith, Glass, & Miller, 1980) that "the average person who had received BMT was better off at the end of treatment than 83% of the people who received either no treatment or a placebo treatment" (p. 443).

BMT has been shown to increase positive behavior while decreasing negative behavior (Baucom, 1982; Jacobson, 1977, 1978). Compared to no treatment or minimal treatment control groups BMT has consistently been shown to be effective (e.g., Baucom, 1982; Hahlweg, Schindler, & Revenstorf, 1982; Jacobson, 1977, 1978, 1984; Margolin & Weiss, 1978; Turkewitz & O'Leary, 1981). There is some evidence that various components of the BMT approach are as effective or nearly as effective in treating marital discord as the multifaceted treatment package as a whole (Baucom, 1982; Jacobson, 1984; Turkewitz & O'Leary, 1981). However, the addition of cognitive interventions has not led to an improvement in BMT's effectiveness (Baucom & Lester, 1986). In addition, Jacobson and associates (Jacobson, Schmaling, Holtzworth-Munroe, Katt, Wood, & Follette, 1989) found that performing BMT in a clinically flexible manner led to longer maintenance of treatment gains than did a more research-structured approach. Several studies have suggested as well that BMT may be delivered in a group setting without diminished effec-

tiveness (Hahlweg et al., 1982; Wilson et al., 1988). However, BMT has continued to evolve to include more than behavior exchange, communication/problem-solving training, and cognitive interventions. Research is needed to evaluate the more clinically flexible, interactionally focused BMT practiced today in order to evaluate whether and how these changes in BMT's practice affect outcome.

BMT has also been employed effectively in treating individual problems in a marital context. For example, BMT was as effective as individual cognitive therapy in the alleviation of depressive symptoms among depressed, married women (Beach & O'Leary, 1986; Jacobson et al., 1990). Finally, components of BMT (communication/problem solving) were used successfully to augment a parent training program (Dadds et al., 1987). In families with marital discord, the augmented treatment led to significant improvements over the standard treatment.

Relationship Enhancement and the Prevention of Marital Distress

Relationship Enhancement

Relationship enhancement programs based on Guerney's (1977) model have generally been effective with both married and premarital *nondistressed* couples (e.g., Ely, Guerney, & Stover, 1973; Jesse & Guerney, 1981; Ridley & Bain, 1983; Ridley, Jorgensen, Morgan, & Avery, 1982). Structured communication training based on this approach has also been investigated as a component of BMT with distressed couples (see above). Communication training alone has been shown to be as effective as BMT (Emmelkamp, van der Helm, MacGillavry, & van Zanten, 1984; Hahlweg et al., 1982; Turkewitz & O'Leary, 1981) with maritally distressed couples.

The efficacy of Marriage Encounter programs has been investigated in a series of studies conducted by William Doherty and associates. Doherty and Walker (1982) analyzed 13 couples whose therapists believed were harmed by their Marriage Encounter experience. They showed increased conflict around their participation in Marriage Encounter, decreased conflict "necessary" for problem resolution, and increased marital enmeshment. Then, Lester and Doherty (1983) retrospectively examined a sample of participants in Marriage Encounter over a 10-year period. Most couples reported their experience as very positive, but the authors found that almost 10% of couples reported several negative consequences of their participation. Finally, Doherty, Lester, and Leigh (1986) followed up the extreme subgroups of their earlier sample (25 couples with prior extreme positive or extreme negative reports) with a more exhaustive interview and assay procedure. They estimated that a small number of couples reported strong positive experiences (5.4%), whereas an equivalent number of couples reported strong negative effects (6.9%). Most couples reported their Marriage Encounter experience as either "somewhat positive" or "neutral." However, given the retrospective nature of this series of studies many couples were not included (such as dropouts), so these proportions must be viewed with caution. The authors note as well that several couples who reported negative effects in the initial survey refused the more detailed follow-up, perhaps leading to underreporting of negative outcomes.

Prevention: Premarital Interventions

Premarital approaches have been shown to be quite effective in a number of studies (Bagarozzi, Bagarozzi, Anderson, & Pollane, 1984; Hahlweg & Markman, 1988; Markman, Floyd, Stanley, & Storaasli, 1988; Ridley et al., 1982). The PREP program developed by Howard Markman and associates (Markman et al., 1986) has perhaps been evaluated the most, and with the longest follow-ups (up to 5 years), so we will focus on these results. The effectiveness of PREP has been quite impressive: both at postintervention and at follow-up, couples who participated in PREP (vs. no-treatment controls) showed increased marital satisfaction, increased sexual satisfaction, and fewer relationship problems (e.g., Markman et al., 1988). In addition, there is some evidence that divorce rates for PREP participants are reduced as well (Markman, 1989).

Emotion-Focused Marital Therapy

The approach of Greenberg and Johnson has been evaluated in two studies of their own, but not by others. In one study they compared EFT with a cognitive-behavioral problem-solving therapy and a wait-list control group (Johnson & Greenberg, 1985a). They found EFT and problem solving to be superior to the no-treatment group, and that EFT showed greater improvements in marital satisfaction and reported intimacy. In another study, using novice therapists to treat wait-list subjects from their first study, Johnson and Greenberg (1985b) found EFT again to be effective, although pre- to postchanges were smaller than in the first study. EFT thus has shown promise as an effective treatment for marital distress and awaits further investigation.

Sex Therapy

Considerable research has documented the efficacy of sex therapy techniques in the treatment of sexual dysfunction (e.g., Heiman et al., 1981; Kaplan, 1974). However, as Heiman et al. (1981) have noted, this literature includes few well-controlled investigations. Thus, some studies have reported impressive results, but with highly selected samples. For example, in clinical practice many couples with sexual dysfunctions have concomitant marital problems in other areas. Yet, often these potentially more difficult couples are excluded from research programs (Jacobson, 1978; Masters & Johnson, 1970).

In general, however, a few conclusions can be drawn. Premature ejaculation can be treated with as high as 90% success. Treatment success for impotence depends somewhat on historical factors: with primary impotence (no history of adequate sexual functioning) success rates are lower (40% to 60%) than with secondary impotence (history of at least some adequate sexual functioning), where success rates are in the 60% to 80% range. With both primary orgasmic dysfunction (never having had an orgasm) and secondary orgasmic dysfunction (at least some orgasmic history) among women, success rates of sex therapy are variable: 85% to 95% will become regularly orgasmic through masturbation, but only half that amount will be orgasmic during sexual intercourse.

Although there has been considerable interest in treating problems of sexual desire (e.g., Kaplan, 1979; Zilbergeld & Rinkleib, 1980), studies evaluating the effectiveness of such treatments are uncommon. One exception is a study by Schover and LoPiccolo (1982), who showed significant treatment gains with a large sample (152 couples). Their multiple intervention program resulted in increased frequency of sexual initiation and interaction, higher sexual satisfaction, and more frequent responsiveness to mates' advances. However, as the authors noted, the absolute (as opposed to comparative) level of frequency and satisfaction after treatment was still quite low.

General Comments

In general, the popularity of marital and family therapy is only partially justified by empirical evidence. However, most approaches to marital and family therapy performed well when subjected to rigorous testing. In fact, some influential reviewers (Gurman et al., 1986) have concluded that after appropriate research has been conducted, "significantly positive, and at times extremely impressive, outcomes have been documented" (p. 594). We agree that most published reports are encouraging, but we are somewhat cautious in our conclusions because (a) there is little agreement with respect to methodology and measurement, making comparisons across studies difficult; (b) most studies are performed by adherents of one approach, which most often is found to be more effective than its comparison; and (c) most bona fide therapies (as opposed to wait-list controls or minimal or nonspecific treatments) are shown to be essentially equivalent in their effectiveness.

Although many improvements in the quality of marital and family therapy research have been suggested (e.g., Jacobson, 1985; Kniskern, 1985), many problems remain. Several exciting new therapies, new research approaches, and heightened awareness of the clinical-research gap suggest a promising future that integrates effective clinical practice with sound research programs.

REFERENCES

Ackerman, N. W. (1958). *The psychodynamics of family life*. New York: Basic Books.

Alexander, J. F., Barton, C., Schiavo, R. S., & Parsons, B. V. (1976). Systems-behavioral intervention with families of delinquents: Therapist characteristics, family behavior, and outcome. *Journal of Consulting and Clinical Psychology, 44*, 656–664.

Alexander, J. F., & Parsons, B. V. (1973). Short-term behavioral intervention with delinquent families: Impact on family process and recidivism. *Journal of Abnormal Psychology, 81*, 219–225.

Alexander, J. F., & Parsons, B. V. (1982). *Functional family therapy: Principles and procedures*. Monterey, CA: Brooks/Cole.

Allen, D., & Harris, F. (1966). Elimination of a child's excessive scratching by training the mother in reinforcement procedures. *Behavior Research and Therapy, 4*, 79–84.

Anderson, C. M., & Steward, S. (1983). *Mastering resistance*. New York: Guilford Press.

Aponte, H. J., & Van Deusen, J. M. (1981). Structural family therapy. In A. S. Gurman & D. P. Kniskern (Eds.), *Handbook of family therapy* (pp. 310–360). New York: Brunner/Mazel.

Arnold, J. E., Levine, A. G., & Patterson, G. R. (1975). Changes in sibling behavior following family intervention. *Journal of Consulting and Clinical Psychology, 43*, 683–688.

Bagarozzi, D. A., Bagarozzi, J. I., Anderson, S. A., & Pollane, L. (1984). Premarital education and training sequence (PETS): A 3-year follow-up of an experimental study. *Journal of Counseling and Development, 63*, 91–100.

Barton, C., & Alexander, J. F. (1981). Functional family

therapy. In A. S. Gurman & D. P. Kniskern (Eds.), *Handbook of family therapy* (pp. 403–443). New York: Brunner/Mazel.

Bateson, G. (1972). *Steps to an ecology of mind*. New York: Ballantine Books.

Bateson, G. (1979). *Mind and nature*. New York: EP Dutton.

Bateson, G., Jackson, D. D., Haley, J., & Weakland, J. H. (1956). Toward a theory of schizophrenia. *Behavioral Science, 1*, 251–264.

Baucom, D. H. (1982). A comparison of behavioral contracting and problem-solving/communications training in behavioral marital therapy. *Behavior Therapy, 13*, 162–174.

Baucom, D. H., & Epstein, N. (1989). *Cognitive-behavioral marital theapy*. New York: Brunner/Mazel.

Baucom, D. H., & Lester, G. W. (1986). The usefulness of cognitive restructuring as an adjunct to behavioral marital therapy. *Behavior Therapy, 17*, 385–403.

Beach, S. R. H., & O'Leary, K. D. (1986). The treatment of depression occurring in the context of marital discord. *Behavior Therapy, 17*, 43–49.

Beck, A. T. (1963). Thinking and depression: I. Idiosyncratic content and cognitive distortions. *Archives of General Psychiatry, 9*, 324–333.

Beck, A. T. (1964). Thinking and depression: II. Theory and therapy. *Archives of General Psychiatry, 10*, 561–571.

Beck, A. T., & Emery, G. (1985). *Anxiety disorders and phobias*. New York: Basic Books.

Beck, A. T., Rush, A. J., Shaw, B. F., & Emery, G. (1979). *Cognitive therapy of depression*. New York: Guilford Press.

Berger, H., Honig, P., & Liebman, R. (1977). Recurrent abdominal pain: Gaining control of the symptom. *American Journal of Disorders of Childhood, 131*, 1340–1344.

Berkowitz, B. P., & Graziano, A. M. (1972). Training parents as behavior therapists: A review. *Behaviour Research and Therapy, 10*, 297–317.

Birchler, G. R., Weiss, R. L., & Vincent, J. P. (1975). A multimethod analysis of social reinforcement exchange between distressed and nondistressed spouse and stranger dyads. *Journal of Personality and Social Psychology, 31*, 349–360.

Bodin, A. M. (1981). The interactional view: Family therapy approaches of the mental research institute. In A. S. Gurman & D. P. Kniskern (Eds.), *Handbook of family therapy* (pp. 267–309). New York: Brunner/Mazel.

Bogard, M. (1986). A feminist examination of family therapy: What is women's place? In D. Howard (Ed.), *The dynamics of feminist therapy* (pp. 95–106). NY: Haworth Press.

Boscolo, L., Cecchin, G., Hoffman, L., & Penn, P. (1987). *Milan systemic family therapy: Conversations in theory and practice*. New York: Basic Books.

Bowen, M. (1978). *Family therapy in clinical practice*. New York: Jason Aronson.

Bower, G. H. (1981). Mood and memory. *American Psychologist, 36*, 129–148.

Breiner, J. L., & Forehand, R. (1981). An assessment of the effects of parent training on clinic-referred children's school behavior. *Behavioral Assessment, 3*, 31–42.

Broderick, C. B., & Schrader, S. S. (1981). The history of professional marriage and family therapy. In A. S. Gurman & D. P. Kniskern (Ed.), *Handbook of family therapy* (pp. 5–38). New York: Brunner/Mazel.

Calvo, G. (1975). *Marriage encounter: Official national manual.* St. Paul, MN: Marriage Encounter.

Cecchin, G. (1987). Hypothesizing, circularity, and neutrality revisited: An invitation to curiosity. *Family Process, 26*, 405–413.

Colapinto, J. (1983). The relative value of empirical evidence. *Family Process, 18*, 427–441.

Dadds, M. R., Schwartz, S., & Sanders, M. R. (1987). Marital discord and treatment outcome in behavioral treatment of child conduct disorders. *Journal of Consulting and Clinical Psychology, 55*, 396–403.

Dicks, H. V. (1967). *Marital tensions.* New York: Basic Books.

Dinkmeyer, D., & Carlson, J. (1986). *Training in marriage enrichment (T.I.M.E.) and time for a better marriage.* Circle Pines, MN: American Guidance Service.

Doherty, W. J., Lester, M. E., & Leigh, G. (1986). Marriage encounter weekends: Couples who win and couples who lose. *Journal of Marital and Family Therapy, 12*, 49–61.

Doherty, W. J., & Walker, B. (1982). Marriage encounter casualties: A preliminary investigation. *American Journal of Family Therapy, 10*, 10–25.

Eisenstein, V. W. (Ed.). (1956). *Neurotic interaction in marriage.* New York: Basic Books.

Ellis, A. (1962). *Reason and emotion in psychotherapy.* New York: Stuart.

Ellis, H. (1936). *Studies in the psychology of sex.* New York: Random House.

Ely, A. L., Guerney, B. G., Jr., & Stover, L. (1973). Efficacy of the training phase of conjugal therapy. *Psychotherapy: Theory, Research, and Practice, 10*, 201–207.

Emmelkamp, P., van der Helm, M., MacGillavry, D., & van Zanten, B. (1984). Marital therapy with clinically distressed couples: A comparative evaluation of system-theoretic, contingency contracting, and communication skills approaches. In K. Hahlweg & N. S. Jacobson (Eds.), *Marital interaction: Analysis and modification* (pp. 36–52). New York: Guilford Press.

Epstein, N. (1982). Cognitive therapy with couples. *American Journal of Family Therapy, 10*, 5–16.

Epstein, N. B., & Bishop, D. S. (1981). Problem-centered systems therapy of the family. In A. S. Gurman & D. P. Kniskern (Eds.), *Handbook of family therapy.* New York: Brunner/Mazel.

Erikson, E. H. (1959). *Identity and the life cycle.* New York: International Universities Press.

Fleischman, M. J. (1981). A replication of Patterson's "Intervention for boys with conduct problems." *Journal of Consulting and Clinical Psychology, 49*, 342–351.

Fleischman, M. J., & Szykula, S. A. (1981). A community setting replication of a social learning treatment for aggressive children. *Behavior Therapy, 12*, 115–122.

Forehand, R. (1977). Child noncompliance to parental requests: Behavioral analysis and treatment. In M. Hersen, R. M. Eisler, & P. M. Miller (Eds.), *Progress in behavior modification* (pp. 111–147). New York: Academic Press.

Forehand, R. L., & McMahon, R. J. (1981). *Helping the noncompliant child: A clinician's guide to parent training.* New York: Guilford Press.

Forehand, R., Sturgis, E. T., McMahon, R. J., Aguar, D., Green, K., Wells, K., & Breiner, J. (1979). Parent behavioral training to modify child noncompliance: Treatment generalization across time and from home to school. *Behavior Modification, 3*, 3–25.

Framo, J. L. (1981). The integration of marital therapy with sessions with family of origin. In A. S. Gurman & D. P. Kniskern (Eds), *Handbook of family therapy* (pp. 133–158). New York: Brunner/Mazel.

Fromm, E. (1941). *Escape from freedom.* New York: Farrar & Rinehart.

Fruzzetti, A. E., & Jacobson, N. S. (1990). Toward a behavioral conceptualization of adult intimacy: Implications for marital therapy. In E. Blechman & M. McEnroe (Eds.), *For better or for worse: How families influence emotions and health* (pp. 117–135). New York: Lawrence Erlbaum Associates.

Gallagher, C. (1975). *The marriage encounter: As I have loved you.* New York: Doubleday.

Goldner, V. (1985). Feminism and family therapy. *Family Process, 17*, 181–194.

Gottman, J. M. (1979). *Marital interactions: Experimental investigations.* New York: Academic Press.

Gottman, J. M., & Krokoff, L. J. (1989). Marital interaction and satisfaction: A longitudinal view. *Journal of Consulting and Clinical Psychology, 57*, 47–52.

Gottman, J. M., Notarius, C. I., Gonso, J., & Markman, H. J. (1976). *A couple's guide to communication.* Champaign, IL: Research Press.

Green, R. J., & Herget, M. (1989a). Outcomes of systemic/strategic team consultation: I. Overview and one-month results. *Family Process, 28*, 37–58.

Green, R. J., & Herget, M. (1989b). Outcomes of systemic/strategic team consultation: II. Three-year follow-up and a theory of "emergent design." *Family Process, 28*, 419–437.

Greenberg, L. S., & Johnson, S. M. (1986). Affect in marital therapy. *Journal of Marital and Family Therapy, 12*, 1–10.

Greenberg, L. S., & Johnson, S. M. (1988). *Emotionally focused therapy for couples.* New York: Guilford Press.

Guerney, B. G., Jr. (1977). *Relationship enhancement.* San Francisco, CA: Jossey-Bass.

Gurman, A. S. (1973). Marital therapy: Emerging trends in research and practice. *Family Process, 12*, 45–54.

Gurman, A. S. (1978). Contemporary marital therapies: A critique and comparative analysis of psycholanalytic, behavioral and systems theory approaches. In T. J. Paolino & B. S. McCrady (Eds.), *Marriage and marital therapy* (pp. 445–566). New York: Brunner/Mazel.

Gurman, A. S. (1983). Family therapy research and the "new epistemology." *Journal of Marital and Family Therapy, 9*, 227–234.

Gurman, A. S., & Kniskern, D. P. (1978). Research on marital and family therapy: Progress, perspective, and prospect. In S. L. Garfield & A. E. Bergin (Eds.), *Handbook of psychotherapy and behavior change: An empirical analysis* (2nd ed., pp. 817–901). New York: John Wiley & Sons.

Gurman, A. S., & Kniskern, D. P. (1981). Family therapy outcome research: Knowns and unknowns. In A. S. Gurman & D. P. Kniskern (Eds.), *Handbook of family therapy* (pp. 742–775). New York: Brunner/Mazel.

Gurman, A. S., Kniskern, D. P., & Pinsoff, W. M. (1986). Research on the process and outcome of marital and family therapy. In S. L. Garfield & A. E. Bergin (Eds.), *Handbook of psychotherapy and behavior change* (3rd ed., pp. 565–624). New York: John Wiley & Sons.

Hahlweg, K., & Markman, H. J. (1988). Effectiveness of behavioral marital therapy: Empirical status of behavioral techniques in preventing and alleviating marital distress. *Journal of Consulting and Clinical Psychology, 56*, 440–447.

Hahlweg, K., Schindler, L., & Revenstorf, D. (1982). Treatment of marital distress: Comparing formats and modalities. *Advances in Behaviour Research and Therapy, 4*, 57–74.

Haley, J. (1963). *Strategies of psychotherapy*. New York: Grune & Stratton.

Haley, J. (1973). *Uncommon therapy*. New York: W W Norton.

Haley, J. (1987). *Problem-solving therapy* (3rd edition). San Francisco, CA: Jossey-Bass.

Hare-Mustin, R. (1980). Family-therapy may be dangerous for your health. *Professional Psychology, 11*, 935–938.

Hazelrigg, M. D., Cooper, H. M., & Borduin, C. (1987). Evaluating the effectiveness of family therapies: An integrative review and analysis. *Psychological Bulletin, 101*, 428–442.

Heiman, J. R. (1986). Treating sexually distressed marital relationships. In N. S. Jacobson & A. S. Gurman (Eds.), *Clinical handbook of marital therapy* (pp. 361–384). New York: Guilford Press.

Heiman, J. R., LoPiccolo, L., & LoPiccolo, J. (1981). The treatment of sexual dysfunction. In A. S. Gurman & D. P. Kniskern (Eds.), *Handbook of family therapy* (pp. 592–627). New York: Brunner/Mazel.

Hoffman, L. (1985). Beyond power and control: Toward a "second order" family systems therapy. *Family Systems Medicine, 3*, 381–396.

Horney, K. (1939). *New ways in psychoanalysis*. New York: W W Norton.

Humphreys, L., Forehand, R., McMahon, R., & Roberts, M. (1978). Parental behavior training to modify child noncompliance: Effects on untreated siblings. *Journal of*

Behavior Therapy and Experimental Psychiatry, 9, 235–238.

Jackson, D. D. (1959). Family interaction, family homeostasis, and some implications for conjoint family therapy. In J. Masserman (Ed.), *Individual and family dynamics* (pp. 79–90). New York: Grune & Stratton.

Jacobson, N. S. (1977). Problem solving and contingency contracting in the treatment of marital discord. *Journal of Consulting and Clinical Psychology, 45*, 92–100.

Jacobson, N. S. (1978). Specific and nonspecific factors in the effectiveness of a behavioral approach to the treatment of marital discord. *Journal of Consulting and Clinical Psychology, 46*, 442–452.

Jacobson, N. S. (1984). A component analysis of behavioral marital therapy: The relative effectiveness of behavior exchange and problem-solving training. *Journal of Consulting and Clinical Psychology, 52*, 295–305.

Jacobson, N. S. (1985). Family therapy outcome research: Potential pitfalls and prospects. *Journal of Marital and Family Therapy, 11*, 149–158.

Jacobson, N. S., Dobson, K. S., Fruzzetti, A. E., Schmaling, K. B., & Salusky, S. (1990). *Marital therapy as a treatment for depression*. Manuscript submitted for publication.

Jacobson, N. S., & Margolin, G. (1979). *Marital therapy: Strategies based on social learning and behavior exchange principles*. New York: Brunner/Mazel.

Jacobson, N. S., & Moore, D. (1981). Spouses as observers of the events in their relationship. *Journal of Consulting and Clinical Psychology, 49*, 269–277.

Jacobson, N. S., Schmaling, K. B., Holtzworth-Munroe, A., Katt, J. L., Wood, L. F., & Follette, V. M. (1989). Research-structured vs. clinically flexible versions of social learning-based marital therapy. *Behavior Research and Therapy, 27*, 173–180.

Jacobson, N. S., Waldron, H., & Moore, D. (1980). Toward a behavioral profile of marital distress. *Journal of Consulting and Clinical Psychology, 48*, 696–703.

Jesse, R. E., & Guerney, B. (1981). A comparison of gestalt and relationship treatments with married couples. *American Journal of Family Therapy, 9*, 31–41.

Johnson, S. M., & Greenberg, L. S. (1985a). The differential effects of experimental and problem-solving interventions in resolving marital conflict. *Journal of Consulting and Clinical Psychology, 53*, 175–184.

Johnson, S. M., & Greenberg, L. S. (1985b). Emotionally focused couples therapy: An outcome study. *Journal of Marital and Family Therapy, 11*, 313–317.

Johnson, S. M., & Greenberg, L. S. (1987). Emotionally focused marital therapy: An overview. *Psychotherapy, 24*, 552–560.

Johnson, S. M., & Lobitz, G. K. (1974). Parental manipulation of child behavior in home observations. *Journal of Applied Behavior Analysis, 7*, 23–31.

Kaplan, H. S. (1974). *The new sex therapy*. New York: Brunner/Mazel.

Kaplan, H. S. (1979). *Disorders of sexual desire*. New York: Brunner/Mazel.

Karoly, P., & Rosenthal, M. (1977). Training parents in behavior modification: Effects on perceptions of family interaction and deviant behavior. *Behavior Therapy, 8*, 406–410.

Kazdin, A. E. (1984). Treatment of conduct disorders. In J. Williams & R. Spitzer (Eds.), *Psychotherapy research: Where are we and where should we go?* New York: Guilford Press.

Kniskern, D. P. (1985). Climbing out of the pit: Further guidelines for family therapy research. *Journal of Marital and Family Therapy, 11*, 159–162.

Lester, M. E., & Doherty, W. J. (1983). Couples' long-term evaluation of their marriage encounter experience. *Journal of Marital and Family Therapy, 9*, 183–188.

Liebman, R., Honig, P., & Berger, H. (1976). An integrated treatment program for psychogenic pain. *Family Process, 15*, 397–405.

LoPiccolo, J., & Friedman, J. M. (1985). Sex therapy: An integrated model. In S. J. Lynn & J. P. Garske (Eds.), *Contemporary psychotherapies: Models and methods* (pp. 459–493). New York: Charles E Merrill.

LoPiccolo, J., & LoPiccolo, L. (Eds.). (1978). *Handbook of sex therapy.* New York: Plenum Press.

Margolin, G., & Wampold, B. E. (1981). Sequential analysis of conflict and accord in distressed and nondistressed marital partners. *Journal of Consulting and Clinical Psychology, 49*, 554–567.

Margolin, G., & Weinstein, C. D. (1983). The role of affect in behavioral therapy. In L. R. Wolberg & M. C. Aronson (Eds.), *Group and family therapy* (pp. 1–38). New York: Brunner/Mazel.

Margolin, G., & Weiss, R. L. (1978). A comparative evaluation of therapeutic components associated with behavioral marital treatment. *Journal of Consulting and Clinical Psychology, 46*, 1476–1486.

Markman, H. J. (1979). Application of a behavioral model of marriage in predicting relationship satisfaction of couples planning marriage. *Journal of Consulting and Clinical Psychology, 47*, 743–749.

Markman, H. J. (1989, November). *Why is a 5 session communication training program associated with the prevention of divorce and marital distress? Results from a 5 year follow-up.* Paper presented at the 23rd Convention of the Association for the Advancement of Behavior Therapy, Washington, DC.

Markman, H. J., Floyd, F., Stanley, S., & Lewis, H. (1986). Prevention. In N. S. Jacobson & A. S. Gurman (Eds.), *Clinical handbook of marital therapy* (pp. 173–195). New York: Guilford Press.

Markman, H. J., Floyd, F. J., Stanley, S. M., & Storaasli, R. D. (1988). Prevention of marital distress: A longitudinal investigation. *Journal of Consulting and Clinical Psychology, 56*, 210–217.

Masters, W. H., & Johnson, V. E. (1970). *Human sexual inadequacy.* Boston: Little Brown.

Meissner, W. J. (1978). The conceptualization of marriage and marital disorders from a psychoanalytic perspective. In T. J. Paolino, Jr. & B. S. McCrady (Eds.), *Marriage and marital therapy: Psychoanalytic, behavioral and systems theory perspectives* (pp. 25–88). New York: Brunner/Mazel.

Minuchin, S. (1974). *Families and family therapy.* Cambridge, MA: Harvard University Press.

Minuchin, S., Baker, L., Rosman, B., Liebman, R., Milman, L., & Todd, T. (1975). A conceptual model of psychosomatic illness in children. *Archives of General Psychiatry, 32*, 1031–1038.

Minuchin, S., & Fishman, H. C. (1981). *Family therapy techniques.* Cambridge, MA: Harvard University Press.

Minuchin, S., Rosman, B., & Baker, L. (1978). *Psychosomatic families.* Cambridge, MA: Harvard University Press.

Mudd, E. H. (1951). *The practice of marriage counseling.* New York: Association Press.

O'Dell, S. (1974). Training parents in behavior modification: A review. *Psychological Bulletin, 81*, 418–433.

O'Leary, K. D., & Turkewitz, H. (1978). The treatment of marital disorders from a behavioral perspective. In T. J. Paolino, Jr., & B. S. McCrady (Eds.), *Marriage and marital therapy: Psychoanalytic, behavioral and systems theory perspectives* (pp. 240–297). New York: Brunner/Mazel.

Papp, P. (1979). Paradoxical strategies and countertransference. *American Journal of Family Therapy, 7*, 11–12.

Parsons, B. B., & Alexander, J. F. (1973). Short-term family intervention: A therapy outcome study. *Journal of Consulting and Clinical Psychology, 41*, 195–201.

Patterson, G. R. (1971). *Families: Applications of social learning to family life.* Champaign, IL: Research Press.

Patterson, G. R. (1974). Interventions for boys with conduct problems: Multiple settings, treatments, and criteria. *Journal of Consulting and Clinical Psychology, 42*, 471–481.

Patterson, G. R. (1982). *Coercive family process.* Eugene, OR: Castalia Press.

Patterson, G. R., Cobb, J. A., & Ray, R. S. (1972). A social engineering technology for retraining the families of aggressive boys. In H. E. Adams & I. P. Unikel (Eds.), *Issues and trends in behavior therapy* (pp. 139–210). Springfield, IL: Charles C Thomas.

Patterson, G. R., & Fleischman, M. J. (1979). Maintenance of treatment effects: Some considerations concerning family systems and follow-up data. *Behavior Therapy, 10*, 168–185.

Patterson, G. R., Reid, J. B., Jones, R. R., & Conger, R. (1975). *Families with aggressive children.* Eugene, OR: Castalia Press.

Penn, P. (1982). Circular questioning. *Family Process, 21*, 267–280.

Rich, M. E. (1956). *A belief in people: A history of family social work.* New York: Family Serivce Association of America.

Ridley, C. A., & Bain, A. B. (1983). The effects of a premarital relationship enhancement program on self-disclosure. *Family Therapy, 10*, 13–23.

Ridley, C. A., Jorgensen, S. R., Morgan, G., & Avery, A.

W. (1982). Relationship enhancement with premarital couples: An assessment of effects on relationship quality. *American Journal of Family Therapy, 10*, 41–48.

Rogers, C. R. (1951). *Client-centered therapy.* Boston: Houghton-Mifflin.

Rosenberg, J. B., & Lindblad, M. B. (1978). Behavior therapy in a family context: Elective mutism. *Family Process, 17*, 77–82.

Sager, C. J. (1966). Treatment of married couples. In S. Arieti (Ed.), *American handbook of psychiatry* (Vol. 3, pp. 213–224). New York: Basic Books.

Sager, C. J. (1976). *Marriage contracts and couple therapy.* New York: Brunner/Mazel.

Satir, V. (1964). *Conjoint family therapy.* Palo Alto, CA: Science and Behavior Books.

Schaap, C. (1984). A comparison of the interaction of distressed and nondistressed married couples in a laboratory situation: Literature survey, methodological issues, and an empirical investigation. In K. Hahlweg & N. S. Jacobson (Eds.), *Marital interaction: Analysis and modification* (pp. 133–158). New York: Guilford Press.

Scharff, D. E., & Scharff, J. S. (1987). *Object relations family therapy.* New York: Jason Aronson.

Schmaling, K. B., Fruzzetti, A. E., & Jacobson, N. S. (1989). Marital problems. In K. Hawton, P. Salkovskis, J. Kirk, & D. Clark (Eds.), *Cognitive-behavioural approaches in adult psychiatric disorders: A practical guide* (pp. 339–369). London: Pergamon Press.

Schover, L. R., & LoPiccolo, J. (1982). Treatment effectiveness for dysfunctions of sexual desire. *Journal of Sex and Marital Therapy, 8*, 179–197.

Selvini Palazzoli, M., Boscolo, L., Cecchin, G., & Prata, G. (1978). *Paradox and counterparadox.* New York: Jason Aronson.

Selvini Palazzoli, M., Boscolo, L., Cecchin, G., & Prata, G. (1980). Hypothesizing-circularity-neutrality: Three guidelines for the conductor of the session. *Family Process, 19*, 73–85.

Skinner, B. F. (1953). *Science and human behavior.* New York: Macmillan.

Skinner, B. F. (1969). *Contingencies of reinforcement: A theoretical analysis.* New York: Appleton-Century-Crofts.

Smith, M. L., Glass, G. V., & Miller, T. I. (1980). *The benefits of psychotherapy.* Baltimore, MD: Johns Hopkins University Press.

Spiegel, J. P., Block, A. D., & Bell, N. W. (1959). The family of the psychiatric patient. In S. Arieti (Ed.), *American handbook of psychiatry* (Vol. 1, pp. 179–201). New York: Basic Books.

Stanton, M. D. (1979). Family treatment approaches to drug abuse problems: A review. *Family Process, 18*, 251–280.

Stanton, M. D. (1981). Strategic approaches to family therapy. In A. S. Gurman & D. P. Kniskern (Eds.), *Handbook of family therapy.* New York: Brunner/Mazel.

Stanton, M. D., & Todd, T. C. (1979). Structural family therapy with drug addicts. In E. Kaufman & P. Kaufman

(Eds.), *The family therapy of drug and alcohol abuse* (pp. 55–69). New York: Gardner Press.

Stanton, M. D., Todd, T. C., & Associates (1982). *The family therapy of drug abuse and addiction.* New York: Guilford Press.

Stuart, R. B. (1980). *Helping couples change: A social learning approach to marital therapy.* New York: Guilford Press.

Sullivan, H. S. (1953). *Interpersonal theory of psychiatry.* New York: W W Norton.

Thibaut, J. W., & Kelley, H. H. (1959). *The social psychology of groups.* New York: John Wiley & Sons.

Thomas, F. N., & McKenzie, P. N. (1986). Prolific writers in marital and family therapy: A research note. *Journal of Marital and Family Therapy, 12*, 175–180.

Tomm, K. (1983). The old hat doesn't fit. *Family Therapy Networker, 7*, 39–41.

Tomm, K. (1984a). One perspective on the Milan systemic approach. Overview of development, theory and practice. *Journal of Marital and Family Therapy, 10*, 113–125.

Tomm, K. (1984b). One perspective on the Milan systemic approach: Part II. Description of format, interviewing style and interventions. *Journal of Marital and Family Therapy, 10*, 253–271.

Tomm, K. (1987). Interventive interviewing: Part II. Reflexive questioning as a means to enable self-healing. *Family Process, 26*, 167–183.

Tomm, K. (1988). Interventive interviewing: Part III. Intending to ask lineal, circular, strategic, or reflexive questions. *Family Process, 27*, 1–15.

Turkewitz, H., & O'Leary, K. D. (1981). A comparative outcome study of behavioral marital therapy and communication therapy. *Journal of Marital and Family Therapy, 7*, 159–169.

Wahler, R. G. (1969). Oppositional children: A quest for parental reinforcement control. *Journal of Applied Behavior Analysis, 2*, 159–170.

Waring, E. M. (1988). *Enhancing marital intimacy through facilitating cognitive self-disclosure.* New York: Brunner/Mazel.

Watzlawick, P., Beavin, J. H., & Jackson, D. D. (1967). *Pragmatics of human communication.* New York: W W Norton.

Watzlawick, P., Weakland, J., & Fisch, R. (1974). *Change: Principles of problem formation and problem resolution.* New York: W W Norton.

Weeks, G. R., & Hof, L. (Eds.). (1987). *Integrating sex and marital therapy: A clinical guide.* New York: Brunner/Mazel.

Weiss, R. L., Hops, H., & Patterson, G. R. (1973). A framework for conceptualizing marital conflict, technology for altering it, some data for evaluating it. In L. A. Hamerlynck, L. C. Handy, & E. J. Mash (Eds.), *Behavior change: Methodology, concepts, and practice* (pp. 309–342). Champaign, IL: Research Press.

Whitaker, C. A., & Keith, D. V. (1981). Symbolic-experiential family therapy. In A. S. Gurman & D. P. Kniskern

(Eds.), *Handbook of family therapy* (pp. 187–225). New York: Brunner/Mazel.

Wile, D. B. (1981). *Couples therapy: A nontraditional approach*. New York: John Wiley & Sons.

Wills, T. A., Weiss, R. L., & Patterson, G. R. (1974). A behavioral analysis of the determinants of marital satisfaction. *Journal of Consulting and Clinical Psychology, 42*, 802–811.

Wilson, G. L., Bornstein, P. H., & Wilson, L. J. (1988). Treatment of relationship dysfunction: An empirical evaluation of group and conjoint behavioral marital therapy. *Journal of Consulting and Clinical Psychology, 56*, 929–931.

Wolpe, J. (1958). *Psychotherapy by reciprocal inhibition*. Stanford, CA: Stanford University Press.

Ziegler-Driscoll, G. (1977). Family research study at Eagleville Hospital and Rehabilitation Center. *Family Process, 16*, 175–190.

Ziegler-Driscoll, G. (1979). The similarities in families of drug dependents and alcoholics. In E. Kaufman & P. Kaufman (Eds.), *The family therapy of drug and alcohol abuse* (pp. 19–39). New York: Garner Press.

Zilbergeld, B., & Rinkleib, C. E. (1980). Desire discrepancies and arousal problems in sex therapy. In S. Leiblum & L. Pervin (Eds.), *Principles and practice of sex therapy* (pp. 65–100). New York: Guilford Press.

Zuk, G. H. (1971). *Family therapy: A triadic-based approach*. New York: Behavioral Publications.

CHAPTER 36

PSYCHOPHARMACOLOGY

Geary S. Alford
Andrew C. Bishop

Although psychoactive drugs have been used for thousands of years for religious, medical, and recreational purposes, the broadscale use of chemical agents in the treatment of psychological disorders is a relatively recent development. Prior to World War II, comparatively few hospitalized psychiatric patients were regularly maintained on psychoactive compounds, although in instances of acute agitation or violent outbursts, a patient might be given a sedating dose of a barbiturate and subsequently confined in a padded room or placed in a straitjacket. Use of pharmacologic compounds for psychiatric outpatients, aside from occasional sleeping pills, was rare indeed and was even opposed by many leading psychoanalysts. To be sure, there were individuals and institutions that experimented with pharmacological agents as part of their treatment of various behavioral disorders, such as the use of heroin or cocaine in treating morphinism or barbiturate-induced prolonged sleep for "irritated nerves." In general, however, the undesirable pharmacological properties of the available drugs outweighed the limited therapeutic benefits.

Modern psychopharmacology and pharmacotherapy really began at the midpoint of this century. In a brief 10-year span between 1950 and 1960, nearly all of the pharmacotherapeutic agents or the prototypes of drugs currently in use were introduced: the first truly antipsychotic compound, chlorpromazine (Thorazine), the first antidepressants, monoamine oxidase inhibitors (MAOIs, e.g., iproniazid) and tricyclic antidepressants (e.g., imipramine), the antimania preparation of the cationic salt lithium carbonate, and the first compound to be more anxiolytic than sedating, meprobamate (e.g., Miltown), and subsequently benzodiazepines (e.g., Librium). Introduction of these drugs met with a mixed reception (Tourney, 1967).

Many traditionally trained psychotherapists tended to ignore what limited clinical pharmacological data were then available. They discounted the utility of pharmacotherapy as treating symptoms but not the true, underlying "intrapsychic" disorder (a reaction curiously recapitulated a decade later in response to the emergence of another empirically based mode of behavior change, behavior therapy). On the other hand, the mid-1950s was the period in which science emerged as the preeminent intellectual force of the 20th century. This was the atomic age, the era of Sputnik, the Salk vaccine, DNA, and the fascination and promises of scientific technology exemplified by the computer and the television set. In this atmosphere of excitement in experimentation and optimism in science, biobehavioral researchers saw the psychoactive drugs as a new and additional means of investigating finer, more subtle brain–behavior relationships. Chemical compounds are real in the material sense. They can be analyzed, formulated, and quantified. As independent variables, they can be experimentally administered and removed or withdrawn. They and their pharmacologic properties can be empirically examined and conceptualized in relation to other physical structures and empirical phenomena: neuroanatomy, neurochemistry, and brain physiology. In addition to their pragmatic clinical potential, it was thought that these new drugs could contribute to the discovery of complex brain processes and perhaps even lead to the identification of underlying biological bases of abnormal behavior.

Chemical compounds that alter not only the arousal level of human beings, but indeed alter mood, thought processes, and even influence content of thinking obviously do so by their chemical action on brain structures and functioning and not by modifying metaphysical constructs like *ego strength* or *ego integration*. This recognition led many behavioral scientists to eschew psychoanalytic formulations of behavior and behavioral disorders and to embrace, perhaps at times equally narrowly, truly biological speculations. Others attempted a rather dissonant integration of biological and psychoanalytic concepts. Picking up on this latter view, pharmaceutical companies throughout the 1960s advertised their drugs with such descriptions as "psychic energizers" (i.e., stimulants and antidepressants), or as "reducing underlying psychic tensions" (anxiolytics), or "ego integrators" (neuroleptics). While adopting somewhat more behavioral terminology in the 1970s, pharmaceutical houses continued this essentially dualistic perspective in part because it reflects the thinking of the majority of practicing clinicians. Nevertheless, the reliance on controlled, experimental investigation, use of measurable dependent behavioral variables, and the conceptualization and interpretation of independent–dependent variable events within the context of empirically derived pharmacological and psychological principles characterizes the core of basic psychopharmacologic research over the last four decades (see Lipton, DiMascio, & Killam, 1978; Meltzer, 1987).

The concurrent clinical use of these compounds, unfortunately, often has not been quite so well guided by either the basic pharmacologic data, controlled clinical research, or a coherent biobehavioral theoret-

ical system. Although new, potentially pharmacotherapeutic compounds must undergo rigorous and extensive tests for safety (i.e., for potentially dangerous and undesirable side effects to the user or offspring) and efficacy before being approved by the Food and Drug Administration (FDA) for general use, actual clinical practices vary greatly among physicians and at times are at variance with basic pharmacological knowledge. This has been most clearly exemplified by the current Zeitgeist of unwarranted pathophysiologizing of behavioral disorders.

Perhaps the most common error in this regard is the post hoc, ergo propter hoc etiologic-pathogenic conclusion. It usually goes something like this: Since drugs affect the biological bases of behavior, if a drug effectively results in altering an abnormal behavior pattern toward the direction of normal functioning, this fact supports or proves a biologic pathogenesis for that abnormal behavior pattern. Although not often articulated this simply, particularly in written material, such notions are quite commonly offered in lectures, grand rounds, and professional convention presentations, and if carefully structured and eloquently delivered may initially appear persuasive. For example, let us assume that we could document that patients who complain of depression and have such symptoms as sleep disturbance, decreased appetite, and crying spells all have decreased central nervous system (CNS) factor-X concentrations. Furthermore, we show that tricyclic antidepressants in fact increase CNS factor-X levels and produce an amelioration of the depression. Here we would have not only the documented clinical effects and probable mechanism of action of these antidepressants, we would also have replicated data that these patients had decreased factor-X concentrations at the time of the depression and that this reversed after drug therapy. Tempting? Yes. Suggestive? Yes. But, of course, not sufficient for any etiologic conclusion. What we would have come close to establishing would be some (possibly *the*) biological correlates of depression but not necessarily the causes of depression. We might very well find—and, indeed, were this relationship between brain factor-X and depression true, reliable, and invariant, we most certainly would find—that individuals profoundly depressed during the grief reaction to the sudden, accidental death of a spouse also had decreased factor-X. The significant and variance-controlling independent etiologic variable then would be the loss and grief reaction, not the biological mechanism or substrate. This is analogous to certain types of hypoglycemia: There are individuals who secrete too much insulin especially in relationship to carbohydrate loads and this is referred to as idiopathic hypoglycemia. The cause of the hypoglycemia is insulin secretion. If one eats a high simple sugar meal at the same time each day, one's pancreas will secrete the same amount of insulin at the same time each day. Then if one misses a day the insulin will be secreted and hypoglycemia will ensue. In the latter case the eating behavior is the "causative" variable although insulin secretion is the final biological or common pathway that gives rise to the symptoms of hypoglycemia.

If we return to the initial syllogism and make a few substitutions of terms, perhaps we can identify some ambiguities that lead some theorists astray. First, drugs affect the biological components (or correlates or substrates or mechanisms) of behavior, not necessarily the bases, in the sense of causes, of behavior. Abnormal behavior does not necessarily imply abnormal physiology. Second, modification of behavior in the direction of desirable overt action by chemicals does not necessarily mean that the underlying biological processes are functioning more normally. Indeed, normal or desirable overt behavior may at times be achieved by chemically inducing abnormal physiological processes. For example, low-level alcohol intoxication may temporarily facilitate a socially anxious (phobic) individual's performance of certain social skills, whereas temporary impairment of normal receptor sensitivity by a topical anesthetic may increase the latency to orgasm in a premature ejaculator. Third, with respect to the initial syllogism, even the identified presence of some abnormal physiological process does not necessarily indicate that this was endogenous and independently produced or caused the abnormal behavior.

A similar fallacy complicating the interpretation and understanding of pharmacotherapeutic–brain–behavior relationships is the tendency to assume that similar abnormal behavior necessarily entails the same biological processes, etiology, and pathogenesis. To return to the hypothetical data and depressed patients, this fallacy is often exemplified as follows: If n number of patients have been found to have a genetically inherited ribonucleic acid controlled, cyclical abnormal production of brain factor-X whose symptoms include feelings of depression, fatigue, and loss of appetite, and Patient A presents complaining of the same symptoms and is also found (at this point in time) to have a lower than normal CNS factor-X concentration, then Patient A has the same genetically inherited depressive disorder. If, however, our Patient A is the same hypothetical patient in the midst of severe grief described earlier, then we can see the fallacy of assuming similar pathogenesis for similar

behaviors even if many of the biological concomitants were found to be the same. Clearly, actual empirical findings analogous to the hypothetical examples described above do raise the possibility of physiological-biochemical pathogeneses. To determine whether such evidence reveals something about pathogenesis as well as about possible biological substrates, converging sources of data would be necessary. From the biochemical-pharmacological point of view, to establish a purely biological pathogenesis it would be necessary to show that some biochemical, metabolic defect exists prior to the molar behavioral symptoms, that this abnormality was truly endogenous, and that it is both necessary and sufficient for the clinical syndrome to appear. Even this would not exclude the possibility that a similar biobehavioral syndrome might arise from external and cognitive-emotional events and share at least part of a final, common, biological pathway.

Given these caveats, it is also important to recognize that the approach to investigating the causes, physiological processes, and potential cures or treatments for abnormal behavior by biological scientists is not on a track tangential to or inconsistent with empirical behavioral sciences. Converging sources of empirical evidence from psychiatric twin studies and family histories, laboratory genetic studies, research in brain chemistry, pharmacobiochemical as well as clinical pharmacotherapeutic investigations are increasingly persuasive that many behavioral disorders, such as major bipolar affective disorders (manic-depressive disease) and schizophrenias, most probably do have a primarily endogenous biological pathogenesis. The point is that this is not an exclusive tract, but one that parallels and interacts with behavioral sciences. Just as early behaviorists tended to ignore, if not dismiss, intraorganismic variables and processes in conceptualizing the development and modification of behavior, many biologically oriented theoreticians tend to ignore the complex, continuous, and inextricable interaction of the internal organism within itself and with its external environment. Such theorists tend to forget that sensory stimuli are not metaphysical constructs but extraordinarily complex physical events that exert a biological influence, at times a profound and enduring impact upon the physiological activity and indeed chemical structures within the organism. Learning and memory are, after all, ultimately subtle and complex biochemical processes. Similarly, the most specific and discrete modification in brain chemistry and function is made not by a drug or an electrode but by a verbal instruction from a therapist.

Finally, and pragmatically most important, whatever the experimental use of pharmacologic compounds in biobehavioral research may or may not tell us about the pathogenesis, etiology, and underlying biological processes or concomitants of behavior, these drugs do exert a variety of potent effects on sensory, perceptual, cognitive, emotive, motoric, and verbal behaviors. Many of these behavioral pharmacologic properties can provide a valuable and crucial contribution to the therapeutic modification of abnormal behavior.

BASIC PHARMACOKINETICS

Psychopharmacological compounds are classified according to (a) their chemical structure, (b) their cellular-physiological action, and (c) their effects on molar behavior. For example, trifluoperazine (Stelazine) and perphenazine (Trilafon) may be classed together because they are both piperazine-phenothiazines (molecular-chemical structure), because they are both dopamine (DA) antagonists, that is, they compete with DA or block DA binding sites (cellular-physiological actions) or because they are both antipsychotic, that is, they affect a reduction of behaviors that are considered symptomatic of schizophrenic psychoses (molar, clinical behavioral effects). Although interrelated, these classifications are not perfectly correlated. Some compounds with similar chemical components and structures may have quite diverse behavioral effects. Similarly, compounds as structurally diverse as ethyl alcohol, phenobarbital, and diazepam (Valium) are all CNS depressants and can, in varying doses, result in behavioral sedation.

In clinical psychopharmacology, compounds are usually classified primarily by their clinical or molar behavioral actions. Secondarily they may be subclassified by their specific cellular-physiological action and by their chemical structure. Thus, the classification "antidepressants" includes the tryicyclic antidepressants that among other actions block the presynaptic reuptake of norepinephrine (NE). Also included are the one- or two-ring MAO-inhibitors, whose mode of action is believed to involve inhibition of monoamine-oxidase (MAO), which breaks down, via oxidative deamination, norepinephrine (NE), and serotonin (SHT). Furthermore, drugs are described in terms of their potency, latency of onset of action, and duration and termination of action. Several factors interact to determine a given compound's potency, latency, and duration, as well as its behavioral action.

The elemental components and molecular structure determine the nature and scope of biochemical reactions a given compound will and will not undergo. This provides a degree of specificity of action on the anatomical structures and neurochemical events that a drug can influence or alter, thereby circumscribing the range of its molar behavioral effects. Furthermore, the chemical structure affects the rate at which a drug is absorbed, metabolized, and degraded, its perfusion and binding properties, whether it is absorbed and stored in various body tissues (hence its bioavailability and duration of action) and the types of cell tissue, in addition to neuronal tissue, upon which it may exert some or even profound effects.

The rate of absorption and speed required for a compound to reach its target organ is partially determined by route of administration. Route of administration can also influence potency and duration of action. The usual routes of administration for psychoactive pharmaceuticals include the following: by mouth (per orram, p.o.), intramuscularly (i.m.), and intravenously (i.v.). In behavioral pharmacological studies with animals, additional routes of administration include intraperitoneal (i.p.), and occasionally intraventricular injections are used. Dosage refers to the amount (usually expressed as weight in milligrams) of the active ingredient being administered, not to the composite weight of the active compound and its vehicle. Dosage is usually considered in relation to body weight of the patient or subject and is commonly expressed as milligrams of drug per kilogram of body weight (mg/kg).

Finally, several idiosyncratic organismic factors interact to influence the nature of drug action. These include (a) the drug history of the patient or subject, (b) the psychophysiological state of arousal of the subject prior to drug administration, (c) the nature and intensity of external stimuli, (d) the type of environment the subject is in during and following drug administration, and (e) any idiosyncratic hypersensitivity, hyposensitivity, or allergic reactivity a given subject may have for a given compound or class of compounds. When working with infrahuman subjects, species differences account for significant variation in dose-response curves and also for the nature of certain drugs' behavior effects. Occasional articles claim to show that expectancy or environmental setting account for an equal if not greater percentage of the variance as a drug compound itself. Such studies, however, have almost always utilized a nonpatient population and/or administered atypically low doses of the drug under investigation. Although expectancy and setting, as noted, can influence behavioral response to a drug, the degree of contribution of such factors is usually inversely proportionate to the potency or dosage of the compound under investigation. In general, as potency or dosage of a psychoactive compound increases, cognitive factors and environmental setting exert proportionately less influence on the central behavioral pharmacologic effect.

HYPNOTICS, SEDATIVES, AND ANXIOLYTICS

Although there are significant differences among the various hypnotic-sedative and anxiolytic drugs, they share many common properties. All drugs of this type are CNS depressants. Their administration produces decreased arousal and motor activity; in larger doses, sedation and sleep induction (hence "hypnotic"); and in still larger doses, general anesthesia, coma, and medullary depression resulting in death. They all have some antianxiety (anxiolytic) effects at varying doses. All compounds of this class induce tolerance and physical addiction, though some much more slowly than others. Abrupt cessation of administration once significant tolerance has developed results in a similar abstinence or withdrawal syndrome, including tremors, hallucinations, delirium, and potentially life-threatening convulsions.

The first drug used medically as a tranquilizer and as a sleep-inducing agent was, of course, ethyl alcohol. There is evidence that alcohol has been produced and used both socially and medicinally for over 8,000 years. In addition to alcohol, extracts of the poppy and *Cannabis sativa* plants have a long history of use as sedatives and hypnotics. In the 19th century a number of compounds were synthesized that had a more specific pharmacologic action as hypnotics and sedatives. This is in contrast to the use of opium or morphine, which we know to be primarily analgesics (pain killers), although in sufficiently high doses they will induce sedation and sleep. These new compounds included the bromide salts (potassium bromide and sodium bromide), the cyclic ether (paraldehyde), and a complex alcohol (chloral hydrate). Although the bromide salts have been abandoned in modern medical practice, paraldehyde and chloral hydrate remain on most hospital formularies and are still administered as sleep-inducing preparations.

In 1864 barbituric acid was first synthesized, and although it has no hypnotic properties itself, it is the core molecule from which numerous effective hypnotics have been prepared. The first of these was diethylbarbituric acid or barbital (Veronal), introduced in 1903 and found to be an excellent hypnotic, though it has a relatively long duration of action. This ushered in the era of modern hypnotic-sedative pharmaceuticals. Over 2,500 barbiturates have been synthesized, but only a few of these have been found satisfactory for clinical use. Today, there are only a dozen or so barbiturates in wide clinical use; the most common of these are presented in Figure 36.1.

The barbiturates have their most profound effect on the mesencephalic reticular activating system, which is extremely sensitive to these compounds. In all areas of the CNS, barbiturates suppress polysynaptic responses. At low nonanesthetic doses proximal inhibitory neurons may be inhibited, thus leading to an initial increase in firing rate. At higher therapeutic doses the postsynaptic neurons are inhibited and the firing rate slows. Molar behavioral effects are easily observed and have been empirically investigated and documented. Although there are individual differences in dose-response reactions, small doses of barbiturates usually result in decreased responsivity to stimulation and subjective feelings of relaxation and tranquilization progressing to sleepiness. Following a somewhat larger dose, a paradoxical state of arousal or excitability is occasionally observed, sometimes having the appearance of drunkenness and, in psychotic patients, agitation or aggressiveness. This "release phenomenon" is presumed to result from depression of higher cortical centers, which are thought to exert an inhibitory control on phylogenetically older, lower-brain structures. Unlike the newer benzodiazepine compounds, barbiturates probably do not have an antianxiety effect apart from their sedative action. Nevertheless, barbiturates have been used clinically not only as hypnotics, but also in the treatment of anxiety.

Since their introduction during the first decade of the 20th century, barbiturates have been used clinically in the treatment of essentially every psychiatric and many neurological disorders. Behavioral disorders for which barbiturates have at one time or another been administered include schizophrenia, manic-depressive disease, alcoholism, insomnia, hyperactivity in children, and all of the neuroses. Aside from their use as anticonvulsants in neurological disorders, barbiturates continue to be used for rapid sedation and occasionally for detoxification from hypnotic-sedatives, for drug-induced hypnotic interviews (e.g., Amytal interview), and for drug-facilitated systematic desensitization and flooding procedures (Alford & Williams, 1980). Because of their significantly increased margin of safety, benzodiazepines have replaced barbiturates as recommended sleep-inducing agents. Similarly, barbiturates are no longer appropriate for use as intermediate or long-action antianxiety agents. Since 1950, barbiturates have been re-

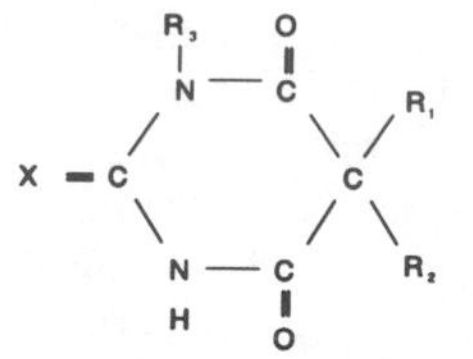

Barbiturate molecule.
Substituents attached at X, R_1, R_2, R_3

Ultrashort-acting Barbiturates

Thiopental (Pentothal)
Thiamylal (Surithal)
Hexobarbital (Sombucaps)

Short-acting Barbiturates

Pentobarbital (Nembutal)
Secobarbital (Seconal)

Intermediate-acting Barbiturates

Amobarbital (Amytal)

Long-acting Barbiturates

Phenobarbital
Mephobarbital
Metharbital
Primidone (Mysoline)

Alcohols

Chloral hydrate
Ethanol (Whiskey, Beer, Wine)

Ethchlorvynol (Placidyl)
Phenaglycodol (Ultran)

Figure 36.1. Hypnotics and sedatives (Trade names given for identification purposes only.)

placed in the pharmacological management of schizophrenia by neuroleptics, in control of mania by lithium carbonate, in reduction of anxiety, and even as sedative-hypnotics by benzodiazepine and related compounds. These latter agents are also excellent drugs for detoxification and rapid sedation when administered intravenously. Most have a potent anticonvulsant action. Except for unusual or special circumstances as noted above, barbiturates, once a mainstay in the psychiatric pharmacy, are obsolete in the management or treatment of behavioral disorders.

ANXIOLYTICS ("MINOR TRANQUILIZERS")

Although anxiolytic or antianxiety agents share many common properties with barbiturates, there are significant differences that distinguish these subgroups of CNS depressors, their depressant effects are generally less potent, and particularly with benzodiazepines (Fig. 36.2), their margin of safety is substantially greater than that of the barbiturates. Moreover, unlike barbiturates, the antianxiety action of benzodiazepines is largely independent of its hypnotic-sedative action (Gilman, Goodman, Rall, & Murad, 1985). Although both barbiturates and benzodiazepines decrease avoidance and escape responding in animals, benzodiazepines can significantly reduce

conditioned avoidance responding without impairing appropriate and adaptive escape behaviors (Iverson & Iverson, 1975). Other animal studies have found that operant behaviors established via positive reinforcement (e.g., food-reinforced lever pressing) but subsequently depressed by punishment display substantial reinstatement of high-frequency response rates following benzodiazepine administration. In contrast, administration of amphetamine stimulants (e.g., Benzedrine) or antipsychotic neuroleptics (e.g., Thorazine) to animals so trained either results in no significant change or even further suppresses response rates (Haefely, 1978). Furthermore, some animal studies have found that anxiolytics given in low, nonsedating doses will nonspecifically increase frequency of previously unpunished operants as well as those suppressed by punishment training (e.g., Kelleher & Morse, 1964).

Not all the behavioral pharmacologic effects of this class of compounds are desirable. CNS depression from overdose, though significantly less with benzodiazepines than with meprobamates or especially barbiturates, is a serious potential hazard. All of these drugs are essentially cross-tolerant with respect to the sedative effects and can potentiate each other. Overdose resulting in death from the ingestion of benzodiazepines alone is extremely rare, with this class of compounds being among the safest in the pharmacy with respect to margin of safety. However, accidental

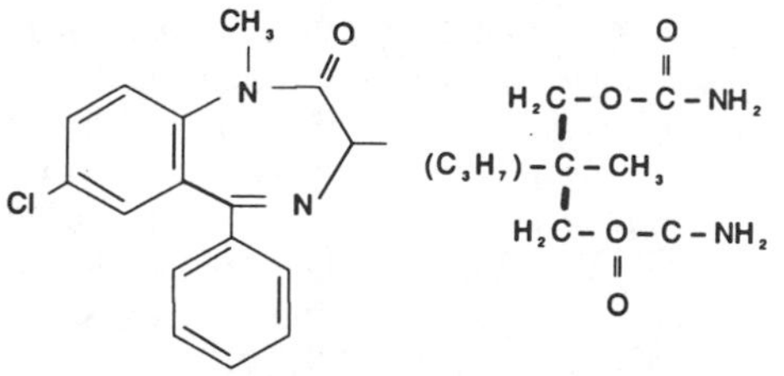

Diazepam
(Valium)

Meprobamate
(Equanil, Miltown)

Anxiolytics

Alprazolam (Xanax)
Chlordiazepoxide (Librium)
Clorazepate (Tranxene)
Diazepam (Valium)
Lorazepam (Ativan)
Meprobamate (Equanil, Miltown)
Oxazepam (Serax)
Prazepam (Centrax)

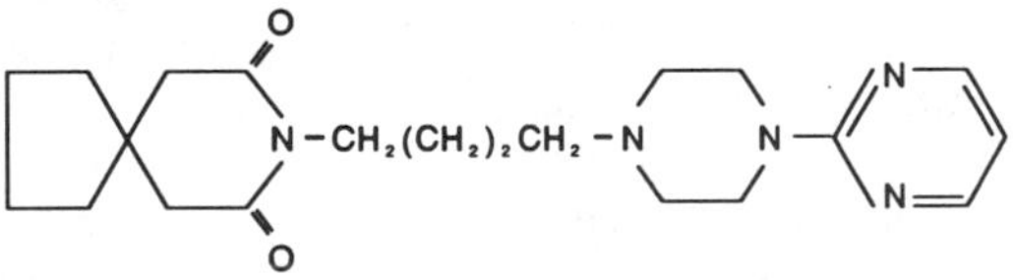

Benzodiazepine Hypnotics

Flurazepam (Dalmane)
Temazepam (Restoril)
Triazolam (Halcion)

Buspirone (BuSpar)

Figure 36.2. Anxiolytics and hypnotics (Trade names given for identification purposes only.)

traumatic injury due to intoxication, particularly when these compounds are mixed with alcohol, are among their most serious liabilities. Abrupt cessation of the prolonged use of benzodiazepines can induce a severe, even life-threatening abstinence syndrome. Intoxication on low to moderate doses resembles intoxication on ethyl alcohol (Smith, Wesson, & Seymour, 1979). And, as with ethyl alcohol, all hypnotic sedative and minor tranquilizers have state-dependent properties (Alford & Alford, 1976; Overton, 1973).

Addiction to and dependency on the benzodiazepines has been felt to be one of the most common and serious forms of addictive behavior (see Alford, 1981). Subsequent studies do not seem to confirm this view for the group of benzodiazepine users as a whole but may be applicable to individuals within the group or to certain subsets of the group. Addiction refers to both the psychological and physiological aspects of the drug-seeking behavior (i.e., the drug is generally pleasurable, increasing doses are needed to obtain the same degree of pleasure or to prevent a withdrawal syndrome, and a withdrawal syndrome exists). When increasing doses of a medication are needed to produce the desired clinical effect this is known as tolerance. Benzodiazepines exhibit a withdrawal syndrome that is basically indistinguishable from other compounds that affect the CNS membranes in a similar manner (barbiturates, alcohol, anticonvulsants). However, the existence of a withdrawal syndrome alone does not prove addiction. Tolerance to the sedative effects of benzodiazepines develops rapidly and the dose must be titrated upward to achieve the same sedative effect. This is the reason for the recommended 14-day limit on benzodiazepine "sleeping pills." Tolerance to the antianxiety effects of benzodiazepines commonly does not develop, and some patients may derive clinical benefits from the long-term administration of these agents. Overall, the risks of dependence and addiction to the benzodiazepines are remarkably low in relation to the massive exposure prevalent in the society (Uhlenhuth, DeWitt, Balter, Johanson, & Mellinger, 1988). The risk of benzodiazepine abuse among alcoholics is commonly considered to be greater than the risk of abuse among the general population, but a critical review of the literature does not fully support this contention for the groups, although individual and subgroup differences in abuse potential may exist (Ciraulo, Sands, & Shader, 1988).

Benzodiazepines and barbiturates exert their effect at the neuronal level through augmentation of the chloride ion flow across the nerve cell membrane. Although both benzodiazepines and barbiturates exert this cellular effect, the benzodiazepines do not decrease excitatory membrane transmission as do the barbiturates which may account for the benzodiazepines ability to exert clinical effect without the marked sedation associated with the barbiturates (Trifilletti, Snowman, & Snyder, 1984). In order for the benzodiazepines to exert their neuronal effect gamma-amino butyric acid (GABA) must be present and the benzodiazepine must bind at the benzodiazepine recognition site which is structurally associated with the GABA site but is chemically distinct from the $GABA_a$ recognition site. Other GABA recognition sites exist but at this time have not been documented to be associated with benzodiazepine action. Because of this structure/function relationship the following parameters concerning benzodiazepine action can be stated: (a) GABA must be present and bind to the $GABA_a$ recognition site, (b) GABA stimulates the chloride anion flow, (c) benzodiazepines augment the GABA stimulated chloride anion flow at synapses where the GABA concentration is insufficient to open all available chloride channels but do not promote receptor function beyond that which is obtained with GABA itself (Enna & Mohler, 1987), (d) benzodiazepines can exert no neuronal or clinical effects without the presence of GABA, (e) there are instances where GABA binding sites may appear without associated benzodiazepine binding sites, but probably no instances where benzodiazepine binding sites occur without GABA binding sites.

Although there has been some decline in the number of anxiolytic prescriptions since a high of 100 million written in 1973, these compounds are among the most prescribed pharmaceuticals in the United States and constitute over 75% of all psychoactive medication prescriptions written. Given the potency of these compounds, the available animal and human research literature, their potential hazards and abuse-dependency liabilities, as well as their apparent popularity with physicians, patients, and abusers, one would think that rather clear indications and guidelines for their clinical use would be recommended in standard psychiatric texts. Recent works have a tendency to be more specific for the recommendations for benzodiazepines. These texts as well as general clinical practice would indicate that benzodiazepines are generally considered appropriate for generalized anxiety disorder, panic disorder, and insomnia (Silver & Yudofsky, 1988). In addition to the above disorders, benzodiazepines are useful in the treatment of muscle spasm, benzodiazepines cross-tolerant withdrawal phenomena, and as anticonvulsants.

Although complete data are hard to obtain, studies of prescribing practices and anecdotal evidence (such as reviewing patients' charts) indicate that, in practice, anxiolytics are frequently used in the treatment of essentially every form of nonpsychotic, psychiatric disorder in which anxiety or agitation are components. Even patients with primary or secondary diagnoses of chemical dependency are frequently prescribed anxiolytics in attempts to reduce their "psychic tensions," which presumably can trigger episodes of drinking or drug abuse. Many alcoholics, for example, are placed on a benzodiazepine even after detoxification. Others go without specific treatment for their alcoholism and, being advised to reduce their drinking, are placed on an anxiolytic to reduce or control the tension and stress that they and their physician erroneously believe cause their excessive drinking in the first place. Since benzodiazepines are cross-tolerant with alcohol (indeed, they are the current drugs of choice for use in alcohol detoxification) and are themselves potentially intoxicating and addicting, this practice is functionally equivalent to methadone maintenance for opiate-addicted patients. Nevertheless, it is true that most anxiolytics, particularly the benzodiazepines, do have a high margin of safety, are used according to prescribed instructions far more often than they are abused, and can be very effective in reducing anxiety.

Historically, it has been the practice to define *anxiety* as separate and distinct from *fear*, primarily on the basis that fears supposedly have identifiable, specific objects, whereas individuals reporting anxiety cannot (or do not) identify specific stimulus triggers. Similarly, fear is sometimes defined as a reaction to a perceived physical threat and anxiety as a reaction to psychological threats, such as loss of self-esteem. Psychophysiologically, such distinctions are unwarranted. The physiological components or concomitants (primary sympathetic hyperarousal and parasympathetic inhibition) of anxiety, fear, severe phobic reactions, and indeed, adaptive in vivo fears of actual danger, are biologically identical. The real issue is the extent to which the patient and therapist can identify or uncover the external or internal factors that evoke this aversive autonomic reaction.

Anxiolytics are but one way of treating anxiety problems and may not be the primary intervention of choice. Abundant evidence now exists empirically documenting the efficacy of such procedures as systematic desensitization, flooding, and various cognitive-restructuring strategies for anxiety and anxiety-mediated problems (Last & Hersen, 1988). Traditionally, clinicians evaluating patients who present with such complaints as nervousness, tensions, agitation, anxiety, fearfulness, or apprehension have determined whether the condition appears as a consequence of current, acute life events or whether it constitutes a more long-term or chronic behavioral reaction pattern. If the former is the case, then a short-term course of anxiolytics may have been indicated to facilitate the patient's postevent adjustment. If, however, the clinical evaluation revealed a more chronic and enduring problem, then appropriate therapeutic intervention aimed at modifying the patient's autonomic and perhaps perceptual-cognitive reaction patterns has generally been the treatment of choice.

Antianxiety agents may well reduce the patient's anxiety and subjective distress. They do not themselves, however, modify the patient's maladaptive cognitive-emotional repertoire, and undesirable emotional reactions can, and indeed theoretically should, be expected to return when anxiolytic pharmacotherapy is discontinued. Although the efficacy of many traditional verbal therapies remains questionable, the evidence documenting the effectiveness of behavioral therapies for anxiety disorders in now voluminous (e.g., see Last & Hersen, 1988). Clinicians who treat anxiety-mediated disorders only pharmacotherapeutically (even if ostensibly combined with "psychotherapy"), without a trial of appropriate behavioral psychotherapeutic intervention, are simply not providing their patients the most effective interventions currently available. Anxiolytic pharmacotherapy may, in certain cases, be effectively utilized as a treatment component of various behavioral anxiety-reduction procedures (Alford & Williams, 1980). In cases involving extremely high-level autonomic arousal, for example, some patients may not be able to attain a sufficient state of relaxation through verbal instruction alone to accomplish systematic desensitization successfully. Similarly, some patients may feel unable or

unwilling to carry out therapeutic tasks designed to extinguish anxiety reactions, and still others may find certain procedures (e.g., in vivo flooding) so aversively anxiety producing as to withdraw from treatment. In such cases, titrated administration of anxiolytics can increase patients' tolerance of previously highly aversive stimulus settings, enhance confrontation and interaction with relevant stimuli, and generally facilitate performance on therapeutic tasks designed to decrease undesirable, disruptive arousal responses. Because of their state-dependent properties, when anxiolytics are used in such therapeutic procedures, it is important to fade drug levels gradually and systematically to zero during active treatment phases (see Alford & Williams, 1980). No matter how carefully planned and conducted, no set of therapeutics is effective for all patients. Unfortunately, treatment failures often do not make it into journals, especially in those publications primarily identified with the form of therapy that failed. The authors have had a number of patients whose chronic and pervasive anxiety failed to respond to any current behavioral, cognitive, or insight-oriented psychotherapeutic intervention, even when anxiolytics were used as adjuncts. On the other hand, some of these patients whose anxiety seriously impaired their vocational, social, or private behavior were able to function at least adequately when maintained on low to moderate dosage regimens of anxiolytic pharmacotherapy. Some authorities have suggested that many patients with various anxiety disorders are being undertreated pharmacologically (Rickels, 1977) and that anxiolytic pharmacotherapy may even be appropriate for individuals who are emotionally overactive to relatively minor, everyday problems in living (Cole & Davis, 1975a). Although there are no large-scale, hard data on the appropriateness of the millions of anxiolytic prescriptions written annually, quite a number of patients are prescribed and maintained on anxiolytics agents in lieu of being treated with appropriate, efficacious anxiety-reduction therapies.

In summary, antianxiety agents, particularly the benzodiazepines, have been demonstrated in both animal and human studies to be deserving of the name anxiolytics. Although substantially safer than barbiturates, they do have liabilities, including abuse potential and addictive properties in some patients. In view of their behavioral-pharmacologic properties together with their liabilities, anxiolytics are indicated where anxiety is at a sufficiently high level to impair an individual's normal behavioral functioning. Mere discomfort is not a primary indication; rather, evidence of significantly impaired or disrupted function should exist. Second, the clinician should be careful to distinguish between a normal behavioral skill repertoire whose performance is disrupted by anxiety versus behavioral deficits or maladaptive behavior that may be problematic independently of significant anxiety. Indeed, such deficits may produce or contribute to anxiety reactions that are secondary to the individual lacking necessary skills in situations that require or demand the missing repertoire. Furthermore, before embarking on a long-term course of anxiolytic pharmacotherapy, the clinician should provide for a competent, systematic course of behavior therapy, such as systematic desensitization, in cases where anxiety appears reflexive to even subtle and obscure stimuli, or cognitive restructuring where anxiety appears to be more the consequence of perceptual and cognitive mediational factors. Where significantly disruptive anxiety exists, anxiolytics are appropriate: (a) for short-term, transient but severe and complicated adjustment reactions; (b) for short-term and gradually reduced or "faded" use, if necessary or significantly facilitory, in systematic anxiety-reduction procedures, or (c) for more long-term use with those few patients who have chronic, disruptively high levels of anxiety and for whom a thorough course of an appropriate, empirically documented anxiety-reduction procedure has failed. Use of a potentially addicting compound to decrease chronic, minor, autonomic discomfort in response to minor, common, indeed, "normal" life stresses or events should be considered unwarranted, if not contraindicated.

Over the past several years other, newer chemical compounds have been formulated to treat anxiety symptoms. Buspirone (BuSpar) was developed in the early 1970s and was brought to market in the mid-1980s. This anxiolytic compound is chemically unrelated to the benzodiazepines or sedatives. Buspirone does not bind at benzodiazepine receptor sites but does bind at 5-hydroxytryptamine (5-HT_{1A} receptors (Peroutka, 1985) and has been demonstrated to potently inhibit the firing of 5-HT dorsal raphe neurons (VanderMaelen & Wilderman, 1984). These neuronal effects may be the anxiolytic mechanism of action but a definitive statement cannot be made at this time.

Clinically, buspirone has been shown to be as effective as benzodiazepine compound in alleviating core anxiety symptoms. In addition, buspirone has fewer detrimental effects on psychomotor function as compared to benzodiazepines, does not seem to interact with alcohol (Mattila, Aranko, & Seppala, 1982), and seems to lack the potential for abuse or to cause physical dependence (Cole, Orzack, Beake, Bird, &

Bar-tal, 1982). Some other clinical investigators have reported that, compared to diazepam, buspirone may be slightly less effective in alleviating somatic symptoms of anxiety while being slightly more effective in relieving symptoms of anger and hostility (Rickels, Wiseman, Norstad, Singer, Stoltz, Brown, & Danton, 1982). Another important clinical effect is that in one prospective study in which the effects of abrupt discontinuation of chlorazepate (a benzodiazepine) and buspirone were compared, the patients on chlorazepate had withdrawal symptoms and rebound anxiety but those patients on buspirone displayed no such effect (Rickels, Csanalosi, Chung, Case, & Schweizer, 1985).

Based on the authors' clinical experience, if buspirone is to be substituted for a benzodiazepine, one should completely discontinue the benzodiazepine prior to instituting buspirone, because buspirone is a behaviorally activating compound and may tend to exacerbate benzodiazepine withdrawal symptoms. In addition, patients who have previously been on benzodiazepine maintenance therapy often request a reinstitution of the benzodiazepine therapy, because buspirone does not impart a feeling of well-being that often accompanies benzodiazepine usage.

Other agents more recently utilized in the treatment of anxiety include nonselective beta-adrenergic receptor blockers (e.g., propanolol), alpha$_2$-adrenergic receptor agonists (e.g., clonidine), tricyclic antidepressants (e.g., imipramine, desipramine), and MAO inhibitors (e.g., phenelzine). Of these compounds only the tricyclic antidepressant imipramine has been shown in a reasonably well-designed study to have antianxiety effects equal to a benzodiazepine (Kahn, McNair, Lipman, Covi, Rickels, Downing, Fisher, & Frankenthaler, 1986). Propanolol appears to possess little intrinsic antianxiety activity but may serve as a useful adjunct to benzodiazepine or antidepressant therapy (Nayes, Anderson, Clancy, Crowe, Slymen, Ghoneim, & Heinricks, 1984). MAO inhibitors have been primarily studied in relationship to panic attacks. Clonidine is useful in the treatment of opiate withdrawal (Gold, Redmond, & Kleber, 1978) where anxiety is a prominent feature, but the use of this compound in generalized anxiety disorders has not been fully investigated. Thus, the benzodiazepines remain the current benchmark against which all antianxiety agents are judged. Although initial studies indicate that at least some of the new, nonbenzodiazepine anxiolytics have comparable effects with fewer liabilities, only continued clinical trials and use along with further controlled research will document and define therapeutic parameters.

DOPAMINE ANTAGONISTIC-ANTIPSYCHOTIC AGENTS

The introduction of phenothiazines into the American psychiatry formulary in 1954 ushered in a new age of pharmacotherapy in treating major psychotic disorders. Their clinical use in France for 2 years before they were approved for use in the United States had already provided some indication of their promise. Dopamine antagonists, such as chlorpromazine, were found to exert such dramatic and generally desirable effects in most hospitalized schizophrenics that truly revolutionary reforms in mental hospital practices became possible. Not only did physical restraints (straitjackets, padded cells, and traditional sedative compounds) become rarely necessary, but many long-term inpatients were sufficiently improved to be discharged to outpatient status. Even those patients who did not improve sufficiently to be discharged were usually able to be managed in much less restrictive and more constructive ward atmospheres.

Structure and Mechanism of Action

Since the introduction of chlorpromazine (Thorazine), a score of neuroleptic, antipsychotic dopamine blocking agents have been developed; the more common of these are listed in Table 36.1. The molecular structure and biological mode of actions of neuroleptics are very different from hypnotic sedatives and anxiolytics. Unfortunately, the terms *major tranquilizers* (neuroleptics) and *minor tranquilizers* (anxiolytics) have, at times, led some erroneously to think of neuroleptics as only more potent forms of a sedative tranquilizer. Most neuroleptics have a tricyclic nucleus in which two benzine rings are linked by a central ring containing a sulfur atom and a nitrogen atom at which side chains are attached. These tricyclic neuroleptics differ by the constituents of side chains attached to the nitrogen or to the benzine rings. More recently synthesized neuroleptics, such as haloperidol (Haldol), have altered the tricyclic structure by bonding cyclic components at different points along an alkane chain. All neuroleptics contain one or two amine functions. These variations affect the potency and, to some extent, the side effects resulting from neuroleptic pharmacotherapy (see Table 36.1).

In spite of a wealth of biochemical research on neuroleptics, the exact mechanisms of action are still unknown. It is known that neuroleptics have multiple biochemical actions in the CNS including effects on alpha-adrenergic, cholinergic, histaminergic, as well as on dopaminergic receptors and on serotonin (5-HT)

metabolism. The midbrain dopamine system is the system most commonly felt to be the site of the antipsychotic effects. Within this system antipsychotic medications exhibit both acute and chronic effects. Acutely, the antipsychotic medications increase the firing rate, especially burst firing, of dopamine neurons in the A9 and A10 cell groups (midbrain dopamine cell body groups). Chronic administration of antipsychotic medications results in a state of "silence" in the same cell groups due to depolarization in activation (Bunney, Sesack, & Silva, 1987). Clozapine does not have this same physiological profile but affects the dopamine system through other mechanisms. In addition, other effects on the dopamine system, such as postsynaptic D_2 receptor blockade, probably play a large role in the clinical effectiveness of antipsychotic medication. Although this partial blockade of dopamine receptors occurs to some extent throughout the brain, a growing body of evidence implicates the mesolimbic dopamine system and its terminals in the paleocortical areas as the critical locus of action (Carlsson, 1978). In regard to biological theories of schizophrenia, it is interesting to note that amphetamines, known to aggravate schizophrenic psychoses and capable of inducing acute organic psychoses indistinguishable from paranoid schizophrenia, stimulate release of dopamine (Carlsson, 1978). Furthermore, administration of neuroleptics will usually reverse stimulant-induced psychoses within a few days of initiating pharmacotherapy, and sometimes within a few hours. Still a great deal remains to be discovered about the biological substrates of major psychoses as well as the complex mechanism of action by which antipsychotic compounds exert their influence.

Behavioral Pharmacology and Clinical Use

All neuroleptics have the capacity to produce sedation. Although this is not their primary behavioral pharmacologic property, sedation is a useful component of neuroleptic action particularly when treating extreme arousal, agitation, or aggressive behavior in a psychotic patient. Unlike the hypnotic-sedatives, neuroleptics produce a relatively easily arousable sedation and usually without the ataxia and intoxication associated with barbiturate sedation. More important, neuroleptics do not have the biphasic action of pseudostimulation or "release phenomenon" preceding sedation that may occur with hypnotic-sedatives. Thus, they can be used to tranquilize psychotic excitement without the risk that the medication may initially

Table 36.1. Neuroleptics (Antipsychotics)

DRUG GROUP		CONVERSION FACTOR[1]	SIDE EFFECTS (1 = LEAST; 4 = MOST)		DOSE (RANGE IN mg/24 HRS.)
GENERIC NAME	TRADE NAME*		EXTRAPYRAMIDAL	AUTONOMIC	
Phenothiazines					
Aliphatic					
Chlorpromazine	Thorazine	1:1	2	4	300–2500 mg/day
Piperazines					
Trifluoperazine	Stelazine	1:20	4	2	10–40 mg/day
Fluphenazine	Prolixin	1:50	4	2	10–20 mg/day
Perphenazine	Trilafon	1:10	4	2	20–80 mg/day
Piperidines					
Mesoridazine	Serentil	1:2	—	—	150–400 mg/day
Piperacetazine	Quide	1:10	1	—	20–80 mg/day
Thioridazine	Mellaril	1:1	—	4	300–800 mg/day
Butyrophenomes					
Haloperidol	Haldol	1:50	4+	1	4–60 mg/day
Thioxanthenes					
Thiothixene	Navane	1:25	4	1	10–60 mg/day
Chloprothixene	Taractan	1:1	4+	1	
Dihydroindolone					
Molindone	Moban	1:5	—	—	
Dibenzoxazepine					
Loxapine	Loxitane	1:6	3–4+	1	
Dibenzodiazepine					
Clozapine	Leponex	1:2	—	4+	

[1]Estimated dosage ratio in relation to Thorazine. For example, 10 mg of Stelazine is equivalent to 200 mg of Thorazine.
*Trade names given for identification purposes only.

aggravate the excitement and agitation prior to sedation. Furthermore, neuroleptics are not physically addicting. It is, however, the antipsychotic action of neuroleptics that constitutes their primary pharmacotherapeutic contribution. Neuroleptics not only reduce arousal symptoms such as agitation, hyperexcitability, and insomnia, but exert a true antipsychotic action on perceptual and cognitive processes. When treated with an adequate dosage of neuroleptics, many, though not all, schizophrenics display a dramatic diminution of cognitive disorganization, looseness of association, thought intrusion or thought derailment, paranoid ideation and general delusional thinking, and remission of bizarre somatic sensation and auditory or visual hallucinations. These effects have been documented in a large number of studies comparing neuroleptics to placebo and other classes of psychoactive compounds. In a survey of 118 clinical studies, Klein and Davis (1969) reported that neuroleptics were significantly superior to placebo in the majority of cases, and that where differences were less striking (particularly in early studies), inadequate dosage had usually been used. In contrast, hypnotic sedatives, such as barbiturates, have consistently failed to produce results superior to placebo in psychotic patients (Baldessarini, 1977). Furthermore, neuroleptic therapy has been shown superior to milieu therapy, group therapy, and individual psychotherapy in schizophrenic populations (Grinspoon, Ewalt, & Shader, 1968; May, 1968). Indeed, the antipsychotic actions of neuroleptics are sufficiently clear and established that it is possible to construct a timetable of therapeutic response; that is, although there is individual variation, the usual timing, nature, and sequence of behavioral change resulting from neuroleptic therapy for schizophrenia has been identified. Maximum therapeutic response to a neuroleptic requires 6 to 8 weeks on an adequate dose (Baldessarini, 1977; Lehmann, 1966, 1975). Because some clinicians tend to initiate treatment with low or conservative dosages, the time from beginning pharmacotherapy until maximum benefit is obtained may be extended. The first behaviors to be modified are usually the arousal symptoms. Agitation, hyperexcitability, aggressiveness, and insomnia display significant reduction or disappear within the first 2 weeks. Within 4 weeks, such affective symptoms as depression, anxiety, and social withdrawal are generally improved. Cognitive and perceptual disturbances, such as hallucinations, delusions, and disorganized cognitive processes (e.g., looseness of association) are usually responsive after 6 to 8 weeks on an adequate dose of a neuroleptic (Lehmann, 1966). In addition to treating the floridly psychotic schizophrenic, neuroleptics have also been shown to reduce the probability of relapse in schizophrenics who are maintained on them. Davis (1975) reviewed 24 controlled studies on drug maintenance and found a relapse rate of only 30% among groups maintained on antipsychotics compared to a relapse rate of 65% among placebo groups. Consistent with these findings, Hogarty, Ulrich, Mussare, and Aristignieta (1976) reported that patients who had been thought suitable for drug discontinuation evidenced a 67% relapse following drug withdrawal.

Like all psychoactive compounds, neuroleptics have a number of undesirable side effects. Among these are dystonias, muscle spasm and stiffness, stooped posture, shuffling gate, masklike faces, and drooling. These Parkinsonian symptoms, which result from postsynaptic D_2 blockade in the nigrostriatal pathway, can usually be reversed or reduced to a minimum by administration of anti-Parkinsonian drugs. Other side effects accounted are dry mouth, blurred vision, and occasionally ejaculatory or erectile impotence. Again, such side effects can usually be minimized by modification of drug dosage or switching to an alternative neuroleptic. The most serious potential neuroleptic side effects are agranulocytosis, tardive dyskinesia, and neuroleptic malignant syndrome.

Neuroleptics are all equally effective and thus are essentially interchangeable. However, there are a number of differences in the incidence and severity of various side effects produced (see Table 36.1). In addition (although there are few research data that speak to or support this statement), many clinicians report that at least some patients who fail to respond to even aggressive neuroleptic pharmacotherapy with one drug display significant improvement on an equivalent dose of an alternative neuroleptic. Studies attempting to determine which patients would respond best to which subclass of neuroleptics have produced essentially negative results. Although apparently only occasionally successful, the clinical finding that at least some patients improve following drug substitution has been observed and anecdotally reported by a sufficient number of careful, competent research clinicians to warrant further investigation. Changing from one neuroleptic to another is commonly employed where a given patient has developed side effects more common to one drug than another or where a patient appears unusually sensitive to a particular neuroleptic.

Clozapine, an antipsychotic medication belonging to the dibenzodiazepine class, is somewhat of an exception to the statements in the above paragraph.

Although the traditional antipsychotic medication loxapine also belongs to this class, clozapine has certain physiological and clinical actions that makes it unique among the antipsychotics. Clozapine binds D_1 and D_2 receptors less strongly than the traditional antipsychotics while having an affinity for serotonergic, alpha-1 adrenergic, and H-1 histaminergic receptors. The antipsychotic effect of clozapine is equal to or greater than the traditional antipsychotics. In addition to affecting a reduction in the positive symptoms of schizophrenia, clozapine has been demonstrated to be particularly effective in reducing the negative symptoms of emotional withdrawal, blunted affect, anxiety, tension, conceptual disorganization, somatic concerns, and mannerisms (Tamminga & Gerlach, 1987).

The side effect profile of clozapine has delayed the distribution of the medication in the United States for several years. Clozapine was related to eight deaths in Finland from agranulocytosis. This resulted in increased hematologic surveillance among those utilizing clozapine. Since this has occurred the cases of bone marrow suppression have decreased from 0.38% to 0.06% and the mortality in this clozapine-treated group of patients with agranulocytosis has dropped from 42% to 19% (Tamminga & Gerlach, 1987). Even though the current rate of antipsychotic-induced agranulocytosis may not be considerably higher than that seen with other phenothiazines, Sandoz, the pharmaceutical company marketing clozapine in the U.S., has established an elaborate patient monitoring system to evaluate potential hematologic side effects. These changes are reversible upon discontinuation of the medication.

In addition to the hematologic side effects of clozapine, the most significant side effects are on the cardiovascular system. This includes a fall in orthostatic blood pressure and electrocardiographic changes. These changes are reversible upon discontinuation of the medication.

Clinically, neuroleptics are indicated and used primarily in the treatment of schizophrenic disorders. These agents also are effective in treating acute, drug-induced psychotic behavior, such as that resulting from stimulant abuse and phencyclodine (PCP or "angel dust") intoxication, in treating hallucinations and agitation in some cases of severe organic brain syndrome, and in acute control of manic behavior in a major affective disorder. Although lithium carbonate is the drug of choice for treating mania in major affective disorder, it requires several days to reach a sufficient serum concentration to exert its behavioral pharmacologic action. During the initial phase, neuroleptics may be used to control the patient's more agitated and psychotic behavior until a therapeutic serum lithium level is achieved. Ideally, in treating an actively psychotic schizophrenic, the patient should be hospitalized and the target symptoms identified and systematically monitored. Unless the patient is highly agitated, poses a threat to himself or others, or has a well-documented history of schizophrenia, it is often advisable to delay pharmacotherapy a few days until a firm diagnosis is obtained. Careful history and drug screening should be obtained routinely, particularly for younger patients. Once a diagnosis of schizophrenic disorder is established, pharmacotherapy is usually instituted rather aggressively. Actively psychotic schizophrenics often have a high tolerance for neuroleptics and frequently require doses two or three times what may eventually be found sufficient for maintenance therapy. Though practices vary, many clinicians prescribe a dosage and schedule that initially results in slightly oversedating the patient. As symptomatic behaviors begin to yield to the pharmacotherapy, dosage is adjusted to reduce signs of oversedation. Starting with a lower dosage may have the advantage of avoiding such sedation but usually requires a significantly longer hospitalization to achieve an adequate dose to impact on the cognitive and perceptual disturbances.

Once maximum pharmacotherapeutic benefit is obtained, which may take several weeks from the time drug therapy is initiated, dosage is gradually reduced to the lowest level at which maximum symptom remission can be maintained. Often, dosage reduction is begun while the patient is still hospitalized, but may be continued on an outpatient basis. During this time, it is essential that the patient be carefully monitored, through frequent and regular outpatient visits. Once patients are well regulated on an appropriate and effective maintenance dose and adjusted and functioning in their home environments, many can be successfully followed over many years with only intermittent office visits. Although long-term neuroleptic maintenance therapy is critical for many schizophrenics, others do quite well over relatively long periods without antipsychotic medication. Unfortunately, no psychological or biological test and no specific symptom or set of symptoms unequivocally predicts which schizophrenic patients can safely discontinue medication. Nevertheless, several factors appear to be correlated with drug-free versus drug-maintenance prognoses. Patients with more gradual and progressive onset of symptoms and poor premorbid levels of function frequently do less well on drug-free follow-up than do patients who evidenced a more abrupt and rapid onset of psychotic symptoms and who responded relatively rapidly to neuroleptic pharmacotherapy. In addition, patients who have a history of relapse shortly after drug discontinuation would, of course, also be candidates for long-term drug-maintenance therapy.

Although neuroleptic pharmacotherapy has been shown to be the single most effective form of treatment for active psychosis in schizophrenia, it does not address the entire symptom profile in most cases. Many people suffering from schizophrenia have severe and debilitating behavioral excesses and deficits that may result from any number of etiological sources. Predictions regarding general long-term outcome have traditionally been considered in reference to a given patient's premorbid personality as well as to the number, frequency, rapidity of onset, and duration of the active psychotic episodes. It is useful to conceptualize "premorbid personality" in terms of performance versus repertoire variables. A careful examination of the patient's prior behavior can yield a great deal of information regarding his or her intellectual, vocational, emotional, and social functioning and skills (i.e., the premorbid repertoire). The best or optimum benefit neuroleptic pharmacotherapy can provide is to ameliorate the biochemical contribution to the individual's impaired cognitive-emotive-verbal-motoric *performance*. Pharmacotherapy cannot, of course, instate behavioral patterns the patient never possessed, or modify those maladaptive patterns acquired through environmental experience (learned), including those developed, in part, in reaction to or as a consequence of their psychoses. Instead, specific psychotherapeutic procedures designed to address those problems are necessary additions to the pharmacotherapy. Such procedures as general ward-token economics aimed at improving patient's self-care, compliance, and general on-ward behavior (see Milby, 1975) and social-skills training (e.g., Hersen & Bellack, 1976) have been found useful. In addition, behavior patterns thought to be the consequence of schizophrenia itself may at times fail to respond to pharmacotherapy, but improve significantly when appropriate psychological procedures are applied. For example, aversion therapy and cognitive restructuring have sometimes significantly reduced or stopped hallucinations in patients with chronic schizophrenia where such behavior persisted in spite of drug treatment, even though most other symptoms had remitted (e.g., Alford, Fleece, & Rothblum, 1982; Alford & Turner, 1976). In treating schizophrenic disorders, psychological interventions are usually best reserved until adequate response to the medication is obtained. In the first place, some of the behavioral symptoms may be primarily performance deficits that, in many but not all cases, medication alone may help. For example, social withdrawal and diminished social responsivity might initially appear to suggest gross social-skill deficits. Some patients exhibiting such behavior will respond to drug treatment alone, and those behaviors disappear or improve significantly (e.g., Liberman et al., 1973). Second, many patients with schizophrenia may initially fail to respond to psychotherapeutic interventions, but begin responding as maximum pharmacotherapeutic benefit is achieved. Hersen and his associates reported a case in which a patient failed to respond to skills-oriented group therapy or even to a simple, clear token program during the first month of hospitalization. Once medication levels were adjusted and the patient began to remit some of the primary symptomatic behaviors (loose associations, flat affect), he also began to respond rapidly to the token program and to the verbal, occupational, and social-skills training designed to ameliorate those repertoire deficits (Hersen et al., 1975). Although, as noted, neuroleptics are often useful in the acute management of psychoses other than the schizophrenias, their use in such cases as drug-induced psychoses is almost always time-limited and discontinued as soon as the major psychotic symptoms remit. Indications for the use of neuroleptics in the treatment of personality disorders or behavioral problems that do not entail clear psychotic symptoms is much less clear.

Clinical Research and Neuroleptics

Clinical researchers often fail to take into account the pharmacokinetics and behavioral pharmacologic properties of various drugs when conducting psychological studies with patient populations receiving medication. This common, though by no means universal, failure probably occurs most often when the drugs involved are neuroleptics. Several factors previously noted need to be kept in mind. Neuroleptic pharmacotherapy usually requires 6 to 8 weeks for full or maximum benefit to be obtained. Likewise, since neuroleptics are tissue-stored, it may take days or weeks for them to be eliminated from the body. Although some patients may relapse within a few days of stopping their medication, others may experience a gradual return of the psychotic behaviors or exhibit a florid psychosis only after several weeks off the medication. Indeed, this is as confusing to many patients as it is to some researchers. In addition, various classes of symptomatic behaviors do not exhibit simultaneous change. Reduction or elimination of delusional and hallucinatory behavior may occur several weeks after a schizophrenic patient has displayed dramatic changes in some of his or her arousal symptoms. Finally, it should go without saying that not all patients with schizophrenia respond well to medication. Although many display a dramatic remission of symptoms, some improve only slightly, and others not at all. Failure to take such pharmacologic properties and effects into account when conducting clinical research can result in very confounded data from which fallacious conclusions may be derived.

LITHIUM CARBONATE

The introduction of lithium carbonate into the American pharmacopoeia has a curious history. In 1949, an Australian psychiatrist named John Cade reported successful treatment of 10 manic patients with lithium carbonate. Shortly after this anecdotal report appeared, controlled studies of lithium treatment for manic psychoses were conducted and confirmed its efficacy. Lithium therapy was rapidly incorporated into Australian, British, and European psychiatric pharmacotherapy. In the United States, however, the Food and Drug Administration did not approve the use of lithium carbonate until 1970. Lithium chloride had long been used as a substitute for common table salt (sodium chloride) by patients on low sodium diets. Unfortunately, at about the time of Cade's original report, several deaths and cases of severe intoxication were reported among individuals using lithium chloride as a sodium-salt substitute (Corcoran, Taylor, & Page, 1949). This occurrence combined with the lack of enthusiasm among pharmaceutical companies (lithium carbonate is a simple, cheap, unpatentable compound) resulted in a 20-year delay in the approval and use of lithium carbonate in America.

Pharmacology

Lithium carbonate is rapidly and almost completely absorbed through the gastrointestinal tract making oral administration as efficient as any other route. Not bound by plasma proteins or metabolized, lithium is excreted unchanged by the kidneys. In solution, such as in CNS extracellular fluid, lithium carbonate yields the cationic lithium ion. Although it is known that the lithium ion is more evenly distributed between intra- and extracellular spaces than is sodium or potassium and is believed to behave like those ions at the cell membrane, it remains unknown how this relates to lithium's effect on molar behavior. Perhaps the lithium ion somehow interferes with the sodium pump (substituting for sodium ions), which would increase the time for cellular repolarization, hence increasing the refractory period between neuronal "firing." But this is still speculation. In addition to its possible direct effect on cellular function, lithium has a number of other CNS effects. It reduces or prevents release of norepinephrine and dopamine at aminergic synapses, it interferes with the production of adenyl cyclase, and it stimulates the synthesis of serotonin while inhibiting its turnover. Just how these properties interact to result in lithium's behavioral pharmacological properties is still unknown. More is known about lithium's more molar and clinical behavioral pharmacologic properties than about its mechanisms of action.

Clinical Efficacy and Use

In a variety of controlled studies, lithium has been shown effective in significantly reducing manic behavior and in preventing recurrence of manic episodes in patients with carefully documented or diagnosed bipolar depressive illness (major affective disorder, manic or bipolar). In a review of the international literature up to 1973, Gershon and Shopsin (1973) found improvement rates between 60% and 100% in studies of lithium treatment for acute mania. The majority of controlled studies comparing lithium to placebo in treating acute mania show lithium distinctly superior (Walker & Brodie, 1978). A large-scale, collaborative study comparing lithium to chlorpromazine found that chlorpromazine was more effective in rapidly quieting highly agitated patients. In less highly agitated manic patients, however, lithium proved superior in diminishing manic behavior, with fewer side effects than chlorpromazine (Prien, Caffey, & Klett, 1971). Although lithium is rapidly absorbed, it usually requires 1 week to 10 days or so before a serum concentration sufficient to control manic behavior is achieved (.5 to 1.2 mEq/liter). Thus, administration of a neuroleptic is often used initially to control the agitated manic patient during the first week after lithium therapy has been initiated. In addition to its efficacy in controlling acute manic behavior, controlled studies have also documented lithium's prophylactic value in preventing or reducing the frequency, intensity, and duration of manic episodes (Baastrup & Schou, 1967; Schou, Baastrup, & Grof, 1970). In reviewing controlled studies from four countries, Davis (1976) calculated the relapse rate (i.e., recurrence of manic episodes) as averaging only 36% among the lithium maintenance groups compared to a 79% relapse rate among placebo groups. Lithium carbonate has also been used adjunctively with tricyclic antidepressants to treat depression in patients who have not responded to antidepressants alone. In such cases, lithium carbonate has been added to the tricyclic antidepressant regimen and maintained for 6 to 8 weeks, then gradually tapered out (de Montigny, Grunberg, Mayer, & Deschenes, 1981; de Montigny, Cournoyer, & Morisette, 1983). The use of lithium carbonate in treating other conditions for which it has sometimes been suggested, such as alcoholism or tardive dyskinesia, does not have adequate controlled empirical documentation and must be assumed for now to be no more than placebo. In patients with a history of manic episodes, lithium maintenance therapy usually is indicated. Maintenance doses vary between 600 mg and 1800 mg a day and are adjusted to each individual patient to maintain a serum lithium concentration between 0.5 and 1.2 mEq/liter. Immediately following discharge from the hospital, blood samples are drawn frequently, usually weekly or biweekly, until a steady state plasma level is reached. Once the patient, having returned to routine daily activities and home diet, demonstrates a stable dose-serum concentration, dosage is maintained and blood samples may be taken at intervals of 1 to 3 months. Still later, if a consistent level has been maintained with no complications, the physician may elect to test even less frequently for serum lithium concentration. Patients and concerned others, such as spouses, are warned of toxic effects of overdose and instructed on the effects of exercise or physical exertion and dietary changes on lithium concentration toxicity. As in the case of schizophrenic disorders, acute manic episodes in major affective disorders usually require medication as the cornerstone of treatment. Systematic psychological evaluation and behavioral assessment may provide means for more careful and objective monitoring of changes in the patient's behavior as pharmacotherapy exerts its effects. However, specific individually tailored psychological interventions are best reserved until maximum medication effects are obtained. Also, like schizophrenic patients, those suffering from cyclic mania or bipolar major affective disorders may appear to have behavioral repertoire excesses or deficits that are, in fact, performance problems resulting from the biological aspects of the psychosis. Careful examination of the patient's history and behavior (e.g., from self-report, siblings, spouses, etc.), as well as from evaluation after the primary psychotic symptoms have remitted, can guide the clinician's planning of specific psychotherapeutic interventions once the patient is pharmacologically controlled. Patients with psychotic disorders commonly exhibit a variety of acquired, maladaptive behavior patterns that are unresponsive to medication and require specific psychotherapeutic procedures. Such problems, unfortunately, are sometimes overlooked by some clinicians who focus on the management of the primary symptoms of the major thought or affective disorder per se.

ANTIDEPRESSANTS

Feelings of depression, sadness, or dysphoria are, like anxiety, universally experienced aversive and disquieting affective states. Most human beings intermittently experience mild degrees of acute and transient depression throughout their lives in response to adverse life events. Similarly, nearly everyone will experience moderate to severe depressive feelings occasionally in the course of life in reaction to personal tragedies, loss of loved ones, or catastrophic events. For most people, such experiences are short-lived and only temporarily disrupt normal functioning. When depressive feelings are chronic, too frequent, too intense, of abnormally long duration, or out of proportion to external precipitants, they are usually considered clinically significant and require professional attention. Two types of pharmacologic compounds effective in treating depression were developed during the 1950s. These are the MAO inhibitors and the tricyclic antidepressants. As in many scientific discoveries, a bit of serendipity intersecting a current theoretical notion played a role in the discovery and development of both classes of compounds.

In 1951, anecdotal reports indicated that some patients who were being treated for pulmonary tuberculosis with isoniazid displayed marked elevation in mood. Initial trials of isoniazid for depression yielded some promising results, but the drug proved to be too hepatotoxic for clinical use. However, molecularly similar compounds were formulated, such as iproniazid, that were less hepatotoxic and were found to have antidepressant properties. Subsequently, the MAOIs that are currently approved for use were developed. These include isocarboxazid (Marplan), phenelzine (Nardil), and tranylcypromine (Parnate). Monoamine oxidase plays a major role in regulating the metabolic degradation of epinephrine, NE, and DA, in addition to oxidatively deaminating serotonin, 5-hydroxytryptamine (5-HT). Put simply, MAO inhibition is known to increase concentrations of norepinephrine in the CNS, and this is believed to be related to reduction in depressive feelings.

Clinical trials produced inconsistent results, but generally supported the antidepressant effects of MAO inhibitors. Unfortunately, MAOIs also interfere with the metabolism of amines involved in blood pressure regulation. Relatively high concentrations of pressor amines are found in a variety of common foods such as cheese, beer, yeast extract, chocolate, red wines, sour cream, broad beans, and raisins, to name a few. This presented a risk of possibly fatal hypertensive crisis, mandating rather strict dietary constraints for patients on MAOIs. Apart from the inconsistent evidence documenting their efficacy, MAOIs fell into disfavor because of these restrictions and side effects and because alternative antidepressants were available: the tricyclic antidepressants. However, the MAOIs have recently come back into favor, especially for treatment-resistant depression (Liebowitz, Quitkin, Stewart, McGrath, Harrison, Rabkin, Tricamo, Markowitz, & Klein, 1984; Pare, 1985) and for atypical depressions (Liebowitz et al., 1984; Quitkin, Rifkin, & Klein, 1979). Other indications include depression associated with panic attack (Sheehan, Ballenger, & Jacobsen, 1980), or to treat prominent anxiety or depression in patients with borderline personality disorder who may be prone to behavioral decompensation on tricyclic antidepressants (Cowdry & Gardner, 1988).

Tricyclic Antidepressants

Like MAOIs, the tricyclics were discovered during a search for something else. The success of the early neuroleptic in the treatment of schizophrenia led pharmacologists to synthesize related compounds in the hope of producing new, more effective, or at least equally effective and patentable antipsychotics. In 1957, Kuhn reported that imipramine was not effective with schizophrenia, but had relieved symptoms in patients suffering from depression (Kuhn, 1957). The era of tricyclic antidepressants was begun.

Structure and Mechanism of Action

Tricyclics (Fig. 36.3), so named because of their three-ring molecular core, are rapidly absorbed after oral administration. They block reuptake of amines at presynaptic nerve endings, which is important since presynaptic reuptake is necessary for in-activation of endogenous sympathomimetic amines (Axelrod, 1971). This is thought to be their primary mechanism of action in relieving depression. Exactly how blockade of amine reuptake relates to relief of depressive behavior remains speculative. The initial CNS physiological event elicited during tricyclic antidepressant (TCA) administration is an increased bioavailability of neurotransmitters NE, DA, and 5-HT. By blocking presynaptic uptake, these amines remain and accumulate in synaptic cleft, thereby increasing their concentration and/or duration of action at postsynaptic receptor sites, facilitating aminergic transmission (Hollister, 1978). After a more sustained administration course, that is, 2 weeks, multiple neurophysiological events are evidenced, including down-

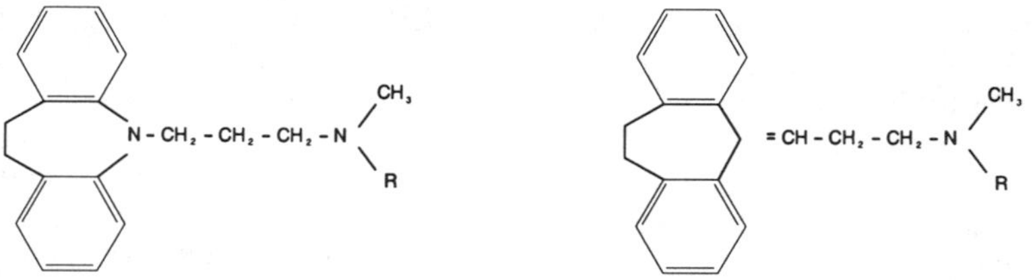

Basic molecules for Tricyclic Antidepressants

Imipramine (Tofranil)
Desipramine (Norpramin, Pertofrane)

Amitriptyline (Elavil)
Nortriptyline (Aventyl, Pamelor)
Protriptyline (Vivactil)

Tetracyclic Antidepressant*
Maprotiline (Ludiomil)

Figure 36.3. Tricyclic antidepressants (Trade names given for identification purposes only.)

regulation of postsynaptic beta receptors, an increase in sensitivity of the postsynaptic alpha-1 receptors, and reduced cyclic-adenosine-monophosphate response to norepinephrine. Serotonin and dopamine effects have been shown to change both in the direction of increased transmission and decreased transmission in different experiments (Heninger & Charney, 1987).

Clomipramine is a tricyclic antidepressant that has been marketed in Europe for many years but has only recently become available in the United States. In addition to the traditional effects on depression as seen with all of the tricyclic antidepressants, clomipramine seems to be particularly effective in the treatment of obsessive-compulsive disorder (Insel & Zohar, 1987). Clomipramine tends to significantly reduce the frequency and severity of obsessive thoughts and rituals but does not, in most cases, totally abolish the symptoms. Also, experimental evidence indicates that the antiobsessional effect is not dependent upon an antidepressant effect. Because clomipramine is a potent blocker of the reuptake of serotonin, and other serotonin reuptake blockers such as fluoxetine have also shown some antiobsessional properties, the antiobsessional effect of these medications has in general been attributed to the effect on the serotonin system. The side effects of clomipramine are generally similar to the other tricyclic antidepressants.

Tetracyclic (four-ring molecular core) antidepressants became available for general clinical usage in the early 1980s. Although initially thought to be faster acting than the tricyclics, recent studies question this claim. There is no compelling evidence that the tetracyclic compounds have beneficial clinical effects substantially different from tricyclic antidepressants.

Fluoxetine (Prozac) was added to the U.S. formulary in the late 1980s. This medication is chemically unrelated to any of the TCA or tetracyclic compounds. The mechanism of action is probably related to its specific and potent serotonin reuptake inhibition (Meltzer & Lowy, 1987). In addition to its antidepressant effect, fluoxetine may possess some benefit as an antiobsessional agent (Fontaine & Chouinard, 1985; Turner, Jacob, Beidel, & Himmelhach, 1985).

Buproprion is a chemically novel antidepressant that was also added to the general U.S. formulary in the late 1980s. Buproprion does not release catecholamines or produce down-regulation of postsynaptic receptors, but it does not block dopamine reuptake and has a direct agonist action on the dopamine receptors (Blackwell & Barry, 1987). The clinical antidepressant effect of buproprion, therefore, cannot be explained by the amine hypothesis. Clinically, the advantage of buproprion is that it has very few side effects.

Buspirone is a compound introduced in the late 1980s as an antianxiety agent. Unlike previous antianxiety agents that primarily affected the GABA system, buspirone primarily affects the serotonin system through agonist effects at the 5-HT 1-A receptors (Peroutka, 1987). Although buspirone has some effects on other 5-HT receptors, the 1-A subtype is generally accepted as the primary site through which this compound exerts its clinical effect. At relatively low doses, that is, about 15 mg per day, buspirone has agonist effects primarily for more sensitive presynaptic 5-HT 1-A receptors. The physiologic effect of buspirone binding to these receptors is to affect a net decrease in impulse flow from the presynaptic neuron. At this dosage, buspirone has been demonstrated clinically to have primarily antianxiety effects. At higher doses, for example, 40–60 mg per day, the presynaptic 5-HT receptors become saturated with buspirone and physiologic effects of binding to the postsynaptic receptors now is primarily evidenced. At these higher doses buspirone has been clinically demonstrated to have antidepressant effects (Rickels, Amsterdam, London, Puzzuoli, & Schweizer, 1989).

Side Effects

If rare and atypical adverse reactions are included, the list of tricyclic side effects is quite long. Fortunately, the more common side effects are usually medically innocuous, though perhaps at times uncomfortable. These side effects may be divided into those associated with the medication's anticholinergic action (dry mouth, constipation, drowsiness, difficulty urinating) and the effect on alpha-adrenergic systems (orthostatic hypotension, dizziness, and possibly mild tremor). The difference in the various TCA's side-effect profile can usually be broken along this dichotomy, and this dichotomy is useful in clinical decision making. Even where one or more of these reactions occur, they usually fade within a few days after treatment. In some cases, the side effects may be useful in the primary treatment. For example, amitriptyline (e.g., Elavil) is known to produce a greater degree of drowsiness, even sedation, than many other tricyclics. Although this side effect is also temporary and diminishes rapidly, it can be useful in facilitating sleep induction in depressed patients who have significant sleep disturbance.

Tricyclics occasionally result in cardiac conduction abnormalities through their quinidine side effect on the conduction system in the heart. Thus, physicians need to assess patients' general physical health and cardiac status carefully, particularly older patients and those patients with a history of cardiac disease, before prescribing tricyclics. In addition, overdose on tricyclics can be fatal. For the average person a fatal dose is usually in the range of 1500 mg per day or about 10 days total daily dosage taken all at once. This does not apply to fluoxetine, which seems to have a very high margin of safety. Because suicidal feelings and ideation are frequent components in severely depressed patients for whom tricyclic antidepressant therapy is being considered, it is usually recommended that such individuals be prescribed the lowest number of doses (or lowest total dosage) practical between office visits.

Fluoxetine has little to no anticholinergic or alpha-adrenergic effect, and therefore the above statements concerning side effects do not necessarily apply to this compound. The most common side effects of fluoxetine include nausea and vomiting in about 20% of patients, a rash in about the same number of patients, insomnia, and weight loss. The nausea and vomiting are usually lessened if the medication is given after breakfast and generally remits within the first week. Insomnia is usually avoided with an A.M. dosing schedule. If the side effects persist, the medication should be discontinued.

Buproprion has few of the side effects associated with the tricyclic antidepressants. The most notable side effect of buproprion is the development of seizures in some patients treated with high doses of the medication. The incidence of seizures seems to depend on the dosage at a given dosing period rather than the total daily dosage; for example, single doses of greater than 150 mg should be avoided (Burroughs Wellcome Co., 1989). This medication should be avoided in patients with a history of a seizure disorder. Buspirone has very few side effects. The side effect noticed most often is an initial increase in agitation.

Clinical Use

Controlled clinical research investigating the efficacy of tricyclics in treating depression (e.g., Bielski & Friedel, 1976), although not uniformly positive, has provided generally strong support for their efficacy, particularly with severe depression (i.e., where vegetative symptoms such as middle and terminal sleep disturbance, poor appetite and weight loss, and psychomotor disturbance are present). In their review of controlled double-bind studies evaluating antidepressants, Cole and Davis (1975b) found that 49 of 65 published reports indicated that tricyclics were significantly superior to placebo in treating depression.

Better performance is seen in trials where less severe depressions are eliminated and adequate dosages are used (Baldessarini, 1977). Depressive disorders associated with neurotic, hysterical, or hypochondriacal traits are often labeled as atypical depressions and consistently respond poorly to tricyclics, but they may respond relatively well to MAOIs. Endogenous depression refers to a depressive disorder with prominent neurovegetative symptoms, whether or not there is an environmental stressor of putative etiologic significance. Depressions cannot be dichotomized into endogenous versus exogenous or reactive solely on the basis of whether particular symptoms are present or absent. Rather severity, duration, and patterns of particular symptoms considered within the context of and in relation to life events provide a more rational basis for such clinical judgment. Symptoms usually considered indicative of severity of depression such as decreased appetite with weight loss, mid-phase and terminal sleep disturbance, psychomotor changes, and the like also occur in some reactive depressions and may persist over several weeks. Current evidence indicates that tricyclic antidepressants are often effective in alleviating these types of depressive symptoms whether they occur as part of a "biological" pathogenesis or a "neurotic-reactive" clinical picture (Hughes, 1981). Thus, rational clinical use of tricyclics at this time is best guided by the symptomatology rather than inferred pathogenesis. For example, a 38-year-old female in the midst of an unwanted and conflictural divorce may suffer from feelings of despair and worthlessness, experience crying spells, sleep disturbance, decreased appetite, anhedonia, and decreased energy. Such symptoms may well endure over several weeks and confound therapeutic procedures designed to reduce the depression. If such symptoms have persisted over several weeks, have not shown evidence of improvement, and appear likely to continue, perhaps impairing the patient's capacity to respond to psychotherapeutic interventions, then a trial of an antidepressant would be indicated. This is so even though the patient's history and current life events suggest that her depression occurred in reaction to the divorce.

Prior to initiating pharmacotherapy, it is important that pretreatment measures be taken along with a careful and detailed history. Assessment instruments useful in determining the nature and severity of depression include the Beck Depressive Inventory (Beck, Ward, Mendelson, Mock, & Erbaugh, 1961), the Hamilton Rating Scale (Hamilton, 1960), the Behavioral Rating Scale (Williams, Barlow, & Agras, 1972), and the Minnesota Multiphasic Personality Inventory (MMPI; Marks, Seeman, & Haller, 1974).

In addition to providing some indexes of depression (particularly the relationship among scales D, Pt, Ma, and Si), other profile features on the MMPI (such as scales Hs, Hy, and Pd) can provide some clues regarding hypochondriacal, histrionic, and other personality features. These may be associated with types of depressive behavior that are generally less responsive to antidepressant pharmacotherapy.

Clinical features usually associated with good drug responses are (a) depression where significant vegetative symptoms are present including two or more of the following—midphase or terminal sleep disturbance, loss of appetite with weight loss, psychomotor retardation, marked diurnal mood variation, anhedonia, and lack of responsivity to environmental and previously reinforcing activities; (b) clear and rapid onset of depressive symptoms; and (c) relatively good premorbid adjustment and functioning. Other factors predictive of good response to antidepressants include prior history of therapeutic response to tricyclics, a family history of affective disorders, and family history of good antidepressant response.

Clinical features frequently associated with poor response to antidepressants are (a) depressive symptoms of longstanding duration; (b) depressive symptoms occurring as part of or an exacerbation of longstanding, chronic negativistic, "depressive" personality; (c) depressive symptoms associated with alcoholism or chemical dependency; and (d) prominent features of hysteria, hypochondriasis, and/or preoccupation with multiple somatic complaints, complaining, blaming others, and strong or rigid externalization of locus of emotional control or "causation." Also, poor previous response to antidepressants, hypersensitivity to side effects, and presence of schizoid or schizoaffective features are typically associated with poor responses to tricyclic pharmacotherapy.

There is, of course, no single pathognomonic sign or symptom of depression that invariably predicts drug response. Likewise, these two sets of clinical features are not mutually exclusive. Patients whose clinical picture is consistent with many of the features enumerated in the second set also may exhibit one or more of the symptoms listed in the first set associated with good antidepressant response. Careful examination of the patient, the patient's history, personality or cognitive behavioral repertoire, response patterns or style, life situation and environmental events, and the interrelationships among such factors can help the clinician determine the relative prominence of good versus poor drug-response features.

Antidepressant pharmacotherapy usually is not recommended as a single modality therapy in treating depression. Rather, where indicated, antidepressants are used in conjunction with psychotherapeutic interventions. Because of the lag between initiating antidepressant therapy and the onset of their antidepressant effects, patients who are severely depressed may require hospitalization or other close supportive measures. Decisions regarding hospitalization should be made on the basis of the patient's current clinical condition rather than on anticipated effects of pharmacotherapy, even if the patient has a history of good or even rapid drug response. Although some patients may respond rather rapidly on an adequate dose, others may not evidence much change for 2 or more weeks. Therefore, if a trial on antidepressants is indicated and elected, the patient should be kept on an adequate dose for a minimum of 3 weeks. Patients need to be informed not only of side effects but that improvement in their mood and feelings may be gradual and may not occur for several days. Furthermore, it is important that patients understand that they should continue taking the medication exactly as prescribed, even if they initially do not feel it is helping them very much. In patients regarded as clinically having a treatment failure, plasma level monitoring of the parent compound and its active metabolite may be of clinical usefulness. If the level of the antidepressant compound is low, even though a usually effective oral dose is being given, the oral dosage should be increased for an adequate time period. If the plasma level is low, perhaps a reassessment of the treatment strategy should be entertained.

When patients do display therapeutic response to antidepressants, the decision of how long to maintain drug therapy is determined by their evolving clinical picture and by etiologic considerations. Where depressive symptomatology has been shown to be cyclic or recurrent off medication, then antidepressant therapy is usually maintained for 6 to 12 months after remission. Clinical follow-up studies indicate that patients on maintenance therapy in such cases do significantly better and experience fewer relapses than similar patients whose medication was discontinued shortly after symptom remission (Klein & Davis, 1969). Alternately, where severe depression occurs in response to an interaction between environmental events and cognitive-emotive or "personality" factors, then reduction of tricyclic therapy is guided by the evolving clinical picture, including both evidence of symptom remission and changes in relevant cognitive-emotional processes. Protracted drug therapy in such cases usually is unnecessary.

In addition to use in treating depression, imipramine has been found to be of value in the treatment of obsessive-compulsive behavior, agoraphobia, and particularly panic attacks. For example, Foa and associates (Foa, Stekett, & Groves, 1979) combined behavioral and pharmacologic treatment for a severe obsessive-compulsive patient. Following behavior therapeutic intervention involving stimulus exposure and response prevention, the patient exhibited a marked reduction in ritualizing but evidenced little change in fear of contaminants, obsessive thinking, or depression. Administration of imipramine resulted in significant improvement in these targeted behaviors. Similarly, Zitrin, Klein, and Woerner (1978) reviewed the use of imipramine in treating agoraphobia, particularly the drug's effect in reducing panic attacks commonly involved in the agoraphobic syndrome. Aside from ameliorating the depressive component frequently involved in these disorders, it remains unclear by what mechanism imipramine's "antiobsessive" and "antipanic" effect is achieved. The utilization of pure serotonergic agents such as fluoxetine has been previously mentioned. Because of the differential pharmacological properties of the various agents used in these disorders, one may speculate that "antiobsessional" qualities may be related to serotonergic effects while the "antipanic" effects may be related to down-regulation of adrenergic receptors.

STIMULANTS

Stimulants are compounds that exert a clinical excitatory effect resulting in an increased molar behavioral activity. Although common stimulants such as nicotine and caffeine have been in use both recreationally as well as medicinally for several hundred years, those of interest here are the more powerful pharmacologic stimulant compounds including amphetamines (Benzedrine, Dexedrine), methylphenidate (Ritalin), and magnesium pemoline (Cylert). The prototypic stimulants are the amphetamines. In the central nervous system, these compounds induce the local release of norepinephrine and dopamine in central synapses. This is thought to be their primary mechanism of action. An oral dose of 10 to 20 mg of amphetamine given to adult subjects usually results in wakefulness, alertness, decreased sense of fatigue, and often increased verbal and motor activity. For these reasons, such stimulant compounds have been popular on college campuses since World War II for the purpose of staying up to cram for exams. High-frequency or chronic use of stimulants in higher doses can produce a schizophreniform psychosis that may initially be clinically indistinguishable from schizophrenia, although the drug-induced psychosis will usually reverse within 1 to 2 weeks upon discontinu-

ation of stimulant abuse, particularly if neuroleptics are used acutely in treatment. Tolerance does develop to stimulants, although marked abstinence symptoms are usually seen only in people taking relatively higher doses. Side effects of stimulants include headache, nausea, insomnia, and anorexia. In long-term and/or high-dosage use, depression and psychosis may develop.

Clinical Use

First used in inhalants for asthmatics, stimulants were subsequently employed in treating morphine addiction, depression, and, because of an anorectic side effect, obesity. Because of their lack of efficacy and the development of more effective alternate therapies, stimulants are no longer appropriate for those disorders. Currently, stimulant pharmacotherapy is approved for narcolepsy (a neurological disorder involving sudden, uncontrollable sleep onset) and attention deficit disorder in children (formerly minimal brain dysfunction or hyperkinetic impulse disorders).

The use of stimulants in the treatment of so-called "hyperactive children" has been and continues to be surrounded by controversy. Fueling this controversy are a variety of factors and complex, emotionally loaded issues. Stimulants have high abuse potential and were among the most misused drugs during the 1960s and early 1970s. Furthermore, the long-term effects of such drugs when taken for protracted periods during childhood are not fully known. For these reasons, parents and professionals express legitimate concerns over forcing young children to take these relatively potent compounds. In addition, the syndrome of behavioral symptoms currently called attentional deficit disorder is poorly understood and is often misdiagnosed. This results in some children being placed on stimulant therapy who could have responded to alternative, drug-free interventions. Finally, some professionals who are untrained in pharmacology and not licensed to prescribe medications often ignore if not dismiss the potential therapeutic contribution of pharmacotherapy. Indeed, there are some who even deny the existence of the disorders. On the other hand, professionals generally untrained in empirically based, efficacious behavioral management procedures often rely solely on drug therapy with such children.

The third edition of the *Diagnostic and Statistical Manual* (DSM-III-R) of the American Psychiatric Association (1987) lists a variety of symptoms under attentional deficit disorders (ADD), including easy distractibility, difficulty concentrating on schoolwork, difficulty organizing work, excessive motor activity, and so forth. These behavioral symptoms were derived from clinical investigators who, over the years, have been struggling to identify the necessary and sufficient symptoms for the diagnostic entity formerly called minimal brain dysfunction (e.g., Wender, 1978). Complicating this process is the fact that all of the behavioral symptoms associated with ADD occur to some extent in normal children. Moreover, most of these behaviors, even in excessive form, can result from maladaptive learning and environmental influences or are associated with other childhood problems (such as childhood grief and situational adjustment reactions). It can be seen, then, how some clinicians may mistakenly overdiagnose ADD, whereas others question its very existence. As Wender (1978) pointed out, and DSM-III-R stipulates, the crucial factor in determining a diagnosis of ADD is not whether one specific symptomatic response class is present or absent. Rather, it is based on the constellation of the various problematic behavioral classes, their history, intensity, and duration, and the absence of alternative etiological evidence that could account for the clinical picture (Cantwell, 1977; Wender, 1978). In clinical studies where child patients who met the diagnostic criteria for ADD served as subjects, results have shown that many of the symptomatic behavioral excesses and deficits do improve with stimulant therapy. Therapeutic improvements resulting from pharmacotherapy have included increased vigilance, time-on-task, accuracy of performance (Sprague & Sleator, 1977), improved reading and arithmetic (Sulzbacher, 1972), significantly increased scores on standard IQ tests (Wiens, Anderson, & Matarazzo, 1971), decreased motor activity such as fewer "out of seats," "jump ups," and "talk outs" (Sulzbacker, 1972; Zike, 1972), and improved social behavior and responsiveness to reinforcement (Sprague & Sleator, 1977; Wender, 1978). By contrast, similar behaviors associated with other childhood disorders such as mental retardation (Lipman et al., 1978) or infantile autism–childhood schizophrenia have not been found to improve with stimulant therapy (Campbell, 1978).

Although nondrug treatments such as various behavioral shaping and contingency-management procedures have been found to be effective in reducing hyperactive behavior, improving scholastic performance, and establishing more adaptive and appropriate social skills (e.g., Ayllon, Layman, & Kandel, 1975), few studies have systematically compared stimulant pharmacotherapy to psychotherapeutic interventions with children who met the criteria for ADD. In one of the better designed and controlled investigations comparing stimulant therapy to behavioral therapy, Gittelman-Klein and her associates compared methylphenidate, placebo, behavior therapy, and combined pharmaco-behavior therapy (Gittelman-Klein, Klein, Abikoff, Katz, Gloisten, & Kates, 1976). Results revealed that although medication alone, behavior therapy alone, and combined pharmaco-behavior therapy were all effective and superior to placebo, methylphenidate was found significantly superior to behavior therapy alone in modifying the targeted problematic behaviors. Teachers who made global, subjective ratings favored the combined therapy. Medication, however, cannot add new components to an individual's behavioral repertoire; it can only influence its performance or help create conditions under which new skills can be acquired. Although clinical studies demonstrate the efficacy of stimulant therapy with respect to hyperexcitability, abnormally short attention span, impaired learning capacity, scholastic performance, and socially disruptive motor-verbal activity, those academic, emotional, and social skills that entail a relatively longer acquisition phase do not show parallel levels of improvement via pharmacotherapy alone. Furthermore, the long-term outcome in the absence of conjunctive psychological therapy is rather poor (Barkley, 1977, 1981).

If stimulant pharmacotherapy is indicated, medication should be used conservatively. It is important to determine which classes of problem behaviors are most serious or crucial and which might be more or less responsive to alternative therapies such as behavior modification. Dose-response studies (e.g., Sprague & Sleator, 1977) have found that positive drug effects on one class of behavior (e.g., scholastic learning) may display optimal response with one dosage, whereas optimal improvement of another class of behaviors (e.g., "hyperactivity") might occur at a higher or lower dosage. Where stimulant therapy proves effective with a specific case, it is not always necessary to maintain drug treatment indefinitely. Pharmacotherapy can sometimes be used to decelerate the rate or intensity of disruptive behaviors to a point where they may be brought under the control of environmental and intraorganismic variables. Similarly, such drug-induced reduction of problem behaviors can allow opportunities for more appropriate behavior to be shaped and instated, thus replacing deviant acts. Because the metabolic turnover rate of stimulants is relatively rapid, medication-reduction trials can be attempted once optimum functioning has been achieved and appears to be stabilized. That is, the pharmacokinetics of stimulants, unlike neuroleptics, allow for relatively shorter and more clearly delineated drug and no-drug treatment-assessment phases. Therefore, clinical case protocols can be planned along programmatic research lines, allowing the clinician to monitor progress systematically over time.

CONCLUSION

Psychopharmacologic research and clinical advances over the past 4 decades have been extensive, at times astounding, and even show signs of further acceleration. Just in the few years between the final drafts of this chapter for the first edition of *The Clinical Psychology Handbook* and the present revision, much more is now known about mechanisms of action of most classes of drugs, and several new forms of psychopharmacologic agents have been formulated, tested, and are entering clinical use. Although pharmacologic "cures" remain elusive, clinical research evidence is clear that properly utilized psychopharmacologic compounds can play an important role in modifying abnormal or maladaptive behavior. In some cases, as with many patients suffering with schizophrenia, pharmacotherapy is crucial; without it environmental or social influence therapies would have little or no impact. In other cases, pharmacologic compounds serve to create or enhance conditions under which psychological interventions can be efficiently applied to attain maximum therapeutic results. Rarely are psychopharmacologic agents appropriate as single modality treatments for behavioral and biobehavioral disorders. Instead, concomitant experiential, learning-based therapeutic programs aimed at behavioral deficits or acquired, maladaptive cognitive, emotive, and overt behavior patterns are usually necessary. Psychological and pharmacological sciences and their respective theoretical as well as clinical therapeutic contributions are not inconsistent, much less incompatible. Traditional behavioral versus physiological and even more traditional mind–body dichotomies both incorporate an implicit metaphysics versus physics distinction. Instead, it is increasingly recognized that behavioral descriptions in contrast to anatomical, chemical, and physiological descriptions of biological structures and physiokinetic events reflect not a different domain of objects and phenomena, but a different level of abstraction, conceptualization, and analysis within the same domain.

Indeed, the depth, breadth, or sophistication of our emerging knowledge base in neurochemistry, physiology, and psychopharmacology has precipitated what amounts to a paradigm shift in how pharmacotherapy is conceptualized and clinically practiced. Psychopharmacologists have already begun to shift away from conceptualizations of chemical compounds as specific treatments for specific psychopathologic disorders. Instead, chemical compounds are increasingly viewed primarily from the perspective of the specific neurochemical-neurophysiological pathways and events they affect and the various sensory-perceptual-verbal-motor systems and behavioral events involved. For example, the constellation of sensory-behavioral events that are considered elemental components of depression involve serotonergic and dopaminergic as well as adrenergic pathways. Rather than simply viewing a patient as suffering from "depression" and prescribing an "antidepressant," psychopharmacologists consider the specific behavioral patterns involved in the particular clinical case and their corresponding neurochemical elements and then select pharmacotherapeutic agents to target those specific classes of events (e.g., neurochemical behavioral targets most associated with, say, serotonergic pathways versus, say, adrenergic activity). At the extreme, there are those who have long argued that all clinically significant abnormal behavior results from some, perhaps subtle, biopathology. However, the approach we are supporting here fully recognizes that many biological events and changes that occur in the brain do so as a consequence of specific sensory event patterns that arise from receptor stimulation in the environment, i.e., from experience. Similarly, it is recognized that such biochemical changes, for now, are most selectively and effectively therapeutically modified by specific, structured experiences; that is, empirically based psychotherapeutic methods. The most specific, circumscribed, and discrete modification in brain neurochemistry, hence in alteration of sensory-perceptual-organizational and effector functions (i.e., modification of *behavior*), is still best accomplished via structured experiences as in learning principle based–psychotherapies. However, although the specificity of biochemical-physiological action and thus the specificity of behavioral systems affected has been significantly enhanced in recent psychopharmacotherapeutics, even the most recently developed chemical agents continue to impact diverse and diffuse structures throughout the nervous system. The emerging paradigm, then, does not conceptualize psychopharmacologic compounds as therapeutic agents for broad diagnostic entities such as "schizophrenic," "depressive," or "anxiety" disorders. Instead, drugs are selected with regard to their biochemical properties, site of action, and biobehavioral systems affected whether those more specific pharmacologic targets occur as components of agoraphobia, chemical dependency, pathological bereavement, or any other disorder. Though this shift may initially appear academic if not only semantic, in fact it reflects the move away from viewing biobehavioral disorders as unitary, closed, and discrete pathologies. Rather, psychologic disorders are conceptualized more as clusters or constellations of interactive but separable biobehavioral processes that, though variable, exhibit sufficient consistency to allow for differential definition and diagnosis. Modern psychopharmacotherapy now involves selective targeting of specific neurochemical axes and increasingly specific, physiological subsystems in biobehavioral disorders.

An important corollary of this approach is that a common language, investigative methodology, as well as fundamental philosophy of science spans, in unbroken linkage, molecular biology to neurophysiology to experimental psychology to clinical therapeutics. Within this framework, new information is more readily disseminated, facilely crossing disciplinary lines. Because of a common empirical conceptual framework and common language (particularly evident among pharmacologist, experimental psychologist, and empirical science-oriented clinicians) the relevance of basic science findings to clinical application is more readily apparent, and thus progress in clinical therapeutic development is enhanced. This continued collaboration between pharmacological and psychological researchers and clinicians is fundamental to advancing the empirical knowledge base from which the best possible therapeutic procedures can be derived for now and for the future.

REFERENCES

Alford, G.S. (1981). Sedatives, hynpotics, and minor tranquilizers. In S.J. Mulé (Ed.), *Behavior in excess: An examination of the volitional disorders* (pp. 39–63). New York: Free Press.

Alford, G.S., & Alford, H. (1976). Benzodiazepine induced state-dependent learning: A correlative of abuse potential? *Addictive Behaviors, 1,* 261–267.

Alford, G.S., Fleece, L., & Rothblum, E. (1982). Hallucinatory-delusional verbal behavior: Modification by self-control and cognitive restructuring. *Behavioral Modification, 6,* 421–435.

Alford, G.S., & Turner, S.M. (1976). Stimulus interference and conditioned inhibition of auditory hallucinations. *Journal of Behavior Therapy and Experimental Psychiatry, 7,* 155–160.

Alford, G.S., & Williams, J.G. (1980). The role and uses of psychopharmacological agents in behavior therapy. In M. Hersen, R.M. Eisler, & P.M. Miller (Eds.), *Progress in behavior modification* (Vol. 10, pp. 207–240). New York: Academic Press.

American Psychiatric Association. (1980). *Diagnostic and statistical manual of mental disorders (3rd ed.).* Washington, DC: Author.

Axelrod, J. (1971). Noradrenaline: Fate and control of its biosynthesis. *Science, 173,* 598–606.

Ayllon, T., Layman, D., & Kandel, H.J. (1975). A behavioral-educational alternative to drug control of hyperactive children. *Journal of Applied Behavior Analysis, 8,* 137–146.

Baastrup, P.C., & Schou, M. (1967). Lithium as a prophylactic agent: Its effect against recurrent depressions and manic depressive psychosis. *Archives of General Psychiatry, 16,* 162–172.

Baldessarini, R. (1977). *Chemotherapy in psychiatry.* Cambridge, MA: Harvard University Press.

Barkley, R.A. (1977). A review of stimulant drug research with hyperactive children. *Journal of Child Psychology and Psychiatry, 18,* 137–165.

Barkley, R.A. (1981). Hyperactivity. In E. J. Mash & L. G. Terdal (Eds.), *Behavioral assessment of childhood disorders* (pp. 127–184). New York: Guilford Press.

Beck, A.T., Ward, C.H., Mendelson, M., Mock, J., & Erbaugh, J. (1961). An inventory for measuring depression. *Archives of General Psychiatry, 4,* 561–571.

Bellack, A.S., & Hersen, M. (1977). *Behavior modification: An introductory textbook.* Baltimore: Williams & Wilkins.

Bielski, R.J., & Friedel, R.O. (1976). Prediction of tricyclic antidepressant response. *Archives of General Psychiatry, 33,* 1479–1489.

Blackwell, B., (1987). Newer antidepressant drugs in psychopharmacology. In H. Meltzer (Ed.), *Psychopharmacology: The third generation of progress,* (pp. 1041–1049). New York: Raven Press.

Bunney, B.S., Sesack, S.R., & Silva, N.L. (1987). Midbrain dopaminergic systems neurophysiology and electrophysiological pharmacology. In H. Meltzer (Ed.), *Psychopharmacology: The third generation of progress,* (pp. 113–126). New York: Raven Press.

Burroughs Wellcome Co. (1989). *Clinical Experience Program Information Package.* North Carolina: Research Triangle Park.

Campbell, M. (1978). Use of drug treatment in infantile autism and childhood schizophrenia: A review. In M.A. Lipton, A. DiMascia, & K.F. Killam (Eds.), *Psychopharmacology: A generation of progress,* (pp. 1451–1461). New York: Raven Press.

Cantwell, D.P. (1977). Drug treatment of the hyperactive syndrome in children. In M.E. Jarvik (Ed.), *Psychopharmacology in the practice of medicine.* New York: Appleton-Century-Crofts.

Carlsson, A. (1978). Mechanisms of action of neuroleptic drugs. In M.A. Lipton, A. DiMascio, & K.F. Killam (Eds.), *Psychopharmacology: A generation of progress* (pp. 1057–1070). New York: Raven Press.

Ciraulo, D.A., Sands, B.F., & Shader, R.I. (1988). Critical

review of liability for benzodiazepine abuse among alcoholics. *American Journal of Psychiatry, 145,* 1501–1506.

Cohen, J.M. (1975). Current status of lithium therapy: Report of the APA task force. *American Journal of Psychiatry, 132,* 997–1001.

Cole, J.O., & Davis, J.M. (1975a). Minor tranquilizers, sedatives, and hypnotics. In A.M. Freedman, H.I. Kaplan, & B.J. Saddock (Eds.), *Comprehensive textbook of psychiatry* (Vol. 2, pp. 1956–1968). Baltimore: Williams & Wilkins.

Cole, J.O., & Davis, J.M. (1975b). Antidepressant drugs. In A.M. Freedman, H.I. Kaplan, & B.J. Saddock, (Eds.), *Comprehensive textbook of psychiatry* (Vol. 2, pp. 1941–1955). Baltimore: Williams & Wilkins.

Cole, J.O., Orzack, M.H., Beake, B., Bird, M., & Bar-tal, Y. (1982). Assessment of abuse liability of buspirone in recreational sedative users. *Journal of Clinical Psychiatry, 433,* 69–74.

Corcoran, A.C., Taylor, R.D., & Page, I.H. (1949). Lithium poisoning from the use of salt substitutes. *Journal of the American Medical Association, 139,* 685–688.

Cowdry, R.W., & Gardner, D.L. (1988). Pharmacotherapy of borderline personality disorder, Alprazolam, Canbumazepine, Trifluoperazine and Tranylcypromine. *Archives of General Psychiatry, 45,* 111–119.

Davis, J.M. (1975). Overview: Maintenance therapy in psychiatry: I. Schizophrenia. *American Journal of Psychiatry, 132,* 1237–1245.

Davis, J.M. (1976). Overview: Maintenance therapy in psychiatry: II. Affective disorders. *American Journal of Psychiatry, 133,* 1–12.

de Montigny, D., Grunberg, F., Mayer, A., & Deschenes, J.P. (1981). Lithium induces rapid relief of depression in tricyclic antidepressant drug non-responders. *British Journal of Psychiatry, 138,* 252–255.

de Montigny, C., Cournoyer, G., & Morissette, R. (1983). Lithium carbonate addition in tricyclic antidepressant-resistant unipolar depression. *Archives of General Psychiatry, 40,* 1327–1334.

Enna, S.J., & Mohler, H. (1987). Gamma-aminobutyric acid (GABA) receptors and their association with benzodiazepine recognition sites. In H.Y. Meltzer (Ed.), *Psychopharmacology: The third generation of progress.* New York, Raven Press.

Foa, E.B., Stekett, G., & Groves, G. (1979). Use of behavior therapy and Imipramine: A case of obsessive-compulsive neurosis with severe depression. *Behavior Modification, 3,* 419–430.

Fontaine, R., & Chouinard, G. (1985). Antiobsessive effect of fluoxetine (Letter). *American Journal of Psychiatry. 142,* 989.

Freedman, R. (1981). Neurochemical and psychopharmacological factors in mental illness. In R.C. Simons & H. Pardes (Eds.), *Understanding human behavior in health and illness* (pp. 513–523). Baltimore: Williams & Wilkins.

Georgotas, A., Friedman, R., McCarthy, M., Mann, J., Krakowski, M., Siegel, R., & Ferris, S. (1983). Resis-

tant geriatric depressions and therapeutic response to monoamine oxidase inhibitors. *Biological Psychiatry, 18,* 195–205.

Gershon, S., & Shopsin, B. (Eds.). (1973). *Lithium ion: Its role in psychiatric treatment and research.* New York: Plenum Press.

Gilman, A.G., Goodman, L.S., Rall, T.W., & Murad, R. (Eds.). (1985). *Goodman and Gilman's The pharmacological basis of therapeutics.* New York: Macmillan.

Gittelman-Klein, R., Klein, D.F., Abikoff, H., Katz, S., Gloisten, A.C., & Kates, W. (1976). Relative efficacy of methylphenidate and behavior modification in hyperkinetic children. An interim report. *Journal of Abnormal Child Psychology, 4,* 361–379.

Gold, M.S., Redmond, D.E., & Kleber, H.D. (1978). Clonidine in opiate withdrawal. *Lancet, 1,* 929–930.

Goodman, L.S., & Gilman, A. (1975). *The pharmacological basis of therapeutics.* New York: Macmillan.

Goodwin, D.V., Powell, B., Bremer, D., Hoine, H., & Stern, J. (1969). Alcohol and recall: State-dependent effects in man. *Science, 163,* 350–360.

Grinspoon, L., Ewalt, J.R., & Shader, R. (1968). Psychotherapy and pharmacotherapy in chronic schizophrenia. *American Journal of Psychiatry, 124,* 1945–1952.

Haefely, W.E. (1978). Behavioral and neuropharmacological aspects of drugs used in anxiety and related states. In M.A. Lipton, A. DiMascio, & K.F. Killam (Eds.), *Psychopharmacology: A generation of progress,* (pp. 1359–1374). New York: Raven Press.

Hamilton, M. (1960). A rating scale for depression. *Journal of Neurology, Neurosurgery and Psychiatry, 23,* 56–62.

Heninger, G.R., & Charney, D.S. (1987). Mechanism of action of antidepressant treatments: Implications for the etiology and treatment of depressive disorders. In H. Meltzer (Ed.), *Psychopharmacology: The third generation of progress,* (pp. 535–545). New York: Raven Press.

Hersen, M. (Ed.). (1986). *Pharmacological and behavioral treatment.* New York: John Wiley & Sons.

Hersen, M., & Bellack, A.S. (1976). Social skills training for chronic psychiatric patients: Rationale, research findings, and future directions. *Comprehensive Psychiatry, 17,* 550–580.

Hersen, M., Turner, S.M., Edelstein, B.A., & Pinkston, S.G. (1975). Effects of Phenothiazines and social skills training in a withdrawn schizophrenic. *Journal of Clinical Psychology, 31,* 588–594.

Hogarty, G.E., Ulrich, R.F., Mussare, F., & Aristignieta, N. (1976). Drug discontinuation among long-term, successfully maintained schizophrenic outpatients. *Disease of the Nervous System, 37,* 494–500.

Hollister, L. J. (1978). Tricyclic antidepressants. *New England Journal of Medicine, 299,* 106–109.

Hughes, J.R. (1981, December). *Interaction between drugs and psychotherapy for depression.* Paper presented at the annual convention of the Association for Advancement of Behavior Therapy, Toronto.

Insel, T.R., & Zohar, J. (1987). Psychopharmacologic approaches to obsessive-compulsive disorder. In H.Y.

Meltzer (Ed.), *Psychopharmacology: The third generation of progress*, (pp. 1205–1210). New York: Raven Press.

Institute of Medicine. (1979). *Sleeping pills, insomnia, and medical practice: Report of a study by a committee of the Institute of Medicine*. Rockville, MD.: NIDA.

Iverson, S.D., & Iverson, L.L. (1975). *Behavioral pharmacology*. New York: Oxford University Press.

Kahn, R.J., McNair, D.M., Lipman, R.S., Covi, L., Rickels, S.K., Downing, R., Fisher, S., & Frankenthaler, L.M. (1986). Imipramine and chlordiazepoxide in depressive and anxiety disorders. *Archives of General Psychiatry, 43,* 79–85.

Kelleher, R.T., & Morse, W.H. (1964). Escape behavior and punished behavior. *Federal Proceedings, 23,* 808–817.

Klein, D.F., & Davis, J.M. (1969). *Diagnosis and drug treatment of psychiatric disorders*. Baltimore: Williams & Wilkins.

Kuhn, R. (1957). Uber die Behandlung depressives Zustande mit eineum Iminodibenzylderivat (G-22355). *Schweizer Medicinischer Wissenschaftschrift, 87,* 1135.

Last, C.G., & Hersen, M. (1988). (Eds.). *Handbook of anxiety disorders*. Elmsford, NY: Pergamon Press.

Lehmann, H.E. (1966). Pharmacotherapy of schizophrenia. In P. Hoch & J. Zubin (Eds.), *Psychopathology of schizophrenia*. New York: Grune & Stratton.

Lehmann, H.E. (1975). Psychopharmacological treatment of schizophrenia. *Schizophrenia Bulletin, 13,* 27–45.

Leitenberg, H. (1976). Behavioral approaches to treatment of neuroses. In H. Leitenberg (Ed.), *Handbook of behavior modification and behavior therapy* (pp 124–167). Englewood Cliffs, NJ: Prentice-Hall.

Liberman, R.P., Davis, J., Moon, W., & Moore, J. (1973). Research designs for analyzing drug-environment behavior interactions. *Journal of Nervous and Mental Disease, 156,* 432–439.

Liebowitz, M.R., Quitkin, F.M., Stewart, J.W., McGrath, P.J., Harrison, W., Rabkin, J., Tricamo, E., Markowitz, J., & Klein, D.F. (1984). Phenelizine V imipramine in atypical depression. *Archives of General Psychiatry, 41,* 669–677.

Lipman, R.S., DiMascio, A., Reatig, N., & Kirson, T. (1978). Psychotropic drugs and mentally retarded children. In M.A. Lipton, A. DiMascio, & K.F. Killam (Eds.), *Psychopharmacology: A generation of progress*. New York: Raven Press.

Lipton, M.A., DiMascio, A., & Killam, K.F. (1978). (Eds.). *Psychopharmacology: A generation of progress*. New York: Raven Press.

Marks, P.A., Seeman, W., & Haller, D.L. (1974). *The actuarial use of the MMPI with adolescents and adults*. Baltimore: Williams & Wilkins.

Mattila, J.H., Aranko, K., & Seppala, T. (1982). Acute effects of buspirone and alcohol on psychomotor skills. *Journal of Clinical Psychiatry, 43,* 56–60.

May, P.R.A. (1968). *Treatment of schizophrenia: A comparative study of five treatment methods*. New York: Science House.

Meltzer, H.Y. (1987). (Ed.). *Psychopharmacology: The third generation of progress*. New York: Raven Press.

Meltzer, H.Y. & Lowy, M.T., (1987). The serotonin hypothesis of depression. In H.Y. Meltzer (Ed.), *Psychopharmacology: The third generation of progress* (pp. 513–526). New York: Raven Press.

Milby, J.B. (1975). A review of token economy treatment programs for psychiatric inpatients. *Hospital and Community Psychiatry, 26,* 651–658.

Nayes, R., Anderson, D.J., Clancy, J., Crowe, R.R., Slymen, D.J., Ghoneim, M.M., & Henricks, J.V. (1984). Diazepam and propranolol in panic disorder and agoraphobia. *Archives of General Psychiatry, 41,* 287–292.

Nicoll, R. (1978). Selective actions of barbiturates on synaptic transmission. In M.A. Lipton, A. DiMascio, & K.F. Killam (Eds.), *Psychopharmacology: A generation of progress*, (pp. 1337–1348). New York: Raven Press.

Overton, D.A. (1973). State-dependent learning produced by addicting drugs. In S. Fischer & A.M. Freedman (Eds.), *Opiate addiction: Origins and treatment*, (pp. 61–76). Washington, DC: Winston.

Pare, C.M.B. (1985). The present status of monoamine oxidase inhibitors. *British Journal of Psychiatry, 146,* 576–584.

Peroutka, S.J. (1985). Selective interaction of novel anxiolytics with 5-hydroxytryptamine 1-A receptors. *Biological Psychiatry, 20,* 971–979.

Peroutka, S.J. (1987). Serotonin receptors in psychopharmacology. In H. Meltzer (Ed.), *The third generation of progress* (pp. 303–312). New York: Raven Press.

Pishkin, V., & Sengel, R.A. (1982). Research in psychopathology, 1972–1980. Unreporting of medication and other relevant demographic data. *The Clinical Psychologist, 35,* 12–14.

Prien, R., Caffey, R., & Klett, C.A. (1971). A comparison of lithium carbonate and chlorpromazine in the treatment of mania. *Cooperative Studies in Psychiatry*. Prepublication Report 86. Perry Point, MD: Center for Neuropsychiatric Research Laboratory.

Prien, R., Caffey, E., & Klett, C. (1972). *Prophylactic efficacy of lithium carbonate in manic depressive illness*. Report of the VA and NIMH collaborative study group. Perry Point, MD: Central for Neuropsychiatric Research Laboratory.

Quitkin, F., Rifkin, A., & Klein, D.F. (1976). Prophylaxis of affective disorders. *Archvies of General Psychiatry, 33,* 337–341.

Quitkin, F., Rifkin, A., & Klein, D.F. (1979). Monoamine oxidase inhibitors: A review of antidepressant effectiveness, *Archives of General Psychiatry, 36,* 749–760.

Rickels, K. (1977). Drug treatment of anxiety. In M.E. Jarvik (Ed.), *Psychopharmacology in the practice of medicine* (pp. 309–324). New York: Appleton-Century-Crofts.

Rickels, K., Amsterdam, J., London, J., Puzzuoli, G., & Schweizer, E. (1989, May). *Buspirone in depressed outpatients: A controlled study*. Poster presented at the 29th annual meeting of the New Clinical Drug Evaluation

Unit, National Institutes of Mental Health Conference, Miami, FL.

Rickels, K., Csanalosi, I., Chung, H., Case, W.G., & Schweizer, E.E. (1985, May). *Psychopharmacology and Anxiety Disorders.* Paper presented at the annual meeting of the American Psychiatric Association, Dallas, Texas.

Rickels, K., Wiseman, K., Norstad, N., Singer, M., Stoltz, D., Brown, A., & Danton, J. (1982). Buspirone and diazepam in anxiety: A controlled study. *Journal of Clinical Psychiatry, 43,* 81–86.

Schou, M., Baastrup, P.C., & Grof, P. (1970). Pharmacological and clinical problems of lithium prophylaxis. *British Journal of Psychiatry, 116,* 615–619.

Sheehan, D.V., Ballenger, J., & Jacobsen, W. (1980). Treatment of endogenous anxiety with phobic, hysterical and hypochondriacal symptoms. *Archives of General Psychiatry, 37,* 51–59.

Silver, J.M., & Yudofsky, S.C. (1988). Psychopharmacology and electroconvulsive therapy. In J.A. Talbott, R.E. Halves, & S.C. Yudofsky (Eds.), *The American Psychiatric Press textbook of psychiatry* (pp. 767–853). Washington, DC: American Psychiatric Press.

Smith, D.E., Wesson, E.R., & Seymour, R.B. (1979). The abuse of barbiturates and other sedative-hypnotics. In R.I. Dupont, A. Goldstein, & J. O'Donnell (Eds.), *Handbook on drug abuse* (pp. 233–241). Washington, DC: U.S. Government Printing Office.

Sprague, R.L., & Sleator, E.K. (1977). Methylphenidate in hyperkinetic children: Differences in dose effects on learning and social behavior. *Science, 198,* 1274–1276.

Stein, L., Wise, C.D., & Berger, B.D. (1983). *The benzodiazepines.* New York: Raven Press.

Sulzbacher, S. (1972). Behavior analysis of drug effects in the classroom. In G. Semb (Ed.), *Behavior analysis and education.* Lawrence: University of Kansas Press.

Tamminga, C.A., & Gerlach J. (1987). New neuroleptics and experimental anti-psychotics in schizophrenia. In H.Y. Meltzer (Ed.), *Psychopharmacology: The third generation of progress* (pp. 1129–1140). New York: Raven Press.

Tourney, G. (1967). A history of therapeutic fashions in psychiatry, 1800–1966. *American Journal of Psychiatry, 124,* 784–796.

Trifilletti, R.R., Snowman, A., & Snyder, S.H. (1984). Anxiolytic cyclopyrolone drugs allosterically modulate the binding of [s] t-butylbicyclophosphorothionate to the benzodiazepine. Aminobuturic acid. A receptor/chloride anionphore complex. *Molecular Pharmacology, 26,* 470–476.

Turner, S., Jacob, R., Beidel, D.C., & Himmelhach, J. (1985). Fluoxetine treatment of obsessive-compulsive disorder. *Journal of Clinical Psychopharmacology, 5,* 207–212.

Uhlenhuth, E.H., DeWitt, H., Balter, M.B., Johanson, C.E., & Mellinger, G.D. (1988). Risks and benefits of long-term benzodiazepine use. *Journal of Clinical Psychopharmacology, 8,* 161–167.

VanderMaelen, C.P., & Wilderman, R.C. (1984). Iontophoretic and systemic administration of the non-benzodiazepine anxiolytic drug buspirone causes inhibition of serotonergic dorsal raphe neurons in rats. *Federation Proceedings, 43,* 947.

Walker, J.I., & Brodie, H.K.H. (1978). Current concepts of lithium treatment and prophylaxis. *Journal of Continuing Medical Education,* 19–30.

Wender, P.H. (1978). Minimal brain dysfunction: An overview. In M.A. Lipton, A. DiMascio, & K.F. Killam (Eds.), *Psychopharmacology: A generation of progress* (pp. 1429–1436). New York: Raven Press.

Wiens, A.N., Anderson, K.A., & Matarazzo, R.G. (1972). Use of medication as an adjunct in the modification of behavior in the pediatric psychology setting. *Professional Psychology, 3,* 157–163.

Williams, J.G., Barlow, D.H., & Agras, W.S. (1972). Behavioral measurement of severe depression. *Archives of General Psychiatry, 27,* 330–334.

Zike, K. (1972). *Drugs in maladaptive school behavior.* Unpublished manuscript, Harbor General Hospital, Los Angeles.

Zitrin, C.M., Klein, D.F., & Woerner, M.G. (1978). Behavior therapy, supportive psychotherapy, imipramine and phobias. *Archives of General Psychiatry, 35,* 307–316.

CHAPTER 37

HEALTH PSYCHOLOGY

Timothy P. Carmody
Joseph D. Matarazzo

As the profession of psychology has evolved, adapting to its own acquisition of knowledge as well as to social and cultural changes, one area that has experienced explosive growth during the past two decades is health psychology. The rapid development of professional and scientific activity in health psychology, reflected in the proliferation of practice, research, training, and employment opportunities, has been due, in part, to the reemergence of the biopsychosocial model in health care. This model holds that health and illness are best understood not only in terms of biological factors, but psychological and social factors as well (Gentry, 1984; Guze, Matarazzo, & Saslow, 1953; Miller, 1987; Rodin & Stone, 1987; Stone, 1987; White, 1988). A plethora of empirical studies have established that life-style, behavioral, and psychological factors affect bodily functioning. This hypothesis first appeared in the earliest writings of Western and Eastern civilizations and has provided the impetus for the modern restatement of this biopsychosocial paradigm (Matarazzo, 1984a; Matarazzo & Istvan, 1988; Miller, 1987; Stone, 1987). Psychologists have played a major role in the reemergence of this biopsychosocial perspective of illness, collaborat-

ing in growing numbers with professionals from a number of other disciplines (e.g., physicians, epidemiologists, public health experts, nutritionists, health educators, biochemists, nurses, etc.) in the rapidly expanding research, training, and practice opportunities that collectively represent the interdisciplinary field of behavioral medicine (Matarazzo, 1980, 1982, 1984b; Schwartz & Weiss, 1978a, 1978b; White, 1988).

At the 1977 Yale Conference on Behavioral Medicine and again at a 1978 conference hosted by the National Academy of Sciences, health experts representing several scientific and professional disciplines met to discuss current issues and future directions in this newly emerging field. Based on these discussions, the following definition of behavioral medicine was formulated and gained wide acceptance:

Behavioral Medicine is the interdisciplinary field concerned with the development and integration of behavioral and biomedical science, knowledge, and techniques relevant to health and illness and the application of this knowledge and these techniques to prevention, diagnosis, treatment, and rehabilitation. (Schwartz & Weiss, 1978a, p. 250; 1978b, p. 7)

Although sister disciplines such as epidemiology and medical sociology have had much to offer to the field of behavioral medicine, psychology has had the longest history of formal research on individual human behavior, a well-established scientific knowledge base, the practical applied experience, and the educational-institutional supports to make substantial early contributions in the field of behavioral medicine. Recognizing this potential, the charter president of the newly established Division of Health Psychology of the American Psychological Association offered the following definition of health psychology encompassing the collective efforts of psychologists:

> *Health Psychology* is the aggregate of the specific educational, scientific, and professional contributions of the discipline of psychology to the promotion and maintenance of health, the prevention and treatment of illness, the identification of etiologic and diagnostic correlates of health, illness and related dysfunction, and the analysis and improvement of the health policy formation. (Matarazzo, 1982, p. 4)

Thus, the activities included within health psychology refer to psychology's contributions as a science and profession to the broad interdisciplinary field of behavioral medicine. According to this definition, health psychology involves not only clinical practice but also teaching, research, and administration. Furthermore, it is meant to encompass all areas of psychology applied to health and illness, for example, clinical, social, industrial, developmental, experimental, physiological, and others (Matarazzo, 1987c).

In the present chapter, the historical emergence of health psychology is first reviewed. Second, the role of psychology in the primary prevention of illness is discussed, focusing on smoking, alcohol and other drug abuse, obesity, coronary risk factors, and stress. Third, examples of the application of the knowledge base of generic psychology in the treatment of physical illness are presented, focusing on chronic pain, cardiovascular disease, neurological disorders, and cancer. The role of psychologists in promoting patient compliance is also examined. Fourth, contemporary issues in the development of training opportunities for health psychologists at both the predoctoral and postdoctoral levels are addressed. Fifth, major scientific and professional issues in health psychology are described, focusing on current professional opportunities in research, teaching, and clinical practice. Finally, we will attempt to offer some predictions about possible future directions for health psychology.

HISTORICAL EMERGENCE OF HEALTH PSYCHOLOGY

A number of factors have contributed to the recent proliferation of scientific and professional activity in health psychology. However, two major historical developments stand out as providing the primary impetus for this increasing application of generic psychology in the health care field: (a) the reemergence of the biopsychosocial paradigm, and (b) the recognition of the increasing role of life-style factors in disease morbidity/mortality.

Reemergence of the Biopsychosocial Paradigm

The recognition of psychological components of health and illness can be traced back to the era of the early Greeks when, for all intents and purposes, health care was practiced by philosophers. References to the influence of the mind on bodily processes date back to the earliest writings of civilization in ancient Greece during the fifth century B.C. (Ehrenwald, 1976; Lipowski, 1977; Rodin & Stone, 1987). In later centuries, mind–body dualism was promoted by the church in its view of physical disease as a breakdown in the biological processes of the body in contrast to sin, which represented corruption of the soul (Engel, 1977). In the 19th and early 20th centuries, the work of Freud, Pavlov, and Cannon set the stage for the heuristically productive empirical study of what was then viewed as mind–body interaction. Decades later in the 20th century, building upon the work of these scholarly pioneers, the field of psychosomatic medicine branched out in two different directions, forming a historical bifurcation that included the work of psychoanalytic clinical investigators such as Franz Alexander, on the one hand, and the human laboratory experiments of psychophysiologists such as Harold Wolff at Cornell, on the other. Applying psychoanalytic theory, Alexander studied the relationship between personality and disease. Wolff and co-workers such as Thomas Holmes and Stewart Wolf, on the other hand, examined the relationship between laboratory-induced stressors and physiological responses.

Until recently, mind–body dualism dominated the perspective of psychosomatic medicine. Diseases were traditionally classified as either psychosomatic (i.e., physical dysfunctions arising from psychological processes) or organic (i.e., physical disorders arising from pathophysiological factors). In contrast, the more recent version of the biopsychosocial paradigm holds that psychosocial factors are involved in all diseases because the individuals in whom they occur not only have a biological make up but a psychological and social make up as well. In the early 1950s, Guze et al. (1953) proposed that physical and psychological factors played a role in varying degrees of prominence in all physical and mental disease states. This view was further developed during the 1960s and 1970s. For instance, Leigh and Reiser (1977), Engel (1977), and Lipowski (1977) offered their criticisms of the organically focused traditional biomedical model of disease, pointing out that it excludes social, psychological, and behavioral dimensions of illness. More recently, White (1988) emphasized that the biopsychosocial model of disease represents a major revision in the health care paradigm because it emphasizes the central role of behavioral, social, and ecological/interactional factors in illness causality.

This biopsychosocial perspective has been supported by numerous empirical demonstrations of the somatic effects of such psychological factors as stress, social isolation, perceived control versus helplessness, hostility, Type A behavior, social support, availability of adaptive (vs. maladaptive) coping responses, and various personality characteristics (Miller, 1987). This evidence has come from clinical and epidemiological studies as well as from well-controlled animal experiments, some of which have examined specific physiological mechanisms underlying the relationship between the brain and bodily health (Krantz & Glass, 1984; Winters & Anderson, 1985). Furthermore, a number of clinical studies have shown that there is a high prevalence of psychological problems among individuals seeking medical care (Olbrisch, 1977). It has been estimated that 60% to 90% of health problems have a significant psychological component (Bakal, 1979) and that at least 50% of the population in the United States suffer from psychophysiologically related symptoms such as recurrent headaches, hypertension, or gastrointestinal diseases (Schwab, Fennell, & Warheit, 1974).

Impact of Life-Style on Disease

The second major factor contributing to the emergence of health psychology is the change that has taken place in the prevalance of illnesses involving life-style factors and the impact of such diseases on escalating health care costs. Developments in the basic and applied health sciences in areas such as infectious diseases, immunology, and epidemiology during the past 80 years have dramatically changed the illness patterns of Americans by reducing or eliminating the incidence of previously highly prevalent conditions such as tuberculosis, influenza, measles, and poliomyelitis (Califano, 1979). The human and dollar toll of these four diseases have been reduced significantly in our lifetime.

As shown in Table 37.1, whereas most deaths and disabilities were caused by infections, now they are caused by chronic diseases in which behavior (life-style) patterns play a major role, including cardiovascular disease (38% of all deaths), cancer (20% of all deaths), and strokes (10% of all deaths; Matarazzo, 1984b). It has been estimated that 50% of mortalities from the 10 leading causes of death in the United States can be traced to behavioral or life-style patterns (U.S. Department of Health and Human Services, 1985). Recognizing this epidemiological trend, Matarazzo (1984a, 1984b) coined the term *behavioral pathogens* to highlight the important role played by disease-producing behaviors and life-style patterns (e.g., high-fat diet, smoking, stress, sedentary life-style, and so forth).

One of the results of these changes in the major causes of morbidity and mortality has been an alarming escalation in the cost of health care in the United States. Between 1950 and 1980, the national total expenditure for health increased from 4.5 of the annual gross national product (GNP) to over 10% of the annual GNP (Vischi, Jones, Shank, & Lima, 1980; Waldo, 1987). Furthermore, the average per capita health expenditure increased tenfold from $82 per capita in 1965 to $968 per capita in 1979, and it is considerably higher today. As shown in Figure 37.1, recent statistics have indicated a steady increase in the share of health care expenses borne by the federal government (Matarazzo, 1984b). The figures for 1987 indicated that the estimated 450.7 billion dollars spent on health care for that year equaled 11.1% of the GNP. Early estimates for 1989 indicate that this upward trend is continuing.

Health analysts have attributed a justifiable proportion of this escalating cost of health care to the willingness of consumers to pay for hospital intensive care units, computerized axial tomography (CAT) scanners, and other very costly technological advances. However, less justifiable have been the rising health costs associated with preventable diseases such as lung cancer, alcohol and other drug abuse, motor vehicle accidents, and cardiovascular disease, which represent a needless waste of human and fiscal resources (Matarazzo, 1982, 1983, 1984a).

Table 37.1. The 10 Leading Causes of Death in the United States: 1900, 1940, and 1980

CAUSE OF DEATH	1900	1940	1980
Pneumonia and influenza	1	5	6
Tuberculosis (all forms)	2	7	
Diarrhea, enteritis, and ulceration of the intestines	3		
Diseases of the heart	4	1	1
Intracranial lesions of vascular origin	5	3	
Nephritis (all forms)	6	4	
All accidents[a]	7	6	4
Cancer[b]	8	2	2
Senility	9		
Diphtheria	10		
Diabetes mellitus		8	7
Motor vehicle accidents		9	
Premature births		10	
Cardiovascular diseases			3
Chronic, obstructive pulmonary diseases			5
Cirrhosis of the liver			8
Atherosclerosis			9
Suicide			10

[a] This category excludes motor vehicle accidents in the years 1900 and 1940, but includes them in 1980.
[b] This category encompasses cancer and other malignant tumors in the years 1900 and 1940 and changes to malignant neoplasms of all types in 1980.

Note: Based on data from Levy and Moskowitz (1982).

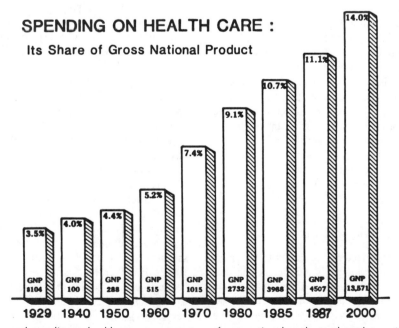

Figure 37.1. Annual spending on health care as a percentage of gross national product, selected years 1929–1985 with projections through the year 2000. Total GNP in billions of dollars. (Compiled from information from D.R. Waldo, 1987, personal communication.)

This fiscal trend has prompted health experts and government officials to support and encourage psychological research and practice in the areas of primary prevention (e.g., to deter children from becoming smokers, to encourage currently healthy Americans to use less salt, to exercise more, to eat foods lower in fat and cholesterol, and so on). This growing need and mandate for primary prevention has contributed significantly to the expanding role of psychology in the health care field and to the expanding role of psychologists as health care providers.

Organizational Emergence of Behavioral Medicine and Behavioral Health

The growth of organized health psychology has been due in part to the recent revitalization of scientific and professional activity in the larger interdisciplinary fields of behavioral medicine and behavioral health (Matarazzo, 1980, 1982, 1983, 1984a). Several developments have contributed to the recent formal recognition of behavioral medicine as a vital field in its own right. Prominant among these developments have been the establishments of the *Journal of Behavioral Medicine,* the Society of Behavioral Medicine, the Academy of Behavioral Research, the Behavioral Medicine Branch of the National Heart, Lung, and Blood Institute (NHLBI), and the Behavioral Medicine Study Section within the Division of Research Grants of the National Institutes of Health (NIH). In addition, both federal and nonfederal sources of monetary support of predoctoral and postdoctoral research training in behavioral medicine as well as basic and applied research in etiology, treatment, and prevention have been increased due to the initiatives of a number of the institutes that comprise the NIH. The NHLBI, for example, has been active in funding predoctoral and postdoctoral research training programs in both health psychology and in other disciplines that collectively constitute behavioral medicine and its sister interdisciplinary field, behavioral health.

APPLICATIONS IN BEHAVIORAL HEALTH

During the past 2 decades, there has been dramatic growth in scientific and professional activity related to primary prevention. Psychologists have played a key role in the development, implementation, and evaluation of intervention programs aimed at keeping healthy people healthy. Almost a decade ago, Matarazzo (1980), wanting to give emphasis to this expanding interdisciplinary endeavor of primary prevention, coined the term *behavioral health* and defined it as follows:

> Behavioral health is an interdisciplinary field dedicated to promoting a philosophy of health that stresses individual responsibility in the application of behavioral science, knowledge, and techniques to the maintenance of health and the prevention of illness and dysfunction by a variety of self-initiated individual or shared activities. (Matarazzo, 1980, p. 813).

Albeit also acknowledging the important role played by federal and state legislation (e.g., laws mandating use of seat belts), the goal of the interdisciplinary field of behavioral health is to promote those life-style practices, or what Matarazzo (1984b) refers to as "behavioral immunogens" in our healthy youth that will help them to maintain their health and prevent illness by sustaining health-engendering behaviors throughout their lifespan. As can be seen in Figure 37.2, a large number of Americans have already eliminated, reduced, or otherwise changed for the better many of those life-style behaviors that constitute risk factors for morbidity and mortality.

Cigarette Smoking

In over 50,000 studies, it has been established that cigarette smoking is still the largest preventable cause of premature death and disability in the United States (U.S. Department of Health and Human Services, 1983). The goal of making the United States a smoke-free nation was proclaimed in 1984 by the Surgeon General. In 1982, the National Cancer Institute initiated a wide-scale smoking intervention research campaign through its Smoking, Tobacco, and Cancer Program (STCP) with the goal of reducing cancer mortality rates by 50% by the year 2000 (Schwartz, 1987). The STCP calls for local, state, federal, and private sector involvement in the establishment of a system of antitobacco measures.

During the past 25 years, there has been a steady increase in research on tobacco addiction and smoking cessation with a focus on the addicting aspects of nicotine, multicomponent intervention strategies using both pharmacological (e.g., nicotine gum) as well as behavioral strategies (Pomerleau & Pomerleau, 1988), the development of methods for validating abstinence, prevention of smoking onset in children and adolescents, and the study of treatment failures, relapse, and methods for maintaining abstinence (Carmody et al., 1988; Schwartz, 1987).

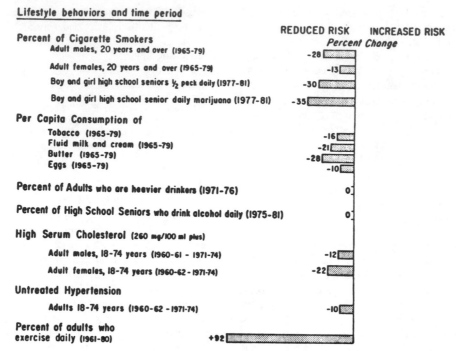

Figure 37.2. Recent changes in life-style behaviors that affect health (Adapted from Harris, 1980, and Johnston Bachman, & O'Malley, 1981.)

During this same period of time, the percentage of smokers has decreased from 42% to 30% (U.S. Department of Health and Human Services, 1983). More than 30 million smokers have quit smoking during the past 25 years. Still, there are over 53 million cigarette smokers, including an increasing number of adult female smokers and 15- and 16-year-old girls who smoke (Califano, 1979; Harris, 1980). Public health statistics indicate that approximately 4,000 children begin to smoke cigarettes each day (U.S. Public Health Service, 1979) and there are approximately 6 million teenage smokers in the United States (Piney, 1979).

Prevention

Given these trends in the epidemiology of smoking onset, a number of programs have been developed to prevent the onset of smoking among preteenage youth. Green (1977), in a study aimed at discerning why children initiate smoking behavior, surveyed 5,200 school-age youths regarding cigarette smoking, factor analyzed their responses, and found that peer pressure and ambivalence toward authority figures were related to the onset of cigarette smoking. Following similar exploratory research in other cities, proto-

typical smoking prevention programs were developed by Evans (1976) and his colleagues (Evans et al., 1978, 1981) using videotaped presentations, peer modeling, group discussion, role-playing ways of resisting social pressures to smoke, and repeated monitoring of smoking and measures of knowledge and attitudes toward smoking. The efficacy of these and related programs has been studied in Stanford, California (McAlister, Perry, & Maccoby, 1979; Perry, Killen, Telch, Slinkard, & Danaher, 1980; Telch, Killen, McAlister, Perry, & Maccoby, 1982), in Minnesota (Arkin, Roemhild, Johnson, Luepker, & Murray, 1981; Hurd et al., 1980), and in New York (Botvin, Eng, & Williams, 1980). In general, the percentages of new smokers in the groups of youths exposed to these interventions has been typically about one half of the percentages of new smokers in the control groups (Carter, Bendell, & Matarazzo, 1985; Flay, d'Avernes, Best, Kersell, & Ryann, 1983).

Treatment

During 1988, the Surgeon General of the United States declared smoking behavior to constitute an addiction. In the treatment of these addicted cigarette smokers, a wide variety of intervention methods have been evaluated in recent smoking cessation research studies, including self-care and educational approaches, clinics, groups, medications, nicotine replacement procedures, hypnosis, acupuncture, physician counseling, risk factor prevention trials, mass media campaigns, community intervention programs, behavioral methods, and worksite policies and programs (Schwartz, 1987). According to a recent review by Glasgow and Lichtenstein (1987), behavioral smoking cessation approaches appear to be more effective than no-intervention control conditions, but no better than alternative treatment approaches, in producing abstinence rates. Programs combining behavioral skills training with nicotine gum appear to be more effective than either of these treatment methods used alone (Carmody et al., 1988; Ockene, 1986). Intensive interventions, particularly those using aversive procedures (e.g., rapid smoking), produce impressive initial abstinence rates, but relapse tends to be substantial (Glasgow & Lichtenstein, 1987). Thus, more recent programs reflect an increased focus on relapse prevention.

In proposing future directions for research in tobacco addiction and smoking cessation, experts emphasize the need for more collaboration between physicians and behavioral scientists because the former have numerous opportunities to influence so many smokers and treatment programs often involve an integration of pharmacological and behavioral approaches. There is also much to learn about how people quit on their own and how best to intervene in the long-term process of smoking cessation in all of its phases (Prochaska, Velicer, DiClemente, & Fava, 1988). Furthermore, there is a continuing need to develop effective mass media campaigns, community-based interventions, and methods of enhancing environmental support for nonsmoking.

Alcohol and Other Drug Abuse

Primary Prevention

Recent studies suggest that the onset of alcohol use occurs at age 13 for over 50% of youths and that problem drinking appears to be quite prevalent among teenage youths (Pandina, 1986). Reports by Galanter (1980) and by Parker, Birnbaum, Boyd, and Noble (1980) revealed that even social drinking among adolescents may produce a marked loss of cognitive functioning. The costs associated with chronic alcoholism across all age groups in the United States have been estimated to approach 42 billion dollars annually

(Vischi et al., 1980). Given these alarming statistics, there has been an increasing emphasis on the prevention of alcohol and other drug abuse among teenage youths. Three strategies have been used in the primary prevention of alcohol abuse: alcohol education classes, public information campaigns, and attempts to modify government policy (Alden, 1980).

Educational programs have included mass media campaigns, community-based programs, parent education, school-based programs, and college campus interventions (e.g., Botvin, Baker, Botvin, Filazzola, & Millman, 1984; Braucht & Braucht, 1984; Engstrom, 1984; Flay & Sobel, 1983; Moskowitz, 1986; Rootman, 1985). Botvin and his colleagues (Botvin et al., 1984) at the American Health Foundation in New York pioneered a health promotion program for school-age youngsters in which drug abuse was one of several target areas of intervention. Traditional alcohol education programs have been shown to be effective in increasing knowledge about alcohol but not in producing attitude or behavior change (e.g., Swisher, Warner, & Hern, 1972; Tennant, Weaver, & Lewis, 1973). As a result, the application of behavioral techniques such as self-management, controlled drinking, and coping-skills training have been implemented (e.g., Berg, 1976; Haggerty, 1977; Tuchfeld & Marcus, 1984) to enhance the effects of alcohol and other drug abuse prevention programs. In a review of such prevention programs, Schaps, Churgin, Palley, Takata, and Cohen (1980) reported almost 10 years ago that over 70% of these behavioral programs had a more positive effect in reducing alcohol consumption than programs that did not use such intervention methods.

The increased sophistication of more recent drug prevention programs reflects the progress that has been made in the study of substance abuse. Regarding the etiology of alcohol abuse, numerous studies have been conducted in an attempt to examine the hereditary and environmental factors involved in the development of alcohol addiction (e.g., Goodwin, 1986; Tarter, 1988). For example, recent studies in Denmark and in the United States have provided further evidence for a familial component of alcoholism (Goodwin, 1986). Other investigators have examined the addictive properties of alcohol (e.g., Nathan, 1988) and the role of learning on the development of tolerance to many of the effects of ethanol (Tiffany & Baker, 1986). Still, there is much yet to learn about the interactions between person, environment, genetic predisposition, and precipitating states in the etiology of alcohol abuse (Abrams, Niaura, Carey, Monti, & Binkoff, 1986).

Treatment

More information is now available regarding the effects of alcoholism treatment (e.g., Sobell, Sobell, & Nirenberg, 1988). Recent reviews of alcohol treatment outcome reveal abstinence rates at 1 year to be approximately 50% (Nathan, 1986). The overall importance of alcohol programs in the health care industry is reflected by recent data from the National Institute of Alcohol Abuse and Alcoholism (1985) showing that health care costs drop significantly for alcohol abusers following participation in alcohol treatment programs. Investigators have begun to examine variables related to treatment outcome including program characteristics, staff functioning, work environment, and treatment components (Moos & Finney, 1986). Inpatient programs do not appear to be any more effective than outpatient programs. Intensity of treatment and theoretical orientation have tended to be poor predictors of outcome. On the other hand, several patient characteristics (motivation, chronicity/severity of alcoholism, age, gender, and personal, interpersonal, educational, and vocational resources) have been shown to be predictive of treatment outcome (Berkowitz & Perkins, 1988). Parsons (1986) recently documented that recovery from neuropsychological deficits can occur in some alcoholics but that some areas of cognitive impairment associated with a positive family history of alcoholism may persist. Such cognitive deficits also affect treatment outcome.

Relapse prevention represents another major area of investigation in the treatment of alcoholism and other forms of substance abuse. Abrams et al. (1986) reviewed important themes in relapse prevention with alcohol abusers. They concluded that much has been learned about the precipitants of relapse, but that an in-depth analysis of the underlying mediating mechanisms is still lacking.

Consistent with an increased emphasis on a public health perspective, various intervention approaches have been aimed at identifying people or groups whose drinking behavior places them at risk or who are in the early stages of dysfunctional drinking practices (Cohen, 1982). To this end, training programs have been developed for primary health care providers including methods for detecting early warning signs of problem drinking, conducting hospital consultations, and developing liaison programs (U.S. Department of Health and Human Services, 1987). Screening procedures are also being studied for early identification of alcohol abuse (e.g., Rosett & Weiner, 1985). Work-based alcohol interventions have increasingly become part of broader employee assistance programs (e.g., Straussner, 1985). Although rigorous scientific study is lacking, occupational alcoholism programs have reported highly positive results. In all of the above-mentioned approaches to alcohol and drug abuse treatment and prevention, psychologists have played a key role in developing them as important areas of behavioral health.

Obesity

Although a successful treatment approach is not yet a reality, much has been learned in the past 20 years about the etiology, treatment, and prevention of obesity. Obesity represents an independent risk factor for cardiovascular disease and is associated with hypertension, hyperlipidemia, and non-insulin dependent diabetes mellitus (NIH Consensus Development Panel on Health Implications of Obesity, 1985). Obese individuals have a higher risk of developing complications related to surgery, a mortality rate 50% greater than for normal-weight people, and a higher incidence of medical problems such as respiratory infections, skeletal-joint dysfunction, hernias, and gall bladder disease (Stuart, 1980; Von Itallie, 1985).

According to recent epidemiological data (Von Itallie, 1985), 26% of adults in the United States or 34 million people between the ages of 20 and 75 are overweight. Of these, 12.4 million adults are categorized as severely overweight (i.e., their weight exceeds the 84th percentile on a body mass index) and the prevalence of moderate and severely overweight adults appears to be increasing slightly. Furthermore, estimates of the prevalence rates of obesity in children in our country range from 10% to 25%, and almost 80% of these overweight youth become obese adults (Coates & Thoresen, 1981; Stunkard, 1979).

Regarding etiological factors, it has been determined that there are both metabolic and behavioral factors involved in the etiology of obesity (Foreyt, 1987; Rodin, Elias, Silberstein, & Wagner, 1988). During the past 2 decades, there have been substantial changes in the conceptualization of the biological aspects of hunger and satiety (Stricker & Verbalis, 1987), including a de-emphasis on the previously popular hypothalamocentric view of overeating. It has been shown that human obesity has a major familial component, both in terms of shared environmental and genetic variables. Research focusing on the familial etiology of obesity has shown that from 20% to 60% of the variation in body fat may be due to genetic factors (Price, 1987). Still, overconsumption, sedentary living, and other life-style habits associated with obesity often can be traced to shared childhood and adolescent food and exercise patterns. These recent developments in the study of obesity clearly indicate the need for a multicomponent treatment approach, given the multiple etiologies and complex pathogenesis of obesity.

Given that childhood life-style habits, familial patterns, and childhood obesity all contribute to the development of obesity in adults, health experts have focused on the early prevention of lifelong patterns of overeating and sedentary living, conducting intervention programs for overweight children and adolescents (e.g., Israel, Silverman, & Solotar, 1988). Given the unnecessarily high incidence of obesity, hypertension, and hyperlipidemia among children in our country, such intervention programs have received considerable governmental support (Connor & Bristow, 1985).

The most pressing challenge in the behavioral treatment of obesity remains the development of methods to facilitate the maintenance of weight loss (Jeffrey, 1987; Perri, McAlister, Gange, Jordan, McAdoo, & Nezu, 1988). In this regard, obesity has come to be viewed as a chronic condition requiring successful early intervention followed by long-term supportive care. Behavioral methods for modifying dietary habits have been combined with supervised physical exercise training, very low-calorie diets, pharmacological agents, and relapse prevention strategies to increase long-term treatment effectiveness (e.g., Rodin et al., 1988).

Severe forms of obesity or morbid obesity (i.e., over 100 lbs. above one's ideal weight) have very serious health consequences and, as the diagnostic label suggests, typically lead to premature death. Morbid obesity is thought by some experts (e.g., Griffen & Printen, 1988; Kral & Kissileff, 1987) to best be treated surgically. Weight losses of 30% to 35% have been achieved using over 27 different surgical procedures that are thought to produce weight loss by altering satiety mechanisms (Kral & Kissileff, 1987). More stringent criteria for patient selection plus modifications of surgical technique are being developed in order to maximize the likelihood of success in the surgical treatment of morbid obesity.

Given the difficulties in successfully treating severe forms of obesity and the prevalence of all forms of obesity, the public health perspective is becoming increasingly emphasized in the treatment of obesity (Jeffrey, 1988). Although approximately one third of adults in the United States are in need of treatment for obesity, very few of these individuals seek help from traditional health care providers (Foreyt, 1987). For this reason, experts in this area are attempting to develop more cost-effective methods of providing treatment to larger numbers of obese individuals as well as focusing more attention on primary prevention. Within the context of these prevention programs, psychologists are lending their expertise in the areas of assessment, research design, behavior change technology, and other areas in the development of more effective approaches to the assessment and treatment of obesity.

Coronary Risk Factors

The cardiovascular diseases (CVD) have been the leading cause of premature death in the United States since the 1930s (Jenkins, 1988). Among the various forms of CVD, coronary artery disease (CAD) has come to be recognized as primarily a behavioral disorder, because so many life-style factors contribute to its etiology. Psychologists possess a unique combination of skills and expertise for investigating these psychosocial risk factors as well as for designing and testing intervention programs at the individual, group, and community levels and developing technologies for such prevention programs that are both effective and economical.

Psychosocial factors

A variety of psychosocial antecedents or correlates of CAD have been investigated. For example, stressful occupational settings characterized by high demands and low levels of control have been shown to be associated with increased coronary risk (Krantz, Contrada, Hill, & Friedler, 1988). Other studies have investigated social stress, Type A behavior, anger and hostility, anxiety and neuroticism, and physiological reactivity in relation to CAD (Contrada & Krantz, 1988; Krantz et al., 1988). In studies of Type A behavior, the hostility dimension has been shown to be predictive of CAD more consistently than any of the other psychological risk factors, including the other dimensions of Type A behavior (Chesney, 1988; Chesney & Rosenman, 1985).

Although further evidence is needed before stress and reactivity can be regarded as proven risk factors for CAD, experimental studies of several animal species have shown that the disruption of the social environment can induce pathology that resembles CAD (Manuck, Kaplan, & Matthews, 1986). Most investigators believe that the activity of the sympathetic adrenal-medullary and pituitary adrenal-cortical systems mediate the relationship between stress and CAD. However, the mechanisms underlying these complex relationships have yet to be fully determined.

Diet

Whereas the study of coronary-prone behavior is still in its early stages, the role of dietary factors in atherosclerosis and CAD has been examined in numerous animal and human studies for the past several decades (Connor & Connor, 1985). As a result of years of basic and applied research, there is a growing consensus among health experts that the typical American diet, which is high in fat, cholesterol, and salt, contributes to our country's increased morbidity and mortality due to cardiovascular disease (Jeffrey, 1988). The most prominent diet-related risk factors for CVD are hypertension, hypercholesterolemia, and obesity.

Strategies for modifying diet have relied primarily on education, skills training, and problem-solving techniques. Recent studies have attempted to demonstrate the effects of modifying diet in entire populations, focusing on diet as a public health issue. Several interdisciplinary teams of investigators have developed a variety of behavioral and community-oriented interventions based on social learning theory and designed to reduce the human and dollar costs associated with these dietary-related coronary risk factors (Carmody, Istvan, Matarazzo, Connor, & Connor, 1986; Carmody, Matarazzo, & Istvan, 1987). At the Oregon Health Sciences University, a 5-year dietary intervention program was conducted by one such team to investigate the acceptance of a low-fat, low-cholesterol, low-sodium "alternative diet" in free living Portland families and to examine the effects of dietary change on plasma lipids, blood pressure, and body weight (Matarazzo et al., 1982). The results are currently being prepared for publication.

Multiple Risk Factor Intervention

Several large-scale community-based projects have been implemented to reduce *multiple* risk factors for coronary heart disease. The Multiple Risk Factor Intervention Trial (MRFIT; Kuller, Neaton, Caggiula, & Falvo-Gerard, 1980) produced significant reductions in plasma cholesterol, hypertension, and cigarette smoking in high-risk male participants. At Stanford, the Three Community Study (Meyer, Nash, McAlister, Maccoby, & Farquhar, 1980) was extended to a more ambitious Five Community Study (Farquhar et al., 1984) aimed at reducing coronary risk factors in whole communities by means of mass media, community networking, and a variety of other creative and innovative behavioral and educational approaches.

Many of these studies targeted at the primary prevention of coronary heart disease (CHD) have emphasized interventions with youth. Perry, Klepp, and Shultz (1988) have recently argued that community-wide strategies with children and adolescents represent the most efficient and efficacious interventions for the primary prevention of CVD. This area of investigation is relatively recent and offers abundant opportunities for interdisciplinary collaboration.

In addition, increasing numbers of worksite health promotion programs are being designed to modify CVD risk factors (Glasgow & Terborg, 1988). Although controlled studies are needed to substantiate the not unexpected initial optimistic claims about the impact of such occupational health promotion programs, research to date has shown that both intrapersonal (e.g., motivational) and organizational factors affect level of participation and work environment intervention outcomes (Glasgow & Terborg, 1988). The political, logistical, organizational, and methodological issues posed by these worksite programs provide unique challenges to the practitioners and investigators working in this growing area of behavioral health and CVD prevention.

Stress and Coping

A recent *Newsweek* article entitled "Stress on the Job" highlighted the impact of stress on health and business productivity (Miller et al., 1988). According to this article, the overall cost of worker stress to the economy is estimated to be as high as 150 billion dollars per year, and some corporate leaders are predicting that the management of stress could become a 15 billion dollar industry within the next decade.

As a scientific construct, stress represents one of the cornerstones of research, clinical practice, and training in health psychology, behavioral medicine, and behavioral health. Of central importance to the study of stress has been the delineation of physiological processes assumed to be related to stress. Mechanisms by which the sympathoadrenomedullary (SAM), hypothalamic-pituitary-adrenocortical (HPAC), and sympathetic nervous system (SNS) mediate the relationship between stress and illness have been explored extensively (Brantley, Dietz, McKnight, Jones, & Tulley, 1988; Cacioppo & Petty, 1982; Hinckle, 1987; McCabe & Schneiderman, 1985). Another important physiological component of stress involves the immune system. There is considerable anecdotal support that psychological factors play a significant role in the etiology of infectious diseases (Ader &

Cohen, 1984; Borysenko, 1984; Kiecolt-Glaser & Glaser, 1987; Pennebaker, Kiecolt-Glaser, & Glaser, 1988). Animal studies provide compelling evidence that environmental factors are capable of modifying immune responses (Monjan, 1981). Immunological competence is of particular relevance in autoimmune diseases such as rheumatoid arthritis and systemic lupus erythematosus (Ader & Cohen, 1984).

In attempting to understand the concept of stress from a psychological perspective, there has developed a "science of coping" (Gentry, 1984; Gentry & Kobasa, 1984); that is, the investigation of the relationship between coping strategies, stressful events, social support, cognitive appraisal, and health status. For example, Antonovsky (1979) proposed a health-related construct that he referred to as the "sense of coherence" (i.e., the pervasive, enduring, dynamic feeling of confidence that one's environment is predictable) and hypothesized that this was one of several "generalized resistance resources" (GRRs) that help protect an individual from a variety of microbiologic pathogens and stress. Kobasa (1982) and her colleagues have studied a personality construct labeled "hardiness," which is similar to Antonovsky's "sense of coherence" and hypothesized that it protects one from the ill effects of stress. Hardiness (Kobasa, 1979, 1982) is defined as a sense of commitment, control, and challenge, and represents a way of internally transforming life events so as to decrease their stressfulness. The transactional model of Folkman and Lazarus (1980) and the taxonomic approach of Billings and Moos (1981) are further examples of attempts to develop theoretical frameworks to define and study the parameters of an individual's coping responses and their effects on adaptational outcomes.

Social support is another important factor that has been shown to influence the relationship between stress and health outcomes (Billings & Moos, 1981; Kaplan & Hartwell, 1987). The buffering effects of social support on health outcome may be the result of a variety of factors, including the relationship between social support and coping competence, the negative effects of illness on social support, the inclusion of losses from one's social network in people's recollections of recent life events, and the assortment of psychological processes engendered by supportive social networks (Cohen, 1988; Cohen & Syme, 1985).

The study of how individuals manage stress has provided an additional opportunity for health scientists to examine the relationship between various coping responses and health. A number of approaches to stress management have been investigated, including relaxation training, meditation, visual imagery techniques, biofeedback, anxiety management procedures, self-regulation, stress inoculation, and numerous other approaches (Anderson, 1988; Meichenbaum & Jaremko, 1983). Such interventions have been designed to modify emotional, behavioral, cognitive, and physiological components of stress.

Behavioral Health: Summary

It is clear from these brief overviews of major areas of the interdisciplinary biobehavioral field that behavioral health-oriented psychologists are making increasingly significant contributions in the development of socially relevant primary prevention programs. Opportunities for psychologists in behavioral health who are working with currently healthy individuals are expanding in such areas as the prevention of smoking, alcohol abuse, obesity, coronary risk, and deleterious effects of stress. Figure 37.3 portrays the relationship between the number of good health practices an individual engages in and future mortality. These results (Belloc, 1973) provide ample evidence from a long-term prospective longitudinal study with healthy individuals that everyday life-style behaviors markedly influence morbidity and mortality (Matarazzo, 1984b). Psychology as a discipline and profession has much to offer to the interdisciplinary field of behavioral health to promote these health-related life-style behaviors.

APPLICATIONS IN BEHAVIORAL MEDICINE

Numerous books, chapters, and journal articles describing recent advances in health psychology attest to the major contributions being made by psychologists collaborating with health professionals from other disciplines in the interdisciplinary field of behavioral medicine (e.g., Gentry, 1984; Schneiderman & Tapp, 1985; Stone, 1987). In the following section, examples of these contributions of health psychologists are described.

Chronic Pain

Interdisciplinary collaboration has led to significant advances in the treatment of chronic pain as well as in the rehabilitation of chronically ill, cognitively impaired, and other disabled individuals. The development of interdisciplinary assessment and intervention programs in the management of chronic pain has been described in detail in several recent texts on behavioral

HEALTH PRACTICES AND MORTALITY

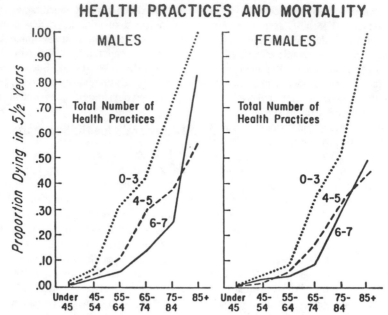

Figure 37.3. Age-specific mortality rates by number of health practices followed by males and females (Adapted from Belloc 1973.)

medicine and health psychology (e.g., Gentry, 1984; Holtzman & Turk, 1986; Pinkerton, Hughes, & Wenrich, 1982; Schneiderman & Tapp, 1985; Turk, Meichenbaum, & Genest, 1983). These interdisciplinary assessment procedures and intervention programs are based on the assumption that chronic pain has multiple components: physiological, motivational, emotional, behavioral, and interpersonal (Turk & Rudy, 1987). Pain as nociceptive tissue damage is distinguished from chronic pain behavior, which is learned and influenced by environmental (social) consequences (Fordyce, 1976a, 1976b; Keefe & Gil, 1986). Fordyce (1988) has recently discussed the importance of distinguishing between pain as nociception versus suffering as an emotional response related to disability. As he stated, "Suffering belongs to the person. Disability is a legal or social judgement, based in part on medical judgements" (p. 276). Thus, pain and suffering behaviors may occur for reasons other than nociception. Many of these programs use extinction and reinforcement contingencies; they are based primarily on operant learning principles and are designed to encourage physical activity and discourage analgesic dependence.

Health psychologists have made significant contributions to the development of these interdisciplinary pain programs. As reviewed by Turner and Romano (1984), psychological treatment methods used in pain

clinics include biofeedback, relaxation, hypnosis, operant conditioning, and cognitive-behavioral therapies (Dobson, 1988) that are designed to enhance control of physiological factors, decrease learned pain behavior by modifying its consequences, and modify cognitive factors in pain (Weisenberg, 1987). Recent controlled studies indicate that each of these treatment methods has merit (Turner & Chapman, 1982a, 1982b), and that cognitive-behavioral therapies may have particular potential for promoting maintenance of treatment gains by providing patients with a wider range of skills for dealing with stress and pain (Turk & Rudy, 1986).

Probably the most common form of chronic pain other than lower back pain is recurrent headaches. Various forms of biofeedback, relaxation training, stress management, and psychotherapy techniques have been used in the treatment of chronic recurrent headaches, both muscle contraction (tension) and vascular (migraine) types, with what appears to be a high level of success (Blanchard et al., 1982; Turner & Romano, 1984). This literature has been reviewed extensively elsewhere (e.g., Blanchard & Andrasik, 1985; Turner & Romano, 1984). Electromyographic (EMG) biofeedback and progressive muscle relaxation training have been shown to produce comparably high levels of pain reduction (Schneider, 1987). In addition, cognitively oriented approaches to the treatment of headaches, based on the assumption that vascular and tension-related headaches are a result of cognitive responses to stressful situations, have been developed and used with high levels of success.

In the treatment of recurrent migraine or vascular headaches, both thermal and EMG biofeedback procedures have been employed with positive results (Blanchard & Andrasik, 1985). Blanchard and his colleagues (Blanchard et al., 1982) have generated an enormous data base to demonstrate the effectiveness of a multicomponent approach to the treatment of tension, vascular, and mixed headaches. Those approaches utilize EMG and thermal biofeedback procedures, as well as cognitive therapies designed to produce changes on both a physiological and psychological level. Blanchard's work exemplifies the contribution of health psychologists to the development of multicomponent assessment and treatment procedures designed to reduce the disabling effects of benign chronic pain problems.

Cardiovascular Disease

More than 4,000 Americans suffer heart attacks each day, with the U.S. incurring an estimated total economic cost of more than 78 billion dollars annually (American Heart Association, 1986). Despite the decline in age-adjusted CHD mortality during the past two decades, CHD remains the leading cause of death in men over the age of 40 and in women over the age of 70. The effects of CHD include substantial physical, social, psychological, and economic morbidity as well as mortality (Blumenthal & Emery, 1988).

Behavioral interventions have been employed in the treatment of a variety of these cardiovascular disorders, including hypertension, cardiac arrhythmias, and postmyocardial infarction rehabilitation (Herd, 1984; Schneiderman & Hammer, 1985). The behavioral treatment of hypertension has included relaxation techniques (progressive muscle relaxation, meditation, yoga, autogenic training) and biofeedback, with the two generally used in combination (Herd, 1984; Pinkerton et al., 1982). However, whereas there appears to be no clear advantage in adding biofeedback therapy in this treatment regimen, home practice of relaxation techniques seems to enhance treatment results. The overall clinical impact of either of these behavioral procedures on lowering blood pressure is still a matter of debate, and it is generally agreed that subtypes of hypertension need to be identified that are most amenable to these behavioral interventions whether used in combination or with other forms of treatment (e.g., weight control, low-salt diet, antihypertensive medications, and so forth).

Cardiovascular arrhythmias represent another common form of cardiovascular disease. They result from abnormalities in the cardiac conduction system and cause several types of symptoms such as premature atrial contractions (PACs), premature ventricular contractions (PVCs), tachycardias (rapid and repetitive heartbeat), and conduction defects (impairment of transmission of impulses within the cardiac conduction system) (Cacioppo & Petty, 1982; Herd, 1984; Pinkerton et al., 1982). Several applications of biofeedback therapy have produced promising results in the treatment of cardiac arrhythmias. For example, certain tachycardias are being treated with biofeedback techniques with some success (Herd, 1984). However, controlled studies are needed to document the clinical efficacy of such behavioral approaches in the treatment of various cardiac arrhythmias.

For postmyocardial infarction (MI) patients, cardiac rehabilitation programs provide formal treatment for the physical and psychosocial sequelae of heart attacks. These programs have primarily focused on physical exercise conditioning with only a few incorporating psychological therapies. Thus far, data on exercise-oriented cardiac rehabilitation programs have not yet demonstrated conclusively that such interventions prolong life or significantly reduce morbidity rates in post-MI patients when compared with routine medical care (Blumenthal & Emery, 1988). However, cardiac rehabilitation programs are generally accepted by the medical community and are providing increasing numbers of opportunities for the application of psychological expertise by interdisciplinary treatment teams of cardiologists, psychologists, nurses, and physical therapists.

Much of the enthusiasm over cardiac rehabilitation programs comes from demonstrations of improvements in quality of life that often result from these programs. Quality of life measures have gained increasing attention and status in studies of the cost-effectiveness of various treatment approaches in cardiovascular disease. Kaplan (1988) and colleagues (Kaplan & Bush, 1982) have developed methods for comparing treatment options in cardiovascular disease, using cost-utility analytic techniques to evaluate hypertension screening and treatment, heart transplant, and primary prevention programs. Thus, psychologists are playing a major role in the development and application of cost-effectiveness analyses. Such analyses are helping to clarify the utility of various intervention approaches in cardiac rehabilitation and in other areas of cardiovascular disease treatment.

Neurological Disorders

Increasing numbers of health psychologists are working in the field of neuropsychology (Bornstein, Costa, & Matarazzo, 1986) and are making major contributions in the treatment and management of a variety of neurological disorders, including traumatic head injury, degenerative neurological disorders, and epilepsy. There has been a growing trend toward the interdisciplinary management of persons with a variety of neurological and neuromuscular disorders involving cognitive, visuoperceptual, and other brain-damage related deficits. Behavioral psychologists and neuropsychologists are collaborating with neurologists, physical and occupational therapists, neurosurgeons, speech therapists, and other rehabilitation specialists on these interdisciplinary rehabilitation teams. This trend is seen, for example, in the developing rehabilitation services being provided for the management of visuoperceptual deficits associated with right hemisphere brain damage, including sensory losses, visual field reductions, hemi-inattention, hemispatial neglect, hemiperceptual deficits, and gaze and visual pursuit disturbances (Gouvier, Webster, & Warner, 1986). Pioneering work in this area has been accomplished at the New York University Institute of Rehabilitation Medicine (Diller, Ben-Yishay, Gerstman, et al., 1974). There is growing evidence that acquired visuoperceptual disorders can be treated and that such treatment gains can make a significant impact on the patient's capacity for independent living.

The applications of these interdisciplinary rehabilitation services are innumerable when one considers that each year approximately 500,000 individuals suffer severe traumatic head injuries that result not only in physical and cognitive impairments, but also in behavioral and emotional sequelae as well (Drudge, Rosen, Peyser, & Pieniadz, 1986). In addition, a number of medical conditions other than head injuries and systemic diseases result in the disruption of normal brain functioning because of cerebrotoxic substances in the circulation, lack of availability of essential substances, and overproduction of certain substances by other organs or systems (Tarter, Edwards, & Van Thiel, 1986). Several other diseases and disorders have potential neurological sequelae (e.g., gastrointestinal disorders, anorexia, acute or chronic liver failure, chronic obstructive pulmonary disease, chronic renal insufficiency, certain diseases of the blood, and myocardial infarction). In addition, there are a number of well-known degenerative neurological disorders that have behavioral and emotional components or sequelae, including multiple sclerosis, Huntington's disease, Parkinson's, Alzheimer's, and cerebrovascular accidents (strokes; e.g., Knight, Godfrey, & Shelton, 1988).

Drudge et al. (1986) have advocated the application of behavioral treatment programs to the chronically brain-impaired individual and the integration of these approaches with the neuropsychological analysis of cognitive deficits. For example, in the case of cerebrovascular accidents (CVAs), strokes are believed to have emotional and behavioral sequelae with both organic and functional components. Decreased social, sexual, and leisure activities after CVAs have been explained in terms of depression secondary to increased dependence, withdrawal, changes in body image, overprotection by family members, and excessive fears about resuming these activities (Drudge et al., 1986). Additionally, the brain damage itself likely has a direct influence on psychological functioning. Tarter et al. (1986) have suggested that impaired cognitive functioning consequential to cerebral pathology can itself affect compliance and adaptive versus maladaptive behavior. For these reasons, health psychologists specifically trained in the areas of rehabilitation and neuropsychology are making major contributions to the management of these brain-damaged patients.

Behavioral (Psychosocial) Oncology

Over the past 2 decades, the role of psychology has expanded significantly in the areas of prevention, treatment, palliative care, and other psychosocial aspects related to oncology (the study and treatment of cancer; Blaney, 1985; Derogatis, 1986). For example, not only are psychologists actively involved in the prevention of lung cancer related to cigarette smoking, but they also serve on interdisciplinary teams addressing psychosocial issues related to cancer treatment, including interventions designed to reduce conditioned aversive responses (nausea and vomiting) to chemotherapy, pain, adjustment reactions to the initial diagnosis of cancer, and adaptation to disability, death, and loss (Meyerowitz, Heinrich, & Schag, 1983).

Many patients receiving chemotherapy develop conditioned aversive responses to this treatment involving nausea and vomiting (Burish & Carey, 1986; Morrow & Dobkin, 1988). Desensitization, counterconditioning, relaxation, cognitive distraction, and self-hypnotic imagery techniques are being used to successfully treat these conditioned aversive responses (Burish & Lyles, 1983). The acute and chronic pain associated with cancer and its treatment has been an additional focus of cancer research and practice (Jay, Elliott, & Varni, 1986). Psychological pain control interventions, including hypnosis, guided imagery, relaxation, biofeedback, cognitive-behavioral methods, and operant approaches have been used with considerable success with cancer patients (Burish & Lyles, 1983).

In studies of the psychological aspects of cancer patients' adaptation to their disease (Koocher, 1986), it has been shown that stressful aspects of some forms of cancer include uncertain prognosis, the aversive nature of treatment, economic burden, and debilitating chronicity of the disease. In one study of the psychological adjustment of patients surviving Hodgkin's disease (Cella & Tross, 1986), greater psychological dysfunction was found in cancer patients than in physically healthy adults (control subjects) even when treatment was successful. For this and other reasons, cancer support groups have come to play a major role in the treatment of cancer. Efforts are underway to ensure that male patients, those from lower socioeconomic groups, and minority patients are better represented in these cancer support groups (Taylor, Falke, Shaptaw, & Lichtman, 1986).

Compliance

Patient compliance to medical regimens has been a major area of emphasis in behavioral medicine and health psychology. Compliance issues are particularly important in the treatment of chronic diseases in which life-style behaviors and self-care activities are emphasized (e.g., CHD, diabetes, hypertension, etc.).

There have been at least three different conceptual models or approaches used to define compliance problems. First, the traditional medical model focuses on the patient as noncompliant and searches for characteristics that differentiate noncompliant patients from compliant ones, usually without much success (Stunkard, 1979). Second, the behavioral perspective emphasizes what people do (i.e., target behaviors and operant contingencies) rather than personal attributes, and it uses operant learning approaches to increase the frequency of compliance behaviors (Epstein & Cluss, 1982). Third, the self-regulation perspective is based on the assumption that a number of factors influence compliance, including the individual's representation of his or her illness, coping strategies, self-competence, and the quality of the patient's relationship with the health care provider (Nerenz & Leventhal, 1983).

The patient–doctor relationship exerts a powerful influence on compliance (DiMatteo & DiNicola, 1982; Suchman & Matthews, 1988). Over 3 decades ago, Szasz and Hollender (1956) outlined three specific role structures or models that define patient–doctor relationships: (a) active doctor—passive patient, (b) guiding doctor—cooperative patient, and (c) mutual participation model. More recently, research has focused on specific characteristics of the patient–doctor relationship that influence compliance (DiMatteo & DiNicola, 1982).

Compliance also involves ongoing decision making both on the part of the patient and the health care provider. Various theoretical decision-making models have been developed and applied to the compliance issue (Janis & Mann, 1977; Janis & Rodin, 1979). Based on these theoretical concepts, a "balance sheet" procedure has been developed to facilitate rational decision making by systematically analyzing possible consequences of different response alternatives.

One of the most widely used intervention strategies for promoting adherence is derived from operant learning and cognitive social learning theories (e.g., Epstein & Cluss, 1982). These techniques have been used to improve adherence rates in the medication management of hypertension, dietary management and prevention of CHD, and self-care activities in the treatment of diabetes mellitus, just to name a few. This area of behavioral medicine represents one of health psychology's major contributions to the health care field today.

TRAINING ISSUES IN HEALTH PSYCHOLOGY

Defining Skill Areas

At the Arden House Conference on Graduate Education in Health Psychology held in New York in 1982 (Belar, 1988; Stone, 1983), leaders in health psychology made several recommendations for developing training opportunities at both the pre- and postdoctoral level. Although Matarazzo (1987c) questioned whether health psychology is a specialty, there was a consensus expressed at that 1982 conference that training in health psychology should begin with education in the broad discipline of generic psychology upon which such specialization could be built. For such careers, it was recommended that psychologists receive additional specialized training in health policy; health care systems and organizations; as well as in the social, psychological, and biological bases of health and illness. The Arden House Conference participants were unanimous in their endorsement of the scientist–practitioner model and emphasized that practitioner training should also include a broad range of clinical and research skills as well as exposure to a wide range of psychopathology, particularly considering the prevalance and severity of various psychiatric disorders in medical patient populations.

In planning training opportunities for health psychologists, leaders in the field have had to confront several important and challenging issues. For example, it has been acknowledged that such training should include opportunities for trainees to develop and maintain their own identities as psychologists while at the same time developing an ability to work with and understand members of other disciplines (Agras, 1982; Altman, 1988). In addition, the issue of the depth versus breadth of knowledge in the psychologist's "second" area of expertise (e.g., cardiology, oncology, immunology, etc.) have been widely discussed. For instance, Levy (1988) and others have argued that research training needs to extend beyond traditional core areas of experimental and clinical psychology to include biomedical science areas such as immunology, endocrinology, cardiovascular pathophysiology, and neurosciences without compromising the traditional field of generic psychology, because researchers in behavioral medicine typically develop scientific identities in more than one field.

Interdisciplinary Training Settings

The crossfertilization between psychology, epidemiology, health education, nursing, public health, and other disciplines has been increasingly fostered in the design and implementation of training programs in health psychology and behavioral medicine (Altman, 1988; Altman & Green, 1988). For example, some training programs in behavioral medicine are housed administratively within schools of public health (Best & Proctor, 1988). Similarly, opportunities are becoming available for doctoral-level training in psychosocial nursing that emphasizes psychosocial and behavioral factors in health care (O'Connell, 1988). Some of the issues relevant to all of these professional health care disciplines include cost containment in health care, the impact of health maintenance organizations, and the efficacy of intervention methods ranging from individual life-style change to worksite and community-wide programs.

Training Experimental Health Psychologists

Basic biobehavioral research forms an important core component of the contribution of health psychology to behavioral health and behavioral medicine. For this reason, predoctoral and postdoctoral graduate training opportunities have been developed in the areas of physiological, psychopharmacological, and experimental psychology as they apply to issues of health and illness. For instance, at the Oregon Health Sciences University in the Department of Medical Psychology, graduate students in the National Institutes of Health (NIH)-funded behavioral cardiology training program receive formal training in the physiological and anatomical aspects of the cardiovascular system, lipid metabolism, nutrition, biochemistry, and the pathophysiology of coronary artery disease. This training effectively prepares students for research careers in both basic and applied aspects of behavioral cardiology (Istvan & Matarazzo, 1987). Health psychologists are receiving similarly patterned training for careers in the neurosciences in that same department in Oregon, in behavioral oncology at Sloan-Kettering, in behavioral immunology at the University of Pittsburgh, and in a growing number of other similar programs.

Expanding Clinical Training Opportunities

Clinical psychologists trained within the guidelines of the 1947 scientist–practitioner (Boulder) model are particularly well suited to make significant contributions in both the basic research and applied areas of health psychology. Their training and experience in the areas of psychopathology, personality, human life-span development, behavior change, human motivation, and psychological assessment and intervention prepare them well to utilize the accumulation of new knowledge in their applied work in the growing numbers of present and potential areas of health psychology discussed in the previous sections of this chapter. Over 3 decades ago, Matarazzo (1955a, 1955b) outlined some of the training opportunities for clinical psychologists working in medical settings. Hartman (1981) repeated these earlier observations and emphasized that psychological intervention techniques applied to the treatment and prevention of medical disorders must be based on rigorous scientific methodology and, therefore, they benefit from the clinical-experimental perspective and expertise of the clinical psychologist. The training that clinical psychologists receive in research design, methodology, and quantitative analysis is being applied to empirical questions pertaining to primary prevention, mechanisms in the etiology of physical dysfunction, the effects of intervention procedures, and a host of other investigative issues in health psychology.

Opportunities for training in applied health psychology have expanded dramatically in recent years. According to a survey by Belar, Wilson, and Hughes (1982), most American Psychological Association–approved doctoral and internship training programs were then offering minimal coursework, practica, and research training in health psychology. A PhD degree in health psychology per se was granted in only three programs: the University of California at San Francisco, Albert Einstein College of Medicine, and the Uniformed Services University of the Health Sciences in Bethesda, Maryland. The most frequently reported training opportunities in health psychology cited in the Belar et al. survey were within portions of clinical psychology programs. Nevertheless, during the past decade, the number of doctoral programs with some specialty training in health psychology has increased dramatically just as has the number of pre- and postdoctoral internship programs with health psychology training (Istvan & Hatton, 1987).

Postdoctoral Training

Most experts agree that the interdisciplinary aspect of training in health psychology should occur at the postdoctoral level after the trainee has received a solid grounding in the traditional discipline of generic psychology (Altman & Green, 1988; Levy, 1988). In this regard, Matarazzo (1987a), albeit acknowledging some remaining problems (Matarazzo, 1987c), and others (Sheridan, Matarazzo, Boll, Perry, Weiss, & Belar, 1988) have advocated a 2-year "generalist" model of postdoctoral training focusing both on a general orientation to health service delivery and on specific proficiency areas whereby the student can interact with members from a number of other health care subspecialties. Matarazzo (1987a) has emphasized that it is in the interdisciplinary health care setting, whether in a hospital, clinic, worksite, school, or other location, that professionally more mature postdoctoral students can acquire the knowledge, skills, techniques, and experience necessary to prepare to become independent licensed practitioners. Unfortunately, there are too few such training sites currently available and there is need for qualified mentors who are themselves trained in the applications of generic psychology in the interdisciplinary fields of behavioral health and behavioral medicine.

RECENT DEVELOPMENTS IN HEALTH PSYCHOLOGY

The following are just a few representative developments that have taken place in the evolution of health psychology during the past 20 years:

Neuropsychology and Health

There has been considerable growth in the subspecialty of neuropsychology and in its relationship to health psychology and behavioral medicine. Several factors have contributed to the recent growth and diversification of clinical neuropsychology, including the increase of knowledge regarding the fundamental bases of cognition, attentional processes, and memory (Bornstein, Costa, & Matarazzo, 1986) as well as improved batteries of tests for neuropsychological assessment, such as the Halstead-Reitan Battery. The increasing availability of CAT scans, magnetic resonance imaging (MRI) technologies, and positron emission tomography (PET) scans have led to an expansion of the role of neuropsychologists in the assessment and treatment of a variety of conditions involving organic brain impairment (Costa, Matarazzo, & Bornstein 1986).

Neuropsychologists have developed a better understanding of the cognitive deficits associated with several neurological conditions including Huntington's disease, multiple sclerosis, Parkinson's disease, head injuries, and the sequelae of alcohol and drug abuse. In addition, neuropsychological evaluations have been found to be helpful in the assessment of cognitive factors influencing compliance by the head-injured patient, health promotion, and life-style change. For this reason, in addition to themselves working on cognitive retraining of brain-damaged patients, neuropsychologists are collaborating with health psychologists in projects aimed at reducing CHD risk, enhancing compliance in the treatment of such conditions as diabetes mellitus and chronic obstructive pulmonary disease (COPD), and in studying newer forms of renal dialysis such as continuous ambulatory peritoneal dialysis (CAPD), which requires more direct patient participation.

Neuropsychology is branching out in other new directions, such as in the investigation of the neuropsychological correlates of several nonneurological diseases including Cushing's, systemic lupus, COPD, renal failure, and hypertension (Drudge et al., 1986; Tartar, Edwards, & Van Thiel, 1986). In addition, new computer-assisted techniques are being studied in the remediation of memory problems, spatial neglect, and other cognitive deficits associated with brain injury and its sequelae (Drudge et al., 1986; Gouvier et al., 1986). Moreover, teams of experts such as Heaton and Pendleton (1981) have begun to examine the use of neuropsychological test data in predicting everyday functioning; for example, whether or not a certain patient should be allowed to drive, cook alone, follow a complex medication regimen, and so on.

Until recently, there was almost no empirical data directly addressing questions regarding which deficits on which tasks affect which daily activities.

Pediatric Issues

Pediatric psychology is playing a major role both in the promotion of health as well as in the management of the psychosocial aspects of illness in children (Carter, Bendell, & Matarazzo, 1985). Regarding primary prevention, behavioral health experts have recommended at least two avenues in which pediatric psychologists can play major roles in promoting behavioral health in children: (a) the demonstration of the long-term impact of interventions on children's health-related behavior, and (b) a greater involvement in the political process at the local, state, and national levels to influence the shaping of health policies regarding children. It has long been recognized that the origins of health habits and practices are in childhood if not even in utero. It is obvious that much of our preventive efforts must be directed at those factors influencing the development of health-related behaviors in children and youth. Margolis, McLeroy, Runyan, and Kaplan (1983) exemplify this approach in their "ecological model" of coronary-prone behavior in children in which they examine psychosocial and cultural factors that influence the development of Type A behavior pattern (including achievement striving, social comparison processes, attribution, competition, role demands, reward systems, time orientation, and industrialization). An understanding of child developmental issues appears to be essential in the investigation of factors involved in the development of healthy versus risk-enhancing behavior patterns in childhood as well as those factors that influence how a child copes with chronic illness and medical interventions (Carter et al., 1985).

Movement Toward Subspecialty Status

As health psychology has continued to develop, some of the early steps involved in its movement toward subspecialty status in the field of professional psychology have already occurred, including the creation of its own national and international associations and the development of its own journals for information dissemination. However, health psychology has not yet been acknowledged as a subspecialty of psychology by its peers in psychology or by colleagues in other professions through mechanisms of designation, accreditation, and licensure. At present, many physi-

cians do not differentiate health psychology from clinical psychology or neuropsychology. Indeed, even within psychology itself, there is considerable overlap among these areas. There are those who even avow that health psychology still currently represents only the application of *generic* psychology to the understanding and promotion of health and prevention of illness (Matarazzo, 1987c); that is, that neither health psychology nor any other area of psychology has yet attained subspecialty status, although some are moving rapidly in that direction.

Evolving Theoretical Perspectives

Both microsystem and macrosystem theoretical models have been recommended to facilitate the development of life-style-change interventions in behavioral medicine and behavioral health. Microsystem models for influencing health behavior focus on individual learning (associative and social) as well as the role of vicarious, symbolic, and self-regulatory processes in the acquisition of new behaviors. On the other hand, macrosystem approaches focus on political, economic, and sociocultural factors that influence health-related behavior patterns of individuals and whole segments of the population. It has been suggested that health psychologists need to apply their efforts on both levels, focusing both on the individual, as Matarazzo (1982, 1984b) has emphasized, and on societal influences and political decision-making processes, as Williams (1982) has discussed.

Leaders in health psychology have continued to advocate a strengthening of the theoretical basis for interventions that attempt to modify life-styles (e.g., Evans, 1988; Leventhal, Meyer, & Nerenz, 1980; Matarazzo, 1984a; Miller, 1987; Stone, 1987). For example, many of the early studies of patient compliance were designed to identify factors that predict compliance despite the absence of a comprehensive theory capable of generating specific hypotheses for integrating numerous and often inconsistent findings. During the past decade, a number of theoretical advances have been made, such as Leventhal's self-regulation model (Leventhal, Zimmerman, & Gutmann, 1984) discussed earlier in this chapter, and Weinstein's recent theory regarding the precaution adoption process (Weinstein, 1988). The construct of self-efficacy (Bandura, 1977, 1982) is another heuristically important theoretical model that has had numerous applications in health psychology within the context of habit change and relapse prevention.

Psychology's several learning theories (i.e., operant, respondent, associative, social, cognitive-social, etc.) have markedly influenced the development of health psychology and behavioral medicine (Agras, 1982; Gentry, 1984; Hunt & Matarazzo, 1982). In their theoretical conceptualization of the psychology of smoking, for instance, Hunt, Matarazzo, Weiss, and Gentry (1979), in considering the most promising methods of intervention, defined the smoking habit as a stable pattern of behavior marked by automaticity, unawareness, associative learning, and reinforcement. As described earlier, a number of behavior therapists also have applied the principles of operant, associative, and social learning to the study of a variety of habit patterns related to compliance, rehabilitation, and chronic pain.

The perspective of human development or life-span psychology (infancy to old age) also has made an important contribution to health psychology. For example, preventive therapeutic programs have been designed to help people cope with difficult transition periods or life events such as marriage, childbirth, graduation, employment, retirement, and so forth (Sank & Shapiro, 1979). Bibace and Walsh (1979) have noted that clinical-developmental psychologists and family-practice physicians share a common interest in normal human (life-span) development. This perspective is also consistent with the formulation of intervention programs designed for particular age groups such as adolescents, elderly, and retirement-age adults (Lebray, 1979). The evolution of the developmental life-span perspective has helped to promote and define productive avenues of research and practice in health psychology.

Similarly, health psychologists are focusing more attention on family systems theory and *family-based* interventions to enhance their understanding of health behavior and to promote life-style changes associated with the treatment and prevention of physical disorders. Examples of family-oriented interventions may be found in community-based primary prevention programs such as the Family Heart–Alternative Diet Study at the Oregon Health Sciences University (Matarazzo et al., 1982), behavioral programs aimed at weight control (e.g., Brownell, Heckerman, Westlake, Hayes, & Monti, 1978), and cardiac rehabilitation (Hoebel, 1976).

FUTURE DIRECTIONS

The fields of behavioral medicine and behavioral health will provide growing numbers of opportunities for psychologists from many areas of generic psychology (e.g., experimental, clinical, social, developmen-

tal, physiological). As detailed previously (Matarazzo, 1982, 1984a, 1987b), every subspecialty of academic, scientific, and professional-clinical psychology has within its ranks psychologists with the potential to contribute to the many emerging frontiers of both behavioral health and behavioral medicine.

Interdisciplinary Collaboration

Psychologists working in academic, medical, and industrial settings who are interested in charting new directions in behavioral health and behavioral medicine have available numerous opportunities to teach, conduct research, and provide direct care in collaboration with other groups of professional colleagues. There is every indication that these collaborative arrangements will continue to grow, prosper, and extend into other areas of preventive medicine and health care. The settings in which this collaboration is taking place will continue to expand beyond the university hospitals and clinics into worksites, schools, military institutions, Veterans Administration medical centers, senior citizen centers, and other community agencies. To such programs, psychologists bring to bear their expertise, knowledge, and skills in the many areas that comprise the core of generic psychology, including an understanding of the biological, social, cognitive, and affective bases of behavior, as well as expertise in research design and methodology and behavior-change modalities.

Changes in disease epidemiology will also continue to impact health psychology as well as the entire health care field. Acquired immunodeficiency syndrome (AIDS) is a highly visible case in point. During the past decade, the AIDS epidemic has captured the attention of growing numbers of health experts and health policy makers across the country and throughout the world. As of September 1986, over 26,000 cases of AIDS among Americans had been reported by the Center for Disease Control, and 56% of these cases were reported to be deceased (Coates et al., 1987). This number had increased threefold (to 78,000) by November 1988. Among adults, approximately two thirds of these 1986 recorded cases have occurred among gay and bisexual men, another 17% among intravenous (IV) drug users, and 8% among gay men who are also IV drug users. Health psychologists are joining the ranks of many other health care disciplines that are actively involved in public health efforts to prevent the further spread of this tragic and fatal disease (Coates, Temoshok, & Mandel, 1984; Coates et al., 1987; Kelly & St. Lawrence, 1988).

Organizational and Institutional Changes

Recent developments suggest that medical school and hospital psychologists continue to represent dominant forces in the fields of behavioral medicine and behavioral health inasmuch as they outnumber other behavioral and social scientists working in such settings and, as licensed health professionals in their states and as voting members of medical staff at some hospitals, they have the unique capacity both to provide direct services to patients and also to do research on health and illness behavior.

Within medical schools in particular, it is possible that there will most likely be a temporary stabilization of growth in the number of psychologists (as well as other specialists) employed on medical school faculties due to present-day consolidations occurring in the health care field, affecting medical schools, community hospitals, and other medical training facilities across the country. Following this temporary plateau, the number of medical school psychologists should again begin to increase. In addition, unlike the 1950–1980 era, which witnessed psychologists administratively housed in departments of psychiatry, recent academic employment patterns suggest that increasingly more medical school psychologists very likely will find themselves housed administratively in departments of pediatrics, medicine, and neurology, as well as in their own departments of medical (or health) psychology. Given the acceleration in the requests for consultations to university hospitals and community hospital-based psychologists from physicians, one also may expect an increase in the number of autonomous departments of psychology in community and university hospitals and in schools of medicine.

Psychotherapeutic Approaches

The 1960s and 1970s witnessed the growth of behavioral and cognitive-behavioral approaches to therapy, along with a proliferation of group and family therapy modalities, as traditional psychoanalytic and psychodynamic therapies took on briefer versions and became integrated with an empirically based understanding of human developmental systems and information processing. Recent trends suggest that traditional individual and group psychotherapy will continue to prosper, although with fewer numbers of sessions per patient on the average. Additionally, well-organized psychoeducational and behavioral group intervention programs will be increasingly utilized in such areas as weight control, smoking cessa-

tion, pain management, cardiac rehabilitation, substance abuse, and stress management. The growth of such programmatic interventions will be limited only by the creativity of health psychologists and their skill at designing well-controlled outcome research documenting the cost-effectiveness of various interventions for specific populations with particular dysfunctions or life-style problems.

Basic and Applied Research

Among the many exciting areas of research in health psychology, investigations of the relationship between personality and disease will continue. The designs and methodologies used in these studies are becoming more sophisticated. For example, in the study of psychological risk factors, investigators are attempting to meet traditionally difficult to satisfy epidemiologic criteria for the consistency, specificity, and reproducibility of the variables used in studying relationships between psychosocial factors and disease.

The development of more sophisticated measurement tools will be an important part of future research in health psychology. Current developments in the measurement of cardiovascular, neuroendocrine, and immune processes are encouraging further investigation of the links between personality and disease. Several psychophysiological measures have been used in the study of cardiovascular reactivity (e.g., heart rate, blood pressure), pain (EMG), and stress response (skin conduction, potential, resistance, impedence, and temperature responses). Furthermore, the development of various self-report and behavioral assessment instruments has played a major role in advancing research and clinical practice in the areas of pain management, treatment of anxiety disorders, stress management, coronary disease prevention, cardiac rehabilitation, weight control, smoking cessation, and others.

The study of stress and coping will continue to be another major area of investigation in health psychology. This area of study appears to have considerable application to the investigation of the links between personality and pathophysiological processes involved in cardiovascular disease (coronary-prone behavior, hostility), various forms of cancer, and immune dysfunction. Coping responses will continue to be scrutinized as they relate to the development of stress management intervention procedures and adaptational outcomes such as morale, social functioning, and somatic indexes of health and illness. More work is needed in the development of a theoretical model for the study of coping, as well as in the creation of methods for assessing coping patterns. Studies are needed to determine how various combinations of coping strategies in certain situations affect particular adaptational outcomes. A "science of coping" will continue to evolve within the context of the study of coping responses, personality patterns, stressful events, social support, and cognitive appraisal in relation to health and illness.

Public Policy Issues

As psychologists seek to become more active in the overall health care arena, increasing numbers of members of our profession are also becoming more involved in *public policy* issues. DeLeon (1988) has long advocated that the discipline of psychology accept more responsibility and involvement in the formation of public policy and related political processes as a sign of our maturity as a profession and, more important, for the public good.

Public policy activity encourages health psychologists to apply their knowledge base to those health issues of most relevance to our society. Such activity also prompts health professionals to develop a clearer definition of health and a better understanding of the health needs of specific segments of the general population (e.g., women, ethnic groups, specific patient populations, and so forth). Although philosophers, theologians, scientists, and other great thinkers have been attempting to define health since ancient times, they have not yet been able to formulate a clear definition of the concept other than suggesting that it is the absence of disease (Stone, 1987). The work of Antonovsky (1979) and cost-utility models of Kaplan (1988) are two examples of scientific inquiries in health psychology that are contributing to the development of a clearer formulation of the concept of health.

To accomplish public policy goals, the symbiotic relationship between the laboratory and the clinic will continue to provide a significant basis for growth and development of health psychology, both in the public and private sectors (Miller, 1987). Clinical work and public policy issues will continue to suggest new problems for laboratory studies and, in turn, the research laboratories will provide empirically based knowledge that can be applied in clinical settings in dealing with public policy issues.

In response to requests to address health-related public policy issues, health psychologists are becoming more involved in applying the principles of generic psychology to the health problems of specific

segments of the overall population, including women (Jansen, 1987), different racial and ethnic groups (Anderson & Jackson, 1987), children (Kurz, 1987), and the elderly (Gatz, Pearson, & Weicker, 1987; Rapp, Parisi, Walsh, & Wallace, 1988). The unique as well as common health care needs and characteristics of these segments of the general population need to be further assessed, as well as the unique patterns of their interactions with the health care system and the consequences of these interactions for both their physical and mental health. For instance, there is considerable collaborative potential between health psychologists and experts in adult development and *aging* for enhancing our understanding of attitudinal factors, health policy issues, prevention activities, and service provision in this important area of geriatric health care.

Recently, the Global Medium-Term Programme of the World Health Organization listed four ways in which psychologists can play a role in the interdisciplinary health promotion field: (a) develop mental health policies, (b) improve our understanding and application of psychosocial factors in health promotion, (c) develop more effective treatment and prevention programs in controlling alcohol and drug abuse, and (d) create prevention and treatment programs for mental and neurological disorders (Holtzman, Evans, Kennedy, & Iscoe, 1987). Supported by such a mandate, psychologists will be increasingly involved in the development of new and innovative service delivery systems, some emphasizing primary mental health care, others devising new behavioral approaches for health promotion and rehabilitation, and still others working in school and industrial settings and in community-wide programs to improve the quality of life.

SUMMARY AND CONCLUSIONS

Health psychology has flourished in the context of the interdisciplinary fields of behavioral health and behavioral medicine. As an application of generic psychology, it has grown within the emerging network of communication and collaborative activity among a number of behavioral, social, and biomedical disciplines that characterize the fields of behavioral health and behavioral medicine. As Gentry (1984) pointed out, the essential nature of behavioral medicine (health) is the integration of empirical knowledge from interdisciplinary research. As such, it functions as a "crucible" providing a forum for many disciplines to collaborate in an emerging network of communication (Agras, 1982), which recognizes the reciprocal nature of relationships between biological, social, and psychological factors in health and illness.

Considering the current economic and political climate in our country, reflected in the federal mandate to reduce government spending and ongoing reformations taking place in the health care industry, both the private sector (business and industry) and governmental agencies are looking to health psychologists and offering them financial support to encourage the application of their expertise and participation in primary prevention efforts. Not only the federal government (National Institutes of Health and National Institute of Mental Health) but corporate leaders as well are becoming increasingly concerned about maintaining the health of their employees and executives to improve the quality of life and increase productivity and profit. More businesses are welcoming psychologists and other health specialists who, for example, conduct health-screening clinics and carry out intervention programs designed to promote healthy behaviors and to prevent, alleviate, or reduce life-style risk behaviors.

World War II and later the Korean and Vietnam conflicts required that our government rehabilitate a large number of disabled veterans and help millions more reassimilate themselves into our nation's colleges and workforce. After 1945, these urgent societal needs helped to rapidly promote the development of modern clinical psychology. Recent advances in behavioral medicine and behavioral health, and revolutionary developments in the health care field have presented psychology with comparable opportunities for rapid growth as a health profession comparable to those faced by clinical psychology in the first years after World War II. The educational, scientific, and professional contributions of health psychology within the broader context of behavioral medicine and behavioral health that were reviewed in this chapter have helped psychologists emerge as full-fledged, well-respected health professionals. In the applied areas of health psychology, examples of the psychologist's expanding role in the treatment and prevention of physical illness can be found in numerous medical, school, academic, community, and workplace settings. What is now required for continued growth is that the leaders in the profession and discipline of psychology, particularly those working in hospitals, medical schools, other health care and academic institutions, as well as those in our scientific and professional societies, and those serving on our state licensing boards, recognize these opportunities and identify ways of expanding them in the service of our society.

References

Abrams, D.B., Niaura, R.S., Carey, K.B., Monti, P.M., & Binkoff, J.A. (1986). Understanding relapse and recovery in alcohol abuse. *Annals of Behavioral Medicine, 8*, 27–32.

Ader, R., & Cohen, N. (1984). Behavior and the immune system. In W.D. Gentry (Ed.), *Handbook of behavioral medicine* (pp. 117–173). New York: Guilford Press.

Agras, W.S. (1982). Behavioral medicine in the 1980s: Nonrandom connections. *Journal of Consulting and Clinical Psychology, 50*, 797–803.

Alden, L. (1980). Preventive strategies in the treatment of alcohol abuse: A review and a proposal. In P.O. Davidson & S.M. Davidson (Eds.), *Behavioral medicine: Changing health lifestyles* (pp. 256–278). New York: Brunner/Mazel.

Altman, D.G. (1988). Looking ahead: Education and training in behavioral medicine. *Annals of Behavioral Medicine, 10*, 3.

Altman, D.G., & Green, L.W. (1988). Interdisciplinary perspectives on behavioral medicine. *Annals of Behavioral Medicine, 10*, 4–7.

American Heart Association. (1986). *Heart facts*. Washington, DC: Author.

Anderson, M.P. (1988). Stress management for chronic disease: An overview. In M.L. Russell (Ed.), *Stress management for chronic disease* (pp. 3–13). Elmsford, NY: Pergamon Press.

Anderson, N.B., & Jackson, J.S. (1987). Race, ethnicity, and health psychology: The example of essential hypertension. In G.C. Stone, S.M. Weiss, J.D. Matarazzo, N.E. Miller, J. Rodin, C.D. Belar, M.J. Follick, & J.E. Singer (Eds.), *Health psychology: A discipline and a profession* (pp. 265–284). Chicago: University of Chicago Press.

Antonovsky, A. (1979). *Health, stress, and coping*. San Francisco, CA: Jossey-Bass.

Arkin, R., Roemhild, H., Johnson, H., Luepker, R., & Murray, D. (1981). The Minnesota smoking prevention program. *Journal of School Health, 51*, 611–616.

Bakal, D.A. (1979). *Psychology and medicine*. New York: Springer.

Bandura, A. (1977). Self-efficacy: Toward a unifying theory of behavioral change. *Psychological Review, 84*, 191–215.

Bandura, A. (1982). Self-efficacy mechanisms in human agency. *American Psychologist, 37*, 122–147.

Belar, C.D. (1988). Education in behavioral medicine: Perspectives from psychology. *Annals of Behavioral Medicine, 10*, 11–14.

Belar, C.D., Wilson, E., & Hughes, H. (1982). Health psychology training in doctoral psychology programs. *Health Psychology, 1*, 289–299.

Belloc, N.B. (1973). Relationship of health practices and mortality. *Preventive Medicine, 2*, 67–81.

Berg, R.L. (1976). The high cost of self-deception. *Preventive Medicine, 5*, 483–495.

Berkowitz, A., & Perkins, H.W. (1988). Personality characteristics of alcoholics: A review. *Journal of Consulting and Clinical Psychology, 56,* 206–209.

Best, J.A., & Proctor, S.P. (1988). Behavioral medicine training from a public health perspective. *Annals of Behavioral Medicine, 10,* 19–22.

Bibace, R., & Walsh, M.D. (1979). Clinical developmental psychologists in family practice settings. *Professional Psychology, 10,* 441–451.

Billings, A.G., & Moos, R.H. (1981). The role of coping responses and social resources in attenuating the stress of life events. *Journal of Behavioral Medicine, 4,* 139–157.

Blanchard, E.B., & Andrasik, F. (1985). *Management of chronic headaches.* Elmsford, NY: Pergamon Press.

Blanchard, E.B., Andrasik, F., Neff, D.F., Arena, J.G., Ahles, T.A., Jurish, S.E., Pallmeyer, T.P., Saunders, N.L., Teders, S.J., Barron, K.D., & Rodichok, L.D. (1982). Biofeedback and relaxation training with three kinds of headaches: Treatment effect and their prediction. *Journal of Consulting and Clinical Psychology, 50,* 562–575.

Blaney, P.H. (1985). Psychological considerations in cancer. In N. Schneiderman & J.T. Tapp (Eds.), *Behavioral medicine: The biopsychosocial approach* (pp. 533–563). Hillsdale, NJ: Lawrence Erlbaum Associates.

Blumenthal, J.A., & Emery, C.F. (1988). Rehabilitation of patients following myocardial infarction. *Journal of Consulting and Clinical Psychology, 56,* 374–381.

Bornstein, R.A., Costa, L.D., & Matarazzo, J.D. (1986). Interfaces between neuropsychology and health psychology. In S.B. Filskov & T.J. Boll (Eds.), *Handbook of clinical neuropsychology* (Vol. 2, pp. 19–41). New York: John Wiley & Sons.

Borysenko, J. (1984). Stress, coping, and the immune system. In J.D. Matarazzo, N.E. Miller, S.M. Weiss, J.A. Herd, & S.M. Weiss (Eds.), *Behavioral health: A handbook of health enhancement and disease prevention* (pp. 248–260). New York: John Wiley & Sons.

Botvin, G.J., Baker, E., Botvin, E.M., Filazzola, A.D., & Millman, R.B. (1984). Prevention of alcohol misuse through the development of personal and social competence: A pilot study. *Journal of Studies on Alcohol, 45,* 550–552.

Botvin, G.J., Eng, A., & Williams, C.L. (1980). Preventing the onset of cigarette smoking through life skills training. *Preventive Medicine, 9,* 135–143.

Brantley, P.J., Dietz, L.S., McKnight, G.T., Jones, G.N., & Tulley, R. (1988). Convergence between the Daily Stress Inventory and endocrine measures of stress. *Journal of Consulting and Clinical Psychology, 56,* 549–551.

Braucht, G.N., & Braucht, B. (1984). Prevention of problem drinking among youth: Evaluation of educational strategies. In P.M. Miller & T.D. Nirenberg (Eds.), *Prevention of alcohol abuse* (pp. 253–279). New York: Plenum Press.

Brownell, K.D., Heckerman, C.L., Westlake, R.S., Hayes, S.C., & Monti, P.M. (1978). The effects of couples training and partner cooperativeness in the behavioral treatment of obesity. *Behaviour Research and Therapy, 16,* 323–333.

Burish, T.G., & Carey, M.P. (1986). Conditioned aversive responses in cancer chemotherapy patients: Theoretical and developmental analysis. *Journal of Consulting and Clinical Psychology, 54,* 593–600.

Burish, T.G., & Lyles, J.N. (1983). Coping with the adverse effects of cancer treatments. In T.G. Burish & L.A. Bradley (Eds.), *Coping with chronic disease: Research and applications* (pp. 159–190). New York: Academic Press.

Cacioppo, J.T., & Petty, R.E. (Eds.). (1982). *Perspectives in cardiovascular psychophysiology.* New York: Guilford Press.

Califano, J.A., Jr. (1979). *Smoking and health: A report of the Surgeon General.* Washington, DC: Superintendent of Documents, U.S. Government Printing Office, Stock No. 017-000-0218-0.

Carmody, T.P., Istvan, J.A., Matarazzo, J.D., Connor, S.L., & Connor, W.E. (1986). Applications of social learning theory in the promotion of heart-healthy diets: The Family Heart Study dietary intervention model. *Health Education Research, 1,* 13–27.

Carmody, T.P., Loew, D.E., Hall, R.G., Breckenridge, J.S., Breckenridge, J.N., & Hall, S.M. (1988). Nicotine polacrilex: Clinic-based strategies with chronically-ill smokers. *Journal of Psychoactive Drugs, 20,* 269–274.

Carmody, T.P., Matarazzo, J.D., & Istvan, J.A. (1987). Promoting adherence to heart-healthy diets: A review of the literature. *Journal of Compliance in Health Care, 2,* 105–124.

Carter, B.D., Bendell, D., & Matarazzo, J.D. (1985). Behavioral health: Focus on preventive child health behavior. In A.R. Zeiner, D. Bendell, & C.E. Walker (Eds.), *Health psychology: Treatment and research issues* (pp. 1–61). New York: Plenum Press.

Cella, D.F., & Tross, S. (1986). Psychological adjustment to survival from Hodgkin's Disease. *Journal of Consulting and Clinical Psychology, 54,* 616–622.

Chesney, M.A. (1988). The evolution of coronary-prone behavior. *Annals of Behavioral Medicine, 10,* 43–45.

Chesney, M.A. & Rosenman, R.H. (Eds.). (1985). *Anger and hostility in cardiovascular and behavioral disorders.* Washington, DC: Hemisphere.

Coates, T.J., Stall, R., Mandel, J.S., Boccellari, A., Sorensen, J.L., Morales, E.F., Morin, S.F., Wiley, J.A., & McKusick, L. (1987). AIDS: A psychosocial research agenda. *Annals of Behavioral Medicine, 9,* 21–28.

Coates, T.J., Temoshok, L., & Mandel, J. (1984). Psychosocial research is essential to understanding and treating AIDS. *American Psychologist, 39,* 1309–1314.

Coates, T.J., & Thoresen, C.E. (1981). Treating obesity in children and adolescents: Is there any hope? In J.M. Ferguson & C.B. Taylor (Eds.), *The comprehensive handbook of behavioral medicine* (Vol. 2, pp. 204–231). New York: Sprectrum.

Cohen, S. (1982). Methods of intervention. In *Prevention, intervention and treatment: Concerns and models* (pp.

127–143). Washington, DC: U.S. Government Printing Office.

Cohen, S. (1988). Psychosocial models of the role of social support in the etiology of physical disease. *Health Psychology, 7,* 269–297.

Cohen, S., & Syme, S. (Eds.). (1985). *Social support and health.* Orlando, FL: Academic Press.

Connor, W.E., & Bristow, J.D. (Eds.). (1985). *Coronary heart disease: Prevention, complications, and treatment.* Philadelphia: JB Lippincott.

Connor, W.E., & Connor, S.L. (1985). The dietary prevention and treatment of coronary heart disease. In W.E. Connor & J.D. Bristow (Eds.), *Coronary heart disease* (pp. 43–64). Philadelphia: J B Lippincott.

Contrada, R.J., & Krantz, D.S. (1988). Stress, reactivity, and Type A behavior: Current status and future directions. *Annals of Behavioral Medicine, 10,* 64–70.

Costa, L.D., Matarazzo, J.D., & Bornstein, R.A. (1986). Issues in graduate and postgraduate training in clinical neuropsychology. In S.B. Filskov & T.J. Boll (Eds.), *Handbook of clinical neuropsychology* (Vol. 2, pp. 652–668). New York: John Wiley & Sons.

DeLeon, P.H. (1988). Public policy and public service: Our professional duty. *American Psychologist, 43,* 309–315.

Derogatis, L.R. (1986). Psychology in cancer medicine: A perspective and overview. *Journal of Consulting and Clinical Psychology, 54,* 632–638.

Diller, L., Ben-Yishay, Y., Gerstman, L., et al. (1974). *Studies in cognition and hemiplegia.* New York: Institute of Rehabilitation Medicine.

DiMatteo, M.R., & DiNicola, D.D. (1982). *Achieving patient compliance: The psychology of the medical practitioner's role.* Elmsford, NY: Pergamon Press.

Dobson, K.S. (1988). *Handbook of cognitive–behavioral therapies.* New York: Guilford Press.

Drudge, O.W., Rosen, J.C., Peyser, J.M., & Pieniadz, J. (1986). Behavioral and emotional problems and treatment in chronically brain-impaired adults. *Annals of Behavioral Medicine, 8,* 9–14.

Ehrenwald, J. (1976). *The history of psychotherapy: From healing magic to encounter.* New York: Jason Aronson.

Engel, G.L. (1977). The need for a new medical model: A challenge for biomedicine. *Science, 196,* 130–136.

Engstrom, D. (1984). A psychological perspective of prevention in alcoholism. In J.D. Matarazzo, N.E. Miller, S.M. Weiss, J.A. Herd, & S.M. Weiss (Eds.), *Behavioral health: A handbook of health enhancement and disease prevention* (pp. 1047–1058). New York: John Wiley & Sons.

Epstein, L.H., & Cluss, P.A. (1982). A behavioral medicine perspective on adherence to long-term medical regimens. *Journal of Consulting and Clinical Psychology, 50,* 950–971.

Evans, R.I. (1976). Smoking in children: Developing a social psychological strategy of deterrence. *Preventive Medicine, 5,* 122–127.

Evans, R.I. (1988). Health promotion—Science or ideology? *Health Psychology, 7,* 203–220.

Evans, R.I., Rozelle, R.M., Mittlemark, M.B., Hansen, W.B., Bane, A.L., & Havis, J. (1978). Deterring the onset of smoking in children: Knowledge of immediate psychological effects and coping with peer pressure, media pressure, and parent modeling. *Journal of Applied Social Psychology, 8,* 126–135.

Evans, R.I., Rozelle, R.M., Maxwell, S.E., Rainer, B.E., Dill, C.A., Guthrie, T.J., Henderson, A.H., & Hills, P.C. (1981). Social modeling films to deter smoking in adolescents: Results of a three-year field investigation. *Journal of Applied Psychology, 66,* 399–414.

Farquhar, J.W., Fortmann, S.P., Maccoby, N., Wood, P.D., Haskell, W.L., Taylor, C.B., Flora, J.A., Solomon, D.S., Rogers, T., Adler, E., Breitrose, P., Weiner, L. (1984). The Stanford Five City Project: An overview. In J.D. Matarazzo, N.E. Miller, S.M. Weiss, J.A. Herd, & S.M. Weiss (Eds.), *Behavioral health: A handbook of health enhancement and disease prevention* (pp. 1145–1165). New York: John Wiley & Sons.

Flay, B., d'Avernes, J., Best, J., Kersell, M., & Ryann, K. (1983). Cigarette smoking: Why young people do it and ways of preventing it. In P. Firestone & P. McGrath (Eds.), *Pediatric behavioral medicine* (pp. 132–183). New York: Springer-Verlag.

Flay, B., & Sobel, J. (1983). The role of mass media in preventing adolescent substance abuse. In T.J. Glynn, C.G. Leukefeld, & J.P. Ludford (Eds.), *Preventing adolescent drug abuse: Intervention strategies* (pp. 5–35). Washington, DC: U.S. Government Printing Office.

Folkman, S., & Lazarus, R.S. (1980). Coping in an adequately functioning middle-aged population. *Journal of Health and Social Behavior, 21,* 219–239.

Fordyce, W.E. (1976a). Behavioral concepts in chronic pain and illness. In P.O. Davidson (Ed.), *The behavioral management of anxiety, depression, and pain* (pp. 117–135). New York: Brunner/Mazel.

Fordyce, W.E. (1976b). *Behavioral methods for chronic pain and illness.* St. Louis: CV Mosby.

Fordyce, W.E. (1988). Pain and suffering. *American Psychologist, 43,* 276–283.

Foreyt, J.P. (1987). Issues in the assessment and treatment of obesity. *Journal of Consulting and Clinical Psychology, 55,* 677–684.

Galanter, M. (1980). Young adult social drinkers: Another group at risk? *Alcoholism: Clinical and Experimental Research, 4,* 241–242.

Gatz, M., Pearson, C., & Weicker, W. (1987). Older persons and health psychology. In G.C. Stone, S.M. Weiss, J.D. Matarazzo, N.E. Miller, J. Rodin, C.D. Belar, M.J. Follick, & J.E. Singer (Eds.), *Health psychology: A discipline and a profession* (pp. 303–320). Chicago: University of Chicago Press.

Gentry, W.D. (1984). Behavioral medicine: A new research paradigm. In W.D. Gentry (Ed.), *Handbook of behavioral medicine* (pp. 1–12). New York: Guilford Press.

Gentry, W.D., & Kobasa, S.C. (1984). Social and psychological resources mediating stress-illness relationships in humans. In W.D. Gentry (Ed.), *Handbook of behavioral medicine* (pp. 87–116). New York: Guilford Press.

Glasgow, R.E., & Lichtenstein, E. (1987). Long-term effects of behavioral smoking cessation interventions. *Behavior Therapy, 18*, 297–324.

Glasgow, R.E., & Terborg, J.R. (1988). Occupational health promotion programs to reduce cardiovascular risk. *Journal of Consulting and Clinical Psychology, 56*, 365–373.

Goodwin, D.W. (1986). Heredity and alcoholism. *Annals of Behavioral Medicine, 8*, 3–6.

Gouvier, W.D., Webster, J.S., & Warner, M.S. (1986). Treatment of acquired visuoperceptual and hemi-attentional disorders. *Annals of Behavioral Medicine, 8*, 15–20.

Green, D.E. (1977). Psychological factors in smoking. In M.E. Jarvik, J.W. Cullen, E.R. Gritz, T.M. Vogt, & L.J. West (Eds.), *Research on smoking behavior* (NIDA Research Monograph No. 17). DHEW Publication 78-581. Rockville, MD: Department of Health, Education and Welfare.

Griffen, W.O., & Printen, K.J. (Eds.), (1988). *Surgical management of morbid obesity*. New York: Marcel Dekker.

Guze, S.B., Matarazzo, J.D., & Saslow, G. (1953). A formulation of principles of comprehensive medicine with special reference to learning theory. *Clinical Psychology, 9*, 127–136.

Haggerty, R.J. (1977). Changing lifestyles to improve health. *Preventive Medicine, 6*, 276–289.

Harris, P.R. (1980). *The health consequences of smoking (the changing cigarette): A report of the Surgeon General*. Washington, DC: Superintendent of Documents, U.S. Government Printing Office, Stock No. 1980-335-339:7063.

Hartman, L.M. (1981). Clinical psychology: Emergent trends and future applications. *Journal of Clinical Psychology, 37*, 439–445.

Heaton, R. K., & Pendleton, M.G. (1981). Use of neuropsychological tests to predict adult patient's everyday functioning. *Journal of Consulting and Clinical Psychology, 49*, 807–821.

Herd, J.A. (1984). Cardiovascular disease and hypertension. In W.D. Gentry (Ed.), *Handbook of behavioral medicine* (pp. 222–281). New York: Guilford Press.

Hinckle, L.E. (1987). Stress and disease. *Social Science and Medicine, 25*, 561–566.

Hoebel, F.C. (1976). Brief family-interactional therapy in the management of cardiac-related high-risk behaviors. *Journal of Family Practice, 3*, 613–618.

Holtzman, A.D., & Turk, D.C. (Eds.). (1986). *Pain management: A handbook of psychological treatment approaches*. Elmsford, NY: Pergamon Press.

Holtzman, W.H., Evans, R.I., Kennedy, S., & Iscoe, I. (1987). Psychology and health: Contributions of psychology to the improvement of health and health care. *International Journal of Psychology, 22*, 221–267.

Hunt, W.A., & Matarazzo, J.D. (1982). Changing smoking behavior: A critique. In R.J. Gatchel, A. Baum, & J.E. Singer (Eds.), *Behavioral medicine and clinical psychology: Overlapping disciplines*. Hillsdale, NJ: Lawrence Erlbaum Associates.

Hunt, W.A., Matarazzo, J.D., Weiss, S.M., & Gentry, W.D. (1979). Associative learning, habit and health behavior. *Journal of Behavioral Medicine, 2*, 111–124.

Hurd, P.D., Johnson, C.A., Pechacek, T., Bast, L.P., Jacobs, D.R., & Luepker, R.V. (1980). Prevention of cigarette smoking in seventh-grade students. *Journal of Behavioral Medicine, 3*, 15–28.

Israel, A.C., Silverman, W.K., & Solotar, L.C. (1988). The relationship between adherence and weight loss in a behavioral treatment program for overweight children. *Behavior Therapy, 19*, 25–33.

Istvan, J.A., & Hatton, D.C. (1987). Curricula of graduate training programs in health psychology. In G.C. Stone, S.M. Weiss, J.D. Matarazzo, N.E. Miller, J. Rodin, C.D. Belar, M.J. Follick, & J.E. Singer (Eds.), *Health psychology: A discipline and a profession*. (pp. 41–59). Chicago: University of Chicago Press.

Istvan, J.A., & Matarazzo, J.D. (1987). Graduate education and training in health psychology. In B.A. Edelstein & E.S. Berler (Eds.), *Evaluation and accountability in clinical training* (pp. 135–149). New York: Plenum Press.

Janis, I.L., & Mann, L. (1977). *Decision making: A psychological analysis of conflict, choice, and commitment*. New York: Free Press.

Janis, I.L., & Rodin, J. (1979). Attribution, control and decision making: Social psychology and health care. In G.C. Stone, F. Cohen, & N.E. Adler (Eds.), *Health psychology*. San Francisco, CA: Jossey-Bass.

Jansen, M.A. (1987). Women's health issues: An emerging priority for health psychology. In G.C. Stone, S.M. Weiss, J.D. Matarazzo, N.E. Miller, J. Rodin, C.D. Belar, M.J. Follick, & J.E. Singer (Eds.), *Health psychology: A discipline and a profession* (pp. 249–264). Chicago: University of Chicago Press.

Jay, S.M., Elliott, C., & Varni, J.W. (1986). Acute and chronic pain in adults and children with cancer. *Journal of Consulting and Clinical Psychology, 54*, 601–607.

Jeffrey, R.W. (1987). Behavioral treatment of obesity. *Annals of Behavioral Medicine, 9*, 20–24.

Jeffrey, R.W. (1988). Dietary risk factors and their modification in cardiovascular disease. *Journal of Consulting and Clinical Psychology, 56*, 350–357.

Jenkins, C.D. (1988). Epidemiology of cardiovascular diseases. *Journal of Consulting and Clinical Psychology, 56*, 324–332.

Johnston, L.D., Bachman, J.G., & O'Malley, P.M. (1981). *Highlights from student drug use in America: 1975–1981*. Rockville, MD: National Institute on Drug Abuse.

Kaplan, R.M. (1988). Health-related quality of life in cardiovascular disease. *Journal of Consulting and Clinical Psychology, 56*, 382–392.

Kaplan, R.M., & Bush, J.W. (1982). Health-related quality

of life measurement for evaluation research and policy analysis. *Health Psychology, 1,* 61–80.

Kaplan, R.M., & Hartwell, S.L. (1987). Differential effects of social support and social network on physiological and social outcomes in men and women. *Health Psychology, 6,* 373–385.

Keefe, F.J., & Gil, K.M. (1986). Behavioral concepts in the analysis of chronic pain syndromes. *Journal of Consulting and Clinical Psychology, 54,* 776–783.

Kelly, J.A., & St. Lawrence, J.S. (1988). AIDS prevention and treatment: Psychology's role in the health crisis. *Clinical Psychology Review, 8,* 255–284.

Kiecolt-Glaser, J.K., & Glaser, R. (1987). Psychosocial moderators of immune function. *Annals of Behavioral Medicine, 9,* 16–20.

Knight, R.G., Godfrey, H.P.D., & Shelton, E.J. (1988). The psychological deficits associated with Parkinsons' disease. *Clinical Psychology Review, 8,* 391–410.

Kobasa, S.C. (1979). Stress life events, personality and health: An inquiry into hardiness. *Journal of Personality and Social Psychology, 37,* 1–11.

Kobasa, S.C. (1982). The Hardy Personality: Toward a social psychology of stress and health. In G.S. Sanders & J. Suls (Eds.), *Social psychology of health and illness* (pp. 3–32). Hillsdale, NJ: Lawrence Erlbaum Associates.

Koocher, G.P. (1986). Coping with a death from cancer. *Journal of Consulting and Clinical Psychology, 54,* 623–631.

Kral, J.G., & Kissileff, H.R. (1987). Surgical approaches to the treatment of obesity. *Annals of Behavioral Medicine, 9,* 15–19.

Krantz, D.S., Contrada, R.J., Hill, D.R., & Friedler, E. (1988). Environmental stress and biobehavioral antecedents of coronary heart disease. *Journal of Consulting and Clinical Psychology, 56,* 333–341.

Krantz, D.S., & Glass, D.C. (1984). Personality, behavior patterns, and physical illness: Conceptual and methodological issues. In W.D. Gentry (Ed.), *Handbook of behavioral medicine* (pp. 38–86). New York: Guilford Press.

Kuller, L., Neaton, J., Caggiula, A., & Falvo-Gerard, L. (1980). Primary prevention of heart attacks: The risk factor intervention trial. *American Journal of Epidemiology, 112,* 185–199.

Kurz, R.B. (1987). Child health psychology. In G.C. Stone, S.M. Weiss, J.D. Matarazzo, N.E. Miller, J. Rodin, C.D. Belar, M.J. Follick, & J.E. Singer (Eds.), *Health psychology: A discipline and a profession* (pp. 285–302). Chicago: University of Chicago Press.

Lebray, P.R. (1979). Geropsychology in long-term care settings. *Professional Psychology, 10,* 475–485.

Leigh, H., & Reiser, M.F. (1977). Major trends in psychosomatic medicine: The psychiatrist's evolving role in medicine. *Annals of Internal Medicine, 87,* 233–239.

Leventhal, H., Meyer, D., & Nerenz, D. (1980). The commonsense representation of illness danger. In S. Rachman (Ed.), *Medical psychology* (Vol. 2). Elmsford, NY: Pergamon Press.

Leventhal, H., Zimmerman, R., & Gutmann, M. (1984). Compliance: A self-regulation perspective. In W.D. Gentry (Ed.), *Handbook of behavioral medicine* (pp. 369–436). New York: Guilford Press.

Levy, R.I., & Moskowitz, J. (1982). Cardiovascular research: Decades of progress, a decade of promise. *Science, 217,* 121–128.

Levy, S.M. (1988). Biomedical science perspectives on behavioral medicine research training. *Annals of Behavioral Medicine, 10,* 8–10.

Lipowski, S.J. (1977). Psychosomatic medicine in the seventies: An overview. *American Journal of Psychiatry, 134,* 233–244.

Manuck, S.B., Kaplan, J.R., & Matthews, K.A. (1986). Behavioral antecedents of coronary heart disease and atherosclerosis. *Arteriosclerosis, 6,* 1–14.

Margolis, L.H., McLeroy, D.R., Runyan, C.W., & Kaplan, B.H. (1983). Type A behavior: An ecological approach. *Journal of Behavioral Medicine, 6,* 245–258.

Matarazzo, J.D. (1955a). Comprehensive medicine: A new era in medical education. *Human Organization, 14,* 4–9.

Matarazzo, J.D. (1955b). The role of the psychologist in medical education and practice: A challenge posed by comprehensive medicine. *Human Organization, 14,* 9–14.

Matarazzo, J.D. (1980). Behavioral health and behavioral medicine: Frontiers for a new health psychology. *American Psychologist, 35,* 807–817.

Matarazzo, J.D. (1982). Behavioral health's challenge to academic, scientific, and professional psychology. *American Psychologist, 37,* 1–14.

Matarazzo, J.D. (1983). Education and training in health psychology: Boulder or bolder? *Health Psychology, 2,* 73–113.

Matarazzo, J.D. (1984a). Behavioral health: An overview. In J.D. Matarazzo, N.E. Miller, S.M. Weiss, J.A. Herd, & S.M. Weiss (Eds.), *Behavioral health: A handbook of health enhancement and disease prevention* (pp. 3–40). New York: John Wiley & Sons.

Matarazzo, J.D. (1984b). Behavioral immunogens and pathogens in health and illness. In B.L. Hammonds & C.J. Scheirer (Eds.), *Psychology and health: The master lecture series* (Vol. 3; pp. 9–43). Washington, DC: American Psychological Association.

Matarazzo, J.D. (1987a). Postdoctoral education and training of service providers in health psychology. In G.C. Stone, S.M. Weiss, J.D. Matarazzo, N.E. Miller, C.D. Belar, M.J. Follick, & J.E. Singer (Eds.) *Health psychology: A discipline and a profession* (pp. 371–388). Chicago: University of Chicago Press.

Matarazzo, J.D. (1987b). Relationships of health psychology to other segments of psychology. In G.C. Stone, S.M. Weiss, J.D. Matarazzo, N.E. Miller, J. Rodin, C.D. Belar, M.J. Follick, & J.E. Singer (Eds.), *Health psychology: A discipline and a profession* (pp. 41–59). Chicago: University of Chicago Press.

Matarazzo, J.D. (1987c). There is only one psychology, no specialties, but many applications. *American Psychologist, 42,* 893–903.

Matarazzo, J.D., Connor, W.E., Fey, S.G., Carmody, T.P., Pierce, D.K., Brischetto, C.S., Baker, L.H., Connor, S.J., & Sexton, G. (1982). Behavioral cardiology with an emphasis on the Family Heart Study: Fertile ground for psychological and biomedical research. In T. Millon, C.J. Green, & R.B. Meagher (Eds.), *Handbook of clinical health psychology* (pp. 301–336). New York: Plenum Press.

Matarazzo, J.D., & Istvan, J.A. (1988). Health psychology. In G. Lindsey, R.F. Thompson, & B. Spring (Eds.), *Psychology* (3rd ed., pp. 586–605). New York: Worth.

McAlister, A.L., Perry, C., & Maccoby, N. (1979). Adolescent smoking: Onset and prevention. *Pediatrics, 63,* 650–658.

McCabe, P.M., & Schneiderman, N. (1985). Psychophysiologic reactions to stress. In N. Schneiderman & J.T. Tapp (Eds.), *Behavioral medicine: The biopsychosocial approach* (pp. 99–131). Hillsdale, NJ: Lawrence Erlbaum Associates.

Meichenbaum, D., & Jaremko, M.E. (Eds.). (1983). *Stress reduction and prevention.* New York: Plenum Press.

Meyer, A.J., Nash, J.D., McAlister, A.L., Maccoby, N., & Farquhar, J.W. (1980). Skills training in a cardiovascular health education campaign. *Journal of Consulting and Clinical Psychology, 4,* 330–334.

Meyerowitz, B.E., Heinrich, R.L., & Schag, C.C. (1983). A competency-based approach to coping with cancer. In T.G. Burish & L.A. Bradley (Eds.), *Coping with chronic disease: Research and applications* (pp. 137–190). New York: Academic Press.

Miller, A., Springen, K., Gordon, J., Murr, A., Cohn, B., Drew, L., & Barrett, T. (1988, April). Stress on the job. *Newsweek.*

Miller, N.E. (1987). Education for a lifetime of learning. In G.C. Stone, S.M. Weiss, J.D. Matarazzo, N.E. Miller, J. Rodin, C.D. Belar, M.J. Follick, & J.E. Singer (Eds.), *Health psychology: A discipline and a profession* (pp. 3–14). Chicago: University of Chicago Press.

Monjan, A. (1981). Stress and immunologic competence: Studies in animals. In R. Ader (Ed.), *Psychoneuroimmunology.* New York: Academic Press.

Moos, R.H., & Finney, J.W. (1986). The treatment setting in alcoholism program evaluation. *Annals of Behavioral Medicine, 8,* 33–39.

Morrow, G.R., & Dobkin, P.L. (1988). Anticipatory nausea and vomiting in cancer patients undergoing chemotherapy treatment: Prevalence, etiology, and behavioral interventions. *Clinical Psychology Review, 8,* 517–556.

Moskowitz, J. (1986). *The primary prevention of alcohol problems.* Berkeley, CA: Prevention Research Center.

Nathan, P.E. (1986). Outcomes of treatment for alcoholism: Current data. *Annals of Behavioral Medicine, 8,* 40–46.

Nathan, P.E. (1988). The addictive personality is the behavior of the addict. *Journal of Consulting and Clinical Psychology, 56,* 183–188.

National Institute of Alcohol Abuse and Alcoholism. (1985). *Alcoholism treatment impact on total health care utilization and costs: Analysis of the Federal Employee Health Benefit Program with Aetna Life Insurance Company.* Washington, DC: U.S. Department of Health and Human Services.

National Institutes of Health Consensus Development Panel on the Health Implications of Obesity. (1985). Health implications of obesity: National Institutes of Health consensus development conference statement. *Annals of Internal Medicine, 103,* 1073–1077.

Nerenz, D.R., & Leventhal, H. (1983). Self-regulation theory in chronic illness. In T. Burish & L. Bradley (Eds.), *Coping with chronic disease: Research and applications* (pp. 13–38). New York: Academic Press.

Ockene, J.K. (Ed.). (1986). *The pharmacologic treatment of tobacco dependence: Proceedings of the World Congress, November 4–5, 1985.* Cambridge, MA: Institute for the Study of Smoking Behavior and Policy, Harvard University.

O'Connell, K.A. (1988). Nursing perspectives on behavioral medicine training: A rose by some other name would be better. *Annals of Behavioral Medicine, 10,* 15–18.

Olbrisch, M.E. (1977). Psychotherapeutic interventions in physical health and economic efficiency. *American Psychologist, 32,* 761–777.

Pandina, R.J. (1986). Methods, problems, and trends in studies of adolescent drinking practices. *Annals of Behavioral Medicine, 8,* 20–26.

Parker, E.S., Birnbaum, I.M., Boyd, R.A., & Noble, E.P. (1980). Neuropsychologic decrements as a function of alcohol intake in male students. *Alcoholism: Clinical and Experimental Research, 48,* 129–142.

Parsons, O.A. (1986). Alcoholics' neuropsychological impairment: Current findings and conclusions. *Annals of Behavioral Medicine, 8,* 13–19.

Pennebaker, J.W., Keicolt-Glaser, J.K., & Glaser, R. (1988). Disclosure of traumas and immune function: Health implications for psychotherapy. *Journal of Consulting and Clinical Psychology, 56,* 239–245.

Perri, M.G., McAlister, D.A., Gange, J.J., Jordan, R.C., McAdoo, W.G., & Nezu, A.M. (1988). Effects of four maintenance programs on the long-term management of obesity. *Journal of Consulting and Clinical Psychology, 56,* 529–534.

Perry, C.L., Killen, B.A., Telch, M., Slinkard, M.A., & Danaher, B.K. (1980). Modifying smoking behavior of teenagers: A school-based intervention. *American Journal of Public Health, 70,* 722–725.

Perry, C.L., Klepp, K., & Shultz, J.M. (1988). Primary prevention of cardiovascular disease: Community-wide strategies for youth. *Journal of Consulting and Clinical Psychology, 56,* 358–364.

Piney, J.M. (1979). The largest preventable cause of death in the United States. *Public Health Reports, 94,* 107–108.

Pinkerton, S.S., Hughes, H., & Wenrich, W.W. (1982). *Behavioral medicine: Clinical applications.* New York: John Wiley & Sons.

Pomerleau, O.F., & Pomerleau, C.S. (Eds.). (1988). *Nicotine replacement: A critical evaluation.* New York: Alan R. Liss.

Price, R.A. (1987). Genetics of human obesity. *Annals of Behavioral Medicine, 9,* 9–14.

Prochaska, J.O., Velicer, W.F., DiClemente, C.C., & Fava, J. (1988). Measuring processes of change: Applications to the cessation of smoking. *Journal of Consulting and Clinical Psychology, 56,* 520–528.

Rapp, S.R., Parisi, S.A., Walsh, D.A., & Wallace, C.E. (1988). Detecting depression in elderly medical inpatients. *Journal of Consulting and Clinical Psychology, 56,* 509–513.

Rodin, J., Elias, M., Silberstein, L.R., & Wagner, A. (1988). Combined behavioral and pharmacologic treatment for obesity: Predictors of successful weight maintenance. *Journal of Consulting and Clinical Psychology, 56,* 399–404.

Rodin, J., & Stone, G.C. (1987). Historical highlights in the emergence of the field. In G.C. Stone, S.M. Weiss, J.D. Matarazzo, N.E. Miller, J. Rodin, C.D. Belar, M.J. Follick, & J.E. Singer (Eds.), *Health psychology: A discipline* and *a profession* (pp. 15–26). Chicago: University of Chicago Press.

Rootman, I. (1985). Preventing alcohol problems: A challenge for health promotion. *Health Education, 24,* 2–7.

Rosett, H., & Weiner, L. (1985). *Identification and prevention of fetal alcohol syndrome.* Brookline, MA: Fetal Alcohol Education Program.

Sank, L.I., & Shapiro, J.R. (1979). Case examples of the broadened role of psychology in health maintenance organizations. *Professional Psychology, 10,* 402–409.

Schaps, E., Churgin, S., Palley, C.S., Takata, B., & Cohen, A.Y. (1980). Primary prevention research: A preliminary review of program outcome studies. *International Journal of the Addictions, 15,* 657–676.

Schneider, C.J. (1987). Cost-effectiveness of biofeedback and behavioral medicine treatments: A review of the literature. *Biofeedback and Self-Regulation, 12,* 71–92.

Schneiderman, N., & Hammer, D. (1985). Behavioral medicine approaches to cardiovascular disorders. In N. Schneiderman & J.T. Tapp (Eds.), *Behavioral medicine: The biopsychosocial approach* (pp. 467–507). Hillsdale, NJ: Lawrence Erlbaum Associates.

Schneiderman, N., & Tapp, J.T. (Eds.). (1985). *Behavioral medicine: The biopsychosocial approach.* Hillsdale, NJ: Lawrence Erlbaum Associates.

Schwab, J.J., Fennell, E.B., & Warheit, G.J. (1974). The epidemiology of psychosomatic disorders. *Psychosomatics, 15,* 88–93.

Schwartz, G.E., & Weiss, S.M. (1978a). Behavioral medicine revisited: An amended definition. *Journal of Behavioral Medicine, 1,* 249–251.

Schwartz, G.E., & Weiss, S.M. (1978b). Yale Conference on Behavioral Medicine: A proposed definition and statement of goals. *Journal of Behavioral Medicine, 1,* 3–12.

Schwartz, J.L. (1987). *Review and evaluation of smoking cessation methods: The United States and Canada, 1978–1985.* Washington, DC: Division of Cancer Prevention and Control, National Cancer Institute.

Sheridan, E.P., Matarazzo, J.D., Boll, T.J., Perry, N.W., Weiss, S.M., & Belar, C.D. (1988). Postdoctoral education and training for clinical service providers in health psychology. *Health Psychology, 7,* 1–17.

Sobell, L.C., Sobell, M.B., & Nirenberg, T.D. (1988). Behavioral assessment and treatment planning with alcohol and drug abusers: A review with an emphasis on clinical application. *Clinical Psychology Review, 8,* 17–54.

Stone, G.C. (Ed.). (1983). National Working Conference on Education and Training in Health Psychology (Special Issue). *Health Psychology, 2* (Supplement).

Stone, G.C. (1987). The scope of health psychology. In G.C. Stone, S.M. Weiss, J.D. Matarazzo, N.E. Miller, J. Rodin, C.D. Belar, M.J. Follick, & J.E. Singer (Eds.), *Health psychology: A discipline and a profession* (pp. 27–40). Chicago: University of Chicago Press.

Straussner, L.A. (1985). The nature and growth of contractual EAPs. *ALMACAN, 15,* 20–23.

Stricker, E.M., & Verbalis, J.G. (1987). Biological bases of hunger and satiety. *Annals of Behavioral Medicine, 9,* 3–8.

Stuart, R.B. (1980). Weight loss and beyond: Are they taking it off? In P.O. Davidson & S.M. Davidson (Eds.), *Behavioral medicine: Changing health lifestyles* (pp. 151–194). New York: Brunner/Mazel.

Stunkard, A.J. (1979). Behavioral medicine and beyond: The example of obesity. In O.F. Pomerleau & J.P. Brady (Eds.), *Behavioral medicine: Theory and practice.* Baltimore: Williams & Wilkins.

Suchman, A.L., & Matthews, D.A. (1988). What makes the patient–doctor relationship therapeutic? *Annals of Internal Medicine 108,* 125–130.

Swisher, J.D., Warner, R.W., & Hern, J. (1972). Experimental comparison of four approaches to drug abuse prevention among 9th and 11th graders. *Journal of Counseling Psychology, 19,* 328–332.

Szasz, T., & Hollender, M. (1956). A contribution to the philosophy of medicine: The basic models of the doctor–patient relationship. *Archives of Internal Medicine, 97,* 585–592.

Tarter, R.E. (1988). Are there inherited behavioral traits that predispose to substance abuse? *Journal of Consulting and Clinical Psychology, 56,* 189–196.

Tarter, R.E., Edwards, K.L., & Van Thiel, D.H. (1986). Cerebral dysfunction consequential to medical illness: Neuropsychological perspectives and findings. *Annals of Behavioral Medicine, 8,* 3–8.

Taylor, S.E., Falke, R.L., Shaptaw, S.J., & Lichtman, R.R. (1986). Social support, support groups, and the cancer patient. *Journal of Conslting and Clinical Psychology, 54,* 608–615.

Telch, M., Killen, J., McAlister, A., Perry, C., & Maccoby, N. (1982). Long-term follow-up of a pilot project on smoking prevention with adolescents. *Journal of Behavioral Medicine, 5,* 1–8.

Tennant, F.S., Weaver, S.C., & Lewis, C.E. (1973). Outcomes of drug education: Four case studies. *Pediatrics, 52,* 246–251.

Tiffany, S.T., & Baker, T.B. (1986). Tolerance to alcohol: Psychological models and their application to alcoholism. *Annals of Behavioral Medicine, 8,* 7–12.

Tuchfeld, B.S., & Marcus, S.H. (1984). Social models of prevention in alcoholism. In J.D. Matarazzo, N.E. Miller, S.M. Weiss, J.A. Herd, & S.M. Weiss (Eds.), *Behavioral health: A handbook of health enhancement and disease prevention* (pp. 1041–1046). New York: John Wiley & Sons.

Turk, D.C., Meichenbaum, D., & Genest, M. (1983). *Pain and behavioral medicine: A cognitive-behavioral perspective.* New York: Guilford Press.

Turk, D.C., & Rudy, T.E. (1986). Assessment of cognitive factors in chronic pain: A worthwhile enterprise? *Journal of Consulting and Clinical Psychology, 54,* 760–768.

Turk, D.C., & Rudy, T.E. (1987). Toward a comprehensive assessment of chronic pain patients. *Behaviour Research and Therapy, 25,* 237–249.

Turner, J.A., & Chapman, C.R. (1982a). Psychological interventions for chronic pain: A critical review. I. Relaxation training and biofeedback. *Pain, 12,* 1–21.

Turner, J.A., & Chapman, C.R. (1982b). Psychological interventions for chronic pain: A critical review. II. Operant conditioning, hypnosis, and cognitive-behavioral therapy. *Pain, 12,* 23–46.

Turner, J.A., & Romano, J.M. (1984). Evaluatng psychologic interventions for chronic pain: Issues and recent developments. In C. Benedetti et al. (Eds.), *Advances in pain research and therapy* (pp. 257–296). New York: Raven Press.

U.S. Department of Health and Human Services. (1983). *The health consequences of smoking: Cardiovascular disease. A report of the Surgeon General* (DHHS Publication No. PHS 84-50204). Washington, DC: Public Health Service, Office on Smoking and Health.

U.S. Department of Health and Human Services. (1985). *Health: United States 1985* (DHHS Publication No. PHS 86-1232). Washington, DC: U.S. Government Printing Office.

U.S. Department of Health and Human Services. (1987). *Alcohol and health: Sixth special report to the U.S. Congress.* Washington, DC: U.S. Government Printing Office.

U.S. Public Health Service. (1979). *Adult use of tobacco.* Atlanta, GA: Center for Disease Control.

Vischi, T.R., Jones, K.R., Shank, E.D., & Lima, L.H. (1980). *The alcohol, drug abuse, and mental health national data book.* Washington, DC: Superintendent of Documents, U.S. Government Printing Office, Stock No. 017-024-00983-1.

Von Itallie, T.B. (1985). Health implications of overweight and obesity in the United States. *Annals of Internal Medicine, 103,* 983–988.

Waldo, D.R. (1987). Personal communication.

Weinstein, N.D. (1988). The precaution adoption process. *Health Psychology, 7,* 355–386.

Weisenberg, M. (1987). Psychological intervention for the control of pain. *Behaviour Research and Therapy, 25,* 301–312.

White, N.F. (1988). Medical and graduate education in behavioral medicine and the evolution of health care. *Annals of Behavioral Medicine, 10,* 23–29.

Williams, A.F. (1982). Passive and active measures for controlling disease and injury: The role of health psychologists. *Health Psychology, 4,* 399–409.

Winters, R., & Anderson, J.B. (1985). The neurologic basis of behavior. In N. Schneiderman & J.T. Tapp (Eds.), *Behavioral medicine: The biopsychosocial approach* (pp. 67–97). Hillsdale, NJ: Lawrence Erlbaum Associates.

CHAPTER 38

MINORITIES

Jack O. Jenkins
Gene A. Ramsey

There are many valid reasons to discuss minority group issues in psychology. Among them are socioeconomic differences that often make the minority individual quite different from the psychologist with whom he or she must interact, cultural differences that affect language usage and therapy expectations, and the value system of the clinician as he or she makes decisions regarding research, assessment, and course of therapy. One problem in gaining widespread acceptance of the importance of minority issues in psychology is that the field is probably considered "soft" by many mainstream psychologists, lacking in the voluminous empirical evidence required to demonstrate that such issues really make a difference in therapy, research, and so forth. In addition, mainstream psychologists, because they can do nothing less, utilize their own value systems as they apply the principles of psychology. To many, discussions of minority issues provoke defensive reactions in which various well-ingrained schemata concerning a certain minority group can come into play. For example, one of the authors marveled at how much time the white members of a student's dissertation committee spent trying to disprove data showing that the white college students in her sample consumed more alcohol than did

the African-American students. The authors' own nonscientific surveys of the offices of many psychologists more often than not fails to find any books directed solely toward minority issues. This suggests both a lack of knowledge as well as a lack of sensitivity. About this point in reading this article a reviewer might be asking—as some of we behavioral types like to ask—"Where's the data for your assertions?" Much will be presented in what follows to validate certain points. However, one should note that it has been minority psychologists who have tended to discuss minority issues from nonmainstream points of view. Because the number of minority psychologists in the United States remains low (Russo, Olmedo, Stapp, & Fulcher, 1981), it comes as no surprise that the total number of studies on minority psychological issues from minority points of views is less than what one would expect.

SOCIOECONOMIC ISSUES

The American dream is still not being realized by large sectors of the American population. Statistics reveal that although the median income for families in in the U.S. in 1986 was $27,735, the medians for

African-American, Mexican-American, and Puerto Rican families were $16,786, $19,400, and $12,865, respectively (see "Statistical Abstracts of the United States," U.S. Bureau of the Census, 1988). While by 1987, 1 in 11 African-American families was in the highest income bracket of $50,000 or more, the percentage of African-American households earning less than $10,000 had risen to 42% (Keller, 1989). Data obtained from the 1979 Census revealed that the median income of Native-Americans was $13,724 and for Asian/Pacific Islander families it was $22,713. One should be aware though that only about half of those who are self-identified as Native-American (American Indian) are usually considered Native-Americans by any conventional definition (Astin, 1982). Similarly, it is difficult to ascertain which groups one has in mind when using the term *Asian-American*. The largest such groups in this country, Japanese- and Chinese-Americans, although having suffered historically from racism and oppression, tend to do at least as well as white Americans in most areas.

The percentage of African-Americans with 4 years of high school has increased from 12.9% in 1960 to 35.6% in 1986 (U.S. Bureau of the Census, 1988). However, figures show that, as of 1986, 39% of whites had 4 years of high school, whereas the total population average was 38.4%. Figures for Mexican-Americans and Puerto Ricans were 27% and 25%, respectively.

By 1986, the percentage of African-Americans with 4 or more years of college had increased from 3.1% in 1960 to 10.9%. The percentage of Hispanics with 4 years or more of college had increased from 4.5% in 1970 to 8.4% in 1986 (U.S. Bureau of the Census, 1988). Nevertheless, the percentages for African-Americans and Hispanics with 4 or more years of college were far less than the 20.1% for whites. In addition, the number of African-American youth attending college has declined since 1980 (Keller, 1989), although figures from Fall 1988 suggest a turnabout.

Unfortunately, many African-Americans who are completing college are not choosing to pursue graduate degrees (Keller, 1989). The number of African-American citizens receiving doctoral degrees from United States universities has declined from 1,116 in 1977 to 765 in 1987, a decrease of 31% (Coyle & Thurgood, 1989). The number of doctorates obtained in 1987 when compared to 1977 is greater for Hispanics, Asian-Americans, and Native-Americans. For white United States citizens the number of doctorate recipients declined from 23,065 in 1977 to 20,358 in 1987. The decline in white doctorate recipients was due solely to fewer white males obtaining degrees. Although white males consistently decreased every year from 1977 to 1987, the number of white female doctorate recipients consistently increased (from 6,054 in 1977 to 8,242 in 1987).

Of concern as well is the fact that a lower percentage of new minority doctorate recipients (except Asian-Americans) indicated commitments to work in academe in 1987 than in 1977. This may mean that even less research on minority issues may be generated by minority researchers in the foreseeable future and fewer minority psychologists will be available to serve as instructors.

In 1986 the total unemployment rate for the country was 7.0%. For whites the figure was 6.0%. However, for African-Americans the percent unemployed was 14.5% and for Hispanics it was 10.6%. Not surprisingly the poverty rate for African-Americans, Hispanics, and Native-Americans remains much higher than the rate for the general population.

A further problem is the high teenage pregnancy rate and large number of births in general to unmarried African-American and Hispanic mothers. The teenage pregnancy rate for African-Americans in 1985 was 23% of all live African-American births. Most African-American births occurred to unmarried mothers (60.1%). For Native-Americans the teenage pregnancy rate was 19.1% and births to unwed mothers 40.7%. Individuals of Hispanic origin averaged a teenage pregnancy rate of 16.5% of live births, with Puerto Ricans displaying a rate of 20.9%, Mexican-Americans a rate of 17.5%, and Cubans 7.1%. Births to unmarried mothers averaged 29.5% for Hispanics, with the rate for Puerto Ricans at 51.1%. Only Asian-Americans had a lower rate than whites, averaging 5.5%. Lowest were Chinese-Americans with a rate of 1.1%. Births to unmarried mothers for Asian-Americans were somewhat higher, but the percentage was still a good bit lower than for all other groups.

Numerous other problems exist, such as the ratio of African-American men to African-American women between the ages of 25 and 44; There are only 86 men for every 100 women. However, the purpose of the foregoing was to illustrate with statistics much of what clinicians already know, that many minority group individuals have severe practical problems in living that make them different from the mainstream therapist. Not even mentioned were the severe problems of crime and drug abuse.

Although each minority group in America has a different history in this country, racism and its effects have played a major role in creating the deplorable state of affairs in which minority group members find themselves today. African-Americans were either slaves or existed in situations where, while free, they were less than equal to whites. The debilitating effects of slavery, including the disintegration of African-American families, cruel treatment, and sexual abuse are well documented (e.g., Saunders, 1974) although not read about widely enough by all Americans. Liberation from slavery did not liberate African-Americans from oppression and prejudice.

Mexican-Americans (Chicanos) are a disadvantaged group who have experienced little social progress, even though they have lived in the United States longer than most other ethnic groups (Acosta, 1984). Mainstream-culture social scientists have explained the lack of social mobility and economic advancement by Chicanos as a result of their approach to life and their distinct cultural values (Madsen, 1964; Saunders, 1954). Their ascribed values, such as greater concern for the present than the future, being more dependent than individualistic, and being more nongoal oriented, are usually viewed as the opposites of Anglo-American values and as impediments to success in the United States (Vaca, 1970).

According to Inclan (1985) Puerto Ricans, as a group, have been involved in a period of very rapid transition. Many migrated to the United States after World War II and, members of a rural and underdeveloped society, experienced culture shock when they settled in industrial centers such as New York City. This culture shock led to the establishment of barrios that served as a buffer between the old society and the new. Some Puerto Ricans, in addition to the survival problems, faced daily suffering at a personal level (Inclan, 1985).

The plight of Native-Americans on reservations is more severe than that suffered by any other minority group in the United States (Levitan, Johnston, & Taggart, 1975). High unemployment, poor educational resources, and alcoholism represent only a few problems of Native-Americans. Native-Americans living on reservations have attempted farming, raising stock, and timber production, but basically they have been unsuccessful. It should be noted that many Native-Americans were not farmers traditionally and had to make tremendous cultural changes when forced to take up farming. At some reservations the people are able to secure jobs nearby. However, many drive themselves or are bused to jobs as far as 60 to 100 miles from the reservation. The economic opportunities available to Native-Americans on reservations are so limited that over a fourth of them are estimated to have left for relocation into urban ghettos, with some overall improvement in their socioeconomic condition (Levitan et al., 1975).

It is clear that many minority group members in America lead lives that are vastly different from mainstream America as in terms of culture, education, and economic resources. However, one should not neglect problems faced by those minority group members who have succeeded as well. Many go to school and work in predominantly white settings and, although successful, may still experience problems in living peculiar to their ethnic identity. Some Hispanics may feel comfortable when being called "Taco" at work and some may not. How should the offended individual express his or her discontent with such teasing in the most socially appropriate fashion? Are others going to be threatened by the assertiveness of a minority group member? Maybe not, but maybe so. Is the mainstream therapist going to tell the individual he or she is being too sensitive?

What is important is that psychologists recognize that the minority group individual may be different from them in many ways. These differences can provoke feelings of disgust, apathy, or sympathy on the part of the therapist, each of which may interfere with the therapeutic enterprise.

PSYCHOLOGY AND MINORITIES: HISTORICAL PERSPECTIVES

Psychology has not always been very sensitive to minority issues. By this we mean that, although psychologists have often seen fit to do experiments with and write about African-Americans and other minorities, the discipline has not always been concerned about taking the perspective of minority group members into account when planning experiments or interpreting results (e.g., Guthrie, 1976; or Thomas & Sillen, 1972). In fact, one might use the discipline of psychology as an example of how current belief systems determine what goes on in a social science discipline. For example, many people during Copernicus's time refused to believe his assertions concerning the universe, and many in Columbus's day firmly believed the earth was flat. These attitudes about minorities influenced their entry into the field of psychology. It is no surprise that the first African-American PhD psychologist was not produced until 1934 (Guthrie, 1976). George I. Sanchez, the father of Chicano psychology, received his doctorate in education from the University of California at Berkeley in 1934 (Murillo, 1984). In 1971, at the second meeting of the meeting of the Association of Psychologists por la Raza, it was estimated that there were no more than 15 doctoral-level Chicano psychologists in the United States.

Psychology was not only affected by the racism that prevailed in many institutions of higher education concerning the admission of minorities as students, but also in terms of the type of theorizing about minorities that occurred. Guthrie (1980) cited a statement by G. Stanley Hall, founding father of the American Psychological Association (APA):

> No two races in history, taken as a whole, differ so much in their traits, both physical and psychic, as the Caucasian and the African. The color of the skin and the crookedness of the hair are only the outward signs of the many far deeper differences, including cranial and thoracic capacity, proportions of body, nervous system, glands, secretions, vita sexualis, food, temperament, disposition, character, longevity, instincts, customs, emotional traits, and diseases. All of these differences as they are coming to be better understood, are seen to be so great as to qualify if not imperil every inference from one race to another, whether theoretical or practical so that what is true and good for one is often false and bad for the other. (pp. 19)

Uninformed statements have been made by other major figures in psychology as well. For example, Carl Jung stated that African-Americans have a whole historical layer less than whites (Thomas & Sillen, 1972). Dr. Jung must not have studied African-American history or spent much time in Egyptian tombs looking at the pictures on the walls. Many of the individuals who appear in the pictures have facial features that are obviously negroid. But then, how many whites, or Hispanics, or Asians takes courses in African-American history? And how many African-Americans, whites, Hispanics, and so on take courses in the history of Native-American tribes?

Although the argument concerning bias in intelligence tests for minorities continues to rage, one cannot dispute the fact that minority populations were not the target for whom the tests were designed. If it were so, logic tells us, Weschler and others would have included them in their original standardization samples. This kind of bias by neglect also occurred for personality tests such as the Minnesota Multiphasic Personality Inventory (MMPI).

The American Psychological Association has become more responsive to minority issues as evidenced by several acts, including the authorization of a Board of Ethnic Minority Affairs and the inclusion of attention to minority issues as a part of the criteria for accreditation of clinical and counseling psychology training programs. Many more doctoral training programs in psychology have now recruited and produced minority PhDs than in the past; traditionally, only a few institutions, such as the University of Michigan, have concerned themselves about minority recruit-

ment. Nevertheless, much more needs to be done, at both the disciplinary and the individual levels.

ASSESSMENT VARIABLES

Assessment is the set of processes used by a person or persons for developing impressions and images, making decisions, and checking hypotheses about another person's pattern of characteristics, which determine his or her behavior in interaction with the environment (Sundberg, 1977). For minority groups, however, the results of assessment may often be biased and could provide an inadequate view of the problem.

Intelligence Testing

The first attempts at mental testing in the United States were in the 1890s. One of the first uses of mental tests was to determine if there were any mental differences that could be attributed to race. The psychologist R.M. Bache tried to measure quickness of sensory perception and compared 12 whites, 11 Native-Americans, and 11 African-Americans. The Native-Americans had the fastest reactions, the African-Americans were second, and the whites were the slowest. These results did not stop Bache, however, from proclaiming that the test proved that whites were the superior group. He maintained that they "were slower because they belonged to a more deliberate and reflective race than did the members of the other two groups" (Berry & Tischler, 1978).

In 1905, Alfred Binet and Theodore Simon, working in France, developed a series of tests designed to measure intelligence. These tests were to be used to distinguish among various levels of "feeblemindedness." Even in these early days of intelligence testing, Binet and Simon admitted that environmental and educational opportunity would invariably affect the scores; they concluded that the tests would only be appropriate for comparing children from closely similar environments (Berry & Tischler, 1978). Unfortunately, many psychologists ignored this warning and viewed the tests as measures of inherited intelligence that were virtually uninfluenced by the environment. When Binet died, the intelligence-testing research laboratories were moved to the United States and came under the control of Lewis Terman.

In 1916, Lewis Terman revised the Binet scales. However, the revisions were overshadowed by his declarations to future psychologists: "Mental retardation represents the level of intelligence which is very, very common among Spanish Indians and Mexican families of the Southwest and also among negroes.

Their dullness seems to be racial" (Terman, 1916, p. 92). He also predicted that there would be significant racial differences when future IQ testing of these groups was done, and that "these racial differences cannot be wiped out by any scheme of mental culture" (p. 92). Finally, speaking of minorities again, Terman (1916) stated: "There is no possibility at present of convincing society that they should not be allowed to reproduce, although from a eugenic point of view they constitute a grave problem because of their unusually prolific breeding" (p. 93).

The Stanford-Binet is still being employed. Of the major intelligence tests currently in use today, only the Wechsler scales for adults and children have provided more normative series for minorities.

The purpose of this chapter is not to pursue any exhaustive argument on this issue. However, because it is clinicians who do a great deal of intelligence testing, it is important that the problems regarding the accurate intellectual assessment of minorities be addressed at least briefly.

Questions have arisen in recent years over the approval passes of intelligence tests. The debate revolves around whether intelligence tests accurately assess the intelligence of African-Americans, Hispanics, and other culturally diverse individuals. There are a number of reasons why the intellectual assessment of many minority group members may lead to erroneous conclusions. One explanation, as indicated earlier, is that normative samples of most intelligence tests do not systematically include minorities (Bernstein & Nietzel, 1980; Berry & Tischler, 1978; Jones, 1980). Second, the items on the tests are not culture-free. Hilliard (1982) defined *culture* as the shared creativities of a group of people, including language, values, experiences, symbols, tools, rules, and so on. Although there are cultural commonalities among American citizens, there are nonetheless a variety of subcultures whose members, for a number of reasons, have some experiences that are different from other individuals in American society. These experiences may be negative in nature and include discrimination, poor school, poverty, unemployment, malnutrition, and the like. On the other hand, these cultures may also manifest variations in the usage of standard English, different values in dressing, and even different cognitive styles in learning and problem solving (Cooke, 1980). Intelligence, according to Hilliard (1982), is reflected in both common and unique cultural behavior.

The dominant intelligence tests in use represent white American middle-class values and culture. Many African-American, Hispanics, and Native-American children have been raised in somewhat different settings than have white middle-class children (Berry & Tischler, 1978; Hilliard, 1982; Jones, 1980; Mercer, 1972). Mercer (1972) and her colleagues found that when they controlled for social background such as occupation, income, and educational level, there were no significant differences in intelligence between whites and African-Americans or Chicanos. In fact, Chicano individuals who had all the sociometric characteristics of their white counterparts actually averaged IQs that were a little higher. No one has yet been able to devise a culture-free test, and there is some doubt as to whether a culture-free intelligence test is even possible. Third, there is the problem in the language of the intelligence tests and the individual taking the test. Many non-English-speaking individuals (e.g., some Hispanics) have been administered intelligence tests in English; those test scores were used to label them as mentally retarded (Acosta, 1977; Jones, 1980). This abysmal situation has recurred more often than one would think. Another issue in the recent intelligence controversy has been the race of the examiner in the testing situation. Some studies over the years have been used to support the notion that African-Americans on the average obtain lower scores when the test is administered by white examiners rather than African-American examiners.

A recent review by Sattler and Gwynne (1982) suggested that the hypothesis that the race of the examiner produces different IQ scores for African-Americans than for whites is a myth. These authors note that of 27 reports, only 4 studies indicate positive results supporting the hypothesis of examiner bias. The authors pointed out that the results of these studies were obviated by methodological problems. Sattler and Gwynne (1982) concluded that there is no substantial evidence that the race of the examiner really has any effect on IQ scores. Although their conclusions may be entirely accurate, it is noteworthy that they did not closely scrutinize the other 23 studies in which the race of the examiner did have significant effect on test results. These authors concluded that the evidence for race-of-examiner effects at this time is equivocal. But, although it may be true that there is no definitive evidence of the race-of-examiner effect, it is also not true that the race-of-examiner effect should be considered merely a myth, as Sattler and Gwynne suggested. Graziano, Varca, and Levy (1982) argued that the reasons for differences observed in African-American and white intelligence scores is a complex issue and that much research remains to be done.

Given the present evidence for the race-of-examiner hypothesis, it would probably be too hasty to dismiss the effect as a myth. It is simply naive to believe that persons high in prejudice who administer intelligence tests obtain the same IQ scores from low socioeconomic status minority individuals as do individuals who are less prejudiced. To believe Sattler and Gwynne (1982) is to believe we should ignore the possibility of the long-term damage that can be done by giving the wrong IQ score. Psychologists of all races and ethnic backgrounds ought to examine their own biases and prejudices when they evaluate culturally diverse populations. Furthermore, Sattler and Gwynne (1982) only addressed obtained IQ scores and not the test reports that are based on such testing.

Hilliard (1982) cogently noted that until the definitive experiment of exposing all individuals to the same environmental variables before testing and then assessing intelligence has been done, there is no evidence to suggest that these tests accurately assess anything except differences in environment. Garcia (1984), cautioning against the use of intelligence tests with Mexican-Americans, asserted that errors are inherent in testing because standard instruments are applied to a culturally diverse population without regard to obvious group differences in practice and motivation.

The National Assessment of Educational Progress (1981) conducted surveys that yielded data from the assessment of reading and writing skills for African-American children at ages 9, 13, and 17 for the years 1969, 1974, and 1979. By 1979 African-American students excelled significantly in the areas of reading and writing. In fact, African-American 9-year-olds improved in reading skills by 9.9% whereas white 9-year-olds improved by 2.8%. According to this organization, the increase in the black 9-year-old's reading skills was one of the largest gains ever reported. In addition, African-American 13- and 17-year-olds improved on almost all of their writing tasks, thus decreasing the gap between their performance and that of the rest of the nation. One may hypothesize that this is because of the integration and exposure of African-American children to the same materials that the average white American child has typically received in public schools.

Although other issues might be discussed, suffice it to say that the clinician must be aware of these issues and also quite careful in the conclusions he or she reaches from reading an IQ report on a minority group member.

Clinical Assessment

Clinical assessment may occur in three spheres: (a) self-report, which is composed of the clinical interview, various pencil-and-paper self-report measures, and self-monitoring, (b) behavioral measures, and (c) physiological measures.

Of self-report measures, the clinical interview represents the most often used method of assessment (Adams, 1981; Bernstein & Nietzel, 1980). According to Yarrow, Campbell, and Burton (1968), in many instances interview data may not always be reliable and valid. These authors found that interview data may be distorted in various ways as a function of (a) characteristics of the interviewer and the questions he or she poses, (b) client characteristics such as memory and willingness to disclose accurate information, and (c) the circumstances under which the interview takes place.

Interviewer error and bias often are problems for the children. Schwitzebel and Kolb (1974) stated that sometimes errors are deliberate. They quoted an interviewer hired to conduct structured inquiries as saying: "One of the questions asked for five reasons why parents had put their child in an institution. I found most people can't think of five reasons. I didn't want [the boss] to think I was goofing off, so I always filled in all five." Bernstein and Nietzel (1980) also stated that personal biases, preferences, and various kinds of prejudice may strongly affect the conclusions reached by clinical interviewers. This view was supported by previous studies (Mehlman, 1952; Temerlin, 1968), in which it was found that interviewers tend to have favorite diagnoses that are applied more often than any others. Temerlin (1968) found that clinicians' diagnoses of a client may be determined by prejudicial information given to them before they ever hear the client speak. Carkhuff and Pierce (1967) assessed the effects of therapist race and social class upon the patient's depth of self-exploration in a clinical interview. These authors found that the patients explored themselves more in the clinical interview when they were more similar to the race and social class of the counselor involved. Patients who were less similar tended to explore themselves less. Hollingshead and Redlich (1958) found that therapists reported greater ease of communication and more positive assessments of clients who were white and middle class. Difference in language, values, and racial prejudice may all lead to less than accurate information being obtained from minority clients by individuals unfamiliar with or perhaps hostile to their subculture. These findings definitely have implications for the psychological treatment of culturally diverse groups.

For example, imagine a therapist, who has ultra-conservative negative opinions of welfare and believes that those on welfare are shiftless and lazy interviewing a poor African-American patient. He ignores the old African-American lady's report of how depressed she is about her state of affairs and concludes it is all her fault. He withholds any kind of psychotherapy and prescribes drugs because "that's all you can do with these people." Any therapist who regularly interviews minority clients should not assume that he or she knows all about these people and should seek out information from appropriate individuals (i.e., minority therapists) about variables important in conducting meaningful interviews with them.

The client's language also is an issue with minority clients. The language barrier makes it impossible for many Spanish-speaking persons to communicate effectively with monolingual therapists (Acosta, 1984; Hilliard, 1982; Olmendo, 1981). Some Asian-Americans may also have difficulty as well as those black Americans who use nonmainstream English in their everyday interrelations.

A few non-Hispanic therapists have probably learned enough Spanish at least to communicate with Spanish-speaking patients, but their numbers are likely to be small and the depth of communication is probably not the same (Acosta, 1984; Olmendo, 1981). Native-Americans, especially those residing on reservations, also may have difficulty because of the almost impossible task of translating some Native-American languages into English while keeping intact the exact meaning of the terms. Other problems in communication occur with African- and Asian-Americans. The therapist should be aware of possible problems in communication with particular members of minority groups.

Other issues therapists should take into consideration include such basics as establishing trust and rapport with the minority client. In many instances, minority clients may not automatically provide the therapist with the detailed information necessary for adequately assessing the problem. This may be attributed to a lack of knowledge in the area of psychological assessment and treatment on the part of the minority client. However, these problems may be alleviated by the sensitivity, interest, and open-mindedness that the therapist shows toward the minority client.

Paper-and-Pencil Self-Report Measures

Paper-and-pencil self-report measures for evaluation of psychopathology primarily have been developed on whites and administered without reservation to minorities. These self-report measures include projective devices, such as the Rorschach and Thematic Apperception Test, trait measures such as the Edwards Personal Preference Scale (Edwards, 1959), empirically derived measures such as the Minnesota Multiphasic Personality Inventory (MMPI; Dahlstrom & Welsh, 1960; Hathaway & McKinley, 1951), and behavioral inventories.

The projective tests (e.g., Rorschach) probably are the most easily abused, because they involve a great deal of subjective interpretation (Adams, 1981; Bernstein & Nietzel, 1980; Jones, 1980). Such a heavy emphasis on subjective interpretation based upon Freudian theory may be easily affected by prejudice (Jones, 1980).

Research with the MMPI comparing the results for African-Americans and whites has found that African-Americans typically obtain significantly higher scores than do whites on scales measuring nonconformity, alienation, and impulsivity (Gynther, 1972). Gynther (1981) stated that clinicians often interpret these differences as indicating that African-Americans are more maladjusted than are whites, but there is no empirical evidence to support this conclusion. Gynther (1981) went on to suggest that misinterpretations could be reduced by developing behavioral correlates of MMPI profiles for African-Americans.

Behavioral self-report measures, such as the Rathus Assertiveness Schedule (Rathus, 1973), Fear Survey Schedule II (Wolpe & Lang, 1964), Fear Survey Schedule III (Geer, 1965), Social Avoidance and Distress Scale, and Fear of Negative Evaluation Scale (Watson & Friend, 1969) are designed to obtain descriptions of an individual's behavior in situations without drawing gross personality interpretations from such data. Although the goal of a quick method of behavioral description is worthwhile, these inventories may or may not be useful for all minority-group members. The normative samples for these measures and the white middle-class perspective from which they were developed may be problematic when administered to minorities.

It is interesting that history does repeat itself. Despite all of the furor over the normative samples of intelligence tests, behavioral self-report measures that have been standardized and validated almost exclusively on white middle-class college subjects continue to be administered to poor and/or minority individuals. Many of the measures do not even provide cautions as to the populations with whom these inventories should be used. Although there may be fewer problems in the use of behavioral tests with various minority clients, we do not know this. It has not yet been documented at this point. For example, the tests may be appropriate for African-American, Chicano, and Native-American college students but not for poor individuals from the same minority groups.

Self-Monitoring

Self-monitoring consists of the detection and tabulation of discrete internal or external behavioral events by an individual. Self-monitoring has proven itself useful as an assessment strategy and occasionally as an intervention strategy (Adams, 1981; Jenkins & Peterson, 1976; Lahey and Ciminero, 1980). It is particularly useful in the assessment of difficult-to-verify covert events (e.g., obsessive thoughts) or behavior, where it is important to detect their occurrence in the natural environment. The problem with self-monitoring may not be self-monitoring per se, but how its usefulness is viewed by poor and minority clients. It may be that the way this middle-class therapist describes the utility of the self-monitoring to his poor and minority clients in no way motivates the individual to believe in the utility of such a strategy. Or, it may be that the way self-monitoring is arranged to occur for this poor, old Native-American is impossible given her environmental constraints. The therapist should utilize a good deal of common sense in applying this useful strategy.

Behavioral Measures

Behavioral measures may be obtained in two ways. The first is through naturalist observations, whereby the therapist observes the behavior as it occurs in the natural environment. The second involves the observation of behavior in the laboratory, in a behavioral analogue. Both types of behavioral observation may have implications for the accurate assessment of minority-client behavior.

During naturalistic observation, the therapist should already be aware of the possible reactivity of his or her presence, regardless of the race or ethnic group of his or her subjects. When the client involved is a minority individual, the observer ought to be aware that not only is his or her presence reactive, but that because the therapist is of one race and his or her clients are of another, his or her presence may be doubly reactive. First, there are some actions that minority individuals will avoid because of their fear that such behavior (while in fact normal) will confirm the prejudices of the observer. Second, there is the natural tendency of any individual to react to being observed.

With analogue situations, the therapist may feel more at ease with his or her client, but there still may be problems. First, the therapist may arrange an analogue situation that does not accurately assess this minority person's behavior. For example, the Chicano client may have excellent assertive skills but not in the presence of whites in authority. These data may be overlooked by the therapist. Another observer may place his or her minority client in a role-play situation to determine conversational skills, but because this African-American male is trying to speak standard English rather than nonstandard English, he gives the impression of being less effective. It is imperative that the therapist take culture into account when arranging behavioral analogues.

Physiological Assessment

Kallman and Feuerstein (1977) stated that the purpose of physiological assessment is to qualify physiological events as they are related to psychological variables. The use of physiological measures, such as the electrodermal response, in cross-cultural studies has not been extensive. Lazarus (1966) and his associates, however, explored this area of research. The research has been based on experimentation with American subjects in which motion picture films are used to produce stress reactions. Lazarus and Opton (1966) presented benign and stressful films to Japanese students and adults and compared their physiological and subjective responses with data from American experiments. The stressful film dealt with subincision rites involving the mutilation of male adolescent genitals. The benign film dealt with rice farming in Japan, which was intended as a Japanese version of a film on corn farming in American studies. The results indicated that in many respects, the Japanese reaction to stress was similar to that of Americans. Unlike Americans, however, the Japanese's skin conductance was almost as high during the benign films as during the stressful film. Lazarus et al. (1966) even suggested that Japanese subjects resembled "high anxious" individuals in American studies. He reported that skin conductance data on Japanese subjects indicated a general state of apprehension, maintained throughout both films, whereas their self-reports reflected small variations in perceived distress. Lazarus hypothesized that lack of experience of Japanese subjects in the laboratory and general apprehension about the total experimental situation produced the variations observed with the physiological measures.

With regard to other ethnic groups, research has shown significant differences between African-Americans and whites in terms of electrodermal-level reactivity. It appears that African-Americans have lower skin conductance than whites when contrasted to the Japanese in Lazarus's study, who manifested higher skin conductance values. Differences have even been found in electrodermal response reactivity between Jewish subjects born in America, Europe, or Israel.

The degree to which genetic factors are operative in addition to cultural processes has not as yet been clarified. It is quite clear that differences in autonomic reactivity may be a function of many social and psychological variables. But until this area is thoroughly researched across ethnic groups, assessment by means of physiological measures may always be interpreted in terms of the race of the subjects being assessed.

The preceding discussion of assessment should be tempered with the knowledge that this discussion is in no way designed to stereotype any minority group or minority clients. Too much of that has been done in the past, and in fact, many liberal white psychologists have avoided considering racial topics for this reason.

The purpose of this section is to delineate some variables that may be important in assessment and ought to be taken into account when evaluating a minority client. We are not suggesting that everything will have to be done differently with a minority client. It is quite likely, however, that therapists will have to attend to more than the usual variables considered to be important in assessment. Because of racism, poverty, unemployment, high levels of stress, language, and other variables, the minority client is almost always different in some manner. These differences may or not be relevant, but they should be given consideration.

PREVALENCE OF MENTAL ILLNESS AMONG MINORITY GROUPS

Given the disproportional representation of many minority group members among the unemployed, the poor, the uneducated, unmarried mothers, and so on, you might expect that the prevalence of psychopathology is greater in this population than in the white population. The epidemiological literature confirms this for all except the major Asian-American groups.

Bulhan (1985), in an excellent article, reviewed the literature regarding the extent of psychopathology in African-Americans. Bulhan's review suggests that African-Americans appear to be much more at risk for certain classes of mental disorders when rates of admission to mental hospitals are examined. The *Task Panel Reports* (1978) submitted to the President's Commission on Mental Health revealed that the age-adjusted rate of inpatient admissions to state and county hospitals for African-American males per 100,000 individuals is 509.4 compared to 213.2 for white males. For African-American females the rate

was 248.5 compared to 110.0 for white females. Kramer et al. (1973) found the age-adjusted rates for schizophrenia for the 1969 national admission rates to psychiatric services in the United States to be 266.6 for nonwhites and 132.2 for whites. Also noted were much higher rates of alcoholism for nonwhites than for whites (90 per 100,000 vs. 27.6).

Given that there have been so few studies of psychological disorder among Mexican-Americans, it comes as no surprise that we still know very little about the phenomenology of various psychiatric syndromes of this population (Cuellar & Roberts, 1984). One study (Fabrega, Schwartz, & Wallace, 1968a, 1968b) examined the manifestation of psychopathology among Mexican-Americans when compared to Anglos and African-Americans. The investigators found the Mexican-American group to be significantly more socially disorganized and regressed on ratings by psychiatrists and observations of ward nurses.

One problem in accurately assessing the degree of psychopathology in African-Americans, Hispanics, Native-Americans, and Asian-Americans may be in the process of diagnosis itself. Bulhan (1985) cited evidence that shows racial bias could enter into the assessment process. Strickland, Jenkins, Myers, and Adams (1988) found that ratings of African-American stimulus patients differed as a function of the race of the rater.

Another factor may be the tendency of certain cultures (at least traditionally) to respond differently to the mentally ill than Western culture does. Kitano (1973) questioned the presence of a "mentally ill role" for Japanese due to the fear of and lack of sophistication regarding the origins and treatment of mental illness and the limited use of psychiatric facilities. Obviously acculturation can and probably has changed some of the practices of Japanese-Americans in this respect.

The clinician should be aware of factors that may affect diagnosis and monitor him- or herself in the labeling of anyone as, for example, schizophrenic. Given the effects of diagnosis on the course of therapy (e.g., administration of powerful drugs), loss of some self-respect, and so on, therapists should be quite careful about attaching any type of diagnosis to clients.

THERAPY ISSUES

Over the years a good bit of theorizing about the mental health of African-Americans has been conducted by psychologists and psychiatrists. According to two psychoanalysts, Kardiner and Ovesey (1962), African-Americans do not have a single personality trait that is not derived from their difficult living conditions (i.e., their life of oppression). In addition, these psychoanalysts believe that psychotherapy or counseling for African-Americans is useless (Maultsby, 1982). Kardiner and Ovesey (1962) believed that the only way to increase the self-esteem of African-Americans is to eliminate all racial prejudice and discrimination in the United States. Although this is a noble ideal, the assertion that African-Americans cannot benefit from therapy is an extremely pessimistic view. It should be noted that Kardiner and Ovesey (1962) drew their conclusions from a limited sample of unsuccessful African-American patients (Maultsby, 1982).

Although Freud himself did not advance conceptualizations of psychopathology that were biased in nature, many American psychoanalytic writers did. In the first issue of their journal, *The Psychoanalytic Review,* White and Jeliffe in 1913 devoted three articles to mental illness among African-Americans. A note by the two editors declared that "the existence side by side of the white and colored races in the United States offer a unique opportunity not only to study the psychology of a race at a relatively low cultural level, but to study their material effects upon one another" (cited in Thomas & Sillen, 1972). Bevis (1921) stated that, "All Negroes have a fear of darkness . . . careless, credulous, childlike, easily amused, sadness and depression have little part in his psychic make-up" (cited in Thomas & Sillen, 1972, p. 11).

The famous European psychiatrist, Carl Jung, on a visit to America, examined African-American patients in a mental hospital. He declared that, "The different states of the mind correspond to the history of the races" and that the Negro "has probably a whole historical layer less" than the white man (cited in Thomas & Sillen, 1972, p. 14). Erikson (1950), a developmental psychologist, observed that "Negro babies often received sensual satisfactions which provide them with enough oral sensory surplus for a lifetime, as clearly betrayed in the way they move, laugh, talk, sing" (p. 214). This "sensory treasure helped to build a slave's identity: mild, submissive, dependent, somewhat querulous, but always ready to serve with occasional empathy and childlike wisdom" (Erikson, 1950, p. 214). Erikson goes on to state the "so-called opportunities offered the migrating Negro often turn out to be more subtly restricted prisons which endangers his only successful historical identity (that of the slave)" (p. 214). Eventually African-Americans would retreat into "hypochondria invalid-

ism," a condition analogous to the safety of being a slave (Erikson, 1950).

Several factors have probably contributed to this depressing state of affairs. The major culprit has been the failure of doctoral clinical programs to recruit, train, and graduate enough minority psychologists. The results of a study published in the *American Psychologist* by Russo et al. (1981) showed that 3.1% of all APA members were members of minority groups. African-Americans constituted 1.2%, Asians 1.0%, Hispanics 0.7%, and Native-Americans 0.2%. Although many schools have made great strides in recent years in the recruitment and training of minority psychologists, the problem of adequate representation remains acute. Problems caused by the paucity of minority psychologists has meant that it has been relatively easy for mainstream psychology to ignore factors related to the treatment of minorities. The modal number of minority faculty for most psychology departments is probably one or zero. Hence, most mainstream psychology members rarely even get to converse with a minority psychologist on a regular basis. Second, the absence of a minority faculty has resulted in fewer courses on ethnic concerns (e.g., African-American psychology or Chicano psychology). Third, minority faculty members could direct mainstream faculty to journals in which many minority psychologists publish (e.g., the *Journal of Black Psychology*). Fourth, minority psychologists often are more vigorous and have the connections to recruit minority students and assist in their retention in graduate programs. Fifth, the culturally aware minority psychologist can generally sensitize other faculty and nonminority students to minority issues.

However, most therapists will continue to be white and most of them will have little or no formal training in working with nonwhite clients. Much more attention needs to be paid to educating present and future nonminority psychologists about minority issues. It should be noted, however, that until substantial curriculum changes are made, even minority graduate students will receive only mainstream-oriented educations. Those minority psychologists who have addressed minority or cultural issues have studied nonmainstream psychology independently and have benefitted from organizations such as the Association of Black Psychologists.

Responsiveness of Minorities to Therapy

Several years ago Sue, McKinney, Allen, and Hall (1974) examined the records of 959 African-American and 1,190 white patients in 17 community mental health centers. Sue et al. found that 50% of African-Americans and 30% of whites terminated therapy in the first session. African-Americans who did attend therapy sessions after the initial visit averaged 4.68 sessions to the 8.68 of whites. Results of a study conducted by Jenkins (1981) found similar results in a community mental health center. Jenkins found that white male and female clients received less severe diagnoses and more psychotherapy than did African-American male and female clients.

Other minorities are similarly affected. According to Padilla, Ruiz, and Alvarez (1975), although highly disadvantaged and subject to multiple stresses, the Mexican-American has been substantially underrepresented among those who receive mental health services. Native-Americans experience similar problems.

A well-researched problem in clinical psychology relates to why clients drop out of therapy prematurely. According to Garfield (1971), premature termination of therapy is a widespread finding across a large number of therapies.

Social class has been established as a very important factor in why clients prematurely terminate therapy. Sue, McKinney, and Allen (1976) reviewed the cases of 13,450 clients in 17 mental health centers and found that individuals with low levels of education and who were members of minority and ethnic groups were more likely to leave therapy early.

It should be noted that several investigators (e.g., Roessler & Boone, 1979) have failed to find any real differences between premature terminators and re-mainers (Sultan, 1982). It may well be that clinics and individual therapists, through their different expectations for success of some clients and their varying levels of ability to provide relevant services, may, in fact, discourage some clients from continuing in treatment (Sultan, 1982).

A major point to be drawn from the literature on dropouts is that there is evidence that socioeconomic status and other variables are related to client dropout rate. There also is other evidence that therapists tend to accept those individuals most like themselves (e.g., Hollingshead & Redlich, 1958; Jenkins, 1981). With African-Americans, Native-Americans, Hispanics, and Asian-Americans constituting a disproportionate number of the lower socioeconomic-status individuals in our society, it is important that therapists address the special needs of such clients in therapy. There are reasons why lower socioeconomic-status clients drop out. Socioeconomic status may account for much of the high dropout rates for minority group members.

However, racial prejudice and failure to understand and to appreciate completely the cultural differences of these minorities most assuredly accounts for some of the dropout rate as well.

The traditional therapies do not hold much promise for many minority group members because of these therapies' long duration, relative ineffectiveness, and select client population. Most traditional therapies are best suited for the YAVIS (young attractive verbal intelligent successful) type of client (Schofield, 1964) and not the HOUNDs (homely old unsuccessful non-verbal dull). Behavior therapy, although lagging in its attention to cultural variables, seems to hold the most promise for minority group members, because of its proven efficacy in the treatment of diverse problems, its heavy emphasis on experimentation, and its pro-pensity to be more flexible in dealing with problems in living. The remainder of this chapter, then, focuses most heavily on the possible utilization of cultural variables to improve and strengthen empirically based treatment strategies.

CLIENT VARIABLES OF MINORITY INDIVIDUALS THAT MAY AFFECT TREATMENT

The first notion that must be advanced here is that the variables we address are those that the therapist needs to take into account when treating minority patients. The goal of this section is not to stereotype the African-American, Hispanic, or Native-American client. The assumption underlying this discussion is that individuals in America who have been forced into different experiences by the dominant culture have both deliberately and inadvertently developed many different cultural values and perspectives from those of mainstream America. The minority client will always be different in some way from his or her white middle-class therapist. It may be that some or all of these differences must be taken into account before maximum success in therapy can be achieved.

African-American Clients

Because most clinical programs do not have re-quired courses addressing issues of culture as they relate to therapy, the non-African-American therapist who sees an African-American client should first assume that he or she does not view them objectively. The therapist should also be aware that all of his or her training (even if he or she has seen some African-American clients) has been white, middle class, and geared to the dominant culture. No matter how liberal the non-African-American therapist, his or her perceptions of the world must be based on past experiences (Maultsby, 1982). These past experiences do not include growing up as an African-American. Cheek (1976) suggested 34 questions African-American and nonblack therapists should ask themselves before assuming readiness to work with African-American clients. The questions are rated on a *very much, somewhat, not at all* format. Nine of the most crucial questions of the 34 that Cheeks suggests are (a) Are you comfortable with African-American language? (b) Do you desire African-American supervision of your work with African-American clients? (c) As a parent, would you approve of your son or daughter dating an average (whatever you consider average) African-American youth? (d) Would you seek out competent African-American consultation or supervision in working with different African-American patients? (e) Have you had exposure to professional training conducted by African-Americans (classes, workshops, seminars)? (f) Have you been exposed to professional views of African-American women as well as African-American men? (g) Are you familiar with the current literature, journals, and periodicals in which African-Americans express their professional views? (h) Have you ever exposed your approach to counseling African-Americans to other African-Americans in the profession (as individuals or in a group) for a response (or advice)? (i) Have you had specific formal training in dealing with ethnic minorities? Cheek (1976) feels that a *not at all* response to any of these questions means that the therapist is not yet ready to counsel African-Americans effectively.

This test should be taken by African-Americans and whites alike. However, since we can safely assume that most non-African-American therapists who work in environments that require they see African-American clients will persist in their attempt to "counsel" or otherwise disposition those clients, a number of variables should be taken into account by such therapists.

First, although discrimination in America has led to similar experiences for many African-Americans, not all African-Americans are alike. Each African-American client is an individual, as is each poor client, each rich client, each Hispanic client, and each Asian-American client.

Second, the fact that this client talks and dresses differently from the therapist has nothing to do with his or her intellect or worth as a human being. Third, characteristics such as poverty, lack of formal education, and poor command of English do not mean that the individual cannot benefit from therapy.

Fourth, cultural variables should be taken into account in assessment and treatment. These cultural variables include the following: (a) Where does this client live and what are the norms of the area? (b) What is the meaning of common expressions in this area? (c) Am I going to be more or less accepted if I use such expressions with this client? (d) How can I enhance the generalization of the effects of therapy to this client's environment? (e) Are the assessment instruments I am using relevant for African-American clients? (f) What is the extent of my knowledge of African-American culture both historically and at present as obtained from African-American writers, not just my mainstream literature? (g) Last, do I have a repulsion to working with or feel ill at ease with African-American clients? If the answer to the last question is yes, then the therapist should seek some assistance in resolving these feelings.

Other Minorities

We will not make the mistake of writing from any supposedly expert sense about other minority clients. What is important is that all of the questions raised in regard to African-American clients may apply to other minority clients. Where we have used the word African-American, the reader may substitute Native-American, Hispanic, Asian-American, or others. Nevertheless, there are other variables that might be taken into account almost entirely within the context of certain groups.

Hispanics

Understanding the role of ethnic and sociocultural variables in psychotherapy with Mexican-Americans and the relevance of psychotherapeutic approaches for Mexican-Americans and other Hispanics continues to be a major challenge for clinicians and researchers in the 1990s (Acosta, 1984). For Hispanics, there is the "problem" of bilingualism. Many Hispanics do not speak fluent English and consequently do not receive maximum therapy benefits from their non-Spanish-speaking therapists. One solution to this problem has been the use of Spanish-speaking interpreters. However, it has been found that some therapists did not think Spanish-speaking patients seen with an interpreter felt understood or helped. This result may have been due to the therapists' anxiety about the situation themselves. Most Mexican-Americans who need psychotherapy do not seek services offered by mental health agencies (Acosta, 1984). In addition, there are numerous stereotypes perpetrated by social scientists and mainstream America in general that therapists should know and scrutinize in him- or herself before beginning therapy. The therapy itself should take into account the cultural heritage of the Mexican-American, Puerto Rican, Cuban, or other Hispanic.

Native-Americans

Historically, Native-Americans are certainly among the most discriminated groups in the United States. Among all the minorities in American society, Native-Americans hold a unique status, in that they were acquired in 1871 as official wards of the federal government. The attitudes of white people toward Native-Americans in the United States have varied widely from disdain to pity. Nonetheless the Native-American, in addition to and because of his or her problems of poverty, poor education, and discrimination, has great need of psychological services.

Dauphinais, LaFromboise, and Rowe (1980) surveyed 150 Native-American and 50 non-Native-American 11th- and 12th-grade students to assess self-reported problem areas and persons perceived as potential sources of help. Although the Native-American students had much in common with the white students in terms of problems most likely to be taken to a counselor, there were differences. Native-American students indicated a large likelihood of talking to no one about getting along with friends, being depressed, and not caring (Dauphinais et al., 1980).

Two other groups of Native-American students (those from boarding schools and metropolitan schools but not those from rural areas) expressed a reluctance to talk to anyone about problems with parents and family members, whether to stay in school, and making a decision. The majority of non-Native-American students indicated that they would talk with some other person about these concerns.

LaFromboise, Dauphinais, and Lujan (1981) investigated verbal indicators of insincerity as perceived by Native-Americans. These authors found that attempting to show affinity, the use of ethnic stereotypes, denial of ethnic differences, displaying a misunderstanding of Native-American-related problems, use of accusatory or derogatory phrases, attempts to gain confidence, displaying a "run-around" or "put off" maneuver, attempting to show an understanding of Native-American experiences, and attempting to antagonize or satisfy curiosity were most often named as indicators of insincerity.

It should be noted that the word *Native-American* must be carefully used and the exact individuals being discussed specified (this is also true for Hispanics).

The variability of individuals within the category called Native-American is great. Our goal of the presentations of the two studies above was to give some information that may prove useful in counseling some Native-Americans. But, as indicated previously, we would caution that each individual—white, African-American, Hispanic, or Native-American—must be viewed as just that—an individual.

Asian-Americans

Asian-Americans should be understood in terms of their specific culture (Chinese, Japanese, Korean, Vietnamese, etc.) and their degree of acculturation to Western values. As with other potential culturally dissimilar clients the therapist should examine his or her own prejudices toward such individuals and do an assessment of his or her degree of knowledge of the client's culture/subculture.

Use of Cultural Variables in Behavior Therapy

Many studies have been conducted demonstrating the efficacy of behavioral strategies (see Rimm & Masters, 1979), but there are very few studies in the behavioral literature that address the systematic assessment and utilization of cultural variables in treatment. The reasons for this oversight vary from an attempt by liberal white psychologists to avoid race in their research as a reaction to previous abuses, to simply viewing race and culture as unimportant variables. It is noteworthy that Kanfer and Saslow (1967), in their article "Behavioral Diagnosis," present a schema for assessment that includes an analysis of the individual's environment. We explore, in the following, the possible use of cultural variables in behavior therapy with regard to well-known strategies.

Systematic desensitization (Wolpe, 1958) now is a standard therapeutic technique principally used to treat maladaptive anxiety occurring in the presence of specific environmental cues. There is no evidence, however, that the technique has been used widely with poor persons and minority group members. The strategy probably does not need any substantial modification with a client who accepts the rationale and is induced to begin.

However, there are some ways in which cultural variables may play an important role. The first concerns getting the client to believe the treatment rationale. The second involves the actual administration of the treatment procedure. The former requires taking into account many of the cultural variables addressed thus far. The latter involves the use of cultural variables in scene preparation (i.e., anxiety and relaxation elicitation stimuli) and scene description (i.e., perhaps the scene is made more vivid by terms more familiar to the client). In some scenes, perhaps an appropriate Spanish accent or African-American voice may facilitate treatment.

Social-skills or assertiveness training (Wolpe, 1958) has been a primary treatment modality for maladaptive anxiety as it occurs in the realm of interpersonal relationships. However, the effects of social-skills or assertive-training procedures have not always generalized to the natural environment (e.g., McFall & Twentyman, 1973) or endured. It is our contention that one major factor in the failure of social-skills training to generalize to the natural environment is that cultural variables have been ignored. (See Caldwell-Colbert & Jenkins, 1982, for a more thorough discussion of these issues.) Many African-American patients have taken part in social-skills training experiments in inpatient settings, but never does the reader see that the client's environmental context was assessed. Moreover, it is not clear that the patient was taught skills most likely to be reinforced in his or her environment. The white middle-class therapist may teach white middle-class social skills to a Mexican-American person who does not use them because they make him or her appear odd in his or her environment. Important variables in social-skills assessment and training may include description of the interpersonal partners and his or her race and sex. Cheek (1976) has argued rather convincingly that the race of a respondent may alter the exact nature of an assertive response.

Lineberger and Calhoun (1983) found that whites and African-Americans altered their responses on a self-report measure when the race of the respondent changed. Garrison and Jenkins (1986) found that African-Americans and whites tended to view the assertive responding of African-Americans differently.

The reader should not assume from this discussion that there are no instances when training in white middle-class social skills is necessary. It may well be the case that the Chicano, African-American, Native-American, or Asian-American individual needs to know more about how to operate effectively in a white middle-class environment. As Cheek (1976) asserted, however, African-Americans and other minorities are raised to be white and not vice versa. Minorities understand the values and skills of the dominant culture much more than the dominant culture understands the values and behavior of its minority members.

With regard to operant strategies, the greater the knowledge the clinician has about the client's culture, the greater the likelihood that he or she will accurately assess potential reinforcers, punishing or negative stimuli, maintaining stimuli, and ways to effect generalization of results. The rationale given to the client should take into account who this client is, how well a treatment rationale will be understood, and the extent to which it is accepted.

CONCLUSIONS

The future status of the treatment of minorities will depend on several factors: (a) Larger numbers of minority clinical psychologists should be trained. The number of minority psychologists in the country (i.e., African-American, Chicano, Asian-American, and Native-American) remains well below what one would expect given their representation in the population of the United States. (b) Larger numbers of minority clinical psychologists should be hired for faculty of academic institutions and community mental health agencies. (c) Larger numbers of nonclinical minority psychologists should be trained. (d) Larger numbers of nonclinical minority psychologists should be hired in appropriate job placements. (e) All psychologists who write about or do research on minority groups but who are not members of such minority groups should consult with appropriate psychologists who are of the minority. If this is not accomplished, then the research should not be undertaken. (f) The APA committee on accreditation should require that all doctoral-level clinical students receive formal instruction in ethnic concerns. (g) Departments of psychology should institute core courses on ethnic concerns taught by minority psychologists and require all of their doctoral (clinical, social, industrial, etc.) students to take them. (h) All students and faculty should be made aware of materials written by minority psychologists on minority concerns that frequently are not found on the shelves of mainstream faculty and college libraries. (i) Research regarding the role of culture in behavior therapy assessment and treatment should be conducted.

If these actions are taken, conditions regarding research, assessment, and treatment of minority group members will surely improve.

References

Acosta, F.X. (1977). Ethnic variables in psychotherapy: The Mexican American. In J.L. Martinez (Ed.), *Chicano psychology*. New York: Academic Press.

Acosta, F.X. (1984). Ethnic variables in psychotherapy with Mexican Americans: Clinical and empirical gains. In J.L. Martinex & R.H. Mendoza (Eds.), *Chicano psychology* (pp. 163–185). New York: Academic Press.

Adams, H.E. (1981). *Abnormal psychology.* Dubuque, IA: WC Brown.

Astin, A.A. (1982). *Minorities in American higher education.* San Francisco: Jossey-Bass.

Bernstein, D.A., & Nietzel, M.T. (1980). *Introduction to clinical psychology.* New York: McGraw-Hill.

Berry, B., & Tischler, H.L. (1978). *Race and ethnic relations.* Boston: Houghton-Mifflin.

Bevis, W.M. (1921). Psychological traits of the southern Negro with observations as to some of his psychoses. *American Journal of Psychiatry, 1,* 69–78.

Bulhan, H.A. (1985). Black Americans and psychopathology: An overview of research and theory. *Psychotherapy, 22,* 370–378.

Caldwell-Colbert, A.T., & Jenkins, J.O. (1982). Modification of interpersonal behavior. New York: Plenum Publishing.

Carkhuff, R.R., & Pierce, R. (1967). Differential effects of therapist race and social class upon patient depth of self-exploration in the initial clinical interview. *Journal of Consulting Psychology, 31,* 632–634.

Cheek, D.K. (1976). *Assertive Black . . . Puzzled White.* San Luis Obispo, CA: Impact.

Cooke, B.G. (1980). Nonverbal communication among Afro-Americans: An initial classification. In R.L. Jones (Ed.), *Black psychology* (2nd ed.). New York: Harper & Row.

Coyle, S.L., & Thurgood, D.H., 1989. *Summary Report 1987, Doctorate Recipients from United States Universities,* Washington, D.C.: National Academy Press.

Cuellar, I., & Roberts, R.E. (1984). Psychological disorders among Chicanos. In J.L. Martinez & R.H. Mendoza (Eds.), *Chicano psychology* (pp. 133–162). New York: Academic Press.

Dahlstrom, U.G., & Welsh, G.S. (1960). *An MMPI handbook: A guide to use in clinical practice and research.* Minneapolis: University of Minnesota Press.

Dauphinais, P., LaFromboise, T., & Rowe, W. (1980). Perceived problems and sources of help for American Indian students. *Counselor Education and Supervision, 20,* 37–44.

Edwards, A.L. (1959). *Edwards Personal Preference Schedule.* New York: Psychological Corporation.

Erikson, E.H. (1950). *Childhood and society.* New York: WW Norton.

Fabrega, H., Schwartz, J.D., & Wallace, C.A. (1968a). Ethnic differences in psychopathology with emphasis on a Mexican American group. *Journal of Psychiatry Research, 6,* 221–225.

Fabrega, H., Schwartz, J.D., & Wallace, C.A. (1968b). Ethnic differences in psychopathology with emphasis on clinical correlates under varying conditions. *Archives of General Psychiatry, 19,* 218–226.

Garcia, J. (1984). The logic and limits of mental aptitude testing. In J.L. Martinez (Ed.), *Chicano Psychology.* New York: Academic Press.

Garfield, S.L. (1971). Research on client variables in psychotherapy. In A.E. Bergin & S.L. Garfield (Eds.), *Handbook of psychotherapy and behavior change* (pp. 271–298). New York: John Wiley & Sons.

Garrison, S., & Jenkins, J.O. (1986). Differing perceptions of black assertiveness as a function of race. *Journal of Multicultural Counseling and Development, 14,* 157–166.

Geer, J.H. (1965). The development of a scale to measure fear. *Behaviour Research and Therapy, 3,* 45–53.

Graziano, W.G., Varca, P.E., & Levy, J.C. (1982). Race of examiner effects and the validity of intelligence tests. *Review of Educational Research, 52,* 469–498.

Guthrie, R.V. (1976). *Even the rat was white: A historical view of psychology.* New York: Harper & Row.

Guthrie, R.V. (1980). The psychology of black Americans: An historical perspective. In R.L. Jones (Ed.), *Black psychology* (2nd ed., pp. 13–22). New York: Harper & Row.

Gynther, M.D. (1972). White norms and black MMPIs: A prescription for discrimination? *Psychological Bulletin, 78,* 386–402.

Gynther, M.D. (1981). Is the MMPI an appropriate assessment device for blacks? *Journal of Black Psychology, 7,* 67–75.

Hathaway, S.R., & McKinley, J.C. (1951). *The Minnesota Multiphasic Personality Inventory Manual* (Rev. ed.). New York: Psychological Corporation.

Hilliard, A. (1982). *IQ thinking as the emperor's new clothes: A critique of Jenson's bias in mental testing.* Unpublished manuscript, Georgia State University.

Hollingshead, A.B., & Redlich, F.C. (1958). *Social class and mental illness: A community study.* New York: John Wiley & Sons.

Inclan, J. (1985). Variations in value orientations in mental health work with Puerto Ricans. *Psychotherapy, 22,* 324–334.

Jenkins, J.O., & Peterson, G.L. (1976). Self-monitoring plus aversion in a case of bruxism. *Journal of Behavior Therapy and Experimental Psychiatry, 9,* 387–388.

Jenkins, J.O. (1981). *An analysis of the delivery of services to black and white individuals in a community mental health clinic.* Unpublished manuscript, University of Georgia.

Jones, R.L. (1980). *Black psychology.* (2nd ed.) New York: Harper & Row.

Kanfer, F.H., & Saslow, G. (1969). Behavioral diagnosis. In C.M. Franks (Ed.), *Behavior therapy: Appraisal and status* (pp. 417–444). New York: McGraw-Hill.

Kardiner, A., & Ovesey, L. (1962). *The mark of oppression.* New York: World Publishing.

Keller, G. (1989). Review essay: Black students in higher education: Why so few? *Planning for Higher Education, 17,* 43–57.

Kitano, H.H.L. (1973). Japanese-American mental illness. In S. Sue & N.N. Wagner (Eds.), *Asian-Americans: Psychological perspectives*. Ben-Lomand, CA: Science and Behavior Books.

Kramer, M., et. al. (1973). Definition and distribution of mental disorders in a racist society. In C. Willie et al. (Eds.), *Racism and mental health*. Pittsburgh: University of Pittsburgh Press.

LaFromboise, T., Dauphinais, P., & Lujan, P. (1981). Verbal indicators of insincerity as perceived by American Indians. *Journal of Non-White Concerns, 9*, 87–93.

Lahey, B.B., & Ciminero, A.R. (1980). *Maladaptive behavior: An introduction to abnormal psychology*. Glenview, IL, Scott, Foresman.

Lazarus, R.S., & Opton, E.M. (1966). The study of psychological stress. In C.D. Spielberger (Ed.), *Anxiety and behavior*. New York: Academic Press.

Lazarus, R.S. Tomita, M., Opton, E.M., & Kodama, M. (1973). A cross-cultural study of stress-reaction patterns in Japan. In W.F. Prokasy & D.C. Raskin (Ed.), *Electrodermal activity in psychological research*. New York: Academic Press.

Levitan, S.A., Johnston, W.B., & Taggart, R. (1975). *Minorities in the United States: Problems, progress, and prospects*. Washington, DC: Public Affairs Press.

Lineberger, M.H., & Calhoun, K.S. (1983). Assertive behavior in black and white American undergraduates. *Journal of Psychology, 113*, 139–148.

Madsen, W. (1964). *The Mexican-Americans of South Texas*. New York: Holt, Rinehart & Winston.

Maultsby, M.C., Jr. (1982). An historical view of blacks' distrust of psychiatry. In S.M. Turner & R.T. Jones (Eds.), *Behavior modification in black populations: Psycho-social issues and empirical findings* (pp. 39–55). New York: Plenum Press.

McFall, R.M., & Twentyman, C.T. (1973). Four experiments on the relative contributions of rehearsal, modeling, and coaching in assertion training. *Journal of Abnormal Psychology, 81*, 199–218.

Mehlman, B. (1952). The reliability of psychiatric diagnosis. *Journal of Abnormal and Social Psychology, 47*, 577–578.

Mercer, J.R. (1972, September). IQ: The lethal label. *Psychology Today*, pp. 44–47, 95–97.

Murillo, N. (1984). The works of George I. Sanchez: An appreciation. In J.L. Martinez and R.H. Mendoza (Eds.), *Chicano psychology* (pp. 23–34). New York: Academic Press.

National Assessment of Educational Progress. (1981). 15(4).

Office of Special Concerns, Office of the Secretary, Department of Health, Education and Welfare. (1974). *A study of selected socio-economic characteristics of ethnic minorities based on the 1970 Census: Vol. 3: American Indians*. Washington, DC: U.S. Government Printing Office.

Olmendo, E.L. (1981). Testing linguistic minorities. *American Psychologist, 36*, 1078–1085.

Padilla, A.M., Ruiz, R.A., & Alvarez, R.A. (1975). Community mental health services for the Spanish-speaking surnamed population. *American Psychologist, 30*, 892–905.

Raines, G.N., & Rohrer, J.H. (1960). The operational matrix of psychiatric practice: II. Variability in psychiatric impressions and the projection hypothesis. *American Journal of Psychiatry, 117*, 33–139.

Rappaport, J. (1977). *Community psychology: Values, research and action*. New York: Holt, Rinehart & Winston.

Rathus, S.A. (1973). A 30-item schedule for assessing assertive behavior. *Behavior Therapy, 4*, 398–406.

Report of the United States Joint Commission on Mental Health (1978). Washington, DC: U.S. Government Printing Office.

Rimm, D.C., & Masters, J.C. (1979). *Behavior therapy: Techniques and empirical findings* (2nd ed.). New York: Academic Press.

Roessler, R.T., & Boone, S.E. (1979) Comparison of rehabilitation center dropouts and completers on demographic, center environmental perceptions, and center problems. *Psychosocial Rehabilitation Journal, 3*, 25–33.

Russo, N.F., Olmedo, E.L., Stapp, J., & Fulcher, R. (1981). Women and minorities in psychology. *American Psychologist, 36*, 1315–1363.

Sattler, J.M., & Gwynne, J. (1982). White examiners generally do not impede the intelligence test of black children: To debunk a myth. *Journal of Consulting and Clinical Psychology, 50*, 196–208.

Saunders, D.E. (1974). *The Ebony handbook*. Chicago: Johnson.

Saunders, L. (1954). *Cultural differences and medical care: The case of the Spanish-speaking people of the Southwest*. New York: Russell Sage.

Schofield, W. (1964). *Psychotherapy: The purchase of friendship*. Englewood Cliffs, NJ: Prentice-Hall.

Schwitzebel, R.K., & Kolb, D.A. (1974). *Changing human behavior*. New York: McGraw-Hill.

Strickland, T.L., Jenkins, J.O., Myers, H.F., & Adams, H.E. (1988). Diagnostic judgements as a function of client and therapist race. *Journal of Psychopathology and Behavioral Assessment, 10*, 141–152.

Sue, S., McKinney, H.L., & Allen, D.B. (1976). Predictors of the duration of therapy for clients in the community mental health system. *Community Mental Health Journal, 12*, 365–375.

Sue, S., McKinney, H., Allen, D., & Hall, J. (1974). Delivery of community mental health services to black and white clients. *Journal of Consulting and Clinical Psychology, 42*, 794–801.

Sultan, F.E. (1982). *Factors contributing to dropout in a psychosocial rehabilitation program for the chronically emotionally disabled*. Unpublished doctoral dissertation, University of Georgia, Athens.

Sundberg, N.D. (1977). *Assessment of persons*. Englewood Cliffs, NJ: Prentice-Hall.

Temerlin, M.K. (1968). Suggestion effects in psychiatric diagnosis. *Journal of Nervous and Mental Disease, 147*, 349–353.

Terman, L.M. (1916). *The measurement of intelligence*. Boston: Houghton-Mifflin.

Thomas, A., & Sillen, S. (1972). *Racism and psychiatry*. New York: Brunner/Mazel.

U.S. Bureau of the Census. (1988). *Statistical abstract of the United States*. Washington, DC: U.S. Government Printing Office.

U.S. Government. (1988). Task panel reports submitted to the President's Commission on mental health, *3*, 820–901.

Vaca, N.A. (1970). The Mexican-American in the social sciences. Part II: 1936–1970. *El Grito, 4*, 17–51.

Watson, D., & Friend, R. (1969). Measurement of social evaluative anxiety. *Journal of Consulting and Clinical Psychology, 33*, 448–457.

Wolpe, J. (1958). *Psychotherapy by reciprocal inhibition*. Stanford, CA: Stanford University Press.

Wolpe, J., & Lang, P.J. (1964). A fear survey schedule for use in behavior therapy. *Behaviour Research and Therapy, 2*, 27–30.

Yarrow, M.R., Campbell, J.D., & Burton, R.V. (1968). *Childrearing: An inquiry into research and methods*. San Francisco, CA: Jossey-Bass.

PART VI

COMMUNITY APPROACHES

EDITORS' COMMENTS

Our introductory comments to this section in the first edition of this book seem to be no less applicable today than they were 8 years ago: "Community psychology has had a remarkably checkered course in its short history. Spurred by the idealistic visions and ample dollars of the Kennedy-Johnson years, community psychology and community mental health began a meteoric rise. There were expectations that the entire mental-health-care delivery system would be transformed from an office-bound resource of the middle class to a truly community-based system. Prevention and social change were seen as the most appropriate province of the new mental-health workers, which included nonprofessional community residents and paraprofessionals, as well as the traditional professional groups. Unfortunately, by the end of the Vietnam era, the proverbial bubble had burst. The flow of dollars to the community mental-health system was dramatically restricted, resulting in a marked curtailment of existing programs, to say nothing about the dashed hopes for expansion. Moreover, much of the early idealism was shattered by the harsh realities of the 'real world.' Prevention was easier said than done and political leaders and community residents had far different ideas about their needs and how they could be met from the ideas of academically trained professionals.

"While some critics have written the epitaph of the community movement, the chapters in this section indicate that it is still alive and well."

In chapter 39, Forgays discusses the thorny issue of primary prevention of psychopathology. He first examines definitional issues and some of the conflicts about the viability of the entire concept. He then describes a variety of imaginative programs that demonstrate that prevention at some level is feasible, even if it does not meet the prototypic definition of "primary" prevention. The remainder of the chapter deals with a variety of conceptual, practical, and economic problems, before closing with some predictions and suggestions for the future. Creativity in the face of limited resources is also a theme of chapter 40, Community Mental Health, by Gonzales, Kelly, Mowbray, Hays, and Snowden. They describe a variety of exciting new programs for underserved populations. They first underscore the vital role of citizen participation. They then describe programs for ethnic minorities, the elderly, women, and AIDS victims. Chapters 39 and 40 both document that significant social problems can be addressed even with limited resources given sufficient enthusiasm, energy, and imagination.

The final chapter in this section, by Clarkin and Hull, covers brief psychotherapies. This chapter could have been included in Part V of the book in that it covers diverse models and strategies for short-term psychotherapy. However, we believe the emphasis on brief treatment fits conceptually with the need for approaches that are economical and more in keeping with diverse ethnic and cultural styles than traditional, longer-term treatments. Clarkin and Hull begin with a review of general features of brief treatment, including issues in setting time limits and goals. They then provide an overview of the predominant theoretical models, followed by a description of some of the numerous variations developed for special populations, including marital and family treatments, and strategies for patients with anxiety disorders, depression, and health-related problems. This section is followed by a discussion of how to determine when brief treatment is appropriate and issues involved in training professionals to conduct brief therapies.

CHAPTER 39

PRIMARY PREVENTION OF PSYCHOPATHOLOGY

Donald G. Forgays

"Words. Words. Words. I'm so sick of words!" In the third act of *My Fair Lady,* Eliza Doolittle expresses this view reflecting her disgust with English reserve and understatement. This passage ends with her singing "Show Me." After looking over the relevant literature in prevention for the past half a dozen years since my last review (Forgays, 1983a), I have found a lot of words and I too have a strong urge for action, or at least more action. Some of the definitional issues I described earlier are still being addressed, alas; some of the problems subverting the effective contribution of community mental health centers (CMHCs) are still in force, if not stronger; and the development of broad programs in primary prevention is still curiously slow in occurring. On the other hand, there is prevention in the land and even primary prevention!

This chapter emphasizes the kinds of programs that have appeared recently that are preventive in nature, although they are not necessarily examples of primary prevention. I emphasize those interventions that work, thereby suggesting models that may be generalized. Before that, however, I return to the definitional issue of what is primary prevention, and discuss the kinds of misconceptions about this area that continue to exist. I also note some of the themes that

appear to underlie the slow development of primary prevention programs.

After this, I review recent prevention programs, take up general problems and issues in prevention, describe the recent happenings associated with the Vermont Conference on the Primary Prevention of Psychopathology, a leader in the field, and, last, comment briefly on the future of primary prevention of psychopathology, both near and far.

DEFINITIONAL AND DEVELOPMENTAL ISSUES

In my earlier review, I spent abundant time defining primary prevention and even suggested a triple classificatory system of primary prevention to include within that rubric some of the intervention programs, extant at the time, which were not quite primary prevention (Forgays, 1983a). I do not wish to retrace those steps, so I will provide here only a straightforward notion of the area. Primary prevention refers to the provision of programs that can be expected to reduce the incidence of psychopathology; such programs are provided to nontargeted groups, that is, groups that are not known to be at high risk for the psychopathology in question. Thus, primary prevention is community oriented, although the community may be quite small; for example, it may be all of the third graders in the city. An example of such a program might be the provision of social skills training for all of the children in an area of a specific age. This training would not only be given to high-risk children but to all children. If the program is targeted to specific children, say to the high-risk group, then it is not, by definition, primary prevention. Rather, it is secondary prevention but, perhaps, of an early variety, in the sense that the children have not yet displayed the active psychopathology.

This definition appears to be clear enough, but there are still misconceptions in the literature about what primary prevention actually is. For example, Albee and Gullota (1986) treat eight common misconceptions concerning primary prevention. The first and foremost is the basic definition of the area. Many do not seem to comprehend that primary prevention is *proactive;* it occurs before the psychopathology is apparent. Of the remaining misconceptions treated here, the most important is their fourth, which suggests that primary prevention does not work. Albee and Gullota strongly challenge this view, as we will also in our review of programs that work.

Cowen (1983) highlighted some of the definitional confusion by suggesting that four different concepts have been used rather indiscriminately and interchangeably in relation to primary prevention: prevention, prevention in mental health, primary prevention, and primary prevention in mental health. Cowen maintains that these are different concepts with different goals and operations. Using his scheme in this chapter, it is only primary prevention in mental health that is of concern. Cowen embellishes our definition by stating that primary prevention is reflected by the development of programs to forestall psychological problems or to build strengths or competencies that favor psychological wellness. Furthermore, it is an intentional outreaching approach targeted to well persons *before* the fact of maladjustment. We agree completely with Cowen's crystalline phrases and continue to wonder why befuddlement is so persistent. It is a puzzlement!

A denouement on this issue is provided by a review of the past 75 years of the *American Journal of Public Health* (Williams & Westermeyer, 1985). These researchers refer to literally hundreds of papers describing the extensive effects of new therapies on public mental health and emphasize that these therapeutic interventions have had their greatest impact in the areas of secondary prevention and tertiary prevention.

In this article, there is *no* mention of *primary prevention.* It can be said, of course, that it is a very brief article.

The real distinctions between primary and other forms of prevention are dealt with by Bower (1987), who claims that the word *prevention* is honored more in word than deed. Secondary and tertiary prevention are *not* prevention, says he, but rather are a contradiction in terms. It is good to see that prevention is being honored in any way, but it is possible to talk about some interventions that are truly secondary as being quite close to primary guidelines (Cowen, 1986; Forgays, 1983a). Bower enjoys frustration equal to my own in reading the literature in this area and bemoans that prevention is being talked to death. He feels that if we persist in dealing with people already targeted as requiring mental health services, then we are not in the "prevention ballpark." The ballpark for prevention programs is not in the clinic but in schools and peer play institutions. Amen.

What has held up the development of primary prevention efforts, in addition to the definitional difficulties? Why hasn't this fourth mental health revolution appeared like the knight on the white charger to win the joust and the day? Forgays (1983b) reviewed prevention programs of the 1970s and early 1980s and sees little evidence that the revolution had yet begun. One of his cited reasons for this sad state was that personnel of the CMHCs did not seem to know what primary prevention was or that they had something to do with it. It was clear at that time that, at least, the fee-for-service mentality of these centers was seriously impeding any preventional efforts that might have been made. The pressure to generate income and to treat large numbers of clients dissipated consultation and educational services, the service category for preventional programs in the CMHC system.

If that commitment level was low around 1980, it seems to be subterranean at the present time. An actual decline in prevention services in recent years in the CMHCs has been reported by Larsen (1987), reflecting major policy and funding shifts. After reviewing the activities of 94 CMHCs in 15 states, she stated that services have become less comprehensive and more oriented toward the chronically and severely ill patient. In her tallies, 57% of the centers report a drop in consultation and education, 48% a drop in prevention services, and 36% a drop in evaluation. Not a happy picture to a preventionist. Nor does it reflect the rosier picture painted by Bloom (1984) in his review of community mental health. In his book, Bloom reported important changes since his 1977 edition, including innovative alternatives to traditional mental health and foci on the prevention of mental disorders and on community change. It would seem to be an error on our part if we relied on the contributions of the CMHCs to produce this relative utopia.

There are some, of course, who oppose developments in primary prevention. Albee (1983) included in this camp those who are committed to organic models of mental disorder, those who feel that one-to-one intervention approaches are the most appropriate, and those who insist that mental health workers should not be involved in social change. Many of these persons help to maintain, deliberately or not, the status quo of problems in our social system, sexual exploitation, and general powerlessness in society. He suggested that these factors may well be the bases of mental disorder to begin with, the causes of the causes.

Another hindrance to greater development of primary prevention relates to one's theoretical approach to preventional interventions. On the one hand, one can take a systems orientation to problems in mental health and emphasize the need for change in important social systems before anything of substance can be done about mental health conditions. On the other hand, one can take a person-centered approach and develop specific programs to enhance the competencies of people. Thus, one can be situation focused and work on programs to provide greater power to persons (Rappaport, 1987; Rappaport, Swift, & Hess, 1984) or one can be person focused and develop skills training programs (Cowen, 1985). Rappaport believed that the person-focused programs are palliative only, whereas Cowen maintained that social change and person-centered approaches are both needed; they are both important primary prevention strategies. He further stated that the situation-focused approach is reactive, whereas the person-centered approach is proactive but that neither competed with social change. The important role of person-centered interventions may be to fill in the period waiting for the social change ideals. This debate is an interesting one, as are most debates on matters of faith.

Finally, there is that old bugaboo of money. The point is made in the edited small book of Hess and Hermalin (1983) that we in prevention have come a long way. The research has been good but we still face the issue of not having adequate resources devoted to prevention programs. When the funding of the CHMCs, for example, was changed to block funding, significant losses occurred in consultation, education, and prevention activities. These authors feel that because of changes such as these, the poor are being left entirely out of prevention programs. The CMHCs are promoting wellness programs in industry where they can be afforded rather than in their own communities where there is no obvious subsidy source. We return to several of these issues toward the end of this chapter.

THE COMMISSION REPORT OF 1986 OF THE NATIONAL MENTAL HEALTH ASSOCIATION

The National Mental Health Association (NMHA) created a panel in 1984 to assess current knowledge about the prevention of mental-emotional disabilities, to assess the application of that knowledge, and to make recommendations about future action in the area. The panel was chaired by Beverly Long and comprised outstanding scientists, professionals, and citizens, along with liaison members from the National Institute of Mental Health (NIMH), the Canadian Mental Health Association, and the World Federation for Mental Health. These many contributors reported on physiological factors, caregiving and parenting, psychosocial competence, special stressors, adolescent issues, family/adulthood problems, aging, problems in the workplace, educational and informational needs and efforts, and the prevention of mental disability.

The Commission made its report in 1986 after 2 years of work. The report is reprinted in a special issue of the *Journal of Primary Prevention* (1987, Vol. 7, Whole No. 4).

The Commission reported that a substantial knowledge base existed, especially on the themes of biological integrity, psychosocial competence, social support, and societal attitudes. Research has identified antecedent stressors for many disabilities, and some of these stressors can be offset through coping skills, social supports, prenatal care, and interpersonal competencies.

As for knowledge application, there has been increased activity reflecting the expanded knowledge base but still few federal funds are appropriated for prevention programs, especially research. Happily, however, a few states have started active prevention programs and there are a few community efforts as well. Certainly relevant are the stress-management training programs occurring in industry that have proliferated. Prevention activities are also taking place in other countries in addition to the United States.

The Commission states that generally speaking "intervention services, although numerous, tend to be scattered, without comprehensive planning and coordination, and are subject to funding cuts. Diversity of programming is fruitful, but coordination of efforts, with a clearer definition of prevention outcomes and improved taxonomy and standards of effectiveness, is needed to move the field forward" (National Mental Health Association, 1987, p. 186). These efforts also frequently require interdisciplinary and interagency planning and coordination.

Program areas identified by the Commission as having immediate potential for prevention research and service include wanted and healthy babies, prevention of adolescent pregnancy, school programs (including academic mastery, development of psychosocial skills, competence building, and mental health strategies), and the provision of support, information and training for individuals experiencing extreme stress.

Recommendations from the Commission include immediate attention to prevention efforts by public and private institutions. Both broad-based research and effective models exist, and thus it would be a prudent investment to provide further prevention research and services to greatly lower the incidence and toll of mental-emotional disabilities. They suggest a representative national group to monitor prevention developments that reflects a partnership of organizations and professions.

The Commission applauds recent changes in prevention, including the opening of the Office of Prevention at NIMH in 1979 and the start of the Center for Prevention Research at NIMH in 1982, the contributions of the Vermont Conference on the Primary Prevention of Psychopathology since 1975, and the efforts of other national organizations and the World Federation for Mental Health.

The report states that there is a need for strong leadership, that NIMH and Alcohol, Drug Abuse, and Mental Health Administration (ADAMHA) should assume more of a leadership role than they have, and that NMHA should form a coalition with nongovernmental groups to establish goals and priorities. States should do their parts and local communities should develop expertise in prevention. Every mental health agency at all levels should spend a *substantial* share of its service, education, and research budgets on *prevention,* increasing it to 15% by 1995. Employers and insurers should also support such activities. Specifically, the panel emphasizes the need for more research on risk factors, coping skills and competence building, on interventions to prevent mental symptoms, and on service delivery systems and information dissemination schemes.

This is a very impressive prevention laundry list, and it is hoped that the prestige of this panel will influence the decision makers who control the funds that are so badly needed. While we await these Elysian changes, we move on to a closer look at prevention programs that have appeared or continued over the past 6 or 7 years.

PREVENTION PROGRAMS TODAY—WHAT WORKS?

I will attempt to provide a rapid overview of the types of programs that have been developed and seem to have produced desirable changes. I have two objectives here. The first is to show clearly that there is a lot of prevention going on, and the second is to indicate that several new areas of prevention intervention have highlighted this progress, likely reflecting the recognition of what is possible to do and replicate, rather than to await what one would wish to do.

I have grouped these interventions roughly into a developmental sequence, starting with programs dealing with problems of infants and young children and coping styles of their mothers, with special attention to child abuse interventions. Then I move on to long-term enrichment effects; programs based in elementary school; preventional efforts directed to adolescents; and issues of separation, divorce, and bereavement in the adult. I end with a section that includes efforts that do not fit easily into the preceding categories.

Infants, Children, and Mothers' Coping Style

Bloom, Siefert, and Akabas (1988) have included in their edited special issue of the *Journal of Primary Prevention* 11 rather general papers dealing with important themes related to problems of women today, including poverty, multiple roles, employment, social competence, empowerment, role stress, consciousness raising, African-American maternal mortality, family planning, and acquired immunodeficiency syndrome (AIDS) prevention. Most of these contributions offer general advice but do not report data based on interventional strategies, with one exception.

A somewhat more specific review has been provided by Osofsky (1986), dealing with programs on infant intervention in high-risk families. These programs are designed to stimulate needed parental adaptive skills and competencies. Osofsky highlights those programs that he considers successful, outlines problems with programs dealing with very young mothers, and suggests future programs and research in this area.

An interesting intervention to provide stress-management training to mothers on public assistance is described by Tableman, Marciniak, Johnson, and Rodgers (1982). This was a 10-week prevention intervention for low-income single mothers experiencing the multiple stressors of little money, heavy responsibilities for young children, and, seemingly, no viable alternatives. The interveners sought to teach concrete life-coping and stress-management skills, to provide psychological support, and to enhance self-confidence. Those mothers in the program improved more than a control group did in self-confidence and ego strength, and also showed improvement on measures of depression, anxiety, and feelings of inadequacy. The intervention was, thus, deemed effective.

How do maternal coping styles relate to adjustment in their children? Atlas and Rickel (1988) reported a study of 186 African-American mothers in Detroit and their preschool children. The researchers employed a variety of scales to measure maternal nurturant and restrictive rearing patterns, life stress, locus of control, and marital status, and the child variables of school adjustment, self-concept, and levels of social problem-solving skills. They reported finding that maternal life stress was significantly related to childrens' lower self-concept, higher aggression, higher "finagling," and nondirective problem-solving strategies. They also reported a significant negative relationship between maternal nurturance and child moodiness and learning problems in school. The authors see these results as clear support for the expansion of the current child developmental focus of preventive parenting programs to include maternal coping strategies. Of these strategies they feel that improved communication and assertiveness training are the best bets to research further.

Child abuse has, at last, become a prominent issue in the public eye. This attention has been reflected by the appearance of a number of prevention programs dealing with the problem. Rosenberg and Rappucci (1985) have summarized several such primary prevention programs, focusing on those that enhance competencies of families, those that prevent the onset of abusive behavior, and those that target high-risk groups undergoing transition to parenthood. Although the programs they describe are a good start to such research, there are many methodological issues in evaluating these child abuse prevention interventions,

including the lack of appropriate control groups, the use of poor outcome measures, and the failure to measure goals. They recommend that future research should focus on proximal objectives and distal prevention goals, should refine their assessment techniques, and should follow a long-term follow-up design.

A recent report on the Child Parent Enrichment Project (CPEP; Barth, Hacking, & Ash, 1988) is of interest here. In this program women are referred to CPEP either during pregnancy or just after delivery if they are identified as at risk of engaging in child abuse. This effort, then, is clearly secondary prevention. In this study 24 of these women received the CPEP program, which included specific training, home visits, and more, whereas 26 others received only traditional community service. The CPEP women proved better than the control subjects in prenatal care, birth outcomes, and child temperament reports. There were also signs of better well-being for the mothers and better indicators of the welfare of their children. However, it is important to note that there were no differences in the amount of child abusive behavior between the two groups for a 6-month period of follow-up after birth. Does this imply that the child abuse problem must be addressed by very specific interventions?

An interesting program to provide primary prevention with children of severely disturbed mothers has been reported by Goodman and Isaacs (1985). The group of concern were poverty-level, inner city mothers who were emotionally disturbed. The program of intervention included regular home visits to help the family with ordinary problems of living, an education component to teach parenting skills, a child interventional aspect, including a simulated day-care exposure for children over 2½ years of age, and an experiential learning component for mother–child groups when the children were younger. They are currently investigating 82 poor families whose mothers are diagnosed as schizophrenic ($N = 56$) or depressed ($N = 26$), and evaluating the efficacy of their program by comparing these program-provided families with 29 other families with well mothers. The evaluation is still going on and we look forward to the results of this fascinating intervention.

Long-Term Enrichment Programs for Young Children

In my earlier review (Forgays, 1983a), I described a few programs in which extensive enrichment programs were provided during early life for children who would be expected to function inadequately later on. Although programs that have been reported in more recent years have not been quite as sweeping, several do qualify as broad enrichment programs. There have also been follow-up evaluations of earlier reported enrichment studies.

Among the newer models is one developed by the Houston Parent–Child Development Center (Johnson & Breckenridge, 1982; Johnson & Walker, 1984; Johnson & Walker, 1987). This project is family-oriented and designed to prepare poor Mexican-American children to enter school, and, therefore, to prevent the poor academic performances and high dropout rates of such children in elementary school. The intervention includes the following: training of the children in social, cognitive, and language skills; parenting services provided to the families; and maternal training for the mother to become a teacher to her child. In the earlier article, the researchers reported up to a 4-year follow-up, wherein they found that the trained parents provide more positive facilitating home environments for their children than did control families; the experimental children, especially the boys, were less destructive, overactive, and less attention-seeking than their control counterparts. In the 1984 and 1987 reports, follow-up through age 11 showed continued positive results, with the experimental children showing important cognitive gains and less impulsive, obstinate, moody, restless, and disruptive behaviors.

Pierson, Klein-Walker, and Tivnan (1984) reported a school-based program from infancy to kindergarten for parents and their children—the Brookline Early Education Program. This intervention includes parental education and support, diagnostic monitoring and feedback, and a variety of educational experiences for the child. Families ($N = 285$) received either mixtures of these components or else were assigned to a nonprogram comparison group. The program began during the infancies of the children involved and continued through enrollment in kindergarten, and it was evaluated at the end of the second grade. In general, it was found that the experimental children were doing much better than the control children, and that the more intense the intervention, the greater the benefits to the children. In comparisons of the two groups of children on standard academic criteria (e.g., reading performance) experimental children had fewer problems than did control children. They were also better in working independently, following directions, and getting along with their peers, and they enjoyed a higher level of participation in classroom activities.

The intervention of the Perry Preschool Program was provided to highly disadvantaged and relatively low IQ (70 to 85) children (Berrueta-Clement, Schweinhart, Barnett, Epstein, & Weikart, 1984). This program has been in effect for about 25 years, and this report provides results for some of the children through the age of 19 years. All of these children were African-American and from a slum area. Each year for 5 years matched subgroups were randomly assigned to experimental or control (no program) conditions. The program itself included preschool experiences in which problem-solving and skill acquisition, interpersonal interactions, and school coping skills were taught in a low teacher-ratio format, and a series of home visits designed to stimulate parents to be aware of their children and for the parents to stimulate them. The researchers repeatedly assessed the intervention over 15 years and found that the children in the experimental program expressed more positive school attitudes and demonstrated higher achievement through the eighth grade, they were rated more positively in school development and their parents were more satisfied with their education, they required fewer special education services, they received more favorable conduct and behavior ratings from teachers, they were kept after school less often, they demonstrated fewer delinquent behaviors, and they had more after-school jobs. More recent results indicate that the experimental children display better academic performance and have lower crime rates and better occupational earnings and prospects. Again, this is a very impressive set of findings on enduring preventive outcomes for those children who are at high risk.

Finally, in this section there is the report of a 20-year follow-up of an early enrichment program provided by Jordan, Grallo, Deutsch, and Deutsch (1985). It is a report of the well-known intervention study of the Institute for Developmental Studies of New York University. The authors examined the long-term effect of the earlier enrichment program. They were able to locate 154 children who had participated, 75 of whom were program children and 79 who were from the comparison group. All of those located were currently living in Harlem. Quite sophisticated analyses of personality and skills measures obtained from them as adults suggested that long-term benefits of the earlier program were still evident for the experimental male children but, unhappily, not for female subjects. However, it is possible that, because only those subjects providing the follow-up data were those who were locatable in Harlem, the outmigration of former subjects might have included persons who had profited more from their previous exposures and that the outmigration included more females. It is also possible that female subjects had received more non-responsive educational experiences at earlier ages from their teachers after the intervention was completed than did male subjects.

Although it would be difficult to evaluate these latter possibilities at present, it seems clear that this interventional program was successful in its long-term goals, at least for male subjects.

Elementary School-Based Programs

Certainly the model for school-based intervention programs for young children is that provided by Emory Cowen of the University of Rochester, New York. This program should be well known to virtually all of the readers of this chapter. It is formally known as the Primary Mental Health Project (PMHP) and has been used in 500 schools in 200 school districts around the world. In general, the program is dedicated to improving the competencies and skills of elementary school children, usually third or fourth graders. It has been tried as a secondary prevention approach with identified risk subjects and as a primary prevention approach with all students of a specific grade within a school system. Early studies have been reviewed by Forgays (1983a) and elsewhere. The program has been very successful to date, with early gains in adjustment and also in the maintenance of these gains across time.

The Cowen group has added information on two factors that are relevant to this type of program. For example, Sterling, Cowen, Weissberg, Lotyczewski, and Boike (1985) studied a large number ($N = 211$) of first- to fourth-grade children who had experienced one or more stressful life events, as rated by teachers, and compared them with a like number of children who had not. The dependent variables were measures of school adjustment and competencies, also provided by the teachers. They found stressful life events to be associated with more serious school adjustment problems and with fewer competencies. These relationships were strongest for children who had experienced multiple recent stress events. Unfortunately, there is a possible contamination in the study because teachers provided the measures for both the independent and the dependent variables of the design. In a second study, Farie, Cowen, and Smith (1986) reported the development and implementation of a rural consortium program to provide early, preventive school mental health services. The program itself is not dissimilar to the general PMHP model except here resources are gathered from various sources. The authors suggest this as a reasonable approach to problems of mental health among children living in underresourced rural school districts, which tend to be unserved and underserved. The program was low in cost especially since the services provided are shared within the consortium. This paper reported a small evaluation of the model with 57 children where generally positive effects were obtained.

A Cowen-type intervention program was recently reported by Nelson and Carson (1988). They reported on two studies describing social problem-solving skills training for third- and fourth-grade students. Because the training was available to entire classrooms of students, the intervention seems clearly to follow the primary prevention model. In the first study, the training was provided 1 hour per week for 18 weeks to 101 children. Those receiving it showed significantly greater improvement in knowledge and performance of social problem-solving skills than did the nonprogram children (controls). However, both positive and negative effects of the intervention were found on behavioral adjustment, self-efficacy, and peer acceptance at the time of 6-months follow-up. In the second study, students receiving social problem-solving training involving teacher–student dialogues, peer pairings, and self-monitoring were compared with students receiving only the training involving student–teacher dialogues. The children in both groups showed significant improvement in their performance of the Social Problem Solving (SPS) skills but no group differences were found for changes in behavior adjustment, self-efficacy, or peer acceptance. They concluded, reasonably enough, that they had failed to support the utility of SPS skills training as a mental health strategy for young children. They suggested that the general premise that SPS skills are relevant to behavioral adjustment is not well supported in the literature and that there may well be severe limitations to cognitively mediated interventions for this age group.

Rebuttal for this position might be expected to come from the Hahnemann Medical Center group. Their program, the Interpersonal Cognitive Problem-Solving (ICPS), is well known; in it an attempt is made to train young children in social or interpersonal cognitive problem-solving skills. The program generally is based on the observation of a relationship between gaps in a family's ICPS skills (e.g., not being able to generate alternative solutions to interpersonal issues or not being able to take the role of others) and maladjustment. Shure and Spivack (1982) summarized much of their work in which they have employed teachers, parents, and college students to train the children. They have reported in several studies that children are able to learn the skills, the skills were generalized to new situations (other classrooms and teachers), and the children improved in behavior adjustment. More recently, Shure (1988) again summarized the earlier work and presented a model for a cognitive approach to prevention. Some cognitively based approaches apparently do work with children and it will be interesting in the future to evaluate why some do and some don't work.

A somewhat similar program offered assertiveness training to fourth- and fifth-grade children (Rotheram, Armstrong, & Booraem, 1982). This was a 12-week program in which the students were trained in eye contact, postural, gestural, and touch cues, giving and receiving compliments, making friends, and in general interaction skills. The attempt was clearly to increase the social effectiveness of the children receiving the program (total N was 343). The experimental students were found to have improved more than did the control students in initiated contacts, teacher behavior ratings, peer popularity, and academic performance. These gains were also maintained when measured 1 year later.

A few skills training programs have been made available to children from some of the higher grade levels of elementary school. For example, Elias, Gara, Ubriaco, Rothbaum, Clabby, and Schuyler (1986) provided social problem-solving skills training to children just before they entered middle school. These students received either a half-year or a full year of training during the school year and were compared with nontrained control children on entry to middle school. The researchers found that the half-year exposure was not as effective as the full year's training, which was itself significantly related to reduced severity of the effects of stressors during the transition to middle school. They concluded that this form of skills training was important as a preventive intervention.

Another project followed up the effect at the seventh-grade level of a primary prevention skills training program provided during the fourth grade to inner-city African-American children. The prevention program was based on the Yale Child Study Center model. In this study, the authors (Cauce, Comer, & Schwartz, 1987) compared 24 children who had the earlier intervention with 24 who had not. They reported that the experimental group is performing significantly better in mathematics and in their overall grade point average, almost better in English, and significantly better in perceived school competence and self-competence.

The use of nontraditional educational formats, including peer counseling and teaching, role-playing, and cooperative learning, have become more popular of late for prevention programs focusing at the elementary school level. For example, Wright and Cowen (1985) reported on the efficacy of peer teaching techniques on elementary student perceptions of class environment, on behavioral adjustment, and on academic performance.

A fascinating use of a cooperative group peer tutoring approach was used by Rooney-Rebeck and Jason (1986) as an attempt to prevent prejudiced behaviors of first- and third-grade students. Second and fourth graders were used as control subjects in this school, which had white, African-American, and Latino students. Direct observation of social interactive behavior in playgrounds was the source of program effect data. These systematic observations were made before and after the 8-week intervention, which was framed around arithmetic and reading skills training. A significant effect was found for the first graders who showed an increase in interethnic interactions and sociometric choices, along with improvement in arithmetic and reading skills. No significant changes were observed in the third-grade students. On this basis, the authors feel that this kind of "preventive" intervention may only be effective when overt ethnic prejudice is not fully ingrained, as is the case in the first grade. These results are interesting, indeed, but we should add a word of caution in generalizing them given that the sample sizes were quite small and there was not random assignment to group.

Finally, it is interesting to note the use of an integrating statistical technique on the results of a large number of school-based prevention interventions, in this case a meta-analysis. Baker, Swisher, Nadenichels, and Popowicz (1984) found that the single largest primary prevention effect size, based on 13 different competence domains, was for *communication skills*.

Transitioning to Secondary School and Other Adolescent Problems

Some have proposed that the special problems and stresses that are associated with transitions in life, such as entry to secondary school or marriage, deserve special attention in prevention. Rutter (1987), for example, suggested that mechanisms operating at these key turning points in people's lives must be examined as an attempt to discover "protective processes" to combat risk trajectories and redirect them to more suitable paths.

Clearly one such period includes the last few years of elementary school and the introduction to secondary school. Experimentation with drugs and alcohol likely occurs then and longer-term patterns may be established. Some research has been directed to this period and this problem. Englander-Golden, Elconin, and Satir (1986) provided assertiveness training to fifth-, sixth-, seventh-, and eighth-grade students as a drug abuse prevention. The program was called "Say It Straight," and it emphasized role-playing situations in which the trainee wanted to say "NO" to alcohol or drugs and also situations in which the trainee is talking to a friend who is "using." They found that their subjects described themselves as feeling good and having high self-respect/esteem only when they said "NO" in an assertive/leveling manner. Only then was their partner surprised, shocked, and respectful. These youngsters felt that the best way to convince their friends to quit or to get help was to express caring and friendship rather than being aggressive or blaming or to be irrelevant or super reasonable. The authors also reported an improvement in assertive skills and significant reductions in alcohol or drug-related referrals and also school suspensions in the program subjects.

Gilchrist and his colleagues have been focusing on this transition period in designing a number of interventional strategies. They feel that the time of junior high school offers many opportunities for primary prevention work. They report on a study with sixth-grade subjects to provide an empirical base for preventive strategies (Gilchrist, Schinke, Snow, Schilling, & Senechal, 1988). Data collected included measures of depression and academic failure associated with this important transition. They have yet to test their model in a systematic way but, on the basis of the data already collected, they have made several recommendations for prevention programs. Because their program would be provided to all students in an age category it would clearly be an example of primary prevention.

In another adolescent-directed program, Gilchrist and Schinke (1983) studied preventive efforts in contraception. Theirs was a multifaceted program to prevent unwanted pregnancy. It involved basically two training thrusts. In one, role-playing and discussion were employed to provide accurate sex information and to help students integrate this new information into their value systems. In the other, training was provided in communication, in social problem solving, and in assertiveness skills. They found that the adolescents did acquire the specific sex information, they improved their social problem-solving skills, they felt more confident, and happily, they began to use more effective methods of contraception.

In yet another prevention program directed to ado-

lescents, and to younger children as well, Schinke and Gilchrist (1985) dealt with tobacco use. This was a prevent-smoking program directed to 193 sixth graders attending three middle-class schools. They were able to enroll 97% of the children eligible for the project, each of whom was assigned to one of three groups: a skills-training group, an attention-placebo group, and a control group. The intervention consisted of 10 1-hour sessions in which films, peer testimonials, and slides were the focus. They reported a significant effect of this intervention for the skills-training group.

Other prevention programs designed specifically to the important transitioning years of adolescence include those of Bry (1982) and Felner, Ginter, and Primavera (1982).

Programs Associated With Separation and Divorce

Certainly the best known research in this area on adults is that conducted by B. Bloom. He has written extensively over the past dozen years or so describing his programs directed toward reducing the stresses of separation and divorce. In 1985 his group submitted a final report on this project (Bloom, Hodges, Kern, and Mcfaddin, 1985). This preventive intervention for 100 newly divorcing adults had two components: support from peers and paraprofessional help agents, and training in specific situationally relevant problem-solving skills. The program lasted 6 months. An earlier report (Bloom, Hodges, & Caldwell, 1982) tracked the subjects at 6 and 18 months. In the 1985 paper they report 30 and 48 months postintervention, and present even better results than at the earlier landmarks. At 30 months, the program subjects were significantly higher than nonprogram control subjects on adjustment measures, they had fewer separation-related problems, and they reported significantly greater separation-related benefits of the program. At 4 years postintervention, subjects in the program continued to report significantly more satisfactory levels of adjustment and quality of life, although the differences from control subjects were not as great as at 30 months. It is a justifiable conclusion that this program *did* reduce psychological problems known to follow marital dissolution. This is not primary prevention, of course, but a good example of an effective secondary prevention program.

Certainly an important group influenced by separation- and divorce-related stressors are the children of the dividing couple. Much attention has been given to this group. One of the earlier studies was that of Rickel and Langner (1985). The data, including follow-up, were collected in the late 1960s and early 1970s and have just been recently reported. It was a long-term (5 years) examination of the psychological adjustment of the children of 1,034 families, of which 25% to 50% experienced marital disruption. The researchers found a significant contribution of the father figure on child adjustment, both at the time of marital disturbance and 5 years later. Children with natural fathers showed the least pathology on the Delinquency measure. Those with surrogate dads showed the most disordered behavior on the Noncompulsivity factor. These differences were stable over the 5-year period.

A very systematic program providing intervention for the children of divorce is called the Children of Divorce Intervention Program (CODIP) which is a school-based program (Pedro-Carroll & Cowen, 1985). This prevention approach has a 10-week group format designed for fourth- through sixth-grade students whose parents had divorced. It provides a supportive group atmosphere in which the children can exchange their divorce-related feelings, common misconceptions concerning divorce are clarified, feelings of isolation are reduced, and competence is enhanced through training in problem solving, communication, and anger-control skills. The sample in this report is 72 children, 40 of whom are assigned to an experimental group that receives the intervention shortly after the divorce and 32 control subjects who receive the program later. The early intervened group showed significantly more improvement than did control subjects on teacher ratings of problem behavior and of competence, on parent ratings of adjustment, and on self-reported anxiety. The intervention group leaders also rated the experimental children as having improved significantly. It should be kept in mind, when considering the results of this intriguing study, that the ratings were done by people with a commitment to the program and, therefore, may reflect their expectancies.

In another CODIP study, the focus was on latency-aged children (Pedro-Carroll, Cowen, Hightower, & Guare, 1986). Again, support, expression of feelings, training in communication, problem-solving and anger-control skills, and enhancement of self-esteem comprised the intervention. The sample consisted of 54 children of divorce whose adjustment levels were compared to 78 matched peers both before and after the 11-session small group program. The authors reported that the children of divorce were less well adjusted than their peers before the intervention, but they improved significantly to a point close to the adjustment levels of their peers. This study also supports the CODIP approach as a meaningful preventive intervention, secondary once more, for this stressed group.

Stolberg and Garrison (1985) reported an evaluation of a prevention program for 7- to 13-year-old children of divorce. They reported here the results of a study undertaken within the Divorce Adjustment Project. The intervention resembles that of the Pedro-Carroll/Cowen group in that it helps the children to better identify, express, and deal with their feelings, it provides support, and it teaches the children communication, anger-control, and problem-solving skills needed to cope with postdivorce realities. The sample consists of 82 pairs of children of both sexes, and mothers who have been separated 33 months or less and have no history of mental health service use. Three conditions were investigated: a child support group (CSG) intervention only, the children intervention coupled with a single-parent support group (SPSG) program, a single-parent support group alone program, and a nonprogram control group. Data were collected before, just after, and 5 months after intervention. They found that children in the CSG alone improved most in self-concept. Mothers in the SPSG alone improved most in adjustment. These improvements were maintained at the 5-month follow-up. The combination training was less effective, curiously. They explain this finding on the basis of these mothers having been separated longer, having lower employment status, and fathers spending less time with their children. Unfortunately, they had recruited subjects group by study group and, thus, subject assignment to a group was questionable.

An intervention program for very young children of separation and divorce is described by Rossiter (1988). Only pilot observations are outlined for this intervention, which attempts to provide to preschoolers practical training and emotional relief within a group setting. The practical training includes such important behaviors as saying hello and goodbye, packing suitcases, using the telephone, and language training in family identity terms. Emotional relief is provided through training in pain acknowledgment, encouragement of play activities, and guilt reduction. Only preliminary data are available for the 6-session intervention and they indicate that the program appears to work well.

Finally, some attention to sex differences in children's responses to parental divorce is shown by Zaslow (1988). She is attempting to examine the generalization that boys are more negatively influenced by divorce than girls. She has made an exhaustive analysis of existing studies and concludes that this generalization is a bromide and that effects depend on conditions of custody, remarriage, and the like.

Prevention Work at the Time of Bereavement

We now come to a sad part of our developmental sequence, the time of bereavement. Most prevention attention has been applied to the most common of bereavement problems, those that occur when a spouse dies. Because in our culture husbands still tend to die earlier than do wives, it is not surprising to find interventions devoted to widows. Early work in this area is summarized by Osterweis, Solomon, and Green (1984). They described the problems and issues in this field and present evidence documenting adverse circumstances of bereavement on physical and psychological well-being. They also describe programs that manipulate factors known to either maximize or minimize these stresses. The described programs include the use of one widow as a "counselor" for another (widow-to-widow), and the use of mutual support group meetings. Follow-up data on such programs suggest better adjustment of program widows for up to 2 years after intervention.

Marmar, Horowitz, Weiss, Wilner, and Kaltreider (1988) reported a controlled study of brief psychotherapy and mutual-help group treatment of bereavement in widows. The sample here consisted of 61 women who sought treatment for grief 4 months to 3 years after their husbands had died. These women were randomly assigned to a condition that provided brief dynamic psychotherapy led by a trained clinician or to a mutual-help group condition led by a nonclinically trained person. They found that both groups experienced reductions in stress-specific and general symptoms and also improvement in social and work functioning. The treatments were found to be equally effective, although there was greater dropout of participants in the self-help groups. The latter is certainly not an unusual finding, and it is assuring that a model that could be generalized reasonably easily does appear to make a significant contribution.

Programs That Do Not Fit into the Above Developmental Paradigm

A few programs remain from my examination of the literature in prevention that do not fit easily into the classificatory schema that I have been using. They are included here as a potpourri because they make distinct contributions to the prevention literature.

In the Roberts and Peterson (1984) book several pieces of research are described that relate to medical problems of children. For example, one by Drotar, Crawford, and Ganofsky (Roberts & Peterson, 1984, pp. 232–265) deals with prevention in chronically ill children. These researchers use expressive and modeling procedures to short-circuit negative effects of anxiety associated with chronic illnesses, and to good effect. Another chapter, by Peterson and Brownlee-Duffeck (Roberts & Peterson, 1984, pp. 263–308), focuses on the special issues of hospitalization and surgery that tend to increase risk for short- and long-term negative psychological consequences. They refer to their own research for reducing such effects. In general this book makes the point clearly that many hospitals around the country today incorporate preventive measures for children experiencing hospitalization and for those looking forward to surgery. Peterson and Mori (1985) are also interested in protecting children by preventing accidental injury; they provide an analysis of objectives, methods, and specific tactics to be used in this area.

Another study of presurgical anxiety and postsurgical pain and adjustment, but this time in adults, is provided by Wells, Howard, Nowlin, and Vargas (1986). There are 24 subjects in this project, mainly adults (ages 14 to 62). A skills training approach to stress inoculation is used, including deep breathing, controlled imagery, and training in monitoring cognitive and physical cues. They reported that their intervention was effective in reducing experiences of pain and anxiety and it also led to improvement in postoperative adjustment, including a reduction of reliance on analgesia and a reduction of postoperative recovery days.

Yet, another quite unrelated study in our potpourri is that of Sweet, Stoler, Kelter, and Thurrell (1989). They dealt with the provision of support groups for veterans who are forced into early retirement, usually because of health reasons, frequently coronary heart disease. The total sample here was 32, broken down into groups of 7 to 12. They were given a small group discussion intervention, which was found to contribute to better postprogram adjustment. There was no control group in this study.

GENERAL PROBLEMS AND ISSUES IN PRIMARY PREVENTION

Throughout my review of the prevention literature, several issues and problems appeared many times. Examples are issues such as powerlessness and resiliency, problems such as finding adequate theoretical models and specific interventional techniques for primary prevention, how to find the money for prevention work, or how to deal with community action. I could hardly leave out these important considerations, even in this brief overview of the field.

The issue of powerlessness and its obverse, empowerment, keeps coming up as central to the problems in society which, in themselves, cause us to have to consider prevention programs. You will recall from material above that Rappaport and Cowen have taken opposite points of view. Cowen feels that while we wait for the great society we should try out a variety of prevention interventional techniques, largely person-oriented ones, if only as temporary fillers. On the other hand, Rappaport et al. (1984) support the notion of the importance of empowerment as a key to achieving the basic goals of primary prevention. Their notion of empowerment is somewhat fuzzy, and it is not clear if it is the same as prevention, or an alternative to it. In this paper they describe nine empowerment-related projects, reflecting a good deal of diversity. More recently, Rappaport (1987) discussed empowerment theory, defined the concept, and suggested much empirical research. He claims that the concept is meaningful for individuals, groups, and communities, and argues that empowerment comes closer to what community psychology should be interested in than positive mental health or competence enhancement, both of which are person oriented.

A study relevant to the powerlessness notion as it may relate to work and to alcohol use is reported by Seeman, Seeman, and Budros (1988). This was a 4-year study of 500 men, and the follow-up data at 4 years replicated the original findings that powerlessness is directly related to drinking and to drinking problems, whereas work alienation and friendship integration are not. These latter variables, however, interact with powerlessness to produce distinctive outcomes. Specifically they report that a change in powerlessness was associated with a change in drinking patterns; if there is intervening stress, then powerlessness can lead to drinking problems. Unemployment does not appear to be one of these intervening or initial stressors.

Resiliency and invulnerability are additional concepts that have been appearing for years whenever positive mental health and prevention programs are considered. Why do some do well in very adverse circumstances? One answer is suggested by the concept of invulnerability, used systematically by Norman Garmezy. A recent review of this construct and relevant literature is provided by Garmezy and Rutter

(1983). Gottlieb (1984) uses the notion specifically with reference to primary prevention interventions. Werner and Smith (1982) reported a long-term study of resilient native children living on the island of Kauai. These children come from dreadful circumstances, but after a 20-year follow-up, Werner and Smith report that many of them are well-adjusted; they are "vulnerable" but invincible. What seems to contribute to their invulnerability, that is, the predisposing factors, include activity, social responsiveness, and autonomy in infancy and early childhood, family closeness and supportiveness, and external support from peers and nonfamily identification models (teachers, neighbors, and ministers).

Cowen and Work (1988) discussed the issue of resilient children and psychological wellness and how the role of primary prevention may be clarified by a consideration of these factors. They suggested that a sharper focus on invulnerable children may help us to develop primary prevention programs for mental health. We should, therefore, emphasize forces that promote wellness and attempt to predict those who are stress resistant and those who are stress influenced.

The notion of invulnerability appears to be related to the protective mechanisms that Rutter (1987) had described and that we referred to earlier. These are "protective processes" that may occur naturally and help the person avoid the risk-pitfalls that may influence others or perhaps they can be promoted in primary prevention interventions. In either case, it seems important that we do focus on those who remain well under adverse conditions as well as on those who do not in trying to develop a theory of positive mental health and in assessing the roles of primary prevention programs.

With respect to community-oriented programs, the worksite health promotion model is one which has expanded greatly of late and this may well be one of the foundations of a new set of feasible approaches to prevention. Fielding and Piserchia (1989) surveyed the field of worksite public health programs and reported a large increase in health promotion activities, especially in smoking cessation, nutritional education, and stress-management programs. There has been a smaller increase in worksite exercise and/or fitness programs and no increase at all in weight control programs. Other evaluations have indicated that these latter programs have not been well attended.

An interesting study that would appear generalizable to an entire community or even larger units is reported by Klingman (1985). It is concerned with the stress and pain associated with inoculations for disease control. Subjects were 51 11- to 12-year-old girls who were randomly assigned to a practice, a no-practice, or a control condition. The practice condition subjects received information that described inoculation and how to cope with this invasion by using cognitive-behavioral coping skills. This group was also encouraged to practice the coping skills described. The no-practice subjects received the instruction but were not encouraged to practice the coping skills. Control subjects received no instruction. Subjects in both the practice and no-practice groups reported less anxiety and exhibited more cooperative behavior during inoculation than did the control subjects. The practice group benefitted the most. It is no surprise that this small intervention did work. What is surprising is that there are not more of these kinds of examples of short-term interventions for minor stressors.

Another example of a community-based and also school-based program of primary and secondary prevention is reported by Toubiana, Milgram, Strich, and Edelstein (1988). The intervention followed an acute bereavement: the death of 19 schoolchildren and 3 adults and the injury of 14 others in a school bus accident. This occurred in June 1985 in a small Israeli city and almost immediatley an intervention program was instituted for the 415 seventh-grade classmates of the dead and injured children. The model for the intervention was based on combat stress reaction programs and emphasized immediacy, proximity, expectancy, and community. They found that the combat principles and techniques were applicable to this particular set of stressors and that the children were better able to integrate the dreadful experiences.

Of course, one can generalize any community-based prevention program to larger and larger units and ultimately think not only of community-wide programs but even of a competent community. This is, essentially, what Rhoads and Raymond (1981) do in their discussion of quality of life and the competent community. Highly speculative but enticing.

Finally, one can get insight into preventional efficacy and also the role of public policy in prevention by making cross-cultural comparisons of programs. This kind of model is suggested in the report of Nikelly (1987). He described pervasive primary prevention programs in Sweden and in Cuba having to do with health, nutrition, and self-injurious behaviors, such as cigarette smoking. These programs appear to work very well in both countries except for smoking cessation efforts in Cuba. Nikelly feels that both Sweden and Cuba have developed a socioeconomic environment that facilitates primary prevention efforts, and furthermore, that conditions in the United States mitigate against the establishment and success of such programs. Here, environmental changes made to enhance mental health are limited and superficial, and "only through the elimination of poverty and unemployment and access to an open national health-care system will the mental and physical well-being of the American population be improved significantly" (p. 130). These statements highlight the distinction between community and policy change versus individual-oriented interventions, which we have raised above more than once.

A practical response to the lack of prevention funding is provided by Fine and Swift (1988) in an article describing an inexpensive technique for identifying at-risk individuals. The technique is a telephone interview that can help to identify risk factors for later handicapping conditions. They proposed that the limited funding available should be spent on those identified as high risk. This proposal for bargain-basement prevention is an interesting one but it raises the thorny issue of whether we should settle on secondary prevention efforts and not strive for primary prevention. Their value scheme would not encourage the kinds of broad community programs described above.

Chronic community strains and their interaction with stressful life events are described by Evans, Jacobs, Dooley, and Catalano (1987). The chronic life strain in question is the smog in Los Angeles. They gave the Psychiatric Epidemiology Research Interview Life Events Scale and the Dohrenwend Demoralization Scales to a large number of LA residents and found that those who had experienced both the smog and the life events exhibited poorer mental health than did those who had experienced only the smog. Happily for the LA residents there were no direct effects of smog on mental health.

Research continues apace within the area of stressful life events, incidentally. However, recent focus is beginning to include, if not substitute, the contribution of daily life events or hassles, as exemplified in the research of Wagner, Compas, and Howell (1988) and many others.

Finally, much of the research above and many other articles not included here make use of support groups as preventive intervention. It is a relatively inexpensive intervention and one that can, at times, be easily generalized. Riessman (1986) provided a good and brief discussion of these groups, distinguishing those that provide self-help mutual aid and those that produce benefit to those who are helping. Riessman feels strongly that support groups both empower individuals and also provide support, and we should not overlook that first benefit. In this chapter, he described a number of support programs for new mothers, for the widowed, for ex-patients, and so on.

VERMONT CONFERENCE ON THE PRIMARY PREVENTION OF PSYCHOPATHOLOGY (VCPPP)

Certainly one of the best sources of information on primary prevention programs is contained in the various products of the Vermont Conference. This group has had a summer conference at the University of Vermont almost each year since 1975. Experts in various subareas of psychopathology gather to present integrative reports as well as to make presentations in primary prevention research, action programs, and policy issues. The annual program has been published through the Conference for the first 10 years or so by the University Press of New England and by Sage Publications in more recent years. In addition, several books published through the Conference are collections of readings based on earlier conferences. The first volume was edited by Albee and Joffe (1977), and it presented a series of papers outlining the basic issues in primary prevention. This was followed by volumes edited by Forgays (1978) on environmental influences, by Kent and Rolf (1979) on social competence in children, by Bond and Rosen (1980) on adult competence and coping, by Joffe and Albee (1981) on the role of political action and social change, by Bond and Joffe (1982) on the facilitation of infant and early childhood development, by Albee, Gordon, and Leitenberg (1983) on the prevention of sexual problems, by Joffe, Albee, and Kelly (1984) on basic concepts (readings), by Rosen and Solomon (1985) on preventing health problems, by Kessler and Goldston (1986) on a review of progress in primary prevention, by Burchard and Burchard (1987) on prevention of delinquent behavior, by Bond and Wagner (1988) on family-oriented prevention programs, and by Albee, Joffe, and Dusenbury (1988) on social change and political action as prevention (readings). All of these books are extremely useful to both the novice and expert in prevention. They represent in many ways the history of this young field.

Special mention is made here of the Bond and Wagner (1988) book, which treats a number of family stress areas, from chronically ill children, maternal competence, family violence, through problems of bereavement and employer-sponsored programs of child care. There is an emphasis on both research and on application, which are especially good regarding getting primary prevention programs instituted. The book ends with a section on the characteristics of primary prevention programs that work. This material includes a description of the general characteristics of such programs, how programs are developed and refined, how resources may be obtained, how prevention and promotion programs can be marketed, and how they can be strengthened. It is a veritable how-to book for preventionists.

In addition to the book series, the *Journal of Primary Prevention* is a product of the Vermont Conference. It is the only journal extant that emphasizes primary prevention and is one of the few that deals exclusively with prevention problems. There are some who may disagree with the first part of that statement, especially those who take an extreme community/social change view of primary prevention.

Last, the Conference publishes the *Prevention Training Clearinghouse*. With support from the NIMH, VCPPP has established the "Clearinghouse to facilitate the exchange of information and resources on training opportunities, courses and/or workshops in primary prevention, or courses that include a prevention component." This newsletter is issued several times a year and includes new books, with frequent reviews, new courses and workshops, lists of available prevention consultants, and other material.

Further information about any of these products of the Vermont Conference can be obtained from VCPPP, Department of Psychology, John Dewey Hall, University of Vermont, Burlington, Vermont 05405.

FUTURE OF PRIMARY PREVENTION

We can see from the foregoing that primary prevention has had a reasonably full past. What do we expect of its future? First of all, since the past is the best indicator of the future we expect that we will continue to see a large number of person-oriented and school-based intervention programs. There probably will be a tendency to include here as subjects those who have been identified as at risk for maladjustment, and therefore secondary prevention. Some programs, it is hoped, will be directed to all persons in a group, before maladjustment has occurred, and without regard to risk factors. These will be the most difficult programs to institute and will be the most critical in the development of a true primary prevention.

Recently, a representative of NIMH made an overview of prevention programs sponsored by that agency (Sargent, 1987). One can reasonably expect that such programs will continue to be sponsored in future by governmental institutions. They include programs dedicated to preventing future problems for high-risk babies, those of preterm mothers who are low-income and live in chaotic homes. Mother support service programs have had positive effects and will likely continue. Interventions that attempt to train children in learning skills as prevention of delinquency, substance abuse, and psychological problems will also likely continue. Some of these are Washington buzzwords and such programs will certainly enjoy future funding. NIMH is also interested in programs that attempt to prevent depression in disadvantaged adults.

We expect to see more research and action programs on the mental and physical effects of unemployment. We outlined one such study above and a prototype might be seen in the work of Linn, Sandifer, and Stein (1985). This was a Veterans Administration study of environmental stress in Miami, Florida, on a sample of 300 men between 35 and 60 years of age. They were followed for several years and over that course of time 30 lost employment. Every 6 months thereafter physical information and scalar information (the Holmes-Rahe Life Events Measure) were obtained. They found that unemployment produces adverse psychological symptoms and increased utilization of health services, if they were available. They also report that people with strong support systems and greater self-esteem seemed to be less stressed by unemployment. We can expect to see more of this kind of study, especially in light of the increasing economic problems that our country will likely experience in the future.

We hope and expect to see a further clarification of the notion of empowerment and research and action studies designed to vary this notion systematically in situations dealing with individuals, groups, and even communities. It is an exciting prospect but one difficult to effect.

Worksite health promotion efforts will continue and likely expand further. The specific preventions included will depend somewhat on the attractiveness of their packaging. An entire recent issue of the journal *Social Science and Medicine* (1988, *26*, pp. 485–575) is devoted to such wellness programs. Several articles therein describe such programs in companies of different sizes. It was generally found that level of participation is not high, as indicated above. The research in this area is really in its infancy. We look forward to many more research efforts here with

special attention to the development of more adequate methodologies than those in studies reported to date.

The community will be much more emphasized in future prevention programs. In an interesting paper by Goldman and Morrissey (1985), they described the first three mental health movements (cf. Forgays, 1983b) and point out that each was promising but that each led to pessimism because of the increase in the number of chronic mental patients. In each case public support turned to neglect. These authors contend that now is the time for the fourth mental health cycle. It will happen because of the failures of community mental health and deinstitutionalization. This "revolution" will involve the creation of effective community support systems and the development of broad networks of mental health and social welfare services. I tend to agree with them. We have already seen a large increase in these services and, of late, some research on their efficacy. I expect these efforts to continue and increase. Sprinthall (1984) appears to agree with this sentiment. In his paper he reviewed programs in which there is active involvement in community helping programs; he calls them *deliberate psychological education*. He finds that this outcome research shows evidence for gains on measures of empathy, ego development, self-reliance, internality, moral judgment, and decreased egocentricity, and he feels that such changes are the whole aim of primary prevention. Cowen (1985) appeared to be making a similar point.

Some of the focus of prevention research and action will be directed to specific subgroups within the culture, rather than to the community at large. For example, Maypole and Anderson (1987) described a substance abuse prevention specific to blacks. They made the point that limited resources will lead to the use of more self-help prevention projects. In this one tailored to the African-American community, plays, skits, and discussions were held in the African-American churches. They found the audience response to be good, much better in the churches than in schools. Bell (1987) described preventive strategies for dealing with violence among African-Americans. He feels that primary prevention is required and that this will include the development of social networks, family support groups, vocational programs, and so on. It is absolutely necessary, he feels, that community development takes place. I expect that we will see many more culturally specific prevention efforts in the future.

Finally, it is important that preventive philosophy invade the territory of the individual clinician in practice. Linn, Yager, and Leake (1988) described a study concerned with preventive activities with high-risk children. The authors developed three scales to measure relevant attitudes of over 200 practicing psychiatrists or those in training. They found that those who were more interested in working with children had more favorable attitudes toward the role of prevention with high-risk children. Those who were intending to enter or were already engaged in full-time private practice were less supportive of prevention efforts. Those whose health beliefs followed a more internal locus-of-control were more favorable to prevention. In general, many felt that there were ethical issues involved in starting prevention programs before an adequate information base was available, and there were also social and financial problems. There are, of course, financial disincentives to practicing clinicians if prevention programs that work are put in place.

The fact is, prevention programs do work. They may not be programs that can be instituted readily in whole countries or even in entire communities. The evidence described above, however, demonstrates clearly that we can prevent the development of some maladjustment (primary prevention) and we certainly can lessen the effects of certain stressors in specific identified groups (secondary prevention). While we search for the causes of the causes and for ways of providing the necessary finances to effect changes in these causes, we must generalize the implementation of prevention programs that have been shown to work.

REFERENCES

Albee, G.W. (1983). Psychopathology, prevention, and the just society. *Journal of Primary Prevention, 4*, 5–40.

Albee, G.W., Gordon, S., & Leitenberg, H. (Eds.). (1983). *Fostering mature sexuality and preventing sexual problems.* Hanover, NH: University Press of New England.

Albee, G.W., & Gullota, T.P. (1986). Facts and fallacies about primary prevention. *Journal of Primary Prevention, 6*, 207–218.

Albee, G.W., & Joffe, J.M. (Eds.). (1977). *The primary prevention of psychopathology: The issues.* Hanover, NH: University Press of New England.

Albee, G.W., Joffe, J.M., & Dusenbury, L. (Eds.). (1988). *Readings in social change and political action as prevention.* Newbury Park, CA: Sage.

Atlas, J.A., & Rickel, A.U. (1988). Maternal coping styles and adjustment in children. *Journal of Primary Prevention, 8*, 169–185.

Baker, S.B., Swisher, J.D., Nadenichels, P.E., & Popowicz, C.L. (1984). Measured effects of primary prevention strategies. *Personnel and Guidance Journal, 62*, 459–464.

Barth, R.P., Hacking, S., & Ash, J.R. (1988). Preventing child abuse: An experimental evaluation of The Child Parent Enrichment Project. *Journal of Primary Prevention, 8*, 201–217.

Bell, C.C. (1987). Preventive strategies for dealing with violence among blacks. *Community Mental Health Journal, 23*, 217–228.

Berrueta-Clement, J.R., Schweinhart, L.J., Barnett, M.W., Epstein, A.S., & Weikart, D.P. (1984). *Changes lives: The effects of the Perry Preschool Program on youths through age 19.* Ypsilanti, MI: High/Scope Educational Research Foundation.

Bloom, B.L. (1984). *Community mental health: A general introduction* (2nd ed.). Monterey, CA: Brooks/Cole.

Bloom, B.L., Hodges, W.F., & Caldwell, R.A. (1982). A preventional program for the newly separated: Initial evaluation. *American Journal of Community Psychology, 10*, 251–264.

Bloom, B.L., Hodges, W.F., Kern, M.B., & McFaddin, S.C. (1985). A preventive intervention program for the newly separated: Final report. *American Journal of Orthopsychiatry, 55*, 9–26.

Bloom, M., Siefert, K., & Akabas, S. (Eds.). (1988). Prevention strategies in the problems of women. *Journal of Primary Prevention, 9*, Whole Nos. 1,2.

Bond, L.A., & Joffe, J.M. (Eds.). (1982). *Facilitating infant and early childhood development.* Hanover, NH: University Press of New England.

Bond, L.A., & Rosen, J. (Eds.). (1980). *Competence and coping during adulthood.* Hanover, NH: University Press of New England.

Bond, L.A., & Wagner, B.M. (Eds.). (1988). *Families in transition: Primary prevention programs that work.* Newbury Park, CA: Sage.

Bower, E.M. (1987). Prevention: A word whose time has come. *American Journal of Orthopsychiatry, 57*, 4–5.

Bry, B.H. (1982). Reducing the incidence of adolescent problems through preventive intervention. *American Journal of Community Psychology, 10*, 265–276.

Burchard, J.D., & Burchard, S.N. (Eds.). (1987). *Prevention of delinquent behavior.* Newbury Park, CA: Sage.

Cauce, A.M., Comer, J.P., & Schwartz, D. (1987). Long-term effects of a systems-oriented school prevention program. *American Journal of Orthopsychiatry, 57*, 127–131.

Cowen, E.L. (1983). Primary prevention in mental health: Past, present and future. In R.D. Felner, L. Jason, J. Moritsugu, & S.S. Farber (Eds.), *Preventive psychology: Theory, research and practice in community psychology* (pp. 11–25). Elmsford, NY: Pergamon Press.

Cowen, E.L. (1985). Person-centered approaches to primary prevention in mental health: Situation-focused and competence-enhancement. *American Journal of Community Psychology, 13*, 31–48.

Cowen, E.L. (1986). Primary prevention in mental health. In M. Kessler & S.E. Goldston (Eds.), *A decade of progress in primary prevention* (pp. 3–45). Hanover, NH: University Press of New England.

Cowen, E.L., & Work, W.C. (1988). Resilient children, psychological wellness, and primary prevention. *American Journal of Community Psychology, 16,* 591–607.

Elias, M.J., Gara, M., Ubriaco, M., Rothbaum, P.A., Clabby, J.F., & Schuyler, T. (1986). Impact of a preventive social problem-solving intervention on children's coping with middle-school stressors. *American Journal of Community Psychology, 14,* 259–275.

Englander-Golden, P., Elconin, J., & Satir, V. (1986). Assertive-leveling, communication and sympathy in adolescent drug abuse prevention. *Journal of Primary Prevention, 6,* 231–243.

Evans, G.W., Jacobs, S.V., Dooley, D., & Catalano, R. (1987). The interaction of stressful-life events and chronic strains on community mental health. *American Journal of Community Psychology, 15,* 23–34.

Farie, A.M., Cowen, E.L., & Smith, M. (1986). The development and implementation of a rural consortium program to provide early, preventive school mental health services. *Community Mental Health Journal, 22,* 94–103.

Felner, R.D., Ginter, M., & Primavera, J. (1982). Primary prevention during school transitions: Social support and environmental structure. *American Journal of Community Psychology, 10,* 277–290.

Fielding, J.E., & Piserchia, P.V. (1989). Frequency of worksite health promotion activities. *American Journal of Public Health, 79,* 16–20.

Fine, M.A., & Swift, C.F. (1988). The prevalence of young children "at risk" for later handicapping conditions. *Journal of Primary Prevention, 8,* 186–200.

Forgays, D.G. (Ed.). (1978). *Environmental influences and strategies in primary prevention.* Hanover, NH: University Press of New England.

Forgays, D.G. (1983a). Primary prevention of psychopathology. In M. Hersen, A.E. Kazdin, & A.S. Bellack (Eds.), *The clinical psychology handbook* (pp. 701–733). Elmsford, NY: Pergamon Press.

Forgays, D.G. (1983b). Primary prevention: Up the revolution. *Journal of Primary Prevention, 4,* 41–53.

Garmezy, N., & Rutter, M. (1983). *Stress, coping and development in children.* New York: McGraw-Hill.

Gilchrist, L.D., & Schinke, S.P. (1983). Coping with contraception: Cognitive and behavioral methods with adolescents. *Cognitive Therapy and Research, 7,* 379–388.

Gilchrist, L.D., Schinke, S.P., Snow, W.H., Schilling, R.F., & Senechal, V. (1988). The transition to junior high school: Opportunities for primary prevention. *Journal of Primary Prevention, 8,* 99–108.

Goldman, H.H., & Morrissey, J.P. (1985). The alchemy of mental health policy: Homelessness and the fourth cycle of reform. *American Journal of Public Health, 75,* 727–731.

Goodman, S.H., & Isaacs, L.D. (1985). Primary prevention with children of severely disturbed mothers. *Journal of Preventive Psychiatry, 3,* 113–121.

Gottlieb, B.H. (1984). *Social support strategies: Guidelines for mental health practice.* Beverly Hills, CA: Sage.

Hess, R., & Hermalin, J. (Eds.). (1983). *Innovations in prevention.* New York: Haworth Press.

Joffe, J.M., & Albee, G.W. (Eds.). (1981). *Prevention through political action and social change.* Hanover, NH: University Press of New England.

Joffe, J.M., Albee, G.W., & Kelly, L.D. (Eds.). (1984). *Readings in primary prevention of psychopathology: Basic concepts.* Hanover, NH: University Press of New England.

Johnson, D.L., & Breckenridge, J.N. (1982). The Houston Parent–Child Development Center and the primary prevention of behavior problems in young children. *American Journal of Community Psychology, 10,* 305–316.

Johnson, D.L., & Walker, T. (1984, September). *The primary prevention of behavior problems in Mexican-American children.* Presented at the annual meeting of the American Psychological Association, Toronto, Canada.

Johnson, D.L., & Walker, T. (1987). Primary prevention of behavior problems in Mexican-American children. *American Journal of Community Psychology, 15,* 375–385.

Jordan, T.J., Grallo, R., Duetsch, M., & Deutsch, C.P. (1985). Long-term effects of early enrichment: A 20-year perspective on persistence and change. *American Journal of Community Psychology, 13,* 393–415.

Kent, M.W., & Rolf, J.E. (Eds.). (1979). *Social competence in children.* Hanover, NH: University Press of New England.

Kessler, M., & Goldston, S.E. (Eds.). (1986). *A decade of progress in primary prevention.* Hanover, NH: University Press of New England.

Klingman, A. (1985). Mass inoculation in a community: The effect of primary prevention of stress reactions. *American Journal of Community Psychology, 13,* 323–332.

Larsen, J.K. (1987). Community mental health services in transition. *Community Mental Health Journal, 23,* 250–259.

Linn, M.W., Sandifer, R., & Stein, S. (1985). Effects of unemployment on mental and physical health. *American Journal of Public Health, 75,* 502–506.

Linn, L.S., Yager, J., & Leake, B. (1988). Psychiatrists' attitudes toward preventive intervention in routine clinical practice. *Hospital and Community Psychiatry, 39,* 637–642.

Marmar, C.R., Horowitz, M.J., Weiss, D.S., Wilner, N.R., & Kaltreider, N.B. (1988). A controlled trial of brief psychotherapy and mutual-help group treatment of conjugal bereavement. *American Journal of Psychiatry, 145,* 203–209.

Maypole, D.E., & Anderson, R.B. (1987). Culture-specific substance abuse prevention for blacks. *Community Mental Health Journal, 23,* 135–139.

National Mental Health Association. (1987). Commission Report on the Prevention of Mental-Emotional Disabilities, 1986. Reprinted in *Journal of Primary Prevention, 7,* Whole No. 4.

Nelson, G., & Carson, P. (1988). Evaluation of a social problem-solving skills program for third- and fourth-grade students. *American Journal of Community Psychology, 16,* 79–99.

Nikelly, A.G. (1987). Prevention in Sweden and Cuba: Implications for policy research. *Journal of Primary Prevention, 7,* 117–131.

Osofsky, J. (1986). Perspectives on infant mental health. In M. Kessler & S.E. Goldston (Eds.), *A decade of progress in primary prevention* (pp. 181–201). Hanover, NH: University Press of New England.

Osterweis, M., Solomon, F., & Green, M. (Eds.). (1984). *Bereavement: Reactions, consequences and care.* Washington, DC: National Academy Press.

Pedro-Carroll, J.L., & Cowen, E.L. (1985). The Children of Divorce Intervention Program: An investigation of a school-based prevention program. *Journal of Consulting and Clinical Psychology, 53,* 603–611.

Pedro-Carroll, J.L., Cowen, E.L., Hightower, A.D., & Guare, J.C. (1986). Preventive intervention with latency-aged children of divorce: A replication study. *American Journal of Community Psychology, 14,* 277–290.

Peterson, L., & Mori, L. (1985). Prevention of child injury. *Journal of Consulting and Clinical Psychology, 53,* 586–595.

Pierson, D.E., Klein-Walker, D., & Tivnan, T. (1984). A school-based program from infancy to kindergarten for parents and their children. *Personnel and Guidance Journal, 62,* 448–455.

Rappaport, J. (1987). Terms of empowerment/exemplars of prevention: Toward a theory for community psychology. *American Journal of Community Psychology, 15,* 121–147.

Rappaport, J., Swift, C., & Hess, R.D. (Eds.). (1984). Studies in empowerment: Steps toward understanding and action. *Prevention in Human Services, 3,* 1–230.

Rhoads, D.L., & Raymond, J.S. (1981). Quality of life and the competent community. *American Journal of Community Psychology, 9,* 293–301.

Rickel, A.U., & Langner, T.S. (1985). Short- and long-term effects of marital disruption. *American Journal of Community Psychology, 13,* 599–611.

Riessman, F. (1986). Support groups as preventive intervention. In M. Kessler & S.E. Goldston (Eds.), *A decade of progress in primary prevention* (pp. 275–288). Hanover, NH: University Press of New England.

Roberts, M.C., & Peterson, L.C. (Eds.). (1984). *Prevention of problems in childhood: Psychological research and applications.* New York: John Wiley & Sons.

Rooney-Rebeck, P., & Jason, L. (1986). Prevention of prejudice in elementary school students. *Journal of Primary Prevention, 7,* 63–73.

Rosen, J., & Solomon, L. (Eds.). (1985). *Preventing health problems and promoting positive health behavior.* Hanover, NH: University Press of New England.

Rosenberg, M.S., & Rappucci, N.D. (1985). Primary pre-

vention of child abuse. *Journal of Consulting and Clinical Psychology, 53,* 576–585.

Rossiter, A.B. (1988). A model for group intervention with preschool children experiencing separation and divorce. *American Journal of Orthopsychiatry, 58,* 387–396.

Rotheram, R., Armstrong, M., & Booraem, C. (1982). Assertiveness training in fourth- and fifth-grade children. *American Journal of Community Psychology, 10,* 567–582.

Rutter, M. (1987). Psychological resilience and protective mechanisms. *American Journal of Orthopsychiatry, 57,* 316–331.

Sargent, M. (1987). Prevention studies focus on infants, schoolchildren, adults. *Hospital and Community Psychiatry, 38,* 455–456.

Schinke, S.P., & Gilchirst, L.D. (1985). Preventing substance abuse with children and adolescents. *Journal of Consulting and Clinical Psychology, 53,* 596–602.

Seeman, M., Seeman, A.Z., & Budros, A. (1988). Powerlessness, work, and community: A longitudinal study of alienation and alcohol use. *Journal of Health and Social Behavior, 29,* 185–198.

Shure, M.B. (1988). How to think, not what to think: A cognitive approach to prevention. In L.A. Bond & B.M. Wagner (Eds.), *Families in transition: Primary prevention programs that work* (pp. 170–199). Newbury Park, CA: Sage.

Shure, M.B., & Spivack, G. (1982). Interpersonal problem solving in young children: A cognitive approach to prevention. *American Journal of Community Psychology, 10,* 341–356.

Social Science & Medicine. (1988). *26,* 485–575.

Sprinthal, N.A. (1984). Primary prevention: A road paved with a plethora of promises and procrastinations. *Personal and Guidance Journal, 62,* 491–495.

Sterling, S., Cowen, E.L., Weissberg, R.P., Lotyczewski, B.S., & Boike, M. (1985). Recent stressful life events and young children's school adjustment. *American Journal of Community Psychology, 13,* 87–98.

Stolberg, A.L., & Garrison, K.M. (1985). Evaluating a primary prevention program for children of divorce. *American Journal of Community Psychology, 13,* 111–124.

Sweet, M., Stoler, N., Kelter, R., & Thurrell, R.J. (1989). A community of buddies: Support groups for veterans forced into early retirement. *Hospital and Community Psychiatry, 40,* 172–176.

Tableman, B., Marciniak, D., Johnson, D., & Rodgers, R. (1982). Stress management training for women on public assistance. *American Journal of Community Psychology, 10,* 359–367.

Toubiana, Y.H., Milgram, N.A., Strich, Y., & Edelstein, A. (1988). Crisis intervention in a school community disaster: Principles and practices. *Journal of Community Psychology, 16,* 228–240.

Wagner, B.M., Compas, B.E., & Howell, D.C. (1988). Daily and major life events: A test of an integrative model of psychosocial stress. *American Journal of Community Psychology, 16,* 189–205.

Wells, J.K., Howard, G.S., Nowlin, W.F., & Vargas, M.J. (1986). Presurgical anxiety and postsurgical pain and adjustment: Effects of a stress inoculation procedure. *Journal of Consulting and Clinical Psychology, 54,* 831–835.

Werner, E.E., & Smith, R.S. (1982). *Vulnerable but invincible: A study of resilient children.* New York: McGraw-Hill.

Williams, C.L., & Westermeyer, J. (1985). Public health aspects of mental health: The last 75 years of the *American Journal of Public Health. American Journal of Public Health, 75,* 722–725.

Wright, S., & Cowen, E.L. (1985). The effects of peer-teaching on student perceptions of class environment, adjustment, and academic performance. *American Journal of Community Psychology, 13,* 417–431.

Zaslow, M.J. (1988). Sex differences in children's response to parental divorce: 1. Research methodology and post-divorce family forms. *American Journal of Orthopsychiatry, 58,* 355–378.

CHAPTER 40

COMMUNITY MENTAL HEALTH

Linda R. Gonzales
James G. Kelly
Carol T. Mowbray
Robert B. Hays
Lonnie R. Snowden

More than a quarter century has passed since John F. Kennedy signed into law the Community Mental Health Systems Act, ushering in an early optimistic expansion of the field. The mission was clear: Serve the people in their communities, with the types of services and programming appropriate to their needs, in order to decrease the prevalence of mental illness and associated dysfunction. In ensuing years two factors have forced tough reappraisal of how best to implement this goal: (a) diminishing fiscal resources, and (b) the complexity of addressing serious mental health problems within the context of the disenfranchising sociopolitical/economic circumstances of clients and communities. In the chapter prepared for the first edition of the *Clinical Psychology Handbook* we emphasized the evolution of specific community mental health services designed to meet community needs. In the present chapter we have included two criteria to guide the selection of specific examples of community-based mental health services. First, we have given special attention to those mental health services that explicitly take into account cultural and social class characteristics of the recipients of the services. Qualities of culture and class create enriched opportunities to deliver *community-based* services. Community-based services dovetail, integrate, and adapt to cultural and class variables. In this way the aspirations of the recipients of services and members of the community can be met through a community approach. Qualities of culture and class are important resources for the development of mental health services, because these topics provide information about the social structures and traditions of communities. Culture and class variables also help sustain and support the efficacy of services.

A second criteria employed to identify exemplary services is the extent to which mental health professionals also serve as advocates to help clients and citizens acquire interpersonal and life skills that can assist them to improve their social and economic roles in the community. The authors believe that reducing the expression of mental illness and promoting mental health includes the acquisition of occupational and social roles. Occupational and social roles provide

Robert Hays's work on this chapter was supported by National Institute of Mental Health/National Institute of Drug Abuse Center Grant No. MH42459.

meaning, orientation, and integration for all of us. The authors have identified community mental health services where mental health professionals have facilitated integration of the delivery of services with the acquisition of social skills. The preferred social skill may be learned in a neighborhood group, a church group, a self-help group, a social support group, via an extended family, or through participation in voluntary activities. In supporting the integration of clients in the community, the providers of service are promoting clients' efforts to learn skills that will help their adaptation to the community. In revising this chapter we have again chosen to focus on exemplary community mental health programs and approaches that have risen to these challenges. The first section, citizen participation, specifically addresses the often-overlooked endeavor of obtaining citizen involvement in the design and critique of community mental health services and systems. In subsequent sections, innovative services are detailed for three specialty populations: ethnic minorities, the elderly, and women. Finally, the use of social support as an alternative type of mental health invervention is discussed, with examples of how this has been used with persons affected by the acquired immunodeficiency syndrome (AIDS) epidemic. Throughout, we attempt to point out unifying principles for community-based, potentially empowering mental health services, as well as ideas for critical evaluation of such approaches.

CITIZEN PARTICIPATION AND COMMUNITY MENTAL HEALTH SERVICES

The development of policies for the improvement of mental health services is directly related to the involvement, persistence, and extensive investment of citizens (Morrison, Holdridge-Crane, & Smith, 1978; Ridenour, 1961). This section of the chapter reports on some of these contributions, where it has been possible for professionals, administrators in mental health programs, and elected officials to jointly affirm that citizens can proactively influence policies and services for the care of the mentally ill in their community.

In looking at citizens' participation in the delivery of mental health services, Kopolow (1981) identified seven benefits: (a) increased sense of self-esteem, (b) increased optimism about recovery, (c) development of innovative programs more responsive to the needs of clients, (d) decreased cost, (e) creation of community-based advocates for improved mental health services, (f) provision of services to underserved popula-

tions, and (g) improved public image of the mentally ill.

These benefits are able to be realized when there is an explicit, palpable commitment for collaborative involvement from the community mental health system of professionals and state and local officials. It certainly has been demonstrated that the degree to which an institution is innovative is associated both with the permeability of its boundaries with the community and with its linkages to external resources (Aiken & Hage, 1968; Katz & Kahn, 1978). There are numerous documented accounts of how mental health services have been influenced by citizens (Bonfield, Olds, Shreve, Smith, & Schoenberger, 1978; Hessler & Walters, 1976; Morentz, 1979), as well as instances in which citizens have made an effective impact upon mental health policy (Burgner, Zinobar, & Dinkel, 1984; Mowbray, Chamberlain, Jennings, & Reed, 1987; Wilson, 1988). There is some evidence that when citizens do participate in the design of community-based activities there is a definite increased sense of personal control for citizens. In addition, social support is created in the process of involvement and participation. In one laboratory and two community studies Zimmerman and Rappaport (1988) reported that greater participation in community activities and organizations is indeed associated with a self-report of empowerment and a confidence in influencing community events. Comparable data are reported by Dundee-Anderson (1985) in an analysis of 164 executive directors, board chairpersons, and board members affiliated with 40 Virginia community service boards.

In a comprehensive review of citizen participation in community mental health, Windle and Cibulka (1981) noted that a major constraint on the involvement of citizens in authoring, enabling, planning, governing, delivering, or evaluating mental health services is presented by the increasing complexity of government operations and the influence of professionals with special expertise about policy formulation not readily available to citizens.

The difficulties and constraints in facilitating citizen participation have been noted by Chu and Trotter (1974) in a critical appraisal of the development of community mental health services funded by the National Institute of Mental Health. The ever-present discrepancy between the intent of federal, state, and local legislation that sanctions citizens to be active partners in the delivery of mental health services but limits their actual participation is frequently noted (Bellin, 1981; Caro, 1981; Cibulka, 1981; Colom, 1981; Eichler, 1978; Kopolow, 1981; Landsberg,

Hammer & Neigher, 1978; Premo, 1972; Riley, 1981; Windle & Cibulka, 1981; Windle & Paschall, 1981). Problems have included lack of consumer representation on boards such that poverty-area mental health centers are given "elitist" boards composed of prominent citizens, and the inability of boards to influence services or policies due to being given neither the legal authority nor the responsibility for programs and services. The remaining portion of this section comments on examples of community mental health programs that have addressed or overcome the barriers between professional and citizen collaboration in the delivery of mental health services.

In the state of Maryland, the power of citizen involvement in the delivery of mental health services was increased in 1983 by forming a coalition of four independent groups. These organizations are The Alliance for the Mentally Ill of Maryland, an association of 18 local self-help groups; On Our Own, an organization of people who have been residents of psychiatric facilities; The Maryland Association of Psychosocial Services, a group representing 40 non-profit providers of services; and The Mental Health Association of Maryland, a voluntary citizens' educational, advocacy, and service agency. This coalition has hired a lobbyist and was successful in increasing the state budget by more than 15 million dollars in appropriations for mental health services in the state between 1985 and 1988 (Cromwell, Howe, & O'Rear, 1988). A coalition of such organizations is a potent method of activating and maintaining ways for citizens to affect policies for services for the mentally ill.

Another example of a method to facilitate citizen participation is a research project reporting techniques for involving citizens in the state of Florida (Burgner et al., 1984). This project involved state mental health facilities, community mental health centers, and mental health clinics. Seventeen citizen review groups were created to meet on a time-limited basis for the purpose of reviewing a facility's evaluative findings and developing written recommendations for improving the facility's operation. These recommendations were presented to the governing board of each facility, each of which was required to respond to the citizen group in writing. The citizen groups were of three types: (a) *homogeneous groups*—made up of one type of citizen, such as former clients, referral agents, and so forth, (b) *heterogeneous groups*—citizens in the community who represented the various subpopulations, or (c) *preexisting citizen groups*. In reviewing the accomplishments of these three groups it was found that, as expected, former clients focused on problem areas specific to service quality much more than other types of citizen groups did. Seven of the 17 groups achieved implementation levels of 75% or greater. An important cautionary feature of the findings was that there was a greater response by the 17 centers to recommendations made by professionals and community members with special expertise than those made by client groups. Follow-up interviews of the center participants indicated that 69% of the centers reported that the research process had been effective in making the centers more responsive to the needs of the community. A discouraging and often cited fact, however, was that although the 17 centers verbally endorsed the citizen review process, only 2 centers formalized procedures to continue the process of citizen review.

The state of Michigan created funds during 1982–1983 for demonstration projects of consumer-run alternative services. Findings related to three projects illustrate that it is feasible to design community-based mental health services and directly involve consumers and citizens (Mowbray et al., 1987). Project Ease Out employed four advocates who were former patients to spend 20 hours per week visiting 25 clients in mental hospitals in rural areas and providing assistance and social support post-discharge. Five of the clients receiving the consumer service were able to survive on their own. In the course of the project one of the four advocates was rehospitalized. A second project was the Companions Program, which matched 10 female volunteers and 2 male volunteers with clients to provide interpersonal relationships in which clients could develop and practice social skills and engage in normal social activities. Over time the companions averaged two social activities per week. Most matches continued beyond the required 6 months. One problem noted was the difficulty in locating male companions. The third project, Project Stay, provided a support network and help with life maintenance skills so that individuals with severe emotional problems could maintain independence in the community. Thirty-seven individuals participated as volunteers. In this program, volunteers had between one and four contacts per day. There was some difficulty in finding volunteers who owned cars, as well as locating housing for clients.

Each of these three Michigan programs illustrates that it is possible to involve consumers and former clients in the delivery of mental health services at a relatively low cost and with relatively positive demonstrated effects. The evidence of these three demonstration projects as well as the pioneering work of Fairweather and colleagues affirms that current clients as well as former patients can be key participants in the design of their own community mental health services (Fairweather, 1964; Fairweather, 1980; Fairweather & Davidson, 1986; Fairweather, Sanders, Maynard, & Cressler, 1969).

The state of Vermont has developed its mental health service delivery system so that citizens, former clients, and advocates for former clients are integral and essential participants in the delivery of mental health services (Wilson, 1988). The Vermont Department of Mental Health has established a Consumer Advisory Committee composed of two consumers from each of the 10 community mental health centers in the state, which advises the department about its policies and procedures. The Vermont Alliance for the Mentally Ill is also very active in working with state employees and local citizens. There has evolved an active collaborative tradition between state program staff, former patients, and advocacy organizations to ensure that the needs of the mentally ill are being served. This collaborative spirit has been a driving force for the development of an array of intensive outreach and case management services that includes attention to housing needs, inpatient care and crisis services.

A defining value for Vermont's efforts to design comprehensive community-based services is the explicit assertion that success of the state mental health program is defined in terms of:

> Its effect on the *lives,* rather than service use of individuals with psychiatric disabilities. . . . The real success should be measured in terms of how well individuals are functioning outside of, but with the support of the service system. Service system comprehensiveness should not preclude the development of natural supports, relationships and activities in the community. (Wilson, 1988, p. 19)

The Vermont program derives from an explicit and deeply held value that affirms that the basis for innovative design and delivery of community mental health services is the participation, collaboration, and ownership of services by citizens at large and former clients of services. The shared affirmation of this value makes it possible to honor, sanction, facilitate, and protect the direct and sustained participation of citizens. When this value is expressed daily in community-based programs like these examples in Florida, Maryland, Michigan, and Vermont the words "community mental health" become real, viable, and inspiring.

The involvement of community members and consumers in the design and evaluation of services is the foundation on which community mental health services should be built. Meeting the needs of special at-risk populations, particularly those who would be ill-served by traditional services, provides the framework for building programs. In the next three sections innovative services pertaining to ethnic minorities, the elderly, and women are discussed. Each of these groups presents particular challenges and concerns that have been successfully addressed.

ETHNIC MINORITIES

A long-standing source of concern in the mental health field has been problems in utilization facing members of ethnic minority groups. The President's Commission on Mental Health (1978) reiterated the call of earlier critics for greater attention to the needs of these special populations. As minority populations continue to grow and face pressures arising from differences in language and culture, poor health, lack of education and income, racism, and discrimination, our need for an understanding of mental health status and service utilization by these groups can only increase.

The evidence suggests that when they appear for formal service by mental health agencies, minority clients are assigned to less desirable forms of care, attend fewer sessions, or receive a lower intensity of services, and are more likely to drop out, in comparison to nonethnic minority clients (Armstrong, Ishiki, Heiman, Mundt, & Womack, 1984; Cole & Pilisuk, 1976; Sue, 1977). These conclusions have remained true in econometrically oriented studies that have used large, representative samples and taken account of need and other factors that predispose and facilitate utilization (Horgan, 1986; Leaf et al., 1985; Williams, 1979).

Barriers to utilization facing minorities may not only limit the extent of their participation in services; they may also prevent some ethnic minority members from entering systems of care in the first place. For Latinos, Asian-Americans, and Pacific Islanders, the picture is relatively clear. Data on admission rates and from community-based surveys converge and point to underutilization relative to whites (Snowden, 1988). Knowledge of Latino help seeking and patterns of utilization has been greatly advanced by the National Institute of Mental Health (NIMH) Epidemiologic Catchment Area (ECA) project, and its Mexican-American oversample at Los Angeles. Comparable data are lacking on Asian-Americans and Pacific Islanders.

The situation of African-Americans, as well as that of Native-Americans and Alaska Natives, appears more complex. For African-Americans, there is evidence both of underutilization of services relative to whites (Sussman, Robins, & Earls, 1987), as well as overutilization (Broman, 1987). To the extent that overutilization occurs, however, it may be attributable to a troubling reliance on inpatient care (Cheung & Snowden, 1990).

Data on Native Americans are sketchy and difficult to interpret. A reservation-based system of care is operated, partly by the Indian Health Service and partly under contract from the Indian Self-Determination Act (Neligh, 1988). Native-Americans living outside reservations use whatever system is at hand. This set of diverse arrangements makes a full accounting of utilization difficult.

How can mental health centers encourage appropriate levels and types of minority utilization? After reviewing the literature, Zane, Sue, Castro, and George (1982) proposed six principles: (a) congruence between services on the one hand, and needs and cultural patterns of clients on the other, (b) an active stance toward prevention and encouragement toward service utilization, (c) integration and linkage of mental health services with other health-related and social services, (d) systems of comprehensive and coordinated services, (e) community control through active advisory board participation with solid community representation, and (f) development of knowledge about effective practices and systems and active attempts at dissemination.

An organization that embodies many of these principles and has maintained an extensive ethnic minority presence is the West Oakland Mental Health Center in Oakland, California. The center is located in a lower-city area, near downtown, and serves a social stratum that has come to be called the "underclass." This community shares a series of problems with many of its urban counterparts: unemployment and a dwindling industrial base, crime, poor public education, and an epidemic of drug abuse. The community mental health center functions as a unit of a larger organization called West Oakland Health Center. That agency originated in the Community Action Program of the Office of Economic Opportunity in the mid-1960s as a neighborhood-based organization that identified needs and created structures to address them. West Oakland Health Center has been described as an example of community action at its best (Pressman & Wildavsky, 1973). West Oakland Health Center, including its community mental health center, is funded from contracts with local government and from collections of fees from public third-party payers (Medi-Cal).

About 80% of clients at West Oakland are African-American. Another 10% are white, and the other 10% are members of other minority groups, mostly Hispanic. The administrative staff of the center are African-American, as are about two thirds of the treatment staff and interns. Its own administrative staff and that of its parent organization include well-known and active figures in community affairs and local government.

The dominant mode of intervention remains office-based, individual psychotherapy. Contact with collaterals (e.g., welfare worker, probation officer, teacher, etc.) is encouraged, however, and represents a significant share of the service effort. In response to a questionnaire, most practitioners described themselves as "eclectic" in their approach to therapy, and as "very knowledgeable" about the culture of African-Americans.

An important feature of West Oakland is that it encourages and facilitates empirical research. One study (Snowden, Storey, & Clancy, 1989) tackled the sensitive but important question of whether in this predominantly African-American setting, clients who were other than African-American were underserved. The data indicated equal withdrawal and dropout rates among racial groups. African-Americans appeared, however, to receive more services overall. This initial difference disappeared when controls were introduced in multivariate analysis for sociodemographic background, diagnosis, and treatment history. The openness to such research and willingness to receive critical evaluation are particularly noteworthy.

West Oakland has principally adapted its services to the needs of the African-American population, but other mental health centers face greater diversity. One such is New Horizons Community Mental Health Center in Miami. This organization must distinguish among groups often lumped together—between Caribbean- and African-Americans; between Cuban-Americans and Puerto Ricans—which make the cultural mosaic that is Miami. Its program of services has been designed to emphasize outreach, cultural responsiveness, and community control.

An important organizational feature has been decentralization within the low-income, inner-city district that makes up the targeted catchment area. Staff are organized into teams, reflecting major sectors of the population; Anglo elderly, Bahamian, Cuban, Haitian, native African-American, and Puerto Rican. Teams are responsible not only for direct provision of mental health services, but also for indirect services, including resource information and outreach, research, consultation and education, and community development. Ethnic matching of team members and community members is emphasized. Referral to collaborating agencies and direct provision of social services accompany biomedical and psychological therapies.

Decentralization is also reflected in the development of community-based miniclinics. Focusing on serving the chronically mentally ill, this network of programs provides assistance in rehabilitation, planning, and monitoring of community living. Miniclinics also sometimes serve as neighborhood centers, sponsoring organized activities for children and youth.

Cultural elements are taken into account in the provision of therapy. Immigration history, socioeconomic standing, and acculturation are considered in the assessment of problems and planning of treatment. In the treatment of an 11-year-old Bahamian girl, for example, "the session involved not only the parents but grandparents, aunts, and uncles. Rituals . . . to keep the spirits away were performed. . . . Thus, our treatment plan grew out of religious practices and beliefs of the immediate as well as extended family" (Bestman, 1986, p. 216). Therapists are aware of indigenous systems of belief (voodoo, obeah, rootwork, santeria, and espiritisimo), understand the practice of traditional healers, and maintain relationships with selected traditional practitioners.

Social action has been another element of service delivery. Projects have included the establishment of a multipurpose service center, a summer employment program for low-income African-American teenagers, and arrangements that resulted in over 1,200 Haitian immigrants receiving social security cards. New Horizons, then, enacts a philosophy of social and political consciousness and cultural awareness.

Both West Oakland and New Horizons in Miami embody many of the principles of service system design discussed previously. Practitioners are culturally aware, and take account of indigenous beliefs and practices. Health and social services are provided in affiliated programs, or through an active network for making referrals. Political involvement in the community makes them visible and open to grass-roots feedback. Research also has been conducted and used for planning and monitoring of services.

ELDERLY PEOPLE AND COMMUNITY MENTAL HEALTH

People 65 and older comprise 12% of the U.S. population, numbering 28.5 million in 1985. The aged population has been growing more rapidly than that of people younger than 65; given current fertility and immigration levels, the only age groups to grow significantly in the next century will be those past age 55 (AARP, 1986). More startling is the fact that the most rapidly growing segment of the aged population is the "oldest old," that is, people 85 years of age or older (Hollenshead & Miller, 1984). However, service utilization data reflect a decided underrepresentation of the elderly as mental health clients. Studies have found the elderly account for only 4% to 6% of community mental health clients and 7% of private mental health professionals' clients (Fleming, Rickards, Santos, & West, 1986; Kermis, 1986). The failure of mental health providers to reach older adults is a complex matter. Consider the following situation: An 86-year-old widow, frail but mentally intact, lives alone on the family farm in rural Kansas. Her only relative is a niece in California. Their contact consists of weekly telephone calls and the niece's annual visit. The niece is concerned because her aunt, who has limitations due to arthritis, diabetes, and cataracts, insists on staying in this isolated situation and will accept little help. However, the aunt states firmly that she prefers things as they are. One winter day she slips on an ice patch, falls, and sustains a hip fracture. Fortunately she is soon found and hospitalized. Against her wishes she is discharged after treatment to a nursing home for rehabilitation. When the niece is able to visit 3 months later she finds her aunt is thinner, apathetic, demonstrating cognitive decline, and completely nonambulatory. Physical therapy had been discontinued due to "resistiveness and lack of motivation." The aunt is clinically depressed. Because this has not been identified or treated, her potentially reversible physical and mental disabilities may become permanent.

This story illustrates several aspects of the difficulties of mental health service delivery to the elderly. First, mental or emotional problems may be unrecognized as such by the elderly person and/or by those around him or her, including the person's physician (German et al., 1987; Waxman, 1986). Second, there are often related social and physical problems that should be addressed in concert with the mental health problems (Lebray, 1984). Third, the older adult tends to be physically isolated from traditional mental health service sites and/or less mobile due to transportation problems, frailty, or health problems (Knight, 1983). Fourth, elderly people may be less willing to seek mental health services, especially as compared to services for health problems (Waxman, Carner, & Klein, 1984).

The widowed aunt's story depicts the worst possible fantasy of many older adults—that of institutionalization and loss of independent functioning. Whereas only about 5% of persons over 65 at any given time live in institutions (primarily nursing homes), the proportion increases with age—for those over 85, the figure is 23% (AARP, 1986). Persons who do live in nursing homes tend to have a higher rate of mental disorders, which may have been associated with the need for institutionalization or which may have followed it. Cognitive impairment appears to be the most frequent, with rates of about 60%; depression is also prevalent, with recent studies finding rates of 12% to 15% for severe depression, either with or without concomitant cognitive impairment (German, Shapiro, & Kramer, 1986; Parmalee, Katz, & Lawton, 1989). A significant minority of nursing home residents, including many older adults, are deinstitutionalized state hospital patients who may have various types of chronic mental illness and "institutional neurosis" (Carling, 1981; Kermis, 1987). Despite the concentration of a resident population with significant mental health needs, the treatment available in nursing homes is generally inadequate to nonexistent (Carling, 1981; Harper & Lebowitz, 1986).

One significant factor in developing successful and well-utilized mental health services for elders is accessibility, both physical and psychological. Indirect methods, such as consultation and education, also play a major role in serving the elderly population as compared to other adult age groups. In the two outreach programs described next, both direct and indirect services are offered for a client population of community-dwelling elderly with the specific goal of maintaining clients' independence.

Elderlink, a program of the Mt. Hood Community Mental Health Center, Gresham, Oregon, and the Elderly Outreach Program, based in Cedar Rapids, Iowa (serving Jones and Linn counties), share a number of common goals and methods. Each seeks to deliver outpatient mental health services to elders who are physically isolated (suburban and rural, respectively), who are at risk of premature institutionalization, and who are unlikely to seek needed services. Both programs offer access to other services besides that of mental health, and both use the coordination of the aging services network with mental health services, based on Raschko's (1985) model. The programs rely on simultaneous intervention at multiple levels in the community rather than on clinical programming alone to reach the target population.

The "gatekeeper" case finding approach (Raschko, 1985) is a component successfully used by both programs for identifying potential clients. Gatekeepers are people who have occasion to observe older adults with actual or emerging problems in the course of their job or community activities. Mail carriers, utility company employees, law enforcement personnel, apartment or mobile home court managers, and others have served as gatekeepers. Their role is not to intervene directly, but simply to identify signs that the older person may need help and to report this to a specific central intake agency. Elderlink trains gatekeepers with an initial single session, a follow-up session every 6 months, and maintains a communication link with a contact person at each gatekeeper agency. The effect is that of casting a wide net; Elderlink has been averaging 20 referrals per month from its 2,230 gatekeepers (J. Applegate, personal communication, October 28, 1988). Once the referral is made, mental health or social service staff contact the identified person, arrange a home visit, and establish rapport before formal services are offered. The objective of maintaining well-being and independence is stressed by the visiting staff. If the elder refuses, reapproach is tried at a later time. Elders may need two or three "friendly visits" to establish adequate trust (T. Schafer-Nelson, personal communication, October 27, 1988; J. Applegate, personal communication, July 23, 1989).

The older person is offered not only mental health treatment if this is indicated, but also any other available needed assistance, including financial help, home health, chore service, home delivered meals, referral to appropriate nursing and medical care, and other services. Elderlink, in particular, conceptualizes its services as interdisciplinary in nature, offering social, health, and mental health services in a coordinated plan. Most of the services, including nursing assessment and mental health services, are delivered at the client's home. Case management is a key component for organizing and following the delivery of such services in both programs. In the design of Elderlink, case management was considered so central that funding was allocated to add one case manager to each of the two involved social service agencies. With reduced case loads more time is spent on training, on health and mental health consultation, and on increased attention for specific clients. Case managers receive ongoing consultation regarding how to address most clients' mental health needs. Goals may include detection of signs of decompensation, with the possibility of proactive intervention; maintaining a communication link with a fearful and withdrawing elder; monitoring the response to pharmacotherapy; and other individualized plans. Clients with more severe problems receive ongoing direct treatment from mental health staff. The availability of several disciplines within mental health has been vital for treatment or consultation for complex cases often encountered.

Education and training is also an essential component for both projects. Elderlink has chosen to emphasize the skill development of 19 case managers with a planned program of continuing education on gerontological health and mental health topics, and case staffings. In contrast, the Elderly Outreach Project has initiated an extensive public education campaign on aging and mental health as well as offering training to persons delivering health and social services. Raising public awareness has gone hand-in-hand with the strategic, consistent efforts of Project staff to gain entree in the rural communities served. It was recognized from the start that the support of community leaders and of other service providers, although essential, would have to be earned over time.

Initial program evaluation studies for both programs show that the appropriate populations are being reached. Clients of the Elderly Outreach Project, in comparison to the general population of older adults in the catchment area, are older, live alone more, and are widowed more, all characteristics of higher risk individuals. In addition, it was found that 26% of the mental health clients could be classified as having severe and persistent mental disorders (Buckwalter, 1987). This was surprising in that aging chronically mentally ill had not been a specific target population. Elderlink is finding that over half of the people referred by gatekeepers receive services for the first time as a result; that is, referred elders were both eligible and previously unserved. Only 6% of those referred were found not to need services, to be ineligible for them, or refused them. Elderlink is also finding a high level of mental health need among the client population. The two programs are in the process of conducting impact studies that will examine the effectiveness of services and their cost-effectiveness.

As noted earlier in this section, the 5% of elderly dwelling in nursing homes are at high risk for mental and emotional disorders and behavior problems. The Outreach Consultation Service of the Geropsychiatric Treatment Program at Oregon State Hospital (Salem, Oregon) provides solely indirect services in the form of clinical (case-centered) consultation, for the target population of long-term care clients at risk for psychiatric hospitalization. The service is provided without charge for appropriate referrals throughout the state of Oregon, and a significant proportion of clients seen are living in rural communities. The mission of the service is to prevent unnecessary commitments of elders to the state hospital by helping caregivers to meet mental health needs in long-term care settings, with the recognition that in many cases the extant health and mental health service delivery system is less than well prepared to do so. Mental health training for nursing home staff is another major component of service.

Members of the Outreach team are a gerontological nurse practitioner, a clinical geropsychologist, and an outreach mental health specialist. Their consultations are conducted at the nursing home or foster home of the referred elder, and rely upon comprehensive investigation of the client's medical and psychosocial history, symptomology, physical and social environment, response to previous interventions, and current mental status. An interdisciplinary approach is used and the team members often discuss the case with professionals from other disciplines before recommendations are formulated. Evaluations are undertaken only after both the primary physician's request and that of the caregiving staff have been received. Recommendations may include medication changes, behavioral interventions, referrals to other specialists, and environmental interventions. A copy of the consultation summary, including practical and "do-able" interventions, is sent to the referring physician, caregiving staff, and to the involved case manager. Follow-up phone calls are made to assess outcome and give additional suggestions. Most of the clients seen are nursing home residents (88%), chronically mentally ill (60%), and three-fourths have three or more medical diagnoses in addition to the presenting mental health problems. In 63% of the cases the client was dangerous to self and/or to others, and in 30% of the cases the client was at risk of being evicted. In one study of 33 consecutive clients followed up for a 6-month period, it was found that in 75% of the cases one or more of the consultant's suggestions were used, and in 68% of these there was improvement in the elderly client's mental health or behavior problems. Twelve percent of the clients were civilly committed despite the consultation.

These three outreach programs illustrate how a high-risk population, unwilling or unable to seek mental health services voluntarily, can nonetheless receive help through varied approaches such as systems intervention, case finding, home visits, holistic, interdisciplinary treatment planning, and the delivery of indirect services such as consultation and education. A balance must be found between paternalistic interference in the lives of older citizens and assertively being available for persons at high risk.

COMMUNITY MENTAL HEALTH SERVICES FOR WOMEN

Unlike older adults and minority group people, women are not underrepresented in community mental health case loads. In fact, numbers indicate an overrepresentation of women in outpatient mental health services (52.4% female, National Institute of Mental Health [NIMH], 1986) compared to population demographics. Women outnumber men in self-reports of mental health symptoms (Goldman & Ravid, 1980; Veroff, Douvan, & Kulka, 1981). Women also outnumber men in mental illness diagnoses in five out of six categories (all except antisocial personality disorders, according to a recent epidemiological study; Myers et al., 1984). Differences in prevalence are particularly striking among the mood disorders, where one out of every four American women will suffer from depression at some point in life, double the rate for men (Landers, 1988).

These differences cannot be attributed to alleged gender differences in response style:

> Sex differences in mental health are not merely a function of men's relative reluctance to see themselves as problematic and/or to report difficulties to a strange interviewer . . . the pattern of results [indicates] that women's life situations confront them with experiences which put them in a more vulnerable position than men, a position that engenders psychological difficulties. (Veroff et al., 1981, pp. 373–374)

Because it is known that high levels of stress contribute to mental health problems, a review of gender differences in risk indicators provides concrete reasons to explain women's greater vulnerability. For instance, women earn only 64 cents compared to every man's dollar. Even in jobs of comparable worth, a substantial disparity remains (79 cents versus a dollar). Female-headed households constitute half of the poverty population but only one seventh of all families. Women are also more subject to victimization: 16 rapes are attempted and 10 women were raped every hour in 1989, according to Uniform Crime Reports and the National Crime Survey (U.S. House of Representatives Select Committee on Children, Youth and Families, 1990).

Although women definitely outnumber men in prevalence of mental health problems (including the more serious mental illnesses) and in service utilization, the treatment programs provided are not necessarily appropriate. To understand the basis for this contention, we need to briefly review theories of sex differences in mental illness. A generation ago, bio-

logical and genetic-based theories were popular. It is now more often acknowledged that the relationship between changes in mood states and specific hormone levels in females is weak and inconsistent and that a biological basis alone is not sufficient to explain sex differences (Weissman & Klerman, 1977). A sociocultural approach, by contrast, emphasizes stress factors in women's environment that adversely affect mental health. These include poverty, lowered social status, women's socialization toward pleasing others rather than independence and achievement, a high incidence of victimization, sex discrimination, stereotypic biases, and the stress of multiple, competing roles. These factors contribute to women's generally lower sense of self-esteem, greater reliance on others in determining adequacy, greater difficulties in identity formulation, self- versus other-directed hostility, and a lower sense of power (Mowbray, Lanir, & Hulce, 1984). Thus, from a sociocultural point of view, women are exposed to higher levels of stress and they possess less adequate coping mechanisms and/or supportive resources to buffer these stresses, thus increasing their risk of psychological impact (Thoits, 1986). The fact that gender interacts with a number of stress-linked demographic factors (such as minority status, older age, marriage, greater numbers of children, etc.) to produce a higher level of mental disorders in women helps corroborate this theoretical approach (Mowbray & Benedek, 1987). That is, these women are more stressed and disenfranchised than are their male counterparts, thus heightening their vulnerability to mental disorders.

Although women are served in greater numbers, the services they receive are not appropriately tailored to reflect the stresses they are under, their coping and resource difficulties, or their unique treatment needs. The issue of sex biases in treatment has been visible and controversial since the Broverman et al.'s study nearly 20 years ago. The results of this research indicated that clinicians of both genders have a double standard of mental health for male versus female clients. The standard for female mental health, but not the male, is different from the standard for a "mentally healthy adult" (Broverman, Broverman, Clarkson, Rosenkrantz, & Vogel, 1970).

Although the Broverman et al. research findings have been questioned on the basis that clinicians' attitudes on paper do not necessarily affect their actual practice, other examples of sex biases in treatment cannot be so easily dismissed. For example, an individual is more likely to be hospitalized when diagnosed as having a disorder usually associated with the opposite sex (Phillips & Seagul, 1972). Treatment to address problems that are sex role incongruent for women (e.g., drug disorders, alcoholism) is usually unavailable and/or inadequate (Mowbray & Benedek, 1987). It has frequently been alleged that clinicians inappropriately stereotype female clients and push them into accepting traditional roles and attitudes as positive therapeutic outcomes. Although these allegations are not proven (methodological issues are horrendous), they are serious enough to require several professional associations to promulgate principles or guidelines for counseling female clients (e.g., Division 17 of the American Psychological Association [APA], see Fitzgerald & Nutt, 1986). And, concerns were serious enough to generate a host of controversy when the American Psychiatric Association proposed adding two new sex-linked diagnostic categories to the *Diagnostic and Statistical Manual,* 3rd edition, revised (DSM-III-R)—paraluteal dysphoric disorder and masochistic personality disorder. Feminists argued that these diagnoses were not founded on research and established practice but merely legitimated a psychiatric label for long-standing negative stereotypes of women.

Other biases are also readily evident: (a) Women are overrepresented in prescriptions for psychoactive drugs, even when number of physician visits is factored out (Eichler & Parron, 1987). (b) Women who are victims of domestic violence, sexual assault, or even incest often find inappropriate "victim-blame" oriented treatment or no treatment at all for their psychological and/or emotional problems. (c) Sexual contacts between male therapists and female patients, by conservative self-reports, involve at least 10% of therapists surveyed (Pope & Bouhoutsos, 1986). (d) Women's access to even traditional community mental health is severely hampered by lack of transportation and the unavailability of child care options. (e) With respect to seriously mentally ill clients, there has been a long-standing assumption that women respond more positively to treatment than do men. A recent review using meta-evaluation statistical techniques shows that this is not the case (Feis, 1987). Bachrach (1984, 1985) has pointed out that unique treatment needs of chronically mentally ill women are not even recognized in community programs.

In contrast to these aspects of community mental health services that are inappropriate or unavailable, we have identified two successful model programs for women that are based on women's strengths (rather than on negative, sex-role stereotypes); tailored to meet their needs by using broad-based modalities and involving the individual's relationship to her family and community; and designed to build coping and

problem-solving skills, thus increasing the individual's belief in her own potential. The models involve two different target groups of women, both of whom have been mis-served, underserved, or ignored: low-income women and seriously mentally ill women who are mothers. Despite the substantially different characteristics and needs of these two subgroups, both interventions share important commonalities in philosophy and treatment approach.

This first model project that we describe, stress-management training (SMT) for low-income women, was initiated as a prevention demonstration project through the Michigan Department of Mental Health but is now in operation nationwide. It was developed out of an interagency needs assessment in a suburban county, which revealed that women on public assistance with family problems were substantial users of community mental health services. An intervention was designed, built on research findings that low-income women often display poor self-esteem and learned helplessness behaviors. Their coping skills and resources are usually low and stress levels are high. SMT, a 10-week multidimensional, structured program uses a psychoeducational approach. SMT differs from other stress-management interventions (usually targeted toward middle class and/or professional groups) in combining training in stress-management behaviors and cognitive restructuring (to change perceptions of worthlessness and lack of control) with an educational program on life planning and problem solving. Sessions are 2½ to 3 hours, involving 6 to 15 group members plus a facilitator. Transportation and child care are provided to facilitate attendance. SMT is held in natural settings in the community. Refreshments are served during the sessions to enhance cohesion and opportunities for socialization. The facilitator leads the group through a set curriculum and also participates as a role model. Participants are provided with take-home materials to increase self-discovery and to keep for future reference.

The first three sessions of this program focus on enhancing self-esteem and identifying stress-producing aspects of personal relationships and ways to minimize these stresses (e.g., responding to negative statements, positive approaches with children). The next five sessions are on life planning, including accepting responsibility for behaviors and techniques for taking control, all of which involve problem solving, decision making, and finding support. The last two sessions provide practice with a variety of stress-management strategies.

The most salient features of this intervention are

that it (a) is time-limited, (b) focuses on low-income women with poor self-images, perceived lack of control, and limited skills and resources, (c) starts with basic issues of self-esteem and life planning before presenting stress-management techniques, (d) occurs in a non-mental health group setting, where women can learn from each other and develop a sense of community, and (e) uses a psychoeducational approach, reinforced by take-home materials.

Evaluation of the original demonstration found that SMT participants, compared to comparison groups, improved significantly on measures of depression, anxiety, inadequacy, ego strength, and self-esteem (Tableman, Marciniak, Johnson, & Rodgers, 1982). SMT also produced positive outcomes according to participants' self-reports, with nearly half making improvements in their vocational or personal situations, one third improving personal relationships, and one quarter increasing their support networks (Tableman, Feis, Marciniak & Howard, 1985). Department of Social Service staff corroborated these findings, indicating that clients who completed SMT made fewer "help me" calls and were more able to participate with their social worker in problem-solving crisis situations (Tableman et al., 1982). An experimental evaluation of SMT as an alternative to traditional outpatient services showed that SMT participants versus control individuals had better outcomes and reduced use of community mental health services, with service costs averaging $200 lower per client (Tableman et al., 1985). SMT has produced similar positive results in other rural, suburban, and urban areas (Tableman, 1989).

Evaluation research findings support the theoretical underpinnings of the stress management model for low-income women which "guides the participant into the belief that she can control her own behavior, training in skills towards effectiveness in handling daily life, and encouragement of the participant's sense of mastery" (Tableman et al., 1985, p. 84).

SMT has been funded as part of education and training for female public assistance recipients. Community implementation requires collaborative referral arrangements between mental health and social service agencies as well as involvement of churches or other community groups in providing a meeting site.

The second model to be described revolves around services available to mentally ill mothers. Although the chronically mentally ill have received expanded attention in the last 10 years, this population has been perceived as almost "genderless" and the significant needs of women have not been recognized (Test & Berlin, 1981). Among these needs is attention to the mothering role. Data suggest that seriously mentally ill women have a greater number of children on average, begin their mothering earlier, are more often divorced or never married, and despite bouts of hospitalization, many still retain child care responsibilities (Rogosch, 1987). Psychiatric histories aside, their demographics alone would put these women at high risk for mothering problems.

The literature on the mothering needs of seriously mentally ill women is sparse and what there is focuses primarily on negative effects on the child from having a disturbed mother. Such research has usually failed to study the mother's feelings and attitudes toward the parenting role and the assistance and support she needs to function as a satisfactory mother to her children, given her psychiatric disability. An exception to this has been the work of Cohler and colleagues on the Thresholds Mother's project in Chicago (Stott et al., 1984) and of Tableman (1987) on the LAMB (Loving Attachment of Mothers and Babies) program in Detroit. The target group for both of these interventions is severely disordered schizophrenic or depressed mothers with young children. For the child the goals of these programs are to minimize the deleterious impact of parental disorder, to stabilize caregiving, and to facilitate normal cognitive and psychosocial development; and, for the mother, to reduce recidivism and increase competence as a parent. Service delivery objects focus on increasing attachment between mother and child; facilitating appropriate child care practices; reducing the mother's psychological distress, social isolation, and environmental stress; increasing social support; maintaining health; and dealing with other problems affecting the child. Women and their children attend an intensive center-based program 3 to 5 days a week, with home visits made at least monthly. Clinical therapeutic and/or rehabilitative services are provided to the women. Services available to the mother include the following: group sessions for mothers that are educational, clinical, and support-focused (e.g., stress management, household management, child development); a nursery and child care setting for the children, which thus provides them with a stable daytime environment, caregiving adults and growth-enhancing activities; child care workers who work with the mother modeling caregiving activities in the nursery; and periodic assessments of the child's development. The program also provides transportation to and from the agency, on-site snacks and lunch times for the mothers and children to be together, and videotaping of mother–child interactions to provide feedback. The program structure provides the mothers with these types of assistance: crisis intervention—alleviating problems brought in by economic deficits or psychiatric illness; supportive treatment for better parenting; insight therapy to resolve issues that interfere with parenting—for example, ambivalence toward the chldren.

An evaluation of the Chicago Thresholds program (Stott et al., 1984) demonstrated that women enrolled in the program showed significant improvement over time in adjustment to work and parenting roles and in cognitive performance. Children showed improvements over time in Developmental Quotient/IQ measures, social competence, and adaptive skills. The evaluation for the LAMB Program in Detroit is still underway.

The mentally ill mothers project demonstrates that seriously mentally ill women can successfully carry out parenting responsibilities, given psychiatric and/ or rehabilitative services for themselves, and support, education, and assistance in their mothering role.

Women have often not been recognized as a population requiring special programming through community mental health. However, the extent of their environmental stress and mental health problems, combined with the biases and inappropriate responses they receive in treatment indicate they should be. The programs reviewed demonstrate how services can be provided appropriately to address women's mental health needs and adaptation problems. Although their settings and target groups differ substantially, the significant operational characteristics of the programs are the same:

- Delivered outside of a traditional clinical or mental health setting.
- Broad-based using modalities other than a one-on-one interaction with mental health professionals.
- Comprehensive, involving all aspects of the individual's life, environment, and social and/or family situation, as necessary.
- Directed at increasing the individual's belief in her own power and potential.
- Provides opportunities and models for problem solving and decision making.
- Provides specific skills to change life situations and address individual deficits.

SOCIAL SUPPORT NETWORKS

An individual's social support network can be defined as those enduring social ties that link the individual to beneficial resources for effective personal adaptation (Cohen & Syme, 1985; Gottlieb, 1981). Components of one's support network may include family, friends, neighbors, work associates, and individuals encountered in social, religious, or organizational memberships. A growing body of research shows that the quality of an individual's social support network is a significant contributor to physical and psychological well-being (Cohen & Wills, 1985; House, Landis, & Umberson, 1988). Social support has been found to be especially valuable in buffering the potentially harmful effects of personal crises and life transitions (Thoits, 1986; Turner, 1983). Although the exact mechanisms by which social support operates are not entirely understood, a number of theorists have described the wide variety of potentially helpful resources that informal personal relationships can offer, including emotional support, task-oriented assistance, communication about expectations and feedback, access to new and diverse information and social opportunities, companionship and recreation, and a sense of belongingness (Cohen & Syme, 1985; Gottlieb, 1981; Thoits, 1986).

Despite the relatively nascent scientific understanding of the social support process, community mental health interventions that use social support have proliferated in recent years (Gottlieb, 1988; Rook & Dooley, 1985). The popularity of social support interventions is understandable. Tapping natural support systems as sources of informal caregiving is much less expensive than drawing on professional services, helps ensure accessible and responsive care that is congruent with the norms of the community, and avoids categorization or stigmatization of the helpee into a formal client role (Collins & Pancoast, 1972; Gottlieb, 1983; Mitchell & Trickett, 1980).

Comprehensive reviews of social support interventions can be found elsewhere (Gottlieb, 1988; Rook & Dooley, 1985). Our goal in this section is to describe the variety of ways in which social support processes can be incorporated into community mental health programs. As a way of illustrating the multiple targets and levels that have been addressed through social support interventions, we use the example of one community, San Francisco, and discuss ways in which community members have instigated social support interventions to cope with the demands of a major crisis, AIDS. The AIDS epidemic presents an especially compelling example for the field of community mental health because of the tremendous numbers of people affected, the severity and wide range of problems associated with AIDS, and the fact that disenfranchised populations (gays, ethnic minorities) have been disproportionately hit by the epidemic. These facts combine to make traditional systems of mental health services less realistic and, in many respects, inappropriate. San Francisco, one of the early epicenters of the AIDS epidemic, has confronted the AIDS crisis with a proactive, compassionate, and resourceful approach that serves as a model for others. The exemplary programs we highlight here are innovative, successful, and cost-effective approaches that tap into the health-promoting resources of social support to deal with a major community crisis. All of them represent grass-roots efforts by community members who identified urgent needs in their community, recognized the potential value of social support in addressing those needs, and took the initiative in bringing a program to life.

A diagnosis of AIDS carries with it multiple and profound stresses, including not only the physical and psychological trauma of having a life-threatening illness, but very realistic fears of discrimination, ostracism, abandonment, and loss of employment and financial resources (Christ & Weiner, 1985; Dilley, Ochitill, Perl, & Volberding, 1985; Nichols, 1983). It is not surprising that depression, anxiety, confusion, anger, and suicidal tendencies are common among people with AIDS, as well as their loved ones (Forstein, 1984; Morin & Batchelor, 1984). A supportive social network can be a critical factor in one's effort to cope with AIDS (Hays, Chauncey, & Tobey, 1990; Hays, Turner, Catania, Mandel, & Coates, 1989). For individuals confronting an intensely stressful predicament such as AIDS, simply meeting others who are going through a similar experience and sharing feelings and information can be extremely valuable (Taylor, Falke, Shaptaw, & Lichtman, 1986). Such is the premise of San Francisco's New Friends Program, in which volunteers who themselves have AIDS visit and assist individuals who are newly diagnosed. Similar to Silverman's (1976) highly regarded "widow-to-widow" program, New Friends volunteers provide emotional support, understanding, and information on practical issues to facilitate the individual's adaptation and basically serve as role models as the newly diagnosed patients come to grips with their illness and begin to develop adaptive coping strategies. Both programs recognize that the empathy and insider's perspective afforded by someone who has surmounted a similar crisis is in many ways much more potent in allaying the worries and sense of alienation accompanying traumatic events than are support attempts by dissimilar others.

Perhaps the classic model of social support intervention is the mutual support group, in which individuals who share a common life crisis meet regularly in an informal group setting to share their feelings and concerns on coping with the unifying experience that binds them (Gartner & Reissman, 1984). For example, San Francisco's AIDS Health Project runs the Positives Being Positive program, which brings together gay men who have tested positive for AIDS antibodies in groups of 8 to 12. Program facilitators provide initial structuring and information sharing about testing positive for human immunodeficiency virus (HIV) and then let group members take the major role in the groups, which meet weekly in members' homes. Investigations into the process by which mutual help groups operate suggest that their effectiveness lies in the sharing of useful information about the problems and effective coping strategies, social support and reinforcement for productive coping efforts, and an improvement in self-esteem through identification with a supportive reference group (Gartner & Reissman, 1984; Killilea, 1976; Levy, 1976). For example, Positives Being Positive participants are encouraged to share their experience with common concerns such as deciding to whom and when to disclose their HIV status to others, decisions about medical treatment options, and issues of dating and sexuality. A major advantage of mutual support groups is that members can progress from helpee to helper (i.e., older members assisting newer members), thus instilling in the individual a new self-image in a way that traditional therapy by a professional can seldom achieve. Furthermore, as Spiegel (1976) noted, whereas traditional psychotherapy tends to isolate individuals in individual treatment, mutual help groups provide an opportunity to draw strength from a collectivity of similar others.

Because the essence of the support group's effectiveness lies in the feeling of mutual understanding and camaraderie among the members, it is not surprising that in San Francisco a plethora of fairly specialized support groups have emerged to address the needs of the diverse populations touched by the AIDS epidemic, including groups for women, African-Americans, and Asian-Americans with AIDS, couples in which one partner has AIDS, parents, friends and lovers of people with AIDS, lovers of people who have died of AIDS, health professionals who work with AIDS, and so on. It is important to note that support groups can be at times anxiety-provoking for people with AIDS, especially the newly diagnosed, who may feel personally threatened confronting group members in the more advanced stages of the illness (Morin & Batchelor, 1984). Likewise, as Gottlieb (1981) discussed, support groups may be detrimental if participants are not equipped to offer support or recommend unproductive coping strategies. Before attempting support group interventions, one should carefully assess the skills, resources, and potential compatibility of those to be involved, and provide some mechanism for the functioning of the group to be monitored.

San Francisco's Shanti Project is a multifaceted, nonprofit organization that provides a wide range of support services for people with AIDS, their friends, family, and loved ones. Shanti (the name is Sanskrit meaning "inner peace") was formed in 1974 to deal with the psychosocial needs of people facing life-threatening illness. In 1984, as the number of AIDS cases in San Francisco began to reach epidemic proportions, Shanti turned its focus entirely to AIDS-related services, illustrating its responsiveness to the emerging needs of its community. In Shanti's Emotional Support Program, community volunteers are matched with a person with AIDS to provide one-on-one peer counseling, companionship, patient advocacy, information, and friendship. Volunteers are carefully screened and must complete an intensive training program prior to being assigned clients. The training emphasizes nonjudgmental, active listening skills, based on the belief that clients can find their own answers to the troubling questions associated with living with AIDS. Volunteers generally meet with their clients once a week according to the client's needs and focus on whatever issues are of concern to the client at that time. Shanti volunteers are also stationed at the AIDS wards of the county hospital to provide supportive counseling to inpatients and their family and friends who visit. Shanti's Practical Support Program operates similarly, except that volunteers focus on the daily living needs of their clients, providing services such as housecleaning, laundry, grocery shopping, cooking, gardening, and running other errands. Such practical assistance allows the client to live at home with dignity, as well as affording more time for the individual to deal with the many psychological issues associated with an AIDS diagnosis. Shanti volunteers are closely supervised and attend weekly support groups in which they can discuss any concerns or stresses that they may be experiencing in their involvement with the program.

An important, though often overlooked, role for community mental health workers is in intervening at an environmental level to optimize or strengthen an individual's interactions with members of his or her social support network. One exemplary program of this nature is the Family Link, which provides housing for friends and family of people with AIDS who are visiting from outside the San Francisco area and provides a contact for informational and emotional support to facilitate the family's visit with their loved

one. Pets are vital elements of many people's social networks, providing companionship, comfort, and opportunities to nurture that may be critical to an individual's self-esteem. The observation that people with AIDS have often had to give up their cherished pets, due to long periods of hospitalization, frailty, or financial strains that made caring for animals difficult, led to the formation of a valuable and popular program known as PAWS (Pets Are Wonderful Support). PAWS provides direct service to help individuals keep their pets, such as financial aid for pet food and veterinary bills, as well as volunteer foster homes while the pet's owner is hospitalized. PAWS volunteers organize a variety of creative fund-raising events throughout the year, such as an annual pet talent show, to furnish the revenues to finance their services.

Given the multiple demands of AIDS, it is not uncommon for people with AIDS to simultaneously draw upon the services of several community programs, in addition to receiving professional mental health services (Morin & Batchelor, 1984). Effective coordination between community programs and professionals is thus essential, as is an understanding of each provider's particular strengths and limitations. Community volunteers must be trained to recognize the limits of their expertise and provide referrals when professional treatment is warranted. Likewise, mental health professionals must educate themselves about the community's informal systems of support and help their clients to utilize the wealth of social support resources available. Although we have focused on AIDS-related interventions here, the types of programs and issues discussed can be applied to social support interventions dealing with any potentially stressful life event. A community's informal social networks offer a wealth of supportive resources that can be tapped in innovative and cost-effective ways to promote psychological adaptation.

CONCLUSION

Community mental health work today in contrast to the 1970s is a less visible but clearly integral component of mental health service delivery. Community mental health services are successful when they are planned, implemented, and maintained by a coalition of mental health professionals, citizens, state and local officials, and clients.

The program examples cited in this chapter illustrate the options, opportunities, and excitement when such coalitions create community-based mental health services. The clinical psychologist as a member of such coalitions generates new professional roles when collaborating with other professions and advocating for the needs of underserved people.

This chapter has presented examples of how the context of the community is considered in the design of services, how collaboration is realized between citizens, professionals, and public officials, and how advocacy roles become an essential part of community mental health. The defining qualities of community mental health work are expressed and elaborated when the clinical psychologist works with citizens for the following shared goals: developing new services; integration of cultural themes and topics in the delivery of services, especially with ethnic minorities; becoming informed about gatekeepers who have access to client groups; and creation of a variety of support and clinical services for such people as seriously mentally ill mothers and their children, as well as people with AIDS. It is this variety and scope of community approaches that express the deeper meaning of community mental health. This deeper meaning is realized when the treatment and prevention of mental illness and the promotion of mental health become interdependent and integrated with the social fabric of the community. Then the clinical psychologist becomes directly a part of the community while creating opportunities for new services to be established and maintained within the community.

In the presentation of the exemplary programs in this chapter several principles have expressed the essence of community mental health work. When citizens, professionals, state and local officials, and clients express these principles they are creating community-based criteria for judging the effectiveness of professional practice.

The community mental health perspective includes the following: (a) designing services with an appreciation and understanding of the culture of the participants, (b) looking for methods and techniques and community processes that help prevent or reduce the incidence of a specific problem, (c) integrating mental health services with other health and social services, (d) working for active community participation in the design of services, (e) creating opportunities for clients to gain control over their treatment plans and services, (f) guiding clients so that skill development and life planning go along with treatment and service, (g) providing crisis services that help focus on environmental, economic, and life cycle stresses, (h) generating educational programs for improved coping, (i) arranging services so that they are located in sites sanctioned as accessible and knowledgeable by citizens, and (j) articulating formal mental health services with the natural support systems in the community. When implementing these 10 principles, the spirit, deep meaning, and validity of community mental health is reaffirmed.

REFERENCES

Aiken, M., & Hage, J. (1968). Organizational interdependence and interorganizational structure. *American Sociological Review, 33,* 912–930.

American Association of Retired Persons. (1986). *A profile of older Americans: 1986* (Research Report No. PF3049, 1086, D996). *Washington, DC: Author.*

Armstrong, H.E., Ishiki, P., Heiman, J., Mundt, J., & Womack, W. (1984). Service utilization by black and white clientele in an urban community mental health center: Revised assessment of an old problem. *Community Mental Health Journal, 20,* 269–280.

Bachrach, L. (1984). Deinstitutionalization and women. *American Psychology, 39,* 1171–1177.

Bachrach, L. (1985). Chronic mentally ill women: Emergency and legitimation of program issues. *Hospital and Community Psychiatry, 36,* 1063–1069.

Bellin, A. (1981). Reaction of a frustrated citizen. *Community Mental Health Journal, 17,* 83–91.

Bestman, E.W. (1986). Cross-cultural approaches to service delivery to ethnic minorities: The Miami model. In M.R. Miranda & H.L. Kitano (Eds.), *Mental health research and practice in minority communities* (pp. 218–230). Rockville, MD: National Institute of Mental Health.

Bonfield, M.B., Olds, M.L., Shreve, B.W., Smith, M., & Schoenberger, V.E. (1978). *Citizen evaluation with program analysis of service systems.* Lancaster, PA: Lancaster County Office of Mental Health/Mental Retardation.

Broman, C. (1987). Race differences in professional help-seeking. *American Journal of Community Psychology, 15,* 473–489.

Broverman, I.K., Broverman, D.M., Clarkson, D.E., Rosenkrantz, P.S., & Vogel, S.R. (1970). Sex-role stereotypes and clinical judgments of mental health. *Journal of Consulting and Clinical Psychology, 34,* 1–7.

Buckwalter, K.C. (1987, December). *The chronically mentally ill in rural environments.* Paper presented at the meeting on the Chronically Mentally Ill Elderly, National Institute of Mental Health, Orlando, FL.

Burgner, L.P., Zinober, J.W., & Dinkel, N.R. (1984). The impact of citizen evaluation review on community mental health center programs. *Evaluation and Program Planning, 7,* 57–64.

Carling, P.J. (1981). Nursing homes and chronic mental patients: A second opinion. *Schizophrenia Bulletin, 1,* 574–579.

Caro, F.G. (1981). Reaction of a skeptical sociologist. *Community Mental Health Journal, 17,* 77–82.

Cheung, F.K., & Snowden, L.R. (1990). Use of inpatient services by members of ethnic minority groups. *American Psychologist, 45,* 347–355.

Christ, G.H., & Weiner, L.S. (1985). Psychosocial issues in

AIDS. In V.T. DeVita, S. Hellman, & S.A. Rosenberg (Eds.), *AIDS: Etiology, diagnosis, treatment and prevention* (pp. 275–279). Philadelphia: JB Lippincott.

Chu, F., & Trotter, S. (1974). *The madness establishment.* New York: Grossman.

Cibulka, J.G. (1981). Citizen participation in the governance of community mental health centers. *Community Mental Health Journal, 17,* 19–36.

Cohen, S., & Syme, L.S. (1985). *Social support and health.* New York: Academic Press

Cohen, S., & Wills, T.A. (1985). Social support, stress and the buffering hypothesis. *Psychological Bulletin, 98,* 310–357.

Cole, J., & Pilisuk, M. (1976). Differences in the provision of mental health services by race. *American Journal of Orthopsychiatry, 46,* 510–525.

Collins, A.H., & Pancoast, D.L. (1972). *Natural helping networks.* Washington, DC: National Association of Social Workers.

Colom, E. (1981). Reaction of an angry consumer. *Community Mental Health Journal, 17,* 92–97.

Cromwell, H.S., Howe, J.W., & O'Rear, G. (1988). A citizens' coalition in mental health advocacy: The Maryland experience. *Hospital and Community Psychiatry, 39,* 959–965.

Dilley, J.W., Ochitill, H.N., Perl, M., & Volberding, P.A. (1985). Findings in psychiatric consultation with patients with acquired immune deficiency syndrome. *American Journal of Psychiatry, 142,* 82–86.

Dundee-Anderson, E.D. (1985). An exploration of the effects of social power on citizen participation in mental health during decision-making processes of Virginia Community Services Boards. *Dissertation Affiliation.* Washington, D.C.: Howard University.

Eichler, A. (1978). The Community Mental Health Center Amendments of 1975 (Title III of P.L. 94-63): *How are new CMHCs doing?* Unpublished report, National Institute of Mental Health, Washington, DC.

Eichler, A., & Parron, D.L. (1987). *Women's mental health: Agenda for research.* Washington, DC: U.S. Department of Health and Human Services.

Fairweather, G.W. (Ed.). (1964). *Social psychology in treating mental illness: An experimental approach.* New York: John Wiley & Sons.

Fairweather, G.W. (Ed.). (1980). The Fairweather lodge society: A twenty-five year retrospective. *New directions for mental health services: A quarterly sourcebook.* San Francisco, CA: Jossey-Bass.

Fairweather, G.W., & Davidson, W.S. (1986). *An introduction to community experimentation: Theory, methods, and practice.* New York: McGraw-Hill.

Fairweather, G.W., Sanders, D.H., Maynard, H., & Cressler, D.L. (1969). *Community life for the mentally ill.* Chicago: Aldine.

Feis, C. (1987). *Qualifying exam for the Ph.D.* Unpublished manuscript, Michigan State University, Department of Psychology, East Lansing, MI.

Fitzgerald, L.F., & Nutt, R. (1986). The Division 17 principles concerning the counseling/psychotherapy of women: Rationale and implementation. *The Counseling Psychologist, 14,* 180–216.

Fleming, A.S., Rickards, L.D., Santos, J.F., & West, P.R. (1986). *Mental health services for the elderly: Report on a survey of community mental health centers* (Vol. 3). Washington, DC: Action committee to Implement the Mental Health Recommendations of the 1981 White House Conference on Aging.

Forstein, M. (1984). Psychological impact of the acquired immune deficiency syndrome. *Seminars in Oncology, 11,* 77–82.

Gartner, A., & Reissman, F. (1984). *Self-help in the human services.* San Francisco, CA: Jossey-Bass.

German, P.S., Shapiro, S., & Kramer, M. (1986). Nursing home study of the eastern Baltimore epidemiological catchment area study. In M.S. Harper & B.D. Lebowitz (Eds.), *Mental illness in nursing homes: Agenda for research* (pp. 27–40). Rockville, MD: National Institute of Mental Health.

German, P.S., Shapiro, S., Skinner, E.A., VonKorff, M., Klein, L.E., Turner, R.W., Teitelbaum, M.L., Burke, J., & Burns, B.J. (1987). Detection and management of mental health problems of older patients by primary providers. *Journal of the American Medical Association, 257,* 489–493.

Goldman, N., & Ravid, R. (1980). Community surveys: Sex differences in mentally ill. In M. Guttentag, S. Salasin, & D. Belle (Eds.), *The mental health of women* (pp. 31–51). New York: Academic Press.

Gottlieb, B.H. (1981). *Social networks and social support.* Beverly Hills, CA: Sage.

Gottlieb, B.H. (1983). *Social support strategies: Guidelines for mental health practice.* Beverly Hills, CA: Sage.

Gottlieb, B.H. (1988). Support interventions: A typology and agenda for research. In S. Duck (Ed.), *Handbook of personal relationships* (pp. 519–542). New York: John Wiley & Sons.

Harper, M.S., & Lebowitz, B.D. (Eds.). (1986). *Mental illness in nursing homes: Agenda for research.* Rockville, MD: National Institute of Mental Health.

Hays, R.B., Chauncey, S., & Tobey, L.A. (1990). The social support networks of gay men with AIDS. *Journal of Community Psychology, 18,* 374–385.

Hays, R.B., Turner, H., Catania, J., Mandel, J., & Coates, T.J. (1989, June). *Social support, HIV symptoms and depression among gay men.* Paper presented at the 5th International Conference on AIDS, Montreal.

Hessler, R.M., & Walters, M.J. (1976). Consumer evaluation research: Implications for methodology, social policy, and the role of the sociologist. *The Sociological Quarterly, 17,* 74–89.

Hollenshead, C., & Miller, J.E. (1984). Behind the myths: A demographic profile of the elderly. *Frontiers of Health Service Management, 1,* 3–12.

Horgan, C. (1986). The demand for ambulatory mental health services from specialty providers. *Health Services Research, 21,* 291–319.

House, J.S., Landis, K.R., & Umberson, D. (1988). Social relationships and health. *Science, 241,* 540–545.

Katz, D., & Kahn, R.L. (1978). *The social psychology of organizations.* New York: John Wiley & Sons.

Kermis, M.D. (1986). The epidemiology of mental disorder in the elderly: A response to the Senate/AARP report. *The Gerontologist, 26,* 482–487.

Kermis, M.D. (1987). Equity and policy issues in mental health care of the elderly: Dilemmas, deinstitutionalization, and DRGs. *Journal of Applied Gerontology, 6,* 268–282.

Killilea, M. (1976). Mutual help organizations: Interpretations in the literature. In G. Caplan & M. Killilea (Eds.), *Support systems and mutual help* (pp. 37–93). New York: Grune & Stratton.

Knight, R. (1983). Assessing a mobile outreach team. In M.A. Smyer & M. Gatz (Eds.), *Mental health and aging: Programs and evaluations* (pp. 23–40). Beverly Hills, CA: Sage.

Kopolow, L.E. (1981). Client participation in mental health service delivery. *Community Mental Health Journal, 17,* 46–53.

Landers, S. (1988, October). Factors confound myths of women, depression. *APA Monitor,* p. 5.

Landsberg, G., Hammer, R., & Neigher, W. (1978). *Analyzing the evaluation activities in CMHCs in National Institute of Mental Health Region II.* Paper presented at the 1987 annual meeting of the National Council of CMHCs, Kansas City, MO.

Leaf, P.J., Livingston, M.M., Tischler, G.L., Weissman, M.M., Holzer, C.E., & Myers, J.K. (1985). Contact with health professionals for the treatment of psychiatric and emotional problems. *Medical Care, 23,* 1322–1337.

Lebray, P. (1984). Providing clinical geropsychology services in community settings. In J.P. Abrahams & V.J. Crook (Eds.), *Geriatric mental health* (pp. 201–216). Orlando, FL: Grune & Stratton.

Levy, L.H. (1976). Self-help groups: Types and psychological processes. *Journal of Applied Behavioral Science, 12,* 310–313.

Mitchell, R.E., & Trickett, E.J. (1980). Task force report: Social networks as mediators of social support. *Community Mental Health Journal, 16,* 27–44.

Morentz, P.E. (1979). A citizen-conducted evaluation of acceptability: The Ronoh School evaluation committee. In G. Landsberg, W.D. Neigher, R.J. Hammer, C. Windle, & J.R. Woy (Eds.), *Evaluation in practice: A sourcebook of program evaluation studies from mental health care systems in the United States* (DHEW Publication No. ADM 80-763). Washington, DC: U.S. Government Printing Office.

Morin, S.F., & Batchelor, W. (1984). Responding to the psychological crisis of AIDS. *Public Health Reports, 99,* 4–9.

Morrison, J.K., Holdridge-Crane, S., & Smith, J.E. (1978). Citizen participation in community mental health. *Community Mental Health Review, 3,* 3.

Mowbray, C., & Benedek, E. (1987, October). *Mental health treatment and services for women.* Paper presented at the Implementing the National Institute of Mental Health Women's Mental Health Research Agenda Conference, Washington, DC.

Mowbray, C., Chamberlain, P., Jennings, M., & Reed, C. (1987). *Consumer-run mental health services: Results from five demonstration projects.* Lansing, MI: Michigan Department of Mental Health.

Mowbray, C., Lanir, S., & Hulce, M. (1984). *Women and mental health: New directions for change.* New York: Haworth Press.

Myers, J.K., Weissman, M.M., Tischler, G.L., Holzer, C.E., Leaf, P.J., Orvaschel, H., Anthony, J.C., Boyd, J.H., Burke, J.D., Kramer, M., & Stolzman, R. (1984). Six-month prevalence of psychiatric disorders in three communities. *Archives of General Psychiatry, 41,* 959–967.

National Institute of Mental Health. (1986). *Specialty Mental Health Organizations, United States, 1983–84* (Series CN No. 11). By R.W. Redick, M.J. Witkin, J.E. Atay, & R.W. Manderschied. (DHHS Publication No. ADM 86-01490). Washington, DC: Superintendent of Documents, U.S. Government Printing Office.

Neligh, G. (1988). Major mental disorders and behavior among American Indians and Alaska Natives. In S.M. Manson & N.G. Vinges (Eds.), *Behavioral health issues among American Indians and Alaska Natives* (pp. 156–186). Denver, CO: National Center on American Indian and Alaska Native Mental Health Research.

Nichols, S.E. (1983). Psychiatric aspects of AIDS. *Psychosomatics, 24,* 1083–1089.

Parmalee, P.A., Katz, I.R., & Lawton, M.P. (1989). Depression among institutionalized aged: Assessment and prevalence estimation. *Journal of Gerontology, 44,* 22–29.

Phillips, D., & Seagul, B. (1972). Sexual status and psychiatric symptoms. *American Sociological Review, 9,* 34–58.

Pope, K.S., & Bouhoutsos, J.C. (1986). *Sexual intimacy between therapists and patients.* New York: Praeger.

Premo, F. (1972). *Overview of CMHC monitoring since decentralization.* Unpublished manuscript, National Institute of Mental Health.

President's Commission on Mental Health. (1978). *Task panel reports: The nature and scope of the problem* (Vol. 2). Washington, DC: U.S. Government Printing Office.

Pressman, J.L., & Wildavsky, A.B. (1973). *Implementation: How great expectations in Washington are dashed in Oakland.* Berkeley: University of California Press.

Raschko, R. (1985). Systems integration at the program level: Aging and mental health. *The Gerontologist, 25,* 460–463.

Ridenour, N. (1961). *Mental health in the United States: A fifty-year history.* Cambridge, MA: Harvard University Press.

Riley, W. (1981). Citizen participation in community mental

center service delivery. *Community Mental Health Journal, 17*, 37–45.

Rogosch, F. (1987). *Casual modeling of parenting attitudes in mothers with severe psychopathology.* Unpublished doctoral dissertation, Michigan State University, East Lansing, MI

Rook, K.S., & Dooley, D. (1985). Applying social support research: Theoretical problems and future directions. *Journal of Social Issues, 41*, 5–28.

Silverman, P.R. (1976). The widow as a caregiver in a program of preventive intervention with other widows. In G. Caplan & M. Killilea (Eds.), *Support systems and mutual help* (pp. 233–243). New York: Grune & Stratton.

Snowden, L.R. (1988). Ethnicity and utilization of mental health services. *Proceedings: Oklahoma Mental Health Institute Professional Symposium, 1988.* Oklahoma City: Oklahoma Mental Health Research Institute.

Snowden, L.R., Storey, C., & Clancy, T. (1989). Ethnicity and continuation at a black community mental health center. *Journal of Community Psychology, 25*, 51–60.

Spiegel, D. (1976). Going public and self-help. In G. Caplan & M. Killilea (Eds.), *Support systems and mutual help.* New York: Grune & Stratton.

Stott, F.M., Musick, J.S., Cohler, B.J., Spencer, K.K., Goldman, J., Clark, R., & Dincin, J. (1984). Intervention for the severely disturbed mother. In B.J. Cohler & J.S. Musick (Eds.), *Interventions among psychiatrically impaired parents and their young children* (pp. 7–32). San Francisco, CA: Jossey-Bass.

Sue, S. (1977). Community mental health services to minority groups: Some optimism, some pessimism. *American Psychologist, 32*, 616–624.

Sussman, L.K., Robins, L.N., & Earls, F. (1987). Treatment seeking for depression by black and white Americans. *Social Science and Medicine, 24*, 187–196.

Tableman, B. (1987). *Project specifications for a center-based family systems service for mentally ill mothers and their infants or preschool children.* Lansing, MI: Michigan Department of Mental Health.

Tableman, B. (1989). Stress management training for low income women. *National Mental Health Association: Eighty Years of Contributions to Prevention* [Special issue]. *Prevention in Human Services, 6*, 259–284.

Tableman, B., Feis, C.L., Marciniak, D., & Howard, D. (1985). Stress management training for low-income women. In B. Tableman & R. Hess (Eds.), *Prevention: The Michigan experience* (pp. 21–85). New York: Haworth Press.

Tableman, B., Marciniak, D., Johnson, D., & Rodgers, R. (1982). Stress management training for women on public assistance. *American Journal of Community Psychology, 10*, 357–367.

Taylor, S.E., Falke, R.L., Shaptaw, S.J., & Lichtman, R.R. (1986). Social support, support groups, and the cancer patient. *Journal of Consulting and Clinical Psychology, 54*, 608–615.

Test, M.A., & Berlin, S.B. (1981). Issues of special concern to chronically mentally ill women. *Professional Psychology, 12*, 136–145.

Thoits, P.A. (1986). Social support as coping assistance. *Journal of Consulting and Clinical Psychology, 54*, 416–423.

Thoits, P. (1986). Position paper. In A. Eichler & D. Parron (Eds.), *Women's mental health: Agenda for research.* Washington, DC: U.S. Department of Health and Human Services.

Turner, R.J. (1983). Direct, indirect and moderating effects of social support on psychological distress and associated conditions. In H.B. Kaplan (Ed.), *Psychological stress: Trends in theory and research* (pp. 105–155). New York: Academic Press.

U.S. House of Representatives Select Committee on Children, Youth, and Families. (1990, June). *Victims of rape fact sheet.* Washington, D.C.: Author.

Veroff, J., Douvan, E., & Kulka, R.A. (1981). *The inner American.* New York: Basic Books.

Waxman, H.M. (1986). Community mental health care for the elderly—A look at the obstacles. *Public Health Reports, 101*, 294–300.

Waxman, H.M., Carner, E.A., & Klein, M. (1984). Underutilization of mental health professionals by community elderly. *The Gerontologist, 24*, 23–30.

Weissman, M.M., & Klerman, G.L. (1977). Sex differences and the epidemiology of depression. *Archives of General Psychiatry, 34*, 98–111.

Williams, S. (1979). Mental health services: Utilization by low income enrollees in a prepaid group practice plan and in an independent practice plan. *Medical Care, 17*, 139–151.

Wilson, S.F. (1988). *Implementation of the community support system concept statewide: The Vermont experience.* Manuscript submitted for publication.

Windle, C., & Cibulka, J.G. (1981). A framework for understanding participation in community mental health services. *Community Mental Health Journal, 17*, 4–18.

Windle, C., & Paschall, N.C. (1981). Client participation in CMHC program evaluation: Increasing incidence, inadequate involvement. *Community Mental Health Journal, 17*, 66–76.

Zane, N., Sue, S., Castro, E., & George, W. (1982). Service system models for ethnic minorities. In L.R. Snowden (Ed.), *Reaching the underserved: Mental health needs of neglected populations* (pp. 229–257). Beverly Hills, CA: Sage.

Zimmerman, M.A., & Rappaport, J. (1988). Citizen participation, perceived control, and psychological empowerment. *American Journal of Community Psychology, 16*, 725–750.

CHAPTER 41

THE BRIEF PSYCHOTHERAPIES

John F. Clarkin
James W. Hull

Comprehensive treatment planning must address five specific facets of intervention: format (individual, group, family and/or marital), strategies and techniques (behavioral, cognitive, dynamic), setting (inpatient, day hospital, outpatient), use or nonuse of medication, and treatment duration and frequency (Frances, Clarkin, & Perry, 1984). With brief therapies the defining emphasis is on the *duration* of treatment. This signifies not an arbitrary fixed number of sessions, but rather an attempt to be time-sensitive, to ration time and "use [it] efficiently, parsimoniously, and in the service of the treatment process" (Budman & Gurman, 1983).

In actuality, surveys of both clinical practice and psychotherapy research indicate that most therapy is brief. Garfield (1986) found that patients usually discontinue treatment before the 20th session, with the median length of treatment being 5 to 6 sessions. In their meta-analysis of 475 psychotherapy studies, Smith, Glass, and Miller (1980) found that the average length of treatment was 16 sessions. Other estimates by Langsley (1978) and Koss (1979) have been similar. As Budman and Stone (1983) noted, one of the resulting ironies is that most planned brief therapy actually is longer than the usual length of "nonbrief" therapies.

A number of reasons have been identified for the recent surge of interest in short-term psychotherapy (e.g., Scheidlinger, 1984). These include a philosophical shift in the mental health profession toward increased pragmatism, eclecticism, and a systems orientation (Marmor, 1979), societal pressures and public policy concerns for more efficient and less costly methods of treatment (Pardes & Pincus, 1981), and a shift in reimbursement toward relatively inexpensive briefer therapies. In addition, almost all existing psychotherapy research focuses on short-term treatment, not because brief therapy is more effective but because it is more easily described, manualized, and investigated. Finally, patients expect treatments to be brief. Surveys indicate that applicants for psychotherapy typically expect significant improvement within five sessions and recovery from their presenting problems within 10 (e.g., Garfield, 1978; Garfield & Wolpin, 1963).

Any attempt to review this area must face the difficult task of delineating the topic so that it does not include the entire contemporary psychotherapy literature. As Budman and Gurman (1988) have noted, the entire body of research on individual psychotherapy outcome might be considered research on "time-unlimited" (i.e., unintended) brief therapy. Other surveys (e.g., Koss & Butcher, 1986; McGee, 1983) have tended to limit the discussion to individual treatment of adult patients, with group and family therapies, brief interventions with children and adolescents, and brief treatment during medical crisis receiving less attention. Because these formats represent important attempts to make psychotherapy more pragmatic, focused, and time-sensitive, we will review not only brief individual therapy, but also group and family and/or marital interventions, short-term individual and group treatment of children, and brief interventions in the area of behavioral medicine.

Another way this review will differ from its predecessors is by focusing on the question: brief therapy for what types of patient problems and/or diagnoses? We have stated elsewhere (Beutler & Clarkin, 1990) that both research and practice in psychotherapy are progressing toward greater specificity. In this advance, there is an increasing concern to match the individual patient and his or her problems with a specific intervention package. In considering brief therapy, one must ask: Brief treatment with what strategies? In what format? For what specific patient problem areas and diagnoses? Thus, we will attempt to specify the kinds of patient problems/diagnoses that lend themselves to the various treatments of relatively brief duration.

We begin with a review of the general features of the brief therapies. This is followed by a discussion of models of brief therapy (the theoretical positions and their related strategies and techniques) and formats of brief intervention. Building upon this common core of shared features, strategies/techniques, and formats, we then review the empirical evidence for those patient problem areas and/or diagnoses that respond to particular types of brief intervention. This information is summarized for the clinician in a section on the current indications for brief therapy. We conclude with sections on clinical evaluation for appropriateness of brief therapy and training in brief therapy.

GENERAL FEATURES OF BRIEF THERAPIES

There are three defining features that characterize most forms of brief psychotherapy. These are (a) a shortened duration of treatment, in which time is "rationed" (Budman & Gurman, 1983), (b) specific areas of therapeutic focus that involve clear and limited goals, and (c) relatively active behavior on the part of the therapist. These features are, of course, intricately intertwined: If the goals of therapy are to be limited so that change may occur within a fixed time

period, therapist and patient must focus on a few central issues, with the therapist frequently taking an active and directive stance. Although these represent the key common elements of all brief therapies, individual authors add to this list in describing their own particular approach. For example, Budman and Gurman (1988) included involvement of relatives and significant others in their list of key features, whereas Flegenheimer and Pollack (1988) specified early transference interpretations as an essential aspect of psychoanalytically oriented brief therapy.

Setting a Time Limit

Establishing a time limit is the central characteristic of all brief therapies. This limit may be fixed at the outset or set along the way as patient and therapist clarify the goals of their work. The fixed time limit imparts to brief therapy a distinctive cast: Short-term treatment is not simply long-term psychotherapy that has been ended prematurely (Dulcan, 1984). The actual number of sessions is arbitrary and has been set variously by different writers. Malan (1963) considered brief focal therapy to have an upper limit of about 40 sessions, whereas Mann (1973) set a limit of 12 sessions, regardless of the patient or the problems presented. There is some evidence of therapeutic effect occurring after just one session (e.g., Malan, Heath, Bacal, & Balfour, 1975).

Although most reviewers (Orlinsky & Howard, 1978) have found a positive relationship between therapeutic benefit and the total number of therapy sessions—that is, the longer the treatment the greater the benefit—recent data suggest it is possible to be more precise about this effect. Howard, Kopta, Krause, and Orlinsky (1986) have demonstrated a dose–effect relationship for psychotherapy based upon a review of a large number of studies of individual psychotherapy. Data from 15 samples covering 2,431 outpatients in individual nonbehavioral therapy were analyzed using a probit analysis. Results suggested that most patients respond to treatment of relatively brief duration. Ten to 18% showed some improvement before the first session. By the eighth session 48% to 58% were measurably improved, and by 26 sessions 75% of the patients had shown improvement. Earlier, Smith et al. (1980) found that the major positive effects of individual psychotherapy occurred in the first 6 to 8 sessions, followed by decreasing impact for the next 10 sessions. These estimates also are consistent with studies of duration of treatment as a main effect, where 60% to 70% rates of improvement were noted among short-term clients (e.g., Butcher & Kolotkin, 1979; Butcher & Koss, 1978). Most relevant for differential treatment planning, however, were the findings by Howard et al. (1986) of localized effects based upon diagnostic category. Patients with anxiety and depression showed the most rapid improvement, with 50% improved by 13 sessions. In contrast, of those patients with borderline-psychotic difficulties, 50% did not improve until 26 to 52 sessions.

In considering the question of a time limit, little attention has been given to the *density* of sessions. Thus, although one might define brief treatment in terms of a certain number of sessions, the duration of the treatment episode will lead to varying levels of intensity, presumably with differential treatment effects. The decision about the distribution in time of a limited number of sessions should not be arbitrary but related to the theory and model of intervention.

Establishing a Focus With Clear and Limited Goals

Budman and Gurman (1988) pointed out that because human behavior is so complex the therapist has almost unlimited choices regarding potential areas of focus in brief therapy. These authors delineate the five most common foci as losses, developmental dissynchronies, interpersonal conficts, symptomatic presentations, and severe personality disorders. They describe a decision tree for setting the focus, suggesting that the therapist first ask why the patient has sought treatment at this time, to determine whether the basic issue involves loss, developmental dissynchrony, or interpersonal conflict. If one of these is present, it becomes the focus of intervention. If these issues are not central, or the patient defines a symptom as the major issue, then the symptom becomes the focus of intervention. Finally, if the patient has repeatedly sought help for his or her difficulties without benefit, or if character issues are most prominent, then the focus of the intervention should be on character pathology. Budman and Gurman (1988) stressed that the chosen focus should have an integrative function within each session: "The theme opens the session, maintains a unity within the session, and closes the session" (p. 67).

Malan (1963, 1976) was one of the first to describe the process of setting a focus with the patient. He utilized both interview and psychological test data to arrive at a focus, and his method of relating crucial dynamic foci in an individual case to desired behavioral changes was classic. More recently, both Strupp and Binder (1984) and Luborsky (1984) have delineated methods for arriving at the foci of a brief

dynamic treatment. Strupp and Binder look for repetitive interpersonal themes in the dialogue of the session, whereas Luborsky examines core conflictual relationship themes as enunciated by the patient that can be reliably scored and evaluated for change over the course of treatment. Because the foci as stated by the patient change with time (Sorenson, Gorsuch, & Mintz, 1985), it cannot be assumed that those issues identified in the first session will be the sole or even the major foci by the end of a brief treatment.

Many of the recent brief therapy manuals have alleviation of a symptom pattern such as depression or resolution of a focal conflict as the focus of change. However, various models identify different intermediate goals to alleviate the symptom. The intermediate goals have more specificity, for example, exposure in vivo or a change in particular cognitions. The cognitive treatment of depression, for example, focuses on the patient's assumptions and negative schemata that are correlated with depressive affect. In contrast, a psychodynamic approach might concern itself with object losses that elicit depressive affect, whereas a behavioral treatment might reinforce the learning of skills that counteract such affective experiences. The nature of these intermediate goals and the way they are negotiated between therapist and patient varies depending on the particular model of brief therapy.

Active Therapist

It is commonly accepted that the practitioner of brief psychotherapy must take a relatively active stance. This is in marked contrast to the dynamic tradition of long-term treatment, where the therapist can afford to be nondirective. When brief therapy involves cognitive-behavioral models, the difference imposed by the brief time limit is less noticeable, because in these approaches the therapist always is actively pursuing certain treatment goals related to behavioral change. Increased activity is necessary for rapid assessment of the patient and identification of the focus of treatment. A working alliance also must be established quickly, so that the time can be spent on problem issues rather than on patient resistance. The early development and maintenance of a positive therapeutic alliance seems crucial, especially in brief dynamic therapy (Gomes-Schwartz, 1978; Hartley & Strupp, 1983; Luborsky, Crits-Christoph, Alexander et al., 1983; Moras & Strupp, 1982).

MODELS OF BRIEF THERAPY

Each of the major theoretical orientations has given rise to brief therapy approaches. Thus, there are models of brief intervention in the dynamic, behavioral, cognitive-behavioral, and developmental traditions. Each model provides a way of conceptualizing change, with implications for short-term intervention including selection criteria, patient and therapist role behaviors, and those problem areas/diagnoses that are most appropriately treated in brief therapy.

Psychodynamic Models

Much has been written about the history and development of brief psychodynamic therapy. Freud's early work involved active intervention on the part of the therapist concentrated within a brief time period (Malan, 1963; Marmor, 1979). As analytic experience accumulated, dynamic treatments became longer. The therapist assumed a more neutral stance, encouraging regressive transference and discovering the importance of progressively earlier memories, patient resistance, the overdetermination of symptoms, and the necessity of working through. The timelessness characteristic of the patient's unconscious became more and more a feature of the sessions themselves.

Flegenheimer and Pollack (1988) have reviewed the course of analytic thinking about brief psychotherapy. One of the earliest pioneers to discuss the importance of the time limit was Rank, who felt that such a limit could help patients understand the necessity of giving up the transference neurosis. Ferenczi's early experiments with an "active technique" had as one goal the shortening of the time required by the analytic process (Dupont, 1988). Later analysts such as Alexander and French (1946) confronted the assumption that longer therapies were "deeper" and led to more desirable results, warning analysts that therapy should end before the gratification of treatment becomes greater than the pain of the symptom.

Recent analytic thinkers have increasingly explored the use of short-term interventions. For example, Mann (1973) offered a theory of brief therapy based on the child's developing sense of time. Arguing that the earliest experience of time is really a sense of timelessness that accompanies the state of fusion, Mann believes that brief therapy with its built-in time limit can be effective because it recreates the experience of separating from the mother, when a reality-based sense of time emerges. He argues that this can help patients confront the unreality of their fantasies about time. Flegenheimer and Pollack (1988) extended this, suggesting that the time limit helps bring into focus the patient's underlying fantasy that if he or she only maintains the symptoms and pathology long enough, the therapist will provide the desired gratifications.

Behavioral and Cognitive Models

Historically, behavioral treatments always have been focused on specific problem areas. There has been little discussion of *brief* therapy per se, but rather a focus on changing specific segments of behavior, with the length of treatment simply the time needed to complete the task. In addition, a hallmark of the behavioral tradition has been to approach empirically the design of treatments and the assessment of outcome empirically. Ironically, just as dynamic treatments started brief and then became longer, the same appears to be happening to behavioral treatments as they are applied to more extensive, difficult, and complex clinical issues (Budman & Stone, 1983).

Recently there has been widespread interest in cognitive and cognitive-behavioral treatments for a variety of specific problems. These treatments share the assumption that the patient has been subjected to faulty learning at some point in his or her development, leading to a distortion in the patient's internalized cognitive-emotional map of the world, which provides a template for all behavior and relationships. Specific features of this map become the target of intervention in brief cognitive-behavioral therapy (Budman & Gurman, 1988).

Developmental Models

In their review Budman and Stone (1983) placed great emphasis on current models of adult development as a theoretical basis for brief interventions. From recent work on normal developmental changes in adult men and women (e.g., Gilligan, 1982; Vaillant, 1977), one may draw a number of implications for how the brief therapist should work. The developmental model holds that people always are in motion, with the potential for change, but that they confront various developmental challenges over the lifespan. The brief therapist does not have to generate the energy for change, but rather must help his or her client to return to a state of action and adaptation. "Cure" is no longer a relevant concept; instead much of the therapist's work may be thought of as helping patients resolve focused "developmental difficulties" (Strupp & Binder, 1984).

SPECIALIZED VARIANTS OF BRIEF INTERVENTION

Brief interventions may vary in terms of their format, strategies/techniques, and foci. It is typically assumed that the major format of the brief therapies is individual treatment. Although individual therapy may remain a predominant mode, there are a number of clinical situations (e.g., marital conflict, child and adolescent problems) and considerations (e.g., therapeutic efficiency) that call for alternative formats such as group and family and/or marital intervention. Each of the theapy strategies and/or techniques (models) discussed above can be used with each of these formats. Because the two are relatively independent, the clinician must make decisions on both axes.

Brief Group Therapy

It would appear that group therapy is one of the most difficult formats in which to carry out brief intervention. Group treatment involves the selection of a number of patients who share some difficulties in common and who can be organized into meeting together regularly. The very task of selecting patients takes time and often cannot be done in a brief time period. Second, once patients are selected it takes time for the individuals to meld into a coherent, cohesive group that can work together toward a common goal.

Despite these difficulties, there is a beginning literature on groups of brief duration (Budman, Bennett, & Wisneski, 1981). Donovan, Bennett, and McElroy (1981), Strickler and Allgeyer (1967), Trakos and Lloyd (1971), and Sadock, Newman, and Normand (1968) have described short-term crisis groups for various types of patients. In addition, Donovan et al. (1981) pointed out that most inpatient units have groups as a regular part of their milieu treatment, so that short-term inpatient group therapy is a very prevalent though largely unstudied treatment modality. Short-term group experiences also are common in the child therapy field. Scheidlinger (1984) reviewed the long history of "therapeutic group modalities" with children, including therapeutic camping, children's diagnostic groups, and short-term group experiences on pediatric services designed to help children cope with medical crises. Also relevant are brief groups emphasizing primary prevention for children at risk, such as those whose parents have been hospitalized or are divorcing. These interventions often are implemented in the schools.

Brief Family/Marital Therapy

Marital and family treatments always have been relatively brief in duration (Gurman, 1981). Judging from reviews of research and reports by practitioners (Framo, 1981), marital and/or family treatments average between 15 and 20 sessions, with most of the positive results achieved in treatments lasting fewer than 20 sessions (Budman & Gurman, 1988). Marital and family treatments may be brief for important reasons inherent in the problems and the assets of individuals who seek such treatments (Gurman, 1981). The marital therapist usually focuses on the problematic aspects of the current situation rather than addressing the historical antecedents of the problem. These patients have shown themselves capable of having at least one (more or less) meaningful relationship, judged by the fact of being married, and in this sense constitute a preselected good-prognosis group. The interpersonal and/or transferential aspects of problems are not only talked about but also enacted in the therapy sessions themselves, lending to family therapy an increased intensity and impact. Finally, the loss of the therapist at termination may not be as threatening as in individual treatment, because the partners (sometimes) leave with each other as company. Brief family treatment methods have been shown to be effective with a variety of problems, including marital discord, conduct disorders in children, juvenile delinquency, adolescent psychiatric disorders, adult anxiety disorders, alcohol and substance abuse, and schizophrenia (Gurman, Kniskern, & Pinsof, 1986).

Crisis Intervention

Crisis intervention is planned, brief treatment in the face of a clearly defined crisis correlated with the onset of symptoms. Lindemann (1944) and Caplan (1964) were pioneers in the development of crisis intervention theory. Following the Coconut Grove fire in the 1940s, Lindemann studied and described the grief of the survivors, noting that although some individuals resolved the crisis in a time-limited period (roughly 6 weeks), others came to a chronic maladaptive resolution. Caplan (1964) expanded Lindemann's model to include all traumatic events and defined the key features of a crisis as follows: an obstacle to important life goals that is not solvable through ordinary coping patterns; a period of disorganization during which the individual tries many forms of coping; and a resolution achieved over time that can be either adaptive or maladaptive. Both Lindemann and Caplan focused primarily on the disequilibrium that follows trauma, and this has become a major theme of most crisis intervention theories (Gilliland & James, 1988).

Brammer (1985) differentiated among normal developmental crises (e.g., birth of a child, graduation from college), situational crises (e.g., automobile accident, loss of a job), and existential crises (e.g., remorse over unmet goals in old age). The general guidelines of the brief therapies are applicable, but in a crisis it may not be possible to gather background data and make a full assessment prior to intervening. Also, at crisis moments it may be necessary to suspend standard therapeutic strategies and shift to a mode of working that involves active intervention in the client's life outside of sessions. The amount of action needed depends on how immobilized the client is at the time and other aspects of the situation, such as imminent threats to safety. It is this readiness to move beyond the confines of the session that distinguishes crisis work.

Recent work has attempted to go beyond psychoanalytic theory as a basis for crisis intervention and include concepts from systems theory, adaptational theory, and interpersonal theory (Janosik, 1984). Gilliland and James (1988) discussed strategies for dealing with specific forms of crisis such as suicide, battering of women, institutional violence, severe physical handicaps, posttraumatic stress disorder, substance addiction, sexual assault, hostage crisis negotiation, and coping with loss and grief. Reviews of the research literature on crisis intervention (e.g., Kolotkin & Johnson, 1983; Koss & Butcher, 1986) provide an impression of overall effectiveness, but the state of research in this area is poor.

The Briefest Therapy

The briefest intervention is a single-session consultation or evaluation. Approximately 30% of all patients who present themselves for treatment are seen for only one session. Bloom (1981) discussed this topic extensively and reviewed the relevant research. Although professionals tend to view early and especially unilateral termination as a sign of client dissatisfaction, empirical studies fail to support this view (e.g., Littlepage, Kosloski, Schnelle, McNees, & Gendrich, 1976; Silverman & Beech, 1979).

Regarding therapeutic effectiveness, the few empirical studies that have been done support the conclusion that a single interview, whether for diagnostic or therapeutic purposes, can have significant positive impact. For example, Getz, Fujita, and Allen (1975) surveyed 104 patients who had made use of a night crisis intervention service connected to a hospital emergency room. Patients generally felt they had been helped, with depressed and anxious patients attributing twice as much helpfulness to the experience as did patients who presented with drug abuse or psychosis. Studies also have demonstrated a dramatic reduction in use of medical care following a single diagnostic or therapeutic interview. In emotionally disturbed patients even one therapeutic interview can reduce medical utilization by over 60% during the following 5 years (Cummings, 1977a, 1977b; Cummings & Follette, 1968, 1976; Follette & Cummings, 1967). Goldberg, Krantz, and Locke (1970) studied patients who had been referred and found eligible for psychiatric care. They found a 31% reduction in office visits and a 30% reduction in laboratory and x-ray visits in the year following referral, whether the patient followed up on the referral or not.

As Bloom (1981), Budman and Stone (1983), and others have noted, the power of a single session may be understandable when viewed from a developmental perspective, assuming that even a single visit helps the client resolve a temporary impasse and resume his or her normal course of adaptation and coping. A very neglected topic is the recommendation by the evaluating consultant or mental health professional that there be *no* treatment following evaluation. Elsewhere we have articulated the indications for no treatment as the recommendation of choice, a course that is rarely suggested by the professional but often initiated by the patient (Frances & Clarkin, 1981; Frances, Clarkin, & Perry, 1984).

MATCHING BRIEF THERAPIES TO PATIENT PROBLEM AREAS

An important consideration for the evaluating consultant is the potential usefulness of one of the brief therapies for a specific patient problem area. As our knowledge increases and we develop specialized intervention packages for specific types of problems, we can no longer refer to brief therapy in general, but rather must specify brief (duration) therapy with specific strategies and/or techniques in a particular format for a particular type of patient.

Process and outcome research on the brief therapies has been extensively reviewed elsewhere (Hollon & Beck, 1986; Koss & Butcher, 1986). Instead of repeating a box-score analysis of the outcome literature, we will summarize those findings most relevant for clinical practice. The clinician needs to know the empirical evidence for (a) patient problem areas that respond to some form of brief (as opposed to longer term) intervention, (b) patient characteristics (in addition to problem area) that are correlated with positive response to brief therapy, and (c) the effective processes of brief therapy with patients experiencing particular types of problems.

What are the patient diagnoses and/or problem areas that are responsive to brief intervention (leaving aside for the moment the question of strategies/ techniques)? Difficulties brought by clients to mental health professionals can be broadly conceptualized as either symptomatic or conflictual in nature (Beutler & Clarkin, 1990). Thus, treatments can be focused on alleviating symptoms (e.g., anxiety, phobias, depression), or targeted to reducing intrapsychic or interpersonal conflicts that lead to symptomatic and troubling behavior. In Table 41.1, we summarize representative empirical studies in major subcategories of these two domains.

Symptoms

Depression

Treatment for depression may be examined as a prototype that illustrates the key issues involved in evaluating the indications for brief therapy. The most salient issues are (a) is brief therapy indicated, or is an open-ended long-term therapy the treatment of choice? (b) If brief therapy is indicated, which model of intervention, with what mediating goals and strategies and/or techniques, should be used?

In evaluating whether brief therapy is appropriate for a particular depressed patient, the duration, severity, nature, and causes of the depression are important considerations. Brief cognitive-behavioral, behavioral, and interpersonal therapies have been shown to be effective in the diminution of mild to moderate depressions in outpatients with at least some functional capacity. When the mediating goals focus on cognitive changes (Rush, Beck, Kovacs, et al., 1977), social skills training (Hersen, Bellack, Himmelhock, et al., 1984), increases in pleasant events (Thompson & Gallagher, 1984), changes in interpersonal problems (Weissman, Prusoff, DiMascio, et al., 1979), and psychodynamic changes (Thompson & Gallagher, 1984), successful brief therapy has been accomplished. Reviews (e.g., Bellack, 1985) suggest that the various models (strategies and/or techniques) are effective but not differentially so. Although this is not clinically satisfying, the most parsimonious explanation may be that different brief therapy models draw upon common change-facilitating elements.

However, a note of caution is in order. A careful reading of studies such as those in Table 41.1 indicates that a sizeable minority of patients do not respond to brief treatment. For example, in the carefully designed study by Hersen, Bellack, Himmelhoch, and Thase (1984), female unipolar depressives responded to all four treatment conditions (social skill, social skill plus amitriptyline, amitriptyline, and psychotherapy) with marked improvement. However, when a conservative cutoff score (below 10 on both the Beck Depression Inventory and Hamilton Rating Scale for Depression) was used, only 23% to 49% of the patients were rated as significantly improved. Thus, as noted by these investigators, a substantial proportion of the patients remained depressed. Although there is no guarantee that such patients would respond to a longer treatment, results such as these suggest that longer and more intensive treatments should be investigated for patients whose depressive symptoms do not substantially remit after brief therapy.

This limitation of therapeutic range may be seen in other studies. Although treatment was effective in the Brown and Lewinsohn (1984) study, at 6-month follow-up, 25% of the patients still met Research Diagnostic Criteria (RDC) criteria for depression. Low responders to this educational treatment (those who needed more treatment and/or another treatment) reported depressions earlier in life, had significant life stresses, and had greater dissatisfaction across more areas of life, especially with friends. Weissman and Klerman (1977) have estimated that 15% of patients will remain depressed or in partial remission following *any* treatment.

Once it has been decided that brief therapy seems appropriate, how does the clinician select the most appropriate mediating goals (e.g., cognitive schema, social skills, interpersonal problems, dynamic conflicts) as the target of intervention? Which area is the most relevant focus for this particular patient? The simplest solution is to endorse only one approach to therapy and give all patients that treatment. Thus, if one is an advocate of brief cognitive therapy of depression and/or has received training in it, all patients who present with depression are given cognitive therapy. This can be easily rationalized by pointing to the outcome literature that suggests comparable effectiveness regardless of the orientation (strategies/ techniques).

However, many clinicians, if not most, seem to be opting for a practical eclecticism (Norcross, 1986) that utilizes techniques from the various manuals and schools of intervention, depending upon the specifics of the individual case. Unfortunately, it is not always clear how the growing number of eclectics choose particular techniques or a certain mix of techniques for the individual case. Other questions raised by the eclectic approach include: How does one assess the outcome of mixed intervention packages? How does one teach an eclectic approach?

The obvious solution (to us, at least) is to assess each individual patient for the presence and/or absence of difficulties in the focal areas posited by the various models of depression, and target those areas

Table 41.1. Representative Studies of Brief Therapy by Problem Area

SYMPTOMS

Depression
- Psychoeducational versus individual tutoring versus minimal contact in 8 weeks of treatment for RDC and DSM-III unipolar depressives (Brown & Lewinsohn, 1984).
- Lewinsohn's behavioral versus Beck's cognitive versus short-term dynamic therapy in 12 sessions for elderly depressed patients (Thompson & Gallagher, 1984).
- Social skills versus social skills plus medication versus medication alone versus dynamic therapy in 12 weeks for treatment for DSM-III major depressives (Hersen et al., 1984).
- Behavioral-cognitive versus insight therapy versus medication versus relaxation training in 10 weeks (McLean & Hakstian, 1979).
- Cognitive therapy versus medication in 12 weeks for major depressives by Feighner criteria (Rush et al., 1977).
- Group cognitive versus individual cognitive versus individual cognitive plus medication in 10 to 12 weeks for Feighner criteria depressives (Rush & Watkins, 1981).
- Cognitive therapy versus cognitive plus medication versus medication in 12 weeks for RDC depressives (Blackburn, Bishop, Glen, et al., 1981).
- Cognitive versus cognitive plus medication versus medication in 12 sessions for RDC depressives (Blackburn & Bishop, 1983).
- Cognitive versus medication versus cognitive plus medication versus cognitive for Feighner criteria depressives (Simons, Murphy, Levine, et al., 1986).
- IPT versus IPT plus medication versus medication versus nonscheduled treatment in 16 weeks for RDC depressives (Weissman et al., 1979).
- IPT versus cognitive versus medication versus placebo in 16 weeks for DSM-III criteria depressives (NIMH collaborative: Elkin, Parloff, Hadley, & Autry, 1985).

Anxiety-Panic
- Treatment of agoraphobia comparing self-instructional training, rational-emotive techniques, and exposure in vivo (Emmelkamp et al., 1986).
- Treatment of agoraphobia with exposure in vivo versus applied relaxation (Jansson, Jerremalm, & Ost, 1986).
- Brief treatment (15 sessions) of panic disorder comparing exposure to somatic cues and cognitive techniques to relaxation therapy (Barlow, Craske, Cerny, & Klosko, 1989).
- Agoraphobic women and their spouses treated in small groups with cognitive restructuring and self-initiated exposure exercises versus same treatment without spouses (Barlow et al., 1984).

Adjustment Disorders, Stress Response Syndrome, Crisis
- Brief (12 sessions) modified dynamic therapy for patients with stress response syndromes involving grief (Horowitz et al., 1984).

INTERNAL CONFLICT AND/OR PERSONALITY DISORDERS

- Focal psychodynamic therapy of nine or more sessions with 39 patients having a range of disorders from depression to anxiety to marital problems to character disorders. Outcome rated for symptom and conflict and/or behavioral change (Malan, 1976).
- Brief dynamic treatment of patients with a variety of conflicts compared to waiting list control subjects treated later with the same dynamic approach (Sifneos, 1972).

INTERPERSONAL CONFLICT

- Component analysis of behavioral marital therapy for distressed couples in 12 to 16 sessions (Jacobson, 1984).
- Behavioral marital therapy versus systematic versus psychodynamic marital therapies (Baucom, 1985).
- Psychodynamic-experiential marital therapy versus behavioral marital therapy (Johnson & Greenberg, 1985).

PHYSIOLOGICAL AND HEALTH PROBLEMS

- Investigated Blue Cross/Blue Shield claims for chronic diseases, comparing medical utilization for patients receiving varying levels of psychotherapy (Schlesinger et al., 1983).
- Compared medical services provided in HMO setting before and after psychotherapy for randomly selected patients receiving varying amounts of psychotherapy (Follette & Cummings, 1967).
- A meta-analysis of 34 studies of brief psychotherapy with heart attack and surgery patients (Mumford et al., 1982).
- For ulcer patients, effects of short-term dynamic psychotherapy combined with medication (Sjodin, 1983).
- Irritable bowel syndrome, treated with short-term dynamic psychotherapy and medication (Svelund, 1983).

Note. RDC = Research Diagnostic Criteria. DSM-III-R = *Diagnostic and Statistical Manual of Mental Disorders,* Third Edition, Revised. IPT = interpersonal psychotherapy. NIMH = National Institute of Mental Health. HMO = Health Maintenance Organization.

where problems are noted. Thus, depressed patients with faulty interpersonal relationships and cognitions will receive treatment focused on these two areas. This demands more of the clinician, who will need to learn a range of strategies and/or techniques in the treatment of depression and be flexible in assessing and treating the individual case. A prime candidate for a central and necessary focus in the brief treatment of patients with mild to moderate depressions is negative cognitions as defined by Beck (1967). The work of Teasdale and colleagues has been most useful in demonstrating the centrality of negative thinking. Initial level of depression and the number of global negative trait adjectives used to describe themselves was predictive of patients' future level of depression (Dent & Teasdale, 1988). In a psychotherapy process study (Teasdale & Fennell, 1982), it was found that thought change procedures produced more change in depressive thoughts than did other aspects of the treatment, which only involved exploring and obtaining more information relevant to the thoughts. This result, although quite preliminary and coming from a small N, does lend support to the notion that the central ingredient in behavioral treatment of depressives is the cognitive techniques aimed at changing negative thought patterns. Such attempts to arrive at the crucial foci of treatment are extremely beneficial to the development of treatments that are brief.

Finally, there has been much debate about the relative effectiveness of brief therapies as compared to or combined with drug treatments for depressions. It is our impression that a debate formulated in an either/or fashion misses the point. Rather, it would seem that brief psychotherapy and medication may be targeted at different aspects of the depressive syndrome.

Anxiety

The application of exposure-based treatments for the alleviation of agoraphobia and avoidance behaviors is unique, in that there seems little doubt that these treatments are effective, and significantly more effective than the alternatives. Cognitive-behavioral treatments of panic and agoraphobia have been successful (Barlow, Craske, Cerny, & Klosko, 1989; Emmelkamp, Brilman, Kuiper, & Mersch, 1986). Spouse-aided treatment of agoraphobia may give additional support to the patient and aid in outcome at follow-up (Barlow, O'Brien, & Last, 1984).

However, as Barlow (1988) indicated, even the exposure-based treatments are limited in their effectiveness, with dropout rates estimated at 12%. In addition, 30% to 40% of all agoraphobics who com-

plete treatment fail to benefit. If panic attacks play a central role in avoidance behavior, then one reason for the less than complete response to exposure treatments may be a lack of direct attention to the panic attacks. Barlow (1988) reported on a combined exposure, cognitive, and relaxation treatment for patients with panic attacks without significant avoidance. Preliminary results are impressive, with an almost total elimination of panic.

Internal Conflict and/or Personality Disorders

Some patients complain less of specific symptoms such as depression and anxiety and more of troubled relationships with others and an overall lack of satisfaction with their lives. Many of these patients are not lacking in social skills (as might be hypothesized by behavioral therapists), but rather are ambivalent and conflicted in the utilization of their capacities. Brief psychodynamic therapies, those using techniques of clarification, confrontation, and interpretation that link early transference themes to the here-and-now relationship with the therapist, have been applied in such cases. Unfortunately, many studies of this approach have nonrandomized, naturalistic designs (Malan, 1976; Sifneos, 1987), making it impossible to adequately evaluate their effectiveness. Some investigators have used brief dynamic treatments as a contrast to other approaches (Hersen et al., 1984; Sloane, Staples, Cristol, Yorkston, & Whipple, 1975) and have found the dynamic approaches comparable to cognitive and behavioral strategies.

A much quoted and well-designed study by Sloane et al. (1975) compared brief behavior therapy to brief dynamic therapy for patients with typical neurotic problems. The few significant differences observed favored behavior therapy. Although it appeared that brief treatment was effective for neurotic conditions, it is interesting to note that sustained improvement at 1-year follow-up was hard to assess because many patients sought further treatment after ending brief therapy. Maybe the patients are telling us something.

Recently developed approaches extend the range of patients for whom brief therapy may be suitable. Examples include Davanloo's (1978, 1980) and Strupp and Binder's (1984) work with severe character disordered patients, Lazarus's (1982) description of a brief psychotherapy approach with narcissistic personality disorders, and Leibovich's (1983) suggestion that short-term treatment may be preferable for some types of borderline patients. Sederer and Thorbeck (1986) also have discussed the advantages and disadvantages of using short-term exploratory psychotherapy with borderline patients in an inpatient setting. To date, these suggested extensions of brief dynamic therapy for more disturbed populations have not received empirical examination.

Interpersonal Conflict and/or Family Problems

Cognitive-behavioral treatments have proven effective in reducing marital conflict and increasing positive marital interaction. For example, Jacobson (1984) compared the effectiveness of brief treatments (12–16 sessions) involving behavior exchange alone, communication and/or problem-solving training alone, and both combined for distressed couples. Using conservative criteria for judging clinical improvement, two thirds of the couples demonstrated improved marital adjustment compared to none of the couples in the waiting list control group.

Patterson's (1982) extensive research on families with acting out preadolescents has been recognized as exemplary (Kazdin, 1988). By systematically observing the family interaction patterns that lead to adolescent acting out, a brief behavioral family intervention has been formulated that has shown positive effects in reducing acting out (Patterson, Chamberlain, & Reid, 1982).

Relatively few research studies can be found in the literature demonstrating the effects of brief interventions with children. An example of the work that has been reported is the study by Fisher (1980). Thirty-seven randomly assigned families were studied, comparing 6-session, 12-session, and unlimited family therapy with a control group that received evaluation and advice. Families that received any treatment improved more than control subjects, but there were no differential effects between treatments. In spite of the dearth of empirical work, a number of authors have argued that short-term work with children may be a meaningful therapeutic endeavor. For example, Turecki (1982) discussed how just experiencing a meaningful therapeutic relationship may provide a "model for future relationships" that can enhance a child's means of coping.

Adjustment Disorders, Stress Response Syndromes, and Crisis Intervention

As noted earlier in this chapter, crisis usually connotes an abrupt change in adjustment concomitant with or subsequent to disruptive external events such

as natural disasters, expectable but sudden life events such as death of loved ones, or acute health problems. There are a predictable group of symptoms and defensive patterns that occur in the so-called stress response syndromes. The work of Horowitz (1988) has been extremely helpful in delineating normal and abnormal responses to stressful life events. The individual typically experiences both denial states (e.g., selective inattention, amnesia, disavowal of the meanings of stimuli, numbness, and withdrawal) and intrusive states (e.g., sleep disturbance, hypervigilance, intrusive and repetitive thoughts and feelings) that may be useful in defining the focus of intervention and setting the duration of the brief therapy and crisis intervention. As noted with other types of problems, in this area there has been a curious lack of either theoretical or empirical determination of the match between specific problem areas and the needed length and intensity of treatment. Stress response syndromes would seem to provide an excellent opportunity to study the natural course of human reaction to aversive stressful events and articulate the needed length of intervention. Horowitz and colleagues (Horowitz, Marmar, Krupnick, Wilner, Kaltreider, & Wallerstein, 1984) have studied a brief treatment for stressful life events (grief upon the loss of a parent) that takes into account the character style of the patient, a very promising clinical approach.

Koss and Butcher (1986) described various levels of crisis intervention from the technical point of view ranging from environmental manipulation to support for the patient through the crisis to understanding what led up to the crisis situation and the patient's response to it. It is quite likely that the more disturbed patients who are most dependent on their environment will need the former, whereas those patients who are well-adjusted prior to the crisis and whose degree of individual distress is mild to moderate will profit most from the latter types of intervention. Research in these areas is typically naturalistic, because it is quite difficult to experimentally study individuals in crisis (e.g., with randomization). Competing and plausible types of intervention could be compared but there seems to be little research of this type.

Physiological and Health Problems

A number of recent investigations have documented the effectiveness of brief psychotherapy in decreasing the use of medical services. This "medical offset" effect was shown in the study by Follette and Cummings (1967) of medical utilization in a health maintenance organization (HMO) setting. Tracking randomly selected groups of emotionally distressed patients who received either no therapy, a single consultation, brief therapy (averaging 6.2 sessions) or longer-term treatment (averaging 33.9 sessions), these authors showed sigificant declines in medical use in all patients who received psychotherapy. Decreases of medical utilization remained constant during the 5 years following the termination of psychotherapy. In a similar study Schlesinger, Mumford, Glass, Patrick, and Scharfstein (1983) investigated Blue Cross/Blue Shield claims for chronic disease (diabetes, asthma, hypertension, and ischemic heart disease) from 1974 to 1978. To explore the possibility of a "dose-response effect," patients were classified into those who received no therapy, a single consultation, brief intervention (2–6 visits), medium-term treatment (7–20 visits), and longer term treatment (21 or more visits). By the third year after intervention the medical costs for patients receiving psychological services had decreased by 39%. When mental health costs were figured in, there was a 5% overall reduction in costs, but a better mix of medical service use was observed, suggesting that the quality of care had improved. A dose-response effect was found in that a minimum amount of mental health care did not lower costs, but with increasingly longer treatments there was greater medical offset. In summarizing this literature VandenBos and DeLeon (1988) observed that most medical offsets are observed *after* the completion of psychological services.

Other studies have focused on specific medical problems, with the beneficial effects of brief therapy frequently demonstrated. In a meta-analysis of 34 controlled experimental studies of brief psychological interventions as an adjunct to medical care for people who had suffered a heart attack or were facing surgery, Mumford, Schlesinger, and Glass (1982) found average effect sizes of .49, indicating that groups who received such interventions did better than control groups by an average of one-half standard deviation. Psychological interventions included a wide range of activities carried out by personnel at various levels, for example, MDs, nurses, and aides providing information, support, or group meetings. Most interventions were modest and *not* tailored to the individual needs of particular patients. The greatest effects were for cooperation with treatment, speed of recovery, lowered requirements for analgesics and sleeping medications, and reduced hospital stays. The authors speculated that the benefits may be even greater when interventions are matched to the needs of patients. Svelund (1983) found that short-term dynamic psychotherapy with medication was significantly more effective with patients suffering from the irritable bowel syndrome than medication alone.

INDICATIONS FOR THE BRIEF THERAPIES

In this section we review and summarize the indications for the brief therapies, drawing as much as possible on empirical literature and supplementing this with clinical wisdom as reported by authors in the field. Budman and Stone (1983) emphasized the dearth of empirical data regarding selection criteria, agreeing with Lambert's (1979) conclusion that, "It does not appear that acute onset, good previous adjustment, good ability to relate, a focal problem, high initial motivation, lower socioeconomic class, a current crisis, or a host of other determining variables . . . have been shown to be any more highly related to outcome in brief therapy than in longer term therapies" (p. 121).

A number of authors suggest that most patients can benefit from brief therapy (e.g., Bennett & Wisneski, 1979; Cummings & VandenBos, 1979) or that most patients should first try brief therapy, with judgments about subsequent treatment based on an evaluation of this "in-basket test" (e.g., Wolberg, 1965). Those advocating this approach tend to exclude only those few patients who met particular exclusion criteria. For example, there are recommendations to exclude patients who cannot attend to the process of verbal interaction, who have diagnoses for which other treatment modalities take precedence, or whose charactererological styles make it unlikely that they can endure the psychological work (MacKenzie, 1988). Narrow sets of exclusion criteria are especially characteristic of nondynamic therapies of depression, for example, behavioral social skills training (McLean, 1982), cognitive therapy (Beck, Rush, Shaw, & Emery, 1979), and interpersonal therapy (Klerman, Weissman, Rounsaville, & Chevron, 1984).

Recommending brief therapy for most patients sidesteps the issue of identifying specific indications for brief intervention. This approach ignores the full range of pathology presented by patients who seek treatment, as well as data suggesting that a sizeable minority of patients do not respond to brief therapy, with up to 60% returning for more treatment later (e.g., Koss & Butcher, 1986). Some disorders, such as schizophrenia, bipolar disorder, and severe character disorders, appear lifelong, and patients with these difficulties probably need either continuous care or multiple episodes of care of varying duration. We do recognize, however, that there is some empirical appeal in the idea of trying most patients in a brief therapy, and then making treatment plans based on the results of that experience. In the hierarchical plan of service delivery that is implicit in the concept of differential therapeutics, brief therapy may at times play an important triage function.

Patient Problem Areas as Indicators

As stated earlier, we think it is extremely important to be aware of the nature of the patient's focal difficulties and whether or not brief intervention has been shown to be effective in treating or alleviating these particular problems. At the present state of our knowledge, it would appear that the following problem areas are likely to respond to brief intervention: intrapsychic conflicts that are focal in nature; marital conflicts; some child, adolescent, and family conflicts; symptoms of mild to moderate intensity such as depression, anxiety, or phobias; and adaptation to some medical disorders. Patients with multiple problem areas and those with chronic difficulties may need either longer-term therapy or repeated episodes of treatment, some of which might be brief in duration.

Treatment Strategies by Enabling Factors as Indicators

Given the above problem areas and/or diagnoses that may respond to brief intervention, a more specific set of indications can be derived by considering the brief therapy model (strategies and/or techniques) to be employed in relation to patient enabling factors. In general, the psychodynamic model of brief therapy specifies the most stringent selection criteria (Budman & Stone, 1983; Clarkin & Frances, 1983). Table 41.2

is a summary of indications for brief dynamic therapy as enunciated by the most prominent writers (Gustafson, 1986; Malan, 1976; Mann, 1973; Sifneos, 1981). Other criteria that have been specified by individual dynamic writers include a clear chief complaint with an oedipal focus (Sifneos, 1981), a capacity for rapid emotional involvement and separation (Mann, 1973), and an adequate response to early "trial interpretations" (Malan, 1976). Budman and Stone (1983) estimated that only about 20% of all outpatients meet such a stringent list of selection criteria.

What the patient brings to the working relationship is only one side of the story, however, and in this sense it is also important to consider therapist enabling factors. The therapist's ability to foster a positive therapeutic alliance is important for any therapy, but the quick development of a good alliance is crucial in brief therapy. The brief therapist must be skilled at rapidly cultivating a good working relationship with a whole gamut of individuals. Strupp (1980) produced some interesting small N process data on nondiagnostic patient issues and aspects of the patient–therapist relationship that have relevance to this point. Two patients treated by the same therapist using the same manualized treatment were studied over the course of their brief dynamically oriented therapy. One of the patients was evaluated as a treatment success, whereas the other was rated as a treatment failure. The process results gathered from objective measures and clinical investigation of the therapy transcripts revealed some plausible conclusions. The patient with positive outcome came to treatment with the ability to engage in the therapeutic relationship and work productively within the framework of the treatment as modeled by the therapist. In contrast, the patient with poor outcome approached the treatment with an attitude of

Table 41.2. Enabling Factors for the Brief Dynamic Therapies

1. Patient reports at least one significant relationship in early childhood.

2. Patient is intelligent and capable of communicating verbally his or her thoughts, feelings, and fantasies.

3. Patient has relatively good ego strength as manifested in satisfactory educational, work, and sexual performance.

4. Patient is motivated to change and understand him- or herself better and is not content with symptom relief. Patient is honest, curious, and realistic about the outcome of therapy.

5. Patient quickly and flexibly relates to the consultant and can freely express feelings.

6. Patient is psychologically minded and willing to study his or her behaviors and feelings, including responses to the therapist that occur during the interview.

7. Patient and therapist can agree to work on a focal area of conflict whose nature becomes increasingly clear as it is explored. The patient responds with further thoughts and feelings to interpretations of the conflict.

8. The patient shows an ability to experience, tolerate, and discuss painful affects.

hostile resistance that did not change. Strupp emphasized that in the case with a poor outcome, "countertransference reactions" interfered with the therapist's ability to effectively confront and resolve the patient's negative transference. We have pointed out in this regard that the patient's reactance level must be low enough to allow him or her to accept help and direction from the therapist (Beutler & Clarkin, 1990).

Even with performance-based screening of patients' suitability for brief treatment such as Gustafson (1986) has described, clinicians cannot always predict accurately. For example, Binder, Henry, and Strupp (1987) noted the difficulty in clinicians' ability to select patients who will respond to brief dynamic therapy. Even when predicting from performance-based assessments, their prognostic ratings correlated with outcome only in the .30 to .40 range. These authors noted two possible explanations for their results: (a) bright, articulate clients may perform well in the initial evaluation but then not respond to the treatment; (b) the therapists's contribution to the therapeutic alliance, and thus outcome, often is ignored in clinical predictions, which are usually based only on patient characteristics and behavior.

Within the child therapy field, Turecki (1982) has suggested that brief therapy is indicated for children at the healthier end of the diagnostic continuum, especially in cases of reactive disorder involving object loss. A history of multiple object losses is a negative prognostic sign, because of difficulties with engagement and the likelihood that the child will experience termination as another instance of abandonment. Turecki feels that an especially good prognostic indicator is the child's ability to delineate the focal issue him- or herself.

TRAINING IN THE BRIEF THERAPIES

Given the increasing prevalence of brief therapy, formal training in this area would seem to be a sine qua non of any clinical psychology training program. Training in the art and science of psychotherapy has been slow to develop, and only now are we beginning to understand the parameters of training and the effectiveness of various procedures (Norcross, 1986). At the present time, training is enhanced by therapy manuals and the rating scales that accompany them for the measurement of adherence and skill. Manualization, which is one manifestation of increasing sophistication in the area of psychotherapy research (Parloff, London, & Wolfe, 1986), has provided the field with de facto brief therapy training manuals because almost all psychotherapy studies focus on short-term interventions. Brief therapies are much easier to manualize and investigate than longer therapies, and with few exceptions, most manuals describe treatments of brief duration.

We would emphasize that training in brief therapy is different from training in therapies that are unintentionally brief. The trainee needs to learn to set and negotiate a time limit with the patient and to actively use this time limit as a context for the treatment. Patients react variously to such limits, and the trainee needs experience in negotiating this. Training should take place in a setting (outpatient clinic, hospital, consortium) that values brief treatments and assigns cases with attention to this dimension of intervention. Also, it is especially important that the trainee have supervisors with experience in and knowledge of planned brief therapies, supervisors who can convey a belief in the efficacy of such treatments.

SUMMARY AND CONCLUSIONS

Brief therapy now is in vogue. At present most treatments are of brief duration, and there is an increasing technology guiding brief therapy that includes more refined diagnostic systems, more precise definition of specific problem areas, and manualization of the brief therapies themselves. Recently there has been a shift of emphasis from the brevity or duration of brief treatment to the focused nature of these interventions. Empirical work has progressed on the focused treatment of specific symptoms such as depression and anxiety, intrapsychic conflicts, interpersonal problems, and coping with medical illnesses. The question of treatment duration and intensity has become a technical issue—what is the appropriate dosage of this particular treatment needed to ameliorate this problem with this particular patient? This progression from a concern with the brevity of treatment to an emphasis on focal interventions is indicative of increasing sophistication in the field, and is consistent with an overall treatment philosophy that emphasizes differential therapeutics.

Most reviews have enthusiastically supported the current state of research and practice in brief therapy. Although also supportive of the vigorous development of these new therapies, we would like to sound a note of caution, because it seems that in the rush of enthusiasm for briefer treatments we are at risk of overlooking some underlying weaknesses and strains. We feel it is time to state some of the difficulties encountered with the brief therapies and readjust our expectations. Without such caution, the brief therapies may suffer under the weight of exalted expectations followed by subsequent disappointment, as have other therapeutic movements.

Brief therapy probably is not as versatile as has been indicated in previous reviews. There are chronic conditions for which this clearly is not the treatment of choice. For conditions such as schizophrenia and severe personality disorders, brief treatment episodes, repeated over a long period of time, may suffice, although it is likely that with many such patients long-term psychotherapy is indicated. Very little attention has been given to the question of which patients in brief therapy should be continued in longer term therapy due to either a lack of response to brief treatment or a fruitful but incomplete response. We also have indicated that in problem areas where brief therapy seems indicated in general and shows much research promise (e.g., depression of mild to moderate severity), a sizeable minority of patients do not respond and may come back for more treatment later. As Binder et al. (1987) noted, the indications for brief treatment, although theoretically elegant, are not equally pragmatic.

Several research questions related to the brief therapies are in need of attention. The growing concern about the clinical significance of therapeutic outcome as opposed to statistical significance suggests that we take a closer look at which brief treatments provide *clinically* effective treatments for which disorders. The numerous studies that compare two active treatments to each other and/or to a placebo condition and simply report statistically significant differences are now out of date; instead, we need reports of effect sizes and the proportion of patients showing clinical change to be convinced of the effectiveness of specific brief interventions. Although there is much speculation as to which patients will profit from brief therapy, especially among the dynamic therapists, the relative lack of research on patient and therapist variables predictive of differential treatment responsiveness regardless of treatment duration is a pressing issue for the field.

In conclusion, we feel that the excitement over brief therapy expressed by previous reviewers should be tempered with clinical realism and the perspective of accumulating research evidence. *Some* brief therapies are effective with *some* patients having *certain* difficulties. Overestimating the effectiveness and applicability of these treatments goes against recent research findings and also carries the danger of fostering unrealistic expectations on the part of insurance companies and third party payers. Even now some providers expect that all therapies will be of brief duration, which is unrealistic and does not match our current

knowledge. Only a sober appraisal of the brief therapies, guided by accumulating research evidence and the overall perspective of differential therapeutics, will place these treatments in their proper context and help ensure their longevity.

References

Alexander, F., & French, T.M. (1946). *Psychoanalytic therapy: Principles and applications.* New York: Ronald Press.

Barlow, D.H. (1988). *Anxiety and its disorders: The nature and treatment of anxiety and panic.* New York: Guilford Press.

Barlow, D.H., Craske, M.G., Cerny, J.A., & Klosko, J.S. (1989). Behavioral treatment of panic disorder. *Behavior Therapy, 20,* 261–282.

Barlow, D.H., O'Brien, G.T., & Last, C.G. (1984). Couples treatment of agoraphobia. *Behavior Therapy, 15,* 41–58.

Baucom, D.H. (1984). The active ingredients of behavioral marital therapy: The effectiveness of problem-solving/communication training, contingency contracting, and their communication. In K. Hahlweg & N.S. Jacobson (Eds.), *Marital interaction: Analysis and modification* (pp. 73–88). New York: Guilford Press.

Beck, A.T. (1967). *Depression: Clinical, experimental, and theoretical aspects.* New York: Hoeber.

Beck, A.T., Rush, A.J., Shaw, B.F., & Emery, G. (1979). *Cognitive therapy of depression: A treatment manual.* New York: Guilford Press.

Bellack, A.S. (1985). Psychotherapy research in depression: An overview. In E.E. Beckham & W.R. Leber (Eds.), *Handbook of depression: Treatment, assessment, and research* (pp. 204–219). Homewood, IL: Dorsey Press.

Bennett, M.J., & Wisneski, M.J. (1979). Continuous psychotherapy within an HMO. *American Journal of Psychiatry, 136,* 1283–1287.

Beutler, L., & Clarkin, J.F. (1990). *Differential treatment assignment: Toward prescriptive psychological treatment.* New York: Brunner/Mazel.

Binder, J., Henry, P., & Strupp, H. (1987). An appraisal of selection criteria for dynamic psychotherapies and implications for setting time limits. *Psychiatry, 50,* 154–166.

Blackburn, I.M., & Bishop, S. (1983). Changes in cognition with pharmacotherapy and cognitive therapy. *British Journal of Psychiatry, 143,* 609.

Blackburn, I.M., Bishop, S., Glen, A.I.M., Walley, L.J., & Christie, J.E. (1981). The efficacy of cognitive therapy in depression: A treatment trial using cognitive therapy and pharmacotherapy, each alone and in combination. *British Journal of Psychiatry, 139,* 181.

Bloom, B.L. (1981). Focused single-session therapy: Initial development and evaluation. In S.H. Budman (Ed.), *Forms of brief therapy* (pp. 167–216). New York: Guilford Press.

Brammer, L. (1985). *The helping relationship: Process and skills* (3rd ed.). Englewood Cliffs, NJ: Prentice-Hall.

Brown, R.A., & Lewinsohn, P.M. (1984). A psychoeducational approach to the treatment of depression: Comparison of group, individual and minimal contact procedures. *Journal of Consulting and Clinical Psychology, 52*, 774.

Budman, S., Bennett, M., & Wisneski, M. (1981). An adult developmental model of short-term group psychotherapy. In S. Budman (Ed.), *Forms of brief therapy* (pp. 305–342). New York: Guilford Press.

Budman, S., & Gurman, A. (1983). The practice of brief therapy. *Professional Psychology, 14*, 277–292.

Budman, S.H., & Gurman, A.S. (1988). *Theory and practice of brief therapy*. New York: Guilford Press.

Budman, S., & Stone, J. (1983). Advances in brief psychotherapy: A review of recent literature. *Hospital and Community Psychiatry, 34*, 939–946.

Butcher, J.N., & Koss, M.P. (1978). Research on brief and crisis-oriented therapies. In S. Garfield & A.E. Bergin (Eds.), *Handbook of psychotherapy and behavior change* (2nd ed., pp. 725–768). New York: John Wiley & Sons.

Caplan, G. (1964). *Principles of preventive psychiatry*. New York: Basic Books.

Clarkin, J.F., & Frances, A. (1983). Brief psychotherapies. In B.B. Wolman (Ed.), *The therapist's handbook: Treatment methods of mental disorders* (2nd ed., pp. 196–221). New York: Van Nostrand Reinhold.

Cummings, N.A. (1977a). The anatomy of psychotherapy under national health insurance. *American Psychologist, 32*, 711–718.

Cummings, N.A. (1977b). Prolonged (ideal) versus short-term (realistic) psychotherapy. *Professional Psychology, 8*, 491–501.

Cummings, N.A., & Follette, W.T. (1968). Psychiatric services and medical utilization in a prepaid health plan setting: Part II. *Medical Care, 6*, 31–41.

Cummings, N.A., & Follette, W.T. (1976). Brief psychotherapy and medical utilization. In H. Dorken & Associates (Eds.), *The professional psychologist today: New developments in law, health insurance, and health practice* (pp. 165–174). San Francisco, CA: Jossey-Bass.

Cummings, N.A., & VandenBos, G. (1979). The general practice of psychology. *Professional Psychology: Research and Practice, 10*, 430–440.

Davanloo, H. (1978). *Basic principles and techniques in short-term dynamic psychotherapy*. New York: Spectrum Books.

Davanloo, H. (1980). A method of short-term dynamic psychotherapy. In H. Davanloo (Ed.), *Short-term dynamic psychotherapy* (pp. 43–71). New York: Jason Aronson.

Dent, J., & Teasdale, J.D. (1988). Negative cognition and the persistence of depression. *Journal of Abnormal Psychology, 97*, 29–34.

Donovan, J., Bennett, M.J., & McElroy, C.M. (1981). The crisis group: Its rationale, format, and outcome. In S.H. Budman (Ed.), *Forms of brief therapy* (pp. 283–304). New York: Guilford Press.

Dulcan, M. (1984). Brief psychotherapy with children and their families: The state of the art. *Journal of the American Academy of Child Psychiatry, 23*, 544–551.

Dupont, T. (Ed.). (1988). *The clinical diary of Sandor Ferenezi*. Cambridge, MA: Harvard University Press.

Elkin, I., Parloff, M.B., Hadley, S.Q., & Autry, J.H. (1985). NIMH Treatment of Depression Collaborative Research Program. *Archives of General Psychiatry, 42*, 305–316.

Emmelkamp, P.M.G., Brilman, E., Kuiper, H., & Mersch, P.P. (1986). The treatment of agoraphobia: A comparison of self-instructional training, rational emotive therapy, and exposure in vivo. *Behavioral Modification, 10*, 37–53.

Fisher, S.G. (1980). The use of time limits in brief psychotherapy. *Family Process, 19*, 377–392.

Flegenheimer, W., & Pollack, J. (1988). The time limit in brief psychotherapy. *Bulletin of the Menninger Clinic, 53*, 44–51.

Follette, W., & Cummings, N. (1967). Psychiatric services and medical utilization in a prepaid health plan setting. *Medical Care, 5*, 25–35.

Framo, J. (1981). Integration of marital therapy with sessions of family of origin. In A. Gurman & D. Kniskern (Eds.), *Handbook of family therapy* (pp. 133–158). New York: Brunner/Mazel.

Frances, A., & Clarkin, J.F. (1981). No treatment as the prescription of choice. *Archives of General Psychiatry, 38*, 542–545.

Frances, A., Clarkin, J.F., & Perry, S. (1984). *Differential therapeutics in psychiatry: The art and science of treatment selection*. New York: Brunner/Mazel.

Garfield, S.L. (1986). Research on client variables in psychotherapy. In S.L. Garfield & A.E. Bergin (Eds.), *Handbook of psychotherapy and behavior change* (3rd ed., pp. 213–256). New York: John Wiley & Sons.

Garfield, S.L., & Wolpin, M. (1963). Expectations regarding psychotherapy. *Journal of Nervous and Mental Disease, 137*, 353–362.

Getz, W.L., Fujita, B.N., & Allen, D. (1975). The use of paraprofessionals in crisis intervention: Evaulation of an innovative program. *American Journal of Community Psychology, 3*, 135–144.

Gilligan, C. (1982). *In a different voice*. Cambridge, MA: Harvard University Press.

Gilliland, B.E., & James, R.K. (1988). *Crisis intervention strategies*. Pacific Grove, CA: Brooks/Cole.

Goldberg, I.D., Krantz, G., & Locke, B.Z. (1970). Effect of a short-term outpatient psychiatric therapy benefit on the utilization of medical services in a prepaid group practice medical program. *Medical Care, 8*, 419–428.

Gomes-Schwartz, B.A. (1978). Effective ingredients in psychotherapy: Prediction of outcomes from process variables. *Journal of Consulting and Clinical Psychology, 46*, 1023–1035.

Gurman, A.S. (1981). Integrative marital therapy: Toward the development of an interpersonal approach. In S.H. Budman (Ed.), *Forms of brief therapy* (pp. 415–457). New York: Guilford Press.

Gurman, A.S., Kniskern, D.P., & Pinsof, W.M. (1986).

Research on the process and outcome of marital and family therapy. In S.L. Garfield & A.E. Bergin (Eds.), *Handbook of psychotherapy and behavior change* (pp. 565–624). New York: John Wiley & Sons.

Gustafson, J.P. (1986). *The complex secret of brief psychotherapy*. New York: WW Norton.

Hartley, D.E., & Strupp, H.H. (1983). The therapeutic alliance: Its relationship to outcome in brief psychotherapy. In J. Masling (Ed.), *Empirical studies of psychoanalytic theories* (Vol. 1, pp. 1–38). Hillsdale, NJ: Analytical Press.

Hersen, M., Bellack, A.S., Himmelhoch, J.M., & Thase, M.E. (1984). Effects of social skills training, amitriptyline, and psychotherapy in unipolar depressed women. *Behavior Therapy, 15,* 21.

Hollon, S.D., & Beck, A.T. (1986). Cognitive and cognitive-behavioral therapies. In S.L. Garfield & A.E. Bergin (Eds.), *Handbook of psychotherapy and behavior change* (pp. 443–482). New York: John Wiley & Sons.

Horowitz, M.J. (1988). Stress-response syndromes: Posttraumatic and adjustment disorders. In R. Michels & J.O. Cavenar, Jr. (Eds.), *Psychiatry* (Vol. 1, pp. 1–16). Philadelphia: JB Lippincott.

Horowitz, M.J., Marmar, C., Krupnick, J., Wilner, N., Kaltreider, N., & Wallerstein, R. (1984). *Personality styles and brief psychotherapy*. New York: Basic Books.

Howard, K.I., Kopta, S.M., Krause, M.S., & Orlinsky, D.E. (1986). The dose-effect relationship in psychotherapy. *American Psychologist, 41,* 159–164.

Jacobson, N.S. (1984). A component analysis of behavioral marital therapy: The relative effectiveness of behavior exchange and communication/problem-solving training. *Journal of Consulting and Clinical Psychology, 52,* 295–305.

Janosik, E. (1984). *Crisis counseling: A contemporary approach*. Monterey, CA: Wadsworth Health Sciences Division.

Jansson, L., Jerremalm, A., & Ost, L.G. (1986). Follow-up of agoraphobic patients treated with exposure in-vivo or applied relaxation. *British Journal of Psychiatry, 149,* 486–490.

Johnson, S.M., & Greenberg, L.S. (1985). Differential effects of experiential and problem-solving interventions in resolving marital conflict. *Journal of Consulting and Clinical Psychology, 53,* 175–184.

Kazdin, A.E. (1988). *Child psychotherapy: Developing and identifying effective treatments*. Elmsford, NY: Pergamon General Psychology Series.

Klerman, G.L., Weissman, M.M., Rounsaville, B.J., & Chevron, E.S. (1984). *Interpersonal psychotherapy of depression*. New York: Basic Books.

Kolotkin, R., & Johnson, M. (1983). Crisis intervention and measurement of outcome. In M. Lambert, E. Christensen, & S. DeJulio (Eds.), *The assessment of psychotherapy outcome* (pp. 132–159). New York: John Wiley & Sons.

Koss, M. (1979). Length of psychotherapy for clients seen in private practice. *Journal of Consulting and Clinical Psychology, 47,* 210–212.

Koss, M., & Butcher, J. (1986). Research on brief psycho-

therapy. In S. Garfield & A. Bergin (Eds.), *Handbook of psychotherapy and behavior change* (3rd ed., pp. 627–670). New York: John Wiley & Sons.

Lambert, M.J. (1979). Characteristics of patients and their relationship to outcome in brief psychotherapy. *Psychiatric Clinics of North America, 2,* 111–123.

Langsley, D. (1978). Comparing clinic and private practice of psychiatry. *American Journal of Psychiatry, 135,* 702–706.

Lazarus, L.W. (1982). Brief psychotherapy of narcissistic disturbances. *Psychotherapy: Theory, Research and Practice, 19,* 228–236.

Leibovich, M. (1983). Why short-term psychotherapy for borderlines? *Psychotherapy and Psychosomatics, 39,* 1–9.

Lindemann, E. (1944). Symptomatology and management of acute grief. *American Journal of Psychiatry, 51,* 141–148.

Littlepage, G.E., Kosloski, K.D., Schnelle J.F., McNees, M.P., & Gendrich, J.C. (1976). The problem of early outpatient terminations from community mental health centers: A problem for whom? *Journal of Community Psychology, 4,* 164–167.

Luborsky, L. (1984). *Principles of psychoanalytic psychotherapy. A manual for supportive-expressive treatment*. New York: Basic Books.

Luborsky, L., Crits-Christoph, P., Alexander, L., Margolis, M., & Cohen, M. (1983). Two helping alliance methods for predicting outcomes of psychotherapy. *Journal of Nervous and Mental Disease, 171,* 480–491.

MacKenzie, K.R. (1988). Recent developments in brief psychotherapy. *Hospital and Community Psychiatry, 39,* 742–751.

Malan, D.H. (1963). *A study of brief psychotheapy*. New York: Plenum Press.

Malan, D.H. (1976). *The frontier of brief psychotherapy*. New York: Plenum Press.

Malan, D.H., Heath, E.S., Bacal, H.A., & Balfour, F.H.G. (1975). Psychodynamic changes in untreated neurotic patients: II. Apparently genuine improvements. *Archives of General Psychiatry, 32,* 110–126.

Mann, J. (1973). *Time-limited psychotherapy*. Cambridge, MA: Harvard University Press.

Marmor, J. (1979). Short-term dynamic psychotherapy. *American Journal of Psychiatry, 136,* 149–155.

McGee, R.K. (1983). Crisis intervention and brief psychotherapy. In M. Hersen, A.E. Kazdin, & A.S. Bellack (Eds.), *The clinical psychology handbook*. Elmsford, NY: Pergamon Press.

McLean, P. (1982). Behavioral therapy: Theory and research. In A.J. Rush (Ed.), *Short-term psychotherapy for depression* (pp. 19–49). New York: Guilford Press.

McLean, P.D., & Hakstian, A.R. (1979). Clinical depression: Comparative efficacy of outpatient treatments. *Journal of Consulting and Clinical Psychology, 47,* 818.

Moras, K., & Strupp, H.H. (1982). Pretherapy interpersonal relations, patients' alliance, and outcome in brief therapy. *Archives of General Psychiatry, 39,* 405–409.

Mumford, E., Schlesinger, H.J., & Glass, G.V. (1982). The effects of psychological intervention on recovery from surgery and heart attacks: An analysis of the literature. *American Journal of Public Health, 72,* 141–151.

Norcross, J.C. (1986). Eclectic psychotherapy: An introduction and overview. In J.C. Norcross (Ed.), *Handbook of eclectic psychotherapy* (pp. 3–24). New York: Brunner/Mazel.

Orlinsky, D.E., & Howard, K.I. (1978). The relation of process to outcome in psychotherapy. In S.L. Garfield & A.E. Bergin (Eds.), *Handbook of psychotherapy and behavior change* (2nd ed., pp. 283–329). New York: John Wiley & Sons.

Pardes, H., & Pincus, H. (1981). Brief therapy in the context of national mental health issues. In S. Budman (Ed.), *Forms of brief therapy* (pp. 7–22). New York: Guilford Press.

Parloff, M.B., London, P., & Wolfe, B. (1986). Individual psychotherapy and behavior change. *Annual Review of Psychology, 37,* 321–349.

Patterson, G.R. (1982). *Coercive family process.* Eugene, OR: Castalia.

Patterson, G.R., Chamberlain, P., & Reid, J.B. (1982). A comparative evaluation of a parent-training program. *Behavior Therapy, 13,* 638–650.

Rush, A.J., Beck, A.T., Kovacs, M., & Hollon, S. (1977). Comparative efficacy of cognitive therapy and pharmacotherapy in the treatment of depressed outpatients. *Cognitive Therapy and Research, 1,* 17–37.

Rush, A.J., & Watkins, J.T. (1981). Group vs. individual cognitive therapy: A pilot study. *Cognitive Therapy and Research, 5,* 95–104.

Sadock, B., Newman, L., & Normand, W.C. (1968). Short term group psychotherapy in a psychiatric walk-in clinic. *American Journal of Ortho-psychiatry, 38,* 724–732.

Scheidlinger, S. (1984). Short-term group psychotherapy for children: An overview. *International Journal of Group Psychotherapy, 34,* 573–585.

Schlesinger, H., Mumford, E., Glass, G., Patrick, C., & Scharfstein, S. (1983). Mental health treatment and medical care utilization in a fee-for-service system: Outpatient mental health treatment following the onset of a chronic disease. *American Journal of Public Health, 73,* 422–429.

Sederer, I., & Thorbeck, J. (1986). First do no harm: Short-term inpatient psychotherapy of the borderline patient. *Hospital and Community Psychiatry, 37,* 692–697.

Sifneos, P. (1972). *Short-term psychotherapy and emotional crisis.* Cambridge, MA: Harvard University Press.

Sifneos, P. (1981). Short-term anxiety-provoking psychotherapy: Its history, technique, outcome and instruction. In S. Budman (Ed.), *Forms of brief therapy* (pp. 45–81). New York: Guilford Press.

Sifneos, P. (1987). *Short-term dynamic psychotherapy: Evauation and technique* (2nd ed.). New York: Plenum Press.

Silverman, W.H., & Beech, R.P. (1979). Are dropouts, dropouts? *Journal of Community Psychology, 7,* 236–242.

Simons, A.D., Murphy, G.E., Levine, J.L., & Wetzel, R.D. (1986). Cognitive therapy and pharmacotherapy for depression: Sustained improvement over one year. *Archives of General Psychiatry, 43,* 43–48.

Sjodin, I. (1983). Psychotherapy in peptic ulcer disease: A controlled outcome study. *Acta Psychiatrica Scandinavica, 6,* 9–90.

Sloane, R.B., Staples, F.R., Cristol, A.H., Yorkston, N.J., & Whipple, K. (1975). *Short-term analytically-oriented psychotherapy vs. behavioral therapy.* Cambridge, MA: Harvard University Press.

Smith, M., Glass, G., & Miller, T. (1980). *The benefits of psychotherapy.* Baltimore: Johns Hopkins University Press.

Sorenson, R.L., Gorsuch, L., & Mintz, J. (1985). Moving targets: Patients' changing complaints during psychotherapy. *Journal of Consulting and Clinical Psychology, 53,* 49–54.

Strickler, M., & Allgeyer, J.M. (1967). The crisis group: A new appication of crisis theory. *Social Work, 12,* 28–32.

Strupp, H.H. (1980). Success and failure in time-limited psychotherapy. *Archives of General Psychiatry, 37,* 947–954.

Strupp, H.H., & Binder, J.L. (1984). *Psychotherapy in a new key: A guide to time-limited dynamic psychotherapy.* New York: Basic Books.

Svedlund, J. (1983). Psychotherapy in irritable bowel syndrome: A controlled outcome study. *Acta Psychiatrica Scandinavica, 67,* 7–86.

Teasdale, J.D., & Fennell, M.J.V. (1982). Immediate effects on depression of cognitive therapy interventions. *Cognitive Therapy and Research, 6,* 343–352.

Thompson, L.W., & Gallagher, D. (1984). Efficacy of psychotherapy in the treatment of late-life depression. *Advances in Behavioral Research and Therapy, 6,* 127.

Trakos, D.A., & Lloyd, G. (1971). Emergency management in a short-term open group. *Comparative Psychiatry, 12,* 170–175.

Turecki, S. (1982). Elective brief psychotherapy with children. *American Journal of Psychotherapy, 36,* 479–488.

Vaillant, G. (1977). *Adaptation to life.* Boston: Little Brown.

VandenBos, G., & DeLeon, G. (1988). The use of psychotherapy to improve physical health. *Psychotherapy: Theory, Research and Practice, 25,* 335–343.

Weissman, M. & Klerman, G. (1977). The chronic depressive in the community: Unrecognized and poorly treated. *Comprehensive Psychiatry, 18,* 523–531.

Weissman, M.M., Prusoff, B.A., DiMascio, A., Neu, C., Goklaney, M., & Klerman, G. (1979). The efficacy of drugs and psychotherapy in the treatment of acute depressive episodes. *American Journal of Psychiatry, 136,* 555–558.

Wolberg, L.R. (1965). The technic of short-term psychotherapy. In L.R. Wolberg (Ed.), *Short-term psychotherapy* (pp. 127–200). New York: Grune & Stratton.

AFTERWORD

EDITORS' COMMENTS

In this large multi-authored volume we have set out to provide the reader with a view of what clinical psychology is like in the 1990s. In so doing we have tried to present as much depth and breadth without the work being an encyclopedia. We must confess, however, that at times this task has been difficult, given the enormous information explosion that has occurred in clinical psychology. The present situation is quite in contrast to how we found the field of clinical psychology in the 1960s.

In the 1960s there were two main journals that were devoted to clinical psychology: *Journal of Consulting Psychology* (renamed the *Journal of Consulting and Clinical Psychology*) and the *Journal of Abnormal Psychology*. There were some others, of course (e.g., *Behaviour Research and Therapy* and *Psychotherapy: Theory, Research and Practice*), but the American Psychological Association publications dominated the field and held the greatest prestige. Because the data and publication explosion had not yet transpired, the specialty journals (such as in assessment, behavior therapy, health psychology, addictions, sports psychology, neuropsychology, epidemiology, computer applications, community psychology, legal and ethical issues, family violence, and child abuse) were only beginning to germinate. Now, of course, even the most avid reader requires *Current Contents* of *PsychSCAN* in order to keep up with the astounding developments.

When we were graduate students in the 1960s our level of sophistication simply was not as high as what we now expect from our graduate students. And that is how it should be. Not only must the diligent clinical psychologist today stay up-to-date with the developments from within the profession, but it is also imperative to maintain the attitude of the "Renaissance Man" (or "Woman"). Clinical psychologists are no longer isolated from the other helping professions or from the basic sciences, for that matter. How can the competent clinical psychologist today ignore computerization, Positron Emission Tomography (PET), computerized axial tomography (CAT), nuclear magnetic resonance imagery (NMRI), genetics, psychopharmacology, psychophysiology, neuroendocrinology, biochemistry, law and psychiatry, medical economics, and the politics of being a mental health provider?

We are proud to say that our eminent contributors have not ignored the important cross-currents and crossfertilization that make being a clinical psychologist in the 1990s exciting, albeit at times overwhelming. We are also delighted to point out that, in spite of the numerous theoretical positions, the acrimonious debates so often seen in the 1960s and 1970s are virtually extinguished. The field has matured to the extent that it has become axiomatic that we all can learn from one another, as long as we are talking about data and science, not groundless speculation. It is now apparent that most of the extreme, single-factor explanations that predominated in the 1970s and 1980s are not viable. No single treatment modality can possibly be effective with the full panoply of psychological-behavioral disorders. Moreover, some disorders (e.g., schizophrenia) may require more than one type of intervention, whereas others (e.g., major depression) may respond equally well to any of a number of diverse psychotherapeutic or psychopharmacologic strategies.

What, then, do we foresee in the future as we travel through the decade of the 1990s? More and better science, more crossfertilization with the other mental health professions, and greater interchange of ideas between clinical psychology and the basic science disciplines. We would argue heartily that this is the blueprint for progress and that we hope to document this when we prepare the third edition of the handbook at the end of the decade.

Author Index

Subject Index

ABOUT THE EDITORS AND CONTRIBUTORS

THE EDITORS

Michel Hersen, Ph.D., is Professor of Psychiatry and Psychology at the University of Pittsburgh School of Medicine. He is Past President of the Association for Advancement of Behavior Therapy. He has coauthored and coedited 78 books, including *Single Case Experimental Designs,* published by Pergamon Press. He has also published more than 179 scientific journal articles and is coeditor of several psychological journals, including *Behavior Modification, Clinical Psychology Review, Journal of Anxiety Disorders, Journal of Family Violence,* and *Journal of the Multihandicapped Person.* He is coeditor of *Progress in Behavior Modification* and Associate Editor of *Addictive Behaviors.* Dr. Hersen is the recipient of several research grants from the National Institute of Mental Health (NIMH), the Department of Education, the National Institute of Disabilities and Rehabilitation Research, and the March of Dimes Birth Defects Foundation.

Alan E. Kazdin, Ph.D., is Professor of Psychology and Professor in the Child Study Center (Child Psychiatry) at Yale University. He is also Director of the Child Conduct Clinic, an Outpatient Treatment Program for Children With Conduct Disorder and Oppositional-Defiant Disorder. He received his Ph.D. from Northwestern University in 1970. He has been Editor of the *Journal of Consulting and Clinical Psychology* and currently is Editor of *Psychological Assessment* and of the Sage Publication Book Series on *Developmental Clinical Psychology and Psychiatry.* In addition, he coedits (with Benjamin Lahey) the annual review series, *Advances in Clinical Child Psychology.* Kazdin's research focuses primarily on the assessment and treatment of childhood disorders, particularly childhood depression and antisocial behavior.

Alan S. Bellack, Ph.D., is Professor of Psychiatry, Director of the Division of Adult Psychology, and Director of the Behavior Therapy Clinic at the Medical College of Pennsylvania at Eastern Pennsylvania Psychiatric Institute. He is also Adjunct Professor of Psychology at Temple University. He is a Past President of the Association for Advancement of Behavior Therapy, and a Diplomate of the American Board of Behavior Therapy. He is a Fellow of Division 12 of the American Psychological Association, the Association for Clinical Psychosocial Research, and the American Psychopathological Association. He is co-author or coeditor of 20 books, including *The Clinical Psychology Handbook, The International Handbook of Behavior Modification and Therapy,* and *Handbook of Clinical Behavior Therapy with Adults.* He has published over 100 journal articles and has received numerous National Institute of Mental Health (NIMH) research grants on social skills, behavioral assessment, and schizophrenia, and is the recipient of a MERIT award from the NIMH. He is editor and founder of the journals *Behavior Modification* and *Clinical Psychology Review.* He has served on the editorial boards of numerous journals, including *Behavior Therapy, Behavioral Assessment,* and the *Journal of Consulting and Clinical Psychology.* He is also a practicing clinician.

THE CONTRIBUTORS

Michael Alessandri, M.S., is an advanced doctoral student in clinical psychology at Rutgers—The State University of New Jersey and Research Coordinator for the Douglass Developmental Disabilities Center. His research interests focus on people with developmental disabilities and their families, with a special focus on the fathers of children with autism.

Geary S. Alford, Ph.D., is Professor of Psychiatry and Psychology and Associate Professor of Pharmacology and Toxicology at The University of Mississippi Medical Center. A former recipient of a Career Medical Teacher Fellowship from the National Institute of Drug Abuse and the National Institute on Alcoholism and Alcohol Abuse, Dr. Alford has published research articles and book chapters on a wide variety of behavioral disorders and therapies. Interests and publications have ranged from pharmacologic animal studies, social learning research, clinical studies involving anxiety, depressive, psychosexual, psychotic and chemical dependent disorders in children and adults, to Zen Buddhism, hedonics, and a chapter on ethics in clinical research. He has been on the editorial boards of *Behavior Therapy* and *Behavior Modification* and has served as editorial consultant for a dozen other national and international journals.

Christopher R. Barbrack, J.D., Ph.D., is a former tenured professor at the Graduate School of Applied and Professional Psychology, Rutgers—The State University of New Jersey. He received a law degree from the University of Pennsylvania. A member of the New Jersey and New York Bars, he currently practices family and matrimonial law, as well as clinical psychology, in Princeton, New Jersey.

Andrew C. Bishop, M.D., is Assistant Professor in the Department of Psychiatry and Human Behavior at the University of Mississippi Medical Center where he also holds a faculty appointment in the School of Pharmacy. Dr. Bishop began his postgraduate education in pediatrics before changing to psychiatry. He has worked in community mental health and private practice as well as in academic settings. Dr. Bishop's primary interests and publications are in biological psychiatry, psychopharmacology, and cognitive-behavior therapy.

Roger K. Blashfield, Ph.D., is Professor of Clinical Psychology in Psychiatry at the University of Florida. Currently his major focus is using the prototype model to study the classification of personality disorders.

Sidney J. Blatt, Ph.D., is Professor of Psychology and Psychiatry at Yale University. He is Chief of the Psychology Section in the Department of Psychiatry and a member of the faculty of the Western New England Institute for Psychoanalysis. He has published extensively on topics in psychopathology, personality assessment, and the integration of cognitive developmental and psychoanalytic theory in the investigation of the development of mental representation, its impairment in psychopathology, especially schizophrenia, depression, and the neuroses, and its changes in the therapeutic process.

William S. Brasted, Ph.D., is the Director of the West Bank Center for Psychotherapy in New Orleans, Director of the Uptown Center for Psychotherapy, and the Director of Psychotherapy for the JoEllen Smith Psychiatric Hospital in New Orleans.

James N. Butcher is Professor of Psychology at the University of Minnesota. He maintains an active research program in the areas of personality assessment, abnormal psychology, cross-cultural personality factors, and computer-based personality assessment. He is a member of the University of Minnesota Press's Consultative Committee, which has worked since 1982 to revise and restandardize the Minnesota Multiphasic Personality Inventory (MMPI). Dr. Butcher is currently an associate editor of *Psychological Assessment: A Journal of Consulting and Clinical Psychology* and advisory editor for *Contemporary Psychology.* He founded the International Conference on Personality Assessment, a program devoted to facilitating international research on personality assessment.

Stephen F. Butler, received his Ph.D., from Emory University in 1981 and is currently Assistant Professor of Psychiatry at the Medical College of Virginia. His clinical specialty is conducting and teaching individual psychodynamic psychotherapy for personality and interpersonal problems. A former recipient of a National Research Service Award from the National Institute of Mental Health, his research interest is in the area of psychotherapy process and outcome. In particular, he is interested in identifying and describing how interpersonal problems of personality-disordered patients affect the relationship with the therapist, improving the training of psychotherapists, and assessing therapists' competence.

Nelson Butters, Ph.D., is Chief of the Psychology Service at the San Diego Department of Veterans Affairs Medical Center and a Professor of Psychiatry at the University of California School of Medicine at San Diego. Dr. Butters is a Fellow of the American Psychological Association (APA) and has served as President of Division 40 (Clinical Neuropsychology) of the APA and of the International Neuropsychological Society. His research for the past 20 years has focused on the memory disorders of amnesic and demented patients.

Timothy P. Carmody, Ph.D., is Acting Chief of the Psychology Service and Director of the Health Psychology Program at the Department of Veterans Affairs Medical Center, San Francisco, California. He is a former recipient of a Research Career Development Award from the National Heart, Lung, and Blood Institute. He has published several articles in the area of health psychology and serves as an editorial consultant for a number of journals. His major areas of interest are tobacco addiction, chronic pain, and behavioral factors in cardiovascular disease.

Robert C. Carson is Professor of Psychology and Medical Psychology at Duke University. He formerly served as Associate Editor of the *Journal of Consulting and Clinical Psychology.* He is author of *Interaction Concepts of Personality* and coauthor of *Abnormal Psychology and Modern Life.* His long-term research interests center on interfaces between social and clinical psychology.

John F. Clarkin, Ph.D., is Professor of Clinical Psychology in Psychiatry at Cornell University Medical College and Attending Psychologist at The New York Hospital. He is also Director of Psychology at The New York Hospital—Westchester Division. His research pursuits include the assessment and psychotherapy of borderline patients and the efficacy of a psychoeducational and behavioral treatment of bipolar patients and their spouses. He has published extensively on the topic of differential treatment planning.

Patrick H. DeLeon, Ph.D., M.P.H., J.D., is administrative assistant to U.S. Senator Daniel K. Inouye. His primary interests are in public service and the interface between psychology and the law. He has served on the American Psychological Association's (APA) Board of Directors and on the Council of Representatives, is past chair of the Board of Professional Affairs, and past president of Divisions 12 (Clinical Psychology), 29 (Psychotherapy), and 41 (Psychology and the Law) of the APA. He is a Diplomate in Clinical and Forensic Psychology, a charter member of the National Academies of Practice, and associate editor of the *American Psychologist.*

Barry A. Edelstein, Ph.D., is Professor and Chairman of the Department of Psychology at West Virginia University. He is also Clinical Professor of Behavioral Medicine and Psychiatry at the West Virginia University Health Sciences Center. He is the former Director of Clinical Training at West Virginia University and is past chair of the Council of University Directors of Clinical Psychology. He has been Associate Editor of *Behavior Therapy* and the *Journal of Child and Adolescent Psychotherapy,* and a member of the editorial boards of *Behavior Modification, The Behavior Analyst,* and the *International Journal of Clinical Neuropsychology.* He currently serves on the editorial boards of the *Clinical Psychology Review* and *Behavioral Assessment.* His research is in the areas of social competence, interpersonal problem solving, and clinical interviewing. His clinical research focuses on the chronically mentally ill and elderly. He is co-editor with Laura Carstensen of the *Handbook of Clinical Gerontology.*

Norman S. Endler, Ph.D., F.R.S.C., is Professor of Psychology at York University, Toronto, Canada, and Senior Research Associate at the Clarke Institute of Psychiatry. His areas of interest include anxiety and stress, depression, electric shock treatment (ECT), social interaction processes, and the interaction model of personality. Among his seven books is *Electroconvulsive Therapy: The Myths and the Realities* with E. Persad, 1988. He has written a description of ECT in *Holiday of Darkness: A Psychologist's Personal Journey Out of His Depression,* which has recently been reissued (Toronto: Wall & Thompson, 1990). Dr. Endler was recently given the award of merit of the Ontario Psychological Association and is a fellow of the Royal Society of Canada. During 1987–1989, Professor Endler was a Killam Research Fellow.

Constance T. Fischer, Ph.D., is Professor of Psychology at Duquesne University, and Director of the Pittsburgh Assessment and Consultation Center, P.C. Her academic interests have been in the development of psychology as a phenomenologically grounded human science, particularly in the areas of qualitative research and psychological assessment. She is author of *Individualizing Psychological Assessment* and co-editor of *Client Participation in Human Services* and of *Duquesne Studies in Phenomenological Psychology* (Vol. 2). She is on the editorial boards of the *Journal of Humanistic Psychology* and *The Humanistic Psychologist.*

Steven T. Fishman, Ph.D., is the Administrative Director of the Institute for Behavior Therapy in New York City, which he co-founded in 1971. Currently, he holds a Diplomate in Clinical Psychology from the American Board of Professional Psychology and is an officer and Diplomate in Behavior Therapy from the American Board of Behavioral Psychology. He is an adjunct faculty member and field supervisor for Yeshiva University. He was a Postdoctoral Fellow in Behavior Therapy at the State University of New York at Stony Brook. He has authored numerous publications in the field of behavior therapy as well as an auditape series, *Multiform Treatment of Agoraphobia,* for Guilford Press.

Stephen E. Finn is Assistant Director of the Clinical Psychology Training Program at the University of Texas at Austin. He received his Ph.D. in 1984 from the University of Minnesota and has served as Consulting Editor for *Psychological Assessment: A Journal of Consulting and Clinical Psychology.* Dr. Finn maintains an active clinical practice and has ongoing research projects in the area of personality assessment.

Donald G. Forgays is Professor of Psychology at the University of Vermont. His major research inter-

ests, in addition to primary prevention of psychopathology, include the use of isolation as a therapeutic intervention, personality relationships to health-injurious behavior, and the etiology and measurement of Type A behavior.

Cyril M. Franks, Ph.D., cofounder and first president of the Association for Advancement of Behavior Therapy, is a Distinguished Professor at the Graduate School of Applied and Professional Psychology, Rutgers—The State University of New Jersey. Dr. Franks is the founding editor of the journal *Behavior Therapy.* His current activities include writing, editing, research, and teaching in the area of behavior therapy, with special relevance to its conceptual foundations and current status.

Richard D. Freund, Ph.D., is Assistant Professor of Counseling at the University of Oregon. He has published articles on the application of mathematical models to human memory and learning, statistical methods for studying parent perceptions of children's behaviors, and the use of multiple regression in psychological research. His current research interests include the teaching of statistical methods and the analysis of clinical supervision.

Alan E. Fruzzetti, Ph.D., is a doctoral candidate in clinical psychology at the University of Washington in Seattle, where he is Research Coordinator at the Center for Clinical Research. He is particularly interested in the interaction between depression and marital and/or family problems.

Anselm George, M.D., is Assistant Professor of Psychiatry at Western Psychiatric Institute and Clinic. His clinical work and teaching focus on the inpatient treatment of patients with mood disorders. He conducts research in the area of borderline personality disorder. After receiving his medical training at the Free University Berlin, West Germany, he obtained a postgraduate fellowship in neurophysiology, and then completed a residency in psychiatry at the State University of New York, Upstate Medical Center, Syracuse, NY.

Linda R. Gonzales, Ph.D., is Assistant Professor of Medical Psychology at the Oregon Health Sciences University, and Clinical Geropsychologist at the Portland Veterans Administration Medical Center. Her major interests are in geropsychology and community psychology, particularly with respect to developing nontraditional approaches to serving older adults' mental health needs and increasing the independence and autonomy of frail elders.

Robert L. Hale is currently an associate professor in the Division of Educational Psychology and Special Education (Program in School Psychology) at the Pennsylvania State University. He obtained his Ph.D. from the University of Nebraska in 1979. His major interest is in classification theory.

Sandra L. Harris, Ph.D., received her doctorate in clinical psychology from the State University of New York at Buffalo. She is currently Professor and Chairperson, Department of Clinical Psychology, Graduate School of Applied and Professional Psychology, Rutgers—The State University of New Jersey. She is also Executive Director of the Douglass Developmental Disabilities Center, a university-based facility for the treatment and study of autism.

Steven C. Hayes is Professor and Director of Clinical Training at the University of Nevada, Reno. An author of five books and over 120 scientific articles, his work focuses on the application of contextualistic psychology to problems of verbal behavior, psychopathology, assessment, and scientific philosophy.

Stephen N. Haynes received his Ph.D. in 1971 from the University of Colorado. He is currently Professor and Director of the Clinical Studies Program in psychology at the University of Hawaii. He has published in the areas of behavioral assessment, experimental psychopathology, psychophysiological disorders, and marital distress.

Robert B. Hays, Ph.D., is Assistant Research Psychologist at the Center for AIDS Prevention Studies at the University of California, San Francisco. Since receiving his doctorate in social psychology from the University of Oregon in 1982, his research has examined interpersonal relationships and their contribution to psychological well-being. His current research focuses on psychosocial aspects of the AIDS epidemic.

James W. Hull, Ph.D., is Assistant Professor of Psychology in Psychiatry at the New York Hospital—Cornell Medical Center, Westchester Division, and a member of the Society for Psychoanalytic Training. His research interests are in patterns of symptom change in borderline inpatients.

Neil S. Jacobson, Ph.D., is Professor of Psychology at the University of Washington in Seattle. His major areas of interest are behavioral marital therapy, depression, psychotherapy research, and clinical research methodology.

Jack O. Jenkins is Professor of Psychology and Dean of the Graduate School at West Georgia College. His major areas of interest are the role of cultural factors in behavioral assessment and therapy and social skills training. Dr. Jenkins has published articles and book chapters on a variety of topics.

Barbara Pendleton Jones, Ph.D., is a neuropsychologist with the Laboratory of Psychology and Psychopathology at the National Institute of Mental Health. She is also Assistant Clinical Professor of Psychiatry and Behavioral Sciences at the George Washington University School of Medicine and Health Sciences, and Assistant Clinical Professor of Psychiatry at the Georgetown University School of Medicine. Dr. Jones's research interests include patterns of neuropsychological impairment in psychiatric disorders and the interface between psychoanalysis and neuroscience.

Martha Kane is a doctoral candidate in clinical psychology at Temple University. She has published in the area of child and adolescent anxiety disorders and has coauthored a manual for the cognitive-behavioral treatment of childhood anxiety and a research report of its evaluation. She is Coordinator at the Child and Adolescent Anxiety Disorders Clinic, Temple University.

James G. Kelly, Ph.D., is Professor of Psychology and Public Health, University of Illinois at Chicago. His published books and articles emphasize the application of ecological theory for community research and preventive mental health programs. He is currently involved in developing a collaborative research method with citizen leaders.

Philip C. Kendall, Ph.D., ABBP, is Professor of Psychology and Head of the Division of Clinical Psychology at Temple University and Professor of Research in Psychiatry at the Medical College of Pennsylvania. He is editor of the *Journal of Cognitive Therapy and Research* and associate editor of the *Journal of Consulting and Clinical Psychology.* Dr. Kendall is President of the Association for the Advancement of Behavioral Therapy and a Fellow of the American Psychological Association and the American Association for the Advancement of Science. He has authored and/or coauthored numerous books, research reports, and monographs. His research interests lie in cognitive-behavioral therapy, assessment, and treatment, especially with children, and in anxiety and depression and research methodology.

Charles A. Kiesler, Ph.D., is Provost at Vanderbilt University and Senior Fellow at Vanderbilt Institute for Public Policy Studies. Formerly the Bingham Professor and Head of the Department of Psychology at Carnegie-Mellon University, Dr. Kiesler has also served as Executive Officer of the American Psychological Association. An experimental social psychologist by training, his recent research interests have been in mental health and public policy. Dr. Kiesler has written numerous books, book chapters, and journal articles related to mental health policy issues.

John F. Kihlstrom, Ph.D., is Professor of Psychology at the University of Arizona, a member of the Committee on Cognitive Science, and an affiliate of the Committee on Neuroscience. His graduate training was in personality and experimental psychology, and he completed a clinical psychology internship in the Department of Psychiatry, Temple University. Currently he pursues research at the interface of cognitive, personality, social, and clinical psychology, with a particular emphasis on the nature and function of nonconscious mental processes.

Benjamin Kleinmuntz received his Ph.D. from the University of Minnesota and is Professor of Psychology at the University of Illinois at Chicago. He was formerly at Carnegie-Mellon University and has published extensively in the domains of judgment and decision making. Currently, he is on the editorial boards of *Computers in Human Behavior* and *Psychological Science*.

Anna C. Lee is currently in independent practice in Cascais, Portugal. Until August 1989 she was an instructor–lecturer in the Department of Psychiatry and Clinical Child Psychologist of the Hospital for Special Surgery of Cornell University Medical Center, and in private practice in New York City. She has published several chapters on such topics as child development, special issues of female therapists, and psychological variables of knee replacement surgery. Her major areas of interests include child and adolescent therapy, psychoanalytic theory and technique, and cross-cultural aspects of personality development.

Christoph Leonhard, B.S.C., received his degree at the University of St. Mary's University, Halifax, Nova Scotia, Canada. He is currently a graduate student in the clinical psychology Ph.D. program at the University of Nevada—Reno. His main interests are program evaluation and the integration of radical behaviorism with outpatient psychotherapy.

Howard D. Lerner, Ph.D., is Assistant Clinical Professor of Psychiatry at the University of Michigan and has a private practice in Ann Arbor, Michigan. His research interests include borderline diagnosis and contemporary issues in psychoanalytic theory. He is coeditor of *Borderline Phenomena and the Rorschach Test* and *Primate Mental States and the Rorschach Test*.

A. W. Logue is Professor of Psychology and Associate Dean of Social and Behavioral Sciences at the State University of New York at Stony Brook. She currently serves on the editorial boards of the *Journal of Experimental Psychology: Animal Behavior Processes,* the *Journal of the Experimental Analysis of Behavior,* and *Behavior Analyst*. Her research interests include self-control, choice, evolutionary theory, and the history of behaviorism. She is also the author of *The Psychology of Eating and Drinking*.

Barry S. Lubetkin, Ph.D., is cofounder and Clinical Director of the Institute for Behavior Therapy in New York City, a position he has held for the past 20 years. He is currently President of the American Board of Behavioral Psychology, and holds a second Diplomate in Clinical Psychology from the American Board of Professional Psychology. He was a National Institute of Mental Health Postdoctoral Fellow in Alcoholism at Massachusetts General Hospital—Harvard Medical School and a Postdoctoral Fellow in Behavior Therapy at the State University of New York at Stony Brook. He is a clinical field supervisor for Hofstra University. He is also coauthor of *Bailing Out: The Action Plan for Getting out of a Bad Relationship and Surviving* (Prentice Hall, 1990).

Brendan A. Maher is Henderson Professor of Psychology and Dean of the Graduate School of Arts and Sciences at Harvard University. He received the B.A. degree from the University of Manchester, England, and an M.A. and Ph.D. in clinical psychology from The Ohio State University. Before coming to Harvard in 1972 he had served as Professor of Psychology and Dean of the Faculty at Brandeis University, and as a faculty member at the University of Wisconsin, Lousiana State University, and Northwestern University, and as Visiting Professor at the University of Copenhagen. From 1973–1978 he was the editor of the *Journal of Consulting and Clinical Psychology*. His research interests focus on language, motor, and thought disorder in schizophrenia, and on the psychopathology of delusions. His books include *Principles of Psychopathology, Introduction to Research in Psychopathology,* and *Delusional Beliefs* (with Thomas Oltmanns). With his wife, Winifred B. Maher, he edited the series Progress in Experimental Personality Research. He served as the charter president of the Society for Research in Psychopathology.

Joseph D. Matarazzo, Chairman, Department of Medical Psychology, School of Medicine, Oregon Health Sciences University, is an academician and practitioner. He is the author and editor of textbooks and many scientific articles. He also has served as president of the American Psychological Association, the Academy of Behavioral Medicine Research, the Association of State Psychology Boards, and the International Council of Psychologists.

Paul McCarthy received his Ph.D. from The Pennsylvania State University and is currently Clinical Director of the BioBehavioral Research Institute in Chester Springs, Pennsylvania. His clinical and research interests include psychophysiology and autonomic and cortical relations in anxiety disorders.

Susan M. McGlynn, M.A., is a graduate student in clinical psychology at the University of Arizona. Her major research interests are in clinical neuropsychology, with an emphasis on the problems of normal and pathological aging.

Scott M. Monroe is Associate Professor of Psychology and Director of the Clinical Psychology Program at the University of Oregon. His major research interests are in psychopathology, with a particular focus on socioenvironmental factors in the etiology and course of mood disorders. Recent research has involved the study of psychosocial factors in relation to biological markers of depressive subtypes and longitudinal research on life stress and recurrent depression.

Teru L. Morton received her Ph.D. from the University of Utah in 1976 and currently serves as Research Associate at Vanderbilt Institute for Public Policy Studies. Formerly the Director of the Graduate Training Program in Clinical Psychology at the University of Hawaii, she has also directed the State Associations Program of the American Psychological Association (APA) and served as APA liaison to such groups as the National Association of State Mental Health Program Directors and the American Association of State Psychology Licensing Boards. Her research interests include diagnostic issues, comorbidity, and special populations, and she has contributed to numerous publications related to these areas.

Carol T. Mowbray, Ph.D., is Director of the Services Research Division for the Michigan Department of Mental Health. She also holds academic appointments at Michigan State University in Ecological Psychology and at the University of Michigan School of Nursing. She has published widely in the areas of women's mental health, evaluation and utilization treatment of the seriously mentally ill, homelessness, and victimization. She chairs the Community Support Program Division of the National Association of State Mental Health Program Directors.

Anne M. Nathan is an advanced doctoral student in clinical psychology at Rutgers—The State University of New Jersey. She has worked as a clinician at the Douglass Developmental Disabilities Center. Her research interests include the treatment of autistic disorder and communication patterns between mothers and fathers of children with developmental disabilities.

Kevin O'Connor is Professor at the California School of Professional Psychology—Fresno, where he directs the Child/Family Proficiency Program. He is the primary investigator for a research program examining child abuse risk in ethnic minority families. Dr. O'Connor is also President of the Association for Play Therapy and the author of the soon to be published *Play Therapy Primer*.

James D. A. Parker received his M.A. degree from York University in 1986 and is currently a Ph.D. candidate in psychology at York University. His research interests include personality assessment, the history of personality psychology, and health psychology. He has published empirical and theoretical papers in each of these areas.

Michael R. Pollard, J.D., is a partner with Michaels and Wishner, P.C., a law firm in Washington, D.C., that specializes in health care and venture capital. He previously was Director of the Office of Policy Analysis at the Pharmaceutical Manufacturers Association. He also served at the Federal Trade

Commission as Assistant Director, Division of Service Industry Practices, Bureau of Consumer Protection, and as Coordinator of Health Policy and Attorney Advisor in the Office of Policy Planning. He received a Juris Doctor from Harvard Law School, and a Master of Public Health from the Harvard School of Public Health. He is a member of the District of Columbia and Commonwealth of Massachusetts bars.

Kenneth S. Pope received advanced degrees from Harvard and Yale, served as chair of the APA Ethics Committee, and is an APA Fellow and Diplomate in Clinical Psychology in independent practice. The books he has coauthored or coedited include *The Stream of Consciousness: Scientific Investigations Into the Flow of Human Experience* and *The Power of Human Imagination: New Methods of Psychotherapy* (both with Jerome L. Singer), *On Love and Loving,* and *Sexual Intimacies Between Therapists and Patients* (with Jacqueline Bouhoutsos).

Howard Rachlin received his Ph.D., from Harvard University in 1965. He taught at Harvard from 1965 until 1969. He is Professor of Psychology at the State University of New York at Stony Brook, where he has been teaching since 1969. His interests include self-control, the interaction of economics and psychology, judgment, decision, choice, and the philosophy of psychology.

James M. Raczynski, Ph.D., is Associate Professor and Director, Behavioral Medicine Unit, Division of General and Preventive Medicine, Department of Medicine, at the University of Alabama at Birmingham. His primary research interests involve health promotion programs, behavioral factors in cardiovascular disorders, and health care in minorities.

Gene A. Ramsey is Program Coordinator for the Mental Hygiene Clinic of the Veterans Administration Medical Center at Tuskegee, Alabama. Dr. Ramsey's areas of interest are cognitive therapy, posttraumatic stress disorder among prisoners of war (from all eras) and Vietnam veterans, and pet-facilitative psychotherapy.

William J. Ray, Ph.D., is Professor of Psychology at The Pennsylvania State University. His research interest involves the interface between clinical psychology and psychophysiology and neuropsychology.

John E. Roberts, M.S., is a graduate student in clinical psychology at the University of Pittsburgh.

His major area of interest is the interface between cognitive processes and the social environment, particularly as related to the affective disorders. Recent empirical studies include a prospective investigation of vulnerable self-esteem and depressive symptoms.

Sheldon D. Rose, Ph.D., is Professor at the School of Social Work, University of Wisconsin—Madison. His major area of research is behavioral and cognitive-behavioral group therapy, about which he has written numerous books and articles. He is on the editorial board of a number of psychology and social work journals.

Ronald H. Rozensky, Ph.D., is Associate Chairman of the Department of Psychiatry, the Evanston Hospital, Evanston, Illinois, where he is also Chief of the Psychology Section. In addition, he is Associate Professor of Clinical Psychiatry and Behavioral Sciences at Northwestern University Medical School and Adjunct Associate Professor of Psychology at Northwestern University. He is a Diplomate in Clinical Psychology from the American Board of Professional Psychology. His teaching activities are in the areas of ethics and professional issues and psychotherapy. He has published articles and book chapters in the areas of self-control, depression, biofeedback, alcoholism, and behavioral medicine. He is coeditor, with Jerry Sweet and Steven Tovian, of the *Handbook of Clinical Psychology in Medical Settings*.

Celeste G. Simpkins received her A.A. in Computer Science in 1982 and is a Research Associate at Vanderbilt Institute for Public Policy Studies. Interested in health policy research, Ms. Simpkins is responsible for computer programming, statistical design, analysis, and developing and maintaining data files. Prior to her appointment as research associate, she served as programmer for the John F. Kennedy Center at Vanderbilt, archiving handicapped child data. Ms. Simpkins has been coauthor on several publications related to the health policy area.

Lonnie R. Snowden, Ph.D., is Professor in the School of Social Welfare at the University of California at Berkeley and Associate Director of the Center on the Organization and Financing of Care for the Severely Mentally Ill. He studies mental service systems emphasizing use of mental health services by ethnic minority populations and by the severely mentally ill.

Andrea L. Solarz, Ph.D., is a Legislative and Federal Affairs Officer in the Science Directorate of the American Psychological Association. As a 1987–1988 APA Congressional Science Fellow, she spent a year as staff to the U.S. Senate Committee on Labor and Human Resources Subcommittee on the Handicapped (now the Subcommittee on Disability Policy). Subsequently, she worked at the U.S. Congress Office of Technology Assessment on a project assessing adolescent health. She received her doctorate in psychology from the ecological psychology program at Michigan State University.

June Sprock, Ph.D., is an Assistant Professor of Psychology at Indiana State University. Her interests are the classification and assessment of psychopathology, especially depression and the personality disorders.

Hans H. Strupp is Distinguished Professor of Psychology in the Department of Psychology at Vanderbilt University. He received his Ph.D. from George Washington University in 1954. His major interest is in psychotherapy research. He has served as president of the Society for Psychotherapy Research.

Jerry J. Sweet, Ph.D., is Director of the Psychological Evaluation and Testing Service at Evanston Hospital, Evanston, Illinois, and Associate Director of Clinical Training for the Clinical Psychology Doctoral Program at Northwestern University. He is Associate Professor of Clinical Psychiatry and Behavioral Sciences at Northwestern University Medical School, Adjunct Associate Professor of Psychology at Northwestern University, and Lecturer at Loyola University of Chicago. He is a Diplomate in Clinical Neuropsychology from the American Board of Professional Psychology. He is on the editorial board of the *Journal of Consulting and Clinical Psychology* and the *International Journal of Clinical Neuropsychology*. He has published articles and book chapters in the areas of clinical neuropsychology, chronic pain, and psychological assessment. He is coeditor, with Ronald Rozensky and Steven Tovian, of the *Handbook of Clinical Psychology in Medical Settings*.

Hugh B. Urban, Ph.D., has been associated with The Pennsylvania State University throughout most of his career, earning both his M.S. and Ph.D. degrees in clinical psychology at that institution and subsequently returning to join its faculty. He has maintained an interest in personality theory, particularly as it applies to treatment and intervention. He has coau-

thored (with D.H. Ford) the book *Systems of Psychotherapy: A Comparative Approach,* and has contributed a number of chapters in edited compendia dealing with psychotherapy and behavior change. He is currently serving as Professor of Human Development and Psychology, with the focus of his work devoted to the analysis of human functioning from a systems perspective, and the use of systems engineering approaches to the design, development, and evaluation of treatment.

Gary R. VandenBos, Ph.D., a clinical psychologist, is currently the Executive Director for Publications and Communications at the American Psychological Association (APA). He previously was a visiting professor of clinical psychology at the University of Bergen (Norway), APA National Policy Studies Director, and Director of the Howell-Area Community Mental Health Center in Howell, Michigan. He is the coauthor (with Bertram P. Karon) of *Psychology with Schizophrenics: The Treatment of Choice* (1981), associate editor of the *American Psychologist,* and editor of the "Psychology Update" column in *Hospital and Community Psychiatry*.

Kelly Bemis Vitousek, Ph.D., is Assistant Professor in the Department of Psychology, University of Hawaii. Her major areas of interest are the eating and anxiety disorders, and cognitive-behavioral theory and therapy. She is on the editorial boards of *Cognitive Therapy and Research, International Journal of Eating Disorders, Journal of Abnormal Psychology,* and *Journal of Consulting and Clinical Psychology*.

Bruce E. Wampold, Ph.D., is Associate Professor and Associate Dean for the Division of Counseling and Educational Psychology at the University of Oregon. He has developed methods to analyze social interactions and has applied these methods to marital and family interactions, counseling and psychotherapy process, and clinical supervision. He serves on the editorial boards of *Behavioral Assessment,* the *Journal of Consulting and Clinical Psychology,* and the *Journal of Counseling Psychology,* and was an associate editor of *Behavioral Assessment*. He is the author (with C. J. Drew) of *Theory and Application of Statistics*.

Richard B. Weinberg, Ph.D., is Director of Psychology Internship Training at the Florida Mental Health Institute of the University of South Florida. He is psychological consultant to the Tampa Metropolitan YMCA, to a publicly funded substance abuse treatment program, and to the Hillsborough and Pasco County Public Schools. He has written various articles on such topics as consulting with nonprofit mental health organizations, coping with stress, health psychology, and communication skills. He received his doctorate in clinical psychology from the University of South Florida.

Irving B. Weiner is Professor and Director of Psychological Services at the University of Florida Psychiatry Center. He has been president of the Society for Personality Assessment and is currently editor of the *Journal of Personality Assessment*. His books in clinical psychology include *Psychodiagnosis in Schizophrenia, Psychological Disturbance in Adolescence, Principles of Psychotherapy*, and *Rorschach Assessment of Children and Adolescents*, and

he edited *Clinical Methods in Psychology* and coedited the *Handbook of Forensic Psychology*.

Arthur N. Wiens is Professor of Medical Psychology at the Oregon Health Sciences University. His interests include professional education and credentialing and certification of psychologists. He is a past president of the American Association of State Psychology Boards, past chair of the Committee on Accreditation of the American Psychological Association, and current chair of the Council for the National Register of Health Service Providers in Psychology. His present research is on assessment and psychotherapeutic interviewing, treatment outcome, and clinical health psychology. He has also published in the area of nonverbal communication.

Pergamon General Psychology Series

Editors: **Arnold P. Goldstein,** Syracuse University
Leonard Krasner, Stanford University &
SUNY at Stony Brook

*Out of print in original format. Available in custom reprint edition.